W9-DIJ-884

THE
THOMAS MERTON
ENCYCLOPEDIA

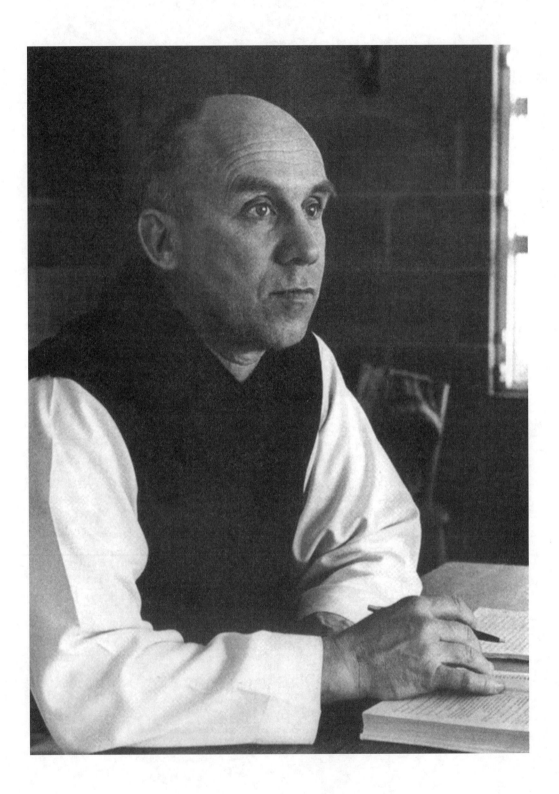

THE THOMAS MERTON ENCYCLOPEDIA

William H. Shannon
Christine M. Bochen
Patrick F. O'Connell

ORBIS BOOKS

Maryknoll, New York 10545

Founded in 1970, Orbis Books endeavors to publish works that enlighten the mind, nourish the spirit, and challenge the conscience. The publishing arm of the Maryknoll Fathers and Brothers, Orbis seeks to explore the global dimensions of the Christian faith and mission, to invite dialogue with diverse cultures and religious traditions, and to serve the cause of reconciliation and peace. The books published reflect the views of their authors and do not represent the official position of the Maryknoll Society. To learn more about Maryknoll and Orbis Books, please visit our website at www.maryknoll.org.

Manufactured in the United States of America

Library of Congress Cataloging-in-Publication Data

Shannon, William Henry, 1917-
    The Thomas Merton encyclopedia / William H. Shannon, Christine M. Bochen, Patrick F. O'Connell.
        p.   cm.
    ISBN 1-57075-426-8 (cloth)
    1. Merton, Thomas, 1915-1968 – Encyclopedias.   I. Bochen, Christine M.
II. O'Connell, Patrick F.   III. Title.
BX4705.M542 S485 2002
271'.12502 – dc21

                                                            2002000770

A Chronology of Merton's Life and Works

1915   January 31. Tom* is born at Prades, France, to Owen and Ruth (Jenkins) Merton —
       Owen an artist from New Zealand, Ruth an artist from America.

1916   The Mertons move to the United States, and live at Douglaston, Long Island, with
       Ruth's parents, Samuel and Martha Jenkins.

1917   The Mertons move to a house of their own at 57 Hillside Avenue in Flushing, New
       York.

1918   November 2. A second son, John Paul, is born.

1919   Tom's grandmother Gertrude Hannah Merton and his aunt Kit visit the Mertons in
       Flushing and stay several weeks. Tom remembered that his grandmother had taught him
       the "Our Father."

1921   Ruth dies of cancer.

1922   Owen takes Tom to Bermuda.

1923   Tom returns to his grandparents' home in Douglaston, while Owen, with Evelyn and
       Cyril Scott, goes on a painting trip to Algeria.

1925   Owen has a successful show at the Leicester Galleries in London, returns to America,
       and on August 25 he and Tom sail to France and settle down in St. Antonin.

1926   Tom is enrolled in the lycée in Montauban, France.

1928   Owen takes Tom to England, where they stay with Aunt Maud Pearce and her husband,
       Ben. Tom goes to Ripley Court School.

1929   Tom enters Oakham School in the English Midlands.

1931   After a prolonged illness, Owen dies of a brain tumor.

1933   February 1. Having successfully completed his studies at Oakham, Tom heads for Italy
       on the day after his eighteenth birthday. He returns to America for the summer, and
       in October he comes back to England to begin his university career at Clare College,
       Cambridge University. This year at Cambridge proves to be a disaster for him spiritually,
       morally, and academically.

1934   May. Tom leaves Cambridge under a cloud. He returns to England briefly in November
       to get the necessary papers to apply for permanent residence in the United States.

---

*Ruth Merton insisted that her son be called "Tom," not "Thomas," and he was so registered at the town hall at Prades.
At Oakham School, at Clare College, and at Columbia he was listed as Thomas Merton. Yet on February 4, 1938, when
he declared his intention to become an American citizen, he signed the declaration: "Tom Merton." On June 26, 1951,
when he became an American citizen, the name on the certificate of naturalization was Thomas Merton. By 1941,
when he entered Gethsemani, he was using the name Thomas James Merton (James being the name he received at his
confirmation).

1935   Thomas Merton enters Columbia University in January. January 31 brings his twentieth birthday. He is impressed by a course on eighteenth-century literature taught by Mark Van Doren. In the summer he and John Paul spend time together. In the fall John Paul enters Cornell, and Merton returns to Columbia.

1936   Merton is editor of the 1937 college yearbook and art editor of the Columbia *Jester*.

        October. Samuel Jenkins dies after a brief illness.

1937   Merton reads, and is impressed by, Etienne Gilson's *The Spirit of Medieval Philosophy*.

        August. Martha Jenkins, who had failed greatly since her husband's death, dies.

1938   Merton graduates from Columbia and begins work on an M.A. degree.

        September. He goes to Corpus Christi rectory to begin instructions.

        November 16. He is baptized by Fr. Joseph C. Moore.

1939   February. Merton receives his M.A. degree in English (thesis on William Blake).

        He moves to Greenwich Village, 35 Perry Street.

        May 25. He is confirmed by Bishop Stephen J. Donahue (confirmation name: James).

        Summer. The summer is spent in Olean, New York, at the cottage of Robert Lax's brother-in-law, Benji Marcus: Edward Rice, Lax, and Merton writing novels.

        October. On Dan Walsh's advice, he applies to the Franciscans, to Fr. Edmund Murphy, O.F.M. (accepted for entrance in August 1940).

1940   Merton teaches spring semester at Columbia Extension School.

        Summer. He reveals scruples about his past to Fr. Edmund and is advised to withdraw his application.

        September. He accepts teaching position at St. Bonaventure College.

1941   Merton is deeply moved by a Holy Week retreat at Gethsemani.

        Assured by Fr. Philotheus Boehner that there is no impediment to his being ordained a priest, he applies to Gethsemani, and on December 10 arrives at the monastery.

1942   February 21. Merton is received into the novitiate and is given the religious name: Brother M. Louis.

        John Paul Merton is baptized at parish church in New Haven, Kentucky, and receives First Communion at the abbot's private Mass at Gethsemani.

1943   April. John Paul is missing in action, as airplane engine fails over the English Channel.

1944   Merton takes simple vows.

        Publication: *Thirty Poems*.

1946   Publications: *A Man in the Divided Sea*; *The Life and Kingdom of Jesus in Christian Souls* (translation); *The Soul of the Apostolate* (translation).

        October. Sends manuscript of *The Seven Storey Mountain* to Naomi Burton, his literary agent.

        December 29. Receives telegram from Robert Giroux, editor at Harcourt, Brace: "Manuscript accepted. Happy New Year!"

1947   Publication: *Figures for an Apocalypse*.

March 19. Merton takes solemn vows.

1948   Publications: *The Seven Storey Mountain; What Is Contemplation?; Cistercian Contemplatives; The Spirit of Simplicity; Exile Ends in Glory; Guide to Cistercian Life.*

August 3. Abbot Frederic Dunne dies.

August 25. Dom James Fox is elected abbot.

1949   Publications: *Seeds of Contemplation; Gethsemani Magnificat; The Tears of the Blind Lions; The Waters of Siloe; Elected Silence.*

May 25. Merton ordained to priesthood.

November. Begins orientation classes for novices.

1950   Publications: *Selected Poems* (foreword by Robert Speaight); *What Are These Wounds?*

1951   Publications: *A Balanced Life of Prayer; The Ascent to Truth.*

June. Merton appointed master of scholastics.

June 26. Awarded American citizenship.

1952   Merton continues to seek transfer to the Carthusians or the Camaldolese; difficulties with censors over *The Sign of Jonas,* finally settled.

1953   Publications: *The Sign of Jonas; Devotions in Honor of St. John of the Cross; Bread in the Wilderness; Trappist Life.*

Merton receives permission to use toolshed in the woods for a hermitage. He names it St. Anne's.

1954   Publication: *The Last of the Fathers.*

1955   Publication: *No Man Is an Island.*

Merton appointed master of novices by Dom James Fox (continues in this office until 1965).

1956   Publications: *The Living Bread; Praying the Psalms; Silence in Heaven; Marthe, Marie et Lazare.*

July. Merton encounters Gregory Zilboorg at St. John's Abbey in Collegeville, Minnesota.

1957   Publications: *Basic Principles of Monastic Spirituality; The Silent Life; The Strange Islands; The Tower of Babel.*

1958   Publications: *Monastic Peace; Thoughts in Solitude; Prometheus: A Meditation; Nativity Kerygma; The Unquiet Conscience.*

March 18. Merton's "Fourth and Walnut" experience.

1959   Publications: *The Christmas Sermons of Bl. Guerric of Igny; The Secular Journal of Thomas Merton; Selected Poems of Thomas Merton* (introduction by Mark Van Doren [expanded edition, 1967]); *What Ought I to Do?*

Begins a revision of *What Is Contemplation?* entitled "The Inner Experience."

December. Merton receives a letter from the Congregation for Religious, refusing him permission to leave Gethsemani and go to Cuernavaca.

1960   Publications: *The Solitary Life; Spiritual Direction and Meditation; Disputed Questions; The Wisdom of the Desert; God Is My Life; The Ox Mountain Parable of Meng Tzu.*

November. Building of the retreat center that would become Merton's hermitage.

1961   Publications: *The Behavior of Titans; The New Man.*

A chapter from *New Seeds of Contemplation,* "The Root of War Is Fear," is published in the *Catholic Worker* in October, signaling Merton's entrance into the struggle for peace. Beginning of the "Cold War Letters."

1962   Publications: *New Seeds of Contemplation; Original Child Bomb; Hagia Sophia; Clement of Alexandria; Loretto and Gethsemani; A Thomas Merton Reader; Breakthrough to Peace; What Think You of Carmel?*

Merton is forbidden by the abbot general, Gabriel Sortais, to publish anything on war and peace.

1963   Publications: *Life and Holiness; Emblems of a Season of Fury; The Solitary Life: A Letter of Guigo.*

January. Circulation of the final version of the "Cold War Letters."

1964   Publications: *Seeds of Destruction; Come to the Mountain; La Révolution Noire.*

June. Merton visits D. T. Suzuki in New York City.

November. Meeting at Gethsemani of leaders of the peace movement.

1965   Publications: *Gandhi on Non-Violence; The Way of Chuang Tzu; Seasons of Celebration; Monastic Life at Gethsemani.*

August 20. Merton becomes a hermit, living on the grounds of the abbey.

1966   Publications: *Raids on the Unspeakable; Gethsemani: A Life of Praise; Conjectures of a Guilty Bystander; Redeeming the Time.*

April. Merton in Louisville hospital for surgery; falls in love with student nurse.

1967   Publications: *A Prayer of Cassiodorus; Mystics and Zen Masters; Monastery of Christ in the Desert.*

December. Meeting at Gethsemani with leaders of women religious from contemplative orders (a second such meeting the following spring).

1968   Publications: *Monks Pond* (four issues, reissued 1989); *Cables to the Ace; Faith and Violence; Zen and the Birds of Appetite; Albert Camus' The Plague.*

October. Merton travels to Alaska, California, Asia.

December. His accidental death, near Bangkok.

Posthumous Publications

1969   *My Argument with the Gestapo; The Climate of Monastic Prayer* (= Contemplative Prayer); *The Geography of Lograire.*

1970   *Opening the Bible.*

1971   *Contemplation in a World of Action; Thomas Merton on Peace; Early Poems: 1940–42.*

1973   *The Asian Journal of Thomas Merton; Six Letters: Boris Pasternak, Thomas Merton.*

1974   *Cistercian Life; The Jaguar and the Moon; A Thomas Merton Reader* (revised edition).

1975   *He Is Risen.*

1976   *Ishi Means Man; Meditations on Liturgy.*

1977   *The Monastic Journey; The Collected Poems of Thomas Merton.*

1978   *A Catch of Anti-Letters: Thomas Merton, Robert Lax.*

1979   *Love and Living.*

1980   *The Nonviolent Alternative; Thomas Merton on St. Bernard.*

1981   *The Literary Essays of Thomas Merton; Day of a Stranger; Introductions East and West: The Foreign Prefaces of Thomas Merton* (revised and expanded reprint in 1989, "Honorable Reader": Reflections on My Work); *The Niles–Merton Songs.*

1982   *Woods, Shore, Desert.*

1983   *Letters from Tom.*

1985   *Eighteen Poems; The Hidden Ground of Love: The Letters of Thomas Merton on Religious Experience and Social Concerns* (Letters, vol. 1).

1988   *A Vow of Conversation: Journal, 1964–1965; Encounter: Thomas Merton and D. T. Suzuki; Thomas Merton in Alaska; The Alaskan Journal of Thomas Merton.*

1989   *"Honorable Reader": Reflections on My Work; The Road to Joy: The Letters of Thomas Merton to New and Old Friends* (Letters, vol. 2); *Nicholas of Cusa: Dialogue about the Hidden God; Thomas Merton: Preview of the Asian Journey.*

1990   *The School of Charity: The Letters of Thomas Merton on Religious Renewal and Spiritual Direction* (Letters, vol. 3).

1992   *Springs of Contemplation: A Retreat at the Abbey of Gethsemani.*

1993   *The Courage for Truth: The Letters of Thomas Merton to Writers* (Letters, vol. 4).

1994   *Witness to Freedom: The Letters of Thomas Merton in Times of Crisis* (Letters, vol. 5).

1995   *Passion for Peace: The Social Essays of Thomas Merton; Run to the Mountain: The Story of a Vocation* (Journals, vol. 1 [1939–41]); *At Home in the World: The Letters of Thomas Merton and Rosemary Radford Ruether.*

1996   *Entering the Silence: Becoming a Monk and Writer* (Journals, vol. 2 [1941–52]); *A Search for Solitude: Pursuing the Monk's True Life* (Journals, vol. 3 [1952–60]); *Turning toward the World: The Pivotal Years* (Journals, vol. 4 [1960–63]); *Thomas Merton's Four Poems in French.*

1997   *Dancing in the Water of Life: Seeking Peace in the Hermitage* (Journals, vol. 5 [1963–65]); *Learning to Love: Exploring Solitude and Freedom* (Journals, vol. 6 [1966–67]); *Thomas Merton and James Laughlin: Selected Letters; Striving towards Being: The Letters of Thomas Merton and Czeslaw Milosz.*

1998   *The Other Side of the Mountain: The End of the Journey* (Journals, vol. 7 [1967–68]).

1999   *The Intimate Merton: His Life from His Journals.*

2001   *When Prophecy Still Had a Voice: The Letters of Thomas Merton and Robert Lax.*

2002   *Survival or Prophecy? The Letters of Thomas Merton and Jean Leclercq.*

Bibliography

Marquita E. Breit and Robert E. Daggy, *Thomas Merton: A Comprehensive Bibliography* (New York: Garland, 1986).

Patricia Burton, *Merton Vademecum: A Quick-Reference Bibliographic Handbook* (Louisville: Thomas Merton Foundation, 2001).

List of Titles

Introduction

Thomas Merton, Cistercian monk and distinguished American author, was born in Prades, France, in 1915 and died near Bangkok, Thailand, in 1968 at the age of fifty-three. Most of the intervening years were lived in America, twenty-seven of them in Kentucky at the Abbey of Gethsemani. The first two decades of his life gave no indication of the amazing influence that he would one day exercise over countless numbers of people throughout the world. He was not yet twenty years old when he returned from Europe and prepared to enter Columbia University in New York City. At Columbia, the teachers he had, the friends he made, the books he read, the soul-searching he did set his life on a new course fraught with excitement and demands. On November 16, 1938, he was received into the Catholic Church. His reflection on the meaning of this conversion eventually led him to the Cistercian monastery of Our Lady of Gethsemani, where he would spend the rest of his life.

Thomas Merton discovered a dimension of human existence that for so long had eluded him (or he had contrived to elude). He discovered spirituality — a very ancient spirituality centered in an awareness of God's presence. This contemplative spirituality was Merton's gift to the Christian community — gift not in the sense that he invented it, but that he rescued it from the marginal place it had occupied for so long a time. Contemplative spirituality is not primarily about prayer or methods of prayer. It is not one single compartment of human life; it embraces each and every aspect of our lives and all our relationships: to God, to others, to the whole created universe. Merton wrote, enthusiastically and frequently, and in many different contexts, about what he was experiencing; and he shared it with an ever growing readership.

It is not too much to say that Thomas Merton has been and continues to be, through his writings, the spiritual director of ever so many people. Merton's literary work opened a whole new way of life for them. It reshaped their spirituality. It enabled them to move from a spirituality centered largely in external practices to one centered in inner awareness of the presence of God. Such a spirituality is the source of the deepest possible happiness: "the happiness," to use his words, "of being at one with everything in that hidden ground of love, for which there can be no explanations" (*Hidden Ground of Love*, 115).

The spirituality that Merton was writing about issued, as all genuine contemplative spirituality must, in compassion. Inevitably, he became involved in efforts for justice and peace. He helped to shape the Catholic peace movement at a time when priests and monks were, by and large, conspicuous by their absence from such social involvement.

A Worldwide Reputation

Merton's writings have been translated into many languages, in both East and West. His reputation as an outstanding writer on spiritual matters was, and still is, commonly, and widely, accepted. To the Dalai Lama (exiled religious and political leader of the Tibetans), Merton was a kind of Christian he had never met before. In his autobiography, *Freedom in Exile*, he speaks of his meetings with Merton in 1968: "I could see he was a truly humble and deeply spiritual man. This was the first time I had been struck by such a feeling of spirituality in anyone who professed Christianity." The much loved Pope John XXIII was fond of Merton's writings. Msgr. Capovilla, secretary to John XXIII, wrote to Merton that when he visited the pope's library, he saw Merton's books there, "one after another" (*l'une après l'autre*). Thich Nhat Hanh (the well-known Vietnamese Buddhist monk, poet, and peace seeker, living in exile in France) saw Merton as a wisdom figure and a peacemaker. He wrote, "Thomas Merton: his life, his feelings, his teachings and his work are enough to prove his courage, his determination, his wisdom. He did more for peace than many who were out in the world." Amiya Chakravarty (distinguished Hindu scholar who taught in several American institutions of learning) pointed out how easily and sympathetically Merton entered into the thinking of people of other religions. In a letter of March 29, 1967, he said, "The absolute rootedness of your faith makes you free to understand other faiths.... Your books have the rock-like inner strength which sustains the Abbey of Gethsemani, which can challenge violence and untruth wherever they may appear." In much the same vein, John Wu Sr. (Taiwanese Catholic, expert on Zen, former ambassador from Taiwan to the Vatican) expressed his admiration for Merton: "It seems to me that you read contemplatively. You are so deeply Christian that you cannot help touching the vital springs of other religions." Sr. Mary Luke Tobin, a sister of Loretto, a highly respected religious leader, the only American woman invited to attend the Second Vatican Council as an official auditor, frequently was in touch with Merton, as the motherhouse of the Loretto Sisters was only twelve miles from Gethsemani. She marveled at Merton's ongoing growth as a world figure with a prophetic voice. She writes in her book *Hope Is an Open Door,* "In my faith-revisioning, it was a privilege to share many of the probings and reflections of Thomas Merton who was exploring the views from his own opening doors. To me he exemplified the evolution from a more privatized spirituality to God-and-person-centered consciousness. Faced by the compelling events of the 1960s, he moved in both private and public expressions to a world-embracing attitude that was truly prophetic."

Merton's Huge Literary Output

On June 11, 1968, in a letter to James Baker, who had written a dissertation on his writings,

Merton expressed surprise that Baker had discovered so many books and pamphlets that he had written. Baker numbered them at fifty. At the same time, Merton confessed, "I must admit that I really wish I had never written most of it."[1] He would be even more surprised to know that the authors of this encyclopedia have discovered that the number of books he wrote is now more than double the fifty noted by Baker. Had Merton known this, would he have, even more forcefully, regretted having written *most* of it? It is a question we cannot answer. Knowing his need to write and his desire to get his material published, one finds it hard to believe that his confession to Baker was much more than a pro forma statement that any author might be expected to make in looking over a lifetime of writing. That he may have regretted *some* of the things he wrote is understandable (that would be true of almost any writer), but *most* of it? Surely, that has to be seen as exaggeration. Merton was too good a writer (and he knew he was a good writer) to disown most of what he had written.

At any rate, whatever Merton's misgivings about his writings may have been, the books, the booklets, the magazine articles, the mimeographed notes are all there. The number of items is staggering. Yet, despite the enormous output of material that came from his pen, publication has not lagged behind. Today, more than thirty years after his death, it is fair to say that most of his writings are available in published form. The appearance of the letters and the journals largely has brought to a conclusion the publication of major Merton works — at least the major works that would interest a general readership.

With this huge amount of material now available, it seemed an appropriate time to try to organize it into some workable, user-friendly form. A number of possibilities suggested themselves. A concordance of the Merton vocabulary, for instance, would be invaluable to all Merton readers, and especially to Merton scholars. This worthwhile (tedious) task we leave to others. We have chosen another route, one that we believe is needed today and will prove most beneficial to today's Merton public: an encyclopedia.

An ordinary dictionary definition of an encyclopedia would describe it as a comprehensive work offering articles on numerous aspects of a particular field, usually arranged alphabetically. The particular field of knowledge this book hopes to present is the literary output of Thomas Merton. The books he published during his lifetime, plus those published posthumously, offer a comprehensive picture of Thomas Merton: the friendships he developed, the books he read, the themes that emerge from his writings. *The Thomas Merton Encyclopedia* attempts to bring together the elements of that picture.

Types of Articles in This Encyclopedia

The types of articles the reader will find in this work cover the following entries: (1) Merton's books; (2) a selection of essential themes that emerge from these books; (3) the persons who were important in his life; (4) the places where he lived out his life. All topics, whatever the category to which they belong, are arranged in alphabetical order. We have limited ourselves to printed materials. Thus, we have not included electronically recorded talks by Merton. We do not presume to identify every edition of a given book, nor do we discuss the many foreign-language translations of his works. Unless otherwise noted, quotations are from the first edition of a book.[2]

Book Articles

In the articles on books, we are dealing with more than one hundred books and booklets that came from Merton's old, battered typewriter. In discussing the books, our intent is to inform, not to critique. We set out to help readers know what issues and topics they will find Merton discussing in a particular work. We eschewed any attempt to evaluate his success or failure in dealing with these issues and topics. An encyclopedia is a place for informative reviews rather than critical ones. It must be said, though, that some critical decisions had to be made: which books needed to be given more space than others. A book's

content, its overall importance in the Merton corpus, its perennial appeal, the interest it arouses in a contemporary readership, as well as a book's amenability to brief summarization — these were some basic criteria for making such decisions. Not everyone will agree with our decisions about space allotment. We can only say that we were under the constraint of keeping this work within reasonable limits, a constraint that sometimes forced us to be more niggardly in allotting space than we would have liked.

Theme Articles

By far the most difficult task in crafting this encyclopedia was choosing what we considered the key themes that surface in Merton's writings and then determining how to deal with them. Merton rarely wrote systematically about any topic. What he had to say about some issue found expression in many different places. Nor did he always agree with himself in what he wrote about some matters of importance, for he was continually rethinking his ideas in particular areas. In early 1964 he wrote, "I am aware of the need for constant self-revision and growth. . . . To cling to the past is to lose one's continuity with the past, since this means clinging to what is no longer there. My ideas are always changing, always moving around one center, and I am always seeing that center from somewhere else. Hence I will always be accused of inconsistency. But I will no longer be there to hear the accusation" (*Vow of Conversation*, 19; *Water of Life*, 67). These words highlight the challenge one faces in trying to pin down what Merton had to say on a particular issue. There are times when Merton's ideas on a particular topic can be clarified by what he said about other topics. We recommend, therefore, that the reader heed the suggestions, appearing at the end of most of the articles, to check other listed related articles.

Persons and Places Articles

Besides the descriptions of books and the themes that emerge from them, which comprise by far the major portion of this work, there are brief biographies of people related to Merton, whether through blood relationship, or the common life of the monastery, or the extensive correspondence he carried on with people from, literally, almost all parts of the world. Besides the biographies, brief notes are made of the various places where he lived or visited.

We hope that this *Thomas Merton Encyclopedia* will find a home, not only with Merton scholars, but also with anyone who has a committed, or even a passing, interest in Thomas Merton. We hope also that it may open a door to Merton studies for those whose first encounter with Merton may be chancing upon this work.

All three authors of this encyclopedia are founding members of the International Thomas Merton Society. Each also has served a term as president of the Society. It is, therefore, with genuine affection and with a deep sense of communion with all the Society's members that we choose to dedicate this book to the members of the International Thomas Merton Society.

WILLIAM H. SHANNON
CHRISTINE M. BOCHEN
PATRICK F. O'CONNELL

Notes

1. Writing six days later (June 17, 1968) to Sr. Joan Marie, Merton makes a similar statement: "Looking back on my work, I wish I had never bothered to write about one-third of it — the books that tend to be (one way or another) 'popular' religion. Or inspirational" (*School of Charity*, 385).

2. Since some of the first editions are out of print and not always easy to locate, we have, in some of our references, given two numbers: the first indicating the first edition; the second, the paperback edition. For example, when we quote *Conjectures of a Guilty Bystander* or *Contemplation in a World of Action,* the second number is from the Doubleday Image paperback: *Guilty Bystander,* 12/21.

A Word of Thanks

The authors of *The Thomas Merton Encyclopedia* wish to express their gratitude and appreciation to the following people:

To Patricia Burton for her bibliographical expertise so well embodied in her *Merton Vademecum;* to Catherine Carlson and the Chester and Dorris Carlson Charitable Trust for making possible Patrick O'Connell's semester at Nazareth College as holder of the William H. Shannon Chair of Catholic Studies and so providing him an opportunity to work closely with his co-authors; to the Killian J. and Caroline F. Schmitt Foundation for the support of the Schmitt Endowed Chair at Nazareth College, which enabled Christine Bochen to go forward with this project; to Roger Collins, Owen Merton's biographer, and to John J. Merton for valuable assistance with the Merton family background and genealogy; to John King for help in locating rare items in the Merton bibliography; to Brother Patrick Hart, for his customary generous support and wise counsel; to Louis Marnella for graciously making available early Gethsemani pamphlets from his own collection; to Robert Mellesh, Gannon University interlibrary loan director for help in tracking down rare materials; to Paul Spaeth, director of the Friedsam Memorial Library of St. Bonaventure University for making available the resources of the St. Bonaventure Merton Collection; to Mary Savoie-Leopold for her faithful assistance in research and related tasks.

Special words of thanks are due to Jonathan Montaldo and Paul Pearson, former and present directors of the Thomas Merton Center at Bellarmine University for going the extra step in offering their generous assistance and collegial support; to Anne McCormick of the Merton Legacy Trust for her help and gracious concern; to Catherine Costello and John Eagleson for their imperturbable patience and careful attention to the details of production; to Wm. Roger Clark for his fine work on the photos and book covers; and, finally, to Michael Leach for his wise advice, his encouragement, and his enthusiasm, which were so helpful in forwarding this work to completion.

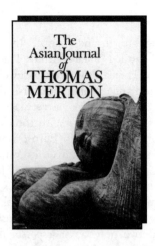

ABBOT

The word "abbot" derives from the Aramaic word *abba*, which means "father." A monastic community forms a family of disciples gathered around an abbot, or "spiritual father." The abbot is more than a juridical head of the community; he also represents Christ. His task is to teach the other monks the ways of holiness (see *Gethsemani*, 2). "The abbot is the superior, a man of God who has been especially endowed with graces and gifts for the sake of the community....He is as it were a 'sacrament' of the Fatherhood of God.... He is 'sent' to the community by Christ, as Christ was sent into the world by the Father. Christ and the Father are therefore hidden in his person, speak in his words, and will what he commands" (*Silent Life*, 48). The abbot must lead his monks to Christian maturity, freedom, and wisdom. This means that he must be mature, free, and wise.

During his twenty-seven years in the monastery, Thomas Merton lived under the guidance and authority of three abbots. Abbot Frederic Dunne (1935–48) received him into the order and encouraged him to write. Abbot James Fox (1948–67) often was at odds with Merton in their understanding of monastic renewal, yet in

Cover for *The Asian Journal of Thomas Merton* reprinted with the permission of New Directions. Cover photograph by Thomas Merton; cover design by Gertrude Huston.

the main he was an important formative figure in Merton's growth as a monk. He was sensitive to Merton's need for more solitude. He showed his confidence in Merton's authentic understanding of monasticism when he appointed him as master of novices, putting into his hands the formation of the monks of the next generation. Dom James resigned in 1967. He was succeeded by Abbot Flavian Burns. Fr. Flavian had been under Merton's direction in the scholasticate (monks preparing for the priesthood). It was he who gave Merton permission to make the journey to Asia in 1968. WHS

ALASKAN JOURNAL OF THOMAS MERTON, THE

Edited by Robert E. Daggy. Isla Vista, Calif.: Turkey Press, 1988. xvii+65 pp.

The Alaskan Journal of Thomas Merton, with an introduction by Robert E. Daggy and a preface by David D. Cooper, was printed in a limited deluxe edition of 150 copies. A single page from Merton's holograph Alaskan journal, dated September 18, 1968, is reproduced opposite the title page. The volume consists of a preface, introduction, prologue, itinerary, the Alaskan journal, epilogue, and what Daggy has called "The Alaskan Letters." In the preface, Cooper emphasizes that this was "an important time" for Merton personally, "a time of

searching, growth and change." In the introduction, entitled "Ideal Solitude: The Alaskan
Journal of Thomas Merton," Daggy characterizes Merton's final year as "a watershed period,"
and the "pre-Asian trips" as very significant to
Merton's quest (xi–xii). With the election of
a new abbot, Fr. Flavian Burns, Merton was
granted permission to travel. In May, he had
visited California and New Mexico.[1] Just a few
months later, he was setting out to explore the
final American frontier. Daggy explains that
he transcribed and compiled the *Alaskan Journal* from two notebooks: a personal journal
(identified as no. 40) and the public journal
(identified as no. 36). "Dovetailing" the two
sources, Daggy merged Merton's notes into a
single journal. He observes that there is little
difference between them except that the public journal is "slightly fuller, more detailed and
perhaps a bit rougher" (xvii). Apart from bringing the two texts together, Daggy did not revise
what Merton wrote, but he did add notes and
also a prologue consisting of several journal entries in which Merton had written about Alaska
(June 7, August 22, 26, 27, 1968).

The itinerary charts Merton's journey: he
flew from Chicago to Anchorage on Tuesday,
September 17, from Anchorage to San Francisco on Wednesday, October 2, and then on to
Santa Barbara on Thursday, October 3.[2] While
in Alaska, he visited a number of sites, including Eagle River — where he stayed at the
Monastery of the Precious Blood — Cordova,
Valdez, Anchorage, Juneau, and Dillingham.

The weeks Merton spent in Alaska were full.
He gave eight conferences (these were taped,
transcribed, and published): six during a workshop for the sisters at the Monastery of the
Precious Blood at Eagle River, one at a day of
recollection for sisters of the Diocese of Anchorage, and one at a day of recollection for
priests.[3] And just as had been the case on his
earlier visit to California, Merton was traveling
with a mission. He was "scouting out" possible
sites for a hermitage for himself and perhaps
for others in the community. Alaska appealed
to him: "If I am to be a hermit in the U.S.,
Alaska is probably the place for it" (*Alaskan
Journal*, 26).

The journal opens as Merton is in flight

from Chicago, where he had visited sisters at a
Poor Clare Convent. The first entry, dated September 17, mixes quotations from his in-flight
reading, *The Tibetan Book of the Dead*, with
recollections of his visit with the Poor Clares,
observations on what he sees on and from the
plane, and his first impressions of Alaska: "First
sight of mountains of Alaska, strongly ribbed,
through cloud. Superb blue of the gulf, inde-
scribable ice patterns. Bird wings, vast, mottled,
long black streamers, curves, scimitars, lyre
bird tails" (10). The entries that follow record
Merton's experiences and impressions during
his days with the sisters at Eagle River and
his travels to various sites in Alaska, as well
as his trip to San Francisco, where he met
Suzanne Butorovich, a young girl with whom
he had corresponded.[4] Merton's reading during
his Alaskan journey continued his preparation
for his upcoming trip to Asia. In addition to *The
Tibetan Book of the Dead*, on which he was making notes on the flight to Anchorage, he was
reading about the First Ecstasy of Ramakrishna
Parahamsa and Hermann Hesse's *Journey to the
East*. He also was reading the Russian Orthodox
theologian Vladimir Lossky, from whose writings Merton drew in his conferences with the
sisters at the Monastery of the Precious Blood.
Daggy includes, by way of epilogue, a last entry, written at Redwoods Abbey in California,
in which Merton reviews his flight to Dillingham, the day of recollection he gave to the
priests, his flight to San Francisco, and his trip
to Santa Barbara, where he spoke at the Center
for the Study of Democratic Institutions.

It is in "The Alaskan Letters" — sixteen
letters written to Abbot Flavian Burns, Br. Patrick Hart, Br. Lawrence Gannon, and Wilbur
"Ping" Ferry — that Merton offers something of
an assessment of his Alaskan experience. "My
feeling at present is that Alaska is certainly the
ideal place for solitude and the hermit life. In
fact it is full of people who are in reality living
as hermits," Merton wrote to Fr. Flavian on
September 26. "I believe," he continued, "that
if nowhere else there is certainly real solitude
in Alaska and that it would be very easy (in
spite of obvious problems, weather, bears, and
all that) to settle here" (48). On October 1,
he wrote that it would be "folly" for him "not

to consider Alaska as one of the best possibilities for a true solitary life" and that he hoped to return to Alaska when he "was through in Asia" (58).

As much as he had enjoyed the trip to the Northwest, he was already heading east, as he confessed to Br. Patrick Hart: "I am getting impatient for India. That is the real purpose of the trip" (51). CMB

SEE ALSO THOMAS MERTON IN ALASKA.

Notes

1. See *Woods, Shore, Desert* for an account of Merton's journey to the American West, which took him to California and New Mexico.
2. For these journal entries, see *Other Side of the Mountain*, 169–99.
3. For transcriptions of the conferences that Merton gave to sisters and priests in Alaska, see THOMAS MERTON IN ALASKA.
4. See *Road to Joy*, 308–14.

ALBERT CAMUS' THE PLAGUE
New York: Seabury, 1968. 43 pp.

This is a pamphlet on Camus's 1947 novel that Thomas Merton wrote as part of the publisher's "Religious Dimensions in Literature" series. It was reprinted in *The Literary Essays of Thomas Merton*. Because it adheres to the series guidelines of "Introduction and Commentary" on the work, its arrangement is somewhat more formally organized than most of Merton's literary essays, but still it manages to convey Merton's sense of the moral and even religious significance of this major work of the French-Algerian Nobel Prize winner.

In the introductory section of the pamphlet Merton stresses the "mythic" dimension of *The Plague*, in which the pestilence that strikes the town of Oran in the novel is seen to represent not only the situation of the French under Nazi occupation but also "the tyranny of evil and of death, no matter what form it may take" (*Albert Camus' The Plague*, 5). He then provides an overview of the author's life and work, with particular emphasis on what he sees as Camus's "almost traditional and classic humanism, with a few significant modern doubts, austerities, and reservations" (9), a stance that resists all dehumanizing structures and institutions, particularly those systems that are willing

to sacrifice the present good of human beings to some yet-to-be-realized ideal.

In his "Introduction to the Book," Merton does not simply summarize the plot of the novel, but begins his consideration of key thematic aspects, emphasizing, "The Plague is not only the physical epidemic but also the moral sickness of men under oppression by a hateful regime — a typological reign of evil" (11). He also introduces the figure of Père Paneloux, the embodiment of the religious issues in the story, who initially preaches that the plague is a punishment for human sinfulness but who then undergoes a change of mind, if not of heart, after witnessing the agonizing death of an innocent child. This religious dimension will continue to be a central concern of Merton throughout his discussion, as one would expect, given the focus of the series and his own interests.

In "Discussion of Themes and Characters," the longest section of the pamphlet, Merton considers the responses of the various characters to the pestilence, with detailed discussion of the theme of "modesty," a refusal to make unjustifiable claims about one's own wisdom, a preference for concrete efforts against evil over abstract theorizing about its causes and its significance; and the theme of "comprehension," an intuitive and experiential recognition of what must and must not be done to defend human dignity when it is threatened. The commitments of those working against the plague are considered both by themselves and by the author not as extraordinary or heroic but simply as decent and human, an attitude that Merton sees as "a fundamentally *optimistic* view of human nature" (18), which regards such commitment not as rare but as normative. Merton situates the book in the ongoing development of Camus's thought, which moves from recognizing "the absurd," to resisting it, to affirming love as a source of meaning. Those who refuse to remain the passive victims of the plague, or worse, to become its accomplices, are motivated by "revolt against the absurdity and arbitrariness of an evil destiny, and determination to give their lives in the affirmation of man, of life, and of love" (20). While Merton sees this stance as intrinsic to an authentic

Christianity, he recognizes Camus's rejection of Christian faith as rooted in his perception that "grace" and "salvation" seem to remove the chosen from the common struggles of humanity and allow them to make their peace with an unjust social order on the basis of an assurance of transcendent happiness — a distortion of true Christian belief but nevertheless one that too many professed Christians accept. Camus, like Kafka, champions a refusal to submit to arbitrary and demeaning demands, even those made in the name of religion. Merton finds Camus to be an advocate of grace, even if an unwitting one, in opposition to those who have subverted grace into law.

In his sketches of the major characters of the novel, Merton compares the stolid, decent Dr. Rieux, who simply tries to be a genuine human being, with the more "romantic" Tarrou, who wishes to become a "saint without God" (13), a desire that Merton sees as not radically different from the ideal of disinterested sanctity, not motivated by a desire for a reward, of a St. John of the Cross. He contrasts the absurd yet touching dedication of Grand, who keeps obsessively rewriting the opening sentence of his novel, with the grandiose machinations of Cottard, a criminal who finds in the plague a reprieve from prosecution and exploits others' sufferings for his own advantage. The journalist Rambert, who relinquishes his plan to escape the quarantined city to be with his beloved wife at the very point when it is about to succeed, represents the perspective of those who come to realize that private happiness cannot be fully realized while others suffer. Finally, the character of Paneloux is analyzed extensively as a representative of a self-assured, militant Christianity that is forced to surrender some of its certitudes in the face of human suffering; but while he too gives his life in the fight against the plague, he does it with a certain willfulness that does not seem to be rooted in love for and solidarity with others.

In his conclusion, Merton sees Camus as both the conscience of his generation and a stumbling block to Christians, affirming many values that are traditionally Christian yet failing to find them embodied by Christians themselves. Merton considers the assertion by some Christian commentators on Camus that he would have been more drawn to Christianity had he been able to encounter the world-affirming vision of a Teilhard de Chardin; but while Merton sees Teilhard as himself in revolt against the kind of negative spirituality of a Paneloux, and sharing with Camus a passionate love of the material world, he ends his commentary by questioning whether Teilhard's evolutionary optimism, which tends to minimize the suffering and death of individuals now in the light of a progress toward future unity, would really have impressed one who "protested vigorously against [the] tendency to sacrifice man as he is now, in the present, for man as he is supposed to be . . . at some indefinite time in the future" (41). Merton suggests that Teilhard's optimism, like Paneloux's pessimism, tends to give in to what Camus sees as "the great temptation" by "attaching more importance to an abstract *idea*, a *mystique*, a *system*, than to man in his existential and fallible reality here and now" (42). Though he does not state it explicitly, Merton leaves the impression that in this regard he is more in sympathy with the concerns of the agnostic Camus than with the assurances of the Christian Teilhard. POC

SEE ALSO *LITERARY ESSAYS OF THOMAS MERTON*.

ALIENATION

In the talk he gave on the morning of December 10, 1968, speaking to monks and nuns in Bangkok, Thomas Merton centered much of his presentation around the theme of alienation. The talk was entitled "Marxism and Monastic Perspectives." The idea of alienation, he told his hearers, is basically Marxist. "What it means is that man living under certain economic conditions is no longer in possession of the fruits of his life. His life is not his. It is lived according to conditions determined by somebody else" (*Asian Journal*, 335). Christianity, Merton insists, is just as much opposed to alienation as Marxism is. Marxism traces alienation to the class struggle between those who own the means of production and those who form the working class. Christianity traces alienation to original sin and the consequent dualism that has separated God from creation and pitted people one against another. Overcoming alienation is a prominent theme in the writings of St. Paul, and the central theme of his epistles *Romans* and *Galatians*. Paul intended that people take very seriously his words "There is no longer Jew or Greek [Gentile]" (Gal. 3:28). There is, for the Christian, no longer Asian or European. "We also have to keep in mind the fact that Christianity and Buddhism, too, in their original purity point beyond all divisions between this or that" (340). So we respect plurality. We work with division. But we seek to go beyond them. Merton points to the idea of compassion that is central to Mahayana Buddhism, and he suggests that it is based on a keen awareness of the interdependence of all these living beings, all of which are part of one another and involved with one another.

Merton concluded his address with the hope that by studying the great Asian traditions, we can come at last "to that full and transcendent liberty which is beyond mere cultural differences and mere externals — and mere this or that" (343).

Merton's most detailed discussion of alienation is found in *The New Man*. The mission of Christ, the second Adam, the New Man, is to recover the unity lost by the first Adam. "Humanity, which was one image of God in Adam, or, if you prefer, one single 'mirror' of the divine nature, was shattered into millions of fragments by that original sin which alienated each man from God, from other men and from himself" (*New Man*, 149). The broken image becomes once again the perfectly united image of God in the recapitulation of all creation achieved by Christ. Christ restores humans to their original existential communion with God, the source of life. "Man was once again able to drink from the inexhaustible spring of truth which God had hidden in the depths of man's own nature at the point where the created image opens out into the uncreated Image of the eternal Reality — the Word of God" (151–52). In Christ we human beings are able to overcome the alienation that a false dualism projects on our consciousness and recover in Christ our unity with God, with others, and, especially, within ourselves.

This recovery signals the demise of the false self in us as we come to know our own identity, an identity that we find in God. For Merton, it is in contemplation that this victory over alienation is accomplished. In moments of contemplation " 'life' and 'reality' and 'God' cease to be concepts which we think about and become realities in which we consciously participate" (18). In contemplation we know the reality of God in an entirely new way. "When we apprehend God through the medium of concepts, we see Him as an object separate from ourselves, as a being from whom we are alienated, even though we believe that He loves us and that we love Him. In contemplation this division disappears, for contemplation goes beyond concepts and apprehends God not as a separate object but as the Reality within our own reality, the Being within our being, the life of our life" (18–19). We experience God's presence within us, not as an object, but as "the transcendent source of our own subjectivity" (19). We lose our false self and discover our true self. We overcome the dualism and the alienation that heretofore have prevented us from viewing reality as it is. We come at last to know our own true identity.

Merton sees the concept of alienation as a point of contact between Buddhism and Christianity. In his dialogue with Suzuki (see *Zen and the Birds of Appetite*), he notes a basic agreement between Buddhism and Christianity "on the point that man, no matter how well balanced, healthy, integrated and sane, is still alienated from his 'true self' " (*Witness to Freedom*, 305). Human beings, even those who are well integrated into family and society, are in exile from their true spiritual homes. "That is to say, according to the Buddhists, that [man] has a basically deceptive and illusory view of life, and according to Christians that he does not 'see God,' does not have access to the ultimate meaning of life and is not in accord fully and deeply with the supernatural love that brought him into existence.... In both religions there tend to be degrees of perfection, an ascent to enlightenment, to union and to fulfillment in self-transcendence" (305). This spiritual breakthrough that overcomes alienation was the topic of Merton's dialogue with Suzuki (the dialogue published in *Zen and the Birds of Appetite*). WHS

SEE ALSO MARXISM; NONDUALISM; SELF.

ALLCHIN, ARTHUR MACDONALD

The Rev. Canon Arthur MacDonald Allchin ("Donald" to his friends), a distinguished Anglican scholar, lecturer, and writer, studied Eastern Orthodoxy in Greece in 1955–56 and was ordained a priest in the Church of England in 1956. He served as librarian at Pusey House, Oxford, and chaplain to the students, later as canon residentiary at Canterbury Cathedral and (his present position) as professor at the university in Bangor, Wales.

A. M. Allchin

His first visit to North America was in 1963 in Montreal for the Faith and Order meeting. Dale Moody, professor at the Baptist Seminary in Louisville, who had come to know Allchin at Oxford, offered to arrange for him to visit Thomas Merton at Gethsemani. Besides this initial visit, there were two others, in 1967 and 1968. During the 1968 visit, they drove to Shakertown at Pleasant Hill in Kentucky. On the way home they heard on the car radio the shattering news of the assassination of Martin Luther King Jr. in Memphis.

Their friendship was a meaningful experience for both of them. Allchin's interests in so many religious and intellectual areas (such as monasticism, spirituality, interreligious dialogue especially with the Orthodox, Celtic literature and culture, the seventeenth-century Anglican divines, to mention a few) sparked similar interests in Merton. He enjoyed Allchin's visits. Merton's last letter to him was a request "to do Wales" in the spring of 1969. The letter came from Delhi on the Asian journey from which Merton never returned. Canon Allchin has continued his interest in Merton. He has lectured on Merton's writings and also written about him. He was one of the leading organizers of the thriving Thomas Merton Society of Great Britain and Ireland. WHS

AMERICAN MYTH

When, in *Conjectures of a Guilty Bystander*, Thomas Merton speaks of the "American myth," he is speaking of a false myth. False myths have lost their creative capacity to mediate reality, and instead of bearing truth, they create illusion and foster evasion. "When a myth becomes a daydream it is judged, found wanting, and must be discarded" (*Guilty Bystander*, 33).[1] "When a myth becomes an evasion, the society that clings to it gets into serious trouble" (34).

What is the American myth? It is a paradise myth: "*America is the earthly paradise*" (34). The American myth grew out of the discovery of a new world full of new beginnings and limitless possibilities. The "New-Found-Land was a world *without history*, therefore without sin, therefore a paradise" unmarred by original sin (34). To those who immigrated to its shores, America offered the opportunity to begin a new life. The American myth became the American dream, with its promise of freedom and prosperity for all. The dream lived on for centuries even though all were not included in its promise. The new frontier guaranteed "more paradise": "There was always a new start, over the mountains, over the plains" in "a great unlimited garden" (35). When the geographic frontier was exhausted, the "frontier" itself became a symbol, as in President John F. Kennedy's proclamation of the "new frontier." Kennedy had found a way to keep the American myth alive.

With insight and accuracy bordering on the uncanny, Merton suggests that the study of American mythology should begin with the car. The car, "with its aggressive and lubric design, its useless power, its otiose gadgetry, its consumption of fuel, which is advertised as having almost supernatural power," is, to Americans, a symbol (76). "Meditation on the automobile, what it is used for, what it stands for — the automobile as weapon, as self-advertisement, as brothel, as a means of suicide, etc. — might lead us at once right into the heart of all contemporary American problems: race, war, the crisis of marriage, the flight from reality into myth and fanaticism, the growing brutality and irrationality of American mores" (76).

Merton's critique of the American myth coincides with his speaking out candidly and passionately on the social issues of his day. In 1962, in a "Cold War Letter" to Leslie Dewart, Merton characterized "the American mentality" as involved in "deep illusions, most of all about itself" (*Witness to Freedom*, 282). The American illusion is rooted in the paradise myth: "The illusion of America as the earthly paradise, in which everyone recovers original goodness: which becomes in fact a curious idea that prosperity itself justifies everything, is a sign of goodness, is a carte blanche to continue to be prosperous in any way feasible: and this leads to the horror that we now see: because we are prosperous, because we are successful, because we have all this amazing 'know-how' (without a real intelligence or moral wisdom, without even really deep scientific spirit), we are entitled to defend ourselves by any means whatever, without any limitation, and all the more so because what we are defending is our illusion of innocence" (282–83). Merton recognized the danger of technological knowledge unbridled by moral sensibility.

A few years later, in 1965, as America was becoming deeply involved in the Vietnam War,

Merton wrote of "the ancient American myth of rejuvenation, justification, and a totally new start. By definition this is the land not only of 'liberty' but also of primeval innocence and indeed complete impeccability" (99). Despite contravening evidence, there is the denial of guilt, refusal of culpability, and the projection of blame onto the enemy. Frequently, in his writings on social issues, Merton exposes and challenges the myths that undergird American self-understanding and are used to justify war and racism. He denounces the myth that "might makes right," played out in the "overwhelming atrocity" of Vietnam (*Faith and Violence*, 93), and the "white Western myth-dream" that feeds a sense of racial superiority (*Love and Living*, 94).

Aware of the complexity of American identity and self-understanding, Merton also recognized that the American paradise myth had some truth in it. In a "Cold War Letter" to M. B. (Mary Childs Black) ca. January 24, 1962, Merton observed that the Shaker "spirit is perhaps the most authentic expression of the primitive American 'mystery' or 'myth': the paradise myth. The New World, the world of renewal, of return to simplicity, to the innocence of Adam, the recovery of the primeval cosmic simplicity, the reduction of divisions, the restoration of unity. But not just a return to the beginning, it is also an anticipation of the end. The anticipation of eschatological fulfillment, of completion, the New World was an earnest and a type of the New Spiritual Creation" (*Witness to Freedom*, 31). For the pioneer and later for the businessman, America held the promise that "all happiness was there for the asking" (31). The Shakers saw both the falseness and the truth of the paradise myth. They recognized "the evil, the violence, the unscrupulousness that too often underlay the secular vision of the earthly paradise" in which the Indian was slaughtered, the Negro enslaved, and the immigrant treated as inferior (31). The Shakers also realized that experiencing the "paradise spirit" in an authentic way required a conversion. "The Shakers apprehended something totally original about the spirit and the vocation of America" that others did not see (31). In so doing, they confirmed the power of myth:

"For myths are realities, and they themselves open into deeper realms" (31). CMB

SEE ALSO RACISM.

Notes

1. Citations are from the Image edition.

ANGLICANISM

SEE ENGLAND, CHURCH OF.

APOPHATICISM

Apophaticism may be viewed as a way of talking about God or a way of relating to God. In both cases it flows from an awareness that human reason never can arrive at a knowledge of God even remotely commensurate with the divine Reality. As a way of talking about God, it is *negative theology*. As a way of relating to God as God is in the divine Selfhood, it is *contemplation*. Negative theology contrasts with affirmative theology. Affirmative theology ascribes to God all the perfections that can be found in creatures. The experiences of fatherhood, motherhood, justice, wisdom, truthfulness, and compassion, which are our human experiences, serve as so many windows whereby we can peer through the created world to the uncreated Reality of God. Yet all these affirmations, as we experience them in creatures, are limited. They can tell us something *about* God, but they can never lead us to God's inmost Reality. Thus, we can speak of wisdom and apply this term to creatures and to God, because there is some sort of similarity. But the similarity is so meager and the dissimilarity so great that we could almost say: God is not wise (in the way that creatures are wise). The Fourth Lateran Council expressed this insight very clearly: "Between the creator and creature there can be noted no similarity so great that a greater dissimilarity cannot be seen between them."[1] God is unnamable: no name we think of fits God. God is unknowable: no concept we devise enables us to know God.

Thomas Merton speaks of the two ways to God: a way of affirmation and a way of denial. He makes clear that we have to use both. "We must affirm and deny at the same time. If we

go on affirming, without denying, we end up by affirming that we have delimited the Being of God in our concepts. If we go on denying, without affirming, we end up by denying that our concepts can tell the truth about Him in any sense whatever" (*Ascent to Truth*, 94). In a helpful analogy, Merton compares the two ways to the takeoff and flight of a plane. Thus we begin with this concept: God exists. This affirmation about God is compared to the plane rolling along the ground. This is affirmation. We use the word "exist" as if it applied to God in the same way it does to us. But then we have to deny that "exist" means the same thing when applied to God and us. "The plane cannot fly unless it 'renounces' its contact with the ground. The theologian cannot reach God in his concepts until he renounces their limits and their 'definitions'" (94–95).

Merton goes on to say, "The Fathers and the great Scholastics agree that the *via negationis* is the way to a true contact with God, a true 'possession' of God 'in darkness.' ... But the *via negationis* of the intellect also requires a *via amoris* for the will; on this dark way both intellect and will must ultimately be possessed and transfigured by the action of divine grace."

Merton never underestimated the value of the affirmative approach to God. God revealed the divine Self to us in the Word made flesh, and in Jesus God took on the limitations of the human condition. But as Merton points out, "The God who has revealed Himself to us in His Word has revealed Himself as unknown in His intimate essence" (*World of Action*, 171/185). That is why the affirmative approach cannot be the ultimate way of speaking about God. The time comes, at least for some theologians and contemplatives, when it must give way to negative theology or the apophatic way. Christian faith, while concerned with certain revealed truths, does not terminate in conceptual formulas of these truths, but attains to God beyond words and ideas. This is to say that ultimately the divine Reality silences the Christian theologian. Likewise, Christian contemplation "experiences the ineffable reality of what is beyond experience. It 'knows' the presence of God, not in clear vision, but 'as unknown' (*tamquam ignotum*)." Hence, Merton is able to say that "in the mystical tradition both of the Eastern and Western Churches, there is a strong element of what has been called 'apophatic theology.'" Like Moses approaching the burning bush, the contemplative, as well as the theologian, must remove the "'shoes' of opinion and rationalization" (173/187). WHS

SEE ALSO CONTEMPLATION; GOD; PRAYER.

Notes

1. Norman P. Tanner, ed., *Decrees of the Ecumenical Councils*, 2 vols. (Washington, D.C.: Georgetown University Press, 1990), 1:232.

ART, THEORY OF

Thomas Merton's understanding of the purpose of art owed a great deal to the beliefs and example of his father, Owen, as Merton perceived them from the time of his own childhood. He writes in his autobiography that he had learned from his painter-father "that it was almost blasphemy to regard the function of art as merely to reproduce some kind of a sensible pleasure or, at best, to stir up the emotions to a transitory thrill. I had always understood that art was contemplation, and that it involved the action of the highest faculties of man" (*Seven Storey Mountain*, 202–3). This insight was confirmed by his reading of Jacques Maritain's *Art and Scholasticism* in 1938 as he was writing his master's thesis on William Blake. For Maritain, art is a "virtue of the practical intellect" (see *Seven Storey Mountain*, 204; *Literary Essays*, 431), by which he means a power that aims not directly at knowledge (the end of the speculative intellect) but at action, specifically the action of making (as distinguished from doing, the sphere of morality). The goal of art is the perfection of the work, but it depends on the formation in the artist of a *habitus*, or stable disposition (see *Literary Essays*, 431–32), a capacity for perceiving genuine beauty, which consists in integrity or completeness, proportion or order, and clarity or intelligibility (what Merton calls "the glory of form shining through matter" [*Literary Essays*, 443]). It is from this perspective that Merton can call art "a natural analogue of mystical experience" (*Seven Storey Mountain*, 202), because art is the ability to see

Watercolor by Owen Merton

not merely what is apparent to the senses but the inner radiance of Being as it is reflected in the particular and concrete. Authentic artistic experience "produced a kind of intuitive perception of reality through a sort of affective identification with the object contemplated — the kind of perception that the Thomists call 'connatural.' This means simply a knowledge that comes about as it were by the identification of natures" (202). This knowledge by imaginative identification or participation in turn gives rise to the work, the concrete expression of this intuitive vision. Consequently, Merton is firmly opposed, on the one hand, to an understanding of art that is crassly objective, merely an imitation of what is perceived by the senses (the literalism and naturalism against which Blake was rebelling [203]), and, on the other hand, to an overly subjective theory of art as simply individual self-expression. The end of art is not to teach a lesson but to create a work that reveals the form, the inner coherence, the "ontological splendor" (*Literary Essays*, 445) of what has been experienced.

This basic perception of art remained central for Merton throughout his life, though at times he shifted the emphasis in one direction or another. For example, in *The Ascent to Truth*, without denying the analogy between art and contemplation, he stresses that analogy is not reducible to identity, so that the "experience of the artist and the experience of the mystic are completely distinct" (*Ascent to Truth*, 62), a focus that probably reflects to some extent his own conflicted experience of living the monastic life with the equipment of an artist. But he also emphasizes that "a true and valid aesthetic formation was necessary for the wholeness of Christian living and worship" (*No Man Is an Island*, 35) because art integrates the material and the spiritual by recognizing in creation an outward sign of the Creator's power and wisdom and love. "Music and art and poetry attune the soul to God because they induce a kind of contact with the Creator and Ruler of the Universe. The genius of the artist finds its way by the affinity of creative sympathy, or connaturality, into the living law that rules the universe" (36). In fact, the cloister may well be, Merton reflects, an ideal place for putting into practice the scholastic ideal of the end of art, where the focus is on "*things to be made* and on the *intention for which they are made* rather than upon the individual artist and upon his subjective emotions in making them," a fidelity to the artistic tradition of the great medieval monasteries and cathedrals (*Silent Life*, 88).

Merton's passionate interest in the intersection of the sacred and the aesthetic led to one of the great unfinished projects of his life. The unpublished manuscript "Art and Worship," which developed from lectures on sacred art given to Merton's students in 1954, was first scheduled for publication in 1958, and was still being worked over by Merton almost to the end of his life. While the reasons for its nonappearance are complicated — including a relative lack of development of material on contemporary sacred art and perhaps a scathing evaluation by an anonymous professional art historian — parts of the manuscript were published as articles, including two chapters in *Disputed Questions*. In "Sacred Art and the Spiritual Life," Merton critiques works of art produced by both the dead conventionalism of conformist piety and the faddism of a superficial attraction to what is new and unusual. He

emphasizes the importance of a commitment to the work itself as the end of art, as well as the power of authentic art to foster an ability "to look, to see, to admire, to contemplate," rather than to be deformed by passive acceptance of conventional clichés and slogans, whether sacred or profane (*Disputed Questions*, 153). He points to the "sacramental" ability of art to function as "a witness to the power of the divine Spirit at work to transfigure the whole of creation and to 'recapitulate all things in Christ,' restoring all material creation to the spiritual and transforming rule of divine love," but warns that this will not happen unless the work of art is "genuinely spiritual, truly traditional, artistically alive" (156), faithful both to artistic form and to religious subject matter. After surveying some of the genuine achievements in sacred art in the past, he concludes by pointing out that any contemporary sacred art that truly is in touch with the horrors of the present era must not flinch from confronting "the violent realities of a cruel age" but must enter into the darkness to provide an authentic and convincing witness to the light (164). In the other article, "Absurdity in Sacred Decoration," Merton contrasts a traditional use of symbolism in sacred art, which "opens the way to an intuitive understanding of mystery — it places us in the presence of the invisible," with the current penchant for pictorial illustration in liturgical art, which "tends to *take the place of* the invisible and obscure it" by keeping attention on the surface, the literal and (to some unformed tastes, at least) emotionally appealing (265). The appreciation of form, of inner clarity, Merton worries, is in danger of being lost in an era when the manipulative techniques of advertising threaten to infiltrate even the sanctuary.

Merton's basic principles remain evident in his "Answers on Art and Freedom," which first appeared in a South American literary magazine and so is less explicitly spiritual in its focus. But Merton continues to emphasize that true art cannot be reduced to any ideological function, whether in support of or in opposition to the established order. The goal of art, he continues to insist almost three decades after first reading Maritain, must be the perfection of the work. Any cult of the artist, even the artist as rebel or nonconformist, distracts from the true aim of art, which is not to call attention to the artist but to serve the integrity of the work. The artist must be deeply conscious of the social and political issues of the age, but art reduced to propaganda, even propaganda for a just cause, is a deformation of art. Insofar as the artist's art is faithful to its own truth, it "will be in harmony with every other kind of truth — moral, metaphysical, and mystical" (Raids on the Unspeakable, 171), but this is an indirect not a direct goal of art. "In the last analysis, the only valid witness to the artist's creative freedom is his work itself. The artist builds his own freedom and forms his own artistic conscience, by the work of his hands. Only when the work is finished can he tell whether or not it was done 'freely'" (175). Fidelity to this belief is a remarkably consistent theme in Merton's theory of art throughout his life, and one he consistently tried to put into practice in his own work as a literary artist. POC

SEE ALSO CREATIVITY; POETRY, THEORY OF.

ARTIST, THOMAS MERTON AS

SEE CALLIGRAPHIES; DRAWINGS, REPRESENTATIONAL; PHOTOGRAPHY.

ASCENT TO TRUTH, THE
New York: Harcourt, Brace, 1951. x+342 pp.

This book offers evidence of Thomas Merton's early interest in the writings of St. John of the Cross, an interest that tended to wane in his later years. In simplest terms, this work attempts to explain the mystical theology of St. John of the Cross in the light of the dogmatic theology of St. Thomas Aquinas. This was a concrete way of doing something that, as he told Sr. Therese Lentfoehr in a letter of February 15, 1949, he felt needed to be done: a setting forth of "the dogmatic essentials of mystical theology."[1] Not many months passed before he realized that this was not the kind of book he ought to be writing. In fact, in the December 1949 revised edition of Seeds of Contemplation, he informs his readers that

henceforth he intends to talk "about spiritual things from the point of view of experience rather than in the concise terms of dogmatic theology" (Seeds of Contemplation, xii). But by this time he had accumulated eight hundred pages in various notebooks. He complains, "I have a huge mass of half-digested notes, all mixed up, and I can't find my way around in them" (Sign of Jonas, 157). But it was too late to turn back. He agonized over all this undigested material and finally got it into some semblance of order.

By his own admission, his efforts were not entirely successful. In a letter to Dom Jean Leclercq, written sixteen years after publication of The Ascent to Truth, he described the book as "unnatural": "I was trying to be academic or a theologian or something, and that is not what I am" (School of Charity, 352). He realized also that the different parts of the book did not hang together well. In sending a copy to Erich Fromm, he tells him that the book may possibly be of some interest, but "it is rather dry reading in patches and badly put together" (Hidden Ground of Love, 312).

Though Merton had begun working on it in 1948, The Ascent to Truth was not published until September 20, 1951. Even the title proved a problem, as the book progressed through a series of names: "The School of the Spirit," "The Cloud and the Fire," and finally, "The Ascent to Truth."[2]

The table of contents includes a prologue and three parts: (1) "The Cloud and the Fire," (2) "Reason and Mysticism in Saint John of the Cross," and (3) "Doctrine and Experience." The book shows signs of the battle scars Merton experienced in writing it: it tends to be repetitious and at times overly abstract. Many readers might well find a bit heady his discussion of the opinions of Suarez and John of St. Thomas on the role of love in the mystical experience (Ascent to Truth, 293–94). Also, some of the religious narrowness that marred The Seven Storey Mountain occasionally appears. See, for instance, chapter 2, which deals with "The Problem of Unbelief," in which he shows little sympathy for those who honestly struggle with the problem of faith.

To suggest that a book has shortcomings

is not to deny that it has value. The importance of the "darkening" of desire (through detachment) and the "darkening" of the intellect (through discernment), the clarification of both the value and the limitations of conceptual knowledge of God, the distinction between faith as assent to propositions and faith as commitment to God, his insistence on the crucial role of reason at all stages of the mystical journey to God, his carefully nuanced explanation of the notion of analogy (so crucial to the theological enterprise), his stress on the ultimate importance of love in achieving mystical union with God — all these are elements of perennial importance in understanding what contemplation is about.

To choose but one of these topics, consider the importance that Merton and St. John of the Cross give to detachment. It must not be thought of as a total withdrawal from creatures. No. What hinders our spiritual progress is not creatures, but the *desire* for creatures. St. John affirms "that the desire of creatures as ends in themselves cannot coexist with the desire of God as our true end" (57). Desire is the culprit. Thus, he does not say: in order to arrive at knowledge of everything, know nothing; but: *desire* to know nothing. It is not knowledge, possessions, pleasures that get in our way. It is desire. When he discusses conceptual knowledge of God, it is the same theme: "It is not so much the presence of concepts in the mind that interferes with the 'obscure' mystical illumination of the soul, as the *desire to reach God through concepts*" (89). Desire locks us in a prison of falsity and unreality, from which we can be delivered only by detachment. Yet for detachment to "function" properly, there is need for discernment in the intellect. Discernment that exposes creatures for what they are and detachment that disarms vain desires that would lead us astray make us capable of the serene and joyful knowledge that is contemplation.

Yet in the end, it must be said that knowledge, whether derived from concepts or received from faith, will not suffice. Concepts tell us of a vast goodness that is beyond their knowledge. Faith tells us of a God whose greatness is beyond all formulations of faith. "But love which transports the soul into the darkness beyond faith, unites our being to the Being of God. . . . Love astounds the intelligence with vivid reports of a transcendent Actuality which minds can only know, on earth, by a confession of ignorance. And so, when the mind admits that God is too great for our knowledge, Love replies: 'I know Him!'" (295–96).

In Merton's 1967 graph evaluating a number of his books on a scale from "best" to "awful," he rates *The Ascent to Truth* "fair." He can hardly be faulted for this evaluation.

The Ascent to Truth was translated into several different languages. When the French translation was published in 1958, it had been edited and cut by Fr. François de Ste. Marie, O.C.D. Extensive cuts were made in part 3; sometimes it is only a word that is changed, but there are instances where an entire paragraph or a whole page is deleted. The total amount cut would represent roughly ten pages. This is a considerable amount in that the cuts cover a section of only fifty-seven pages (258–315). Some of the cuts are clarifying; others appear to be an attempt to avoid statements that seemed to blur the distinction between God and the contemplative. In the brief introduction he wrote for the French translation, Merton stated that he himself had made additional cuts and revisions. He also made clear that "the French edition henceforth replaces all others (including the English) as the final version. It contains all that the author desires to retain of the original. The rest can profitably be forgotten" (*"Honorable Reader,"* 28). This definitive edition is not available in English. whs

Notes

1. Archives of the Thomas Merton Center, Louisville, Kentucky. Unfortunately, this letter was not included in *The Road to Joy.*

2. Merton had some misgivings about this title, fearing that some readers might take it to mean "Assent to Truth." But this was the publisher's choice, and the publisher prevailed.

ASCETICISM

Thomas Merton's first contact with asceticism came when, as a student at Columbia, he read a book recommended to him by his friend

Robert Lax. The book was Aldous Huxley's *Ends and Means*. It made a deep impression on him. What Huxley suggested was that there existed — beyond the reprobate world committed to greed, violence, ambition, and materialistic values — a realm with very different values, spiritual values. Moreover, this higher realm, Huxley intimated, was accessible to experience and could be reached by prayer and detachment and love. Merton's eyes were opened and his heart was touched (see *Seven Storey Mountain*, 184–87). This was in 1937, a year before his conversion to the Catholic Church. Four years later he would be on his way to a Trappist monastery in search of those values and that higher realm of reality.

Asceticism derives from the Greek word *askesis*, which means "practice." In Christian spirituality it refers to those practices or disciplines whereby we uproot sin and foster virtue. It embraces concepts such as self-denial, mortification, humility, and renunciation. "The real purpose of asceticism is to disclose the difference between the evil use of created things, which is sin, and their good use, which is virtue" (*No Man Is an Island*, 106). It is important to distinguish between sin, which is something negative, and pleasure, which is a positive good. There is no necessary link between sin and pleasure.

Asceticism is about the struggle between the flesh and the spirit. Yet we must be careful not to fall into the error of thinking of the flesh as evil and the spirit, considered separate from the body, as good. This dualism, which often has surfaced in Christian thought, Merton totally rejects. "When the Bible speaks of flesh and spirit, it does not mean to oppose the material element in man to his spiritual element, as if the body were evil and only the soul were good. On the contrary both terms refer to the whole man, body and soul" (*Monastic Spirituality*, 18/64).[1] It is the whole person who is "flesh" if his or her life is dominated by selfishness and self-centeredness — what St. Paul calls "the cravings of the flesh" (Gal. 5:16). The whole person is "spirit" if he or she is subject to the Spirit of Christ. "The Benedictine ascesis of silence, obedience, solitude, humility, manual labor, liturgical prayer is all designed to unite us with the Mystical Christ, with one another in charity, and its aim to bring our souls under the complete dominance of the Holy Spirit" (19/64).

It should be clear, then, that the ascetic life is not just negative (denying ourselves, overcoming the sins and faults that hamper our union with Christ); it is, more importantly, something very positive: the living of the new life in the Spirit, which develops in us in proportion as we empty ourselves. The fruit of ascesis is that purity of heart which brings the freedom of the children of God and the joy and peace that are the fruits of the Holy Spirit. WHS

SEE ALSO *BASIC PRINCIPLES OF MONASTIC SPIRITUALITY*; DETACHMENT; PURITY OF HEART.

Notes

1. In this article, the first page citation number refers to the Abbey of Gethsemani edition (1957), and the second to the Templegate edition (1996).

ASIAN JOURNAL OF THOMAS MERTON, THE

Edited by Naomi Stone, Patrick Hart, and James Laughlin. New York: New Directions, 1973. xxix+445 pp.

The journal notes that Thomas Merton kept during his Asian trip comprise part 5 of volume 7 of the Merton journals (published in 1998 under the title *The Other Side of the Mountain*). Except for a few corrections in spelling and in words that had been misread in the earlier publication, the texts of volume 7 dealing with Merton's Asian journey are the same as those in *The Asian Journal*. There is considerable difference, however, between the two volumes. While *The Other Side of the Mountain* has much journal material that preceded the Asian journey, *The Asian Journal* has a wealth of material other than journal notes.

The Asian Journal begins with a preface by Amiya Chakravarty, eight pages of editors' notes explaining the process of putting the book together, and a foreword by Br. Patrick Hart, Merton's secretary, which details Merton's preparations for the trip to Asia.

Part 1 is made up of seven sections, all except the first identified by place names.

1. The Eastward Flight, October 15–18 (1968). The journal begins with Merton's sense of destiny, "of being at last on my true way after years of waiting" (*Asian Journal*, 4). This man who had never had a home (he denied that the monastery was a home[1]) writes ecstatically, "I am going home to the home where I have never been in this body" (5). There was a brief stay in Bangkok, where he met with a Buddhist abbot who spoke with him about Theravada Buddhism. (All through his journey Merton sought out native religious leaders to meet.) He reports their conversation and his own reflections. This he will continue to do. From this point on, the journal will abound with quotations from the conversations he had and from the books he was reading. His enthusiasm to learn more and more continued unabated.

2. Calcutta, October 19–27. At Calcutta, Merton was met by Susan Hyde, secretary of Peter Dunne, who was secretary of the Temple of Understanding in Washington, D.C., the sponsoring organization of the Spiritual Summit Conference that Merton would address on October 23 (see on appendices 3 and 4, below). He records his impressions of Calcutta: "Calcutta has the lucidity of despair, of absolute confusion, of vitality helpless to cope with itself. Yet undefeatable.... An infinite crowd of men and women, camping everywhere, as if waiting for someone to lead them ... into a world that works, yet knowing ... that in the end nothing really works and that life is all *anicca, dukkha, anatta,* that each self is the denial of the desires of all the others — and yet somehow a sign to others of some inscrutable hope" (28). On October 21, in company with Amiya Chakravarty, he visited Jamini Roy, a creator of remarkable iconlike paintings of both Christian and Hindu subjects.

3. New Delhi, October 28–31. At New Delhi, Merton was met by Harold Talbott, an American student of Buddhism, who had been baptized as a Catholic at the Abbey of Gethsemani. He was in India studying with the Dalai Lama. He arranged Merton's meetings with the Dalai Lama.

4. The Himalayas, November 1–25. Traveling by train and jeep, Merton and Talbott arrived at the latter's cottage in Dharamsala, where Merton stayed and from which he climbed up the mountain to Upper Dharamsala for his three audiences with the Dalai Lama. These occurred on November 4, 6, and 7. Merton was most impressed with this Tibetan leader of a people in exile. After the first meeting he wrote, "The whole conversation was about religion and philosophy and especially ways of meditation. He said he was glad to see me, had heard a lot about me" (101). All three audiences were lively and enjoyable. Merton inquired about Tibetan schools of Buddhism. The Dalai Lama was interested in learning more about Western monasticism.

The next stop on the journey was Darjeeling, where he and Talbott arrived on November 13 to stay at the Windamere Hotel. At a nearby Loretto convent Merton arranged to say Mass. (It is worth noting that throughout his trip Merton made sure he said Mass whenever possible and also read the monastic office daily.) On November 18 Merton went to the Mim Tea Estate above Darjeeling (with a fine view of Mount Kanchenjunga) for a couple days of retreat. Now a month into his Asian trip, he reflects on where eventually he might take up residence as a hermit (Alaska? California?), though without ever completely separating himself from Gethsemani. "I ought eventually to end my days there.... It is my monastery and being away has helped me see it in perspective and love it more" (149).

5. Madras, November 26–28. During a brief stay in Madras, Merton visited St. Thomas Mountain, where, legend has it, the apostle Thomas, after preaching the gospel in India, was martyred. Merton spent time with Dr. V. Raghavan, an eminent Sanskrit scholar, professor emeritus at the University of Madras.

6. Ceylon (Sri Lanka), November 29–December 6. Brief stays at Colombo and Kandy prepare the way for his visit to the Buddhist shrine in Polonnaruwa, an ancient ruined city sacred to both Buddhists and Hindus. Among the ruins of temples and palaces are three colossal figures of the Buddha carved out of huge stones. Merton was deeply moved by these huge Buddha figures. "I am able to approach the Buddhas barefooted and undisturbed, my feet in wet grass, wet sand. Then the silence

of the extraordinary faces. The great smiles. Huge and yet subtle. Filled with every possibility, questioning nothing, knowing everything, rejecting nothing.... Looking at these figures I was suddenly, almost forcibly, jerked clean out of the habitual, half-tied vision of things, and an inner clearness, clarity, as if exploding from the rocks themselves became evident and obvious.... The thing about all this is that there is no puzzle, no problem and really no 'mystery.' All problems are resolved and everything is clear, simply because what matters is clear.... Everything is emptiness and everything is compassion" (233–34).

7. Bangkok, December 7–8. After a brief stay at Singapore, Merton arrived at Bangkok on December 7. He took an enchanting walk through the city and in the evening went to see an Italian movie. The next day, the Feast of the Immaculate Conception, he said Mass at St. Louis Church. One cannot help but think: how appropriate the church! In the afternoon he moved to the Red Cross meeting place where two days later he would deliver the talk he had come half way around the world to give. The last words in his journal are "on to the Red Cross place this afternoon" (254).

The journal items are followed by Br. Patrick's postscript telling of Merton's untimely death and the return of his body to Gethsemani.

Merton quoted frequently from various books he was reading while in Asia. Some of the texts were too long to include in the body of *The Asian Journal*. They have been placed in part 2, called "Complementary Reading."

There are nine appendices. Three are letters: two circular letters from Merton to friends (appendices 1 and 6 [also published in volume 2 of his letters, *The Road to Joy*]) and one letter to Merton's abbot, Fr. Flavian Burns, from leaders at the Bangkok meeting informing him of Merton's death (appendix 8). Appendix 2 is an article on mindfulness by Bhikkhu Khantipalo.

Appendices 3 and 4 have to do with Merton's talk in Calcutta at the Temple of Understanding meeting. Appendix 3 is the talk he actually gave, which concludes with the moving words "My dear brothers [and sisters] we are already one. But we imagine that we are not. And what we have to recover is our orig-

Thomas Merton in Bangkok, Thailand, December 10, 1968

inal unity. What we have to be is what we are" (308). Appendix 4 consists of the notes he prepared for that talk, but did not use. They include five helpful principles to guide interreligious dialogue (316–17).

Appendix 5 is a prayer Merton offered at the Calcutta meeting. Appendix 9 is an article on the Bhagavad Gita that Merton wrote originally as a preface to *The Bhagavad Gita As It Is*, by Swami A. C. Bhaktivedanta (New York: Macmillan, 1968).

Appendix 7, "Marxism and Monastic Perspectives," is the talk Merton had come to Bangkok to deliver at the meeting of monastics in Asia. It was his first time on television and his last talk. It is a talk with flashes of insight. At one point he discusses the ideal of Marxist communism, which would promote a society "where each gives according to his capacity and each receives according to his needs" (334). This goal, he maintains, cannot be achieved in communism, but can be achieved in a monastery, for the whole purpose of the monastic life is to teach people how to love. This goal was expressed in the Augustinian formula of the translation of *cupiditas* into *caritas*, "of self-centered love into an outgoing, other-centered love. In the process of this change the individual ego was seen to be illusory and dissolved itself, and in place of this self-centered ego came the Christian person, who was no longer just the individual, but was Christ dwelling in each one" (334). It is worth noting that in this, his final talk, he returns to a subject he had written so much about: the distinction between the false self (the individual) and the true self (the person). That afternoon, he departed this mortal life and joined the company of the "burnt men."

There are several pages of bibliography and a detailed (fifty-five pages), almost overkill, glossary of terms, most of them relating to Eastern religions. An extensive index of twenty-two pages concludes the volume. WHS

Notes

1. See *"Honorable Reader,"* 65.

ATHEISM

In August 1964 Thomas Merton wrote a letter to an Indian student in which he explained that the "phenomenon of atheism today is quite ambiguous." He went on to say that this remains "the naïve atheism of nineteenth-century scientism," which resulted in "a scientific myth" that attempted to replace "the religious myth." This "atheism" regards the God in whom religious people believe as "a God who is simply 'a being among other beings,' an 'object' which can be discovered and demonstrated" (*Hidden Ground of Love*, 452). This concept of God is not only inadequate; it is false.

In 1967, Merton sounded a similar chord when he wrote to Carlton Smith, a friend of Cardinal Koenig, archbishop of Vienna, who then was head of the Secretariat for Non-Believers. Merton's letter to Smith followed up on conversations they had had at Gethsemani. Merton observed that "organized atheism is negligible" in the United States and thus "dialogue with non-believers" will be different in the United States from what it is in Eastern

Europe. "What we do have . . . is a great deal of indifference to religion" (556). Merton points out that any dialogue with nonbelievers will have to begin by taking into account "the pragmatic 'sociologism'" of Americans and even of the American church as illustrated by Cardinal Spellman's attitude toward the war in Vietnam: " 'Now we are in it, we had better get it done with in the most efficient possible way'" (557). To understand the American indifference to God, Merton suggests that Cardinal Koenig should talk to people "to find out what they all think" — scientists and intellectuals, believers and nonbelievers alike. But Merton warns that the discussion ought not to focus on a discussion of " 'God' as a theoretical problem with no attention to the urgent existential problem of man and his survival and the humanization of his technical society . . . this technological society is dangerously indifferent to authentic human values, and dangerously, indeed naively, obsessed with efficacy as an end in itself" (558). The two letters surface Merton's concern about what might be described more accurately not as atheism but as indifference: a circumstance in which people are not against God but indifferent to an image of God that is far removed from the reality of God.

This theme resounds in much of what Merton wrote in the late 1960s when he addressed belief and unbelief in a way that tried to take into account the experience of persons who found themselves unable to believe in God. In the 1960s, Merton was returning to a topic that he had addressed earlier in *The Ascent to Truth* as he considered the predicament of those persons unable to believe in God and concluded that the roots of the problem lay, at least in part, in the believers who are "merely apologetes" when they ought to be "Apostles" (*Ascent to Truth*, 43–44). In an essay published in *Harper's Magazine* in 1966, entitled "Apologies to an Unbeliever," Merton acknowledges that the religious problem of the twentieth century is shared by unbelievers and believers: neither knows the reality of the Living God — a God sometimes mysteriously experienced in absence. In other essays written in the late 1960s and also published in part 4 of *Faith and Violence*, Merton explores the challenges to faith in God expressed in the writings of radical theologians such as J. A. T. Robinson, Dietrich Bonhoeffer, and the "Death of God" theologians, which Merton characterizes as "a new atheism" whose religionless Christians are "Christian atheists" (*World of Action*, 173/187).

Mindful of the need to open communication with those who struggle with belief, Merton saw this responsibility to be a dimension of his contemplative vocation. The Christian contemplative, by his or her very existence, points to the reality of God known and experienced as mystery and presence, a God who paradoxically can be known in God's absence. This is at the very heart of the Christian mystical experience. Contemplatives witness to the reality of a God beyond concepts. In an essay entitled "The Contemplative and the Atheist," Merton concluded that the special task of contemplatives is "to keep alive and to deepen the 'intimate understanding' of and 'experience' through which divine revelation is handed down not merely in Christian preaching but as a living and experienced reality" (194). CMB

SEE ALSO FAITH.

AT HOME IN THE WORLD:
The Letters of Thomas Merton and Rosemary Radford Ruether
Edited by Mary Tardiff. Maryknoll, N.Y.: Orbis Books, 1995. xix+108 pp.

Edited with a preface by Mary Tardiff, O.P., introduction by Rosemary Radford Ruether, and afterword by Christine Bochen, *At Home in the World* is one of several volumes, published to date, that feature an exchange of letters between Thomas Merton and one of his many correspondents. This exchange between the famous Trappist monk and the theologian who would become a leading Catholic voice in feminism consists of forty letters, the first written by Ruether on August 12, 1966, and the last by Merton on February 18, 1968. Each wrote twenty letters, but Merton's number includes two circular letters.[1] All but one of Merton's letters to Ruether were published in *The Hidden*

Ground of Love, edited by William H. Shannon, and Merton's circular letters were published in *The Road to Joy,* edited by Robert E. Daggy. Ruether's letters to Merton had not been published previously. In addition to the letters, two other pieces by Merton are reprinted in this book: Merton's "Campaign Platform" (his thoughts on the abbatial election in 1968) and a poem, "A Round and a Hope for Smith Girls." Also, one of Merton's abstract drawings/calligraphies is reproduced in the volume.[2] Both the footnotes and the index are helpful.

The photographs reproduced on the book's cover help to contextualize this exchange of letters. Merton, middle-aged and grinning, wears the work clothes that were his favored attire during the hermitage years (1965–68); Ruether, smiling demurely, is some twenty years younger. She was only twenty-nine when their correspondence began. Merton was a well-published writer; Ruether was just beginning her career as a theologian, professor, and writer. She had just completed her Ph.D. in classics and patristics at Claremont Graduate School and was moving, together with her husband and three children, to Washington, D.C., where she was about to begin teaching historical theology at Howard University. Merton and Ruether were an unlikely match and yet, despite the difference in age and experience, for a time they shared an intense and lively correspondence. Ruether found Merton very receptive. Even though he was a "seasoned thinker" and she was "a neophyte," Ruether notes that Merton addressed her "as an equal," even occasionally assuming "the stance of a subordinate, asking me to be his teacher or even confessor" (*At Home in the World,* xv). In her introduction, Ruether recalls that the question for her "was not simply historical truth, but truthful living.... Could Catholics speak the truth and be Catholics?... In 1966 Merton was my 'test case' for whether integrity was possible for Catholics" (xvii). And, for his part, Merton responded with candidness, a willingness to engage the issues, and a spirited enthusiasm that was his hallmark. Merton was supportive of her work and impressed by the articles she sent him and the manuscript of *The Church Against Itself* (New York: Herder and Herder, 1967).

He proclaimed himself in need of a theologian like her.

In her preface, Mary Tardiff sets the exchange of letters within the historical, theological, and ecclesiological context of the 1960s, in which a number of factors were at play: the spirit of the Second Vatican Council, the rise of secular theology, the struggles of the civil rights movement, the protests against the war in Vietnam, and "a general upheaval of established values" (viii). Tardiff also introduces Ruether and points to the interrelationship of biography and theology evident on her side of the correspondence. Ruether draws on her own experience as a Christian living in the world and introduces into the conversation a range of theological topics she deems to be urgent issues for the church: "ecclesial renewal, radicalism, sexuality, racism, ecumenism, and poverty." While Tardiff's preface focuses on Ruether, Bochen's afterword recaps Merton's story in order to situate this exchange of letters in the context of Merton's life as a monk and hermit. She emphasizes that one of the subjects uppermost on Merton's mind at this time was monastic renewal, and in the course of talking about monasticism, Merton continued to develop his understanding of what it meant for him to be a monk.

When it came to monasticism, Merton and Ruether held widely divergent views. Ruether challenged Merton's commitment to monastic life in the light of her own commitment to respond to the needs of justice and the world. Living in the city and witnessing the pain and struggle of people in the world, Ruether was unable to understand or affirm Merton's monastic vocation. Ruether's critique of monasticism was direct and uncompromising: "Monasticism, no longer today standing for radical Christianity, has indeed lost its soul." Monasticism, she continued, "not only today, but always was a misunderstanding of the gospel ... monasticism, no matter how much it tempers its language and mixes itself up in 'openness' to the world, is rooted in a view of the gospel that makes salvation a salvation *from* the world and not the salvation *of* the world" (28). And while she did believe that persons continued to need contemplation and solitude,

she saw "temporary withdrawal for inner deepening" not as an end in itself but "directed back towards the real action" (29). To Merton, Ruether's view of monasticism was "abstract" and "poles apart" from the lived reality. For him, monastic life "is in closer contact with God's good creation" (34). Rather than cutting one off from "created things and other people," the purpose of asceticism is to normalize and heal those relationships. "The contemplative life, in my way of thinking (with Greek Fathers, etc.), is simply the restoration of man, in Christ, to the state in which he was originally intended to live" (35). And, although Merton was quick to dissociate himself with the stereotypical concept of a monk and claim himself to be a nonmonk, living a sort of hippie life in the woods, he was, Bochen notes, adamant that "the monastic life — for all its struggles and ambiguities — was nevertheless the place for him" (105).

Although the two-page index does not include subject headings, the listing of names of persons and books mentioned serves to illustrate the range of topics Merton and Ruether discussed. For example, the entries under the letter A alone include Dietrich Bonhoeffer's *Art and Being*, Fr. Robert Adolfs (author of *The Grave of God*), Pope Alexander VI, "Death of God" theologian Thomas J. Altizer, and Sts. Ambrose, Anthony, Athanasius, and Augustine. References to classical figures and contemporary voices fill their exchange. Although it was brief in duration, lasting only eighteen months, the exchange of letters between Merton and Ruether reveals much about both. The correspondence serves as a point of entry into what was for Merton a complex and challenging time in his own life.

It was a time when Merton was particularly attuned to women's voices, and in Rosemary Radford Ruether he had encountered a woman who would challenge and enrich his own thinking. One indication of how seriously he took their exchange is that he reflected on it in his journal. This was somewhat unusual for Merton. The fact that he did so in this case was an indication that what they were discussing mattered deeply to him. On February 7, 1967, Merton wrote, "In her letter Rosemary challenges my solitude, but not understanding it, I think. She is very Barthian — which is why I trust her. There is a fundamental Christian honesty about her theology — its refusal to sweep evil under the rug and its 'No' to phony incarnationalism. And above all she knows where the real problem lies: the Church" (*Learning to Love*, 195).[3] Theirs was a brief but meaningful encounter. CMB

SEE ALSO CALLIGRAPHIES.

Notes

1. Merton occasionally wrote what have been called "circular letters," letters that he sent to many of his friends to update them on his activities. The circular letters eased the burden of keeping up with his correspondence.

2. Merton had asked Ruether to take care of some of his calligraphies (black ink Zen brush paintings). After his death, she felt committed to carrying out his request that "they not be exploited commercially, but used for some social good." They were auctioned to raise money for a defense fund for Daniel and Philip Berrigan. Ruether kept one, which is reproduced in *At Home in the World* (see xix, xx).

3. For references to Ruether, see *Learning to Love*, 101, 194, 195–97, 207, 219, 276.

AWARENESS

The word "awareness" appears frequently in Thomas Merton's presentation of contemplation. It describes an experience or a state of heightened consciousness. Merton uses various synonyms to describe it: awakening, attentiveness, alertness, realization. To cultivate awareness requires a sense of inner silence, inner unity. The noisiness, the flood of words with which our culture inundates us, makes any kind of awareness, let alone awareness of God, difficult for us. So often, we are not fully present to what is right before us, and yet we are not entirely absent. "We just float along in the general noise. Resigned and indifferent, we share semi-consciously in the mindless mind of muzak and radio commercials which pass for 'reality'" (*Love and Living*, 40–41).[1]

The awareness of which Merton speaks is not so much something we *do* as something we *are*. Awareness is not the same thing as thinking. Thinking tends to divide: it implies a subject thinking and an object that is thought about. Awareness, on the other hand, reduces the distance between me and what I am aware

of. A deep sense of attentive awareness closes the gap between me and that of which I am aware. It brings together and unites. In fact, in a deep experience of attentive awareness the subject-object dichotomy disappears. I am not aware *of something*. I am *simply aware*. This is Merton's understanding of contemplation. As he writes in *New Seeds of Contemplation*, "In the depths of contemplative prayer there seems to be no division between subject and object, and there is no reason to make any statement either about God or about oneself. He IS and this reality absorbs everything else" (267). Similarly, he says in *The New Man*, "We fully 'realize' ourselves when we cease to be conscious of ourselves in separateness and know nothing but the one God Who is above all knowledge" (122).

In volume 6 of the journals, Merton is talking about the same issue when he writes about the distinction between realizing and knowing. "In realization the reality one grasps, or by which one is grasped, is actualized in oneself, and one becomes what one realizes, one is what he realizes. Knowing is just a matter of registering that something is objectively verifiable — whether one bothers to verify it or not. Realization is not verification but isness" (*Learning to Love*, 321).

On March 27, 1968, Merton responded to a Carmelite superior who had asked him about the meaning of "continuous prayer." He pointed out that, while such prayer is firmly fixed in the contemplative tradition, it is often misunderstood. "What it really means," he wrote, "is continuous openness to God, attentiveness, listening, disposability, etc." He continued, "In terms of Zen it is not awareness *of* but simple awareness. If one deliberately cultivates a distinct consciousness *of* anything, one tends to frustrate one's objectives — or God's objectives. If one just thinks of it in terms of loving God all the time in whatever way is most spontaneous and simple, then perhaps the error can be avoided."[2]

A proper understanding of awareness helps us to see the difference between meditation and contemplation. Meditation[3] (understood as discursive meditation) involves thinking. One reflects on the Scriptures and their application to life here and now. A person thinks about the truths of faith to deepen penetration into their meaning. But the real end of meditation is, Merton tells us, "to teach you how to become aware of the presence of God; and most of all it aims at bringing you to a state of almost constant loving attention to God, and dependence on Him" (*New Seeds of Contemplation*, 217). Here, Merton is speaking not of discursive meditation but of meditation leading to contemplation. For the time comes when images and concepts are no longer enough to satisfy your desire for God. Then it may be mean that you have reached the point where "you relax in a simple contemplative gaze that keeps your attention peacefully aware of Him hidden somewhere in this deep cloud into which you also feel yourself drawn to enter" (219). WHS

SEE ALSO CONTEMPLATION; GOD; MEDITATION.

Notes

1. From Merton's essay "Creative Silence," originally written for *The Baptist Student* in 1968.

2. Unpublished letter to Mother Mary Therese, in the archives of the Merton Center, Bellarmine University.

3. Merton is not always consistent in his use of the term "meditation." At times he equates it with contemplation. This may be due to the influence of Zen, in which meditation is more akin to what Western spiritual traditions would call contemplation.

AZIZ, ABDUL

A Sufi scholar who has lived all his life in Karachi, Pakistan, Aziz was educated at the University of Karachi, where he received the degrees of M.S. and LL.B. He worked in government service, retiring as a collector of customs in 1974. Of major interest to him were his spiritual aspirations that led to a lifetime study of mysticism, especially Sufism. Impressed by Thomas Merton's *The Ascent to Truth* and encouraged by Louis Massignon, he wrote to Merton on November 1, 1960. From then until 1968 the two exchanged letters and books. Merton's side of the correspondence is found in *The Hidden Ground of Love* (43–67). Of special interest in this correspondence is Merton's description, at Aziz's request, of his way of prayer (63–64). WHS

SEE ALSO PRAYER; SUFISM.

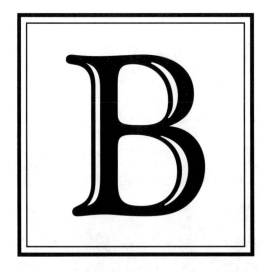

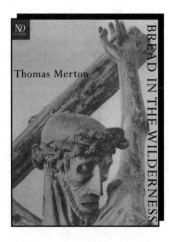

BALANCED LIFE OF PRAYER, A

Trappist, Ky.: Abbey of Gethsemani, 1951.
21 pp.

This small booklet (three by six inches) is divided into four main sections: (1) The Object of the Life of Prayer, (2) Obstacles to the Life of Prayer and How to Overcome Them, (3) Public Prayer and Sacrifice, and (4) Mental Prayer and Contemplation.

In section 1, Merton begins with St. Paul's directive calling us "to pray without ceasing" (1 Thess. 5:17). Prayer ought to be as instinctive as breathing. Had Adam not fallen, prayer would be second nature to us. Christ, the new Adam, has restored us to the life of grace, making it possible for us to breathe with the breath of God, the Holy Spirit. "It is by prayer that we lay our souls open to God and seek to 'breathe' His life. The supreme object of prayer is the fulfillment of God's Will" (*Balanced Life of Prayer*, 2/5).[1]

A life of prayer is a necessity and a possibility for all peoples. Merton quotes Pope Pius XII's encyclical *Mediator Dei*, which says that the Christian ideal is union with God in the closest and most intimate manner. Our work, our duties, and all our interests must be trans-

figured by a supernatural intention, divinized by charity, so that our most common and routine actions can become a sacrifice of praise to God.

Yet there are obstacles to the life of prayer, as discussed in section 2. Some people are ignorant of what prayer is really meant to be. Prayer involves our intellect and will; it must be intelligent and a sincere act of love. This calls for constant purification of our thoughts and loves. Merton uses a parable that will become a theme of later writings — Jesus' Parable of the Sower and the Seed — to describe different levels of cooperation with God's grace in prayer. A mere formalism (which makes prayer a thoughtless routine) as well as a weak and artificial sentimentality (which makes prayer maudlin and egocentric) must be avoided.

A balanced life of prayer will include the following: (1) the prayer of the liturgy, particularly the Mass, (2) public prayer for certain needs or times (e.g., various public devotions, such as stations of the cross and the like), and (3) mental prayer, contemplation, and a life of sustained personal union with God (see 10–11/12).

Section 3 discusses liturgical prayer. Merton speaks about active participation, but he is writing before Vatican II, when the term "active participation" took on new meaning. Participation, as he saw it then, meant above all conformity with Christ as priest and victim. "This participation means conforming our minds and hearts to the obedience and the humility and the total self-oblation of our divine Redeemer in His death on the cross for love of us" (13–14/14).

In section 4, we learn that while liturgical prayer is essentially vocal prayer, it does stimulate acts of the mind and affections of the heart that turn into mental prayer and even contemplation. Pope Pius XII speaks about the importance of meditation in the Christian life. Meditation is a quest for the truth that we find in the tradition of faith. But it is a quest that "springs from love and ends in greater love" (19/19). The peculiar value of mental prayer, or meditation,[2] is that it is more personal and private and therefore allows us to develop our spirituality in terms of our own character, temperament, and needs. The proximate end of mental prayer is "loving awareness of the presence of God" (21/20).

The practice of mental prayer is not always full of sweetness and consolation. The Holy Spirit seeks to purify our souls by detaching them from such interior consolations. "The secret of progress in mental prayer lies above all in the humble acceptance of spiritual dryness and interior trial. But here we are close to the heart of the matter, because in mental prayer, more than any other, the way to perfection is the way of the Cross" (21–22/20–21). WHS

SEE ALSO MEDITATION; PRAYER.

Notes

1. In this article, the first page citation number refers to the original booklet, and the second to the reprint of this work in volume 8 of *The Merton Annual*.

2. In this booklet Merton treats mental prayer and meditation synonymously. There is at least a hint that meditation leads to contemplation.

BAMBERGER, JOHN EUDES

After serving in the navy, and while at medical school, Bamberger read *The Seven Storey Mountain* and was impressed by it. Finally, when working his internship, he decided that he was being called to the monastic life. He entered Gethsemani in 1951. While in the scholasticate (where young monks are prepared for ordination to the priesthood), he

studied with Thomas Merton, whom he described as the best teacher he ever had. In 1956 Fr. John Eudes, O.C.S.O., accompanied Merton to St. John's Abbey in Collegeville, Minnesota, where Merton had an unpleasant encounter with psychiatrist Gregory Zilboorg. Merton was stunned, but rather quickly he recovered and found a more congenial therapist in James Wygal, whose office was in Louisville.

Abbot John Eudes Bamberger, O.C.S.O.

The abbot, Dom James Fox, decided that a psychiatrist was needed at the abbey, and Fr. John Eudes was sent to study this field in Washington, D.C. When he returned from his studies, he joined Merton, now master of novices, and Fr. Matthew Kelty to screen candidates who applied for admission to the monastery.

In 1971 Fr. John Eudes was chosen as abbot for the recently founded Abbey of Our Lady of the Genesee near Rochester, New York. He continued in this office for thirty years, resigning in 2001. He has been remarkably helpful to Merton scholars and devotees in his willingness to share his perceptive insights into Gethsemani's most distinguished monk. WHS

BAPTISM

Thomas Merton's first discussion of baptism is found in the vivid account of his own reception of the sacrament at Corpus Christi Church in Manhattan on November 16, 1938, as told in

The Seven Storey Mountain (222–23). There is relatively little analysis of the theological significance of the sacrament in his straightforward description of the ceremony, though he does mention the renewal of "the inward vision of God and His truth" in the profession of the creed; the symbolism of the salt and its association with wisdom, "the savor of divine things"; and the significance of the exorcism, the gift of the Spirit of God and the expulsion of impure spirits that had dominated his life before his conversion. His concern that his newly enlightened soul not be repossessed by darkness is echoed in subsequent comments about the need for perseverance: the awesome responsibility, initially unfulfilled, to live out the new life in the Spirit begun in baptism (226–27, 229).

In his discussion of baptism in numerous later writings, Merton particularly stresses that it is the gift of a new identity through a participation in the death and resurrection of Christ. The paschal meaning of the sacrament is rooted in the Pauline doctrine of baptism as an immersion in the death of Christ so as to share in the life of the risen Savior: "The Passion of Christ is communicated to us in Baptism, as a remedy for our sins as if we ourselves had died on the Cross. At the same time, in Baptism, the power of the Resurrection flows out into our souls bringing us a new life in Christ" (*New Man*, 204) (cf. Rom. 6:3–11). This identification with Christ also can be understood as sharing in a new creation with the new Adam, as passing from enslavement to liberation in a new exodus with the new Moses, as being drawn into "all the great works of God from the Creation to the Last Judgment" (203). Merton repeatedly emphasizes that this union with Christ is made possible by the gift of the Holy Spirit breathed out by Jesus on his followers on Calvary and in the Upper Room on Easter night: "Without the invisible mission of the Holy Spirit into the soul there would be no Baptism" (220). With the gift of the Spirit come the gifts of the Spirit, particularly wisdom and understanding, "part of the normal equipment of Christian sanctity... given to all in Baptism" (*What Is Contemplation?* 3), empowering one first of all to "prudent conduct of one's life, more than the repose of contemplation" (*New Man*, 218), but ultimately orienting the Christian toward a full participation in the Trinitarian life of selfless love. The ancient association of baptism with illumination focuses on the power to see reality as it actually is, "deep perceptions of the reality of spiritual things" (217), of the spiritual dimension of all created things, which have "recovered their translucency in the eyes of man made innocent and spiritual once again" (213). This restoration of spiritual sight can be extended to encompass a recovery through baptism of all the "spiritual senses," by which one is enabled "to penetrate, by mystical experience, through the veil of darkness and mystery that separates us from God" (215).

By sharing in the paschal mystery, Merton writes, one becomes oneself, discovers one's authentic identity in Christ: "The most fundamental question raised by Baptism is *man's true identity*" (211). This "new" identity is actually the self that one has been created to be by God but that had been obscured by the illusory disguises of self-created existence. Baptism "tells us we must become ourselves in Christ. We must achieve our identity in Him, with whom we are already sacramentally identified by water and the Holy Spirit" (*No Man Is an Island*, 134). Paradoxically, this self-discovery involves identification with the person of the risen Jesus: "We must be ourselves by being Christ," imaging the perfect image of God "by knowledge and by love" (134). At the same time, this connection with Christ in baptism is also a connection with all those other persons who likewise are joined actually or potentially with Christ. "We too, all of us, have been baptized into a single body by the power of a single Spirit, Jews and Greeks, slaves and free men alike.... And every man is, to the Christian, in some sense a brother. Some are actually and visibly members of the Body of Christ. But all men are potentially members of that body, and who can say with certainty that the non-Catholic or the non-Christian is not in some hidden way justified by the indwelling Spirit of God?" (*Life and Holiness*, 42–43). Thus, baptism has a profoundly social dimension that creates community, enlightens the baptized to recognize that community, and empowers them to live it out in their daily lives.

Merton often warns that the transformation brought about by baptism takes effect only with the willing cooperation of the one being baptized. He writes, "Baptism is not fruitful unless one means thereby to receive new life in Christ and to give himself forever to Christ....It means living up to the dignity of our new being in Christ. It means living as sons of God" (79). This involves, then, a process of growth and transformation, a lifelong, progressive actualizing of the gift that has been given once for all in the sacrament: "The rebirth of which Christ speaks is not a single event but a continuous dynamic of inner renewal. Certainly, sacramental baptism, the 'birth by water,' can be given only once. But birth in the Spirit happens many times in a man's life, as he passes through successive stages of spiritual development" (*Love and Living*, 199).

An extrinsic and largely moralistic understanding of baptism as a ritual necessary for salvation that entails following certain ethical precepts is considered by Merton to be a "naive" and immature grasp of the meaning of the sacrament and its place in Christian life. "The true Christian rebirth is a renewed transformation, a 'passover' in which man is progressively liberated from selfishness and not only grows in love but in some sense 'becomes love....' In the language of the mystics, there is no more ego-self, there is only Christ; self no longer acts, only the Spirit acts in pure love" (199). Here, the full meaning of baptismal participation in the redemptive passage of Christ through death to new life, "the maturity of the 'New Man,'" is described as unconditional availability to the action of the Spirit, "the illumination of Love shining by itself" (199). POC

SEE ALSO REDEMPTION; SACRAMENT.

BASIC PRINCIPLES OF MONASTIC SPIRITUALITY

Trappist, Ky.: Abbey of Gethsemani, 1957. 35 pp.

This booklet, published in 1957 as an Abbey of Gethsemani publication, was included in *The Monastic Journey* (1977) and published

again (with Merton photos illustrating the text) by Templegate in 1996. It represents Thomas Merton's effort to express the mystery of the monastic life. "The purpose of these notes," he tells us, "is to examine briefly the great theological principles without which monastic observance and monastic life would have no meaning" (*Monastic Spirituality*, 10).[1] He does suggest, though, that nonmonastics might well profit from the fundamental spiritual principles set forth in the book.

There are six chapters, with a foreword and an epilogue. The chapter headings are (1) "Whom Do You Seek?" (2) "The Word Was Made Flesh," (3) "The Word of the Cross," (4) "Children of the Resurrection," (5) "Sons and Heirs of God," and (6) "Spouse of Christ." The foreword is untitled; the epilogue is called "The Monk in a Changing World."

Monks spend their whole lives entering deeper and deeper into the mystery of the monastic life without ever fully exhausting its meaning. "The monk who ceases to ask himself: 'Why have you come here?' has perhaps ceased to be a monk" (15). According to St. Benedict, a monk is one who seeks God. He seeks God in Jesus Christ, who gives the power to become God's children. The meaning of the monastic life, therefore, flows from the mystery of the incarnation. For in Christ, God has revealed and given Godself to us. Because of the incarnation, we all live in a new world, a world that has been recapitulated in Christ. Because Christ entered into the world of God's creation, we must be able to see Christ in creation, "in the hills, the fields, the flowers, the birds and animals that He has created, in the sky and the trees" (32).

Creation is good, yet people have fallen from grace and the world has fallen with them. Sin has entered the world. Men and women have gone astray. Hence, we must seek Christ "not only as the Creator and exemplar of all things, but far more as the *Redeemer*, the Savior, of the world" (43). As Christ died on the cross to save us from sin, so we must accept the cross. St. Paul tells us that we seek Christ crucified as our redemption, our strength, our wisdom, our life in God (1 Cor. 1:23–24).

Redeemed by Christ, who died on the cross

and was raised for our salvation, we share in his risen life and therefore are "children of the resurrection." Still, while Jesus has delivered us from sin, we are not free from the weaknesses and concupiscence of the flesh. Having died to sin in baptism, we still must "put to death sin in our flesh by restraining our evil desires and bad tendencies. This is the basis for the life of monastic asceticism" (60). Yet asceticism is not merely negative. "The Benedictine ascesis of silence, obedience, solitude, humility, manual labor, liturgical prayer, is all designed to unite us with the mystical Christ, with one another in charity, and its aim to bring our souls under the complete dominance of the Holy Spirit" (66–67).

Thus the positive side of monastic asceticism is to empty oneself in order to arrive at purity of heart and life in the Holy Spirit as children of God and heirs of the kingdom. Liturgy, silence, manual labor, *lectio divina*, private contemplative prayer — all work together to deepen our life in Christ. "No one of them, by itself, can satisfy all the interior needs and aspirations of the monk's soul. No one of them must ever be allowed to crowd out the others. In all of them the monk seeks and finds Christ" (84).

The positive and negative aspects of monastic asceticism are summed up in the monastic vows. Merton speaks of five vows. Three are explicit: (1) stability, which binds a monk to a particular monastery and means renouncing the freedom to travel; (2) conversion of manners (*conversio morum*), which calls for a complete change of one's attitudes from those of the world to those of the cloister; and (3) obedience, whereby the monk renounces his own will in order to carry out the will of another who represents God. Implicit in the vow of *conversio morum* are the vows of poverty and chastity.

In chapter 6 Merton speaks of the monk as spouse of Christ, by which the monk seeks to live a virginity of spirit. "The virginity of spirit which keeps us united to the Word is the perfection of the monastic life. By it the monk not only renounces human marriage, but rather lays hands upon the supernatural and mystical reality of which marriage is only an external symbol — the union of love which joins the soul to God 'in one spirit'" (92). Spiritual virginity involves total acceptance of ourselves as God wills us to be and at the same time an emptiness and forgetfulness of oneself. "In order to be perfectly what God wants us to be, we must be truly ourselves. But in order to be truly ourselves, we must find ourselves in Christ — which can only be done if we lose ourselves in Him" (98–99).

In the epilogue Merton makes clear that the monk, even though he has left the world, cannot be completely unrelated to, or uninfluenced by, the world. Without belying the necessary withdrawal from the world implicit in the monastic vocation, Merton expresses the firm conviction that life in the cloister does not exempt the monk from responsibility for the world in which he lives. What this responsibility amounts to and how it is to be carried out will be a frequent theme in Merton's later writings. WHS

SEE ALSO PURITY OF HEART; VOWS, MONASTIC.

Notes

1. In this article, page citation numbers refer to the Templegate edition, which uses a larger type and runs to 125 pages.

BEHAVIOR OF TITANS, THE
New York: New Directions, 1961. 106 pp.

This book marks a definite departure from the content and tone of Thomas Merton's earlier works. Published by New Directions in 1961, it prepares the way for later works such as *Raids on the Unspeakable* and some of his later poetry. It contains literary works of different types, including myth, parable, a broadside, and reflective essay. The book is divided into three parts. Part 1, "The Behavior of Titans," consists of (1) "Prometheus" and (2) "Atlas and the Fat Man." Part 2, "The Guilty Bystander," includes (1) "Letter to an Innocent Bystander" and (2) "A Signed Confession of Crimes against the State." Part 3, "Herakleitos the Obscure," contains (1) "Herakleitos: A Study" and (2) "The Legacy of Herakleitos."

To the two titans of Greek mythology, Merton adds a modern titan, "Fat Man," the name given to the second atomic bomb dropped by the United States, the one on Nagasaki. The titans are at war with the established Olympian order where Zeus reigns supreme and where "no bird may chirp and no flower may look at the sun without the permission of the jealous father" (*Behavior of Titans*, 12). The titans and the Fat Man are archetypal figures of the struggle between the superpowers with results unknown and terrifying to reflect on.

The meditation on Prometheus is preceded by a brief note in which Merton contrasts the different ways in which Prometheus is portrayed by Hesiod, the Greek poet of the eighth century B.C.E., and Aeschylus, the Greek dramatist of the fifth century B.C.E. For Hesiod, Prometheus is the villain because he is a threat to the static order established by the patriarchal god, Zeus. In the Aeschylus version of the myth, it is Zeus, not Prometheus, who is the usurper. Prometheus's rebellion is "the rebellion of life against inertia, of mercy and love against tyranny, of humanity against cruelty and arbitrary violence" (14). "The Prometheus of Hesiod," Merton tells us, "is Cain. The Prometheus of Aeschylus is Christ on the Cross" (14). In his meditation, Merton presents Hesiod's view in order to reject it.

"Prometheus: A Meditation" was first privately published in a limited edition of 150 copies (1958) by Victor Hammer at the King Library Press, University of Kentucky, in Lexington. In Merton's meditation Prometheus becomes a type of all human beings, facing the abyss of their nothingness, the terror they face at having to be something. Thus, "the fire Prometheus thought he had to steal from the gods is his own identity," his own spiritual freedom. "Guilty, frustrated, rebellious, fear-ridden, Prometheus seeks to assert himself and fails. His mysticism enables him to glory in defeat. For since Prometheus cannot conceive of a true victory, his own triumph is to let the vulture devour his liver: he will be a martyr and a victim because the gods he has created in his own image represent his own tyrannical demands upon himself. There is only one issue in his struggle with them: glorious defiance in a luxury of despair" (18). To Prometheus the gods are enemies. The fire he must have to give

to humankind can be obtained only by stealing it from the gods. He did not realize that fire was his for the asking. It was a gift of the living and true God.

"No one," Merton writes, "was ever less like Prometheus on Caucasus than Christ on His Cross. For Prometheus thought he had to ascend into heaven to steal what God had already decreed to give him. But Christ, Who had in Himself all the riches of God and all the poverty of Prometheus, came down with the fire Prometheus needed, hidden in His Heart. And He had Himself put to death next to the thief Prometheus in order to show him that in reality God cannot seek to keep anything good to Himself alone" (21–22).[1]

In the essay "Atlas and the Fat Man," the titan, Atlas, who holds up the pillars of the universe and also of the mountain in Libya that was regarded as supporting the heavens, is a mythical and archetypal figure of Nature in its relationship to humans. People too often take the things of Nature for granted. Atlas speaks: "I do not tire easily, for this is the work I am used to. Though it is child's play, sometimes I hate it. I bear with loneliness for the sake of man. Yet to be constantly forgotten is more than I can abide" (29). The Fat Man, representative of the nuclear age, symbolizes the spiritual predicament of alienated humanity, a self-complacent and materialistic society that so often is terrifyingly abusive of Nature. Hiroshima, Nagasaki, and the Holocaust are examples of the grosser workings of the Fat Man. "Sad is the city of the fatman, for all his industry. Snow cannot make softer the city of the fatman, which is always black in its own breath. Rain cannot wash clean the city of the mercenary, which is always gray with his own despair. Light cannot make fair their houses or wine their faces, though they swim in millions they have won. The fatman with his inventions is propping up a fallen heaven" (38–39).

Yet the Fat Man's triumph is illusory. The time will come when "Life shall wake under ground and under the sea. The fields will laugh, the woods will be drunk with flowers of rebellion, the night will make every fool sing in his sleep and the morning will make them stand up in the sun and cover themselves with water and with light" (45).

The meditation on Prometheus and the myth of Atlas and the Fat Man are thoughtful poetic pieces that need to be revisited and savored.

"Letter to an Innocent Bystander" anticipates by two years Merton's "Letters to a White Liberal," and by five years his *Conjectures of a Guilty Bystander*. Addressed to intellectuals, it is a call for a dialogue that will face this question: Is nonparticipation a viable option in contemporary society? Merton puts the question this way: "Does the fact that we hate and resent tyranny and try to dissociate ourselves from it suffice to keep us innocent?" (55). Recalling the story "The Emperor's Clothes," he suggests that the very condition of our innocence requires that we speak out like the child and keep on saying that the king is naked.

The broadside, "A Signed Confession of Crimes against the State," is a delightful, whimsical piece in which Merton reduces to absurdity the power of the state over free persons. He confesses to being the worst kind of traitor to the state. For he dares to sit under a tree simply enjoying himself. He takes off his shoes and listens to a mockingbird. Sitting silently in the grass, he watches the clouds go by. Mockingly, he begs forgiveness of the state and signs a confession acknowledging his crimes.

The essay on Herakleitos the Obscure[2] picks up once again the theme of fire. This obscure fifth-century B.C.E. native of Ephesus left no writings of his own, but is quoted by later Greek writers. For him, fire was the primary substance of the cosmos. But it is more than material; it is spiritual and divine. "Our spiritual and mystical destiny is to 'awaken' to the fire that is within us, and our happiness depends on the harmony-in-conflict that results from this awakening" (76). The "philosophical viewpoint [of Herakleitos] is that of a mystic whose intuition cuts through apparent multiplicity to grasp underlying reality as *one*" (79). No wonder that Clement of Alexandria, Justin, and other early Christian writers saw him as "a 'Saint' of pre-Christian paganism" (77).

Merton closes his reflection on Herakleitos with his own version and arrangement of twenty of the "Fragments" composed by this obscure Ionian figure. Here is one example.

> xiii *All things change.*
> The sun is new every day.
> You cannot step twice into the same stream;
> for fresh waters are ever flowing upon you.
> (101)

WHS

SEE ALSO *PROMETHEUS: A MEDITATION; RAIDS ON THE UNSPEAKABLE.*

Notes

1. This quotation is strophe 7 in the meditation; the quotation in the previous passage is strophe 4. In August 1958 Merton sent a copy of the limited edition of "Prometheus" to Boris Pasternak. In October Pasternak responded, thanking Merton for the book and expressing his reaction that "strophes 4 and 7 are the most succeeded [sic], the last one containing fine individual Christosophical touches" (*Six Letters*, 8).

2. Czeslaw Milosz, in a letter to Merton in late 1960, expresses his "astonishment" at Merton's essay on Herakleitos and, having himself written about this Ionian figure, sees the essay as a "proof of our deep spiritual affinity" (*Striving towards Being*, 100).

BENNETT, THOMAS IZOD

Dr. Thomas Izod Bennett, a successful London physician, was a classmate of Owen Merton at Christ's College in Christchurch, New Zealand. In 1915 he visited Ruth and Owen Merton in Prades. Ruth mentions in "Tom's Book" that Bennett circumcised baby Tom (Ruth insisted that his name be "Tom," not "Thomas"), but she says nothing of baptism. Bennett was Owen's physician when he was hospitalized in London with an incurable brain tumor. After Owen's death, Bennett became Thomas Merton's guardian. When rumors reached him of Thomas's unruly life at Cambridge, he reprimanded him and eventually suggested that he return to America and to his maternal grandparents. WHS

BERRIGAN, DANIEL J.

Daniel J. Berrigan was born in Virginia, Minnesota, in 1921. His family moved to Syracuse, New York, where he received his early education. He joined the Society of Jesus and was appointed to Le Moyne College in Syracuse, where he taught from 1957 to 1963. Following a trip to Europe, he worked for three years as associate editor of *Jesuit Missions*. He helped found the Catholic Peace Fellowship in 1964. That same year he participated in a meeting of peace activists invited to Gethsemani by Thomas Merton. He and Merton had met and corresponded several years before this meeting. His radical involvement in antiwar activities earned him a period of "exile" in Latin America. On his return, his antiwar activities took him to Hanoi in 1968 to bring back three prisoners of war. That same year in May at Catonsville, Maryland, he participated, with his brother, Philip, and seven others, in the burning of draft records. The nine were imprisoned and then released on bail, with a trial set for October 5, 1968. Philip Berrigan wrote to Merton, who was in Alaska at the time, asking for his presence at the trial as a witness. In October 1968 the nine were convicted. Daniel Berrigan went underground for a time. He was apprehended by federal agents in August 1970, and was paroled in February 1972. Still very much involved in the cause of peace, Berrigan is in residence at a Jesuit house in New York City. WHS

SEE ALSO *HIDDEN GROUND OF LOVE.*

BIBLE

Thomas Merton's years in the monastery coincided with the remarkable renewal of Scripture studies in the Catholic Church, particularly in the post–World War II era. Merton's appreciation of this movement was somewhat slow in developing, but became quite marked in the final decade of his life. He was, of course, immersed in the Scriptures through the readings of the divine office and *lectio divina*, and made a special effort, during some periods at least, to read the Scriptures in conjunction with the cycle of the liturgy, so that the entire Bible would be read during the course of the year (*Entering the Silence*, 133). But as a student he was initially somewhat resistant to a focus on the literal sense, preferring the figurative readings of the patristic and monastic tradition. In November 1947 he observed, "Fr. Anthony [Chassagne] got to talking with impassioned emphasis in Theology class about

the great importance of the literal sense of Scripture, and I dare say he is right except that his stress seemed to throw the Fathers, and the *interesting* senses of Scripture, out the window. So it depressed me." He adds that if this approach requires that one pay attention to the minutiae of Hebrew and Greek grammar, then he wanted no part of it, and concludes, "Do you mean to say that the *literal* sense is what we have to look for in the Old Testament? It would make strange food for spiritual reading" (138–39). He is somewhat bemused by the advice of the Abbé Fillion, a Scripture scholar whose work he is reading in 1949, to study Hebrew, Greek, Aramaic, Itala, Arabic, Syriac, Assyrian, Ethiopian, Coptic, Armenian, Persian, Slavonic, Gothic, and the three principal Egyptian dialects, noting that after all that "you will come to the conclusion that Jonas in Nineveh sat down under a castor oil plant and became attached to its shade" (357). He is more receptive to the suggestion of "My pious Abbé Fillion" that when one is "stumped" about the meaning of a passage, one should pray to the sacred author for enlightenment, remarking that he feels closer to the biblical authors than to virtually any other writers (362). His typical, very traditional approach during this period is exemplified by his comments on the Book of Josue (Joshua), in which the five kings hung by Josue are equated to the disciplining of the five senses during Lent, and the stopping of the sun to the delay of the Final Judgment. The violence of the invasion of the Holy Land (the literal level) causes him no qualms, and he is able to say, "Josue is my favorite epic," preferred to Homer, Virgil, and *The Song of Roland* (413).

But there are signs of change in the early 1950s. Merton includes a section in *The Ascent to Truth* on "The Battle over the Scriptures" between the conservative "scholastics" and the progressive "scriptural" party in sixteenth-century Salamanca regarding the importance of the literal meaning of the Bible, and notes that St. John of the Cross, though not taking a direct part in the controversy, clearly sided with the scripturalists. "The most important effect of this," according to Merton, "was that Saint John of the Cross took great pains to respect the literal meaning of Scripture," though he was not technically trained in biblical languages and made mistakes at times, and though he continued to be interested in the "spiritual" sense of biblical passages (*Ascent to Truth*, 142). It would not be stretching a point too far to see Merton finding in John a model in this regard as in so much else. In his book on the psalms, *Bread in the Wilderness*, Merton cites approvingly the directive of Pope Pius XII in his groundbreaking encyclical *Divino Afflante Spiritu* (considered the charter for modern Catholic biblical studies) to use all available tools to determine what the biblical authors intended to say. "The chief task of the exegete is, of course, to discover the literal sense of the Scriptures," though always directed toward the purpose of leading "to a deeper and more accurate understanding of what God has revealed, for our salvation" (*Bread in the Wilderness*, 34). Throughout the book Merton distinguishes between the imaginative flights of allegory, which discards the literal sense, and the more sober approach of typology, which respects both the literal sense (of an Old Testament text) and its fulfillment in the new dispensation.

By the late 1950s Merton had become quite enthusiastic about the ways in which biblical scholars open up the text to new insights, citing with approval Catholic exegetes such as Gillet (*Search for Solitude*, 135) and Boismard (*Turning toward the World*, 71), and, beginning in 1960, Protestant scholars including C. H. Dodd (63), G. E. Wright (171), Werner Kümmel (*Water of Life*, 45), Amos Wilder (86), and particularly Rudolf Bultmann (52–53; *Opening the Bible*, 75). He has high praise for Old Testament theologians Gerhard von Rad and Walther Eichrodt, who are beginning to make evident "the greatness of the Old Testament" (*Guilty Bystander*, 121). Commenting on Heinrich Schlier's article "Eleutheria" in Kittel's *Theological Wordbook of the New Testament*, he calls it a "superb investigation of the relation of sin, death and works" (*Water of Life*, 91). By the mid-1960s he clearly has come to recognize that the sense of personal involvement he valued so highly in the traditional patristic and monastic exegesis is not neces-

sarily absent from a more critical approach to the Scriptures. He still finds a place for the traditional approach, but has come to recognize the "prophetic" dimension of Scripture, in the sense of "typology," as operating in a much looser way: "as witness to a central truth, rather than as linear prediction. If you say 'Because God first said this would happen, then made it happen, and because I can prove this from Scriptures, I am convinced,' you may have the whole thing backwards. ... On the other hand: 'This is what happened, and it is what God everywhere pointed to, it is the central event and all others gain their true meaning when this is seen,' then you have an access to the Scriptures in peace and contemplation" (247).

In a 1965 article for *The Bible Today* (a Catholic magazine begun three years earlier for a nonscholarly audience), Merton spells out his mature attitude toward the Scriptures. He rejects both a narrowly "scientific" approach that provides "a low-protein diet" for spiritual nourishment, and a fundamentalist literalism that ultimately distorts and confuses the Christian message. His point is that the best of both traditional and contemporary commentators treat the Scriptures not "as strict scientific history but as kerygmatic recitals embodying the inerrant truth of revelation" (*Love and Living*, 221). It is this focus on the kerygmatic, the proclamation that challenges the reader to respond not just intellectually but with the whole self, that Merton finds at the heart of any authentic reading of the Scriptures. He makes similar points in greater detail in *Opening the Bible*, written in the last year of his life as an introduction to the never published *Time-Life Bible*. He admits that the allegorical explanations of previous ages often had little objective validity, yet maintains that the commentaries of the church fathers "have a creative value of their own and often arrive at astonishing insights by roundabout ways" (*Opening the Bible*, 60). The influence of the Vatican II Constitution on Divine Revelation (*Dei Verbum*) is evident in his endorsement of the need to "respect the wide variety of literary forms and historical backgrounds, which give special characters to the separate books," and at the same time to "remember that the Bible as a whole can and should be seen as imparting a unified, or unifiable, theological message" (60–61). He respects the contributions of "the historico-critical method" in clarifying the meaning of the texts themselves, but warns that if one remains on this level and does not "make contact, by living commitment, with the challenging word that is addressed to us," the Bible will remain "curiously alien," a relic from a past and very different culture (62). Merton's response to the Bible thus shows a considerable evolution throughout his life; what remains constant, however, is his belief that "the Holy Spirit enlightens us, in our reading, to see how *our own lives* are part of these great mysteries — how we are one with Jesus in them" (*Monastic Journey*, 29). POC

SEE ALSO *BREAD IN THE WILDERNESS; OPENING THE BIBLE; PRAYING THE PSALMS.*

BOEHNER, PHILOTHEUS

A Franciscan priest, teaching philosophy at St. Bonaventure University, Fr. Boehner was a gifted scholar in biology and also in Franciscan philosophy and theology. He introduced Thomas Merton to Ockham's philosophical writings, and also to the writings of St. Bonaventure and Duns Scotus. In December 1941 he assured Merton that, contrary to what Fr. Edmund Murphy had said to him earlier in New York City, the moral lapses of his past life did not constitute an impediment that would prevent him from being a monk and a priest. This freed Merton to go to the Abbey of Gethsemani. On December 10, 1941, Merton took the train, bus, and taxi that brought him to the abbey. WHS

SEE ALSO MURPHY, EDMUND.

BRAMACHARI, MAHANAMBRATA

Bramachari (1904–99) was a Hindu monk sent by his monastery to the World Congress of Religions held in conjunction with the Chicago World's Fair. After the fair, he earned a doctorate in philosophy at the University of Chicago.

Seymour Freedgood's wife, who met him in Chicago, invited him to the family home on Long Island. He left there to come to New York City and Columbia. It was June 1938: Freedgood, Robert Lax, and Thomas Merton met him at Grand Central Station. In his autobiography Merton describes this meeting with this unconventional monk (*Seven Storey Mountain*, 194–98). Merton was struck by the fact that Bramachari never attempted to explain his own religion to him; and when Merton asked him about mystical writings, Bramachari told him, "There are many beautiful mystical books written by the Christians. You should read St. Augustine's *Confessions* and *The Imitation of Christ*." Looking back at this event, at the time he wrote *The Seven Storey Mountain*, Merton saw his contact with Bramachari as a special grace from God. They became friends, and when Merton traveled to Asia in 1968, he tried, but unsuccessfully, to get in touch with his Hindu friend of college days. WHS

BREAD IN THE WILDERNESS
New York: New Directions, 1953. 146 pp.

Thomas Merton first explored the relationship between the psalms and contemplation in a three-part series published in *Orate Fratres* (now *Worship*) in 1950.[1] These articles, revised and expanded, became a chapter in *Bread in the Wilderness*. Although Merton had completed the manuscript in 1950, New Directions did not publish *Bread in the Wilderness* until 1953. Contractual difficulties accounted for the delay. Harcourt, Brace had just published *The Ascent to Truth* and held rights for the publication of Merton's next book. Nevertheless, Merton promised and sent the manuscript to his friend James Laughlin at New Directions, then had to lobby for postponing publication until *The Sign of Jonas* had been published and marketed.[2] It was not the last time that Merton's inattention to contractual obligations created difficulty.

Merton's initial enthusiasm for the book seems to have dimmed by the time it appeared in print. In a letter to James Laughlin, written on September 28, 1952, Merton shared his doubts about the book: "Frankly I think I am wasting my time writing books like *The Ascent to Truth*. There are plenty of other people who can do that a lot better than I can. As for *Bread*, it looks to me like a botched piece of work, now that I see it all in one piece. . . . Your job of presentation will make up for most of its defects — I hope" (*Thomas Merton and James Laughlin*, 95). Indeed, it was a handsomely designed volume, printed in two colors, with text complemented by photographs (by J. Comet) of *Le Devot Christ*, a crucifix from a chapel adjoining the Perpignan cathedral in southern France. In a page-long reflection, Merton identifies this image of Christ suffering with the Christ of Isaiah and of Psalms; it is Christ of the Dark Night of John of the Cross, the Christ who "shares His agony with the mystics." It is also "the Christ of our own time — *the Christ of the bombed city and of the concentration camp. We have seen Him and we know Him well*" (*Bread in the Wilderness*, 1). Five full-page photographs of *Le Devot Christ*, each focused on part of the image and each marking the beginning of a chapter, keep drawing the reader back to the image of the suffering Christ. The stark images underscore Merton's reading of the Hebrew psalms as Christian prayer.

In addition to a prologue and an epilogue, the book contains five chapters: (1) "Psalms and Contemplation," (2) "Poetry, Symbolism and Typology," (3) "*Sacramenta Scripturarum*," (4) "The Perfect Law of Liberty," and (5) "The Shadow of Thy Wings." Each chapter is further divided into titled sections, thus creating a series of short reflections on each chapter topic. A final "Author's Note" contains a disclaimer. Merton writes that he intended to follow the norms of *Divino Afflante Spiritu*, the encyclical on biblical studies issued by Pope Pius XII. If, through "ignorance" or "stupidity," he has misinterpreted church teaching, he renounces the error. And he cautions his reader to regard any "spiritual" interpretations of Scripture with which they disagree as "a pious application of the text." Such caution and deference appear to characterize Merton's approach in the late 1940s and early 1950s. Uncharacteristic of Merton and so worth noting is the use of endnotes in this volume.

In the prologue, Merton extols the Book of Psalms as "the most *significant and influential collection of religious poems ever written*" and likens the psalms to bread given those who have followed Christ into the wilderness (3). The eucharistic analogy suggested by the title is intentional. Both word and sacrament feed and nourish those who consume them. Merton expects that the book will be of most value to those who pray the psalms as part of the divine office.

The book shows Merton linking two aspects of the monastic life: *opus Dei* (the divine office and liturgy) and contemplation (the intimate knowledge and experience of God). Praying the Psalter (commonly called the divine office) is as much *opus Dei* (work of God) as is the liturgy (celebration of the Eucharist). *Opus Dei* "opens to us the deep springs of interior contemplation" (13). Though the psalms do not "produce" contemplation, praying the psalms is a way to open one's self to God's gift of contemplation. In contemplation one knows God, intimately and experientially. The Psalter is "a school of contemplation" (107). The psalms "dispose" one for contemplation.

Merton distinguishes between the literal meaning of the psalms and their typical or typological sense. Though exegetes employ the tools of critical study to discover the literal meaning of the text, a fuller reading of the text requires the discovery of its spiritual sense revealed by God. Attention to typology leads to recognition of symbolism and identification of the types in Scripture — for example, David as a type of Christ. Merton sees that such a reading is appropriate because the psalms are poetry and, more particularly, because they are "religious" poetry, poetry that "springs from a true religious experience" (55). In the words of St. Augustine, the Scriptures are "sacraments" of God's word.

Merton's approach to the psalms is rooted in his firsthand experience of praying them in the weekly cycle required by the Rule of St. Benedict. When he wrote, "We bring our sorrows, our problems, our difficulties, and immerse them in the Psalms," he was reflecting his own experience of finding "all our spiritual problems mirrored" in the words of the psalmist (73). Entering into the psalms, a person is transformed by the Spirit, who speaks in them. The experience of the psalmist not only becomes but is our experience: "It is in chanting the Psalms that we too are leaving Egypt" (89). The inner transformation is reflected in our relationships with others: "We begin to see Christ now not only in our own deep souls, not only in the Psalms, not only in the Mass, but everywhere, shining to the Father in the features of men's faces. The more we are united to Him in love the more we are united in love to one another, because there is only one charity embracing both God and our brother" (92). "The secret of our fulfilment," Merton writes, "is charity." "The discovery of our true selves" is the discovery of our unity with Christ and with one another in Christ (93). This insight informs much of Merton's later writing on contemplation and in support of peace and justice.

Nevertheless, *Bread in the Wilderness* remains the work of the "early Merton." Merton was just beginning to become acquainted with the new biblical scholarship and still employed a reading of the Bible he learned from his reading of the church fathers.[3] His ecclesiology appears narrow,[4] as does his understanding of Eastern religions.[5] CMB

Notes

1. "The Psalms and Contemplation," *Orate Fratres* 24, no. 1 (July 1950): 341–47; no. 2 (August 1950): 385–91; no. 3 (September 1950): 433–40.

2. See "Letter to Sr. Therese Lentfoehr, S.O.S., November 28, 1950," in *The Road to Joy*, 205; *Thomas Merton and James Laughlin: Selected Letters*, passim.

3. Note Merton's use of a hermeneutic of typology. Also note that although Merton states that the inspired authors wrote in the language of their time and culture, he blurs the insight in this sentence: "When God inspired the author of *Genesis* with the true account of the creation of the world, the writer might, by some miracle, have set the whole thing down in the vocabulary of a twentieth-century textbook of paleontology" (59). Furthermore, the reference to the "true account of the creation" is unnuanced by any mention of myth.

4. For example, Merton proposes, "The whole meaning of human existence is in the hands of the Church" (41).

5. For example, see Merton's reference to the "pessimism" of the Buddha (61).

BREAKTHROUGH TO PEACE:
Twelve Views on the Threat of Thermonuclear Extermination
New York: New Directions, 1962. 253 pp.

Published in September 1962, this book was conceived by Thomas Merton and James Laughlin, publisher of New Directions, as a book by well-known authors that would highlight the danger and even the imminent possibility of nuclear war. Merton was to be the editor. Although he carried out all the responsibilities of an editor, he changed his mind about being so designated. The reason: in April of 1962 he had been ordered by the abbot general to cease writing about war and peace. As a result of this precaution the book has no editor. Merton contributed an introduction and an essay entitled "Peace: A Religious Responsibility."

In the introduction, Merton states that these essays, each in its own way, approach "the problems related to nuclear war with a freely questioning mind, in search of facts and principles." "They all share a common note of urgency and protest, and by that very fact alone they manifest their intention to continue fighting in defense of genuine democracy, freedom of thought and freedom of political action" (*Breakthrough to Peace*, 13–14).

The essay Merton contributed is actually one of a number of rewrites of what is perhaps the clearest statement of his position on nuclear war, "Nuclear War and Christian Responsibility," which appeared in *Commonweal*, February 9, 1962, and is published in *Passion for Peace*.

Other authors and their essays included in the volume: Lewis Mumford ("The Morals of Extermination"); Tom Stonier ("What Would It Really Be Like? An H-Bomb on New York City"); Norman Cousins ("Shelters, Survival and Common Sense"); Erich Fromm and Michael Maccoby ("The Question of Civil Defense: A Reply to Herman Kahn"); Howard E. Gruber ("Man or Megaperson"); Gordon C. Zahn ("The Case for Christian Dissent"); Walter Stein ("The Defense of the West"); Herbert Butterfield ("Human Nature and the Dominion of Fear"); Alan Forbes Jr. ("An Essay on the Arms Race"); Joost A. M. Meerloo ("Can

War Be Cured?"); Jerome D. Frank ("Breaking the Thought Barrier: Psychological Challenges of the Nuclear Age"). WHS

BUDDHISM

Although Thomas Merton frequently emphasized that Zen was not exclusive to Buddhism (see *Birds of Appetite*, 4, 45), his attraction to Zen led him to a sympathetic interest in and a deep sense of affinity for Buddhism in general. He writes to a correspondent in 1964, "I have no hesitation in saying that the 'Buddhist' view of reality and of life is one which I find extremely practical and acceptable. . . . It is by no means foreign or hostile to the spirit of Christianity, provided that the Christian outlook does not become bogged down in a slough of pseudo-objective formalities" (*Witness to Freedom*, 167–68). Part of the reason for this sense of compatibility is that Buddhism prescinds from the notion of positive revelation, so that there is no cause for conflict on the doctrinal level. The basic orientation of Buddhism is "toward an enlightenment which is precisely a breakthrough into what is beyond system, beyond cultural and social structures, and beyond religious rite and belief" (*Birds of Appetite*, 4–5). Buddhist concepts need to be approached, therefore, not in abstract metaphysical terms but in the context of concrete spiritual experience (*Mystics and Zen Masters*, 16). One needs to focus on the experience more than on the explanation (*Birds of Appetite*, 38).

Merton rejects and refutes stereotypes of Buddhism as quietistic, atheistic, and world denying. He points out the distortion of considering Buddhism "selfish" when the whole aim of Buddhism is to "overcome that attachment to individual self-affirmation and survival which is the source of every woe" (*Mystics and Zen Masters*, 8). He questions how a religion that "forbids the taking of *any* life without absolute necessity" can be considered life denying (*Birds of Appetite*, 16). He points out that the charge that Buddhism is either atheistic or pantheistic is beside the point, since "God is neither affirmed nor denied by Buddhism, insofar as Buddhists consider such affirmations and denials to be dualistic, therefore irrelevant to the main purpose

of Buddhism, . . . an ontological awakening to the ultimate ground of being" (*Mystics and Zen Masters*, 282). Much of the problem, according to Merton, came from poor early translations of Theravada Buddhist texts, which seemed to suggest that "the ideal is to spend one's earthly existence in a trance in order that after death one may pass away into pure nothingness" (*Birds of Appetite*, 81), a notion embraced and idealized by fashionable nineteenth-century Western pessimism. In fact, the Buddhist perception of emptiness is properly understood as limitlessness, and nirvana as the goal of the Buddhist path is not negation but "pure presence" (81), "the void which is Absolute Reality and Absolute Love" (86).

Merton considers the Buddhist diagnosis of the human dilemma to be remarkably insightful and accurate. It shares with Christianity the realization that people build their lives on a false relation to things, the *avidya*, or ignorance, that puts the ego at the center of its world and "refer[s] all things to it as objects of desire or of repulsion" (82). This fatal tendency to treat the empirical self as an absolute and to subordinate all other objects to it inevitably leads to suffering (*dukkha*) because it demands of things more than they can give (83). This craving or desire (*tanha*), including even the desire to attain *nirvana*, is the root of suffering, founded as it is on illusion (*Mystics and Zen Masters*, 239), above all the illusion of a "self" that is confirmed in its sense of its own being by the attainment of its desires: "The basic tenet of Buddhism is that an identity built on this kind of consciousness is false. Such a 'self' has no metaphysical status" (239). The Four Noble Truths of Buddhism are intended to show how to escape from this web of self-deception and "rediscover [one's] real roots in the true ground of all being" (*Birds of Appetite*, 84). In Merton's view, the Buddhist notion of *anatta*, the denial of selfhood, may well be understood in a way that is not incompatible with Christian personalism. He writes to Jacques Maritain in 1964, "I think that one of the most crucially important subjects to investigate today is the Buddhist metaphysic of the 'person,' which claims to be non-personal (*anatta*) but as a matter of fact might well be something completely unique and challenging. The *anatta* idea is simply a 'no' to the Hindu Atman as a pseudo-object or thought" (*Courage for Truth*, 45). While this interpretation may be open to question, it does provide an entry point for dialogue on a deep and meaningful level.

It is significant that when Merton selects texts to demonstrate that Buddhism is far from life denying, he chooses excerpts from all three major traditions, the Mahayana, the Theravada, and the Tibetan (*Birds of Appetite*, 93–95). Merton's acquaintance with the Mahayana tradition is most extensive, since that is the approach out of which Zen develops. He highlights the Mahayana emphasis on compassion (*karuna*), exemplified by the figure of the bodhisattva, who chooses to remain in the world of rebirth (*samsara*) until all sentient beings are saved, a focus that comes to the paradoxical recognition that the bodhisattva finds nirvana here and now, transcending the dualism between *nirvana* and *samsara*, by identifying everyone with the Buddha, whose nature, knowingly or unknowingly, they share (38, 87). His friend the Vietnamese monk Nhat Hanh articulates this insight that "Nirvana is not an escape from life, but is to be found right in the midst of 'life, suffering and death.' This is, of course, a modern expression of the pure Mahayana ideal, that of the Bodhisattva" (*Mystics and Zen Masters*, 287). It is this ideal that Merton evokes as he leaves for Asia when he prays that he may not return without having found "the great compassion, *mahakaruna*" (*Other Side of the Mountain*, 205), and that he realizes before the statues of the Buddha at Polonnaruwa: "Everything is emptiness and everything is compassion" (323).

Merton had much less contact with the more conservative, southern, Theravada tradition before coming to Asia, though in a May 20, 1964, letter to James Forest he does say, "The Hinayana (pardon, Theravada) group is getting into the picture with books now, Ceylon etc., they have the advantage of being clearer and less cloudy than Mahayana, serve as good starting points" (*Hidden Ground of Love*, 280). It was with monks of this tradition that he came in contact in Thailand and again in Ceylon, whereas he never got to Mahayana Japan. He

Standing Buddha at Polonnaruwa, photograph by Thomas Merton

does see some affinities between the Theravada emphasis on "being one's own lamp" and Zen's independence from the structures of tradition and ritual, though in both cases he emphasizes that this attitude is far from Western notions of self-reliance (*Mystics and Zen Masters*, 218–19). His contacts with Theravada monks lead to discussion and reading on mindfulness or insight meditation (*satipatthana, vipassana*) (*Other Side of the Mountain*, 211, 216), with which he had some previous acquaintance (*Learning to Love*, 95), and certainly deepened his respect for the Theravada tradition, though there does not seem to be a sense of profound engagement and excitement in these encounters; it is perhaps somewhat ironic, then, that the great experience at Polonnaruwa takes place in Ceylon, a Theravada nation.

The real discovery and excitement of the Asian pilgrimage, of course, is Merton's interaction with Tibetan Buddhism, which some consider a branch of Mahayana and others a third "vehicle," Vajrayana, the "Diamond Way." Though he had some personal contacts with this tradition and had done some reading on it, as late as July 1968 he writes in his journal, "As for Nepalese Buddhism, if it is like that of Tibet it is not exactly the kind I myself am most interested in, ferocity, ritualism, superstition, magic. No doubt many deep and mysterious things, but maybe it *needs* to disappear"; although he immediately adds, "I'd better suspend judgment on that. I hope to meet the Dalai Lama or someone like that at Darjeeling and find out more about it" (*Other Side of the Mountain*, 145–46). Having prepared himself by a rapid immersion course of reading, he does of course meet and bond deeply with the Dalai Lama. He establishes a warm rapport with numerous other Tibetan monks as well, particularly Chatral Rinpoche, with whom he "started talking about *dzogchen* and Nyingmapa meditation and 'direct realization' and soon saw that we agreed very well... all leading back to *dzogchen*, the ultimate emptiness, the unity of *sunyata* and *karuna*" (278) — again a discussion pointing forward to Polonnaruwa.

It is telling that in a dream a little more than a month before his death, Merton finds himself back at Gethsemani "dressed in a Buddhist monk's habit, but with more black and red and gold, a 'Zen habit,' in color more Tibetan than Zen.... I was a kind of Zen monk and Gelugpa together" (255) — but, significantly, back at his own monastery. For ultimately, Merton's encounter with Buddhism did not conflict with but deepened his own Christian identity, fulfilling the prediction he had written years earlier: "Properly understood, Buddhist concept of liberation should open me to Xt" (*Turning toward the World*, 212). As he put it in the final words of his Bangkok address, "The combination of the natural techniques and the graces and the other things that have been manifested in Asia and the Christian liberty of the gospel should bring us all at last to that full and transcendent liberty which is beyond mere cultural differ-

ences and mere externals — and mere this or that" (*Asian Journal*, 343). POC

SEE ALSO INTERRELIGIOUS DIALOGUE; MYSTICS AND ZEN MASTERS; VOID; ZEN; ZEN AND THE BIRDS OF APPETITE.

BURNS, THOMAS (FR. FLAVIAN)

Thomas Burns was born in Jersey City, New Jersey, on December 23, 1931. Some time after finishing high school, he read Thomas Merton's *The Seven Storey Mountain*. Like many young men of his time, he was deeply influenced by the book, and on January 30, 1951, at the age of nineteen, he became a monk of Gethsemani and received the religious name "Flavian." He was in the scholasticate when Merton was master of scholastics. He became a strong admirer of Merton and a friend. Ordained a priest in 1959, he was sent by the abbot, Dom James Fox, to study at Gregorian University in Rome. After his return, he was appointed master of scholastics and eventually prior of Gethsemani. In January of 1968, when Dom James retired as abbot, Fr. Flavian was called from his hermitage on the Gethsemani grounds (to which he had moved in 1966) to become Gethsemani's seventh abbot.

It was Fr. Flavian who gave Merton permission to go to Asia to address a gathering of monks and nuns at Bangkok. Eventually this permission was extended to enable him to visit India (where he visited the Dalai Lama) and other places in Asia. This was the trip that ended so abruptly and tragically with Merton's death in Bangkok on December 10, 1968. It was Fr. Flavian who received the news of Merton's death and gave the homily at the funeral mass, when the body was returned to Gethsemani.

On January 31, 1973, he resigned as abbot to return to his hermitage. In 1980 he was called to be temporary superior at the Berryville, Virginia, monastery of the Holy Cross. After a brief return to his hermitage, he was called to be acting superior at Ava, Missouri. Soon after, the monks at Berryville elected him as their abbot. He served there for six years, and in 1996 he resigned to become chaplain of the Trappistine monastery in Crozet, Virginia. WHS

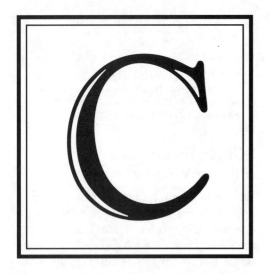

CABLES TO THE ACE,
or Familiar Liturgies of Misunderstanding
New York: New Directions, 1968. 60 pp.

A long sequence of eighty-eight numbered sections, with prologue and epilogue, half in verse and half in prose, published in the year of Thomas Merton's death, this work focuses particularly on the use and especially the abuse of language in an increasingly depersonalized, manipulative, coercive modern culture. Drawing on the theory and practice of his contemporary, the Chilean poet Nicanor Parra, some of whose work Merton had translated, much of *Cables to the Ace* consists of what Parra called "anti-poetry," an ironic, parodic feedback of the essentially meaningless jargon that passes for information and communication in modern, or perhaps early postmodern, mass society.

The poet immerses his readers in the cacophony of seemingly pointless verbiage in order to convince them, or rather allow them to convince themselves, that language has been violently wrenched from its true function to reflect and interpret reality; too often it has become a substitute for reality, all appearance

Cover for *The Collected Poems of Thomas Merton* reprinted with the permission of New Directions. Cover photograph by John Howard Griffin; cover design by Hermann Strobach.

and no substance, in order to facilitate social control and political oppression. But within the sequence itself there is a countermovement, tentative and hesitant at first but growing in clarity and intensity as the poem moves toward its conclusion, that suggests that a recognition of the distortions and manipulation of language can lead to a realization of the need for a contemplative stillness, which in turn makes it possible for words of truth, indeed for the Word who called himself the Truth, to be heard and answered.

The first half dozen sections serve as a kind of overture, introducing motifs that will be elaborated in greater detail as the sequence proceeds. Following the concluding sentence of section 2, "The sayings of the saints are put away in air-conditioned archives," that is, have been rendered safe and irrelevant to contemporary, desacralized society, section 3, a series of staccato comments suggesting one of the meanings of the term "cables" in the title, goes on to describe and exemplify the reductive functions of language that have replaced "the sayings of the saints." Rather than a medium for developing relationships and expressing personal commitment, language has been reduced to a self-referential, closed system of passive impersonality in which "The saying says itself" and "No one need attend" (i.e., "be present" and/or "pay attention"). The result is fragmentation and isolation, emblematized by the enclosed space of the automobile, the "small blue capsule of indignation" that is both protection from the outside world and at least potentially a weapon against it. That this hostility can be turned against language itself is suggested by the final parenthetical comment, "Some of the better informed have declared war on language," an uncannily prophetic foreshadowing of the age of deconstruction still to come.

While the poet sees the distortion and manipulation of language as a primary characteristic of the contemporary world, it is by no means unique to the present but endemic to the human condition. In section 7, a lyric lament entitled "Original Sin (A Memorial Anthem for Father's Day)," the poet both satirizes the pretensions of scientific rationalism, which tries to find the answers to the human predicament in an exclusively materialistic examination of human origins, and suggests an alternative, mythic explanation of the fall as the degradation of the Edenic ability to *name,* symbolized by Adam's beating of "the words he offended." The fall is a descent into deception, illusion, and incoherence, aptly represented by the babble of commercial and bureaucratic jargon of the modern wasteland that dominates the sections that follow, ranging from the sinister demands of totalitarian dictators for complete conformity (no. 21) to the apparently more trivial but ultimately just as dehumanizing cultural conformity of advertising, with its claims to sell not only a product but an identity (no. 43).

In the midst of this continual verbal overstimulation that characterizes the modern world, the poet makes repeated efforts to recover a sense of authentic meaning. In section 38, he counsels a journey of self-discovery that rejects conformity and recognizes and cherishes the mystery of personal identity: "Follow the ways of no man, not even your own. The way that is most yours is no way." But at this stage the power of social control is still too strong to sustain this independence; the banality of the social world reasserts itself in the nonsensical memo of section 40, "Good Morning! Address more inspections to the corporate tunnels. Yours truly," and the voice of

the poet is once again submerged in the noise that surrounds him. In section 53, poetry itself is proposed as an antidote to the misuse of language: "I think poetry must / I think it must / Stay open all night / In beautiful cellars." But art by itself is not strong enough to support meaning; it is too easily co-opted by commerce, as the phrase "beautiful cellars" degenerates into "the crowd of beautiful callers" found "in this temple of spenders," and again "one more wild hope dies of affliction" (no. 58).

Despite the frustration that results from these attempts to escape, articulations of this countermovement increase in frequency in the final third of the sequence. In section 62 the speaker quotes the instructions of the Zen master Dōgen to clear oneself of the clutter of distractions, becoming "empty of your own will and of your own ideas," only to remark ruefully, in a passage that almost certainly reflects Merton's ironic sense of his own limitations, that "He claims his light is out and secretly turns it on again to read novels. He builds a big fire to keep beginners warm: give him credit for his kindness." Again the breakthrough is abortive, but the potential for transcending the pseudo-meanings of a packaged culture more and more take over the poem as it moves toward its conclusion. In section 74 the possibility of authentic poetic expression is once more raised, first negatively, a rejection of the stereotypical picture of the poet as someone who "captures" external reality in words and images ("O God do I have to be Wordsworth / Striding on the Blue Fells / With a lake for sale and Lucy / Locked in the hole of my camera?"), and then positively as an exploration and articulation of mystery: "Better to study the germinating waters of my wood / And know this fever: or die in a distant country / Having become a pure cone / Or turn to my eastern abstinence / With that old inscrutable love cry / And describe a perfect circle." The reference to the "inscrutable love cry" leads in turn to a series of meditations on love as pathway to freedom and transcendence, though an ambiguous one, as it is left unclear whether the lovers who "teach April stars / To riot rebel and follow faithless courses" (no. 78) are to be understood as preaching liberation from a counterfeit or an authentic order. Love in and of itself is not a self-sufficient guide in a fallen world. It is not until section 80 that a definitive turning point is reached, as "Slowly, slowly / Comes Christ through the garden," both Eden and Gethsemane, to arouse the "lost disciple," who "will awaken / When he knows history," when he no longer confuses illusion with reality.

The sequence itself has functioned as the instrument of such an awakening: by pushing the abuse of language to the point of absurdity, by exposing, not just parodying, the meaningless babble of contemporary discourse, the poet has cleared the way for a movement into the silence and emptiness of contemplation. The poem has demonstrated that the failures of language, once recognized, can prove to be as adequate a starting point for contemplative realization as any other. If symbolism is a kind of *via positiva* that points beyond itself to transcendent experience, "anti-poetry" can function as a *via negativa* that impels one to silence by inducing revulsion from its meaningless cacophony. Yet in this silence, the true word once again can be heard and spoken, and one can discover anew one's own true name. This is what takes place in the concluding sections of the sequence.

The very next section affirms both the value and the limitation of language: words are a necessary but insufficient path to meaning: "Not to be without words in a season of effort. Not to be without a vow in the summer of harvest. What have the signs promised on the lonely hill? Word and work have their measure, and so does pain. Look in your own life and see if you find it" (no. 81). The active dimension, "word and work," is balanced by the passive, the necessity of suffering, reflected particularly by the signs on the "lonely hill" of Calvary, where the Christ who first appeared in the previous section provides the pattern of self-emptying, the paschal *kenosis* that leads to the fullness of life. The difficulties and possibilities of an authentic response to this invitation are exemplified in section 82, which describes the futile efforts of "the prelates, mayors, and confessors" to institutionalize the mystical love of Teresa of Avila, who, "Forgotten by these entranced jokers turned her

heart into a dove" that "had flown into the fiery center of the vision." Here, then, is the paradigm of self-transcendence that is also a transcending of all the limitations imposed by a society devoted to control by deception and illusion.

In the section entitled "Solemn Music" that follows, an opening has been created in which authentic voices, speaking true words, once again can be heard: "And go to meet / In the wet estranged country / The midnight express / Bringing Plato, Prophets, Milton, Blake." But ultimately the guidance and wisdom of others cannot substitute for one's own solitary exploration: "But use your own numbered line / To go down alone / Into the night sky / Hand over hand / And dig it like a mine" (no. 83). Only in this way will one encounter the "Total poverty of the Creator . . . a point of nowhereness in the middle of movement, a point of nothingness in the midst of being: the incomparable point, not to be discovered by insight" (no. 84). Only in this way can one hear the "true word of eternity" that "is spoken only in the spirit of that man who is himself a wilderness" (no. 86). Only in this way can one discover that one already holds the winning card, the lowest that is also the highest, and with the poet "walk away from this poem / Hiding the ace of freedoms" (no. 87). POC

CALLIGRAPHIES

Thomas Merton produced a series of abstract drawings, with brush and black ink, twenty-six of which were first exhibited at Catherine Spalding College in Louisville in November 1964. "I gave them names and prices, not without guilt feelings (perpetuating a hoax?). But the drawings themselves I think are fairly good," Merton wrote in his journal (*Water of Life*, 157). He intended funds earned from sales of the drawings to support a scholarship "for a Negro girl student," as he explained to his friend Ping Ferry (*Hidden Ground of Love*, 220). However, sales were less than brisk and the monastery funded the scholarship (see *The Road to Joy*, 133).

Merton's drawings — it is unclear just how many he made — also were exhibited in cities across the country, including New Orleans, Atlanta, Milwaukee, St. Louis, Santa Barbara, and Washington, D.C. The Washington exhibit, arranged by a local poet, was to have included some welded sculptures made by prison inmates. When Rosemary Radford Ruether reported that the poet's "elaborate plans" for the exhibit had not materialized by the end of 1967, Merton gave the drawings to Ruether's parish "to do what you want with them" (*Hidden Ground of Love*, 515; *At Home in the World*, 96). Ruether picked up twenty-nine drawings and, after Merton's death, arranged for them to be sold. "Feeling committed to carry out his request that they not be exploited commercially, but used for some social good, I used most of them for an auction to raise money for the Berrigan Defense Fund that was defending Dan and Phil Berrigan against an absurd U.S. government effort to indict them on conspiracy charges" (*At Home in the World*, xix). Ruether kept one of the drawings, which has been reproduced in *At Home in the World*, a collection of the Merton/Ruether letters.

Calligraphy by Thomas Merton

Both Merton's delight in the calligraphies and the fact that he did not take them too seriously are apparent in his comments about the drawings in letters to friends. In a letter to James Forest in December 1963, Merton mentioned sending him a few "scrawls," noting that "they may or may not look good" but "make sense" for him to do (*Hidden Ground of Love*, 278). He told Forest that "the scrawls"

are "some strictly safe abstract art" in which he can say what he wants "perfectly freely because nobody knows what any of it means anyway (for the simple reason that none of it has that kind of a meaning)" (277–78). Encouraging Ethel Kennedy to try to arrange a showing in Washington of "forty-three extremely way-out and abstract drawings," Merton argued, "With the drawings in Washington you can go and see them and thus you can pick one, and then you will have the non-distinction of owning 'a Merton.' And if you have a good attic, you will not have too much trouble storing it" (448). But when it came to his friend Victor Hammer, Merton worried that the artist would be "shocked" if he heard news of the exhibition. "I feel like writing to him and saying: If you heard I had taken a mistress you would be sad but you would understand. These drawings are perhaps worse than that. But regard them as a human folly. Allow me at least, like everyone else, at least one abominable vice etc." (*Water of Life*, 162). Merton was much more subdued and a bit apologetic in the letter he actually wrote to Hammer, telling his friend to "ignore" the news of his "exhibiting strange blobs of ink in Louisville. . . . I think I have made it plain to all concerned that I do not regard it as 'art' and that they are not supposed to either" (*Witness to Freedom*, 10).

Merton had been modest about calligraphies from the first. He had entitled some calligraphies "Shamanic Dictation" when he sent them to Meg Randall and Sergio Mondragón, editors of *El Corno Emplumado* in Mexico, in 1963 and then asked them to drop the "rather cheap and misleading" title (*Courage for Truth*, 216). The calligraphies "should lay no claim to being anything but themselves. . . . Each time one sees them is the first time. Each stroke is so to speak first and last, all goes in one breath, one brushful of ink, and the result is a statement of itself that is 'right' insofar as it says nothing 'about' anything else under the sun . . . just call them calligraphies" (217).

Fifteen calligraphies were reproduced in *Raids on the Unspeakable*, published in 1966. "Signatures: Notes on the Author's Drawings," written in 1964 to accompany the exhibition at Catherine Spalding College in Louisville and originally entitled "Notes by the Artist for an Exhibit of His Drawings," is included in *Raids on the Unspeakable*. "These abstractions — one might almost call them *graffiti* rather than calligraphies — are simple signs and ciphers of energy, acts or movements intended to be propitious" (*Raids on the Unspeakable,* 180). They are not conventional signs and have no assigned reference. They simply "came to life when they did" as "notes of harmony" and "Summonses to awareness, but not 'awareness *of*'" (181). Merton concludes simply, "The only dream a man seriously has when he takes a brush in his hand and dips it into ink is to reveal a new sign that can continue to stand by itself and to exist in its own right, transcending all logical interpretation" (181–82). CMB

SEE ALSO DRAWINGS, REPRESENTATIONAL.

CAMALDOLESE

A few weeks before his Easter retreat at Gethsemani in 1941, Thomas Merton went to the library to read about the Trappists. From the *Catholic Encyclopedia* he not only learned that the Trappists were Cistercians but also "came across the Carthusians" and saw "a great big picture of the hermitages of the Camaldolese" (*Seven Storey Mountain,* 316). Although Merton decided to become a Cistercian, he continued to be attracted to eremitical orders such as the Carthusians and the Camaldolese.

In the late 1940s Merton had thought about being a Carthusian; in the mid-1950s he was considering the possibility of joining the Camaldolese. In a letter to Fr. Barnabas M. Ahern, C.P., Merton summarized his situation this way: "I have been fretting over this question for some nine years, Father. No matter how hard I have tried to convince myself, I have never really succeeded in quite believing that the ordinary routine of Trappist life is exactly what I am called to. It is just 'not *it.*' With me it does not *work*" (*School of Charity,* 51). Merton longed for deeper solitude: "To be alone, with real silence, real solitude without material responsibilities, and able to really sink into God, straightens everything out" (51).

In April 1955 Merton had written to Dom Jean Leclercq, telling him that the community at Camaldoli d'Arezzo was willing to receive him, but he feared that his abbot, Dom James Fox, would block the move. He peppered Jean Leclercq with questions such as whether the monks "truly live a contemplative life at Camaldoli," whether it would be better to go to Camaldoli or Frascati or, if not to either, where he could "find an analogous eremitical life" (84). In May 1955 Merton actually applied for a *transitus,* or transfer, to Camaldoli. When Dom Jean Leclercq discouraged the idea, Merton said he "practically gave it up, making a grab instead for Frascati" (*Search for Solitude,* 311). On June 3, 1955, he wrote to Jean Leclercq that Dom James "proposed to place before higher Superiors the possibility of my becoming a hermit in the forest here" (*School of Charity,* 85). On the same day, he wrote to Dom Maurizio Levy-Duplatt, E.C., at Sacro Eremo Tuscolano at Frascati, Italy, to inquire whether he would be accepted there (87). In August 1955 he reported to Jean Leclercq that Frascati would be willing to receive him and that there is a "real chance of my being allowed to live in solitude here," perhaps in a small cabin at the foot of a fire tower to be erected on one of the monastery's hills. Merton's request for a *transitus* to Camaldoli was denied, permission to go to Frascati was refused, and in September 1955 Merton was appointed master of novices. The crisis of stability was resolved (for the time being), as Merton indicated in a letter to Dom Gabriel Sortais, the Cistercian superior general: "I am now quite convinced that God does not want me to be a Camaldolese" (92).

In July 1959, as Merton was considering going to Latin America to live as a monk in simplicity and greater solitude, he looked back at his efforts, four years earlier, to go to Camaldoli. Reading his correspondence of 1955, he realized that it was "a frightening and disheartening mess . . . What could have been very simple was turned into a sickeningly complicated and futile jamboree, partly through my own fault and partly through the stubborn and adroit politics of my superiors" (*Search for Solitude,* 311). He thought that his superiors were ready to let him be a hermit at Gethsemani, "but I realized that this would never work" and the appointment as novice master was "a compromise" (311).

Now, as he was making plans to go to Latin America, he drew a lesson from his experience in 1955: to "keep my mouth shut, not write a lot of letters, pray and *wait*" (311).

Merton wrote about the Camaldolese in *The Silent Life,* published in 1957, devoting a chapter to the eremitical order founded by St. Romould in 1012 in a high valley in the Appenines. The monks' cells, set at a distance of twenty or thirty feet from one another, are clustered around a church. "The hermits live, read, work, eat, sleep and meditate in their cells but gather for the canonical hours in the Church" (*Silent Life,* 149). Like the Carthusians, the Order of Camaldoli realizes that "the best way to foster interior silence is to preserve exterior silence, and the best way to have interior solitude is not to be alone in a crowd but to be simply and purely alone" (149). The Camaldolese hermit may even be permitted to become a recluse, to live "absolutely alone and undisturbed" (153), joining the community only three times a year. Merton was intent on pointing out that the Camaldolese are "true sons of St. Benedict" (154) and on showing that the hermit life, rooted in the tradition of the desert fathers, has a legitimate place in contemporary monastic life. CMB

SEE ALSO CARTHUSIANS.

CAMBRIDGE, UNIVERSITY OF

This renowned institution of higher learning is located in the city of Cambridge, Cambridgeshire, in central England on the Cam River. It is made up of faculties, departments, and colleges. The university carries out many of the administrative functions. The colleges provide students with rooms and meals, tutors, and a variety of social, cultural, and athletic events. The academic year has three terms of eight weeks each. Three years of residency are required to earn a degree of Bachelor of Arts. The university also confers a number of graduate degrees.

Cambridge was a center of Renaissance learning and of Reformation theology. In modern times it has excelled especially in science.

One of its outstanding colleges is King's. Behind King's and to its left is Clare College,

Clare College Court, Cambridge, England

where Thomas Merton spent the academic year of autumn 1933 to spring 1934. WHS

CARDENAL, ERNESTO

Nicaraguan poet, priest, and revolutionary Ernesto Cardenal was a novice under Thomas Merton at Gethsemani in 1957–59. Through conversation with Cardenal, Merton deepened his understanding of Latin American culture, literature, and politics and developed contacts with a host of Latin American writers, including Pablo Antonio Cuadra. Merton and Cardenal began corresponding in 1959 after Cardenal returned to Latin America, and the two continued exchanging letters until Merton's death in 1968. Merton's letters to Cardenal document Merton's ongoing fascination with Latin America, his dream of going to live there as a monk, and his enthusiasm for Our Lady of Solentiname, the contemplative foundation that Cardenal founded in Nicaragua in 1965. Merton's letters to Ernesto Cardenal are published in *The Courage for Truth* (110–63). "A Selection of Letters from the Earliest Correspondence of Thomas Merton and Ernesto Cardenal" appears in *The Merton Annual* 8 (1995): 162–200. In 1998 Cardenal published his exchange of letters with Merton in *Del Monasterio al Mundo: Correspondencia entre Ernesto Cardenal y Thomas Merton (1959–68).*[1] CMB

Notes
1. Santiago: Editorial Curato Propio, 1998.

CARTHUSIANS

While he was making his Easter retreat at the Abbey of Gethsemani in April 1941, Thomas Merton talked with a Carmelite priest who told him about the Carthusian monks at Parkminster Abbey in England. "There were no longer any pure hermits or anchorites in the world: but the Carthusians were the ones who had gone the farthest, climbed the highest on the mountain of isolation that lifted them above the world and concealed them in God" (*Seven Storey Mountain*, 327). Merton goes on to compare the communal life of the Cistercians with the solitary life of the Carthusians, who worked, slept, and ate alone: "All day long and all night long, except for the offices in choir and other intervals, the Carthusian was with God alone. *O beata solitudo!*" (327). Citing the war and his own "lack of a vocation," Merton declared the Carthusians "doubly out of reach" (328). Back in New York, Merton returned to the Carthusian "dream." But there was no Carthusian monastery in America and going to Europe was out of the question.

The "dream" became a "temptation" for the young Trappist monk, who in the late 1940s and early 1950s struggled with whether he should remain at Gethsemani or leave to join the Carthusians or the Camaldolese. Merton's journal, including the selections he himself made for *The Sign of Jonas,* and his correspondence record his attraction, preoccupation, and attempts to become a Carthusian. Merton himself characterizes his thoughts and efforts as "temptations" against stability, the vow by which a monk promises to remain in one monastery for the rest of his life. His hunger for ever deeper solitude fueled the temptation to join an order in which he might live the life of a hermit. By comparison with the Carthusians and the Camaldolese, the Abbey of Gethsemani was, in the later 1940s, overcrowded and afforded Merton little of the solitude he was seeking.

In the opening pages of *The Sign of Jonas,* which begins in December 1946, Merton is already reporting his complaints to Dom Frederic Dunne that he is making no progress at Gethsemani and thinking he ought to be a Carthusian or "an outright hermit" (*Sign of Jonas,* 19). Dom

Frederic counsels him to read Carthusian writers and "make use of anything of value that they say," and, if he is tempted "to run off to the Charterhouse," to "treat that desire like any other movement of disordered appetite and not get upset about it" (20).

On April 29, 1947, Merton reports that he has been corresponding with a Carthusian from Parkminster, and on May 23 he notes that he has received from Parkminster three volumes of the meditations, which he later remarks are "full of simple and practical ideas about the contemplative life" (44, 49, 54). On August 15 he is enthralled with pictures of Charterhouses that he finds in the library and learns that a former retreat master had become a Carthusian (61). But in December 1947 Merton reports, "At the end of the retreat I had suddenly lost all taste for becoming a Carthusian. . . . It is no longer permitted to me to waste, in such a dream, the precious hours of my monastic life, given me by God" (79). However, in October 1948 Merton is again confiding "his temptations to become a Carthusian" to Dom Frederic, who tells Merton that "he doesn't see why things can't be fixed up right here" (123). In December 1948 Merton says that the temptations have "more or less subsided." Dom James Fox, the new abbot, exacted a formal declaration that Merton would not "run off and be a Carthusian" before his ordination to the subdiaconate (137) and arranged for him to do his work in the rare book vault with "a spark of encouragement, 'Maybe this is the solution to your problem,' i.e., the Carthusians" (147). In the spring of 1949 Merton was corresponding with Dom Porion, the procurator general of the Carthusians in Rome,[1] about the possibility of an American foundation and found himself "accepting the idea that perhaps I do not have a purely contemplative vocation. I say 'accept.' I do not *believe* it" (175). At the end of 1949 he declared his dream of becoming a Carthusian "all over now" (261). A little more than a year later, when he was appointed master of scholastics, Merton saw that resisting the temptation to become a Carthusian was a way "to learn how to help all the other ones who would be one way or another tempted to leave the monastery" (329).

The Carthusians were founded by St. Bruno, who in 1084, with six companions, moved to a site in the Alps near Grenoble. There they built the first Carthusian monastery, the Grande Chartreuse. Merton makes passing reference to the Carthusians in *The Waters of Siloe*, published in 1949, and he devotes an entire chapter to a description of the Carthusian life in *The Silent Life*, published in 1957. Merton's description of Carthusian life reflects his own enthusiasm. St. Bruno and the group he led became "hermits who would bring back to life something of the forgotten purity of the contemplative life as it was once led in the deserts of Egypt" (*Silent Life*, 127). As he notes the "special peculiarities" of Carthusians, Merton points to elements of Carthusian life that especially appealed to him. Carthusians live almost entirely in "the solitude of the monk's cell," which are hermitages or small cottages united by a common cloister of the Charterhouse. Merton describes the monk's cell and routine in such detail that one can imagine Merton living the life. The Carthusian spirit is one of "solitude, silence, simplicity, austerity, aloneness with God" (135). And although Carthusians have eschewed any work that would bring them into contact with the world, they have engaged in copying manuscripts and writing books. Merton names two great Carthusian writers, Guigo and Denis the Carthusian, who wrote some forty volumes and who, Merton observes, "could write a book on any subject, much as a pious housewife might knit a sweater or a pair of socks" (138). Might not the same be said of Merton? Merton concludes his chapter with a few paragraphs on the American Carthusian foundation at Whitingham, Vermont, called Sky Farm, founded in 1951. He warns that it will have to "meet the great temptations which this country offers to all the monastic orders — publicity, technology, popularity, commercialism, machines and the awful impulsion to throw everything overboard for the sake of fame and prosperity" (144). CMB

SEE ALSO CAMALDOLESE; MONASTICISM.

Notes

1. For Merton's letters to Dom Porion, and also to Dom Humphrey Pawsey, see *The School of Charity*.

CATCH OF ANTI-LETTERS, A: *Thomas Merton, Robert Lax*

Kansas City, Mo.: Sheed, Andrews and McMeel, 1978. viii+128 pp.

This is a collection of sixty-six letters from the 1960s between Thomas Merton and Robert Lax that Merton gathered and edited, but which did not find a publisher until ten years after his death. The two friends had corresponded since shortly after their graduation from Columbia in 1938, but were able to exchange letters only infrequently from the time Merton entered Gethsemani in December 1941 through the late 1950s. But over two hundred letters (of a total of 346, now published complete in *When Prophecy Still Had a Voice*) survive from the last decade of Merton's life, most marked by witty allusiveness and obscure wordplay as well as by the friends' deep love for the world and one another, shared concern for spiritual and social transformation, and common commitment to avant-garde poetry.

As early as February 1965 Merton proposed collecting a representative sample of their letters for possible publication in a *New Directions Annual* (*When Prophecy*, 295). He first mentions the project to James Laughlin in a February 25 letter (*Thomas Merton and James Laughlin*, 260), though the letters still have not been sent by March 19 (261). By April 28 Merton has sent the typescript to Laughlin (*When Prophecy*, 301), but in May Merton responds to Laughlin that he trusts the latter's judgment about "not publishing the letters to Lax" (*Thomas Merton and James Laughlin*, 263; see *When Prophecy*, 305). But the project does not die. In June 1967 Merton writes that he has sent the letters to another prospective publisher (*When Prophecy*, 365, 366), and a selection of the letters appeared in the journal *Voyages* in January 1968 (380). This encouraged the duo to keep trying, and in February Merton reports that Teo Savory of Unicorn Press might be interested in publishing a small edition of fifteen hundred copies, but that it would need to be subsidized (382, 384). Lax still hoped for a more commercially viable publishing arrangement (*When Prophecy*, 385, 386–87, 402; *Thomas Merton and James Laughlin*, 339), but none emerged before Merton's death, though the project is still being discussed as late as August (*When Prophecy*, 409, 410).

The title of the volume provides a good indication that this is no ordinary collection of correspondence. "Anti-Letters" indicates a comparison with the aesthetically subversive "anti-poetry" that Merton was translating from the Chilean poet Nicanor Parra and composing himself in what would become *Cables to the Ace*; "Catch" suggests something that might be fished up, or perhaps caught "on the fly," but also probably a pun on "cache," a hidden treasure trove where one would need to dig beneath the surface to find what is of value. The letters, filled with aliases and pseudonyms, invented and stolen, such as "Captain Belsford," "Commodore Perry," "Moon Mullins," "Chretien de Troyes," "Harpo," and "Henry Clay," certainly "cast our awful solemnity to the winds," as Merton recommends in the final chapter of *New Seeds of Contemplation* — though whether the sometimes hermetically obscure references could be considered part of "the general dance" is more problematic (297).

As finally published, the collection is composed of two parts: twenty-seven letters from 1962–64 (thirteen by Merton) and thirty-nine letters from 1965–67 (eighteen by Merton). This constitutes somewhat less than half of the letters exchanged between the two friends during these years (a total of 151), though in some cases parts of the letters were omitted for reasons of privacy or in certain instances "delicacy." The exchange begins about the time of Lax's removal to the Greek islands. Much of the early correspondence included in the collection concerns this relocation. Lax had applied for a Guggenheim grant (which he did not receive) to fund his original stay in Greece, and asked Merton for a letter of recommendation (*Catch of Anti-Letters*, 3), which leads to a good deal of high-spirited badinage in which Merton demands bribes, in increments of fifty dollars, for concealing Lax's supposed scorn for formal education and "contempt for the Greed's eppig Homware, Suffoelits, Europates, Askils" (i.e., the Greeks' epic Homer, Sophocles, Euripides, Aeschylus), and claims to think that Lax, then at the Athens home of art historian Alexan-

der Eliot, is "staying with the very Eliot of cats. No, no. it has not come to this!" (a reference to T. S. Eliot's *Old Possum's Book of Practical Cats*, much later to achieve fame in another form on Broadway) (4, 5). This first exchange of letters sets the tone for much of what follows. Lax continues to report on his stay in the islands, which is to last until almost the end of his life ("this patmos is a splendid place. at first you wld think so, then you would not, then you would think so again" [14]), while Merton provides news from the monastery (e.g., his recuperation from a disk operation, reading George Herbert while lying on a hot water bottle [22]) and the country (e.g., the 1963 march on Washington for civil rights [17, 26]). They exchange reports about old friends and classmates, reminisce about the past and commiserate about the present, and continually encourage one another in the creative work that they pass back and forth enthusiastically — all communicated in doublespeak of various degrees of intelligibility.

The second part is largely more of the same, though the tone darkens somewhat. Merton reports on various inanities of popular culture, often accompanied with cuttings from newspapers and magazines, but also on the threats to peace in world and church ("Tomorrow Mass for the peace, but the mists of bad feeling are all over this country let me tell you it smell bad here in Denmark" [63]; "I am truly spry and full of fun, but am pursued by the vilifications of progressed Catholics. . . . The Ottavianis was bad but these are infinitely worse. You wait and see" [110]). Yet he refuses to give in to the "gloom" that he finds pervading the monastery, the church, and the country: "I resist the weltschmerz with secret rum and other pursuits. . . . Let joyous Greece shake it all off, there is still plenty of room for joy at least in Greece" (85). But "weltschmerz" seems finally to catch up with the pair despite their best efforts. The collection ends with increased awareness of mortality as Columbia friends Ad Reinhardt and John Slate die ("It is never a limit to the laments of Old Slates and Old Reinhardt. Truly the bloom has faded," Merton writes in the final letter of the series [125]), to be followed soon by the death of Seymour

Freedgood and, before the end of the following year, by Merton's own death.

But the zany poem entitled "Western Fellow Students Salute with Calypso Anthems the Movie Career of Robert Lax," commemorating Lax's appearance in an extremely obscure film and included as the appendix (even though this may not have been Merton's own idea), provides an appropriately humorous and upbeat last word, with verses such as these: "While you are portrayed in love with a stellar pulchritude / All for the visions of the less fortunate / Who lurk in the shadows of the cinema and view / (As once you did The Marx Brothers) who else but You? / This is principally (you must admit it) due / To the radical and wholesome influence of creative Columbia U" (127). Certainly, the friendship represented in these pages provides testimony of a lasting influence on the two men and their group that was indeed radical, wholesome, and creative. POC

SEE ALSO *WHEN PROPHECY STILL HAD A VOICE.*

CELIBACY

In the 1960s, when clerical celibacy was hardly an issue up for discussion in the Roman Catholic Church, Thomas Merton did speak, briefly, about the possibility of optional clerical celibacy and married priests. His remarks are found chiefly in "An Interview with Thomas Merton," given to Thomas P. McDonnell (in *U.S. Catholic* of March 1968),[1] and in a statement he made in April 1967[2] as he accepted the invitation to become an adviser of the National Association for Pastoral Renewal.[3]

In the whimsical work *Day of a Stranger,* Merton wrote, "All monks, as is well known, are unmarried; and hermits more unmarried, than the rest of them" (49). His own commitment to celibacy, despite his brief struggle over the issue in the summer of 1966, was strong. He saw celibacy as an important charism in the life of the church, but one for monks, members of religious institutes, and "those of the secular clergy who wish freely to remain celibate" (April 1967 statement). He saw no necessary link between celibacy and the charism of priesthood. What

alone should link them, he believed, was the free choice of the person.

He saw no theological problem in accepting a married clergy. After all, "the first Pope was a married man and St. Paul seems to assume that Bishops will be married" (April 1967 statement). He did see, however, a psychological problem. The reality of celibacy seemed so rooted in the Catholic cultural heritage that many see it as an element of Catholic identity.

This notion of a celibate clerical caste had nothing to do with orders as such, but rather was wrapped up in a bigger package handed down to us from medieval times: the myopic view of sexuality that mars the writings of so many of the church fathers. "The notion that priests *must* be celibate forms part and parcel of a deep-rooted general attitude toward man, the flesh, and the world. It implies . . . a suspicious fear of marriage and the flesh and it suggests that the perfect Christian life is reserved for virgins" (April 1967 statement).

This uneasiness with marriage and the flesh meant inevitably a division of Christians into two classes: (1) those who "take their faith seriously" and consequently are celibate, and (2) second-class Christians unable to live the life of celibacy. These second-class citizens of the kingdom could make up to some degree for their more lowly state by bringing some elements of monastic spirituality into lay life. It also helped if they raised a child or two for the priesthood or the cloister.

This idea, Merton suggests, may have worked within the framework of a feudal society wherein a celibate clerical caste system was taken for granted. The breakdown of such a feudal society had its effect on church order. The position of Vatican II in *Lumen Gentium* — about the universal call to holiness of life — tolled the death knell to the notion of superior and inferior classes of membership in the church. The fundamental call to holiness comes not from orders or celibacy but from baptism, which makes us all one in Christ.

Many people have accepted this change in thinking, but not its inevitable consequence, that celibacy no longer can be seen as a "better" way of living out one's Christian commitment. As a matter of fact, it is important to understand, as Merton puts it, that "to undertake [celibacy] in a spirit of perfectionism is a blasphemous waste of time. That is why it makes so much sense for many priests today to prefer a serious married life to a futile perfectionism in celibacy."[4]

Speaking with a prophetic voice, Merton saw that the issue of a married secular clergy was critical. Some people, he realized, would try to ignore it in the hope that it would go away by itself. But that is not possible. "It will become," Merton said in 1967, "more and more urgent from day to day . . . and it involves the future of the Church in the modern world" (April 1967 statement).

Merton expressed his solidarity with fellow priests, for whom he felt the prevailing attitude in the church caused unnecessary anguish and emotional upheaval. "Though I myself as a monk am dedicated to the solitary and contemplative ideal, and have no intention whatever of getting married, I feel deeply involved in this question which affects so many of my fellow priests and has such profound implications for the self-understanding of all Catholics today" (April 1967 statement).

Merton was not afraid to face the issue of celibacy straight on and affirm that it is not the normal way of human living. In fact, in the interview with Thomas P. McDonnell, he does not hesitate to call the celibate life one of "radical absurdity." When Merton speaks of absurdity, he is not intending to say that celibacy is foolish or stupid. His remark must be understood in the context of other writing that he was doing at the time, especially his writing on Albert Camus. For Camus, the absurdity of human existence was a given. Here, the word "absurdity" means living in a world in which one recognizes at once both the nobility and the poverty of human freedom. Merton writes in his splendid introduction to Camus's *The Plague*, "Camus is sometimes represented as having preached 'the absurd.' Nothing could be more mistaken. He wants his readers to recognize 'the absurd' in order to resist it" (*Albert Camus' The Plague*, 5).

The aspect of absurdity of which Merton speaks when he talks of celibacy is especially that of loneliness. One way of resisting lone-

liness is through relationship. The God-given human relationship for overcoming loneliness is marriage. To quote Merton:

> Man without woman is absurd. He experiences in himself the fact of his incompleteness. If he is honest, he will realize his creaturely limitations in all their poignancy. It is not merely a matter of "interpersonal relations." I certainly agree that the real point of marriage is not just sexual fulfillment but a communion of persons. But the communion of persons in marriage cannot merely bypass the fact that the two persons in communion are man and woman, and that as man and woman they complete one another to make "one, as Christ and the Church are one."[5]

Yet at the same time, Merton points out, marriage does not always (maybe not even frequently) create the completeness that should come from their relationship. "Even in the best of relationships between man and woman [there is] loneliness. . . . There are moments in human love in which loneliness is completely transcended, but they are brief and deceptive, and they can point only to the further and more difficult place where two lonely and helpless people elect to save one another from absurdity by being absurd together."[6]

There is another way of dealing with loneliness, and that is to embrace it with a willingness to live that incompleteness, but to do so precisely as a witness to the fact that there is a form of communion, transcending existence in the world, that alone can overcome the sometimes terrifying loneliness of human existence. This embracing of loneliness, in an act of faith and eschatological witness, is at the heart of what Merton meant when he called the celibate life one of "radical absurdity." Celibate persons freely embrace the limitations that human existence imposes and the kind of "death" that these limitations imply, simply because they experience that they are called to do so. For Merton in his own life, this meant especially the life of the celibate monk or hermit. Monks witness to what transcends absurdity, not in words, but simply in being who they are. It is not so much that their lives necessarily overcome absurdity; they are, for a world embedded in absurdity, quite simply living witnesses to a belief that it can be transcended.

Merton did not discuss a topic that has been more widely aired in the twenty-first century: the meaning of celibate sexuality and the need of celibate persons for deep personal relationships. WHS

SEE ALSO MARRIAGE.

Notes

1. This interview was previously published in *Motive* (October 1967).
2. This statement was written in April 1967 and first published in Portuguese in Brazil. In 1979 it appeared in the autumn issue of *The Merton Seasonal*.
3. The National Association for Pastoral Renewal took a poll on clerical celibacy. Cardinal Francis Spellman was opposed to the poll, and Merton was reported to the apostolic delegate because of his membership in the NAPR. See *Learning to Love*, 241.
4. Thomas P. McDonnell, "Interview with Thomas Merton," 30.
5. Ibid.
6. Ibid.

CENSORSHIP

"I am having a bit of censor trouble," Thomas Merton wrote to his friend Ping Ferry on December 21, 1961 (*Hidden Ground of Love*, 203). In a few months Merton would be experiencing more than "a bit" of trouble. In late April 1962 his superiors would forbid him to publish on the subject of war. That would not be Merton's first experience with censorship. Censorship was a fact of life for Catholics writing on religious matters in Merton's day. In addition, as a Trappist, Merton was required to submit his books to appointed censors of the order, who granted the *nihil obstat*, after which Merton's abbot gave the *imprimi potest*. Then the book was subjected to a second review by the *censor librorum* of the church in a particular area, who granted another *nihil obstat* and forwarded it to local ordinary for the *imprimatur* — the final permission to publish the work. While ecclesiastical authorities were concerned about maintaining orthodoxy on matters of faith and morals, the order's censors were motivated by additional concerns, such as maintaining a sense of monastic propriety, which dictated what was and was not appropriate form and content for a monk.[1]

The censors of the order "bother their heads about everything," Merton remarked to poet Lawrence Ferlinghetti, "because they have been given the task of judging whether or not a piece of work is *opportune*." Merton went on to explain that the "word *opportune* covers a lot of ground. First of all, it is intended explicitly to discourage new writers from arising in the Order. Secondly, it is concerned with how the work of an established writer may be imagined to affect the reputation of the Order. This extends to some very picayune things. . . . In a word these cats are obsessed with a certain image they have of themselves and they don't want anyone disturbing it" (*Courage for Truth*, 267).

Sometimes the censors of the order also functioned as writing critics. The case of *The Seven Storey Mountain* illustrates this point. On April 16, 1947, Merton wrote in his journal that the censor "flung back *The Seven Storey Mountain*, refusing his *nihil obstat* with caustic remarks about my style, suggesting that I was not yet capable of writing such a book 'with his present literary equipment,' and suggesting that I take a correspondence course in grammar. He also objected to my frankness about my past" (*Entering the Silence*, 63). In a few weeks the situation sorted itself out, and Merton conceded that "now that he has given the *nihil obstat*, I am glad to take advantage of all his other observations because the book needs much cutting, and besides that, he has caught a lot of errors and lazy writing" (72).

As he was revising his autobiography in May 1947, Merton reveals that, to an extent, he had made the censors' concerns his own. "I am trying to tone down *The Seven Storey Mountain*. When I wrote it three years ago, I don't know what audience I might have been thinking of. . . . But not everything that I remember will please — or help — everyone who may happen to read the book. Now I have suddenly thought of all the different kinds of people who may some day read it: men riding on the Long Island Railroad, nuns in Irish convents, my relatives, secular priests, communists . . . and young girls in boarding schools, whom the censors are afraid to scandalize" (*Sign of Jonas*, 50–51). Merton's growing sense of audience was coupled with a sense of what the censors did and did not deem appropriate. He actually was censoring himself. Michael Mott notes a passage in one of Merton's typescripts of *The Seven Storey Mountain* in which, at the beginning of his account of his time at Cambridge, Merton says, "There would certainly be no point whatever in embarrassing other people with the revelation of so much cheap sentimentality mixed with even cheaper sin. And besides, I have been told not to go into all that anyway. So that makes everything much simpler."[2]

Not infrequently, after running into trouble with the order's censors, Merton would plead his case directly to Dom Gabriel Sortais, abbot general of the order, as he did in 1952, when after *The Sign of Jonas* was in galleys, the English-language censor of the order refused approval of the book, taking issue with the "trivialities" recounted there (*School of Charity*, 34–39). The situation was resolved and the book was published after Jacques Maritain intervened. He wrote a letter to Robert Giroux, which was passed on to Dom Gabriel, arguing that the journal actually would help people "in understanding the reality of the monastic existence and vocation" (*Courage for Truth*, 26).

Troubles with the order's censors were a constant in Merton's life even when he was writing about subjects such as monasticism and solitude, as evidenced by the problems he had with *Silence in Heaven, The Silent Life,* and *Thoughts in Solitude.* Merton's attempts to explain and defend himself to the abbot general make for interesting and, occasionally, amusing reading. In 1956 the book in question was *Thoughts in Solitude.* Insisting that he had "no grudge" against the censors, that he was "grateful to them," and that he regretted any "hurt" he may have caused one of the censors, Merton nevertheless held his ground: "Many a time he interpreted me in an unfavorable sense and he demanded clarification the context provided in abundance. I am always quite willing to render my text clearer, but when a censor asks me to qualify the phrase 'without Christ there is no salvation' — then I insist all the same on saying that this seems to me slightly idiotic" (*School of Charity*, 98). In the same letter, he asked the reverend father to forgive him "this fuss" and

insisted that he actually had very little to do with the censors. "I write next to nothing," he demurred (97–98).

The difficulties continued. In 1959 the censors refused to permit the inclusion of an introduction by Buddhist monk and scholar D. T. Suzuki in *The Wisdom of the Desert.* In January 1960 Merton reported to Killian McDonnell, O.S.B., that the censors had demanded "a lot of picayune corrections" in *Spiritual Direction and Meditation,* and he went on to describe his problems with the book on the desert fathers. Suzuki's essay was "thrown out of the book by the censors, on the ground that all my readers would instantly become Buddhists" (128). Although by no means exhaustive, these examples offer a glimpse into what it meant for Merton to be subject to censorship.

Merton's most serious problem with censorship occurred in 1961 and 1962 when he began writing on the subject of war. "Everybody wants me now to say something, except the censors who want me to shut up," he wrote in his journal on February 13, 1962 (*Turning toward the World,* 203). But it is clear that Merton's writing on war and peace was not a response to external pressure. It was something he felt he had to do. "I don't feel that I can in conscience, at a time like this, go on writing just about things like meditation. . . . I think I have to face the big issues, the life-and-death issues," he had written to Dorothy Day in September 1961 (*Hidden Ground of Love,* 140).

As he had explained to James Forest in November 1961, Merton had found a way to deal with censorship. There was a "loophole in the censorship statute" that left him "a little liberty of action" and enabled him to bypass the bottleneck created by things getting "jammed up" in the censors' offices. "When a publication is very small and of very limited influence (and this is not defined), articles for it do not need to be censored" (258). Merton and his abbot, Dom James Fox, agreed that *Fellowship* magazine and Robert Lax's *Pax* fell into this category. It is well worth noting that Dom James was assisting Merton in getting out what he had to say.

On April 26, 1962, Dom James Fox communicated to Merton that his superiors in the order were directing him to stop writing antiwar articles. Although Merton accepted the restriction imposed on him, he could not help voicing his frustration privately in letters to friends. What concerned Merton was not so much the fact of censorship — he had learned to live with that — but that writing about war and peace was deemed inappropriate for a monk. On April 29, 1962, Merton wrote to tell James Forest of the ban: "here is the ax. . . . The orders are, no more writing about peace . . . please do not under any circumstances publish anywhere anything I write to you on this subject or on non-violence etc. It will only make it impossible to do whatever still remains possible." Merton explains that the "reason given is that this is not the right kind of work for a monk, and that it 'falsifies the monastic message.' Imagine that: the thought that a monk might be deeply enough concerned with the issue of nuclear war to voice a protest against the arms race, is supposed to bring the monastic life into *disrepute*" (266–67).

Again Merton found a loophole. He mimeographed (rather than published) and distributed a selection of letters that he entitled "Cold War Letters," 111 letters he had written between October 1961 and October 1962. A few years later the ban on Merton's publishing antiwar writings was lifted. With the publication of Pope John XXIII's peace encyclical, *Pacem in Terris*, the climate in the Catholic Church had changed.

By the late 1960s censorship was much less an issue than it had been in Merton's earlier years in the monastery. Reassured by Fr. Paul Bourne, Merton's chief censor, who on June 28, 1967, wrote, "Don't fret about censorship. I've about reached the point where I consider it 'inappropriate,'" Merton responded on June 30, 1967, saying, "I do hope we can reach some kind of real openness in the Order as regards things like censorship — and a lot of others too. It is pointless to try to keep up this farce of rigid control. . . . My feeling nowadays is to just go ahead as much as one can and wait until they feel they *have* to object. I am not going to try to get diocesan censorship for 'Cables' — I gave that up on the poetry etc. books four or five books ago. It's absurd to send a book

like that to Spellman's boys, and distract them from moneymaking activities" (*School of Charity*, 335–36). Nevertheless, he continued to send material to Fr. Bourne "only to have it sent back with the reassurance that the 'green light' was now on permanent until he sent his old novel, at which point Father Paul said he was not even allowed to read novels, so he could certainly not censor one!"[3] CMB

SEE ALSO "COLD WAR LETTERS"; PEACE; *SILENT LIFE*; WAR.

Notes

1. Although the process outlined above describes the procedure for books, Merton also had to submit articles to the order's censors.

2. See Michael Mott, *The Seven Mountains of Thomas Merton* (Boston: Houghton Mifflin, 1984), 77.

3. Ibid., 490. Fr. Bourne's letter was dated August 31, 1968.

CHAKRAVARTY, AMIYA

Indian philosopher, poet, and world scholar Amiya Chakravarty was born in Serampore, West Bengal, India, on April 10, 1901. He studied in India at the University of Patna and in England at Oxford University, where he earned a Ph.D. in 1936. He taught in the United States at Boston University, Smith College in Northampton, Massachusetts, and the State University of New York at New Paltz. He served as adviser to the Indian delegation at the United Nations.

He corresponded with Thomas Merton from 1966 to 1968.[1] On March 14, 1967, while teaching at Smith College, he organized a "Merton Evening," at which the students read and discussed some of Merton's writings. He wrote to Merton, "The young scholars here realize that the absolute rootedness of your faith makes you free to understand other faiths" (*Hidden Ground of Love*, 115). Some of the students wrote to Merton, and he responded to them through Chakravarty.

Chakravarty helped Merton plan his visit to Asia and met him in Calcutta in October 1968 (see *Hidden Ground of Love*, 121). WHS

Notes

1. Merton's letters to Chakravarty are published in *The Hidden Ground of Love*.

CHRISTMAS SERMONS OF BL. GUERRIC OF IGNY, THE

**Trappist, Ky.: Abbey of Gethsemani, 1959.
62 pp.**

This book contains five sermons of Blessed Guerric of Igny translated by Sr. Rose of Lima and with an introduction by Thomas Merton. No publisher is listed, but the book was copyrighted in 1959 by the Abbey of Gethsemani. Guerric (d. 1157) was one of four writers known as the "four Cistercian evangelists." The greatest of the four was St. Bernard, the other two being William of St. Thierry and Blessed Aelred of Rievaulx. Guerric was the second abbot of Igny, a monastery founded by St. Bernard in France's Marne Valley. As abbot of Igny he was the spiritual father of three hundred monks, for whom he provided spiritual nourishment in the daily Latin sermons delivered at chapter. Merton sees these sermons as a true witness to the spirit of simplicity of the Cistercian monks.

The first three of these Christmas sermons begin with the same text, a verse from Isaiah: "A child is born for us." The fourth sermon is called "The Fullness of Time," and the fifth, "God's Providence in the Birth of Christ." Various themes are developed in the five sermons. They offer a positive Christology that contrasts with much of the medieval emphasis on punishment and fear of God. They tell of the lowliness of the child who comes as savior, not as judge. He brings us divine mercy. "Guerric considers above all the special *delicacy* with which God made Himself a little one in order to become most easily accessible to us" (*Christmas Sermons*, 3).

Another theme is the Pauline notion of our rebirth in Christ: "He is born in Bethlehem in order that he may be born in us. . . . He is born 'Son of Man' in order that we may be born sons [and daughters] of God, our souls being Bethlehems in which He is born 'for us'" (6–7).

Guerric insists that if we understand the meaning of Christmas, we can never be discouraged or distressed except, perhaps, in a superficial way. We may *feel* sad, but we can never give in to that, we cannot take it seriously. If we turn our eyes to the mercy of God

shown to us at Bethlehem, then all our burdens will be lightened. Our hearts will be filled with a spirit of joy. After all, in the fullness of time Christ brought heaven with him. "Precious and costly as it is, Christ has set it at a very low price. In two minutes, whether with a cup of cold water or with the mere intention, one may buy the kingdom of heaven" (49).

In the fifth sermon Guerric takes us into the mystery of silence. "This Word which in such great silence leaped from the throne of the Father down to the manger of animals, speaks now to us in silence" (57). "The true grace of Christmas is to be found, not in listening to a message of words about the Word, but in silent contemplation of the Word made Flesh" (23).

Despite the many beautiful things he says about the incarnation, it must be admitted that Guerric's sermons are marred by a hostile, bitter anti-Semitism. One passage from the second sermon (easily matched by other passages) is sufficient to make the point: "The Church, rejoicing this day in thanksgiving for the Son given to her, fills the heavens with the voice of praise; but the Synagogue sits mute in the darkness or wearies the lower world with her lamentations. Miserable and blind, why does she not notice how manifestly her God has passed to us, how plainly she is repudiated? . . . The Spouse has transferred her whole dowry to the new bride. In our hands is the marriage contract of the two testaments" (35). Merton, without comment, takes note of Guerric's contrast between synagogue and church. "[Guerric] goes on to show that the Synagogue sits alone, clinging to the Law which merely proves her an adulteress, while the Church has all the adornments of the true Bride" (8).

It is puzzling that Merton seems to have had no problems with this blatant anti-Semitism. One has to wonder whether this work was written much earlier than its publication date of 1959. Merton's contacts with Rabbi Abraham Joshua Heschel show deep sympathy with him and his people.

In fairness to Merton, it needs to be noted that soon after the publication of the book, Merton realized his mistake in overlooking Guerric's anti-Semitism and ordered the book withdrawn from sale. (Br. Patrick Hart, O.C.S.O., Merton's secretary, has testified to this fact.) WHS

SEE ALSO HESCHEL, ABRAHAM JOSHUA; VATICAN COUNCIL, THE SECOND.

CHRISTOLOGY

One would look in vain for a systematic presentation of Christology in Thomas Merton's writings. Like many Catholics before Vatican II, he used the name "Jesus" somewhat sparingly, preferring the title (seemingly turned into a name) "Christ" or "Jesus Christ." If his understanding of God was strongly apophatic, it might be said that his Christology was clearly cataphatic: Christ is the revealer and manifestation of the hidden God. Merton's Christology is one of light.

In the spring of 1933, while visiting in Rome, the young Merton (eighteen at the time) discovered the Roman churches and their Byzantine mosaics, and for the first time, he tells us, he began to find out something about the person whom people called Christ. "It was in Rome that my conception of Christ was formed" (*Seven Storey Mountain,* 109). "These mosaics," he reflects, "told me more than I had ever known of the doctrine of a God of infinite power, wisdom and love Who had yet become Man *and revealed in His Manhood the infinity of power, wisdom and love that was His Godhead*" (110 [italics added]). The humanness of Jesus sheds light on the incomprehensible mystery of God's presence and action in the world.

This is Merton the monk writing some thirteen years after the Roman experience. But it expressed the "high" Christology — the Christology of light — that would dominate his thinking and teaching about Christ. Some twenty years later, in a letter of June 1967 to John and June Yungblut, he comments on a chapter of a book that John Yungblut was in process of writing.[1] Christ for Yungblut is "God in human guise," yet "no longer to be thought of as coextensive with the Jesus of history." "He can be known in the depths of our own being and we may catch glimpses of him in one another" (27). Merton writes that Yungblut's Christology is lost on him because he

(Merton) is "hung up" on that of the Councils of Nicaea and Chalcedon. Harking back to his Roman experience, he tells John that his Christ is the Christ of the icons (*Hidden Ground of Love,* 637). In a later letter (March 29, 1968) Merton attempts to clarify what he means by the "Christ of the icons." The attempt is not entirely successful. The icon represents, he suggests, not the world of empirical data, but that world transformed and transfigured by the divine light shining through the icons. That is why the Christ of the icons is reached "not through any scientific study, but through direct faith and the mediation of the liturgy, art, worship, prayer, theology of light, etc." (643). When one looks at an icon, one sees not an external representation of a person (such as you might see in Western Renaissance art), but an interior presence of the glory of the risen and transfigured Christ.

Different from the Christ of historical criticism, the Christ of the icons is linked with a contemplative theology of light. What is important is not Christ as an object of study, but Christ as the center in whom and by whom we are illuminated. This event in Rome in 1933 and the letter in 1968, just a few months before his death, frame his Christology as one of transcendent light and transfigured beauty — what Paul would describe as "the glory of God shining in the face of Christ" (2 Cor. 4:6). In this context it may be said that, like St. Paul,[2] Merton's interest is not so much in the "historical Jesus" as in the risen Jesus transfigured and active in the life of God's people. Thus, in an essay on "The Humanity of Christ in Monastic Prayer," which appears in *The Monastic Journey,* he discusses the role of Christ's humanity in the prayer of the monk (or of any Christian). One must distinguish, he points out, being human in mortal life from another way of being human, namely, in risen, immortal life. The early church fathers, Merton points out, reflected on Jesus' earthly life much as they reflected on the Hebrew Scriptures: as something that had been radically changed and brought to perfection. "They meditated on the Passion as a past event in order to come to contemplation of Christ in His present glory" (*Monastic Journey,* 98). In contemplation the light of Christ is "the light of His personal presence, not the presence of the divine essence in its immensity, but the presence of the God-Man in His transcendent glory" (103).

In a chapter on "The Mystery of Christ" in *New Seeds of Contemplation,* he makes the point that the only reason we use our imagination in reflecting on the events of Christ's life is to prepare ourselves for a more intimate contact with him through love. "Therefore when His love begins to burn within us, there is surely no strict necessity for using our imaginations any more. Some may like to, some may not, and others have no choice, one way or another." Thus, his admonition is simply this: "Use whatever helps you, and avoid what gets in your way" (*New Seeds of Contemplation,* 155). As he says in a poem in *A Man in the Divided Sea,* "Make ready for the Christ, Whose smile, like lightning, / Sets free the song of everlasting glory / That now sleeps, in your paper flesh, like dynamite" (*Collected Poems,* 115).

Drawing of Christ by Thomas Merton

It should be added that Merton admitted the ambiguity of using the icon as a starting point for his Christology. There is the danger that the pantocrator icon, for example,

might be identified with the emperor, as if he were the locus of divine manifestation and as if the icon were seen as justifying Byzantine theocratic imperialism. When he speaks of the Christ of the icons, Merton has in mind "the Christ of immediate experience" — something found throughout the mystical tradition, such as the Christ born in us in poverty as in the writings of Eckhart or the Christ of Julian of Norwich's *Showings.*

An important insight into Merton's christological thinking is found in a section of *The New Man* entitled "The Second Adam." It is about the re-creation of humanity in Christ. Merton appropriates the Pauline parallel of Christ and Adam, while making clear the subordination of Adam to Christ. The incarnation was not an afterthought on God's part, following a failed creation. Rather, "The far ends of time meet in His hands" (*New Man,* 132). Christ is the beginning of creation and its fulfillment. Christ is the uncreated image of God, whereas Adam was created as the image of the image of God. Apart from Christ, Adam has no meaning. "In his very creation, Adam is a representation of Christ Who is to come. And we too, from the very moment we come into existence, are potential representations of Christ simply because we possess the human nature which was created in Him and was assumed by Him in the Incarnation, saved by Him on the Cross and glorified by Him in His [Resurrection and] Ascension" (134).

Would the incarnation have taken place if Adam and Eve had not sinned? Over the centuries this question has been debated by theologians. Merton clearly supports the view that it was God's love, not human sin, that prompted God to enter into the human situation. Thus, in the final chapter of *New Seeds of Contemplation,* he makes this clear. "The Lord made the world and made man in order that He Himself might descend into the world, that He Himself might become Man" (*New Seeds of Contemplation,* 290). Again, he writes, "The Lord would not only love His creation as a Father, but He would enter into His creation, emptying Himself, hiding Himself, as if He were not God but a creature. Why should He do this? Because He loved

His creatures, and because He could not bear that His creatures should merely adore Him as distant, remote, transcendent and all powerful" (292). Still more: "In becoming man, God became not only Jesus Christ but also potentially every man and woman that ever existed. In Christ, God became not only 'this' man, but also, in a broader and more mystical sense, yet no less truly, 'every man'" (see 294–95).

Christ comes as our mediator. He not only teaches us what the Christian life should be; he restores that life to us through the action of his Spirit. The action of Christ through the Spirit "re-centers" our life in God. Jesus Christ, whom the liturgy praises as the "Key of David," "alone has the power to enter into the depths of our being, into those depths which lie far beyond our own domination, [and] unlock an ontological abyss that opens out within us upon the darkness of the Beginning, the Source, the Father" (*New Man*, 174–75). This opening up of ourselves to God is what happens in baptism, the sacrament of illumination. In baptism we discover (recover) our true identity. The fire that is divine grace makes us members of the risen Christ, uniting us with him and with one another in God. This grace, reestablishing humankind in existential communion with God, is God's gift. "We have not stolen it like Prometheus. It has been given to us because the Father wanted us to have it, in order that we might find ourselves and become His [Children]" (223). Exultantly, we can say with St. Paul, "All praise to God through Jesus Christ our Lord!" (Rom. 7:25). Borrowing Irenaeus's theme of recapitulation, Merton sees Christ in terms of the cosmic vision of Paul's epistles to the Colossians and the Ephesians. Thus,

> With perfect wisdom and insight
> God freely displayed the mystery
> of what was always intended:
> a plan for the fullness of time
> to unite the entire universe through Christ.
>   (Eph. 1:8a–10)

It is thus the risen Christ (especially the Christ of the Pauline epistles), rather than the Jesus of the Gospels, who is most prominent in Merton's writings.[3] This is not to deny that the mysteries of Christ's life were important to Merton's spirituality. In *Seeds of Contemplation* he writes,

> As a magnifying glass concentrates the rays of the sun into a little burning knot of heat that can set fire to a dry leaf or a piece of paper, so the mysteries of Christ in the Gospel concentrate the rays of God's light and fire to a point that sets fire to the spirit of man. And this is why Christ was born and lived in the world and died and returned from death and ascended to His Father in heaven.... Through the glass of His Humanity He concentrates the rays of His Holy Spirit upon us so that we feel the burn, and all mystical experience is infused into the soul through the Man Christ. (*Seeds of Contemplation*, 91)

Note how this text moves from the mysteries of Christ to the action of the risen Christ who comes to us through the Spirit. A few pages later he writes, "We read the Gospels not merely to get a picture or an idea of Christ, but to enter in and pass through the words of revelation to establish, by faith, a vital contact with the Christ Who dwells in our souls as God" (94).

The Risen One is all-pervasive in the life of the monk (and the Christian). In a poem in *A Man in the Divided Sea* he pictures the risen Christ walking into the physical reality where the monks are at work, and their workplace becomes a monastic "church":

> Walk to us, Jesus, through the wall of trees,
> And find us still adorers in these airy
>   churches,
> Singing our other Office with our saws
>   and axes. (*Divided Sea*, 61; *Collected Poems*, 96)

It is this personal encounter with Christ present through the Spirit in all aspects of our lives that counts more than the doctrines and speculations of theologians.

Nor can we forget that the exaltation of Christ comes through his emptying of himself. Again, it is the Pauline message of the hymn of chapter 2 of Philippians:

Though in the form of God, Jesus did not claim
equality with God, but *emptied himself,*
taking the form of a slave, human like one of us.
Flesh and blood, he humbled himself,
obeying to the death, death on a cross.
For this very reason
God lifted him high and gave him the name above all names. (Phil. 2:6–9 [italics added])

George Kilcourse, author of a full-length study of Merton's Christology, has emphasized the kenotic[4] approach of Merton's writing about Christ.[5] In *Conjectures of a Guilty Bystander* Merton, borrowing from St. Anselm, makes clear that human salvation was not the result of Christ satisfying the injured justice of God. For although Christ could have saved the human race by a use of power, Christ chose instead the way of renunciation of power. God sent Christ into the world, Merton writes, *"to use his freedom to save man."* Christ freely chose "the way of total poverty, humiliation, self-emptying, since in this way He was most completely identified with man" (*Guilty Bystander,* 312).

In another passage in the same book Merton reflects on the moving words about the Suffering Servant in Isaiah 53:2.

"There is in Him no comeliness." Christ came on earth, not to wear the awful cold beauty of a holy statue, but to be numbered among the wicked, to die as one of them, condemned by the pure, He Who was beyond purity and impurity. If Christ is not really my brother with all my sorrows, with all my burdens on His shoulder and all my poverty and sadness in His heart, then there has been no redemption. (127)

In a moving passage found in volume 3 of the Merton journals, he speaks again of the fullness with which God in Jesus entered into the human situation. "In emptying Himself to come into the world, God has not simply kept in reserve, in a safe place, His reality and manifested a kind of shadow or symbol of Himself. He has

emptied Himself and is *all* in Christ....Christ is not simply the tip of the little finger of the Godhead, moving in the world, easily withdrawn, never threatened, never really risking anything. God has acted and given Himself totally, without division, in the Incarnation. He has become not only one of us but even our very selves" (*Search for Solitude,* 381).

On July 11, 1967, Merton wrote to a man who found it difficult to square his understanding of Christ with the seeming abandonment that Christ experienced on the cross. Merton suggests that the problem comes from imposing on the Bible the demands of a nonbiblical Christology. "I have no explanation of how He was able to feel such dereliction, but the fact that He did so does not trouble me because it reminds me that He shared a lot of my own kind of feelings and was therefore closer to me: is closer" (*Witness to Freedom,* 334). WHS

Notes

1. John R. Yungblut published his book in 1974: *Rediscovering the Christ* (New York: Seabury, 1974), x, 180.
2. See, for example, 2 Cor. 5:16b: "Even though we once knew Christ from a human point of view, we know him no longer in that way."
3. Philip Burnham, who reviewed *Seeds of Contemplation* in the *New York Times Book Review,* noted that "Merton does not dwell on the Gospel stories." This is a helpful insight that, with some exceptions in the early poetry, generally applies to most of Merton's writings.
4. The Greek word *kenōsis* means "emptying." In the text of Philippians, the verb *ekenōsen* means "he emptied himself."
5. George Kilcourse, *Ace of Freedoms: Thomas Merton's Christ* (Notre Dame, Ind.: University of Notre Dame Press, 1993), xii–273.

CHURCH, ROMAN CATHOLIC

The church that Thomas Merton entered on November 16, 1938, was one whose roots and outlook went back four centuries to the sixteenth-century Council of Trent. Highly structured and hierarchically organized, it prided itself on being the one true church of Christ, offering its members teachings that were certain and unchangeable. As a young man whose early years lacked any deep sense of meaning and purpose, Merton found in this pre–Vatican II mentality, initially at least, what he thought he was searching for. He had long admired Catholic culture, but, having been given a skewed understanding of Catholics, he had always been afraid of the Catholic Church (*Seven Storey Mountain*, 172). But the instructions he received before his reception into the church cleared up his misgivings and misinformation. He embraced Roman Catholicism with eagerness and gratitude. A couple of months before his entrance into the monastery, he wrote that the Vatican probably was the only place where freedom and justice could be found (*Hidden Ground of Love*, 5).[1]

Merton was too intelligent to remain committed lengthily and unquestioningly to a church order that at the time discouraged dialogue and expected complete compliance with its teachings. The author's note to *Seeds of Contemplation* expresses the hope that "it does not contain a line that is new to Catholic tradition or a single word that would perplex an orthodox theologian" (14). That was 1949. Thirteen years later, in *New Seeds of Contemplation*, a very different hope is expressed: that the book "does not contain a line that is new to Christian tradition" (xiv). He was no longer fearful of challenging theologians, and his understanding of tradition had considerably broadened.

His most detailed description of the reality of the church is an essay (written in 1961, before the Second Vatican Council) entitled "Church and Bishop in St. Ignatius of Antioch." This early second-century Christian, on his way to martyrdom in Rome, writes to the local churches of Asia. His theology of the church is not a doctrinal treatise but a liturgy, a hymn of praise surrounding an act of sacrifice. "He sings the praises of the Church, the Body of Christ, born from His true Body in His true Passion." The reality of Christ is to be found "in His historical presence, in His eucharistic presence, and His real presence in His Body the Church" (*Seasons of Celebration*, 29). Ignatius sees Christ in every local church as it gathers around its bishop and as it witnesses to God's merciful and salvific love. Significantly, his emphasis is on the local church united with its bishop. For him, the "Catholic Church" (he was the first to use the term "catholic" in reference to the churches) is the

unity of all the local churches. "The Church is presided over by Christ Himself, Who also presides over each local Church. Christ is the Bishop of the whole Church and the Bishop of each local Church. But each Church also has its 'visible bishop' who is simply the representative of Christ, invisibly present wherever the bishop himself is" (37–38). This ecclesiology, which sees the reality of the universal church present in each local church and the bishop as vicar of Christ in that church, is an insight that was recovered at the Second Vatican Council.[2]

Merton makes clear that the invisible union of the faithful with Christ cannot be separated from their visible union with one another in the day-to-day structure of the church. "There is for Ignatius no contradiction between the 'spiritual' and the 'institutional' aspects of the Church" (38). All are called to build up the unity of the church and to struggle against those forces that would endanger that unity.

The faithful are called to be saints (and in one sense already are saints), yet we struggle against our own sinfulness. Thus, Merton can write that the church is "what the Gospel said it is: the communion of saints in the Holy Spirit" (*Hidden Ground of Love*, 580), albeit saints conscious of their own proneness to evil. The church is a redeemed community, yet there is much in it that is as yet unredeemed (see *Water of Life*, 266). Still, though sinners, we are at the same time saints because of the immense riches that come to us in, from, and with Christ. We are continually being called to holiness of life, a holiness that proves its authenticity by becoming incarnate in our behavior. This is a consistent theme in what Merton wrote about the church: it exists to make possible for us an interior life and a commitment to justice called for by that interior life. Writing in his journal under the date of February 24, 1959, he speaks of his great discovery of his need for the church. He then proceeds to clarify what he means by the church: "the Holy Spirit dwelling and acting in the Mystical Christ" (*Search for Solitude*, 263). To E. I. Watkin he writes, "There is no question that the mystics are the ones who have kept Christianity going, if anyone has" (*Hidden Ground of Love*, 583).

To carry out this role of deepening our spirituality and motivating us to works of justice and peace, the church has to deal with radical problems. "The great problem is the fact that the Church is utterly embedded in a social matrix that is radically unfriendly to genuine spiritual growth because it tends to stifle justice and charity as well as genuine inner life" (581). This statement may be seen as something of a call — not just from Merton, but from many others in the church — for the document that eventually emerged from the Second Vatican Council in its last days: the Constitution on the Church in the Modern World (*Gaudium et Spes*). Merton followed the development of that document with keen interest. He wrote an article about it when it was in its preliminary stages (at that time it was called Schema 13). "Schema 13 on the Church in the Modern World," he wrote, "is, from a pastoral viewpoint, of such unique importance that one may believe the whole work of the Council stands or falls with it."[3] The heart of his article was a call to the bishops to condemn nuclear war. He sent copies of his article to a number of bishops. In addition, copies of a number of his articles on peace, which were put together in a book called *Peace in a Post-Christian Era* and which his superiors had forbidden him to publish, were assembled in mimeograph form and sent to some of the bishops. He sent copies to a number of women, including Dorothy Day and Hildegard Goss-Mayr, who had gone to Rome to lobby the bishops for a strong statement of condemnation against war, especially nuclear war.

The presence of these women in Rome and their efforts to influence the bishops deepened Merton's realization of the importance of what Cardinal John Henry Newman had written about in his essay "On Consulting the Laity on Matters of Doctrine." He wrote to Bishop John J. Wright of Pittsburgh, "There is such a thing as public opinion in the Church and now, if ever, is the time for it to be articulate" (*Hidden Ground of Love*, 610). Later, in 1967, he would write to Dorothy Day, "But what is a Church after all but a community in which truth is shared, not a monopoly that dispenses it from the top down. Light travels on a two-way

street in our Church; or I hope it does" (152). On June 11, 1962, he wrote to a woman who had just become a Catholic. He admonishes her that coming into the church means there is work to be done. You should have a sense, he tells her, that "the Catholic laity are an important, very important part of the people of God. The Church is not just an institution for the benefit of priests and nuns, with lay people around to fill in the background" (110). He was writing in 1962, the year in which the Second Vatican Council began. He expressed the hope that the Council would give "some light and direction in these matters." The task ahead, he points out, is not an easy one. You may have at times, he tells her, the feeling "that you are just scrambling up the gangplank into the ark, and be prepared at times to wonder if the ark itself is going to leak. Ultimately our trust has to be in God."

In 1967 Charles Davis, the best-known British Catholic theologian, chose to leave the Catholic Church precisely because the abuse of authority had become intolerable to him. Merton understood the position Davis had taken and stated that "his points are unassailable. Authority has simply been abused too long in the Catholic Church and for many people it just becomes utterly stupid and intolerable to have to put up with the kind of jackassing around that is imposed in God's name" (230). On November 11, 1963, he had written to Czeslaw Milosz about the deepest reality of the church: "The Church is fortunately a mystery that is beyond the reach of bureaucracy, though sometimes one is tempted to doubt it" (*Courage for Truth*, 82).

Some seven months later, in June of 1964, he confided to Pablo Antonio Cuadra, a Nicaraguan poet, journalist, and editor, "I personally think that we are paralyzed by institutionalism, formalism, rigidity and regression. The real life of the Church is not in her hierarchy, it is dormant somewhere" (192). He expresses the conviction that the areas of new life will be Latin America, Africa, and perhaps Asia. Moreover, the real movement, when it comes, will start of itself.

Still, despite his misgivings about the intransigence that he saw in the church, Merton saw great hope for church renewal in the document on the church (*Lumen Gentium*). In an article published in *The American Benedictine Review* in 1965, he noted the shift in emphasis from the church as hierarchy to a deeper understanding of the church as being, first of all, the community of God's people. He wrote, "Instead of considering the Church primarily and principally as a hierarchical society and a strictly organized institution, [the Constitution] affirms that the Church is the community of the faithful."[4] It thus affirmed the primacy of an interior life, ready to reach out in social action for the sake of the world, over organizational rigidity. The organizational structures of the church, while having their own importance, are not ends in themselves; they exist for the sake of love and life. "They exist to safeguard the freedom of the Spirit within the framework of earthly society." The true end of the church is the transformation of its members and of society and the consecration of all life to God. The static concept of the church that prevailed since the Council of Trent is replaced by "a dynamic concept of the Church as a living Body moved by the invisible and divine Spirit of Truth and Love imparted to her by the Risen Christ." He also welcomed the new emphasis in *Lumen Gentium* on collegiality of the bishops as a happy balance to an overly centralized understanding of lines of authority in the church. Writing in November 1963 to the Russian Orthodox scholar Sergius Bolshakoff, he sees collegiality as a move in the direction of the Russian theological doctrine of *sobornost*:[5] "I am very drawn to the Russian idea of *sobornost* which seems to me to be essential to the notion of the Church, in some form or other.... Collegiality is a step in that direction" (*Hidden Ground of Love*, 104).

In 1965 Merton wrote to a woman who was a new convert and who experienced difficulty with some of the changes made by the Second Vatican Council, especially those in the liturgy. He admits to her that he himself has been obliged to let go of matters that were important to him, such as the value of Latin and Gregorian chant in the liturgy. Yet he believes that the changes in liturgy and in other matters will bring "a true deepening of faith" (*Witness to Freedom*, 324). After all, he tells her, the heart of our religion is love, and there are times when we may have to sacrifice our own desires for the common good. And we can never underestimate the importance of the sacraments of the church. And "whatever may happen, let us remember that persons are more important than opinions."

In this same letter Merton offers a significant statement about what he sees as his role in the church: "I still want above all to try to be a bridge builder for everybody, and to keep communication open between the extremists at both ends" (324–25). His approach was to search for common ground that would unite people and help them understand one another. WHS

SEE ALSO ECUMENISM; INTERRELIGIOUS DIALOGUE; VATICAN COUNCIL, THE SECOND.

Notes

1. In a letter to Catherine de Hueck Doherty, October 6, 1941.
2. "The Church of Christ is truly present in all legitimate local congregations of the faithful which, united with their pastors, are themselves called churches in the New Testament" (*Lumen Gentium*, 26). "Bishops govern the particular churches entrusted to them as vicars and ambassadors of Christ" (*Lumen Gentium*, 27).
3. "Schema 13: An Open Letter to the American Hierarchy," *Worldview* 8 (September 1965): 4–7.
4. Published also in *World of Action*, 117/135.
5. *Sobornost* (from a Russian word meaning "catholic") is an ideal of ecclesiology that would combine collegial and conciliar elements and would see the Holy Spirit acting and leading the whole church into the truth.

CISTERCIAN CONTEMPLATIVES: A Guide to Trappist Life

Trappist, Ky.: Gethsemani Abbey, 1948. 62 pp. 25 black-and-white photographs.

The first of several books (booklets) that Thomas Merton wrote on Gethsemani,[1] *Cistercian Contemplatives* also includes information on the founding of two daughter monasteries: Our Lady of the Holy Ghost in Conyers, Georgia (founded in 1944), and Our Lady of the Most Holy Trinity in Huntsville, Utah (founded in 1947). This expansion was a result of a re-newed vitality at Gethsemani due to the influx of postulants who, in the wake of World War II, were seeking a different way of life or, as Merton puts it, "[having] had more than their fair share of the 'world' and its ways, . . . have sought a peaceful habitation in a more lasting city" (*Cistercian Contemplatives*, 7).

The booklet begins by introducing the reader to the three monasteries (7–8). Following this introduction there are eight chapters (though not numbered as such). First is a chapter on "The Contemplative Life" (9–15). Written in 1947, this is one of Merton's earliest statements about contemplation. It is a fine expression of the contemplative ideal, more clearly stated, perhaps, than in his book *What Is Contemplation?* which was written around the same time. He describes a contemplative as one whose whole life is directed toward emptying and purifying the mirror of the soul in order that it may be filled with the radiance of the divine. Contemplation reduces the multiplicity that so easily characterizes human life to unity — the unity of one desire, one striving: the love of God. To achieve this unity demands asceticism, though asceticism is never an end in itself. "The contemplative refuses himself natural satisfactions and pleasures and comforts not merely in order to punish his flesh, but in order that the energy that wasted itself in seeking happiness where it could not be found may now be checked and diverted into the one all-absorbing occupation of loving God" (10). "The perfection of the contemplative life is to be found neither in the experiences we receive from God nor in the sacrifices we make for Him nor in the works we perform for Him, but in the *all-absorbing ardor of our love for Him*" (14).

The second chapter, "The Cistercian Ideal" (16–21), makes clear that the goal of the Cistercian reform, as expressed by the late eleventh-century founders in the *Exordium Parvum*, was simply to live the Rule of St. Benedict to the letter. It was a reaction against the Cluniac monasteries that had tipped the simple balance of the Rule by emphasizing long and elaborate liturgical services that left little room for other elements of the Rule. Merton quotes St. Bernard as an expression of the Cistercian ideal: "Our life is the practice of silence, fasting, vigils, prayers, manual labor, and ABOVE ALL TO FOLLOW THE MORE EXCELLENT WAY WHICH IS CHARITY and to progress in all these things from day to day and persevere in them until the last day" (21).

The third chapter, "A Hundred Years of History" (23–29), speaks briefly of Armand-Jean de Rancé and the renewal of the Cistercians at La Trappe, and then tells the story of the Abbey of Gethsemani, as it was entering upon its centenary. This history may be found in more detail in *Gethsemani Magnificat: Centenary of Gethsemani Abbey* (1949).

The fourth chapter (30–32), "Our Lady of the Holy Ghost," and the fifth chapter (33–36), "Our Lady of the Most Holy Trinity," tell the stories of the first two foundations made as daughterhouses of Gethsemani. The sixth chapter (37–42), "A Visit to the Abbey of Gethsemani," details what a visitor to the monastery in 1948 would see. The grounds and the buildings are described, as well as the abbey church (as it was before the renovation that was completed in 1967).

The seventh chapter (43–56) details the three specific observances that characterize Cistercian life: (1) the *opus Dei*, the praise of God in the liturgy; (2) manual labor, which takes the monk into the fields or workshops for five hours a day; and (3) *lectio divina*, spiritual reading and private contemplation. Each of these is discussed in some detail. Finally, there is a brief eighth chapter, "The Joy of Austerity" (57–62), in which he shows that the penitential life of the Cistercians, with its strict fasts, hard labor, and uninterrupted silence, is not the cheerless, unhappy existence that some might imagine. Quite the contrary, by detaching the monk from life's trivialities and from his own self-centeredness, the life of austerity unites him to God, the source of all happiness and joy. WHS

Notes

1. He also wrote *Gethsemani Magnificat: Centenary of Gethsemani Abbey* (1949); *God Is My Life: The Story of Our Lady of Gethsemani* (1960); *Monastic Life at Gethsemani* (1966); *Gethsemani: A Life of Praise* (1966).

CISTERCIAN LIFE

Spencer, Mass.: Cistercian Book Service, 1974.
56 pp. (unnumbered); 20 photographs.

Cistercian Life is a reprint of a booklet that Thomas Merton originally wrote for St. Benedict's monastery in Snowmass, Colorado. The earlier booklet was called *Come to the Mountain*. In this reprint the last section (about St. Benedict's monastery) is omitted. WHS
SEE ALSO *COME TO THE MOUNTAIN*.

CISTERCIANS

Soon after he became a Roman Catholic in 1938, Thomas Merton began to think of joining a religious order. It was Daniel Walsh who mentioned to him the Cistercians of the Strict Observance. "The very title made me shiver, and so did their commoner name: The Trappists," Merton confessed in *The Seven Storey Mountain* (263). He recalled that six years earlier when he had seen Tre Fontane, outside Rome, the fancy of becoming a Trappist had entered his adolescent mind — but it was little more than a day-dream. "Now when I was actually and seriously thinking of entering a monastery, the very idea of Trappists almost reduced me to a jelly" (263). Walsh, who had made a retreat at Gethsemani, told Merton about the abbey in Kentucky and described the life of silence, prayer, work, and fasting. To Merton, who at the time was considering becoming a Franciscan, Cistercian life sounded "cold and terrible" (264). Recalling his arrival at Gethsemani in 1941 for a Holy Week retreat, Merton wrote, "I felt the deep, deep silence of the night, and of peace, and of holiness enfold me like love, like safety. The embrace of it, the silence! I had entered into a solitude...that enfolded me, spoke to me, and spoke louder and more eloquently than any voice" (321). When, in December 1941, Merton arrived at Gethsemani to stay and the gate was locked behind him, he felt that he was "enclosed in the four walls of my new freedom" (372).

In the years that followed, through his writings, Merton would introduce countless readers to the Cistercian order and Cistercian life. In autobiographical writings such as *The Seven Storey Mountain* and *The Sign of Jonas*, he would share his own experience of life as a Cistercian monk. In a host of other writings — pamphlets and books — he would tell and retell the Cistercian story, its beginnings and its history, in Europe and in America. He would describe the basic elements of Cistercian life, introduce readers to the life and thought of Cistercian writers and saints, and present the themes of Cistercian spirituality. Through his writing on Cistercian themes and his own life as a Cistercian, he would contribute to the growth and the renewal of the order.

The story of the Cistercians has its roots in the witness and wisdom of the desert fathers of the third and fourth centuries, which laid the foundations of Christian monasticism; the vision of monastic life expressed in the sixth-century Rule of St. Benedict, which defined the balance of prayer, manual labor, and study that comprises the monastic life; and the tenth-century reform at Cluny, which established monasticism as an influential reality in medieval society. The Order of Citeaux was founded in 1098 as a reform of Cluny, whose monks had strayed from the balance of the monastic path set by the Benedictine Rule. Robert of Molesmes and twenty-one monks who left Cluny to found a monastery at Citeaux were reclaiming a life of poverty and simplicity. Led by Sts. Robert, Alberic, and Stephen Harding, and later by St. Bernard of the Abbey of Clairvaux, the Cistercians grew. By 1153, when Bernard died, there were more than three hundred Cistercian houses of men and of women. The first Cistercian abbey for women had been founded in 1135 at Tart. With growth came power, influence, and a way of life that compromised the charism of the founders of Citeaux. In 1623 the Cistercians of the Strict Observance were founded in France, and in 1664 Armand-Jean de Rancé became the abbot of La Trappe. Under his leadership the Trappist life became strictly disciplined and deeply ascetic. But, as Merton pointed out, while La Trappe "reestablished in a clear light the full claims of penance in Christian spirituality," there was something lacking at La Trappe: a contemplative dimension (*Waters of Siloe*, 49). When the French Revolution led to the dispersal of

Cistercians, some went to Switzerland, some stayed in France, and others made their way to the United States, the first group arriving there in 1803. The first permanent foundation of Trappists was made in 1848 at the Abbey of Gethsemani by monks who came from the Abbey of Melleray, a daughterhouse of Citeaux.

Merton tells the story of monasticism in *The Silent Life*, and he recounts the story of the Trappist arrival in the United States, the founding of Gethsemani, and the new foundations that followed in *The Waters of Siloe*. In these books and in others, including *Cistercian Contemplatives*, Merton attempts to communicate something of the Cistercian spirit. Above all, Merton emphasizes that the Cistercian life is a contemplative life. "Contemplation... demands silence, solitude, poverty, detachment. And the contemplative life is a life which is organized with one end alone in view: to isolate man from the noise and bustle of temporal activity and to establish him in the profound peace of the presence of God" (*Cistercian Contemplatives*, 10). Cistercian observance includes three complementary parts: *opus Dei*, manual labor, and *lectio divina* (43). Cistercian monks take three vows: obedience, stability, and *conversio morum* (conversion of manners). The latter embraces poverty and chastity. CMB

SEE ALSO *CISTERCIAN CONTEMPLATIVES*;
GETHSEMANI MAGNIFICAT; VOWS, MONASTIC.

CIVIL RIGHTS MOVEMENT

Thomas Merton's sensitivity to the issue of racial injustice in the United States dates back to his time in the summer of 1941 working at Catherine de Hueck's Friendship House in Harlem, which he describes in his autobiography as "a living condemnation of our so-called 'culture'... a divine indictment against New York City and the people who live downtown and make their money downtown" (*Seven Storey Mountain*, 345). Thus, his deep interest in the movement for civil rights in the 1960s, like his concern for other social issues such as war and poverty, is a return to commitments from his premonastic years, now viewed through the lens of contemplative

identification with and compassion for all humanity, particularly those most excluded and oppressed.

Merton first mentions his "great admiration and compassion for the Negroes" in his journal of March 1961 (*Turning toward the World*, 99), where he is both impressed by their dedication to nonviolence and aware of the ambivalence of an approach that could simply invite a violent response from those whose status is challenged. In encountering three significant authors over the next couple of years, Merton discovers important principles of the contemporary struggle for racial justice. Reading Martin Luther King's *Stride toward Freedom*, on the first major campaign of the movement, the Montgomery bus boycott, he recognizes the intrinsically Christian dimension of the movement in King's description of his own spiritual development (119); in March 1962 he is "moved and disturbed" by the experiences of John Howard Griffin (soon to become a close friend) as described in *Black Like Me*, Griffin's memoir of dyeing his skin and traveling through the South, and concludes, "What there is in the South is not a Negro problem but a white problem" (213); after finishing two books by James Baldwin he comments in February 1963 on two of Baldwin's key ideas, that "liberation of the Negroes is necessary for the liberation of the whites" and that little is to be expected from "white liberals, who sympathize but never do anything" (297). All these ideas will show up in Merton's own writings on the civil rights issue, beginning with his review of William Melvin Kelley's novel *A Different Drummer* in September 1963 and his "Letters to a White Liberal" two months later (both reprinted in *Seeds of Destruction*, published in November 1964).

In the review of Kelley's novel, he first raises the idea that the movement for racial justice is an expression of *kairos*, a time of crisis and decision that calls for a radical change of heart and change of direction (*Seeds of Destruction*, 76). Consequently, Merton insists, the call for integration cannot simply mean the inclusion of blacks into an otherwise unchanged social structure, but rather, a renewal of fundamental human values of liberty and community that will bring all, black and white, beyond "passive subjection to the lotus-eating commercial society that [the white man] has tried to create for himself, and which is shot through with falsity and unfreedom from top to bottom" (86). The same message is developed at greater length in the "Letters to a White Liberal," which situates the freedom struggle both in the context of the Christian responsibility to manifest the love of Christ and the truth of human dignity to all, and in relation to "liberal" idealism that approves of social reform so long as it does not adversely affect one's own comfortable living arrangements. Merton points out the inadequacy of a shallow optimism that can easily harden into opposition to social change if it threatens to get out of hand. He notes the insufficiency of legal changes that are not reflected in changes in attitude, and disagrees with those "who blithely suppose that somehow the Negroes (both north and south) will gradually and quietly 'fit in' to white society exactly as it is" (29). He characterizes a genuinely Catholic attitude toward racial justice as one that considers different races as correlative and mutually complementary, each contributing different gifts to a fully formed humanity (61). Again he calls for recognition of "the providential 'hour,' the *kairos* not merely of the Negro, but of the white man" (65), which is revealed in the nonviolent and deeply Christian movement for liberation led by Martin Luther King. The purpose of the movement is not only to secure social, political, and economic rights for oppressed blacks, but also to "awaken the conscience of the white man to the awful reality of his injustice and of his sin, so that he will be able to see that the Negro problem is really a *White* problem: that the cancer of injustice and hate which is eating white society and is only partly manifested in racial segregation with all its consequences, *is rooted in the heart of the white man himself*" (46).

Merton is not optimistic that whites will respond to this moment of decision, and he finds the subsequent shift away from nonviolence toward the more confrontational and even violent approach of the Black Power movement to be largely a consequence of white failure to heed the summons to redemptive transfor-

mation of individuals and society. In "Religion and Race in the United States," which first appeared in September 1964, he praises the movement led by King as "the greatest example of Christian faith in action in the social history of the United States" (*Faith and Violence*, 131), but he considers that the moment of *kairos* has passed, and a more destructive ethos has taken the lead. He nevertheless concludes that the failure of white Christianity to respond adequately to the invitation to conversion can actually be a purificatory experience, a dispelling of triumphalist illusions, a humbling admission that "we are not a special kind of privileged being, that our faith does not exempt us from facing the mysterious realities of the world with the same limitations as everybody else, and with the same capacity for human failure" (142). If the turn to violence on the part of blacks can lead to an awareness of the structural violence built into the social fabric of American institutions, Merton believes, then ultimately it can bring about authentic social transformation, though he is far from certain when or how this could happen.

In his final extended discussion of the civil rights struggle, "The Hot Summer of Sixty-Seven," Merton sees the nihilism and racism of black militants as at least in part a consequence of the violence of American power in Southeast Asia, as well as a violent reaction to civil rights struggles at home. He considers "the new segregationism" of the Black Power movement as "no improvement" on other racialist ideologies (177), though he is able to understand and even to empathize to some extent with the frustration and anger that prompted it. His conclusion is that Christianity by its very nature transcends all racial divisions in Christ, and that the task of the Christian is to "live up to what we ourselves profess to believe" regardless of how it is received (179). As he writes in his introduction to the section on the race issue in *Faith and Violence*, the Christian is called to "seek out effective and authentic ways of peace in the midst of violence," to identify the causes of injustice that fuel violence both in racial unrest and in war, and to critique the ways in which even religious institutions might consciously or unconsciously be profiting

Entering class, Clare College, 1933

from structures of injustice. He concludes this final statement on racial justice and injustice by declaring, "I for one remain *for* the Negro. I trust him, I recognize the overwhelming justice of his complaint, . . . I owe him support, not in his ranks but in my own, among the whites who refuse to trust him or hear him, and who want to destroy him" (129). One gesture of such support was a retreat planned for Martin Luther King and his associates in the spring of 1968 at Gethsemani, which was postponed because of the trip to Memphis from which King never returned — a tragedy that put a definitive end to the predominantly Christian and nonviolent phase of the civil rights movement and confirmed for Merton "the feeling that 1968 is a beast of a year" (*Other Side of the Mountain*, 78). POC

> SEE ALSO *FAITH AND VIOLENCE; RACISM; SEEDS OF DESTRUCTION.*

CLARE COLLEGE, CAMBRIDGE

Clare College was founded by Elizabeth de Clare. The Clares were a family of English nobles who go back to Richard Fitz-Gilbert, the first earl of Clare, who participated in the Norman invasion of England (1066). The college was founded in 1326. A small college, standing

somewhat in the shadow of the imposing structure of King's College, it backs up to the Cam River and is noted for its beautiful gardens.

Thomas Merton attended Clare College from autumn 1933 to spring 1934. He writes of his stay there in *The Seven Storey Mountain* (118–30). It was a disastrous year for him, as he neglected his studies, drank too much, and carried on with women. In his autobiographical novel, "The Labyrinth," he describes the year at Cambridge as the fall of a symbolic night into his life. "The year had already made its decision to fill itself full with night as early as October. It had that early started into a dive. From Rome as zenith, you could take your compasses and draw the track of my sun about in a sweeping half circle that falls and falls to this nadir: Cambridge."[1] At the end of spring term he left England with rumors of a paternity suit hanging over his head.

In November 1934 he returned to England briefly to get the necessary papers to apply for permanent residence in the United States. He was never to see England again. WHS

Notes

1. "The Labyrinth," chapter 4 ("The Party in the Middle of the Night"), first page. (The pages are unnumbered.)

CLEMENT OF ALEXANDRIA:
Selections from the Protreptikos
New York: New Directions, 1962. 27 pp.

In August of 1961 Thomas Merton wrote to Edward Deming Andrews, a scholar on Shaker beliefs, "I am currently very interested in Clement of Alexandria, one of the earliest Christian 'Gnostics,' and his spirit has much in common with that of Shaker simplicity and joy" (*Hidden Ground of Love*, 35; see also *Courage for Truth*, 239). His interest, quite predictably, turned into a book that New Directions published in January 1962. It bore the title *Clement of Alexandria: Selections from the Protreptikos*, an essay and translation by Thomas Merton. It is a small book, undersized and only twenty-seven pages, but it shows, in the space of a thirteen-page introduction, Merton's remarkable ability to sum up the ideas of an early Christian thinker in a way that makes them both clear and attractive.

It is a happy, joyful book. Merton admires Clement and is eager to share his admiration with others. Born about 50 C.E. in Athens and educated in the Greek classics, Clement spent his early life looking for a teacher and a doctrine. He found them in Christ and in the Christian faith. He became a teacher of what he had discovered. His was not a catechetical school or a school of theology. His teaching appealed to the cultured pagan: the intellectual, the poet, the lawyer, the businessperson. Merton writes, "Clement is unique and there is no substitute for his combination of innocence, erudition, faith, and joyous understanding of the great mystery of Christ. His is a wisdom that has no equal because he is the first of his kind: the first to embrace with his whole heart the new and dangerous vocation of teaching Christianity to the intellectuals and society people of a great cosmopolitan city" (*Clement of Alexandria*, 6).

Clement had no hesitation about quoting Homer, Plato, Aeschylus, Sophocles, and the other authors he had studied in his youth. Indeed, he quotes them with the same familiarity with which he quotes the prophets or the apostles. This does not mean that he put the writings of Plato on the same level as the Bible.

But the serene confidence of his faith made it possible for him to see that Plato's works and the other Greek classics could serve as a preparation for the gospel. "He knows that Classical culture is, itself, perishable, limited and unsatisfactory. But, baptized by the divine Light, it is transformed and elevated, to take its proper place in the splendor of a world made new by the mystery of the Incarnation" (9). Christians of later centuries would argue, sometimes quite acrimoniously, with one another. That would never have occurred to Clement, and if he argued with pagans, he did so with serenity and confidence. He understood the meaning of authentic dialogue.

His surviving writings have to do with teaching Christian faith. The one that interests Merton in this little book is called the *Protreptikos*, a Greek word which means "discourse" or "persuasion." Its intent is to awaken the pagan to the mystery of Christ. Merton has chosen four sections from this work: (1) "The New Song," (2) "Diatribe against the Old Gods," (3) "The Logos Our Teacher," and (4) "Soldiers of Peace." A couple of quotations from Merton's nine pages of Clement's text will suffice to give the flavor of the book. The first quotation anticipates much later discussions of the feminine in God; the second foreshadows a basic principle of present-day ecumenism and feminism.

> God in his great love for humans stays very
> close to them
> Like the mother bird when the fledgling
> falls from the nest.
> God the Father seeks His creature, heals it
> when it falls,
> Chases away the wild beast, picks up the
> little one
> And encourages him to fly back into the
> nest. (21)

> For we hold in trust the only true wisdom
> Which the greatest philosophers have
> barely glimpsed
> But which the disciples of Christ have
> received and announced to the
> world.
> And indeed the whole Christ, if I may say
> so, is not divided.

He is not Barbarian or Jew or Greek, not
   man or woman.
He is the "new man," made over entirely
   by the Holy Spirit of God. (23) WHS

CLIMATE OF MONASTIC PRAYER, THE

Spencer, Mass.: Cistercian Publications, 1969.
154 pp. Also published under the title
Contemplative Prayer. New York: Herder and
Herder, 1969. 144 pp.

In 1964 Thomas Merton wrote an article called
"The Climate of Monastic Prayer." First circulated privately, it was published in 1965 in the
international Cistercian journal, *Collectanea
Cisterciensia.* That same year the original article of fifteen pages was expanded to a booklet
of fifty-eight pages that also circulated privately. Some time after October 1965 Merton
expanded the booklet into a reasonably sized
book, retaining the original title. The way he
expanded it was curious and probably illegal. At
various points in the fifty-eight-page booklet he
inserted sections of a manuscript he had written in 1963. This manuscript, called "Prayer as
Worship and Experience," Merton had offered
to Macmillan Publishing Company. Macmillan
paid an advance royalty of ten thousand dollars.
A problem arose. Merton was under contract
with Farrar, Straus and Giroux, who, when they
heard of the Macmillan deal, threatened a suit
against the monastery. The book was withdrawn, the royalty returned, and Merton agreed
not to publish this book elsewhere. Now in
1965, wanting to make a book out of "The Climate of Monastic Prayer," Merton used parts 3
and 4 of this four-part manuscript that he was
not supposed to publish. Naomi Burton Stone,
who had acted on his behalf and gotten him "off
the hook" with Macmillan, had high praise for
the new book, not recognizing that substantial
pieces of it were taken from the "forbidden"
manuscript.

In reading this book it is helpful to know that
between chapters 5 and 11 are five chapters
that intrude on the continuity between these
two chapters by inserting material from "Prayer
as Worship and Experience" that discusses the

history of private prayer in the Benedictine tradition. Chapter 11 picks up where chapter 5
left off. Besides this insertion, chapters 12, 13,
15, and 19 also are intrusions into the text.[1]

The Climate of Monastic Prayer was also
published under the title *Contemplative Prayer.*
The intent of this new title was to encourage a readership beyond the cloister. In both
editions Merton writes, "A practical, non-
academic study of monastic prayer should be
of interest to all Christians, since every Christian is bound to be in some sense a person of
prayer" (*Climate of Monastic Prayer,* 30; *Contemplative Prayer,* 19).[2] Actually, except for the
different title and the occasional substitution
of "prayer" for "monastic prayer," little change
from the original text was made in the Herder
edition.

The "climate" of monastic prayer is the
desert, both historically (in that the monastic life traces itself back to the monks of the
Egyptian desert) and existentially (in that the
monk, though living in community, must explore the inner reality of his own being as a
solitary). "The dimensions of prayer in solitude
are those of man's ordinary anguish, his self-
searching, his moments of nausea at his own
vanity, falsity and capacity for betrayal.... The
way of prayer brings us face to face with the
sham and indignity of the false self that seeks
to live for itself alone.... This 'self' is pure illusion and ultimately he who lives for and by
such an illusion must end either in disgust or
madness" (35–36).

The monastic prayer that Merton writes
about is not community prayer, but personal
prayer: the ensemble of the varied ways in
which the monk seeks God and rests in the
divine presence. It includes psalmody, *lectio
divina,* meditation, and contemplation — all
as elements of a unified and integrated spiritual life. Yet his emphasis in this book is on
meditation. He does not, however, mean discursive meditation, but rather, an experience
akin to authentic Zen meditation, in which
one goes beyond the dualities of life and finds
one's "original self." Linking meditation with
the practice of the desert monastics, Merton
understands it as "prayer of the heart," or the
"return to the heart." The heart is the deep-

est ground of one's being, "the inner sanctuary where self-awareness goes beyond analytical reflection and opens out into metaphysical and theological confrontation with the Abyss of the unknown-yet-present-One who is 'more intimate to us than we are to ourselves'" (48). For this reason, "Our knowledge of God is paradoxically a knowledge not of him as the object of our scrutiny, but of ourselves as utterly dependent on his saving and merciful knowledge of us" (113–14).

Returning to the heart calls for "purity of heart," which involves total surrender to God and complete acceptance of our situation in life as willed by God. We must not think, however, that purity of heart builds a wall between our inner world and the world of external realities. "Meditation has no point and no reality unless it is rooted in *life*" (55). Prayer thus is intended to unite the entire day's activities into an organic whole. It helps us to see that love for others and openness to them remains the condition for a vital and fruitful inner life. "The love of others is a stimulus to interior life, not a danger to it, as some mistakenly believe" (56).

In the mid-1960s, when Merton was writing the material of this book, he had been reading Søren Kierkegaard, Jean Paul Sartre, Albert Camus, and other existentialists. This book clearly shows their influence. Merton writes a great deal about the existential dread that one encounters when confronting the mystery of the self and the mystery of God in prayer. Dread means coming face to face with our finiteness and realizing that it cannot sustain us. Dread is the experience of our poverty as contingent beings. But it is more than that. We are not merely creatures, but creatures in rebellion. What we have to face up to is not only our *nothingness*, but also our *falsity*. Dread differs from fear. Fear is the anxiety caused by an object that is known. Dread has no such specificity. It is "the deep, confused metaphysical awareness of a *basic antagonism between the self and God* due to estrangement from him by perverse attachment to a 'self' which is mysterious and illusory" (132). Meditation is the scene of this struggle, which ceases when we find our authentic reality in God. "Without dread, the Christian cannot be delivered from the smug

self-assurance of the devout ones who know all the answers in advance, who possess all the clichés of the inner life, and can defend themselves with infallible ritual forms against every risk and every demand of dialogue with human need and human desperation" (146). We can arrive at spiritual maturity only when we pass through dread and anguish and the fears that accompany the inner "crisis of death" and finally abandon our attachment to our exterior self and surrender completely to Christ (147–48). At last we come to an awareness of God and of ourselves that enables us to see that the dread was not a punishment, but a purification.

The material taken from "Prayer as Worship and Experience" may be read as a history of spirituality in the Benedictine tradition and can easily be read as separate from the chapters into which this material has been inserted.

The book has a helpful foreword by the Quaker scholar Douglas V. Steere. He builds his remarks around a text from William Blake: "We are put on earth for a little space that we may learn to bear the beams of love" (13). WHS

Notes

1. For a detailed discussion of the organization of this book, see William H. Shannon, *Thomas Merton's Paradise Journey: Writings on Contemplation* (Cincinnati: St. Anthony Messenger Press, 2000), 183–206, 292.

2. From this point on in this article, page citation numbers refer to *The Climate of Monastic Prayer*. Those reading *Contemplative Prayer* will be able to locate the texts without difficulty.

"COLD WAR LETTERS"

The term "Cold War Letters" is used by Thomas Merton to designate some of the letters he wrote during a period of one year — not a calendar year, but one that extended from October 1961 to October 1962. They were selected by Merton from the many letters he wrote during this period of time. He chose to begin these letters with October 1961, since this month coincided with his first published article on war and peace, an article that appeared in the *Catholic Worker* under the title "The Root of War Is Fear."

The term "Cold War" that Merton used to designate these letters described an international confrontation that was of great concern to the whole world at the time he wrote. Originally coined by the distinguished American columnist Walter Lippman, the term "Cold War" designated the "power struggle" between the United States and the Soviet Union that emerged after World War II. It was called a "cold" war because little military combat occurred. But each of the superpowers poured immense resources into building up its military, especially its nuclear, arsenal. This power conflict was aggravated by the ideological struggle: the Communists claimed to follow the teachings of Karl Marx as elaborated by Lenin, and the United States promoted "liberal democratic political theory." Merton was well aware of both the arms race and the ideological face-off.

He conceived of the "Cold War Letters" as a way of getting his message out on issues of war and peace without having to go through the censors. They were mimeographed and distributed privately by and among his friends.[1] The first edition of the "Cold War Letters" appeared in the spring of 1962 and included forty-nine letters. January 1963 saw the printing of the complete version, which comprises 111 letters, mimeographed and put together with a spiral binding. In addition to the letters it has a preface by Merton. A bright yellow cover helped to identify the volume.

The "Cold War Letters" are arranged in chronological order, and taken together they give us a reasonably good image of Merton the peacemaker. Merton, whether by intent or not, gives some care to protecting the identity of the particular correspondents. At the head of each letter he gives only the person's initials and place of residence. The letters are numbered, but no date is indicated. Thus, determining names and dates called for a good bit of detective work. Since the letters were taken from letters that Merton wrote to various correspondents, a date can be ascertained once the person has been identified if that letter in its earlier form is still extant. Enough dates were established in this way to give reasonable certitude that the letters are in chronological order.[2] All the letters have been identified except for one. Letter no. 50, addressed to W.D., Oyster Bay, L.I., has escaped detection so far.

These letters also are in the five volumes of the Merton Letters. Volume 5 of the Merton Letters, *Witness to Freedom,* has a section devoted to the "Cold War Letters." It places all 111 letters in chronological order and includes in that order the texts of fifty-eight of the letters. The other fifty-three are identified and placed in that order, but the texts are not given, since they are already contained in the previously published volumes: thirty-seven in *The Hidden Ground of Love,* ten in *The Road to Joy,* one in *The School of Charity,* and five in *The Courage for Truth.*[3] whs

Notes

1. See, for instance, his letter of December 21, 1961, to Wilbur H. Ferry (*Hidden Ground of Love,* 203).

2. See the editor's note in *Witness to Freedom,* 65–66.

3. See Particia Burton, *Index to the Published Letters of Thomas Merton* (Rochester, N.Y.: Thomas Merton Society, 1996).

COLLECTED POEMS OF THOMAS MERTON, THE

New York: New Directions, 1977. 1048 pp.

This work comprises the nine volumes of poetry published by New Directions during or immediately after Thomas Merton's lifetime (including the book-length prose poem *Original Child Bomb*) as well as *Early Poems: 1940–42* (which appeared posthumously from Anvil Press in 1971), along with eight appendices.

The contents of the previously published volumes are reproduced with certain variations in *Collected Poems.* The reappearance of *Thirty Poems* (1944) as an appendix to Merton's second volume, *A Man in the Divided Sea* (1946), is, of course, not duplicated. "Poetry and the Contemplative Life," the essay appended to *Figures for an Apocalypse* (1948), is not reprinted. The translations that formed part of *Emblems of a Season of Fury* (1963) are included elsewhere in the volume. The "Notes on Sources" for *The Geography of Lograire* (1969) are slightly more complete than in the original edition. The text of *Thirty Poems* follows that of the original 1944 publication rather than that of *A Man in the Divided Sea,* which has a slightly different ordering of the poems and a few slight verbal differences. The texts of two of the *Thirty*

Poems and seven poems from *A Man in the Divided Sea* include a few readings different from the original volumes, based on Merton's handwritten alterations in a copy of *A Man in the Divided Sea* (now at the Thomas Merton Center of Bellarmine University).

The appendices, which occupy about 40 percent of the volume, vary considerably in length and in importance. The first consists of "Sensation Time at the Home," the collection of shorter poems written subsequently to *Emblems of a Season of Fury* and assembled by Merton for publication, but in the aftermath of Merton's death never issued separately.

The second and longest appendix, "Uncollected Poems," includes a heterogeneous collection of fifty-nine items of various types from all periods of Merton's career, only thirty-five of which are dated, although in some cases a date can be deduced from previous publication. Two of the poems are erroneously included duplications of pieces in published collections.[1] Three items ("Atlas and the Fatman," "Martin's Predicament," and "The Early Legend") are prose pieces from *Raids on the Unspeakable* and/or *The Behavior of Titans* (the last, subtitled "Six Fragments of Work in Progress," does include verse in its fourth and fifth sections). "Readings from Ibn Abbad" (first published in *Raids on the Unspeakable*) and "The Legacy of Heraclitus" (first published in *The Behavior of Titans*) are reworkings of material by these authors similar to the "translations" of Chuang Tzu and Clement of Alexandria included in appendix 6; one poem on the cross is a translation from the Latin liturgy, not an original poem, as is evident from its previous appearance in *Conjectures of a Guilty Bystander*. Eight of the poems comprise the "Freedom Songs" Merton wrote to be set to music in 1966 (in the paperback edition of *Collected Poems* these are identified on page 668; this list is not included in the original cloth edition). Of the remaining forty-three items, six are early premonastic poems published in *Columbia Poetry* of 1939 and not subsequently reprinted; four come from the earlier years of Merton's monastic life, between 1942 and 1953. The rest of the dated poems come from the final five or six years of Merton's life: two each from 1963 and

1964, three from 1967, and eight from 1968, six of these composed on his final Asian trip; most if not all of the remaining eighteen undated pieces clearly belong to this same late period.

Appendix 3, "Humorous Verse," includes fifteen pieces, such as the well-known satiric thrust at Gethsemani business, "CHEE$E" ("Poems are nought but warmed-up breeze, / *Dollars* are made by Trappist Cheese" [*Collected Poems*, 800, ll. 11–12]); three pieces addressed to his friend Robert Lax in Merton's customary "anti-letter" style; "A Practical Program for Monks," which is more satiric than humorous; and "Never Call a Babysitter in a Thunderstorm," which will turn up again in Merton's collection of love lyrics, *Eighteen Poems*.

Appendix 4 consists of a single poem in French, entitled "Les Cinq Vierges" ("The Five Virgins") and dedicated to Jacques Maritain. It was written after Maritain's visit to Merton's hermitage with John Howard Griffin in 1966 and is a truly humorous poem about five modern bridesmaids who run out of gas (instead of oil) but are allowed to come to the wedding feast of the Lamb anyway because they are able to dance well, so that actually there were "dix vierges" at the wedding.

Appendix 5 consists of a translation of the four poems of Merton written in French, "Je crois en l'Amour" from *The Tears of the Blind Lions*, "Le Secret" from "Sensation Time at the Home," section 35 of *Cables to the Ace*, and "Les Cinq Vierges."[2]

Appendix 6, "Translations," includes 163 pieces from twenty sources. These can be separated roughly into two groups. First, there are the genuine translations from original languages, including four Latin sources (or six, as three anonymous pieces are counted together as one group), eight Spanish sources, and two sources each from Portuguese and French (all or most of the translations of six of these modern poets originally were included in *Emblems of a Season of Fury*; the rest were collected here for the first time). Second, the "translations" from Persian ("The Tomb Cover of Imam Riza") and from Chinese (the "Ox Mountain Parable" of Mencius and the fifty selections from Chuang Tzu) are renderings adapted from existing translations in European languages, since Merton did not know the original languages.[3] The selections from Clement of Alexandria occupy a middle ground, since Merton translated from the original Greek with the assistance of a French translation; it should also be noted that the *Protreptikos*, from which Merton adapted his versions, is a prose work, though he has selected passages suitable for verse renderings. Neither the headnotes of the modern poets from *Emblems of a Season of Fury* nor the extensive introductions from the original volumes of Chuang Tzu and Clement are included with the poems themselves in this appendix.

Appendix 7 is comprised of fourteen "Drafts and Fragments," eight of them untitled. Of these the most interesting are the "Prayer of Thanksgiving Written for Victor Hammer" (Merton's friend the artist-printer), a Latin quatrain with its English translation; and "April 4th, 1968," a thirty-two-line poem in honor of Martin Luther King, a stark description of the scene at the Lorraine Motel that concludes, "And on the balcony / Said the minister / We found / Everybody dying" (1006, ll. 29–32).

The final appendix, "A Selection of Concrete Poems," includes a dozen samples of Merton's experiments with verse governed by typographical patterning, the repetition of a word or phrase in varied disarrangements and rearrangements, perhaps best approached as a verbal analogue to his experiments with Zen-like calligraphic "signatures" during the same period.

It should be noted in conclusion that *Collected Poems*, although very full, is not exhaustive. A small but not insignificant number of Merton's poems have been omitted from the collection, either deliberately or inadvertently. In the first category are the poems Merton wrote to or for the student nurse with whom he fell in love in 1966, which later were published in a limited edition as *Eighteen Poems* in 1985 (although three of the eighteen actually do appear in *Collected Poems*).

Aside from this group of poems, intentionally withheld at the time of the publication of *Collected Poems*, the collection apparently was intended to contain all of Merton's work in

verse, as indicated by the inclusion even of a section comprised of "Drafts and Fragments." There are, however, a number of additions to be noted. In the mid-1950s, as Merton began to return to writing verse after a number of years, he included in his journals various examples of what he typically entitled "exercises"; of the thirteen of these found in *A Search for Solitude*, three are preliminary versions of poems eventually published, but the other ten, generally "drafts and fragments," are not included in *Collected Poems*. In addition, about two dozen other poems not included in separate volumes of Merton's verse and evidently overlooked in the process of assembling *Collected Poems* have come to light; these otherwise unpublished poems have appeared at various times since the late 1980s, almost all in *The Merton Seasonal*.[4]

Given the prolific nature of Merton's writing, it is not surprising that even the thousand-plus pages of *Collected Poems* do not contain every example of his work in this genre. It is not unlikely that additional fugitive pieces will be discovered in coming years. But *Collected Poems* certainly provides weighty evidence that Merton, particularly in the early and in the final years of his writing career, devoted a considerable part of his time, attention, and energy to writing verse, and suggests that a full understanding of Merton's vision and achievement is impossible without taking into account this dimension of his work. POC

Notes

1. "Poem in the Rain and the Sun" (741–42) is a slightly different version of "In the Rain and the Sun" from *The Tears of the Blind Lions*; "[Untitled] ('O small Saint Agnes dressed in gold')" (789–90) is a variant version of "A Prelude: For the Feast of St. Agnes" from *The Strange Islands*.

2. The poems have been retranslated in the limited edition of *Thomas Merton's Four Poems in French* issued by Anvil Press in 1996. The translations in the *Collected Poems* are notably unreliable. For example, "Je crois en l'Amour / qui dort et vit, caché dans les semences" (ll. 1–2) ("I believe in Love, / which sleeps and lives, hidden in the seed(s)") is rendered "I believe in the love / which sleeps and wakes up, caught in the sperm of the seasons"; in the same poem, "L'émoi s'éveille au plus profond / De mon être mortel" (ll. 6–7) ("Emotion awakes at the very depths / Of my mortal being") becomes "The anxious essence of my being / awakens with gaping yawns"; the breast ("sein") of the ocean (l. 9) becomes "the womb of the ocean"; "Les cloches légendaires" (l. 8) ("the legendary bells") becomes

"the legendary clocks"; "c'est là mon chant, mon capital, / Ma louange de Notre Dame!" (ll. 12–13) ("My song is there, my wealth, my praise of Our Lady") is translated "my song is pure, / this skeletal praise of Our Lady is my money." The allusion to Song of Songs 2:14 in the final lines, "Dans le creux de mon coeur d'homme, / Et dans le sein de mon rocher fendu!" (ll. 19–20) ("In the cleft of my human heart / And in the breast of my riven crag") is lost by "in the hollow heart of a man / and in the breast of my own broken rock." Similar problems exist with the translations of the other three poems.

3. Only those selections from *The Way of Chuang Tzu* that are at least partially in verse are included; twelve selections in prose have been omitted.

4. See *The Merton Seasonal* 12, no. 2 (1987): 4–9; 21, no. 1 (1996): 7–8; 23, no. 2 (1998): 11–12; 24, no. 1 (1999): 12–14; 25, no. 1 (2000): 6–8; 25, no. 2 (2000): 5–8; 25, no. 3 (2000): 7–9; 25, no. 4 (2000): 12–18. One other previously unpublished poem appeared in *Kentucky Poetry Review* 28, no. 1 (1992): 92.

COLUMBIA UNIVERSITY

This institution of higher learning, with a long history reaching back to pre-Revolutionary days, is located in New York City, Morningside Heights at 116th Street and Broadway. Thomas Merton became a student at Columbia in January 1935. He was "turned on" by Columbia. In an essay written some twenty-five years later, he said, "The thing I always liked best about Columbia was the sense that the university was on the whole glad to turn me loose in its library, its classrooms, and among its distinguished faculty, and let me make what I liked out of it all. I did. And I ended up by being turned on like a pinball machine by Blake, Thomas Aquinas, Augustine, Eckhart, Coomaraswamy, Traherne, Hopkins, Maritain, and the sacraments of the Catholic Church" (*Love and Living,* 13). It was at Columbia that he met lasting friends: Mark Van Doren, Daniel Walsh, Robert Lax, Edward Rice, to name a few. It was while he was at Columbia that he was baptized into the Roman Catholic Church. In 1939 he received his M.A. degree. His thesis was entitled "Nature and Art in William Blake: An Essay in Interpretation."[1]

In 1961 Merton was awarded the University Medal for Excellence. Mark Van Doren accepted it for him at the commencement. The citation, signed by President Grayson Kirk, read, "Gifted master of language, in poem and prose, light-hearted as you are grave, you have

Thomas Merton as a Columbia University student

reached out with winged words to the world you left. In the phrase of one who was your beloved teacher in days on Morningside, you are much less lost to the world than many who insist they are still in it. To his hand, for early conveyance to you, I entrust the University Medal for Excellence as a testimonial of your Alma Mater's admiration and enduring respect" (see *Road to Joy*, 41). WHS

Notes

1. The thesis published in *The Literary Essays of Thomas Merton*.

COME TO THE MOUNTAIN

Snowmass, Colo.: St. Benedict's Monastery, 1964. 66 pp. (unnumbered); 22 photographs of various monasteries, 10 of St. Benedict's.

Thomas Merton was not happy with the first draft of the booklet he had agreed to write for St. Benedict's Monastery in Snowmass, Colorado.[1] "It is the worst piece of writing I have done in years," he wrote on May 1, 1964 (*Water of Life*, 102). He managed to complete it a day or so later, hopefully more to his satisfaction.

Following an introduction, in which he describes the book as a meditation on the mystery of monastic life in its twentieth-century context, there are six sections: (1) "Monastic Renunciation," (2) "The Contemplative Community," (3) "Observance and Change," (4) "The Way of Silence," (5) "Vocation," and (6) "St. Benedict's Monastery Today." Each section begins with a text from the Bible or from ancient monastic sources.

The monk answers a call from God to leave the world of familiar patterns of human and social life to enter into the unfamiliar desert of solitude and renunciation. Monks become strangers in the world, "living apart, consecrated to silent meditation and liturgical praise, to poverty, manual labor, solitude, sacred study, and spiritual discipline" (*Come to the Mountain*, 17). In solitude the monk experiences, at least to some degree, that "the chaos of greed, violence, ambition and lust which the New Testament calls 'the world' is to a great extent the reign of untruth. It is a place of confusion and falsehood where the spirit is enslaved and

where one does not easily learn God's ways" (16). Yet the monk's renunciation of the world must preserve a sense of balance. He must have the virtue of hope that brings a deep awareness of the goodness in God's creation, the good in men and women made in the image of God. The monk must never lose sight of the mercy of God in the mystery of redemption. Evagrius said, "The monk is one who is separated from all and united to all" (28).

Cistercian monks since the twelfth century have lived the contemplative life in community,[2] thus combining the advantage of life apart from the world with the values of living together. Monks share in a common task of praise and work and a common search for truth. Monasteries, however, are never "finished products"; each generation of monks has to build and rebuild community anew. "The joy of the monastic life is ultimately based on the truth and sincerity with which the life is lived by the monks" (27).

The monastic observances, involving discipline and asceticism, are essential instruments for the spiritual formation of the monk. They help the monk acquire an outlook on life radically different from that which he had before entering the monastery. These observances include (1) *opus Dei*, the communal office of prayer; (2) manual labor (at times combined with intellectual work); and (3) *lectio divina*, the meditative reading of Scripture that leads to prayer and in due time to contemplative absorption in God. There must be a balance among these three observances, with no single one allowed to usurp the place rightfully belonging to the others. Moreover, the observances are carried out in the context of solitude and in obedience to a monk chosen to be abbot, the "father" of the community.

Solitude is especially important. One of the problems of modern life is the ceaseless flow of words, sounds, and images. Silence enables us to listen to God's word, for it opens our hearts to the message of the sacred text. Silence calls for an attitude of detachment that makes the monk free to ignore what is irrelevant to the monastic life and what is unrelated to the monk's responsibility to the world in which he lives. "The chief function of monastic silence is then to preserve the *memoria Dei*, which is much more than just 'memory.' It is a total consciousness and awareness of God which is impossible without silence, recollection, solitude and a certain withdrawal" (46). Such silence is not just a monastic practice; it is a gift of God.

In the final section of the booklet Merton speaks of the qualities that one would expect to find in someone who seeks entrance into the monastery. It must be a free choice that brings him to the monastery, and he must come with a certain degree of maturity.

Section 6 is something of an appendix to the booklet, detailing the history and observances of the monastery of St. Benedict at Snowmass, Colorado.

A later edition of this booklet included "A Declaration of the General Chapter of 1969 on the Cistercian Life." WHS

Notes

1. St. Benedict's Monastery was founded in 1956 from St. Joseph's Abbey in Spencer, Massachusetts.

2. Merton makes clear, however, that the life of the solitary has always been a part of Cistercian life.

COMMUNISM

In the pages of his autobiography, Thomas Merton details his brief flirtation with communism as a Columbia undergraduate. He describes it both as evidence of immaturity and as "about as sincere and complete a step to moral conversion as I was then able to make" (*Seven Storey Mountain*, 131), motivated as it was by a revulsion from his own hedonism and an aversion to bourgeois complacency that was more aesthetic then economic. But there is also a strong awareness of social injustice evident in Merton's reflections on this period of misplaced idealism, a recognition that while the communist solution was as mired in materialism as the system it intended to replace, the evils it identified were real, and were indeed "the fruits of an unjust social system, a system that must be reformed and purified or else replaced" (135). Merton never succumbed to the temptation to draw a neatly Manichaean dichotomy between capitalism and communism, America and Russia, light and darkness (see *Witness to Freedom*, 20). Like his mentor Catherine de Hueck, he was too aware of Christian failures to live the gospel as a reason for communist influence to point a self-righteous finger of condemnation toward "the Reds" as the source of all evil (*Seven Storey Mountain*, 340–41). The fact that his friend Ad Reinhardt considered himself communist yet clearly was motivated by high ideals also must have contributed to a nuanced perspective (see *Run to the Mountain*, 128–31). On the other hand, Merton did not minimize the repression and brutality of the communist system as it revealed itself in, for example, the destruction of the Cistercian monastery of Yang Kia Ping by the Chinese Communists, which he describes in detail in *The Waters of Siloe* (249–61).

When Merton begins again to think seriously, and eventually to write, about communism in the mid-1950s, he recognizes both the threat of communism and its distorted but revelatory reflection of tendencies found in the West as well. In November 1957 he wrote in his journal that communism is one of the "things a religious person needs to think about" because it is "one of the keys to the mystery of Providence in our time" (*Search for Solitude*, 136), by which he means that it is one of the "Signs of the Times" (133) that indicate how the Christian message needs to be communicated. He is struck by the fact that "one of the most interesting things about Marxist-Stalinist authoritarianism is the likeness to our authoritarianism" (136), "our" in this case referring to the "closed system" of monasticism (though he quickly modifies his comparison by saying that monastic discipline is actually closer to old-fashioned liberalism). He is already appalled by the lack of communication between communism and the West, which fosters a crusading mentality comparable to medieval Christendom versus Islam (134), a mentality that he will repeatedly try to counter in the years ahead.

Merton's admiration for Boris Pasternak certainly was a major influence in his mature response to communism and the Soviet Union. On the one hand, he was appalled by the Soviets' treatment of the author of *Doctor Zhivago*, and spoke out against it both privately (see *Courage for Truth*, 93–95) and publicly. But on the other hand, he admired and sought to emulate Pasternak's refusal to be co-opted by one side or the other in the Cold War, and his determination to maintain an independent stance in favor of humanity and humane values, which were being subverted and manipulated by both sides. "The liberty that Pasternak defends is a liberty of the spirit which is almost as dead in the West as it is behind the Iron Curtain" (*Disputed Questions*, 28). He similarly identifies with the stance of the exiled Polish poet Czeslaw Milosz, who became a friend and frequent correspondent. After reading his book *The Captive Mind*, Merton wrote to Milosz, "There *has to be* a third position, a position of integrity, which refuses subjection to the pressures of the two massive groups ranged against each other in the world. It is quite simply obvious that the future, in plain dialectical terms, rests with those of us who risk our heads and our necks and everything in the difficult, fantastic job of finding out the new position, the ever-changing and moving 'line' that is no line at all because it cannot be traced out by political dogmatists" (*Courage for Truth*, 54). Albert Camus's philosophy of revolt, which refused allegiance to either "a stagnant and ineffectual bourgeois culture" or "a fanatical and arbitrary totalism" (*Literary Essays*, 234) because each was compromised by a willingness to sacrifice human lives to preserve and extend its respective system, also won Merton's admiration. He writes in a 1967 letter, "My attitude to Communism has remained substantially the same as that of Albert Camus who saw that Communism is a form of political absolutism that always sacrifices human values to abstract political principles, and depends on force and violence to attain its ends. But incidentally this is not a monopoly of Communism and the western democracies are just as bad. I seriously believe that a radically new form of political life needs to be discovered to fill the needs of twentieth century man" (*Road to Joy*, 348).

Despite his comment here that "western democracies are just as bad," Merton did not generally subscribe to a reductive "moral equivalency" argument that saw no difference between capitalist democracy and Soviet autocracy, but he refused to see the abuses of the one as an excuse for minimizing the failures of the other, much less as a justification for destroying the one to preserve the comfortable way of life of the other. Praying for peace, he writes in *New Seeds of Contemplation*, means praying "to be protected not only from the Reds but also from the folly and blindness of my own country." It means praying that both sides "may somehow be restored to sanity and learn how to work out our problems, as best we can, together, instead of preparing for global suicide" (*New Seeds of Contemplation*, 121). He resists the simplistic yet seductive tendency to project onto the enemy a demonic image that suggests that all will be well if only the incarnation of evil is eliminated, an attitude that marks both armed camps. "For the West, this one Antichrist is Communism. For the Communists it is capitalist imperialism. Not even the obvious divisions within the two camps can persuade men to drop this paranoid obsession with *one* presumed source of all evil!" (*Guilty Bystander*, 61–62). The most significant aspect of Pope John XXIII's encyclical *Pacem in Terris*, in Merton's opinion, is its encouragement of dialogue and cooperation with communists as the way to a lasting peace (*Turning toward the World*, 315; *Witness to Freedom*, 285). This certainly is the course that Merton advocates in his own writings on the threat of nuclear war. He is willing to admit that "Christianity is not only opposed to Communism, but in a very real sense, at war with it," but he immediately adds that the weapons it must employ are spiritual, the same weapons by which the early church conquered the Roman world (*Breakthrough to Peace*, 98–99). He emphasizes, however, that politically one must choose between "the arduous and sacrificial path of negotiation and the insane course of destruction" (*Witness to Freedom*, 33). Rather than adopt the same ruthless methods that one ascribes, rightly or wrongly, to the enemy, Merton counsels, "What is needed is moderation, rationality, objective thought, and above all a firm continued reliance on the very things which are our strength: constitutional processes of government, respect for the rights we want to defend, rational discussion, freedom of opinion, and a deep loyalty to our inherited ideals" (43). It is precisely this approach that

Merton finds so lacking in the policy of the United States in Vietnam, which he repeatedly criticizes for driving the Vietnamese into the arms of the communists by its brutality and stupidity (118). Ultimately, Merton insists, the loyalty of Christians cannot be reduced to being for or against any ideology, cannot identify itself unreservedly with any social, economic, or political system: "The Christian responsibility is not to one side or to the other in the power struggle: it is to God and truth, and to the whole of mankind" (*Seeds of Destruction*, 98). POC

SEE ALSO MARXISM.

COMMUNITY

SEE PERSON.

COMPASSION

To have compassion literally means "to suffer with" someone. It is an attitude of mind and heart whereby, moved by the suffering or distress of another, one desires to enter into the situation of that other and do all one can to relieve that suffering. The suffering may be that of an individual or a social group. "The natural law recognizes in every other human being the same nature, the same needs, the same rights, the same destiny as in ourselves" (*New Seeds of Contemplation*, 76). But if I am to treat other human beings as human beings, I must have compassion for them. "I must have at least enough compassion to realize that when they suffer, they feel somewhat as I do when I suffer" (76). One way of putting this is to say that my desire to help makes sense of the contemplative vision of our oneness with one another in God. In fact, Thomas Merton specifically links compassion with contemplation. "Contemplation," he tells us, "is out of the question for anyone who does not try to cultivate compassion for other [people]" (77).

This was a vision that gradually emerged in Merton's life. During his early years in the monastery he sought to be alone with God. By 1961 he was ready to speak out against war and violence and for peaceful settlement of differences and conflicts. The solitude in which he had found God in contemplation had issued in what all contemplative solitude must eventually become: compassion. Finding God in his contemplation, he found God's people, who are inseparable from God and who, at the deepest level of their being (a level that only contemplation can reach), are one with God, the Hidden Ground of Love of all that is. "I must," he tells himself and us also, "learn to share with others their joys, their sufferings, their ideas, their needs, their desires" (77). True compassion, moreover, must be inclusive. It must have an ecumenical thrust. It must extend not only to those who are "the same class, the same profession, the same race, the same nation as myself," but also to people who suffer and belong to other groups, even groups that may be hostile to us. Nor is compassion simply a nice thing for me to offer if I feel so inclined. It is an essential element of our commitment to God. "If I do this I obey God. If I refuse to do it, I disobey Him. It is not therefore a matter left open to subjective caprice" (77).

Once he had immersed himself in the study of Buddhism, Merton discovered the centrality of compassion (*karuna*) to the Buddhist way of life. It is prominent in the stories about the Buddha. Once he had achieved enlightenment, he had to decide whether to be a Buddha just for himself or for others. All at once he experienced an overpowering flood of *karuna*, compassion, a deep experience of love for all sentient beings and chose to be a Buddha for others; thus, he spent forty years preaching the Four Noble Truths to bring people an understanding of the path for overcoming the universal condition of suffering (*dukkha*). Out of early Buddhism developed the Mahayana tradition, in which the ideal is the bodhisattva, who, once enlightened, chooses to stay in the world and identify with all who suffer. In *Zen and the Birds of Appetite*, Merton writes about the Mahayana tradition and points out that *karuna*, compassion, is an intuition into the human condition that leads to a paradoxical reversal of what that intuition might seem to imply: "Instead of rejoicing in his escape from the phenomenal world of suffering, the Bodhisattva elects to remain in it and finds in it his *Nirvana*, by reason not only of the metaphysic which identifies the phenomenal and the noumenal, but also of the compassionate love which identifies all the sufferers in the round of birth and death with the Buddha, whose enlightenment they potentially share" (*Birds of Appetite*, 38). WHS

SEE ALSO BUDDHISM; CONTEMPLATION; MERCY; NONVIOLENCE.

CONFUCIANISM

While not as extensive or as enthusiastic as his writing on Buddhism and Taoism, Thomas Merton's discussion of Confucianism is an integral part of his overall engagement with Eastern thought. He emphasizes that Confucianism is less a distinct religion than a "sacred philosophy, . . . the natural law expressed in a sacred culture" (*Mystics and Zen Masters*, 46–47), and hence able to coexist with other religious traditions, not only those of ancient China, but also those of Christianity. He stresses the sacred humanism and personalism of Confucian or "Ju" philosophy, with its focus on the social nature of the person, on relationships grounded in a respect for human dignity, and on the belief that rightly ordered government can bring out the basic goodness of its subjects (see 51–52). He contrasts the basically optimistic and democratic outlook of Confucianism with the pessimism and rigidity of the Legalist school, which believed that only the application of severe sanctions would prevent social upheaval (see 54–57). In discussing the Confucian spirit (58ff.), Merton notes that it is practical without being utilitarian, and that it is based on "the *Tao* itself, but the ethical *Tao*, the way of man, rather than the metaphysical *Tao* or the inscrutable way of God. The main difference between the *Ju* school and the Taoists is that the latter are concerned with the metaphysical, the former with the ethical *Tao*" (58). He points out that it is not merely a doctrine but a wisdom, a way of life in which one comes to know its truth by committing oneself to it and living it out. He considers the "four-sided mandala of basic virtues" as the key to the character of the "Superior" or "Noble Minded" person and the heart of the Confucian ethic: compassion (*jen*), justice (*yi*), ritual (*li*), and wisdom (*chih*) (*Way of Chuang Tzu*, 18–19). He pays

particular attention to the four Confucian classics, especially *Great Learning* (*Ta Hsio*), which he sees as the key to the Confucian ethic, which is not simply conformity to rules but "the *fruit of spiritual awareness*" (*Mystics and Zen Masters*, 61) in which one recognizes and acts out one's responsibilities to the community.

Merton is especially interested in the interaction of Christian missionaries with the Confucian culture in China in the sixteenth century, and is very sympathetic to the efforts of Matteo Ricci and other Jesuit scholars to integrate Christianity and Confucianism, an enterprise he considers analogous to that of St. Paul and other early Christian missionaries to preach the gospel in Hellenistic society. He rejects the accusations made against the Jesuits that they made compromises with "paganism" in allowing Confucian converts to continue to reverence their ancestors and sees the suppression of their mission as a tragic instance of cultural misunderstanding, ending what he calls "a kind of brief epiphany of the Son of Man as a Chinese scholar" (90).

While he is largely sympathetic to Confucianism, he also is aware of its limitations and potential for declining into a kind of formalism based on external behavior that does not express interior attitudes. He sees the Taoist stress on inner spontaneity and creativity as both a complement and a challenge to the clearly defined patterns of behavior spelled out by Confucianism with its "self-conscious virtuousness" (*Way of Chuang Tzu*, 26). While it produced "well-behaved and virtuous officials, . . . it nevertheless limited and imprisoned them within fixed external norms and consequently made it impossible for them to act really freely and creatively in response to the ever new demands of unforeseen situations" (20). The Confucian reliance on the "ethical Tao," the "Tao 'that can be named,'" was critiqued by the Taoists Lao Tzu and Chuang Tzu as neglecting the "Eternal Tao . . . the nameless and unknowable source of all being" (20–21). While Merton notes the tendency in later Confucianism for the ethical Tao to be subdivided into numerous "ways" of behaving properly in various social roles, he does note that "these various human taos could and did become fingers pointing to the invisible and divine Tao" (21), thus allowing for a synthesis rather than an irreconcilable opposition between Confucianism and Taoism.

Probably the Confucian text to which Merton responded most wholeheartedly was the "Ox Mountain Parable" of Meng Tzu (or Mencius), the fourth-century successor of Confucius, which he versified from a literal translation and published both in a limited edition printed by his friend Victor Hammer and in *Mystics and Zen Masters* (66–68). He saw it as a "parable of mercy" in which the devastated mountain, symbolizing the mind, has the potential to be restored by the " 'night spirit,' the merciful, secret, and mysterious influence of unconscious nature which . . . as long as it is not tampered with, heals and revives man's good tendencies, his 'right mind' " (*Mystics and Zen Masters*, 66). This parable provides the title for the third section of *Conjectures of a Guilty Bystander*, "The Night Spirit and the Dawn Air," in which Merton summarizes the message of Mencius and reveals the affinity of this Confucian story with his own belief in the absolute necessity of silence and solitude: "Without the night spirit, the dawn breath, silence, passivity, rest, man's nature cannot be itself" (*Guilty Bystander*, 123). POC

SEE ALSO INTERRELIGIOUS DIALOGUE; *OX MOUNTAIN PARABLE OF MENG TZU*; TAOISM.

CONJECTURES OF A GUILTY BYSTANDER

Garden City, N.Y.: Doubleday, 1966.
328 pp. (cloth); 360 pp. (paper).

The cloth-bound edition of this book, published in 1966 by Doubleday, is out of print. The book is available in the Image paperback (1968).[1] The title bears analysis. It is a book of "conjectures." Conjectures are more than guesses, but less than definitive positions. Thomas Merton describes himself as a "bystander," though this was more a designation of where he had come from than where he was when he wrote the book. He saw himself as having been a "guilty" bystander because for too long he had remained aloof from conscious

efforts to probe the issues of the day. This aloofness of his earlier years had generated a kind of existential guilt.

The subject matter of *Conjectures of a Guilty Bystander* is taken from journals that Merton kept from 1956 until the time the book was finished. None of the items is dated, though for some a date can be inferred from the context. Nor are the items identical with journal entries; at times they contain reflections on journal material — for example, the narrative of the famous "Fourth and Walnut" experience, where the journal entry is reflected upon and considerably augmented. The items are too long to be *pensées*, too short and unfinished to be called essays. They may be compared to the parables of Jesus, not in terms of their form (generally, they are not stories), but in terms of their basic thrust: they tend to invite the reader to involvement in the question being addressed.

The book's preface offers an important clarification of the author's intent. It is his own personal view of the world in the 1960s, intended not as a soliloquy, but as a dialogue with his readers about the challenges offered by the world of which he is a part just as much as they are. He refuses to offer ready-made answers to current questions. The book has an ecumenical thrust, yet it is not a book of professional ecumenism. More than anything it is about life and openness and growth. Thus he writes, "If the Catholic Church is turning to the modern world and to the other Christian Churches, and if she is perhaps for the first time taking seriously note of the non-Christian religions in their own terms, then it becomes necessary for at least a few contemplative and monastic theologians to contribute something of their own to the discussion. This is one of the things this book attempts to do. It gives a monastic and personal view of these contemporary questions. The singular, existential, poetic approach is proper to this monastic view" (*Guilty Bystander*, 7).

Conjectures of a Guilty Bystander is divided into five parts: (1) "Barth's Dream" (see 11–12); (2) "Truth and Violence: An Interesting Era" (see 66); (3) "The Night Spirit and the Dawn Air" (see 137, 207); (4) "The Fork in the

Road" (see 249); (5) "The Madman Runs to the East" (see 285). The pages noted in parentheses suggest the reason for the title of each part. The content of each of the five parts is so diverse that it defies summarization, as each covers such a variety of overlapping subjects that the titles are of little help as leads into the content of each of the five sections.

Part 1: "Barth's Dream"

The first part begins with the story of Karl Barth's dream. Barth, one of the great theologians of the twentieth century, loved Mozart's music, and every morning before going to work on his dogmatic treatises, he would listen to a Mozart piece. Staunch Protestant that he was, he never got over his annoyance that Mozart was Catholic. In his dream, Barth tells us, he was appointed to examine Mozart's theology. Deliberately he centered his questions about the Mozart Masses. But Mozart refused to answer a single question. Barth came to understand that Mozart was not a theologian and that it was not a theologian who spoke in his music. Instead, he tells us, "It is a child, even a divine child, who speaks to us in Mozart's music." Merton comments on Barth's dream, "Fear not, Karl Barth! Trust in the divine mercy. Though you have grown up to be a theologian, Christ remains a child in you. Your books (and mine) matter less than we might think! There is in us a Mozart who will be our salvation" (12).

In the rest of this section there are but two further brief references to Barth: his comment on revelation as the "opening of a door that can only be unlocked from the inside" (18), and his words about Judaism: "Barth sees clearly that the Nazi anti-Semitism was also an attack *on Christ*" (19).

A wide variety of subjects is touched upon. Judaism is one of them: "One has either got to be a Jew or stop reading the Bible.... The spiritual sense of the Old Testament is not and cannot be a simple emptying out of its Israelite content.... The New Testament is never therefore a denial of Judaism, but its affirmation" (14).

The references to Barth (as well as other Christian writers) and to Judaism suggest the strong desire Merton had to search out the unity that exists in various religions, as he hoped to unite in himself the thought, devotion, and mysticism of Western and Eastern Christendom as a way to prepare in himself the reunion of divided Christians (21).

He writes of Marx ("an ersatz for religion" seeking vainly for "a paradise on earth") (2), and of the American myth that sees America as the earthly paradise. Those who came to these shores were baptized in the Atlantic and came to a place with no history and therefore with the possibility of a new start, with always a new frontier to move to by going west. Today those frontiers have all been used up. The only possible frontier is a spiritual one (34–35).

There are thoughts on technology (25) and racism (31–33). Over several pages Merton offers trenchant reflections on the meaning of monastic *contemptus mundi* and a proper understanding of the Christian approach to the "world" (45–47). He makes the point that, when he came to the monastery, he left behind an *understanding of himself* that he had developed in civil society — a society that "is happy because it drinks Coca Cola or Seagrams or both and is protected by the bomb" (47), a society "imaged in the mass-media and in advertising, in the movies, in TV... in all the pompous and trifling masks with which it hides callousness, sensuality, hypocrisy, cruelty, and fear" (48). He goes on to insist that becoming a monk means that his whole life is a protest against and a nonacquiescence in all such false values. "Before we can properly estimate our place in the world, we have to get back to the fundamental Christian respect for the *transciency* of both the world and the institutional structure of the Church. True *contemptus mundi* is rather a *compassion* for the transient world and a humility which refuses arrogantly to set up the Church as an 'eternal' institution in the world" (53). The church, he is, in effect, telling us, must not be confused with the kingdom of God.

Part 2: "Truth and Violence: An Interesting Era"

The subtitle derives from Albert Camus, who writes of an oriental wise man who asks the

Divinity to spare him from living in an interesting age. "As we are not wise, the Divinity has not spared us, and we are living in an interesting era" (63). In this section Merton sees the time in which he lived as a time of crisis, revealing the chaotic forces boiling over in everybody. There is so much cynicism, violence, and self-contradiction. It is a time of excitement, as we move at a maddening pace toward greatness or destruction. He deals with some of the crucial situations of our age: the crisis of faith, the Gandhian commitment to truth and nonviolence, the ambiguities of a technological age, religion as a source of spiritual freedom, and Christian social action.

Speaking of Christian faith, he points out that it is matter of questioning and doubting before it becomes a matter of certitude and peace. "One has to doubt and reject everything else in order to believe firmly in Christ, and after one has begun to believe, one's faith itself must be tested and purified. Christianity is not merely a set of foregone conclusions" (70). Merton quotes Gandhi on nonviolence. Lying, Gandhi says, is the mother of violence. A truthful person cannot long remain violent. Nonviolence seeks the salvation, not the humiliation, of the opponent (see 84–86).

Running through this section is Merton's evaluation of technology. Some have seen technological progress as the beginning of the golden age of plenty and perfect freedom. "I am," Merton writes, "as ready as the next man to admire the astonishing achievements of technology" (72). Yet he goes on to speak of the unbalance that technology has brought to other aspects of human existence. "It does us no good to make fantastic progress, if we do not know how to live with it.... Never before has there been such a distance between the abject misery of the poor (still the great majority of mankind) and the absurd affluence of the rich" (73).

Part 3: "The Night Spirit and the Dawn Air"

The title of this section (borrowed from Mencius [see 137]) suggests the atmosphere that is necessary to achieve true humanness and to deepen our understanding of our inner depths where we meet God. We need the quiet, the silence, the unhurriedness so essential for a true spiritual life. He appeals to St. Thomas Aquinas: "His understanding, which is clear as day, owes much also to the 'night spirit' which communes with what he did not know.... The force of his words comes from his silence and his respect in the presence of what could never be said" (207). Key to this section is the well-known experience of March 18, 1958, that took place at Fourth and Walnut Streets, where Merton reflects on his oneness with all the people he saw coming out of stores in a Louisville shopping center. He sees the beauty in them and revels in the joy of just being a human being. As in the other sections of this book, there is a potpourri of various issues: the religious genius of the Protestant Reformation (168–69), a visit from his aunt Kit from New Zealand (200), the originality of Thomas Aquinas (206–8), Julian of Norwich and her eschatological secret (211), and many other topics.

Part IV: "The Fork in the Road"

The title comes from Merton's reflection on Thoreau: "He went his way, without following the advice of his neighbors. He took the fork in the road" (249). The sentence is a bit confusing. Presumably, Merton meant that when he came to the fork in the road, he took the path less traveled. One way of looking at this section is to see it as being about the importance in human life of being willing to change: one's ideas, one's plans, one's way of dealing with people. There is reflection on a theme frequent in his writings: the ever growing possibility of nuclear war (258–59); and on the need to discover one's true self (265–66). There are also autobiographical elements (as he recalls events from the past), his sense of joy in life (262), reflections on the Second Vatican Council (269), and so forth.

Part 5: "The Madman Runs to the East"

This catchy title comes from a Zen proverb: "The madman runs to the East / And his keeper runs to the East: / Both are running to the East, / Their purposes differ" (275). It needs to be remembered that this book was written and published before Merton had any inkling that he would be "running" to the East in 1968. Those who would, understandably, expect this section to deal with Eastern thought will be disappointed. Apart from several brief references to Zen, this section, like the others, covers a wide variety of topics. There is, however, an important statement on the reason that people in the West have been attracted to Zen: "The taste for Zen in the West is in part a healthy reaction of people exasperated with the heritage of four centuries of Cartesianism: the reification of concepts, idolization of the reflexive consciousness, flight from being into verbalism, mathematics and rationalization. Descartes made a fetish out of the mirror in which the self finds itself. Zen shatters it" (285). There are comments on such diverse people as Nicholas of Cusa, Fenelon, Eichmann, Hannah Arendt, Pope John XXIII, Bonhoeffer, Paul Evdokimov (the Orthodox theologian), and St. Anselm (an important section on Anselm's *Proslogion* expressing Merton's conviction that Anselm starts not from a notion of God, but "from the direct awareness of God as the ground of being that cannot-not-be" [327]; also a fine reflection on the *Cur Deus Homo* and Anselm's [often misunderstood] explanation of God's plan of redemption). There are reactions to Bishop John A. T. Robinson and his book *Honest to God*, which was so popular in the mid-1960s; references to the Second Vatican Council; thoughts on the relation of the church to the world (Merton writes, "My conversion to Catholicism began with the realization of the presence of God *in this present life*, in the world, and in myself" [320]). The book ends on a note of Christian hope: "There is the hope, there is the world that remakes itself at God's command without consulting us" (349).

This attempt to sum up the material in the five parts of *Conjectures of a Guilty Bystander* is a demanding undertaking (trying to say a little about so much) that almost certainly is doomed to inadequacy. One way of seeing a path through this work is to note three points that Merton makes in the preface: First, "the book attempts to show how in

actual fact a Catholic monk is able to read Barth and identify with him in much the same way as he would read a Catholic author like Maritain — or indeed a Father of the Church" (6). He does say, however, that his book is "not a critical analysis of Protestant thought by a Catholic, but a Catholic sharing the Protestant experience — and other religious experiences as well" (6). Second, this book has certain things to say about the contemplative life, the most important being that it is *life*, and life implies openness, growth, and development. Third, there is in this book a conscious reaching out not only to other Christian churches, but also to non-Christian religions. Clearly, Merton is pleased that the church, for the first time perhaps, is "seriously taking note of non-Christian religions in their own terms" (7), and he wants to be a part of the dialogue.

Finally, it remains to point out that the book has an excellent index of ten pages that will help the reader find material that he or she may be looking for. The following examples will give the reader some idea of how reflections on various subjects keep coming up again and again (and many more similar examples could be cited).

1. autobiography (5–7, 89, 156–58, 180–89, 193, 200, 214, 245, 249, 257, 261–62, 280, 312, 320, 324)

2. racism, violence, nonviolence, peace (31–33, 41, 58–59, 68–69, 84–85, 86, 109–12, 117, 200, 227–28, 269–70, 301–2, 317, 343)

3. the self (7, 14–15, 45–48, 50–51, 53, 125–28, 156–58, 194–95, 223, 253–54, 256–57, 283–84, 312–14, 316–21)

4. technology (25, 67, 75–77, 220–23, 230–32, 251, 253, 296–97, 308)

5. the world (7, 14–15, 45–48, 50–51, 53, 125–28, 156–58, 194–95, 223, 253–54, 256–57, 283–84, 312–14, 316–21)

There are many references to nature and Merton's enjoyment of the birds, the trees, and the whole ecological system that surrounded him and of which he was a part (29, 131–32,

137, 146, 148–49, 179, 201–2, 246–47, 249, 280, 284–85, 294, 296, 304, 306). WHS

SEE ALSO *DANCING IN THE WATER OF LIFE; TURNING TOWARD THE WORLD*

Notes

1. In this article, page citation numbers refer to the Image edition.

CONSCIENCE

Thomas Merton's *No Man Is an Island* has a detailed discussion of conscience in chapter 3 (24–51), entitled "Conscience, Freedom and Prayer." Conscience governs the free choices a person makes. It teaches us how to make right choices. Prayer assists conscience-formation by helping people develop and deepen their consciences. A mature conscience gives an accurate account of the moral judgments a person makes. It clarifies the motives, the intentions, and the moral actions for which one takes personal responsibility. An immature conscience, on the other hand, bases its judgments, partly or wholly, on the decisions made by others. "Therefore, it does not make real moral decisions of its own, it simply parrots the decisions of others" (*No Man Is an Island*, 28).

Conscience is closely akin to consciousness. In fact, it could be called moral consciousness, as distinguished from psychological consciousness. Psychological consciousness makes us aware of what we do; it reports to us the action we perform. Moral consciousness or conscience "tells us not only *that* we act and *how* we act, but *how well* we act" (30). Conscience goes beyond a simple awareness of what we have done to a judgment about the values or disvalues embodied in our actions.

"We do not have to create a conscience for ourselves," Merton says. "We are born with one, and no matter how much we may ignore it, we cannot silence its insistent demand that we do good and avoid evil" (41–42). Maturing our consciences requires translating this general moral demand into what we are able to discern as the living, concrete manifestation of God's will in our own lives. "The moral conscience, by showing us the way of obedience to the inspirations of actual grace, *grasps and pos-*

sesses at each moment of time the living law that is the will and love of God for ourselves" (38–39).

Merton warns against ignoring the subconscious dimension of our lives. It is wrong to think of the subconscious as "an old attic that is not worth visiting, full of the rubbish from which we make our dreams" (36). On the contrary, it is "a storehouse of images and symbols" providing "more than half the material of what we actually experience as 'life.' Without our knowing it, we see reality through glasses colored by the subconscious memory of previous experiences." Indeed, it often happens that a person's true self is buried in the subconscious, where it can only express itself "in symbolic protests against the tyranny of a malformed conscience that insists on remaining immature" (37–38).

In his correspondence (e.g., letters to John Heidbrink, Hildegard Goss-Mayr, and others, including especially the "Cold War Letters") he asserts that war and much public policy on war can lead to a deadening of conscience. Again and again he defends "the right of the individual conscience to dissociate itself from irresponsible public action" (*Hidden Ground of Love*, 332). He expresses his conviction that "a Catholic must decide for himself, in the forum of conscience, how far he can participate in dubious policies proposed by military men" (331). WHS

SEE ALSO AWARENESS; UNCONSCIOUS.

CONTEMPLATION

It is reasonably safe to say that there is no theme more prominent in Thomas Merton's writings, no subject he wrote more about and in more detail, than contemplation. He expressed his commitment always to remember contemplation in *The Tears of the Blind Lions* (a 1949 book of poems), wherein he prays, in an image borrowed from Psalm 137,

> May my bones burn and ravens eat my
>   flesh,
> If I forget thee, contemplation!
> May language perish from my tongue
> If I do not remember thee, O Sion, city of
>   vision. (*Collected Poems*, 212)

Books on Contemplation

The number of books explicitly written about contemplation and the frequent reflections on contemplation in his other writings, including his letters and journals, clearly witness his fidelity to that commitment. His first book on the subject was called *What Is Contemplation?* It is a small book, written in 1948 in response to a letter from a student at St. Mary's College, Notre Dame, Indiana, who put to him the question that became the title of the book. This initial effort showed little indication of what was to come, as in his later writings Merton would radically reshape American Catholic spirituality. More promising was a book published the next year, 1949. Called *Seeds of Contemplation,* it was widely read and established Thomas Merton as someone who chose to write about contemplation for people who were not monks. He had something to say to those people who perhaps had hardly heard of contemplation and who certainly never thought of it as an option in their lives. Surely, a new phenomenon: a contemplative monk extending the invitation to contemplation to everyone. Yet Merton himself had to grow into a deeper understanding of what that meant. In these earlier works there is an ambiguity about this universal call, for, while he addresses it to all, he seems to be saying that the only environment where this call can effectively be responded to is a monastery (or a place similar to it). This seems to be his position, though he is not entirely consistent. There are times when his enthusiasm to share contemplation with those outside the monastery seems to belie this elitist view of contemplation.

In 1959 Merton almost completed a fine but fragmented book on contemplation called "The Inner Experience," which moves in a different direction, as his vision of the contemplative life begins to extend beyond the monastic walls. The same thing may be said of the extensive revision of *Seeds of Contemplation* published in 1962. *New Seeds of Contemplation* probably can be called Merton's most popular work on contemplation. It may well be remembered as Merton's clearest and most poetic presentation of his understanding of contemplation and all that the experience of it involves. "The Inner Experience" and *New Seeds of Contemplation* clearly show the influence of Zen on Merton's thinking. This emerges even more obviously in *Zen and the Birds of Appetite* (1968), which, while somewhat loosely organized, contains some of Merton's most mature reflections on Christian spirituality. At the same time, it opens new pathways to the spirituality of the East.

The Meaning of Contemplation

Contemplation is a gift of God. It "utterly transcends everything" we are, yet it is "the only meaning" for our existence (*Seeds of Contemplation,* 176). These few words establish for Merton the fundamental paradox of contemplation: it is above our capabilities to achieve, but it is the destiny for which we were created. Merton expresses this in a statement that is about as close to a "definition" of contemplation that he probably would ever want to come. "Contemplation, by which we know and love God as He is in Himself, apprehending Him in a deep and vital experience which is beyond the reach of any natural understanding, is the reason for our creation by God" (144). It would be possible, of course, for him to go on and say that this experience, which is at once pure gift and at the same time our only destiny, is achieved after death. And he does say that this is true for many (perhaps even for the majority of people?). But he also insists that there are many others who are destined to "breathe this new atmosphere while they are still on earth" (144).

This contrast between gift and our "natural" capabilities can be understood in two different ways. It can be viewed dualistically, as distinguishing what is natural from what is supernatural. Another way of looking at this contrast is to see that in reality there is no such contrast, for everything is gift. Contemplation in this sense may be seen as the fullness of what comes with the gift of creation. Merton struggled with this seeming dichotomy for a long time. He was not entirely consistent, as he sometimes moved from one position to the other. Still it may be said that the basic thrust of his thought is generally in the direction of nondualism.

In his "definition" of contemplation (given above), Merton speaks of knowing and loving God in the divine Selfhood, a knowledge and love that are experienced. For most people, knowledge of God is thought of as coming to us from the outside, from the Scriptures and from reason. Thus, in the 1940s and 1950s, proofs for the existence of God, as well as theological reflections on God's attributes, were "in." Experiential knowledge of God, which Merton began to write about, was considered "out," except, of course, for those few extraordinary saints whom we looked up to as mystics we could admire, but never as models we could imitate. Merton's unique contribution to American spirituality was to make contemplation an "in" subject for all who were willing to undergo the spiritual discipline it called for.

Merton wrote so much about contemplation that it is difficult to summarize his ideas in a brief article. In a circular letter written to his friends in 1963 (Road to Joy, 89), he wrote on the theme "What the contemplative life means to me." "It means to me," he stated, "the search for truth and for God. It means finding the true significance of my life and my right place in God's creation." Contemplation, then, is more than an exercise of prayer; it involves the experience of (1) seeking God, (2) coming to know one's true self, and (3) learning one's relationship to the world.

Change of Consciousness

All this means that contemplation calls for a change of consciousness. It means seeing God and self and creation at a different and deeper level of reality. It means delving beneath the surface level of our existence in order to find our inner world: that level of reality that exists below and above and beyond our ordinary, everyday experience. In Figures for an Apocalypse Merton writes, "But in the dazzled, high and unelectric air / Seized in the talons of the terrible Dove, / The huge unwounding Spirit, / We suddenly escape the drag of earth / Fly from the dizzy paw of gravity / And swimming in the wind that lies beyond the track / Of thought

and genius and of desire, / Trample the white, appalling stratosphere" (Collected Poems, 159). Reaching this higher realm of experience is no easy task today. Our culture, with its emphasis on speed, productivity, and profit, longs to grab all our attention (and all too often succeeds in doing so) and thus inhibit us from seeking the deeper realities of life or even knowing that they exist.

Seeking God

Merton speaks of seeking God. It should be clear that this seeking is unlike any other that we undertake. We may seek for something we have lost or we may seek to meet a person we have never met before. Seeking in such contexts always means the quest for something that is not present. Clearly, this is not the meaning of seeking God, for God is everywhere. God is present to and in and for everything that exists. In fact, all else exists only because it receives its existence from God and is sustained in existence by God. At a meeting that Merton held at Gethsemani in December of 1967 for superiors of women's contemplative communities, Merton was asked, "What is the best way to help people attain union with God?" His answer was, "We must tell them they are already united with God. *Contemplative prayer is the coming into consciousness of what is already there.* God is so close!"[1]

Awakening to God

Contemplation, therefore, is becoming aware of something that already is: our oneness with God at the deepest level of our being. Merton is fond of using the term "awareness" (or equivalents such as attentiveness, awakening, alertness, realization) to describe this experience. This is most emphatically asserted in the first chapter of New Seeds of Contemplation, which is entitled "What Is Contemplation?" and which repeats over and over the word "awareness" or one of its synonyms. It begins with these words: "Contemplation is the highest expression of man's intellectual and spiritual life. It is that life itself fully awake, fully active, fully aware that it is alive. . . . It is gratitude for life, for awareness and for being." Merton keeps reaching for other ways of expressing this awareness. It is a "vivid realization of life and being" proceeding from "a transcendent and infinitely abundant Source." It is, above all, "awareness of the reality of that Source." Again and again in this chapter he returns to the word "awareness." "Contemplation is a sudden gift of awareness, an awakening to the Real within all that is real. . . . An awareness of our contingent reality as received, as a present from God, as a free gift of love." It is being awakened, being enlightened, at a new level of consciousness, "the amazing intuitive grasp by which love gains certitude of God's creative and dynamic intervention in our daily life" (*New Seeds of Contemplation*, 5).

Contemplation is not an intellectual accomplishment. It is not something we learn from textbooks. It is more than theological insights about God. It would be incorrect to think that the awareness or awakedness that contemplation brings enables us to find a clearer idea of God and then to confine God within the boundaries of that idea and "hold God there as a prisoner to Whom we can always return." On the contrary, in contemplation we are carried away by God "into His own realm, His own mystery, and His own freedom" (5). One way of putting this is to say that contemplation moves us from where we are, namely, in God, to an *awareness* of where we are, namely, in God. To paraphrase a well-known verse from T. S. Eliot: In contemplation we return to the place where we always were, but come to know it for the first time.

In an essay on "The Gift of Understanding" Merton writes, "There is no awareness like the awareness of the contemplative who suddenly wakes up to the fact that this whole being [i.e., all of reality] is full of God, and that the universe is swimming in meaning." Nothing can compare, he asserts, "with the intense and vivid and magnificent expansion of sight which lifts the mind of the contemplative beyond the complex pictures and images and notions contained in the created universe, into a cloud of obscurity charged with the glory of God."[2]

Notice how Merton suggests that the contemplative "suddenly wakes up." Awakedness is a synonymous concept that he often used for awareness. Contemplation is like waking up from a dream state. Think of a dream you have had recently. If the dream was especially vivid, you might say to a friend, "I had a dream last night. Everything seemed to be so real." But now that you are awake, you are aware that the dream objects were not real, but only seemed to be so. But to realize that they were not real, you had to pass to another state of consciousness: waking consciousness. Contemplation awakens us to yet another, deeper state of consciousness, at which we come to realize that the objects of waking consciousness are not unlike the objects of dream consciousness. Just as the objects of dream consciousness exist only as long as the dream exists, so too the objects of waking consciousness have only a limited existence. Their reality ceases for us when we depart the mortal phase of our existence. Only in heaven do we see reality as it truly is. This is why contemplation is so great a gift: in a sense it anticipates this ultimate transformation of consciousness, for it puts us, while still in this mortal life, in touch with the truly Real.

Thus it is that contemplation takes us into the very mystery of God. "Mystery" is another important word in Merton's contemplative vocabulary. In 1961 he put together for the novices at Gethsemani a book of prayers from a variety of Christian sources. The selected prayers are preceded by a single page in which Merton manages to express a whole theology of prayer. While accepting the standard definition of prayer as "the lifting up of the mind and heart to God," he adds a much deeper understanding of prayer: "the response to God within us," which "leads ultimately to the discovery and fulfillment of our own true self in God." In this kind of prayer we come to know that we do not know ourselves and that we know God even less. We do not know our own needs and desires; much less do we understand God's desires in our regard. "Prayer then is always shrouded in mystery. To pray is to enter into mystery, and when we do not enter into the unknown, we do not pray. If we want everything in our prayer-life to be abundantly clear at all times, we will by that very fact defeat our prayer-life."[3]

The Ineffability of God

Because contemplation seeks to know God in God's very divine being, our human words can never express in any adequate way what the contemplative experience is — not that people through the centuries have not tried to put the ineffable into words. The road toward contemplation is strewn with fallen idols, the false images of God that we have created for ourselves or those images given to us by our culture or religion: the god "out there" or "up there," the god who is white, male, and paternalistic, the god whose all-seeing eye is ever upon me watching to catch me in sin, the god who rewards and punishes. All these have to go. Even apparently holy understandings of God must be consumed in "a purification of the sanctuary, so that no graven thing may occupy the place that God has commanded to be left empty" (*New Seeds of Contemplation*, 13). No words, thoughts, or images of ours can convey the Reality of God. A contemplative who speaks about his or her experience of God is forced to use terms that describe created reality (for we have no language to describe uncreated Reality). The best a contemplative can do is describe the experience (and even that only obscurely); he or she cannot describe the Reality experienced. Paradoxically, the evidence of God's "everywhereness" blinds us. In a poem in *Figures for an Apocalypse* Merton writes, "Not in the streets, not in the white streets / Nor in the crowded porticoes / Shall we catch You in our words, / Or lock you in the lenses of our cameras, / You Who escaped the subtle Aristotle, / Blinding us by Your evidence, / Your too clear evidence, Your everywhere" (*Collected Poems*, 179).

For the would-be contemplative this can be a terrible anguish, for he or she no longer knows what God is. But ultimately, this anguish is a freeing experience. It makes clear that God is not an object. God is not one existent alongside many other existents. God is not to be found among the things God has created. That is why God cannot be named. Having let go of all the things that substitute for God, the contemplative is able to experience God not in created words and images, but in the silence of the very divine Selfhood.

Coming to Know One's True Self

Experiencing the Reality of God in contemplation makes it possible for the contemplative to experience created reality as it truly is. As Merton expressed it, "Contemplation is an awakening to the Real within all that is real." In every human creature there is something of God. It is that "something of God" that alone is real. In discovering the real in ourselves, we discover God, who is Reality itself. That is why Merton can describe contemplation not only as seeking God, but also as coming to know my true self in God. In contemplation, as we let go of words and concepts as a way of relating to God, we enter God's own silence in the depths of our being. There we discover and experience God in a relationship so direct that we discover our own true selves in God. A remarkable passage in *The New Man* (19) expresses this truth in a profound way.

> The experience of contemplation
> is the experience of God's life and presence
>   within ourselves
> not as an object, but as the transcendent
>   source of our own subjectivity.
> Contemplation is a mystery
> in which God reveals Himself to us
> as the very center of our own most intimate
>   self—
> *Interior intimo meo* as St. Augustine said.
> When the realization of His presence bursts
>   upon us,
> our own self disappears in Him,
> and we pass mystically through the Red
>   Sea of separation
> to lose ourselves (and thus find our true
>   selves) in Him.[4]

These words call for careful reading and serious reflection. They are in reality another way of expressing the gospel paradox that to find ourselves we have to lose ourselves. We come to know our true self only by letting go of a self that is false and in ultimate terms unreal.

Learning Our Relationship to the World

When we find God in contemplation, we find the rest of reality, especially our fellow human beings. We discover them not as a faceless mass, but as individual persons, each distinct and unique in the eyes of God, yet not separate from God or from one another. All are bound together in a network of interlocking relationships, and each finds his or her identity and uniqueness in God, who is for all the Hidden Ground of Love. When we become aware of our total dependence on God and the same dependence of all reality on God, we experience a sense of interdependence with all God's people and a sense of the responsibility we have toward them. Thus, true contemplation increases our sense of social justice and concern. It also increases our ecological consciousness and concern to use but not abuse the good things of creation that God has given to us. WHS

Notes

1. This comes from notes taken at Merton's retreat for superiors of contemplative nuns given at Gethsemani in December 1967. These notes were thus identified and were in the collection of Sr. Therese Lentfoehr, though they do not appear in the published version of that retreat, entitled *Springs of Contemplation.*

2. This is a Merton essay whose source I have not been able to locate. *Seeds of Contemplation* and *New Seeds of Contemplation* have chapters with the same title and with some similar material, but this essay is significantly different from those chapters.

3. See William H. Shannon, *Thomas Merton's Paradise Journey: Writings on Contemplation* (Cincinnati: St. Anthony Messenger Press, 2000), 148–49.

4. For an easier appreciation of this important paragraph, it has been spread out in sense lines. Augustine's words mean that God is more intimate to me than my most intimate self.

CONTEMPLATION IN A WORLD OF ACTION

New York: Doubleday, 1971. xxii+384 pp.

Published posthumously, with an introduction by Jean Leclercq, O.S.B., "most of the material" in this collection of essays was "put together" by Thomas Merton before he died in December 1968 (*World of Action*, xxi/19).[1] In her editorial note, Naomi Stone reports that Merton, in his last letter to her, written on September 6, 1968, indicated that "the Monastic Essays" should be published after *My Argument with the Gestapo.* That novel, which Merton wrote in 1941 and originally called "The Journal of My Escape from the Nazis," was released in July 1969. Stone notes that she did "as little editing as possible" and removed one repetitive chapter (xxi; 19).

In his introduction, Jean Leclercq, O.S.B., introduces Merton, whom he knew well in several different ways: through extensive correspondence, thorough familiarity with his writings, and as a personal friend. Moreover, as a monk himself, Leclercq shared Merton's love for the monastic life. Leclercq appreciated Merton's longing for ever deeper solitude and understood Merton's vision for the renewal of monasticism.

Contemplation in a World of Action is comprised of twenty-two essays written in the mid- and late 1960s, most of which had been previously published elsewhere. Although the essays are focused on monastic renewal, the collection lives up to the title, taken from the one of the essays. Together the essays explore the reality of "contemplation in a world of action" — inside the monastery and outside it. The essays also reveal Merton's thinking on a host of issues relevant to Christian faith and life: images of God, contemplation, prayer, church, faith, belief and unbelief, justice, ecumenism, identity, and wholeness. The essays represent Merton's attempt to frame these spiritual issues in a way fitting for the times and for his diverse audiences.

The book is divided into three parts: (1) "Monastic Renewal," (2) "The Case for Eremitism," and (3) "Contemplative Life." The section on "Monastic Renewal" consists of thirteen essays and two appendices. The essays include (1) "Problems and Prospects," (2) "Vocation and Modern Thought," (3) "The Identity Crisis," (4) "Dialogue and Renewal," (5) "Renewal and Discipline," (6) "The Place of Obedience," (7) "Openness and Cloister," (8) "Is the World a Problem?" (9) "Contemplation in a World of Action," (10) "The Contemplative and the Atheist," (11) "Ecumenism and Renewal," (12) "The Need for a New Education," and (13) "Final Integration — Toward a 'Monastic Therapy.'" Part 1 also includes two appendices: "Notes on the Future of Monasticism" and "The Monk Today."

In the first essay, written in 1967 and previously unpublished, Merton tackles the "Problems and Prospects" of monastic life. While, in the light of the Second Vatican Council, religious have begun to question the basic institutional structures of religious life, others continue to reduce monasticism to the role of a "spiritual dynamo," generating results from God. But the monk is not "defined by his task, his usefulness" (7/27). The monk lives to cultivate "a certain *quality* of life, a level of awareness, a depth of consciousness, an area of transcendence and of adoration which are not usually possible in an active secular existence" (7/27). Monasticism calls for a "true creative spirit ... fired with love and with *an authentic desire of God*" (23/43). Nurturing creativity will require openness to new forms.

In the next two essays, "Vocation and Modern Thought" (written in 1964) and "The Identity Crisis" (published in *Spiritual Life* in 1968), Merton draws on knowledge gleaned from his experience as a monk and novice master and his reading of contemporary psychologists, philosophers, and theologians to better understand the forces that influence young men coming to the monastery and their responses to monastic life. Recognizing that postulants come out of a society that fosters alienation rather than identity, monastic renewal must "aim at authenticity" (73/92). "Our first task," Merton concludes, "is to be fully human, and to enable the youth of our time to find themselves and develop as men and as sons of God.... Monastic spirituality today must be a personalistic and Christian humanism that seeks and saves man's intimate truth, his personal identity, in order to consecrate it entirely to God" (82/100).

The next four essays, "Dialogue and Renewal" (*Spiritual Life*, 1968), "Renewal and Discipline" (*Cistercian Studies*, 1970), "The Place of Obedience" (*American Benedictine Review*, 1965), and "Openness and Cloister" (*Cistercian Studies*, 1967), surface themes that are central to the renewal of monastic life. Merton states that religious themselves must take an active part in the work of renewal.

Merton asks what aggiornamento means for contemplatives. "Should contemplatives be 'open to the world'?" (130/147). What does openness to the world mean? "First of all, being 'open to the world' means being aware of and responsive to the real situation of people in the world, the critical problems of the world" (138/155). It means "being more accessible to people of flesh and blood who are brought by God, in one way or another, to our doorstep. The poor, materially and spiritually" (139/156). Contemplative communities can provide opportunities for people to experience quiet. And monks "might in exceptional cases travel to engage in ecumenical dialogue or discussions where their presence would be really useful" (140/157). Finally, openness should characterize relations within the community itself. "The real purpose of openness is to renew life in the Spirit, life in love" (142/158).

Perhaps the best-known essays in this book are "Is the World a Problem?" and the title essay, "Contemplation in a World of Action." "Is the World a Problem?" was published in *Commonweal* in June 1966 under the title "Ambiguities in the Secular." The essay contains some signature passages. For example, Merton tells how "a book [he] wrote thirty years ago" contributed to "a sort of stereotype of the world-denying contemplative — the man who spurned New York, spat on Chicago, and tromped on Louisville, heading for the woods" (143/159). He assures his reader that he is not speaking as the author of *The Seven Storey Mountain* or as "the official voice of Trappist silence, the monk with his hood up and his back to the camera, brooding over the waters of an artificial lake," but rather as "the voice of a self-questioning human person who, like all his brothers, struggles to cope with turbulent, mysterious, demanding, exciting, frustrating, confused existence in which almost nothing is really predictable, in which most definitions, the explanations and justifications become incredible even before they are uttered, in which people suffer together and are sometimes utterly beautiful, at other times impossibly pathetic" (144/160). Merton says that he speaks "as a man in the modern world" who recognizes that he is very involved in the world:

"That I should have been born in 1915, that I should be the contemporary of Auschwitz, Hiroshima, Viet Nam and the Watts riots, are things about which I was not first consulted. Yet they are also events in which, whether I like it or not, I am deeply and personally involved" (145/161). In developing his response to the question posed in the title of the essay "Is the World a Problem?" Merton contrasts two views of the world. The first is the Carolingian worldview, in which the "world" was "identified simply with the sinful, the perilous, the unpredictable (therefore in many cases the new, and even worse the free), and this was what one automatically rejected" (147/163). Christian society or Christendom "conceived itself as a world-denying society in the midst of the world" (147/163). In contrast, the world can once again become an object of choice in which the Christian chooses the attitude he or she will take toward the world. "To choose the world," Merton writes "is to choose to do the work I am capable of doing, in collaboration with my brother, to make the world better, more free, more just, more livable, more human" (149/165). The Christian cannot turn his or her back on Auschwitz or Vietnam or Watts. However, "turning to the world" cannot simply mean affirming it uncritically and adopting its patterns of thought and its structures. "Turning to the world" involves a spiritual dimension: "The way to find the real 'world' is not merely to measure and observe what is outside us, but to discover our own inner ground.... When I find the world in my own ground, it is impossible for me to be alienated by it" (154/170). For the Christian, the choice is not between choosing Christ and choosing the world, but "choosing the world" as it really is in Christ. "The world cannot be a problem to anyone who sees that ultimately Christ, the world, his brother and his own inmost ground are made one and the same in grace and redemptive love" (156/171).

In "Contemplation in a World of Action," published in *Bloomin' Newman*, a student publication at the University of Louisville, in April 1968, Merton opens with a critical question: "What does the contemplative life or the life of prayer, solitude, silence, meditation, mean to man in the atomic age?" (157/172). Merton ex-

plains that by the "contemplative life" he does not mean "the institutional cloistered life, the organized life of prayer." Instead, he says he is talking about "a special dimension of inner discipline and experience, a certain integrity and fullness of personal development, which are not compatible with a purely external, alienated, busy-busy existence" (157/172). Merton is critical of a view of the contemplative life that perceives the universe as "a cause-and-effect mechanism with a transcendent God 'outside' and 'above' it ... regarded as a Supreme Engineer" (159/174) and a view of prayer ordered to influence God's action. Merton contrasts this transcendent view of God with "the immanentist approach, which sees God as directly and intimately present in the very ground of our being" (160/175). Becoming aware of God in this way means entering into "a whole new kind of existence.... Call it faith, call it (at a more advanced stage) contemplative illumination, call it the sense of God or even mystical union: all these are different aspects and levels of the same kind of realization: the awakening to a new awareness of ourselves in Christ, created in Him, redeemed by Him, to be transformed and glorified in and with Him" (161/176). Although this awareness and vision is "not produced by technique," meditation and prayer are ways of preparing ourselves for the experience. Merton insists, "Real Christian living is stunted and frustrated if it remains content with the bare externals of worship, with 'saying prayers' and 'going to church,' with fulfilling one's external duties and merely being respectable" (163–64/178). Persons are called to experience the very reality of God. From this experience will come the capacity for meaningful action for others and for the world.

The next two essays, "The Contemplative and the Atheist" (*Schema XIII*, 1970) and "Ecumenism and Renewal" (*Journal of Ecumenical Studies*, 1968), broaden the context of the discussion of contemplative life. The contemplative life, centered on the experience of God, points to the possibility of experiencing God in a world that questions the reality of God and where some proclaim the "the death of God." Merton urges a dialogue between monasticism and the Reformation. At the heart of the Reformation experience was "the discovery of a more immediate and radical commitment to God's unfailing promises in faith," which "called into question the highly institutionalized and mediate structure of monastic dedication which came down from the Middle Ages" (196/209).

"The Need for a New Education" considers what is essential to the monk's theological formation. Merton identifies a number of components that should be part of the monk's curriculum, including an understanding of the non-Christian traditions, especially of Asia; familiarity with mystical literature of Christianity, Eastern and Western; and an ability to understand the crucial problems of our times: "race, war, genocide, starvation, injustice, revolution" (203/216).

In "Final Integration" Merton explains that the ideas of rebirth and new life are central to the understanding of the Christian life and of monastic life and have their parallels in other religious traditions — Zen Buddhism and Sufism. In Reza Arasteh's model of "final integration" Merton recognized an explication of transformed identity. "Final integration is a state of transcultural maturity far beyond mere social adjustment.... The man who is 'fully born' has an entirely 'inner experience of life.' He apprehends his life fully and wholly from an inner ground.... He is in a certain sense 'cosmic' and 'universal man.'... He is in a certain sense identified with everybody.... He is able to experience their joys and sufferings as his own, without however becoming dominated by them. He has attained to a deep inner freedom" (211/225). The person who has achieved final integration is "no longer limited by the culture in which he has grown up" (212/225). He accepts all people and is "fully 'Catholic' in the best sense of the word" (212/226). He is a peacemaker.

Part 2, "The Case for Eremitism," consists of five essays: (1) "Christian Solitude," (2) "The Cell," (3) "Franciscan Eremitism," (4) "The Spiritual Father in the Desert Tradition," and (5) "The Case for a Renewal of Eremitism in the Monastic State." In these essays Merton focuses on solitude as an essential element of the monastic life and on the hermit life as a valid way of living the monastic vocation. He

suggests that the new emphasis on community and on the person has also meant "a new awareness of the seriousness of *solitude,* not simply as an expression of man's existential plight, but as a Christian value, a challenge, and even as a vocation" (237/251). Merton attempts to show there has been "a constant tradition, in Western monasticism, and even within the Cistercian Order, which has not only recognized the rights of the solitary vocation in theory, but has even permitted certain simple, concrete solutions within the juridical and institutional framework of the monastic state" (324/336).

Part 3, "Contemplative Life," consists of a single piece entitled "Is the Contemplative Life Finished?" published in *Monastic Studies* in 1969. It is comprised of notes from taped conferences and consists of a series of reflections on various aspects of the contemplative life. The subtitles offer an indication of the range of topics addressed by Merton: "Prayer," "Good Souls," "The Sacrifice of Security," "Contemplative Life," "The Imagination," "Liberating the Imagination," "Catholic Pessimism," "Natural Problems," "What Is Monastic?" "A Life of Charismatic Freedom," "Asceticism," "Martha and Mary," "The Discipline of Listening," "Contemplative and Mystic," "Christian Community," "Active Service," "Attentiveness to God," "Deviations," "Penance," and "Prayer for Faith."

Reissued as the first work in the Gethsemani Studies in Psychological and Religious Anthropology Series, *Contemplation in a World of Action* was published by the University of Notre Dame Press in 1998 with a foreword by Robert Coles. This edition of the book differs from the 1971 edition in that three sections included in the 1971 edition have not been reprinted here. Not included in the 1998 edition are the original introduction by Jean Leclercq, O.S.B.; two essays presented as appendices to the original part 1; and the original part 2, consisting of five essays that appeared under the heading "The Case for Eremitism." CMB

Notes

1. In this article, the first page citation number refers to the Doubleday hardcover edition, and the second to the Image paperback edition.

CONTEMPLATIVE PRAYER

SEE *THE CLIMATE OF MONASTIC PRAYER.*

CONVERSION

The story of Thomas Merton's conversion is told, in part, in *The Seven Storey Mountain,* in which Merton recounts his spiritual awakening, his reception into the Roman Catholic Church, and his becoming a Trappist monk. Although Merton knew moments of spiritual awareness during his youth and adolescence, it was while he was a student at Columbia that he experienced conversion. It is clear from his account that he saw his conversion as a process rather than as a single event, and he recognized that it was a process in which God took the initiative. Being at Columbia had a place in "the providential designs of God" (*Seven Storey Mountain,* 177) where "God brought me and a half dozen others together" (178). With a deeply incarnational theological perspective, Merton recognized that salvation "begins on the level of common and natural and ordinary things. . . . Books and ideas and poems and stories, pictures and music, buildings, cities, places, philosophies were to be the materials on which grace would work" (178).[1]

Among books, Merton's most significant find was Etienne Gilson's *Spirit of Medieval Philosophy,* in which Merton discovered an idea: "an entirely new concept of God" (172). "What a relief it was for me, now, to discover not only that no idea of ours, let alone any image, could adequately represent God, but also that we *should not* allow ourselves to be satisfied with any such knowledge of Him" (174–75). Reading Aldous Huxley's *Ends and Means,* Merton learned about mysticism and "the possibility of real, experimental contact with God" (186). Like many other converts, Merton hungered for a spiritual life. "My hatred of war and my own personal misery in my particular situation and the general crisis of the world made me accept with my whole heart this revelation of the need for a spiritual life, an interior life, including some kind of mortification" (187). He began reading about Eastern mysticism and then, at the suggestion of the Hindu monk Bramachari,

turned his attention to Christian classics such as St. Augustine's *Confessions* and Thomas à Kempis's *The Imitation of Christ.* "Now that I look back on those days, it seems to me very probable that one of the reasons why God had brought him all the way from India, was that he might say just that" (198). Merton's comment reveals his deep conviction that God was acting in his life, mindful of "all the external graces that had been arranged, along [his] path, by the kind Providence of God" (204).

Finding his way to a Catholic church, Merton was moved by the people he found there. "What a revelation it was, to discover so many ordinary people in a place together, more conscious of God, than of one another" (208). His reading became "more and more Catholic" as he discovered Gerard Manley Hopkins (211). He decided to take instructions, and on November 16, 1938, he was received into the Catholic Church. Merton concludes his account of his sacramental initiation with a statement that captures what he realized to be at the heart of his conversion: "I had entered into the everlasting movement of that gravitation which is the very life and spirit of God: God's own gravitation towards the depths of His own infinite nature, His goodness without end. And God, that center Who is everywhere, and whose circumference is nowhere, finding me, through incorporation with Christ, incorporated into this immense and tremendous gravitational movement which is love, which is the Holy Spirit, loved me. And He called out to me from His own immense depths" (225).

Embraced by God's love and drawn to the center that is God, the new convert began living the life of faith. Conversion was not simply an event that had marked his entry into the Catholic Church. Conversion became, for him, a way of life, as a Christian, monk, and contemplative. As a Christian, he heard himself called, as all Christians are, to heed the Gospel imperative of *metanoia,* the change of heart, the change of consciousness. As a monk, he committed himself to *metanoia* in an intentional and explicit way: through the vow of *conversio morum,* one of three vows taken by Trappist monks. *Conversio morum,* which literally means "conversion of manners" and is also translated as "conversion of life," is a commitment to inner transformation. As a contemplative, he knew that inner transformation involved awakening to his true identity in God. "We are not 'converted' only once in our life but many times, and this endless series of large and small 'conversions,' inner revolutions, leads finally to our transformation in Christ" (*Life and Holiness*, 159). CMB

SEE ALSO CONTEMPLATION; GOD; *SEVEN STOREY MOUNTAIN*; VOWS, MONASTIC.

Notes

1. For an in-depth discussion of conversion and Thomas Merton's conversion in particular, see Walter Conn, *Christian Conversion: A Developmental Interpretation of Autonomy and Surrender* (New York: Paulist Press, 1986).

CORPUS CHRISTI CHURCH

Corpus Christi Church is located at 529 West 121st Street, New York. In September of 1938 Thomas Merton made the decision to go to the Corpus Christi rectory to ask for instructions

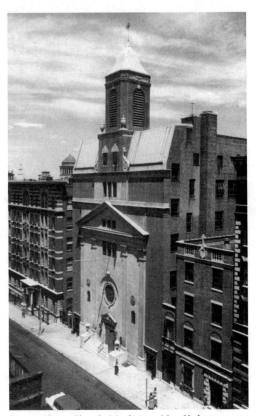

Corpus Christi Church, Manhattan, New York

about the Catholic Church. On November 16, 1938, Fr. Joseph C. Moore, who had given the instructions, received him into the Roman Catholic Church. Edward Rice was his godfather. It was also at Corpus Christi Church that he was confirmed, on May 25, 1939, by Bishop Stephen J. Donahue. He took James as his confirmation name. For some time after, he signed himself Thomas James Merton. It was the name he used on June 26, 1951, when he became a naturalized American citizen. WHS

COURAGE FOR TRUTH, THE:
The Letters of Thomas Merton to Writers

Edited by Christine M. Bochen. New York: Farrar, Straus and Giroux, 1993. xiv+314 pp.

This volume of Thomas Merton's letters to writers, the fourth of five volumes of letters published under the general editorship of William H. Shannon, spans the period from 1948, when Merton's autobiography became an instant bestseller, until 1968, when he died in Bangkok.[1] For twenty years Merton corresponded with an ever widening circle of writers — many prominent, some less well known — all over the world. The letters reflect his kinship with all writers and his special sense of solidarity with those resisting forces of social oppression and political tyranny. The title of the volume reflects Merton's conviction that writers, especially poets, must speak the truth. Merton was convinced that poets "remain almost the only ones who have anything to say" and that they have "the courage to disbelieve what is shouted from every loudspeaker; and it is this courage that is most of all necessary today" (*Courage for Truth*, 172). Fidelity to truth requires courage, and those who speak truth can find strength when they are "guided by a common inspiration and a communion in truth" (159).

The volume is divided into five parts. Part 1 contains the earliest letters in the volume, Merton's letters to Evelyn Waugh, which reveal a young and enthusiastic, if somewhat naive, monk and writer, delighted to be exchanging letters with the renowned man of letters. "I am in a difficult spot here as a writer," Merton wrote to Waugh. "I am told to 'write' and so I cover pages and pages with matter and they go to several different censors and get lost, torn up, burned, and so on. Then they get pieced together and retyped and go to a publisher who changes everything and after about four years a book appears in print" (4). Feeling isolated because he was unable to discuss his work with fellow writers, Merton proclaimed himself to "need criticism the way a man dying of thirst needs water" (4). Waugh, who edited *The Seven Storey Mountain* for publication in England, where Merton's autobiography was published as *Elected Silence,* was more than willing to comply and issued critical comments on *The Seven Storey Mountain, The Waters of Siloe,* and *Seeds of Contemplation,* which Merton received with humility, grace, and gratitude.

The letters in part 2 celebrate Merton's friendships with Jacques Maritain and Czeslaw Milosz and testify to Merton's profound connection with Boris Pasternak. Merton's correspondence with these three writers easily bridged the distance of geography. With each, Merton exchanged ideas, but more importantly, he shared something of himself. With French philosopher Jacques Maritain, Merton shared a common Catholic heritage, love for the contemplative tradition, and concern for the issues facing the church. Even though they did not always see eye to eye on those issues, Merton knew that Maritain understood his hunger for solitude, his desire to get free of illusions, and his determination to "try to forget the more obvious entanglements with all that is trivial and passing, and to get more into the heart of things" (44). In Czeslaw Milosz, Merton found a writer who taught him about the predicament of writers in totalitarian regimes and about writing as an act of resistance. If Merton found in Milosz a kindred spirit, he also found him to be an honest critic whose experiences, so different from Merton's, made Milosz especially critical of Merton's romantic views of nature and his antiwar stand. Merton's brief correspondence with Boris Pasternak reveals Merton's admiration and affection for Pasternak. "Although we are separated by great distances and even greater barriers it gives me

pleasure to speak to you as to one whom I feel to be a kindred mind.... With other writers I can share ideas, but you seem to communicate something deeper. It is as if we met on a deeper level of life on which individuals are not separate beings ... it is as if we were known to one another in God" (87–88). While Merton reached out to encourage Pasternak, he also shared himself to the point of telling Pasternak about his dream about Proverb (the feminine embodiment of divine Wisdom). Also included in this section of the book are several letters relevant to Merton's correspondence with Pasternak: a letter that Merton wrote to Aleksei Surkov, head of the Soviet Writers Union, to protest the union's expulsion of Pasternak after he was named to receive the Nobel Prize for literature, and letters to Helen Wolff at Pantheon Books, Pasternak's American publisher, who shared news of Pasternak with Merton.

Merton's letters to Ernesto Cardenal, written between 1959 and 1968, appear in part 3. Their correspondence began in 1959 when Cardenal, who had been a novice at Gethsemani, returned to Nicaragua, and Merton, his novice master, wrote to offer him support and encouragement. At the same time, Merton was making plans to leave Gethsemani to live as a monk in Latin America, and Cardenal was Merton's enthusiastic source of information. Not only do Merton's letters to Cardenal record Merton's crisis of stability in 1959 and its resolution (Merton stayed at Gethsemani), but also they document Merton's life through the 1960s with remarkable completeness. In Ernesto Cardenal, Merton had found someone with whom he could honestly share what was on his mind and in his heart as a contemplative, social critic, and writer. Cardenal was Merton's primary contact in Latin America and instrumental in promoting Merton's Latin American connections.

Part 4, which includes Merton's letters to sixteen other Latin American writers — including Pablo Antonio Cuadra, Miguel Grinberg, Nicanor Parra, Ludovico Silva, José Coronel Urtecho, and Victoria Ocampo — reveals the breadth and depth of Merton's Latin American connection. Merton repeatedly proclaimed his sense of kinship with Latin American writers. In a letter to University of Hawaii professor of literature Stefan Baciu, published as a postscript to Merton's letters to Latin American writers, Merton expressed his deep sympathy with these writers and poets, who seem "to be alive, to have something honest to say, to be sincerely concerned with life and with humanity" (241).

The fifth and last part of the book is devoted to Merton's letters to a host of North American writers, including James Baldwin, Cid Corman, Guy Davenport, Clayton Eshleman, Lawrence Ferlinghetti, Julien Green, Henry Miller, Walker Percy, Jonathan Williams, William Carlos Williams, and Louis Zukofsky. These letters situate Merton in the company of American writers in the 1960s. A number of letters are related to the publication of *Monks Pond*, the literary magazine Merton edited in the last year of his life.

This volume of Merton's letters to writers enables the reader to view Merton as a writer among other writers, some of whom he counted among his close friends, and as a citizen of the world engaged in the dialogue that he saw to be his mission when, in December 1958, Merton wrote to Pope John XXIII, "It seems to me that, as a contemplative, I do not need to lock myself into solitude. . . . I also have to think in terms of a contemplative grasp of the political, intellectual, artistic, and social movements in this world — by which I mean a sympathy for the honest aspirations of so many intellectuals everywhere in the world" (*Hidden Ground of Love*, 482). Merton reported that his efforts had already, in 1958, "produced striking effects among artists, writers, publishers, poets, etc. who have become my friends without my having to leave my cloister" (482). Merton could not have foreseen the profound effect that his contacts with writers all over the world would have on him, but *The Courage for Truth* shows that this indeed was the case. CMB

SEE ALSO LATIN AMERICA.

Notes

1. Selections from the volume are included in an Italian edition entitled *Il Coraggio Della Verità*, edited and introduced by Mirco Scaccabarozzi (1997).

CREATION

The Christian doctrine of creation, according to Thomas Merton, has a much more profound significance than simply providing a solution to the puzzle of where the world came from. It is not restricted to the level of efficient causality, "merely an answer to the question of how things got to be what they are by pointing to God as a cause" (*Guilty Bystander*, 200). It is less a matter of cause and effect than of participation in absolute Being, or rather, Be-ing, the Pure Act, the inexhaustible Source, from which all contingent reality receives its existence. The starting point for the Christian understanding of creation is not a process of logical inference but an existential awareness, an insight into what it means to be, and at the same time a realization that one's being does not derive from oneself. Merton writes, "The doctrine of creation as we have it in the Bible and as it has been developed in Christian theology (particularly in St. Thomas) starts not from a *question about being* but from a *direct intuition of the act of being*" (200). Creation is not a completed act of the primordial past but an ongoing, ever present reality, since there is never a moment when contingent beings are not being called into life and filled with life by their divine Source and Goal. "My act of being is a direct participation in the Being of God. God is pure Being, this is to say He is the pure and infinite Act of total Reality. All other realities are simply reflections of His pure Act of Being, and participations in it granted by His free gift" (201). This is, of course, not pantheism, the identification of contingent reality with God, but panentheism, the awareness that nothing is, nothing can be, unless it is grounded in that which alone is Being in the true sense, *ens a se*, Being that is its own source, as Merton was astonished and overjoyed to discover in Gilson's *Spirit of Medieval Philosophy* back in February 1937 (*Seven Storey Mountain*, 171–74).

Thus, there is no opposition between Creator and creation unless the Absolute is relativized or the relative is absolutized. Merton expresses his disagreement with Karl Barth's rejection of natural theology by maintaining that "our very creation itself is a beginning of revelation" (*Water of Life*, 279). Creation is an epiphany of the divine Wisdom "playing before God the Creator in His universe.... The beauty of all creation is a reflection of Sophia living and hidden in creation" (*Witness to Freedom*, 4–5). This belief has profound implications for dialogue with non-Christian religions, which can be recognized as responses to this primordial cosmic revelation. The cosmos is a window (see *Bread in the Wilderness*, 60) through which shines the light of the Logos, the Word through which all things came, and come, to be (cf. John 1:1–3): "God creates things by seeing them in His own Logos" (*New Seeds of Contemplation*, 291). Thus, Merton sees an intrinsic relationship between creation as an epiphany of the divine Word and the incarnation as the culmination of this revelatory self-disclosure of God, the perfect manifestation of Creator in creation. "The whole character of the creation was determined by the fact that God was to become man and dwell in the midst of His own creation. Creation is therefore not a preestablished fact into which the Word will come and fit Himself as best He can at the appointed time. Creation is created and sustained in Him and by Him. And when He enters into it, He will simply make clear the fact that He is already, and has always been, the center and the life and the meaning of a universe that exists only by His will" (*New Man*, 137). Here, Merton seems clearly to be identifying with the teaching of Duns Scotus that the incarnation would have taken place even without the fall, that, as he puts it in the final chapter of *New Seeds of Contemplation*, "The Lord made the world and made man in order that He Himself might descend into the world, that He Himself might become Man" (290).

Merton draws on the traditions of Eastern Christianity to show that the apprehension and appreciation of the presence of God in God's creatures is an authentic dimension of contemplative awareness. "Natural contemplation" (*theōria physikē*, or in its Latinized form, *physica*) is not "natural" as distinguished from "supernatural" (see "Inner Experience," 4:298), but "a kind of intuitive perception of God as He is reflected in His creation" (*Ascent to Truth*, 27). It is the awareness that "Everything that is, is holy" (*New Seeds of Contemplation*, 21), and that each created being reflects the Being and holiness of God in its own unique way, the infinity of God giving rise to an innumerable variety of ways of mirroring the divine goodness and love. Echoing the poet Hopkins (and indirectly, Duns Scotus), Merton writes, "Each particular being, in its individuality, its concrete nature and entity, with all its own characteristics and its private qualities and its own inviolable identity, gives glory to God by being precisely what He wants it to be here and now.... Their inscape is their sanctity. It is the imprint of His wisdom and His reality in them" (30).

Of course, Merton is aware that this contemplative perception of the created universe is by no means automatic; it can be distorted either by despising the material world and embracing "an exaggerated asceticism that tries to sever the soul entirely from the rest of creation" (*Seasons of Celebration*, 136) or by demanding more from creation than it can provide, by turning it into an end in itself or a means to glorify the self rather than God: "The fulfillment we find in creatures belongs to the reality of the created being, a reality that is from God and belongs to God and reflects God. The anguish we find in them belongs to the disorder of our desire which looks for a greater reality in the object of our desire than is actually there: a greater fulfillment than any created thing is capable of giving. Instead of worshipping God through His creation we are always trying to worship ourselves by means of creatures" (*New Seeds of Contemplation*, 26). Thus, redemption in Christ is also a restoration of a right relationship with creation as it was meant to be, and an anticipation of the ultimate fulfillment of the cosmos in the glorified Christ, the first-born of the whole creation. "This new creation begins with the Resurrection of the Lord and will be perfected at the end of time.... The recapitulation of the work of creation sublimated and perfected in Christ is a communion in the divine life, an infusion of the life and glory and power and truth of God not only into man's spirit but also, ultimately, into all the material creation as well" (*New Man*, 150).

Redeemed humanity is called to participate in this process of extending the effects of Christ's saving work to the rest of creation. "If man's eye is 'lightsome' with the spiritual beauty of grace, wisdom, understanding and divine sonship, then light will pass through him to pervade and transfigure the whole of creation . . . by the creative work of man's own spirit, a work born out of love for God the Creator and for our fellow man. Work that springs from this creative love is patterned on the truth implanted in our very being, by nature, and in our redeemed spirit by the Pneuma who is given us by the Risen Christ" (*Seasons of Celebration*, 167–68). POC

SEE ALSO CHRISTOLOGY; CREATIVITY; ECOLOGY; NATURE.

CREATIVITY

For Thomas Merton, human creativity is a participation in the creative power and activity of God. "Our power to create is a power to consent in creation, or to work in common with the creative will that transcends both our freedom and our world" (*Water of Life*, 41). Apparent creativity that is divorced from its ground in the divine is ultimately illusory and self-contradictory, a kind of idolatrous divinization of the self as its own god, its own independent source of life and energy. "The supposed 'creativity' claimed by the untrammeled subjectivism of men who seek complete autonomy defeats itself, because man centered on himself inevitably becomes destructive" (*Faith and Violence*, 65). What is not the self, rather than being respected and cherished in its own right, is reduced to raw material for achieving the fantasies of the autonomous ego. Creativity is confused with one's own accomplishments, "a kind of semi-Pelagian productivism which is obsessed with visible results and enamored of technological prowess" (*Love and Living*, 177). From this distorted perspective, creativity is simply equated with power, the exercise of power over matter, which ironically becomes readily identified with the power to destroy, to demonstrate and so to prove one's control over nature and even other humans. It is a kind of declaration of independence: "Our power to

destroy . . . seems to us more of a power because it seems to be more unique, more personal, more autonomous. It seems to be uniquely *ours*. . . . We destroy in order to affirm our freedom and our 'reality.' The more we doubt our freedom and our identity, the more we are impelled to destroy" (*Guilty Bystander*, 315). Though Merton points out that the power is an illusion, the "destruction itself can be very objective and real" (315).

Thus, the starting point for any authentic human creativity must be an acceptance, at least implicitly, of one's total dependence upon God, and a restraint that refuses to turn one's own creativity against creation either through subjugation or destruction. True creativity is first of all a participation in the task of creating one's own identity, of becoming one's true self. Since this cannot be done in isolation, one is drawn into a partnership with others that is simultaneously a process of self-creation and a participation in the ongoing process of creating the world: "It is through our struggle with material reality, with nature, that we help one another create at the same time our own destiny and a new world for our descendants." This uniquely human vocation "is a prolongation of the creative work of God" and thus in a profound sense a fulfillment of the command to adore God the Creator by sharing and so imaging God's creative activity (*Love and Living*, 177–78). Human creativity is not an act of self-assertion but a recognition and acceptance of one's own nothingness apart from God (*Learning to Love*, 356) that is simultaneously a recognition and acceptance of "the only true power," which is never a possession, always a gift: "We are truly powerful when our autonomy is lost in Him" (*Guilty Bystander*, 316). Merton situates the "creativity in monastic life" as a particular manifestation of this self-surrender to and in love. "True monasticism is nothing if not creative" because it seeks to lose itself in union with God and so to find "a *totally new way of being in the world*" (*World of Action*, 22–23).

In his most extensive discussion of the topic, the 1960 essay "Theology of Creativity," Merton first critiques glib and superficial uses of the word: to describe the manipulation of language for pragmatic ends, as in "creative" advertising or salesmanship (*Literary Essays*, 355); creativity as a negation of itself, in which the unmaking of the old becomes its own end and the depiction of destructiveness too often becomes complicity in destructiveness (356); and the equation of creativity with frenetic activity with no clear direction or goal, a kind of primal urge that actually is considered subhuman, a welling up of subconscious energy unrestricted by the exercise of intelligent discrimination and formal shaping (356–58). He critiques four current conceptions of creativity, all of which resist "lifeless formality and aesthetic cliché" (358), but in incomplete or inadequate ways: creativity as spontaneous self-expression, not grounded in a sense of discipline and responsibility (358–59); creativity as conformity to the hidden dynamism of history, as interpreted by social or political authority, the "realism" of communist collectivism that has its capitalist equivalent in loyalty to the organization, the "team" (359–60); creativity as productivity, the quantitative criterion that dominates a consumerist culture (360); creativity as the achievement of the artist as hero, the high priest of a cult that substitutes itself for religion (360–61).

As a corrective for these distorted conceptions of creativity, Merton turns to the insights of four contemporary thinkers whose views of creativity are grounded in a recognition of the primacy of the spiritual dimension in humanity and in the world. Paul Tillich encourages the artist to recognize and wrestle with the threat of meaninglessness in a world alienated from its true ground, so that a depiction of the contemporary situation becomes an expression not of pride and revolt but of existential anguish and of humility before the mystery of life (362). From a Zen Buddhist perspective, D. T. Suzuki undermines the cult of the artist as isolated genius by abolishing the "self" as the subject of experience — the work of art is "a concretized intuition: not however presented as a unique experience of a specially endowed soul, who can then claim it as his own" but as a spontaneous expression of "emptiness" and "suchness" (364). Ananda Coomaraswamy (along with Eric Gill) emphasizes the necessity

of discipline and craftsmanship, a sense of responsibility to the work, as an antidote to the "modern heresy of a pseudo-personalist art cult in which the genius is hero and high priest" (365). Jacques Maritain's articulation and defense of the "creative intuition" of the artist reconciles the drive for self-expression and the revelation of the "hidden mystery of things" by recognizing that mystery in the depths of the authentic self, which is intrinsically related to a society and world to which the artist has "loyalties and obligations" (366).

Drawing on these thinkers, Merton sketches in a theology of creativity that contrasts authentic creativity as collaboration with God with the futile attempt at autonomous creation, a "magical" manipulation of reality that is both "absurd and servile" (367). True creativity is the renunciation of a spurious autonomy and the recovery of authentic human identity as made in the image of God and therefore participating in the creative activity of Trinitarian love, pure and disinterested self-donation. "Creativity becomes possible insofar as man can forget his limitations and his selfhood and lose himself in abandonment to the immense creative power of a love too great to be seen or comprehended" (368). A theology of creativity would at once be an affirmation of the infinite value of the person and a proper situating of the person in the dynamic vitality of the entire creation. Creativity is not the preserve of an elite, the talented few: "Every Christian has his own creative work to do, his own part in the mystery of the 'new creation'" (370). The vocation of the artist is a privileged expression of the vocation of every Christian, of every human, to participate in the ongoing task, centered in and flowing from the cross and resurrection of Christ, of redeeming the time, of renewing the face of the earth. Merton concludes his essay by focusing on the "eschatological dimensions of Christian creativity," reminding his reader of St. Paul's assertion that "'all creation is groaning' for the final manifestation of this finished work, the only work that has an eternal importance: the full revelation of God by the restoration of all things in Christ" (370). POC

SEE ALSO ART, THEORY OF; POETRY, THEORY OF.

CULTURE

Thomas Merton was both committed to the values of his own culture and open to the contributions of other cultures and an advocate of what he called "transcultural consciousness." He declared himself to be "deeply in sympathy with . . . the traditional religious culture of the West" (*Guilty Bystander*, 293), and this sympathy extended beyond the religious to the broader cultural milieu of Europe. Some of the most lyrical pages in *Conjectures of a Guilty Bystander* are those in which he reflects on the roots of his own intellectual and spiritual inheritance, as when he speaks of Paris as the cultural capital of Western Christendom, and remarks, "The sign of Paris is on me, indelibly!" (163), both because it was there that his parents first met as art students, and because of the varied streams of tradition — Dionysian, Victorine, Franciscan, Thomistic — that converged there and influenced his own formation. It is of these and the tradition they represent that he writes, "I know I must keep alive in myself what I have once known and grown into: and if anyone else wants a part of it, I can try to pass it on" (169). Merton does not come to an encounter with other cultures empty-handed; his own tradition is vitally present in him and available to be communicated to others. Secure in his own cultural identity, he was not threatened by different ideas or customs, and so was able to respond to them creatively rather than to react defensively.

But if Merton is no rootless, alienated wanderer in search of a replacement for a culture he had rejected, or felt had rejected him, neither is he an apologist for Western hubris, a cultural imperialist bent on proving the superiority of his own position and determined to impose it on others. To become thoroughly conversant with one's own culture is to recognize its shortcomings and distortions, its past sins, its current problems, its future threats. This self-critical attitude is itself one of the strengths of Western culture, in Merton's opinion, though one increasingly endangered by a conformist, materialist, and totalitarian mindset (62). Thus, Merton's prophetic critique of the crimes and the follies of his own country

and his own culture is an expression of fidelity and commitment to the best and most genuine impulses of that culture. It is, of course, no less critical for that. His analyses of the depersonalization that he discovers at the heart of the problems of war, of racism, of colonial exploitation, of quantified, technological, soulless mass society are all the more powerful for his belief that these evils are antithetical to the authentic genius of the West, albeit they reflect strands of thought and behavior present from the earliest days of European civilization. Merton displays a profound yet healthily realistic ambivalence toward his own tradition. He recognizes that any Westerner encountering other cultures brings a double heritage, representing both the admirable and the shameful aspects of white, European civilization. To neglect or deny either of these dimensions is to doom any encounter to frustration, since it will be based not on honesty but on either self-hatred or an unwarranted, self-satisfied complacency. By acknowledging the full impact of Western culture on its own people and the rest of the world, Merton positions himself for a mutually beneficial contact with non-Western cultures.

It is particularly important, in Merton's view, to comprehend other civilizations on their own terms, not to make any premature attempt at assimilation, to reject the temptation to incorporate congenial elements of another culture into one's own worldview and to discard the rest. Such an approach simply would be colonialism in another guise. There must be a willingness to recognize and respect the integrity of another culture, to respond to it, as best one can, as a whole. "One cannot arrive at an understanding of any 'wisdom,' whether natural or supernatural, by arguing either for or against it. Wisdom is not penetrated by logical analysis" (*Thomas Merton Reader*, 302). What is needed, rather, to appreciate the core values of another tradition, is the sympathetic effort to perceive the world from the standpoint of the other, to enter as far as possible into that framework. On its deepest level, this receptivity is an openness to the divine present within the other: "God speaks, and God is to be heard, not only on Sinai, not only in my own heart, but in the *voice of the stranger*.... We must, then, see the truth in the stranger, and the truth we see must be a newly living truth, not just a projection of a dead conventional idea of our own — a projection of our own self upon the stranger" (*Collected Poems*, 384–85). To do this is to take a risk, to put in jeopardy the comfortable, secure conception of truth one already has, but it also is to make possible a widened, broadened, deepened awareness of truth that is pure gift, grace, revelation.

Having made the commitment to patient listening, one then is able to relate new insights to his or her own tradition, to move from comprehension to convergence and synthesis, as one sees the strengths and weaknesses of one's own culture from a new standpoint, through the eyes of the other. That the questions raised and the insights offered by another worldview are profoundly relevant to the development of one's own tradition was a truth known by the early generations of Christians, for whom Platonism provided "a language and a sensibility that were equipped to penetrate in a specially significant way the depths of the revealed mystery of Christ" (*Thomas Merton Reader*, 303). It characterized the flowering of medieval Christian society, which was enriched by "turning to the non-Christian world — to Aristotle and to Islam" (*Guilty Bystander*, 186). This same cross-pollenization, Merton maintains, is needed today if the West, if the world, is to surmount its crises: "The cultural heritage of Asia has as much right to be studied in our colleges as the cultural heritage of Greece and Rome.... If the West continues to underestimate and to neglect the spiritual heritage of the East, it may hasten the tragedy that threatens man and his civilizations. If the West can recognize that contact with Eastern thought can renew our appreciation for our own cultural heritage, a product of the fusion of the Judeo-Christian religion with Greco-Roman culture, then it will be easier to defend that heritage, not only in Asia but in the West as well" (*Mystics and Zen Masters*, 45–46).

Besides considering another culture on its own terms, and discovering how to integrate it with one's own tradition, there is a further step in which the artifacts of another cul-

ture become part of one's own heritage. One recognizes a kinship that transcends cultural differences and grounds itself in what all human beings share, precisely their humanity. Thus, in the preface to *Mystics and Zen Masters* Merton announces that the aim of someone like himself is "not merely to look at these other traditions coldly and objectively from the outside, but, in some measure at least, to try to share in the values and the experience which they embody. In other words, he is not content to write about them without making them, as far as possible, 'his own'" (ix). While acknowledging that it is perhaps impossible fully to achieve this transcultural appropriation, Merton nevertheless is convinced that in the emergent global society it is crucially important to go beyond a narrow, parochial conception of culture: "We hopefully look forward not to an age of eclecticism and syncretism, certainly, but to an age of understanding and adaptation that will be able to synthesize and make use of all that is good and noble in all the traditions of the past.... We must hope for a new world culture that takes account of all civilized philosophies" (65).

It is this capacity to transcend the limitations of one's own worldview, to become "in a certain sense identified with everybody" (*World of Action*, 211), that Merton, drawing on the Persian-American psychoanalyst Reza Arasteh, calls "final integration." "The man who has attained final integration is no longer limited by the culture in which he has grown up.... He accepts not only his own community, his own society, his own friends, his own culture, but all mankind.... He is fully 'Catholic' in the best sense of the word. He has a unified vision and experience of the one truth shining out in all its various manifestations, some clearer than others, some more definite and more certain than others. He does not set these partial views up in opposition to each other, but unifies them in a dialectic or an insight of complementarity" (212). Merton believes that this vision can no longer be the preserve of a few, but is now "becoming a need and aspiration of mankind as a whole" (216), a necessity if humanity is to surmount the "existential crisis" in which it finds itself.

Yet, as critically important as this mutual

interpenetration of various traditions certainly is, Merton reminds us that absolute loyalty is due neither to a single culture nor to a synthesis of all cultures. The ultimate stage of transcultural consciousness transcends the very category of culture itself. "The path to final integration for the individual, and for the community lies, in any case, beyond the dictates and programs of any culture ('Christian culture' included)" (217), because all culture, all human achievement, is provisional, partial, a limited approximation of the divine design for humanity, the fullness of truth, the reign of God. "For a Christian," Merton writes, "a transcultural integration is eschatological. The rebirth of man and of society on a transcultural level is a rebirth into the transformed and redeemed time, the time of the Kingdom, the time of the Spirit, the time of 'the end.' It means a disintegration of the social and cultural self, the product of merely human history, and the reintegration of that self in Christ, in salvation history, in the mystery of redemption, in the Pentecostal 'new creation'" (216). POC

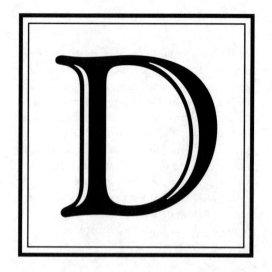

DALAI LAMA (TENZIN GYATSO)

Tenzin Gyatso, born July 6, 1935, in a small village in northeastern Tibet of a peasant family, was recognized at the age of two as the fourteenth Dalai Lama, the reincarnation of his predecessor and an incarnation of Avalokitesvara, the Buddha of Compassion. His enthronement took place on February 22, 1940. He was educated in Tibet and at the age of twenty-five he completed the Doctorate of Buddhist Philosophy. In 1950 he was called to assume full political power, as Tibet was invaded by Chinese soldiers. His efforts to achieve a peaceful solution were thwarted by Beijing. A revolt sprang up in Tibet and was brutally crushed by the Chinese army. The Dalai Lama escaped to Nepal, where he was given political asylum. Tibetan refugees followed him. As many as 120,000 live there in exile. In 1989 he was awarded the Nobel Peace Prize, to the plaudits of the whole world, China alone excepted. The Nobel Prize Committee cited his consistent opposition to the use of violence and his efforts to seek peaceful solutions, based on tolerance and mutual respect, in order to preserve the historical and cultural heritage of his people.

Cover for *Dancing in the Water of Life* reprinted with the permission of HarperSanFrancisco.

Harold Talbott, an American student of Buddhism (at the time studying with the Dalai Lama) met Thomas Merton at New Delhi and brought him to his bungalow in Dharamsala. Talbott arranged for Merton to meet the Dalai Lama. Merton reports on their conversations in *The Asian Journal* and in volume 7 of the journals, *The Other Side of the Mountain*. At their first meeting (November 4, 1968), the conversation was about religion, philosophy, and ways of meditation. Merton was impressed by the Dalai Lama. Clearly, the feeling was mutual, as the Dalai Lama invited him to return for a second discussion. The second audience was on November 6. They talked about the freedom and transformation of consciousness that comes with meditation. Merton wrote, "I like the solidity of the Dalai Lama's ideas.... His ideas of the interior life are built on very solid foundations and on a real awareness of practical problems. He insists on detachment, on an 'unworldly life,' yet sees it as a way to complete understanding of, and participation in, the problems of life and the world. But renunciation and detachment must come first" (*Asian Journal*, 113; *Other Side of the Mountain*, 258–59). The third visit, on November 8, was in many ways the best, Merton felt. They talked about Western monasticism, Marxism, and more abstruse topics relating to Buddhism. "It was a very warm

The Dalai Lama and Abbot Timothy Kelly, O.C.S.O., at Thomas Merton's grave.

and cordial discussion," Merton wrote, "and at the end I felt we had become very good friends and were somehow quite close to one another" (125/266).

In his autobiography, *Freedom in Exile* (New York: HarperCollins, 1990), the Dalai Lama spoke of his meetings with Merton: "I could see he was a truly humble and deeply spiritual man. This was the first time I had been struck by such a feeling of spirituality in anyone who professed Christianity" (189). In 1995 the Dalai Lama came to Gethsemani and visited Merton's grave. He sat in silence for a few moments by the cross that marked the place where Merton's mortal remains had been buried. After rising from prayer, he said, "I am now in touch with his spirit" (from a videotape of the Dalai Lama's visit). WHS

DANCING IN THE WATER OF LIFE: *Seeking Peace in the Hermitage*

The Journals of Thomas Merton, vol. 5: 1963–65. Edited by Robert E. Daggy. San Francisco: HarperSanFrancisco, 1997, xviii+363 pp.

This fifth of the seven volumes of Thomas Merton's complete journals covers a period of almost two and one-half years, from August 1963 through the end of 1965.[1] Its title is taken not from the journal itself but from "Message to Poets," sent to a gathering in Mexico City of young, mostly Latin American poets in February 1964, which concludes with the invitation "Come, dervishes: here is the water of life. Dance in it" (*Raids on the Unspeakable*, 161).

The subtitle refers to the single most significant event of Merton's life during this period, the beginning of his full-time commitment to the solitary life in August 1965; the peace which he sought suggests both the inner tranquillity of what he called, in his farewell conference as novice master, "a life free from care," and his continued commitment as a hermit to the cause of world peace.

The period also is marked by significant social and political events such as the assassination of John F. Kennedy, the escalation of the Vietnam War, and continued racial unrest, including the Birmingham church bombing; by important developments in ecclesial and monastic life, including the last three sessions of the Second Vatican Council, promulgation and beginnings of implementation of Council documents, particularly the Constitution on the Sacred Liturgy (Sacrosanctum Concilium) and the Constitution on the Church in the Modern World (Gaudium et Spes), and the death of the Cistercian abbot general, Dom Gabriel Sortais, and the election of his successor, Dom Ignace Gillet; by significant events in Merton's own life, including his fiftieth birthday, two extended hospital stays, the opening of the Merton Room at Bellarmine University, where his papers would be housed, visits from friends such as Rabbi Abraham Heschel and Marco Pallis and from survivors of the Hiroshima bombing, as well as Merton's own trip to New York City to see the aged Zen scholar D. T. Suzuki, the memorable retreat with peace activists on "The Spiritual Roots of Non-Violence," and numerous publications, including books on Gandhi, Chuang Tzu, and liturgy, his first volume of poetry in six years, and the long-delayed appearance in book form of his writings on peace and justice issues. Commentary on these events and many others appear in the journal, as well as reflections on reading, writing, living alone in the midst of nature, and living in solidarity with everyone else in a world both lovely and threatened.

The journal is divided by the editor into five sections plus an appendix, though the bulk of the material comes from a single manuscript notebook. The first section is given the title "Living as a Part-time Solitary" and covers the

period from August 3, 1963, through June 13, 1964, with a total of 141 entries. During these months Merton continues to serve as novice master while also spending time in solitude in the cinder block cabin on Mount Olivet that already he is calling the hermitage. His reflections on his life at this time include strong self-criticism for what he calls "my lack of seriousness, my triviality, my dilettantism," though at the same time he notes his resistance to "merg[ing] them in a triviality and false seriousness that are general and canonized by the fact that they are common to many and officially approved" (Water of Life, 69). Despite his reference to "dilettantism," clearly he realizes that his breadth of interests is intrinsic to his vocation, writing: "I know I should equally well read Sartre and Ammonas or Theodoret on Julian Saba. Both are relevant to me at the same time. To pretend otherwise would be to lie" (68). This simultaneous commitment both to the tradition and to the present is evident throughout this period, as he compares the late eleventh-century philosophy of St. Anselm to that of Jean-Paul Sartre (12, 16), writes on the same day to the cloistered English Benedictine Dame Hildelith Cumming about his work on Guigo the Carthusian and to Meg Randall, the editor of the avant-garde literary magazine El Corno Emplumado, on his abstract drawings (24), and expresses enthusiasm in the same entry for the monastic letters of Abelard and for Walker Percy's novel The Moviegoer (63–64); at the same time as he is writing articles on Zen (33) and "The Black Revolution" (24), he is beginning novitiate conferences on Cîteaux and Cluny (20); he writes of mailing off the text for a pamphlet on monasticism for the abbey at Snowmass in Colorado in the same entry that he mentions sending the typescript of Gandhi on Non-Violence to New Directions (102).

The second, brief section, "The Suzuki Visit," which details in four entries Merton's trip to New York in June 1964, is taken from a small reading notebook he had brought with him. Along with his descriptions of the two talks he had with Suzuki, which he calls "very pleasant, and profoundly important to me" (116), because of the rapport he felt with someone whom he respected highly and whose

affirmation confirmed his sense of the validity of his own studies of Zen, Merton records
his unexpected feelings of warmth and appreciation for New York (114, 116), visits to
a restaurant and the Guggenheim Museum
(117), and the "deeply mov[ing]" experience
of saying Mass at the altar of Corpus Christi
Church, where he had made his profession of
faith at his baptism (117).

The third section, entitled "The Joy and Absurdity of Increasing Solitude," consists of 145
entries from June 23, 1964, through the end of
April 1965. Summarizing his life at this time,
he writes, "Literature, contemplation, solitude,
Latin America — Asia, Zen, Islam, etc. All
these things combine in my life. It would be
madness to make a 'monasticism' by simply excluding them. I would be less a monk. Others
have their own way, I have mine" (125). To
these subjects might be added photography
(149), abstract drawings (175), and Orthodoxy
(181), as well as stinging social commentary on
race, technology, and war. On the occasion of
his fiftieth birthday he takes stock of his past,
reflecting, "No matter what mistakes and illusions have marked my life, most of it I think
has been happiness and, as far as I can tell,
truth"; he considers that both the "profound-
est and happiest times of my life" and "some of
the most terrible" have been at Gethsemani,
recalling times in the woods and at the hermitage, work with the novices, and visits with
friends as examples of the former; he begins
to list friends old and new, only to conclude,
"Why go on? *Deo gratias* . . . for all of them"
(199). During the fall he had begun to sleep
on occasion at the hermitage (153), and even
to spend full days there (179); by the spring
he is reflecting both on the joy and peace of
solitude (209) and the challenge to a fidelity
that is neither passivity nor activism (224) and
that will lead to a proper sense of detachment
by which one is enabled "to love and serve the
man of the modern world, but not simply to
succumb, with him, to all his illusions about
his world" (226).

Such reflections lead up to Merton's essay
"Day of a Stranger," the first version of which,
written in May 1965, is included as part 4 of
the journal. Though considerably less devel-

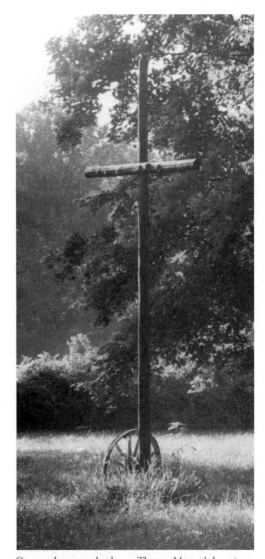

Cross and wagon wheel near Thomas Merton's hermitage

oped than, and to some extent different from,
the final essay, this preliminary draft introduces
the contrast between the natural and cultural
ecology of life in the hermitage and the unbalanced "non-ecology" of war and pollution and
inequality; it takes the narrator through his
day from predawn prayer and the coming of
the light, to the return to the abbey and duties
of the novitiate, then back to the hermitage,
identifying with the political prisoner, unable
to escape the constrictions of a powerful and
destructive society, and with the poet, speaking a word of freedom from others' illusions and

freedom from self, to be found only "under the dark tree that springs up in the center of the night and of silence, the paradise tree, the *axis mundi*, which is also the Cross" (242).

The final section, "Hermit in the Water of Life," includes 105 entries dating from May through December 1965. It focuses above all on preparation for the permanent move to the hermitage and the early months of solitary life, which he calls "a revelation, . . . what I have always hoped it would be and always sought. A life of peace, silence, purpose, meaning" (283), and also "a 'return to the world,' not a return to the cities, but a return to direct and humble contact with God's world, His creation, and the world of poor men who work" (293). But it is not an escape from the problems of the world of "the cities" either, as Merton learns from the controversies in which he becomes embroiled over the use of his "Freedom Songs" (325) and his relations with the Catholic Peace Fellowship in the aftermath of the suicide of protester Roger LaPorte (314); there is even a brief reprise of wanderlust as Merton toys for a last time with the idea of going into "exile" in Nicaragua (308–9). But there is also contentment and enrichment in reading Rilke (305) and Isaac of Stella (298), and working what will become *Conjectures of a Guilty Bystander* into final form (297). Merton concludes the year by wondering what the following year will bring, conjecturing illness, war, less writing, more meditation. He concludes, "But I have no real plans, except to live and free the reality of my life and be ready when it ends and I am called to God. Whenever that may be!" (329).

The appendix, taken from one of Merton's working notebooks, consists of a lengthy reflection followed by two entries dated December 2 and 4, from a section Merton called "Some Personal Notes, End 1965–Beginning 1966." The reflection, evidently written over a period of some weeks, is a critical self-examination of his hermit life after the first bloom has passed, warning himself against the delusions of taking on an objectivized identity, a "role," of hermit (335), or attaching himself to some "cause," even a good and just one (343), or looking for satisfaction in his work: "My own personal task is not simply that of poet and writer (still

less commentator, pseudo-prophet), it is basically to *praise* God out of an inner center of silence, gratitude and 'awareness'" (347). The same basic theme occupies the two dated entries, the last of which concludes with a reflection on his own work in the light of Rilke's distinction between art sprung from necessity and unnecessary work that is therefore not art, concluding with a saying from Abba Arsenius that the monk should "not occupy himself with anything and he will find rest" (349), an encouragement to radical detachment that would remain for Merton an unfulfilled ideal through his remaining three years. POC

SEE ALSO DAY OF A STRANGER; VOW OF CONVERSATION.

Notes

1. A considerably revised and abridged version of some of this material, entries from January 1, 1964, through September 6, 1965, shortly after his removal to the hermitage, was prepared by Merton in 1968 for publication under the title A *Vow of Conversation*, though it did not finally appear until 1988, after the death of Dom James Fox (see Naomi Burton Stone's preface to the volume, ix–x).

DARJEELING

A famous Himalayan hill station, Darjeeling is also a tourist center with excellent views of Mount Kanchenjunga and Mount Everest. WHS

DARK NIGHT, THE

For St. John of the Cross the spiritual journey to God involves two ascents into darkness, which he calls, respectively, "the night of the senses" and "the night of the spirit." Thomas Merton describes them thus: "The mind must detach itself from sensible appearances and seek God in those invisible realities which the intellect alone can apprehend. . . . This darkening of the senses is like a cloud in which the soul becomes accustomed to traveling blind, without relying on the appearances of changing things or on the emotional import of experience in its judgments of truth and falsity, of good and evil." The night of the spirit is an even deeper darkness. "Before the spirit can see the Living God, it must be blind even to the highest perceptions and judgments of its natural intelligence.

It must enter into pure darkness. But this darkness is pure light — because it is the infinite Light of God Himself. And the mere fact that His Light is infinite means that it is darkness to our finite minds" (*Ascent to Truth*, 50).

In his poem "The Dark Encounter," Merton speaks of the wordless silence of this "dark night" encounter with Reality itself: "O Silence with no syllable for weapon, / . . . Slaying the meaning of the mind's alarums, / . . . Our eyes are wider than the word: 'Aware,' / O darkness full of vision, vivid night, / Defying the frontier. / O silence full of execution, / All intuition and desire lie destroyed / When Substance is our Conqueror." In this encounter the mystic, touched by the divine light of God's very Self is born into new life "full of sweet delight! / What secret and intrepid Visitor / Has come to raise us from the dead? / He softly springs the locks of time, our sepulchre, / In the foretold encounter" (*Collected Poems*, 112–13).

For these two nights of darkness described by St. John of the Cross, Merton finds early patristic authority. In his *Life of Moses*, Gregory of Nyssa (335–95) describes the contemplative approach to God in terms of the three movements of Moses toward God. Moses first experiences light in the burning bush (Exodus 3). Then there are two ascents, each time into a deeper darkness (see Exodus 19, wherein Moses ascends into the cloud on the mountain, and Exodus 33, wherein he sees the glory of God). In Merton's words, "These degrees of the ascent to God were symbolized, thought St. Gregory, in the degrees of illumination and darkness through which Moses journeyed to God. Moses first saw God in the burning bush. Then he was led by God across the desert in a pillar of cloud. Finally he ascended Sinai, where God spoke to him 'face to face,' but in the divine darkness" (*Ascent to Truth*, 50–51). In the night of the senses a person approaches God by letting go of images and concepts (thus entering darkness by turning off its own lights) and is actively open to receive God's gifts of grace. In the night of the spirit one enters into the habitual practice of the Prayer of Quiet in which God acts and unites the person to the divine Self in mystical union. Into the abyss of the blazing glory that is God, so infinitely

bright as to be pure darkness to our intelligence, the mystic enters (i.e., is led by the touch of God), "in order to be transformed like a bar of iron in the white heat of a furnace. The iron turns in fire. The mystic is 'transformed' in God" (261).

This transformation into God takes place in a context of love. Faith gives us title to this divine treasure that is ours to possess in darkness. "Love enters the darkness and lays hands upon what is our own" (295). Faith makes clear that the divine Reality is so great that no words of ours can contain its meaning. "But love, which transports the soul into the darkness beyond faith, [unites our being to the Being of God in such a way that we seem to be annihilated and to vanish out of existence, so that nothing remains but the power and the glory of God]. It is in this way that love astounds the intelligence with vivid reports of a transcendent Actuality which minds can only know, on earth, by a confession of ignorance. And so, when the mind admits that God is too great for our knowledge, Love replies: 'I know Him!'" (295–96).[1] WHS

SEE ALSO APOPHATICISM; CONTEMPLATION; MYSTICISM.

Notes

1. *The Ascent to Truth*, 295–96. It is worth noting that the words in brackets was eliminated from the French edition of *The Ascent to Truth*. Moreover, it should be pointed out that Merton declared the French edition to be the only definitive edition. For information regarding other deletions in this work, see ASCENT TO TRUTH.

DAY, DOROTHY

When Dorothy Day (1897–1980) was received into the Catholic Church in 1927, she brought with her a strong commitment to social justice, a deep concern for the poor, and an uncompromising pacifist attitude toward war. Indeed, she found many of the radical positions she had shared with socialists, anarchists, and communists in her earlier years to be in harmony with Catholic social teaching and with the gospel.

One of the truly prophetic voices in the history of the Catholic Church in the twentieth century, she managed to combine radical views on social issues with a conservative and unquestioning theology of church and sacraments. She lived at the Catholic Worker House in New York City, a poor woman among the poor. She inspired a whole generation of Catholic social activists, Thomas Merton among them. She was an able writer, doing regular columns for the *Catholic Worker*. She wrote several books, including *From Union Square to Rome*, her autobiography; *The Long Loneliness*, which retells her story; and *Loaves and Fishes*, which tells of her meeting with Peter Maurin and their founding of the Catholic Worker movement.

On the jacket of *Loaves and Fishes*, Merton wrote, "Poverty for Dorothy Day is more than a sociological problem, it is also a religious mystery." He had great respect, even a reverential awe, for this remarkable woman, who was for him a symbol of the deepest meaning of the Christian gospel: concern for the poor, the neglected, and the homeless. He admired her unrelenting opposition to war, and although he refused to call himself a pacifist, his commitment to nonviolence brought him very close to her position on war.

Between July 9, 1959, and July 25, 1968, Merton wrote twenty-nine letters to her. In a letter of December 29, 1965, he wrote, "If there were no *Catholic Worker* and such forms of witness, I would never have joined the Catholic Church" (*Hidden Ground of Love*, 151). WHS

DAY OF A STRANGER
Salt Lake City: Gibbs M. Smith, 1981. 63 pp.

This is a short essay describing a "typical day" in Thomas Merton's life in the period just before he retired as novice master at the Abbey of Gethsemani and became a full-time hermit. It was written in May 1965 at the request of his friend the Argentinian poet and editor Miguel Grinberg and first appeared in a South American journal. It was published in *The Hudson Review*, no. 20 (1967), and reprinted posthumously in book form with numerous photographs by Merton and a helpful introduction by Robert E. Daggy. An earlier version of the essay is now available in *Dancing in the Water of Life*, the fifth volume of the complete Merton journals.

The essay reveals the essential elements of the life of solitude as Merton had already begun to experience it. In describing his day, Merton presents his life as a unique way of experiencing a common humanity. The word "stranger" in the title might initially suggest someone whose way of life is strange or exotic, but eventually it takes on the connotations of one who does not fit in, whose identity cannot be defined by a public role, a recognized place in society at large or monastic society in particular, cannot, in fact, be defined at all. Merton takes pains to dispel the impression of strangeness in the first sense by emphasizing that in fundamental ways his life is no different from anybody else's, but this very ordinariness protects and nurtures the mystery of identity that unfolds throughout the description of the day.

The essay is simply structured in two main sections: the first part provides an overview of Merton's way of life and introduces key themes, while the second, somewhat longer, part moves chronologically through the day. He begins (as he will end) with a focus on planes flying overhead, first a passenger jet with its pseudomystical elevation ("contemplation that *gets you somewhere!*" [*Day of a Stranger*, 29]), then "the SAC plane, ... the metal bird with a scientific egg in its breast" (31). Merton immediately reminds himself and his reader that withdrawal into solitude cannot mean escape from the perils that human society has created for itself: "Like everyone else, I live in the shadow of the apocalyptic cherub" (31). Yet at the same time his vocation is a sign of contradiction to the pervasive power of technology, an assertion of an identity that cannot be reduced to a number.

This focus on personal identity is immediately complemented by a sense of immersion in the natural world, of being part of a larger whole, of forming "an ecological balance" (33) with the trees and birds amidst which he lives. This responsiveness to nature is not intended to substitute for or to exclude human contact. The natural world provides a context in which the wisdom of the human world can be properly heard and appreciated, and the ecological balance of his physical environment provides a pattern for "a mental ecology, too, a living balance of spirits in this corner of the woods. There is room here for many other songs besides those of birds" (35), voices of poets singing in many languages, voices of Eastern sages and Western church fathers, voices of Hebrew prophets and women artists and visionaries.

Using the terminology of Marshall McLuhan, Merton describes the hermit life as "cool" (37), not filled with the intensity of questions to be answered and problems to be solved, and thus a sign of contradiction not only to the busyness of the secular world but also to the projects and questions and obligations of monastic community life. Yet this is not a claim for a moral or spiritual elitism. He pointedly and humorously demythologizes any mystique of the hermit as superior to or set apart from ordinary people: "This is not a hermitage — it is a house. ('Who was that hermitage I seen you with last night? . . .') What I wear is pants. What I do is live. How I pray is breathe" (41).

With this declaration of ordinariness the opening section of the essay concludes, and the description of the events of his day begins, with his rising "at two-fifteen in the morning, when the night is darkest and most silent" (43). He describes the interpenetration of the words of the psalms prayed in the divine office with the words of the broken, suffering world in which he lives, "blood, guile, dark, anger, death. Selma, Birmingham, Mississippi, . . . the atomic city" (43). The final word is "mercy," but its power is revealed not by refusing to hear the other words, but by confronting them and realizing that through no merit of one's own there is a deeper, more lasting reality than hate and death.

After a short, sardonic self-interview in which intrusive questions about the author's motives for living alone are parried, there follows a rich meditation on the call to solitude as an invitation to recognize and embrace the Love hidden in the depth of all that is real, to "marry the silence of the forest" and hear "the secret that is heard only in silence" (49). This secret, "the virginal point of pure nothingness which is at the center of all other loves," is an awareness that each particular love, insofar as it is authentic, shares in the one all-encompassing Love, that all particular surrenders are concrete ways of participating in the primal and primary surrender of self to Absolute Reality, of embracing "the primordial paradise tree, the *axis mundi,* the cosmic axle, . . . the Cross" (49).

As the day unfolds, the speaker is present at the coming of dawn, able to hear "the one word 'DAY,' which . . . is never spoken in any known language" (51). He attends to the ordinary rhythms and routines of everyday life, from which the hermit is not exempt. Merton deliberately, and slyly, uses the term "rituals," with its associations with religious rites, to describe the most "secular" of activities, not excluding even a visit to the outdoor privy, as a reminder that grace builds on nature but does not replace it. Human life is inescapably incarnate, fleshly, and part of the value of even the most ordinary activities is to keep one rooted in concrete actuality, to guard against the fatal self-deception that the "religious" person lives on a different plane of reality from everyone else.

He describes his descent through the woods to the monastery, where "I have duties, obligations, since here I am a monk. When I have accomplished these, I return to the woods where I am nobody" (57). After his conference with the novices, chanting the office with the community, lunch in the refectory, where a message from the pope is read "denouncing war, denouncing the bombing of civilians, reprisals on civilians, killing of hostages, torturing of prisoners (all in Vietnam)" (59), he returns at noon to the hermitage to sit in silence in the cool back room and experience "the *consonantia* of heat, fragrant pine, quiet wind, bird song and one central tonic note that is unheard and unuttered . . . to which every other meaning aspires, in order to find its true fulfillment" (61). As the day draws to a close, so does the essay, and the peace of "silent Tzu's and Fu's (men without office and without obligation)" is placed in final juxtaposition to "the metal cherub of the apocalypse [which] passes over me in the clouds, treasuring its egg and its message" (63), a final recognition of living in a world that is both saved and in need of salvation, a repository of wisdom and an arena of mortally dangerous folly. POC

SEE ALSO *DANCING IN THE WATER OF LIFE;* HERMITAGE.

DEATH

Thomas Merton experienced death early in his life: he was six when his mother died of cancer in 1921 and not quite sixteen when his father died of a brain tumor in 1931. Twelve years later he lost his brother, John Paul, who died at sea when his military plane went down in the English Channel. Other deaths followed — his grandfather Samuel Jenkins died in 1936; his grandmother "Bonnemaman" died the following year — but none had the impact on his life that the deaths of his parents had. The death of Ruth Jenkins Merton changed her son's life. Informed by mail that his mother was about to die, he was left in the car while his father, grandparents, and uncle went to the hospital. When they returned to the car, they were "shattered by sorrow" (*Seven Storey Mountain*, 15). The young boy saw his father and his grandmother weeping, but he never saw his mother again. Her body was cremated. Years later he would speak of his "desperate, despairing childhood" (*Learning to Love*, 111) after his mother died. Writing in his journal in March 1941, before his Easter retreat at Gethsemani, Merton admits that his father's death was something he did not understand. "His illness ... was being 'kept from me,' that is, how bad it was. I knew all along father would die, but didn't reflect upon it, because I couldn't: I mean I didn't know how" (*Run to the Mountain*, 327). His father's death left him "sad and depressed for a couple of months" (*Seven Storey Mountain*, 85), and then for the next five or six years he imagined that he was free, only to discover that he had got himself into "a frightful captivity" (85). Looking back on the deaths of his parents, Merton writes that he "never doubted the fact that father's soul, or mother's, were immortal" (*Run to the Mountain*, 327). But as a child and adolescent he did not experience the comfort that religion can offer in the face of death. When he learned that his mother was dying, it never occurred to him to say a prayer. Years later when John Paul died, it was different. Merton's faith enabled him to place his brother's death in a context of meaning. A poem he wrote as a memorial to John Paul begins with the lines "Sweet brother, if I do

not sleep / My eyes are flowers for your tomb." The closing stanza proclaims, "In the wreckage of your April Christ lies slain / And Christ weeps in the ruins of my spring ... The silence of Whose tears shall fall / Like bells upon your alien tomb. / Hear them and come: they call you home" (*Seven Storey Mountain*, 404). Merton's grief perhaps was mitigated as he framed John Paul's death in the context of Christian faith, in which death no longer appears as a wall but a door. Viewed in the light of the death and resurrection of Jesus Christ, death is a homecoming.

As a monk, Merton was taught how to live *and* how to die. He learned how to meditate on death and face its reality. In the Middle Ages, monks had been instructed to meditate on a human skull — a graphic reminder that life would end. In striking contrast to the death-denying attitudes of American society, death is accepted as natural and inevitable in a monastery. The bodies of monks are not embalmed. Corpses are not disguised by cosmetics intended to make them look lifelike. Burial is simple. Death is experienced directly, without pretense.

Merton not only learned to face death; he anticipated its coming and even seemed to have had premonitions that he would die young. Although he was by no means obsessed with death or even preoccupied with the fact that he would die, Merton felt a growing sense of urgency to prepare himself for death. In December 1962 he writes that by God's grace, he must "see at last that *everything* now leads in one direction: all the water is heading for the falls, and for my death, so that I must want all, eagerly, to be part of my ultimate and complete offering of my whole life in His beloved will" (*Turning toward the World*, 281). On August 4, 1963, Merton is thinking, "How insufficient are conventional meditations on death! I have the *responsum mortis* [answer of death] in me, and have spontaneously been aware of death as a kind of presence several times today" (*Water of Life*, 3). In December 1964 he writes, "How often in the last years I have thought of death. It has been present to me and I have 'understood' it, and known that I must die. Yet last night, only for a moment, in passing, and so to speak without grimness or drama, I momentarily experienced the fact that I, this self, will soon simply not exist. A flash of the 'not-thereness' of being dead" (173). When he wrote this, Merton was living part of the time in the hermitage, and he counted his insight as one of the first fruits of solitude. Some months later, in July 1965, Merton asked himself whether his solitude "meets the standard set by [his] approaching death" (264). He feared that it did not. "Solitude is not death, it is life. It aims not at living death but at a certain fullness of life. But a fullness that comes from honestly and authentically facing death and accepting it without care, i.e., with faith and trust in God" (264). Facing his "untruth in solitude" was "preparation for the awful experience of facing it irrevocably in death" (264–65). Living solitude was a way of "preparing for death" (*Learning to Love*, 26).

In March 1962 Merton was reading "a most exciting book," Karl Rahner's *On the Theology of Death* (*Turning toward the World*, 211). He found himself resonating with Rahner's ideas. Death is not simply "suffered and undergone"; by grace, death becomes an *act* (Merton underlined the word twice) of faith and submission "in fulfillment and self-transcendence" (212). It strikes Merton that Rahner's view of death as act is in sync with a Buddhist approach to death: "Death can and should be an act of complete liberation, a going forth, an *act* by which one freely and completely leaves behind all that is not definitive, and the affirmation of the meaning hidden in all one's other acts" (*Witness to Freedom*, 47).

Death is "a critical point of growth, or transition to a new mode of being, to *maturity* and fruitfulness that I do not know (they are in Christ and in His Kingdom). The child in the womb does not know what will come after birth. He must be born in order to live. I am here to learn to face death as my birth" (*Water of Life*, 333). The images that Merton uses to speak of death, "a new mode of being" and a new birth, are images that he also uses to speak of contemplation. Implicit in his understanding of contemplation is the ultimate awakening to the presence of God that happens in death. It

is in death that a person realizes the true self in God.

In a short essay on death written in 1966 as part of "Seven Words for Ned O'Gorman,"[1] Merton critiques what he calls "a death-oriented society," which grants death a power of its own and leaves people living "as if death were always ready to exercise this inescapable power over us" (*Love and Living*, 98). A death-oriented society promotes "an essentially meaningless life-drive that demands to continue in spite of everything" (99) and seeks to destroy those weaker than ourselves to assure ourselves of our power to survive. A death-oriented society is fascinated with death. Death becomes life's goal. In contrast, a Christian view of death sees dying as a dimension of life in which one dies "to self in order to give to others" and so affirms life (102). The end of life becomes "a *culminating gift*, the last free perfect act of love which is at once surrender and acceptance: the surrender of his being into the hands of God, who made it, and the acceptance of death which in its details and circumstances is perhaps very significantly in continuity with all the acts and incidents of life — its good and its bad, its sins and its love, its conquests and its defeats. Man's last gift of himself in death is, then the acceptance of what he has been. . . . It is the final seal his freedom sets upon the love and the trust with which it has striven to live" (103).

The death of Jesus Christ — a "total renunciation of power . . . by total poverty, annihilation and death" — has transformed death, leaving persons "free to choose, within the limits of truth." Christ's death "is anything but blind and desperate subjection to an irreversible decree of death" (*Water of Life*, 28). Christ's death makes it possible for a person to die "with an act of glad acceptance and of love which transcends death and carries him over into eternal life with the Risen Christ" (*Love and Living*, 103). Eternal life in Christ is not simply interminable life; it is "*pure reality*, the total compact fulfillment of man in love and in vision, not measured out in infinitely extended time, but grounded in the depths of the personal life of God and the inner dynamic of love" (104). In death, a person enters into "the hidden ground of love" that is God. CMB

Notes

1. "Death" is one of the words on which Merton reflects in "Seven Words for Ned O'Gorman," published in its entirety in *Love and Living*, 97–105.

DESERT

"The 'desert' of contemplation," according to Thomas Merton, "is simply a metaphor to explain the state of emptiness which we experience when we have left all ways, forgotten ourselves and taken the invisible Christ as our way" (*Contemplative Prayer*, 115–16). But the effectiveness of the metaphor is dependent on the resonances it has taken from the tradition. The earliest monks of the fourth and fifth centuries went out into the actual deserts of Egypt and Syria to confront themselves, their fears, their mortality, and learn to trust only in God. They saw themselves as following in the footsteps of Christ, who was tested in the desert and so entered fully into the human condition. "From the moment Christ went out into the desert to be tempted, the loneliness, the temptation and the hunger of every man became the loneliness, temptation and hunger of Christ." As Christ shared our state, so by sharing his desert sojourn one is led to see reality and so to accept salvation. "But in return, the gift of truth with which Christ dispelled the three kinds of illusion offered him in his temptation (security, reputation and power) can become also our own truth, if we can only accept it" (*Raids on the Unspeakable*, 18). Christ's forty days in the desert in turn recapitulate the forty years of Israel in the wilderness, where they learned to love God because they were stripped of all other sources of support and consolation. "The forty years in the desert came to be regarded as the golden age of the history of Israel, the age of Israel's nuptials with the Lord — the pattern of all future perfection" (*Disputed Questions*, 224). It is also the desert of which Isaiah writes, which shall be transformed into a garden, which in some sense will be transformed into paradise.

The desert, then, is a profoundly ambiguous symbol, a place where one is able to meet the Creator and Divine Lover without disguises (*World of Action*, 229), but also the place where one confronts the power of the Evil One with no defenses but those of faith. It is a place "for risk, for walking with God in the wilderness, and wrestling with Satan in vulnerable freedom" (186). This desert, then, is not a location on a map but the landscape of the human heart: "The real desert is this: to face the real limitations of one's own existence and knowledge and not try to manipulate them or disguise them." When one adopts this "radical desert perspective... a new dimension opens up" (*Learning to Love*, 309–10); by letting go of the limitations of narrow hopes and fears and expectations, one is drawn into a realm of existence where all limits are transcended in a present moment of grace and love. Such a realization generally involves a certain degree of withdrawal and physical solitude, but does not necessarily have to do so. "It does not matter what kind of a desert it may be: in the midst of men or far from them. It is the one vast desert of emptiness which belongs to no one and to everyone. It is the place of silence where one word is spoken by God. And in that word are spoken both God Himself and all things" (*Disputed Questions*, 197).

The desert, then, is the true home of contemplatives, "a desolation where there is no food and no shelter and no refreshment for their imagination and intellect and for the desires of their nature" (*New Seeds of Contemplation*, 235). It is a realm of dryness and aridity where nevertheless one experiences a peace that is on a level deeper than the intellect and the affections (275–76). "Contemplative prayer," according to Merton, is "simply the preference for the desert, for emptiness, for poverty" (*Contemplative Prayer*, 111). It is the willing renunciation of all that is not God, including even legitimate but limited concepts, images, and experiences of God. The silence and darkness and emptiness become the revelation of a Presence that cannot be comprehended: "The contemplative... has risked his mind in the desert beyond language and beyond ideas where God is encountered in the nakedness of pure trust" (*Monastic Journey*, 173). And unaccountably, one finds oneself restored to unity with God, creation, and oneself: "What the Desert Fathers sought when they believed they could find 'paradise' in the desert was the lost innocence, the emptiness and purity of heart which had belonged to Adam and Eve in Eden . . . the recovery of that 'unity' which had been shattered by the 'knowledge of good and evil' " (*Birds of Appetite*, 117).

For Merton, the monastic vocation is intrinsically a call into the desert, not only because its historical roots are in the Egyptian wilderness, but also because the monk is one who has publicly renounced the fictions of a collective social existence in which success is equated with power and pleasure and wealth. "When the windows of the monastery no longer open out upon the vast horizons of the desert, the monastic community inevitably becomes immersed in vanity" (*Disputed Questions*, 175), becomes, in other words, a mirror image of the world whose values have infiltrated the cloister (*World of Action*, 228–29). The monk is called to be a sign that the enticements and the demands of a world of competing egos are fraudulent. "The monk, by the simplicity, the poverty, the detachment of this naked 'desert life' and solitude — or by his obedience in the poor community of laborers which is the monastic family — bears witness to the fact that the happiness of the Christian *does not depend* on the promises of this world" (230).

The solitary, the hermit, is the figure who incarnates the desert life most starkly and uncompromisingly, by "an advance into solitude and the desert, a confrontation with poverty and the void, a renunciation of the empirical self, in the presence of death, and nothingness, in order to overcome the ignorance and error that spring from the fear of 'being nothing.' " In this confrontation with emptiness the solitary is not escaping from the condition of other human beings but embracing it in its most elementary form. "The solitary, far from enclosing himself in himself, becomes every man. He dwells in the solitude, the poverty, the indigence of every man. It is in this sense that the hermit . . . imitates Christ. For in Christ, God takes to Himself the solitude and dereliction

of man: every man" (*Raids on the Unspeakable*, 17–18).

Thus, the true solitude of the desert is the very opposite of isolation and alienation. It is a profound identification with and empathy for the sufferings and struggles of all other persons. Like the original hermits of Nitria and Scete, the true desert solitary is able to be filled with "charity and discretion . . . because he [is] completely empty of himself" (*Disputed Questions*, 191–92). The desert provides the proper detachment to see others as well as oneself with a vision undistorted by passion or prejudice. "Go into the desert," Merton advises, "not to escape other men but in order to find them in God" (*New Seeds of Contemplation*, 53). Even when alone, one always travels, like Israel, through the desert as part of the community of faith, the pilgrim people of God, "some members" of which "are bound to have a special consciousness of this wilderness and exiled aspect of the Christian life" (*World of Action*, 238). This sense of communal responsibility was made vividly clear to Merton himself when he became master of students, responsible for the formation of young professed monks, as he explains in what is perhaps the most celebrated "desert" passage in his writings: "What is my new desert? The name of it is *compassion*. There is no wilderness so terrible, so beautiful, so arid and so fruitful as the wilderness of compassion. It is the only desert that shall truly flourish like the lily. It shall become a pool, it shall bud forth and blossom and rejoice with joy. It is [in] the desert of compassion that the thirsty land turns into springs of water, that the poor possess all things" (*Entering the Silence*, 463). POC

SEE ALSO *WHAT OUGHT I TO DO?*; *WISDOM OF THE DESERT*.

DESPAIR

Thomas Merton defines despair as a perverse form of pride. "Despair is the absolute extreme of self-love. It is reached when a man deliberately turns his back on all help from anyone else in order to taste the rotten luxury of knowing himself to be lost" (*New Seeds of Contemplation*, 180). It is the result of the inevitable failure of a delusory autonomy, a refusal to admit one's own contingency and therefore one's need for an unearned mercy: "It selects the absolute misery of damnation rather than accept happiness from the hands of God and thereby acknowledge that He is above us and that we are not capable of fulfilling our destiny by ourselves" (180). The antidote to despair, therefore, is humility, which cannot coexist with the self-pity on which despair thrives, and therefore overcomes the tendency to despair that is endemic to the condition of fallen humanity.

But such humility requires one to let go of the image of the self so laboriously constructed over time, the only "self" one knows. Such self-surrender appears more perilous than clinging desperately to one's image even as it plunges into the abyss. This is, Merton says, the "Promethean" stance that "makes a victory out of defeat and glories in its own despair" in order to retain the delusion of its own independence (*New Man*, 23). It is the despair of Milton's Satan, "the absolute refusal to let anyone else change your mind for you, by any means, reasonable or otherwise" (*Literary Essays*, 256). Yet paradoxically, Merton says, the pride that leads to despair is also a kind of "servility," an obsession with doing and making and achieving that is in fact a kind of enslavement, a grim ethic of productivity that leaves no room for spontaneity and play and joy. "The fruit of our servility is the despair that no one can admit — unless of course he is a monk or a beatnik" (*Guilty Bystander*, 283).

Another path that can only lead to despair is to place one's reliance on anything less than God; it is building one's house on sand. "Be careful," Merton warns, "of every vain hope: it is in reality a temptation to despair," because it creates expectations that will not be fulfilled. "Then, when it dissolves into air, everything else dissolves along with it" (*New Seeds of Contemplation*, 186). Even the gifts God has given to lead to himself, "my own intelligence, my own strength, and my own prudence," inevitably fail: "To place your trust in visible things is to live in despair" (*No Man Is an Island*, 16).

There are, of course, all sorts of ways of masking one's despair, even from oneself: the pretensions of the intellectual who has "clever answers to clever questions — none of which have anything to do with the problems of life"; the pseudoprophetic visionary who condemns the world so as to avoid having to face his or her own inner emptiness (xiii); the conformist who clings to delusions at all costs, for "such delusion . . . is the merciful form which cowards give to their despair" (*New Man*, 4); the facile optimist who is content with shallow hopes that are not hopes at all, for according to St. Paul, "A hope that is seen . . . is no hope" (5). To avoid despair, Merton warns, is to be possessed by despair. Only by confronting despair, by facing the reality of the temptation to despair, can despair be overcome. "How much better and saner it is to face despair and not give in than to work away at keeping up appearances and patching up our conviction that a bogus spirituality is real" (*Guilty Bystander*, 147). The mercy of God is experienced only by those who recognize their need for mercy, who reach the edge of the abyss and suddenly find themselves "instead of falling over the edge, . . . walking on the air" (*No Man Is an Island*, 206) through a mysterious power not their own. "It is better," Merton says, "to find God on the threshold of despair than to risk our lives in a complacency that has never felt the need of forgiveness. A life that is without problems may literally be more hopeless than one that always verges on despair" (21–22). It is in the "dread" that reaches the point "where the void seems to open out into black despair" (*Contemplative Prayer*, 28) that one encounters the figure of the crucified Jesus and passes with him through the ultimate self-surrender of death into new life with and in God. To flee the abyss of despair is to miss the invitation to salvation. To face despair is to find the authentic ground for both contemplation and action. "The contemplative life," Merton writes, "begins with the acceptance of my own self in my poverty and my nearness to despair, in order to recognize that where God is there can be no despair, and God is in me even if I despair: that nothing can change God's love for me, since my very existence is the sign that God loves me and the presence of His love creates and sustains me" (*Monastic Journey*, 172–73). Likewise, the foundation for Christian action in the world, especially for a nonviolent witness to the victory of the reign of God, is to recognize all the reasons to despair and refuse to do so, because one has experienced in one's own life the transforming power of the cross and resurrection. "Despair is not permitted to the meek, the humble, the afflicted, the ones famished for justice, the merciful, the clean of heart and the peacemakers. All the beatitudes 'hope against hope.'...They refuse to despair of the world and abandon it to a supposedly evil fate which it has brought upon itself. Instead, like Christ himself, the Christian takes upon his own shoulders the yoke of the Savior, meek and humble of heart...the burden of the world's sin with all its confusions and all its problems...[which] are our very own" (*Faith and Violence*, 26). POC

SEE ALSO HOPE; MERCY.

DETACHMENT

Detachment (or nonattachment) means separation. In the spiritual journey it means separating myself from creatures in order to find in God alone the goal for which I was made and the happiness for which I am destined. In the *Summa Theologiae* of Thomas Aquinas, Thomas Merton had read question 2 of the Prima Secundae, in which the "angelic doctor" parades before the reader all created things, such as material possessions, honor, fame, power, and bodily health. They are all found wanting. None can bring total fulfillment to human persons. To achieve the true happiness for which we were made, not even the possession of the highest good in the created order will do. One must move out of the realm of created reality to achieve fulfillment and happiness where alone it can be found: in God.

Detachment, therefore, is the refusal to let any person or thing in God's wonderful creation take the place of God. Detachment frees me from any attachment to any created thing, to any gift of God (even the highest and most supernatural), indeed even from attachment to my very self. Only a person with this freedom that detachment brings is able to see reality as it truly is. Only this person has let go of all illusions.

Are there any persons who have this degree of total detachment? In both *Seeds of Contemplation* (124) and *New Seeds of Contemplation* (203), Merton wonders if there are even twenty such persons in the world. The problem he sees is that even our virtuous actions are so easily tainted by (often, unconscious) forms of selfishness and therefore some element of attachment.

These were Merton's thoughts in 1949, when he wrote *Seeds of Contemplation*, and also in 1962, when he published *New Seeds of Contemplation*. Years later (in November 1968), while he was in India, he wrote much the same thing, though in another context: "Compassion is proportionate to detachment; otherwise we use others for our own ends under the pretext of 'love'" (*Other Side of the Mountain*, 287). Only a person of detachment is able perfectly to fulfill the law of love of God above all things and love of neighbor as oneself.

Levels of Detachment

What are the levels of detachment we must learn to master? Quite understandably, one who seeks holiness of life must give up attachment to material things and to physical and sensual pleasures. But that is not enough; Merton takes us to another level. One must be free, he tells us, from attachment even to spiritual goods (prayer, contemplation, virtue, delight in God). For, after all, as he points out, "recollection is just as much a creature as an automobile" and interior peace is "no less created than a bottle of wine" (*New Seeds of Contemplation*, 205). But there is yet another level. To achieve perfect detachment one must let go of the need to be a separate self. For a separate self (a self without relationship to others and especially to God) is an illusory self. It does not really exist. Merton writes, "It is only when we are detached from ourselves that we can be at peace with ourselves" (*No Man Is an Island*, 121).

Detachment and Joy

Some might think that a life of detachment, as just described, would be a gloomy, somber, joyless existence. But this would be to misunderstand Merton. What he is saying is just the opposite. His problem is not with the good things of creation, but with *attachment* to them. For when we are attached to them, they enslave us. We cling to them. We fear their loss. The problem that creatures pose for us lies, therefore, not in their goodness, but in our *desire* for them. For desire is at the heart of attachment. It is not creatures, therefore, but the *desire* for them that stands as a barrier between God and us. As Merton writes in his book on John of the Cross, "The desire of creatures as ends in themselves cannot coexist with the desire of God as our true end" (*Ascent to Truth*, 57). It is only when we are detached from creatures that we are free to enjoy them.[1]

Once we let go our desire for creatures, we can see their goodness simply as they are and not in terms of how they benefit us. And because we are seeing them for what they truly are — no more, no less — we can enjoy in them precisely the proper goodness God has put into them. We are freed from illusions that becloud our vision of things. Things cease to be rivals to God. We enjoy them all the more.

Detachment and Results

In *No Man Is an Island*, in a chapter on "Being and Doing," Merton points out that there are times when, through no fault of our own, we cannot be pleased with what we have done. "We must learn," he says, "to be detached from the results of our own activity. We must withdraw ourselves, to some extent, from effects that are beyond our control." We must be content "to work without expecting an immediate reward, to love without an instantaneous satisfaction, and to exist without any special recognition" (*No Man Is an Island*, 106–7).

This form of detachment became especially important to Merton once he began writing on social issues. Because results are inevitably so uncertain, a spirit of detachment from results, from the fruits of one's labors, is especially important for a person's well-being. When I work for peace and justice, my task is to embody the truth in my actions in a prudent and discerning way. But once the actions I perform get into the public arena, they mingle with the actions of others (over which I may have little or no control) and may be diverted into directions I

never intended. They may be prevented from achieving the purpose I had in mind in performing them. This failure to achieve results, especially results that I know are good and important, can easily lead to discouragement. But, if I have reached a point in my growth where I am not attached to results, such discouragement will not prevent me from continuing to do what I see needs to be done.

Detachment from the results of my actions must be carefully understood. It does not mean that I am indifferent to results. If my actions are to oppose war and work for peace, detachment does not mean that I do not care whether there is war or peace. Detachment means that I do what I must do because of the truth. I must always act for the truth.

On February 21, 1966, Merton wrote a long letter to James Forest (widely circulated under the title of "A Letter to a Young Activist"). His letter is a reply to a rather despondent letter from Forest in which Jim wrote that he was in a bleak mood: his actions for peace and justice seemed to be going nowhere. Merton responded with sympathy and understanding. But he tells Forest not to depend on the hope of results. "When you are doing the sort of work you have taken on, ... you may have to face the fact that your work will be apparently worthless, and even achieve no result at all, if not perhaps results opposite to what you expect. As you get used to this idea you start more and more to concentrate not on the results, but on the value, the rightness, the truth of the work itself... as gradually you struggle less and less for an idea and more and more for specific people" (*Hidden Ground of Love*, 294).

Detachment is important throughout our lives. It is equally important in death, for death is the moment of enlightenment, when we let go our attachment to mortal existence. It is the final act of self-surrender (see *Love and Living*, 102–3). It is, therefore, the final expression of detachment. WHS

Notes

1. Buddhism, as Merton came to understand, teaches that the root of suffering (*dukkha*) is desire or craving (*tanha*). One of the steps to overcoming suffering is to rid oneself of craving.

DEVOTIONS IN HONOR OF SAINT JOHN OF THE CROSS

Compiled by a Cloistered Religious.
Philadelphia: Jefferies & Manz, 1953. 8 pp.

This small booklet is intended for congregational use at a service commemorating St. John of the Cross, presumably for his feast day, November 24, indicated on the title page. Though issued anonymously, it is listed as Thomas Merton's in Frank Dell'Isola's bibliographies.[1] The text assigns the prayers to "Priest," "People," and "Priest and People." After introductory prayers, the priest asks for the grace "that we may praise Thee in the wisdom and sanctity of Thy servant, Saint John of the Cross" (*Devotions in Honor*, 3), and the people respond with a prayer that through St. John's intercession they may learn the ways of prayer and come to know "how to find joy in desolation and light in darkest night" (4); there is also opportunity to "secretly mention a special favor desired" (4). After singing the "Vexilla Regis," priest and people briefly pray to St. John directly; then a prayer to Christ by the priest asks that they may learn to live as true Christians through John's teaching and intercession, and priest and people together read two brief selections from the saint's Maxims. The priest then reads the collect from the Mass of St. John, and priest and people together pray to St. John for the grace to "endure all tribulations and adversities with dauntless courage" (8) in imitation of his virtues so as to be with him "a lover of the Cross and of suffering and thus...merit to be thy companion in glory" (8). A brief prayer to Mary concludes the service, for which three hundred days' indulgence is given. These devotions may have been a by-product of Merton's introduction to St. John's *Counsels of Light and Love* (from which the Maxims are taken), published the same year.[2] POC

Notes

1. It appears as item A16 in Frank Dell'Isola, *Thomas Merton: A Bibliography* (Kent, Ohio: Kent State University Press, 1975).
2. Introduction to St. John of the Cross, *Counsels of Light and Love* (Wheeling, W.Va.: Monastery of St. Theresa, 1953). This introduction is included as "Light in Darkness: The Ascetic Doctrine of St. John of the Cross" in *Disputed Questions* (208–17).

DISPUTED QUESTIONS

New York: Farrar, Straus and Cudahy, 1960.
xii+297 pp.

The title page of *Disputed Questions* has the name under which Merton almost always wrote (Thomas Merton); the preface, however, somewhat unusually, carries his religious name, Father M. Louis, O.C.S.O.

The book covers a wide variety of articles, most of them written in 1959 or 1960, but two (one on St. John of the Cross, the other on St. Bernard) date from 1953. It is not unusual for Merton to bring disparate subjects together to form a book. The book has three parts. Part 1 has three articles: (1) "The Pasternak Affair," (2) "Mount Athos," and (3) "The Spirituality of Sinai (John Climacus)." Part 2 includes (1) "The Power and Meaning of Love" and (2) "Christianity and Totalitarianism." Part 3 has seven articles: (1) "Sacred Art and the Spiritual Life," (2) "A Renaissance Hermit (Blessed Paul Giustiniani)," (3) "Notes for a Philosophy of Solitude," (4) "Light in Darkness (St. John of the Cross)," (5) "The Primitive Carmelite Ideal," (6) "Absurdity in Sacred Decoration," and (7) "St. Bernard: Monk and Apostle."

The words of the title, "disputed questions," are not intended to suggest the disputations in medieval universities, but simply questions that to a greater or lesser degree will appear controversial and, hopefully, relevant in one way or another to the spiritual and intellectual life of modern people. Merton suggests in his preface that one theme, more or less, runs through the whole book. "It is a philosophical question: the relation of the *person* to the social *organization*. Sometimes the question takes the shape of a more ancient one: solitude versus community, or the hermit versus the cenobite. At other times, as in the Pasternak essays, it takes an acutely concrete and actual form, in discussing the struggle of one outstanding and gifted person isolated in the presence of a huge antagonistic totalitarian machine which turns against him the full force of its disapproval and stops short only of physical destruction" (*Disputed Questions*, viii–ix). This is a familiar Merton theme: the contrast between a mass society made up of disconnected individuals and the community made up of persons who cooperate with one another in a communion of love.

With this theme as guide, it seems clear that the key articles are (1) the Pasternak essays, (2) the two articles of part 2, and (3) part 3's article on a philosophy of solitude.

Merton's writings on Pasternak glow with enthusiasm. He corresponded with the Russian author[1] and read *Dr. Zhivago* as soon as it was available in English. He saw Pasternak as a sign of contradiction "in our age of materialism, collectivism and power politics" (10). Courageously and independently loyal to his own conscience, he refused to compromise with slogans or rationalizations. Merton likens him to Gandhi: though there are obvious differences between the two, both stood for basic human values over theories and programs. Both chose to be judged by their commitments to these values. Pasternak's novel *Dr. Zhivago* is rich with an overpowering symbolism. Whether he realized it or not, his writing plunged him fully into the mainstream of "the lost tradition of 'natural contemplation' which flowed among the Greek Fathers" (17). Like Dostoyevsky to whom he has been compared, he has the vision of a mystic, yet his mysticism is "more latent, more cosmic, more pagan, if you like" (13). His witness is essentially Christian, but it is a Christianity "reduced to the barest and most elementary essentials: intense awareness of all cosmic and human reality as 'life in Christ' and the consequent plunge into love as the only dynamic and creative force which really honors this 'Life'" (12). It is a Christianity that is primitive, rudimentary, almost pre-Christian in its character. It is almost as if Pasternak has discovered Christianity all by himself.

Merton sees Yuri Zhivago and Lara Antopova as cosmic figures. He is Adam; she is Eve, the figure of wisdom, the mother of all the living. They are prototypes, however, not ideals. In the end, Lara vanishes without trace, probably into a concentration camp. Zhivago is neither saint nor perfect hero.[2] "He is weak-willed and his life is a confused and unsatisfactory mess" (48). He knows that his life is not a success. He knows also that the circumstances in which he lives make a successful life impossible for him. He does the only honest thing he can do: he faces the meaninglessness and failure with humility and makes out of it the best he can. Merton makes the shrewd comment that the vilest person in *Dr. Zhivago* "is not one of the Communist automatons, but the shrewd, lecherous business man, Komarovsky" (28).

In many ways the article "The Power and Meaning of Love" makes clear the personalist understanding of humans that is at the heart of this book. Love is possible only between persons as persons. It is not a subject-object relationship. It is a subject relating to a subject. It is a creative, self-transcending reality that is "able to bridge the gap between subject and object and *commune in the subjectivity of the one loved*" (103). Only in such self-transcendence can one discover the full meaning of Christ's command to love.

"Christianity and Totalitarianism" is closely linked with the previous article. It is a challenging, insightful look into the conscience of the modern age, in which many people are afraid of love and do not dare to be persons. The members of a totalitarian society easily become units of a mass movement in which they lose their own personal freedom. The solidity of the Christian community is based on the Christian awareness that the church's mission is not to proselytize, but to bring God's forgiveness and peace to all peoples. "A mass-movement is a pyramid at whose summit a few powerful men thrive and grow stronger on the labors of the huge anonymous mass.... The Kingdom of God is just the opposite: it is the Kingdom of One who being equal to God took the form of a servant and suffered the death of the Cross that the love and life of God might descend and reach out into the lowest depths and bring light to all who are sitting in darkness, poverty, hopelessness, and the shadow of death" (144).

Part 3's "Notes for a Philosophy of Solitude" went through several stages before it assumed its present form. The first stage is a French version called *Dans le desert de Dieu*, published in 1955 in *Temoignages* (the journal of the French Benedictines of La Pierre-qui-Vire). Merton's

English version has never been discovered; a translation was published in the spring 1993 issue of *The Merton Seasonal*. The article is a spirited defense of the hermit life. The second stage is an expanded version in English of the French text. It failed to receive the approval of the censors of the order. While waiting for that approval, Merton had a limited edition (sixty copies) of it published in 1960 by Victor Hammer with the title *The Solitary Life* (it appeared in 1977 in *The Monastic Journey*). The third stage is a yet longer version, which, after struggles with the censors and some compromises with them, was finally permitted publication.

Merton considered this article one of his most important writings. He says as much in the journal he was keeping when *Disputed Questions* was published. "[It] is perhaps the best thing of the sort I have ever written" (*Turning toward the World*, 40). In a letter of December 20, 1962, he tells John Wu, "I am glad you liked 'Philosophy of Solitude.' It is one of the things I have most wanted to say, perhaps the only thing I have said that needed to be said" (*Hidden Ground of Love*, 624). On March 6, 1968, to June Yungblut, who was preparing to do postdoctoral work on Merton's writings, he wrote, "The 'Notes on the Philosophy of Solitude' is very central" (642).

Merton intended the article in this final stage to be not so much a defense of the hermit life as an explanation of the solitariness that is part of every human life. Yet he is not entirely consistent. He vacillates between the terms "solitary" and "hermit," using the latter at least nine times. Is this his way of hinting, if only subliminally, that the hermit is the prototype of the solitary life and a normal element of the Cistercian tradition?

It would be a mistake to see this article as a full-blown thesis on solitude; rather, it offers notes (as the title suggests) out of which such a philosophy can be constructed. There are three parts: (1) "The Tyranny of Diversion" (177–85), (2) "In the Sea of Perils" (185–200), and (3) "Spiritual Poverty" (200–206). There is also an important conclusion, which seems to belong to part 3, but is not to be found in any of the early drafts. This could indicate that

it was written in the summer of 1960 (without having been seen by the censors?).

Merton suggests three possible levels at which humans can live their lives. The first level is the *phenomenal*, the level of what appears to be. Here, a person lives at the surface of reality, finding a superficial harmony in life or, if that is lacking, diverting oneself from life's disharmony by turning to planned distractions and meaningless activities. This is the level of diversion. Merton borrowed this notion from Blaise Pascal, who writes about *divertissement*, by which he means engagement in empty and inane actions that makes it possible to ignore the true realities of human life. Diversion is a tyranny because it controls our lives and deprives us of the freedom to be ourselves.

Merton uses revealing terms to describe diversion: "illusion," "fiction," "stupor." They evoke a picture of persons in a daydream or a daze. They may function well at the surface, but they never touch the deeper realities of life. "The function of diversion is simply to anesthetize the individual as individual, and to plunge him in the warm apathetic stupor of a collectivity which, like himself, wishes to remain amused" (*Disputed Questions*, 178). The soap operas and situation comedies of today's television easily can become diversionary addictions.

A second level at which a person can choose to live is the *existential*. Such a person chooses to plunge below the surface realities of life. There, one senses the rumble of chaos and comes into direct contact with life's complexities, incongruities, contradictions, and absurdities. Alienation seems to be at the heart of human existence. Philosophers have confronted this sense of alienation in various ways. Some, for instance, have chosen to live with it and accept the meaninglessness of life. The solitary chooses to explore this level and refuses to be diverted from doing so.

The third level is the *contemplative*. The contemplative realizes his or her potential as a contemplative and breaks through that level of seeming meaninglessness to enter the mystery of self, and in doing so enters at the same time the mystery of God. It is at this level that life's contradictions and absurdities find their resolution. This is what Merton means when he refers, in *Conjectures of a Guilty Bystander,* to Julian of Norwich and her eschatological secret: her conviction that "All shall be well. All manner of things shall be well." God comes to us with the final answer to the world's anguish. The "Last Day" will bring not destruction and revenge, but mercy and life. "All partial expectations will be exploded and everything will be made right" (*Guilty Bystander,* 192/212).

This does not mean that the solitary faces no perils. There is the danger of choosing the solitary life for the wrong reason: separating oneself from society not for a deeper understanding of one's responsibility to society, but in order to be noticed and praised by society. This is a sham solitariness and, in fact, another form of diversion. The true solitary witnesses to the primacy of the spiritual and of the mystical character of the church. "A Christian hermit can, by being alone, paradoxically live even closer to the heart of the Church than one who is in the midst of her apostolic activities" (*Disputed Questions,* 192).

Yet, one must not conclude that the solitary is someone who has reached the heights and joys of mystical contemplation. Such solitude does not deliver the solitary from distractions, worries, and concerns. These persons face doubts, as they live with questions that reach to the very roots of their own existence. It is doubt that finally reduces them to silence, where they cease to ask questions and are satisfied with the only certitude they know: the presence of God in the midst of uncertainty and nothingness. The solitary knows peace. "He knows where he is going, but he is not 'sure of his way,' he just knows by going there. He does not see the way beforehand, and when he arrives, he arrives. His arrivals are usually departures from anything that resembles a 'way.' That is his way. But he cannot understand it. Neither can we" (203).

Merton concludes this article with four stunning, poetic paragraphs on the distinction between the false, ephemeral self that must disappear and the true, enduring self that must emerge. Without solitude there can be no such emptying of false self and renewal of true self.

This distinction between the ephemeral and the enduring in us is a theme he had hinted at in *Seeds of Contemplation* and developed at much greater length in his unpublished work "The Inner Experience" (1959). Later, he will take it up with even greater emphasis in *New Seeds of Contemplation* (1962). whs

SEE ALSO ALIENATION; SELF; SOLITUDE.

Notes

1. See *The Courage for Truth* and *Six Letters: Boris Pasternak, Thomas Merton.*
2. On May 5, 1959, Merton replied to a letter from an English correspondent, John Harris, "As for Dom Hubert Van Zeller's saying that he dropped *Zhivago* when adultery came into the picture: he is a good man and I respect him, but I do not agree with everything he says. By this standard he would have to close *Genesis* as soon as bigamy reared its ugly head, or as soon as Abraham palms Sarah off on Pharaoh as his 'sister'" (*Hidden Ground of Love,* 389).

DISTRACTIONS

Thomas Merton devotes a chapter in *New Seeds of Contemplation* (221–24) to the subject of distractions, a slightly modified version of the material that appeared in *Seeds of Contemplation* (140–43) more than a decade earlier. Merton's chapter on "Distractions" is one of several in the two books in which Merton offers readers practical advice on the practice of meditation and contemplative prayer.

Merton's message is clear and direct. Distractions in contemplative prayer are natural and "often unavoidable" in the life of prayer. "If you have never had any distractions you don't know how to pray" (*New Seeds of Contemplation,* 221). Persist in prayer and do not use books to stave off distractions. "If your book merely becomes an anesthetic, far from helping your meditation it has probably ruined it" (222). Merton explains that distractions emerge because the mind, memory, and imagination have "no real job to do" in contemplative prayer when the will is occupied in "obscurely and mutely loving God" (222). He advises readers not to pay them any mind: "remain in simple attention to God" (222). Some distractions are like "the intermittent shadows" of "an annoying movie" (222). Others — and these are more harmful — focus on work and projects we have under way. Merton adds what appears to be a lesson drawn in large measure from his own experience: there is a danger that our meditation "will break down into a session of mental letter-writing or sermons or speeches or books or, worse still, plans to raise money or to take care of our health" (223).

What matters are the "will to pray" and "the desire to find God, to see Him and to love Him" (224). In the concluding paragraph of the chapter on distractions in *New Seeds of Contemplation*, Merton invites his readers to the simple practice of resting in God's presence: "No matter how distracted you may be, pray by peaceful, even perhaps inarticulate, efforts to center your heart upon God, Who is present to you in spite of all that may be going through your mind. His presence does not depend on your thoughts of Him. He is unfailingly there; if He were not, you could not even exist" (224). In these few lines Merton captures what is at the heart of contemplation: awakening to the presence of God, in whom we have our very being.

In 1949 Merton had shared with his friend Sr. Therese Lentfoehr some similar thoughts and suggestions on how to deal with distractions in prayer. He recommended that she take fifteen minutes or a half hour in a garden "to walk up and down among the flower beds" and offer the walk as "a meditation and a prayer to Our Lord. Do not try to think about anything in particular and when thoughts about work, etc. come to you, do not try to push them out by main force, but see if you can't drop them just by relaxing your mind. Do this because you 'are praying' and because Our Lord is with you. But if thoughts about work will not go away, accept them idly and without too much eagerness with the intention of letting Our Lord reveal His will to you through these thoughts" (*Road to Joy*, 195).

In his essay on "Notes for a Philosophy of Solitude," Merton takes up the subject of distractions, not just in prayer, but in life. Speaking of *divertissement,* or diversion, Merton warns against the activities that "anesthetize" individuals and keep them from ever moving beyond the illusions and fictions that abound on the surface of life and present themselves as counterfeit reality (*Disputed Questions*, 177–85). Such "distractions" keep individuals from

experiencing the deeper realities of self, other, and God. Merton strikes a similar chord in "Creative Silence," an essay he wrote for students at the University of Louisville: "When we live superficially, when we are always outside ourselves, never quite 'with' ourselves, always divided and pulled in many directions by conflicting plans and projects, we find ourselves doing many things that we do not really want to do, saying things we do not really mean, needing things we do not really need, exhausting ourselves for what we secretly realize to be worthless and without meaning in our lives" (*Love and Living*, 43). Such is the price of diversion and distraction. CMB

SEE ALSO CONTEMPLATION; *DISPUTED QUESTIONS*; SELF.

DOCTRINES

Doctrines are official statements of the teachings of the church. Doctrines that are taught irrevocably and infallibly are called dogmas. Doctrines are attempts to put into human words God's self-revelation. They express the faith of the church. Because human words can never express fully the divine Reality, doctrines are open to development and reformulation. They cannot tell us everything about God; rather, they point to mystery that is invisible and incomprehensible. "The object of our faith is not a statement about God, but God Himself to Whom the statement points and Who is infinitely beyond anything the statement might lead us to imagine or understand" (*Redeeming the Time*, 26).

Doctrinal formulations must not be seen as attempts to resolve the mystery of God's reality, much less to reduce it to our level of intelligibility. They are ways of saying something of what we can experience of the One who never can be totally experienced. They help us understand and express the experience of God going on in the Christian community.

Reverence for the truth demands that we express the doctrinal formulations of faith in language that is as clear and as accurate as we can make it. "They must be clean windows, so that they may not obscure and hinder the light that comes to us. They must not falsify

God's truth. Therefore we must make every effort to believe the right formulas. But we must not be so obsessed with verbal correctness that we never go beyond the words to the ineffable reality which they attempt to convey" (*New Seeds of Contemplation*, 129). In his essay "A Christian Looks at Zen," Thomas Merton stresses the importance of remembering that Christian faith is first and foremost about living experience. "This obsession with doctrinal formulas, juridical order and ritual exactitude has often made people forget that the heart of Catholicism, too, is a *living experience* of unity in Christ which far transcends all conceptual formulations" (*Birds of Appetite*, 39).

In the preface to the Japanese edition of *Thoughts in Solitude*, Merton tells us, "While these doctrines may be very true, yet they cannot be understood if we think that the only purpose of faith is multiple information communicated in many complex doctrines. In fact the object of faith is One — God, Love. And though the revealed doctrines about Him are true, yet what they tell us of Him is not fully adequate as long as we grasp them only separately, incoherently, without living unity in Love." He uses two metaphors (spokes of a wheel, window frames) to clarify what he means. "[The doctrines] must converge upon Love as the spokes of a wheel converge upon a central hub. They are window frames through which the One Light enters our houses" ("*Honorable Reader*," 114).

In a somewhat whimsical statement in one of his holographic journals that did not make it into the published journal texts, Merton suggests the "problem" that arises in efforts to enflesh the Word of God in human language:

> In the beginning was the Word. The Word was made flesh. The Word was banished from the flesh by doctrine. The Word attempted to re-enter the world as history. But history had become a program; and the Word was made chatter.[1]

Is he saying that the Word, stripped of its concreteness by the abstractions of doctrinal formulations, tried to become flesh once again in history — the history of the Christian community — but because the Word had become overly programmed in formulas that tried to capture God's self-revelation, it lost some of its intelligibility? Does he mean that at times expressions of faith became superficial or, as he put it, little more than idle talk or "chatter"? WHS

Notes

1. *Working Notebook: Holographic Journal*, no. 43 (March 26, 1968).

DOHERTY, CATHERINE DE HUECK

Born into a wealthy family in 1900, Catherine married Baron Boris de Hueck at the age of fifteen. Five years later she and her husband were forced to flee Soviet Russia and arrived penniless in Canada. Good fortune and astute management made them wealthy again. But she was haunted by the gospel call to give up all and follow Christ. In 1930 she made the decision to live and work among the poor and established the first Friendship House in the slums of Toronto, then later in New York City's Harlem. In 1943 she married a well-known journalist, Eddie Doherty. Together they founded Madonna House in Combermere, Ontario. It became a place of prayer and retreat and a center of training for the lay apostolate.

In 1941 Thomas Merton met her when she came to speak at St. Bonaventure College, where he was teaching at the time. He volunteered to work at Friendship House in Harlem. This was the beginning of their friendship. His letters to her (see *The Hidden Ground of Love*) reveal a young man searching for his place in God's plan and finally making the decision to enter the Abbey of Gethsemani. He continued corresponding with her with some regularity, the last letter of his dated January 12, 1966. WHS

DOHERTY, FRANK

Headmaster at Oakham School during the years that Thomas Merton studied there (1929–32). WHS

John Paul and Tom Merton

DOUGLASTON

In this section in Queens, New York, Thomas Merton's maternal grandparents, Samuel and Martha Jenkins, resided at 50 Virginia Street. Owen and Ruth Merton lived with them temporarily until they were able to get a home of their own. The Virginia Street residence was home for John Paul for much of his life and for Tom whenever he was in New York. WHS

DRAWINGS, REPRESENTATIONAL

It is not surprising that Thomas Merton, the son of artists, showed facility in visual as well as verbal artistry. There is evidence of his interest and skill in drawing from various periods throughout his life, including a collection of eight hundred drawings now housed at the Thomas Merton Center at Bellarmine University.

In his autobiography Merton speaks of writing novels in French while a student at the Lycée Ingres in Montauban, "scribbled in exercise books, illustrated in pen and ink — and the ink was generally bright blue" (*Seven Storey Mountain*, 52). While these early works have not survived, stories that Merton wrote as a

teenager for his young cousins, illustrated with line drawings, are extant and show his interest in combining the verbal and the visual.[1] During his senior year at Columbia, Merton became art editor of *Jester*, the campus humor magazine, where his drawings and cartoons had already been appearing regularly. Forty-seven original drawings from this period have survived, ranging from captioned cartoons to female nudes (one a sketch obviously modeled on Botticelli's Three Graces in his *Primavera*) to figures in which the outlines are made up of words appropriate to the picture (e.g., "Dame Winning a Lottery" with hair saying "Zowie! I'm rich! Have a cigar!").[2] He was considered talented enough to provide illustrations (at six dollars per drawing) for an advertising campaign for paper cups, in which, he says, "I did cartoons that said you would surely get trench mouth if you ever drank out of an ordinary glass" (*Seven Storey Mountain*, 156).

At the time of Merton's conversion or shortly afterward, the subjects of his drawings changed, and line drawings of saints, Madonnas, and crucifixes begin to appear, many of them drawn during his time at St. Bonaventure College.[3] (Interestingly, he does not completely abandon his use of verbal outlines:

a drawing of the angel Gabriel is preserved in which the outline of the angel includes phrases from the "Angelus" and the wings are formed by the words of the "Hail Mary" followed by John 1:14; another of St. Thérèse is outlined in French and Latin words.) He continued to make drawings of this type at least from 1947 on (see *Entering the Silence*, 130, 146), including heads and full figures of Christ, Mary, and the saints, as well as drawings of monks, panoramic views of the monastery, and occasional still lifes. While many of these are line drawings, some of the monastic drawings are made with a considerably thicker outline than the earlier drawings, and some are quite detailed.[4]

On October 28, 1960, Merton records in his journal, "Tried some abstract-looking art this week" (*Turning toward the World*, 60). Two weeks later he speaks of "spending some work time on abstract drawings for a possible experimental book" (63). These references mark a new phase in Merton's experiments with the visual arts, brush-and-ink drawings that later he will call "calligraphic abstractions" (*Water of Life*, 20) and "abstract calligraphies" (139) (or more dismissively, "strange blobs of ink" [*Witness to Freedom*, 10]). Some of these drawings are quasi-representational, such as the rectangular design filled with irregular shapes entitled "Jerusalem" and dated "[19]60." But most of them are completely abstract, particularly those done by a method of "crudely printing" his designs on the "thin, almost transparent beautiful Japanese paper" that his friend the abstract painter Ad Reinhardt sent at the beginning of 1964 (58), after a begging letter from Merton (*Road to Joy*, 281). POC

SEE ALSO CALLIGRAPHIES; PHOTOGRAPHY.

Notes

1. See the foreword by Paul M. Pearson to one of the stories, "The Black Sheep," in *The Merton Annual* 11 (1998): 12–16, in which he notes that the other three of the four stories shown him by Merton's cousin, Frank Merton Trier, were illustrated by Merton. Subsequently, a fifth story, "The Great Voyage," was found, and published in *The Merton Seasonal* 24, no. 4 (1999): 3–6, along with its two illustrations. Like "The Haunted Castle," one of the first group of four, which was published (without its illustrations) in *The Merton Seasonal* 19, no. 1 (1994): 7–10, this is a variation on the "Winnie the Pooh" stories of A. A. Milne, and the illustrations reflect those of Ernest Shepherd for the originals.

gallant fox

Published in *Jester*, February 1940

2. Eleven of these drawings, all of which were from the collection of Edward Rice, are included in Rice's memoir of Merton, *The Man in the Sycamore Tree* (Garden City, N.Y.: Doubleday, 1970).

3. Thirty-four drawings are included in the "Fitzgerald File," materials Merton gave to seminarian Richard Fitzgerald before leaving for Gethsemani in 1941, and returned to St. Bonaventure in 1975.

4. *The 1979 Thomas Merton Appointment Calendar* (Kansas City, Mo.: Sheed, Andrews and McMeel, 1978 [repeated in 1980]) contains a total of fifty-two Merton drawings of various types. *The Merton Annual* 3 (1990) includes nine drawings as section dividers (see "A Note on the Merton Drawings in This Volume," x). *Dialogues with Silence: Prayers and Drawings*, ed. Jonathan Montaldo (San Francisco: HarperSanFrancisco, 2001) includes close to one hundred drawings, almost all representational.

DREAD

Dread is a condition of human existence that has been explored at length by existential thinkers, notably by Søren Kierkegaard[1] in his book *The Concept of Dread* (1844). Dread must be distinguished from fear. Fear is the anxiety about some specific object or experience that threatens a person. It may be a particular illness that a person is unable to be rid of. It could be the fear of loss of employment in a company that is drastically reducing the number of workers. In each of these cases the person knows the object of his or her fear.

Dread, on the other hand, has no such specificity. It is about human freedom faced with life's uncertainties, ambiguities, absurdities, and contradictions. Thomas Merton writes, "underlying all life is the ground of doubt and self-questioning which sooner or later must bring us face to face with the ultimate meaning of our life. This self-questioning can never be without a certain existential 'dread' — a sense of insecurity, of 'lostness,' of exile, of sin. A sense that one has somehow been untrue not so much to abstract moral or social norms but to one's own inmost truth" (*Climate of Monastic Prayer*, 36).

Merton contrasts dread with "remorse." Like fear, remorse is directed toward some specific object or action, but with the added dimension of sinfulness or guilt. As he puts it, "*Remorse* is easier to bear than *dread*, for it is at least centered on something definite" (133). Dread, on the other hand, cannot be assigned to a definite cause or attributed to a particular action. It is not something we can repent of, but an experience we must face and struggle with. He links dread with the "fear of God" of the desert fathers and the "dark night" of St. John of the Cross. Dread is an awareness of our absolute contingency, our finiteness. But there is more: the poverty of our creatureliness is compounded by the fact that we are sinners alienated from God and from our own true selves. We are not simply creatures, but creatures in rebellion. We have acted contrary to the truth of who we are. We have failed to meet the challenge of our own life situation. The realization of our failure to measure up begets a sense of guilt — guilt that is real and not a mere neurotic anxiety. "*It is the sense of defection and defeat that afflicts a man who is not facing his own inner truth and is not giving back to life, to God and to his fellow man, a fair return for all that has been given him*" (131). More than that, dread is "an awareness of infidelity as unrepented and without grace as *unrepentable*. It is the deep, confused, metaphysical awareness of a *basic antagonism between the self and God*" (132). This estrangement is due to a perverse attachment to a self that is false and illusory. The estrangement can be removed juridically by receiving the sacraments of the church with the proper dispositions. Then one can believe that he or she has been restored to God's good graces. "But this will not liberate him from 'dread' and 'night' as long as he tends to cling to the empty illusion of a separate self, inclined to resist God" (132).

The context in which we struggle with this illusion of separateness finally to discover that it is not there is our prayer, our meditation.[2] "Only when we have descended in dread to the center of our own nothingness, by [God's] grace and his guidance, can we be led by him, in his own time, to find him in losing ourselves" (137). When finally we relax our determined grasp of a self that is an empty illusion and come to understand that our only hope is in God, we begin to see that the dread we experienced was not a punishment but a purification. Though the experience of dread may have seemed like a kind of "hell," it turns out to be, in the curious words of the twelfth-century Cistercian Isaac of Stella, "a hell of mercy, and not of wrath." "To be in a 'hell of mercy,' " Merton writes, "is to fully experience one's nothingness, but in a spirit of repentance and surrender to God with desire to accept and do His will." In this "hell of mercy," we find ourselves lost in and liberated by the infinite fullness of God's love. "We escape from the cage of emptiness, despair, dread and sin into the infinite space and freedom of grace and mercy" (138). WHS

SEE ALSO CONTEMPLATION; SELF.

Notes

1. Merton refers briefly to Kierkegaard in "The Inner Experience" (99).
2. Merton tends to use the term "meditation" to designate what elsewhere he prefers to call "contemplation."

DUNNE, FREDERIC

Dom Frederic Dunne was Gethsemani's fifth, and first American-born, abbot (1935–48). A kindly and gentle leader, he steadfastly held himself and his monks to the strictest observance of the monastic rule. He was fond of books, and before entering the monastery, he had helped with his father's printing and bookbinding business. He encouraged the intellectual growth of his monks and welcomed the writings of two resident authors:

Fr. Raymond Flanagan and Fr. Louis (Thomas) Merton. It was he who directed Merton to write his autobiography, the book that made Gethsemani known throughout the country and even throughout the world. During his time as abbot Gethsemani's community grew in size so that Dom Frederic was able to establish two daughter houses: Our Lady of the Holy Ghost at Conyers, Georgia (March 1944), and Our Lady of the Most Holy Trinity near Huntsville, Utah

(1946). On August 4, 1948, he died on the train en route to Conyers to visit the monastery there. In a journal entry of August 12, 1948, Merton notes that he had had a long talk with Dom Frederic the day before he left. "He said earnestly that he wanted me to start planning a book on the spiritual life, 'a book to make people love the spiritual life.' I asked could I narrow it down to contemplative life and he was pleased" (*Entering the Silence*, 26). WHS

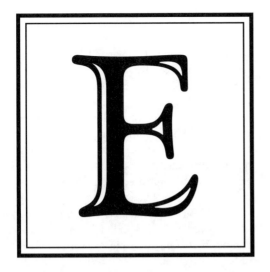

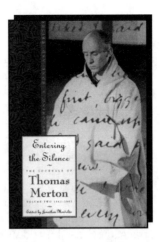

EARLY POEMS: 1940–42

Lexington, Ky.: Anvil Press, 1971. 26 pp.

This is a posthumous collection of Thomas Merton's verse with a foreword by poet Jonathan Greene. These are not the earliest of Merton's poems; they are a further selection of poems contemporaneous with most of those found in *Thirty Poems* (1944) and in the first half of *A Man in the Divided Sea* (1946). All but two of the sixteen items included in the collection were written before Merton's entrance into the monastery in December 1941. While the years 1940–42 are included in the title, at least one of the poems, "The City's Spring" (no. 6; 9 ll.) dates from 1939, and the length (72 ll.) and tone of "Sacred Heart," the unpublished poem from which the last item, "Sacred Heart 2" (no. 16; 14 ll.), was excerpted, suggest that it may have been written as late as 1944 or 1945, contemporary with the final poems of *A Man in the Divided Sea*, which are noticeably longer than poems written earlier.

The decision to publish these poems some three decades after they had been written, and particularly after they had been omitted from two previous collections, may appear somewhat problematic. But they should not simply be considered lesser efforts that merited publication only in the aftermath of their author's death.

Cover for *Entering the Silence* reprinted with the permission of HarperSanFrancisco.

Merton himself was apparently involved in the process of selection (though one poem, "Hymn to Commerce" [no. 10; 23 ll.], actually had been published in an almost identical version as "The Dreaming Trader" in *A Man in the Divided Sea*, an error that may have been caught had Merton himself been able to check the final draft). Part of the answer is that this volume was planned as a limited edition (only 150 copies were printed) to be published on a hand press by Merton's friend Carolyn Hammer, the collaborator and widow of Victor Hammer, who had printed a number of limited editions of Merton works in the 1960s. But many of these poems also represented a side of Merton's work that might not have been considered appropriate from a monk in the early 1940s. For example, the lines "While up and down the perjurer goes, / Picking his nose, picking his nose. / The weary thief, the limping whore / Lie down upon the windy shore" (ll. 21–24) from "Dirge for the City of Miami" (no. 7; 35 ll.) or "Your shoes untie, your mantle you untwitch / Your stocking is all runs, you gaudy bitch" (ll. 15–16) from "From the Second Chapter of a Verse History of the World" (no. 11; 196 ll.) probably would not have passed the censors. More generally, the political themes, as well as the play with language and literary allusion, in a number of these poems, represent interests of the early Merton that had resurfaced in his final years. The publication of *Early Poems: 1940–42* is to

123

a certain degree analogous to the posthumous publication of My Argument with the Gestapo, Merton's novel written during the same period, which also exhibited both theme and style that recur to some degree in Merton's late work.

The collection as a whole has a rather somber tone to it. The first poem, "The Philosophers" (no. 1; 19 ll.), concludes with the word "graves," and five of the remaining fifteen (including three of the next four) end with the word "dead." The first five poems in various ways present a quite critical view of the world at the outset of the Second World War. In "The Philosophers" the speaker (apparently in the grave, though awaiting "the Easter rains" [l. 3] and "Enfolded in my future leaves" [l. 17]) hears two mandrakes (traditionally held to have a human shape [cf. Donne's "Get with child a mandrake root"]) twist the final lines of Keats's "Ode on a Grecian Urn" into perverted parodies representing contemporary materialism ("Body is truth, truth body. Fat is all / We grow on earth, or all we breed to grow" [ll. 10–11]) and militarism ("Beauty is troops, troops beauty. Dead is all / We grow on earth, or all we breed to grow" [ll. 14–15]). In "Dirge for the World Joyce Died In" (no. 2; 16 ll.), where the love of money and prestige is supreme, anyone who is able to see and speak the truth, "Proud spy in the cursing kingdom of the dead" (l. 16), is to be blinded. The long history of war is epitomized in "Two British Airmen" (no. 3; 26 ll.), where the dead pilots of the title are buried alongside Roman soldiers whom they had previously encountered as schoolboys in the pages of Tacitus. In "Poem" ("Here is the man of the islands") (no. 4; 18 ll.), the first of three poems inspired by Merton's Cuban trip in the spring of 1940, human alienation from the natural world — symbolized by "the crested sun" (l. 7) — is presented in images of a cockfight. In "Poem" ("Light plays like a radio in the iron tree") (no. 5; 23 ll.) the scene of war is obliquely suggested as "lightnings race across the western world" (l. 3), probably a reference to the German blitzkrieg, and "a noise of tractors" (l. 9) in actuality turns out to be the sound of tanks; Life itself is imaged as a woman fleeing from impending destruction, but in vain, as the poem concludes, "The woman I saw fleeing

through the bended wheat: / I know I'll find her dead" (ll. 22–23).

Four of the other poems (five counting the redundant "Hymn to Commerce") continue this critical portrait of modernity. "Dirge for the City of Miami," another product of Merton's visit to Cuba, is filled with gangsters, forgers, drunkards, thieves, and whores, with only death as a release, as "all the downcast palms recall / The tears that Magdalen let fall" (ll. 29–30, 34–35), though here there is no sign of the repentance that led to Magdalene's redemption. A companion piece of sorts is "Hymn of Not Much Praise for New York City" (no. 12; 43 ll.), in which the war that has brought low the cities of Europe has elevated New York to be "Queen among the cities of the Earth" (l. 9), a status that is all surface and no substance, as the "hymn" suggests New York to be a modern embodiment of biblical Babylon, where "even the freshest flowers smell of funerals" (l. 39) and no one looks closely enough to discover "Which of the rich men, shivering in the overheated office, / And which of the poor men, sleeping face-down on the Daily Mirror, / Are still alive, and which are dead" (ll. 41–44). The following poem, "Tower of Babel" (no. 13; 29 ll.), subtitled "The Political Speech," actually is the germ of Merton's later (1957) verse drama of the same title: reordered and slightly rewritten, these lines become the speech of the Professor in part 1, scene 2, of the longer work. They focus on the misuse of language to conceal, distort, and manipulate reality rather than reveal the truth, and conclude with the ominous transformation of the image of the web, from "The backward-forward working of the web" (l. 28) by which words are said to create the only reality there is, to "The movement into the web" (l. 29), which implies the ultimate purpose of the web and the ultimate fate of those trapped by it. The longest poem of the collection, "From the Second Chapter of a Verse History of the World" (there is no evidence that there was ever a first chapter), is a reworking of the classical myth of the sacrifice of the Athenian maidens to the minotaur to represent the contemporary destruction of innocence (a theme treated more briefly in "Iphigenia: Politics" in Thirty Poems). It is presented as the increasingly disintegrating commentary on the scene of "some poet, but I don't know which" (l. 17) and includes distorted echoes of "Lycidas" ("your mantle you untwitch" [l. 15]), Scott's "Breathes there the man" ("Unweft, unbuckled and unstrung" [l. 21]), and even "The Star Spangled Banner" ("Starspeckled sweaters" [l. 22]); deliberately singsong rhymes: "The jaunty ship shall hop to Crete where all the monsters are. / The roaring poet sun shall play the hot sea like a lyre, / And twang the copper coastal ridge like any vocal wire: / And then our exile daughters lift their voices in a choir" (ll. 103–6); extreme variations in language and tone: "O see the little jailbait dames are carried off to Crete!" (l. 102); "Standing at the edge of the crowd I saw a subaltern / Discuss with little acumen a target / Painted upon the red-as-welcome gunwales / Of this expensive vessel" (ll. 143–45); "Bend, bend my pretty boughs / And throw my sighs away like leaves. / Scatter upon the land my tears like rain, / Soften the hard earth where no pity lives" (ll. 148–51) — all in the service of a scathing critique of public willingness to acquiesce in blatant injustice in the name of public order. It is not surprising that the Merton of the late 1960s, the author of *Cables to the Ace* and *The Geography of Lograire*, would have been interested in bringing this youthful effort into print.

Of the remaining poems, "The City's Spring" is a short lyric with a completely positive vision of "air . . . full of courtesies" (l. 3), "Flowers and friendly days" (l. 6), and "sweet songs and strawberries" (l. 9) that vividly contrasts in tone and content with the volume as a whole and with the other city poems in particular. "La Comparsa in Oriente" (no. 8; 33 ll.) is a colorful description of a Cuban religious procession that concludes with an invocation recalling the much better known "Song for Our Lady of Cobre": "Then pray for us, Mother of Jesus, / Caridad, Merced, / Queen of Cobre and of the three towers / That watch over Camaguey: / The ten angels are playing gangarias / And the comparsa goes away" (ll. 33–38). "The Strife between the Poet and Ambition" (no. 9; 55 ll.) is a dialogue between Money and Fame, who urge the poet to produce something quickly that

will burnish his reputation, and the poet himself, who claims that his "whole menagerie of verse" (l. 35) has been released so that he is left empty; "Nombril Walketh on the Loam" (no. 14; 33 ll.) is a kind of "calypso" version of the same scenario, in which the aggressive "Nombril" plays the role of Money and Fame and the poet basically reprises the same excuses for his writer's block.

The two final poems, "Lent" (no. 15; 15 ll.) and "Sacred Heart 2," are both subtitled "A Fragment"; the second is, and the first may be, an excerpt from a longer poem.[1] They are radically different in perspective from the preceding group and represent a shift in tone and subject matter that perhaps deliberately reflects the move from the world into the monastery. "Lent" leads the soul into the desert, where "Senses will seem to perish" (l. 2) and thoughts, finding nothing to provide nourishment, vanish; it is a foretaste of the apophatic way of emptiness that will mark much of Merton's later verse and prose. "Sacred Heart 2" opens with four lines, also used as an epigraph for the entire volume, that suggest the central Mertonian theme that it is the inner landscape that must ultimately be explored: "Geography comes to an end, / Compass has lost all earthly north, / Horizons have no meaning / Nor roads an explanation" (ll. 1–4). With its vision of death and resurrection, the final lines of the fragment recall the contrasting images of burial in the opening poem, and so bring the volume to an appropriate conclusion: "Here will I love and praise You in a tongueless death, / Until my white devoted bones, / Long bleached and polished by the winds of this Sahara, / Relive at Your command, / Rise and unfold the flowers of their everlasting spring" (ll. 10–14). POC

Notes

1. Two versions of the complete "Sacred Heart" have been published in *The Merton Seasonal* 25, no. 4 (2000): 12–16.

ECOLOGY

Thomas Merton's attraction to and appreciation of the natural world led him to endorse the growing ecological consciousness of the 1960s.

He first writes in his journal on December 11, 1962, of his interest in reading Rachel Carson's *Silent Spring*, with its revelations of the effects of indiscriminate pesticide use on bird populations. His response to the objection that one should be concerned about people rather than about nonhuman creatures is that it is not a question of either/or but of both/and: "We are in the world and part of it and we are destroying everything because we are destroying ourselves, spiritually, morally and in every way. It is all part of the same sickness" (*Turning toward the World*, 274). After reading the book, he wrote an appreciative letter to Carson linking her analysis of contemporary disregard for the environment to other manifestations of the same technological hubris, particularly the threat of atomic destruction. "The awful irresponsibility with which we scorn the smallest values is part of the same portentous irresponsibility with which we dare to use our titanic power in a way that threatens not only civilization but life itself" (*Witness to Freedom*, 70). He finds a subconscious hatred of life itself buried beneath the superficial optimism of an affluent society that utterly fails to satisfy the deepest human desires for interior unity and a sense of connectedness with all life. The separation from one's own deepest identity results in an alienation from the rest of creation as well. "The whole world itself, to religious thinkers, has always appeared as a transparent manifestation of the love of God, as a 'paradise' of His wisdom, manifested in all His creatures, down to the tiniest, and in the most wonderful interrelationship between them.... That is to say, man is at once a part of nature and he transcends it. In maintaining this delicate balance, he must make use of nature wisely" (71). But it is this sense of balance that is lost in human estrangement from God, creation, and the true self, and the unifying vision of wisdom is replaced by the analytic, dominating attitude of scientistic and technical control. The vocation of modern humanity, Merton concludes, is to rejoin technics and wisdom, though he is not optimistic about the willingness to do so.

Merton sees ecological awareness as part of an authentic contemporary monastic spirit, in continuity with traditional Benedictine respect

Photograph by Thomas Merton

for the land. The development of "a tradition that opens out in *full continuity* into a wisdom capable of understanding the mystery of the contemporary world" must include, along with commitment to peace and racial justice, awareness of and responsiveness to "the great spiritual problem of the profound disturbances of ecology all over the world, the tragic waste and spoilage of natural resources" (*Turning toward the World*, 330). In his description of his own life at the hermitage in *Day of a Stranger*, he emphasizes a sense of being a part of a larger whole: "I know there are trees here. I know there are birds here. I know the birds in fact very well, for there are precise pairs of birds (two each of fifteen or twenty species) living in the immediate area of my cabin. I share this particular place with them: we form an ecological balance. This harmony gives the idea of 'place' a new configuration" (*Day of a Stranger*, 33).

In his 1968 review of Roderick Nash's *Wilderness and the American Mind*, Merton stresses the importance of the environmental ethic of pioneer ecologist Aldo Leopold as a guiding principle for the present and future. A concept of freedom that has in practice led to ruthless exploitation of the environment by industrial and military institutions has reached the point of threatening the foundations of life on earth. "Leopold brought into clear focus one of the most important moral discoveries of our time. This can be called the ecological conscience, which is centered in an awareness of man's true place as a dependent member of the biotic community" (*Preview of the Asian Journey*, 105–6). The utilitarian and pragmatic attitude that sees the natural world principally as a potential source of profit must be countered by this ecological conscience if the process of environmental degradation is to be reversed. In a February 1968 letter to Barbara Hubbard, Merton contrasts ecological consciousness with what he calls millennial consciousness: the latter is oriented completely toward a vision of a utopian future brought about by technological mastery that tends to "destroy and repudiate the past" (*Witness to Freedom*, 74). Merton's response to this attitude is to warn of unintended or disregarded consequences: "We must not try to prepare the millennium by immolating our living earth, by careless and stupid exploitation for short-term commercial, military, or technological ends which will be paid for by irreparable loss in living species and natural resources" (74). He sees humanity at a crossroad, where it can "be dominated by millennial thinking or by ecological thinking" (75). He concludes that it is crucial "to avoid a shallow millenarianism as we enter the space age, and retain a solid ecological consciousness" (75). Despite the slowness of the Christian community to respond to this critical issue, Merton does see an awareness of the interconnectedness of all creation and a sense of environmental stewardship as an intrinsic element of an authentic Christian and religious consciousness: "How absolutely true, and how central a truth, that we are purely and simply *part of nature*, though we are the part which recognizes God" (*Turning toward the World*, 312). Appreciation of this fact, Merton believes, can have profound consequences for the future of Christianity and the future of the earth. POC

SEE ALSO CREATION; NATURE.

ECUMENISM

The Roman Catholic Church into which Thomas Merton was baptized could hardly be called ecumenical. Basking in the certitude of its conviction that it alone was the true church of Christ, it had no inclination to enter into dialogue with other Christians. If there

was any conversation at all, it was only to convince the others that they were wrong and that the only way to salvation open to them was to accept the authority and teachings of the one true church of Christ. Merton embraced this mentality, and his autobiography, *The Seven Storey Mountain*, is, in its ecclesiology, a monument to this Catholic triumphalism.

With his cosmopolitan background and his keenness of mind, he could hardly be expected to maintain so narrow a view for a very long time. As a contemplative, he came to experience a oneness with people at a level of being that is far deeper than the issues that divide them. At least by 1958 Merton was eager to enter into dialogue with others and began meeting with Protestant groups that came to visit at the abbey of Gethsemani (see *Hidden Ground of Love*, 396). Many of his longer correspondences were with people of diverse religious backgrounds — not just other Christians, but adherents of Judaism, Islam, and the religions of the East.

It is important to make clear that Merton's perspective on interreligious dialogue differed from what could be called "professional" ecumenism. Ecumenical dialogue, as it is generally understood, is concerned with refining doctrinal language for the purpose of identifying points of agreement and disagreement, with the hope, at least among Christians, of narrowing differences and working toward eventual reunion of the separated churches.

Certainly Merton saw the value of this sort of dialogue, but his own interests lay elsewhere. Leaving to the "professional" ecumenists the task of recovering a unity that had been lost because of human frailty, weakness, and intolerance, he directed his search toward a unity that had never been lost, because it is beyond the reach of human weakness. It can be discovered only at the level of the religious experience — something that can never be adequately expressed in doctrinal formulations. To Etta Gullick, an English woman who lamented the lack of unity between Catholics and Anglicans, Merton wrote that he was not terribly anguished about the difference. "To me," he wrote, "it is enough to be united with people in love and in the Holy Spirit" (*Hidden*

Ground of Love, 378), in spite of what may seem to be momentous doctrinal and institutional differences. His desire to look for what unites rather than what divides is expressed with a touch of wry humor in a letter to John Harris, a British school teacher: "My concept of Christianity is far from being an old-maidish theology of hiding in a corner of the house and standing on chairs for fear of heretical mice" (390). In a revealing letter to Dona Luisa Coomaraswamy, written in January of 1961, the year before the Second Vatican Council met, he speaks of a vision of peace that can be achieved only by women and men who, without belonging to any movement, "are able to unite in themselves and experience in their own lives, all that is best and most true in the various great spiritual traditions" (126). This was his approach to ecumenism: to seek out what was best and true in all religious traditions. In an oft-quoted statement Merton says, "If I can unite *in myself* the thought and the devotion of Eastern and Western Christendom, the Greek and the Latin Fathers, the Russians with the Spanish mystics, I can prepare in myself the reunion of divided Christians" (*Guilty Bystander,* 12/21). He also speaks of the importance of keeping alive a continuous sense of what has been valid in the past: "I am more and more convinced that my job is to clarify something of the tradition that lives in me, and in which I live: the tradition of wisdom and spirit that is found not only in Western Christendom, but in Orthodoxy, and also, at least analogously, in Asia and Islam" (176/194).

Wherever he looked in the various fields of religious thought and experience, he sought areas of common affirmation rather than points of disagreement. He would be a better Catholic, he was convinced, not by being able to refute Protestant beliefs, but by being able to affirm the truth of Protestantism wherever he could. This was true, he felt, not only about other Christian traditions, but also about other religions — the two other Abrahamic religions: Judaism and Islam; as well as the great religions of the East: Hinduism, Taoism, and Buddhism.

This must not be taken to mean that Merton favored a kind of vapid indifferentism or a syncretism that somehow made everything one.

No, he realized well the rules of interreligious dialogue.[1] Prayer and spiritual discipline are of crucial importance. One must be well grounded in and faithful to one's own tradition. This means that there will be things in other religious traditions that as a Catholic he could not accept and affirm. But first, he would say, one needs to say yes to all the things one can. "If I affirm myself as a Catholic merely by denying all that is Muslim, Jewish, Protestant, Hindu, Buddhist, etc., in the end I will find that there is not much left for me to affirm as a Catholic, and certainly no breath of the Spirit with which to affirm it" (129/144). WHS

SEE ALSO CHURCH, ROMAN CATHOLIC; ENGLAND, CHURCH OF; INTERRELIGIOUS DIALOGUE.

Notes

1. See the statement of the principles of monastic interreligious dialogue that he prepared for a talk he gave to the Temple of Understanding meeting in Calcutta on October 23, 1968 (*Asian Journal,* 309–17).

EIGHTEEN POEMS
New York: New Directions, 1985. 62 pp.

A posthumous collection of poems written by Thomas Merton in 1966 to and for the student nurse with whom he had fallen passionately in love, *Eighteen Poems* has been published only in an expensive limited edition of 250 copies. It did not appear until 1985, two years after Michael Mott's biography had first revealed the details of the relationship, though three of the poems already had been included in *The Collected Poems:* "The Harmonies of Excess" is section 78 of *Cables to the Ace;* "With the World in My Bloodstream" is the third poem of "Sensation Time at the Home"; "Never Call a Babysitter in a Thunderstorm" is found in appendix 3, "Humorous Verse." (Five of the remaining poems are also included in *Learning to Love,* the sixth volume of the complete journals.)

The opening poem, "With the World in My Blood Stream" (no. 1; 97 ll.), the only piece in which the nurse does not appear, provides both the chronological and thematic setting for the subsequent poems: it details the sense of mental and spiritual disorientation (presumably due in part to medication) that the speaker experiences in his hospital bed after a back operation, "searching the impossible ceiling / For the question and the meaning" (ll. 51–52). A paradoxical answer is found in Meister Eckhart's image of the *scintilla animae*, the spark of the soul that is one with God even as all other marks of personal identity fall away, leading to participation in the sufferings of Christ and to a "Love without need and without name" (l. 94) that both foreshadows and remains in tension with the human love of the subsequent poems in the sequence.

"Untitled Poem" (no. 2; 92 ll.), beginning "All theology is a kind of birthday" (l. 1), is a meditation both on the fact (mentioned in Merton's journals) that M. (as the nurse is called) had just been born near Cincinnati shortly before Merton passed through the city on his way to Gethsemani in 1941 ("Across the river my meaning has taken flesh" [l. 20]) and on the themes of paradise and exile that will run through the entire sequence: "The ground of birth is paradise / Yet we are born a thousand miles / Away from our home" (ll. 7–9). The experience of human love is envisioned as a true theology, a genuine word of God, that provides "A way home to where we are / Epiphany and Eden" (ll. 83–84).

"I Always Obey My Nurse" (no. 3; 48 ll.) is built on the analogy between the healing power of God and the nurse's vocation of healing, and between the poet's physical recuperation and a deeper healing of his own brokenness, the brokenness of the nurse herself, and the brokenness of the world. To obey his nurse is to "obey the little spark [Eckhart's *scintilla* again] / That flies from fracture to fracture / And the explosion / Where God did not make death [a repeated assertion throughout the poem] / But only vision" (ll. 23–27).

"Louisville Airport" (no. 4; 56 ll.), subtitled "May 5, 1966," describes the experience of sitting on the grass in the evening watching jets land as a kind of return to Eden ("this paradise of grass / Where the world first began" [ll. 23–24]), in which the couple's love is a participation in the creative love of God and the sunset is revealed as the "One Flame" (l. 45) in

which all reality is clearly seen and "the whole world" (l. 49) is recreated. The "foolish grass" (ll. 1, 8, 53) on which the lovers sit, symbolizing a wisdom that the pragmatic world cannot comprehend, is contrasted with the materialistic hopes of "the foolish rich" (l. 22), who are oblivious to the revelation of the divine that surrounds them and is visible only to those who have become like little "children permitting God / To make again that love / Which is His alone" (ll. 12–14).

"May Song" (no. 5; 63 ll.), the most sensuous of the poems, describes an experience of getting "lost" in the monastery woods (ll. 13–14) as being truly "found" in one another; but even as the speaker prays, "In this heaven let me lie down / Under the fragrant tent / Of your black hair" (ll. 23–25), even as he pleads to be carried away from the isolation and loneliness of "too much perfection" (l. 53) by "Your lifeboat / Your saving body" (ll. 48–49), there is a realization that "In the imperfect wood / In the land of bodies" (ll. 56–57) such a heaven is impermanent. The Edenic moment has passed, and they must struggle with the conflicts between love and other responsibilities in a "part of the wood" (perhaps Dante's wood) where "nothing can ever be / Consistent" (ll. 14, 17–18).

"The Harmonies of Excess" (no. 6; 30 ll.) uses the imagery of the germination of seeds as a symbol of breaking through conventional categories into new life. Yet there is perhaps an ambivalence in the statement that "the lovers teach April stars / To riot rebel and follow faithless courses" even though the speaker asserts "it doesn't matter" (ll. 18–20) since the seed is able to endure both the burial of winter and "the terrible sweetness / Of spring's convivial nightmare" (ll. 22–23) (another ostensibly positive yet problematic metaphor). The poem ends with the speaker sending his beloved "this burning garden / My talkative morning-glory / My climbing germ of poems" (ll. 28–30), making the works of art an expression of his love but perhaps also a sublimation of it, as the poems rather than the lovers themselves become identified with the garden and its flowers.

The physical separation accepted with equanimity in the previous poem is a matter of anguish in "Aubade on a Cloudy Morning" (no. 7; 54 ll.). The poet uses the traditional term for "dawn poem," when lovers greet one another and the new day, to reflect on his own absence from that "distant room / Which I have never entered" (ll. 3–4) where his beloved awakens. Though he declares, "I am at war with my own heart / Because I am never by your side / When those eyes first open / To recognize the new day" (ll. 44–47), he concludes on a note of acceptance: so long as it is a day that she sees and knows, even a day without sunlight, "I am satisfied with it / I look for no other" (ll. 53–54) — surely a statement that conveys an attitude not only toward this one day but also toward their relationship as a whole.

"Certain Proverbs Arise out of Dreams" (no. 8; 63 ll.), a prose poem arranged in fourteen paragraphs rather than in sense lines, implicitly relates the beloved to the figure of Proverb, the feminine embodiment of divine Wisdom, who first appeared in a Merton dream in 1958 and who was the subject of his earlier prose poem "Hagia Sophia." "Certain dreams" are seen as providing access to a level of reality deeper than rational thought, to "a day which is not on the calendar" (l. 9), to "the first day of creation" (l. 51). They open out onto the inexplicable realm of mystery, and so transcend the more limited and rationalistic dimension of problem: "My sin was this: I wanted to understand my own problem. In punishment for which I was instantly given a problem to understand. All understanding then became impossible until, in my sleep, I turned again to you" (ll. 34–37). The problem, in one of its dimensions at least, surely is the conflict between his monastic commitment and his love, while the mystery that dissolves the problem is the paradox of a commitment that is also a detachment: "I will no longer burn your wounded body. We do not need to weary ourselves grasping anything, even love: still less the bloody jewel of desire" (ll. 52–54).

"Never Call a Babysitter in a Thunderstorm" (no. 9; 35 ll.) is a raucous piece of fantasy in which the "baby" in question holds the babysitter hostage as he launches an anarchic revolution with ever increasing levels of mayhem that make communication impos-

sible. The baby ultimately is equated with love (presumably based on the traditional figure of Cupid or Eros), and the addressee of the poem ("my boy") finally is advised to sell his worldly goods (car, golf clubs, tennis racket, TV) "And pay the baby to set her free" (l. 35); though the nature of this "freedom" is left undefined, the implication seems to be that it is a love in which *agape* is liberated from *eros*.

"Two Songs for M." (no. 10; 32 ll.) consists of two separate poems, of eighteen and fourteen lines, respectively. The first, with its epigraph from Camus, "*L'amour avait pris chez eux la forme de l'obstination*" ("Love had taken among them the form of obstinacy"), is a reflection on the "absurd" situation (another Camusian term) of continuing to be faithful to a love with no likelihood of bodily fulfillment; this "obstinate" (l. 12) fidelity is reflected in the very form of the poem, which concludes as it began, with the words "Love is the non-stop body of believing" (ll. 1, 18). In the second song the physical absence of the beloved is balanced and complemented by an interior presence that creates a spiritual landscape of love: "Deep inside me / Is your lovely hill / Deep inside me / Your silken cry" (ll. 11–14).

"Cherokee Park" (no. 11; 85 ll.) brings the lovers together for the first time since "May Song." The location of the title is an actual park in Louisville where the couple find themselves "In the wooded hollow" (l. 6) on a hillside, no longer in Eden but "Half way between / Heaven and hell / Zion and the green river" (ll. 31–33). As they foresee her departure "To that other city where the cosmic fires / Are out" (ll. 41–42), they experience "The dry rapture of hopelessness / Purer than any joy" (ll. 54–55). Even as they cling to one another, they come to acknowledge, in an echo of Dante, that "In this unspeakable denial / Is our peace" (ll. 80–81).

"Gethsemani" (no. 12; 50 ll.), dated "May 19, 1966," is a striking expression of the poet's own subconscious ambivalence. It combines a description of the "half destroyed" (l. 7) abbey church (in the process of renovation) with a reflection on the many monks who have left the monastery, in particular Fr. John of the Cross, "A taut, embittered / Young Christ" (ll. 29–

30), who returns in a dream to tell the speaker, "Now many priests will tell lies / In order to marry" (ll. 37–38). This serves as an ironic counterpoint to the earlier dream poem, as the declaration is described as "the local theology / Reduced to a proverb" (ll. 45–46). Though the words are intended to be "funny" (ll. 42, 43) since they are spoken "By one who has met liars / Everywhere" (ll. 47–48) and who is thus not a spokesperson for the narrow vision of "the local theology," ultimately this recognition is no consolation for the speaker: the ubiquity of liars does not provide any easy solution to or escape from his own contradictory situation as a monk in love.

In "Evening: Long Distance Call" (no. 13; 41 ll.) the conversation only calls attention to the distance between the lovers: "You might as well be gone / Into another country where love's language / Has never been spoken" (ll. 14–16). In contrast, the following poem, "A Long Call is Made out of Wheels" (no. 14; 62 ll.), is marked by a willingness to be content with and grateful for the present moment of contact, even if from a phone booth with the rumbling of trains in the background: "There is no time / Table for the unforeseen / Connection" (ll. 44–46). The poet is able to conclude that "The edge of this hot town / Is still the edge of Eden" (ll. 61–62).

"Cancer Blues" (no. 15; 68 ll.), as the title suggests, is written to suggest both the rhythms and the tone of a blues song. The speaker laments his own "cancer of the heart" (l. 8) and cries out for his "sweet Babe" (l. 4) (the language of this poem is considerably more colloquial and "jazzy" than any of the others), who apparently is working on an Indian reservation, to heal him with "her fiery gentle healing light" (l. 28); she has "become a lucky Indian / star" (ll. 58–59) who is able to "point right down to the / root cure / All the way down in the sweet summer earth to clean / The hunted heart of the hell-blues because you are grown / Into a healer" (ll. 61–65).

"Six Night Letters" (no. 16) actually consists of six full-length poems that provide a kind of retrospective survey of the relationship. The first (45 ll.) evokes the peacefulness of "secure night" (l. 18) in which the beloved comes to the speaker in a dream "Bringing the truth I need" (l. 42) yet causing him to awaken "with a cry and loud tears" (l. 44). The opening line of the second letter (40 ll.), "Every beautiful day," echoes and complements the line "Every beautiful night" that opened the first. Again the Eden myth is evoked as the speaker recalls "the morning when God / Takes you out of my side" (ll. 6–7) and declares, "O my divided rib / It is good to be willing / To be taken apart / To come together" (ll. 10–13). Yet he realizes that their experience of the "paradise wood" (l. 20) puts them at odds with a fallen world marked by "dead heart / And sick intelligence" (ll. 36–37), so that the final affirmation that "every beautiful day / Is our invention" (ll. 39–40) seems less than totally affirmative. The third letter (28 ll.) develops this tension between their love and the outside world: they are both "free / Of its hold" (ll. 5–6) and responsible to and for it, since "the whole world's / Greatest need" (ll. 15–16) is their love, which is both "The newest love in the world" (l. 23) and a participation in the creative Love that is the very foundation of the universe "In the unheard of beginning" (l. 25). In the fourth letter (53 ll.) the speaker lies awake at night reflecting on the new depth of revelation that had occurred that day as the lovers opened their lives to each other: "Now we know each other / We need never be afraid / Of telling too much / But only of not telling / Everything" (ll. 22–26). But in the fifth letter (27 ll.) there is a recognition of the fragility of love, an awareness that it is beyond human control, that "Love runs best / When it seems to break down / . . . / Loves runs well / When it runs by itself" (ll. 14–15, 20–21). The final letter (19 ll.) both affirms the identity of the lovers ("You are myself" [l. 10]) and locates that identity in their common loneliness: "The loneliness here . . . / Envelops me / Like your own loneliness / Exploring my dark wood / And my lost house / To find itself" (ll. 11, 15–19). Thus, the six letters as a group recapitulate the phases of the relationship from initial ecstatic wonder to final paradoxical recognition of unity in shared separation.

The final two poems look back on the relationship with a mixture of detachment and longing. "For M. in October" (no. 17; 36 ll.)

consists largely of a litany of "If..." clauses culminating with the rueful yet resigned acknowledgement "If only you and I / Were possible" (ll. 30–31), followed by the affirmation that even though apart, they are not separate, as they are able to "watch [the full moon] rise together" (l. 36). The concluding poem,[1] "For M. on a Cold Grey Morning" (no. 18; 34 ll.), takes place even later, on a morning of "rain / And melting snow" (ll. 1–2). While it testifies to a continuing longing without any prospect for further direct contact, it affirms the beloved's continuing presence within the speaker, "nearer than we know" (l. 27), so that the sequence ends on a note of tenderness expressing both ongoing separation and ongoing unity: "You wake in another room / And the bed where you slept / Is a nest in my heart" (ll. 32–34).

Thus, the sequence as a whole traces the pattern of the relationship from an initial experience of holistic "paradise-consciousness," a sense of oneness not only with one another but also with the natural world and with its divine source, through a period of anguish caused by the fact of physical separation and by the tension between commitment to another person and commitment to a solitary vocation, to a tenuous yet genuine resolution that both embraces the bond of shared experience and accepts the necessity of letting go of the other and of the possibilities she embodies. POC

Notes

1. This poem was not part of the original group given by Merton to James Laughlin; it was added from a handwritten version discovered by William H. Shannon in a notebook at Syracuse University Library and is dated October 1966.

ELECTED SILENCE

London: Hollis and Carter, 1949. iv+381 pp.

This volume, the British edition of Thomas Merton's *The Seven Storey Mountain*, under a new title, was edited and introduced by Evelyn Waugh. Robert Murray Davis, in an article entitled "How Waugh Cut Merton,"[1] describes Waugh's editing as "intelligent and ruthless." He eliminated repetitions, seemingly irrelevant material, entries that were overly pious or that

expressed what Waugh considered anti-British and anti-Protestant prejudices. In a letter of August 29, 1949, to Merton, Waugh mildly reproves the young Trappist writer for his habit of "scatter" bombing rather then "precision" bombing. "You scatter a lot of missiles all round the target instead of concentrating on a single direct hit. It is not art. Your monastery tailor and bootmaker could not waste material. Words are our materials."[2]

Waugh cut more than one-fifth of the original text, focusing the book, as the new title suggests, on a central theme: Merton's movement from the secular world to the life of contemplation. No doubt the book is improved as a literary work. But, as Michael Mott has pointed out, "It lacks the flavor of the original. A few important sections are no longer in Merton's voice."[3]

In 1973 *The Seven Storey Mountain* was published in England by Sheldon Press. WHS

SEE ALSO *SEVEN STOREY MOUNTAIN*.

Notes

1. Robert Murray Davis, "How Waugh Cut Merton," *The Month*, April 1973.
2. *The Letters of Evelyn Waugh*, ed. Mark Armory (New York: Ticknor and Fields, 1986), 308. See also Merton's letters to Waugh in *The Courage for Truth* (3–21).
3. Michael Mott, *The Seven Mountains of Thomas Merton* (Boston: Houghton Mifflin, 1984), 248.

EMBLEMS OF A SEASON OF FURY

New York: New Directions, 1963. vi+149 pp.

This is Thomas Merton's sixth book of verse, the last volume of shorter poems to be published before his death. It consists of thirty pieces, a number of them prose poems; the essay "A Letter to Pablo Antonio Cuadra Concerning Giants"; and translations of six poets, each preceded by a short biographical and critical profile. The title, which parallels that of the early volume *Figures for an Apocalypse* (1947), reflects the considerable number of poems in the collection that deal with the critical social issues of the period, including racism, war, and political oppression; these are complemented by other poems that reflect Merton's continuing commitment to the Christian contemplative tradition and his openness to the insights of other religious traditions.

Among the most prominent poems of social criticism are "And the Children of Birmingham" (no. 16; 45 ll.), in which the "fairy tale" of Red Riding Hood becomes terrifyingly real in the civil rights marches in Alabama in 1963 as young children face police dogs, and language is perverted to mask rather than reveal reality, with hostility and threats disguised as care and concern; "A Picture of Lee Ying" (no. 11; 34 ll.), prompted by a newspaper photograph of a young refugee forced to return to communist China, in which Merton once again highlights the distortion of language, both in the bureaucratic indifference to the nineteen-year-old girl's plight and in the reporting of her situation (the tragically inapposite caption *"Point of no return"* [l. 4] beneath the photo); and "Chant to Be Used in Processions around a Site with Furnaces" (no. 22; 35 secs.), a self-justifying monologue by a concentration camp commander that ends with the chilling statement "Do not think yourself better because you burn up friends and enemies with long-range missiles without ever seeing what you have done" (l. 35).

Among other poems with contemporary social relevance are "Why Some Look up to Planets and Heroes" (no. 1; 44 ll.), a satiric look at the American space program as an exercise in fatuous self-promotion; "The Moslems' Angel of Death" (no. 2; 32 ll.), a reflection on the Algerian war of liberation against France; "And So Goodbye to Cities" (no. 3; 37 ll.), a somber meditation on the catastrophic threat of nuclear war (likened to the destruction of Sodom in its reference to "Lot's wife, sleeping at the switch" [l. 23]); "There Has to Be a Jail for Ladies" (no. 14; 48 ll.), a recognition and assurance of the presence of God even among those poor imprisoned women in whose curses "God and Hell are rusted together in one red voice" (l. 19); "Advice to a Young Prophet" (no. 18; 39 ll.), apparently a critique of those whose protests against American society take the ineffectual form of dropping out and seeking a drug-induced "mysticism": "Pretty big prophets whose words don't burn" (l. 32).

Critiques of violence, technology, and ma-

terialism also appear, though more obliquely, in "Song: In the Shows of the Round Ox" (no. 5; 42 ll.), in which personal identity is reduced to financial worth as "The first-last dollar's number / Is my own name" (ll. 30–31); in "Gloss on the Sin of Ixion" (no. 6; 42 ll.), in which the myth of Ixion's passion for Juno is transformed into modern humanity's lust for material success, and his punishment is imaged as the violence that is the consequence of greed: "Giant war Ixion / Rolling and fighting on the red wheel" (ll. 41–42); in "A Dream at Arles on the Night of the Mistral" (no. 15; 27 ll.), in which the hot south wind blows men toward "Mars / Dark commander" (ll. 1–2), and "Two twisting armies / Wound the incurable mind" (ll. 13–14); and in "Seven Archaic Images" (no. 20; 66 ll.), in which the innocence of a prehistoric procession to the "Womb of a secret hill / Paradise / Covered inside with animals" (ll. 7–9) is soon replaced by "Man-eating war," which "Shakes the land with drums" as the cave is transformed into "The sacred enclosure / The house of omens and weapons" (ll. 51–54).

The essay, "A Letter to Pablo Antonio Cuadra Concerning Giants," which likens the two world powers of the Soviet Union and the United States to the figures of Gog and Magog in Ezekiel, and looks to the "Third World," particularly to Latin America, as providing hope for renewal should the two giants destroy each other, takes a similar perspective to these poems of social criticism. Despite its use of symbolism, it clearly is an essay rather than a poem; it remains from an earlier conception of *Emblems of a Season of Fury* as a combination of verse and prose, perhaps because it serves as a kind of transition to the group of translations, the first of which are of poems by Cuadra. Except for the French verse of Raïssa Maritain, wife of Merton's friend the philosopher Jacques Maritain (seven poems), all the poets translated in this volume were from Central and South America and wrote in Spanish (Cuadra: ten poems; Ernesto Cardenal: fifteen poems; Jorge Carrera Andrade: five poems; Cesar Vallejo: four poems; Alfonso Cortes: nine poems), thus reflecting Merton's growing interest in Latin America during the final decade of his life.

Less easily classified poems in the volume include "An Elegy for Five Old Ladies" (no. 4; 9 ll.), an affectionate yet ironic tribute to residents of a rest home who were drowned when the car in which they were sitting rolled into a lake ("Let the perversity of a machine become our common study" [l. 9]), and elegies written for Ernest Hemingway (no. 7; 7 secs.), which weaves references to his books into prayers for his soul at monastic liturgy, and for James Thurber (no. 8; 13 ll.), whose death is described as the death of humor as well since "The great dogs of nineteen sixty-one / Are nothing to laugh at" (ll. 6–7). "To Alfonso Cortes" (no. 27; 27 ll.) is addressed to the Nicaraguan poet (one of those translated by Merton in this volume), who is seen as a kind of holy fool, "the mad / Saint of a hot republic!" (ll. 7–8). Two poems are the fruit of Merton's studies of the medieval Platonic school at Chartres. The whimsical "News from the School of Chartres" (no. 28; 78 ll.) consists of a series of seven (presumably authentic) versified extracts from letters to teachers, parents, and friends, requesting money, books, news, and "Good chalk. / The chalk here won't write" (ll. 46–47). More ominous is the prose poem "What to Think When It Rains Blood" (no. 29; 16 secs.), based on a letter of Fulbert of Chartres to the French king, which sees such an event as a portent of calamities (and evidently is presented by Merton as a medieval analogue to modern catastrophes such as nuclear fallout).

The remaining poems concern themselves in one way or another with the contemplative dimension of life. Two poems look back to the desert father tradition. "Macarius and the Pony" (no. 9; 48 ll.) retells an anecdote of parents who brought to the elder their daughter, whom they thought had been transformed into a pony, but whom Macarius recognized in her true form and identity, prompting the warning "Your own ill-will . . . / Peoples the world with specters" (ll. 46, 48). "Macarius the Younger" (no. 10; 57 ll.) actually is composed of three related stories: the first on the saint's home in the desert of Scete, to which "No road, no path, / No land marks / Show the way" (ll. 6–8); the second on an incident in which a precious bunch of grapes is successively given

to and given away by each of the hermits at Scete; the last about a soldier who sees the two Macarii, "ragged bums, having nothing, / Free men" (ll. 47–48), on a boat and as a result "gave away all that he had / And enlisted in the desert army" (ll. 56–57). The Islamic tradition is drawn upon in "Song for the Death of Averroës" (no. 12; 46 secs.), in which the great philosopher encounters the Sufi mystic Ibn Al Arabi and comes to realize the insufficiency of an exclusively rationalist view of reality.

Many of the remaining poems are among the best known that Merton wrote. "Grace's House" (no. 13; 50 ll.), based on a drawing by a young girl (appropriately named Grace) sent to Merton by her father, describes the "child's world" as a "paradise . . . / Where all the grass lives / And all the animals are aware" (ll. 37–39) and concludes with the rueful recognition that for those who have lost their innocence, "Alas, there is no road to Grace's house!" (l. 50). "Song for Nobody" (no. 17; 17 ll.) describes the simple beauty of a flower as beyond all usefulness and therefore an implicit analogue for contemplative awareness. "Song: If You Seek . . ." (no. 19; 28 ll.) reveals solitude as guide to authentic self-discovery, and indeed as identified with the true self: "I, Solitude, am thine own self: / I, Nothingness, am thy All. / I, Silence, am thy Amen!" (ll. 26–28). "O Sweet Irrational Worship" (no. 21; 31 ll.) presents the loss of the ego-centered self as leading to identification with all creation and with creation's hymn of praise to the Creator. "A Messenger from the Horizon" (no. 23; 42 ll.) describes the naked messenger as "A mute comet, an empty sun" (l. 14) whose message is paradoxically to be found in his silence and his renunciation. In "Night-Flowering Cactus" (no. 24; 28 ll.) the plant that blooms only once a year in the darkness is a symbol of contemplative realization, as the cactus shows its "true self only in the dark" (l. 4) and so reveals the Word issuing from the silence: "The all-knowing bird of night flies out of my mouth" (l. 25). In "Love Winter When the Plant Says Nothing" (no. 25; 21 ll.) the apparently dead landscape actually hides the vital fire of life deep within, identifying "the house of growth" (l. 4) with what from another perspective is "A house of nothing" (l. 16).

"The Fall" (no. 26; 23 ll.) contrasts the total self-emptying, the surrender of all self-created identification, which brings about a return to paradise, with the exile from Eden in a world of organized routines and recorded identities, concluding that only those who have been liberated from oppressive social identities truly are able to live in the social world creatively, because "They bear with them in the center of nowhere the unborn flower of nothing, /... the paradise tree" (ll. 22–23). The four-part prose poem "Hagia Sophia" (no. 30; 39 secs.), the last of the original poems in the volume, uses the pattern of the liturgy of the hours to structure a meditation on Holy Wisdom, "an invisible fecundity, a dimmed light, a meek namelessness, a hidden wholeness" (sec. 1), encountered in creation and creativity, in the nurturing presence of women and of God, in the self-donation of the Virgin Mary and the human pilgrimage of her son, "a destitute wanderer, ... A homeless God, ... a frail expendable exile" (sec. 39) who has fully entered into the condition of "the least of these." This "sophianic" presence, which recognizes how creation already manifests the presence of God, balances and is balanced by the more "prophetic" poems, which call attention to the ruptured bonds that have frustrated the divine design for unity between creation and Creator. Thus, the volume as a whole is representative of the simultaneous embrace and critique of the world: the commitment to both contemplative silence and prophetic speech that characterizes Merton's vision in the final decade of his life. POC

SEE ALSO HAGIA SOPHIA.

ENCOUNTER: THOMAS MERTON AND D. T. SUZUKI

Edited by Robert E. Daggy. Monterey, Ky.: Larkspur Press, 1988. xx+104 pp.

Following an introduction by Robert E. Daggy explaining the genesis of the book, there are two parts: (1) the Merton-Suzuki letters and (2) the account of the Merton-Suzuki meeting in New York City in June 1964. There is also a selection of notes compiled by Daggy.

Part 1 contains the exchange of letters between these two men: some letters from the Merton Center at Bellarmine University in Louisville, the others from the University of Kentucky's King Library in Lexington. There are eight letters from Merton to Suzuki (March 12, 1959, to May 3, 1965),[1] and five letters from Suzuki to Merton (March 31, 1959, to November 22, 1959). In addition, there is one letter (June 1, 1964) from Suzuki's secretary, Mihoko Okamura, to Merton, in which she invites him to meet with Suzuki at Columbia University's Butler Hall.

The meeting of these two men is told with selections from Merton's journals, which in the same year as the publication of *Encounter* appeared in *A Vow of Conversation*. Pages 75–90 (June 12, 1964, to July 10, 1964) correspond to the same entries in *A Vow of Conversation*, 54–62. This account of the Merton-Suzuki encounter differs somewhat from what appears in volume 5 of the Merton journals (*Water of Life*, 108–25).

A limited edition of 1060 copies of this volume was printed, of which sixty are special, with their own particular paper and cover. WHS

Notes

1. The Merton letters to Suzuki also are in the first volume of the Merton letters, *The Hidden Ground of Love* (560–71).

ENGLAND, CHURCH OF

Thomas Merton's New Zealander father belonged to the Church of England. As a baby, young Thomas had an appointed godfather, Dr. Thomas Izod Bennett, who circumcised him. But there is no mention of his ever having been baptized into the Anglican Church.

His evaluation of the Church of England in *The Seven Storey Mountain* is unremittingly harsh and, by his own admission, probably unfair.[1] He sees its doctrines, as taught from their pulpits, as vague and without substance. But the core problem, the reason it was, in his eyes, sterile and inefficacious, was "its lack of vital contact with the Mystical Body of the True Church" (*Seven Storey Mountain*, 66). Moreover, it was "a class religion, the cult of a special society and group, not even of the whole nation, but of the ruling minority in a nation." It represented "the solidarity and conservatism of the English ruling class" (65).

This obviously prejudiced opinion of the Church of England was written by a young monk who had so wholeheartedly accepted the narrow exclusiveness of the Catholicism of the 1940s. It was a Catholicism that claimed to be the one true church and refused to acknowledge that other Christian bodies were churches or even Christian. The Second Vatican Council distanced itself considerably from this mentality, as it recognized other Christian bodies as churches or ecclesial communities. Merton had begun to move in this direction even before the Council met.

In an essay on ecumenism, written on the Feast of St. George, 1965, and entitled "The Poorer Means: A Meditation on Ways to Unity," Merton commends the Church of England for the special respect it gives to the dignity of the personal conscience. "This," he says, "is something born of no 'revolt' but on the contrary [is] rooted in the most authentic Catholic and monastic past of Anglo-Saxon and medieval England."[2] He points out to the members of his own church their need to understand that it is this respect for personal conscience that accounts for the repugnance of Anglo-Catholics for what they perceive as an excessive and arbitrary authoritarianism often manifested in the Catholic Church. (It should be mentioned, though, that in this same article Merton deplores the frank agnosticism of some Anglican writers and speakers about fundamental theological principles. He probably is referring to the debate that followed the publication in 1963 of Bishop John A. T. Robinson's book *Honest to God*.) In a letter to his aunt Kit of May 27, 1964, Merton attempts to clarify the difference in perspective between the Church of England and the Roman Catholic Church: "Anglicanism assumes a great deal and takes a lot for granted: first of all that you are able to do most of it on your own, so to speak. The Roman Church goes to the other extreme and tries to push you into everything and do it all for you, including all your thinking (and some of us don't take too kindly to this, as you may imagine)" (*Road to Joy*, 62).

Writing again to Aunt Kit on June 1, 1966, Merton describes some of the ecumenical contacts he had at Gethsemani. He especially mentions those with Anglicans. "I have lots of Anglican contacts, convents in England, a good friend at Pusey House, Oxford [A. M. Allchin], some people in Boston (Cowley Fathers) and so on. All High Church, as you might well imagine. But I am a pretty liberal bloke myself, if not radical. Actually I feel very much at home with the C. of E., except when people are awfully stuffy and insular about it" (75). Pointing to his own Welsh background and British upbringing, he assures Aunt Kit, "I have never been and will never be aggressively Roman, by any means. It would not be possible for a Merton to go too far with a really 'popish' outlook. We are all too hard-headed and independent" (75).

This same spirit of independence is expressed in a letter of November 24, 1966, to Etta Gullick, who, among other things, was involved in the training of young men for the Anglican priesthood. She had written lamenting the fact that there seemed little likelihood of "institutional or sacramental reunion" between Rome and Canterbury. He was not as anguished as she. Leaving the ecumenical task to others, he says, "To me it is enough to be united with people in love and in the Holy Spirit.... Where there is a sincere desire for truth and real good will and genuine love, there God Himself will take care of the differences far better than any human or political ingenuity can" (*Hidden Ground of Love*, 378). This is a clear statement of Merton's ecumenical approach. He does not discount the importance and necessity of discussing the doctrinal differences that separate the churches, but his own interest lay elsewhere: in discovering the elements of unity in which people already were one.

In a letter of April 25, 1964, to Canon A. M. Allchin, he expresses the hope that in the liturgical renewal going on in the Roman Catholic Church, Catholics just entering upon the use of the vernacular in worship might learn a great deal from the Anglican Church, for "the best of Anglicanism," he says, "is unexcelled." And for his part, he continues, "I will try to cling to the best and be as English a Catholic as one in my position can be" (26).

Clearly, the mature Merton has repudiated the rigidly critical attitude toward the Church of England so strongly expressed by the youthful Merton in *The Seven Storey Mountain*. He made this very clear in an April 2, 1965, letter to Mrs. Mycock:[3] "Your supposition that if I wrote that book (*The Seven Storey Mountain*) again today I would speak differently of Anglicans was both charitable and correct. My thought at the time of writing was hardly matured and I just said what came to mind, as people so often do, and more often did in those days. It is, unfortunately, so easy and so usual simply to compare the dark side of someone else's Church with the bright side of one's own. Thank heaven we are getting over that now, I hope" (*Witness to Freedom*, 319). WHS

SEE ALSO CHURCH, ROMAN CATHOLIC; ECUMENISM.

Notes

1. See *The Seven Storey Mountain* (176), where Merton describes his feeling about the Zion Episcopal Church, where his father had played the organ.
2. "The Poorer Means: A Meditation on Ways to Unity," Haywards Heath, England, Holy Cross Convent, 1965.
3. Not otherwise identified.

ENTERING THE SILENCE: Becoming a Monk and Writer

The Journals of Thomas Merton, vol. 2: 1941–52. Edited by Jonathan Montaldo. San Francisco: HarperSanFrancisco, 1996. xvii+501 pp.

This second and longest volume of Thomas Merton's complete journals begins with the day of his official reception into the Abbey of Gethsemani as a postulant and concludes over a decade later with the famous "Fire Watch" passage, in which Merton, now Fr. Louis, master of the newly professed monks, journeys literally through the darkened monastery and metaphorically through his own history as a member of the Gethsemani community.

In actuality, however, the journal does not cover this entire period. The first of the volume's three parts consists of a mere six entries

between December 13, 1941, and April 3, 1942, fragments saved from an otherwise destroyed novitiate journal,[1] for the sake of the seven poems recorded on these pages, although the adjacent prose material, fortuitously preserved, does provide some interesting observations, as when on December 18 Merton reflects that the meaningfulness within the monastery lends meaning to the larger world (*Entering the Silence*, 4), prays on January 9 to be lost in God (5), and on Good Friday meditates on seeking obscurity and letting go of results (10–11).

There is no journal material between April 1942 and sometime early in 1945, when "A Journal-Memoir: Dom Frederic Dunne" begins.[2] This is a gathering of entries, most of them dated, written over the course of three years, all focused in some way on Merton's first abbot and intended to serve as notes for whoever would one day write Dom Frederic's biography; they were discovered among the papers of Fr. Raymond (Flanagan), who did indeed write a memoir of the abbot after his death and to whom Merton must have given the material.[3] The reflections make clear Merton's respect and affection for the abbot who admitted him to the monastery and encouraged his writing.

The third, major part of the journal, entitled "The Whale and the Ivy" after the tentative title of what eventually would be published as *The Sign of Jonas* (see 237), runs from December 10, 1946, the fifth anniversary of Merton's entrance into Gethsemani, through July 5, 1952, the date given for the fire watch. The main lines of this material have long been familiar from *The Sign of Jonas*, but the previously published journal contains only about half of the original material, much of it revised and polished. Eighty-eight of the 405 dated entries of the original journal were omitted completely (including twenty-five consecutive entries from December 31, 1947, through March 12, 1948), but the more typical strategy was to cut material within an entry, as with the two sentences on surface distractions and underlying recollection and the entire following paragraph on Duns Scotus from the first, December 10, 1946, entry. The complete journal for this period is more mundane, containing many details of ordinary daily routine, Merton's readings, and so forth not found in *The Sign of Jonas,* and also more conflicted, more frank about Merton's struggles to reconcile his desire for solitude with the busyness of Trappist life in an overcrowded monastery and his dual vocation as monk and writer.

These years are marked by a number of significant milestones in Merton's monastic life, beginning with his profession of solemn vows on March 19, 1947 (49), and culminating with his ordination to the priesthood on May 26, 1949 (317). In November of the same year he begins giving classes in Scripture and in monastic history and spirituality to novices and young monks (372), and in May 1951 he is appointed the first master of students at Gethsemani, in charge of the education and formation of newly professed monks (459).

Important events in the life of the monastery also have their impact on Merton, particularly the death in August 1948 of Dom Frederic (222) and the election of Dom James Fox (227–28), who will be Merton's abbot for most of the remaining two decades of his life; the arrival of Dom Gabriel Sortais to supervise the election also results in Merton's first trip to Louisville in the seven years he has been at Gethsemani (223–24). The celebration of the abbey's centenary at the beginning of June 1949 not only leads to various writing projects (96, 272), but also coincides closely with the time of his ordination (320–21). Growth in the size of the community (339), up over two hundred by September 1949 (369), is relieved somewhat by new foundations in Utah (87) and South Carolina (372).

These are also, of course, the years when Thomas Merton suddenly became a household name. No less than nine books, along with a number of shorter booklets, appeared during the period of this journal, most significantly *The Seven Storey Mountain,* which is accepted for publication shortly after the journal begins (34) and "change[s] a lot of things" (102), as Merton suspected it would, when it is published, leading the way for various other books, among them *Seeds of Contemplation, The Waters of Siloe,* and *The Ascent to Truth,* over which Merton agonized for many months (282).

The journal records not only these and many other events, but also Merton's complex response to them. The two major, and intertwined, issues that he wrestles with throughout these years are his desire for deeper solitude, which periodically prompts him to consider joining a more eremitic order like the Carthusians (33, 141), and the difficulty of trying "to live the spiritual life with the spiritual equipment of an artist" (371). While neither of these issues will ever be resolved completely for Merton, eventually he is able to recognize that no simple answer can do justice to the complexity of a truly spiritual life, a fully human life. He writes in February 1950, "The difference between the moral life and the mystical life is discovered in the presence of contradiction. When we move ourselves as men, morally... we end up by choosing one horn of the dilemma and hoping for the best. But when we are moved by God, mystically, we seem to solve the dilemma in ease and mystery by choosing at the same time both horns of the dilemma and no horn at all, and always being perfectly right" (412). A year later he comments on the journal itself in the same vein: "It is useless to drop the thing and say I am solitary just because I am not writing a *Journal,* when, in fact, the writing could help me find my way to where I am supposed to be traveling. So I read about forgetting and write down all I remember. And somehow there is no contradiction here. It is simply a somewhat particular way of becoming a saint" (453). Similarly, he reflects after his first six months as master of students, a responsibility he feared would detract from his solitude, that it "is, in fact, the only true path to solitude," because solitude is no longer seen as an object to be attained or possessed: "Do you suppose I have a spiritual life? I have none, I am indigence, I am silence, I am poverty, I am solitude, for I have renounced spirituality to find God" (463).

Already the neat division between monastery and world is beginning to break down in this vision of a reconciliation of opposites, a process that will propel Merton back into the heart of human struggles and social conflicts by the end of the decade. Speaking of Louisville after a visit to the doctor in November 1950, he reflects, "There is no reason why a monk should not have a definite attitude toward the place which, in relation to his monastery, is 'town.' I do not think that being a monk means living on the moon" (440). While the major breakthrough experience in Merton's turn toward the world is usually associated with his vision on March 18, 1958, at the corner of Fourth and Walnut Streets in Louisville, which he described as "like waking from a dream of separateness, of spurious self-isolation in a special world, the world of renunciation and supposed holiness" (*Guilty Bystander*, 140), in fact a very similar insight had already marked the visit to Louisville to procure naturalization papers seven years earlier. On March 3, 1951, he writes in his journal,

> I have come to the monastery to find my place in the world, and if I fail to find this place, I will be wasting my time in the monastery.... Coming to the monastery has been, for me, exactly the right kind of withdrawal. It has given me perspective. It has taught me how to live. And now I owe everyone else in the world a share in that life. My first duty is to start, for the first time, to live as a member of a human race which is no more (and no less) ridiculous than I am myself. And my first human act is the recognition of how much I owe to everybody else. There is a world which Christ would not pray for.... But the world also was made by God and is good, and, unless that world is our mother, we cannot be saints, because we cannot be saints unless we are first of all human. (*Entering the Silence*, 451)

It is this project of being human, and thus holy, that Merton has come to recognize in the early 1950s as the meaning of his life as monk and writer, and that he will continue to explore in subsequent years and subsequent journals. POC
SEE ALSO *SIGN OF JONAS*.

Notes

1. After the publication of this volume, a nine-page typescript entitled "Meditations, December 23–30, 1941," consisting of five dated entries from Merton's first month at Gethsemani, was discovered in the Mark Van Doren Collection in the Columbia University Library; it has been published in *The Merton Seasonal* 25, no. 4 (winter 2000): 3–11.

2. The date assigned by the editor to the first entry in this group is October 1946, but it is clear from Merton's statement that "Next year (1946)" will be the fiftieth anniversary of the abbot's simple profession (17) that it must have been written sometime in 1945, and the references to "This Advent" and "this Thanksgiving" as apparently recent suggest early 1945.

3. Raymond cites Merton explicitly on page 206 of his book (*The Less Traveled Road: A Memoir of Dom Mary Frederic Dunne, First American Trappist Abbot* [Milwaukee: Bruce, 1953]), and seems also to have borrowed from Merton's notes in detailing Dom Frederic's frugal eating habits (205–6, 208–9), in his remark that Utah seemed to be possessed by the devil (228), and perhaps his remark that CARE packages were being sent overseas to Jesus Christ (though Raymond claims to have witnessed this himself) (224).

ESCHATOLOGY

Eschatology is the branch of theology concerned with the "last things," traditionally listed as death, judgment, heaven, and hell. It might also be defined as the theology of ultimate things, definitive realities, not necessarily confined to the end of one's life or of historical time. For Thomas Merton, "Eschatology ... is not simply an 'end of the world' belief, but, in the light of the New Testament, a belief in the decisive and critical breakthrough in man's destiny" (*Witness to Freedom*, 337). Like many modern Christian thinkers, he emphasizes both final and realized eschatology, both the absolute future consummation of the divine plan for creation and the fact that the world already has entered the new age with the incarnation, death, and resurrection of Christ.

Belief in the general resurrection and eternal life is essential to the Christian vision. "Indeed," Merton writes, "Christianity without this fabulous eschatological claim is only a moral system without too much spiritual consistency" (*New Man*, 6). The doctrine of the parousia, the return of Christ in glory, is an affirmation of the eventual perfect fulfillment of God's design for creation: "The Last Judgment will be the final consummation and revelation of the 'Mystery' — the re-establishment of all things in Christ, that is being accomplished in secret beneath the surface of human history.... The Parousia is the great event which will not destroy human history but fulfill it, explaining everything that was not clear, showing how all things worked together for the good of Christ and fulfilled the purposes of the Father" (*Living Bread*, 152–53).

But the dynamism of this process already has been inserted into history by the salvific work of Christ. The new era, the "time of the end," already has been inaugurated by the coming of the Word made flesh: "The message of Christmas is eschatological: it is the revelation and celebration of the new age in which we live, in which our humanity has been restored to us untrammeled and disentangled, in Christ" (*Love and Living*, 225). The decisive breakthrough already has taken place, and the vocation of the Christian is to respond to this revelation of new life by living out this radically transformed existence here and now, by refusing to give allegiance to the sovereignty of sin and death. "The restoration of the whole world in Christ . . . is envisaged not as a future prospect but as a present *fact*. The 'last things' are already present and realized in a hidden manner" (*Seasons of Celebration*, 63–64). But this means that the "crisis" of accepting or rejecting the inbreaking of the reign of God demands decision and commitment in this present. To live in the "end time" is to be required to align oneself for or against the new era; the "judgment" is something that takes place here and now. "A Christian is, or should be, one who has 'decided for' the Parousia, for the final coming of the Kingdom. His life is oriented by this decision. His existence has meaning in so far as the Parousia is crucial to him" (*Guilty Bystander*, 108). The Christian is one who is committed not to escaping the present for the future but to living the future in the present, to being a sign of union with God and the unity of all humanity, of all creation, which is brought about by Christ's reversal of the effects of the fall.

A proper understanding of eschatology as having a present as well as a future dimension, therefore, has profound consequences for the meaning and methods of Christian witness in the world. Merton writes, "Eschatological Christian hope is inseparable from an incarnational involvement in the struggle of living and contemporary man" (*Love and Living*, 156), because the Christian affirms that Christ already has triumphed over the forces of alienation and division. This perspective is at the heart of Merton's own commitment to issues of peace, racial reconciliation, and justice for the poor in the last decade of his life. He writes in his journal in March 1964, "I am coming to see clearly the great importance of the concept of 'realized eschatology' — the transformation of life and of human relations by Christ *now*. . . . Realized eschatology is the heart of genuine Christian humanism and hence its tremendous importance for the Christian peace effort for example" (*Water of Life*, 87). With faith in the ultimate victory of Christ, the Christian can stand as a sign of contradiction to institutions and practices that deny the infinite value of the human person by war or prejudice or oppression. Authentic nonviolence is grounded in this eschatological consciousness, with its reliance on a strength that is manifested in the "weakness" of the cross, and its faith in a hidden dynamism that will culminate in the full revelation of *shalom*. "Christian meekness, which is essential to true non-violence, has this eschatological quality about it. It refrains from self-assertion and from violent aggression because it sees all things in the light of the great judgment" (*Faith and Violence*, 17).

An eschatological perspective also is essential to contemplation. Merton writes, "If it were a matter of choosing between 'contemplation' and 'eschatology' there is no question that I am, and would always be, committed entirely to the latter" (*Water of Life*, 181). That is, he believes in the dynamic presence of the divine in history rather than in an escape from the demands and opportunities of incarnate existence into some timeless sphere of pure transcendence, as contemplation sometimes is interpreted. In fact, of course, authentic Christian contemplation is intrinsically eschatological; it is part of the whole process of anticipating the fullness of life here and now. "Christian contemplation is not merely lost in God. It also includes in its vision an eschatological understanding of the world redeemed in Christ. It sees the world transformed in the divine light, it sees all things recapitulated in Christ" (*World of Action*, 179–80). Merton claims, "Because my faith is eschatological it is *also* contemplative, for I am even now in the Kingdom and I can even now 'see' something of the glory of the Kingdom and praise Him who is King.... Thus contemplation and eschatology are one, in Christian faith and in surrender to Christ. They complete each other and intensify each other" (*Water of Life*, 182).

Because it is oriented to contemplation, monasticism therefore is also intrinsically eschatological. "The monastic community is a covenant community whose gaze ... is fixed on the definitive eschatological truth: the *emeth* of God, the unfailing promise that is obscurely apprehended by faith as already fulfilled" (*World of Action*, 192). The vows are understood as a public and definitive commitment to seek fulfillment nowhere but in this promise, this divine fidelity. This "prophetic and eschatological awareness" (187) is a witness to the rest of the church and to the world at large of the true source and goal of creation.

Finally, an eschatological perspective entails the relativizing of all human ideologies and institutions. Nothing is definitive, exempt from judgment, except the transforming power of Christ. The "end time" marks the end of all idolatries. The "final integration" that transcends all culturally constructed identities "is eschatological.... It means a disintegration of the social and cultural self, the product of merely human history, and the reintegration of that self in Christ, in salvation history, in the mystery of redemption, in the Pentecostal 'new creation'" (216). POC

SEE ALSO DEATH; KINGDOM OF GOD; REDEMPTION; SALVATION.

EUCHARIST

In a June 1960 letter to Jacques Maritain, Thomas Merton briefly reflects on the central role played by the Eucharist in his own spiritual development. He writes, "My own first experience of understanding & ... wisdom (??) was all connected with Mass & the Holy Eucharist. To me the Eucharist has always been light, illumination. Not sensible.... It should be so simply obvious that the Eucharist *is* light, union, joy. Especially light" (*Courage for Truth*, 31–32). The first major step in his movement toward entrance into the Catholic Church was taken when he attended Mass at Corpus Christi Church near Columbia University (*Seven Storey Mountain*, 206–11), and even though he left before the consecration and communion, he felt as though he "walked in a new world" in which even the "ugly buildings of Columbia were transfigured" (211). He describes his own first communion as an experience of "the One Eternal and Pure Sacrifice ... offered up to the God dwelling in me: the sacrifice of God to God, and me sacrificed together with God, incorporated in His Incarnation. Christ born in me, a new Bethlehem, and sacrificed in me, His new Calvary, and risen in me: offering me to the Father, in Himself, asking the Father, my Father and His, to receive me into His infinite and special love" (224–25).

Thus, from the very outset of his life as a Catholic, Merton places a strong stress on the paschal reality of the Eucharist, not merely as a doctrine but as an experience. This continues to be the most important focus of his writing on the sacrament. The Eucharist is to be understood not merely as a formal act of worship, not as a ritual commemoration of a past event, but as a "re-presentation" of the paschal mystery (*Spiritual Direction and Meditation*, 54), a privileged locus of encounter with the events of redemption: "Our life in Christ comes from our participation in His death and resurrection. But the Cross and Resurrection of Christ are something more than a historical memory. They are a present fact, mystically actualized by the Liturgy, or the 'sacred action' which we call the Mass" (*Monastic Journey*, 8–9). Communion in the body and blood of Christ unites the believer to Christ and through Christ to his Father, in the Holy Spirit poured out by the crucified Christ and breathed upon the apostles by Christ risen. The Eucharist is the normative way in which one enters into the life of divine love. "Receiving the Sacred Body of the Savior in the consecrated Host the believer affirms his union with Christ in His Passion, Death and Resurrection from the Dead. He becomes one heart, one mind and one spirit with the Blessed Savior. He becomes lost in the Mystical Christ as a drop of water becomes lost in a chalice of wine. The mystery of the Eucharist

Altar in Thomas Merton's hermitage

Mass as meal. In reflecting on the Holy Thursday liturgy he notes, "The liturgy reminds us that every Mass is a representation not only of Calvary but also of the Last Supper" (*New Man*, 239). In his book-length study of the Eucharist, *The Living Bread*, he begins with a focus on the sacrificial character of the Mass, but concludes by emphasizing the Eucharist as nourishment and celebration: "In such a time as ours it is therefore most important to remember that the Eucharist is a *convivium*, a sacred banquet" (*Living Bread*, 129). While he strongly emphasizes the contemplative dimension of the Eucharist, as "one of the most normal ways of entering into infused prayer" ("Inner Experience," 4:294), a development that takes place when the sacramental union of the communicant and Christ is "prolonged in silent and solitary adoration" (*Silent Life*, 150), he also is very much aware of the communal and social dimensions of the Eucharist, which draw each communicant into union with all those who are similarly joined to Christ. "The communion of the faithful in the Body and Blood of the Saviour not only really joins them to Him in a sacramentally mystical union but also unites them to one another in Christian charity and in the Holy Spirit" (*New Seeds of Contemplation*, 165). The Eucharist is preeminently the sacrament of unity, of love; it effects the unity of those who receive it and makes their union a sign of Christ's presence to the wider world. As early as 1953, Merton stresses the importance of experiencing the Eucharist as "a feast of love, an *agape*," and quotes Thomas Aquinas that the "matter" (*res*) of the sacrament "is *the unity of the Body of Christ*" (*Bread in the Wilderness*, 83). He emphasizes that the Eucharist and the church are not two separate manifestations of the body of Christ; rather, the "Eucharist, which prolongs the Incarnation among us, is the sign and cause of the Mystical Body which Christ has taken to Himself" (*Living Bread*, 133). The love of and for Christ and one another in the Eucharist is not confined to the church itself but overflows to witness to that love in the wider world: "The eucharistic life by its very nature is orientated towards an apostolate of charity which will effect a visible union of all mankind" (156), though how this unity will ul-

both symbolizes and effects the mystical union of the believer with Christ by charity" ("Inner Experience," 4:293–94). The purpose of the Eucharist, therefore, is to transform the Christian into Christ, which is at the same time a discovery of one's own deepest identity: "By our union with Christ in the Eucharist we find our true selves" (*Living Bread*, 119). With identity comes vocation: to receive communion is to participate fully in the paschal victory that definitively establishes God's reign (*Seasons of Celebration*, 8) and to accept the responsibility to spread the good news of the kingdom of God.

Given this paschal focus, Merton of course places a good deal of emphasis on the sacrificial character of the Eucharist, particularly in his earlier works. For example, he calls the Eucharist "the Sacrifice of praise and thanksgiving" and adds that "in the Sacrifice Jesus, giving thanks to the Father, offers and immolates Himself entirely for His Father's glory and to save us from our sins" (*Thoughts in Solitude*, 40). But he regularly complements the focus on the Mass as sacrifice with an awareness of the timately be manifested is a mystery hidden in the mind of God.

In addition to his focus on the sacramental celebration of the Eucharist, Merton gives a good deal of attention to the reservation of the consecrated host and nonliturgical worship of the Blessed Sacrament, particularly in *The Living Bread*, which focuses in its prologue on the Society for Perpetual Adoration of the Blessed Sacrament, a priest's group, and the Priests' and People's Eucharistic Leagues (*Living Bread*, xxiv–xxx). But as early as Holy Thursday 1948, in a long reflection in his journal, Merton emphasized that adoration of the Blessed Sacrament must not be detached from the dynamic presence of Christ in the Mass: "The heart of all life is not merely in the static presence of the Blessed Sacrament, although Christ is truly living in our tabernacles, but above all in the *action* of the Mass that is the center of all contemplation, an action in which the Christian family is gathered around Christ and in which Christ in His Body glorifies His Father.... When the Mass discovers its meaning, then devotion to the Blessed Sacrament reserved in the Tabernacle acquires its own true meaning also and begins to live" (*Entering the Silence*, 192).

In his final extended statement on the Eucharist, in response to a question asked at one of the conferences given to sisters in Alaska in mid-September 1968, Merton returns to the issue of praying before the Blessed Sacrament, a matter of some controversy at the time, and considers it a matter of personal preference, one that he himself continued to find valuable, as he rediscovered when a chapel was added to his hermitage.

> I moved into my hermitage and was not allowed to have the Blessed Sacrament. This went on for a couple of years, and I didn't even think about it really until somehow or other the issue came up again and I was given permission to have the Blessed Sacrament reserved at the hermitage. I found it was a great help. One of the things that was nicest about it — well, I would lie in bed and if I woke up, there was the tabernacle. This is a real, simple, naive sort of thing, but actually it made me feel quite differ-

ent at night, just the sense of this Presence. (*Thomas Merton in Alaska*, 90–91)

This comment indicates Merton's continued commitment to living "a full and well-integrated eucharistic life" in which "communion, adoration, fraternal charity, and active participation in the liturgy" are all "drawn together in one supremely relevant focus upon the central Mystery of our faith — our sharing in the death and resurrection of Jesus Christ" (*Living Bread*, 14). POC

SEE ALSO LITURGY; *LIVING BREAD*; SACRAMENT.

EVANS, MARGARET MAY

Margaret May Evans, a typist who had enlisted in the British armed forces, met John Paul Merton in London. They fell in love and were married, in February 1943, at St. Laurence Church in Birkenhead (her hometown) by Canon William Griffin. They spent their honeymoon in the Lake District. Two months after their wedding she became a widow, when John Paul died in a plane crash in the English Channel. WHS

EXILE ENDS IN GLORY: The Life of a Trappistine, Mother M. Berchmans, O.C.S.O.
Milwaukee: Bruce Publishing Company, 1948. xii+311 pp.

Begun in 1944 and dedicated to the "American Cistercian Pioneers" — founders of Our Lady of the Holy Ghost in Georgia in 1944 and Our Lady of the Most Blessed Trinity in Utah in 1947 and to the Cistercian nuns founding the first convent of Trappistines in America at Wrentham, Massachusetts — this story of Mother M. Berchmans is one of two accounts of the lives of Cistercian women that Thomas Merton wrote in the mid-1940s. The other, *What Are These Wounds?* tells the story of the mystic St. Lutgarde of Aywières. In 1967, when he evaluated his work, he ranked *Exile Ends in Glory* "very poor," a higher ranking than that of "awful," which he gave to *What Are*

These Wounds? Merton's reservations about *Exile Ends in Glory* already were apparent when the book was being read in the refectory. Although "people in general seem to accept it all right," Merton confided in his journal, "there are parts of it that make my stomach turn somersaults. Where did I get all that pious rhetoric? That was the way I thought a monk was supposed to write, just after I had made simple profession" (*Entering the Silence,* 217–18). In the preface to *Exile Ends in Glory,* Merton suggests that Mother Berchmans's story can be an inspiration to contemporary Cistercian "pioneers." God purifies souls through trials that we find hardest to understand and accept. For Mother Berchmans, the trial was exile.

Fr. Robert Lepasquier, Mother Berchmans's spiritual director in Japan, left an eight-hundred-page biography of her life. Merton drew from that account and from documents from the archives of Our Lady of the Angels Monastery in Japan, where Mother Berchmans lived. In constructing his own narrative, Merton includes numerous quotations from Mother Berchmans's own journal and from her letters. The book includes a preface, eighteen chapters, and an epilogue. There are also six pages of photographs of Mother Berchmans and of the convents at Laval and Japan. Chapter titles indicate how Merton framed Mother Berchmans's story along chronological and thematic lines and reveal some aspects of her life experience that Merton thought important to highlight: (1) "The Convent of the Redemption," (2) "An Interval in Lyons," (3) "The Convent at Laval," (4) "The Novice," (5) "Sentence of Exile," (6) "The Journey," (7) "Another Orphanage," (8) "At Work in the House of God," (9) "The Chicken Coop," (10) "New Stability," (11) "A Vocation within a Vocation," (12) "The Child of Mary," (13) "At the Gate," (14) "A Canticle of Gratitude," (15) "Mistress of the Novices," (16) "Via Crucis," (17) "Via Crucis" (continued), and (18) "Calvary."

In 1880 four-year-old Mary Piguet's mother left her to the care of the nuns at the Convent of the Redemption. Mary lived there, quite happily, until 1897. The twenty-one-year-old Mary spent "an interval in Lyons," supporting herself by doing needlework, then as a governess, be-

fore entering the Cistercian convent at Laval, where the life was demanding and the discipline strict — "The tradition of De Rancé indicated merciless humiliation as the most merciful and charitable form of correction" (*Exile Ends in Glory,* 29) — but Mary did not find the life hard. In 1899 Sr. Berchmans was received into the community at Laval. As a novice, Sr. Berchmans "was burning with a desire of sacrifice" (42). She experienced trials — singing the psalms was one, as she could not sing, did not understand Latin, and even in French the psalms were incomprehensible to her. "For her, to pray meant to pour out her heart.... Hers was the piety that would easily burst into flame before a life-size statue of a Jesus with brown and flowing locks and large tender eyes and a most natural seeming red-and-white complexion; and the plaintive, rather sentimental hymns that congregations of the faithful usually sing to Jesus at Benediction, in the present day, were all that was needed to stir up her feelings to a great warmth of love" (46).

Her time at Laval ended with a "sentence of exile" when her confessor instructed her to volunteer to be one of two women from Laval sent to Our Lady of the Angels Monastery in Japan. The self-sacrifice, immolation, and holocaust she so earnestly desired took the form of exile. After a painful departure and a difficult journey, Sr. Berchmans and six nuns, together with the two priests who accompanied them, arrived in Japan in February 1902. The convent was a little wooden building that had been built to house an orphanage. The accommodations were dire, the diet spare (even by Cistercian standards), and the climate harsh. But Sr. Berchmans bore the hardships of life in Japan with good humor, as evidenced by her humorous description in her letters of the rats with which the nuns shared living quarters. Though she suffered from ill health, aggravated by her living conditions, she remained committed to her vocation of prayer and sacrifice. She even applied herself to learning Japanese, an effort that was, for her, another trial. During this time she had continued to be a nun of Laval, but in 1906 she vowed stability to the community of Our Lady of the Angels. Her exile became permanent.

In 1907 the nuns received a copy of the autobiography of St. Thérèse of the Child Jesus. *The Story of a Soul* made its way around the convent. St. Thérèse's "Little Way" resonated with Mother Berchmans and became for her, in the words of Fr. Robert Lepasquier, "a vocation within a vocation" (162). Merton observes that Thérèse's "life and even her character closely resembled Mother Berchmans' own. She never did anything extraordinary. She simply lived the normal, everyday life of her convent. She kept her rule, she performed all her duties as well as she could — not always to the perfect satisfaction of everybody else either" (156). And, like Mother Berchmans, St. Thérèse embraced exile: "I dream of a monastery where I should be unknown, where I should have to suffer *exile of the heart*" (157).

In 1907 Mother Berchmans consecrated herself to Mary. Merton writes, "In all her actions, everything she did during the day, she strove faithfully to preserve in her mind the habitual intention of asking Mary to do what was to be done in and for her" (179). Despite her poor health, Mother Berchmans had numerous responsibilities in the monastery. In February 1907 she "found herself holding the positions of sacristan, sales manager of the cheese department, portress, guest mistress and cellarer" (183). When she was assigned to instruct the oblates — in Japanese — she shared the spirituality that nurtured her. "She preached the love of our own helplessness, of our own weakness. She preached a spiritual childhood" she had learned from St. Thérèse (194). In 1910 she was named mistress of novices and once again faced the challenges of language and culture. Now she began to understand Japanese customs and attitudes. "In consequence of her sympathy, she was quickly able to distinguish what would be necessary in their formation — that is, what was strictly Cistercian and Benedictine — and what was unnecessary, or, more plainly, what was merely in tune with her French training and blood" (226). And she learned not to impose on them "what appealed particularly to herself in the spiritual life" (231).

Merton characterizes the final years of her life as "Via Crucis" and her death as "Calvary." Through her illness she accepted her suffering as she had all her life and continued her duties as best she could for as long as she could. In the epilogue Merton notes that after her death, her community and other Trappistines and Trappists experienced healings and favors after praying to her. Among them was a monk at Gethsemani — surely, it was Merton — who was cured of an attack of stomach trouble after praying to Mother Berchmans and, on another occasion, "made the best monthly day of recollection he had made in over a year when he put the day under her protection" (309).

In July 1953 Merton wrote a preface for the French edition of *Exile Ends in Glory*. Only one page long, the preface offers "an apology or at least an explanation" for *Exile Ends in Glory* and for *What Are These Wounds?* "Convinced that the book would remain anonymous and would attract hardly any attention, [the author] attempted to write a pious memoir similar to other pious memoirs. But, once the work of the book was underway, the author found himself with a problem. To do justice to the saintliness of Mother Berchmans — which was certainly authentic and profound — it became necessary to rewrite the biography and even to do so in a different style. For several reasons this was impossible" ("*Honorable Reader,*" 11). Merton gratefully acknowledges revisions in the French edition done by the Carmelite nun who translated the book into French, and he concludes the preface with the "hope that, in making available the life of a humble Trappistine contemplative, we have added another testimony to the essential apostolic character of all Christian life and, particularly, of contemplative life which cannot exist without our speaking at the same time with eloquence, even with silence, of the mystery of Christ" (11). CMB

SEE ALSO *WHAT ARE THESE WOUNDS?*

EXPERIENCE

Theology in the mid-twentieth century tended to be largely deductive in its methodology. The starting point of the theology manuals of the time was the doctrinal thesis that was accepted as true and then proved from Scripture, tradition, and reason. Thomas Merton would have studied these manuals when he was preparing for ordination to the priesthood. In 1949 *Seeds of Contemplation* was published. His dissatisfaction with it was expressed in a slightly revised edition that began with the seventh printing. The revision was not extensive (that was to come later in *New Seeds of Contemplation*), but it contained an important preface in which he wrote, "The author is talking about spiritual things from the point of view of experience rather than in the concise terms of dogmatic theology or of metaphysics" (*Seeds of Contemplation*, xii).

Three years later, in the prologue to *The Sign of Jonas*, Merton says much the same thing. "I have attempted to convey something of a monk's spiritual life and of his thoughts, not in the language of speculation, but in terms of personal experience" (*Sign of Jonas*, 8). He admits that this may be a bit hazardous because it leaves "the sure plain path of an accepted terminology" and travels "in byways of poetry and intuition." Yet he justifies this change of course by remembering an earlier book of his that he was not happy with. "I found in writing *The Ascent to Truth* [1951] that technical language, though it is universal and certain and accepted by theologians, does not reach the average man and does not convey what is most personal and most vital in religious experience" (8–9).

In 1952, the year before *The Sign of Jonas* appeared, Merton produced a manuscript that he called "Sentences,"[1] in which there are several references to experience. In Sentence no. 79 he speaks of the capacity we have for "vision and disinterested love." This capacity, which he calls "the summit of the spirit in us," is brought to perfection in us only through experience. It is impossible to reach this summit "by retiring from experience." In Sentence no. 80 he identifies that summit with the image of God. "When the summit of my being lies open to consciousness, I know by experience that I am the image of God."

In 1955 "Sentences" became *No Man Is an Island*. Here is a full-blown understanding of the importance of experience. "It seems to me that the first responsibility of a man of faith is to make his faith really part of his own life, not by rationalizing it [as he had done in *The Ascent to Truth?*], but by living it" (*No Man Is an Island*, xiv). To live one's faith is to refuse to accept prepackaged answers unexamined. It calls for personal struggle and a willingness to live with questions when clear-cut answers are not yet available. Living with questions makes for a certain amount of insecurity; still, it is preferable to "a far worse insecurity, which comes from being afraid to ask the right questions — because they might turn out to have no answer." He paints the dark picture of people "huddling together in the pale light of an insufficient answer to a question we are afraid to ask" (xiii).

The word "experience" appears prominently in Merton's later works on contemplation as well as in his writings on Zen. Thus, it threads its way through *New Seeds of Contemplation*: "Contemplation reaches out to the knowledge and even to the experience of the transcendent and inexpressible God" (2); it is an awareness summed up "not in a proposition, but in an experience: 'I Am'" (4); it is "an experience beyond the reach of verbalization and of rationalization" (6). These are examples, but throughout this work readers will find the word expressed or implied.

Necessarily, the word "experience" occurs frequently in Merton's writings on Zen, for, as he writes in his introduction to John Wu's book, *The Golden Age of Zen*, Zen is nothing other than "the quest for direct and pure experience, liberated from verbal formulas and linguistic preconceptions" (*Birds of Appetite*, 44). In this same essay he makes clear that Christianity is also at its deepest level about experience: "a living experience of unity in Christ which far transcends all conceptual formulations" (39). This is what the first epistle of John is concerned to make clear: Christian faith is about "what we have seen and heard and announce to you in order that you also may have fellowship with us and that our fellowship may be with the Father and with His Son Jesus Christ" (39–40 [cf. 1 John 1:2–3]). WHS

SEE ALSO AWARENESS.

Notes

1. "Sentences" (unpublished typescript in the archives of the Merton Center at Bellarmine University), dated on the concluding page: Feast of the Sacred Heart, 1952.

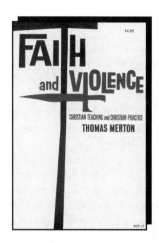

FAITH

Thomas Merton's conversion, recounted in *The Seven Storey Mountain,* is a discovery of faith; his life is a story of faith lived; and his writings are an exploration of the reality of faith and its meaning in the twentieth century. Merton's idea of faith is grounded in his experience and understanding of contemplation: it is a contemplative vision of faith.[1] Writing about contemplation provided a context for writing about faith. Merton devotes a chapter to faith in *Seeds of Contemplation* that grows to two chapters in the revised and expanded *New Seeds of Contemplation.* He opens the chapter by asserting, "The beginning of contemplation is faith" (*Seeds of Contemplation,* 77; *New Seeds of Contemplation,* 126), and goes on to explain what faith is not: an emotion, a feeling, an elemental need, or a conviction that one is saved. Nor is it an opinion or a "conviction based on rational analysis" (*Seeds of Contemplation,* 77–78). Faith is "first of all an intellectual assent" that accepts the truth of propositions God has revealed. But, most important, faith is "the way to a vital contact with a God Who is alive, and not to an abstract First Principle worked out by syllogisms" (78). Above all, faith is an assent

to God. In faith, one knows and is known by the loving God. Concepts about God remain what they are: merely *concepts about* God. In the end, language about God gives way to silence. Merton's path to God is a dark one.

Building on his treatment of faith in *Seeds of Contemplation,* in *New Seeds of Contemplation* Merton elaborates on three aspects of faith: faith as communion, dimension of life, and realization of the true self. First, he emphasizes that faith is more than an intellectual assent: it is "a grasp, a contact, a communion of wills." In faith one "*receives* God. One says 'yes' not merely to a statement *about* God, but to the Invisible Infinite God Himself" (*New Seeds of Contemplation,* 128). Merton insists that "faith goes beyond words and formulas and brings us the light of God Himself" (129). Words and formulas have their use, but they "must be clean windows" through which God's light can shine. But, Merton emphasizes, faith is a not a matter of clinging to the right words: "Above all, faith is the opening of an inward eye, the eye of the heart, to be filled with the presence of Divine light" (129–30). Second, Merton presents faith as "that acceptance of God which is the very climate of all spiritual living," which gives "a dimension of simplicity and *depth* to all our apprehensions and to all our experiences" (135). Faith concerns the whole of life; it cannot be relegated to a "spiritual" compartment. Third,

Cover for *Faith and Violence* reprinted with the permission of the University of Notre Dame Press. Cover design by Andre Chappaz.

faith opens up to us "the true depths of reality, even of our own reality" (137), bringing us "into contact" with our own inmost spiritual depths and "with God, Who is present within those same depths" (139). In faith, we discover "our unknown and undiscovered self" (137). In other words, in faith, we discover our true selves.

Merton's vision of faith is a contemplative vision. Faith opens the door to an awakening to the presence of God within that is contemplation. However, for Merton faith is not simply an interior reality. Faith finds expression in the way we live. Just as for Merton contemplation leads to compassion, so too faith's inner awakening must lead to faithful living. Merton reflected this conviction in a letter he wrote, in 1965, to Ludovico Silva, a Latin America poet: "One's whole being must be an act for which there can be found no word. This is the primary meaning of faith. On this basis, other dimensions of belief can be made credible. Otherwise not. My whole being must be a yes and an amen and an exclamation that is not heard. Only after that is there any point in exclamations. . . . One's acts must be part of the same silent exclamation" (Courage for Truth, 225).

Merton's way of keeping faith was to speak out, through his writings, on a host of social issues. Beginning in 1961, when his passion for peace moved him to speak out against war and the proliferation of weapons, and through the 1960s, when he addressed the urgent issues raised by racism, genocide, and the war in Vietnam, Merton viewed his writing as a way of keeping faith. Merton recognized that the time and circumstances of his birth were not just a fact of chronology but a matter of kairos: "That I should have been born in 1915, that I should be the contemporary of Auschwitz, Hiroshima, Viet Nam and the Watts riots, are things about which I was not first consulted. Yet they are also events in which, whether I like it or not, I am deeply and personally involved" (World of Action, 145/161). Making peace was, for Merton, a way of taking responsibility and of "keeping faith." Rather than functioning as an escape or a diversion, faith demands acknowledgment and response to the urgent life-and-death issues of the day. This stance is illustrated in

Faith and Violence, a collection of essays subtitled Christian Teaching and Christian Practice, which presents a vision of faith rooted in the gospel and engaged in the struggle for justice, and which offers models of faithful resistance in the examples of individuals such as Fr. Alfred Delp, Franz Jägerstätter, and Simone Weil. In the preface Merton writes that faith must not be "a kind of drunkenness," a narcotic or an anesthetic, but rather, must function as "an awakening" (Faith and Violence, x). In a similar way, in Life and Holiness, Merton contrasts "a human, limited, external faith in human society" with "a faith in the transcendent and invisible God . . . that demands an interior revolution of one's whole self and a reorientation of one's existence in a contrary sense to the orientation taken by mundane prejudice" (Life and Holiness, 96–97).

In a booklet written in 1962 to commemorate the 150th anniversary of the Sisters of Loretto, Merton reflected on what he called "the ideal of 'keeping the faith,' " noting that it "can sometimes dwindle into something very negative, resentful, and obtuse: a mere 'no' to everything that we do not agree with" (Loretto and Gethsemani, 7). But faith calls for a "yes" to God and "to all that is valid in human culture and civilization" (7). "Keeping the faith," Merton urged, entails a contemplative dimension that expresses itself in responsible and compassionate action. Merton expressed this conviction in the title of an essay that became the title of a book: Contemplation in a World of Action, a collection of "monastic essays," some of which, paradoxically, explored the links between contemplation and action as they situated the contemplative in the modern world.

Although Merton was adamant when, in 1965, he wrote in his journal that for him, "There is nothing more important than the gift of Catholic faith — and keeping that faith pure and clear" (Water of Life, 317), he was empathetic with those who struggled with faith. In the 1960s he returned to the subject of belief and unbelief, which he had addressed in 1951 in The Ascent to Truth, where he had observed the problem of unbelief for which believers share responsibility: "We are merely apologetes when we ought to be Apostles" (*Ascent to Truth*, 41) who proclaim the "word of faith" (43–44). He took seriously the new theologies (radical, death of God, religionless Christianity) and responded critically, as the essays in part 4 of *Faith and Violence* illustrate. In a particularly significant essay entitled "Apologies to an Unbeliever," Merton directs these words to unbelievers: "If I, as a Christian, believe that my first duty is to love and respect my fellowman, in his personal frailty and perplexity, in his unique hazard and his need for trust, then I think that the refusal to let him alone, the inability to entrust him to God and to his own conscience, and the insistence on rejecting him as a person until he agrees with me, is simply a sign that my own faith is inadequate" (*Faith and Violence*, 208). But Merton had a message for believers as well: it is their faith that has "grown cold" and has "too often become rigid, or complex, sentimental, foolish, or impertinent" (213). Merton reminds his readers that faith requires listening: listening to "the inscrutable ground" of one's own being, listening to God in silence, and listening to the world in which we live. In a world in which some find themselves unable to hear God and are experiencing God's "absence" rather than knowing God's "presence," Merton sees his "own peculiar task" as that of "a solitary explorer" who "is bound to search the existential depths of faith in its silences, its ambiguities, and in those certainties which lie deeper than the bottom of anxiety. In these depths there are no easy answers, no pat solutions to anything. . . . On this level, the division between Believer and Unbeliever ceases to be so crystal clear. . . . Everybody is an Unbeliever more or less! Only when this fact is fully experienced, accepted, and lived with, does one become fit to hear the simple message of the Gospel — or of any other religious teaching" (213). CMB

SEE ALSO CONTEMPLATION; GOD.

Notes

1. For an extended discussion of faith, see Christine M. Bochen, " 'The Eye of the Heart': Thomas Merton on Faith," in *The Vision of Thomas Merton: Essays in Honor of Robert E. Daggy*, ed. Patrick F. O'Connell, to be published by Cistercian Publications.

FAITH AND VIOLENCE:
Christian Teaching and Christian Practice
Notre Dame, Ind.: University of Notre Dame Press, 1968. x+290 pp.

"By Way of Preface" to this collection of essays and reviews, Thomas Merton offers a story by a Hasidic Rabbi, Baal-Shem-Tov. Two men, one drunk and one sober, were attacked by robbers as they were traveling through the woods. They were beaten and robbed. When questioned, the drunken man insisted that everything was fine. The sober man said, "Do not believe him: he is drunk. It was a disaster. Robbers beat us without mercy and took everything we had. Be warned by what happened to us, and look out for yourselves" (*Faith and Violence*, ix). "For some 'faithful' and for unbelievers too — 'faith' seems to be a kind of drunkenness, an anesthetic, that keeps you from realizing and believing that anything can ever go wrong," Merton observes (ix). Is faith a "narcotic dream" or "an awakening?" he asks. "What if we awaken to discover that *we* are the robbers, and our destruction comes from the root of hate in ourselves?" (x).

This book, dedicated to Philip Berrigan and James Forest (Merton had just dedicated a pamphlet on Camus to Daniel Berrigan), is divided into four parts: part 1 is focused on nonviolence, part 2 on the war in Vietnam, part 3 on race and black power, and part 4 on unbelief and the death of God. The seven essays in part 1, all previously published, include "Toward a Theology of Resistance," "Blessed Are the Meek," "Non-Violence and the Christian Conscience," "Peace and Protest," "The Prison Meditations of Father Delp," "An Enemy of the State," and "Pacifism and Resistance in Simone Weil." In a circular letter written before Lent in 1968, Merton characterizes his soon-to-be-published book as "a tract for the times" and predicts that "it will make a lot of people mad." With typical humility he adds, "I don't claim to have final answers to contemporary problems: just opinions, which are subject to modification. And maybe by the time the book is out I will have changed many of them myself" (*Road to Joy*, 111). Although Merton maintained his fundamental convictions about peace and non-violence, he recognized that "things are so fluid and so uncertain that an opinion loses its significance in three weeks" (*Witness to Freedom*, 49). In such circumstances he realized that all he could do was to say what he thought.

In "Toward a Theology of Resistance" Merton insists that theology "needs to focus carefully upon the crucial problem of violence" which "is not the problem of a few rioters and rebels, but the problem of a whole social structure which is outwardly ordered and respectable, and inwardly ridden by psychopathic obsessions" (*Faith and Violence*, 3). Merton insists that the problem of violence must be "traced to its root . . . the massively organized bands of murderers whose operations are global" (4). Critical of Catholic moral theology that concerns itself "chiefly with casuistical discussion" of state use of force and supportive of the message of *Pacem in Terris*, Merton insisted that the reality of violence in contemporary society must be a subject of theological concern. "The theology of violence must not lose sight of the real problem which is not the individual with a revolver but death and even genocide as big business" (6). A theology of love must seek to deal "realistically with the evil and injustice in the world" (9). A theology of love is "a theology of *resistance*" (9). This opening essay serves as an introduction to the book and to this section, where Merton elaborates on nonviolence and offers examples of resistance in the stories of Fr. Delp, Franz Jägerstätter, and Simone Weil.

The next three essays, "Blessed Are the Meek," "Non-Violence and the Christian Conscience," and "Peace and Protest," make a case for the Christian commitment to and practice of nonviolence. "Blessed Are the Meek," first published in *Fellowship* in 1967, establishes the Christian basis of nonviolence as "faith in Christ the Redeemer and obedience to his demand to love and manifest himself in us by a certain manner of acting in the world" and in relation to others set forth in the Sermon on the Mount (16). Merton identifies seven conditions for the practice of Christian nonviolence: nonviolence must (1) "be free from all occult, unconscious connivance with an

unjust and established abuse of power"; (2) "be not for [oneself] but *for others*, that is for the poor and underprivileged"; (3) "*avoid a facile and fanatical self-righteousness*, and refrain from being satisfied with dramatic self-justifying gestures"; (4) establish itself "as a desirable alternative"; (5) use means that manifest truth; (6) be "willing to *learn something from the adversary*"; and (7) maintain hope in humanity (21–25). "Non-Violence and the Christian Conscience" originally was published as a preface in *Nonviolence and the Christian Conscience* (1966) by Raymond Régamey, a Dominican active in the French Gandhian nonviolence movement. Merton argues that the image of nonviolence commonly held in America is "*largely negative and completely inadequate*" (35). The witness of genuine nonviolence, such as that demonstrated by Régamey, exposes the difference between *nonviolence* and *nonresistance* and makes it clear that nonviolence is "*the only really effective resistance to injustice and evil*" (39). In "Peace and Protest," which first appeared in *Continuum* in 1966, Merton questions "the validity of the protest as communication" and asks whether current protest is "making any real headway in re-educating us, in giving us a new attitude towards war" (43). He states his opposition to the burning of draft cards. "What is needed is a constructive, consistent and clear dissent that recalls people to their senses, makes them think deeply, plants in them a seed of change, and awakens in them the profound need for truth, reason and peace which is implanted in man's nature" (44).

The three essays that complete this section of the book highlight three stories of nonviolent resistance. "The Prison Meditations of Father Delp" was written as an introduction to Fr. Delp's book.[1] Delp was executed by the Nazis in February 1945. "His prison meditations are a penetrating diagnosis of a devastated, gutted, faithless society in which man is rapidly losing his humanity because he has become practically incapable of belief. Man's only hope, in this wilderness which he has become, is to respond to his inner need for truth, with a struggle to recover his spiritual freedom" (52). Fr. Delp recognized that what is needed is not simply goodwill and piety, but "truly religious men *ready to cooperate in all efforts for the betterment of mankind and human order*" (57). In "An Enemy of the State" Merton reviews *In Solitary Witness* by Gordon Zahn, published in *Pax Bulletin* in 1965. Zahn tells the story of Austrian Catholic peasant Franz Jägerstätter, who "was beheaded by the German military authorities as an 'enemy of the state' because he had repeatedly refused to take the military oath and serve in what he declared to be an 'unjust war'" (69). Merton takes issue with the bishop who termed Jägerstätter "a completely exceptional case" (74) and concludes that the "real question raised by the Jägerstätter story is not merely that of the individual Catholic's right to conscientious objection (admitted in practice even by those who completely disagreed with Jägerstätter) but the question of the church's own mission of protest and prophecy in the gravest spiritual crisis man has ever known" (75). Reviewing *Simone Weil, a Fellowship in Love* (1964) by Jacques Cabaud in "Pacifism and Resistance in Simone Weil" (*Peace News*, 1965) provided Merton with an opportunity to challenge Cabaud's "cliched identification of pacifism with quietist passivity and non-resistance" (79). When Germany overran France, Weil joined the French resistance to affirm "human liberty against the abuse of power" (83). Weil realized that "effective non-violence ('the non-violence of the strong') is that which opposes evil with serious and positive resistance, in order to overcome it with good" (83).

Part 2, focused on the war in Vietnam, consists of five essays, beginning with "Vietnam — An Overwhelming Atrocity" (*Catholic Worker*, 1968), which calls attention to women and children burned by napalm and the continuous "bombing, burning, killing, bulldozing and moving people around while the numbers of plague victims begins to mount sharply and while the 'civilization' we have brought becomes more and more rotten" (90), in light of which Merton calls for the abolishment of the draft law. Four essays follow. "Is Man a Gorilla with a Gun?" first published as a review of Robert Ardrey's *African Genesis* in 1964 in *Quest*, exposes and opposes the author's philosophy of determinism that issues in the

belief that humankind is predetermined to be a killer — "a gorilla with a gun." Merton wrote "Nhat Hanh Is My Brother" (*Jubilee*, 1966) after meeting Nhat Hanh at Gethsemani. Merton pleads for the safety of Nhat Hanh, who, by deploring "the needless destruction, the fantastic and callous ravaging of human life, the rape of the culture and spirit of an exhausted people," has incurred the wrath of the Vietcong (106). "Taking Sides on Vietnam" is a short statement published in *Authors Take Sides on Vietnam*, edited by Cecil Woolf and John Bagguley (1967). Merton writes, "I am on the side of the people who are being burned, cut to pieces, tortured, held as hostages, gassed, ruined, destroyed.... The side I take is then the side of the people who are sick of war and want peace in order to rebuild their country" (109–10). In "A Note on the Psychological Causes of War by Eric Fromm,"[2] Merton bemoans "the overwhelming and almost totally neglected importance of exploring this spiritual unconscious of man" — the ground of man's being, "the spiritual self, beyond and above the level of mere empirical individuality" (112).

Part 3 addresses the racial crisis in America. The first essay, "From Non-Violence to Black Power," sets the context for this section as Merton attempts to understand the Black Power movement while reaffirming his commitment to nonviolence. He writes, "I do believe that the Christian is obligated, by his commitment to Christ, to seek out effective and authentic ways of peace in the midst of violence. But merely to demand support and obedience to an established disorder which is essentially violent through and through will not qualify as 'peace-making'" (128–29). "Religion and Race in the United States" (*New Blackfriars*, 1965) represents Merton's overview of the racial situation in 1964, which he characterizes as "provisional" (127).

In "Events and Pseudo-Events" (*Katallagete*, 1966) Merton exposes the inability "to distinguish the real happening from the pseudo-event. Nine tenths of the news, as printed in the papers, is pseudo-news, manufactured events. Some days ten tenths" (151). We are unable to see the world as it is or ourselves as we are. "*We no longer communicate. We abandon com-*

munication in order to celebrate our own favorite group-myths in a ritual pseudo-event" (159). Merton emphasizes two points in "The Hot Summer of Sixty-Seven" (*Katallagete*, 1967–68 Supplement): first, violence will continue, and this fact "demands great realism and foresight" (167); second, the racial conflict is a symptom of a deeper problem, "It is a spiritual and psychological problem of a society which has developed too fast and too far for the psychic capacities of its members, who can no longer cope with their inner hostilities" (174). In "The Meaning of Malcolm X" (*Continuum*, 1967), a reflection on *The Autobiography of Malcolm X*, Merton recounts Malcolm X's story and traces his life through the Negro ghetto, as a Black Muslim, and in his emergence as "a completely new person" transformed by his experience of a hajj to Mecca (187).

Part 4 addresses another kind of crisis: belief and unbelief. It opens with "Violence and the Death of God: or God as Unknown Soldier," which functions as an introduction to the essays that follow. Merton asserts that the "Death of God" theologians deserve to be taken seriously and that their challenges cannot be evaded. "The Unbelief of Believers," a review of Martin E. Marty's *Varieties of Unbelief* (*Commonweal*, 1965), focuses on "the phenomenon of a general pervasive indifference and complacency which are spread out among believers and non believers alike" (199). Marty is right to be concerned "by the real unbelief of apparent believers" (199).

"Apologies to an Unbeliever," published in 1966 in *Harper's Magazine*, is, as the title suggests, an apology to unbelievers for what has been inflicted upon them by believers. At the same time, it sends a message to believers. Merton describes his "peculiar task" as "that of the solitary explorer who ... is bound to search the existential depths of faith in its silences, its ambiguities, and in those certainties which lie deeper than the bottom of anxiety. In these depths there are no easy answers, no pat solutions to anything" (213). In "The Contemplative Life in the Modern World," written as the preface to the Japanese edition of *Seeds of Contemplation*, Merton explores the necessity and the reality of con-

templation, defining it as "a living contact with the Infinite Source of all being" (222). Contemplation, Merton explains, is "an extreme intensification of conscious awareness, a kind of total awareness ... which attains the totality of meaning beyond all limited conceptions" (223). "Honest to God: Letter to a Radical Anglican" (*Commonweal*, 1964) is a personal and critical response to Bishop J. A. T. Robinson, author of *Honest to God*. Merton concludes that the issues Robinson raises are not new and that Robinson has failed to shed light on them. The last two articles, "The Death of God and the End of History" (*Theoria to Theory*, 1967) and "Godless Christianity?" (abridged from *Katallagete*, 1967–68 Supplement), continue Merton's response to the new radical theology. In the first, Merton describes the "Death of God" theology as he understands it and discusses some of the problems it raises. In the second, Merton responds to the radical theologians, including J. A. T. Robinson and Dietrich Bonhoeffer, in the context of the contemplative and mystical tradition. He proposes that "what is required of Christians is that they develop a completely modern and contemporary *consciousness* in which their experience as men of our century is integrated with their experience as children of God redeemed by Christ. The weakness of our Christian language lies not so much in the theology and formulated belief as in the split which has hitherto separated our Christian faith from the rest of our lives" (279). Merton mentions Rilke and Teilhard de Chardin as witnessing in different ways to modern religious consciousness that is not godless. The final sentence of the essay recaptures a major theme of part 4: "It is unfortunately true that for many 'believers' the God they believe in is not the living God but an apologetic hypothesis" (287). CMB

Notes

1. *The Prison Meditations of Father Delp* (New York: Herder and Herder, 1963). Merton simultaneously published the same piece in three periodicals: *Jubilee* (May 1963), *Way* (May 1963), and *Continuum* (spring 1963).

2. This article was first published as "Comment on War within Man" in Erich Fromm's *War within Man: A Psychological Enquiry into the Roots of Destructiveness* (Philadelphia: American Friends Service Committee, 1963), 44–50.

FALL

The biblical story of the fall is a key element of Thomas Merton's spiritual teaching
throughout his career. It can be traced from
his premonastic journals, where he speaks of
original sin as a love of independence (*Run to
the Mountain*, 141–42), to the talk he gave on
the final day of his life, in which he suggests
that "our experience of ourselves as absolutely
autonomous individual egos" is central both
to the Buddhist concept of *avidya* and to the
Christian "myth of original sin" (*Asian Journal*, 332). He draws on traditional patristic
and medieval exegesis of the opening chapters of Genesis, particularly Augustine (*New
Man*, 114; *Birds of Appetite*, 126–27), Gregory
of Nyssa (*New Man*, 128), and Bernard (*Spirit
of Simplicity*, 93, 106–7; *New Man*, 104ff.), but
he reformulates it in contemporary terms as
the loss of "existential communion" (*New Man*,
105), the working title of the volume published
as *The New Man*, in which he discusses the
theme of the fall in greatest detail.

Merton views original sin not simply as disobedience, certainly not as disobedience to
some arbitrary divine command, but as an
attempt to usurp the position of God: "The fundamental temptation, the one to which Adam
owes his fall, is the temptation to be 'like unto
God'" (*Disputed Questions*, 100). The tragic
irony, of course, is that this is a desire to gain
what is already given, for humans are already
like God, made in the divine image and likeness. But the temptation is to possess this divine
likeness "as if it were *something more* than God
had already given him, as if it were something
that could be his apart from a gift of God, apart
from the will of God, or even against the will of
God" (101). Thus, the fall is a choice of illusion
in place of reality, as one cannot be Godlike
apart from God, in the place of God. It is the
choice of the self I create in preference to the
self God has created: "To say that I was born
in sin is to say I came into the world with a
false self. I was born in a mask. I came into
existence under a sign of contradiction, being
someone that I was never intended to be and
therefore a denial of what I am supposed to be"
(*New Seeds of Contemplation*, 33–34). It is this

state of sin, this ontological lie, that is at the
root of all particular sinful acts: "All sin starts
from the assumption that my false self, the self
that exists only in my own egocentric desires, is
the fundamental reality of life to which everything else in the universe is ordered" (34–35).
Thus, the embrace of a false identity, "man's
alienation from himself" (*Birds of Appetite*, 64),
entails a false relationship to the rest of reality.
"The self must be treated as if, not merely in
feeling but in actual fact, the whole universe
revolved around it. . . . If I am the center of the
universe, then everything belongs to me" (*New
Man*, 102). But of course the universe does not
and will not revolve around the self, does not
conform to the desires and fantasies of the individual, so that such a perspective inevitably
leads to frustration, to futile efforts to bend
things and even people to one's own will; it
results in further alienation from reality and
a deeper plunge into illusion. Here, Merton
finds significant analogies between Christian
teaching on original sin and the fundamental
Buddhist doctrines of *avidya*, or ignorance, "a
disposition to treat the ego as an absolute and
central reality and to refer all things to it as objects of desire or of repulsion" (*Birds of Appetite*,
82), and *dukkha*, or suffering, the inevitable
frustration of self-centered desire that "tends
to bear ultimate fruit in pain rather than lasting joy, in hate rather than love, in destruction
rather than creation" (83).

The primordial human vocation to contemplation, to experiencing the unity of all
being with its divine ground, is blocked by
the fall. "The story of Adam's fall from Paradise says, in symbolic terms, that man was
created as a contemplative. The fall from Paradise was a fall from unity. . . . Man fell from
the unity of contemplative vision into the multiplicity, complication and distraction of an
active, worldly existence" ("Inner Experience,"
3:201). This rejection of simplicity is rooted in
the choice of Adam to know evil as well as
good, to gain "an existential knowledge of evil.
He wanted not only to know evil by theoretical
inference from good (which he could well have
done without sin) but he wanted to know evil
in a way in which it was not even known by
God: that is to say, by *experience*" (*New Man*,

106). But rather than knowing more, he knew less by tasting of the fruit of the tree of good and evil, since evil is a diminishment of the good, not a reality in itself, and in experiencing evil he cut himself off from good, that is, from reality as created by God.

This loss of contemplative vision was at the same time a loss of fruitful action, "a perversion of man's active instincts, a turning of man's creativity away from God so that he produces and creates not the society and the temple which God's own creation demands as its fulfilment, but a temple of man's own power. The world is then exploited for the glory of man, not for the glory of God" (59–60). The consequence is exploitation, waste, violence, destruction, the denial of all common good in an insatiable search for the satisfaction of a limitless private good (115). The desire to raise oneself above the human ironically reduces one to a level below the human, to a kind of enslavement to material things, a compulsive need to satisfy one's appetite for pleasure and control, a servitude that masks itself as domination. The consequences of the fall — the loss of immortality, the exile from the Edenic state of inner wholeness and unity with all creation — were not arbitrary punishments but "were inherent in the very attitude and act which constituted Adam's sin" (110). In separating himself from the source of life, in choosing "to become his own poor fallible little god" (111), Adam was left to his own pathetically inadequate resources, which did not open out onto the infinite and eternal but isolated him even from the authentic created order so that "he found himself surrounded not with supports but with so many reasons for anxiety, insecurity, and fear" (111).

Yet at the same time as this pull toward self struggles to rearrange reality on its own behalf, there remains a deep, often unacknowledged awareness of the true order of things, of God's will for creation. Fallen humanity is simultaneously pulled in opposite directions: toward self and toward God. "The human soul is still the image of God, and no matter how far it travels away from Him into the regions of unreality, it never becomes so completely unreal that its original destiny can cease to torment it with a

need to return to itself in God, and become, once again, real" (112). Consequently, Merton can describe the doctrine of original sin as fundamentally optimistic, since it "does not teach that man is by nature evil, but that evil in him is unnatural, a disorder, a sin" and cannot bring lasting contentment (*Guilty Bystander,* 72); the restlessness of the human search for authentic meaning can be satisfied only in a return to the divine source. Merton echoes the traditional teaching that regards the fall as a *felix culpa,* a happy or fortunate fault, since it can lead to an awareness of the need for divine mercy (*New Man,* 95) and has led to the revelation of the "infinite love" of God for humanity in sharing the human condition through the incarnation of the Son and providing "its most striking proof and manifestation in Christ's death on the Cross" (245). POC

SEE ALSO ALIENATION; ORIGINAL SIN; PARADISE; REDEMPTION; SALVATION.

FERLINGHETTI, LAWRENCE

Lawrence Ferlinghetti owned the City Lights Bookstore and was editor-publisher of City Lights Books in San Francisco. Thomas Merton stayed with him prior to his departure for Asia. He published Merton's "Auschwitz" poem in 1961. He not only published poetry, but also was a poet and novelist in his own right. Merton's letters to him are found in *The Courage for Truth.* WHS

FERRY, WILBUR H.

Wilbur H. ("Ping") Ferry was vice-president of the Center for the Study of Democratic Institutions at Santa Barbara, California, from 1954 to 1969. In a letter of September 18, 1961, Thomas Merton made the initial contact of what was to become an important and lasting friendship. Ferry furnished him with much helpful reading material and introduced him to the writings of authors such as Lewis Mumford, Jacques Ellul, and I. F. Stone. Merton's correspondence with Ferry was substantial, eighty-five letters in all. The letters cover a wide range of topics — for example, the problem of war and the ways to work for peace, the issue of racism and politics, and the church and the Roman curia. Ferry visited a number of times at Gethsemani, including the 1964 meeting of people involved in the peace movement. On October 3, 1968, as Merton was preparing to leave for Asia, Ferry brought him to the Santa Barbara Center, where he carried on a lively dialogue with scholars gathered at the Center (see *Preview of the Asian Journey*) in which he discussed his plans and hopes for his Asian trip. One of Merton's hopes for this time away from Gethsemani was finding a new location for a hermitage. With this goal in view, he accepted Ferry's offer to drive him along the California coast to check possible sites. The trip up the coast lasted for several days. Then on October 15, 1968, Ferry saw Merton off on the plane that would take him to Asia. Merton's last letter to Ferry was a lighthearted note written in Singapore on December 5, 1968, five days before his tragic death in Bangkok.

The Merton letters to Ferry are found in *The Hidden Ground of Love* (203–45). In addition, Ferry published a private edition of selected letters called *Letters from Tom*. WHS

SEE ALSO LETTERS FROM TOM.

FIGURES FOR AN APOCALYPSE
Norfolk, Conn.: New Directions, 1947. 111 pp.

This is Thomas Merton's third published book of verse, appearing a year after *A Man in the Divided Sea* and three years after *Thirty Poems*. It is the first of Merton's volumes in which all the poems were written in the monastery, dating from 1946 and perhaps early 1947. The volume consists of the title poem, an eight-part sequence, and twenty-six other poems, followed by the essay "Poetry and the Contemplative Life," which had first appeared in the July 4, 1947, issue of *Commonweal*.

The opening sequence, as the title suggests, is an imaginative vision of the end of the world, drawing heavily on the imagery of Revelation, but also reflecting Merton's early awareness of the destructive power of atomic weapons. The "figures" of the title seemingly refer to symbolic representations (i.e., "figures of speech") rather than to human figures, presumably an indica-

tion that the poet did not intend his scenario to be taken as a literal description of future events. The untitled opening section (47 ll.) is a call for the "Beloved" Bridegroom (drawing both on Matthew 25 and Revelation 21) to come forth "Clad in the wrath of Armageddon" (l. 32) and "Lead out Thy Bride" (l. 40) from the earthly cities (Sidon and Tyre) that are imaged both as set aflame and as cast into the "foaming seas" (l. 47). The second section (33 ll.), likewise untitled, alternates between addresses, in the manner of Amos and Isaiah, to the "rich women" (ll. 1, 8, 30) caught up in their own luxurious self-absorption, and reflections by these "spurious queens" (l. 24) themselves, who realize too late the emptiness of their lives. The third section (55 ll.), with its parenthetical subtitle "(Advice to my Friends Robert Lax and Edward Rice, to get away while they still can)," exchanges scriptural diction for a quasi-surreal informality: in three fantastic settings ("Hotel Sherlock Holmes" [l. 1], "Fauntleroy Bar" [l. 12], and "Hotel Wonderland" [l. 26]) the friends observe signs of the coming end, finally recognizing that it is time to "fly … to the mountains" (ll. 44–45) and prepare for their own climactic battle, to be fought only with spiritual weapons, in "the pathless wood" (l. 49) (where Dante encountered the beasts of sensuality, violence, and fraud). The fourth section (35 ll.) is preceded by the scriptural reference to "Apoc. XIV, 14," in which one like a "son of man" is seen on a cloud with a sickle in his hand; this image of the final harvest dominates the poem, which concludes with the first personal reference of the sequence, in which the sound of the trumpet "bites my soul with lightnings live as steel!" (l. 35). In the fifth section (44 ll.), entitled "Landscape, Prophet and Wild-dog," the prophet in question is successively communism (ll. 6–13) and capitalism (ll. 17–26); in each case the prophecies are unfulfilled and the fleeing prophet is run down, killed, and buried by the "wild-dog," the pitiless forces of nature that destroy human illusions before the final end. The sixth section, "In the Ruins of New York" (87 ll.), adapts prophetic imagery (particularly Isaiah on the fall of Babylon [Isaiah 13]) to the destruction of New York City, presumably in an atomic attack, "When flames out of the clouds burned down your cariated teeth" (l. 12), envisioned as punishment for the "callous" disregard "of her six million poor" (ll. 42, 45); in this intermediate period, the city is reclaimed by nature, as "doves' nests, and hives of bees" take over "the cliffs of the ancient apartments" (ll. 60, 61) and "some hermit" may build a cell from "the stones of the city hall" (ll. 72, 73). The seventh section, "Landscape: Beast" (39 ll.), envisions those marked with the sign of the beast waiting for their Lord to arise from the sea both on the east coast and the west, failing to recognize that the "ordinary dragon, ... as usual as sin" (ll. 29, 30), is already present in the center of the land, and failing to notice the avenging angels gathering to the north. The final section, "The Heavenly City" (28 ll.), addresses the new Jerusalem as the culmination of human history (l. 17) and the dawn of the new creation (l. 19); its final line, in which the city is described as crowned "In nine white diadems of liturgy" (l. 28), perhaps suggests that this eschatological consummation is anticipated and even mystically experienced by the church at prayer. Despite the positive conclusion, the perspective of this ambitious sequence (363 ll. total) is almost unrelievedly negative and judgmental toward contemporary society, viewing it as doomed by its own materialism and addiction to violence.

A similar perspective is present in some of the other poems in the volume. "A Letter to America" (no. 4; 42 ll.) contrasts the original promise of the "new world" with its present degeneration, and considers hopes for its renewal as "wishful lies" (l. 19). "Three Postcards from the Monastery" (no. 5; 61 ll.) presents the monastic life as a salutary escape from the illusions of contemporary life, though also as a way of discovering the "new, true name" (l. 20) of America. "The Song of the Traveller" (no. 14; 29 ll.) views the "cities full of sorcery" (l. 15) from the serene heights of the hill of the Lord, but with the warning that to turn back on the road of pilgrimage is to court the fate of "Mistress Lot ... on the stony road from Sodom" (ll. 28–29). "Pilgrims' Song" (no. 25; 30 ll.) likewise escapes the "Stepmother city" (l. 3) through the darkness of the cross, rejecting

the overtures of the city with its "imitation arms" (l. 17) because "We are in love with your antagonist" (l. 21).

In contrast to the artificiality of life in the "the world," many of the poems in this volume depict the monastic life as one both in harmony with and transcending the natural order. "Landscape: Wheatfields" (no. 2; 42 ll.) compares gathering the harvest with final judgment, when the fruitfulness of the monks' lives will be weighed in the balance. "Spring: Monastery Farm" (no. 12; 27 ll.) sees the liturgy of the abbey as complementing and completing the "deep, uncomprehending choirs" (l. 24) of all creation at the time of its seasonal rebirth. "Evening: Zero Weather" (no. 15; 34 ll.) recognizes that "Christ, our August" (l. 29) is continually present, even "in the zero days before Lent" (l. 30).

While less specifically monastic, in "The Transformation: For the Sacred Heart" (no. 16; 42 ll.) the poet, aware that too many people "Bide in their January ice / And keep the stubborn winter of their fruitlessness" (ll. 17–18), prays that he may "leave the frosts (that is: the fears) of my December" (l. 26) and experience even in times of apparent anguish the work of Christ, who "makes these new green blades / In the transforming of my soul" (ll. 35–36). In "Winter Afternoon" (no. 22; 22 ll.) the end of the old year and advent of the new is seen as a portent of the new creation, while in "The Sowing of Meanings" (no. 24; 37 ll.), with its echoes of Hopkins, the coming of spring is a prophetic foreshadowing of the coming of the Lord as "Creation finds the pressure of His everlasting secret / Too terrible to bear" (ll. 26–27) and new life bursts forth "every way we look" (l. 28), even, or especially, within the self. "A Mysterious Song in the Spring of the Year" (no. 8; 37 ll.) sees the paschal pattern of dying and rising with Christ as breaking through the rigidities of temporal patterns and slipping "Sidelong into eternity, between the angular hour" (l. 18).

Nature is related more specifically to contemplation in "Two States of Prayer" (no. 3; 32 ll.), in which the autumn colors of October and the bleak bareness of December are compared, respectively, to exultant affective prayer and the quieter, deeper prayer of the apophatic way. "Natural History" (no. 20; 52 ll.) finds in caterpillars' cocoons along the sheltered wall beside the cemetery an emblem of "Two figures, death and contemplation" (l. 40). Symbolic use of natural imagery is found as well in "The Landfall" (no. 26; 48 ll.), in which a vivid tropical landscape suggests the classical myth of the islands of the blessed, and Shakespeare's *The Tempest* is echoed in the final lines' allusion to resurrection as "the strange tale / Of the drowned king (our nature), his return!" (ll. 47–48). In "Song: Contemplation" (no. 7; 47 ll.) the natural world is seen as a sacrament revealing the divine presence, but ultimately is left behind by a prayer that "lies beyond the track / Of thought and genius and of desire" (ll. 45–46), while in "Theory of Prayer" (no. 18; 56 ll.) the insufficiency of natural paths to the divine, whether external ("the flowering green groves / Where the pretty idols dwell" [ll. 8–9]) or internal ("Logic . . . Theorems . . . Economy" [ll. 35–37]), finally reveals that only total self-surrender releases the "ocean of peace" (l. 42) deep within and plunges the believer into "those soundless fathoms where You dwell" (l. 56). "Freedom as Experience" (no. 23; 30 ll.) takes a more cosmic perspective as interior order mirrors the order of the universe and (in a Copernican updating of Dante) "Our loves revolve about You as the planets swing upon the sun" (l. 15). The cosmic and the homely are juxtaposed in "A Christmas Card" (no. 21; 22 ll.) as hills and stars that offer adoration to the Christ Child are joined by shepherds who "Stamp and shake out their hats upon the stable dirt" and kneel "to look upon their Life" (ll. 21–22).

Saints are the subjects of a number of the poems. "St. John's Night" (no. 13; 44 ll.) takes as its point of departure the traditional midsummer bonfires in southern France (Merton's birthplace) as images of the purifying and pentecostal flames promised by the Baptist, to be brought by the one who would baptize with the Holy Spirit and with fire. "Duns Scotus" (no. 10; 43 ll.) presents the Franciscan theologian as the chivalric champion of his lady the Virgin Mary, who is unappreciated by a prosaic age that prefers law to freedom. "Two Desert Fathers" (no. 11) focuses first on St. Jerome

(30 ll.) as master both of the language of Scripture and of the language of searing social critique, "most learned, mad / And immaculate indignation" (ll. 25–26); the second part addresses the legendary "St. Paul the Hermit" (88 ll.), known only through Jerome's *Vita*, who is praised as a model of solitary contemplation, "Saint, who of all great saints, oh! I most envy!" (l. 36). "Rievaulx: St. Aelred" (no. 17; 51 ll.) adapts the biblical story of Judith and Holofernes as a pattern for the foundation of the abbey of Rievaulx, a beautiful, "feminine" presence that puts to death the pride represented by the Scottish court where Aelred had spent his early life. In a very different key, the subsequent history of another twelfth-century Cistercian monastery is explored in "Clairvaux Prison" (no. 19; 39 ll.), which considers the odd fate of St. Bernard's abbey during the French Revolution, when it was used as a jail rather than being destroyed, and thus was preserved as "so true an image of a world / That was untrue to Him" (ll. 27–28).

A more personal note is struck by "On the Anniversary of My Baptism" (no. 6; 46 ll.), which juxtaposes the poet's safe passage in his many ocean crossings with the salvific dying and rising from the waters of baptism, "my world's end and my Genesis," when the Lord "drowned me in the shallow font" (ll. 36, 41) and so "charged my sinews with His secret life" (l. 41). "Canticle for the Blessed Virgin" (no. 9; 84 ll.) also includes a personal element, as the poet prays that he might receive the grace of priesthood, but asks that even if his past has made him "too unworthy of the Liturgy" (l. 65), he might present his entire life and activity to be transformed into Christ, and thus (echoing Hopkins's "As kingfishers catch fire") "bring forth new Incarnations / Shining to God with the features of His Christ" (ll. 75–76). Finally, "The Poet, To His Book" (no. 27; 24 ll.) suggests the increasing ambivalence with which Merton regarded his verse: he questions whether it is a positive activity, a labor on behalf of Christ, or an intruder stealing "prayers and joys" (l. 15) from time that would otherwise be devoted to meditation, and so adding to his time in purgatory; he sends the book out into the world to stand on "the loud world's corners" (l. 18) in the hope that at least "some one prisoner" (l. 23) will be ransomed from the "Christless avenues" (l. 22) by "the rhythms that upset my silences" (l. 20). This ambivalence continues in the essay that follows, "Poetry and the Contemplative Life," in which Merton suggests that at a certain point in the process of spiritual development poetry can interfere with contemplation; it also foreshadows the (temporary) renunciation of poetry after his next volume, *The Tears of the Blind Lions* (1949).

This restlessness may have influenced Merton's own dissatisfaction with *Figures for an Apocalypse*, both at the time of its publication and later. Reading proofs for the volume, he describes himself as "disgusted with the verse I have been writing" (*Entering the Silence*, 128), and later says that he should have "pulled the stuffing out of" some of the poems (170); when the book appears, he describes it as a "child's garden of bad verses," and continues, "I should have pulled out a lot of weeds before I let that stuff get in print, but the damage is done now. May God have mercy on me. The reviewers won't. I hope this time Reverend Father will let me look at the reviews — I might learn something" (179). This immediate negative reaction is endorsed twenty years later in the graph that Merton made for his books, in which *Figures for an Apocalypse* is ranked "poor," the lowest of any of his books of verse, though this evaluation may be prompted at least in part by the rejection and condemnation of the world beyond the monastery that marks the title sequence in particular and to some extent the volume as a whole, and that contrasts so markedly with the openness of the later Merton.

Though its copyright is dated 1947, the volume was apparently published only in early 1948 (see *Entering the Silence*, 170). POC

SEE ALSO POETRY, THEORY OF.

FOREST, JAMES H.

Born in 1941 in Salt Lake City, James Forest went to school in California and later in New York City (at Hunter College). He entered the U.S. Navy, but he was discharged as a conscientious objector in 1961, the same year that he became a Roman Catholic. He joined the Catholic Worker movement and became editor of the *Catholic Worker* paper. This was the beginning of a lifelong commitment to the cause of peace and nonviolence. He published articles by Thomas Merton in the *Catholic Worker* and visited him at Gethsemani. Thus began a friendship and a substantial exchange of letters: Merton's letters to him number seventy-two. (The originals of this correspondence are available to scholars in the Merton Room of the Nazareth College library in Rochester, New York.)

Forest was much involved in the Catholic peace movement and was several times imprisoned for his peace activities. In 1973 he became editor of *Fellowship*, a publication of the Fellowship of Reconciliation (FOR), whose headquarters are at Nyack, New York. Four years later he became general secretary of the International Fellowship of Reconciliation (IFOR), whose offices are located in Alkmaar, Holland, where Forest and his wife, Nancy, now live. He has written several books on Merton, including *Living with Wisdom: A Life of Thomas Merton*. Forest is now a member of the Orthodox Church and has made a number of visits to Moscow. There he has met with people interested in Merton. His biography of Merton has been translated into Russian. WHS

"FOURTH AND WALNUT" EXPERIENCE, THE

On March 19, 1958, Thomas Merton wrote in his personal journal about an experience he had while he was in Louisville the previous day. Merton begins his entry by noting that he is writing it in St. Anne's. "How rich for me has been the silence of this little house which is nothing more than a toolshed." In 1953 Abbot James Fox had given Merton permission to spend time there. Notably, it is in the solitude of the toolshed become hermitage that Merton records and reflects on a spiritual experience that took place not at Gethsemani but in the middle of Louisville, and yet gave him new insight into the meaning of his vocation to solitude. He writes, "Yesterday, in Louisville, at the corner of 4th and Walnut

I suddenly realized that I loved all the people and that none of them were, or, could be totally alien to me. As if waking from a dream — the dream of my separateness, of the 'special' vocation to be different. My vocation does not really make me different from the rest of men or put me in a special category except artificially; juridically. I am still a member of the human race — and what more glorious destiny is there for man, since the Word was made flesh and became, too a member of the Human Race!" (*Search for Solitude*, 181–82). Full of gratitude to God that he is "only another member of the human race," Merton celebrates the "immense joy of being a man! As if the sorrows of our condition could really matter, once we begin to realize who and what we are — as if we could ever begin to realize it on earth" (182).

Merton begins the next paragraph by reflecting on the women he saw. "It is not a question of proving to myself that I either dislike or like the women one sees in the street" (182). He is "keenly conscious, not of their beauty... but of their humanity, their womanness." He observes that his vow of chastity makes their "secret beauty" accessible to him. "It is as though by chastity I had come to be married to what is most pure in all the women of the world and to taste and sense the secret beauty of their girl's hearts as they walked in the sunlight — each one secret and good and lovely in the sight of God." Their womanness brings "the image of God into the world" and "each one is Wisdom and Sophia and Our Lady" (182).

What follows is a note, addressed to Proverb, the young Jewish girl of whom he dreamed in late February and to whom he wrote a letter in his journal on March 4, 1958 (176). Merton writes to tell Proverb that he saw her yesterday "in a different place, in a different form, in the most unexpected circumstances. I shall never forget our meeting yesterday. The touch of your hand makes me a different person. To be with you is rest and truth. Only with you are these things found, dear child sent to me by God" (182). Although the women he saw in Louisville, especially Proverb, appear to be significant aspects of his experience at

Fourth and Walnut, Merton does not comment on them in *Conjectures of a Guilty Bystander*, where he writes not of the secret beauty of women or of his meeting with Proverb, but of "the secret beauty" of all hearts (*Guilty Bystander*, 142/158).

In the second account of his experience at Fourth and Walnut, expanded to more than two pages in *Conjectures of a Guilty Bystander* (140–42/156–58), Merton writes, "In Louisville, at the corner of Fourth and Walnut, in the center of the shopping district, I was suddenly overwhelmed with the realization that I loved all those people, that they were mine and I theirs, that we could not be alien to one another even though we were total strangers. It was like waking from a dream of separateness." He labels the idea of "a separate holy existence" an illusion: "the illusion that by making vows we became a different species of being, pseudoangels, 'spiritual men,' men of interior life, what have you." This "sense of liberation" came as a "relief" and a "joy." "Thank God, thank God that I am like other men." He celebrates the "glorious destiny" of being "a member of the human race," a race "in which God himself became incarnate." "And if only everybody could realize this! But it cannot be explained. There is no way of telling people that they are all walking around shining like the sun" (158).

In the light of the experience at Fourth and Walnut, Merton reinterprets his solitude. His solitude does not belong to him alone. Although solitude implies a responsibility to be alone, "When I am alone they are not 'they' but my own self. There are no strangers" (158).

Plaque at Fourth and Walnut site, Louisville, Kentucky

Returning to his vision, Merton writes, "Then it was as if I suddenly saw the secret beauty of their hearts, the depths of their hearts where neither sin nor desire nor self-knowledge can reach, the core of their reality, the person that each one is in God's eyes" (158). Merton uses a phrase, borrowed from Louis Massignon, to express what he saw to be the deepest reality of the human person: *le point vierge*. Literally, the phrase means "the virgin point," but noting that it cannot be translated, Merton writes, "At the center of our being is a point of nothingness which is untouched by sin and by illusion, a point of pure truth, a point or spark which belongs entirely to God... this little point of nothingness and of *absolute poverty* is the pure glory of God in us" (158). Comparing this point or spark to "a pure diamond, blazing with the invisible light of heaven," Merton proclaims that it is "in everybody, and if we could see it we would see these billions of points of light coming together in the face and blaze of a sun that would make all the darkness and cruelty of life vanish completely" (158).

Merton's vision at the corner of Fourth and Walnut in Louisville, on March 18, 1958, expressed and has come to symbolize his transformed understanding of humanity, of monks, and of himself. For Merton, this experience was a moment of epiphany, a realization of the divine made manifest in the midst of the human. Merton's vision of a shared common humanity clarified his understanding of what it meant for him to be a monk and what kind of monk he was meant to be. The experience symbolized a turning point in Merton's life. Coupled with his increased contacts with thinkers and writers all over the world, it marked the beginning of Merton's "return to the world" that he thought he had left behind when he entered the monastery. In the years that followed the Louisville vision, as he continued to be nurtured by contemplation and fired by compassion, Merton began to write on a host of social issues, including war and racism. He had realized not only that he was not separate from the human race, but also that he, like everyone else, shared responsibility for the future of humankind. CMB

SEE ALSO *POINT VIERGE*; PROVERB; WOMEN.

FOX, JAMES

Dom James Fox was born in 1896 and grew up in Dedham, Massachusetts. A graduate of Harvard Business School, he entered the Abbey of Gethsemani in 1927. In 1941, when John Paul Merton came to visit Tom at the abbey, Dom James was guestmaster and arranged for John Paul's baptism into the Catholic Church. In 1946 he became superior of the new foundation in Conyers, Georgia, and in 1948 he was chosen to succeed Dom Frederic Dunne as abbot of Gethsemani. Dom James mechanized much of the work at Gethsemani, tractors replacing horse-drawn wagons. To increase the monastery's meager income, he established Gethsemani Farms, which proved highly successful in raising funds from the sale of Kentucky bourbon fruitcake and Gethsemani cheese. In 1960 Dom James invited Merton's Columbia friend Daniel Walsh to come to the monastery to reorganize the program of studies for the priesthood.

Much has been written about Dom James's relationship with the most famous monk in the monastery, Fr. Louis Merton. There is no doubt that Merton had his problems with Dom James, though the diatribes against his abbot that appear in his journals are excessive and unappreciative of the important role Dom James played in his life. Though they differed in their understanding of the monastic and Christian life, Dom James displayed a remarkable insight into Merton's needs in ways that one could hardly have expected.

It was Dom James who gave Merton more time for solitude in the Gethsemani woods in the early 1950s and eventually got approval for him to live as a hermit in 1965. It was Dom James who had sufficient confidence in the authenticity of Merton's understanding of the monastic life to appoint him in 1955 as master of novices, thus placing the formation of the next generation of Gethsemani monks in his hands. It was Dom James's sensitivity to Merton's need to get as much as possible written about war and peace that moved him in 1962 to postpone for three months notifying Merton that the abbot general in France had forbidden Merton to write on such subjects.

Dom James Fox, O.C.S.O.

His firm yet gentle handling in 1966 of the delicately difficult issue of Merton's relationship with a student nurse helped Merton to move out of a situation that he was neither emotionally nor rationally equipped to handle. All in all, Dom James displayed a shrewdness of insight into the complexities of a highly gifted monk whom almost any religious superior would have found difficult to deal with. His choice of Merton as his personal confessor for the last fifteen years of Merton's life is one further testimony to his belief that, despite his vagaries and wanderings, Merton understood deeply what monastic life was all about, even if by his own admission he, more often than he wished, failed to live the ideal he professed.

When he resigned as abbot in 1967, Dom James followed Merton's example and became a hermit. His life as a hermit came to an abrupt end on April 16, 1977, when his hermitage was vandalized and he himself brutally beaten by two men who broke into his hermitage and became angry when they found nothing of monetary value there. He moved to the infirmary, where he would live for ten more years. He died on Good Friday, 1987, at ninety-one years of age. WHS

FRANCISCANISM

Certainly one of the most familiar and most significant episodes in Thomas Merton's premonastic life was his decision to join the Franciscans, his initial acceptance, and subsequent rejection after he disclosed the irregularities of his past (see *Seven Storey Mountain*, 261–62, 265–66, 288–92, 294–98). What is much less familiar but perhaps equally significant is the fact that Merton actually did become a Franciscan, not only in spirit but literally. During the ten months preceding his entrance into Gethsemani, Merton was a member of the Franciscan Third Order at St. Bonaventure College (*Seven Storey Mountain*, 300, 343). The journal from this period includes numerous entries reflecting the intellectual, devotional, and personal influence of Franciscanism on Merton at this time.

During the 1940–41 academic year Merton was immersing himself in early Franciscan texts under the direction of Fr. Philotheus Boehner (333, 337). From December 1940 through March 1941 he was systematically working his way through the *Itinerarium Mentis in Deum* of St. Bonaventure, generally considered the most significant work of Franciscan spiritual theology; during May he was studying Bonaventure's *Collationes de Septem Donis Spiritus Sancti*, a series of sermons on the gifts of the Holy Spirit. While the journal entries on the *De Septem Donis* are limited to a thorough outline of the work,[1] those on the *Itinerarium* include lengthy quotations as well as comments and reflections that provide some indication of the impact that this work had on Merton. Among the dozen or so passages quoted by Merton in the journal, some are particularly evocative of his later spiritual teaching, including the first citation, an outline of the entire journey, which moves from encountering God as reflected in the outside world to discovering the divine image and likeness within, to contemplative union with God as God is *in se* (*Run to the Mountain*, 270). Another passage which attracted Merton's attention says that the human person was created for contemplation — the true paradise life — and that original sin entailed a fall from contemplative unity into ignorance and concupiscence (275). In the epilogue to *The Seven Storey Mountain* he calls the contemplative vision of God in the final chapter of the *Itinerarium* "one of the best descriptions ever written of this highest of all vocations" (*Seven Storey Mountain*, 418).

Merton's comments on Francis of Assisi himself complement his discussions of the Franciscan intellectual tradition. An extended meditation from late November 1940 on the meaning of the stigmata is among the most powerful in the entire journal and does not suffer by comparison even with journal material from the last decade of Merton's life. Of Francis after his descent from Mount Alverna Merton writes, "*He is no longer a dramatic figure. He is no longer a colorful, lovable figure, no longer charming, romantic, no longer the St. Francis who preached to the birds, who played on the fiddle with two sticks and made songs for the Lord in French. On the contrary, he is a strange, colorless, hunched up little man, silent, seeming to be sick*" (*Run to the Mountain*, 266). Merton's point here is that in bearing the marks of the Crucified One, Francis is sharing in the shame, the stigma, of the passion: "Saint Francis' greatness is in this, that he bore the same insult as Christ — an insult beyond all comprehension, beyond all drama, beyond all speech, so extreme as to seem utterly neutral" (266). It is impossible after reading a passage such as this to assume that Merton had a naive and romantic notion of what the Christian spiritual life entailed when he entered the monastery.

Merton's reception into the Third Order on February 19, 1941, is invested for him with a very deep spiritual significance (309–11). It is evident that he regarded it at the time as a turning point in his life as a Catholic. It expressed his need to move beyond a conceptual approach to God; it also is a response to the call to follow the way of the cross, and a confession of his inadequacy in doing so; finally it shows an awareness, perhaps still subconscious, that simply to give away a symbol of his possessions, as he did in the ceremony, is not going to be enough for Thomas Merton. This act of becoming a Franciscan then, albeit a Third Order Franciscan, crystallizes issues of identity and vocation that were so crucial for

Merton both then and later. While not providing a resolution to these issues, this event, two months before Merton's first visit to Gethsemani, emerges from the journal as an important stage in the process leading to the monastery.

On September 6, 1941, at the Trappist monastery of Our Lady of the Valley in Rhode Island, Merton writes a long prayer addressed to "Holy Father Saint Francis," in which he grapples with his unresolved vocational perplexities (405–7). The appropriateness of addressing it to St. Francis soon becomes very evident: his humility and simplicity model the virtues that Merton finds so deficient in himself, and his commitment to gospel poverty is directly pertinent to the immediate question that Merton is wrestling with, whether to work full-time at Friendship House, a vocation that clearly is attractive to Merton because of its Franciscan dimension, closer to the spirit of Francis than the life of friars running churches and colleges. He writes, "Pray for me that I may give as much as I can to the poor. And that soon I may be able to go hungry so that someone else may eat. And that soon I may be able to suffer so that someone else may not suffer. And that I may laugh and sing when I am despised for God's love, and that I may dance and play when I am reviled for God's love, and called a madman, and a fool and a crook" (407). It is quite clear from the references to dancing and singing and playing, to being considered a madman, a fool, and a crook, that Merton sees in Francis the pattern for his own life. Ultimately, this pattern is not just that of the attractive, romantic image of God's troubadour, but that of conformity to Christ and absolute fidelity to his teaching: "Pray for me to be poor, meek; to hunger and thirst for justice and be merciful; to be a peacemaker, clean of heart, to be reviled, to be persecuted for God's sake" (407). Though unstated, the context of these words is undoubtedly Merton's effort to discern whether he should return to Harlem and Friendship House permanently. Since this is not the vocational path Merton eventually took, it might be concluded that the influence of Francis was not decisive. But the final paragraph of the prayer suggests that the other option, represented not by the place he had just come from but by the place where he now was, was at least in the back of Merton's mind as well: "Only pray for me, my Father Saint Francis, to give up everything for My Lord, to be the least of His children and the most insignificant of the poor for love only, and that in all things I may have grace to pray meekly and patiently and happily, and not in the confusion of pride, and the scruples pride puts in our heads and the fears pride freezes us with. Pray for me for enough humility to always pray for humility, poverty, and tears" (407).

While the Franciscan influence should not be overestimated, neither should it be neglected. Merton's interest was not simply a nostalgic attraction toward a life from which he had been excluded. It was a mature commitment involving rigorous study as well as personal devotion. Nor was it simply a passing enthusiasm to be abandoned in favor of the Cistercian approach. In many ways the Franciscan emphasis on experiencing God through love was an adaptation of monastic theology to a new, more scholastic era. The two traditions are not so much alternatives as ramifications from the same root source, so that Merton's Franciscan studies served as an excellent preparation for his monastic life. In fact, the Franciscan tradition made a lasting impression on Merton, and its central themes and figures continued to be significant throughout the rest of his life. It could be argued that in becoming a Cistercian, Merton did not cease to be Franciscan.

Francis and the Franciscan tradition continue to be important for Merton after his entrance into Gethsemani, particularly in the years of formation leading to his ordination in 1949. He records praying to Francis for more objectivity in his spiritual life in September 1947 (Entering the Silence, 111), and a year later he writes, "Day and night I think about St. Francis and about poverty as I reread the seventh chapter of St. Bonaventure's Itinerarium" (233). In August 1949 he notes that "the Franciscan side" of his spiritual life "continues to grow" (343). For a time he is particularly enthusiastic about Duns Scotus, the thirteenth-century Franciscan theologian whom he had begun to study at St. Bonaventure, saying, "He always shows me the way

to great heights by showing me Christ and Our Lady in a light in which nobody else manages to see them" (136), though eventually he worries that "too much technical theology (Scotus) is deadening my interior life" (162) and decides that he prefers Denis the Carthusian to Scotus, commenting, "I am finished with subtleties" (240); however, Scotus's influence certainly remains in Merton's conviction that the incarnation would have taken place even without the fall (see New Seeds of Contemplation, 290).

Merton's most extensive discussion of Francis is as a model for the apostolic vocation, which combines contemplative and active dimensions, in No Man Is an Island (159–63). He also sees Francis as a model of the peacemaker, especially in an ecumenical context (Seeds of Destruction, 181–83). His attraction to both the poet Zukofsky and Albert Camus is related to the Franciscan qualities he finds in each of them (Literary Essays, 130–31, 239–41). In his search for models of the hermit life, one of the places he looks to is "Franciscan Eremitism" (World of Action, 260–68). Thus, a Franciscan thread continues to run through the varied interests of Merton's mature spirituality, providing support for his statement in 1966, "I . . . will always feel that I am still in some secret way a son of St. Francis. There is no saint in the Church whom I admire more than St. Francis" (Road to Joy, 298). POC

Notes

1. These notes were omitted from Run to the Mountain.

FREEDGOOD, SEYMOUR

One of Thomas Merton's closest friends at Columbia, Seymour (Sy) Freedgood (1915–68) is described in The Seven Storey Mountain as "full of a fierce and complex intellectuality which he sometimes liked to present in the guise of a rather suspicious suavity" and as one who "had carried the mendacium jocosum or 'humorous lie' to its utmost extension and frequency" (182). Though Freedgood was perhaps the least religiously inclined of Merton's college friends, it was through him that Merton encountered the little Hindu monk Brahmachari, who was to play an important role in Merton's own growing interest in Catholicism (*Seven Storey Mountain*, 191–99). Seymour was one of the group of Merton's friends who was present for his ordination (*Entering the Silence*, 318), as he had been a witness at his baptism more than a decade earlier (*Seven Storey Mountain*, 222). He worked as a journalist throughout his life, including a stint editing an army newspaper in India during World War II (*Seven Storey Mountain*, 409), and for the last decade of his life was associate editor at *Fortune* magazine. He also wrote occasional short stories, including a lightly fictionalized account of Brahmachari's encounter with his Jewish family entitled "Grandma and the Hindu Monk," which has been widely anthologized.[1] In March 1967, he visited Merton at Gethsemani for the first time since the 1949 ordination, a lively encounter despite an auto accident on the way from Louisville to the monastery (*Learning to Love*, 206). Freedgood died in January 1968 in a fire at his home on Long Island. Merton's letters to Freedgood are found in *The Road to Joy* (123–31). POC

Notes

1. See Milton Crane, ed., *50 Great American Short Stories* (New York: Bantam, 1965), 460–79; the story first appeared in the May 1951 issue of *Harper's*.

FREEDOM

One way of viewing Thomas Merton's story is to see it as a gradual growth toward authentic freedom. The fifth volume of the Merton letters, *Witness to Freedom*, suggests three stages in his growth to freedom. In the early stage — his youthful years, highlighted by the tragic year at Clare College, Cambridge — freedom meant for him doing whatever it pleased him to do. The restraints of rules and regulations, from whatever source they might come, he viewed as hindrances to freedom.

The second stage of his growth toward true freedom came with his entrance into the monastery of Gethsemani in 1941 (prepared for by his conversion to the Roman Catholic Church in 1938). He offers an interesting description of this new freedom in narrating the story of his arrival at Gethsemani. With an obvious sense of joyfulness he tells us how Br. Mat-

thew met him at the monastery gate, led him through the gate, and then locked it. "I was enclosed," he tells us, "in the four walls of my new freedom" (*Seven Storey Mountain*, 372). These words, after Merton's years of misspent youth, ring out with a sense of anticipated joy. Yet one cannot help but wonder: surely this a curious way of defining freedom — enclosure behind four walls. The freedom of "the four walls" was the freedom to do what he was told, the freedom to keep the rules. A favorite monastic attitude in his early days in the monastery was "Obey your superiors and you will be using your freedom properly. You will be carrying out the will of God." Such a view, which in effect reduces freedom to obedience, can keep a person perpetually immature. It can stifle any kind of personal growth.

For these two stages keeping rules are central. In the first stage, the rules are the problem; in the second, the solution. The first stage could lead to moral depravity; the second, to moral rigidity. Merton had too fine a mind to allow himself to be stuck for very long in a mold of rigidity. As he grew in the monastic life and in contemplative spirituality, his understanding of freedom underwent drastic modification.

At this third stage he saw freedom as an inner reality guided much more from within than from without. To one of his correspondents Merton wrote, "A contemplative is one who has God's will bearing right down upon him often in the most incomprehensible way" (*Hidden Ground of Love*, 362). In contemplation we encounter God and in the encounter discover our deepest freedom. Authentic prayer, of which contemplation is the flowering, enables us to emerge from our servility into freedom in God. We experience our true identity in God. In his notation for July 31, 1961, Merton remarks that during the night office and the morning meditation, "[I saw] that my whole life is a struggle to seek the truth...and that the truth is found in the reality of my own life as it is given to me and that it is found by complete consent and acceptance...by 'creative' consent in my deepest self to the will of God which is expressed in my own self and my own life. And indeed there is a sense in which my own deepest self is in God and even expresses Him, as 'word' " (*Turning toward the World*, 146).

To be free and to experience "our deepest self," our own identity, in God means to rid our lives of the illusions and fictions we so often live by. We begin to live in the real world instead of one constructed by our own or other people's fantasies and expectations. This means taking responsibility for our own lives, standing on our own feet, and making our own decisions of conscience. This is much harder than simply living by the rules, but it is also more truly human and surely more mature. It is the way of imitating Jesus, the perfect example of one whose decisions came from within. Merton came to see this as the only authentic way of living as a free person in the monastic life, and indeed in any form of the Christian life. To what degree he achieved this authenticity in his own life is difficult, perhaps impossible, for us to judge. But that he strove for it is undeniable.

Persons achieve this third degree of freedom to the degree that they rid themselves of the illusions that distort reality for them. On June 11, 1963, Merton wrote to Jacques Maritain and spoke of these illusions. He was readying himself, he confides to Maritain, for the final journey to God, yet he realized that there was much work yet be done in his life. "There are," he wrote, "great illusions to be got rid of and there is a false self that has to be taken off. . . . There is still much to be changed before I will really be living in the truth and in nothingness and in humility and without any more self-concern" (*Courage for Truth*, 39).

First of all, there is need to rid ourselves of the illusion that beclouds our perception of God. The God whom illusion projects on the screen of my consciousness is a God who is seen as an "Object" alongside of other objects, as a "Being" among other beings, whose existence can be discovered and demonstrated. This is a false notion of God. For God is the Absolute: the Source and Ground of all existing beings. God is not to be sought among the creatures God has made. God, the Hidden Ground of Love, from whom all things come and in which all things are sustained (see *Hidden Ground of Love*, 115, 452), is the deep Source of all freedom. "The only true liberty,"

Merton writes, "is in the service of that which is beyond all limits, beyond all definitions, beyond all human appreciation: that which is All, and which therefore is no limited or individual thing: the All is no-thing, for if it were to be a single thing separated from all other things, it would not be All. This precisely is the liberty I have always sought: the freedom of being subject to no-thing, and therefore to live in All, through All, for All, by Him Who is All. In Christian terms, this is to live 'in Christ' and by the 'Spirit of Christ,' for the Spirit is like the wind, blowing where He pleases, and He is the Spirit of Truth. 'The Truth shall make you free' " ("*Honorable Reader*," 64).

The truth that delivers me from the illusions that make God into an idol is the same power that delivers me from the illusion that makes me into a being who is shadowed by a false self (see *Seeds of Contemplation*, 28; *New Seeds of Contemplation*, 34). The false self arises from the condition of alienation in me that prevents me from realizing that I am the image of God. The false self, veiling as it does that likeness to God in which I was created, hides from me the true identity I have only in God. The false self is "created" by my self-centeredness and self-seeking activities. It is a straw self without substance because it is built of bits and pieces of superficiality and rooted in unreality. "When we live superficially, when we are always outside ourselves, never quite 'with' ourselves, always divided and pulled in many directions by conflicting plans and projects, we find ourselves doing many things that we do not really want to do, saying things we do not really mean, exhausting ourselves for what we secretly realize to be worthless and without meaning in our lives" (*Love and Living*, 43). This false self drugs my true self, so to speak, so that I do not know who I really am. In narcissistic love it feeds on itself and imagines that it is experiencing God when in actual fact it is only experiencing its own vacuity and nothingness. It may say "I" on ever so many occasions, but unfortunately, there is really no one there to say it. In "The Inner Experience" Merton warns that the first thing a would-be contemplative must do is "to recover your basic natural unity. . . . This means that you have to bring back together the fragments of your distracted existence so that when you say 'I' there is really someone present to support the pronoun you have uttered" ("Inner Experience," 3).

My true self, which is as secret as God and which, like God, eludes every concept that seeks to seize hold of it, sleeps meanwhile in the depths of my spirit, waiting to be awakened by "the promptings of a Superior Freedom" (5).[1] This true self is "our entire substantial reality itself on its highest and most personal and most existential level" (6).

The true self is the *point vierge* at the center of our being. Compared to God, it is "a point of nothingness which is untouched by sin and by illusion." Compared with the false self, it is "a point of pure truth, a point or spark which belongs entirely to God and which is never at our disposal." It is nothing less than the emergence of the image of God in which we were created. It is our reflection of God's glory. In the same text Merton continues, "This little point of nothingness, and of *absolute poverty* is at the same time the pure glory of God in us. It is, so to speak, His name written in us" (*Guilty Bystander*, 142/158).

It is God's "I Am" dwelling in me and enabling me to say my "I am" in God. "It is keeping [myself] in the presence of God and of reality, rooted in [my] own inner truth" (*Climate of Monastic Prayer*, 34). It is that inner truth[2] that is God's gift. It is my identity that is God's image. It is my center that is the "place" where I am I and God is God. It is my nothingness experiencing the touch of God's transcendence. It is my being grounded in God, my personhood realized in God. It is only this true self that can be free, for it is unshadowed by the illusions that describe the false self.

To be fully free I also must be liberated from the illusions that mark my relationships with my fellow human beings and with the rest of God's creation. When I find the center of my own being and meet God there, I realize that the Source and Ground of my own being is at the same time the Source and Ground of everything. I am yanked out of the false dualism that my illusions projected onto the world and find myself able to see all of God's creation in unity and communion rather than in isolation,

separateness, and competition. I come to know that I must love my neighbor as myself, not simply because God commands it, but because my inner truth demands it. For my neighbor is no longer "the other," but in a true sense she or he is my self, for we all find our identity in God.

The road to true freedom, then, is strewn with many false idols: the false god, the false self, the false image of God's creatures. I become free only when I have unmasked the illusions that falsify my vision of what is. I become free when I see God, my self, and my fellow creatures as they truly are. It is not enough, however, to be told that I must be delivered from illusions, not enough even to identify what these illusions are: to become free I must experience that deliverance in my own life.

Responding to my inner truth means saying yes to God and to my own identity realized in God. It also means saying no to all that is illusory, false, and less than human. It should be clear that freedom for Merton is "freedom of spontaneity," not "freedom of contrariety." The first means the freedom to choose the good; the second, the freedom to choose between contrary realities — for example, between good and evil. Merton writes, "Freedom of choice is not, itself, the perfection of liberty. But it helps us take our first step toward freedom or slavery, spontaneity or compulsion. The free man is the one whose choices have given him the power to stand on his own feet and determine his own life according to the higher light and spirit that are in him" (*New Man*, 178–79). Merton also says, "The mere ability to choose between good and evil is the lowest limit of freedom, and the only thing that is free about it is the fact that we can still choose good. To the extent that you are free to choose evil, you are not free. An evil choice destroys freedom.... Perfect spiritual freedom is a total inability to make any evil choice" (*Seeds of Contemplation*, 120; *New Seeds of Contemplation*, 199). WHS

SEE ALSO ALIENATION; GOD; ORIGINAL SIN; POINT VIERGE; SELF; SIN.

Notes

1. Cf. *New Seeds of Contemplation*, 10: "It is not we who choose to awaken ourselves, but God who chooses to awaken us."

2. Merton's use of the term "inner truth" seems to have meanings similar to the term "fundamental option," used today by ethicists to describe that accumulation of values and principles that persons have so appropriated and made their own that they become a center of unity in their lives from which their actions flow and their lives take direction.

"FREEDOM SONGS"

The "Freedom Songs" are eight poems in the "Negro spiritual" idiom that Thomas Merton composed in 1964 for Robert Lawrence Williams. A young African American tenor, Williams hoped to have the poems set to music and to sing them in various places throughout the country in order to raise scholarship money for seminarians in Africa. Four of the poems ("Sundown," "All the Way Down," "The Lord Is Good," "Earthquake")[1] eventually were put to music by Alexander Peloquin. Williams never got to sing them. The four were sung at the 1968 Liturgical Conference in Washington, D.C., by the Ebenezer Baptist choir and members of Peloquin's choir from Providence, Rhode Island. The songs were presented as a memorial tribute to Martin Luther King Jr., who had been assassinated on April 4, 1968.

The songs are based on scriptural themes: (1) "Sundown" (Micah 3); (2) "Evening Prayer" (Psalms 140–41); (3) "All the Way Down" (Jonah 2); (4) "I Have Called You" (Isa. 43:1); (5) "Be My Defender" (Psalm 4); (6) "The Lord Is Good" (Psalm 7); (7) "There Is a Way" (Isa. 35:8–10); (8) "Earthquake" (Isaiah 52).

The eight songs were published privately by Robert Lawrence Williams in a booklet of limited circulation entitled *Reflections on Love.* They are found in *The Collected Poems of Thomas Merton,* published by New Directions, in appendix 2[2] ("Uncollected Poems"). They are scattered throughout this appendix, but a note on page 668 directs the reader to the pages where they can be located.[3] WHS

Notes

1. They were published by G.I.A. Publications, Chicago, under the title *Four Freedom Songs.*
2. This is found only in the paperback edition of *Collected Poems,* not in the hardback.
3. For further information, see *Hidden Ground of Love,* 587–607. See also *Water of Life,* 73, 80, 136, 148, 158.

FROMM, ERICH

Erich Fromm (1900–1980) was born in Frankfurt, Germany. Trained in psychoanalysis at the University of Berlin, he came to the United States in 1934 to escape Nazi Germany. After teaching in several universities, in 1951 he became professor of psychoanalysis at the National University of Mexico at Cuernavaca, while retaining an office in New York City. Following the lead of Karl Marx, he saw alienation as the great problem in human society.

Erich Fromm

His strong opposition to modern warfare resonated with Thomas Merton's views on the subject. Merton wrote twelve (some quite lengthy) letters to him over a period of twelve years, from October 2, 1954, to October 13, 1966. The letters between them are a fine example of dialogue between two persons of very different background who were able to share with one another in the context of a growing friendship that left them free to speak to one another in genuine honesty. Merton's letters to Fromm are published in *The Hidden Ground of Love.* WHS

GANDHI ON NON-VIOLENCE:
A Selection from the Writings of Mahatma Gandhi

Edited, with an introduction, by Thomas Merton. New York: New Directions, 1965. 82 pp.

Thomas Merton wrote two articles on Mohandas Gandhi. One became part of Merton's *Seeds of Destruction* with the title "A Tribute to Gandhi." It also appeared as "The Gentle Revolutionary" in the December 1964 issue of *Ramparts*.[1] The other, published in the January 1965 issue of *Jubilee* under the title "Gandhi and the One-Eyed Giant," became the introduction to this book of selections from Gandhi's writings.

In the *Ramparts* article he indicates that his interest in Gandhi goes back to his school days at Oakham, where (in 1930 or 1931) he defended Gandhi's right to demand British withdrawal from India. This event from his boyhood he recalls in the *Ramparts* article.

Merton's twenty-page introduction to the Gandhi book is followed by five groupings of selections taken from Gandhi's *Non-Violence in Peace and War*: (1) "Principles of Non-Violence" (eleven pages), (2) "Non-Violence: True and False"(seven pages), (3) "The Spiritual Dimensions of Non-Violence" (eight

pages), (4) "The Political Scope of Non-Violence" (twelve pages), and (5) "The Purity of Non-Violence" (ten pages). The book has a three-page index.

In his introduction Merton shows how Gandhi initially was enamored with Western ways. But becoming acquainted with Western writers such as Tolstoy and Thoreau and (perhaps especially) reading the New Testament enabled him to rediscover his own tradition and in that tradition the importance of nonviolence in the human struggle to achieve freedom.

Gandhi had great admiration for the Christian gospel and for the person of Jesus Christ. Jesus embodies the ideal of nonviolence. "Jesus," Gandhi says, "was the most active resister known perhaps to history. This was non-violence *par excellence*" (*Gandhi on Non-Violence*, 40).

Gandhi saw the Indian notion of *ahimsa* as a fundamental principle in human life and action. The Sanskrit word *himsa* means "injury." *Ahimsa*, therefore, means "noninjury." *Ahimsa* is based on the realization of the unity of all reality. For this reason it is a very positive notion, calling us to love all, as we are one with all. But since the word seems to convey a negative meaning, Gandhi invented a new word to describe what he meant by nonviolence: *satyagraha*. The word has been variously translated: "firmness in the truth, persistence in the truth."

Merton suggests that it may be seen as a way of life "in which the *satyagrahi* is totally dedicated to the transformation of his own life, of his adversary, and of society by means of love" (35). It must be distinguished from the nonviolence of the weak, which simply submits to violence without resistance. To that kind of nonviolence Gandhi would prefer an honest resort to violence, for it is a fundamental principle of Gandhi's thought that violence always must be resisted. But to resist it violently simply brings more violence into the world. Hence, Gandhi's choice for combating evil always is nonviolence.

This is a spiritual principle, not merely a political stance. The attitude that nonviolence is good only if and when it works is a betrayal of the very meaning of nonviolence. The nonviolent person refuses to accept the attitude that sees an irreversible character of evil, an attitude that would have us believe that change is impossible. Those who are nonviolent seek to find the goodness in the adversary, a goodness that is there but often lies hidden. This means not only expressing love, but also looking for love in the adversary.

The measurement of nonviolence is not the degree of success that results, but the completeness of one's commitment that refuses to waver. Such a commitment "demands nothing short of the ability to face death with complete fearlessness and to suffer without retaliation" (43). For nonviolence seeks to liberate not only the oppressed but also the oppressor. "The only way truly to 'overcome' an enemy is to help him become other than an enemy. This is the kind of wisdom we find in Gandhi. It is the wisdom of the Gospels" (15).

There is a universality about nonviolence. We do not pick and choose the situations in which we will be nonviolent. It would be a caricature of nonviolence, for example, to be violent in interpersonal or family relationships but nonviolent regarding certain issues, such as war or capital punishment. Gandhi's nonviolence is "a creed which embraces all of life in a consistent and logical network of obligations" (51). WHS

SEE ALSO *PASSION FOR PEACE*; *SEEDS OF DESTRUCTION*.

Notes

1. This article also appeared in *The Nonviolent Alternative* and in *Passion for Peace*.

GEOGRAPHY OF LOGRAIRE, THE

New York: New Directions, 1969. 153 pp.

The last of Thomas Merton's books of poetry, published the year after his death, is a single unified work, epic in scope, alternating sections of verse and prose, which Merton himself describes in his introductory author's note as "this wide-angle mosaic of poems and dreams [in which] I have without scruple mixed what is my own experience with what is almost everybody else's." Its theme is both the global unity of humanity and the ways in which that unity has been violated, particularly by Western assertions of cultural and moral superiority. While Merton claims that the individual poems that make up the work "incidentally are never explicitly theological or even metaphysical" and that his methodology is "on the whole that of an urbane structuralism," the spiritual implications of the work are never far beneath the surface, and the objective detachment implied by the phrase "urbane structuralism" in actuality masks a focused if largely unexpressed outrage at the dehumanization described repeatedly throughout the work.

According to Merton's friend Sr. Therese Lentfoehr in her contribution to the lengthy "Notes on Sources" appended to the work, Merton invented the name "Lograire" based on "Des Loges," the alternate surname of the medieval French poet (and sometime outlaw) François Villon. The French word *loge* means "rustic hut or cabin," and thus suggests Merton's own hermitage, reinforcing the connection with Villon to present the poet as both an outsider able to recognize the flaws of his society and yet as someone who is himself implicated in certain ways in these flaws (a "guilty bystander" figure). Since much of the poem deals with the power of language both to reveal and to conceal or distort reality, there may also be a connection to the Greek *logos*, meaning "word" (and thus also to Christ as Logos, the Word of

God). There may also be an allusion to Logres, the name associated with the Arthurian realm (and therefore with the theme of quest) and with the story of the wasteland and the fisher king (and so reflective of connections between wounded humanity and devastated land).

The work is divided into four cantos based on the four compass points, preceded by a prologue. Each of the cantos is subdivided into individual poems or sections, many of which depend closely on the historical and anthropological sources that Merton consulted. Because of the relative unfamiliarity of the incidents and movements described, the frequent lack of explicit comment on the material that is quoted and rearranged, and the obscurity of some of the more personal sections, this book probably makes greater demands on the reader than any other of Merton's works, whether poetry or prose.

The prologue, entitled "The Endless Inscription" (107 ll.; 18 secs.), provides an overall orientation to the work. It introduces the theme of voyage and search as the poet seeks a place of peace and refuge first in Wales (home of Merton's ancestors) but realizes that even here there is no unfallen world, unmarked by the division between Cain and Abel; there is no hope in the illusion of an idealized past but only in an honest recognition and acceptance of the unvarnished truth of past and present, which brings the poet back to his actual location in Kentucky with its legacy of enslavement and civil strife (the twin themes of racism and violence that were so central to Merton's prose writings on social issues in the last years of his life and that will be central throughout the poem). But it also discloses a belief in the salvific power of suffering love, of "Lamb Son's Blood" (l. 76) made one with the blood of Abel and all history's victims and promising the ultimate victory of *shalom*, of reconciliation and community of all humanity: "Sign Redeemer's 'R' / Buys Mars his last war" (ll. 106–7). While these words of hope that conclude the prologue are infrequently echoed in the body of the poem, they remain the implicit frame into which the diverse and disturbing materials of the four cantos are placed.

The opening "South" canto consists of

eleven sections (thirty pages). The first four focus on the southern United States, the next three on Africa, and the final four on Mexico. The opening poem, "Will a narrow lane save Cain?" (62 ll.), applies the Cain and Abel imagery of the prologue to the racial oppression of the American South, and reflects the belief of Martin Luther King and his movement of nonviolent liberation that ultimately this question can be answered affirmatively, that even the oppressor can be redeemed, that "One narrow lane saved Lamb's friend Paschal Cain" (l. 62). This optimism will be severely tested but never repudiated throughout the rest of the poem. The second section, "Roar of red wood racer eats field" (eighteen prose sections), describes the American obsession with speed and with winning and relates it to military exploits, represented by Fort Knox; it concludes with the enigmatic line "A ghost dancer walks in a black hat through gates of horn" (i.e., the path of true dreams), which foreshadows the final sections of the poem, which focus on the Native American ghost dance movement. "III. Hymns of Lograire" (25 ll.) parodies hymns and popular songs to satirize the comforts of popular religion, which is seen as "Wishing everybody well" (l. 7) but failing to challenge militarism, indicated by the sign on the church dome, "Don't tread on the marine" (l. 11). The last of the American sections of "South," entitled "Miami You Are about to Be Surprised" (49 ll.), presents the city as a symbol of materialism, consumerism, and the pursuit of pleasure and suggests it will be inundated by the sea, an intimation of mortality that also may be a suggestion of possible rebirth "out of the stream / Of cold function" (ll. 40–41).

From the southernmost point in the United States the poem travels to southern Africa. "V. Two Moralities" juxtaposes a "Thonga Lament" (25 ll.), in which worshipers seek to make contact with their ancestors through sacrifice, with the Hottentot prose tale "Hare's Message," in which the hare fails to communicate the moon's message of rebirth and so is rejected as food: "They do not eat Hare the runner for the runner is death." The two following sections reflect the negative effect of Western culture, specifically Western Christianity, on indigenous African spirituality. "VI. A Clever Stratagem: or, How to Handle Mystics" is a first-person prose account of a missionary who deals with reports of supernatural experiences among his congregation by administering "a stiff dose" of medicinal salts, at which point the visions ended and "a sweetly reasonable piety that disturbed no one" ensued. "Notes for a New Liturgy" (47 ll.) describes a native African pastor who adopts all the worst characteristics of white churchmen and merges them with questionable indigenous practices to create a sham ritual that promotes only his own self-glorification.

This African "liturgy" is then juxtaposed with the first of the Latin American sections, "Ce Xochitl: The Sign of Flowers" (51 ll.; 7 secs.), in which the invading Spaniards condemn the Native American rituals, centered on gathering flowers to make garlands for the gods, as "the services which their demons commanded them" (l. 51). In "The Ladies of Tlatilco" (103 ll.; 14 secs.) the beauty and delicacy of early Mexican art is compared to the vulgarity of contemporary American advertisements, and the straightforward nakedness of "The ladies of Tlatilco" who "Wore nothing but turbans" (ll. 23–24) with the seductive poses of models, commodifying the body to sell products. The final two poems of "South," "Chilam Balam" (69 ll.; 10 secs.) and "Dzules" (129 ll.; 27 secs.), describe the process of degradation of the native cultures from the perspective of the Indian prophet Chilam Balam. In the first poem the oppression of one indigenous group by another is recounted, while in the second the conquest of the Spaniards is related. At the conclusion of the latter poem there intrudes the unmistakable voice of a policeman on a bullhorn giving orders to protesters in the contemporary American South, returning the poem to the present and reflecting the belief that the historic struggle between oppressors and oppressed still continues.

The second canto, "North" (thirty-eight pages), has its own prologue followed by four sections. The prologue, entitled "Why I Have a Wet Footprint on Top of My Mind" (33 ll.), is about memory, the journey back in time that is both intensely personal and a link to universal experience; it concludes with the programmatic declaration: "*Geography.* / *I am all (here)* / *There!*" (ll. 31–33). This short poem is a prelude particularly to section 1 of "North," "Queens Tunnel" (fifty prose paragraphs), the longest single section of the poem, which Merton himself describes as a "long meditation on Eros and Thanatos, centering in the New York City Borough of Queens" written in a "surrealistic" style. Its most prominent symbols are the "funnel house" (probably a Joycean conjunction of amusement park fun house, funeral home, and Dante's Inferno), which is both the mortuary in which Merton's mother and grandparents were cremated and an Orwellian observation post watching every movement of those on the streets below; and the tunnel itself, another symbol of the descent into death but one that may allow for a reemergence into light at its end. (Christ appears in Harlem at the conclusion of this section, though his acceptance there is problematic because of his appropriation by white society.)

Section 2, "There is a grain of sand in Lambeth which Satan cannot find" (26 ll.), is also autobiographical, ringing changes on the opening line (quoted from Blake's *Jerusalem*) to reflect on early, unsatisfactory experiences of sexuality and of school, and concluding somewhat ambivalently by repeating the opening line but following it with the less confident modification, "While deep in the heart's question a shameless light / Returns no answer" (ll. 25–26).

Section 3, "The Ranters and Their Pleads" (ten subsections of mixed prose and verse), echoes the theme of religious persecution from the previous canto by examining the treatment of the antinomian sect of Ranters by orthodox Puritans in mid-seventeenth-century England, in which the offending heretics are burned through the tongue for saying such things as that all people will be saved, that God is the life and being of all things, "that there is neither heaven nor hell / But what is in man" (no. 10, ll. 1–2) (as well as, at least according to their accusers, that someone who is moved to commit adultery or murder should do it [no. 3]).

Section 4 of this canto moves further north: "Kane Relief Expedition" (nine subsections of mixed verse and prose) reworks the journal entries of a member of an arctic exploration team sent in search of an earlier expedition led by Dr. Elisha Kane (whose name may have been particularly attractive to Merton as a homonym of "Cain"). It begins with imagery of austere and awe-inspiring beauty in the arctic icescape, but moves toward expressions of sexual desire for Eskimo women, narration of senseless slaughter of tame birds, and eventual destruction of the ship by an iceberg (though the parenthetical final line notes that both the relief expedition and Kane's own group eventually "reached safety").

The "East" canto (thirty-six pages) includes ten sections, preceded by a brief anecdote of a slave who beheaded himself for love of the sultan, an emblem of self-destructive behavior on behalf of another person considered superior that will be echoed in subsequent sections. It is taken from the record of the fourteenth-century Muslim traveler Ibn Battuta, which is also the source of the first section, entitled "East with Ibn Battuta" (seven subsections, six in verse). This geographical survey of the principal sites of medieval Islam reveals a preoccupation with materialistic display, harsh persecution of deviants, and ostentatious religiosity (levitation!) similar to that displayed by Western Christians in the previous two cantos, until the disillusioned Ibn Battuta (after having been robbed of his slave girls by the king of Sumatra) retires to the Maldive Islands, where the natives are all Muslims who "Use sandalwood and do not fight / Their armor is prayer" (no. 7; ll. 17–18).

This is followed by the similarly titled "East with Malinowski" (46 ll.), in which the early twentieth-century anthropologist Bronislaw Malinowski describes his sense of disorientation (and implied cultural superiority) on his first arrival in Melanesia. Malinowski's reminiscences continue to be interspersed throughout the next section, "Cargo Songs" (twenty-one subsections of mixed verse and prose), including his climactic comment when the natives refuse to stand still for a photograph: "My feelings toward them: exterminate the brutes" (no. 19). This section begins a sequence of eight sections (the rest of the "East" canto)

that focus on the Cargo movements of New Guinea and the South Sea islands, which Merton himself describes (in a letter quoted in the notes) as "a messianic or apocalyptic cult movement which confronts a crisis of cultural change by certain magic and religious ways of acting out what seems to be the situation and trying to get with it, controlling the course of change in one's own favor." In particular, it reflects the desire of indigenous peoples to receive "cargo" — material goods such as whites have in abundance — from a divine source. It represents for Merton a profoundly ambiguous and very revealing development, reflecting both the debasement of authentic religiosity through contact with materialism, recognized to be the "true faith" of the West, and an authentic assertion on the part of "primitive" peoples of their essential dignity and equality with the European colonizers. "Cargo Songs" begins with the violent act of the English governor in Papua physically dethroning the "Paramount Chief" (no. 1, l. 3) and moves toward the withdrawal of the natives from contact with whites while awaiting the arrival of cargo prophesied by their visionaries. "Place Names" (41 ll.) is a series of laconic records of Europeans renaming Polynesian sites after themselves, their patrons, and their ships. "Tibud Maclay" (50 ll.) describes imperialist rivalries as Maclay (one of the place namers of the previous section), "A culture hero / From the land of figureheads" (ll. 11–12), warns the islanders against the arrival of "very bad" whites (l. 25), especially *"Djamans"* (Germans), only to have "A decent *Djaman*" (l. 36) claim to be Maclay's brother and so win acceptance, paving the way for "all the others" (l. 43) who "went into business / Taking over the country" (ll. 46–47). In the sixth section, "Sewende" (three subsections, two in verse), the islanders look with hope to the far country of "Sewende" (i.e., "Seven Day") for gifts of cargo; in the following section their prophet Kaum prays from jail for divine help from "Father Consel," noting that the Kanakas have "Nothing at all because Whiteman / Steals everything and you are so sorry / O Father Consel / Now you send / Something" (no. 3; ll. 12–16), only to have the poem end with the ironically echoed reply "(So sorry!)" (l. 17). "Cargo Catechism" (nine prose sections) is a reworking of the Genesis story of the fall and Noah, in which the offending Ham, who saw his father, Noah, naked, is identified with New Guineans who are deprived of cargo, but the Bible itself is criticized as incomplete because "All the instructions about Cargo torn out" (no. 5). "John the Volcano" (nine subsections of mixed prose and verse) describes one of the most influential Cargo cults, the John Frum movement, of which the most notable act of resistance was to tear the price tags off items for sale in the white man's store in preparation for the arrival of John Frum and his free cargo. In "Dialog with Mister Clapcott" (26 ll.) one of the cults turns violent and murders a planter, who had "messed with all our women" (l. 2), in an effort to usher in an eschatological era when the dead will rise, blacks will become white, and cargo finally will arrive. Finally, in "And a Few More Cargo Songs" (five subsections, four in verse) the waning of the movement is recorded with the capture of John Frum (though true believers denied it was the real John Frum who "Had gone to America / To confer with Rusefel [Roosevelt] / To get a Black American Army" [no. 3, ll. 4–6]), and devotees are left pleading for just enough paper and tobacco to roll a cigarette, but are willing to "Trade me a houseful of rifles / For a new white skin /.../ For Whiteman good times" (no. 5, ll. 11–12, 15), an acknowledgement of total cultural subjugation.

The final canto, "West" (nineteen pages), is the shortest of the four, with only four sections. The first, "Day Six O'Hare Telephane" (220 ll.) is a long, ironic meditation on the Chicago airport and a subsequent flight to the west coast, in which the human pilgrimage is seen as trivialized, depersonalized, and secularized (Mt. Rushmore as the American shrine), but the frenetic business of the airport and the superficial friendliness of the flight attendants are punctuated by lines from a Hindu sutra that counsel authentic self-surrender, and the speaker has a vision of possible human solidarity prompted by the sight of wheat fields far below: "hosts of (soon) Christ-Wheat / Self-bread which could also be / Squares of Buddha-Rice / Or Square Maize about those

pyramids" (ll. 115–18). This vision of shared communion leads to identification with all the victims of injustice past and present: "I am one same burned Indian / Purple of my rivers is the same shed blood / All is flooded / All is my Vietnam charred" (ll. 122–25). This is, literally and figuratively, the high point of the entire poem, but it is not the conclusion; the subsequent sections make clear just what such identification entails. "At This Precise Moment of History" (seventeen sections of mixed verse and prose) uses the congressional candidacy of former child star Shirley Temple ("Goody-two-shoes" [no. 1, l. 2]), who is described first as a child sitting on President Roosevelt's knee and then, by association, as a kind of ventriloquist's dummy mouthing dangerous platitudes about the Vietnam conflict first voiced by then-Governor Ronald Reagan, to epitomize the sorry state of political discourse at a moment of supreme crisis.

From this contemporary situation the final two sections of the poem look back to the last major struggle of Native Americans for spiritual and cultural independence, the Ghost Dance movement of the late nineteenth century. "Ghost Dance: Prologue" is a short summary from 1890, after the movement had waned, by the Sioux leader American Horse, of the consistent pattern of deceptions and broken promises by the American government toward the Indians. It is followed by "Ghost Dance" (thirty-one prose subsections), later reminiscences by Native American participants in the Ghost Dance religion, which began in the 1870s when visionaries predicted a return of the dead as a result of the ecstatic dancing of their descendants. The ensuing result was first described in terms of genuine equality: "No distinction would exist any more between races" (no. 7). Later manifestations predicted the disappearance of the whites and the death of all mixed-breed children, but eventually the motives for the dance became corrupted by desire for gain: "Annie Peterson said Coquille Charlie carried the dance around only to make money.... Nobody had any visions at Charlie's dance" (no. 30). The final words of this section, and thus of the poem as a whole, express the disillusion of a failed movement, and once again the triumph of the dominant culture: "After a while the dreaming stopped and the Dream Dance turned into a Feather Dance. It was just a fun dance. It was mostly a white man's show" (no. 31). Thus, the poem seems to end on a pessimistic note, an awakening from a vision of unity, justice, and equality to the harsh reality of alienation and oppression. While in one sense this is certainly accurate, as Merton refuses to conceal the victims' sufferings or palliate the oppressors' offenses, or to indulge in a facile fantasy of human progress, part of the point of the poem's structure is that it is not linear, that no point on this moral compass is uniquely privileged, that it is up to the reader to choose not how the story is to end, but how it is to continue beyond the confines of the poem: whether with "a white man's show" or with a sharing of "Christ-wheat, Buddha rice, Square Maize"; whether with "the dreaming stopped" or with "A ghost dancer [who] walks in a black hat through gates of horn"; whether with Cain continuing to murder Abel or with the choice of the narrow gate that leads to life, the "One narrow lane [that] saved Lamb's friend Paschal Cain."

Merton described *The Geography of Lograire* in his author's note as "a purely tentative first draft of a longer work in progress, . . . only a beginning of patterns, the first opening up of the dream." One certainly could envision additional sections added to each of the cantos, particularly the last ("West"), which is considerably shorter than the others. There is indeed a sense in which a mosaic poem of this sort can never be regarded as definitively finished, since it is intended to encompass the entire world in space and time, to "include everything," as Merton once said of his journals. But it is equally evident that the essential pattern of the poem is present in the work as it actually exists, that the central insight "that this world is at once his and everybody's" has been articulated, and that the work, if not "finished," is nevertheless an integral, unified whole. POC

GERDY, ROBERT

A younger contemporary of Thomas Merton at Columbia, Robert Gerdy (1919–65) is de-

scribed in *The Seven Storey Mountain* as "a very smart sophomore with the face of a child and a lot of curly hair on top of it, who took life seriously" (183). It was he who recommended that Merton take a course in scholastic philosophy from Dan Walsh (*Seven Storey Mountain*, 218). He was one of the large group of friends who spent the summer of 1940 at the Olean, New York, cottage owned by Bob Lax's brother-in-law, and the memorable hitchhiking trip of that summer from Olean to Cleveland (see *Run to the Mountain*, 313) was to visit one of Gerdy's relatives. Though Jewish, like many of Merton's Columbia friends, he was a witness at Merton's baptism and became a Catholic himself in September 1943, while in the army. For the last thirteen years of his life he worked as a highly respected editor at the *New Yorker*. He suffered a fatal heart attack on a Manhattan sidewalk a short distance from his home on December 23, 1965 (see *Learning to Love*, 6), the first among Merton's college friends to die. POC

GETHSEMANI, ABBEY OF

This Cistercian monastery near Bardstown, Kentucky, was founded in 1848 by Cistercian (Trappist) monks coming from France under the leadership of Fr. Eutropius Proust. At the time of its centenary, Thomas Merton would be called upon to write the story of Gethsemani (*Gethsemani Magnificat*). Merton first heard of Gethsemani from his teacher and friend Daniel Walsh. In the spring of 1941, during Holy Week, Merton made a retreat there that changed his life. On December 9 of that year he took the train for Kentucky and asked to be accepted into the order. He lived the last half his life (twenty-seven years) as a monk of Gethsemani. Struggling at times to seek greater solitude elsewhere, he obeyed his superiors when they told him that his vocation was at Gethsemani. In 1965 he became a hermit on the grounds of the abbey. Following his accidental death in Bangkok, his remains were returned to Gethsemani and rest in the abbey cemetery adjoining the monastery church. WHS

Drawing of Gethsemani by Thomas Merton

GETHSEMANI: A *Life of Praise*

Trappist, Ky.: Abbey of Gethsemani, 1966.
64 pp. (unnumbered); oversized (11 x 8 in.).

This volume is a book of photos of the Abbey of Our Lady of Gethsemani, with four sections of text by Thomas Merton: (1) "Monastic Life" (three pages), (2) "The Spirit of Gethsemani" (three pages), (3) "Monastic Work" (two pages), and (4) "The Life of Praise" (two pages). There are multiple photographs by Art Filmore, Brother Ephrem, and Brother Pius. These black-and-white photographs show the buildings and grounds at the monastery, as well as photos of monks at work, at prayer, and at study. The book was intended as a replacement for Shirley Burden's book *God Is My Life*.

In his discussion of the monastic life Merton makes clear that a contemplative monastery exists for "no other purpose than the praise and love of God." It does not exist to carry out some task, such as teaching or working in parishes. He traces the monastic life back to the early fourth-century Christians who withdrew into the deserts of Egypt and Syria to live alone with God. Sometimes they formed communities and offered hospitality to the rare visitor. Their prayer and sacrifice and "being alone" they saw as the best way to face the deepest realities of life and give themselves entirely to God.

Later monasticism developed into institutions of various forms. One form emphasized pure solitude, and practitioners were known as hermits. Others, called cenobites, lived a "common life" marked by asceticism, liturgy, and work. Such a community formed a family of disciples gathered around an abbot, or spiritual father. The abbot was not simply the juridical head of the community; he represented Christ and was expected to teach the other monks the way of holiness. The community is committed to self-support through manual labor and to a simple life of poverty and prayer, silence and separation from the world.

In the Middle Ages some monasteries became involved in the social, political, and cultural history of the time and often became learning centers for bishops, scholars, and religious leaders. Other monasteries rejected such a role as interfering with the solitude and silence of the monastic life.

Merton distinguished four kinds of monasteries existing in the Western world today: (1) semieremitic communities; (2) cenobitic communities emphasizing silence, prayer, and manual labor; (3) communities dedicated, within the context of monastic solitude, to liturgical prayer and the intellectual life; and (4) communities devoting themselves almost entirely to pastoral care and educational work.

In the section on "The Spirit of Gethsemani" Merton gives a brief history of his own monastery. Founded in 1848 from the Abbey of Melleray in France, it struggled for survival in its earliest years. He discusses the role of three of Gethsemani's abbots: Dom Edmond Obrecht (1898–1935), Dom Frederic Dunne (1935–48), and Dom James Fox (1948–67). Significant changes in the monastic life took place in the wake of the Second Vatican Council.

St. Benedict insists in his Rule that monks live by the labor of their hands. "Hard work in the fields, gardens, and shops of the monastery, or in the necessary maintenance of the monastery itself, keeps the monks' prayer-life in touch with everyday reality." The monk also is obliged to study, reading, and reflection in order to seek a deeper understanding of the mysteries of faith and of the monastic life itself. Thus, manual labor and intellectual work take up the time that the monk does not spend in choral or secret prayer.

Today the monastery is highly mechanized, but still there are many jobs: Gethsemani Farms, dairy and cattle barns, carpentry, shoemaking, and so forth. There is also a guesthouse

to maintain. Many of the photos illustrate these various tasks at the monastery.

The whole life of the monastery is dedicated to love and praise of God. Central to this dedication is liturgy, the common worship of the community. The night vigils begin at 2:30 in the morning, and the whole day is consecrated by times set apart for the psalms and hymns in praise of God. Besides this communal prayer, silent secret prayer and meditation occupy an important place in the life of the monk. WHS

GETHSEMANI MAGNIFICAT:
Centenary of Gethsemani Abbey
Trappist, Ky.: Abbey of Gethsemani, 1949. 72 pp. (unnumbered); 200 photos.

This centenary book of seventy-two (unnumbered) pages with two hundred photos is dedicated to the Blessed Virgin Mary. Following letters of blessing and congratulation from Pope Pius XII, Cardinal Denis Dougherty, Archbishop Amleto Giovanni Cicognani (apostolic delegate), Archbishop John A. Floersh of Louisville, and Dom Dominique Nogues, O.C.S.O. (abbot general of the order), there is an introduction by Dom James Fox, O.C.S.O., who at the time was abbot of Gethsemani. The rest of the book presents a detailed history of Gethsemani and two of its daughter houses, as well as an understanding of the meaning of the Cistercian life and vocation. Both the history and the life of the monastery are amply illustrated with helpful photos.

The History of Gethsemani (14 pages)

The history begins in France at the Abbey of Melleray, founded in 1134. Seven centuries later the French Revolution brought an end to the life of religious orders in France. In 1803 a group of Trappists, fleeing France, came to America and eventually to Kentucky. Sadly, their monastery was unable to survive. Meanwhile, the Abbey of Melleray was refounded in 1817. The revolution of 1848, again disrupting religious life in France, occasioned another attempt to found a monastery in the United States. A group of monks led by Fr. Eutropius Proust left Le Havre in November 1848, landed at New Orleans, and traveled by boat to Louisville, where they were welcomed by Bishop Flaget on December 21, 1848. From Louisville they journeyed to their final destination a few miles southwest of Bardstown, Kentucky, where they would build their monastery.

The history of the monastery they founded is told in five sections, one for each of the first five abbots.

1. Dom Eutropius Proust (1848–59): the first abbot of any order or congregation in the New World. Under him the construction of the monastic buildings was begun, at times Trappist priests working side by side with black slaves loaned by a local planter.

2. Dom Benedict Berger (1859–89): abbot for thirty difficult years, when there were few postulants and superiors in Europe were not sure that Americans could live the rigors of Cistercian life. During his administration the new buildings were completed and the abbatial church dedicated (November 15, 1866). The monks built a boys' school that survived but a short time.

3. Dom Edward Chaix-Bourbon (1890–98): much admired for his piety and humane direction, but ill health and the weight of cares and the anxieties of his office led to his decision to return to France.

4. Dom Edmond Obrecht (1898–1935): a clear-sighted, energetic leader with a wealth of experience and resourcefulness, he not only oversaw the growth of Gethsemani but also visited monasteries in remote parts of the world. Despite his many travels, he was never more delighted than when he was at home with his monks at Gethsemani.

5. Dom Frederic Dunne (1935–48) the first native-born American to be abbot. A kindly and gentle abbot, he steadfastly held himself and his monks to the strictest observance of the Rule. He is said to have remarked, "Where the Rule is well kept, there will never be any lack of vocations." He died on the train on August 4, 1948, on his way to visit the daughterhouse of Gethsemani in Conyers, Georgia, the monastery of Our Lady of the Holy Ghost. Dom James Fox, who had been abbot at Conyers, was elected to succeed him.

The first daughterhouse of Gethsemani at Conyers was founded in 1944. In 1947 a second foundation was made at Huntsville, Utah. By 1948 there were some sixty monks at Conyers, more than forty in Utah, and a large community of 160 at Gethsemani. It would be Dom James Fox who would modernize and mechanize the monastery, but that belonged to the future.

Background of the Gethsemani Story
(6 pages)

The Cistercian-Trappist life traces itself back to St. Benedict (d. 547) and the Rule he drew up. Benedict established a community in which charity was to govern all hearts. All things were to be held in common (Rule, ch. 33). All were to be one in Christ (Rule, ch. 2). The dignity of work and intellectual labor was stressed, but above all was the liturgical praise of God that framed the horarium of the monks. At the beginning of the ninth century Charlemagne imposed the Rule of St. Benedict on all monasteries in the empire.

In the tenth and eleventh centuries Cluny and its monasteries became known for their concentration on communal prayer and elaborate liturgies that made such demands on their time that there was little left for manual labor (feudal serfs were employed in the service of the more than a thousand Cluniac monasteries).

In 1098 the Cistercian reform was begun by St. Robert of Molesme and continued by St. Alberic and St. Stephen Harding. Their aim was a restoration of the primitive simplicity of monastic and Christian life. The liturgy was considerably simplified. The strict fasts prescribed by the Rule were restored, and the monks labored with their own hands to support themselves. At first, life was difficult for them. In 1112 new life was infused into the struggling monastery when a group of thirty-one postulants arrived, among them St. Bernard, who became a leading light in the development of the Cistercian way of life.

As time went on, the White Monks (as the Cistercians were called because they wore a white habit) came to control huge tracts of land and became an important economic factor in European life. The eventual result was a worldly spirit that corrupted the purity of their monastic and contemplative life.

Once again there was a reform in the Benedictine world. In 1664 Armand-Jean de Rancé, a young French nobleman, godson of Cardinal Richelieu, worldly minded and marked for a brilliant ecclesiastical career, experienced a deep conversion and entered one of the monasteries under his, de Rancé's, control. As abbot of La Trappe, he took the habit of the monks of the Strict Observance and gave meaning and vitality to the reform. His study of the desert fathers moved him to believe that the best way to train his monks was to subject them to stinging humiliations and to encourage them to practice many works of severe penance not prescribed by the Rule. It was the spirit of La Trappe that was brought to America at Gethsemani. Called Trappists, they are more correctly named Cistercians of the Strict Observance.

The Cistercian Vocation

From two o'clock in the morning until seven or eight o'clock in the evening the monk devotes himself to prayer, penance, work, and study for the glory of God. Besides the "night office" of psalms and readings, there is the daily celebration of Eucharist, as well as the "day hours," in which the monk stops work or study to stand in choir for the canonical office. The most solemn of these is vespers, which closes the exterior activity of the monastery. Shortly after sundown, compline is the final communal prayer, concluding with the beautiful hymn "Salve Regina." The meaning of this life of prayer may be summed up in one thought: continual praise and adoration of God. The Trappist-Cistercian lives for God alone, immersed in the light of God's presence. The monk assumes the task of praising God and interceding for the sins of the world.

During the day there are also times for meditation, reading, and study, as well as several hours of manual labor. St. Benedict called for monks to live by the labor of their own hands. Labor for the monk is more than a penance; it refreshes the soul and enables it to return to prayer purified and invigorated. The monks are also dedicated to study. The purpose of the study is to deepen the monk's knowledge of God and of the divine ways in order that he may achieve communion with God in contemplative prayer. The monk's reading and study include Scripture, theology, and the fathers and doctors of the church, as well as their own Cistercian fathers, especially the writings of St. Bernard. There are full courses in philosophy, theology, and Gregorian chant. There is also Cistercian literature on the spiritual life by contemporary Cistercian authors, among whom may be mentioned Frs. Ailbe Luddy, Eugene Boylan, Raymond Flanagan, and Thomas Merton.

One of the characteristic statutes of the Cistercian order is that monasteries are to be built in remote and solitary places, not in towns and villages. "The traditional Cistercian monastery is one that lies hidden in a wooded valley, far off the beaten track, where the songs of birds mingle with the sounds of simple labor, and the hours of the day are counted by bells from the abbey tower and chanting in the abbey choir.... The Cistercian soon acquires such a familiarity with the earth and its creatures that he feels that sense of kinship and brotherhood with all living things, which was the glory of St. Francis of Assisi.... A soul that matures in humble soil in fields, barns and woods soon develops a beautiful and mellow spirituality.... The ancient legends of the Order tell us that Jesus sometimes appeared and joined in the work of the monks, taking the reins from their hands, or guiding the plow in their stead" (*Gethsemani Magnificat*, from the section "The Monk and Nature"). WHS

GIBNEY, ROBERT

One of Thomas Merton's closest friends at Columbia, Bob Gibney is described in *The Seven Storey Mountain* as having "an attitude that would be commonly called impious" but that "covered a sense of deep metaphysical dismay," and as "always holding out for some kind of a 'sign,' some kind of a sensible and tangible interior jolt from God, to get him started" (183, 184). Like Merton, he filed for noncombatant conscientious objector status at the outset of World War II, but unlike Merton he was drafted. After the war he married Nancy Flagg, a Smith graduate from Boston who was part of the circle of Merton's friends, and the couple moved to the Virgin Islands. Though Merton was not directly in touch with Gibney after entering the monastery, their mutual friend Bob Lax kept Merton informed about the Gibneys (see *When Prophecy*, 108, 132, 153, 189). POC

GIROUX, ROBERT

Robert Giroux was born in New Jersey on April 8, 1914. He attended Regis High School in New York City and went on to Columbia College. One of his schoolmates there was Thomas Merton. The two of them worked on the college publications: Giroux on the literary publication, the *Columbia Review*, and Merton, predictably, on the humor magazine, *Jester*. In 1939 Giroux became a junior editor at Harcourt, Brace. After Giroux had rejected several novels of Merton that, he said, went nowhere, Naomi Burton sent him the manuscript of *The Seven Storey Mountain*. He felt that it had possibilities and recommended that it be published. As is now well known, the book had phenomenal success and established Merton as a writer of importance. Giroux did some judicious editing that in no small measure contributed to the book's popularity. In the copy of *The Seven Storey Mountain* that Merton autographed for Giroux, he wrote, "+ for Bob Giroux. We didn't see this coming, twelve years ago when you printed that little one page sketch about an auto accident in the *Columbia Review!* But anyway — thanks for a fine job of editing and 'pushing.' God bless you. In Corde Jesu, Fr. Louis Merton, O.C.R."

Merton was not the only author of note for whom Giroux was editor. He worked with such masters as T. S. Eliot, Carl Sandburg, Edmund Wilson, Flannery O'Connor, and numerous others. He moved from Harcourt, Brace to Farrar, Straus, and in 1964 he became a full partner in the firm still known as Farrar, Straus and Giroux. Roger W. Straus Jr., who founded the firm, once said of him, "He is a great editor, probably the best in the United States."

Following the success of *The Seven Storey Mountain*, Giroux edited and published a number of Merton's books — *The Sign of Jonas, Thoughts in Solitude*, and *Disputed Questions* among them.

Robert Giroux, photograph by Arthur Wang

In 1967 Merton had established the Merton Legacy Trust to administer his estate and take charge of his publications, past and future. As trustees he chose James Laughlin of New Directions, Naomi Burton Stone, who had been his literary agent, and Tommie O'Callaghan (Mrs. Frank O'Callaghan), a longtime friend from Louisville. When Naomi Stone resigned as trustee, Robert Giroux was chosen to take her place. Since then, his has been an active involvement in the workings of the Trust. He continues his work at Farrar, Straus and Giroux, but in a more limited capacity. WHS

GLORY

In the Scriptures glory is the outward manifestation of divinity, as when the glory of God shines around the shepherds in the nativity story (Luke 2:9), or the glory of God is seen in the Word become flesh in the prologue to John's Gospel (John 1:14). According to Thomas Merton, "The glory of God is the effulgence of His own presence manifested in mystery" (*Seasons of Celebration*, 10).

The creation itself is a revelation of the divine glory, as in the opening verse of Psalm 19: "The heavens declare the glory of God, and the firmament proclaims the work of his hands" (see *Bread in the Wilderness*, 56). Merton identifies the glory of God present in creation as the freedom with which creatures are allowed to manifest God by being themselves. "God's glory is God in them without possessing them. God in them without touching them. God in them without being touched by them. God giving them everything and retaining His own infinite separation. God being their Father without being related to them. They are related to Him, but never come near Him Who is within them. God's glory and God's shyness are one. His glory is to give them everything and to be in the midst of them as unknown" (*Entering the Silence*, 475). Thus, he identifies God's glory as an immanence that does not compromise the divine transcendence, that both reveals and conceals God. He continues, "God never seeks glory except by *giving glory*" (475); that is, God, precisely by the divine life and love with creatures, makes Godself visible and tangible in the world. It is God's gifts that make God's presence known. Human glory points back to the self; divine glory flows outward to the other, who glorifies God by living as a sign of the presence of God. The rest of creation does this simply by being what it is. The human part of creation does it by a free decision to be what they are created to be, by discovering and living out their authentic identity as made in the divine image. "Men 'give Him glory' by the sacred awe and the spontaneous exultation, with which they recognize and acclaim His presence in fear, trembling and holy joy. It is the freedom of man and his free submission to God in love that 'give glory to God.' What glorifies God, in man's submission to God, is not the fact of submission alone, but the far deeper truth that by submitting to God man gains his freedom. By 'renouncing' his private and 'economic' self for love of God man finds his true self" (*Seasons of Celebration*, 10). The gifts of wisdom, knowledge, and power "manifest in the world the glory of God" only if they are united to God's

merciful love, only, that is, if their exercise truly images God (*Disputed Questions*, 98); otherwise they become means of glorifying the self apart from and rather than God, and so inevitably lead to misery and frustration. "The greater our capacity to receive His mercy, the greater is our power to give Him glory, for He is glorified only by His own gifts, and He is most glorified by those in whom His mercy has produced the greatest love" (*Thoughts in Solitude*, 57–58).

To give God glory, then, is to direct attention through and beyond the self to the Source and Goal of all reality. To call attention to oneself in the guise of glorifying God is to risk turning God into "nothing more than a shadow" (*No Man Is an Island*, 256), that is, substituting an idol of one's own creation for the living God. One glorifies God most fundamentally not by what one says or does but by who one is, by simple presence, in which silence can communicate more than speech. "The mere fact that you wish to give God glory by talking about Him is no proof that your speech will give Him glory. What if He should prefer you to be silent? Have you never heard that silence gives Him glory?" (256). Thus, "the thirst for the manifestation of God's glory" is a fundamentally contemplative (as well as eschatological) aspiration; unless it is rooted in this contemplative dimension, Merton warns, "our apostolate is more for our own glory than for the glory of God" (*Contemplative Prayer*, 144).

Though one is able to show forth the glory of God only by freely uniting oneself to God, there is a sense in which one whose eyes have been illuminated by the grace of God is able to perceive the glory of God in people even when they themselves may not be aware of it. This is a central point of what is certainly the most familiar and significant of Merton's comments on glory, in the "Fourth and Walnut" passage of *Conjectures of a Guilty Bystander*, where he speaks of watching the passersby and suddenly recognizing "the secret beauty of their hearts, the depths of their hearts where neither sin nor desire nor self-knowledge can reach, the core of their reality, the person that each one is in God's eyes." This innermost identity, Merton says, "this little point of nothingness and of *absolute poverty* is the pure glory of God in us. It is so to speak His name written in us, as our poverty, as our indigence, as our dependence, as our sonship." To perceive this glory, Merton says, is to see a billion points of light shining so brilliantly that "all the darkness and cruelty of life" would completely disappear. There is no way, he concludes, to insure this vision, to make it happen. "It is only given. But the gate of heaven is everywhere" (*Guilty Bystander*, 142). POC

GOD

In *The Silent Life* Thomas Merton describes the monk as "a man who has been called by the Holy Spirit to relinquish the cares, desires and ambitions of other men, and devote his entire life to seeking God" (*Silent Life*, vii). This description can be said to define Merton's life from the time he entered Gethsemani (December 10, 1941) to the fateful day of his mysterious death in Bangkok twenty-seven years later.

This is not to say that his perception of what the seeking meant and how it was to be articulated did not change. It did indeed change, and quite substantially. But there was no wavering in the seeking itself. Merton was a man afire to know God, but he had to purify his perception of what it means "to know God."

His earliest writings reveal an attraction for the scholastic approach to God that places special emphasis on the role of human reason in coming to know God. In his autobiography Merton sees the beginning of that interest emerging from the classes he took at Columbia from Mark Van Doren. His teaching, Merton writes, prepared "my mind to receive the good seed of scholastic philosophy." For "the truth is that Mark's temper was profoundly scholastic in the sense that his clear mind looked directly for the quiddities of things and sought being and substance under the coverings of accidents and appearances" (*Seven Storey Mountain*, 140).

Merton's first venture into a reading of scholastic philosophy came almost by chance. One day in February 1937 he was passing Scribner's bookstore on New York City's Fifth Avenue and noted in the window a book called *The Spirit of Medieval Philosophy* by Etienne Gilson. Thinking it would be helpful for a course he was taking at Columbia on French medieval literature, he bought the book.

What he read revolutionized his life. Up to that time (he was twenty-two years old), he had never, on his own admission, "had an adequate notion of what Christians meant by God" (174). Reading Gilson introduced him to a completely new and highly credible concept of God. Gilson's presentation of God was neither vague nor superstitious nor unscientific. One word flew off the page and quite literally opened a whole new world to him. The word was Latin: *aseitas*. It means — this is Merton's own definition, though based on Gilson's — "the power of a being to exist absolutely in virtue of itself, not as caused by itself, but as requiring no cause, no other justification for its existence except that its very nature is to exist. There can be only one such Being: that is God" (172–73).

The God of Reason

What impressed him so profoundly about Gilson's book was that it made sense of the notion of God. The Christian concept of God was intelligent and reasonable. God was not what he had so long thought: a mere projection of people's fears and desires and ideals. God was real. To accept God's existence was intellectually acceptable.

Without doubt it was Merton's discovery of scholasticism and the reasonableness of Christian faith in God that helped him take the steps that led to his conversion to the Catholic faith and eventually brought him to the monastery, where he could continue and deepen his search for God. His admiration for the teachings of scholastic philosophy bore fruit in some of his earlier writings, such as *What Is Contemplation?* and *The Ascent to Truth*. In the latter work he makes quite clear his conviction that "there can be no sanctity that is not intelligent" (*Ascent to Truth*, 325).

Though all his life Merton was, in his own words, "infected with an incurable sense of metaphysics,"[1] there are indications, very early in his writings actually, of a growing dissatisfaction with the categories of scholastic thinking and a desire to move to a more simple, more existential approach to the reality of God. Significantly, the book that is the most systematically scholastic of all his writings was the one that caused him the most anguish in writing: *The Ascent to Truth*. In *The Sign of Jonas* he details the mental and emotional travail he suffered in bringing this book to birth (157, 161, 178).

The God of Revelation

In this context it is important to point out that the God of scholasticism — at least that of the twentieth century — seemed to be more a God of reason than of faith. What soon came clear to him is that he was not in the monastery simply to seek a God whose existence he could prove and whose nature he could speculate about. It was not proving the existence of God that mattered so much as experiencing God's presence. It was not enough to find a God who answered his mind's questions. He sought a God to whom his heart could respond. "It is unfortunately true," he writes, "that for many 'believers' the God they believe in is not the living God, but an apologetic hypothesis" (*Faith and Violence*, 287). Elsewhere he writes, "I have attempted to convey something of a monk's spiritual life and of his thoughts, not in the language of speculation, but in terms of personal experience" (*Sign of Jonas*, 8). All his life Merton remained faithful to this intuition. In talking about God we have to rely on experience and we must not be afraid to trust that experience. If Merton is to be called a theologian in any sense at all, it is preeminently as a theologian of experience. In a letter written to him in February 1967, Rosemary Radford Ruether made this affirmation: "I distrust all academic theology. Only theology bred in the crucible of experience is any good" (*At Home in the World*, 25). Merton would not have brushed academic theology aside so readily and completely; yet her statement would have struck responsive chords in him. He certainly would have said that academic theology needs to be tested in the crucible of experience, for a God who is known only to exist as an "apologetic hypothesis" can be kept at arm's length. A God who is experienced as present is a God who calls for a response. In 1967, in one of his reading notebooks, Merton wrote, "At the heart of philosophy is a secret 'nostalgia for revelation.'"[2]

Very early in his monastic life Merton experienced this nostalgia. The God he sought was not the "mute" God of reason, but the God of revelation, who speaks to people.

The very structure of the monastic life directed him toward the God of revelation, the God who speaks in the Scriptures. Each day in the communal office Merton prayed the psalms. Part of each day was devoted to *lectio divina*, that daily meditative reading of Scripture that leads to prayer and in due time to contemplative absorption in God. Since he sought the God who reveals the divine Self in many ways, but especially in Scripture, Merton attached great importance to the third chapter of Exodus, in which God speaks to Moses and reveals the divine name. He writes, "The third chapter of *Exodus* is one of the most important texts in the Bible. It forms the basis not only for the Christian and Jewish theology, but also for the whole religious concept of Islam. It is a text that must be known, meditated and absorbed by a believer in any one of these religions" (*Seasons of Celebration*, 192).

In the episode of the burning bush, Moses hears a voice calling him to lead the Israelite out of Egyptian slavery. Realizing that the people will want him to identify the God who is offering this deliverance to them, Moses asks the voice, "If the people want to know who sent me, what name shall I give them?" The response is the mysterious Tetragrammaton (four letters) of Exodus 3:14: YHWH. This generally is translated as "I am who am" (in Latin, "Ego sum qui sum"). Traditional Roman Catholic theology has generally inclined to a metaphysical understanding of this holy word and seen it as a declaration of the absolute aseity of God. Though this interpretation may have developed over time, it could scarcely have been the meaning it would have conveyed to the unlettered Israelite slaves who first received the revelation.

The Tetragrammaton has been interpreted in many ways. Most of them seem to suggest that it has something to do with the divine Presence to the people. "Yahweh is saying that he *will be* present, because He is the one who *is* present. . . . Moses is aware of the altogether extraordinary and gratuitous reality of God's presence to him here at Horeb. This in itself constitutes and implies a promise of that same presence and powerful protection in the future. Thus the reality of Yahweh's presence . . . is not an *awareness of nature,* but a *personal relationship* of a supremely religious kind. . . . [Martin] Buber brings this out in his translation: 'I will be there as the *I* that will be there'" (195).

The full significance of the Tetragrammaton of the second book of the Bible, whose original meaning seems irrevocably lost in the details of Israel's long history, comes to light (for the Christian), Merton believes, in the last book of the Bible, Revelation. The martyrs who "hold fast to the name" (Rev. 2:13) have "the name" written on their foreheads (Rev. 14:1). And "it is the name which was given by Joseph to Mary's child, at the command of an angel (Mt. 1:21): 'Ye-shuah,' 'Yahweh saves,' or in the form familiar to us, 'Jesus.' . . . Thus the name which is said, in *Hebrews,* to be 'inherited' by the incarnate Word is the same 'I Am' revealed to Moses, present in the midst of the people of God throughout salvation history. That is why Jesus said, 'Before Abraham was, I Am' (John 8:58). The Christian faith, then, sees in the Person of Jesus the living actual presence of the ineffable Name" (203).

Thus, Merton's theology of "the Name" slips into Christology. In the ancient hymn in Philippians 2, Paul speaks of Jesus' emptying himself and becoming obedient even to death on a cross, for which God gives to Jesus the name that is above all names: the name found in Exodus 3. The many words of Scripture find their fullness in the Word who became flesh among us.

The God of the Mystic

Besides the tradition that experiences God as the "One who is present" through the words of Scripture and especially through the Name, there is another, though subordinate, tradition also associated with Moses: the tradition of "the Face." In Numbers, Moses is described as one to whom God speaks face to face (Num. 12:8). The tradition of the Face does not loom large in the Bible. Even Moses is allowed only to see God's "back" (Exod. 33:23). In fact, there is the contrary tradition in the Bible that human eyes cannot look upon the Holy God without perishing. The biblical emphasis clearly is on a God who is heard rather than seen. In the Bible "seeing God" is an eschatological experience. Only in the "last days" will the glory of God, as Isaiah describes it, shine upon us and make us radiant with what we see (Isa. 60:2). Since the last days have already begun with the risen Jesus, the New Testament can proclaim what the Old could not: "that which we have seen with our eyes" (1 John 1:1). Paul could sum up the New Testament "theology of the Face" by saying that we come to know the "glory of God shining in the face of Christ" (2 Cor. 4:6).

The tradition of the Face is quite congenial to the mystical and contemplative tradition. Since contemplation is viewed as in some sense an eschatological experience (it is a "return to paradise"), the contemplative speaks with much less uneasiness about "seeing God."

Merton's well-known predilection for the apophatic way attracted him to the theology of the Face. His contacts in the last decade of his life with Zen and Sufism deepened that attraction. The *satori* experience in Zen is described as "seeing one's original face" (*Mystics and Zen Masters,* 17). In one of his holographic journals Merton quotes with some enthusiasm a Muslim hadith: "God hides himself behind seventy-thousand veils of light and darkness. If he took away the veils, the penetrating light of his Face would at once destroy the sight of any creature who dares to look at it."[3] Merton comments, "And of course if he took away the veils, there would be no choice but to 'look at' His Face, for one would see it unveiled in oneself. One would no longer 'be' a veil, but 'be' the Face. Total disappearance of the non-face. Would this be so 'terrible'? Let it come!"[4]

In a rare revelation written in 1966 to Abdul Aziz, his Sufi friend in Pakistan, Merton describes his own prayer life "as centered entirely on attention to the presence of God." He goes on to say, "It is not 'thinking about' anything, but a direct seeking of the Face of the Invisible which cannot be found unless we become lost in Him who is invisible" (*Hidden Ground of Love,* 63–64). This attraction to the "theology of the Face" was something Merton had written about much earlier. Twenty years earlier, on December 13, 1946, he wrote in his journal, "I have only one desire and that is the desire for solitude — to disappear into God, to be submerged in His peace, to be lost in the secret of His Face" (*Entering the Silence*, 32).[5]

To be lost in God, to disappear into God — these are expressions that are most congenial to the Sufi tradition. But they also belong to the mystical vocabulary of the West. They occur frequently in Merton's discussion of contemplation. Here are a few examples: "If I am true to the thought of [God] I was meant to embody, I shall be full of His actuality and find Him everywhere in myself, and find myself nowhere. I shall be lost in Him: that is, I shall find myself" (*New Seeds of Contemplation*, 37). "I who am without love cannot become love unless Love identifies me with Himself. But if He sends His own Love, Himself, to act and love in me and in all that I do, then I shall be transformed, I shall discover who I am and shall possess my true identity by losing myself in Him" (63). Pure and unselfish love "empties the soul of all pride and annihilates it in the sight of God, so that nothing may be left of it but the pure capacity for Him" (182). "For in the depths of contemplative prayer there seems to be no division between subject and object, and there is no reason to make any statement either about God or about oneself. He IS and this reality absorbs everything else" (267).

This brief sampling of quotations (many more could be cited) indicates how far Merton has moved away from the Cartesian mentality that for so long dominated the language of philosophy and even of faith. For the Cartesian person, another subject can be seen only as an object viewed subjectively and therefore always as "other," always as separate. Cartesianism, in other words, is a dualistic understanding of reality that ultimately separates God and God's creation. For Cartesian thinking, even God becomes an object that can be reached only by concepts. Merton points out how the taste for Zen that has developed in the Western world is a healthy reaction against four centuries of Cartesian heritage, which he defines as "the reification of concepts, the flight from being into verbalism, mathematics and rationalization" (*Guilty Bystander*, 260/285).

Merton's thinking moves consistently in the direction of nondualism and a holistic understanding of reality. It is not the thinking self that is at the center of reality, but God, the one center of all, who is everywhere and nowhere, from whom all proceed and in whom all are related and encountered. Merton writes about the moving experience of his baptism: being drawn into the very life of God, "that center Who is everywhere, and whose circumference is nowhere" (*Seven Storey Mountain*, 225).

The human search for God — of the monk and also of the nonmonastic Christian — a search built into our very creatureliness, becomes the yearning to achieve or, better, to experience, oneness with God. On April 13, 1967, Merton wrote about that oneness to a group of Smith College students who had spent an enjoyable evening reading and discussing some of his writings. He tells them that he believes that they have understood what he had written and have shared with him something most precious and most available too: "The reality that is present to us and in us: call it Being, call it Atman, call it Pneuma . . . or Silence. And the simple fact that by being attentive, by learning to listen (or recovering the natural capacity to listen which cannot be learned any more than breathing) we can find ourself engulfed in such happiness that it cannot be explained: the happiness of being at one with everything in that hidden ground of Love for which there can be no explanations" (*Hidden Ground of Love*, 115).

The "hidden ground of Love" is a moving description of the One from whom we all come, by whom we are all sustained, in whom we all live. But we must not overlook the modification Merton adds to that description: this hidden ground of Love cannot be explained. This is an important warning: be wary of what you say about God. Do not try to explain God. Do not try to prove God's presence in the world. "His presence cannot be verified, as we would verify a laboratory experiment" (*Contemplative Prayer*, 79/99).

Talking about God

We must be very careful how we speak about God. We must not reduce God to the level of an object, as if God were a thing, such as a book or a house, that we can possess. God is infinite (i.e., without limits). Hence, we cannot define God. The word "define" means "to place limits" (the Latin *finis* means "limit"). But God has no boundaries, no limits. God is the center that is everywhere and the circumference that is nowhere. God is the All who is beyond all beings. "He transcends them all and hence is not to be sought among them."[6] If we were able to parade before us all created things that are or ever have been or will be, God would not be among them. This is simply to say that the Creator is not to be sought among the things or objects that God has created. In *New Seeds of Contemplation* Merton writes, "There is 'no such thing' as God, because God is neither a 'What' nor a 'thing,' but a pure 'Who.' He is the 'Thou' before whom our inmost 'I' springs into awareness [and love. He is the living God, Yahweh, I Am, who calls us into being out of nothingness, so that we stand before Him made in His image and reflecting His infinite being in our littleness, and reply: 'I am,' and so with St. Paul we awaken to the paradox that beyond our natural being we have a higher being 'in Christ' which makes us as if we were not and as if He alone were in us]" (*New Seeds of Contemplation*, 13).[7]

This paradox ("as if we were not and as if He alone were in us") may be expressed in this way: God is not to be found among the creatures God made, yet these creatures cannot be separated from the God who created them. In one of his reading notebooks Merton quotes one of his favorite writers, Meister Eckhart. "The Divine One, Eckhart says, is a negation of negations and a denial of denials." He goes on to explain, "Every creature contains a negative: a denial that it is the other. God contains the denial of denials. He is the one who denies of every other that it is anything except Himself."[8]

Eckhart's point is that creatures are finite, limited. A particular creature is "this," not "that." The very limitation of their being distinguishes them, one from another. To say that a horse is a horse is to deny that it is a house. This is what Eckhart means when he says, "Every creature contains a negative: a denial that it is the other."

But God, he goes on to say, contains a denial of denials. Thus, God is denial: God is "not this" and "not that." And yet, God is at the same time a denial of denials; that is, God is a *denial* that God is "not this" and "not that," for every "this" and "that," namely, all creatures that are, find their being and identity in God. To put this seeming paradox in other words: God is transcendent, which means that God is not "this" and not "that"; at the same time, God is immanent, which means that God is in all creatures as the source and ground of their being.

How can we talk about God? We have no divine language, only the human language that describes our experience of created things. Since created things participate in a limited way in the qualities and perfections of the One who alone is absolutely Real, we can draw on our experience of them and use these experiences as metaphors or symbols to express our experience of God. Thus, we see justice and mercy and goodness in wonderful people and we are able to say, "God is like this and, indeed, in the fullest and highest possible way." The experiences of motherhood, fatherhood, joyfulness, truthfulness, which are our experiences of created things, serve as windows through which we can look upon the Reality of God. All this is wonderful knowledge that can bring joy, peace, and happiness to us.

But the time comes (for some people at least) when we begin to realize that the Reality of God we have experienced completely outstrips the language we use to express that experience. However glorious the concepts and images we have of God may be, the tremendous Reality of God infinitely transcends them. Our concepts of God are as tiny matches lighted to try to look at the sun. "As soon as we light these small matches which are our concepts: 'intelligence,' 'love,' 'power,' the tremendous reality of God Who infinitely exceeds all concepts suddenly bears down upon us like a dark storm and blows out all their flames!" (*Ascent to Truth*, 106).

Our knowledge of God through concepts is always, therefore, a mediated knowledge. This is not to deny its value.[9] The rich images that the Bible and our culture offer us are not to be underestimated. The richer the imagery, the more deeply we will be able to know about God through God's creation. Still, there is a huge difference between *knowing about God* and *knowing God as God is in the divine Self.* Knowledge *about* God is knowing God indirectly, that is, through an intermediary. Instinctively we realize that this is insufficient.

There must be a way in which we come to know God directly, as God is in the divine Self. Most people are content to think of such knowledge as eschatological, that is, as belonging to eternal life. This is what is meant by the beatific vision. Yet there is a long tradition — the mystical, contemplative tradition — that claims that, besides our knowledge of God through concepts, we can get to know God *immediately*, as God is in the divine Self. This can be done only by going beyond concepts and images. This means turning off the lights of reason and imagination and entering into the darkness. Merton describes what it means to seek God perfectly: "Since God cannot be imagined, anything our imagination tells us about Him is ultimately misleading and therefore we cannot know Him as He really is unless we pass beyond everything that can be imagined and enter into an obscurity without images and without the likeness of any created thing" (*New Seeds of Contemplation*, 131). In the same vein he writes about the need "to cultivate an intellectual freedom from the images of created things in order to receive the secret contact of God in obscure love" (45–46).

It should be noted that when we enter into the darkness, it is love that makes this secret contact with God. Merton distinguishes love from faith and hope. Faith and hope are able to reach God only at a distance, as the revealer of truth and the rewarder of goodness, but "love goes straight to the depths of the Divine Substance and rests in God for His own sake alone, taking us, so to speak, out of ourselves and making us live entirely in Him" (*Ascent to Truth*, 295). Thus it is that love astounds the intelligence "with vivid reports of a transcendent Actuality, which minds can only know, on earth, by a confession of ignorance. And so, when the mind admits that God is too great for our knowledge, Love replies: 'I know Him!'" (296).

Thus, while eluding our efforts to contain the divine Reality within our feeble reasonings, God responds to the yearnings of our hearts. In one of his working notebooks, Merton says, "The heart only is capable of knowing God."[10] In the context of this statement he quotes a saying of Allah attributed to Muhammad:

My earth and heaven cannot contain me,
But the heart of my believing servant
    contains me.

The human heart, Merton comments, is the only place strong enough to bear the divine secret. And the divine secret is that the Ground of all that exists is the Hidden Ground of Love. In Jesus, God has revealed to us that God is love. Love is not a moral quality in God, not something God has; it is the divine life. In God there is no shadow of *eros* (need-love); there is all *agape* (gift-love).

It is by love that we most truly share in the life of the One God in Three Persons. Thus Merton writes, "The One Love of the Three Persons is an infinitely rich giving of Itself which never ends and is never taken, but is always perfectly given, only received in order to be perfectly shared and returned. It is because this circulation of the Love of God never finds a *self* that is capable of halting and absorbing it, but only another principle of communication and return, that the Life and Happiness of God are absolutely infinite and inexhaustible (*Seeds of Contemplation*, 52).[11]

We enter into that circulation of Love that constitutes the divine Reality. This circulation of Love envelopes the whole universe. It is, to paraphrase Merton, the Love that feeds me when I am hungry and nourishes me at a deeper level when I fast, the Love that sends the winter days that make me cold and the hot summers that make me sweat, the Love that speaks to me in the birds, in the gentle breezes, in the streams, in the woods, in the clamor of the cities. This Love, which circulates in the whole universe, throbs in my heart and with its gentle but mighty power invades my whole being (see *Seeds of Contemplation*, 18).[12] WHS

SEE ALSO CHRISTOLOGY; HOLY SPIRIT; TRINITY.

Notes

1. *Working Notebook: Holographic Journal*, no. 43 (1968).

2. *Working Notebook: Holographic Journal*, no. 28 (1967): 12.

3. Ibid.

4. Ibid. In another of his reading notebooks Merton quotes a pertinent passage from Martin Lings, *A Sufi Saint in the Twentieth Century* (University of California Press, 1961), 123: "Ghazali says: 'Each thing hath two faces, a face of its own, and a face of its Lord; in respect to its own face it is nothing, and in respect to the Face of God it is Being. Thus there is nothing in existence save only God and His Face, for everything perisheth but His Face, always and forever.'"

5. See also *Sign of Jonas*, 17–18.

6. *Working Notebook: Holographic Journal*, no. 28 (1967).

7. The section in brackets was added by Merton to the French edition. See unpublished letter to Marie Tadie, November 22, 1962, Merton Center, Bellarmine University, Louisville, Kentucky.

8. *Working Notebook: Holographic Journal*, no. 43 (October 9, 1968).

9. See *Ascent to Truth*, 292–93, for the difference between the "mysticism of light" and the "mysticism of darkness."

10. *Working Notebook: Holographic Journal*, no. 18.

11. See also *New Seeds of Contemplation*, 68–69.

12. See also *New Seeds of Contemplation*, 16–17.

GOD IS MY LIFE: The Story of Our Lady of Gethsemani

Photographs by Shirley Burden, introduction by Thomas Merton. New York: Reynal and Company, 1960. 94 pp. (unnumbered). 69 photos.

Invited by Edward Steichen, curator of photography for the Museum of Modern Art in New York City, to photograph life at Gethsemani, Shirley Burden produced not just a book of photographs, but a work of art. Thomas Merton writes in his introduction, "Now for once, almost for the first time, the camera has caught sight of [the] fugitive and symbolic beauty in the very heart of all that is, to us, most ordinary.... For this book is not intended as documentation. It is a work of art, and in a work of art what is not said is just as important, if not more so, than what is explicit.... What we have [here] is a Trappist monastery, the oldest and largest one in the western world, seen not as a sociological phenomenon but as a religious mystery."

In the perceptive postscript to the book, Shirley Burden speaks in much the same vein.

From the outside Gethsemani is neither ugly, nor is it beautiful. The buildings you see and the many daily jobs you watch the monks perform, have little to do with its meaning. What transforms it is an overpowering desire on the part of these men to be with God now, and for all eternity. You cannot see it, but you can feel it, and it surrounds you in a wonderful way. I believe I was aware of this some time before I really understood it. One night I woke about 2 a.m. From somewhere far away, I could hear the sound of chanting voices. As I lay in the darkness, listening, the real meaning of Gethsemani came over me.

Each of the photographs is accompanied by a brief text, generally from Scripture, to help create the mood suggested by the photograph. In addition, Merton's introduction acts as a guide, walking us through them, as he describes in vivid prose the hidden beauty manifested in them. The following words from the introduction furnish a helpful path through the photographs:

Under the wonderful, moving mountains of cumulus cloud, amid the tall grasses and the shallow waters of the creeks, in the hayfields, the barns, the shops, the young monks work and sweat and laugh and are bewildered. The old monks plod on in emptiness, saying nothing, now no longer because it is the rule but because they have lost interest in speech. The young ones and the old ones go into the church and pray, perhaps, leaning sadly against a brick wall. Or they go meditate under a tree. Or they read by a pond. Or they find for themselves corners and sit in them, face to face with questions that have no answer.

Meanwhile, the water moves, the leaves move, things grow in silence, life reaches out all around us. The silence of God embraces us, consoles us, answers our questions (once we have the sense to stop asking). And the flowers bloom everywhere, the high weeds wave in the sun, the birds chant in the swinging green heavens which are the trees; and all this has much to say to anyone able to listen. It is all liturgy because it is all mercy. Then, at the height of the summer, with the sun boiling the creeks and baking the cow-trampled mud as hard as rock, the liturgical life of the monastery bursts into its own most luxuriant flower. It is the Feast of Corpus Christi. The feast of that inexpress-ible Sacrament of Divine Mercy in which Christ dwells in our midst in lowliness and splendor. The feast of that Sacrament which is made of the wheat of our fields, changed into the Body of the Son of God. To honor Him, the fields are ransacked of flowers, the gardens are stripped. Even the weeds come into their own: they have their place in the flower mosaics on the cloister floor where the hidden Christ will pass by, secret in His obviousness, King and Host.

The book concludes with this reflection of the artist: "When I finished I was sad. I must leave men I could not soon forget, and a way of life few understand, and fewer would have the conviction and courage to live." WHS

GOSS-MAYR, HILDEGARD

Born in Vienna in 1930, Hildegard was strongly influenced by her father, Kaspar Mayr, who, in the wake of the First World War, had become a strong advocate of nonviolence. He founded what was to become a small but influential jour-nal promoting peace activities, *Der Christ in der Welt.* In 1958 Hildegard married Jean Goss, who had been a prisoner during the Second World War and who in his imprisonment experienced a deep religious conversion in which he came to see Jesus Christ as "absolute Love." Their mar-ried life became a commitment to the practice and teaching of nonviolence.

In the year following their marriage, Pope John XXIII announced that a Council of the Catholic Church would be held and invited suggestions for the agenda. They took him at his word and went to Rome, where Jean managed to get an audience with Cardinal Ottaviani, a well-known conservative in the Roman curia who nonetheless was a strong op-ponent of war. Ottaviani put him in touch with Sebastian Tromp, S.J., who was in charge of the preparatory theological commission. Thus

they were able to get their peace materials to theologians and the Council fathers.

During the Council a group of women, including Hildegard Goss-Mayr and Dorothy Day, were in Rome seeking to contact the bishops and pleading with them for a strong statement against war, especially nuclear war, as well as a recognition of the right of con-scientious objection. Thomas Merton was in touch with these women and sent them various articles he had written on war and peace.

The Goss-Mayrs have been active in pro-moting peace and teaching nonviolent strate-gies in eastern and western Europe as well as in Latin America and the Philippines. In 1965 Hildegard, in company with Jim Douglass, visited Thomas Merton at Gethsemani.

Merton wrote twelve letters to Hildegard, the first in January 1962, the last on April 22, 1967. He had great respect for this petite, quiet-mannered, dynamic woman. In Septem-ber 1966 he sent a letter to William Robert Miller, who was then editor of *Fellowship,* the journal of the American Fellowship of Recon-ciliation. He spoke of the need for a training center for teaching the principles and strate-gies of nonviolence. "Hildegard Goss-Mayr," he wrote, "would be the one to really do something with it. She is my candidate for sainthood in this day (along with Dorothy Day and a few others like that)" (*Witness to Freedom,* 252). WHS

GRIFFIN, JOHN HOWARD

John Howard Griffin, social activist, photogra-pher, and novelist, was born in Dallas, Texas. As a young man he joined the French Resis-tance. For many years he was blind as a result of injuries sustained in World War II. During this period, despite his blindness, he studied philos-ophy under Jacques Maritain. Recovering from his illness, he became actively involved in the civil rights movement in the United States. A frequent visitor to Gethsemani, he was a con-tact person for Thomas Merton with others involved in that movement. The author of two novels (*The Devil Rides Outside* and *Nuni*), he is perhaps best known for his book *Black Like Me,* an account of his trip to the South with his skin pigment darkened so that as a white man he could experience the discriminations that were the constant lot of black people. Perhaps the best cataloging of his relationship with Merton is the book *The Hidden Wholeness: The Visual World of Thomas Merton*, which he published in 1970. It contains photographs by Merton and Griffin, with text by Griffin. The camera that Merton used for the many photographs he took at Gethsemani and on his Asian trip was loaned to him by Griffin, who also had the films developed for him.

The year following Merton's death, Griffin was appointed by the Merton Legacy Trust as the "official" biographer of Thomas Merton. Ill health prevented him from completing the biography. He resigned as biographer in 1977.[1] In 1978 Michael Mott was appointed by the Trust to do the biography. It was published in 1984. WHS

Notes

1. His account of the last three years of Merton's life was published by Orbis in 1993 under the title *Follow the Ecstasy: The Hermitage Years of Thomas Merton*.

GRINBERG, MIGUEL

Born in 1937, Miguel Grinberg studied at the University of Buenos Aires School of Medicine. In 1961 he turned to literary works and began editing *Eco Contemporáneo*, a literary magazine published in Buenos Aires, to contribute to "knowledge between people interested in the same subjects and troubled by the same problems" (letter to Merton, May 5, 1963). Thomas Merton was enthusiastic about *Eco Contemporáneo* and also about *Acción Interamericana*, founded by Grinberg to promote cultural exchange in the Americas. In 1964 Grinberg visited Merton at Gethsemani. He invited Merton to a meeting of poets in Mexico City. Merton was not allowed to go to the meeting, but he did write "A Message to Poets." In a remarkable essay he writes of the importance for poets of "fidelity to *life* rather than to artificial systems. The solidarity of poets is an elemental fact like sunlight, like the seasons, like the rain. It is something that cannot be organized, it can only happen. It can only be 'received'" (*Raids on the Unspeakable*, 156). Later

he says, "Let us be proud of the words that are given to us for nothing; not to teach anyone, not to confute anyone, not to prove anyone absurd, but to point beyond all objects into the silence where nothing can be said. We are not persuaders. We are children of the Unknown. We are the ministers of silence"(160). WHS

GUIDE TO CISTERCIAN LIFE
Trappist, Ky.: Abbey of Gethsemani, 1948. 15 pp.

This brief, pamphletlike booklet (13 cm.), printed without indication of its author, provides an overview of monastic life in the Cistercian Order. It begins with brief references to the founding of Cîteaux at the end of the eleventh century and to the Trappist reform in the seventeenth, and indicates that Cistercians have no direct apostolate. A discussion of "Cistercian Austerities" points out that the soul and God work together, God doing more in the later stages of spiritual development, the soul itself in the earlier stages, marked by austerities. "Silence, Separation from the World" explains that Trappist silence is for the sake of recollection, as is the minimal contact with the outside world — no access to newspapers, rare visits with family, letters only four times a year. "Fasting and Abstinence" describes the Trappist diet — no meat, fish, eggs — as reparation for the excess of the outside world. A description of "Vigils," the common dormitories, the rising at two o'clock in the morning, is followed by discussions of "Clothing," made by the monks themselves and worn even to bed, and "Manual Labor," four to five hours per day for choir monks, generally farm work, viewed principally as penance. A section on "Obedience, Community Life" emphasizes detachment from one's own will and the need for patience, along with "Poverty," in which all property is held in common and the simplicity of the monks' lives keeps them at the level of the humble and underprivileged of society. Description of the "Life of Prayer" focuses on the celebration of the divine office, the Mass as the center of Cistercian life, moments of silent thanksgiving as the secret of contemplation, and devotion to Mary as characteristic of Cistercian life. A section on "Studies" describes both preparation for priesthood and the need for ascetical and mystical theology as preparation for a truly contemplative life. A short section on "The Laybrothers" describes their way of life, with more manual labor, a simpler prayer life, and less fasting, as its own road to sanctity. Finally, a section on "Admission to a Cistercian Monastery" lists requirements for acceptance as a member of the order (unmarried Catholic without debts, aged at least fifteen, with a high school education if entering the choir, good physical and spiritual health); after a one-month trial (six months for brother candidates), the prospective monk is admitted to a two-year novitiate, followed by three years of temporary vows and then solemn vows of obedience, poverty, chastity, conversion, and stability. In conclusion, the monk is promised a hundredfold return for the sacrifice of taking up his cross daily and following Christ.

The contents of the pamphlet make clear that its purpose is to provide in brief compass all necessary information about the nature of Cistercian life both for the curious and particularly for anyone who might be interested in joining the order. The pamphlet's "voice" is very much that of the order in general rather than the author in particular, though occasional glimpses of Merton's own perspective might be found in the emphasis on the need to study the psalms and to participate fully in the chanting of the office, or in the mention of the singing of the "Salve Regina" at the close of each day, or in the praise of the simple life of the lay brothers working outdoors under God's sky. POC

GULLICK, ETTA

Etta Gullick first contacted Thomas Merton in 1960 about a project she had been given by her spiritual guide, Dom Christopher Butler, abbot of Downside. He had suggested that,

with her interest in spirituality, she might find it helpful to prepare an English edition of the third part of the *Rule of Perfection* of Benet of Canfield, a sixteenth-century Capuchin. That part of his Rule was not available in English. She asked Merton to read her manuscript and possibly prepare an introduction. A delightful correspondence (including forty-two letters from Merton) ensued, during which Benet of Canfield, for all practical purposes, disappeared from the scene (she never completed her edition, Merton never finished his introduction). The correspondence (i.e., Merton's letters to her,[1] published in *The Hidden Ground of Love*) branched off into discussions of many other topics: other spiritual writers, problems of prayer, the joys and sufferings of a dedicated life of spirituality, ecumenical problems, issues of war and peace.

Married to a lecturer in geography at St. Edmund's Hall, Oxford, Etta traveled quite extensively and delighted Merton with accounts of her travels, especially when she told of visits to places in England and on the continent that he had visited himself. Expressing his appreciation of the news she kept sending him about England and people and places he knew there, he says, "It is really almost as if I had a sister still living [in England]. I never had a sister, and really I have felt this as a kind of lack" (*Hidden Ground of Love*, 353). This correspondence, regular and consistent over a period of eight years, between an Anglican woman and a Roman Catholic monk makes fascinating reading, offering wonderful insights into Christian life and spirituality.

In April 1967 Etta and her husband visited Merton at Gethsemani and enjoyed a picnic with him at Monks Pond. WHS

Notes

1. Etta Gullick's letters to Merton are extensive and worth reading. They are housed at the Thomas Merton Center at Bellarmine University in Louisville, Kentucky. Unfortunately, they are written in longhand and are not always easy to decipher.

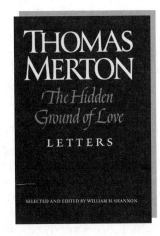

HAGIA SOPHIA

Lexington, Ky.: Stamperia del Santuccio, 1962.
8 pp.

This is a prose poem on divine Wisdom as the feminine manifestation of God. ("Hagia Sophia" means "Holy Wisdom" in Greek and is feminine in gender.) It was first printed in a limited edition on Victor Hammer's hand press and later included in *Emblems of a Season of Fury* (1963).

Its composition was prompted by a painting by Hammer that Thomas Merton saw when visiting him early in 1959, in which the boy Christ is being crowned by a woman. Hammer said that the painting began as a Madonna and Child, but that he was no longer sure of the identity of the woman. Merton identified her as Holy Wisdom, whom Mary represented in bestowing the crown of human nature upon Christ. In a May 14, 1959, letter to Hammer (*Witness to Freedom*, 4–6), Merton explains that Wisdom is the feminine dimension of God, not another "person" but God's *ousia* (being or substance), the "pivot" of all being and creativity, the mercy of God in and toward the creation, identified particularly with the Virgin Mary, who gives the Word his human nature

and sends him forth on his redemptive mission of mercy, and with the church, which shares this mission of mercy. These themes, and even many of the phrases of the letter, will reappear in the poem, which draws on the figure of Wisdom from Proverbs 8, on reflections of the Russian theologians Soloviev and Bulgakov, on the writings of the fourteenth-century English recluse Julian of Norwich, and even on Merton's own recurring dreams of Proverb, the young Jewish girl who loves him with the merciful love of God.

The prose poem is structured in four parts, based on the canonical hours of prayer: (1) "Dawn: The Hour of Lauds," (2) "Early Morning: The Hour of Prime," (3) "High Morning: The Hour of Tierce," and (4) "Sunset: The Hour of Compline. Salve Regina." It should be noted that Merton does not include the full pattern of seven canonical hours: the hours of sext, nones, and vespers, which come between tierce and compline, are omitted, perhaps because Wisdom is understood as less easily recognized in the full light of day, perhaps because the incompleteness of the pattern symbolizes the incompleteness of the human response to the presence of Wisdom.

The first part, "Lauds," is the longest. It begins with an introductory paragraph identifying the "hidden wholeness" of the visible creation as the presence of Wisdom, which also is to be experienced in the depths of the self as both "my own being / my own nature" and as a divine gift (*Hagia Sophia*, 1). Then the setting is specified: it is July 2, the Feast of the Visitation, called a Feast of Wisdom, thus suggesting that Mary (carrying the unborn Christ) is a manifestation of Wisdom, a theme to be explored later in the poem. The speaker is in the hospital and is awakened at dawn by the gentle hand of a nurse. (Note that this poem was written about seven years before Merton fell in love with a student nurse in 1966.) This experience is successively described as the awakening of humanity from dreams to reality, of a fragmented human race to the unity of love in the One Christ, of Adam to the first morning of life in Eden, of the world to the final morning of eschatological restoration. The gentleness and mercy of the nurse who calls the speaker back into consciousness is likened to being awakened by Eve or by the Virgin Mary: it is an experience of paradise and of a redeemed world. It is given above all to the least ones, represented by the man in the hospital, a man in need of healing, a man who in his vulnerable state is summoned to trust, to give up defensiveness and self-assertion. To respond to this invitation to awake, to live, is to recognize Hagia Sophia, to respond to the presence of Wisdom.

The second part, "Prime," is the shortest. It focuses on the usual failure to hear the voice of Wisdom though it speaks everywhere, the failure to recognize the manifestation of Wisdom in gentleness, mercy, yielding love (Sophia as nonviolence, or the Tao). Only those who realize and accept their own helplessness can respond to Sophia and awake not to a desire for power and conquest but to an acceptance of the primordial unity of creation, "to the impeccable pure simplicity of One consciousness in all and through all: one Wisdom / one Child / one Meaning / one Sister" (4). The coming of daylight symbolizes the coming of Sophia, and going forth to make a new world each day is a way of sharing in the work of Sophia.

In the third part, "Tierce," Sophia is described as mediating and diffusing the full light of divinity, as the light of God shining within

Woodcut of Hagia Sophia by Victor Hammer

the "ten thousand things" (4) of creation (recalling the "ten thousand places" in which Christ "plays" in Hopkins's sonnet "As Kingfishers Catch Fire"). God is seen both as the solitary Father transcending creation and as the Mother, the "glory" of God embracing all creatures with tenderness and light, allowing the divine power to be experienced as mercy and love, as "Jesus our Mother," in the words of Julian of Norwich (5). This Wisdom perhaps is to be identified with the divine *ousia*, but in any case is the manifestation of divinity, the female child playing in the world from Proverbs 8, who delights to be with the children of men, "God-given and God Himself as Gift," most hidden and yet filled with light, "inexhaustible nothingness" that is the source of all that is (6). Sophia is the source of beauty and creativity, but glimpsed by few if any in a fallen world that turns away from the light and loves darkness. Wisdom therefore must be the agent not only of creation but also of redemption, of transformation, the tenderness and mercy of a forgiving God.

Thus, the third part leads to the need for

the incarnation, the focus of the final section, "Compline." Since the "Salve Regina" ("Hail, Holy Queen") is sung at this last of the periods of prayer, the focus here on Mary as a revelation of Sophia is particularly apposite. She is the perfect embodiment of redeemed human nature and the source of human nature for the incarnate Word, thus "crown[ing]" the Logos (as in Hammer's painting). In Mary, God enters the broken world through and as Sophia; in the person of Jesus, God is revealed in poverty, in weakness (an expression of the self-emptying, the *kenosis,* of Philippians 2). The final scene of the poem, as evening falls, is of the "homeless God" who lies down and, like the hospital patient of the opening section, "entrusts Himself to sleep" (8). In identifying fully with the human condition, Christ is the perfect epiphany of Sophia, embodying and extending to all the redemptive mercy of God. POC

SEE ALSO WISDOM.

HAMMER, VICTOR

Born in Vienna on December 9, 1882, Victor Hammer entered the Vienna Academy of Fine Arts at the age of sixteen. He became proficient in painting and in typography. When Hitler came to power, Hammer was a professor at the Academy. He resigned his position and came to the United States, where he taught art at Wells College in Aurora, New York, and founded a college press there. In 1948 he retired from Wells and took the position of artist-in-residence at Transylvania College in Lexington, Kentucky. He and his wife, Carolyn, whom he married in 1955, lived in a historical mansion in Gratz Park in Lexington. A number of his paintings hung on the walls of their residence. One of them was the painting of mother and child that Thomas Merton named *Hagia Sophia.* One of his presses was brought from Florence and became the King Library Press. Under the imprint he had used in Italy, *Stamperia del Santuccio,* he printed special limited editions of several of Merton's books, including his long poem *Hagia Sophia,* which grew out of his reflection on Hammer's painting. On several occasions Merton received permission to visit the Hammers. They in turn came to Gethsemani to visit him.

Merton's letters to him are published in *Witness to Freedom.* On July 10, 1967, Victor Hammer died in Lexington. WHS

HART, PATRICK

Born in Green Bay, Wisconsin, Br. Patrick Hart, O.C.S.O., did his university studies at Notre Dame University and became a Holy Cross brother. He taught in secondary schools in Monroe, Michigan. In June 1951 he entered the Abbey of Gethsemani. Secretary to Abbot Dom James Fox from 1957 to 1966, he spent two years at the Trappist headquarters in Rome. Returning to Gethsemani in 1968, he became Thomas Merton's secretary, a position that he held at the time Merton traveled to Asia. Br. Patrick received a number of letters from Merton while he was in Asia (see *School of Charity,* 411–17). In the last letter, written on December 8, 1968 (the Feast of the Immaculate Conception and just two days before his unexpected and mysterious death), Merton wrote, "I think of you all on this Feast Day.... Also with Christmas approaching, I feel homesick for Gethsemani.... Best love to all" (*School of Charity,* 417).

Brother Patrick Hart, O.C.S.O.

Br. Patrick has edited books by, and written books about, Thomas Merton. He also has contributed book reviews and book endorsements in abundance. His most recent work was acting as general editor of the seven volumes of Merton journals, personally editing the first and seventh volumes. A founding member of the International Thomas Merton Society, he continues to be the voice of the Abbey of Gethsemani on issues that relate to Thomas Merton. WHS

HEART

The heart, as Thomas Merton points out, traditionally is used to symbolize the innermost self, though because of its associations in other contexts there is always a danger of a more superficial interpretation that does not go beyond the level of the emotions and associates the heart with the sentimental or the erotic ("Inner Experience," 2:129). But for the Christian contemplative tradition, as well as analogous traditions such as Sufism, the heart is "a traditional and technical term" (*Birds of Appetite*, 72). The heart is "the root and source of all one's own inner truth" (*Contemplative Prayer*, 22); it is used to refer to "the deepest psychological ground of one's personality," where one encounters not merely one's inner self but the "Abyss of the unknown yet present," who can be described in Augustine's terms as the one "more intimate to us than we are to ourselves" (38). To find one's heart, then, is to recover an awareness of one's deepest identity as grounded in the divine (87). In biblical terms this self-discovery entailing a death to the superficial self is the essence of *metanoia*, conversion, a change of heart profound enough "to transform our spirit and make us 'new men' in Christ" (89). The discipline of meditation is aimed at overcoming hardness of heart and becoming supple to God's grace (87). Faith can be described as the opening of the eye of the heart in order to receive the divine light (*New Seeds of Contemplation*, 130). It is the experience of the disciples on the road to Emmaus, which progresses from the awareness of the heart burning within to a recognition of the risen Christ (*Thomas Merton in Alaska*, 162). Genuine spiritual renewal, Merton believes, depends on a rediscovery of "the inner discipline of 'the heart,' that is to say, of the 'whole man' — a discipline that reaches down into his inmost ground and opens out to the

invisible, intangible, but nevertheless mysteriously sensible reality of God's presence, of His love, and of His activity in our hearts" (*World of Action*, 113).

Genuine monastic formation is "education of the heart," a rediscovery of the affirmation and acceptance of God that is the innermost truth of one's being, a recognition Christianity shares, Merton says, with Sufism and the Hasidic tradition of Judaism. "Deep in our hearts is the most profound meaning of our personality, which is that we say 'yes' to God, and the spark is always there. All we need to do is to turn towards it and let it become a flame" (*Thomas Merton in Alaska*, 153–54). This reawakening of contact with one's own heart is at the same time an experience of being plunged into the heart of the world, becoming aware of "the deepest and most neglected voices that proceed from its inner depth" (*Contemplative Prayer*, 25), as Merton himself experienced most notably in his "Fourth and Walnut" experience, when he was able to identify with the people around him, "as if I suddenly saw the secret beauty of their hearts, the depths of their hearts where neither sin nor desire nor self-knowledge can reach, the core of their reality, the person that each one is in God's eyes" (*Guilty Bystander*, 142). POC

SEE ALSO HESYCHASM; PURITY OF HEART.

HE IS RISEN

Niles, Ill.: Argus, 1975. 59 pp.

In a journal entry under the date of September 14, 1967, Thomas Merton writes, "Today I finished that Easter Homily for the Argus recording" (*Learning to Love*, 291). Reflecting that it had been hanging over him for several weeks, he says that his first draft had been a poor job, but he hopes he could improve it before having it typed. The very next day in his hermitage Merton was recording a tape for the Carmelite monastery in Savannah, Georgia. He tells them that he had been asked to write an Easter homily that was to be recorded (by someone else). He decided to read it into the tape recording that he was preparing for the nuns. No evidence has been found that the homily was recorded, but eventually it was published (1975) by Argus Communications (Niles, Illinois) in a small booklet, with contemporary colored photos, and called *He Is Risen*. This booklet-homily is Merton's most extensive reflection on the resurrection of Jesus. WHS

For a summary of those reflections, see RESURRECTION OF JESUS CHRIST.

HERMIT

During the years that eventually led to permission to live as a hermit, as well as during his time at the hermitage itself, Thomas Merton did a great deal of research and writing, both popular and more technical, on the role of the eremitical life in monasticism and in the church as a whole. The consistent theme of all this writing is that the hermit vocation is intrinsic to and essential for the life of the body of Christ, and more particularly for the monastic community. It is properly understood as existing not exclusively or even primarily for the personal sake of the hermit, but as an essential, if relatively uncommon, contribution to the entire Christian community.

In his overview of monasticism in an early section of *The Silent Life* (1957), Merton calls the presence of eremitical members in a monastic community "quite logical" because it gives witness to values of contemplation and solitude that are important for all monks and so is a contribution to the common life (*Silent Life*, 40). In describing the eremitical lives of Carthusians and Camaldolese later in the same work, he emphasizes that while the Benedictine Rule (which governs the lives of the latter though not the former) is written for cenobites, it contains an "implicit orientation . . . towards eremitical solitude" (148), and he cites Peter Damian's assertion that the hermit's life is itself an expression of the unity of the mystical body of Christ, which is present in charity in the soul of the hermit — "The whole Church is present in the cell where he is alone" (151) — and is strengthened by the intensity of his love of Christ and the body of Christ. Merton will express the same idea in a chapter added to *New Seeds of Contemplation* in which he repudiates the notion that becoming a hermit

is a way to sanctity because it is an escape from other people. In his view, "The only justification for a life of deliberate solitude is the conviction that it will help you to love not only God but also other men" (52). Physical separation does not imply metaphysical isolation, much less a narcissistic dialogue with oneself. The true solitary is not an individualist defining self in the separation from others, but an authentic person whose identity is constituted by relationality, who is able to find others in God and to "care for all beings made by God and loved by Him," an ability inhibited, even destroyed, by the impersonality and conformity of modern technological society (*New Seeds of Contemplation*, 53).

The eremitical life, Merton repeatedly emphasizes, makes no sense except as a way of following Christ. "The hermit, like the martyr, is the most eloquent witness of the Risen Christ" (*Disputed Questions*, 165) because the hermit is moved by the Spirit, breathed out upon the apostles on Easter night, to journey into the desert, to confront personal inner demons and the evils of the entire world, in imitation of Christ. The hermit models for the entire church the search for God alone that may be less visible in the midst of society. "The exigencies of Christian life *demand* that there be hermits," Merton writes in his introduction to the life of Blessed Paul Giustiniani. "The Kingdom of God would be incomplete without them, for they are the men who seek God alone with the most absolute and undaunted and uncompromising singleness of heart" (166). And in finding God, the solitary finds all other people and all creation in God. "Loving God in God, the solitary is perfectly united to that infinite Love with which God loves all things in Himself" and so participates in the calling of every Christian to share in the work of restoring all things in Christ (174). In his essay "Rain and the Rhinoceros" Merton cites the early Syrian hermit Philoxenos, who emphasizes that the solitary "becomes every man" in his union with Christ in the desert, because with Christ he takes upon himself "the solitude, the poverty, the indigence of every man" (*Raids on the Unspeakable*, 18). Thus, properly understood, the eremitic vocation is an expression of profound solidarity with the human condition, as recognized and embraced in the human figure of Christ. Here can be seen the spiritual and theological foundation for Merton's own deepened sense of compassion for others as his experience of and commitment to the eremitic life developed.

At the same time, the hermit is a sign of contradiction, even a scandal, to a society that calculates worth in terms of achievement and measurable accomplishment. The hermit can be considered a "failure" only in the eyes of a status-conscious society, since the hermit has no clear function, makes no easily defined contribution. "He is outside all our projects, plans, assemblies, movements" (*Disputed Questions*, 199). The hermit therefore is a living reminder to Christians in general and other monks in particular that the ways of the world and the ways of God's kingdom are not identical or even compatible, that followers of Christ are pilgrims and wayfarers on the earth. "The hermit remains there to prove, by his lack of practical utility and the apparent sterility of his vocation, that cenobitic monks themselves ought to have little significance in the world, or indeed none at all," Merton writes in his "Notes for a Philosophy of Solitude." "The monk has all the more of a part to play in our world, because he has no proper place in it" (200).

Merton's most developed treatment of the hermit life comes in his long essay "The Case for the Renewal of Eremitism in the Monastic State," first published in early 1965, the year in which Merton himself would become a hermit. He provides a very detailed historical survey of the presence of hermits both in the earliest days of monasticism and throughout the Middle Ages, in support of his thesis that eremitic vocations should be allowed within existing cenobitic orders (Benedictine and Cistercian), as an alternative to proposals current at the time that canonical regulations should be changed to permit prospective hermits to transfer freely to eremitic orders within the *ordo monasticus*, or that the eremitical state should be canonically distinguished from the monastic state (*World of Action*, 318–22). The evidence that Merton assembles demonstrates that there has been a consistent, if little-known, tradition

in Western (Benedictine) monasticism allowing for the practice of solitary vocations "within the juridical and institutional framework of the monastic state." He concludes that a revival of this approach "remains in itself the simplest, the most practical and the most traditional monastic solution" to the dilemma of eremitic vocations within cenobitic monasticism, though he warns of the need for "a great deal of prudence, tact, charity and understanding" in implementing the proposal (324). The thoroughness of his discussion is both a reminder of deep-seated opposition to the hermit life within Cistercianism, which had resulted in virtually as much censorship of Merton's writings on solitude as of those on war, and a foreshadowing of the change in policy about to take place in Cistercian life that would allow Merton to put his proposal into practice within a matter of months after it was published.

A final discussion of the eremitic state that should be noted is the essay "Christian Solitude," originally subtitled "Notes on an Experiment" and first published in February 1967, a year and a half after Merton's permanent move to the hermitage. Here Merton is able to declare, "A place has . . . been made for Christian eremitical solitude within the monastic institution" (240), the solution he had proposed in the earlier article, and to provide a preliminary evaluation of its success in the context of its implementation at Gethsemani. He draws together many of the themes of earlier discussions of solitude, including the idea that the solitary is in some sense the norm for monasticism (239); that the life of solitude "was a particular charismatic way of participating in the death and resurrection of Christ" (239); that the eremitic state must not be an eccentric or theatrical affectation but an experience of "the ordinary values of a life lived with a minimum of artificiality" (241); that the hermit's life is lived for the sake of the community as a whole, not as an escape from the community, and that "his solitary life with its depth of prayer and awareness is his contribution to the community, something that he gives back to his 'monastic Church' in return for what has been given him," so that "monastic solitude retains its fully communal and Christian character"

(242). He recognizes the risks of a life alone, where the solitary struggles with the mystery of human identity by entering into the mystery of Christ (244), and sees the hermit as a sign to the wider community that their monastic, Christian, and human identity is not dependent on structures and institutions but on God alone (245). He emphasizes both the eremitic "grace of independence: a breaking away from certain exorbitant claims of society and of institutions" and the fact that the hermit remains subject to the monastic rule, the vows, and the abbot (246). Referring to the situation at Gethsemani, with its two hermits (at that time), he stresses the "new and special relationship" (248) between hermit and community, the mutual respect and mutual obligations, and the need for — and presence of — charity on both sides. He emphasizes that the life of solitude must be a life of love, not in an abstract sense but as "a concrete, existential good" (249), and concludes that the freedom of the hermit "is never a freedom *from* the Church but always a freedom *in* the Church and a contribution to the Church's own charismatic heritage" (251). If Merton's journals and letters from this period reveal that he was not always able to live up to the ideals he outlines in this essay on the eremitic state, the essay indicates that these were indeed the ideals he had committed himself to, and if he acknowledges that the hermit "retains his human defects, he remains capable of failure and error, and like everyone else in such a case he depends on the understanding and love of his brothers," he sees this state of life as above all "a response to a personal call from God in Christ" and "a contribution to the life and faith of the community and of the Church as a whole" (250–51). POC

SEE ALSO CAMALDOLESE; CARTHUSIANS; HERMITAGE; MONASTICISM; MONK; *SOLITARY LIFE*.

HERMITAGE

Thomas Merton's dream of a hermitage on the Gethsemani property can be traced all the way back to 1949. On June 27 of that year, after a long reflection on his first day in the woods outside the monastery enclosure, he writes, "Last night in my imperfection, I came out of meditation with a wild scheme for starting a sort of Carmelite Desert out there. I know I'd never be allowed a one-man hermitage, but perhaps one might start a little house for special retreats, where Priors and Guestmasters and what not could escape for a little recollection. Where one could go for a month at a time or even more and get in some real and solid contemplation" (*Entering the Silence*, 330). This plan foreshadows remarkably the actual development of the building on Mt. Olivet that became Merton's hermitage. Though he adds, "I can imagine no project less likely to meet with the favor of our General Chapter" (330), in a September 10, 1949, letter to Abbot James Fox, then attending the chapter, he submits a proposal for "a little chapel" in the woods, "a center where one might have little retreats in solitude and silence." He gives three models for such a chapel, the third, and most developed, being a "regular little *grange . . .* something like a Carmelite Desert," which would have "a monk permanently in residence (guess who??)." He adds, "I am really deadly in earnest about this" (*School of Charity*, 15–16). Nothing came of this scheme at the time, of course, but it would resurface in strikingly similar form a decade later.

After signing a contract for four books at the beginning of 1950, Merton writes of this commitment as meaning "the final renouncement forever of any dream of a Charterhouse or a hermitage," saying that his work would be his hermitage because his writing was actually what allowed him to be solitary and contemplative in the context of life at Gethsemani, though he adds, "God will prepare for me His own hermitage for my last days" (*Entering the Silence*, 400). Similarly, when he becomes master of students in 1951, he writes that anything can contribute to a life of solitude "as long as you do not insist on doing the work yourself and building your own kind of hermitage" (463). Nevertheless, in late December 1952 he writes a letter to the abbot requesting to be a hermit after three years, at Gethsemani or elsewhere, though it was not sent due to the abbot's illness (*Search for Solitude*, 27). But an interim solution was begun at exactly this point for time in solitude in "the fixed-up shanty" (27), an old toolshed (first mentioned on September 3 [14]) that Merton was to rename St. Anne's and call his "hermitage" for the next seven years.

Though he was hoping to spend "a week at a time" at St. Anne's, in fact he generally was limited to spending afternoons there. His journal entries for the next couple months are filled with detailed descriptions of inner peace and the quiet beauties of the natural surroundings (29–41), with Merton saying, "I was clothed in this hermitage eleven years ago without even knowing it. The black and white house indeed is a kind of religious habit" (35). Though the journal breaks off shortly after this point (in March 1953) and does not resume until July 1956, there are occasional glimpses of Merton at St. Anne's in his letters from the intervening period (see Road to Joy, 25; Witness to Freedom, 184), and soon after the journal resumes, he describes "a quiet morning at St. Anne's," though mentioning that he is there for the "first time in months" (Search for Solitude, 64). On March 19, 1958, he returns to St. Anne's for the first time in "I can hardly tell how long" and reflects retrospectively on the "graces, here in St. Anne's, that I did not know about, in those years when I was here all the time, when I had what I most wanted and never really knew it. . . . How rich for me has been the silence of this little house which is nothing more than a toolshed" (181). He then goes on to describe his experience of the previous day — at the corner of Fourth and Walnut in Louisville — a significant juxtaposition of experiences of solitude and solidarity.

Of course, the toolshed was never more than a stopgap measure, however long it lasted. It did not keep Merton from planning various other scenarios for living in deeper solitude, most of them elsewhere than at Gethsemani. The more permanent solution surfaces in June 1960 with the development of plans for "the retreat house . . . on Mt. Olivet" (390). A year earlier Merton had decided to request to live as a hermit on the Gethsemani grounds, sure that he would be refused by the abbot (289–90). When he broached the idea a month later, Dom James actually seemed quite receptive (303), though Merton did not pursue it further at the time, still thinking about becoming a hermit else-

where. When that option was refused by Rome in December 1959 (358–59), the "dream" of a solitary life at Gethsemani itself (343) began to move toward reality. While the original reason for the building on the hill in back of the monastery ostensibly was to host the ecumenical gatherings that Merton had begun to hold, and while Merton calls the building "the retreat house" during the planning process (Turning toward the World, 6, 14, 20, 40), he already is reflecting in June that "if the worst came to the worst they would let me live alone here, if I wanted to. . . . It seems to me that it is quietly working itself out in its own way" (14). When the actual decision is made as to the building's shape and size, it is clear that it is not suited for large gatherings, and when the foundation of the building is actually staked out on October 3, Merton refers to "the place on the hill — let's be frank: the hermitage" (55). The building is completed on November 30 and christened St. Mary of Carmel (71); and while it occasionally is used to host Protestant seminarians (Turning toward the World, 109; Water of Life, 169), its primary purpose, as even the visiting abbot general recognizes (Turning toward the World, 97), is to provide a solitary environment for Merton. Looking at the evening sky from the hermitage, Merton sums up his early experience there by calling it Janua Coeli, the gate of heaven, and prays that he may be faithful to the "great gift" he has been given (108).

For the next five years there is a process of gradually increased time at the hermitage. On March 20, 1962, Merton spends his first full day there (212), something he will do regularly for the next three years when his duties as novice master permit. On October 13, 1964, Merton receives permission to sleep there, "without any special restriction, though not necessarily all the time" (Water of Life, 153). "Only here," he reflects the following month, "do I feel that my life is fully human. And only what is authentically human is fit to be offered to God" (170). On December 10, 1964, he celebrates the twenty-third anniversary of his arrival at Gethsemani by cooking supper for the first time at the hermitage (179), and six days later he sets up the schedule that he will follow after

Thomas Merton's hermitage

becoming a full-time hermit, returning to the monastery at midday for his private Mass and dinner but spending the rest of the day in solitude (179–80). Just before Christmas, plans are made to wire the cottage (183), and on February 16 he is able to turn on the electric light for the first time (207); a small refrigerator arrives a week later (209). "One thing the hermitage is making me see," Merton writes at the beginning of March, is "that the universe is my home and I am nothing if not part of it" (212).

The question of a change in novice masters is first raised in June (258) and decided by early July (265). The change is made on the Feast of St. Bernard, August 20, 1965, when Merton is relieved of all responsibilities at the monastery and becomes a full-time hermit. Five days later he writes, "This life is what I have always hoped it would be and always sought. A life of peace, silence, purpose, meaning" (283). His life in the hermitage is described as a dynamic, indefinable "eschatological gift. I have never before really seen what it means to live in the new creation and in the Kingdom. Impossible to explain it. If I tried I would be unfaithful to the grace of it — for I would be setting limits to it. It is *limitless*, without determination, without definition. It is what you make of it each day, in response to the Holy Spirit" (276). It also was a life of struggle, as he would come to

realize over the following three years; and even though in February 1967, after the turbulence of the previous summer, he can say, "Maybe the hermit life is another kind of defeat," he immediately adds, "I certainly feel that here I am relatively more honest and more true than anywhere else" (*Learning to Love*, 199).

He continues to return to the monastery once a day for Mass and a meal until July 16, 1967, when an altar is set up in the main room of the hermitage and he says his first Mass there (*Learning to Love*, 265). The foundation for the bathroom and chapel to be added to the hermitage is laid in February 1968 (*Other Side of the Mountain*, 56), and the chapel is completed on April 26 (86), the bathroom a few days later (87). By this time, however, Merton's sense is that the hermitage is too easily accessible to both friends and strangers (129), and the search for an alternative site, whether in Alaska, California, or elsewhere, begins. In his final reflections on the hermitage while in Asia, Merton writes, "I am beginning to appreciate the hermitage at Gethsemani more than I did last summer when things seemed so noisy and crowded" (252), comparing his situation to that of the Tibetan monks whose dwellings were considerably more accessible than his own was, though at this point he is considering Alaska as perhaps the best site, and reflects that a pattern of periods of solitude alternating with times of "coming 'out' for a while" seems optimal (252). Two weeks later he returns to the question and writes, "Though I fully appreciate the many advantages of the hermitage at Gethsemani, I still have the feeling that the lack of quiet and the general turbulence there, external and internal, last summer are indications that I ought to move," but he goes on to express his affection for "my monastery" and adds, "I suppose I ought eventually to end my days there" (*Other Side of the Mountain*, 282). Exactly one month later he was buried in the abbey cemetery. POC

SEE ALSO HERMIT; MONASTICISM; MONK.

HERSCHER, IRENAEUS

Born in Haute-Alsace, France, Herscher came to the United States in 1924, joined the Franciscan order, and was ordained in 1931. After receiving his B.A. and M.A. from St. Bonaventure, he earned a master's degree in library science at Columbia. He served as librarian at St. Bonaventure's Friedsam Memorial Library from 1937 to 1970. Herscher was a friend and adviser to Thomas Merton. They shared walks on the campus while Merton was teaching at the college. Herscher familiarized him with St. Thérèse of Lisieux, a saint very popular at the time. Merton kept in touch with Herscher after his entrance into the monastery. The journals that enter into the first volume of the Merton published journals, *Run to the Mountain*, are housed at the Friedsam Memorial Library. WHS

HESCHEL, ABRAHAM JOSHUA

Abraham Joshua Heschel (1907–72) was born in Warsaw and received his higher education at the University of Berlin. His doctoral thesis on the prophets was published and became a classic study of the prophetic writings. Merton wrote of this work of Heschel, "You take exactly the kind of reflective approach that seems to me most significant and spiritually fruitful, for after all it is not the Prophets we study but the word of God revealed in and through them" (*Hidden Ground of Love*, 431).

For a time Heschel taught at Frankfurt as successor to Martin Buber. The Nazis forced him out of Germany. He returned briefly to Warsaw, then had to flee from his native country. From 1940 to 1945 he taught at Hebrew Union College (Cincinnati), then in the Jewish Theological Seminary in New York City, where he completed his teaching career.

His writings (*No Man Is Alone, Man's Quest for God,* to name just a couple) are much admired and widely read. His writings exhibit a poetic sensitivity toward God and people together with a prophetic stance toward a world filled with stress and turmoil.

On July 13, 1964, he visited Thomas Merton to express his fears about the forthcoming Vatican II document on the relation of Christians and Jews. Deeply affected by this visit, Merton wrote a spirited letter to Cardinal Bea of the Secretariat for Christian Unity. For further information on Heschel's concerns and Merton's response, see VATICAN COUNCIL, THE SECOND. Merton's letters to Heschel are published in *The Hidden Ground of Love.* WHS

HESYCHASM

The Hesychast movement of the Eastern church was associated particularly with the "Jesus Prayer" or "prayer of the heart." Thomas Merton first discusses it on his thirty-fifth birthday as "my latest discovery," focusing on its importance for understanding the desert fathers, its similarities to St. Bernard's devotion to the name of Jesus, and its integration of bodily, mental, and spiritual dimensions in prayer (*Entering the Silence*, 404–5). He traces the origin of the term to the rest or tranquillity (*hesychia* in Greek, *quies* in Latin) that was a principal goal of early desert spirituality (*World of Action*, 272). Rest in this context was not inactivity but a spiritual repose in God and in the divine will, a liberation from worldly anxieties and cares, from the demands of the ego and from the subsequent illusions intrinsic to such a self-centered life. It was the calmness of a heart not roiled by passionate upheavals (the *apatheia* of Evagrius Ponticus). Such a state was not achieved by ascetical austerity alone, but was the gift of God: "*quies* is not something in ourselves, it is God the Divine Spirit. Thus we do not 'possess' rest, but go out of ourselves into him who is our true rest" (275).

From early in the monastic tradition this rest was associated with recollection of the name of Jesus, "since the sacramental power of the Name of Jesus is believed to bring the Holy Spirit into the heart of the praying monk" (*Contemplative Prayer*, 23). The simple "repetitive invocation of the name of Jesus in the heart emptied of images and cares" (103), typically integrated with an echo of the words of the publican of the Gospel, "Lord Jesus Christ, Son of the Living God, have mercy on me a sinner" (see *Disputed Questions*, 78), was considered the key to banishing distraction and temptation and to praying in the midst of other activities of the day. This prayer of the heart was preeminently "a way of keeping oneself in the presence of God and of reality, rooted in one's own inner truth" (*Contemplative Prayer*, 24). It was prayer on a deeper level than the mind or the affections, an encounter with the presence of God in the very center of one's self (34), "the ground of our identity before God and in God" (87).

This emphasis on contemplative repose centered on the recollection and repetition of the name of Jesus underwent a revival in Greek monasticism of the Middle Ages, associated particularly with the figure of St. Gregory Palamas, a monk of Mount Athos who later became archbishop of Salonika, who taught that Hesychasts could experience in this life the "divine energies," the light manifested to the disciples in the transfigured Jesus (see *Mystics and Zen Masters*, 179–80; *Disputed Questions*, 77–78). Merton points out that this movement was controversial in its own time and aroused suspicion in Western Christian writers for centuries. He rejects what he calls the "outraged platitudes" of those who dismissed the Jesus Prayer as self-hypnosis (*Mystics and Zen Masters*, 180) and defends Hesychasm as "an authentically Christian and deeply simple way of prayer" (*Disputed Questions*, 78). In more recent times Hesychast prayer flourished in Russia, nourished by the translation of the *Philokalia*, the anthology of passages from Eastern monas-

tic sources concerned with prayer, above all the prayer of the heart (*Contemplative Prayer*, 22–23). Of particular significance in Russia was the way in which this typically monastic form of prayer was adopted by the laity, particularly the poor peasantry, as described, for example, in *The Way of a Pilgrim*, which Merton calls "surely one of the great classics of the literature of prayer" (*Mystics and Zen Masters*, 180).

While Merton is both an enthusiastic expositor and exponent of the authenticity of Hesychasm, he nonetheless is quite restrained when it comes to recommending this method of prayer for his contemporaries. He notes that it was not practiced in Russia except under the guidance of a *staretz*, or elder, and warns that it "is not safely to be followed by us in the West without professional direction" (180). Writing in 1963 to a fellow monk who had been reading *The Way of a Pilgrim*, he remarks that "it is all very well for a hard-headed nineteenth-century Russian moujik to do that all day and all night, but it is not going to work for Americans today" (*School of Charity*, 176). He comments that "this repetition of the prayer is useful at certain times" and mentions that he uses it himself, especially when he finds himself distracted or too tired to pray in other ways, but recommends the Bible as "a much better source of light than the Jesus Prayer" (177). He is particularly wary of too much attention to the Jesus Prayer as technique, the concentration on breathing, as well as of too much expectation of psychophysical consequences, "the inner warmth around the heart, as a result of pushing the prayer" (177). In a later letter to another monk he summarizes his attitude: "I favor the Prayer of Jesus only in cases where it comes rather spontaneously and I do not think that our monks ought to make a deliberate project out of it with a great deal of concentrated introversion. This will do more harm than good. But the prayer is good on and off, when needed and when one feels it is helpful" (226). This corresponds to Merton's general teaching that methods of prayer must not become "projects," quasi-Pelagian techniques to reach God by human effort,[1] but should simply be used as ways of reminding oneself that God is always already present within and beyond oneself in gracious love. POC

SEE ALSO HEART.

Notes

1. See, for example, his comment on Western and, particularly, Benedictine indifference to techniques in comparison with Eastern and Orthodox mysticism in *Entering the Silence*, 402.

HIDDEN GROUND OF LOVE, THE: *The Letters of Thomas Merton on Religious Experience and Social Concerns*
Edited by William H. Shannon. New York: Farrar, Straus and Giroux, 1985. xiv+669 pp.

This first volume of the Thomas Merton letters was published by Farrar, Straus and Giroux, 1985 (cloth), 1985, 1986, 1989 (paperback); by Collins Flame, England, 1990 (paperback); by Harcourt, Brace, 1993 (paperback). It is the longest of the volumes of the letters, running to 669 pages.

The title comes from a letter written to the young students of Smith College in Northampton, Massachusetts, in which Merton spoke of "the happiness of being at one with everything in that *hidden ground of Love* for which there can be no explanations" (*Hidden Ground of Love*, 115). The subtitle makes clear that the letters are about spirituality (prayer, contemplation, love, compassion, etc.) and its relationship to social issues (war, nonviolence, racism, anti-Semitism, etc.). Linking spirituality and social concerns helps to unify the Merton story. Expressing his conviction of that link, he writes to a Brazilian nun, Sr. Emmanuel, that we must take responsibility for the problems of our own country, while at the same time "recognizing our higher responsibility to the whole human race." And yet, he says, "I remain a contemplative. I do not think there is a contradiction, for I think at least some contemplatives must try to understand the providential events of the day. God works in history, therefore a contemplative who has no sense of history, no sense of historical responsibility, is not a fully Christian contemplative" (186–87).

The letters are arranged alphabetically in sets according to the names of the correspondents. Each set of letters to a particular individual is, in turn, arranged in chronological order.[1] Especially in the longer sets of letters, this arrangement helps the reader to view the development and growth of so many friendships that became important realities in the life of this Trappist monk. Friendships did indeed develop through these letters, for Merton displays in them an extraordinary sensitivity to the needs, the problems, and the life situations of the people to whom he writes.

He wrote to an amazingly large number of people. More than seventy different correspondents are represented in this volume. They range from Allchin to Zahn. They cover categories from Allah to Zen. Some of the well-known persons included in this volume are Daniel Berrigan, Amiya Chakravarty, Catherine Doherty, Dorothy Day, John Tracy Ellis, Wilbur H. Ferry, James Forest, Erich Fromm, Thich Nhat Hanh, Abraham Joshua Heschel, Pope John XXIII, and D. T. Suzuki. There also are letters to persons less familiar to the reader, which contain valuable insight into Merton's life and thought. For instance, his correspondence with Abdul Aziz, a Sufi scholar in Pakistan, offers a unique look into Merton's own prayer life (63–64). His letter of a contemplative to the world, written at the behest of Pope Paul VI, combines literary elegance and authentic spirituality in a way that is breathtakingly moving and beautiful. To quote just one small part: "The contemplative is not a man who has fiery visions of the cherubim, carrying God on their imagined chariot, but simply he who has risked his mind in the desert beyond language and beyond ideas where God is encountered in the nakedness of pure trust.... The message of hope the contemplative offers you ... is that, whether you understand it or not, God loves you, is present in you, lives in you, dwells in you, calls you, saves you and offers you an understanding and light which are like nothing you ever found in books or heard in sermons" (158).

There are lengthy correspondences with people opposed to war who advocated nonviolence as the only authentic way of resolving conflict situations. Writing to John Heidbrink in October 1961, he says, "I am very anxious to be in touch with anyone who is working for peace at this hour" (402). He was in touch with many such people. It is helpful to indicate a few of them. Wilbur H. Ferry, at the Center for the Study of Democratic Institutions in Santa Barbara, was most faithful to Merton in sending books and articles that helped him keep abreast of what was happening in the world. Ferry visited Merton and they became good friends. Ferry also became something of a "distributor" of the *samizdat*[2] articles (especially the "Cold War Letters") that Merton wrote to a kind of "underground" readership — a tactic that enabled him to get around the censors. Merton's letters to "Ping" (as Ferry was called) number at least eighty-five. James Forest, at the *Catholic Worker,* was the recipient of seventy-two letters from Merton, letters in which Merton, acting as spiritual guide, helped Forest and others in launching the Catholic Peace Fellowship and became more and more linked with the Fellowship of Reconciliation. In a letter of February 6, 1962, Merton warned of the subtle dangers that threatened people in the peace movement: "One of the most problematic questions about non-violence is the inevitable involvement of hidden aggressions and provocations" (263). In a letter of February 21, 1966, that has become something of a classic, Merton addresses himself to a despondent Forest, who lamented that the peace movement seemed to be going nowhere. "Do not depend on the hope of results," Merton told him. "When you are doing the sort of work you have taken on . . . you may have to face the fact that your work will be apparently worthless and even achieve no result at all. As you get used to this idea, you start more and more to concentrate not on the results but on the value, the rightness, the truth of the work itself. . . . You struggle less and less for an idea and more and more for specific persons" (294). Twelve letters were written to Hildegard Goss-Mayr, a remarkable woman who dedicated her life, as did her husband Jean, to teaching the principles and tactics of nonviolence as the only way to peace. During the Second Vatican Council Merton wrote to her, Dorothy Day, and other women who had come to Rome to lobby the bishops for the cause of peace and nonviolence. He also sent them some of his peace writings, which they were able to get into the hands of some of the bishops at the Council.

It should be remembered that Merton wrote most of his letters in the tumultuous 1960s. At times he yielded to the temptation to be different, glib, and offbeat. Yet, as the preface to the volume points out, "He was essentially a man of tradition, striving to recover authentic Christian and monastic values in a time of change and upheaval, during which he often read the signs of the times better and more clearly than others. He never claimed to have the answers to all questions. He did feel certain that he had some of the right questions; and he probed them relentlessly with a greater sense of freedom in his letters than elsewhere. He wrote at a time when the very foundations of Christian life and culture were being shaken. One of the reasons he was sometimes misunderstood was that he was doing a bit of the shaking himself" (vii). WHS

Notes

1. The Farrar, Straus and Giroux edition failed to give a list of the correspondents. The publishers deemed this unnecessary because the letters were arranged in alphabetical order by correspondents. The Harcourt, Brace edition does give, on pages 657–58, a helpful listing of the names of the correspondents, and with each, the number of letters and the time span over which they were written.

2. *Samizdat* originally referred to the secret publication and distribution of government-banned literature.

HINDUISM

Thomas Merton's earliest interactions with Hinduism took the form of "encounters" with two extraordinary Hindus. Merton was a student at Oakham when, in 1931, he first became aware of Mahatma Gandhi. Although the young Merton never met Gandhi, news reports of Gandhi's visit to England apparently made an impression on Merton. He recalled arguing about Gandhi with the head prefect and insisting that "Gandhi was right, that India was, with perfect justice, demanding that the British withdraw peacefully and go home;

that the millions of people who lived in India had a perfect right to run their own country" (*Seeds of Destruction*, 222). Years later Merton's reading of Gandhi would inspire and sustain his own commitment to nonviolence. From Gandhi, Merton would learn the Hindu principles that inform the practice of nonviolence: a commitment to the force of truth (*satyagraha*), to noninjury (*ahimsa*), and to action without attachment to results (*nishkama karma*). In "A Tribute to Gandhi" and in "Gandhi and the One-Eyed Giant" (the introduction to *Gandhi on Non-Violence*), Merton celebrated Gandhi's wisdom and witness. "Gandhi's whole concept of man's relation to his own inner being and to the world of objects around him was informed by the contemplative heritage of Hinduism, together with the principles of Karma Yoga which blended, in his thought, with the ethic of the Synoptic Gospels and the Sermon on the Mount" (227).

While Merton was a student at Columbia University, he met Dr. Bramachari. The Hindu monk, at once learned, wise, and kind, made a deep impression on Merton and his friends. It was Bramachari who suggested that Merton read the *Confessions of St. Augustine* and the *Imitation of Christ*. In so doing, the Hindu monk played a role in Merton's conversion to Catholicism. Later in his life Merton would continue to find that encounters with persons of deep faith, whatever their religion, would serve to deepen his own faith.

Merton's interest in Eastern religions, already in evidence before his conversion as he read about Christian and Eastern mysticism in the writings of Aldous Huxley, grew in the 1950s and 1960s, when Merton immersed himself in the writings of Asian religions. Personal contacts continued to play a role as Merton deepened his understanding of Eastern religions: Buddhism, Taoism, Confucianism, and Hinduism.

One such contact with Indian thought, although Merton neither met him nor corresponded with him, was Indian scholar and philosopher Ananda Coomaraswamy. Ananda died in 1947, but in 1961 Merton wrote to his widow, Dona Luisa Coomaraswamy, to share his admiration for and interest in her hus-

band's writings. "Ananda Coomaraswamy is in many ways to me a model: the model of one who has thoroughly and completely united in himself the spiritual tradition and attitudes of the Orient and of the Christian West, not excluding also something of Islam.... Such men can become as it were 'sacraments' or signs of peace, at least. They can do much to open up the minds of their contemporaries to receive, in the future, new seeds of thought" (*Hidden Ground of Love*, 126). In the same letter he tells Dona Luisa Coomaraswamy that he had enjoyed a record of Indian religious music. The "chanting of the Vedas, of which a sample is given, was the thing that really first opened up the Upanishads to me. The *way* in which the words are chanted shows the spiritual character of Hindu singing and reflects the spiritual understanding of breath that is exposed in the Upanishads. I am now finishing the Brihad Aranyaka Upanishad and it is tremendous" (128).

In 1966 Amiya Chakravarty, Indian poet, philosopher, and scholar, who then was teaching at Smith College, wrote to ask Merton to inscribe some copies of his books for his students who had held a "Merton reading" at the college.[1] In a letter to Chakravarty and his students Merton wrote, "I do really have the feeling that you have all understood and shared quite perfectly. That you have seen something that I see to be most precious — and most available too. The reality that is present to us and in us: call it Being, call it Atman, call it Pneuma... or Silence. And the simple fact that by being attentive, by learning to listen (or recovering the natural capacity to listen which cannot be learned any more than breathing), we can find ourself engulfed in such happiness that it cannot be explained: the happiness of being at one with everything in that hidden ground of Love for which there can be no explanations" (115). Merton was grateful for the books Chakravarty sent to him. "I am especially glad to have the ones on India, and I am bent on continuing to read about Hindu thought and deepening my appreciation of it" (113).

In 1968, Merton published a preface to *The Bhagavad Gita As It Is*, with an introduction and translation by Swami A. C. Bhaktivedanta. Entitled "The Significance of the *Bhagavad Gita*," the piece was reprinted in *The Asian Journal*. Merton sees the Bhagavad Gita as fusing "worship, action, and contemplation in a fulfillment of daily duty which transcends all three by virtue of a higher consciousness: a consciousness of acting passively, of being an obedient instrument of a transcendent will" (*Asian Journal*, 348). With its emphasis on inner consciousness, the Gita, Merton wrote, exposes the inadequacy of "our highly activistic and one-sided culture" (349). Merton also focuses attention on two themes in the Gita: God and war. While the Upanishads focus on the formless, unconditional Godhead, the Gita directs attention to the Godhead made manifest in Krishna. "Conditioned brahman, then, appears in the world of nature and time under personal forms (various incarnations for Hinduism, one incarnation only for Christianity)" (350). The superior reality is manifest in countless forms, "in the million-formed inexhaustible richness of beings and events" that make up the cosmic dance (350). Living in consciousness of the cosmic dance, "our life attains its true dimension" (350). Observing that the Gita "appears to accept and justify war" as Arjuna "is exhorted to submit his will to Krishna by going to war against his enemies, who are also his own kin" and thus "do his duty as a warrior" (351). Merton points out the danger of a myth of war "willed by God," but he explains that the Gita "is not a justification of war, nor does it propound a war-making mystique" (350–51). War, in the ancient context of the Gita, was accepted, but with clearly defined limitations. The Gita does not glorify war; it emphasizes the importance of duty done with the right intention, not directed "by one's own selfish interests, still less by cruelty, sadism, and blood-lust" (352–53).

Merton's trip to Asia in 1968 provided him with the opportunity for a brief but intense immersion in Indian culture. Merton visited Calcutta, New Delhi, and Madras. *The Asian Journal* is full of vivid descriptions of what he saw — images of deities, pujas, and devotees — and what he was reading and thinking, including eighth-century Hindu philosopher

Sankaracharya's studies of atman, brahman, and karma.[2] CMB

SEE ALSO BRAMACHARI, MAHANAMBRATA; CHAKRAVARTY, AMIYA; *GANDHI ON NON-VIOLENCE*; NONVIOLENCE.

Notes

1. Among the students who wrote to Merton was Diana Eck, who went on to become an Indologist and is currently a professor at Harvard University.
2. The journal that Merton kept during his Asian journey has also been published as *The Other Side of the Mountain*.

HIROSHIMA

The atomic bombings of Hiroshima and of Nagasaki were important for Thomas Merton because of their intrinsic horror, but also as paradigmatic events for the subsequent development of the arms race and the threat of nuclear destruction. They constituted the climax of the erosion through the course of World War II of any ethical limitations to a policy of total war, an acceptance of the "systematic terrorism" (*Breakthrough to Peace*, 8) of attacks on civilians as a tactic for gaining military and political objectives. The fact that Hiroshima was chosen as a target primarily because it was largely undamaged by previous attacks and therefore would provide unambiguous evidence for the effectiveness of the newly developed weapon was for Merton a particularly blatant example of the way "a calculated project of terror and annihilation" could be determined without "the remotest reference to morality" (106). Hiroshima represented the total abdication of adherence to traditional principles of the just war in favor of "pragmatic principles" and "more or less opportunistic choices" (*Passion for Peace*, 33).

In addition to his prose poem *Original Child Bomb*, an ironic "meditation" that Merton describes as "a deadpan thing, a simple chaining together of clichés" representing the way the human race regarded the bombing at the time, "its pitiful and sudden attempts to exorcise the horror with cheap symbols" (*Road to Joy*, 40), Merton's most significant reflections on the horror of Hiroshima were expressed in his 1962 letter to the mayor of Hiroshima and in connection with the visit to his Gethsemani hermitage in 1964 of a group of "Hibakusha," survivors of the atomic bombing. The letter to Mayor Shinzo Hamai expressed Merton's "conviction that the people of Hiroshima stand today as a symbol of the hopes of humanity" because of their witness for peace and disarmament, a witness that he feared the wider world would not really accept because "it cannot face the truth which you represent" (*Hidden Ground of Love*, 380–81). Two years later, on May 16, 1964, the vigil of Pentecost, Merton hosted the group of atomic victims whom he describes in his journal as "signed and marked by the cruelty of the age, signs on their flesh because of the *thoughts* in the minds of other men" (*Water of Life*, 104). He juxtaposes the abstract "logic" of the atomic attack with the concrete reality of the human beings whose sufferings had been imposed by this logic. He provides concrete descriptions of each of the visitors as a kind of witness to their unique and irreplaceable humanness. "The most valid statement of the whole afternoon" (105) for Merton was made by Mrs. Tayoshi, who did not say a word but left behind a folded paper crane in response to Merton's reading of his poem "Paper Cranes" (subtitled "The Hibakusha Come to Gethsemani") (*Collected Poems*, 740), in which the innocent creation of a child's hand and heart and eye is proclaimed to be wiser and ultimately more powerful than the hawk's and eagle's aggression.

Merton remained in contact with Hiromu Morashita, a leader of the group, writing to him in 1965 shortly before the anniversary of the bombing that present American policy in Vietnam bore unsettling similarities to the "logic" that led to the attacks on Hiroshima and Nagasaki. The root of the problem, Merton wrote to Morashita, "is that those in power do not think in terms of human beings and living persons, but in terms of political abstractions which tend to become more and more unrelated to human reality" (*Hidden Ground of Love*, 460). The purpose of protest is precisely to keep this human reality, the human cost of war, in plain view, and Merton declares his own unity with Morashita and the other survivors "in concern and protest at this time when once again violence seems to be usurping the place of reason and humane understanding" (460). POC

SEE ALSO *ORIGINAL CHILD BOMB*.

HOLOCAUST

As a "contemporary of Auschwitz, Hiroshima, Viet Nam and the Watts riots," Thomas Merton saw himself as "deeply and personally involved" in the events that had shaped the twentieth century (*World of Action*, 145/161). When, in the summer of 1961, he began to speak out on the issues of genocide, war, and racism — issues that would continue to claim his attention during the 1960s — he wrote two poems: "Original Child Bomb" on the bomb detonated at Hiroshima and "Chant to Be Used in Processions around a Site with Furnaces" on the atrocity of Auschwitz (*Collected Poems*, 293–302, 345–49). In both poems Merton drew on published accounts, rife with double-talk, to expose the reality that the accounts themselves distorted and obscured. In a letter to Nicanor Parra in June 1965, Merton identifies the source for "Chant": "In truth this poem is composed almost in its entirety from the very words of the commanders of Auschwitz. It would be impossible to invent something more terrifying than the truth itself" (*Courage for Truth*, 213). Merton was bothered by the fact that the "sardonic" tone of the poem appeared, at least to one reader, "noncommittal and callous (apparently)" (268).

In the years that followed Merton wrote two articles on the Holocaust: "A Devout Meditation in Memory of Adolf Eichmann" and "Auschwitz: A Family Camp." The Eichmann essay was first published in the 1964 issue of *New Directions Prose and Poetry* and later appeared in *Ramparts* (October 1966) and also in *Raids on the Unspeakable*. Merton himself described the essay as "a mosaic of Eichmann's own doubletalk about himself" (248). Examined by a psychiatrist at his trial, Eichmann was pronounced "sane." "All along, the terrible thing about the Eichmann case," Merton wrote in his journal in March 1963, "was the fact that his motives were always *motives of conscience* and duty, not of fanaticism" (*Turning toward the World*, 308).

"Auschwitz: A Family Camp," a review of *Auschwitz: A Report on the Proceedings against Robert Karl Ludwig Mulka and Others before the Court of Frankfurt*[1] by Bernd Naumann, was published in the *Catholic Worker* (November 1967). After listing horrific examples of atrocities of Auschwitz that surfaced in twenty months of the trial — only to be "confidently and consistently denied" by the defendants (*Passion for Peace*, 276) — Merton turns his attention to the language of Auschwitz: "In destroying human beings, and human values on a mass scale, the Gestapo also subjected the German language to violence and crude perversion" (281). Secrecy, cryptic and evasive records, double-talk and double-think, officialese — all served to create and maintain a demonic reality. " 'Disinfectants,' 'materials for resettlement of Jews,' 'ovaltine substitute from Swiss Red Cross' — all references to Zyklon B!" (282). Merton concludes that "the incredible brutality and inhumanity of Auschwitz" was perpetrated by "ordinary respectable people"; "Auschwitz worked because these people wanted it to work" (285). The whole bureaucracy was involved — police and party members, managers and employees. "Almost all of them committed gratuitous acts of arbitrary cruelty and violence which were forbidden even by the Gestapo's own rules" (286). Merton warns that what happened at Auschwitz could happen again if "one basic principle" is affirmed: "ANYONE BELONGING TO CLASS X OR NATION Y OR RACE Z IS TO BE REGARDED AS SUBHUMAN AND WORTHLESS, AND CONSEQUENTLY HAS NO RIGHT TO EXIST. ALL THE REST WILL FOLLOW WITHOUT DIFFICULTY" (285–86).

A third essay, "The Trial of Pope Pius XII: Rolf Hochhuth's *The Deputy*," became the occasion for raising the subject of the church and the Holocaust. Reviewing Hochhuth's play in 1963, Merton characterized it as "an attack, a passionate aggression on the character and reputation" of Pope Pius XII, whom the playwright places "on the same plane as Hitler" (*Literary Essays*, 162, 163). Although it is "a bad play," it raises a serious question (162). The question, however "crudely stated" by Hochhuth, is this: "When the Church is faced with a critical choice between the most basic of all its moral laws, the law of love for God and for man, and the practical, immediate options of power politics, is she now so accustomed to choosing the latter that she is no longer able to see the former?" (164). Is the church concerned with preserving its power "at any cost?" (164). Although he defends Pius XII against Hochhuth's vitriolic attacks, Merton questions the church in the light of its continuing silence on a host of political situations. Silenced himself when it came to writing about war, Merton observed in his journal, "It seems strange that a monk should be forbidden to stand up for the truth" (*Water of Life*, 84). Appalled by the "stupor of the Church," he lists as examples "Pope Pius XII and the Jews, the Church in South America, the treatment of Negroes in the U.S., the Catholics on the French right in the Algerian affair, the German Catholics under Hitler" (84). Admitting that "we in the Church are deluded and complacent about ourselves" (93), Merton was opening the door to a critical examination of the Church's actions and failures to act in the face of genocide and injustices that threaten human lives. CMB

SEE ALSO JUDAISM.

Notes

1. London: Pall Mall Press, 1966.

HOLY SPIRIT

Thomas Merton's appropriation of the Western, Augustinian explanation of the Holy Spirit as the bond of mutual love between Father and Son grounds his understanding of the role of the Spirit in uniting persons to the Father through the Son, as the bond of unity in the church, and as the dynamic power of re-creation transforming the face of the earth. "The Holy Spirit is the bond of union between the Father and the Son, their 'peace,' their 'love,' their 'unity' " (*Thomas Merton on St. Bernard*, 35). Therefore the gift of new life in Christ is the gift of the Holy Spirit, which makes a person one with Christ and so draws the person into the intimacy of the divine life of Trinitarian love. "The mystery of our sanctification in Christ is, then, that the love of God, the bond of the Father and the Son, the Holy Spirit, reaches out to us from within

Christ, and brings to life divine love, the likeness of Christ in us" (*Seasons of Celebration*, 43).

The gift of the Spirit is poured out in the death and resurrection of Christ and draws the Christian into a participation in that death and resurrection by a total self-surrender in which the spurious identity of the false self is given up so that the true person created by God and redeemed by Christ can live in and as Christ. "The Holy Spirit, therefore, is at work in us, not just to remind us to look back to the Passion and remember where it all started, but to communicate to us the fruits of the Passion and of the Resurrection and to create in us the risen life or the victory over death" (*Thomas Merton in Alaska*, 84). This is the essential meaning of redemption, and is the heart of the experience of Christian contemplation. "The work of the Holy Ghost," Merton writes, is to confer on us the reality of divine Sonship, "identifying us, each individually, with the only-begotten Son of God, Christ, the Incarnate Word" (*No Man Is an Island*, 175). There are not many sons (and daughters) of God, but all are one in the risen Christ and all come into the presence of the Father with and in the glorified Son: "It is not Christ that we see but Christ who sees in us: this is based on a theology of the Spirit" (*Witness to Freedom*, 336). Yet, this is not the extinguishing of true selfhood but its fulfillment. "Each one of us becomes completely himself when, in the Spirit of God, he is transformed in Christ" (*No Man Is an Island*, 175).

Thus, Merton sees the role of the Spirit in Christian life as leading the believer through the paschal transformation that recovers the true self in Christ and draws the person into the eternal life of Trinitarian love. "The Christian life is a return to the Father, the Source, the Ground of all existence, through the Son, the Splendor and the Image of the Father, in the Holy Spirit, the Love of the Father and the Son. And this return is only possible by detachment and 'death' in the exterior self, so that the inner self, purified and renewed, can fulfil its function as image of the Divine Trinity [and can] return to the Father in Christ" ("Inner Experience," 3:202). This is the reality that has already taken place once for all in the paschal mystery and that all the redeemed will experience fully in the final resurrection, but it is also a present reality that all believers experience in faith and that is revealed in an unmediated way in contemplative prayer: "Contemplation is an intuition of love recognizing our union by grace and gift with the indwelling Holy Spirit 'in whom we cry Abba Father.' Properly speaking, Christian contemplation is Trinitarian, and sees the connection of our own inner life with the inner life of the Three Divine Persons since we are united to the Father, in the Son, by the Holy Spirit" (*Witness to Freedom*, 195).

But this is not a process that takes place in isolation from the rest of humanity and the rest of creation. To be united to Christ in the Spirit is to be joined to all others who are likewise made one with Christ. "After all, transformation into Christ is not just an individual affair: there is only one Christ, not many. He is not divided. And for me to become Christ is to enter into the Life of the Whole Christ, the Mystical Body, made up of the Head and the members, Christ and all who are incorporated in Him by His Spirit" (*New Seeds of Contemplation*, 156–57). Thus, the Spirit is the "soul" (*Life and Holiness*, 66), the animating principle of the church, "the principle of life, unity, and action which draws the souls of men together to live as one in the 'Whole Christ'" (*No Man Is an Island*, 177). The church cannot be regarded simply as an institution, an external structure (*Life and Holiness*, 66); it is a "living and organic" unity (45) constituted by the gift of the Spirit to the community of disciples gathered together at Easter and empowered to preach the good news by the descent of the Spirit at Pentecost. "The Holy Spirit, Who is the bond of union between the Father and the Son, is also the bond of union between the faithful who have been reconciled to the Father through the Son, and with one another in the Church" (*Seasons of Celebration*, 218). It is thus through the mediation of the church that the gift of the Spirit is regularly transmitted. Baptism is the normal way in which the believer receives the Holy Spirit by entering "into the Mystery of the Passion and Resurrection of Christ" (*No Man Is an Island*, 178). It is through the power of the Spirit that failure to fully enflesh the new identity in Christ is pardoned and forgiven sinners are invited to participate in the Eucharist, the sacrament of unity and "the celebration of our reconciliation in Christ and in His Spirit" (*Seasons of Celebration*, 227).

But the Spirit of love is not only centripetal, drawing members of the body of Christ into deeper unity with one another; it also is centrifugal, a dynamism that extends the power of God's love to the ends of the earth. The Spirit of creation who hovered over the waters at the beginning of Genesis is the same Spirit who impels redeemed humanity to participate in the ongoing act of renewal and transformation of the world. "Our life," Merton writes in his journal, "is a powerful Pentecost in which the Holy Spirit, ever active in us, seeks to reach through our inspired hands and tongues into the very heart of the material world created to be spiritualized through the work of the Church, the Mystical Body of the Incarnate Word of God" (*Search for Solitude*, 86). The ongoing work of the Spirit takes place through those in whom the Spirit dwells. Life in the Spirit is a life of hope and freedom and love, a life that is willing to obey the inspiration of the divine breeze that blows where it wills. Whereas for the "old man" any change is a threat even though he realizes what he has cannot satisfy him, so that he lives in an agony of self-division, "for the 'new man' — everything is new. Even the old is transfigured in the Holy Spirit and is always new. There is nothing to cling to, there is nothing to be hoped for in what is already past — it is nothing. . . . The new man lives in a world that is always being created, and renewed. He lives in this realm of renewal and of creation. He lives in life" (269). He is not only able to recognize the new but also to act as the instrument of renewal, of re-creation. "The true responsibility" of the Christian, Merton believes, is "to receive the Holy Spirit and cooperate with His transforming work in time now" (*Turning toward the World*, 274).

Thus, Merton's work in monastic renewal, in advocating for racial justice and for peace, and in challenging injustice and deadly conventions in society and even in the church are ways of being faithful to the gift of the Holy Spirit. As he notes, "When custom and law systematically conceal rights and truth, then the Holy Spirit inspires men to carry out actions that violate custom and law in order to bear witness to truth" (*Guilty Bystander*, 207). There is a need to discern what the Spirit is saying to the churches, and to obey the Spirit even when the more comfortable course is to prefer the old to the new. Merton is aware of the constant temptation to domesticate the Spirit. As he wrote in October 1957, well before Angelo Roncalli became pope and made the same image famous, "The fresh air we need is the air of the Holy Spirit 'breathing where He pleases' which means that the windows must be open and we must expect Him to come from any direction. The error is to lock the windows and doors in order to keep the Holy Spirit in our house. The very action of locking doors and windows is fatal" (*Search for Solitude*, 130).

This willingness to expect the Holy Spirit to come from any direction extended for Merton even beyond the confines of the Christian community. He came to recognize that "God must be allowed the right to speak unpredictably. The Holy Spirit, the very voice of Divine Liberty, must always be like the wind in 'blowing where he pleases' " (*Collected Poems*, 384). This means that the role of the Christian is not only to witness to the presence of the Spirit to those outside the church, but also to look for and to find the Spirit already present in other cultures, other religious traditions, and other human beings, also made in the image of God. The Spirit "certainly inspires and protects the visible Church, but if we cannot see him unexpectedly in the stranger and the alien, we will not understand him even in the Church. We must find him in our enemy, or we may lose him even in our friend. We must find him in the pagan or we will lose him in our own selves, substituting for his living presence an empty abstraction" (384). It is this recognition that is evident in Merton's spontaneous closing prayer at the Calcutta Spiritual Summit Conference: "Oh God, in accepting one another wholeheartedly, fully, completely, we accept You, and we thank You, and we adore You, and we love You with our whole being, because our being is in Your being, our spirit is rooted in Your spirit. Fill us then with love, and let us be bound together with love as we go our diverse ways, united in this one spirit which makes You present in the world, and which makes You witness to the ultimate reality that is love" (*Asian Journal*, 318–19). POC

SEE ALSO GOD; REDEMPTION; TRINITY.

"HONORABLE READER":
Reflections on My Work
Edited by Robert E. Daggy.
New York: Crossroad, 1989. 172 pp.

This book, originally published as *Introductions East and West: The Foreign Prefaces of Thomas Merton,*[1] is a unique work, for it represents Thomas Merton's later thinking about some of his books that had been translated into other languages. Fifteen prefaces are included, three not in the original edition. Editor Robert E. Daggy provides brief, helpful introductory words with each of the prefaces. The book contains Merton's 1967 graph evaluating his books and a list of the books translated into other languages. The title of the book is taken from the concluding paragraph of the introduction to the Japanese edition of *The Seven Storey Mountain.*

The foreign prefaces were written between 1953 and 1967. They are, Daggy tells us, unique to the Merton corpus and an important resource for future study of Merton. They vary in length and quality. In them we see him "thinking about the themes in the books he is introducing. In his attempts to convey aspects of Western idealism to the East, we glimpse his hope for understanding between peoples" ("*Honorable Reader*," 5).

These fifteen prefaces were written for translations into seven different foreign languages: five in French, four in Japanese, two in Spanish, one each in Catalan, Korean, Portuguese, and Vietnamese. The following five may serve as representative examples of Merton's afterthoughts about some of his books.

Preface to the Argentine Edition of The Complete Works of Thomas Merton (April 1958)

This preface of six pages speaks of the importance of the contemplative life. It finds its place

wherever there is life and love and pain and ideals and aspirations for the future. To understand the significance of life, one needs to enter life's interiority.

Merton speaks of his vocation to be a contemplative, a Christian, and an American. He is not just a North American, for the North is incomplete without the richer part of the hemisphere, the roots of the old America: the America of Mexico and the Andes, of Brazil and Argentina. "I cannot," Merton writes, "be a partial American and I cannot be, which is even sadder, a partial Catholic. For me Catholicism is not confined to one culture, one nation, one age, one race" (41). It is not simply the culture of Irish America, or the culture of his native France, or the Spanish culture of Latin America. "My Catholicism is not the religion of the bourgeoisie nor will it ever be. My Catholicism is all the world and all ages" (41). Nor can it be simply a relic of the past. The past does not depend on us, but the future does. The church must open its eyes to the future. Contemplation will not construct the future; without contemplation, however, we easily can succumb to narrow groups and selfish interests and in the end betray the Christ we pretend to serve. The joyous reign of God can come only when people, made in the image of God, achieve unity with one another through the power of the cross and the victory of the resurrection. Then will Christ have come to full maturity in the whole hemisphere of a whole New World.

Preface to the Japanese Edition of The Seven Storey Mountain (August 1963)

Reflecting on his autobiography, Merton declares that it is a youthful book that no longer belongs exclusively to him. Nor would he choose to tell it differently. Yet he faces this question: Has the author changed? Certainly there has been no change in his conviction to be a Christian, a monk, and a priest, but the assumptions and attitudes behind that conviction have changed in many ways. He looks to the world in which he lives with greater compassion. While refusing to live with its delusions, he nonetheless identifies with its struggles and its hopes for happiness.

The only true liberty, he affirms, "is in the service of that which is beyond all limits, beyond all definitions, beyond all human appreciation: that which is All and which therefore is no limited or individual thing: the All is nothing, for if it were to be a single thing separated from all other things, it would not be All." To achieve such freedom, "I must let go my hold upon myself also and not retain the semblance of a self which is an object or a 'thing.' I too must be no-thing. And when I am no-thing, I am in the All and Christ lives in me" (64–65).

His monastery, he insists, is not a home, but a place where he can disappear from the world as an object of interest in order to be everywhere in the world by hiddenness and compassion. By his monastic life and vows he says no to the crimes of injustice and war, to economic tyrannies, to racial discrimination, "to the whole socio-economic apparatus which seems geared for nothing but global destruction in spite of its fair words in favor of peace" (65–66). At the same time, he says yes to all that is good in humans, to all that is beautiful in nature, to all his brothers and sisters in the world.

"Therefore, most honorable reader," he concludes, "it is not as an author that I would speak to you, not as a friend only; I seek to speak to you, in some way as your own self. But if you listen things will be said that perhaps are not written in this book. And this will be due not to me, but to One who lives and speaks in both!" (67).

Preface to the Japanese Edition of Seeds of Contemplation (March 1965)

Merton laments that our modern technological society has lost its sense of the importance of the way of wisdom, which alone can lead to the inner meaning of life. "This way of wisdom is no dream, no temptation and no evasion, for it is on the contrary a return to reality in its very root" (86). Throughout this preface Merton uses the word "way," clearly with the Tao of Eastern thought in mind. The way of wisdom is the contemplative way, a way that renounces the obsession with the triumph of the individual or the collective will to power. "The life of the collective mass is such that

it destroys in man the inmost need and capacity for contemplation" (89). The mission of the contemplative is to seek the true way to human unity and peace. This means keeping alive in the world an awareness of God living in people and thereby establishing a living contact with the infinite Source of all being. This the contemplative seeks to achieve by a surrender of love. For God is not only pure being but also pure love, and to know God is to become one with God in love.

Preface to the Japanese Edition of Thoughts in Solitude (March 1966)

This preface is a remarkable essay on solitude that deserves to be read and studied on its own, quite apart from the book it is intended to introduce. Two quotations will whet the reader's interest. "Where is silence? Where is solitude? Where is Love? Ultimately, these cannot be found anywhere except in the ground of our own being. There in the silent depths, there is no more distinction between the I and the Not-I. There is perfect peace because we are grounded in infinite creative and redemptive love" (114). "Often our need for others is not Love at all, but only the need to be sustained in our illusions, even as we sustain others in theirs. But when we have renounced these illusions, then we can certainly go out to others in true compassion" (117).

Preface to the Japanese Edition of The New Man (October 1967)

Building on Jesus' words to Nicodemus (John 3:5–8), Merton speaks of the need to be reborn. To be born again involves a change from within. It does not mean becoming somebody else, but becoming ourselves. "To be born again is to be born beyond egoism, beyond selfishness, beyond individuality, in Christ" (133). Yet it is important to realize that far from being a once-and-for-all event, rebirth calls for "a continuous dynamic of inner renewal" (133). A Western world that has lived under the sign of Prometheus, "the fire-stealer, the man of power who defies heaven in order to get what he himself desires," needs to learn that there is another side to Christianity: "the interior, the silent, the contemplative, in which hidden wisdom is more important than practical or-ganizational science and in which love replaces the will to get visible results. . . . This aspect of Christianity will perhaps be intelligible to those in an Asian culture who are familiar with the deeper aspects of their own religious tradition. For the religions of Asia also have long sought to liberate man from imprisonment in a half real external existence, in order to initiate him into the full and complete reality of an inner peace which is secret and beyond explanation" (136). WHS

Notes

1. Greensboro, N.C.: Unicorn Press, 1981.

HOPE

Christianity, according to Thomas Merton, is preeminently "a religion of hope," founded on the belief that human beings are created in the image and likeness of God and that di-vine mercy and goodness are more powerful than human evil (*Monastic Journey*, 52). The basis for Christian hope, then, is God's love and acceptance, as revealed in the cross of Christ (*Thoughts in Solitude*, 38–39), and in the new life bestowed by "the great feast of Christian hope: the Resurrection" (*Road to Joy*, 99). Merton emphasizes both that hope has a transcendent dimension, pointing toward the ultimate fulfillment of the world to come (*Thoughts in Solitude*, 38), the eschatological kingdom (*Seasons of Celebration*, 60), and that it has profound effects on the way one's life is lived here and now. The "problem of hope," Merton writes, is "to establish a right relation-ship between the past and the future, which give spiritual solidity to the *present*" (*Search for Solitude*, 354).

Hope is the heart of genuine asceticism (*No Man Is an Island*, 18) because it demands total reliance on the unseen God and total detach-ment from all that is not God. It frees one from unrealistic desires and expectations of oneself and of the rest of creation, but at the same time makes possible an authentic and vital re-lationship with created reality, including the self. Merton writes that hope "is the virtue that strips us of all things in order to give us

possession of all things. . . . Hope deprives us of everything that is not God, in order that all things may serve their true purpose as means to bring us to God" (14–15). Hope recognizes the true end of creation in the eschatological new heaven and new earth (19), and at the same time, creation itself provides evidence of God's fidelity to the divine promises and thus a reason for hope (20). Hope undermines all spurious autonomy, all reliance on oneself independent of God: "The more our hope is based on our own virtues and resources, the less we are able to face the truth" (*Search for Solitude*, 157). True hope is intrinsically linked with self-forgetfulness and love of other people rather than depending on an illusory founda-tion of past achievements and the even less substantial base of future expectations (*Learn-ing to Love*, 361). Hope is able to acknowledge even the darkest places in one's own soul when the light of God shines on them, though it does not indulge in excessive self-examination and self-abnegation (*Guilty Bystander*, 14). It does not ignore or reject God's gifts of intelligence and free will, but makes confident use of them as faculties that image God and lead to God. "Some who think they trust in God actually sin against hope because they do not use the will and the judgment He has given them" (*No Man Is an Island*, 16). In the exercise of hope, the conflict between grace and free will is re-solved by freely accepting that even this act of hope itself is God's gift: "Hope is the wedding of two freedoms, human and divine, in the ac-ceptance of a love that is at once a promise and the beginning of fulfillment" (22).

Though he sometimes equates optimism and hope (see, e.g., *Seasons of Celebration*, 88; *Monastic Journey*, 52), Merton typically distin-guishes between them (see *Turning toward the World*, 236); too often hope is reduced to "a kind of pious optimism that 'everything will be all right,' presumably because it is just some-how the nature of things to be all right" (*Hidden Ground of Love*, 533). Authentic hope is based not on trust in some sort of static "metaphysi-cal immobility but in the dynamism of unfailing love" (*Seeds of Destruction*, 184). Hope is an act, not a state; Merton contrasts "the work of *hope*" with "the stupid, relaxed, self-pity of *acedia,*" the lethargic torpor that fails to live out professed beliefs (*Water of Life*, 278). Hope puts its trust in the power of love more than in law, in freedom more than in structures, in people more than in institutions, in the mystery of grace rather than in a "cult of success and visible results" (*Seeds of Destruction*, 323). It rejects blind faith in the power of technology and "secular progress," what Merton describes as "a false eschatology of the 'new heaven and new earth' which places its hope in the power of science to transform earth and heaven into places of happiness and bliss" (*Water of Life*, 228). It relies not on "the system" but on the free gift of transforming grace: "Christian hope" must be "hope in the Cross and Victory of Christ, not hope in Catholic organizations" (*Seeds of Destruction*, 323).

Authentic hope develops not by avoiding the darkness and apparent emptiness of life but by entering into the depths of human suffering and discovering life and meaning where from the outside an observer sees only death and absurdity: "Perfect hope is achieved on the brink of despair when, instead of falling over the edge, we find ourselves walking on the air" (*No Man Is an Island*, 206). A facile optimism must not be maintained "by the mere *suppression* of tragic realities"; hope is valid only when it confronts "darkness, desperation and ignorance" and overcomes them in Christ (*Seasons of Celebration*, 88). Hope is therefore profoundly paschal, "a communion in the agony of Christ . . . the identification of our own *agonia* with the *agonia* of the God Who has emptied Himself and become obedient unto death. It is the acceptance of life in the midst of death, not because we have courage, or light, or wisdom to accept, but because by some miracle the God of Life Himself accepts to live, in us, at the very moment when we descend into death" (*New Man*, 5); it is pure gift, not the result of merely human effort or persistence, which can only end in delusion or despair. Thus, hope is a desert virtue, discovered in solitude (*Thoughts in Solitude*, 109; *No Man Is an Island*, 253), in silence (*No Man Is an Island*, 259; *Love and Living*, 42). "It springs out of nothingness, completely free. But to meet it, we have to descend into nothingness" (*New Man*, 4–5).

Though hope points beyond the limitations of a transient world, it exists as a sign of ultimate meaning within that world. "Christian hope in God and in the world to come is inevitably also hope in man, or at least *for* man. How can we despair of man when the Word of God was made man in order to save us all?" (*Disputed Questions*, 193). Merton looks to Pope John XXIII as a model of genuine Christian "hope in the goodness placed in human nature by God the Creator. Only if human nature is radically good can a concept of authority based on the natural law and on human liberty be conceived as also at the same time rooted in the will of God" (*Seeds of Destruction*, 174). A confidence in ultimate human destiny leads to the affirmation and protection of human dignity in the concrete circumstances of the present: "Eschatological Christian hope is inseparable from an incarnational involvement in the struggle of living and contemporary man" (*Love and Living*, 156). At the same time, hope that is not naive optimism recognizes the capacity of human beings to deny their own goodness and refuse to recognize the goodness of others. An "almost despairing refusal to accept the myths and fictions with which social life is always full" may well be "a sign of hope" because it refuses acquiescence to "fiction, especially political and demagogic fiction" that is actually evidence of hopeless capitulation to unreality (*Monastic Journey*, 152). Thus, hope demands resistance to all the forces that deny authentic human dignity and destiny. Hope is a sign of contradiction to illusion and oppression and is therefore an essential element of Christian nonviolence, which depends on "an eschatological Christian hope which is completely open to the presence of God in the world and therefore to the presence of our brother who is always seen, no matter who he may be, in the perspectives of the Kingdom" (*Faith and Violence*, 26).

A steadfast witness to hope is one of the gifts that the contemplative gives to the world inasmuch as authentic contemplation is inseparable from hope. In his 1967 "Letter on the Contemplative Life," Merton describes the contemplative as one who "has risked his mind in the desert beyond language and beyond ideas where God is encountered in the nakedness of pure trust," and describes "the message of hope the contemplative offers" as the assurance "that whether you understand or not, God loves you, is present to you, lives in you, dwells in you, calls you, saves you, and offers you an understanding and light which are like nothing you ever found in books or heard in sermons," an experience of "the intimate union in the depths of your own heart, of God's spirit and your own secret inmost self, so that you and He are in all truth One Spirit" (*Monastic Journey*, 173). POC

SEE ALSO DESPAIR.

HUMANISM

The word "humanism" is an ambiguous and problematic one. In its origins, as Thomas Merton notes in passing (*Mystics and Zen Masters*, 114), it referred to Renaissance scholars of the humanities, dedicated in particular to recovering classical culture. Its more usual contemporary usage often connotes a rejection of the supernatural, in which the human rather than the divine is considered the primary source of value and meaning. Merton is skeptical of what he considers a reductive humanism unmoored from any transcendent ground, in which the human person is in danger of being subordinated to ideology and in fact is easily dehumanized. He writes, "The great error and weakness of our time is the delusion of 'humanism' in a culture where man has first been completely alienated from himself by economic individualism, and then precipitated into the morass of mass-technological society which is there to receive us in an avalanche of faceless 'numbers'" (*Disputed Questions*, xi). If he is mistrustful of the capitalist tendency to turn the person into a consumer, not only of commodities but also of preformed ideas, he is equally uneasy with the dogmatic Marxist approach that too often is willing to sacrifice actual human beings to an abstraction, the ideal human being of the future who is to emerge from the revolutionary process. "The Marxian dialectic of historical determinism, its humanism without the human person, leaves man powerless to transcend the forces of the social process in which he is immersed" (*Seeds of Destruction*, 161). Thus, Merton applauds

Pasternak's commitment to genuine freedom and creativity "against the false and empty humanism of the Marxists — for whom man does not yet truly exist," but sees his protest as equally applicable to "the technological jargon and the empty scientism of modern man" in the West as in the East (*Disputed Questions*, 31). He summarizes his judgment of the inadequacies of secular humanism in a 1963 letter: "The Cold War is a struggle between two kinds of humanism which I regard as more or less gross and ineffective: the liberal kind and the totalist kind. Neither is, to me, an effective and realistic humanism at all" (*Witness to Freedom*, 101).

Merton believes that authentic Christian humanism is, or at least should be, a paramount safeguard of the essential dignity of the human person because it "is the full flowering of the theology of the Incarnation. It is rooted in a totally new concept of man which grew out of the mystery of the union of God and man in Christ.... It is the full realization of man's dignity and obligations as son of God, as image of God, created, regenerated, and transformed in the Word made Flesh" (*Mystics and Zen Masters*, 114–15). A Christian humanism, therefore, is committed not to some abstract ideal of the human but to the human person "in his personal and existential actuality" (*Love and Living*, 149). Christian humanism is dynamic, affirming the transforming power of forgiveness and merciful love to allow persons to grow into full humanity (145).[1] It recognizes the true identity of the person, whose selfhood is intrinsically bound up with freely chosen relationships with others, in contrast both to the solipsistic narcissism of the individual (146) and to the absorption of the self in the collectivity or mass society. For the Christian, sanctity is simply the full realization of the potential of the human person as made in the image of God and recreated in Christ, himself the person who was most perfectly human (*Thoughts in Solitude*, 24; *Life and Holiness*, 20). It is the recognition and acceptance of the responsibility to take on the obligations of true freedom, as contrasted with a kind of relaxed, undemanding attitude that "sometimes usurps the name of 'humanism'" (*Seasons of Celebration*, 136).

While strongly affirming the centrality of

genuine humanism to Christianity and professing his own determination to be an authentic Christian humanist (*Search for Solitude*, 374), Merton in his most extensive discussion of the subject recognizes that Christian humanism in the contemporary world is both a problem and a temptation. The problem arises from the fact that the wider culture neither recognizes nor accepts Christianity as truly humanistic. The temptation is simply to assert a traditional articulation of Christian humanism in terms that will continue to be meaningless to a world that is desperately in need of the wisdom that Christian humanism can provide (*Love and Living*, 135). Christianity must reject a nostalgic desire to return to a pre-Enlightenment "Christendom" in which society is unified under the leadership of the church. It must be willing to enter dialogue with contemporary cultures in order to find common ground, and must recognize that it has the opportunity to learn as well as to teach, with an honest and humble admission of its own failures and infidelity as a prerequisite to any fruitful exchange (*Hidden Ground of Love*, 542).

Merton finds this openness to the world in the "personalistic . . . humanism" of the Second Vatican Council, particularly the Constitution on the Church in the Modern World (*Gaudium et Spes*), with its central affirmations of the value and dignity of each human being and of the unity of all humanity as a single family (*Love and Living*, 151), and its willingness to work together with science and technology to improve the conditions of life for humanity, even as it realistically confronts the crisis and potential for disaster in a world divided between rich and poor and threatened with annihilation by the power of technology untethered from the wisdom of authentic respect for every human person. In the current state of the world, Merton asserts "the urgent need for Christian humanism," for "the fully Christian notion of man" as of infinite value because created and loved by God (*Hidden Ground of Love*, 541), as a sign of contradiction to all systems that subordinate the person to the institution, but also as a sign of new possibilities, of an alternative vision that points out a way to avoid self-destruction.

Merton sees the necessity for a dialogue between Christian and secular humanism that may draw out potential elements in the latter that can break through its own reductivist limitations. He advocates an interchange between Christian humanists and Marxists, based on "the inner spiritual potentialities hidden under the surface of the Marxian dialectic," with its protest against human alienation, as discovered particularly in the early essays of Marx in which "there is a very clear demand for the kind of dimension that can only be supplied by wisdom." Likewise, he sees the possibility of a "collaboration between the Christian humanist and the technological humanist, based on the latter's realization of the need for wisdom" (544–45). He finds in this "religious humanism," present in all authentic spiritual traditions, with its "appeal to the deepest moral idealism of a civilized tradition," the best hope for a resolution of the violence that is pervasive in foreign war and domestic unrest, yet confesses in a statement written for the National Commission on the Causes and Prevention of Violence that the general disregard for such a tradition, for "the classic way of religious humanism and nonviolence exemplified by Gandhi," leaves him less than optimistic about the future (*Nonviolent Alternative*, 227, 230). POC

Notes

1. See also Merton's assertion that traditional Christian humanism elevated the status of women in comparison with their position in pagan society, with its "humanism for men only" (*Mystics and Zen Masters*, 119).

HUMILITY

Humility, according to Thomas Merton, is based on a true awareness of who we are and where we stand. We are creatures totally dependent on God and therefore we stand always in need of God's sustaining power. We have nothing that we have not been given. So precarious is our existence as a self that apart from God we would simply cease to be. Our situation of total dependence is further complicated by the fact that we are sinners, estranged from God and needing God's saving grace. We have no claim on God's mercy. Recognizing our dependency and our sinfulness leads us to the realization that "we are not capable of fulfilling our destiny by ourselves" (*Seeds of Contemplation*, 108; *New Seeds of Contemplation*, 180).[1]

Humility, deriving as it does from *humus*, which means "ground" or "soil," is the firm base on which the spiritual life is built, for it involves a true grasp of the truth about ourselves and our utter need of God. In perfect humility selfishness disappears and we are transformed into God in a pure and selfless love that "empties the soul of all pride and annihilates it in the sight of God, so that nothing may be left of it but the pure capacity for God" (*New Seeds of Contemplation*, 182). Such self-emptying brings joy, for "humility alone can destroy the self-centeredness that makes joy impossible" (181).

A humble person is one who has ceased paying attention to self. Such persons, because they are in God, have no need to be concerned about themselves. Humility detaches them from "that absorption in [themselves] which makes [them] forget the reality of God. ... It gradually pulls down the edifice of illusory projects which [they] have erected between [themselves] and reality" (*Silent Life*, 4). They are no longer self-conscious: their thoughts and concerns are not about themselves. They can, therefore, accept their incompleteness with joy, knowing that such completeness comes from God. That is why a humble person can do what a prideful person cannot: accept praise graciously and without fuss, knowing that it belongs to God. "The humble person receives praise the way a clean window takes the light of the sun. The truer and more intense the light is, the less you see of the glass" (*New Seeds of Contemplation*, 189).

The humble person is able to accomplish great things for God and for people, because "living no longer for himself or on the human level, the spirit is delivered of all the limitations and vicissitudes of creaturehood and of contingency and swims in the attributes of God, whose power, magnificence, greatness and eternity have, through love, through humility, become our own" (181). In Jesus' words, "Those who exalt themselves will be humbled, and those who humble themselves will be exalted" (Luke 14:11). WHS

Notes

1. In both these books this statement occurs in a chapter entitled "Humility against Despair" (pages 183–86 in *New Seeds of Contemplation* is new material).

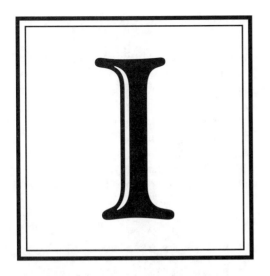

ILLUSION

On April 27, 1966, when he was living in the hermitage, Thomas Merton wrote to Erich Fromm of his need for this solitary kind of life: "I need this delving into reality, this sweating out of illusions and desires." On August 25, 1966, Fromm wrote that he very much understood what Merton had written about delving into reality: "I am sometimes surprised how, even at my age of 66, and after so many years of being occupied with the analysis of others and myself, I still discover the many veils and blindfolds and the increasing happiness when more and more falls off" (*Hidden Ground of Love*, 322).

Illusion is the failure to see reality as it is. It means seeing what is not there or not seeing what is there. Since contemplation is awareness of "the Real within all that is real" (*New Seeds of Contemplation*, 3), it should be clear that contemplation can be experienced only by a person who is free from illusions. There are many illusions with which we must deal: illusions about God, about ourselves, about people, about all created reality. Especially we need to rid ourselves of the illusion of being a separate self existing apart from God and from the rest of

reality. True freedom involves liberation from everything that is illusory. WHS

SEE ALSO CONTEMPLATION; FREEDOM; SELF.

INDIVIDUAL

SEE PERSON.

"INNER EXPERIENCE, THE"
Unpublished manuscript, 1959, 1968. 150 pp.

In the summer of 1959 Thomas Merton started out to revise an earlier work, *What Is Contemplation?* It turned out to be in many ways an entirely new full-length book, which he called "The Inner Experience."[1] Not completely satisfied with it, he kept intending to return to it to revise it. There is no evidence, however, that he ever did so, until 1968, when just before leaving for Asia, he made some brief changes.[2] The largest was the insertion of a paragraph of 125 words. The other changes were minor: a word, phrase, or sentence here or there. Altogether the changes amounted to 450 words, just one hundred words more than one of the manuscript pages — hardly a substantial change.[3]

"The Inner Experience," though not completed to his satisfaction, is an important work in the Merton corpus. Dealing as it does with the subject of contemplation, it is a transitional

Cover for *Ishi Means Man* reprinted with the permission of Unicorn Press. Woodblock by Rita Corbin.

work between the earlier works on contemplation, such as *Seeds of Contemplation,* and his later works, beginning with *New Seeds of Contemplation* and extending to works such as *Zen and the Birds of Appetite.* The book has a broader focus than those earlier writings and introduces themes that will be further developed in the later ones. Of particular interest is the introduction of elements of Eastern thought to help understand the Christian experience of contemplation. Merton stresses the unity that contemplation can bring to human life and also the way in which it affects the totality of life. Do not set aside another compartment in your life and call that "contemplation," Merton warns us; rather, get rid of compartments and unify your life. There is an extensive discussion of an important issue in the spiritual life that he had hinted at ten years earlier (see *Seeds of Contemplation,* 28): the difference between the true self and the false self. This is a topic he will develop even further in *New Seeds of Contemplation.* Merton discusses the change that occurs in a person's life when he or she makes the move from an exterior life (centered largely in external practices) to an interior life in which the "inner and spiritual consciousness has been awakened" (85). He also anticipates his later, more detailed discussions of the relation of contemplation with the world of technology.

In a remarkable letter of September 12, 1959, to Czeslaw Milosz, he sums up the book's contents: "I have just been finishing another book, 'The Inner Experience,' a wider deeper view of the same thing, contemplation, with more references to Oriental ideas. There is to me nothing but this that counts, but everything can enter into it" (*Courage for Truth,* 63).[4] Note the four points he makes: (1) "The Inner Experience" is about contemplation; (2) it offers a "wider deeper view" of the subject than do his earlier writings; (3) it will enrich the topic by linking it with Eastern thought; (4) it will show how contemplation is connected with and unifies the totality of human life: nothing counts more and everything enters into it. The reader is advised to keep these four points in mind when reading "The Inner Experience."

The typescripts of "The Inner Experience"

are located at the Thomas Merton Center at Bellarmine University in Louisville, Kentucky. The text also is available in offprints from eight issues of *Cistercian Studies.* The texts of the initial four of these offprints are found in Lawrence S. Cunningham's book *Thomas Merton: Spiritual Master.* In April of 2001 the Merton Trust authorized the full publication of "The Inner Experience." This is expected to appear in 2002 or 2003. WHS

Notes

1. See letters to Sr. Therese Lentfoehr, July 4, 1959, and September 29, 1959, in *Road to Joy,* 233–34.
2. Before leaving for Asia, he gave Daniel Walsh a copy of the manuscript, telling him, "It's something I wrote a *long time ago,* but wondered what the response would be if it were published. I had previously decided against it [in a provision in his will stipulating that it was not to be published as a book]. But *recently* I reread it and made some corrections and additions which you will note. Give it to the Carmelite nuns to read and one day tell me what they think" (letter of Daniel Walsh to Abbot Flavian Burns, May 6, 1972, archives, Abbey of Gethsemani).
3. See *Thomas Merton's Paradise Journey,* 115–16; also 150, nn. 6–10.
4. For an extended study of "The Inner Experience," see *Thomas Merton's Paradise Journey,* 113–52.

INTERNATIONAL THOMAS MERTON SOCIETY, THE

In the spring of 1987 Robert E. Daggy, Br. Patrick Hart, O.C.S.O., and William H. Shannon agreed that the time had come to organize an international Thomas Merton Society. Accordingly, an invitation was extended to a number of Merton scholars to meet at Bellarmine College, May 29–30 of that year. Fourteen women and men were able to accept the invitation and became the "Celebrate Merton 88" committee.

The first meeting was held at 10:30 a.m. May 29, 1987, in Bonaventure Hall of Bellarmine College. After a welcome and opening remarks by Robert Daggy, William Shannon gave the background/genesis of the present committee. On the tenth anniversary of Merton's death, in 1978, commemorations had been held in a number of places. A Vancouver meeting brought together a number of scholars who had been working independently on Merton's writings. Few of them had met one another before. On that occasion a proposal was made that a Merton Society be formed. Nothing came of this proposal. The time had not yet come.

Since then, much work had been done in Merton studies. Scholars were better acquainted with one another. In 1987, therefore, the time seemed ripe for such a society; and because of the Canadian involvement and a rekindled interest developing in England, it should be an international society.

The "Celebrate Merton 88" committee floundered a bit, momentarily, about how actually to bring such a society into existence. At first there was discussion about a "founding meeting," which, it was agreed, should be held in 1989, with 1988 as a "Celebrate Merton" year to prepare for that general meeting. What eventually surfaced was a dilemma: to make plans for a general meeting, it would seem necessary to have the society already in existence. The obvious way out of the dilemma was to found the society then and there. Thus it was that on May 30, 1987, the International Thomas Merton Society (ITMS) came into existence with fourteen members. The founding members were Christine Bochen, David Cooper, Lawrence Cunningham, Robert E. Daggy, Br. Patrick Hart, Glenn Hinson, Dewey Kramer, Victor Kramer, Patrick O'Connell, Anthony Padovano, Ron Seitz, William Shannon, Bonnie Thurston, and Sr. Mary Luke Tobin. William Shannon was elected president, Robert Daggy vice-president, Christine Bochen corresponding secretary, Glenn Hinson recording secretary, and Bonnie Thurston treasurer.

During the two-day meeting a tentative constitution was drafted, and an initial general meeting was decided upon for late spring of 1989. In addition, a "Celebrate Merton 88" year was proclaimed, beginning January 31, 1988, ending December 10, 1988. A text for announcing the formation of the Society (to be sent to various newspapers and journals) was agreed upon. It read as follows:

A group of representative Merton scholars, meeting in Louisville, Kentucky, on May 29–30, 1987, under the leadership of Msgr. William H. Shannon, Dr. Robert E. Daggy and Brother Patrick Hart, announce the formation of the International Thomas Merton Society (ITMS) to promote an understanding and appreciation of the multifaceted character of Thomas Merton and to encourage research and study in relation to his work. Inquiries concerning membership should be addressed to: The International Thomas Merton Society, Thomas Merton Studies Center, Bellarmine College, Louisville, KY 40205.

It was agreed that letters of invitation to membership should be sent to prospective members, and that *America* and *Commonweal* should be invited to do a "Merton issue" sometime in 1988. *America* devoted its entire October 2, 1988, issue to a series of essays on Thomas Merton, with the schedule for the first general meeting of the Society appearing on the back page. The meeting's theme was announced: "The Pattern in the Seed: Thomas Merton's Glimpse of the Cosmic Dance." The meeting was scheduled for May 25–28, 1989, at Bellarmine College. *Commonweal,* in its December 2, 1988, issue, published an article

William H. Shannon, founder of the ITMS

titled "The Future of Thomas Merton: Sorting Out the Legacy."

The final task of the "founding fourteen" was to make plans for the 1989 meeting. After some discussion, the officers were appointed, as was a program committee. In later meetings, held in Rochester, New York, the committee came up with the substance of the program, which took final shape by the spring of 1988. It was published in the October 2, 1988, issue of *America,* as mentioned above.

The ITMS meets every two years. Thus far there have been meetings in Louisville, Kentucky (1989), Rochester, New York (1991), Colorado Springs, Colorado (1993), Allegany, New York (1995), Mobile, Alabama (1997), Waterloo, Ontario (1999), and Louisville, Kentucky (2001). The 2003 meeting is scheduled for Vancouver, British Columbia.

The official publication of the ITMS is *The Merton Seasonal.* WHS

INTERRELIGIOUS DIALOGUE

Thomas Merton emphasized repeatedly that it is "absolutely essential" for contemporary society to recover "a dimension of *wisdom* oriented to contemplation as well as to wise action," and that to develop this sapiential awareness "it is no longer sufficient merely to go back over the Christian and European cultural traditions. The horizons of the world are no longer confined to Europe and America. We have to gain new perspectives, and on this our spiritual and even our physical survival may depend" (*Mystics and Zen Masters,* 80). Interreligious dialogue has a crucial role to play in this process, Merton believes, because "the values hidden in Oriental thought actually reveal themselves only on the plane of spiritual experience, or perhaps, if you like, of aesthetic experience" (*Thomas Merton Reader,* 302). Interreligious dialogue is at the heart of Merton's contemplative alternative to cross-cultural misunderstanding or to a soulless global "culture" dedicated to efficiency, pragmatism, and profits. He considered the final decades of the second millennium to be a time of "crisis, a moment of crucial choice," when the potential loss of humanity's "spiritual heritage" could result in a world fragmented into hostile segments or regimented into sterile conformity. "We are witnessing the growth of a truly universal consciousness in the modern world. This universal consciousness may be a consciousness of transcendent freedom and vision, or it may simply be a vast blur of mechanized triviality and ethical cliché" (*Asian Journal,* 317). Those committed to spiritual values and discipline have a responsibility to form this universal consciousness through dialogue. While he had no grandiose expectations of "visible results of earth-shaking importance," Merton stated that nevertheless he was "convinced that communication in depth . . . is now not only possible and desirable, but most important for the destinies of Twentieth-Century Man" (313).

The same principles that mark Merton's conception of nonviolence are essential to interreligious dialogue: a respect for the humanity and dignity of the other, a recognition that no single point of view has a monopoly on the truth, a willingness to learn from the other, a commitment to truth rather than to defending one's own position, a "person-oriented" approach that "does not seek so much to *control* as to *respond,* and to *awaken response,*" which promotes an "openness of free exchange in which reason and love have freedom of action" (*Faith and Violence,* 28). It is a model of "dialogue as compassion, substitution, identification" (*Guilty Bystander,* 132). On its deepest level it is an openness to the divine present within the other: "God speaks, and God is to be heard, not only on Sinai, not only in my own heart, but in the *voice of the stranger.* . . . We must, then, see the truth in the stranger, and the truth we see must be a newly living truth, not just a projection of a dead conventional idea of our own — a projection of our own self upon the stranger" (*Collected Poems,* 384–85).

Dialogue both assumes and confirms that what unites is more significant, ultimately more powerful, than what divides. To recognize affinities with other traditions is to deepen one's own spiritual insight: "If I affirm myself as a Catholic merely by denying all that is Muslim, Jewish, Protestant, Hindu, Buddhist, etc., in the end I will find that there is not much left for me to affirm as a Catholic: and certainly no breath of the Spirit with which to affirm it"

(*Guilty Bystander*, 129). While acknowledging the very real and substantial differences among religions on the level of concepts and doctrines, Merton maintained that the "great similarities and analogies in the realm of religious experience . . . a very real quality of existential likeness" (*Asian Journal*, 312) could provide mutual support and mutual insight across confessional boundaries and thereby shape a global consciousness oriented to wisdom rather than to technique and control. For Merton, contact with other spiritual traditions reinforces a conviction that contemplative awareness is fundamental to authentic human fulfillment. For example, the "discipline of simplicity, of silence, of self-effacement, of contemplation" (*Mystics and Zen Masters*, 9) at the foundation of Zen practice preserves essential values common to all authentic religious traditions: "The capacity for contemplative experience and the fact of its realization . . . are therefore implicit in all the great religious traditions, whether Asian or European, whether Hindu, Buddhist, Moslem, or Christian" (209). Liberation is the common aim of "the great contemplative traditions of East and West"; they concur that "by spiritual disciplines a man can radically change his life and attain to a deeper meaning, a more perfect integration, a more complete fulfillment, a more total liberty of spirit than are possible in the routines of a purely active existence centered on money-making" (viii). On this level the wisdom of East and West can and should be mutually affirming and supportive.

This dialogue not only creates insights; it creates relationships. Authentic dialogue, according to Merton, offers the possibility of transcending communication to reach the deeper dimension of communion, an experience of "original unity" that "is beyond words, . . . beyond speech, . . . beyond concept" (*Asian Journal*, 308). This existential identification with another, even with someone of a different culture, faith, tradition, is the most profound level of solidarity. It can be observed in Merton's correspondence with his Muslim friend Abdul Aziz (*Hidden Ground of Love*, 43–67), or in his account of his visit with the aged Zen master D. T. Suzuki (*Water of Life*, 115–17). It revealed itself in profound ways

during his Asian pilgrimage: he summarizes his three meetings with the Dalai Lama by saying, "I felt we had become very good friends and were somehow quite close to one another. I . . . believe, too, that there is a real spiritual bond between us" (*Other Side of the Mountain*, 206); and of his encounter with another lama, Chatral Rinpoche, he comments, "It was a grace for us to meet one another" (278). This sense of spiritual unity across confessional lines is perhaps articulated most memorably in his statement on behalf of Thich Nhat Hanh, the Vietnamese Buddhist monk exiled from his war-torn country: "I have said Nhat Hanh is my brother, and it is true. . . . I have far more in common with Nhat Hanh than I have with many Americans, and I do not hesitate to say it. It is vitally important that such bonds be admitted. They are the bonds of a new solidarity and a new brotherhood which is beginning to be evident on all the five continents and which cuts across all political, religious and cultural lines to unite young men and women in every country in something that is more concrete than an ideal and more alive than a program" (*Faith and Violence*, 108).

Yet, while he strongly affirmed the spiritual experience that all people have in common and the benefits of seeing one's own tradition through the eyes of another, Merton did not hesitate to articulate what he saw to be the uniqueness of his own Christian heritage. He writes in his journal for June 26, 1965, "I may be interested in Oriental religions, etc., but there can be no obscuring the essential difference — this personal communion with Christ at the center and heart of all reality, as a source of grace and life. 'God is love' may perhaps be clarified if one says that 'God is void' and if in the void one finds absolute indetermination and hence absolute freedom. (With freedom, the void becomes fullness and $0=\infty$.) All that is 'interesting' but none of it touches on the mystery of personality in God, and His personal love for me. Again, I am void too — and I have freedom, or *am* a kind of freedom, meaningless unless oriented to Him" (*Water of Life*, 259). While admitting the past abuses and present dangers of a Christian triumphalism, he maintains the uniqueness of Christ and Christian revelation even in the face of his beloved Gandhi's question, "How can he who thinks he possesses absolute truth be fraternal?" (*Turning toward the World*, 122) — the answer for Merton being not a "vague indifferentism" (123) but a humble recognition that the fullness of revelation does not entail a fullness of possession, that it is a matter of relationship, above all of love, of God and of all those made in the image of God, rather than of "knowing" absolute truth as some sort of definitive collection of concepts. From this perspective, sharing the vision of other traditions can enrich one's own faith by unveiling neglected or undervalued aspects of what it means to be fully human. Without compromising his belief in Catholicism in the confessional sense, Merton aspires to a catholic, universal vision, an inclusivity that embraces the truth wherever it is to be found: "The more I am able to affirm others, to say 'yes' to them in myself, by discovering them in myself and myself in them, the more real I am. I am fully real if my own heart says yes to everyone" (*Guilty Bystander*, 129). POC

SEE ALSO BUDDHISM; CONFUCIANISM; HINDUISM; JUDAISM; *MYSTICS AND ZEN MASTERS*; SUFISM; TAOISM; ZEN; *ZEN AND THE BIRDS OF APPETITE*.

INTIMATE MERTON, THE: *His Life from His Journals*

Edited by Patrick Hart and Jonathan Montaldo. San Francisco: HarperSanFrancisco, 1999. xvii+374pp.

The Intimate Merton is a series of selections from the seven published Thomas Merton journals, presenting in a single volume what the editors chose as the major themes of the journals (some minor themes also are included). The editors, both well-known Merton scholars, make clear that the selections are theirs, not Merton's. The seven chapters correspond to the seven volumes of the journals and have as their names the subtitles of the respective journals: (1) "The Story of a Vocation (1939–1941)," (2) "Becoming a Monk and Writer (1941–1952)," (3) "Pursuing the Monk's True Life (1952–1960)," (4) "The Pivotal Years (1960–1963)," (5) "Seeking Peace in the Hermitage (1963–

1965)," (6) "Exploring Solitude and Freedom (1966–1967)," (7) "The End of the Journey (1967–1968)."

In an illuminating introduction, called "A Path through Thomas Merton's Journals," the editors set forth their (fairly modest) goals. Making no claim to offer "the essence" or "the best" of the journals, they simply plot one path through them, while admitting that readers might choose to travel through the same journals by another way. The editors have selected what they consider most readable in the journals and most revelatory of their subject. Wisely they have chosen to bypass material in the original journals that at times causes the story to lag and the reader to lose interest. By the sheer necessity of space this book moves through the Merton story at a faster pace than that set by the journals. This is all to the good, for it gives a liveliness to the story that one misses at times in the individual journal volumes. It also makes certain moments in the story stand out in greater relief, moments whose importance might not have been so clearly grasped in the wider contents of an individual journal. Sometimes less can mean more: less detail, more insight; less repetition, more clarity. The paring down of the story gives an insight into Merton's life and struggles that is more direct and more intimate. This more than justifies the editors' choice of *The Intimate Merton* as the book's title.

This is not in any way to minimize the value of the seven journal volumes and their importance for anyone who wants to understand the Merton story. It is simply to point out the uniqueness of *The Intimate Merton*. The editors have called this single volume a "translation," a helpful description of the selected choices and the extensive cuttings of the journals that constitute, in the editors' words, a revisioning of the Merton story. WHS

INTRODUCTIONS EAST AND WEST: *The Foreign Prefaces of Thomas Merton*

Greensboro, N.C.: Unicorn Press, 1981. 147 pp.

SEE "*HONORABLE READER.*"

ISHI MEANS MAN:
Essays on Native Americans
Edited by Teo Savory. Greensboro, N.C.:
Unicorn Press, 1976. 71 pp.

This book brings together five essays, four of
which originally were published in the *Catholic
Worker* in 1967 and 1968, a fact that Dorothy
Day notes, with pride, in her one-page foreword. Day admits to feeling a sense of guilt
because she knew so little about the people
whose story remained untold in history books.
It was reading John Collier's book on the Indians of the Americas that brought her out of
"abysmal ignorance," and it is her hope that
Thomas Merton's book will have far-reaching
influence.

This handsome volume, with an original
woodblock by Rita Corbin on its cover, was
published as volume 8 in the Unicorn Keep-
sake Series, dedicated to modern classics of
poetry, prose, and the visual arts. Teo Savory,
to whom Merton sent for publication one of the
essays included in this book, "Cross-Fighters,"
edited the series and this volume. Merton's
essay appeared in 1968 in the first number
of the *Unicorn Journal*. *Ishi Means Man* is divided into two parts. Part 1 gathers together
three essays on North American Indians: "The
Shoshoneans," "War and Vision," and "Ishi: A
Meditation"; part 2 includes two essays on Indians of Central America: "The Cross-Fighters"
and "The Sacred City."

Appropriately, the title of this book focuses
attention on the story of Ishi, whose story is
related in one of the essays. It was Merton's
reading, in January 1967, of Theodora Kroeber's *Ishi in Two Worlds: A Biography of the Last
Wild Indian in North America* that prompted
Merton to read and write about the injustices
perpetrated upon Indians. Although the subtitle of the book speaks of Native Americans,
Merton, writing about a decade earlier, speaks
of Indians. In a review of *Ishi Means Man*, published in *America* in 1976, Br. Patrick Hart
recalls Merton's visits to New Mexico in May
and September 1968: "From his first trip to
New Mexico in May 1968, he brought back to
his hermitage at Gethsemani several beautiful
hand-woven Navajo rugs, which he placed in

his hermitage chapel where they still remain.
To me, they are symbolic of Merton's deep admiration of the Native American Indian and
burning concern for his plight."[1]

Merton's interest in the plight of indigenous
peoples already is evident in his correspondence with Ernesto Cardenal, a Nicaraguan
poet who was for a time in the late 1950s
a novice under Merton at Gethsemani. In
1958 Merton was reading translations of Mayan
and Aztec poems and wrote to Pablo Antonio
Cuadra to say that he would very much like to
have a collection of Indian poems in Spanish
(*Courage for Truth*, 180).

In 1963 Merton wrote to Cardenal about the
anthology of indigenous American literature
that Cardenal was completing. "Your poems
about the Indians have been simply superb. I
am sure your whole book [*Literatura indígena
americana: Antología*] will be splendid and look
forward to seeing it. You have a very great deal
to say and I know it is most important. This
is something far deeper than *indigenismo* with
a political — or religious — hook inside the
bait. This is a profound spiritual witness. Also
a reparation, and a deep adoration of the Creator, an act of humility and love which the
whole race of the Christian conquerors has
been putting off and neglecting for centuries.
It reminds me that some day I want to write
something about Vasco de Quiroga. I have not
forgotten about the Indians and all that they
mean to us both" (136). A few weeks later, in
November 1963, in another letter to Cardenal,
Merton observed that Cardenal's book was a
very important project: "Coming just at the
right time it can have a decisive effect, both
spiritual and cultural, throughout Latin America" (142). Merton reminded Cardenal that he
had shown him *The Sacred Pipe* by Black Elk
when Cardenal was at Gethsemani.

The three essays in part 1 of *Ishi Means Man*
express Merton's outrage at the mistreatment
of American Indians. In the first essay Merton reviews *The Shoshoneans*, by Edward Dorn,
with photographs by Leroy Lucas.[2] As was often
the case for Merton, this book review grew
into a reflection on the issues raised by the
book and provided Merton with an opportunity to express his own views on the subject at

hand. Merton begins this essay with a quotation from a government mimeographed sheet about the Indians of Fort Hill Reservation, Idaho. It reads, "Indians who are now principally on the reservation were the aboriginal owners of the United States. Placing them on reservations was an act to protect the white settlers from acts of depredation, which became more common as the Indians were pushed further back out of their original holdings" (*Ishi Means Man,* 5). The "crass and impenetrable complacency" (5) of the statement exposes the government's blindness to the abhorrent treatment of Indians by whites. This inability to "see" the Indian is in stark contrast to the notes and photos that Dorn and Lucas share with their readers. Their pilgrimage to Nevada and Idaho brought them face to face with Indians, and their book shows the true face of Indians, "a face marked with suffering, irony, courage, sometimes desperation: always with a human beauty which defeats sometimes obvious degradation" (7). Merton's analysis of the white man's treatment of the Indian parallels his analysis of the white man's treatment of the Negro.[3] "The real confinement, the real reduction and unmanning of the Indian is the reduction to a definition of him not in terms of his essential identity, but purely and simply in terms of his relations with us. More exactly, a definition of him in terms of a relationship of absolute tutelage imposed on him by us" (9). In the last three pages of this essay Merton quotes extensively from a statement by Clyde Warrior, a young Ponca Indian from Oklahoma. Originally written as a speech for a conference on the "War on Poverty," a speech that was never delivered, Clyde Warrior's statement gives voice to the story of his people and to their hopes. For example, he writes, "The indignity of Indian life, and I would presume the indignity of life among the poor generally in these United States, is the powerlessness of those who are 'out of it,' but who yet are coerced and manipulated by the very system which excludes them" (14).

In the second essay, "War and Vision," Merton explores the North America Indian practices of the vision quest and of "fasting for vision." First he describes and reflects on the meaning of the vision quest as a rite of passage, which involves an encounter with a "vision person" that "set the young Indian upon his life's way" with the support and guidance of the community (18). Then Merton turns his attention to the biography of a Crow Indian visionary recounted by Peter Nabokov in *Two Leggings: The Making of Crow Warrior.*[4] Nabokov edited and set in context "the record of his conversations, taken down with an interpreter fifty years ago" and made available "one of the most fascinating autobiographies published in this century" (21).

The third essay, "Ishi: A Meditation," grows out of a review of Theodora Kroeber's *Ishi in Two Worlds,* which tells the story of Ishi, the last survivor of the Mill Creek Indians. The Yana Indians, who lived around the foothills of Mount Lassen, east of the Sacramento River (not far from the Trappist monastery at Vina), were driven into the hills by white settlers and eventually destroyed. A small remnant (about twenty), determined to keep away from the white population, disappeared into the hills, where they lived and died until finally Ishi, the last survivor, was taken into captivity by the scholars who "saved Ishi and learned from him his language, his culture, and his tribal history" (26). Merton remarks on the similarity between the wars against the Indians and the war in Viet Nam. "The jungles are thought to be 'infested' with communists, and hence one goes after them as one would go after ants in the kitchen back home. And in this process of 'cleaning up' (the language of 'cleansing' appeases and pacifies the conscience), one becomes without realizing it a murderer of women and children. But this is an unfortunate accident, what the moralists call 'double effect.' Something that is just too bad, but which must be accepted in view of something more important that has to be done" (32). It is a continuation of "the cowboys-and-indians game which seems to be part and parcel of our national identity" (32). Merton concludes the essay with an ironic observation: "In the end, no one ever found out a single name of the vanished community. Not even Ishi's. For Ishi simply means MAN" (32).

The first of the two essays in part 2, "The Cross-Fighters," is subtitled "Notes on a Race War" and consists of six numbered sections.

The essay recounts the conflict between the Mayans and the Ladinos in Yucatan in the middle and late 1800s. Merton notes that it was "more properly a cultural and a caste war rather than a battle between two races" in a society in which persons of mixed blood were able to choose one side or another and generally chose the side of the Ladinos (36). When the Indian rebellion of 1848 failed, it was because the Mayans "were still too willing to listen to the voice of peaceful and constructive human instinct — a voice which has to be silenced if efficiency is to be total" (42). With the Mayan population reduced by half, those remaining formed a resistance movement centered around a shrine called Chan Santa Cruz, where they experienced the "Speaking Cross," which they believed made possible direct contact with God. Chan Santa Cruz resembled Cargo cults, which are characterized by "an intense *will to believe* in prophetic promise, which are often, from our viewpoint, wildly irrational and utterly hopeless" (46). But Merton counters, "we would do better to consider the phenomenon — in this case the Speaking Cross — as a spontaneous living expression of the new sense of community and identity which has been called into being by a spirit of resistance" (46). The Cruzob, the people of the cross, were able to retain their identity "for over fifty years as a *de facto* separate nation" (49). Merton sees the rebellion of the Maya Cruzob as "a paradigm of literally thousands of sectarian eschatological movements which spring up spontaneously and independently everywhere today" (51).

The final essay, "The Sacred City," explores the ancient Zapotecan culture of the Oaxaca Valley in Mexico and celebrates the achievements of the ancient city of Monte Alban (53). The essay reflects Merton's intense interest in anthropology, archeology, and history, and demonstrates how his reading of the past sheds light on his understanding of the present. Comparing a "sacred city" such as Mount Alban to our own culture serves to highlight distinguishing features of the ancient culture: "the indifference to technological progress, the lack of history, and the almost total neglect of the arts of war. The three things go together, and

are rooted in an entirely different conception of man and of life" (63). Their culture, "as a network of living interrelationships, can be called synthetic and synchronic," while our culture today is "analytic and diachronic" (63). Knowledge of another way of life can illuminate our own. "In other words, it is important that we fit the two thousand war-less years of Monte Alban into our world-view. It may help to tone down a little of our aggressive, self-complacent superiority, and puncture some of our more disastrous myths" (70). CMB

Notes

1. Patrick Hart, review of *Ishi Means Man*, by Thomas Merton, *America* 135 (September 18, 1976): 152.
2. New York: William Morrow, 1967.
3. See "Letters to a White Liberal" in *Seeds of Destruction*.
4. New York: Thomas Y. Crowell, 1967.

ISLAM

Thomas Merton's interest in the tenets and practices of the world's religions included an interest in Islam. When in November 1960, Merton responded to a letter from Abdul Aziz, a student of Sufism living in Pakistan, and began what was to be an extensive and substantial exchange of letters, Merton spoke of his interest in al-Hallâj, "that great saint and mystic, martyr of truth and of love" (*Hidden Ground of Love*, 44), and of his familiarity with the mystical poetry of Rûmî. Merton told Aziz that he was "tremendously impressed with the insights into the mysticism of Islam" (44) that he had come to through a reading of Louis Massignon's work.

In the letters he received from Abdul Aziz, Merton learned in some detail about the beliefs and practices of Islam. His own reading of the modern scholarship in Islam, for example the work of Sayyed Hossein Nasr, deepened his knowledge. Merton read the Qur'an and was even momentarily tempted to learn Arabic in order to read the Qur'an as it was recorded and is recited by Muslims. However, when Abdul Aziz suggested that Merton himself recite the Qur'an, Merton explained that, although he read the Qur'an "with deep attention and reverence" (61), he considered it inappropriate to recite the sacred book of Islam. He did not know how to do so "properly" and believed that it was his task "to chant the sacred books of [his] own tradition" (61). Yet Merton was deeply moved by "the intensity of Moslem piety toward [God's] Names, and the reverence with which He is invoked as the 'Compassionate and the Merciful' " (48) and felt himself united with his Muslim brother, remembering him in prayer always and especially during the holy month of Ramadan. In 1965, Merton asked Abdul Aziz about the dates of Ramadan because he wanted to "join spiritually with the Moslem world in this act of love, faith and obedience toward Him Whose greatness and mercy surround us at all times" (60). Later in 1965, Merton wrote words that sound as though they could have been written at the dawn of the twenty-first century: "My friend, we live in troubled and sad times, and we must pray the infinite and

merciful Lord to bear patiently with the sins of this world, which are very great. We must humble our hearts in silence and poverty of spirit and listen to His commands which come from the depths of His love, and work that men's hearts may be converted to the ways of love and justice, not of blood, murder, lust and greed. I am afraid that the big powerful countries are a very bad example to the rest of the world in this respect" (61–62).

Merton was also deeply interested in and became quite well acquainted with the writings of such intellectuals of the Islamic tradition as al-Ghazâlî, Ibn Averroës, Ibn Sina, and Ibn al-'Arabi. But it is not surprising that Merton's interest in Islam centered on its mystical expression in Sufism — an expression that resonated so readily with his own way of life. CMB

SEE ALSO SUFISM.

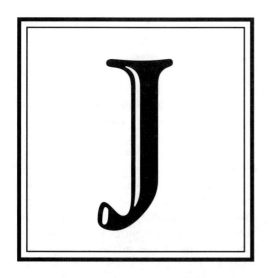

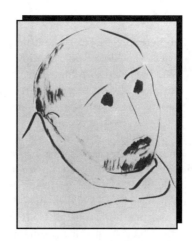

JAGUAR AND THE MOON, THE

Translated from the Spanish with an introduction by Thomas Merton. Greensboro, N.C.: Unicorn Press, 1974. 39 pp.

In his journal for May 3, 1958, Thomas Merton writes of meeting the Nicaraguan poet, editor, and social critic Pablo Antonio Cuadra (1912–2002), who had come to Gethsemani to visit his cousin Ernesto Cardenal. He notes, "Read me some very fine poems — his latest — *El jaguar y la luna* — after showing me some Indian ceramic designs by which they were inspired. Fine short poems with a very high degree of mystical quality and power." He adds, "All the poems had very impressive titles. Were at once very Asiatic and very American. This is the voice of the true America" (*Search for Solitude*, 200). He quickly set to work translating some of the poems, and by October 13 he could write to Cuadra that a selection would be published in the *New Directions Annual* and that a complete book of translations with the originals was in the planning stage as part of the New Directions World Poets series (*Courage for Truth*, 180; see also *Thomas Merton and James Laughlin*, 135, 138). In the event the series was discontinued and the volume never appeared, but translations of ten of the volume's thirty-three poems were included in Merton's 1963 collection *Emblems of a Season of Fury*. A bilingual edition of

Drawing of John of the Cross by Thomas Merton.

the same ten poems,[1] in a somewhat different order,[2] with the introduction found in *Emblems of a Season of Fury*, the Nicaraguan author's illustrations from the original volume, and a brief biography of Cuadra at the conclusion finally was published six years after Merton's death by his friend Teo Savory of Unicorn Press. POC

Notes

1. Merton actually translated fourteen poems from the collection. One, "Faces of Girls Looking at Themselves in the River," originally was among those to be included in *Emblems of a Season of Fury* but was omitted, probably for reasons of space; the other three, "Meditation Before an Ancient Poem," "Nahoa Urn, For a Woman," and "Written Next to a Blue Flower," are found only in *Collected Poems* and may have been translated after the publication of *Emblems of a Season of Fury*. Presumably, the existence of these additional translations was not known to the Unicorn Press editors at the time of publication.

2. Neither the order in *Emblems* nor the order in this volume corresponds to the sequence of the poems in Cuadra's original collection (nor does the alphabetical arrangement in *Collected Poems*).

JAZZ

When, in 1963, Thomas Merton wrote a form letter to be sent to students requesting information about his life and writings or, as he wrote to Tommie O'Callaghan, "to High School kids who want me to write essays for them," he said about jazz, "I like it" (*Road to Joy*, 88, 90). That was an understatement. As a teenager, Merton spent hours in a record shop listening to jazz — Duke Ellington, Louis Armstrong, and

Hot Club de France.[1] At Oakham he played jazz — loud — on his record player. Merton's love for jazz remained with him all his life. He listened to jazz in clubs in New York. In his later years he enjoyed jazz records at the home of his friend Jim Wygal. And on occasion he filled the air with the sound of jazz while he was living in the hermitage, where he also listened to Bob Dylan records. Responding to John Wu Jr., then a student at Seton Hall in New Jersey, Merton said that he liked Ornette Coleman and Jackie McLean and that he had heard Coltrane and admired him but "I am still more inclined to the old jazz of my own day, not because it is better but because I hear it better" (354).

In February 1968 Merton wrote in his journal about two visits to a new jazz club in Louisville. On his first visit to the Washington Street club, in the company of Tommie O'Callaghan and friends, Merton was frustrated that not everyone in the group was "really interested in jazz." But he and a few others listened appreciatively and "it was good." He was struck by the "power and seriousness of the jazz. As if they were playing for their own sake and for the sound's sake and had no relationship to the people around them. And yet for the most part everyone seemed to like it. Without understanding that here was one place in Louisville where something was definitely being done and said" (Other Side of the Mountain, 54). A week later he again went to the club with Tommie and some of her relatives. Although he felt ambivalent about going out and losing the night and then trying to "salvage something from the next day" after getting in late, the jazz was great: "The combo turned on and really played. . . . Power and unity and drive. It was very fine, very real" (56).

Merton appreciated all kinds of music. Gregorian chant moved him deeply, as did classical music. Merton knew that the language of music expressed deep reality, and he found that musical metaphors helped him to speak about other realities. Recalling that to Cardinal Newman, Clement of Alexandria was "like music," Merton noted that he now wanted to listen to "all the music of Clement" and Newman too. His favorite writers resonated in his spirit like fine music did. "Resonances: one of the 'choirs.' Maritain, Van der Meer de Walcheren, Bloy, Green, Chagall, Satie — or a string sextet! Another earlier music: Blake, Eckhart, Tauler (Maritain got in here too), Coomaraswamy . . . etc." (Turning toward the World, 149). He describes his favorite writers as a kind of chorus whose voices he hears in the silence of the hermitage — with "clanging prose," "voluble dissonances," and "golden sounds" (Day of a Stranger, 35). He also discovers that the language of music enables him to speak of the inner unity of contemplation: "Chanting the alleluia in the second mode: strength and solidity of the Latin, seriousness of the second mode, built on the Re as though on a sacrament, a presence. One keeps returning to the re as to an inevitable center. Sol-Re, Fa-Re, Sol-Re, Do-Re. Many other notes in between, but suddenly one hears only the one note. Consonantia: all notes, in their perfect distinctness, are yet blended in one" (59). Absorbed in the "one central tonic note that is unheard and unuttered," he writes, "In the silence of the afternoon all is present and all is inscrutable in one central tonic note to which every other sound ascends or descends, to which every other meaning aspires, in order to find its true fulfillment. To ask when the note will sound is to lose the afternoon: it has already sounded, and all things now hum with the resonance of its sounding" (61).

Merton appreciated and enjoyed all kinds of music. He understood the language of music. But most of all he loved jazz. CMB

Notes

1. See Michael Mott, The Seven Mountains of Thomas Merton (Boston: Houghton Mifflin, 1984), 55.

JENKINS, HAROLD BREWSTER

Born to Samuel and Martha Jenkins in 1889, Harold was Ruth's brother and therefore Tom Merton's maternal uncle. Harold lived with his parents in Douglaston until their deaths and his late marriage to Elsie Hauck Holahan. He was Tom's American guardian as Tom Bennett had been his English guardian. Harold was bitterly disappointed when he heard that Tom was entering the Abbey of Gethsemani. WHS

JENKINS, MARTHA CAROLINE BALDWIN

Born in 1863, Martha married Samuel Adams Jenkins in 1885. Their daughter, Ruth, married Owen Merton. She was, therefore, Tom's maternal grandmother. (Tom and John Paul called her "Bonnemaman.") She died in August 1937. WHS

SEE ALSO JENKINS, SAMUEL; MERTON, RUTH.

JENKINS, SAMUEL ADAMS

Born in Ohio in 1862, Samuel Adams Jenkins married Martha Caroline Baldwin in 1885. Their two children, Ruth Calvert and Harold Brewster, were born in Zanesville, Ohio. The family moved to Philadelphia and then eventually to New York, where Samuel worked for the publishing house of Grosset and Dunlap. He made a comfortable salary and was able to build a house in Douglaston, Long Island. When the Mertons (Owen, Ruth, and son Tom) came from France on August 15, 1916, they stayed with the Jenkinses for a time until they got their own home. John Paul, who was born in 1918, spent considerable time during his younger years at the Jenkinses' home. The same was true of Tom until 1925, when his father took him to France. On the several occasions that Tom returned to America from England, he too resided with his mother's parents, who were affectionately called "Pop" and "Bonnemaman." Pop was generous to his grandchildren. In 1930 he set up funds that would enable them to be financially independent. While Tom was at Oakham School, he returned to New York and Douglaston during the summers and finally returned to America permanently in 1934.

Samuel Jenkins died October 27, 1936. Tom thought well of his grandfather, though they differed in many ways and interests. He admired his simplicity and ingenuousness. It was, he writes, "something peculiarly American. Or at least it belonged to the Americans of his generation, this kind and warm-hearted and vast and universal optimism" (*Seven Storey Mountain*, 159). WHS

JESUS CHRIST

SEE CHRISTOLOGY.

JOURNALS

Thomas Merton kept journals for most of his adult life. Journal writing was for him a mode of self-expression as well as a tool for self-discovery and spiritual growth. Following the enthusiastic reception of his best-selling autobiography, *The Seven Storey Mountain*, Merton selected entries from his journals (1946 to 1952) and published them in 1953 under the title *The Sign of Jonas*. In 1959 he published entries selected from his premonastic journals in *The Secular Journal*, and in 1966 he drew from journals he had kept during much of the previous decade in *Conjectures of a Guilty Bystander*. Editions of Merton's journals were published posthumously, including *The Asian Journal; Woods, Shore, Desert; A Vow of Conversation; The Alaskan Journal* (published in a limited edition of 150 copies); and *Thomas Merton in Alaska*, which includes the text of the Alaskan journal and talks Merton gave to women religious and priests in Alaska.

In planning for his literary estate, Merton directed that his personal journals be made available to his appointed biographer and allowed for the publication of the journals twenty-five years after his death. Between 1995 and 1998 Merton's complete journals, spanning the period from May 1939 to December 1968, were published by HarperSanFrancisco in seven volumes under the general editorship of Br. Patrick Hart. Transcribed from Merton's own hand, each volume was titled by its editor. The volumes are *Run to the Mountain: The Story of a Vocation (1939–1941); Entering the Silence: Becoming a Monk and Writer (1941–1952); A Search for Solitude: Pursuing the Monk's True Life (1952–1960); Turning toward the World: The Pivotal Years (1960–1963); Dancing in the Water of Life: Seeking Peace in the Hermitage (1963–1965); Learning to Love: Exploring Solitude and Freedom (1966–1967);* and *The Other Side of the Mountain: The End of the Journey (1967–1968).* An eighth volume, *The Intimate Merton: His Life from His Journals,* comprised of selec-

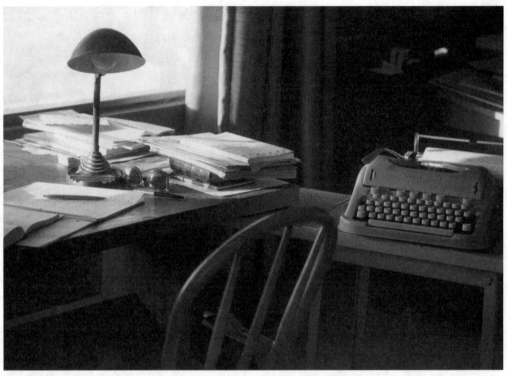

Merton's desk in the hermitage

tions from all seven volumes, was published in 1999.

Even as Merton was keeping a journal, he was reflecting on the meaning of doing so. "Journals take for granted that every day in our life there is something new and important," wrote the young Merton in December 1940 (*Run to the Mountain*, 133). A few weeks later he observed that the entries of a journal "investigate what differences there are between one day and the day before it" (138). Even after he embraced the regimen of monastic life, in which one day was in many ways the same as the day that preceded it, Merton found much to write about. And, from the beginning, he admitted that he was writing for publication: "Why would I write anything, if not to be read? This journal is written for publication. It is about time I realized that, and wrote it with some art. . . . If a journal is written for publication, then you can tear pages out of it, emend it, correct it, write with art. If it is a personal document, every emendation amounts to a crisis of conscience and a confession, not an artistic

correction" (271–72). On June 11, 1941, Merton wrote that he had "three journals going at once": *The Journal of My Escape from the Nazis* (thinly disguised fiction published in 1969 as *My Argument with the Gestapo*), what he was writing on the typewriter, and the longhand book in which this note was made and which is "to be more private, more nondescript, and more religious — more personal, I guess" (375). In later years Merton himself would make the private journals public as he edited parts for publication.

In 1947, as he was beginning to fill a new notebook with journal entries, Merton explained that he is writing "in obedience" and "in spite of my own personal disinclination for it." But, he candidly observes, "If it is tedious to keep a journal, it is more tedious to keep wondering whether or not I should give the thing up" (*Entering the Silence*, 41). And when, in 1960, he worried that he was writing too much, not well enough, and telling people what to think, he decided that he should "cut down on publication" and "put more feelings into this

Journal which is not for publication" (*Search for Solitude*, 392).

The publication of Merton's personal journals provides his readers with more than a record of his life; the journals offer an entrée into the life itself — Merton grappling with the meaning of faith and vocation, contemplation and compassion, solitude and love. Merton's candidness reveals the complexity of his personality, its strengths and weaknesses. What he wrote about in other books — prayer, contemplation, social responsibility, monastic life, ecumenical vision — came out of lived experience, and the journals are a record of that experience viewed through a poet's eye and expressed with a writer's skill. Not everything one finds in the journals is lofty and inspiring — Merton can be petty and even bitter at times — but the journals, taken as a whole, tell a bigger story and one that is worth telling: God encountered and embraced; faith found, lived, and kept. In his journals, Merton tells the story well. Perhaps he realized this when, in April 1966, he wrote, "The bad writing I have done has all been authoritarian, the declaration of musts, and the announcement of punishments. . . . The best stuff has been more straight confession and witness" (*Learning to Love*, 371). CMB

JOY

Joy is perhaps not one of the first themes one associates with Thomas Merton, but nonetheless it is extremely significant throughout the corpus of his writings. It is prominent from the very earliest of his publications. The final chapter of his 1948 work *Cistercian Contemplatives*, subtitled *A Guide to Trappist Life*, is entitled "Joy in Austerity" and emphasizes that the strict regimen of the monastic life actually creates an atmosphere of deep joy, since Cistercians are removed from the disputes and wrangling of secular society, are willing to accept sacrifice for the sake of others, and are under the special protection of the Mother of God (*Cistercian Contemplatives*, 57–59). In his biography of Mother Berchmans he explains that "the Cistercian life is a life of superabundant joy. . . . The very function of the silence, the fasting, the

hard labor, the long offices chanted in the night, and so on, is to liberate the souls of the monks and nuns from all the cares and burdens that make people unhappy. The Cistercian is joyful because he is free — delivered from the crushing anxieties that are bred of selfishness and passion" (*Exile Ends in Glory*, 17).

These comments, of course, present an idealized picture marked by the fervor of a monk who still is in, or at least remembers vividly, the "honeymoon" phase of his monastic life. But the theme of joy also runs like a leitmotif through *Seeds of Contemplation*, where the focus is not specifically on the monastic life. In the third chapter he prays that his use of created things may be for the purpose of finding joy in glorifying God (*Seeds of Contemplation*, 35). In the following chapter he emphasizes that the joys of heaven are increased because they are shared with all the saved: "The more of us there will be to share it the greater will be the joy of all" (48). (A similar point is made about the joys of the eschatological banquet in *The Living Bread* [126].) In one of the central chapters he emphasizes the joyful nature of mystical love and union (*Seeds of Contemplation*, 110), while each of the final four chapters is filled with references to joy, beginning with the emphatic statement "Do not look for rest in any pleasure, because you were not created for pleasure: you were created for JOY" (172). The following chapter points out that the beginning of joy is found in the helplessness of inward destitution, a rejoicing in one's own nothingness (177), while the chapter on sharing the fruits of contemplation declares, "When we have been delivered from every other desire we shall taste the perfection of an incorruptible joy" (182). The final chapter describes the "tide of quiet, unutterable joy" often associated with the experience of union with God (192), and on the last page Merton declares that those who have surrendered completely to the will of God "are the only ones capable of understanding joy. Everybody else is too weak for joy. Joy would kill anybody but these meek" (200). All these passages are retained in the revised text, *New Seeds of Contemplation*.

In his journal from this same period Merton writes of speaking on joy at a day of recollection and reflects, "The chief reason why we have so little joy is that we take ourselves too seriously. Joy can only be real if it is based on truth, and since the fall of Adam, all man's life is shot through with falsehood and illusion." He refers to St. Bernard's teaching that only realizing "the truth of how utterly unimportant we are ... can set us free to enjoy true happiness" (*Entering the Silence*, 406).

Further spiritual maturing leads Merton to a greater appreciation of the paradoxical nature of true joy. In a December 1952 journal entry on the surrender of one's own desires and plans (in Merton's case, for a more solitary life), he reflects, "Our joy is to be led by Him to the thing He desires, even though that thing be in some way terrible" (*Search for Solitude*, 26). Elsewhere he cites St. John of the Cross's teaching that one finds true joy only by surrendering all desire for joy (*Ascent to Truth*, 54), a point made again in his essay "The Primitive Carmelite Ideal": "In order to seek true joy, the joy of God in all things, renounce joy in all things. That is, do not trouble and distract your soul with a concern that yearns for this or that limited joy.... Renounce the vain quest, give your whole heart to God, and He Himself in return will give you joy in all things" (*Disputed Questions*, 250). The same point, from the same source, recurs in a work written toward the very end of Merton's life: "The purpose of the dark night, as St. John of the Cross shows, is not simply to punish and afflict the heart of man, but to liberate, to purify and to enlighten in perfect love. The way that leads through dread goes not to despair but to perfect joy, not to hell but to heaven" (*Contemplative Prayer*, 138). The reference to "perfect joy" recalls not only the story given that title in the *Little Flowers of St. Francis*, where the Poverello defines true joy as experiencing rejection, in union with Christ, even by one's own brothers, but also the similar passage from Chuang Tzu that Merton gives this title, in which the message is "Perfect joy is to be without joy" (*Way of Chuang Tzu*, 101), which Merton explains as a renunciation of "the way of conscious striving" (24).

But the other side of the paradox, the unexpected and uncalculated experience of the gift of joy, also is evident in Merton's experience and writing. It is, of course, there at the corner of Fourth and Walnut, where the "sense of liberation from an illusory difference was such a relief and such a joy to me that I almost laughed out loud.... I have the immense joy of being *man*, a member of a race in which God Himself became incarnate" (*Guilty Bystander*, 141). This association of joy with the incarnation recurs throughout the later writings. It appears again in a journal entry for August 1965, perhaps stimulated by rereading the 1958 "epiphany" passage while preparing the text of *Conjectures of a Guilty Bystander*, and perhaps contributing something to its final form: "The joy that I am *man*! This fact, that I am a man, is a theological truth and mystery. God became man in Christ. In the becoming what I am He united me to Himself and made me His epiphany" (*Water of Life*, 279). Both the Christmas essays "The Time of the End Is the Time of No Room" and "The Good News of the Epiphany" stress the coming of Christ as the time of the "Great Joy," the former focusing on the fact that only the shepherds, dwelling "in silence, loneliness and darkness," are not too preoccupied to hear the good news of great joy (*Raids on the Unspeakable*, 69), while the latter is somewhat more upbeat with its statement "The Nativity message is the message not only of joy but of *the* joy: the GREAT JOY which all the people of the world have always expected without fully realizing what it was ... the joy of eschatological fulfillment which we seek, in the depths of our hearts, from the moment that we are beings endowed with conscious life" (*Love and Living*, 224).

Associated specifically in the scriptural text with the nativity, joy reaches its culmination in the resurrection, as Merton points out in quoting the greeting of one of his favorite Russian saints, Seraphim of Sarov: "Christ is risen, my joy!" to which Merton himself responds, "Encounter — Truth — the Joy of the Spirit, the presence of the Risen Kyrios" (*Water of Life*, 334). Though the phrase is young Grace Sisson's rather than Merton's own, the title given to the second volume of his letters, *The Road to Joy*, is an apt description of his own convictions about the way and the goal of the Christian life, and indeed of all human life. POC

JUDAISM

Thomas Merton's attitude toward Judaism can best be understood in terms of both his contact with Jewish thinkers and his appreciation of Jewish thought. His expressed desire "to be a true Jew under my Catholic skin" (*Hidden Ground of Love*, 434), written at a time of great strain in Roman-Catholic-Jewish relationships, gives some measure of his deep appreciation of the relationship of the church and the synagogue.

Merton had a deep reverence and respect for the Jewish Scriptures, especially Psalms and the Prophets. Writing to Erich Fromm in December 1961, he reflects on the global sickness of a world seemingly bent on self-destruction. "The situation certainly makes the psalms we chant in choir each day most eloquent. Erich, I am a complete Jew as far as that goes: I am steeped in that experience of bafflement, compunction and wonder which is the experience of those who have been rescued from tyranny, only to renounce freedom and in confusion and subjection to worse tyrants, through infidelity to the Lord. For only in His service is there true freedom, as the Prophets would tell us" (317).

There are notable and extensive correspondences with three Jewish scholars: Rabbi Abraham Heschel, Hasidic scholar Zalman Schachter, and author-psychoanalyst Erich Fromm.[1] Although Fromm was not a practicing Jew, his values and insights into the dignity of the human person and the importance of true freedom belong to the Jewish heritage that was his. Fromm acquiesced when Merton described him as an "atheistic mystic" (308). Merton also wrote to him, "Your writing shows you to be one who has a very real sense of the God of Abraham and Isaac and Jacob.... [Your writings] would not be comprehensible ... without an implicitly *monotheistic* foundation" (314).

The Mystery of Israel

The "mystery" of Judaism fascinated Merton. Yet he approached the subject with a sense of diffidence, not because he lacked interest, but because he felt inadequate to deal with the issues involved. In a letter to Rabbi Steven

Schwarzschild he writes, "I am not worthy yet to write about the mystery of Judaism in our world. It is too vast a subject. I wish I could. Maybe someday. If there is anything I say en passant that happens to make sense to you, you can quote it if you like. The article will have to be a thing of the future" (*Witness to Freedom*, 36).

Merton had a unique sensitivity toward the Hebrew Scriptures that also form part of the Christian Bible. He respected the Jewish tradition enshrined in these books, not as something crypto-Christian but as first and foremost a heritage that belongs to the people of Israel. On February 15, 1962, he wrote to Zalman Schachter, "I have sat on the porch of the hermitage and sung chapters and chapters of the Prophets in Latin out over the valley, and it is a hair-raising experience is all I can say" (*Hidden Ground of Love*, 535).

Many Christians have lost the sense that they *share* a heritage with the Jews, a heritage that they received from the Jews and would not have except that the Jewish people had preserved it. Thus, Merton writes,

> One has either got to be a Jew or stop reading the Bible. The Bible cannot make sense to anyone who is not "spiritually a Semite." The spiritual sense of the Old Testament is not and cannot be a simple emptying out of its Israelite content. Quite the contrary! The New Testament is the fulfillment of that spiritual content, the fulfillment of the promise made to Abraham, the promise that Abraham believed in. *It is never therefore a denial of Judaism, but its affirmation.* Those who consider it a denial have not understood it. (*Guilty Bystander*, 5–6/14 [italics added])

A Shared Heritage and Destiny

Merton believed too that a shared heritage suggested a shared destiny. He refused to consider the *election* of the "New Israel" as a *repudiation* of the "old Israel." "The Jews were and remain the people especially chosen and loved by God." In an entry in one of his reading journals — dated July 1964, the very time that Rabbi Abraham Heschel, distraught by what was happening at the Second Vatican Council on the "Jewish statement," had visited him — he writes, "[The Jews] remain the people of God, since His promises are not made void nor are they being transferred *en bloc* to the Church without further ado, the Jews . . . are still the object of His special mercy and concern, a *sign* of his concern."[2]

The Holocaust

The entire Bible is full of eschatological expectations. For Christians, the death and resurrection of Jesus signal the beginning of the eschatological age. Is it possible, Merton wonders, that for the Jews the terrible experience of the Holocaust (climaxing centuries of anti-Semitism) may be seen as a national death and the rise of the state of Israel, not primarily as a political event but as a religious experience, as a new beginning that in some sense may be seen as an eschatological fulfillment? He writes to Zalman Schachter that the Holocaust is a sign making clear to Christians what they had lost sight of for centuries: we cannot separate Israel and Christ. The Suffering Servant of the songs of Isaiah is Israel and is also Christ. The wedding feast to which God calls God's people is a single wedding feast (see *Hidden Ground of Love*, 535).

In the same letter he suggests that Christian anti-Semitism became a problem when Christians began to think of Christ as Prometheus. Then it was, he says, that they justified wars and crusades and pogroms and the bomb and Auschwitz. Michelangelo's *Christ of the Last Judgment* in the Sistine Chapel is precisely this Promethean Christ. "He is," Merton writes, "whipping sinners with his great Greek muscles." He goes on: "All right, if we can't make it to the wedding feast (and we are the ones who refused), we can blow up the joint and say it is the Last Judgment." Merton comments, "Well, that's the way it is the Judgment, and that's the way men judge themselves, and that's the way the poor and the helpless and the maimed and the blind enter into the Kingdom: when the Prometheus types blow the door wide open for them" (*Hidden Ground of Love*, 536).

Writing to Rabbi Schachter in Advent of 1961, he speaks of Jewish and Christian expectation. "We need to make straight the paths for the coming of the Consoler. And I think the Christian needs to wait with the longing and anguish of the Jew for the Messiah, not with our foregone-conclusion, accomplished-fact-that-justifies-all-our-nonsense attitude" (534). Each of us, he says, on our own side and in our own way, must prepare for the great eschatological feast on the mountains of Israel. In addition, Christians must accept their responsibility for the anti-Semitism that prevailed for so long in the church, an anti-Semitism that climaxed in the Holocaust. In a 1966 *Commonweal* article Merton wrote, "That I should have been born in 1915, that I should be the contemporary of Auschwitz, Hiroshima, Viet Nam and the Watts riots are things about which I was not first consulted. Yet they are also events in which, whether I like it or not, I am deeply and personally involved" (*World of Action*, 145/161).

Merton and Pius XII

If Christians have sometimes used Christ to justify war and persecution, they also have used him to protect institutional power. In 1963 Merton wrote an article entitled "The Trial of Pius XII." The article was about Hochhuth's play *The Deputy*, though it is more a reflection on the deeper meaning of the play than a review of it.

To say anything about Hochhuth's play put Merton in an awkward position. He was still "under the ban," imposed by the abbot general of the Cistercians, forbidding him to write about war and peace. Hochhuth's play touched closely on these issues. Clearly it was an attack on Pius XII and, more than that, on the institution of the papacy. The pope was accused in the play of sacrificing the entire Jewish people in order to achieve a policy of coexistence with Hitler.

Without doubt the play was white-hot with partisanship. Nothing is said about the quiet and unofficial aid given secretly and effectively to thousands of individual Jews by the pope himself. Instead, Hochhuth portrays Pius XII as a hypocrite, ambitious and obsessed with his own power.

Merton views the play as an instance of anti-Catholic or at least antipapal propaganda. At the same time, however, he refuses to dismiss it out of hand. For he feels that despite its "vulgar polemic," *The Deputy* does raise an issue that must be taken seriously, even though the play seldom rises to the level of that issue. "Crudely stated (and Hochhuth states it crudely) the question is this: when the Church is faced with a critical choice between the most basic of all its moral laws, the love for God and for man, and the practical, immediate options of power politics, is she now so accustomed to choosing the latter that she is no longer able to see the former?" (*Literary Essays*, 164).

Merton believed that *The Deputy* was unfair to Pius XII, and he offers some of the reasons why the pope did not speak out against Hitlerism. But he also suggests that Hochhuth's pope is not a person but an institution, and that he is more than the institution of the papacy. He stands, Merton says, for "*all* Fatherhood" (165) or, as we might want to express it today, for all paternalistic ways of exercising authority. It is the papacy as this kind of institution that is on trial in the play. Merton asks, "Is it a completely unwarranted reaction to the use of the 'Papal image' to enlist blind obedience to all kinds of temporal and expedient causes that are by no means divine, but which are put forward as if they were God's will, without alternative, because they have been presented in close association with the magic image? Is it not the habit both of some who speak officially in the name of the Church, and even of some who cannot, to evoke this image in support of interests and projects which are not, to put it mildly, those of God and of the Church?" (167).

The Second Vatican Council and the Document on the Jews

The very next year, following the writing on *The Deputy*, the same issue — the proper exercise of ecclesiastical power — occupied Merton's attention in connection with another matter deeply affecting the Jews. The matter at stake was the Second Vatican Council's declaration on the relationship of the church to the Jews. An original statement was hailed by the Jews as a break-through in Jewish Christian relations. But the statement had a stormy journey through the Council. Some of the Council

fathers voiced a concern that was principally political: the fear of giving offense to the Arab people of the East and making the lot of Christian Arabs more difficult. The possibility of a statement unacceptable to the Jews loomed as a threat to Jews who looked to the Council for a statement of repentance for the anti-Semitism of so many centuries. Rabbi Abraham Heschel was deeply disturbed by what might emerge from the Council. He visited Merton on July 13, 1964, and expressed his anguish and outrage. That very day Merton wrote a strong letter of appeal to Cardinal Bea, in which he pointed out the moral loss that would come with a watered down statement on the Jews. (For the details of the Merton-Heschel conversation, see VATICAN COUNCIL, THE SECOND.)

At the heart of Merton's concern for a dramatic change in Christian-Jewish relations was his deep realization of the horrible and terrifying eschatological event of the Holocaust. During Easter week of 1964, he wrote in his journal, "Can one look attentively at Christ and not also see Auschwitz?" (*Vow of Conversation*, 42).[3] WHS

SEE ALSO FROMM, ERICH; HESCHEL, ABRAHAM JOSHUA; HOLOCAUST; VATICAN COUNCIL, THE SECOND.

Notes

1. See *Hidden Ground of Love*, 308–24 (Fromm); 430–36 (Heschel); 533–41 (Schachter).
2. *Working Notebook: Holographic Journal* (July 1964).
3. This line is slightly different in *Water of Life*, 98.

JUST WAR, THEORY OF

Thomas Merton consistently states that he is not a pacifist, though usually with provisos that bring him close to a pacifist position in practice. For example, in a 1965 statement sent to a Louisville journalist he begins, "If a pacifist is one who believes that all war is always wrong and always has been wrong, then I am not a pacifist," but then he adds that he believes war to be "an avoidable tragedy" and that the major problem of the age is to find solutions to international conflicts that do not resort to violence (*Witness to Freedom*, 114). Four years earlier he had written to his (pacifist) friend James Forest, "Technically I am not a pure pacifist in theory, though today in practice I don't see how one can be anything else since limited wars (however 'just') present an almost certain danger of nuclear war on an all-out scale" (*Hidden Ground of Love*, 259). This comment indicates Merton's usual approach to the traditional Catholic ethical teaching on war, the so-called just war theory, which Merton basically accepts as legitimate but which he believes leads logically to a rejection of virtually all war in the modern era.

Merton based his own decision to seek noncombatant conscientious objector status in World War II on the application of just war principles, as he explains in his autobiography. Basically, he is willing to accept that the war conforms to the criterion of just cause (i.e., is defensive not aggressive) and if declared would be done so by competent authority; he is somewhat less certain if it would be waged as a last resort but is willing to give the government the benefit of the doubt. Thus, he accepts the legitimacy of the war according to what is traditionally called *jus ad bellum*, the justice of entering into war. Where he has a serious problem is with what is termed *jus in bello*, just methods of waging war. He writes, "To my mind, there was very little doubt about the immorality of the methods used in modern war. . . . Methods that descend to wholesale barbarism and ruthless, indiscriminate slaughter of non-combatants practically without defense are hard to see as anything else but mortal sins" (*Seven Storey Mountain*, 312). It is this perspective that leads him to seek noncombatant objector status (though he also approaches the question from the more evangelical perspective of bringing "the charity and mercy of Christ" to an experience of "human misery" [313]). In the event, his entrance into the monastery rendered the issue moot before he learned if his request would be granted.

Two decades later, in writing a letter of support for a young man seeking conscientious objector status, Merton relies on a somewhat similar argument, still based on just war principles. His four points are first, that the church allows for the possibility of a just war of defense even today, but that for a war to be just, only just means must be used, a criterion that

many moralists consider to have been violated in World War II; second, the position of the church (at that time, 1962) is that citizens are obligated to serve their country if all conditions for a just war are fulfilled; third, papal statements consistently "cast great doubt" upon the possibility that any use of atomic, biological, or chemical weapons can be considered just means; and fourth, given the fact that any war is likely to escalate to include use of weapons of mass destruction, *"there is every reason why a Catholic should be prevented by reasons of conscience from serving in the armed forces"* (*Road to Joy*, 322–23). (Merton does not deal with the fact that such an argument could be construed as a defense of *selective* conscientious objection — not to all war anywhere at any time but only to wars as currently fought — which was not permissible under the Selective Service Act.)

Merton's consistent position is that it is virtually inevitable that modern warfare will be unjust, and therefore that a Catholic in good conscience cannot participate in war. He associates this stance with the availability of atomic weapons but traces the massive disregard of just war principles back to the Second World War, which the allies entered with justice on their side but in which they progressively used more and more unjust methods, culminating with the dropping of the atomic bombs on Hiroshima and Nagasaki, which he calls "a dire injustice and an atrocity" (*Passion for Peace*, 34). He points out that the two criteria for waging a war justly, discrimination (observing the distinction between combatants and non-combatants in battle) and proportionality (the intended good clearly outweighs the collateral evil), were completely disregarded, and that in fact terror bombing intentionally targeted civilians to an effort to break the enemy's will. The unjust methods of the enemy in fact were adopted by the Allies, whose criteria were no longer ethical but pragmatic and opportunistic (28–29, 33). Merton's conclusion is that there has been a complete breakdown in the traditional just war position, which is generally considered irrelevant by policymakers and is often manipulated by the casuistry of "realist" moralists to allow for what in fact is clearly immoral. The result has been the development of what Merton calls the "relative pacifist" position (often called "nuclear pacifism" by others), "which would outlaw all nuclear war and work for disarmament as the course of action most consistent with Christian morality" (36).

Merton often suggests that "in practice the just war theory has become irrelevant" (*Nonviolent Alternative*, 90), by which he means that it no longer has any usefulness in determining if a particular war is or is not just, because modern warfare by its very nature is unjust. In a 1965 letter to John Heidbrink of the Fellowship of Reconciliation (an interreligious pacifist organization to which Merton belonged, despite his "non-pacifist" position), Merton agrees with Heidbrink that "if the logic of the just war were followed, it would lead in practice to a 'pacifist' position, and that is in fact what the Popes have actually done, especially Pope John in *Pacem in Terris*. His reasoning here is simply that new developments in war technology and the present political condition of the world have conspired to make the conditions of the just war practically unfulfillable" (*Hidden Ground of Love*, 421). This actually is the approach that Merton typically takes: though he calls the just war theory "irrelevant," he in fact uses it in an effort to convince those who accept the validity of the theory that it leads to a virtually complete rejection of modern warfare. Thus, not only in dealing with the threat of nuclear war but also in responding to the situation in Vietnam he can write, "In terms of the traditional Catholic just war theory (which is also insufficient, but let that pass) when a war produces only massive slaughter out of proportion to any good that can conceivably come of it, it is unjust and immoral" (*Witness to Freedom*, 118).

Finally, it should be noted that when Merton discusses the origins of the just war theory in Christianity in the writings of St. Augustine, he is quite willing to criticize what he sees as its twofold weakness: its stress on subjective purity of intention and its tendency to pessimism about human nature and the world as a justification for recourse to violence (*Seeds of Destruction*, 150–51). In comparing the Augustinian position to the more evangelical and eschatological witness of Origen to Christian nonviolence, Merton clearly is more in sympathy with Origen's perspective. While he concedes that in the context of the times "the theory of the just war was not altogether absurd" (148), he suggests that "if there are to be significant new developments in Christian thought on nuclear war, it may well be that these developments will depend on our ability to get free from the overpowering influence of Augustinian assumptions and take a new view of man, of society and of war itself" (145). He identifies this "new view" with the more evangelical position of the early church ("though not necessarily a return to an imaginary ideal of pure primitive pacifism," he adds) and with the more optimistic view of human nature taken by John XXIII (145). Thus, while Merton never disavows the just war theory outright, and finds it useful in providing a logical argument against modern war that is in some continuity with the past, his passionate advocacy of gospel nonviolence in an essay such as "Blessed Are the Meek" (*Faith and Violence*, 14–29), while it is not incompatible with the just war theory, is much closer to the pacifist position that Merton theoretically disavows but in practice embraces. POC

SEE ALSO NONVIOLENCE; PEACE; WAR.

KANCHENJUNGA

This mountain peak in the Himalayas, rising to 28,208 feet, is the third highest in the world. During his brief retreat at the Mim tea estate, Thomas Merton had unrivaled views of Kanchenjunga. He reflected on the mountain, "O Tantric Mother Mountain! Yin-yang palace of opposites in unity! Palace of *anicca*, impermanence and patience, solidity and nonbeing, existence and wisdom. . . . The full beauty of the mountain is not seen until you too consent to the impossible paradox: it is and is not. When nothing more needs to be said, the smoke of ideas clears, the mountain is SEEN" (*Asian Journal*, 156–57; *Other Side of the Mountain*, 286). WHS

KATAPHATICISM

The affirmative way (*via affirmationis*) of speaking about and experiencing God. It both complements and contrasts with apophaticism (*via negationis*). For a detailed approach to both, see APOPHATICISM. WHS

KINGDOM OF GOD

For Thomas Merton, the revelation and establishment of the kingdom of God is central to

Mount Kanchenjunga, photograph by Thomas Merton.

the life and mission of Jesus: in his birth, in his preaching of good news to the poor, and above all in his death and resurrection, the transforming power of God's reign is released into the world. The birth of Jesus ushers in the reign of God because in Jesus the will of God, the divine plan for creation, is fully present in an absolutely faithful human being, who came "not merely to seek and save that which was lost, but to establish his Kingdom, the eschatological Kingdom, the manifestation of the fullness of time and the completion of history" (*Love and Living*, 223). Thus, the mission of Christ is not only the healing and redeeming of individuals but also the renewal of all humanity. In his preaching Jesus reveals the kingdom to be a sign of contradiction to the illusory perception that wealth or social status or political power confers or connotes superiority before God. In Merton's view "the sign *par excellence*" of the presence of the kingdom is Jesus' identification with the poor: "The prophetic message of salvation, the fulfillment of the divine promises is now formally announced to the *anawim*, to those who hungered and thirsted for the Kingdom because they had no hope but the Lord" (*Seasons of Celebration*, 98). Jesus' arrest, torture, and execution are an attempt to silence and discredit the proclamation of the reign of God, an attempt proven futile by Jesus' divine vindication, his triumph over the forces of sin and death. Thus, in the crucifixion and resurrection of the Lord the disclosure of the kingdom of God reaches its climax. Because Christ is risen, sin has been defeated and the kingdom has become present: "For with the death and resurrection of Christ we are in a new world, a new age. The fulness of time has come. The history of the world has achieved an entirely new orientation. We are living in the Messianic Kingdom" (*New Man*, 148).

For Merton, the contemporary disciple of Christ is one who is able to perceive with the eyes of faith "the victory of Christ and the reality of his Kingdom in the world even now, in all the confusion, the chaos and the risk of this historical and revolutionary time of crisis which we call the atomic age" (*World of Action*, 180). But Christians are not called merely to observe the kingdom but to incarnate it: the same reality definitively manifested in Jesus must be made visible and tangible in those who claim to be his followers. Merton writes, "The great historical event, the coming of the Kingdom, is made clear and is 'realized' in proportion as Christians themselves live the life of the Kingdom in the circumstances of their own place and time" (*Faith and Violence*, 16). By serving as a sign of contradiction to the power of sin and death and a sign of invitation to the fullness of human life, which ultimately is the fullness of divine life, Christians resolve the tension between commitment to the present reality of the kingdom and recognition of the continuing power of darkness and division.

The vocation of the Christian community and each of its members, therefore, is to be a sign of the kingdom's transforming presence and an instrument of its further unfolding. While the church cannot simply be identified with the kingdom, the kingdom, the full expression of God's will for creation, is both its origin and its goal: "The Church, by celebrating the death and resurrection of Christ, enters into the Kingdom of Life which He has established once for all by His definitive victory over sin and death" (*Seasons of Celebration*, 113). The Christian community continually is summoned to move with humility and with confidence toward an ever deeper yet never perfected incarnation of the essential values that constitute God's reign, to model the love and peace and unity that are God's will for history. Merton is not so naive, of course, as to think that the Christian community has been or will be completely faithful to this mission. The community and its members are called to an ongoing conversion, a recognition and confession of failure to live as citizens of the new creation, a death to self on ever deeper levels of one's being (130). This does not mean that Merton would restrict the working of the Spirit, and so the presence of the kingdom, to the formal activity of the church: the "immensity and power of the Kingdom that is established, in mystery" (*Search for Solitude*, 143) may be glimpsed beyond the boundaries of the Church, for God's Spirit blows where it wills. Yet encounters with the kingdom beyond the boundaries of the church do not lessen the responsibility of those within the church to serve as the primary witnesses of the good news that the reign of God is at hand, and to call the world to conversion and fidelity by their own faithfulness to the message they proclaim.

For Merton, the reality of the kingdom is at the heart of both the contemplative and the active dimensions of the Christian life. As an experience of the divine presence and a foretaste of eternal union with God, contemplation is a way of participating in the kingdom: "Because my faith is eschatological," Merton writes in his journal, "it is *also* contemplative, for I am even now in the Kingdom and I can even now 'see' something of the glory of the Kingdom and praise Him who is King." It is through the presence of the Holy Spirit that this "union of contemplation and eschatology" is brought about, for in the Spirit the first fruits of resurrected life, "that Truth which is the end," is already disclosed: "We are already fully and eternally alive. Contemplation is the loving sense of this life and this presence and this eternity" (*Water of Life*, 182). Contemplation not only serves as a guard against false or inadequate expressions of the kingdom motivated by fear of failure or by a desire for measurable results rather than by selfless love, but also acts as invitation and encouragement for authentic incarnation of the kingdom. "The most important need in the Christian world today," Merton writes, "is this inner truth nourished by this Spirit of contemplation: the praise and love of God, the longing for the coming of Christ, the thirst for the manifestation of God's glory, his truth, his justice, his Kingdom in the world" (*Contemplative Prayer*, 144).

If in contemplation the kingdom as gift is experienced, Christian action carries out the responsibility of discipleship to make the reality of the kingdom more evident in the world. While the kingdom has been definitively established in the life, death, and resurrection of Jesus, in its temporal, human dimension it is always partial and provisional: "The earthly manifestation of the Kingdom of God is still only a shadow of the eternal Kingdom that is to come." But the realization that the perfection of God's reign will come only in God's good time "cannot be made into a pretext for ignoring the temporal happiness and welfare of man in this present life" (*Disputed Questions*, 127); whatever protects and enhances the essential dignity of human beings, made in the divine image, conforms to God's will for creation and therefore contributes to the revelation of God's reign. "The Kingdom is already established; the Kingdom is a present reality. But there is still work to be done. Christ calls us to work together in building his Kingdom. We cooperate with him in bringing it to perfection" (*He Is Risen*, 9). In what does this work consist? Merton looks to the great judgment scene of Matthew 25 for the most concise and meaningful answer: "Those who have fed the hungry and given drink to the thirsty, given shelter to the stranger, visited the sick and the prisoner, are taken into the kingdom: for they did all these things to Christ himself" (*Life and Holiness*, 115). To see and serve Christ in, and to be Christ for, other people, particularly those most neglected and despised, is to live the will of God for humanity, to allow God to reign on earth as in heaven, to act as God's instruments in the ongoing task of transforming the world.

For this reason, a commitment to nonviolent resistance to evil becomes central to Merton's understanding of the kingdom, which is preeminently the reign of *shalom*. As Jesus released the transforming power of the kingdom by fidelity to his mission of sacrificial, redemptive love, even in the face of hatred, rejection, and murderous violence, the Christian community and its members testify to the same transforming power operative in the world today by conforming to the pattern set by their Master, by taking up their cross and following him, with no assurance of immediately observable results but with confidence of sharing in the mystery of the ultimate victory of love. "The religious basis of Christian non-violence is then faith in Christ the Redeemer and obedience to his demand to love and manifest himself in us by a certain manner of acting in the world and in relation to other men. This obedience enables us to live as true citizens of the Kingdom, in which the divine mercy, the grace, favor and redeeming love of God are active in our lives. Then the Holy Spirit will indeed 'rest upon us' and act in us, not for our own good alone but for God and his Kingdom" (*Faith and Violence*, 16).

For Merton, as for the entire tradition of Christianity, the kingdom is the secret hidden in the heart of creation that gives meaning and direction to all that is of permanent value in human life: "The world was created without man, but the new creation which is the true Kingdom of God is to be the work of God in and through man. It is to be the great, mysterious, theandric work of the Mystical Christ, the New Adam, in whom all men as 'one Person' or one 'Son of God' will transfigure the cosmos and offer it resplendent to the Father" (*Birds of Appetite*, 132). POC

SEE ALSO ESCHATOLOGY; REDEMPTION; SALVATION.

KNIGHT, W. JAMES

A red-haired Atlantan and classmate of Bob Gerdy and Ed Rice in the Columbia Class of 1940, Jim Knight (b. 1918) was a member of the literary group that coalesced around *Jester* and other publications on the fourth floor of John Jay Hall. He spent the summer after his graduation with Merton and many other Columbia friends at Bob Lax's brother-in-law's cottage and was Merton's companion on the memorable hitchhiking trip from Olean to Cleveland that summer (see *Run to the Mountain*, 313) that resulted in Merton's poem "Aubade: Lake Erie." He served in the army in North Africa and Europe during World War II, concluding his service in command of a company of African American soldiers. After the war he worked as a newspaperman in Paris, eventually becoming news editor of the Paris edition of the *New York Herald Tribune,* and as an official in the International Labor Organization, an agency of the United Nations. He is also the author of a novel, *The Master of Chambord* (1995). His own reminiscences of Merton and his Columbia friends can be found on the Internet at *www.therealmerton.com.* POC

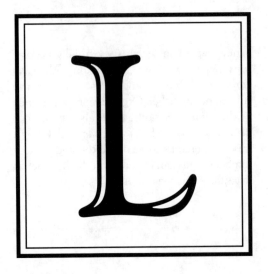

"LABYRINTH, THE"

SEE NOVELS, UNPUBLISHED.

LANGUAGE AND PROPAGANDA

As a poet and writer, Thomas Merton not only appreciated the power of language to communicate truth, create community, and even express something of deepest reality, but he also recognized that language has the potential to deceive, manipulate, and control human beings and to distort and obscure reality itself. Especially in the 1960s, as he spoke out against war, racism, and the oppression imposed by totalitarian governments, Merton called attention to the abuse of language and the role of propaganda.

It is significant that *Original Child Bomb* and "Chant to Be Used in Processions around a Site with Furnaces" — two poems that Merton wrote in the summer of 1961, inaugurating his vocal and public opposition to war — both exposed the use of language to conceal rather than to reveal reality. Employing the words used by the participants themselves to describe the testing, deployment, and explosion of the atom bomb at Hiroshima and the atrocities

Cover for *Learning to Love* reprinted with the permission of HarperSanFrancisco.

committed at Auschwitz, Merton exposes what the participants skillfully hid with language.

In the late 1960s, Merton returned to a discussion of the language of Auschwitz and war in two important articles. In the first article, "Auschwitz: A Family Camp"[1] — a review of Bernd Naumann's *Auschwitz* — as Merton turns his attention to the language of the Gestapo, he observes, "Language itself has fallen victim to total war, genocide and systematic tyranny in our time" (*Passion for Peace*, 281). A preeminent example is the language employed by the Gestapo, which, with its emphasis on secrecy and evasion, "subjected the German language to violence and crude perversion" (281). Employing a variety of strategies for circumlocution — understatement, double-talk, doublethink, and officialese — the Gestapo recognized the power of language even as they abused it. In the second article, "War and the Crisis of Language," written in 1968 and published posthumously,[2] Merton identifies himself as a poet, noting that poets "are perhaps the ones who, at the present moment, are most sensitive to the sickness of language" that is symptomatic of "a national — indeed worldwide — illness," of which race riots and assassinations are also symptoms (300, 301). Lamenting the "gap between words and actions," Merton notes the "spastic upheaval" of theological language and the absurdity of advertising claims (301, 302). But it is the language of war — the war in Vietnam — that Merton finds most appalling: "The burned huts become 'enemy structures'; the dead men, women, and children become 'Vietcong,' thus adding to a 'kill ratio' that can be interpreted as 'favorable'" (305). The "practical language of the battlefield" is matched and perhaps surpassed by "the much more pompous and sinister jargon of the war mandarins in government offices and military think-tanks" (307). Language becomes a sinister element in the game of war and "an instrument of manipulation" (309). "The illness of political language — which is almost universal and is a symptom of a Plague of Power that is common to China and America, Russia and Western Europe — is characterized everywhere by the same sort of double-talk, tautology, ambiguous cliché, self-righteous and doctrinaire pomposity, and pseudoscientific jargon that mask a total callousness and moral insensitivity, indeed a basic contempt for man" (313).

Merton had long recognized the capacity of mass media to create false images and the power that those images exert. He knew how the interplay of words and images shapes the way in which a society sees itself and supports values that promote servitude rather than freedom. This fabrication of false images is the purpose of propaganda, which spreads ideas and information to serve its cause. In journal entries written during an earlier war Merton recorded two examples of how propaganda had affected him personally. He saw two films of the war. The first focused on the Germans, the second on the Allies. In September 1940 Merton saw a film of the war in Poland, made a year earlier. "The Germans took a lot of trouble to get those pictures.... It showed no dead men, nobody getting killed, nobody even getting roughed up ... there were hundreds of feet, it seemed, of destroyed material and houses. All this destruction was completely dehumanized. You saw a lot of razed buildings, blasted bridges, wrecked trains, piles of captured guns ... when they did show men, even the men looked dehumanized, and appeared to be nothing more than equipment. The Germans looked like good equipment, the Poles looked like cheap equip-

ment, slightly spoiled" (*Run to the Mountain*, 236). The effect of the film was not terror but drabness: "a lot of tired soldiers and a lot of rubble and garbage" (237). Merton especially was struck by the ugliness of the war, particularly the bombers: "The most actively obscene shot in the whole picture was one of a bomber releasing a stick of bombs which fell away from under its belly in a group: it was like some vile beetle laying eggs in the air, or dropping its filth" (237). While the film favored war, it is clear that Merton, even then, saw through it. But a few weeks later he saw a movie of London under bombing, and he says, "For the first time in my life, I think, I momentarily wanted to be in the war" (244). What he saw was a hole blasted out of the store in Oxford Circus where he had bought a suit when he was sixteen, up the street from a bar where he used to drink beer, and not far from the cinema where he had enjoyed movies he still remembered. He saw people going into the air-raid shelter and the empty streets and heard the sound of an alarm. "This, for the first time, made me want to fight. Of course it was propaganda, and good propaganda" (245).

Years later, Merton had much more to say about propaganda. In *Conjectures of a Guilty Bystander* Merton analyzes the genre, observing that we make the mistake of thinking propaganda false and fictitious, "a malicious and systematic misrepresentation of truth" (*Guilty Bystander*, 214/235). But it need not be "blatantly false." Although propaganda is "*irrational*," it is "not necessarily *untrue*" (215/236). Employing facts, propaganda thrives on innuendo and insinuation; or it simply overwhelms the listener with a "mass of information" — "statistics, editorial opinions, the results of opinion polls, the decisions of statesmen" (215/236). There is too much information to assimilate, and so the listener makes "an act of faith in his government or his political party" (215/237). In a "labyrinth of information" one does not have a choice. Although there is too much information, there is also too little. Important facts are withheld. The violence exerted by propaganda is real: "by means of apparent truth and apparent reason, it induces us to surrender our freedom and self-possession" (216/237). Others make up our minds or, rather, we are left with "the mass mind" (217/238).

Hitler and the Nazis were expert propagandists, announcing their plans and describing their actions in forms they thought people would find acceptable. Writing about the horrors of Auschwitz in "Chant," Merton found that all he needed to do was to repeat the utterances of the propagandist: that was enough to expose their mentality and their atrocities. But Merton was not simply concerned to expose past uses of propaganda; he was intent on showing that the manipulation of language and images continues to enslave humankind. CMB

SEE ALSO HOLOCAUST; *ORIGINAL CHILD BOMB*; TRUTH.

Notes

1. Published in *Catholic Worker* 33 (November 1967): 4–5, 8.
2. Published in Robert Ginsberg, ed., *The Critique of War: Contemporary Philosophical Explorations* (Chicago: Henry Regnery Company, 1969), 99–119.

LAST OF THE FATHERS, THE: *St. Bernard of Clairvaux and the Encyclical, Doctor Mellifluus*
New York: Harcourt, Brace, 1954. 123 pp.

On January 18, 1950, Thomas Merton records in his journal that he had signed a contract with Harcourt, Brace to write four books for them, one on St. Bernard (see *Entering the Silence*, 399). On May 24, 1953, Pope Pius XII wrote an encyclical commemorating the eighth centenary of St. Bernard's death. Dom James Fox asked Merton to translate the document and write a commentary on it (see *School of Charity*, 64). This was the origin of *The Last of the Fathers*.

The book has four parts: (1) a biographical note about St. Bernard and his times (23–44); (2) a brief discussion of his writings (47–67); (3) Merton's notes on the encyclical (71–90); and (4) Merton's translation of the encyclical. In addition, the book has a preface, a bibliography, and a brief index.

In the first part of the book Merton attempts to present St. Bernard as the person he actually was to counteract in the different biographies of him, which tend to single

out one aspect of his person: "history celebrating one side of him, theology another, piety a third, his own monastic Order a fourth" (*Last of the Fathers*, 9). Merton tries, as he suggests the encyclical does, to bring these fragments together. He warns against any overly literal understanding of the title of the encyclical, *Doctor Mellifluus*, which literally suggests that his writings were "as sweet as honey." Merton warns that this does not mean that Bernard's writings are "sugary," sentimental; rather, they embody the sweetness, freshness, and gentleness of Christian love. And yet, it is true to say that Bernard was not all sweetness and light; when the occasion demanded it, he could be angry and belligerent.

In 1115 Bernard, a young monk at Cîteaux, was made abbot of a new foundation, Clairvaux, the "Valley of Light." Eventually he founded seventy other monasteries. He was in close touch with the papacy when one of his monks became Pope Eugenius III. Indeed, he worked with the pope in what proved to be a tragic collaboration: the Second Crusade (1147–49), which had neither the enthusiasm nor the success of the First. It failed in its effort to recapture Edessa. "As it was, the armies of the Cross converged on Constantinople and gave the impression that the capital on the Bosporus was the real objective of their Crusade. Manuel Commenius, the Basileus, did what he could to make sure that there would not be a victorious army of Crusaders returning through the city. This meant, in fact, that he made sure there would be no victorious army" (43). Bernard had conceived the crusade as a manifestation of Christian unity; it was not, and to Bernard this was why it failed. Merton reminds his readers that Bernard's motives for the crusade were mystical (saving the holy places in Palestine), whereas the motives of the crusaders were very different. Remember, he tells us, that Bernard belonged to the twelfth century, not to ours.

Though Bernard wrote voluminously, most of his works are quite short. Only one of them, the *De Consideratione*, would exceed the length of a long article in a literary magazine. Best known are his sermons (about 350 in number) and his many letters. Several of his writings may be singled out as especially important:

(1) a group of eighty-six sermons on the Song of Songs (the best articulation of his mystical teaching); (2) the treatise *De Diligendo Deo* (*On the Love of God*), on the four degrees of love (loving ourselves, loving God and others for our own sake, loving God for God's own sake, and loving ourselves for God's sake); and (3) sermons on the Virgin Mary (*Homiliae super Missus Est*),[1] in which he speaks of the mystery of redemption in terms of the incarnation rather than the passion.

Speaking of the *De Diligendo Deo*,[2] Merton sees it as "the high point of Bernard's Christian humanism. It shows that the fulfillment of our destiny is not merely to be lost in God, as the traditional figures of speech would have it, like 'a drop of water in a barrel of wine or like iron in the fire,' but *found* in God in all our individual and personal reality" (52).

Merton expresses his satisfaction with the texts that Pius XII chose to illustrate Bernard's teaching. He sees as the principal theme of *Doctor Mellifluus* "Saint Bernard's teaching on charity and on the elevation of the soul to divine union by the mercy of Him who has 'first loved us'" (74).

Fittingly, the book is dedicated to Étienne Gilson, author of *The Mystical Theology of St. Bernard*. His book *The Spirit of Medieval Philosophy* was a decisive influence on Merton during his Columbia days. WHS

SEE ALSO *THOMAS MERTON ON ST. BERNARD*

Notes

1. These are homilies on the Gospel of the annunciation that begins "Missus est."
2. During his Holy Week retreat at Gethsemani in 1941, Merton had read *De Diligendo Deo*. See *Seven Storey Mountain*, 331; *Run to the Mountain*, 337–54.

LATIN AMERICA

"I have never for a moment questioned the vocation to be a monk, but I have had to settle many other questions about ways and means, the where and the how of being a monk," Thomas Merton wrote to Robert Menchin on January 15, 1966 (*Witness to Freedom*, 255). Merton's restlessness and craving for solitude led him, at different times in his monastic life, to consider leaving Gethsemani to go elsewhere

to live as a monk. In the late 1940s he was tempted to become a Carthusian; in 1955 he considered joining the Camaldolese; and in 1959 he planned to go to Latin America to live as a monk.

Merton's attraction to Latin America was not new. In 1940 the young Merton traveled to Cuba, where he experienced an instant affinity for the culture and the people, as is apparent in the accounts of his trip in his journal and autobiography. Havana "overwhelms you, and you are overcome by its brilliance and the lights and shadows and the noise and the cries and the colors and the smells and the tremendous vitality" (*Secular Journal*, 56).[1] The Cuban people are "astonishingly . . . beautiful people . . . full of joy and kindness and grace" (73). Merton's enthusiasm for Cuba soon grew into a passion for Latin America fueled, in the late 1950s, by personal connections. There were several Spanish-speaking novices in the monastery; there was talk of a new Trappist foundation in Ecuador; and in July 1957 Ernesto Cardenal, a young Nicaraguan poet, came to Gethsemani as a postulant. Cardenal's influence on Merton was especially significant. In something of a reversal of roles, Cardenal found that his novice master was eager to learn all he could about Latin American history, culture, and literature from his Nicaraguan novice.[2] Cardenal introduced Merton to the work of Latin American poets and writers with whom Merton felt an immediate connection. In 1958 Merton began corresponding with Pablo Antonio Cuadra, Nicaraguan writer and editor of *La Prensa*; in 1957, after Cardenal left Gethsemani, he and Merton began exchanging letters; and during the 1960s Merton corresponded with poets and writers throughout Latin America.[3]

The idea of a Trappist foundation in Latin America appealed to Merton and in July 1959 he wrote to Dom Gabriel Sortais volunteering "to help make a foundation in South America, if it is God's will," convinced that a "quite poor, quite simple" monastery in Ecuador, Peru, or Colombia could do much good (*School of Charity*, 104). But at the same time, Merton was exploring other options that would enable him to live as a hermit in Latin America. One possibility was Cuernavaca, Mexico, where Dom Gregorio Lemercier, O.S.B., was prior of Our Lady of the Resurrection, an experimental Benedictine community. Lemercier visited Gethsemani several times in late spring and summer of 1959 and encouraged Merton to consider Cuernavaca. But Merton also wrote to several bishops in his search for a location suitable for a hermit. He contacted Bishop James P. Davis of San Juan, Puerto Rico, who suggested Tortola in the Dutch West Indies, a community with some fifty Catholics where Merton would not "be burdened" with pastoral concerns.[4] He wrote to Carthusian Bishop Matthew Niedhammer of Bluefields, Nicaragua, who confirmed that Big Corn Island, an island off the coast of Nicaragua that Cardenal had suggested, would be a good choice. By late September Merton seemed to have settled on Cuernavaca. Merton wrote to Msgr. Larraona at the Sacred Congregation for Religious in Rome requesting an indult that would permit him to transfer to another monastery.

In October Merton's enthusiasm for the move was running high, as was his confidence that the indult would be granted. Merton began making plans. In a "conscience matter" letter to Cardenal, Merton talked about how he would travel to Mexico via Albuquerque, New Mexico, where he planned to look at Indian pueblos and maybe "make a kind of retreat in the desert" (*Courage for Truth*, 115). He wondered about what kind of paperwork would be required, and he alerted Cardenal to expect packages of books to be held for his arrival and informed him that he planned to dress as a layman. While he was hospitalized for surgery in mid-October — Merton's health was "a small trial" — he wrote to reassure Cardenal that he was still very much looking forward to going to Mexico. And, although he dreaded "going off with imprecations hurled" after him and "being treated as a traitor, etc.," Merton told Cardenal that a "work of God can often and usually does demand a complete uprooting that is extremely painful and disconcerting, and which requires great fidelity in the one called to do the work" (117). It appears that Merton saw Cuernavaca as something of a temporary arrangement, since he continued to speak of possible sites for a monastic foundation in Nicaragua, perhaps

Ometepe or Corn Island. Merton was interested in a site that would provide opportunities for immersion in Latin America: "I feel, as does Pablo Antonio," he wrote to Cardenal, "that one must . . . be rooted in the Indian and Latin cultural complex in a very definite way" (117). It was important that he "not simply be a gringo tourist" (118). Merton wanted to get free of the "inertia of conventional religious life, . . . it is true that God works here also but there are so many influences to deaden and falsify the interior life. A kind of perpetual danger of sclerosis" (120). Merton was intent on recovering what he saw to be essential to monastic life: "It is not a question of building a great edifice, but of living a simple life and preserving as much as possible of the values we already have found, in experience, here and elsewhere — eliminating as far as possible the great defects and obstacles of a highly organized life" (118).

On December 17, 1959, Merton notified Cardenal that a decision had been rendered: "a letter from Rome has given absolutely final negative decision of my case. Or at least, a decision so final that I am not at liberty to take any further steps on my own behalf, but can only accept and obey. I must stay here until the Church herself places me somewhere else. I still believe that the mercy of God can and perhaps will accomplish this, but I can only wait in darkness and in faith, without making any move. I have hopes that Dom Gregorio will still be able to do something for me. But what?" (121). Merton received the news with striking equanimity and affirmed his obedience: "I can only obey the Congregation and remain passive and I have no hope of making any move to leave this Order. I have in fact promised not to leave, but will only await the action of the Church to move me elsewhere if she sees fit" (122).

Merton was coming to realize that ultimately, solitude was not a matter of place. Writing in his journal on December 17, 1959, Merton put it this way: "Actually, what it comes down to is that I shall certainly have solitude but only by miracle and not at all by my own contriving. Where? Here or there makes no difference. Somewhere, nowhere, beyond all 'where.' Solitude outside geography or in it. No matter" (*Search for Solitude*, 359).

But Merton's dream of going to Latin America was not set aside for ever. In October 1965 Ernesto Cardenal visited Merton at Gethsemani and invited Merton to join him in Nicaragua, where Cardenal was founding an experimental community at Solentiname. Since August 20, 1965, Merton had been living in a hermitage on the grounds of the monastery. His longing for a hermit life was being satisfied but something of his earlier "restlessness" persisted, intensified perhaps by the isolation he began to experience now that he was living in the hermitage. So there began, for Merton, a brief flirtation with the idea of going to live in Latin America. Merton wrote to Archbishop Paul Phillippe, secretary of the Sacred Congregation of Religious, requesting to "be loaned by my community to his community, either with leave of absence, or, if your Excellency thought necessary, an exclaustration. The idea would be for me to continue my monastic life in his community while remaining a member of my own Order canonically."[5] Although Merton continued to give thought to Cardenal's proposal, his approach to the possibility was much more realistic than it had been in 1959. He carefully considered the pros and cons of going to Nicaragua[6] and concluded, "my only job is to make my own decision and it is 'yes' to the project as far as I am concerned. I will go if I am sent. I consent to it gladly if it is God's will, in so far as this will be a chance to leave everything and give myself to God in such a way as to live for others, and bring the contemplative life to Central America, and so on" (*Learning to Love*, 4). Merton concludes the entry on a telling note: "It would be a real sacrifice to leave this hermitage and the real security I have here. And a real risk with my back as it is and my guts as they are" (4). A week later Merton realized that his connection to Latin America was more than a matter of geography: "Yesterday p.m. (January 19) realized importance of a definite relationship of response to my Latin American friends, poets etc. Whether I ever go to Solentiname is accidental" (*Learning to Love*, 353).[7] He resolved to answer letters and read more in Spanish and to "really know" Latin

American literature, poetry, history, and so on (354). Merton would stay at Gethsemani. But his "restlessness" would surface again in the summer of 1968, when he would be scouting out California and Alaska for possible sites for a hermitage. CMB

SEE ALSO CAMALDOLESE; CARTHUSIANS; LATIN AMERICAN WRITERS.

Notes

1. For the full journal account of Merton's Cuban interlude, see *Run to the Mountain*, 170–219. See also *Seven Storey Mountain*, 278–85.
2. See "Ernesto Cardenal," in Paul Wilkes, ed., *Merton, by Those Who Knew Him Best* (San Francisco: Harper & Row, 1984), 35–39.
3. For Merton's letters to Latin American writers, including Ernesto Cardenal and Pablo Antonio Cuadra, see *The Courage for Truth*.
4. Michael Mott, *The Seven Mountains of Thomas Merton* (Boston: Houghton Mifflin, 1984), 328.
5. See ibid., 630 n. 456.
6. See notes Merton made in "Notebook 17," published, in part, in *Water of Life*, 343–45.
7. Merton wrote this entry in "Notebook 17," the second half of which is published in *Learning to Love*, 351–67.

LATIN AMERICAN WRITERS

"I feel myself clearly much more in sympathy with the Latin America poets today than with those of North America," Thomas Merton wrote to Stefan Baciu in May 1965 (*Courage for Truth*, 241). Merton's letter to Baciu expressed Merton's sense of kinship with Latin American poets, who "seem to me to be alive, to have something honest to say, to be sincerely concerned with life and with humanity" (241). Merton goes on to name the poets whom he counts among his favorites and poets whose work he admires, as well as his contacts in Nicaragua (Ernesto Cardenal, Pablo Antonio Cuadra, José Coronel Urtecho, Ernesto Mejía Sanchez, and Alfonso Cortés), Ecuador (Jorge Carrera Andrade), Chile (Nicanor Parra), Peru (César Vallejo), Argentina (Victoria Ocampo and Miguel Grinberg), Mexico (Octavio Paz), Uruguay (Esther de Cáceres and Susana Soca), and Brazil (Jorge de Lima and Carlos Drummond de Andrade).

Merton's writings were being read throughout the Spanish-speaking world. When, in 1958, Editorial Sudamericana in Buenos Aires approached Merton to propose publishing *The Complete Works of Thomas Merton*, fifteen of Merton's major writings already had been translated into Spanish and published in Spain, Chile, Argentina, and Mexico.[1] For his part, Merton translated selected works of Spanish-speaking poets, including Ernesto Cardenal, César Vallejo, Alfonso Cortes, Pablo Antonio Cuadra, and Jorge Carrera Andrade.[2] But Merton's connection with Latin America ran deeper than reading Latin American writings and being read by Latin Americans.

In the late 1950s Merton was, as he put it, discovering "the whole Western Hemisphere" (*"Honorable Reader,"* 40). In the silence of the monastery he heard "the voice of all the hemisphere... a voice that speaks from the depths of my being with a clarity at once magnificent and terrible.... It seems that entire cities with great opulence and terrible indigence side by side live inside me" (40). The voice of ancient civilizations and the cries of indigenous peoples resonated within his heart so much so that he defined his own identity not as a North American but as a citizen of the hemisphere, and his vocation in it "to know America in its totality, to be a complete American, a man of the whole hemisphere, of the whole New World; to be a complete Christian, a complete contemplative, and through this, to help others to know Christ in the fullness of maturity, in all His universality" (43).

What Merton discovered and admired in Latin American writers was that they spoke the truth against injustice and with a prophetic voice exposed the "lies and hypocrisy" of established powers. They manifested "a new spiritual consciousness" that is hopeful and has the power to give a voice to people who have been silenced (*Courage for Truth*, 144). In 1964 Miguel Grinberg invited Merton to a meeting of poets in Mexico City. Unable to attend, Merton sent a "Message to Poets" expressing his sense of solidarity with the new Latin American poets gathered in Mexico. His words to them are words of conviction and of hope that they all may continue to speak truth with courage. "If we are to remain united against these falsehoods, against all power that poisons man, and subjects him to the mystifica-

tions of bureaucracy, commerce and the police state, we must refuse the price tag" (*Raids on the Unspeakable*, 158).

Merton's letters to Ernesto Cardenal, Pablo Antonio Cuadra, and other Latin American writers, published in *The Courage for Truth*, reveal his solidarity with Latin Americans in their struggle to speak out for truth and justice. But, as Merton recognized, they were able to speak because they had heard "the voice of the new man who is rooted in the American earth" (*Courage for Truth*, 146). Grateful for what Cardenal had written about the San Blas Indians, Merton told him that he had "a providential task in this work of understanding and love, a profound work of spiritual reconciliation, of atonement... true atonement, a redemptive and healing work, that begins with *hearing*" (146). That, as Merton saw it, was the task of the poet, and it was not unlike the task that he knew was his as a monk. CMB

SEE ALSO *COURAGE FOR TRUTH*; LATIN AMERICA.

Notes

1. See Robert Daggy's introduction to the "Preface of the Argentine Edition of the Complete Works of Thomas Merton" (April 1958), in *"Honorable Reader,"* 37.
2. See *The Collected Poems of Thomas Merton.*

LAUGHLIN, JAMES

Born in Pittsburgh, Pennsylvania, in 1914, James Laughlin decided very early that he did not want to enter the steel business that had enabled his family to amass a huge fortune. This did not, however, prevent him from enjoying the family wealth and putting it to good use. He attended Choate School in Wallingford, Connecticut, and in 1933 entered Harvard. In the middle of his sophomore year he took a leave of absence and visited France and Italy. In Rapallo, Italy, he stayed with Ezra Pound for six months. Pound became his hero and changed his interests and his outlook on literature. After reading Laughlin's poetry, Pound told him that he would never be any good as a poet and encouraged him instead to publish worthwhile books.

When he returned to Harvard and while still a student, he followed Pound's advice and started New Directions Publishing in a building near his aunt's home in Norfolk, Connecticut, and with a little help from family. In 1939, when he graduated from Harvard, he received a family gift of one hundred thousand dollars, which he invested in a ski lodge in Utah (skiing was one of his lifelong passions). The principal from this earned him enough to keep New Directions solvent. From the beginning he published young, modernist writers, often working in innovative literary forms.

In 1944 he published a book of Thomas Merton's poems delivered to him by Mark Van Doren. Called *Thirty Poems*, the book initiated a relationship between monk and publisher that would grow over the years, as Laughlin visited at Gethsemani and published essays, poems, and books from Merton's pen, among them several volumes of poems: *Raids on the Unspeakable, The Wisdom of the Desert, The Way of Chuang Tzu*; as well as his poems in a new idiom: *Cables to the Ace* and *The Geography of Lograire*.

A genuine friendship and lifelong affection developed between the two, as they shared — through the mail and Laughlin's visits to Gethsemani — their ideas on political, social, religious, and literary issues. The extent of that conversation can be seen in the volume edited by David Cooper, *Thomas Merton and James Laughlin: Selected Letters*.

They kept in touch while Merton was in Asia. After Merton's untimely death, Laughlin worked with Naomi Stone and Br. Patrick Hart in editing *The Asian Journal of Thomas Merton*. James Laughlin died on November 12, 1997. WHS

SEE ALSO *THOMAS MERTON AND JAMES LAUGHLIN: SELECTED LETTERS.*

LAX, ROBERT

Robert Lax was born in Olean, New York, on November 30, 1915. During his youth he moved to New York City with his family. In the 1930s he attended Columbia University, where he became a friend of Thomas Merton and an influence leading Merton toward a spirituality that eventually led him into the Catholic Church and, soon after, into a Trap-

pist monastery. Some years later Lax, of Jewish background, followed Merton into the Catholic Church. After graduation from Columbia he worked for a time on the staff of the *New Yorker*, and did screenwriting for Hollywood and freelance writing for a variety of journals, including *Jubilee*, edited by another Columbia friend, Ed Rice.

Lax figures prominently in *The Seven Storey Mountain*. He visited Merton several times at Gethsemani, including May 1949, when Merton was ordained to the priesthood. In 1962 Lax went into a self-imposed exile in the Greek islands, eventually settling on the isle of Patmos. He achieved fame as a major poet noted for his simplified, pared-down poetic style. Among his books of poems are *Circus of the Sun, New Poems, Love Had a Compass*, and *A Thing That Is*.

In the summer of 2000 he returned to his American home in Olean, New York. He died in his sleep on September 26, 2000, and was buried in the St. Bonaventure Cemetery. WHS

SEE ALSO *WHEN PROPHECY STILL HAD A VOICE.*

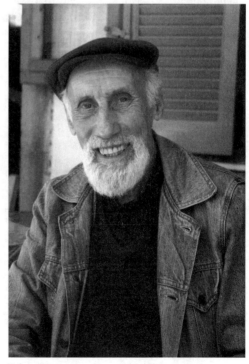

Robert Lax

LEARNING TO LOVE:
Exploring Solitude and Freedom
Edited by Christine M. Bochen. San Francisco: HarperSanFrancisco, 1997. xxiv+382 pp.

Learning to Love, the sixth volume of Thomas Merton's journals, spans the period between January 1966 and October 1967 and documents "a tumultuous and unsettling period" in Merton's life after he fell in love with a student nurse, identified in the journal simply as "M." (*Learning to Love*, xiv).[1] The introduction sets the journal in context and previews its contents. The editor points out that although the journal tells the story of a relationship, it actually presents a one-sided account of the relationship between Merton and M. Merton was determined to be "completely open" about the relationship (and even gave permission for his journals to be published twenty-five years after his death): "I have no intention of keeping the M. business entirely out of sight. I have always wanted to be completely open, both about my mistakes and about my effort to make sense out of my life. The affair with M. is an important part of it — and shows my limitations as well as a side of me that is — well, it needs to be known too, for it is part of me. My need for love, my loneliness, my inner division, the struggle in which solitude is at once a problem and a 'solution' " (234). This journal entry, written in May 1967, months after "the affair" was over, underscores the fact that the story we hear is Merton's. M.'s story emerges, insofar as it does, only in the context of Merton's own story and is, of course, told from his point of view and in his words.

Although there is much more to this journal than the account of Merton's love story, that story dominates a substantial part of the journal and provides a lens through which to read what comes before and after. The editor divides the journal into four parts: (1) "Being in One Place" (January 1966–March 1966), "a period of relative tranquillity" during which Merton is enjoying his life of solitude in his hermitage; (2) "Daring to Love" (April 1966–September 1966), "a time of emotional intensity during which Merton experiences himself as 'a monk in love'"; (3) "Living Love in Solitude" (September 1966–December 1966), "a time of recommitment" to his life as a monk living and loving in solitude; and (4) "A Life Free from Care" (January 1967–October 1967), "a time during which Merton settled once again into the routine of life as a hermit and writer" (xiv). Each of the parts is preceded by an epigraph chosen by the editor, who also selected a passage that Merton wrote on April 14, 1966, to serve as an epigraph for the journal: "One thing has suddenly hit me — that nothing counts except love and that a solitude that is not simply the wide-openness of love and freedom is nothing. Love and solitude are the one ground of true maturity and freedom. . . . True solitude embraces everything, for it is the fullness of love that rejects nothing and no one, is open to All in All" (vii, 40). As Merton began writing in this journal, he inscribed lines from Latin American poet César Vallejo on the opening page: "*Tu pobre hombre vives, no lo niegues / Si mueres, no lo niegues / Si mueres de tu edad! ay! y de tu época*" ("You poor man, you live; don't deny it, / if you die; don't deny it, / if you die from your age, ay! and from your times") (xxv).

The volume also includes three appendices. "A Midsummer Diary for M." (June 1966) is discussed below in the context of part 2. "Some Personal Notes" (January 1966–March 1966) consists in a section of "Notebook 17," one of many spiral notebooks that Merton filled with reading notes, ideas, and, occasionally, as in the case of "Notebook 17," more personal entries.[2] A postscript (April 1966) appears in "Notebook CI" (March 1966–July 1966), located in the George Arents Research Library, Syracuse University, Syracuse, New York. In this passage Merton offers an incisive assessment of himself as a writer: "The bad writing I have done has all been authoritarian, the declaration of musts, and the announcement of punishments. Bad because it implies a lack of love, good insofar as there may yet have been some love in it. The best stuff has been more straight confession and witness" (371).

The title of the journal, *Learning to Love*, a word play on Merton's essay "Learning to Live" and the subtitle of the journal, *Exploring Solitude and Freedom*, capture the dynamic of this time in Merton's life. Although the title calls attention to Merton's relationship with M. and suggests that the relationship was significant to Merton's life and growth, *Learning to Love* has a broader and deeper meaning. The monastery, as Merton knew so well, is itself a school of charity in which monks learn to love God, self, and others. In this volume Merton continues to learn monastic lessons of charity in the special circumstances of solitary life in the hermitage.

As the journal opens on January 2, 1966, Merton is enjoying life in the hermitage on the grounds of Gethsemani, where he had been living full time since August 1965. Part 1, "Being in One Place," provides a picture of the monk at prayer and at work. Merton's heightened sense of place permeates his entries in early 1966 as he relishes his solitude. Merton's entries reveal his attention to the world around him: the cold and snow, the first hints of spring, the "dark scudding clouds and moments of brightness" (24). We find Merton listening to the "song of robins and cardinals in pre-dawn dark" and studying constellations in the night sky (31).[3] And, although he was deeply disturbed by the escalation of the war in Vietnam, sometimes frustrated by the abbot, and concerned about his health, Merton was grateful for the opportunity to live in solitude — at long last. "To go out to walk slowly in this wood — this is a more important and significant means to understanding … than a lot of analysis and a lot of reporting on the things 'of the spirit' " (23). He also was becoming aware that "the solitary life is fraught with problems and 'dangers,' " but saw that it was "necessary" for him "to meet these precisely" as they came to him "in solitude" (22).

Day by day, the entries that make up part 2, "Daring to Love," recount Merton's love story. Most unexpectedly, fifty-one years old and some twenty-four years a monk, Merton fell in love with a woman in her mid-twenties. This segment of the journal is a record of several emotionally charged months, from April through August, during which Merton was at once aware of his commitment to his life as a monk living in solitude and swept away by the intensity of his feelings for M. His journal entries capture powerful and, often, conflicting responses: amazement, passion and

gratitude, confusion and regret, and the "self-questioning, anxiety and guilt" that became so apparent to him when he read his journal at the end of the summer (126). The spring and summer of 1966 were like riding a roller coaster of emotions. Gradually he moved from elation and clarity born of passion — "Now I see more and more that there is only one realistic answer: Love. I have got to dare to love, and to bear the anxiety of self-questioning that love arouses in me, until 'perfect love casts out fear' " (44) — to more sober and realistic assessments as he admitted "that there was a very powerful drag of passion at work" and recognized their "completely unrealistic, impetuous willingness to consider absurd possibilities" (122–23). Inspired by his love for M., Merton wrote eighteen poems, five of which he copied into this journal and four of which (all written in May 1966) appear in part 2: "Louisville Airport, May 5, 1966," "I Always Obey My Nurse," "Aubade on a Cloudy Morning," and "Certain Proverbs Arise out of Dreams." A fifth poem, "A Long Call Is Made out of Wheels," written in September 1966, appears in part 3. These poems, and the remaining thirteen published in a limited edition entitled *Eighteen Poems*, comprise another record of Merton's experience of being in love and his attempts to express that love and to understand it.[4]

Integral to part 2 is "A Midsummer Diary for M.," which Merton wrote in June 1966 and which appears as an appendix. Although Merton called it a diary, it reads, alternately, like a love letter and a journal. Merton began "A Midsummer Diary for M." on June 17 and wrote through the following week, producing what was "practically a book" (87). The diary "presents a picture of Merton as M.'s *lover*: passionate, tender, vulnerable, melancholy, full of longing, lonely, confused, and anguished" and as a "*hermit monk* struggling to make sense of this passionate love and searching for ways to reconcile love and solitude, turning his loneliness for M. into a dimension of 'a general loneliness' that is his 'ordinary climate' and insisting that 'love and solitude must test each other' in one who seeks solitude" (xxi). In "A Midsummer Diary for M." Merton writes with eloquence and insight about solitude: " 'The only solitude is the solitude of the frail, mortal, limited, distressed, rebellious human person, made of his loves and fears, facing his own true present' and opening himself to others and to God. At the heart of solitude is mystery and the solitary is called to 'return to the heart of life and oneness, losing himself not in the massive illusion but simply in the root reality . . . plunging through the center of his own nothingness and coming out into the All which is the Void and which is . . . the Love of God' " (xxi).

On September 8, 1966, Merton reaffirmed, in writing, his commitment "to live in solitude for the rest of [his] life" (129). His abbot, Dom James Fox, cosigned the statement. This declaration signaled a new phase in his relationship with M. He was clearer about his monastic commitment: "I know in my heart that my true call is to solitude with God, however much I may love her," and, he adds, "She knows this too" (162). But still he felt that he could have both love *and* solitude. "Somehow in the depths of my being I know that love for her can coexist with my solitude, but everything depends on my fidelity to a vocation that there is no use trying too much to rationalize. It is *there*. It is a root fact of my existence" (162), he wrote on November 16, 1966. Although he saw M. a few times in October when he was again in the hospital, things were different between them. The relationship had lost some of its intensity and Merton was beginning to recover his monastic bearings. On December 31, 1966, as the old year ended, Merton was still struggling with the knowledge that "it has to *all* end" (176). He calls M. twice and later writes, "I am still so powerfully held by her love and she seems to be by mine also. It is going to be a struggle to get all this straight" (177) — but made easier, perhaps, by M.'s leaving Louisville.

The title of part 4, "A Life Free from Care," taken from Merton's talk to the community before he moved to the hermitage in August 1965, captures Merton's resolve "to get back to right order" (181). As the new year opens, he observes that he experiences "the whole M. thing as something that is credible — and acceptable — in the past tense" (181). The "love affair" becomes, in Merton's words, "a friendship that does not need that much passion —

and is perhaps free of complication" (181–82). Unlike the entries in part 2 and, to some extent, part 3, the entries in part 4 show Merton recovering the tranquillity and equilibrium that characterized his life in the early months of 1966. Once again Merton is writing about his work, his reading, and his prayer, revealing a broad spectrum of interests that includes anthropology, Cargo cults, and the plight of indigenous peoples in the past and present,[5] as well as poetry, philosophy, and literature. "The struggles of the 1960s — the war in Vietnam, racial conflicts, changes in the church, monastic reform" — all continued to capture Merton's attention (xx). On September 10, 1967, Merton ominously observes, "A feeling of great violence is in the air everywhere" (288). In October, as this volume of the journals comes to an end, Merton, influenced by his reading of Bachelard, is thinking about places — Gethsemani, the hermitage, and the "Merton Room" at Bellarmine College — "a place where I store away endless papers, in which a paper-self builds its nest to be visited by strangers in a strange land of unreal intimacy" (296).

On October 7, 1967, Merton dreams of a woman and himself: "M. and I, I guess" (299). It is one of only a few references to M. in part 4. His relationship with M. is more a matter of the past than the present. Merton the monk and writer continues to eclipse Merton the lover, and the eclipse seems quite complete in volume 7 of the journals, *The Other Side of the Mountain,* in which Merton reports burning M.'s letters. On August 20, 1968, Merton writes, "Today, among other things, I burned M.'s letters. Incredible stupidity in 1966! I did not even glance at any one of them. High hot flames of the pine branches in the sun" (*Other Side of the Mountain,* 157). Merton's comment fuels the discussion promoted by the publication of volume 6 of the journals and puts into question just how well Merton learned to love. CMB

SEE ALSO *EIGHTEEN POEMS;* NATURE; SEXUALITY; WOMEN.

Notes

1. The editor notes that an initial was used for certain names "to protect the privacy of the individuals involved." For the same reasons, several lines of Merton's journal

were omitted from the published text. See *Learning to Love*, xxiii–xxiv.

2. "Notebook 17" can be found at the Thomas Merton Center, Bellarmine University, Louisville, Kentucky. The first part of "Notebook 17" has been published in *Dancing in the Water of Life*.

3. Merton's attention to and affinity for the natural world first became evident to readers in *The Sign of Jonas*. With the publication of his complete journals, readers have access to the range of Merton's descriptive passages noting and responding to his environment and the creatures that inhabit it with him. See ECOLOGY; NATURE.

4. For an analysis of Merton's love poems, see EIGHTEEN POEMS.

5. For a discussion of essays that grew out of Merton's reading in 1967, see ISHI MEANS MAN.

LECLERCQ, JEAN

SEE *SURVIVAL OR PROPHECY?*

LECTIO DIVINA

Lectio divina (often referred to simply as *lectio*) is prayerful reading of, generally, the Scriptures, leading to prayer and directed toward union with God. Literally, it means "divine reading" or "holy reading." Thomas Merton suggests that it is called "divine" "because it calls to mind divine truths and prolongs itself by prayer in God" (*Silence in Heaven*, 48). This approach to prayer has a long history in Christian spirituality. It involves four steps: (1) reading (*lectio*), (2) meditation (*meditatio*), (3) prayer (with words) (*oratio*), and (4) contemplation (*contemplatio*). They were given classical expression by Guigo II (d. 1188), the ninth prior of the Grand Chartreuse, in a work called *Scala Claustralium* (*The Ladder of Monks*).[1] The ladder image, a familiar one in mystical writings, is taken from the biblical story in which Jacob sees a ladder reaching from earth to heaven (Gen. 28:10–19). The ladder that Guigo speaks of, though having only four rungs, wondrously reaches from earth to heaven. *Reading* is thoughtful, slow, reflective perusing of the scripture text. *Meditation* involves memorizing, repeating, ruminating (chewing) on the text. *Prayer* is the turning toward God in words of praise, thanks, sorrow, and petition. *Contemplation* is God's gift enabling us to experience God directly beyond words and concepts and images.

It is interesting to note the ways in which Guigo relates the four steps to one another. In the case of the first three he says that one sends you to the other (the Latin word he uses is *mittit*). Step four is different. Thus, while reading sends you to meditation and meditation sends you to (vocal) prayer, prayer does not send you to contemplation. Contemplation is different from the other rungs of the ladder; it is in a class by itself. The first three are about things we can do; contemplation is something God does. When he introduces it, Guigo simply says that contemplation, "when it comes," takes us out of our realm of doing and enables us simply *to be* in the presence of God. Contemplation is a gift of God that comes to us when we are ready to receive it. As Merton states, "Contemplation reaches out to the knowledge and even to the experience of the transcendent and inexpressible God. It knows God by seeming to touch Him. Or rather it knows Him as if it had been invisibly touched by Him.... Touched by Him Who has no hands, but Who is pure Reality and the source of all that is real! Hence contemplation is a sudden gift of awareness, an awakening to the Real within all that is real" (*New Seeds of Contemplation*, 2–3).

In a book on the monastic life, *Silence in Heaven* (for which Merton wrote an introduction), there is a section called "Lectio Divina." The unidentified author of the text in this book writes, "The ineffable sweetness [of the monastic life] is sought in *reading* and found in *meditation*, called for by *prayer* and savoured in *contemplation*" (*Silence in Heaven*, 45 [italics added]). He goes on to say, with Guigo, that all four "steps" are linked with one another. The first two are without value without the second two, and the second two cannot be attained except through the first two. Thus, reading without meditation will be barren. Prayer without meditation will be lukewarm. Meditation without prayer will be fruitless. Prayer opens the heart to contemplation, which is God's gift. "The important thing to notice," Merton points out elsewhere, "is that the contemplative has a special way of reading. He does not devour books, he savors them. Or rather, he uses them as intermediaries to arrive at the *sapida scientia*, that experimental[2] knowledge of God which tastes the sweetness of His infinite goodness. Often the mere reading of a few lines will suffice to establish this contact, and the monk may spend the rest of his reading moments in a contemplation whose simplicity strikes deeper than reasoning and affective acts can reach" (*Cistercian Contemplatives*, 54).

The practice of *lectio* was an integral part of the monastic life. It would have been part of Merton's training as a novice and also the training he would have given as a novice master. It would have been a daily practice that is so much a part of the monastic life that he seldom mentions it. One has to search for references. For instance, there is a passing reference in a letter he wrote to Dame Marcella Van Bruyn in August 6, 1966. He speaks of some of the practices he has preserved in the Latin. "I am going to keep the office in Latin *usque ad mortem*. I read the Vulgate[3] for my *lectio divina*" (*School of Charity*, 311).

There is an unpublished and undated typescript by Merton called "Lectio Divina." It is not clear to whom this material originally was addressed, but it seems to be the kind of writing he would have done for the Gethsemani novices. Interestingly, its thirty-eight pages are concerned solely with reading, though it is reading directed toward prayer. It might just as easily have been titled "Spiritual Reading." He indicates the goal of all such reading. "All our reading, in general, whether it be scriptural or otherwise, should tend to enrich our awareness of the reality of God in Himself and in His creation and in us."[4] In this article Merton refers explicitly to *lectio divina*, as Guigo understood it, only once. He writes of the purposes for reading: (1) to find out facts, (2) to study, (3) for recreation, (4) for edification, and (5) for *lectio divina*, which he describes as *lectio divina* properly so called, for it is reading mingled with prayer.[5]

The three main subjects of monastic reading are (1) God: who God is; the divine holiness and greatness as mirrored in creation; (2) humans: their original dignity, the fall, the present state of people — illusions, powers, threats to integrity; and (3) the history of God's way with people: God's plan, the mystery of salvation, the merciful Savior in dynamic relationship with fallen human beings, the church, the last things, the parousia, the eternal destiny of God's people.

The sources of monastic reading are the Scriptures above all, but also early Christian writers, doctors of the church, and the lives of holy men and women in whom God manifests what humans can become. Merton recommends reading writers of our own time who would share our language and our preoccupations, especially monastic writers. Nor would he exclude writers who have developed other forms of spirituality.[6]

The personal motive for reading should be to open oneself up to real contact with God. "By reading I can give myself to God, give my mind to the light of His truth in order that I may serve Him with all the love of my heart."[7] Opening our hearts to God's presence in what we read will give glory to God.

Reading helps us to absorb ideas and values into a meaningful interior life of our own that will have vital significance for the way we live our lives. Yet, Merton cautions, a "meaningful interior life of our own should not mean a purely subjective activity, for we share in the common interior life of redeemed humanity, the life of the church, the mind of Christ."[8] WHS

SEE ALSO CONTEMPLATION; MEDITATION; PRAYER.

Notes

1. Merton's appropriation of Guigo's understanding of *lectio* can be found in appendix 1 in the notes of Merton's lectures to the novices, "Introduction to Christian Mysticism," written in 1961 and, as of the year 2002, unpublished. Merton uses Guigo's very words and comments on them.

2. In his earlier writings Merton uses the word "experimental" to designate what we would call "experiential." He is describing what comes from experience, not from experiment.

3. The official Latin translation of the Bible.

4. "Lectio Divina," 5 (unpublished, undated, archives of the Thomas Merton Center, Louisville, Kentucky).

5. Ibid., 10.

6. One wonders if he is here referring not only to Christian spirituality but also to spirituality outside Christian faith, such as Taoism or Buddhism. If so, then it might indicate as a possible date for this work the late 1950s or early 1960. This may have been written for the novices in his care.

7. "Lectio Divina," 6.

8. Ibid., 7.

LENTFOEHR, THERESE

Sr. Therese Lentfoehr, S.D.S., was born in 1902 in Wisconsin and lived most of her life there. A poet and a teacher, she had a long and unusual friendship with Thomas Merton. Their first contact was in 1939 when she wrote to commend him for one of his poems. The second was in 1948 when she wrote to take him to task for his criticism of her collection of Marian poems, *I Sing of a Maiden*. This began a twenty-year-long exchange of letters. She typed manuscripts for him, and in return he gave her manuscripts and other materials he had written. She became an avid collector of any materials by or about Merton. As a result, she possessed the largest private collection of Merton materials. The collection includes one of the three copies of the original script of *The Seven Storey Mountain*. In her will she left the collection to Paul Dinter, the Catholic chaplain at Columbia University. Subsequently the collection was given to the Columbia University archives, where it is presently stored.

Sr. Therese and Merton met at a picnic at Gethsemani in November 1967. He was somewhat overwhelmed by her exuberant spirit, but their correspondence continued, as did her collecting of Merton material. His last letter to her came November 21, 1968, just about three weeks before his death. Merton's letters to Sr. Therese are published in *The Road to Joy*. She died in 1981. WHS

LETTERS

When Thomas Merton came to Gethsemani Abbey, Trappists were allowed to write four letters per year. With the publicity surrounding his best-selling *Seven Storey Mountain*, Merton received much fan mail. Most of these letters could be answered with a simple form letter of thanks, but some of the letters concerned spiritual problems about which correspondents were seeking Merton's counsel. Especially in the late 1950s and the 1960s serious correspondences began with people all over the world. Some of these resulted in an exchange of many letters. We cannot tell with certainty how many letters Merton wrote. Four thousand would be

a conservative figure; probably, the number is much higher.

The scope and variety of Merton's correspondents, and the range and contents of his letters are staggering. There is quality too. Many of the letters are skillfully, if almost always hurriedly, crafted. His talent for letter writing was recognized early on by Evelyn Waugh, who suggested that he give up writing books and confine himself to writing letters. Actually, he did both.

Letters are important sources of knowledge about a person and also about the age in which that person lived. "The true life of a person," John Henry Newman said, "is found in his letters." In reading letters, one meets persons in their full humanness; they reveal secret desires and ambitions. Often they uncover fears, imperfections, faults, and concerns. Merton's letters (as well as his journals) were the only bit of his writing that did not have to be submitted to the censors; hence, he could be his own uninhibited self. That self could be profound, radical in its thinking, witty, and at times hilariously funny.

Virginia Woolf has called letter writing "the humane art that owes its origin to the love of friends" — an interesting perspective, though of course not all letters fit this category. Some letters can be angry, hostile, sarcastic in tone. By and large, most of Merton's letters do fit Woolf's definition: they rise out of friendship and are indeed means of sustaining friendships. This is especially true in Merton's case, since he did not have open to him all the ways that people outside the monastery have of building and sustaining friendships. If he wanted to keep his friends, he could not ordinarily visit them. He had to write.

Letters have a relational character and a particularity about them. Normally they are written not for a general audience, but for a special person. There is therefore an intimacy and a particularity about letters that belongs to no other form of writing. Generally a letter is written in some kind of quiet atmosphere and is read, preferably, in a place of quietness. In letter writing, one person's solitude communicates with that of another. It is a unique way of combining solitude and company.

There is a fragility about letters. One puts a letter in a not so durable envelope, secures it with glue that may only half stick, and entrusts it to a good but surely imperfect mode of transportation. Once it reaches its destination, it is committed to the care of someone who may treasure it or who may be careless and unappreciative of it. If it survives at all, it is left to the mercy of future generations. It may easily be the victim of removals, of housecleaning, or mere ignorance of its value. Not until 1963 did Merton make any systematic effort to preserve his letters. The fact that so many of them survived is a tribute to the perceptiveness of the recipients of his letters.

Sometimes Merton's letters seem to have been overshadowed by the published journals. Yet there is an important difference between these two similar forms of writing. Merton's journals often tend to be overly introspective and self-occupied. In his journals he is necessarily talking to himself (though he certainly saw the real possibility that these journals would be published), whereas in his letters he is talking to, and building a relationship with, another person. In both these forms of writing he was able to be himself without fear of interference from the censors. But the letters not only tell us what he thought at a particular time; they also show his concern for the effect his letters would have on their recipients. He cherished friendships. His letters show that the love of friendship was important to him. He saw his letters as a way of building and deepening friendships.

Five volumes of selected letters were published between 1985 and 1994: vol. 1, *The Hidden Ground of Love*; vol. 2, *The Road to Joy*; vol. 3, *The School of Charity*; vol. 4, *The Courage for Truth*; vol. 5, *Witness to Freedom*. (See the entries on the individual volumes for further information.) WHS

SEE ALSO "COLD WAR LETTERS."

LETTERS FROM TOM:
A Selection by Wilbur H. Ferry
Scarsdale, N.Y.: Fort Hill Press, 1983. 73 pp.

This is a selection from the many letters that Thomas Merton wrote to Wilbur H. Ferry. Five hundred copies were privately printed. Fort Hill is the name of the street in Scarsdale where Ferry lived. The book comprises about one-third of the total number of letters that Merton wrote to Ferry. All of Merton's letters to Ferry are published in *The Hidden Ground of Love*. WHS

LETTERS OF CONSCIENCE

During most of Thomas Merton's years at Gethsemani Abbey his letters, like those of other monks, routinely were opened by the abbot, who sometimes answered them himself and without always passing them on to the addressee. If, however, letters were marked "conscience matter" by the correspondent (indicating a personal problem about which he or she wished to consult a particular monk), almost always they were given to the monk unopened. Merton not infrequently suggested to some of his correspondents that they mark "conscience matter" on any letters that they wanted to be sure actually got to him. Merton learned more than one way of getting around Trappist censorship! WHS

SEE ALSO CENSORSHIP.

LIFE AND HOLINESS
New York: Herder and Herder, 1963.
xii + 162 pp.

This book is a collection of five essays published in *Sponsa Regis* between November 1961 and March 1962. Thomas Merton revised and expanded the essays, originally intended for an audience of women religious, to appeal to a wider audience of readers. In the introduction he indicates that he intended *Life and Holiness* to be "a very simple book, an elementary treatment of a few basic ideas in Christian spirituality" and, more precisely, "a meditation on some fundamental themes appropriate to the active life" (*Life and Holiness*, 7).[1] Merton understands action "not in opposition to contemplation, but as an expression of charity and as a necessary consequence of union with God by baptism" (viii). All Christians, including contemplatives, are called to a life devoted to "the spiritual and material development of the whole human community" (8). Christian action is rooted in grace and interiority, guided by the Holy Spirit, and lived out in daily life. "The spiritual life," Merton cautions, "is not a life of quiet withdrawal, a hothouse growth of artificial ascetic practices beyond the reach of people living ordinary lives. It is in the ordinary duties and labors of life that the Christian can and should develop his spiritual union with God" (x). Drawing inspiration from the words with which Pope John XXIII opened the Second Vatican Council in 1962, Merton writes, "Christian holiness in our age means more than ever the awareness of our common responsibility to cooperate with the mysterious designs of God for the human race" (10) ever responsive to God's grace, which is "the power and light of God in us" (vii). Fittingly, *Life and Holiness* is dedicated in memory of Louis Massignon (1883–1962), a scholar of Islam whose work and Christian witness deeply moved Merton.

The book is divided into five chapters: (1) "Christian Ideals," (2) "The Testing of Ideals," (3) "Christ, the Way," (4) "The Life of Faith," and (5) "Growth in Christ." Each chapter is further divided into several subtitled sections, each of which stands as a reflection in its own right.

Chapter 1, "Christian Ideals," consists of four sections: "Called Out of Darkness," "An Imperfect Ideal," "The Plaster Saint," and "Ideas and Reality."[2] Christians are called out of darkness and into light; they are called to renounce sin and embrace sanctity. Citing St. John Chrysostom, Merton explains, "There is only *one* morality, one holiness for the Christian — that proposed to all, in the Gospels" (13). Clerics, religious, and lay — all are called to holiness and to love, although the "religious takes on a more radical and more total commitment to love God and his fellow man" (14). What matters for all Christians, religious and lay, is the perfection of their love. The Christian life must not be reduced to "propriety" (18) and "superficial religiosity" (19). The way of Christian holiness is hard and demanding; it involves fasting, prayer, and sacrifice. It demands "the gift and commitment of our inmost self" (19). "Superficial religiosity" and "pious

gestures" (19) are not enough. "Our time needs more than devout, Church-going people who avoid serious wrongs . . . but close their eyes to all kinds of evil" and injustice (20). We need saints who model sanctity, not the "plaster saints" of hagiography but genuinely "human saints." Sanctity "is not a matter of being *less* human, but *more* human," as manifested by Jesus Christ, who was "the most deeply and perfectly human being who ever lived" (24). The saint is "a window through which God's mercy shines on the world" (24). There is no formula for sainthood except in the Scriptures: "Repent and be baptized." "Be perfect." "Keep the commandments" (26–27, 28). But each person must respond to these gospel imperatives in his or her own way. The spiritual life, Merton insists, is always "a dialectic between ideals and reality" in which "each one becomes perfect, not by realizing one uniform standard of universal perfection in his own life, but by responding to the call and the love of God, addressed to him within the limitation and circumstances of his own peculiar vocation" (29).

In chapter 2 Merton explores "The Testing of Ideals" in five short reflections: "The New Law," "What Is the Will of God?" "Love and Obedience," "Adult Christians," and "Realism in the Spiritual Life."[3] The way of perfection begins with a call, a vocation, to follow Christ and become a saint. "Our reply to this call of Christ does not consist in saying many prayers, making many novenas, lighting vigil lights before the statues of the saints, or in eating fish on Friday. It does not merely consist in attendance at Mass, or the performance of certain acts of self-denial" (34). Our response consists in taking up our cross and seeking to do the will of God in all things. The Christian discovers God's will in community; God's will is "mysteriously communicated to us through one another" (38). The will of God is "that each one should, according to his capacity, according to his function and position, devote himself to the service and salvation of all his brothers, especially of those who are closest to him in the order of charity . . . parents, children, dependents, friends: but eventually his love must reach out to all" (40). Christians are called to love and to obedience. "Love is something much deeper than obedience, but unless obedience opens up those inner spiritual depths our love will remain superficial, a matter of sentiment and emotion, little more" (40). "Objective norms" help us to channel our love. Adult Christians must confront "inadequate ideas of God and the Church" (46) and face the imperfection and the real abuses in the church. Realism in the spiritual life means that we must face reality: "We can only become saints by facing ourselves, by assuming full responsibility for our lives just as they are, with all their handicaps and limitations, and submitting ourselves to the purifying and transforming action of the Savior" (51).

In chapter 3, "Christ, the Way," Merton explores the meaning of sanctity in relation to Christ and the church in five sections: "The Church Sanctifies Her Members," "Sanctity in Christ," "Grace and the Sacraments," "Life in the Spirit," and "Flesh and Spirit."[4] Sanctity involves becoming a "new being," a new creation in Christ. It is a gift of God "drawing the soul into the hidden abyss of the divine mystery" (58). The Christian life is "deeply mystical," which means that it is also sacramental. Sacraments are "mystical *signs* of a free spiritual work of divine love in our souls." Sacraments are signs of God's gift of grace. "The sign," Merton observes, "is necessary for us," not for God (61). Merton cautions that sacraments "produce no fruit where there is no love" (62). The "code of love" defines Christian morality, which is not "legalistic" but "eucharistic" (64). Christians are called to live according to the spirit and not the flesh. Flesh is not to be understood as "bodily life" but as "*mundane* life" in which persons "follow the norms of prejudice, complacency, bigotry, group-pride, superstition, ambition or greed" (67). The "flesh" is "our external self, our false self. The 'spirit' is our real self, our inmost being united to God in Christ" (67).

In chapter 4, "The Life of Faith," comprised of four sections — "Faith in God," "The Existence of God," "Human Faiths," "New Testament Faith" — Merton develops several ideas that are central to his understanding of faith.[5] "By faith Christ becomes the 'power of God' in our lives" (72). Without faith, a person is a nominal Christian, merely conforming to

norms. Faith is not merely a matter of intellectual assent or acceptance of truths; "it is the gift of our whole being to *Truth itself*" (73). Persons must choose between two kinds of faith: "One, a human, limited, external faith in human society with all its inert patrimony of assumptions and prejudices, a faith based on fear of solitude and on the need to 'belong' to the group and to accept its standards with passive acquiescence. Or, in the second place, a faith in what we do not 'see,' a faith in the transcendent and invisible God, a faith that goes beyond all proofs, a faith that demands an interior revolution of one's whole self and a reorientation of one's existence *in a contrary sense* to the orientation taken by mundane prejudice" (76). New Testament faith calls for the rejection of all that is not Christ in order that all may be found "in Christ."

Chapter 5, "Growth in Christ" — with sections on "Charity," "Social Perspectives of Charity," "Work and Holiness," "Holiness and Humanism," "Practical Problems," and "Abnegation and Holiness" — contains Merton's most compelling writing in the book.[6] Taking inspiration from Pope John XXIII's encyclical *Mater et magistra*, promulgated in 1961, and his own commitment to human dignity and justice, Merton writes with passion. "Without love and compassion for others, our own apparent 'love' for Christ is a fiction" (87). Charity is more than "being nice to" people. Charity demands justice and calls for action for justice. A Christian has to "face the fact" that "the misery that exists everywhere in the world, even in the richest nations," is not God's will but "the effect of incompetence, injustice, and the economic and social confusion of our rapidly developing world" (90). Faith must inform action in the world in which we live. The "Christian life" cannot be "confined, in practice, to the pews of the parish Church and to a few prayers" (93); it must be lived. Inspired by *Mater et magistra*, which teaches that work is "not a commodity but an expression of the human person" (100), Merton calls for the restoration of work to its proper place and an understanding of work and of Christian humanism that is grounded in the incarnation. Holiness and humanism are inextricably linked: "There is no genuine holiness without this dimension of human and social concern" (100). Christians must "help defend and restore the basic human values without which grace and spirituality will have little practical meaning" (101). Christians cannot take refuge in a "spirituality of evasion." They must recognize that all are implicated "in the problems and responsibilities of the nuclear age" (103).

In the conclusion Merton recalls that Christians are called to die and rise with Christ. "We are not 'converted' only once in our life but many times, and this endless series of large and small 'conversions,' inner revolutions, leads finally to our transformation in Christ" (117). In the "Preface to the Korean Edition of *Life and Holiness*," written in July 1965, Merton returns to this theme as he speaks of the "interior revolution" in which what seems to be the "self" is "gradually destroyed and exchanged for another deeper self, the Spirit of Christ" ("*Honorable Reader*," 99).[7] It was the only preface Merton wrote to a foreign language edition of *Life and Holiness*, even though the book was translated into nine foreign languages during his lifetime. Writing prefaces to the foreign language editions of his books provided Merton with opportunities to revisit earlier works and offer his new readers fresh perspectives on books he had written some years ago. In this case it was an opportunity to call attention to what was essential to Christian holiness: "simple fidelity and love in the ordinary life of every day" or, put another way, "liv[ing] as Christ" (99). CMB

Notes

1. In this entry, page references are to the Image edition of *Life and Holiness* (Garden City, N.Y.: Doubleday, 1963).

2. Chapter 1 is an expansion (by 30 percent) of "Out of Darkness," *Sponsa Regis* 33 (November 1961): 61–71.

3. In chapter 2 Merton builds on the essay by the same title, retaining both the opening and closing sections, deleting the segments addressed specifically to religious, and adding substantial sections of new material. Sixty percent of the material is added. See *Sponsa Regis* 33 (December 1961): 95–100.

4. Chapter 3 is an only slightly revised and expanded version of "Christ, the Way," *Sponsa Regis* 33 (January 1962): 144–53.

5. Chapter 4 represents a 30 percent expansion of "The Life of Faith," *Sponsa Regis* 33 (February 1962): 167–71.

6. For chapter 5, Merton added a substantial amount of new material (more than 50 percent) to "Growth in Christ," *Sponsa Regis* 33 (March 1962): 197–210.

7. "*Honorable Reader*" editor Robert Daggy notes that although Merton rated the book only "fair," it was one of his "more successful books," and "the American paperback edition (1964) has remained consistently in print" (95).

LIFE AND KINGDOM OF JESUS IN CHRISTIAN SOULS, THE:
A Treatise on Christian Perfection for Use by Clergy or Laity, by St. John Eudes

Translated from the French by a Trappist Father in the Abbey of Our Lady of Gethsemani. With an Introduction by Fulton J. Sheen. New York: P. J. Kenedy & Sons, 1946. xxxv+348 pp.

This is the first of a six-volume collection of the selected works of St. John Eudes, under the general editorship of two Eudist fathers and issued by the publisher between 1946 and 1948. Only this volume was translated by Thomas Merton, who is simply identified as "a Trappist Father" (even though he was still three years from ordination at the time). Unlike any of Merton's other translation work, this volume contains no further contributions from him; the introduction was written by then-Monsignor Fulton Sheen, who was much better known at that time than Merton, who then was the author only of a single volume of poetry. The English version, which Sheen calls "so ably translated" (xix), was completed sometime before October 2, 1944, the date of the *imprimi potest* (permission to publish from the Eudist religious superior); Sheen's introduction is dated June 20, 1945.

St. John Eudes (1601–80) was an exponent of the so-called French school of spirituality, a seventeenth-century movement of religious and pastoral renewal associated particularly with Cardinal Pierre de Bérulle (1575–1629). Born into a peasant family, Eudes entered the Oratorian Congregation founded by Bérulle and studied under him. After ordination in 1625 he engaged in pastoral and missionary work throughout France, and eventually (in 1643) founded his own order of priests, the Congregation of Jesus and Mary (known as Eudists), as well as two religious congregations for women. He was particularly well known for developing a theology and spirituality centered on the sacred hearts of Jesus and Mary. He was beatified in 1909 and canonized in 1925.

The Life and Kingdom of Jesus in Christian Souls, completed by 1637, is considered the major work of Eudes' early period. It is strongly representative of the Christocentric spirituality of the French school, emphasizing that each Christian, as a member of the mystical body of Christ, "continues and accomplishes, by every act he does in the spirit of Jesus Christ, the actions which Christ Himself performed during His earthly life" (6). The work, arranged in seven parts, is strongly devotional in character. Part 1 focuses on what is to be done "during the whole course of your life to make Jesus live and reign within you" (xxxiii), and includes instruction on prayer and practice of Christian virtue; part 2 provides various devotional exercises to be undertaken throughout the day, including instructions for confession and receiving communion; part 3 outlines a pattern for sanctification of daily actions, including sections on Mass, the divine office, and the rosary; part 4 outlines a series of meditations arranged according to the days of the week; part 5 presents monthly, and part 6 yearly, devotional exercises, while part 7 offers exercises for commemorating the anniversaries of birth and baptism and for preparing for death. While the highly structured devotional emphasis of the work has little in common with Merton's own contemplative focus, Eudes does share with Merton a strongly Pauline emphasis on identifying with the person of Jesus Christ as the central spiritual dynamic not just for professed religious but for all Christians. POC

LITERARY ESSAYS OF THOMAS MERTON, THE

Edited by Patrick Hart. New York: New Directions, 1981. xvi+549 pp.

This volume gathers together virtually all of Thomas Merton's writings on literature, both as critic and as theoretician. Material both from published books and uncollected pieces, a few of which had not previously been printed, is included. It consists of four major sections and three lengthy appendices. The first section includes seventeen essays on various writers, all composed over the final decade of his life, when he increasingly came to agree with his friend Jacques Maritain "that perhaps the most living way to approach theological and philosophical problems in our day was in the form of 'creative writing and literary criticism'" (*Literary Essays,* xv). The second section is devoted completely to Merton's writings on Albert Camus, a figure whom he found particularly significant in the final years of his life. The third section is a series of nine short introductions to poets, the majority of them Latin American, most of whom Merton had translated. The fourth and final section includes six pieces of a more theoretical nature, written between 1953 and 1968, which consider the purpose of art and its relationship to a life of faith and contemplation.

The first of the three appendices contains Merton's master's thesis on William Blake, written at Columbia University and submitted in February 1939. The second includes fourteen book reviews written by Merton before entering the monastery. The final appendix consists of two transcriptions of Merton's informal talks to the Gethsemani community on William Faulkner.

The essays in part 1 are not presented in any discernible order, either of composition, of chronology, or even of the alphabet. Five of the seventeen had appeared in earlier Merton books: "The Pasternak Affair" in *Disputed Questions* (1960); "William Melvin Kelley — The Legend of Tucker Caliban" in *Seeds of Destruction* (1965); "'To Each His Darkness': Notes on a Novel of Julien Green" and "Flannery O'Connor — A Prose Elegy" in *Raids on the Unspeakable* (1966); and "The Answer of Minerva: Pacifism and Resistance in Simone Weil" in *Faith and Violence* (1968). Of the remaining twelve, all but two can be described as review essays, in which Merton does not simply summarize and evaluate the work he is reviewing but enters into a kind of dialogue with it to comment on key issues raised by the author. Three of these are examinations of

secondary sources: "Blake and the New Theology" considers "Death of God" theologian
Thomas Altizer's *The New Apocalypse* and finds
it a significant work, though Merton questions Altizer's Hegelian and process-oriented
approach both as a key to Blake and as an
adequate lens for viewing Christianity; "News
of the Joyce Industry" takes a skeptical view
of academic writers on James Joyce, particularly those who use reductivist approaches
that fail to recognize and respect Joyce's own
ambivalences; "Faulkner and His Critics" surveys the changing attitudes toward the novelist
with particular attention to what he considers
to be a representative and well-selected collection of reprinted critical essays. The other
seven look at novels, a play, poetry, correspondence, and a work of literary theory. In
"*Morte d'Urban*: Two Celebrations" Merton
praises J. F. Powers's novel and warns against
a superficial reading that fails to recognize
the protagonist's development from a "superficial self" to "a deeper, more noble, and more
spiritual personality" (147); he is more critical of William Styron's *The Confessions of Nat
Turner*, in which he finds distortion of historical
fact that reduces religious inspiration to ab-
normal psychology. A previously unpublished
review of Rolf Hochhuth's play *The Deputy*
considers it both as "a bad play" and "a significant phenomenon" (162), a crude, poorly
written attack on Pope Pius XII that nevertheless raises important questions about the role
of the church in speaking out, or failing to
speak out, for the defenseless. Both reviews
of poets are highly laudatory: "The True Legendary Sound: The Poetry and Criticism of
Edwin Muir" uses the occasion of the publication of Muir's prose essays to survey his
work as a whole, finding him to be a poet
who penetrates to the depths of being and
expresses that being in its concrete manifestations; "Louis Zukofsky — The Paradise Ear"
finds in the purity of language of this contemporary poet a kind of return to paradise,
a participation in the process of naming that is
a quintessential human act. "Pasternak's Letters to Georgian Friends" is a kind of pendant
to Merton's long essay on Pasternak and *Doctor Zhivago*, focusing both on his loyalty to

poet friends from the southern Soviet region
of Georgia, his translations from the Georgian
language, and the "asceticism" of his commitment to his art. "Roland Barthes — Writing
as Temperature" examines an early work of
the French literary theorist that privileges the
act of writing over the urge to communicate a
message and finds in it a kind of austerity comparable to that of his friend Ad Reinhardt in
painting. The two remaining essays of this section differ considerably in focus and tone: "A
Footnote from *Ulysses*: Peace and Revolution"
considers the Cyclops episode of Joyce's novel
not as a model for genuine nonviolence but as
an example of "the nonviolence of the weak"
that "is merely another, more equivocal form
of the language of power," as contrasted with
authentic nonviolence, which "is not primarily
the language of efficacy, but the language of
kairos" (28). "'Baptism in the Forest': Wisdom
and Initiation in William Faulkner," written as
an introduction to a collection of essays on
religious themes in literature, emphasizes the
"sapiential" dimension in Faulkner's work, particularly "The Bear," with its recognition of
"the wilderness as an epiphany of the cosmic
mystery" (104).

"The Plague of Camus: A Commentary and
Introduction," the first of the "Seven Essays
on Albert Camus," was published separately as
Albert Camus' The Plague in the Seabury "Religious Dimensions in Literature" series (1968).
The remaining six appeared in various periodicals during the last three years of Merton's life.
They approach Camus's work from a wide variety of perspectives. "The Stranger: Poverty of
an Antihero" counters what Merton considers
a simplistic reading of Camus's first novel by
considering the response of Meursault, its main
character, to his predicament as incomplete,
still mired in an "absurd, solipsistic loneliness"
(301) that did not develop into solidarity with
others. "Three Saviors in Camus" examines
characters in three Camus works, two short stories and a play, who in one way or another take
on the role of "savior," in each case with tragic
or at best ambiguous results. "Camus: Journals
of the Plague Years" actually spends more time
considering three secondary works on Camus
than the English translations of his notebooks

referred to in the title. "Terror and the Absurd: Violence and Nonviolence in Albert Camus" focuses particularly on the long philosophical essay *The Rebel*, in which Camus both distances himself theoretically from a position of absolute nonviolence, which he sees as an essentially religious stance not available to a nonbeliever, and comes in practice "very close to the nonviolent position" (250) in his "resolute refusal to accept any system which rests directly and essentially on the justification of killing, especially mass killing, whether by war or by more subtle forms of destructive domination" (251). "Prophetic Ambiguities: Milton and Camus" examines the figures of Milton's Satan and Camus's Sisyphus as inadequate heroes who ultimately fail to embody their authors' choice of "authentic rebellion" rather than "totalist nihilism" (257). "Camus and the Church" focuses particularly on Camus's address to a Dominican audience in which he calls for Christians "*to speak out clearly and pay with their own person*" (267) in defense of human dignity whenever it is threatened.

All but two of the short biographical and critical presentations on modern foreign-language poets served to introduce Merton's own translations, hence the (not completely accurate) section title "Introducing Poets in Translation." Six of these first appeared in *Emblems of a Season of Fury*: Pablo Antonio Cuadra, Ernesto Cardenal, Jorge Carrera Andrade, Alfonso Cortes, César Vallejo, and Raïssa Maritain. One other brief introduction, on Fernando Pessoa, remained unpublished, along with the translations, at the time of Merton's death. The other two pieces actually were written and published as essays in their own right: the short appreciation of Rubén Darío (whom Merton never translated) was written in 1966 to commemorate the centenary of the Nicaraguan poet's birth; the essay on the Spanish poet Rafael Alberti (originally published as "Raphael Alberti and His Angels") surveys his career with particular focus on what Merton agrees to be "one of the greatest poetic works of the twentieth century" (317), Alberti's sequence "Concerning the Angels," recently translated into English for the first time (not by Merton, who did,

however, translate a handful of other poems by Alberti).

Of the six pieces included in part 4, four already had appeared in previous Merton books: "Poetry, Symbolism and Typology" was a chapter of Merton's book on the Psalms, *Bread in the Wilderness* (1953); both "Message to Poets" and "Answers on Art and Freedom" were included in *Raids on the Unspeakable* (1966); "Poetry and Contemplation: A Reappraisal," first published in *Commonweal* in 1958, was incorporated into the first edition of Merton's *Selected Poems* but was replaced by new poems in the second edition. Only "Theology of Creativity" and the previously unpublished "Why Alienation Is for Everybody" had not appeared before in book form. The former, part of a symposium in *American Benedictine Review* from 1960, critiques fashionable but inadequate explanations of creativity as individualistic self-expression, teamwork, productiveness, and the cult of the artist as hero; it briefly summarizes theories of creativity put forward by Tillich, Suzuki, Coomaraswamy, and Maritain, and concludes with reflections on a theology of creativity that recognizes all authentic creation as a participation in the divine creativity. The latter, which was written to introduce a selection of work by Louisville writers but was never previously published, declares that the theme of alienation, of detachment from one's true identity, is both a perennial subject for human thought and art and one particularly prominent in contemporary writing, because of the number of different and mutually incompatible roles the modern person is required, or tempted, to play.

Merton's master's thesis consists of a short preface and two chapters. The first chapter, "Background and Development," surveys Blake's intellectual and artistic background and influences, both as writer and painter/engraver, with emphasis on his hostility toward rationalism and empiricism and defense of imagination and inspiration. The second chapter, "Blake's Ideas on the Place of Nature in Art," contrasts nature as seen by the senses with nature transfigured by the imagination, and looks to insights from Thomist and Indian theories of art, as represented by Maritain and Coomaraswamy, not as influences on Blake but as a framework for understanding the nature of authentic artistic creativity.

Six of Merton's book reviews appeared in the *New York Herald Tribune*, five in the *New York Times*, two in the *Columbia Review*, and one in the *Catholic World*.[1] The three earliest appeared before his entrance into the Catholic Church, the fourth four days after his baptism; all but the last were published while Merton was still in New York City. The majority of the books Merton reviewed are literary criticism, either of a broad range of materials (John Crowe Ransom, John Cowper Powys, E. M. W. Tillyard and C. S. Lewis, Hoxie Lee Fairchild, G. Wilson Knight) or on a specific writer (William Nelson on Skelton, William York Tindall [one of Merton's Columbia teachers] on D. H. Lawrence); he reviews two novelists, Nabokov and Richard Hughes (the latter a kind of review essay of Hughes's work in the *Review*); miscellaneous reviews treat Christine Herter's art criticism, Agnes Addison's book on the influence of Gothic architecture on romanticism, and R. H. S. Crossman's discussion of the contemporary relevance of Plato's *Republic*. Perhaps the two most significant pieces for Merton's own development are the earliest and the latest, both on Aldous Huxley, whose turn to asceticism and metaphysics in *Ends and Means* he finds profoundly significant in March 1938, and whose "theosophic" ideas he is much less enthused about in November 1940 as he finds them in Huxley's novel *After Many a Summer Dies the Swan*.

The final appendix contains transcriptions of two sets of talks given by Merton on Faulkner. "Time and Unburdening and the Recollection of the Lamb: The Easter Service in Faulkner's *The Sound and the Fury*" sets the sermon of the Rev. Shegog both in the context of the overall plot of Faulkner's novel and particularly in relation to the theme of time, finding that Dilsey's experience of the resurrection is a genuine experience of *kairos*, of the fullness of time. "Faulkner Meditations: *The Wild Palms*" explicates the interwoven stories of the convict and the pregnant woman in "Old Man" and of the doomed lovers in "Wild Palms" as a contrapuntal presentation of contrary movements of creativity and sterility, acceptance and denial

of life, converging in the "monastic" setting of a Mississippi penitentiary. POC

SEE ALSO *ALBERT CAMUS' THE PLAGUE*; ART, THEORY OF; *BREAD IN THE WILDERNESS*; CREATIVITY; *DISPUTED QUESTIONS*; *FAITH AND VIOLENCE*; *RAIDS ON THE UNSPEAKABLE*; *SEEDS OF DESTRUCTION*.

Notes

1. An additional early review, of Milton O. Percival's *William Blake's Circle of Destiny*, published in *The Nation* in July 1938, has been reprinted in *The Merton Seasonal* 26, no. 2 (2001): 3.

LITURGY

Liturgy, Thomas Merton emphasizes, is fundamentally a paschal experience, "a ritual participation in the death of Christ (by which all our sins are expiated) and in His glorious Resurrection (by which His divine life is made our own) and in His Ascension (by which we enter with Him into heaven and sit at the right hand of the Father)" (*Seasons of Celebration*, 133). In the sacred ritual of the Eucharist, the saving events of redemption are not merely remembered but re-presented: "In the Liturgy the 'then' of the salvific actions of Christ is 'now' in the redemptive mystery of the Church's prayer. . . . It is not *out of time*, not an escape from the flux and fall of life, but an affirmation of the fulness of life, present 'now' as it was 'then,' neither in time nor out of it" (47). It brings worshipers into union with the Father in the Spirit through identification with Christ crucified and risen, and into unity with one another through sharing in the common experience of worship. "Liturgy is . . . the celebration of our unity in the Redemptive Love and Mystery of Christ. It is the expression of the self-awareness of a redeemed people" (2–3). Thus, liturgy properly heightens the community's awareness of its oneness in and through Christ, in order that it can make the Love on which that unity is founded active and effective in the wider world.

Though in its origins monasticism was rather isolated from the liturgical life of the broader church, "liturgy soon came to be regarded as a specialty of monks and canons" (*Contemplative Prayer*, 20). In one of his earliest works Merton writes, "The principal function of monks in the Church is to offer to God public praise, adoration, thanksgiving, reparation, and petition, in the name of the whole Christian family" (*Cistercian Contemplatives*, 45). He goes on to point out that one of the principal reasons for the Cistercian reform was to purify the monastic liturgical life, as practiced by the Cluniac Benedictines, of the excrescences that had grown over the centuries to a point where the monks spent almost the entire day in choir, and so to restore a proper balance between public prayer, private prayer, and manual labor according to the primitive Benedictine vision (46). Thus, the emphasis in Merton's own monastic tradition was on the integration of liturgy with the rest of life, a balance he consistently advocates in his writings on liturgy throughout his life.

The liturgical life of monks extends beyond the Mass to the chanting of the divine office, which Merton sees as an extension of the pattern of worship throughout the day. "From this great centre of the Mass, the Liturgy reaches out to sanctify every moment of the Christian day, by the canonical hours of the Divine Office — the Church's sacrifice of praise" (*Monastic Journey*, 9). In a similar way the entire year is drawn into the pattern of redemptive transformation by participation in the liturgical cycle. "The liturgy makes the very passage of time sanctify our lives, for each new season renews an aspect of the great Mystery of Christ living and present in His Church. . . . Each new feast draws our attention to the great truth of His presence in the midst of us, and shows us a different aspect of the Paschal Mystery in our world" (*Seasons of Celebration*, 52).

Merton stresses repeatedly that there is no conflict between the public, communal prayer of the liturgy and personal, contemplative prayer. Liturgy and sacraments must have a contemplative dimension to be meaningful, while contemplative union with God in Christ is the completion, the full personal actualization, of the paschal mystery encountered liturgically and sacramentally. A contemplative appreciation of and participation in the mysterious transforming action of the liturgy will in turn provide the insight and impetus

for authentic Christian action in the world. "Without the spirit of contemplation in all our worship — that is to say without the adoration and love of God above all, for his own sake, because he is God — the liturgy will not nourish a really Christian apostolate based on Christ's love and carried out in the power of the *Pneuma*" (*Contemplative Prayer*, 143–44).

Much of Merton's public and private writing on the liturgy during the last years of his life came in response to the liturgical reforms of the Second Vatican Council. In theory he was very supportive of the liturgical renewal emanating from the Council. He calls the Council's Constitution on the Sacred Liturgy (*Sacrosanctum Concilium*) "a splendid and lively document" (*Seeds of Destruction*, 317), "most exciting and very rich" (*School of Charity*, 188), and adds, "If it is properly understood and implemented, it will amount to a revolution in the sense of a metanoia for the whole Church" (188). On the other hand, he is already concerned before the reforms have begun to be implemented that monasteries may embrace changes that have not been thoroughly considered, with questionable results. "Our great danger," he writes to a Carthusian friend, "is to throw away things that are excellent, which we do not understand, and replace them with mediocre forms which seem to us to be more meaningful and which in fact are only trite" (187). His comments about concelebrated Mass in his journal are ambivalent, though finally supportive (*Water of Life*, 196, 264, 269, 273). He is unimpressed by the English translations of the scriptural readings, which he calls "extremely trite and pedestrian" (227), and while he regards much of the conservative opposition to the changes as "pretty neurotic," he can see some of the reasons for the criticism (*Learning to Love*, 13). He writes in 1966 that at the hermitage "I still say the old office. . . . I am going to keep the office in Latin *usque ad mortem*. I read the Vulgate for my *lectio divina*. I am horribly conservative in these respects" (*School of Charity*, 311). While able to appreciate the freewheeling Mass he concelebrated with Daniel Berrigan, with its "very moving simple English text" (not officially approved and evidently "borrowed" from the Anglicans), he also liked the "sober, austere, solemn, intense" Mass he had celebrated for Jacques Maritain the previous week, "old style." He concluded, "Somehow I think the new is really better," but added, "I have nothing against the old" (*Learning to Love*, 149).

In his principal articles on liturgical reform he is encouraging about its potential. "Liturgy and Spiritual Personalism" (1963) emphasizes the need for "intelligent and active participation" in the redemptive process that will be communal rather than collective, active "work" rather than passive observation (*Seasons of Celebration*, 6). "Liturgical Renewal: The Open Approach" (1965) acknowledges some of the problems that have surfaced in connection with the "new Mass," and notes the tendency of both conservatives and progressives to rely on constraint, whether juridical or psychological, to push their own agendas. He counsels patience, mutual respect, and a willingness to be flexible, and finally recommends approaching liturgy "in a spirit of *play*," for "it is in play that the human heart is at once open, engaged, joyous, serious and self-forgetful" (248), the very qualities needed to make liturgy truly a celebration. POC

SEE ALSO EUCHARIST; SACRAMENT; *SEASONS OF CELEBRATION*.

LIVING BREAD, THE

New York: Farrar, Straus and Cudahy, 1956. xxxi + 157 pp.

This book opens with an introductory note by Gregory Peter XV Cardinal Agagianian, patriarch of Cilicia and of Armenia, who explains that the book was written "at the request and suggestion" of leaders of a movement dedicated to "Daily and Perpetual Adoration of the Most Blessed Sacrament of the Eucharist among Priests of the Secular Clergy." In his prologue Thomas Merton recalls the history of the Society for Perpetual Adoration of the Blessed Sacrament, developed in the Italian Alps during World War II by priests of the region who took turns spending time in adoration of the Blessed Sacrament. A Eucharistic League was established in France in 1879 and brought to the United States in 1894. At the time of writing, Merton noted that about 80 percent of the

U.S. clergy belonged to the Priests' Eucharistic League, whose members were committed to spending time in prayer and silence before the Eucharistic Christ. A People's Eucharistic League also was founded in France. Its members around the world are obligated to spend at least one hour a month in adoration of the Blessed Sacrament.

Merton describes the purpose of the book in theological terms, explaining that the "book was written primarily as a summary of the Church's teaching on the Eucharist." The "central theme" of the book is "the intimate connection between the two mysteries of the Eucharist and of the Church" (*Living Bread*, xxx). Merton explains that the purpose of "a life of prayer before the Blessed Sacrament is not only that we may ourselves become men of prayer or holier priests, but above all that we may become men of charity, peacemakers in the world" (xxx). This emphasis on Christian action is consistent with the opening lines of the prologue: "Christianity is more than a doctrine. It is Christ Himself, living in those whom He has united to Himself in one Mystical Body" (ix). The Eucharist is "the very heart of Christianity since it contains Christ Himself, and since it is the chief means by which Christ mystically unites the faithful to Himself in one Body" (ix–x). The "Mystery of the Eucharist" can "only be penetrated by being lived and loved" (xii). But the "problem of love" is "the whole problem of our time" (xii). Materialism, with its "exorbitant optimism" (xiv), and totalitarianism, with its "techniques of degradation" (xiii), erode the human spirit. "Passive and despairing, we allow ourselves to sink back into the inert mass of human objects that only exist to be manipulated by dictators, or by the great anonymous powers that rule the world of business" (xv).

It is in this context that Merton writes about the Eucharist, the celebration of the sacrament of the body and blood of Jesus Christ. The liturgy and the devotional practices of prayer and adoration before the Blessed Sacrament make possible "contacts" that "deepen our awareness of the great mystery" (xix). Although Merton is mindful of the times in which he is writing, he draws on very traditional sources, including Scripture, the church fathers, St. Thomas Aquinas, St. Bonaventure, St. Bernard, encyclicals of Pope Pius XI and Pope Pius XII, and early twentieth-century theologians such as E. Mersch and Scheeben. Merton also brings to the topic his own growing realization of the integral relationship between cultivating an interior life in contemplation and becoming an instrument of peace in a life of charity and compassion. Mindful of the priests for whom this book apparently was written, Merton nevertheless appears to be writing for a broader audience in much of the book.

The Living Bread is divided into five parts: (1) "Unto the End," (2) "Do This in Memory of Me," (3) "Behold I Am with You," (4) "I Am the Way," and (5) "O Sacrum Convivium." Part 1 consists of two sections: "Christ's Love for Us" and "Our Response." In the words of John's Gospel, Jesus loved his disciples "unto the end" (John 13:1). The Eucharist expresses "the love with which he died for us" (6), makes Christ present until the end of time, and enables "mysterious participation in His own divine life" (11). "Our communions are more truly and more perfectly what they are called when they are a sharing in the divine life of contemplation and love which Christ lives in the Blessed Trinity" (12). Eucharistic adoration and mental prayer are a way of "prolonging our communion" (13). A "full and well-integrated eucharistic life" is a response to Christ's love for us manifested in the Eucharist (14). Contemplation is a form of worship.

Part 2 consists of four sections — "The Christian Sacrifice," "Worship," "Atonement," and "Agápe" — in which Merton focuses attention on the Eucharist as the sacrifice that makes present Christ's death on the cross. Sacrifice is an act of worship, an act of atonement (prompted not by guilt but by a need for reconciliation), and an act of agape in which a person enters into God's love. "We enter into the Mystery of the Holy Trinity not so much by thinking and imagining, as by loving" (51). Merton quotes from the Gospel of John and the letters of Paul, from St. Irenaeus and St. Cyril of Jerusalem, and from St. Thomas.

There are three sections in part 3: "The Real Presence," "Sacramental Contemplation," and "The Soul of Christ in the Eucharist." Merton's focus is on the presence of Jesus Christ in the Eucharist, a "real" and "integral" presence. Quoting the Council of Trent and then Dom Anscar Vonier, Merton reiterates and attempts to explain how Christ is present in the Eucharist through transubstantiation and then to describe the Christ who is present in the Eucharist. He writes, for example, "Not only are the divinely illumined intelligence and will of Christ living and active in this Sacrament, but also His memory" (73). Merton cites Pope Pius XI's encyclical Miserentissimus Redemptor (1928) to explain how the soul of Christ in the agony sorrowed for our sins and received solace from our acts of reparation. Merton concludes part 3 by admonishing readers to free themselves "from the narrow limitations of an individualistic piety which treats Communion as a refuge from the troubles and sorrows of communal living" and which "ends by cutting us off, spiritually, from the Mystical Christ" (85–86). Communion ought not to be treated "uniquely as a source of personal consolation" (86). Putting the point in another way, Merton writes, "Communion is not a flight from life, not an evasion of reality, but the full acceptance of the responsibilities of our membership in Christ and the total commitment of ourselves to the lives and aims of the Mystical Body of Christ" (86–87).

Part 4 is divided into three sections: "Our Journey to God," "The Bread of God," and "Communion and Its Effects." Merton characterizes "every sacramental action performed by the Incarnate Word in and with His Church" as "a direct, supernatural intervention of God in the affairs of man and of time" (89). Sacraments "lightly touch our several senses with their simple meanings, and thereby release in the depths of our souls the secret fire of God" (91). We are taken out of the world while remaining in it. Our liberation is "not an escape from a material universe which is regarded as evil, but an escape from the blindness and illusion and evil that were in our own heart, and which made us unable to see and appreciate the good that is in the world, and even the true good that is in ourselves" (92–93). Just as the Passover is a reminder to Jews of their deliverance from Israel, so the Mass "perpetu-ates for us the great 'intervention' of God in our world by His Incarnation, Passion, Death and Resurrection" (96) and reminds us of our deliverance into the freedom of the children of God. Inspired by the Bread of Life discourse in John 6, Merton emphasizes the relationship be-tween keeping the commandments and loving one another. "If we do not love one another, we cannot eat the Bread of Life, we cannot come to the Father. It is only by loving one another that we allow the Father to draw us to Christ, for it is by love that we become one Mystical Body, one Christ. And only by 'being Christ' can we come to the knowledge of Christ" (106). As St. Augustine wrote, "The faithful know the Body of Christ if they do not neglect to be the Body of Christ" (106). There is, then, an "inseparable connection between the Eu-charist and the Church" (106). The Church is the "Body of Christ." To explain how the Eucharist affects those who receive it, Merton draws on and quotes from a variety of sources: St. Ambrose, St. Cyprian, Pope Pius XII, the Council of Trent, Ignatius of Antioch, St. Ire-naeus, St. Thomas, and Scheeben as well as collects and postcommunion prayers.

Part 5 includes five sections: "Come to the Marriage Feast!" "The Eucharist and the Church," " 'I Have Called You My Friends,' " "The New Commandment," and "Toward the Parousia." Merton describes communion as a sacrum convivium, a sacred banquet. "To call a feast a 'convivium' is to call it a 'mystery of the sharing of life' " (127). Individualism and the emergence of a mass society have corrupted this natural sense of convivium. To show that there is an intimate connection between the mys-tery of the Eucharist and the mystery of the church, each of which is the body of Christ, Merton marshals quotations from the writings of St. Augustine, St. John Chrysostom, and St. Thomas. "The 'sacred banquet' is then the banquet of charity, of fraternal unity in Christ. It is the sharing of Christ's love with one an-other: so that the strong help the weak to find Christ and the weak, in their turn, give the strong an opportunity to love Jesus more by loving Him in His members" (139). The Last Supper discourse in John 15 provides a manual

of priestly spirituality. "The whole program of the priestly life, as Jesus has exposed it here, is summed up in these two ideas: love Me as I have loved My Father — love one another as I have loved you. And the two can be reduced to one: Abide in my love (John 15:9)" (141). "We are priests not for ourselves but for Him. Therefore we are priests also for one another" (144). As Merton completes his meditations on the Eucharist, he reflects on the parousia, when what is hidden will be revealed. "The Parousia will indeed be the manifestation of Christ in us and of us in Christ" (154). "Our life in Christ . . . calls for a fully eucharistic aposto-late — a far-seeing and energetic action, based on prayer and interior union with God, which is able to transcend the limitations of class, and nation, and culture and continue to build a new world upon the ruins of what is always falling into decay" (155).

The Living Bread represents a very tra-ditional approach to the Eucharist with its emphasis on devotion, encouraging prayer and adoration of the Blessed Sacrament; and on dogma, exploring the Real Presence and tran-substantiation. But the book also reflects Mer-ton's growing awareness of the centrality of contemplation, compassion, and community in the Christian life and their significance for an understanding of the Eucharist. CMB

SEE ALSO EUCHARIST; LITURGY.

LORETTO AND GETHSEMANI: In Commemoration of the 150th Anniversary of the Founding of the Sisters of Loretto at the Foot of the Cross, 1812–1962

Trappist, Ky.: Abbey of Gethsemani, 1962. 8 pp.

In this eight-page commemorative booklet Thomas Merton highlights the intersecting histories of Loretto and Gethsemani, both "children of exile and of revolution" and neigh-bors "hidden in the same mystery of Our Lady's Sorrow and Solitude in the Lord's Passion," and explores their shared prophetic vocation to reconciliation and unity (Loretto and Geth-semani, 3). Founded in 1812 by Fr. Nerinckx, the Sisters of Loretto established a school in a house on Pottinger's Creek, donated to them by the Dant family. They called the school Gethsemani and ran it for thirty years. In 1848 the sisters sold the land on which the school stood to the Trappists of Melleray for their new foundation. Gethsemani had passed from one community to another. While the Lorettines moved west and south, the Trappists remained in one place, until after World War II, when they founded houses in the south, west, and north.

Loretto and Gethsemani share "a secret that reveals itself only partially even to those who live for a long time in our valley" (5). The two communities share "a wise madness," not "altogether part of" the world. Both are *"engagés"* in a world that identifies "holiness with prosperity" (5, 6). Both are called to prophetic witness. "We who are consecrated to Christ retain the dubious privilege of acting as a kind of conscience in a confused and increasingly conscienceless world of pragmatism and *laissez faire*. In this society of ours we must frankly admit a tragic intellectual and moral incoherence where the only universal principle is 'whatever works is right.'...Our Christian ethic is not based on any such relativism" (6). Accepting that we are "in some sense exiles at odds with materialism, commercialism, and secularism," we can "begin to be fully faithful to Christ" (7).

We have the duty, Merton writes, to preserve the purity of faith, but doing so does not require that we exclude dissent. The "ideal of 'keeping the faith' can sometimes dwindle into something very negative, resentful, and obtuse: a mere 'no' to everything that we do not agree with" (7). Rather than barricading ourselves in a Catholic world, "we are obliged by our faith and by our love of truth to commit ourselves humbly and completely, not only to the message of Christ, but also to all that is valid in human culture and civilization" (7). Prayer and work are not opposed. "Keeping the faith" entails recognizing the paradoxical nature of the cross, which is "the sign of contradiction, but also and above all the sign of reconciliation" (7). The cross "reminds us of the contradictions within ourselves, and within our society, only in order to resolve them all in unity in love

of the Saviour" (7). Loretto and Gethsemani share a vocation to unity. "This unity in Christ is the true secret of our Christian and religious vocations, whether our lives be active or contemplative." While false unity is the "work of force," true unity is "the work of love" (8).

The "vocation to love the truth is also a vocation to love the Cross" and to live under the sign of the cross (8). "The Christian life is not an enclosed garden in which we can sit at ease, protected by the love of God. It is, alas, a wilderness into which we can be led by the Spirit in order to be tempted by the Devil. Or, a garden where, while Christ sweats Blood, in an agony beyond our comprehension, we 'struggle to keep awake under the moonlit olive trees'" (8).

In 1992 *Loretto and Gethsemani* was published as an appendix in *The Springs of Contemplation* (277–85). CMB

LOVE

When Thomas Merton spends Holy Week 1941 on retreat at the Abbey of Gethsemani, he not only participates in the Trappist liturgy during this most meaningful period of the Christian year, but also he reads, meditates, and reflects on what is perhaps the most characteristic work of the most significant figure in Cistercian history, the *De Diligendo Deo* (*On Loving God*) of St. Bernard of Clairvaux. He quotes and comments on the treatise extensively in his journal throughout his stay at the monastery, beginning with the provocative assertion in the opening chapter that the reason for loving God is because God is God and the way to love God is without limit (*sine modo*), the concise statement that is then "unpacked" throughout the rest of the work (*Run to the Mountain*, 337). Thus, Merton's contact with the Cistercians, the order whose "specialty was love" (*Waters of Siloe*, xxiii), is intimately connected from the very outset with Cistercian teaching on love, and his own reflections on love, as rich and varied as they are throughout his life, are deeply grounded in his Cistercian heritage.

From Bernard and the other Cistercian fathers (and the Augustinian tradition to which

Bernard belongs) Merton learns that as there is in this life no direct knowledge of God as God actually is, only love can attain to God directly, not conceptually but "with an intimate experimental knowledge of God as he is in Himself, by virtue of the immediate contact which it establishes with Him" (*Spirit of Simplicity*, 99). But this love is a response to and a participation in God's love for us, the love that created us with the capacity to love, so that our love for God is in fact God's love working in us (*Cistercian Contemplatives*, 9; *Waters of Siloe*, 290). Pure love, which is a perfect union of wills with God (*Spirit of Simplicity*, 125), alone makes us equal to God (*Last of the Fathers*, 82), one spirit with God (*Thomas Merton on St. Bernard*, 188). According to St. Bernard, love is our whole reason for existing, and growth in the spiritual life is a process of reeducation that redirects fallen humanity's love away from self and toward God in a four-stage development that begins with a self-love that motivates a person to seek salvation for one's own sake, moves through love of other people and of God for one's own sake, to love of God for God's own sake, and culminates with a love of ourselves for God's sake, which Merton calls "the high point of Bernard's Christian humanism," since it reveals that ultimately we are not lost in God but "*found* in God in all our individual and personal reality, tasting our eternal happiness not only in the fact that we have attained to the possession of His infinite goodness, but above all in the fact that we see His will is done in us" (*Last of the Fathers*, 52). This disinterested love, in which all creation and even the self is loved for God's sake alone, is made possible only through the ultimate sign and instrument of divine love, Jesus Christ, above all the crucified Jesus (*Waters of Siloe*, 291), in whom human love for God and for humanity is poured out in total self-sacrifice. The monastic life, according to this understanding, is thus truly a school of charity (*Cistercian Contemplatives*, 20) in which selfless love is learned and practiced in community in union with Christ. "You came to the monastery," Merton writes, "to learn, or rather to relearn, the love whose seeds were implanted in your very nature" (*Waters of Siloe*, 291). Contemplative life is simply

a life of love, "a life that is devoted before all else to the knowledge and love of God and to the love of other men in Him and for His sake" (xix).

Merton continued to draw on this Cistercian legacy, directly or indirectly, until the end of his life. Virtually every statement on love in *Seeds of Contemplation* (and repeated in *New Seeds of Contemplation*) can be linked to teachings by Bernard and his contemporaries. In *No Man Is an Island* he repeats Bernard's assertion that we must love God "without measure" (*No Man Is an Island*, 18), and later in the book he explores extensively what it means to say that love is without limit (164ff.) — with no explicit mention of his source. His consideration of the progressive nature of the "law of love" in *Conjectures of a Guilty Bystander* also depends on Bernard, again without attribution: "We begin by loving life itself, by loving survival at any price. Hence, we must first of all love ourselves. But as we grow we must love others. We must love them as our own fulfillment. Then we must come to love them in order to fulfill them, to develop their capacity to love, and finally we must love others and ourselves in and for God" (*Guilty Bystander*, 106). In his dialogue with D. T. Suzuki he cites Bernard's teaching on "pure love" as analogous to the Zen notion of original emptiness: "He loves with a purity and freedom that spring spontaneously and directly from the fact that he has fully recovered the divine likeness, and is now fully his true self because he is lost in God. He is one with God and identified with God and hence knows nothing of any ego in himself. All he knows is love. As St. Bernard says: 'He who loves thus, simply loves, and knows nothing else but love'" (*Birds of Appetite*, 129–30). On his trip west in May 1968 he writes of "a love for God that knows no reason because He is God; a love without measure" (*Other Side of the Mountain*, 102). Even on the final day of his life he will refer to the teaching on "monastic therapy" of the early Cistercian abbot Adam of Perseigne, in which the purpose of the monastic life is understood as being "to teach men to live by love," to transform "*cupiditas* into *caritas*, . . . self-centered love into an outgoing, other-centered love" by dying to self and being resurrected in, and as, Christ (*Asian Journal*, 333–34).

But Merton realized that to reach a modern audience it was not enough simply to repeat, or even to explain, medieval expositions of love. He writes in his journal in 1957, "Love is the only answer. But medieval talk about love solves nothing. What does love mean today? What is its place in the enormous dimensions of the modern world?" (*Search for Solitude*, 150). Hence, while continuing to draw on traditional sources, Merton more and more frames his discussions of love in terms of contemporary issues such as alienation and authenticity, personalism and individualism. But he still situates love in the context of the central Christian mystery of fall and redemption. "All sin is simply a perversion of that love which is the deepest necessity of man's being: a misdirection of love, a gravitation toward something that does not exist, a bond with unreality" (*Disputed Questions*, 102). The fall is both the result and the cause of turning love, which has its source and its end in God, back toward the self; it is an attempt to claim an autonomy that is illusory and can lead only to frustration, misery, and an alienation from self and others as well as God. *Agape*, the love that seeks the good of the other, is reduced to *eros*, desire to possess the loved object for one's own satisfaction. "Man is divided against himself and against God by his own selfishness, which divides him against his brother. This division cannot be healed by a love that places itself only on one side of the rift. Love must reach over to both sides and draw them together" (*No Man Is an Island*, xx).

But having rejected the love of God, human beings are incapable of reorienting themselves from an exclusive to an inclusive love. This is the mission of Christ, who is perfectly united in love with his Father and with his fellow humans. To respond to the love of God in Christ is to renounce one's spurious autonomy and live once again in divine love. Consequently, "True love is a death and a resurrection in Christ. It has one imperious demand: that all individual members of Christ give themselves completely to one another and to the Church, lose themselves in the will of Christ and in the good

of other men, in order to die to their own will and their own interests and 'rise again' as other Christs" (*Disputed Questions*, 100). Participation in the paschal mystery is the restoration of the power to love rightly. It is the recovery of one's authentic self: "Love is my true identity. Selflessness is my true self. Love is my true character. Love is my name" (*New Seeds of Contemplation*, 60). One learns once again to love oneself, not because one is worthy of love, but because in the mercy of God one experiences love that is totally undeserved. Love is sheer gift, yet love is the deepest dimension of personal identity; the gift of love is inseparable from the gift of life, the gift of being, which ultimately is a participation in the Being, the love of God. The true goal of life once again is revealed and made available: to become a manifestation of divine love in the world through union with the source and goal of love. Contemplation is nothing other than sharing fully in the life of God, which is love. "What happens is that the separate entity that is *you* apparently disappears and nothing seems to be left but a pure freedom indistinguishable from infinite Freedom, love identified with Love. Not two loves, one waiting for the other, striving for the other, seeking for the other, but Love Loving in Freedom" (283).

But this love of God alone is by no means a diminution of love for others. God is not an object alongside other objects. To love God is to love all reality in God. "The man who loves God alone loves all men in God and for God. He does not have to leave Him to find them in Him, and his love for them is no distraction from his love for God" (*Monastic Journey*, 56). True love does not treat God as an object, nor does it objectify other people. "Love means an interior and spiritual identification with one's brother, so that he is not regarded as an 'object' to 'which' one 'does good.' . . . Love takes one's neighbour as one's other self, and loves him with all the immense humility and discretion and reserve and reverence without which no one can presume to enter into the sanctuary of another's subjectivity. From such love all authoritarian brutality, all exploitation, domineering and condescension must necessarily be absent" (*Wisdom of the Desert*, 18). Love that is a participation in God's love shows the same disregard of "worthiness" in the neighbor as Christ showed toward oneself (*New Seeds of Contemplation*, 74–75; *Guilty Bystander*, 156–57). It indulges neither in the "romantic" quest for the perfect object of love, which refuses all responsibility to love people as they actually are in all their frailty, nor in authoritarian coercion that forces others to meet certain standards to be considered lovable (*Disputed Questions*, 106–7). Yet authentic love of others is rooted in truth and calls others to fulfill their true identities even as it loves them in their brokenness (*No Man Is an Island*, 5), since "love without truth is mere sentimentality" (*Life and Holiness*, 52).

Love is a creative force, a participation in the divine power to redeem and transform the world by loving creation as God loves it (*Disputed Questions*, 99). Therefore, love is inseparable from justice, from a recognition and a defense of the dignity, the infinite worth of every other human being as created in the image of God (*Life and Holiness*, 115). Genuine love includes even the love of enemies as "one of the crucial ways in which we give proof in practice that we are truly disciples of Christ" (*Passion for Peace*, 241). Yet love of enemies, like the love of one's neighbor, is inseparable from truth, which means a nonviolent resistance to evil even as one refuses to demonize and hate the evildoer: "Participation in the sufferings of Christ, in order to vanquish the enemy of Christ by the power of Christ's love . . . is of the very essence of the Christian life, a proof of one's Christian faith, a sign that one is a follower and an obedient disciple of Christ" (246). Thus, love in action is not a sentimental acceptance of the status quo, of "established power and legalized violence against the oppressed" (*Faith and Violence*, 8). Love is both a sign of contradiction to injustice and an invitation to conversion, reconciliation and an end to enmity and alienation. "Love is measured by its activity and its transforming power. Christianity does not teach man to attain an inner ideal of divine tranquillity and stoic quiet by abstracting himself from material things. It teaches him to give himself to his brother and to his world in a service of love in which God will manifest his creative power through men on earth" (*Love and Living*, 150). POC

LOVE AND LIVING

Edited by Naomi Burton Stone and Patrick Hart. New York: Farrar, Straus and Giroux, 1979. vii+232 pp.

This posthumously published collection of essays, edited by Thomas Merton's literary agent and his personal secretary, includes twenty-one essays of varying length that Merton wrote between 1965 and 1968. These essays, some of which were published during his lifetime, others posthumously, appear under three headings: "Love and Living," "Seven Words," and "Christian Humanism."

Part 1, "Love and Living," consists of seven essays. In the opening essay, "Learning to Live," first published in a collection of essays honoring Columbia University, Merton not only articulates his philosophy of education but also shares something of his own experiences as a student at Columbia University.[1] The purpose of education, Merton writes, is "to show a person how to define himself authentically and spontaneously in relation to his world" (*Love and Living*, 3), and the purpose of the university is "first of all to help the student to discover himself" (4). Merton likens the university to the monastery, both of which are, or ought to be, directed toward the "activation of that inmost center . . . that 'apex' or 'spark' which is a freedom beyond freedom, an identity beyond essence, a self beyond all ego, a being beyond the created realm, and a consciousness that transcends all division, all separation" (9). In the last part of the essay Merton celebrates his experience as a student at Columbia: "The thing that I always liked best about Columbia was the sense that the university was on the whole glad to turn me loose in its library, its classrooms, and among its distinguished faculty, and let me make what I liked out of it all. I did" (13).

The next two essays explore the subject of love. "Love and Solitude" is one of two essays included in this book that originally were written as prefaces to foreign editions of his books (the other being "Rebirth and the New Man

in Christianity," 192–202). This essay was written as a preface to the Japanese translation of
Thoughts in Solitude in March 1966 and revised
and expanded in April 1966 in light of a new
and deep personal experience of love. Merton
was revising the piece shortly after he had returned to Gethsemani following hospitalization
for back surgery. While in the hospital he had
fallen in love with a student nurse assigned to
his care. Writing in his journal, Merton observes that he thinks he has "deepened and
improved" the essay: "One thing has suddenly
hit me — that nothing counts except love and
that a solitude that is not simply the wide-
openness of love and freedom is nothing. Love
and solitude are the one ground of true maturity
and freedom" (*Learning to Love*, 40). Merton
again revised and expanded the piece for publication in *The Critic* in November 1966 "to
form an essay on the solitary life, on contemplation, and on basic monastic values which
are today called into question even by monks
themselves" (*Love and Living*, 15). It is this last
version that is reprinted in this book.

The "peculiar" English phrase "falling in
love" catches Merton's attention in "Love and
Need: Is Love a Package or a Message?" (25).[2]
"To consider love merely as a matter of need
and fulfillment, as something which works itself
out in a cool deal, is to miss the whole point
of love, and of life itself. The basic error is
to regard love merely as a need, an appetite,
a craving, a hunger which calls for satisfaction" (33). Merton critiques the facile attitude
toward love in contemporary society and celebrates love's power to transform persons and
make them over into "new beings": "I cannot
find myself in myself, but only in another" (35).
Merton concludes that it is "the mission of the
poet, the artist, the prophet," who are "themselves taught and inspired by love" to teach us
to love (37).

"Creative Silence" represents one of Merton's attempts to express the themes of contemplative spirituality for a new audience in
the late 1960s. First published posthumously
in *The Baptist Student* in 1969, the essay calls
Christians to "periods of silence, reflection,
meditation, and 'listening'" (39). Such practice is key to awakening the "silent self within

us" that cannot be known when persons are
"immersed in a flood of racket and words" (40)
and escape in a search for stimulation: "a distraction, a drink, a drug, a gimmick, a game,
a routine of acting out our sense of alienation
and trouble" (41). Merton explains that "a God
who is made up of words, feelings, reassuring slogans . . . can become a substitute for the
truth of the invisible God of faith" — the God
with whom "our deepest encounter" becomes
possible in silence (42).

Merton continues his critique of contemporary culture in "The Street Is for Celebration."[3] Reflecting on space, Merton contrasts
"alienated space," where people "submit," with
"inhabited space," where people actually live
(48). *"Living is more than submission: it is creation"* (49). Our streets have become scenes of
violence, which is a kind of submission, unlike the streets of the first cities of the North
American continent (e.g., the Mayan cities of
Guatemala and the Zapotecan city of Mount
Alban), which were places of celebration. *"Can
the street become an inhabited space? Yes, when it
becomes a space for celebration"* (53).

In "Symbolism: Communication or Communion?"[4] Merton describes and decries the
loss of the sense of symbolism in modern society. "The death of symbolism is itself the most
eloquent and significant symbol in our modern cultural life" (56). "Though he now has
the capacity to communicate anything, anywhere, instantly, man finds himself with *nothing
to say*" (64). The very technology that has made
communication possible has contributed to the
degeneration of the symbols that make communion possible. Signs communicate. Symbols
embody and make possible participation in that
which they symbolize. Symbols "aim not at
communication but at communion. Communion is the awareness of participation . . . in the
mystery of being, of human love, of redemptive
mystery, of contemplative truth" (68).

"Cargo Cults of the South Pacific," an
edited and shortened version of a taped conference prepared for publication in *America*
in 1977, reflects Merton's growing continued
interest in primal religions and his growing
interest in anthropology. In this essay he compares the mythology that promised salvation

in the form of cargo ("kago") to the native people of the South Sea Islands (and in variant forms to the people of Africa and Southeast Asia) with the false promises of Western social and political movements. "Is there really much difference . . . between kago and the coming of the good life promised in our fabulous modern consumer advertising" (83) or "myth-dreams" (93) that inform the ideology of white supremacists and the antiguerilla forces in Bolivia supported by the CIA? "Both the white man's and the native's myth-dreams are only partial and inadequate expressions of the whole truth. . . . Each needs the other, to cooperate in the common enterprise of building a world adequate for the historical maturity of man" (94).

In 1966 Merton wrote the seven short articles that appear in part 2 as "Seven Words." Entitled "Seven Words for Ned O'Gorman" in draft, each short piece explored a word and so a theme: death, theology, divine, purity, world, ethics, and war. Two of the articles, "Purity" and "Death," were published in *Prophetic Voices: Ideas and Words on Revolution.*[5] The other five pieces appeared for the first time in this book. Although the brevity of these pieces (they range in length from three to five pages) precludes much development of the themes, Merton's reflections on each theme provide insight into his thinking and, at points, his personal story. Merton's reflections on death, theology, and purity can serve of examples of his approach in the "Seven Words."

Although Merton speaks about death in other writings, particularly in his journals, this is his only attempt at an essay on the subject. Merton's monastic perspective is evident in statements such as "Death contributes something decisive to the meaning of life" (97–98). He contrasts a "death-oriented society," in which "*death becomes the end of life in the sense of its goal,* and this is made at least symbolically evident by the fact that money, machines, bombs, etc., are all regarded as more important than living people" (101), with a view of death as "the last free culminating gift in a fruitful life oriented to ultimate truth in God" (103), a life that already has involved a "'dying' to self in order to give to others" (102). Writing

about theology, Merton builds on the classic definition of "*credo ut intelligam,* I believe in order to understand," by calling attention to the dynamic aspect of faith by which a person "not only hears *about* God but enters into a personal relationship of obedient love with God" (105). In light of this understanding of faith, theology ought not "merely to improve our scientific understanding of dogmas but to deepen and enlighten our personal relationship with God in the Church" (105). Theology must also point out how the church "may exercise her mission" to serve humanity "in [its] most pressing and authentic needs" in the face of injustice and the threat of destruction (107). Merton's reflection on purity might well be read along with "Love and Solitude" and "Love and Need," since all three pieces were written after Merton fell in love with M. in the spring of 1966 and bear the stamp of personal experience. Merton describes an approach to purity in which the emphasis "will be not so much on law as on love, not so much on what happens to nature or to the parts of the body as to what develops in the person (though in this case the two are manifestly inseparable)" (119).

Part 3 gathers together seven essays under the title of "Christian Humanism." In the title essay of this section Merton explains the "heart of true Christian humanism" is to be sought in the incarnation.[6] "The Church is the center and focus of this incarnational and redemptive humanism because it is in her that Christ dwells, and the transforming power of the Holy Spirit makes men into sons of God" (144–45). Forgiveness, then, is at the very heart of Christian humanism: "it is a life of dynamic love which *forgives* evil and, by forgiving, enables love to transform evil into good" (145). Christian humanism calls persons to "a service of love," sorely needed in the world today (150). The second essay, "Christian Humanism in the Nuclear Era,"[7] begins by pointing to the personalistic character of humanism put forward in the Second Vatican Council's insistence on the "the value and dignity of the human person in his relation with other men and with God, and the unity of the human family, which is made up of these human persons" (151). Merton quotes at length from the Council's

Constitution on the Church in the Modern World (*Gaudium et Spes*) to demonstrate its "deeply traditional Christian humanism which is willing and able to collaborate with modern science and technology in building a new world" for persons (169). But Merton also notes the Council's commendation of nonviolence, its insistence on the obligation to work for world peace, and its condemnation of total war. A "whole new attitude toward war is demanded. The Council solemnly affirmed that all men must take seriously and personally the obligation incumbent on the entire human race to abolish war" (168).

Two essays concern the writings of French Jesuit paleontologist Teilhard de Chardin. In "The Universe as Epiphany" Merton takes up Teilhard's spiritual vision as expressed in *The Divine Milieu*, leaving it to others to assess its relationship to Teilhard's scientific vision. Merton essentially restates what he sees to be Teilhard's key themes, showing them to be consistent with Christian theology and spirituality. Merton, along with Teilhard, dispels "the false notion of a *disincarnate* or *disembodied* Christianity which, in fact, is not Christian at all" (174). Merton affirms Teilhard's view of the "'divine milieu' which surrounds, sustains, and embraces" persons "together in harmony and in unity" (175), noting how Teilhard mirrors St. Paul's teaching of the recapitulation of all things in Christ. Teilhard "sees far beyond the supposed contradiction between action and contemplation" (177) and recognizes that the Christian life must be rich in contemplation and in action. Merton explains Teilhard's concern with the "passive realm": "the passivities of growth . . . of diminishment, which include all possible obstacles, frustrations, and evils, even death itself" (179–80). The Christian is not called to "stoic indifference" or mere endurance but to "consciously and freely working to bring out of evil that good which is willed by God" (181). Merton concludes that "this scientist and priest is speaking above all as a mystic" (183). The second essay on Teilhard de Chardin, "Teilhard's Gamble," is a review of Henri de Lubac's *The Religion of Teilhard de Chardin*.[8] Merton characterizes the book as "a summa of Teilhard's spiritual doctrine: his

teaching on the ascetic and mystical life in the context of his evolutionary and incarnational cosmogony" (188). Merton describes de Lubac as intent on showing that Teilhard's statements "can be understood in a perfectly traditional sense, or at least in a way that does not contradict Catholic tradition" (188). But Merton also critiques Teilhard's optimism. "Clearly, the Teilhardian wager is as much a gamble as Pascal's. Perhaps it is more of a gamble. . . . Teilhard has hocked everything and bet it on the human species. . . . Teilhard does not seem to notice the wounds of mendacity and hatred which have been inexorably deepened in man by his practice of technological warfare, totalitarianism, and genocide" (190).

"Rebirth and the New Man in Christianity" is a revision and expansion of Merton's preface to the Japanese edition of *The New Man*, which Merton wrote in October 1967.[9] Merton reflects on the "new birth," "the new being," and the "new creation" as "at the very heart of Christianity" (193). Being born again is an awakening, a "deep spiritual consciousness" (198). Spiritual rebirth is "an awareness that we are not merely our everyday selves but we are also one with One who is beyond all human and individual self-limitation" (198).

In "The Climate of Mercy," dedicated to Albert Schweitzer, Merton writes that becoming "a new man" and "a new creation" is "the work of mercy" (203).[10] Mercy is "an event in which God reveals himself to us in His redemptive love and in the great gift which is the outcome of this event: our mercy to others" (203), and the "climate of mercy" is the "the climate of the new creation" that "depends on the realization that *all men are acceptable before God*" (212). It is this realization that roots out colonialism and racism. In this essay honoring Albert Schweitzer, Merton writes, "The grace of the word preached to Africa is perhaps the paradoxical realization of our own sin, our own need to be pardoned, and in particular our immense need to be pardoned by Africa" (215).

"The Good News of the Nativity" offers "a monastic reading" of the nativity of Christ, a reading that seeks to hear "the plain message of the Gospel" (222).[11] The gospel of the nativity is "not merely the gentle, comforting story of a Virgin Mother and a sweet Babe lying in the manger.... It is a solemn proclamation of an event which is the turning point of all history: the coming of the Messiah, the Anointed King and Son of God, the Word-made-Flesh" (223). The nativity gospel "remains a Gospel of renewal...a Gospel of *aggiornamento*" (231). CMB

Notes

1. In draft, the essay was entitled "Learning to Learn." "Learning to Live" was published in Wesley First, ed., *University on the Heights* (New York: Doubleday, 1969), 187–99.

2. This essay was published as "A Buyer's Market for Love?" *Ave Maria* 104 (December 24, 1966): 7–10, 27.

3. This essay first appeared in *Mediator* 20 (summer 1969): 2–4.

4. This essay was first published in India in *Mountain Path* 3 (October 1966): 339–48.

5. Ned O'Gorman, ed. (New York: Random House, 1969), 164–72; 230–38.

6. This essay first appeared in *Spiritual Life* 13 (winter 1967): 219–30.

7. This essay was published in altered form in *Katallagete* (summer 1967): 30–36.

8. Merton drafted the piece as "The Teilhardian Wager" in July 1967. It was published in *Commonweal* 87 (October 27, 1967): 109–11.

9. See *"Honorable Reader,"* 130–36.

10. This essay was first published in *Cord* 15 (April 1965): 89–96.

11. This article was first published as "The Good News of the Nativity: A Monastic Reading of the Christmas Gospels," *Bible Today* 21 (December 1965): 1,367–75.

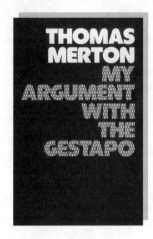

M.

M. is the initial used by the editor of the sixth volume of Thomas Merton's journals to refer to the student nurse with whom Merton fell in love in the spring of 1966 during a hospitalization for back surgery. He records the story of their relationship in his journal, posthumously published under the title *Learning to Love*. This volume includes four of the eighteen poems Merton wrote for M. and "A Midsummer Diary for M." — a diary or journal which Merton wrote during a week in June 1966 and which he gave to M. In his biography, *The Seven Mountains of Thomas Merton*, Michael Mott identifies the young woman as S. Both Michael Mott and Christine Bochen, editor of *Learning to Love*, chose to refer to the student nurse by initial rather than by name in order to honor her privacy. It should be noted that what is known of M. and of Merton's relationship with M. is derived from Merton's own writings and from the accounts of Merton's friends who shared their memories with Mott. CMB

SEE ALSO *EIGHTEEN POEMS*; *LEARNING TO LOVE*; WOMEN.

Cover for *My Argument with the Gestapo* reprinted with the permission of New Directions. Cover design by Gertrude Huston.

MAN IN THE DIVIDED SEA, A

New York: New Directions, 1946. 155 pp.

This, Thomas Merton's second published book of poetry, is considerably the longest collection of his verse. It is comprised of fifty-six poems, not including the text of his previous collection, *Thirty Poems* (1944), which is printed in a slightly revised and reordered version as an appendix to this volume. The title, which refers, of course, to the exodus, the escape of the Israelites from Egypt through the parted waters of the Red Sea, reflects Merton's sense of the meaning of his own spiritual journey — the soon to be well-known story of his conversion to Catholicism and entrance into monastic life — as a passage from enslavement to freedom. But the title also represents the contents of the book quite accurately in another way: unlike his first book of poems, only six of which were written after he had joined the Trappists, *A Man in the Divided Sea* can be divided into two approximately equal groups of poems, the first half written before he entered the monastery, the second in the early years of his monastic life.

Because many of the premonastic poems with explicitly religious themes had already appeared in *Thirty Poems*, the contrast between the two parts of the volume is somewhat more striking than it would otherwise be. As in the previous volume, classical and mythological themes are prominent, here in four variations of a common situation: a woman's response to the arrival of a male hero. In "Ariadne" (no. 4; 29 ll.) the Cretan princess is presented as a bored, jaded aristocrat who is jolted out of her lethargy by the arrival of "the black-eyed captain" Theseus (l. 27). In "The Greek Women" (no. 15; 24 ll.) news of the end of the Trojan War sparks anticipation in those women who do not yet realize they are widows, but a very different reaction in Clytemnestra, whose husband, Agamemnon, "Bleeds in her conscience, twisting like a root" (l. 24). In "Calypso's Island" (no. 16; 19 ll.) the arrival of Odysseus is depicted as an event that "Wakes from a dreaming lifetime" (l. 12) the isolated queen (whose divine status is not mentioned) and suggests both the passion ("the flame-feathered birds" that "Shout their litany in the savage tree" [ll. 15, 16]) and the suffering ("the red red wound / Of the sweet pomegranate" [ll. 17–18]) that this encounter will bring her. "A Song" ("When it was day . . . ") (no. 13; 30 ll.) implicitly likens the initial enthusiasm and eventual disillusion experienced at the arrival of spring to the story of Dido and Aeneas.

The coming of spring is depicted in different form in "The Man in the Wind" (no. 3; 16 ll.), which focuses on the personified figure of "Captain April" (l. 2), who strides down the New York City streets only to disappear and reappear repeatedly, reflecting the weather of the season. In "April" (no. 14; 18 ll.) the season is compared to a leopard which "Sports with the javelins of the weather" (l. 2) but cannot be captured or controlled. A more conflicted view of the encounter between the human and the natural is found in "Tropics" (no. 6; 16 ll.), in which guards "Arrest the four footed wind" (l. 4) and prisoners are "Building a cage for the devouring sun" (l. 7). The "Penal Island" (l. 2) of this poem reappears in "Crusoe" (no. 11; 18 ll.), where "the last man" (l. 13) shipwrecks there "like the wiseguy Crusoe" (l. 18) after failing to guide his journey by the pattern of "the stars' unending Lent" (l. 12). A similar tropical setting, undoubtedly reflecting Merton's 1940 visit to Cuba, marks "Fugitive" (no. 7; 25 ll.), a quasi-surrealist portrait of "a mad half-Spaniard" (l. 1) who tries to escape his

nightmarish visions in which "Bones had begun to turn to money" (l. 9) and whose "paper mask plays (always), dead" (l. 20). A very different view of dreams and the subconscious is found in the opening poem, "Song (from Crossportion's Pastoral)" (no. 1; 17 ll.), which is about the process of getting in touch with the deeper reaches of the psyche and therefore with one's creativity (associated with mermaids and their music, found in the depths of "my room, the sea" [l. 10], where limits, boundaries, and distinctions are dissolved in order to identify fully with a nonfinite reality).

Several of the poems reflect the early stages of the Second World War, beginning with "Poem: 1939" (no. 2; 12 ll.), which contrasts the order of nature (the "wheeling ring" of the stars [l. 2]) with the violence of the human world, in which "Towns dry up and flare like tongues / But no voice prophesies" (ll. 11–12). "The Pride of the Dead" (no. 17; 24 ll.) suggests that the shades of long-dead generals and emperors have reemerged to demand a dirge in the midst of "your burning country" (l. 22). "The Bombarded City" (no. 18; 79 ll.) declares that the "Curse of the little children killed" (ll. 14, 15) will continue even when field flowers and weeds have grown from the dead leader's corpse. "Dirge for a Town in France" (no. 25; 38 ll.) recalls a prewar carnival and laments the loss of childhood innocence in the midst of adult violence and destruction.

Social themes also are found in "The Ohio River — Louisville" (no. 20; 25 ll.), in which the noise of the city is contrasted with "the tremendous silence" (l. 2) of the river, which in turn is disturbed only by swimmers and "The thin, salt voice of violence, / That whines, like a mosquito, in their simmering blood" (ll. 24–25); in "The Dreaming Trader" (no. 21; 23 ll.), whose ambitions for material success are doomed to "founder in the dark Sargassos of your own intolerable dream / And never be heard of again" (ll. 22–23); in "Aubade: Harlem" (no. 23; 24 ll.), in which the oppression of ghetto residents by the white power structure is likened to Christ's betrayal and crucifixion; and in "Aubade: The City" (no. 26; 40 ll.), in which the alienation of the modern city from the natural order parallels the alienation of its residents from one another and from their authentic selves.

The religious dimension of many of these early poems is allusive, oblique, or an unexpected contrast to the rest of the poem. In "The Oracle" (no. 5; 25 ll.) the materialistic "prophet" of the title, who predicts worldly success or failure for two groups of young girls, is suddenly confronted with "The stern, astounding angel" (l. 23) who bears "a truer message" (l. 24) as he descends "down the far, fast ladders of light" (l. 22). The title of "Ash Wednesday" (no. 8; 19 ll.) seems to have little connection with the bleak landscape of the poem itself until it is realized that the "naked traveller" (l. 1) who "Starves on the mad sierra" (l. 3) is a model of failed asceticism, as he makes the traditional Lenten journey into the desert but tries, unsuccessfully, to survive on his own resources, unaided by grace. "Song" ("Come where the grieving rivers of the night") (no. 9; 17 ll.) uses the imagery of Psalm 137 ("Let grow our harps in windy trees" [l. 6]) to suggest the modern experience of spiritual exile. "Some Bloody Mutiny" (no. 10; 25 ll.) contrasts the pseudoresurrections of contemporary life, in which "We time our Easters by the rumpus / In our dancehall arteries" (ll. 15–16) but "there's no Good Friday" (l. 20), no preceding death to self, with the genuine rebirth in which heaven "flower[s] for us / Upon the bonebranch we made dead" (ll. 24–25). "Dirge" (no. 12; 22 ll.) notes that the noise of contemporary life makes it almost impossible to "hear our Messenger come home from hell / With hands shot full of blood" (ll. 16–17). "The Storm at Night" (no. 19; 20 ll.) recognizes the failure of many in the midst of their crises to cry out, as the disciples did to Jesus, "Oh save us, in the dark tornadoes of Genesareth!" (l. 12). "The Peril" (no. 27; 20 ll.) contrasts anticipated disaster with the sudden arrival of "the Bridegroom [who] comes like lightning where we never looked" (l. 9) and prays "Stab me and save me with the five lights of Your Crucifixion!" (l. 17).

Only in poems written just before (or possibly, immediately after) the entrance into Gethsemane do religious themes become the focus of entire poems. "The House of Caia-

phas" (no. 22; 24 ll.), a meditation on Peter's betrayal, implies the continuing relevance of the scene as the line "And the gates of night fall shut with the clangor of arms" (l. 12) is changed to the concluding statement, "And the gates of night fall shut with the thunder of Massbells" (l. 24). "Aubade — The Annunciation" (no. 24; 27 ll.), juxtaposing the renewal of spring, the scene of the angel's message to the Virgin, and the "world of March" (l. 23), the Lenten world, serves as a reminder that the harvest is produced only because the seed falls into the ground and dies (John 12:24): even at the glorious moment of the dawn of salvation, the darkness of Calvary cannot be ignored. "Advent" (no. 28; 19 ll.) evokes the peace of outer and inner landscapes in anticipation of the incarnation, as "We have become more humble than the rocks, / More wakeful than the patient hills.../ And intellects are quieter than the flocks that feed by starlight" (ll. 10–11, 15).

The second half of the volume, the poems written between the end of 1941, when Merton entered the monastery, and early 1946 (the date of the final seven pieces), is more overtly and consistently religious in tone and subject matter. Most striking are the poems on the monastic life itself, beginning with "Trappists, Working" (no. 36; 15 ll.) of early 1942, in which the monks are envisioned as encountering Jesus not only in the church but also in the woods and fields, "Singing our other Office with our saws and axes" (l. 6). "After the Night Office — Gethsemani Abbey" (no. 46; 36 ll.) explores the congruence between the divine darkness of contemplative awareness and the natural darkness, the time of quiet recollection and receptivity, when there is nothing to distract the senses so one can more readily direct one's focus to God within. "The Trappist Cemetery — Gethsemani" (no. 51; 69 ll.), addressed to the monks in the abbey graveyard, combines an apophatic focus on the darkness of contemplation and of death with a holistic, sacramental, "Franciscan" appreciation of creation, which converge in a final vision of eschatological fulfillment: "The beasts and trees shall share your resurrection, / And a new world be born from these green tombs" (ll. 68–69).

"Clairvaux" (no. 55; 96 ll.) sees the monastery built by St. Bernard as "model of all solitudes" (l. 3), with its central pool and garden as participating in the identity of the enclosed garden of the Song of Songs (subject of Bernard's great series of sermons), its archways as symbolizing complete dependence of the monks on "their key, / Who is their Christ and Father, their superior" (ll. 61–62), and its bells summoning the monks to their office as signs of eternity in time.

Participation in the liturgical cycle is reflected in "The Candlemas Procession" (no. 32; 22 ll.), in which the monks "come, / New Simeons, to kindle, / Each at Your infant sacrifice his own life's candle" (ll. 3–5); in "Song for the Blessed Sacrament" (no. 47; 30 ll.), as the change of seasons parallels the passage through Lent to Easter, and the returning birds are addressed as "you wild Cistercians" who "tune your praises / To our Latin, with your native liturgy" (ll. 18–19); and in "A Whitsun Canticle" (no. 52; 88 ll.), a Pentecost hymn that concludes by asking the Holy Spirit to "Build us a monastery . . . / In the full fields of gentle Heaven. / Build us our cells forever in Your Mercy's woods" (ll. 78, 81–82).

Many of the poems are meditations on scriptural themes, reflecting the young monk's immersion in the Bible in both public and private prayer. "Carol" (no. 29; 18 ll.), probably the first of the monastic poems, brings the speaker and his audience, "we unnumbered children of the wicked centuries" (l. 15), before the Christmas crib with shepherds and magi to offer "our penances and prayers" (l. 16) to the child "in the sweet-smelling hay" (l. 17). "How Long We Wait" (no. 30; 22 ll.) likens the monks both to the watchmen of Psalm 129 and to the shepherds and magi of the Christmas story, as their waiting for the coming of day is symbolically likened to waiting for the mystical and eschatological coming of Christ the Bridegroom. "Cana" (no. 33; 18 ll.) both personalizes Christ's first miracle, seeing it as filling "our earthen vessels, waiting empty" (l. 13), and universalizes it, recognizing it as a gift of "Wine for old Adam, digging in the briars!" (l. 18). In "The Widow of Naim" (no. 34; 35 ll.) the miracle is applied "to all the widow-Church's

risen children" (l. 35), who are called to "read the Cross and Easter in this rising" (l. 33). "The Snare" (no. 37; 21 ll.), dedicated to "St. Benedict, in thanksgiving," uses the imagery of the psalms in likening the monks to birds that have escaped the traps of sin set by the fowler. In "The Betrayal" (no. 44; 23 ll.) the speaker identifies successively with Judas and the crowd in Gethsemane, with the crowd crying out for Jesus' death before Pilate, and with the executioners on Golgotha, but also, finally, with those forgiven by Christ's words on the cross, healed in their five senses by the five wounds of Christ. "Rahab's House" (no. 45; 41 ll.) uses the traditional typological interpretation of the scarlet cord in the harlot's window at Jericho as an image of "the red of our Redemption" (l. 7) and reminds the reader of Rahab's place among the ancestors of Christ: "A rod will grow / From Jesse's tree, / Among her sons, the lords of Bethlehem, / And flower into Paradise" (ll. 28–31). "The Word — A Responsory" (no. 48; 40 ll.) literally "responds" to the psalm verse "*My heart hath uttered a good Word*" (ll. 8, 27) by reflecting on its meaning and praying that the "Word / . . . Whose Name is: 'Savior'" (ll. 32, 34) might "Burn in our hearts, burn in our living marrow, own our being" (l. 36).

Participation in the paschal mystery of dying and rising with Christ is the theme of a number of poems. In "The Image of True Lovers' Death" (no. 41; 45 ll.) the monk escapes the "stern, accusing" (l. 4) reminders of his past life and "bleeds . . . on a daily Cross, / With Christ" (ll. 44–45). In "The Fall of Night" (no. 42; 40 ll.) the "homeward farmers" (l. 10) pray that the "tree of Jesse growing in our garden" (l. 19) will not recall "the arbors where we hid, in Eden" (l. 24) but the tree of Calvary, so that "these cross-branch fruits [might] transfigure us / And makes us gods" (ll. 25–26) — a gloriously ironic fulfillment of the distorted promise of the serpent's temptation. In "The Biography" (no. 43; 52 ll.), the most personal poem in the volume, the speaker moves from identification with the crucifiers to identification with the Crucified, and so discovers a new identity: "If on Your Cross Your life and death and mine are one, / Love teaches me to read, in You, the rest of a new history" (ll. 42–43).

In "The Dark Encounter" (no. 49; 36 ll.) a "secret and intrepid Visitor / Has come to crack our sepulchre" (ll. 4–5), "Has come to raise us from the dead" (l. 34), while in "The Victory" (no. 50; 64 ll.) the humble, undramatic death to self of authentic monastic life nevertheless reveals "beneath the rags of our disguise / The Christ Who died for us" (ll. 48–49).

Poems on the saints are another prominent category in this part of the volume. The speaker in "Saint Paul" (no. 35; 19 ll.) identifies with the sinful Saul and prays for a like conversion through participation in the death and resurrection of Christ (a key Pauline theme). "An Invocation to St. Lucy" (no. 38; 20 ll.), recalling Donne's "Nocturnal on St. Lucy's Day" in its reflections on her name (meaning "light" [l. 2]) and the mid-December date of her feast ("in our darkest season" [l. 1]), prays for the transformation of darkness into light through her intercession. "St. Thomas Aquinas" (no. 39; 28 ll.) reflects both the intellectual achievement of the great Dominican and his childlike piety, which finds creation "Full of the Child Who consecrates the universe, / Informing all with power and meaning, like a Sacrament" (ll. 20–21). "St. Alberic" (no. 40; 28 ll.) celebrates one of the Cistercian founders, who experienced both exile and a return to paradise in the cloisters of Cîteaux. "St. John Baptist" (no. 54; 114 ll.) addresses the forerunner of Christ as "the first Cistercian and the greatest Trappist" (l. 102) because in his eremitic simplicity he "laid down for us the form and pattern of / Our love for Christ" (ll. 105–6).

After bidding farewell to "those crowded ruins, /... you woebegone, sad towns" (ll. 12, 13) in "A Letter to my Friends" (no. 31; 29 ll.), written immediately after coming to "This holy House of God" (l. 1), the poet looks once again at the world beyond the monastery only toward the end of the volume; he is not impressed with what he sees. "Ode to the Present Century" (no. 53; 33 ll.) castigates the "prudent citizen" (l. 2) for spiritual emptiness and materialistic rapacity and urges, "Forsake your deserts of centrifugal desire" (l. 30) in order to penetrate "the depths of life" (l. 31) within and so to discover "the image of all Mercy's Sovereign" (l. 28). "La Salette" (no. 56; 43 ll.),

the final poem in the volume, describes the apparition of the Virgin to two French peasant children "a hundred years" (l. 7) earlier, and considers the disasters of the present century a result of humanity's failure to heed her call to repentance; the final image of an "inexorable" (l. 37) Christ who has "roused, with His first two great thunderbolts, / The chariots of Armageddon" (ll. 42–43) projects a dark vision of the future, foreshadowing the title sequence of Merton's next volume of verse, *Figures for an Apocalypse*. POC

"MAN IN THE SYCAMORE TREE, THE"

SEE NOVELS, UNPUBLISHED.

MARITAIN, JACQUES

Jacques Maritain (1882–1973), a French neo-Thomist philosopher and writer, first met Thomas Merton when Merton was a student at Columbia University. The introduction was made by Daniel Walsh. Maritain visited Merton at the Abbey of Gethsemani in 1966. Their correspondence, which spans the period 1949–67, reflects Merton's affection for Jacques and his wife, Raïssa. Merton's letters address many topics of mutual concern, including contemplation, suffering, and death; changes in the church occasioned by the Sec-

Jacques Maritain

ond Vatican Council; and social issues such as violence, war, and the proliferation of nuclear weapons. Merton not only shares ideas in this correspondence; he also reveals himself, as in this passage: "There are great illusions to be gotten rid of, and there is a false self that has to be taken off, if it can be done" (*Courage for Truth*, 39). For Merton's letters to Maritain, see *Courage for Truth*, 22–53. CMB

MARRIAGE

As a celibate monk, Thomas Merton does not give a great deal of attention to married life, but he does touch on it in a number of places in his writings. In his early monastic journals he presents a somewhat idealized and unrealistic picture of the possibilities of living a contemplative existence in the midst of family life, recommending that "Catholics inside and outside of cloister — form *casas* [houses] of silence" (*Entering the Silence*, 440) — the Spanish word no doubt intended to recall the "*casa*" that St. John of the Cross leaves in quiet at the beginning of his poem "The Dark Night." In the revised version of this passage he goes on to say, "Bring up their kids not to yell so much. Children are naturally quiet — if they are left alone and not given the needle from the cradle upward, in order that they may develop into citizens of a state in which everybody yells and is yelled at" (*Sign of Jonas*, 311–12).[1] In *The Ascent to Truth* Merton cites St. Teresa of Avila, who distinguishes between cloistered and married spirituality by recounting an example of what Merton calls "stupid" spiritual direction: a confessor advises a married woman drawn to a life of prayer "to drop her work and to pray when she ought to be doing the dishes." Merton comments, "Her life of prayer at once becomes an obstacle to her happiness as a wife, and her marriage, at the same time, erects a barrier between herself and God" (*Ascent to Truth*, 80). Implicitly, he suggests that this does not have to be and should not be the case, that prayer and marriage are by no means incompatible, that married love is indeed a way to God.

He discusses this relationship between marriage and holiness more specifically in *No Man Is an Island*, in which he declares that of course many more married people than celibates will become saints, since many more people are married. He maintains that the success of married life "presupposes the capacity for a deeply human love which ought to be spiritual and physical at the same time," and points out that the sacramental status of marriage is a strong affirmation of the holiness of the body: "The 'flesh' spiritualized by prayer and the Holy Ghost, yet remaining completely physical, can come to play an important part in our sanctification" (*No Man Is an Island*, 99–100). Later in the same work he writes that in marriage "divine love is more fully incarnate than in the other vocations," though he goes on to say that it is also more limited in its focus on one's immediate family and circle of friends. But his emphasis is mainly on the way in which natural affections can serve as "a sign of divine love and an occasion of divine grace" when consecrated to God (154). In his journal he endorses Kierkegaard's perception of marriage as the free choice of the spouse as one's neighbor, in the biblical meaning of neighbor as one to be loved as oneself, and reflects that when "two consciously make this choice, this spiritual choice, with regard to one another, then a great mystery and transformation takes place in the world and God is present in this mystery" (*Search for Solitude*, 259).

Perhaps the most "theological" discussion of marriage by Merton comes in *The New Man*, in the context of his exploration of the significance of the relationship of Adam and Eve, in which the fruitful union of man and woman symbolizes both the fecundity of divine love, "the infinite giving and diffusion of goodness which is the inner law of God's own life," and the loving bond of Christ and the church: "The married love that is transfigured by the Church's sacrament reproduces something of this love by which Christ sanctified His Church, and the natural mystery of the communication of life by love becomes a supernatural mystery of the communication of holiness by charity" (*New Man*, 92–93). In "The Inner Experience" Merton warns married Christians against being "influenced too much by a virginal or priestly spirituality that has nothing to do with [their] state and only blinds [them] to its essential dignity," and calls for "a contemplative spirituality centered in the mystery of marriage" that will focus on the need for "keeping the Christian mind fully and sanely *incarnate*" ("Inner Experience," 7:282). In *Life and Holiness*, while maintaining the traditional idea that vowed life is intrinsically a "higher" because a "more radical" commitment, he again emphasizes "that the married state is also most sanctifying by its very nature" and may well require self-sacrifices that are more demanding and more effective than those of vowed life (*Life and Holiness*, 7). Part of the problem, Merton notes toward the end of the same book, is that married people are not made aware that theirs is "a truly spiritual vocation" (147–48). Here he is anticipating the teaching of the Second Vatican Council on the universal call to holiness. In *Redeeming the Time* he refers to the teaching of the Council's Constitution on the Church in the Modern World (*Gaudium et Spes*) that marriage is a relationship that has a profoundly spiritual dimension: "In authentic married love, two persons become not merely well-adjusted sexual partners, but they complete one another spiritually, they bring meaning and fulfilment to one another's lives by a unity which cannot be accounted for by the human and biological needs of the natural species" (*Redeeming the Time*, 57). In one letter of "spiritual direction" concerned with marriage, he warns against a myth of marriage, of perfect sexual and social adjustment, a glamorization of sexual fulfillment in contemporary culture that almost inevitably leads to disillusionment with one's own actual relationship. His concluding advice is that the "great thing in marriage is not an impossible ideal of fulfillment and exaltation but a mature rational Christian acceptance of the responsibilities and risks of human love" (*Witness to Freedom*, 310). POC

SEE ALSO SACRAMENT.

Notes

1. This passage is added to the original discussion in the journal; "*casas*" are not mentioned in *The Sign of Jonas*, which simply says, "Christians should have quiet homes" (311) and interestingly adds a reference to television, absent from the original journal passage — not surprisingly, since it dates from November 1950 — making the reference in *The Sign of Jonas* somewhat anachronistic.

MARRIED PRIESTS

SEE CELIBACY.

MARTHE, MARIE ET LAZARE
Paris: Desclée de Brouwer, 1956. 145 pp.

This book is a translation of a somewhat expanded version of "Action and Contemplation in the Doctrine of Saint Bernard," published in three parts in *Collectanea Ordinis Cisterciensium Reformatorum* in 1953. The title comes from the traditional association of the three vocations, active, contemplative, and penitential, with Martha, Mary, and Lazarus, respectively, a major focus of St. Bernard's teaching and of Merton's article. Plans to publish the material in book form in English remained unfulfilled during Merton's lifetime; it became part 1 of *Thomas Merton on St. Bernard* only in 1980. The preface, originally written in April 1954 for the projected English-language edition and published in the French volume, is available in English only in *Honorable Reader* (17–22). It emphasizes Bernard's traditional teaching that contemplation is rooted in the mystery of Christ and of the church as the bride of Christ and warns against distorting Bernard's teaching on the relationship of action and contemplation by quoting passages out of context in support of the superiority of one aspect or the other of Christian and monastic life. POC

SEE ALSO *THOMAS MERTON ON ST. BERNARD*.

MARXISM

Although Thomas Merton is no Marxist, and is extremely critical of communist ideology as it was put into effect in the Soviet Union and elsewhere, he recognizes Marx's significance as a thinker and finds that he raises significant issues that must be addressed not only to meet the challenge of communism but also to be faithful to Christian principles. He sees communism, as it then existed, as being in some ways a betrayal of authentic Marxism ("Do they still imagine that Russia is Marxist?" he asks [*Witness to Freedom*, 296]) and in other ways a taking of Marxist principles to their ultimate conclusions. "Marx is one of those who cannot be dismissed," he writes in his journal in May 1957. "We have to listen to his tune and understand it. Because it does not mean exactly what Marx himself thought it would mean or what the communists made it mean (for Marxism, in a sense, is dead. But the unintentional consequence of Marxism lives on and their work is terrible)" (*Search for Solitude*, 90). He sees Marx's great gift as "diagnosis." He recognized and critiqued the great flaw in capitalist society: the readiness to make commodities more important than people, and in fact to turn people into commodities, into means of production. But he failed to recognize, Merton continues, that this tendency would not be eliminated but in fact would be exacerbated by the so-called dictatorship of the proletariat, which Merton says "is more than anything else a tyranny of 'things' and 'commodities' over human values" (91). The great irony is that Marx identified the process of the reification of the human and the animating of the material, yet he has been the thinker who in the past two centuries has been most responsible for the spread of this process, which is even worse in communist countries than in capitalist ones. "The thing most significant about the genius of Marx," Merton believes, "is the ambivalence and internal contradictions which are bearing fruit monstrously in the world of our time" (92). This ambivalence is particularly acute in the matter of human rights, since the whole dynamism of Marx's philosophy is aimed at vindicating the rights of the proletariat, yet he is willing to deny the rights of people in the present for the sake of creating a just society in the future (92).

Merton considered Marx's critique of religion to be in part misplaced, a reductivist attempt to provide an economic solution to a spiritual problem, yet he also finds something prophetic about it, in the scriptural sense, Marx as "an heir of Ezechiel and Jeremias," even if an unconscious one (90): any attempt to justify the inequalities of society by referring to the will of God and promising redress in eternity is indeed a perversion of revelation and a futile attempt "to give . . . hopelessness a transcendental justification" (*Monastic Journey*, 73). The question Marx raised, "How shall we face the contradiction between the ideal and the real in our society, the ideal and the concrete in ourselves" (74), is indeed a valid one, a crucial one, and the "bourgeois paternalism, the flaccid humanitarianism" that Marx equated with religion provides no sufficient answer. The challenge of Marx to Christians is to show by the commitment of their lives that religion is not a force for alienation but for integration and liberation, but this can be done not by "merely 'going through the motions'" but by responding to grace with generosity and humility (75). Yet ultimately, Merton maintains, Marx's "idea of man's alienation by religion, economics, politics and philosophy" is less to be feared than redirected, since it serves as a potent critique of those who claim to be the heirs of Marx: "The most ironical fact about the twentieth century is that Atheistic Communism has finally realized, in its ultimate perfection, the economic alienation of man which Karl Marx ascribed in part to religion" (*Disputed Questions*, 146, 147), though Merton hastens to add that this is not an excuse for complacency or self-congratulation, since the "same errors are all too likely to be our own," and "Christian circles are by no means immune from the contagion of totalitarianism" (147).

Merton is particularly impressed with the writings of the early Marx as he encountered them in his friend Erich Fromm's book *Marx's Concept of Man* in 1961. He mentions in his journal that he has become more aware of the biblical roots of Marx through this work, not only the messianism, but particularly the concept of alienation, which Fromm rightly likens to idol worship (*Turning toward the World*, 151). Merton finds "inner spiritual potentialities hidden under the surface of the Marxian dialectic," precisely in this awareness of alienation from one's authentic identity by the "subordination of man to the technological process." The early Marx recognized that "the ultimate challenge was for man to free himself of his machines and gain control over them, thus breaking the bonds of alienation and making himself the master of his history." While Merton considers Marx's own presentation of this issue "uncertain and ambiguous," he himself sees the need for spiritual wisdom, not simply the working out of a dialectical process, to overcome this alienation and restore true identity to the human person (*Hidden Ground of Love*, 544–45). Clearly, he finds an opportunity for fruitful dialogue between the Christian and the revisionist Marxist on this point. As he writes to Fromm, "I think Marx needs a little clearer kind of personalism to fully clarify his idea of unalienated man. This is the realm of investigation that seems important to me. Especially since the only society so far more alienated than that of the Marxists is our own, where, however, we like to talk of personalism" (315).[1]

When it arrives in the mid-1960s, Merton welcomes the advent of the Christian-Marxist dialogue, but he remains rather skeptical of its focus, which seems to require the Christian to accept the Marxist ground rules (as represented by the French Marxist Roger Garaudy), so that only a Teilhardian worldview, with its historical dynamism, provides an adequate conversation partner for the Marxist. A more contemplative focus, which would take into account basic questions of identity, seems to be left aside. Merton worries that such a dialogue may simply result in "a transition from the rigidity of curial-control to the political rigidity of party control," and adds, "I can imagine nothing more futile!" (*Learning to Love*, 31–32). (He is more impressed, as he mentions in his Bangkok talk, by the fact that Garaudy is interested in the writings of Teresa of Avila [*Asian Journal*, 328].) Given the focus of his own interest in Marx, it is not surprising that he is very positive toward the work of the neo-Marxist thinker Herbert Marcuse, whose book *One-Dimensional Man* focuses on precisely the issue of alienation that Merton found so important in his reading of the early Marx. Merton says that he finds Marcuse to be closer to a monastic perspective than are many theologians (*School of Charity*, 392), and uses his work to anchor his discussion of "Marxism and Monastic Perspectives," his presentation at the Bangkok conference on the final day of his life. Merton suggests to his audience that their relevance in a world of Marxism lies not in becoming "pseudo-Marxists or semi-Marxist monks" — the danger he saw in the Christian-Marxist dialogue as it was being conducted in the nonmonastic world — "but in proportion as we are simply monks" (*Asian Journal*, 328). His point is that precisely as monks, as those who are called to "experience the ground of [their] own being" in such a way that they come to know the "secret of liberation" (333), monks have something to contribute to a dialogue on alienation and authenticity, where Merton sees the real value of Marxian analysis to lie. He summarizes Marcuse's theory as claiming that "all highly organized technological societies, as we have them now, all so-called managerial societies, as found both in the United States and in the Soviet Union, end up by being equally totalitarian in one way or another" because "significant choices can no longer be made in the kind of organized society you have either under capitalism or under Soviet socialism" (334–35). Hence, people are deprived of any true freedom; they are alienated from themselves because, as Erich Fromm points out, their life "is lived according to conditions determined by somebody else" (335). Here Merton finds the key point of intersection between Christianity and Marxism, between monasticism and Marxism, since "Christianity is against alienation," and the whole New Testament can be read as "a protest against religious alienation" (335, 336). As an ironic aside he notes that monastic regimentation can actually promote alienation precisely by removing all meaningful choice from the monk, but he clearly sees the charism of the monastic vocation as a healing of alienation, the restoration of genuine human identity, the attainment of "full realization" (333). Such realization, Merton suggests, empowers the monk to deal creatively with whatever circumstances present themselves, whether to engage in Marxist dialogue, or to endure Marxist persecution: "If you once penetrate by detachment and purity of heart to the inner secret of the ground of your ordinary experience, you attain to a liberty that nobody can touch, that nobody can affect, that no political change of circumstances can do anything to" (342). POC

SEE ALSO ALIENATION; COMMUNISM.

Notes

1. It is clear from the context of this letter that Merton is referring to Fromm's book *Marx's Concept of Man*, not *Sigmund Freud's Mission*, as indicated in the bracketed annotation.

MARY

In his autobiography Thomas Merton writes that the most serious deficiency in his spiritual life during the first year after his conversion was a lack of devotion to Mary, who "occupied in my life little more than the place of a beautiful myth" (*Seven Storey Mountain*, 229). This defect was soon remedied, as the Mother of Jesus came to take a central place in his spirituality that would last until the end of his life. A key turning point was his visit to Cuba in April 1940, which was a kind of Marian pilgrimage, though he is rather reticent about this aspect of the trip in his journal. But in retrospect he focuses on his visits to the shrines of La Soledad, Our Lady of Solitude, whom he calls "one of my big devotions" (281), and of course to the Patroness of Cuba, Our Lady of Cobre, whom he promises to honor in his first Mass should he become a priest (282; see *Entering the Silence*, 304, 314, 318), and who inspires him to write the "Song for Our Lady of Cobre," which he calls "the first real poem I had ever written" (*Seven Storey Mountain*, 283) and which is the first of a number of Marian poems. The reflection of the statue of Our Lady of Mt. Carmel in the mirror of his Havana hotel room (*Run to the Mountain*, 219) remained an experience that had deep resonances for him many years later (*Search for Solitude*, 46).

In the closing pages of his premonastic journal he writes of dedicating the whole of Advent 1941 to the Blessed Virgin to ask her aid in entering Gethsemani, and the monastic journals of the next decade are filled with reflections and prayers that express an ongoing intensity of devotion to Mary. For example, on the Feast of the Visitation in 1947 he speaks of Mary visiting him, bringing health and light into his life (*Entering the Silence*, 88). After being ordained deacon in March 1949, he writes of Mary having "taken possession of my heart.... She was given to me with the book of the Gospels which, like her, gives Christ to the world. I wonder what I have been doing all my life not resting in her heart which is the Heart of all simplicity" (296). Although the intensity and frequency of his journal references to Mary decrease in later years, they still are present and

significant. In December 1959, in the midst of his recurring vocation crisis, he writes, "Hope in Our Lady. Today at Mass I thought: If I have Her, nothing else matters. But it does matter because this desire for solitude is part of my love for her, her will for me" (*Search for Solitude*, 352). At the beginning of 1965, the year in which he will move permanently into the hermitage named for Our Lady of Carmel, he writes of the important yet elusive presence of Mary at the hermitage, adding, "I need her and she is there. I should perhaps think of it more explicitly more often" (*Water of Life*, 197). A year later, on the day following the Feast of the Presentation, he writes of praying to Mary after Mass, of recognizing her "immense importance" in his life and of rededicating himself to her: "I have a great need to 'belong' to her" (*Learning to Love*, 16–17), he writes, a statement that echoes much earlier statements (see, e.g., *Entering the Silence*, 141, 253, 296), though now he focuses on the mystery of what this self-donation really means. In the midst of his intense relationship with the nurse, he even thanks Mary for "for the pure gratuitousness of this love" (*Learning to Love*, 74). Almost a year later, on the vigil of Pentecost 1967, he speaks of his "sense of the nearness and mercy of Mary" in the context of reports of apparitions at Garabandal in Spain, which he regards as "for the most part genuine" and as a summons to deeper repentance for himself (234).

Merton's personal devotion to the Virgin is closely bound up with the tradition of Cistercian Marian piety. Both during his initial visit to Gethsemani in Holy Week 1941 and when he is at the monastery of Our Lady of the Valley later in the year he speaks of entering the court of the Queen of Heaven (*Run to the Mountain*, 333, 393). Later he will explain to his Pakistani Muslim correspondent Abdul Aziz that all Cistercian monasteries are dedicated to Mary, and that he understands this to mean that "each monastery dwells so to speak surrounded and protected by the maternal love of Mary, and by her prayers in heaven," identifying his own monastery of Gethsemani particularly with the Virgin's compassion for the suffering of her abandoned Son in the Garden of the Agony

(*Hidden Ground of Love,* 47). His early books and pamphlets on Cistercian life and saints emphasize Mary as "Mother of Cistercian charity and of the monks' contemplation" (*Cistercian Contemplatives,* 59), "the key to Cistercian mysticism as she is, indeed, to Christian spirituality" (*What Are These Wounds?* 119). In particular, all of Merton's writings on St. Bernard emphasize the central role of Mary in his teaching, especially the sermons on the *Missus Est,* the Gospel text of the annunciation to Mary, "a small but complete treatise in Mariology" (*Last of the Fathers,* 36), which focuses on both the freedom of Mary's consent as the supreme example of action and her receptivity to the indwelling of the Word as a model of contemplation (*Thomas Merton on St. Bernard,* 82); according to Bernard, Mary's intense desire for the incarnation of the Word is cause as well as model for Christians' hunger and thirst for union with Christ, made possible only through Mary's *fiat* (Luke 1:38) (*Disputed Questions,* 288–89), which restores to humanity a taste for divine realities (*Seasons of Celebration,* 84–85).

The theological focus of Merton's own Mariology shifts noticeably over the course of time. In his earlier discussion of Mary there is a good deal of stress on her intercessory role (see *Run to the Mountain,* 31, 136) and on the figure of Mary as mediatrix of all graces (*Exile Ends in Glory,* 178; *What Are These Wounds?* 118; *Seven Storey Mountain,* 322; *Disputed Questions,* 288; *Last of the Fathers,* 89; *Thomas Merton on St. Bernard,* 84). In later years he will distance himself from what he calls "the medieval idea of *Mediatrix apud mediatorem*... (without prejudice to her motherhood which is a much better statement and truth)" (*Water of Life,* 197). His mature focus is less on Mary as intermediary than as model of perfection in her simplicity and hiddenness: "She was in all things human and ordinary, close to her fellow men, simple and unassuming in her way of life, without drama and without exaltation" (*Disputed Questions,* 227). This is the person revealed in the statue of the Mother and Child that Merton commissioned for the novitiate library in 1958 from the Ecuadorian sculptor Jaime Andrade, the "Holy Mother" as "the Indian woman of the Andes, the representative of all that is most abject,

Sculpture of Mother and Child by Jaime Andrade, photograph by Thomas Merton

forgotten, despised, and put aside" (*Witness to Freedom,* 264).

Yet there are continuities as well. Merton's pages in *Seeds of Contemplation* on the hiddenness of Mary and on true devotion to her as the desire to share her "absolute emptiness, this poverty, this obscurity" (*Seeds of Contemplation,* 103) are amplified by the addition of three new paragraphs on the importance of recognizing her role in salvation in order for faith to be complete in what is now a separate chapter in the revised version of *Seeds of Contemplation* published later the same year with the title "Electa ut Sol," which can be translated "Shining Like the Sun"; all this is taken over into *New Seeds of Contemplation* in a chapter now entitled "The Woman Clothed with the Sun," which adds more than three pages (*New Seeds of Contemplation,* 170–73) clarifying Catholic devotion to Mary not as an attempt to divinize her but as a recognition of her total availability to God and the divine will: "The glory of Mary is purely and simply the glory of God in her, and she, like anyone else, can say that she has nothing that she has not received from Him through Christ. As a matter of fact, this is precisely her greatest glory: that having nothing of her own, retaining nothing of a 'self' that could glory in anything for her own sake, she placed no obstacle to the mercy of God and in no way resisted His love and His will" (170–71).

Merton's devotion to La Soledad, Our Lady of Solitude, in whom, he writes in 1947, his "whole interior life is summed up" (*Entering the Silence*, 112), only deepens as the years pass. "She is the Virgin of Solitude," he writes, "Whom God called His hermit" (*Ascent to Truth*, 317), discovered by the angel praying alone in "virginal silence and solitude," which is completely receptive to the coming of the Word (*Seasons of Celebration*, 85). Perhaps even more central for Merton is the ongoing identification of Mary as "the most perfect expression of the mystery of the Wisdom of God" (*Hidden Ground of Love*, 392) in whom shines "the light of God's own wisdom, the reflection of His own truth, indeed His truth itself" (*Seasons of Celebration*, 164), an identification that culminates in the final section of the prose poem "Hagia Sophia," which is set on the Feast of the Visitation: "Now the Blessed Virgin Mary is the one created being who enacts and shows forth in her life all that is hidden in Sophia. Because of this she can be said to be a personal manifestation of Sophia, Who in God is *Ousia* rather than Person. . . . It is she, it is Mary, Sophia, who in sadness and joy, with the full awareness of what she is doing, sets upon the Second Person, the Logos, a crown which is His Human Nature. Thus her consent opens the door of created nature, of time, of history, to the Word of God" (*Collected Poems*, 369–70). POC

MASSIGNON, LOUIS

Louis Massignon, who was to become one the outstanding scholars of Islam of the twentieth century, was born July 25, 1883, in a suburb of Paris. His father was a sculptor and an agnostic, his mother a Catholic who brought him up in the traditional piety of nineteenth-century Catholicism. Profoundly French, he had a deep respect for Islamic culture. Very early on he was attracted to the famous ninth-century Sufi mystic of Baghdad, al-Hallaj, who was put to death for claiming identification with the divine Reality. Massignon identified with this mystic, and his dissertation at the Sorbonne was "The Passion of al-Hallaj."

Massignon was in contact with Charles de Foucauld, who, after a military career and a brief time in a Trappist monastery, became a hermit in the Algerian desert. Massignon also was in close association with the leaders of the Catholic renascence in France: J. K. Huysmans, Teilhard de Chardin, Gabriel Marcel, Georges Bernanos, François Mauriac, and Jacques Maritain. Married and the father of three children, he was given permission by Pope Pius XII to become a priest in the Melkite rite. This enabled him to align himself more easily with Arab Christians living in Muslim countries. One of his deep commitments was to the concept of "substitution mystique": compassion taking on the sufferings of another and transferring them to oneself. Hallaj gave the name *badal* to this notion. Massignon's interest in this spiritual practice led to the formation of a sodality of the Badaliya. One of the illustrious members of that sodality was Pope Paul VI.

Thomas Merton's contact with Massignon was brought about by Herbert Mason, a young American writer doing research in Paris. Mason became friends with Massignon and urged him to write to Merton. He did so in 1959, thanking Merton for his articles on Pasternak. Their correspondence seems to have been fairly extensive, even though it covered a relatively brief period of time, as Massignon died in 1962. But it is clear that Massignon had a deep influence on Merton, who looked upon him as a spiritual mentor. He wrote to Abdul Aziz (whom Massignon had introduced to Merton), "The departure of Louis Massignon is a great and regrettable loss. He was a man of great comprehension and I was happy to have been numbered among his friends" (*Hidden Ground of Love*, 53). *Witness to Freedom* carries a selection of Merton's letters to Massignon, the only letters available at the time of publication (1994). WHS

MASTER OF NOVICES

In October 1955 Thomas Merton was appointed master of novices at the Abbey of Gethsemani, replacing Fr. Walter Helmstetter, who had been elected abbot of Gethsemani's daughterhouse, Our Lady of the Genesee, in upstate New York. In one way, Merton was a logical choice for the office, having already served since 1951 as master of students, in charge of the training of newly professed monks. But there was an element of unexpectedness and perhaps even of risk in his volunteering to take on the position, as well as in his abbot's acceptance of the offer, for Merton had been going through a recurring "vocation crisis" since the late 1940s, periodically seeking to transfer to an order, such as the Carthusians or Camaldolese, that would satisfy his longing for greater solitude. Immediately before this new development, a tentative compromise solution had been worked out between Merton and Abbot James Fox, and approved by the Cistercian abbot general, Dom Gabriel Sortais, whereby Merton would continue as a Cistercian but live a more solitary life as a fire-watcher atop a tower a few miles from the abbey. Instead Merton decided, as he put it to Dom Gabriel, "to reimmerse myself completely in the true spirit of my vocation" (*School of Charity*, 93) by taking responsibility for the formation of the young men just beginning their monastic life. While his restlessness did not disappear, Merton continued in this demanding position for almost a full decade before leaving in August 1965 for the hermitage where he would spend the final three years of his life.

Merton himself evaluates his decision and its results some four months after becoming novice master in a letter to Dom Jean Leclercq: "My new life as master of novices progresses from day to day. It is an unfamiliar existence to which I often have difficulty in adapting myself. I sometimes feel overcome with sheer horror at having to talk so much and appear before others as an example. I believe that God

is testing the quality of my desire for solitude, in which perhaps there was an element of escape from responsibility. But nevertheless the desire remains the same, the conflict is there, but there is nothing I can do but ignore it and press forward to accomplish what is evidently the will of God" (95). As he writes to Jacques Maritain in the spring of 1956, he takes an interest in the psychological aspect of novitiate formation (*Courage for Truth*, 27), though after his chastening experience with psychiatrist Gregory Zilboorg during the following summer (*Search for Solitude*, 59–60), and what he judged to be a rather unsuccessful attempt to evaluate a disturbed novice (69), he seems to have left psychological analysis to professionals.

Writing to the abbot general in July 1957, he says that he finds the position "a quite comforting office," and adds that his fears that the work would "eventually ruin my famous 'contemplative life'" have not materialized (*School of Charity*, 103), though he does have to remind himself in his journal that his responsibilities to the novices must come first (*Search for Solitude*, 175), and that he must sacrifice his privacy when they need him, and even when they do not (*Turning toward the World*, 86). By the end of 1960 he writes of being drawn to the newly built hermitage but reaffirms the importance of remaining as novice master for the time being (74).

One of the significant dimensions of his responsibilities was the preparation and presentation of conferences for the novices on monastic life and history. In becoming novice master Merton pledged to represent fairly and fully the authentic Cistercian tradition, not an idiosyncratic personal vision. As he wrote to Dom Gabriel, "I have made a vow...not to say anything to the novices that would diminish their respect for the Cistercian cenobitic life and orientate them towards something else" (*School of Charity*, 93). In a letter to a Brazilian monk, written some ten months after he had left the novitiate for the hermitage, Merton outlined the course of studies as it had developed during his tenure as master: "During the novitiate, courses were given on the vows, on Cassian, on Monastic History, on Cistercian

Fathers and history, on ascetic theology, Scripture and the Monastic Fathers, Liturgy, chant. All this was spread over two years" (305). Except for the training in chant, Merton taught all these courses himself for much of his tenure, eventually turning over the Scripture courses to a monk trained in this field (185). Merton also added conferences on modern literature to the program in the final two years of his tenure (305).

The Cistercian novitiate lasted for approximately two years, so the conferences were generally repeated, as Merton notes, according to a two-year cycle, but since there was no common time for beginning the novitiate, individual novices simply joined the ongoing sequence of the conferences at whatever points coincided with their own entry into the novitiate. Generally the young professed monks continued to attend the conferences as part of their ongoing training. The potential awkwardness of this arrangement was reduced by the orientation of the conferences, which was predominantly practical rather than academic. While packed with factual and interpretive material, the conferences' focus was on formation rather than information. Their purpose was not to have the novices master a body of knowledge but to immerse them in a tradition, to allow them to become acclimated to a way of life that reached back in a continuous line to the early centuries of the church. Merton's primary concern for the contemporary pertinence of the material and its application to the lives of his novices is already evident in his carefully prepared notes, which usually were multigraphed for distribution to the novices, and even more so in the tapes of the actual conferences that were recorded in the later years of Merton's tenure (1962–65). While Merton occasionally expressed doubts about the value of the conferences, particularly in the later years of his mastership (*Turning toward the World*, 257, 326), he does acknowledge that his teaching "has been more interesting and has taken a broader view, covered more ground, perhaps gone a little deeper than was usual" (257), and that he has worked hard to make sure the conferences were well prepared.

One of the significant events of the later

years of Merton's time as novice master was the merger of the novitiates of the choir monks and the brothers at the beginning of 1963. This turned out to be a very positive experience that infused Merton with a renewed sense of his contributions in this position. "With the Brothers now in one novitiate with the choir, I certainly have a whole new view of life. There is no question they are 'poorer,' simpler, more vulnerable" (286). As the numbers of people attending his conferences increased, he comments, "My attitude toward the monastery changes. They have need of me and I have need of them. As if without this obedience, and charity, my life would lack sense" (288). Thus, even after his withdrawal to the hermitage Merton would continue to give a weekly conference to the novices and young professed (and anyone else who wished to attend).

Merton's deep love for the novices in his charge is most vividly expressed in a journal entry from late November 1961, when he enters the novitiate scriptorium during a fire watch and experiences the empty room as "full of their hearts and their love." He reflects, "To have been appointed by God to be their Father, to have received them from God as my children, to have loved them and been loved by them with such simplicity and sincerity, without nonsense or flattery or sentimentality; this is completely wonderful and is a revelation, a parousia, of the Lord of History" (183).[1] POC

SEE ALSO MASTER OF STUDENTS.

Notes

1. A revised version of this passage forms the final entry of part 3 of *Conjectures of a Guilty Bystander* (193–94).

MASTER OF STUDENTS

In May 1951, on Trinity Sunday (*Entering the Silence*, 459), Thomas Merton became the first master of students (or scholastics) at the Abbey of Gethsemani. After the regular visitation by the abbot of Melleray in France, Gethsemani's motherhouse, it was decided that the young professed monks (those in simple vows preparing for the priesthood) should have a more organized program of formation. Since November 1949 Merton had been teaching courses to novices and young professed in monastic orientation, Scripture, and mystical theology (372, 375), so that he was a logical choice for the position, which included acting as spiritual director as well as teacher for the group (see *Sign of Jonas*, 303), generally numbering between twenty-five and forty young monks. Six volumes of orientation notes from conferences that Merton presented to the scholastics on Scripture, liturgy, and monastic history and values subsequently were collected and circulated through a number of the houses of the order but remain unpublished. Merton continued as master of students until September 1955; originally he had planned to resign in order to live in greater solitude, but instead he became master of novices when the current master was elected abbot of Gethsemani's daughterhouse, the Abbey of the Genesee in upstate New York.

Merton explains in a 1953 letter that the term "scholasticate" generally was avoided in deference to the reservations of the French abbot, who did not approve of treating the young professed as "a separate group within the community" (*School of Charity*, 56); hence, "master of students" probably is a term preferable to "master of scholastics," though Merton uses both. Actually, one of the plans Merton formulated during the early part of his tenure as master was to establish a separate house of study (in the Colorado Rockies) for the young professed from all or many of the American Cistercian monasteries, an idea that received strong endorsement from the secretary of the Vatican Congregation of Religious when he visited Gethsemani in August 1952 (*Search for Solitude*, 10–11) and that Merton discussed in letters to the abbot general of the order (*School of Charity*, 36–39), but that did not materialize.

Merton initially viewed this position as a providential answer to much of his own vocation struggles of the preceding years, and he considered these struggles as good preparation for working with the young monks. He saw the mastership as an opportunity to be re-formed in Cistercian ideals as "a grown-up monk" who had passed beyond the "monastic adolescence" of his own time as a scholastic (*Entering the Si-*

lence, 460). After six months in the position he evaluated his relationship with his "children" in one of the most celebrated passages of the journals from this period, in which he concluded that this work that he had feared would interfere with his quest for solitude was in fact "the only true path to solitude." As long as there was a prior commitment to solitude, "the care of souls can serve to lead one further into the desert," which he goes on to describe as "the wilderness of compassion, . . . the only desert that shall truly flourish like the lily" (463). Commenting on his charges some weeks later, he says, "They refresh me with their simplicity," and cautions himself about imposing his own "theological complications" on them (466).

Typically for Merton, he eventually (September 13, 1952) questions his role after being advised by another monk that he should be living a more solitary life; he considers his interest in the scholastics as "uselessly human" and now locates the complexity in the job more than in himself: "an occupation that complicates my mind too much for the simplicity of God" (*Search for Solitude*, 15). Yet in mid-February 1953 he expresses his gratitude to the scholastics for simply being who they are and to God for putting him in their midst as their master. He takes a more balanced view that recognizes both the times when he fails to know himself while with them and also the times when he is able to find himself with and in them, times when both he and they come to a deeper self-discovery and "God recognizes Himself in us" (30). It is this view of the position that seems most representative of his general attitude toward his experience as master. POC

SEE ALSO MASTER OF NOVICES.

MCCORMICK, ANNE

Anne McCormick, living in New York City, has for many years been secretary of the Merton Legacy Trust. After James Laughlin's death she was chosen to take his place as one of the trustees. She continues in her role as secretary of the Trust. WHS

MEDITATION

Thomas Merton seems at times to equate meditation and mental prayer, though generally he sees the latter term as misleading, since "we rarely pray with the 'mind' alone" (*Contemplative Prayer*, 34). Sometimes meditation may be the equivalent of what is sometimes called "spiritual reading." A book of "meditations" can prove helpful as a prod to our reflection, but we should not fear to set a book aside. We need, however, to be on the alert when grace calls us to our own reflections and beyond.

When he speaks of meditation, Merton hardly ever intends "discursive meditation," which, since it consists of "busy discursive acts, complex logical reasoning, active imagining and deliberate stirring up of affections," is liable to "conflict with our silent and receptive attention to the inner working of the Holy Spirit" (51). What he normally would intend by the word is the second of the "rungs" on the spiritual "ladder" of *lectio divina*: the resting in the sacred text of Scripture that moves one to reach beyond the levels of imagination and rationalization.

Meditation is not a "place" where we should stay in our life of prayer. It has two purposes: (1) to give us sufficient control over our minds and our wills so that we can be recollected and withdrawn from other concerns, and (2) to help us become aware of the presence of God. "Most of all," Merton says, "it aims at bringing you to a state of almost constant loving attention to God, and dependence on Him" (*New Seeds of Contemplation*, 217). It seems clear that meditation, as Merton sees it, is intended to lead us to contemplation. He writes, "When [meditation] gets beyond the level of your understanding and your imagination, it is really bringing you close to God, for it introduces you into the darkness where you can no longer think of Him and are consequently forced to reach out for Him by blind faith and hope and love" (219). At this point you may be led to "a completely simple form of affective prayer, in which your will with few words or none reaches out into the darkness where God is hidden," or perhaps it may happen that "you relax in a simple contemplative gaze that keeps your attention peacefully aware of Him hidden somewhere in this deep cloud into which you also feel yourself drawn to enter" (219).

In fact there are times when Merton appears to use meditation as synonymous with contemplation. A case in point: *The Climate of Monastic Prayer* (= *Contemplative Prayer* published a year after Merton's death), although clearly concerned with what in his earlier works Merton called "contemplation," consistently uses the term "meditation" instead. Why this change in terminology? It seems plausible to say that he used the term "meditation" in this later work because in the mid-1960s, when he was putting this work together, meditation as a practice borrowed from Eastern religions enjoyed a wide popularity in the West among Christians and non-Christians alike. To such people Merton wanted to make clear that meditation (or contemplation) was more than a psychological exercise aimed at bringing an element of quiet and peace into a person's life, more than a way of relaxing from the cares and problems that life brings. Moreover, he wanted to say that it should not be seen as something new imported from the East. On the contrary, it is a practice deeply rooted in the earliest Christian tradition of prayer, represented, for example, in the prayer of the early desert fathers and mothers and in the mystics of Eastern and Western Christianity. WHS

SEE ALSO CONTEMPLATION; *LECTIO DIVINA*; PRAYER.

MEDITATIONS ON LITURGY
London and Oxford: Mowbrays, 1976. vi+171 pp.

This abridged version of *Seasons of Celebration* was published in Great Britain with an introduction by Basil Hume, archbishop of Westminster. Four essays, published in *Seasons of Celebration*, were deleted: "Liturgy and Spiritual Personalism," "Church and Bishop in St. Ignatius of Antioch," "The Sacrament of Advent in the Spirituality of St. Bernard," and "In Silentio." The remaining eleven essays, slightly rearranged and reordered, include "Liturgical Renewal: The Open Approach," "Time and the Liturgy," "Advent:

Hope or Delusion?" "The Nativity Kerygma,"
"A Homily on Light and the Virgin Mary,"
"The Name of the Lord," "Ash Wednesday,"
"Christian Self-Denial," "Community of Par-
don," "Easter: The New Life," and "The Good
Samaritan." CMB

SEE ALSO SEASONS OF CELEBRATION.

MERCY

Mercy is not something we deduce from our
knowledge of the divine essence; rather, it is revealed in God's relationships with people. This
is the point of the Hebrew word that we translate as "mercy," *chesed*. Thomas Merton writes
of *chesed* in some detail in *Seasons of Celebration*. He sees the Parable of the Good Samaritan
as a revelation of what the prophet Hosea says
about God: "I will have mercy and not sacrifices" (Hos. 6:6). This is the reading of Hosea
that Merton would have found in the Douai-
Rheims translation of the Bible. More recent
translations tend to give a wider meaning to
chesed. The New American Bible renders it as
"love" ("It is love I desire, not sacrifice"). Better
still is the New Revised Standard translation:
"I desire steadfast love and not sacrifice."

Merton's reflection on mercy does tend to
see it in this more expansive sense. "*Chesed*
(mercy) is also fidelity. It is also strength.... It
is ultimate and unfailing love because it is the
power that binds one person to another, in a
covenant of wills" (*Seasons of Celebration*, 175).
Mercy is the covenant promise that binds God
to us and us to God. It is evident in the incarnation of the Word, which is God's irrevocable
expression of the divine love for people. "The
power of His mercy has taken hold of us and
will not let go of us" (181). *Chesed* knows no
classification of good and evil, just or unjust. It
"declassifies" us of both our sins and our virtues.
"God makes his sun rise on the evil and the
good, and sends rain on the righteous and the
unrighteous" (Matt. 5:45). God's love is gratuitous (i.e., pure grace): it does not depend on
our worthiness or our return of love. Merton
writes, "Revelation of the mercy of God makes
the whole problem of worthiness something
almost laughable" (*New Seeds of Contemplation*, 75). But *chesed* also binds us as covenant

partners with God. We express our *chesed* by
showing mercy to our neighbor irrespective of
his or her dignity or merit.

For Merton, mercy is closely linked with
forgiveness, forgiveness being mercy's most
characteristic expression. Yet, mercy is "more
than forensic absolution from sin." It is "an
event in which God reveals himself to us in His
redemptive love and in the great gift which is
the outcome of this event: our mercy to others"
(*Love and Living*, 203). Mercy in God helps us to
understand our restoration to the divine likeness — a truth that is so central to the teaching
of the early church fathers. Mercy in us enables
us to give full expression to the freedom in us
that flows from that divine likeness restored.[1]

God's mercy penetrates to a depth of our
being that is beyond our sinfulness and un-
worthiness. When we ask God for mercy,
we ask God "to be just with a justice so
holy that it knows no evil and shows mercy
to everyone who does not fly from Him in
despair" (*No Man Is an Island*, 210). In a
chapter entitled "The Climate of Mercy" in
Love and Living, Merton quotes a fourteenth-
century English mystic's description of God's
mercy: "He abideth patiently, he forgiveth easily, he understandeth mercifully, he forgeteth
utterly."[2] Merton comments,

> In these simple and profound words mercy is
> identified with God's knowledge of the sin-
> ner. It is not only that God, looking down
> on the sinner as a wretched object, de-
> crees forgiveness, but that He *understands
> mercifully*. His mercy is not merely an an-
> nulment of unpleasant facts, a refusal to see
> an evil that is really there. It is more: it
> is a seeing of the inner meaning of evil,
> not as an entity in itself, but as an inci-
> dent in a saving event, as the *felix culpa*
> of the paschal "Exultet."... God does not
> gaze with grim and implacable revulsion into
> the heart of the sinner to discern there the
> "thing" or the "being" [sin] which He hates.
> He understands the sinner mercifully, that
> is to say, that His look penetrates the whole
> being of the sinner with mercy from within
> so that the inmost reality of the sinner[3] is
> no longer sinfulness but sonship. Then the

power of mercy is free to draw the sinful existent into identity with his inmost being. Alienation is overcome. The sinful consciousness becomes capable of seeing itself face to face with the truth. . . . The mercy of God shows the sinner to himself . . . as having an inner being in which truth is present. (*Love and Living*, 205)

Thus it is that we are able to see ourselves as capable of a grace-filled existence, in which outward behavior is reconciled with our inmost self. And once we have discovered ourselves in God's mercy, we are able to understand others in mercy. Our self-centeredness, which so often makes us pitiless toward others, is dispelled by our trust in the divine mercy. We "are ready to accept our own boundless need in a merciful exchange with others whose poverty is as great as our own!" (207).

In an Ash Wednesday meditation, written in 1958, Merton says that the God of Ash Wednesday is "like a calm sea of mercy." God " 'hides' our sins, . . . like a mother making quick and efficient repairs on the soiled face of a child just before entering a house where he ought to appear clean. . . . He is everywhere shown to us as plenteous in mercy — *multum misericors*" (*Seasons of Celebration*, 120).

Thomas Merton was a man who knew he was a sinner. But he never saw his life (as some have suggested he did) as one long act of penance for his sins. He found joy in the realization that his life was the fruit of divine mercy. At the end of *The Sign of Jonas*, the voice of God is heard in paradise: "*I have always overshadowed Jonas with my mercy, and cruelty I know not at all. Have you had sight of Me, Jonas My child? Mercy within mercy within mercy!*" (*Sign of Jonas*, 362). WHS

SEE ALSO COMPASSION.

Notes

1. In a letter to Lawrence Ferlinghetti, in which Merton denies that he is trying to preach to him, he nevertheless encourages his friend to be faithful to the inner voice of conscience. And he tells him that he does not need to look around for a place to start. It all begins and ends in mercy. Thus he writes, "The mercy of God, unknown and caricatured and blasphemed by some of the most reputable squares, is the central reality out of which all the rest comes and into which all the rest returns" (*Courage for Truth*, 269).

2. Merton does not identify this mystic. A good guess would be Julian of Norwich.

3. The reader might compare this with Merton's "Fourth and Walnut" experience, in which he "suddenly saw the secret beauty of their hearts, the depths of their hearts, where neither sin nor desire nor self-knowledge can reach, the core of their reality, the person that each one is in God's eyes" (*Guilty Bystander*, 142/158).

MERTON, AGNES GERTRUDE STONEHEWER

Agnes Gertrude Stonehewer Merton (1889–1968) was Owen Merton's sister, Tom's aunt "Kit." Together with Gertude Hannah Merton, Owen's mother, she visited the Mertons in Flushing, New York, in June 1919. They stayed several weeks. In November 1961 she visited Tom at Gethsemani. From her he learned a great deal about the family history. On April 25, 1968, Merton learned that fifteen days earlier Aunt Kit had died when the ferryboat *Wahine* sank between the two main islands of New Zealand. The lifeboat she was getting into capsized. Later he heard of the details from his aunt Ka. Nine Merton letters to Aunt Kit are published in *The Road to Joy*. WHS

MERTON, BEATRICE KATHARINE

Born to Alfred and Gertrude Merton in 1891, Beatrice Katharine Merton was Owen Merton's sister, Tom's aunt "Ka." A nurse, she lived in Christchurch, New Zealand. She visited her brother and his children at Douglaston, Long Island, and on Cape Cod in 1922. She died in 1972. Two Merton letters to Aunt Ka are published in *The Road to Joy*. WHS

MERTON, GERTRUDE HANNAH (GRIERSON)

The Grierson family had immigrated to New Zealand in 1864. The father, John Grierson (a Scot), married Elizabeth Bird (Welsh). Gertrude was nine years old when the family came to New Zealand. On December 18, 1882, Gertrude Hannah Grierson married Alfred Merton. (The Merton family had immigrated to New Zealand several years before the Griersons.) Gertrude and Alfred had six children, including Beatrice Katharine (Tom's aunt Ka), Agnes Gertrude Stonehewer (Tom's aunt Kit), Owen Heathcote Grierson (Tom's father), and Gwynedd Fanny Merton Trier (Tom's aunt Gwyn).

In 1920 Gertrude Merton, accompanied by Aunt Kit, visited Owen and Ruth Merton and their two sons, Tom and John Paul. Thomas Merton recalls that visit in *The Seven Storey Mountain* (9). He speaks of her gentleness and affection and remembers that she put salt on her oatmeal and taught him the say the Lord's Prayer. Writing to Sr. Therese Lentfoehr on August 5, 1955, he asks her to pray for his "New Zealand grandmother who is really OLD. She is going to be a hundred on that day" (*Road to Joy*, 220). She died the next year at the age of 101. WHS

MERTON, GWYNEDD FANNY

SEE TRIER, GWYNEDD FANNY MERTON.

MERTON, JOHN PAUL

John Paul Merton, Thomas Merton's only sibling, was born in Flushing, Queens, in the city of New York on November 2, 1918. John Paul was a month under three when his mother died in the hospital. At the time of Ruth's death, he and Tom and Owen were living with the Jenkinses in Douglaston. Both boys eventually were registered at Public School 98 in Douglaston. In 1925 Owen took Tom with him to France. John Paul was left with the Jenkinses. He attended the choir school at the cathedral of St. John the Divine. Later he entered the military academy at Gettysburg, Pennsylvania, where he graduated with the academy's last class in 1935. By this time Tom had returned from England and was registered at Columbia. In October 1935 John Paul matriculated at Cornell University in Ithaca, New York. In Ithaca he got to know the Miscall family. Leonard and Rovere Miscall, who had a son and daughter more or less John Paul's age, "adopted" him, and he came to consider the Miscalls rather than the Jenkinses as his family. He gave their

address as his home address and made Rovere Miscall the executrix of his will.

In June 1940, after classes were over, he drove to Mexico in his Buick with plans to live there. These plans were short-lived. After a brief stay he returned to Ithaca and once more lived with the Miscalls. That, too, was a short stay. In September 1940, the time that Tom took a teaching position at St. Bonaventure, John Paul went to Toronto and enlisted in the Royal Canadian Air Force. He listed his occupation as "photographer."

In July 1942, on embarkation leave, John Paul visited his brother (now a monk at Gethsemani). They spoke about John Paul's baptism into the Catholic Church. (John Paul became interested in Catholicism while at Cornell, where he had taken up flying together with Fr. Donald Cleary, the Catholic chaplain.) With only a week remaining before he had to return to Canada, he was given instructions by Tom and by Dom James Fox and was baptized on the Feast of St. Anne (July 26, 1942) at the Church of St. Catherine of Alexandria in New

John Paul Merton

Haven, Kentucky. Rocco Dawson, son of Senator Edwin Dawson, was godfather. He took his conversion seriously, much to the joy of his brother. Then it was back to Canada and off to England.

In late August John Paul arrived in Liverpool at the bomber command in Buckinghamshire. From there he went off to Bournemouth for training. On his disembarkation leave he took the train to London, where he visited the American Eagle Club, set up for Americans in the RAF. While in London he met Margaret May Evans, a typist, who had enlisted in the British armed forces. They fell in love and were married, February 1943, at St. Laurence Church in Birkenhead (her hometown) by Canon William Griffin. They spent their honeymoon in the Lake District.

On April 16 "Mert" (as John Paul was called) took off in a crew of five in a Wellington bomber. For a reason that has never been discovered, the plane began to lose altitude and finally crashed into the English Channel. Two members of the crew were able to get into the inflated dinghy. They managed to pull Merton on board. His back was broken in the fall. He was conscious for a while and spent much of his time praying. Finally he died in the early hours of Saturday, April 17, the Saturday of Passion Week. They watched over his body for two days, hoping for rescue. Eventually it came, but too late for Merton. His two comrades had buried him at sea, in as Christian a manner as possible, according to Eric Hadingham, one of the two members of the crew who survived. They were rescued on Holy Thursday, April 22, 1943. On Easter Tuesday, Thomas Merton was called to the abbot's office to be informed that his brother had been killed in action. Thomas Merton's sorrowing response was his poem (the poem that originally closed *The Seven Storey Mountain*) "For My Brother Reported Missing in Action, 1943." WHS

SEE ALSO *SEVEN STOREY MOUNTAIN; THIRTY POEMS.*

MERTON, OWEN

Owen Heathcote Grierson Merton was born in Christchurch, New Zealand, May 14, 1887, to Alfred Merton and Gertrude Grierson. Alfred Merton was music master at Christ's College and organist at the cathedral of Christchurch. Owen attended Christ's College. (A classmate at the college, Thomas Izod Bennett, immigrated to England and became a distinguished surgeon in London. Later Bennett attended Owen in London during his long agony from a brain tumor. After Owen's death Bennett became Tom Merton's guardian.) Owen showed early signs of talent in both music and painting. The latter became his life's work. In 1904 he visited London for a two-year stay and created a favorable impression as a young watercolorist. In 1909 he left New Zealand for good. In September of 1910 he moved to Paris and began studying under Percyval Tudor-Hart, a wealthy Canadian who had set up his own art school and who became Owen's longtime patron and friend.

In Paris he fell in love with Ruth Jenkins, and on April 7, 1914, they were married in St. Anne's Church in the Soho district of London. The five persons listed as witnesses included Owen's sister Gwyn and his aunt Maud and her husband, Benjamin Pearce. Immediately after the wedding they returned to Paris and then made their way to southern France, where they settled in the town of Prades in French Catalonia. On January 31, 1915, their son Tom was born. War conditions in France moved them to make their way to America. They sailed from Bordeaux on the SS *La Touraine* and arrived in New York on August 15, 1916. Ruth's parents, Sam and Martha, were at the pier waiting for them. Initially the Mertons stayed with Ruth's parents at Douglaston, but within the year they moved to a small house of their own at 57 Hillside Avenue. Merton remembered it as "a small house, very old and rickety, standing under two or three high pine trees, in Flushing, Long Island" (*Seven Storey Mountain*, 7). Owen set to work as a landscape gardener. He also was organist in Zion Episcopal Church and sometimes played the organ at the local movie house.

On November 2, 1918, Ruth gave birth to a second son, John Paul. The following year Owen's mother, Gertrude Hannah Merton, visited them and stayed for several weeks. Owen and Ruth had not lost their love for France. They spoke French in the house and yearned to return to France. That yearning would never be satisfied for Ruth. In 1920 she became very ill and was diagnosed with stomach cancer. She was taken to the Bellevue public hospital, where her condition rapidly worsened. From one of his visits to her Owen brought back a letter from her to Tom telling him he would never see her again. The letter left the young lad puzzled and grieving. Ruth died on October 3, 1921.

In the winter of 1921–22 Owen went to Bermuda alone; in October 1922 he returned to Bermuda, this time taking Tom with him and leaving John Paul with the Jenkins grandparents. It was a short stay, but while there Owen managed to fall in love with Evelyn Scott, a novelist who probably deserves better notice as a novelist than she ever received. Evelyn's husband, Cyril Kay-Scott, seemed to have known of the affair, but looked at it with a benign indifference. In fact, in 1923 the three of them traveled to France, where they stayed for some months, crossing over to Algeria in

Owen Merton

October 1923 and then returning to France in the spring of 1924. Owen did some of his best painting during this period. In 1925 he had a successful show at the Leicester Galleries in London.[1] He was able to return to his children (both staying with the Jenkinses) with money in his pocket.

In August 1925 Owen and his elder son left New York and in September arrived in France, where they took up residence in St. Antonin in southern France. In January 1926 Owen purchased land and made plans to build a home for himself and his two boys. That same year Sam and Martha Jenkins, with John Paul, came to St. Antonin for a visit, and all five did a quick tour of Europe under Sam's leadership. It was then that the decision was made that Tom would study at the Lycée Ingres at Montauban. The time at Montauban was not easy for this eleven-year-old boy. He was lonely and desolate and sad, but eventually he adjusted. Two years later, in 1928, Owen announced that they were going to England. Tom was overjoyed that he suddenly was free. The house that Owen had intended to build remained unfinished. Owen wanted to be a good father, but he also wanted to be distinguished as a painter. All too often the artist role won out over that of the father.

In England they stayed at Ealing with Aunt Maud (Maud Mary Grierson Pearce) and Uncle Ben (Benjamin Pearce). Tom spent a year at Ripley Court School, a much gentler place than the French lycée. In the fall of 1929 he was ready to enter the Oakham public school. Before completing his studies at Oakham, he learned that his father was seriously ill. Uncle Ben told him the sad truth that Owen had a malignant tumor on the brain. Tom visited his father in the hospital. Owen told him that the doctors (including Tom Izod Bennett, his one-time schoolmate in New Zealand) were doing all they could for him. "Pray for me," he said. In the summer of 1930 the Jenkinses, with John Paul, came to England and spent much of their time at the hospital, where Owen's health was rapidly failing. They often were in touch with Tom Bennett. Sam Jenkins liked him and saw him as a role model for his grandson and a good choice to be his guardian in the event of Owen's death.

On January 18, 1931, Owen Merton died at the Middlesex Hospital of a brain tumor. It was just thirteen days short of Thomas Merton's sixteenth birthday. WHS

Notes

1. Owen had an equally important exhibit at the Leicester Galleries in 1928, and earlier had had solo exhibits at the Daniel Gallery, New York, in 1923 and 1925.

MERTON, RUTH CALVERT JENKINS

Ruth, daughter of Samuel Adams Jenkins (1862–1936) and Martha (Mattie) Caroline Baldwin, was born in Zanesville, Ohio, in 1887. Her brother, Harold Brewster Jenkins, was born two years later in 1889. The family moved to Philadelphia in 1898, where Sam set up a stationery store. Within the year they were in New York City, where Sam joined the publishing house of Grosset and Dunlap as editor and publicist. The family lived in Manhattan near St. John the Divine Cathedral until 1913, when they built a house at 50 Virginia Road in Douglaston, Queens. Ruth attended various schools, public and private. In 1909 she graduated with distinction from Bradford Academy in Haverhill, Massachusetts. Her interest was in art and she chose to study in Paris at L'École National des Arts Decoratifs.

While in Paris she met Owen Merton, who had come from New Zealand and was studying art with Percyval Tudor-Hart, a wealthy Canadian who had established his own art school in the French capital. Ruth and Owen fell in love and were married in London at St. Anne's Church, in Soho, in April 1914. They left immediately after the wedding, taking boat and train to Paris, and then went on to Prades in French Catalonia, where they settled down and where Tom Merton was born on January 31, 1915 (Ruth insisted that his name be "Tom," not "Thomas"). In 1916, with a war raging in Europe, they sailed from Bordeaux to New York. Eventually they took a house in Flushing, New York, near Douglaston.

On November 2, 1918, a second son, John Paul, was born. The Mertons led a penurious existence, Owen working as a landscape gar-

Ruth Jenkins Merton

dener and sometimes playing the organ at Zion Church and at the local movie house. At home Ruth and Owen always spoke French to one another and longed to return to Paris. But that was not to be. Ruth's health deteriorated, and in the summer of 1921 she was taken to Bellevue, the huge public hospital in the city. She was suffering from stomach cancer. On one of Owen's visits to the hospital Ruth gave him a letter to give to Tom telling him that she would never see him again. She died on October 3, 1921. WHS

SEE ALSO "TOM'S BOOK."

MERTON LEGACY TRUST, THE

This trust agreement, made on the 14th day of November 1967, established as Trustees Naomi Stone, James Laughlin, and Thomasine O'Callaghan. The trustees were given responsibility for Thomas Merton's literary estate and for any future publication of his works, it being understood that all income from these publications belongs to the Abbey of Gethsemani.

Bellarmine College (now University) was named as the depository for all Merton's manuscripts, tapes, drawings, photographs, and kindred items, to be kept in the Merton Room of Bellarmine College. The trustees are to set the policies for dealing with these materials.

All drafts of books existing in manuscript and not yet published may be published with the exception of two books: "The Inner Experience" and "The School of the Spirit." These are not to be published as books. The trustees may permit qualified scholars to quote from said works.

The trustees may publish essays, poems, and other unfinished material. They may make available to Merton's biographer his letters, holographic notebooks, journals, and diaries marked "private" and "not for publication."

After the biography is completed and after twenty-five years from the date of Merton's death, the trustees are to publish such holographic notebooks, journals, and diaries, in whole or in part, as they see fit.

They may determine the appropriateness of publishing a selection or collection of Merton letters.

They may make available to qualified persons his nonconfidential notes, reading notes, and typed or handwritten notes of conferences.

They shall be responsible for making all contracts regarding the copyright and general promotion of all his published works, including the selection of the publisher and promoter. They are to promote a general public interest in all his works.

They will grant written permission to copy or publish or exhibit his drawings, paintings, and photographs.

They are never to make a contract that will lead to autobiographical materials about Merton or materials of his about Gethsemani being filmed or dramatized on radio or presented on television.

At the end of the trust agreement there is list of places where Merton collections are held: Bellarmine College, St. Bonaventure University, Boston University, Boston College, and Columbia University. Also listed are private collections, such as those of Sr. Therese Lent-

foehr (now at Columbia), Ed Rice, Naomi Stone, and James Laughlin.

Also given is a list of items that are to be physically transferred to the official collection at Bellarmine College: collections of essays (which mostly have appeared in magazines); manuscripts of unpublished books, such as "The Inner Experience" and "Prayer as Worship and Experience"; other manuscripts, such as notes of "Rilke" and "Art and Worship"; and some personal notes and "Sentences."

When Naomi Stone resigned as trustee, Robert Giroux was chosen to take her place. When James Laughlin died, Anne McCormick, longtime secretary of the Merton Trust, was appointed as trustee in his place. Mrs. McCormick remains as secretary of the Merton Trust. John Ford is the lawyer of the Merton Trust, a position he has held since the trust agreement went into effect. WHS

MILOSZ, CZESLAW

Born in Lithuania in 1911, Nobel Prize winning author Czeslaw Milosz was active in the resistance in Poland during World War II and published an anthology of resistance poetry. After the war Milosz worked for the Polish diplomatic service and in 1951 sought political asylum in France, where he wrote several novels and published several volumes of poetry. In 1953 he published *The Captive Mind,* an exploration of the plight of Polish intellectuals in a repressive regime. When Thomas Merton read the book several years later, he wrote to Milosz, initiating a correspondence that continued for a decade until Merton's death in 1968. Though they lived quite different lives — Merton a monk in rural Kentucky and Milosz an expatriate living in Paris and then a university professor at Berkeley — they had much in common. Both were prolific working writers and insightful critics of contemporary society and American culture — though they did not always see eye to eye, which makes their correspondence all the more interesting.[1] They not only exchanged and debated ideas — about books and writers, war and freedom, faith and church — but also shared a deep friendship. Merton's regard for Milosz was evident from the start: "Sense of dealing, for once, with a real person, with one who has awakened out of sleep" (*Search for Solitude*, 264). They met twice: in September 1964 at Gethsemani, and in October 1968 in California, just before Merton left for Asia.

For Merton's letters to Milosz, see *Courage for Truth*, 53–86. For their exchange of letters, see *Striving towards Being*. CMB

Notes

1. Milosz was critical of Merton's writings on peace, which he read in the light of his own experience of life in a totalitarian regime. See *The Courage for Truth* (esp. 79–81) and *Striving towards Being* (esp. 138–40). Milosz also characterized Merton's views on nature, as expressed in *The Sign of Jonas*, as romantic.

MIM TEA ESTATE

This tea plantation, reached from Darjeeling, has a wonderful view of Mt. Kanchenjunga. Thomas Merton stayed here in a bungalow from November 17 to 19, 1968. It was a time of retreat for him and an opportunity to evaluate what his Asian trip had meant to him up to that point (*Other Side of the Mountain*, 279–87). WHS

MONASTERY OF CHRIST IN THE DESERT

Abiquiu, N.Mex.: Monastery of Christ in the Desert, 1967. 16 pp.

This illustrated pamphlet, issued by the Primitive Benedictine monastery in New Mexico, provides a brief description of the abbey (*Christ in the Desert*, 2–3), founded from Mount Saviour Monastery in 1964, followed by Thomas Merton's short essay "Christ in the Desert," the main text of the volume. Merton begins by noting that it may be misleading to call Christian monastic life "contemplative," a term more Platonic than biblical, associated with an aristocratic form of intellectual life for a privileged elite. Christian monasticism is, rather, an experience of the wilderness, the desert associated with the exodus, Christ's temptations, and John the Baptist, which includes but transforms the *bios theoretikos* (the life of vision) of Greek philosophy. It entails

not speculation but experience, not philosophy but worship, not gnostic illumination but humility and love. It is one form of the universal Christian vocation to leave all and follow Christ. Merton points out that the New Mexico monastery is a perfect expression of the "desert" character of monasticism, in its isolation, its setting in the pueblo country, and its buildings, well integrated into the stark landscape. It is a place for both the community and guests to readjust their perspective. "While not blindly rejecting and negating the modern world, the monastery nevertheless retains a certain critical distance and perspective which are absolutely necessary as mass society becomes at once more totally organized and more mindlessly violent. In its firm assertion of basic human values as well as of God's message of salvation, the monastery bears witness to the most fundamental and most permanent truths of life" (12). Christ in the Desert is a small seed seeking to plant its roots in the rocks and sand of its setting, with no great ambitions except to live out the complete simplicity of Benedictine monasticism in its most authentic primitive form — a communal life a prayer, study, work, and praise in the silence of the desert. Though Merton wrote this essay without having been

Monastery of Christ in the Desert, photograph by Thomas Merton

to the monastery (he would have seen the photographs included in the pamphlet), he visited Christ in the Desert twice the following year, in the spring during his first trip to the West (May 16–20) (*Other Side of the Mountain,* 103–8) and again in mid-September at the beginning of the journey that would take him to Asia (174–77). POC

MONASTICISM

In considering Thomas Merton's response to monasticism and to his own monastic vocation, it is helpful to think in terms of four broad phases. The first phase extends from his entrance into the Abbey of Gethsemani in December 1941 through the late 1940s, when he takes his final vows (March 1947), publishes his autobiography (October 1948), and is ordained a priest (May 1949). A major element of this period is his desire to recover what he considers the authentically contemplative character of Cistercianism. It is marked by intense study of St. Bernard and other early Cistercian fathers, and it results in the publication of three volumes toward the end of this period that indicate his perspective on the order he has joined. *The Spirit of Simplicity* is a hybrid book, in which the translation of the official 1925 document on Cistercian simplicity, which Merton considered too focused on externals (*Spirit of Simplicity,* ii), is supplemented by his own collection of texts from St. Bernard on interior simplicity, along with his own commentary. He suggests that "due to ignorance or lack of contact with the sources of Cistercian spirituality" (iii), many members of the order may not be fully aware of the significance of this theme, which is aimed above all at *"getting rid of everything that did not help the monk to arrive at union with God by the shortest possible way"* (iii). Thus, his emphasis is on the intrinsically contemplative character of Cistercian spirituality: "St. Bernard does not hesitate to promise, as the *normal term* of the Cistercian life of simplicity, a perfect union of wills with God, by love, which he calls the Mystical Marriage" (80). But it is essential in attaining this simplicity to "enter into contact, directly or at least indirectly with the sources from which it flowed" (138). In his pamphlet

Cistercian Contemplatives, the title is a significant indicator of Merton's perspective. He is interested in showing that Cistercians are contemplatives not merely in the juridical sense, members of a cloistered contemplative order, but that the true charism of the order is to produce genuine contemplatives, men drawn to intimate union with God in silence and solitude (*Cistercian Contemplatives,* 9). While he acknowledges that "the uninterrupted community life of the Cistercian doubtless deprives him of certain consolations and of a certain facility in contemplation which will be arrived at more easily by the pure solitary" (19), it also protects against the dangers of eccentricity and delusion. In touching on what he calls the "providential" reform of the Abbé de Rancé in the seventeenth century, he claims that "de Rancé himself never arrived at a full appreciation of the contemplative spirit of the first Cistercians" (23). This assertion of the inadequacy of the Trappist reform becomes a major theme of his history of the order, *The Waters of Siloe,* in which he states that "unless a Trappist is a Cistercian, he is not quite what he ought to be" (*Waters of Siloe,* xxii). His point is that "the contemplative life, in the strict sense of the word, seems to have remained abortive at La Trappe," where the atmosphere "was one of athletic activity rather than of contemplative detachment and peace" (46). The antidote to the "patchwork" character of Trappist life (300), in which contemplation was regarded as a means to penance rather than vice versa — "Never was a cart put more squarely before the horse," Merton comments (301) — is a return to the original vision of the founders of the order and the great saints of the twelfth century, who saw the essence of their monastic life as intimacy with God and stressed love rather than self-abasement as the center of Cistercian spirituality. In concluding the book Merton cites the proverb *"Bibe aquam de cisterna tua* ('Drink the water of thy own well')" (350) to emphasize his commitment to a process that already had begun in the order but that he thinks still has a long way to go, the recovery of the sources of authentic Cistercian life and teaching. Even so, it is already evident in *The Seven Storey Mountain* that Merton's yearning for a more solitary vocation is exerting its influence. When he confesses to his novice master that Carthusian solitude still attracts him, the only answer he receives is that the Carthusian life is less penitential, a more "Trappist" than "Cistercian" response (*Seven Storey Mountain*, 384). He is surprisingly frank in his criticism of the busyness he finds at Gethsemani. "For it seems to me that our monasteries produce very few pure contemplatives. The life is too active. There is too much movement, too much to do. That is especially true of Gethsemani. It is a powerhouse, and not merely a powerhouse of prayer. In fact, there is an almost exaggerated reverence for work in the souls of some who are here.... It goes by the name of 'active contemplation.' The word active is well chosen. About the second half of the compound, I am not so sure" (389).

The second phase runs from the end of the 1940s to about the end of 1957. During this period Merton's own restlessness about his vocation leads him to make repeated, if somewhat sporadic, efforts to transfer to a more solitary order, the Carthusians (especially in mid-1949) or the Camaldolese (particularly in mid-1955). At the same time, he is quite involved in the process of training young monks at Gethsemani to become good Cistercians, first as a teacher, then from 1951 to 1955 as master of students, and at the end of this period as master of novices. So there is a definite tension between his public role and his private yearnings during this time. The characteristic monastic writings from this period are *The Sign of Jonas* from the early part, and *The Silent Life* and *Basic Principles of Monastic Spirituality* from the end. The first, his edited journal from the years 1946 to 1952, presents a period he describes in the prologue as "an unusual moment of crisis and transition" in which a house designed to hold seventy monks is filled and overfilled with 270. He writes of "traveling toward my destiny in the belly of a paradox" (*Sign of Jonas*, 11), both his attempt to combine the vocations of writer and monk and his search for solitude in the midst of a monastery bursting at the seams. In particular, "the vow of stability has been the belly of the whale" (10) because "God pointed one way and all my 'ideals' pointed in another"

(10). Though he indicates that the theme of the book is his discovery of "[his] own solution to this problem" (10), in fact the problem will recur in various forms throughout his life. In *No Man Is an Island*, from the middle of this period, the chapter on vocation includes an extensive discussion of monasticism, with a strong emphasis on the monastic life as a life of complete interior conversion leading to interior and fraternal peace (*No Man Is an Island*, 144–46). He considers both the centrality of life under a rule and "the relative unimportance of exterior observance when it is compared with the interior spirit and the real essentials of the monastic life" (149). Likewise, he stresses the importance of tradition, of a life in direct continuity with the rich wisdom handed down from the past, but warns that this must not be confused with dead conventionalism, a passive acceptance of routine and external practices that leads not to creativity and vitality but to slavish imitation (149–50). In *The Silent* Life he describes the varieties of monastic life, Benedictine, Cistercian, Camaldolese (which also follows the Benedictine Rule in a more eremitic fashion), and Carthusian (which has its own rule). In a sense this work is both an expression of his attraction toward other, more solitary forms of monasticism, and perhaps to some extent a way of exorcising it, of entering into the Carthusian and Camaldolese life in a literary rather than a literal way. *Basic Principles of Monastic Spirituality*, an overview of monastic life as a specific way of following Christ, "sharing His life, participating in His action, united with Him in His worship of the Father" (*Monastic Journey*, 15),[1] does not focus on the varieties of expression (being written primarily for young monks at Gethsemani) and so represents a view that to some extent transcends the conflicts that Merton himself feels about the best way for him to be a monk. Near the conclusion of the pamphlet he emphasizes that the traditional monastic theme of flight from the world is by no means to be interpreted as a diminishment of the monk's "love for and concern with all those souls redeemed by Christ ... and above all for those who, loved and sought by Christ, never think of Him and have never, perhaps, heard His holy name" (34–35). In the epilogue,

"The Monk in a Changing World," he also distinguishes between the "many secondary and transient aspects of the Christian and monastic lives," which will have to be adapted or even discarded, and the essentials of monastic spirituality, "solitude, poverty, obedience, silence, humility, manual labour, prayer and contemplation," which will remain at the center of any authentic monastic vocation (36). In this focus on relations with the wider world and on the process of monastic renewal he introduces themes that will continue to engage his attention for the rest of his life.

The third period, extending from early 1958 through August 1965, corresponds to most of Merton's term as Gethsemani's novice master, but also is the time when he opens up to the world again and becomes involved in social and political issues, symbolized most vividly by the "Fourth and Walnut" experience of March 1958. The temptation of this period is not to join an already existing order but to become part of some sort of less structured eremitical life, whether associated with Dom Gregorio Lemercier's experimental Benedictine monastery in Cuernavaca, Mexico, or with Ernesto Cardenal's development of a new form of monastic life on the island of Solentiname in Nicaragua, or as a hermit in Nevada, or on the island of Tortola, or elsewhere (see especially the letters collected in the section entitled "Vocation Crisis: 1959–1960" [*Witness to Freedom*, 200–230]). Merton's monastic writings during this period are marked by concern with monastic renewal, eventually in the context of the call for renewal of religious life during the Second Vatican Council. In *Monastic Peace*, a pamphlet from early 1958, he begins, significantly, by situating monasticism in the context of the universal Christian call to be a peacemaker. He goes on to speak of cenobitic monastic discipline as "not the submersion of a personality in the social whole . . . but the emancipation of the person through his full and mature participation in the common life" (*Monastic Journey*, 53). He warns of the danger of juridical rigidity, and stresses that authentic obedience must be an expression of freedom rather than its abdication (65), and that spiritual maturity is "the ability to govern one's own life from

within, and not merely to conform to exterior standards" (77).

He writes repeatedly about how the structure needs to serve the spirit rather than vice versa. Monastic observance must never be reduced to "the maintenance of an institution whose function is to proclaim the superiority of the feudal and hierarchical way of life as that which is fully and authentically 'Christian' because it bears witness to the days when the Church enjoyed uncontested temporal power" (*Seeds of Destruction*, 205). Any hint of a "ghetto" spirit, concentrating too exclusively on a return to the letter rather than the spirit, is unfaithful to the true Benedictine charism (*Guilty Bystander*, 6). In particular, a "glorification of monasticism as part of the glorification of an essentially medieval culture has been, in fact, disastrous for monks" (162) because it preferred anachronistic "accidentals" to perennially valid charisms, and so too often stifled the Spirit. Merton's vision for monasticism in the contemporary world is of a life "of complete liberty from the pressures and confusions of 'the world' in the bad sense of the word, and even from the more 'worldly' side of the Church, so that the monk, isolated and at liberty, can on the one hand give himself to God and to the Word of God, attain to a truly Christian understanding of the needs and sufferings of the men of his time (from his special vantage point of poverty, labor, solitude and insecurity) and also enter into dialogue with those who are not monks and not even Christians" (*Seeds of Destruction*, 319). This certainly describes elements of monastic life that he tried to live out himself during this period.

The fourth phase of his monastic life is spent, of course, in the hermitage, from August 1965 until his departure for Asia in the fall of 1968. The great temptation during this period is, of course, to abandon eremitic and monastic life altogether because of his love for the nurse he met during the spring of 1966, but by the fall of that year he had taken his vow to remain a Cistercian hermit until his death, health permitting (see *School of Charity*, 419). His many essays on monastic renewal during this period continue to emphasize the relationship of monasticism to the whole church and to the wider world. The purpose of monastic life is to serve as a privileged, though by no means exclusive, witness to the contemplative and eschatological dynamism of the church as a whole. "The monastic life," when it is truly faithful to its essential charism, "is alive with the eschatological mystery of the kingdom already shared and realized in the lives of those who have heard the Word of God and have surrendered unconditionally to its demands in a vocation that (even when communal) has a distinctly 'desert' quality" (*World of Action*, 199). As with the church as a whole, the monastery will not fulfill this role as eschatological sign simply by its institutional functioning; it must have a dynamic rather than a static relationship to the kingdom: "The monastic community does not effectively act as a sign of God's presence and of His kingdom merely by the fulfillment of certain symbolic functions" (207). Whenever the charismatic freedom of the contemplative is replaced by "an organizational mystique, so that in effect it is the institution itself that becomes definitive," there is a danger of confusing means with ends, of considering the structures or rules "as the incarnation of God's definitive truth, as the practical realization of the Kingdom" (193). If the monk is one who "sees and experiences the Kingdom of Promise as already fulfilled" (188), it is not due to formal arrangements, those, for example, which "keep the monks strictly enclosed and remote from all external activity — this does not by itself constitute a sign of the eschatological kingdom" (207–8); rather, it is the spiritual gift of charismatic solitude that makes possible "a recovery of paradisal simplicity, of wilderness obedience and trust, and an anticipated completion in blessed light" (188). POC

SEE ALSO ABBOT; CAMALDOLESE; CARTHUSIANS; CISTERCIANS; CONTEMPLATION IN A WORLD OF ACTION; HERMIT; MONASTIC JOURNEY; MONK; *SILENT LIFE*.

Notes

1. Both *Basic Principles of Monastic Spirituality* and *Monastic Peace* are included in *The Monastic Journey*, the posthumous collection of a number of Merton's monastic essays.

MONASTIC JOURNEY, THE

Edited by Patrick Hart. Kansas City, Mo.: Sheed Andrews and McMeel, 1977. xii + 187 pp.

Thomas Merton wrote books on the monastic life (e.g., *The Waters of Siloe*, *The Silent Life*), but also many articles. In this volume Br. Patrick Hart has gathered articles written between 1957 and 1967 (all but two in 1964 or later), some already published, a few unpublished. The book has three parts and three appendices.

Part 1, "The Monastic Vocation," is made up of three essays that had previously been published, in pamphlet form, at the Abbey of Gethsemani: (1) "What Is the Monastic Life?" ([1965] 3–10); (2) "Basic Principles of Monastic Spirituality" ([1957] 11–38); and (3) "Monastic Peace" ([1958] 39–84).

Part 2, "Monastic Themes," also has three essays: (1) "The Humanity of Christ in Monastic Prayer" ([1964] 87–106); (2) "Conversion of Life" ([1966] 107–20); and (3) "Monastic Attitudes: A Matter of Choice" ([1967] 121–32).

Part 3, "The Solitary Life," likewise has three essays: (1) "Project for a Hermitage" ([draft 1964, unpublished] 134–43); (2) "Wilderness and Paradise" ([1967, review of two books] 144–50); and (3) "The Solitary Life" ([previously published 1960, limited edition by Carolyn and Victor Hammer] 151–62).

The three appendices are (1) "Monastic Renewal: A Memorandum" ([draft February 1964] 165–68); (2) "A Letter on the Contemplative Life" ([written at the request of Pope Paul VI and sent to Dom Francis Decroix, August 21, 1967] 169–73); and (3) "Contemplatives and the Crisis of Faith" ([a collaborative text, by Dom J.-B. Porion, Dom André Louf, and Thomas Merton, sent to the synod of bishops meeting in Rome, October 1967] 174–78).

The book concludes with four pages of notes and a select bibliography (179–85).

The theme of the book could be summed up in the title of the first article: "What Is the Monastic Life?" It is a question asked by "outsiders" who visit a monastery and wonder why monks live the way they do: in silence, in an enclosure that severely limits their contact with people outside the monastery. Are they happy? Do they find their lives meaning-ful? What people do not always realize is that these are questions that monks have to face too. In the religious void of today's world the monk must deal with the doubts and struggles that all men and women are obliged to face. A monk knows all too clearly in his own life "the possibility of infidelity and failure" (*Monastic Journey*, 5). He also knows that he is called to hear the gospel with the utmost seriousness. "He is bound, by his faith in Christ, to develop a *special awareness* of the spiritual possibilities and hazards of human life" (6–7).

The monk must live by the word of God, as he seeks to penetrate the words of Scripture, reflecting on them in *lectio divina*, celebrating them in liturgy, keeping them in his heart day and night. This means living "consciously in an atmosphere of prayer" (60). The monas-tery should be a place of peace where monks surrender "their minds and wills to the call of Christ" and find their reality in him (40). "The monastery remains in the world, but not of the world, as a vision of peace, a window open-ing on the perspectives of an utterly different realm, a new creation, an earthly paradise in which God once again dwells with men and is almost visibly their God, their peace and their consolation" (43).

The Cistercian monk takes three vows: obedience, stability, and conversion of life (*conversio [conversatio] morum*, literally, "con-version of manners"). He "makes no explicit vows of poverty and chastity, for they are con-tained implicitly in the vow of 'conversion of manners,' which covers all the peculiar means by which the monk seeks God in the mon-astery" (64). Merton discusses obedience on pp. 64–66, and stability ("permanent and life-long attachment to the monastery of one's profession") on pp. 66–68. *Conversio morum* is given a whole chapter in part 2. Poverty and chastity, as elements of *conversio morum*, are dealt with on pp. 62–63.

The term *conversio morum*, Merton sug-gests, is "both ambiguous and quaint" (108). It involves a commitment to make constant progress in virtue. The monk can never say that he has done enough. It means following the Sermon on the Mount and renouncing all care

in complete dependence on God. "It is the vow to respond totally and integrally to the word of Christ, 'Come, follow Me' by renouncing all that might impede one in following Him un-trammelled, all that might obscure one's clarity of intent and confuse one's resolve" (110). Such a vow is a source of peace. It is the peace of Christ, which comes where there is a "will-ingness to renounce our petty selves and find our true selves beyond ourselves in others, and above all in Christ" (40).

Part 2 has a helpful chapter on the humanity of Christ in monastic prayer. What role does the humanity of Christ play in the prayer of the monk (or of any Christian)? In dealing with this question, one must distinguish being human in mortal life from another way of being human: in risen, immortal life. The early fathers, Mer-ton points out, reflected on Jesus' earthly life much as they reflected on the Hebrew Scrip-tures, as something that had been radically changed and brought to perfection. They med-itated on events in the historical life of Jesus as past events "in order to come to contemplation of Christ in His present glory" (98).

Part 3 is largely concerned with a monastic reality close to Merton's heart: the hermit life. The third essay, "The Solitary Life," is a spirited defense of the hermit life that ran into trouble with the censors. WHS

MONASTIC LIFE AT GETHSEMANI

Trappist, Ky.: Abbey of Gethsemani, 1965.
29 pp. (unnumbered); 19 photographs.

Texts and photos in this booklet are as-cribed to "monks of Gethsemani." These monks included Thomas Merton, Br. Pius, and Br. Ephrem. The booklet endeavors to offer visitors to the monastery some clarifica-tion for questions they might have about who the monks are and why they are there.

Personal encounters, Merton asserts, can lead to a discovery of something of the mystery of the identity of another person, and in the process may help us to understand the mys-tery of our own identity. People who arrive at a monastery may come for a momentary visit, for a retreat, or as a postulant seeking entrance into the community. It is perhaps only the last of these who can encounter the monastic community in any real depth. Others may have questions about why these men refrain from talking to outsiders, why they stay in their enclosure instead of preaching or teaching or performing other active works generally associated with a life of dedication to God.

The booklet is an attempt to help such guests arrive at some encounter with and understanding of what the monastic life is all about. It has nine brief sections: (1) "Encounter and Questions," (2) "Monasticism Today?" (3) "What Is a Monk?" (4) "Purity of Heart," (5) "Praise, Prayer and Labor," (6) "The Monastic Family," (7) "The Abbey of Gethsemani," (8) "Vocation to Silence," and (9) "Novices."

In all the major religions one will find men and women who separate themselves from the ordinary life of society in order to seek a deepened consciousness about basic human realities. It is true that all Christians are called by the gospel to be disciples of Jesus; the monk takes the gospel call with the utmost seriousness. In a monastery, separated from the ordinary life of society, he explores the deeper realms of the human spirit, seeking to arrive at an awareness of the spiritual possibilities as well as the hazards of human life. The monastic life calls him to a simple life of purity of heart. This is possible only where there is a spirit of inner solitude.

The monk belongs to a community of praise focused on the worship of God in common prayer that St. Benedict called the *opus Dei*. At the center of this life of prayer and praise is the Mass, around which revolve the various liturgical hours of prayer. Of no less importance for understanding the monastic life are the hours of manual labor and the time that monks give to personal prayer and contemplation (*lectio divina*).

A brief history of the Abbey of Gethsemani is included, with emphasis on the monastery as a place of discipline, renunciation, humility, silence, and prayer. The booklet closes with a statement of the qualities expected in one who applies to the monastery to become a postulant. WHS

MONASTIC PEACE

Trappist, Ky.: Abbey of Gethsemani, 1958.
58 pp.

Monastic Peace, in contrast to the rather austere appearance of *Basic Principles of Monastic Spirituality*, an otherwise similar pamphlet issued the previous year,[1] is handsomely designed, and illustrated with drawings by liturgical artist Frank Kacmarcik and photographs by Shirley Burden, with whom Thomas Merton was collaborating on the monastic picture book *God Is My Life*. The work consists of five chapters.

Chapter 1, "Blessed Are the Peacemakers," situates monastic life in the context of the general human and Christian search for both inner and social peace, a topic that would, of course, become central to Merton's writings in the final decade of his life. Here he reminds the reader that there can be no authentic and lasting peace that is not based on a recognition of the spiritual dimension of the human person, and he considers the role of the monastery to be a sign of peace, a model for the rest of the church and for the world of unity in charity. "The monastery remains in the world, but not of the world, as a vision of peace, a window opening on the perspectives of an utterly different realm, a new creation, an earthly paradise in which God once again dwells with men and is almost visibly their God, their peace and their consolation" (*Monastic Peace*, 7–8). Chapter 2, "Action and Contemplation," emphasizes that the role of the monk is not primarily to perform a certain work or fulfill a certain function, not even the *opus Dei* of liturgy, but to be a monk, a Christian, "a member of a little 'Mystical Body,' the Monastic Community" that together forms " 'one Person' — the mystical Christ" (10–11). Monastic life includes the activity of conversion and ascetical purification, as well as the activities necessary for a fruitful communal life, but always oriented toward contemplative union with God, or, more precisely, toward the awareness that one is already united with God. The monk comes to the monastery simply to live the Christian life in its fullness, "to realize and to appreciate all that any good Christian already has ... [to] see and understand that *he already possesses everything*" (14).

Chapter 3 (the longest chapter), "The School of Charity," follows St. Bernard in describing the monastic life as a reorientation of the self that enables the monk to love God, others, and even himself with God's own love. By living for God alone, one discovers all things in God. This chapter explores how the basic elements of monastic life, public and private prayer, the life of detachment symbolized and effected by the vows — poverty and chastity (incorporated in the Benedictine vow of conversion of manners), obedience and stability — effect this reorientation by liberating the monk from his own self-centeredness through the power of the Holy Spirit and so drawing him "most fully into the mystery of Christ, which is the restoration of the world to God in Christ" (35). Chapter 4, "The Vision of Peace," emphasizes that monastic peace is not found by avoiding conflict, whether interior or social, but by confronting and transcending it in Christ. "The secret of monastic peace is therefore not to be sought on the shallow level of psychological tranquillity, but in the infinitely deep abyss which men call the divine mercy" (43). This chapter also features a comparison of this monastic recovery from alienation with the prescriptions of Marx, who proposed economic solutions for what was at root a spiritual problem — a notable anticipation, if in more conventional terms, of Merton's talk in Thailand on "Marxism and Monastic Perspectives" on the last day of his life. Chapter 5, " 'I Have Chosen You,' " is directed primarily at prospective candidates for the monastic life. It describes St. Benedict's four signs of a monastic vocation: the desire to seek God; the surrender of one's own self-sufficiency through obedience; a commitment to the life of prayer; and an appreciation of humility and poverty (along with normal physical and mental health). Merton concludes by pointing out that the Benedictine life is one of a balance of work and prayer in a communal setting, and that "those who seek total physical silence and solitude must go elsewhere" (!) (57), but that genuine adaptability is signaled not by an absence of frustration with the life but by an ability to cope with normal frustrations creatively. In his final sentence he turns to address the reader directly in the second

person for the first and only time in the work: "The mere desire to pray for a vocation may be a sign that God has already decreed a favorable answer to your prayer" (57). Thus the evocation of monastic peace throughout the pamphlet leads to at least an implicit invitation to experience it. While largely traditional in its description of monastic life and the monastic institution, the treatise has a number of indications of a developing receptivity to the world and its problems. Merton writes, "The monk is immersed in history, and forms just as much a part of it as the communist. His role in history, though more hidden, is just as decisive. The fate of man is in the balance, and the monk has just as much to say as anyone else, perhaps more, as to how the question is to be weighed" (45). Such a statement forms a kind of prelude to Merton's own "weighing in" on the fateful questions of his era of history in the years just ahead. POC

SEE ALSO *BASIC PRINCIPLES OF MONASTIC SPIRITUALITY*; *MONASTIC JOURNEY*; MONASTICISM; MONK; *SILENT LIFE*.

Notes

1. Both are included in *The Monastic Journey*, the posthumous collection of a number of Merton's monastic essays.

MONK

In the glossary appended to *The Waters of Siloe*, Thomas Merton provides a standard definition of a monk as "a religious dedicated to God by vow in the monastic life," distinguishing the monk, committed to a contemplative life, from friars involved in preaching and teaching and from members of other active religious orders, such as the Jesuits, who generally do not celebrate the divine office in common (*Waters of Siloe*, 364). But in the opening sentences of the book's first chapter Merton's description of the monk is considerably less straightforward, more paradoxical: "A monk is a man who has given up everything in order to possess everything. He is one who has abandoned desire in order to achieve the highest fulfilment of all desire. He has renounced his liberty in order to become free" (3). The monk is one who empties himself in order to make room for the Spirit of God, who

is the only genuine fulfillment of human potential. It is this more spiritually oriented, more
experiential approach to the monastic vocation
(based in large part, ironically, on the writings
of the Carmelite friar St. John of the Cross),
rather than a precise canonical definition, that
will continue to characterize Merton's ongoing
exploration of what, and who, a monk is. To
chart his efforts to discover and articulate the
qualities of an authentic monk is to recognize
both the continuities and the development in
his understanding of what a monastic identity
entails.

In the first sentence of the prologue to *The
Silent Life* Merton answers the question of his
subtitle, "What Is a Monk?" by stating, "A
monk is a man who has been called by the
Holy Spirit to relinquish the cares, desires and
ambitions of other men, and devote his entire
life to seeking God" (*Silent Life*, vii). But he immediately qualifies the apparent clarity of this
explanation by pointing out that in fact what
it means to "seek God" cannot be determined
a priori, but rather, is discovered only by setting out on this quest without really knowing
where one is going. Yet, again paradoxically,
one sets out only because in some sense one
has already begun to find what one seeks, or
rather because one has been found by the One
who is sought. The monastic calling is a summons to plunge into mystery. He goes on to
point out that since all are called to seek God,
this cannot be the distinguishing mark of the
monk, but the monk has no other obligations
or responsibilities except to seek and find God
directly, and to seek and find and love other
people and all creation in God.

In his writings on monastic life from the late
1950s Merton makes three main points about
the monk. First, and foremost, the vocation
of the monk is profoundly paschal. "The monk
seeks to *become* Christ by sharing in the passion
of Christ" (9). Again, this is not an exclusively
monastic trait but is the essential mark of any
and all Christians, but the monastic qualities of
humility and obedience are the monk's way of
dying to himself and being raised with Christ.
Merton writes that "the basis for our life of monastic asceticism" is "to reproduce in our life
the cross of Christ so that having died sacra-

Drawing by Thomas Merton

mentally to sin in baptism and penance, we may
also put to death sin in our flesh by restraining
our evil desires and bad tendencies" (*Monastic
Journey*, 24). In doing so the monk can be described as "a man of paradise," one who lives,
by faith, in the new Eden, the new creation
revealed in the risen and glorified Christ, even
as he remains in the desert of a world that does
not recognize its redemption, "the sandy wastes
of the human spirit deprived of God" (*Seasons
of Celebration*, 207). The monk is called to be
a sign of new life to and in a world that clings
obsessively to death and sterility.

Thus, the second essential quality of a monk
that Merton emphasizes is his solidarity with
the rest of humanity. Separation from the world
and its delusions does not mean abandonment
of others: "The monk is inextricably involved
in the common suffering and problems of the
society in which he lives" (*Silent Life*, 172).
Precisely because he has a certain degree of
distance, a freedom from direct involvement
in "the maze of political entanglements which
is only on the surface of history," the monk
"will have a different, and perhaps more accu-

rate, perspective" (*Monastic Journey*, 35). But because he has identified himself fully with Christ, he also has identified himself completely with all other human beings, whom he finds in and through Christ. "Their needs are his own, their interests are his interests, their joys and sorrows are his, for he has identified himself with them not only by a realization that they all share one human nature, but above all by the charity of Christ, poured forth in our hearts by the Holy Spirit who is given to us in Christ" (35). A monk must not be regarded, or regard himself, as a member of a spiritual elite, as "a different species of being," as Merton realizes at the corner of Fourth and Walnut (*Guilty Bystander*, 141). Rather, "The monk is just an ordinary Christian who lives, in the monastery, the ordinary Christian life: but he lives it in all its perfection. He lives it to the full" (*Monastic Journey*, 48). The monk comes to the monastery not to acquire something he does not already have as a baptized Christian, but to commit himself to living out the meaning of his baptism, his membership in the Body of Christ, his participation in the life of God. "He comes in order that he might see and understand that *he already possesses everything*. This is the true secret of the monastic life. This is what it means 'to be a monk'" (48). This is what is meant by seeking the God who already has been found.

This also is why Merton can say that the monk is defined not by what he does but by who he is, the third essential characteristic of a monk. The "scandal" of the monastic life is that the monk produces nothing, accomplishes nothing, achieves nothing. "His life appears to be completely useless" (*Silent Life*, viii). But because he cannot be defined by his function, he witnesses to the fact that no one's identity is reducible to whatever work is performed. "'Being' always takes precedence over 'doing' and 'having'" (*Monastic Journey*, 44). This does not mean that the monk does nothing, but that whatever the monk does flows from who he is, from his identification with Christ, and with the community formed by Christ, first the monastic community in which he lives and then the wider community of church and world.

These key themes continue in Merton's reflections on monastic identity in the final decade of his life, but they are sharpened by an emphasis on the freedom of the monk to reject the absolute claims that any institution or structure or authority makes about itself. The monk is one "who at once loves the world yet stands apart from it with a critical objectivity which refuses to become involved in its transient fashions and its more manifest absurdities" (*World of Action*, 227). Hence Merton's description of a monk as "a marginal person, ... essentially outside of all establishments" (*Asian Journal*, 305), at the periphery of contemporary "mass society" with its tendency to depersonalize and dehumanize, yet thereby in a unique position not simply to withdraw from society but to offer it a challenging and life-affirming critique — the vision of authentic humanity rooted in the dignity of the person as image of God. Thus, Merton can write in his preface to the Japanese edition of *The Seven Storey Mountain* that his monastic life, "a life that is essentially non-assertive, non-violent, a life of humility and peace," is his way to "take my true part in all the struggles and sufferings of the world ... to make my entire life a rejection of, a protest against the crimes and injustices of war and political tyranny which threaten to destroy the whole race of man and the world with him" (*Honorable Reader*, 65). In his final talk at Bangkok, Merton goes so far as to define a monk as "essentially someone who takes up a critical attitude toward the world and its structures, ... somebody who says, in one way or another, that the claims of the world are fraudulent" (*Asian Journal*, 329).

If from one perspective, that of status, efficiency, and productivity, the monk is marginal, from another he is at the very heart of the human enterprise. "The monk," Merton said in Bangkok, "dwells in the center of society as one who has attained realization — he ... has come to experience the ground of his own being in such a way that he knows the secret of liberation and can somehow or other communicate it to others" (333). In discovering his own true center he is in communion with all other human beings through compassionate identification. The monk affirms authentic human values by incarnating them himself and by recognizing and defending them in others, especially when they are threatened or violated. "The monastic life today stands over against the world with a mission to affirm not only the message of salvation but also those most basic human values which the world most desperately needs to regain: personal integrity, inner peace, authenticity, identity, inner depth, spiritual joy, the capacity to love, the capacity to enjoy God's creation and give thanks" (*World of Action*, 81). Thus, the monk's most essential gift to the world is to live out fully his own identity and vocation as a monk. "The monk belongs to the world," Merton says in his final talk, "but the world belongs to him insofar as he has dedicated himself totally to liberation from it in order to liberate it" (*Asian Journal*, 341). POC

SEE ALSO HERMIT; MONASTICISM.

MONKS POND

Four issues, 1968; facsimile edition, Lexington: University Press of Kentucky, 1989. xv+351 pp.

This is the little magazine edited by Thomas Merton in 1968 and "devoted," in his words, "to poetry and to some unusual prose" (*Monks Pond*, 5). The acquisition in 1967 of an offset printing press by the monastery was the external event that made possible the founding of the magazine, and Merton's increasing contact with avant-garde poets and his own experimental verse in his last years evidently prompted this venture into editing, which mixes contributions by established writers with those of relative newcomers, some known to Merton personally, others "friends of friends." From the outset it was designed to have a short run: Merton mentions in the first number that only four issues were planned, though he leaves open the possibility of a fifth or sixth if enough good material is available. By the third issue he has decided to limit the number to four and requests that no more material be sent. Material for the fourth and last issue was selected and typed before Merton left on his Asian trip, but he never saw a printed copy before his death. The facsimile publication, issued with a helpful introduction by Robert E. Daggy and a short, appreciative afterword by Br. Patrick Hart, is

identical to the original except for its continuous pagination (and the reset tables of contents reflecting this) and its somewhat reduced size (7″ x 10″ from 8½″ x 11″).

The first issue, spring 1968, is sixty-four pages and includes four prose pieces and thirty-two poems by eight poets. Merton's brief introduction notes the ephemeral nature of the venture, mentions that future issues will include translations, "concrete poetry," and additional Asian material, invites submissions, and states that the magazine is free of charge, though donations to defray expenses would be accepted. Among the contributors to the first issue are poets Jonathan Greene, Jonathan Williams, and Keith Wilson, all of whom Merton would cite in the final issue as particularly supportive, as well as his correspondent Margaret Randall de Mondragón, editor of *El Corno Emplumado*, the bilingual Mexican journal to which Merton contributed. The issue also features a reprint of his late friend Ad Reinhardt's "Art as Art" manifesto, selections from eighth-century Zen master Shen Hui, and a chapter (on Pai-Chang) from John Wu's *The Golden Age of Zen*. Merton's own contribution was the "Kane Relief Expedition" section from the "North" canto of the yet unpublished *Geography of Lograire*, as well as a calligraphic fish drawing (with a quotation from Thoreau) and two photographs of roots, one on the cover.

The second issue, summer 1968, is the shortest, only forty-eight pages, but includes twenty-one contributors, all but three of them new. There are forty-six poems by eighteen authors, and three prose pieces, including a piece by Louis Zukofsky, whose poetry Merton admired, and an overview of Sufism by Persian American psychoanalyst Reza Arasteh, whose book had prompted Merton's seminal essay "Final Integration." Among the poets represented are Jack Kerouac, whose two brief pieces are dedicated to Merton, Wendell Berry, priest-poet Raymond Roseliep, Russell Edson, and Merton's Louisville friend Ron Seitz; the painter Paul Klee appears in translation with four poems and two prose selections from his journal; Jonathan Greene reappears with translations of three poems from Chinese. A concrete poem by Merton's friend Robert Lax concludes the volume. Merton's own contribution is limited to his translation of what he calls "Found Macaronic Antipoem," fifteen lines in alternating Latin and German from a 1514 anthology, and a calligraphy accompanied by a short quotation from Goethe. The cover photograph is by Merton's Lexington friend Ralph Eugene Meatyard, who also contributes four other photographs inside the issue. This is the only issue without a prefatory note by the editor.

The size of the third issue, fall 1968, jumps to ninety-eight pages. Merton notes in his short introduction that "the Pond is overflowing" and that the editor is somewhat overwhelmed with his duties; the decision has been made to limit the number of issues to four, and thus the attempt to include as much as possible in this issue (and in the next). There are thirty-seven contributors to this issue, eleven of whom had appeared in one or both of the previous issues. There are six prose pieces and about seventy poems, not including the seven samples of concrete poetry inserted in a special section. Merton's friend and correspondent June Yungblut contributed an article on Samuel Beckett, although Merton's introductory note says that the magazine "exclud[es] all forms of critical writing" (116); she probably was also responsible for the inclusion of a barely literate but deeply moving telegram sent to the widow of Martin Luther King that is printed on the inside front cover. Among the poets making their initial appearance in this issue are Mark Van Doren, who contributes a poem on Merton's hermitage, Charles Simic, Czeslaw Milosz, Francis Ponge (in a translation by Merton's sometime correspondent Cid Corman), and David Ignatow. Ted Enslin is represented by a couple of poems and excerpts from his Thoreau-like journal. The youngest contributor is Christopher Meatyard, thirteen-year-old son of Gene Meatyard (who appeared in one of his father's photographs in the previous issue). Ron Seitz's five short poems were misattributed to Robert Bonazzi, evidence perhaps of the harried state of the editor. Merton's presence is more in evidence in this issue than in the previous one, with the inclusion both of the verse preface to The Geography of Lograire, "The End-

less Inscription," and of a prose section from the still unpublished My Argument with the Gestapo (written in 1941), as well as a concrete poem, the cover photo, and six other photographs inside the issue.

The final issue, winter 1968, is the largest, running 148 pages (longer than the summer issue and either of the other two issues combined). "The Pond has frozen over," Merton says in his introductory note (aptly illustrated by a photo, presumably of the pond — indeed frozen — on the monastery property that gave the magazine its name). He expresses satisfaction that the cycle of the seasons has been completed and the magazine has run its course, amused consternation at "the hell of editors" in misplacing material, forgetting to send out notifications, and so forth; and gratitude to contributors, supporters, and workers (Jesuit scholastic typist Phil Stark, monastery printer Br. Cassian) who "made MONKS POND something unusual in little magazines" (212).

Fifty-one contributors are included in this final issue, thirty-two of them new to this issue (including three genuine poems by Robert Bonazzi). Among the six prose selections are additional material from Enslin's journal, a paraphrase by Richard Chi of a "Humorous Discourse" from an early Chinese Zen master, and a translation of excerpts from a German Benedictine on Tibetan Buddhist perspectives on health and well-being. About 125 poems are included, among them translations of the Chilean Nicanor Parra and the Brazilian Carlos Drummond de Andrade (both of whom Merton had translated, though not these poems). Merton's friend Sr. Therese Lentfoehr is represented by two poems, one dedicated to Merton and the other to Robert Lax (who contributes a cryptic "play" in four acts — slightly over a page in length and consisting of twenty-eight words of dialogue composed of five different words: "ow," "oh," "ik," "ok," and "zow"). Two of Merton's fellow monks, Matthias Gill and Augustine Wulff, are included (both of whose names are misspelled, an error that perhaps can be laid at the feet of the typist rather than Merton), as well as novice Alan Abele (Br. Carl) and one-time novice Nels

Richardson. Christopher Meatyard reappears, but loses the youngest-poet title to eleven-year-old Ira Livingston, whose four contributions are by no means the least estimable in the issue (and whose mother, Clare, also is a contributor). Merton may have been particularly struck by W. W. Pemble's poem "Morro Castle," with its evocation of the landmark sighted when entering the Havana harbor, remarked on by Merton himself on his trip to Cuba in 1940 (see *Run to the Mountain*, 172). Merton's own contributions include "Proverbs" (dedicated to Lax), two concrete poems, and the two adapted "African Religious Myths" that would reappear in the "South" canto of *The Geography of Lograire*, as well as material (including two sections later omitted) from the "Queens Tunnel" section of the "North" canto. Four photographs, including the cover, were taken by Merton; four others, including one of Wendell Berry working on his farm, by Gene Meatyard. The last piece in the issue, placed after the contributors' notes, is the "spring fever bear post-hibernation poem" of Anglo-Finnish poet Anselm Hollo (contributor as translator and original composer to two of the previous issues), suggesting that while the magazine has come to its end, the cycle of creativity it represented and contributed to will continue. POC

MONTAUBAN

This town in the south of France, about ten miles southwest of St. Antonin, is where Thomas Merton entered the Lycée Ingres in the fall of 1926, when he was eleven years old. He was unhappy there and often lonely, though after a time he seemed to have adapted to a situation that was not to his liking. When his father came in the spring of 1928 to inform him that they were going to England, he saw this as a wonderful experience of freedom from the tedious discipline of this French school. WHS

MURPHY, EDMUND

Fr. Edmund Murphy, O.F.M., provincial secretary of the Franciscans, was in residence at the Church of St. Francis of Assisi on Thirty-first Street in New York City when Thomas Merton visited him in October of 1939. On the advice of Daniel Walsh, Merton had come to talk with him about the possibility of becoming a Franciscan. The interview went well. Merton was invited to enter the novitiate in August 1940. In the summer of 1940, while staying with friends in Olean, New York, Merton had scruples about whether or not the moral lapses of his past life would bar him from the priesthood. He took the train to New York, and went to see Fr. Murphy. After hearing his story, the priest advised him to withdraw his application from the Franciscans and apparently gave him the impression (whether the priest had intended this or not) that what he had disclosed about his past (presumably, that he had fathered a child while a student in England) would constitute an impediment to his ever becoming a priest. See *Seven Storey Mountain*, 265, 296–98. WHS

MY ARGUMENT WITH THE GESTAPO
Garden City, N.Y.: Doubleday, 1969. 259 pp.

This book, Thomas Merton's only published novel, was written in the summer of 1941, while Merton was teaching at St. Bonaventure College, but only appeared in print twenty-eight years later, a year after Merton's death. Its subtitle, "A Macaronic Journal," refers to the author's frequent introduction of snatches of dialogue in a mixture of various European languages, and links the work to one of Merton's favorite literary genres, also indicated by the original title, *Journal of My Escape from the Nazis*. The book describes a fictional journey back to wartime England and France by a character with the same name and the same history as its author, and includes numerous autobiographical reminiscences of youthful experiences in both countries. It could be argued that "novel" is in fact a somewhat misleading genre classification for this work, which actually is a kind of imaginative reflection on the state of the world and of the author's own soul, in which the fictional elements are simply the framework for a very factual examination of conscience. In the preface Merton wrote in January 1968 he says, "This novel is a kind of sardonic meditation on the world in which I then found myself: an attempt to define its predicament and my own place in it" (*My Argument with the Gestapo*, 6). With its frequent reminders of Blake, Eliot, Joyce, Kafka, Evelyn Waugh, and, above all, Dante, the book creates a spiritual landscape in which its narrator grapples with the tragedy and the absurdity of the Second World War and with his own moral responsibility for its eruption. In deciding to have the book published so many years after its composition, Merton indicated his own belief in its continued pertinence for the era of Vietnam and the nuclear threat. He concludes his preface by calling for an "awareness that, though one may or may not escape from the Nazis, there is no evading the universal human crisis of which they were but one partial symptom" (6).

The story begins with the narrator's return to London during the blitz and his attempts to find its reality beneath the projections of bluff heartiness and wry humor that mark the British endurance of German attacks. He views London through the lens of St. Augustine's two cities. After describing the first city, the "city of angels" (33) with its well-mannered children, its parks and galleries, he continues, "Until, suddenly, sometime, not for everybody, and never for the innocent, the masks fall off the houses, and the streets became liars and the squares become thieves and the buildings become murderers" (34). This is the London against which Blake railed, with its great dark areas of slums; it is the "unreal city" of Eliot's *Waste Land*, a term borrowed, of course, from Dante's *Inferno*. It is, quite clearly, a vision of hell itself, as was indicated on the very opening pages of the novel, when the narrator is forced to go "downward into the earth," into the underground station that serves as a bomb shelter for the poor, where suddenly he has a vision of "people sitting along the platforms, down below, like souls waiting for the boatman Charon, by the black river of hell" (18). The implications of these images, and the many similar ones of death and disintegration, are quite evident: the hellish conditions that England is enduring

are not simply the result of external forces, not merely the consequences of the blitz, but the result also of inner rot, of a culture based on deception and superficiality and pervasive bad faith, a society that had lost its values without realizing it, that mouthed its platitudes without believing them — and without realizing it no longer believed. Merton clearly is indicting not Germany alone for the war, but Western civilization as a whole.

This does not mean that other nations are treated less harshly than England. The narrator's journey to occupied France (after being expelled from England as a putative spy) brings him into direct contact with Nazism in Paris, which is described as "the artificial city...like something I have dreamed up, in bed, in the early hours of the morning when dreams are most vivid" (181). The detectives who harass the author are "big, thick-necked brutal men, Frenchmen that look and behave exactly like Germans" (184). To some extent, then, the conquered are indistinguishable from, or have taken on the characteristics of, their conquerors. The young Merton refuses to divide the world dualistically into good and bad, heroes and villains. Even the Americans are included in the criticism, by way of the description of the trivial contents of a time capsule, which becomes the symbol and substance of the ultimate bankruptcy of modern Western materialism (126).

But the pilgrim Merton is not simply an objective observer, self-righteously flaying the crimes of others. In his comments on the two cities he had said that the innocent alone are spared the sight of the decay beneath the placid surface: he who has seen this rot sees a reflection of his own evil. In a scene near the middle of the novel the narrator slips into a London church for early morning Mass. In the midst of the silence a kind of dialogue begins, as the light of the flickering candles on the altar draws his attention, and probes his motives for returning to a Europe beset by war. To the question "You who went away from here lost, would you ever have returned here if you had been lost still?" he responds, "I make this journey for the reasons Dante made his" (137) — an attempt to find the right way, to find the true self. It is a journey not only into the maelstrom of Europe at war, but also back into his own past, the years of growing up in England and in France, in an effort to identify and acknowledge his own responsibility for the conditions that made the war possible. As Dante journeys through hell so as to recognize and reject sin, so Merton returns to Europe to confront and repent of his own sinfulness.

This central theme is articulated throughout the book, most successfully in two crucial scenes. The first is Merton's meeting with an old girlfriend, a kind of Beatrice figure appropriately known only as "B." Their conversation turns to questions of the loss and recovery of identity, the conformity and regimentation both symbolized and required by putting on a uniform. B. admits that while in uniform she shared the general suspicion of her old friend's motives and actions: "It was not until I dressed as myself, and remembered who I was, that I remembered who you are also" (115). She is repelled by the casual, cynical attitudes of soldiers who pick her up, the "persistent and studied love-making that the world seemed to believe in" (116), which she identifies with the war. But Merton replies that such attitudes are not only the effect but also, in some sense, the cause of the war. He continues: "I am in no way superior to them because they fight the war and I try to understand the war. Their pride is no greater than mine, and they are no further than I am from the Kingdom of God. Suppose you believe, as I do, that the war is, in some way we cannot understand, a retribution for the acts of men; my life has probably been much worse than most of theirs" (118). He recalls that even with B. herself, in the past, his interests had been base and selfish: "Therefore, when you compare me with them, now, I cannot speak for shame, because I remember the way it was when I myself made love to you" (119). This scene is in many ways reminiscent of the meeting of Dante and Beatrice in the Garden of Eden atop Mt. Purgatory, where Dante is forced to acknowledge his own evasions, infidelities, and mixed motives, and in confessing them truly becomes himself, assumes his true identity. Here, in this garden, with this still quite earthbound B., there is a sort of mutual

confession and absolution. Though this is the last time they see each other, they have been able to be themselves in one another's presence, to recognize themselves both as sinful and redeemed. This same theme concludes the scene in the church, as the suffering of the war is identified with the passion of Christ: "Your pride was not the world's fault, but yours, because you were the one who finally consented to be, also, proud. Look now where the Crucifixion flowered in London like a tree, and the wounds were made in Cambridge, red as oleanders" (138). Merton's journey in spirit to a world at war is not to apportion blame to others but to see that his own inner war has been both mirror and even cause of the present cataclysm.

Though the upward path is less evident than the downward one in this book, it is nonetheless there, waiting to be found. It may be associated in particular with the mysterious Madame Gongora, in whose house, a kind of repository of authentic European culture, Merton stays while in London. He writes her from Paris, "I invite your inspirations, madama, living in your otherworldly house, not out of the bombed city, not in the eighteenth century, not in the sentimental minds of the moralizing communists, but in and out of the world, knowing the illusion from the truth. Teach me, teach me" (188). She, and soon Merton himself, say they are citizens of Casa, that is, of that otherworldly house that nevertheless is not out of the bombed city but within it — borrowed from the opening stanza of St. John of the Cross's poem "The Dark Night," in which the speaker, inflamed by love, leaves his quiet house unobserved ("estando ya mi casa sosegada"). This poem serves as the text commented on by John in his *Ascent of Mount Carmel*, the symbolic equivalent of Dante's ascent of Mt. Purgatory. Madame Gongora is the inspiration not only for the narrator's writing, then, but also for his ascent to God. In fact, the two are identified when Merton writes in his letter to her the macaronic verse "Toute lettera se fait un Jacob's Ladder, / Hasta el ciel, desde la lousy terre: / Laquelle habemos, con nos vils orgueils / Hecho la casa di folor y guerre!" ("Every letter becomes a Jacob's Ladder, up to the heavens from the lousy earth, which we with our base pride have made the house of folly and of war") (189). He intends his writing to be an instrument of ascent to God, presumably not only for himself but also for the reader. There is at least an implicit invitation to participate in the process of radical purification and regeneration that the speaker is undergoing.

It is not clear at what stage of the spiritual journey the book concludes. The pattern definitely is left open-ended, as indeed Merton's own life certainly was at the time he wrote the book. While there are intimations of further spiritual development, the emphasis has been on purification and renunciation. Yet in the very last words of the book the speaker says, "I think suddenly of Blake, filling paper with words, so that the words flew about the room for the angels to read, and after that, what if the paper was lost or destroyed? That is the only reason for wanting to write, Blake's reason" (259). Here, at least in desire, is envisioned the ultimate goal of writing as of life, total self-surrender for the glory of God. POC

SEE ALSO NOVELS, UNPUBLISHED.

MYSTICISM

The term "mysticism" is not an easy one to clarify, for, as Thomas Merton notes, "mystical experience has been confused with every kind of emotional, pseudo-religious, aesthetic or supposedly extra-sensory perception."[1] The confusion has been accentuated by the introduction into the West of Eastern religions, which have brought with them a mysticism that, unlike Western mysticism, is unrelated to dogma or sacraments. Even when properly understood, mysticism often is greeted with some uneasiness by people sincerely committed to a life of the spirit. The reason for this uneasiness is that the mystical experience is outside of a person's control. "The mystic must surrender to a power of love that is greater than human and advance toward God in a darkness that goes beyond the light of reason and of human conceptual knowledge."[2]

One of the difficulties in summing up Merton's understanding of mysticism is that apart from the few times when he explicitly is using the term "mysticism," he seems to prefer the term "contemplation." In an essay bearing the title "The Contemplative and the Atheist" he uses "contemplative" and "mystic" interchangeably. Thus, he writes: "The *Christian contemplative* is aware that in the *mystical tradition* both of the Eastern and Western Churches there is a strong element of what has been called 'apophatic theology.' . . . The heart of the Christian *mystical experience* is that it experiences the ineffable reality of what is beyond experience. It 'knows' the presence of God, not in clear vision but as 'unknown.' . . . Now, while the *Christian contemplative* must certainly develop, by study, the theological understanding of concepts about God, he is called mainly to penetrate the wordless darkness and apophatic light of an experience beyond concepts" (*World of Action*, 172/185–86 [italics added]). Like Moses approaching the burning bush, the *contemplative* must remove "the 'shoes' of opinion and rationalization" (173/187).

To grasp the meaning of "unknowing" one must let go of any notion of God conceived of as a definite (i.e., "defined," or limited) object. "Any experience of God as possessing some finite form or idea which we can grasp is an experience not of God but only of something that remotely resembles Him in an analogical way. There is nothing whatever in existence that even remotely resembles God as He is in Himself. And yet the 'knowing' of God in 'unknowing,' far from being unreal and uncertain, possesses the highest reality and certainty of any experience accessible to man."[3]

The mystic (contemplative) arrives not at a clear idea of God, but a pure love, a complete abandonment to the One known to be beyond understanding. It is the experience of presence that removes the dichotomy of subject-object. It is a union of essential love in which God and humankind, "while remaining no doubt metaphysically distinct, are practically and experientially 'one Spirit' in the words of St. Paul (1 Cor. 6:16), quoted in this sense by Christian mystics down the centuries."[4]

In the 1960s Merton was deeply impressed by his reading of texts of Eastern religions (texts that in *The Seven Storey Mountain* he had dismissed as "simply more or less useless" [188]). On September 11, 1962, he wrote to E. I. Watkin, "I am most impressed with the depth and subtlety of Oriental texts on mysticism, and I have no doubt that it is urgent for us to come to understand them and to see the correspondences between our thought and theirs. There can be no question in my mind that what is often passed off with a shrug as philosophical pantheism is in reality something quite different, an expression of a profound religious experience" (*Hidden Ground of Love*, 579). He was drawn especially to Zen as offering insights most congenial to the Christian mystical experience. WHS

SEE ALSO APOPHATICISM; CONTEMPLATION; ZEN; *ZEN AND THE BIRDS OF APPETITE*.

Notes

1. Thomas Merton, foreword to William Johnston, *The Mysticism of The Cloud of Unknowing* (New York: Desclée, 1967), vii.
2. Ibid.
3. Ibid., ix.
4. Ibid., vii.

MYSTICS AND ZEN MASTERS
New York: Farrar, Straus and Giroux, 1967.
x+303 pp.

This is a collection of sixteen essays, all but two previously published in periodicals, often in somewhat different form, dating between 1961 and 1966; many of the chapters are developed from review essays on current books. The title is drawn from the opening essay, but also represents in a general way the contents of the entire volume, all of which focus in some way upon religious experience East and West (though not all the essays on Western topics are concerned with mysticism and not all those on Eastern topics are concerned with Zen, or indeed with Buddhism). In his brief preface Merton suggests that what holds the book together is its concern with "a wider 'oikoumene' " — an ecumenism that extends beyond the bounds of Christianity to all those seeking the "ultimate purpose" of life. "All these studies are united by one central concern: to understand various ways in which men of different traditions have

conceived the meaning and method of the 'way' which leads to the highest levels of religious or of metaphysical awareness" (*Mystics and Zen Masters*, x).

While the volume is perhaps best known for containing Merton's earlier essays on Eastern religions, these articles constitute less than half the total (though about half the number of pages). The first three essays ("Mystics and Zen Masters," "Classic Chinese Thought," and "Love and Tao") focus on the East; they are followed by two transitional essays that link East and West ("The Jesuits in China" and, to a lesser extent, "From Pilgrimage to Crusade"); then come three essays focused on the Catholic spiritual tradition ("Virginity and Humanism in the Western Fathers," "The English Mystics," and "Self-Knowledge in Gertrude More and Augustine Baker") and three more on other Christian traditions ("Russian Mystics," "Protestant Monasticism," and "Pleasant Hill"); "Contemplation and Dialogue" serves as a bridge back to Eastern material; of the last four essays, three ("Zen Buddhist Monasticism," "The Zen Koan," and "Buddhism and the Modern World") are concerned with the East; the penultimate essay, "The Other Side of Despair," subtitled "Notes on Christian Existentialism," seems rather oddly placed, though it suggests implicitly (and in one place explicitly) a standpoint for dialogue with the East.

"Mystics and Zen Masters" is largely a reflection on Heinrich Dumoulin's *History of Zen Buddhism*, though it also brings in a work by R. C. Zaehner and a new translation of the Platform Scripture of Hui Neng, the sixth Chinese Zen patriarch. It wrestles with the meaning of Zen, providing a definition as "the ontological *awareness of pure being beyond subject and object,* an immediate grasp of being in its 'suchness' and 'thusness' " (14). Much of the essay is taken up with a defense and explication (based on the work of D. T. Suzuki) of the approach to Zen of Hui Neng, toward whom Merton finds Dumoulin rather unsympathetic, though there is also considerable discussion of Dōgen, the Japanese founder of the Soto school of Zen, whose approach Dumoulin finds more congenial.

The two following essays are concerned with non-Buddhist Chinese thought. After a brief discussion of the call of Taoism for "a complete transformation, a change of heart, which Christianity would call *metanoia*" (50), "Classic Chinese Thought" focuses mainly on Confucianism, which is described as fundamentally humanistic: "The foundation of Confucian system is first of all the *human person* and then his relations with other persons in society" (51); Merton goes on to provide a brief overview of the Confucian classics and key Confucian terms, and concludes with his own version of the "Ox Mountain Parable" of the later Confucian Meng Tzu, with its evocation of the restorative "night spirit" that brings the exhausted mountain (likened to the mind) back to life. "Love and Tao" discusses two Chinese works, the foundational text of Taoism, the *Tao Te Ching*, which promotes "the way of supreme spontaneity, which is virtuous in a transcendent sense because it 'does not strive'" (74), and the more practical *Hsiao Ching*, a primer of Confucian ethics, in which Merton once again finds evidence of a personalistic (rather than simply a rule-based) approach to life. The essay concludes with Merton's insistence on the necessity to restore an emphasis on wisdom in education, and on the importance of seeking this wisdom in Eastern as well as Western sources.

"The Jesuits in China" looks at the brief period in the seventeenth century when the possibility of a genuine dialogue between Christianity and the East developed, especially through the work of Jesuit missionary Matteo Ricci, only to be thwarted by narrow vision and ecclesial politics; Merton sees this history as "the story of Christ in China: a kind of brief epiphany of the Son of Man as a Chinese scholar" (90), and implicitly as an object lesson for the new age of dialogue he sees beginning. "From Pilgrimage to Crusade" surveys the history of the "sacred journey" in Christianity, with particular attention to the Irish tradition of "*peregrinatio*" and to journeys to the Holy Land, which eventually were transformed into the armed invasions of the Crusades; Merton's conclusion is that for contemporary pilgrims, the "task now is to learn that if we can voyage to the ends of the earth and there find *ourselves* in the aborigine who most differs from ourselves, we will have made

a fruitful pilgrimage. . . . We have to come to the end of a long journey and see that the stranger we meet there is no other than ourselves — which is the same as saying that we find Christ in him" (112).

"Virginity and Humanism in the Western Fathers" finds in the writings of Sts. Cyprian, Ambrose, and Jerome on virginity not a rejection of the world and the flesh but a "most uncompromising . . . defense of basic human values" (114), rooted in the doctrine of the incarnation and looking both back to the unfallen world and forward to eschatological fulfillment. "The English Mystics" surveys the major tradition of English spirituality, with particular emphasis on the fourteenth century, and finds in it "a 'paradise spirituality' which recovers in Christ the innocence and joy of the first beginnings and sees the world . . . in the light of Paradise" (152). "Self-Knowledge in Gertrude More and Augustine Baker" looks at those two seventeenth-century English Benedictine exiles as true successors of the fourteenth-century mystics, retaining a more contemplative practice and theory in an age of discursive meditation and introspective analysis.

"Russian Mystics" (written as an introduction for a book by Sergius Bolshakoff not published until 1976) surveys the important figures and movements in Russian spirituality, with particular attention to the Jesus Prayer and to St. Seraphin of Sarov, and finds that the central strand of the tradition "is a theology not of suffering but of transfiguration" (183); Merton finds in Pope John XXIII's optimistic attitude toward the world and in his love for the Eastern church a basis for further dialogue with and appreciation for Orthodoxy. "Protestant Monasticism" looks at the surprising recent growth of monasticism in the Reformed churches, represented particularly by Taizé, as a sign of ecumenical convergence and a witness to the Roman Catholic Church, in the words of Taizé founder Roger Schutz, "to recenter their attention on the essential treasures which it has always possessed" (192). "Pleasant Hill," subtitled "A Shaker Village in Kentucky," reflects Merton's deep attraction to the quasi-monastic way of life of the Shakers and to the purity and simplicity of their craftsmanship, rooted in a belief that "their work was a worship offered to God in the sight of his angels" (198), an attitude that Merton finds quite Benedictine.

"Contemplation and Dialogue" suggests that the current momentum toward interreligious dialogue both within and beyond Christianity is best carried out not on the level of doctrine but on the plane of religious experience, since "in all religions it is more or less generally recognized that this profound 'sapiential' experience, call it gnosis, contemplation, 'mysticism,' 'prophecy,' or what you will, represents the deepest and most authentic fruit of the religion itself" (204), so that dialogue can best be carried out by those who have not lost a sense of this "sapiential" dimension in their own tradition.

"Zen Buddhist Monasticism" (which had not appeared previously) describes Zen as "an Asian form of religious existentialism" (219) and Zen monasticism as an environment in which one is enlightened by "completely [dying] to one's empirical 'I'" under the direction of the *roshi*, "who is himself enlightened and who knows exactly how to bring one through the perilous ways of transformation and enlightenment" (225). "The Zen Koan" examines the most famous method of breaking through the tendency to objectification "to a state of pure consciousness which is no longer a 'consciousness of'" (252), and which Merton compares to the "out-gazing" of Rilke (244), which likewise transcends "self-consciousness, separateness, and spectatorship" (245) to discover a state of identification with all reality.

"The Other Side of Despair" looks at the Christian dimension of existentialism, a philosophy popularly considered to be atheistic, and finds it "associated with the return to a Biblical mode of thought which is entirely concrete and personal and, in fact, much more fundamentally Christian than the rather abstract and intellectualist approach that has been accepted as the 'only' Catholic approach for almost seven hundred years" (270); he finds a Christian existentialism not only in the meditations of a Kierkegaard but also in the fiction of Flannery O'Connor, and sees "genuine existentialism," with its "non-objective, elusive, concrete, dynamic" qualities, "like Zen Buddhism and like apophatic Christian mysticism, hidden in life itself" rather than available in neat "verbal formulas" (258).

The final essay, "Buddhism and the Modern World," sees the emancipation from duality as the great contribution of Buddhism in general and Zen in particular to contemporary humanity, while raising the question of how this insight and experience can be communicated beyond the limited circle of those who have engaged in the discipline traditionally leading to enlightenment. In the final part of the essay Merton turns to his Vietnamese Buddhist friend Thich Nhat Hanh's program of engaged Buddhism, in which correct action proceeds from correct perception, a transformation from within, rather than what Masao Abe describes as the characteristically Western "will to transform others" (287), a distinction Merton finds, in the final words of the volume, as adumbrating "an ontology of nonviolence, which requires further investigation" (288). POC

SEE ALSO BUDDHISM; CONFUCIANISM; INTERRELIGIOUS DIALOGUE; TAOISM; ZEN; *ZEN AND THE BIRDS OF APPETITE.*

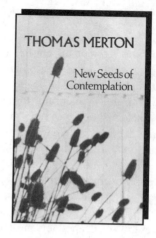

NATIVITY KERYGMA

Trappist, Ky.: Abbey of Gethsemani, 1958.
14 pp. (unnumbered).

This is a Christmas homily, which was presumably preached to the Gethsemani community, perhaps in 1956.[1] It was published as an oversized gift book[2] in a limited edition that Merton considered "very beautifully done," which arrived in time for Christmas 1958 (*Search for Solitude*, 240). After a brief prefatory note declaring that "Christianity is not so much a body of doctrine as the revelation of a mystery" (*Nativity Kerygma*, [3]), the salvation proclaimed by the church and its preachers, and explaining that the word "kerygma" means "proclamation," the homily itself interweaves a number of themes associated with the Feast of the Nativity. Prominent among them is the theme of proclamation itself, as the annunciation of the good news by the angels is echoed by the words of the Scriptures and the liturgy, quoted liberally throughout the homily. The content of the message is that the salvation brought by the birth of Jesus is a present reality, "not merely an old thing which happened long ago, but a new thing which happens today" ([5]). In the liturgy the church sings a new

Cover for *New Seeds of Contemplation* reprinted with the permission of New Directions. Cover design by Gilda Kuhlman.

song, a celebration of the renewal of all creation. Drawing on the Gospel reading of the third Mass of Christmas, the Johannine prologue, and other readings for the feast, Merton emphasizes the birth of Christ as the illumination of the world and of humanity. "Christ, light of light, is born today, and since He is born to us, He is born in us, and therefore, we also are born today" ([7]).[3] This light is manifested in praise of God and in charity toward one another, which come together in the Mass and are revealed in all the sacraments. Yet the homily also points out that the coming of the heavenly light into the darkness through the incarnation is also a veiling of that light, which would otherwise be blinding to sinful humanity. Here the final important theme of *kenosis*, the revelation of the divine majesty in the humility and hiddenness of the child in the stable, is introduced: "In 'emptying Himself' and taking the form of a servant that is human nature, the Lord laid aside His majesty and His divine power, in order to dwell among us with all His divine goodness and mercy" ([10]).[4] The Word of God identifies completely with the human condition in order to draw those whom he has come to save into the fullness of divine life, a passage that can take place only through the mystery of the cross. Thus, the celebration of the birth of Jesus cannot be separated from awareness of and participation in the death and resurrection of the Savior: "If we wish His light to shine on our darkness and His immortality to clothe our mortality, we must suffer with Him on earth in order to be crowned with Him in Paradise" ([12]). Finally, the union of humanity with Christ made possible by the incarnation is to be lived out by those who believe in Christ so that the entire creation, which groans in expectation for the revelation of the children of God, will be drawn into the saving events initiated on Christmas day. "The mystery of Christmas therefore lays upon us all a debt and an obligation to the rest of men and to the whole created universe. We who have seen the light of Christ are obliged, by the greatness of the grace that has been given us, to make known the presence of the Savior to the ends of the earth" ([13]). This proclamation of the message of salvation is to be made not only through what one says but also by how one lives, so that Christians themselves become a manifestation, an "Epiphany" of Christ to the world.[5] POC

Notes

1. In the author's note to *Seasons of Celebration*, in which the *Nativity Kerygma* was reprinted, Merton states that most of the pieces "had been delivered to . . . a group or congregation" (*Seasons of Celebration*, vii); in the final paragraph of the piece there is a direct address to "my brothers" (*Nativity Kerygma*, [13]) (omitted in the *Seasons of Celebration* version). If the date 1956 affixed to the end of the homily (*Seasons of Celebration*, 112) is not a mistake for the date of publication, presumably it refers to the date of composition and presentation; since the imprimatur for the book was granted on December 19, 1957 (*Nativity Kerygma*, [2]), the homily probably was not preached that year.

2. In the final paragraph of the author's note (omitted in *Seasons of Celebration*) Merton writes, "Such a message, such an *Evangelium*, coming from God rather than from men, should be uttered with all solemnity, printed with seriousness and splendor. It is not fitting that pages like these should be bought or sold, and therefore, they are not offered for sale, they can only be given as a present. They have no price and neither has salvation" (*Nativity Kerygma*, [3]).

3. In *Seasons of Celebration* this sentence reads, "Christ, light of light, is born today, and since He is born to us, He is born in us as light and therefore, we who believe are born today to new light" (104). There are some three dozen textual differences (omissions, additions, alterations) between the two versions, none longer than a few words.

4. The *Seasons of Celebration* version omits "that is human nature" and concludes "in goodness and mercy" (108).

5. This homily can be compared profitably to later discussions of the mystery of the nativity in "The Time of the End Is the Time of No Room" (*Raids on the Unspeakable*, 65–75) and "The Good News of the Nativity" (*Love and Living*, 220–32).

NATURE

Thomas Merton's love of the natural world was closely bound up with his sense of religious vocation from the time of his conversion. One of his attractions to the Franciscans, the religious order he originally intended to join, was Francis of Assisi's sense of kinship with all creation, and when he was debating with himself about entering the Cistercians, he questioned whether he would be cut off somehow from the natural world: "telling myself some absurd thing about the necessity to love God's creatures — nature etc. The only answer to that is: there is nothing in the Trappist discipline to prevent you loving nature the way I meant it then and do now: loving it in God's creation, and a sign of His goodness and Love" (*Run to the Mountain*, 399). As his vocation to solitude deepened, so did his contact with and appreciation for nature. In June 1949, when he was given permission to spend time alone meditating in the woods, a sense of liberation, contentment, and heightened awareness radiates through his description of his first afternoon outside the monastic enclosure. Every detail he sees and hears emerges with vivid clarity: "Right under me was a dry creek, with clean pools lying like glass between the shale pavement of the stream, and the shale was as white and crumpled as sea-biscuit" (*Entering the Silence*, 329). The sights and sounds of birds combined the familiar and the unknown: "Down in the glen were the songs of marvelous birds. I saw the gold-orange flame of an oriole in a tree. Orioles are too shy to come near the monastery. There was a cardinal whistling somewhere, but the best song was that of two birds that sounded as wonderfully as nightingales and their song echoed through the wood. I could not tell what they were. I had never heard such birds before. The echo made the place sound more remote and self-contained, more perfectly enclosed, and more like Eden" (329). The hills provide Merton with a new perspective on the monastery itself: "It made much more sense in its surroundings. We do not realize our own setting and we ought to: it is important to know where you are put on the face of the earth" (329); from this vantage

Photograph by Thomas Merton

poplar, and short leaf pine, and loblolly pine" with the novices, going on to describe the last as having "the most curious name and the most interesting smell," and adding, "I like the red and purple tinge on the end of their needles" (470). Merton will continue to be attentive to the particular in nature. Being able to recognize and identify natural phenomena is not merely a way of labeling and cataloguing, and so somehow controlling, living things, but rather is part of a fundamental discipline of respect for the created world.

A second approach to nature that recurs frequently in Merton's journals is the emblematic application of a natural fact or event to a human situation, finding in nature a moral or spiritual lesson. For example, on March 10, 1951, Merton reflects on his experience burning brush and almost starting a forest fire and finds an application to his inner life: "Wind . . . flames springing up in the leaves across the creek like the spread of attachments in an unmortified soul! . . . Many lights are burning that ought to be put out. Kindle no new fires. Live in the warmth of the sun" (453). One of the most striking examples in his journals dates from February 1950, when Merton, from his "observation post" in the garden house attic, where he frequently went to meditate, sees a hawk descend "like a bullet" on a flock of starlings, "a terrible and yet beautiful thing, that lightning flight, straight as an arrow, that killed the slowest starling." Though so thoroughly disconcerted as to be unable to pray, Merton perceived in the hawk's unwavering intensity of purpose not only an analogy to "the terrible fact that some men love war" but also an example, even an inspiration, for his own vocation: "In the end I think that hawk is to be studied by saints and contemplatives because he knows his business. I wish I knew my business as well as he does his" (407–8).

point he sees as well the community's failure to appreciate fully the gift of this environment: "We huddle together in the midst of it and jostle one another like a subway crowd and deafen ourselves with our own typewriters and tractors" (329).

It is in the context of these periodic forays into the countryside, these encounters with the "sweet scent of the woods — the clean stream, the peace, the inviolate solitude!" (329), that four interrelated dimensions of Merton's writing about nature become evident. Merton became much more interested in the particularities of natural phenomena. For example, traveling into Louisville on June 22, 1951, to become an American citizen, he is particularly aware of the varieties of flowers along the roadside in what he now "could definitely speak of . . . as 'my country' "; he writes, "The ditches along the road were full of cornflowers and hollyhocks, and there were tiger lilies everywhere. Wild roses were climbing over the fences of the farms and were in bloom, and the trumpet vines were putting fourth [sic] their dull red soundless horns" (460–61). After being appointed the abbey forester in 1951, Merton procured books on identifying trees, and he will confidently speak of planting seedlings of "yellow

Thirdly, it is in recognizing the full significance of the relationship between the natural and the human that Merton shows his awareness that nature requires not simply investigation and analysis but participation. So Merton can say, reflecting on a day spent amidst "the ceremonies of the birds" at the hermitage, "How absolutely true, and how central a truth, that we are purely and simply *part of nature*," although, he adds, "we are the part which recognizes God" (*Turning toward the World*, 312). For Merton this holistic consciousness is, or should be, something intrinsic to monastic life. He writes in March 1951, "How necessary it is for monks to work in the fields, in the rain, in the sun, in the mud, in the clay, in the wind: these are our spiritual directors and our novice masters. They form our contemplation. They instill into us virtue. They make us as stable as the land we live in" (*Entering the Silence*, 450). When he becomes master of students a short time later, in charge of the training of the newly professed monks, one of his innovations is to put them to work in the woods planting thousands of seedlings — sharing with them his own love and respect for nature and implanting in them the recognition that stewardship and renewal of the natural environment is a spiritual discipline, long before this connection becomes widely acknowledged.

A sense of unity with nature is for Merton an antidote to the "post-Cartesian technologism that separates man from the world" (*Turning toward the World*, 312). A true appreciation for creation can be found only from within the continuum of nature. While scientific experimentation and analytical investigation have their place, Merton acknowledges, such an approach has its limitations: "It is misleading, because with this kind of knowledge you *do not really* know the beings you know. You only know *about* them" (*Search for Solitude*, 190). He continues, "I want not only to observe but to *know* living things, and this implies a dimension of primordial familiarity which is simple and primitive and religious and poor" (190). It is such an experience of "connatural" knowing, a "mode of apprehension" that "reaches out to grasp the inner reality, the vital substance of its object, by a kind of affective identification of itself with it" (*Literary Essays*, 347), that he describes in September 1965, during his first month living at the hermitage, when deer appear in the evening in an adjacent field: "The thing that struck me most: one sees, looking at them directly in movement, just what the cave painters saw — something that I have never seen in a photograph. It is an awe-inspiring

thing — the *Mantu* or 'spirit' shown in the running of the deer, the 'deerness' that sums up everything and is sacred and marvelous. A contemplative intuition! Yet perfectly ordinary, everyday seeing. The deer reveals to me something essential in myself! Something beyond the trivialities of my everyday being, and my individuality" (*Water of Life*, 291). It is this experience of interrelatedness that characterizes his life as a hermit: "I exist under trees. I walk in the woods out of necessity. . . . I know there are trees here. I know there are birds here. I know the birds in fact very well, for there are precise pairs of birds (two each of fifteen or twenty species) living in the immediate area of my cabin. I share this particular place with them: we form an ecological balance" (*Day of a Stranger*, 33).

Finally, for Merton an appreciative and responsible integration with the natural world is an essential component of any authentic human life, but especially of one that aspires to some sort of contemplative awareness, for the natural world in Merton's view is ultimately a source of revelation, a manifestation of the divine Ground of all created reality, which nevertheless infinitely transcends it: "When your mind is silent, then the forest suddenly becomes magnificently real and blazes transparently with the Reality of God. For now I know that the Creation, which first seems to reveal Him in concepts, then seems to hide Him by the same concepts, finally *is revealed in Him*, in the Holy Spirit. And we who are in God find ourselves united in Him with all that springs from Him. This is prayer, and this is glory!" (*Entering the Silence*, 471). Merton owed this recognition of creation as a window on God largely to the teachings of the Greek patristic writers on *theōria physikē*, or "natural contemplation, which beholds the divine in and through nature" ("Inner Experience," 4:298).

Concepts, logical explanations, are not enough to disclose what Merton called this "epiphany of the cosmic mystery" (*Literary Essays*, 104); such awareness is not available to the detached, "objective" observer but only to one who has what Merton liked to describe as a "sapiential" or "sophianic" consciousness, an intuitive, participatory awareness of the "hidden wholeness" (*Collected Poems*, 363) of all reality, "a kind of knowledge by identification, an intersubjective knowledge, a communion in cosmic awareness and in nature . . . a wisdom based on love" (*Literary Essays*, 108). For those whose inner eye has been opened, the very existence, order, life, and beauty of the universe, and of each creature within it, reflect and participate in the mystery of the divine Wisdom who made it. As Merton would say from the hermitage, "Up here in the woods is seen the New Testament: that is to say, the wind comes through the trees and you breathe it" (*Day of a Stranger*, 41). POC

SEE ALSO CREATION; ECOLOGY.

NEW MAN, THE

New York: Farrar, Straus and Cudahy, 1961. 248 pp.

On November 23, 1959, Thomas Merton confided to his journal that that very day he had "finished editing and correcting" *The New Man*. He says that it was written in five weeks in 1954 during the fall vacation. He declares himself happy with the book and adds that there are few other books of his he could read with satisfaction after five years. Interestingly, he inserts in brackets after the title the name he had given the book at an earlier date: *Existential Communion* (*Search for Solitude*, 348).[1]

At the Merton Center at Bellarmine University in Louisville, Kentucky, there is a draft of a typescript bearing the title *Existential Communion*. A cover sheet calls the text a draft, gives as its title "*Existential Communion* (i.e., The New Man)," and dates it 1960. This cover sheet, in a different type font from the typescript, must have been written by the curator at the Merton Center. The date, 1960, is incorrect. It conflicts with Merton's journal statement mentioned above. The top of page 1 of the typescript has the inscription "jhs Maria." This was characteristic of Merton in 1954,[2] but not in 1960.[3]

The text of *Existential Communion*, while having undergone some omissions and additions in the process of becoming *The New Man*, is still easy to recognize in the final product. The two texts are substantially the same. Here are the chapter headings with the chapters of *Existential Communion* in brackets: "The War within Us [Existential Communion]"; "Promethean Theology [Prometheus: A Promethean Theology]"; "Image and Likeness [Adam in Paradise]"; "Free Speech: *Parrhesia* [Parrhesia]"; "Spirit in Bondage [The Spirit in Exile]"; "The Second Adam [same]"; "Life in Christ [same]"; "Sacramental Illumination [Wisdom in Mystery]"; "Called Out of Darkness [same]." In *The New Man* paragraphs or groups of paragraphs are numbered: 1–161. This numbering is lacking in *Existential Communion*.

One way of looking at *The New Man* is to see it as an extensive paraphrase of Genesis 1–3 and Romans 6–8. Merton sees the book as a series of meditations in which he talks about "man 'finding himself in God'" (*New Man*, 67). After an introductory chapter ("The War within Us"), which briefly previews the book's contents, these meditations cover three main topics: (1) the primal state of humankind before the fall, (2) the fall and its consequences, and (3) the new creation in Jesus Christ, which reestablishes communion between God and humankind. Or to put it in other terms: "existential communion" given, lost, restored.

The primal state of humankind is discussed in two chapters: "Image and Likeness" and "Free Speech: Parrhesia." The creation of the first human beings was an awakening of their own reality to the fact that they were loved by Reality itself, that their existence was an overflow of the abundant joy of God's own existence. This is the life of contemplation, wherein God's human creatures can see God not as a separate object but "as the Reality within our own reality, the Being within our being, the life of our life" (19). Merton uses the Greek word *parrhēsia* — used in the Acts of Apostles to express the boldness and freedom with which the apostles preached the gospel — to express the existential communion between God and human creatures. They were able to communicate freely and familiarly with God. Genesis stresses the active life of Adam in paradise. But "even his activity had an essentially contemplative character, since it was entirely impregnated with light and significance by his union with God" (78).

The fall and its consequences are discussed in two chapters: "Promethean Theology" and "Spirit in Bondage." The fall is described in various ways. It was "the wilful acceptance of unreality." Illusion entered into the story to disrupt the communication between Adam and God. "*Parrhesia* was at an end not because God no longer consented to speak with Adam, but because Adam, stripped of his sincerity, ashamed to be what in fact he was, determined to fly from God and from reality, which he could no longer face without a disguise" (77). Thus it was that Adam withdrew from God, who had been the center of Adam's existence, and put himself at the center of reality. In effect he put "himself" (i.e., the false self that he had constructed) between himself and God. "Adam's sin was a double movement of intraversion and extraversion. He withdrew from God into himself and then, unable to remain centered in himself, he fell beneath himself into the multiplicity and confusion of exterior things" (114). Yet the original fall did not destroy human nature; rather, it weakened it. It still retains its innate capacity for union with God. "The human soul is still the image of God, and no matter how far it travels away from Him into the regions of unreality, it never becomes so completely unreal that its original destiny can cease to torment it with a need to return to itself in God, and become, once again, real" (112). This is the special anguish and restlessness of spirit that burdens us all: we can find rest only in God. "The spiritual *anguish of man*," Merton tells us, "has no cure but mysticism" (114).

These words may serve as an entry into the third part of the book: the re-creation of humanity in Christ. Merton discusses the Pauline parallel of Christ and Adam, but makes clear his position that Adam is subordinated to Christ. The incarnation was not an afterthought following a failed creation; rather, Christ is the beginning of creation and its fulfillment. "The far ends of time meet in His hands" (132). Christ is the uncreated Image of God, whereas Adam was created as the image of the Image of God. Apart from Christ, Adam has no meaning. "In his very creation, Adam is a representation of Christ Who is to come. And we too, from the very moment we come into existence, are potential representations of Christ simply because we possess the human nature which was created in Him and was assumed by Him in the Incarnation, saved by Him on the Cross and glorified by Him in His [Resurrection and] Ascension" (134).

Christ comes as our mediator. He not only teaches us what the Christian life should be; he restores that life to us through the action of his Spirit. The action of Christ through the Spirit "re-centers" our life in God. Jesus Christ, whom the liturgy praises as the "Key of David," "alone has power to enter into the depths of our being, into those depths which lie far beyond our own domination, [and] unlock an ontological abyss that opens out within us upon the darkness of the Beginning, the Source, the Father" (174–75). This opening up of ourselves to God is what happens in baptism, the sacrament of illumination. In baptism we discover (recover) our true identity. The fire that is divine grace makes us members of the risen Christ, united with him and one another in God. This grace, reestablishing humankind in existential communion with God, is God's gift. "We have not stolen it, like Prometheus. It has been given to us because the Father wanted us to have it, in order that we might find ourselves, and become His [Children]" (223). Exultantly, we can say with St. Paul, "All praise to God through Jesus Christ our Lord!" (Rom. 7:25). WHS

SEE ALSO CHRISTOLOGY; FALL; ORIGINAL SIN; REDEMPTION; SALVATION.

Notes

1. There is ample evidence of the earlier title: the expression "existential communion" occurs twelve times in the text of *The New Man*.

2. *The School of Charity* includes a letter that Merton wrote to Dom Gabriel Sortais on May 21, 1960, in which he tells the abbot general that *The New Man*, just that day approved by the censors, had been written in 1955. Thus, 1954 or 1955 seems a reasonable date for the first draft of what became *The New Man*.

3. On p. 105 Merton speaks of Adam possessing "experimental" knowledge, where in later writings he uses the more correct term "experiential" knowledge. Yet note that on p. 185 he does use the word "experiential," and this is also found in the draft text of *Existential Communion* and it is not a correction.

NEW SEEDS OF CONTEMPLATION

New York: New Directions, 1962. xv+297 pp.

In 1949 Thomas Merton had been dissatisfied with *Seeds of Contemplation* and was planning to revise it. In December 1949 he produced an edition with a new preface and a few minor revisions. It was not until 1961 that he did a revision extensive enough to justify adding *New* to the title. In the twelve years that elapsed between the original and the full revision many things had changed in Merton's life. *Seeds of Contemplation* was the work of a young monk glorying in the fact that he had "left the world." *New Seeds of Contemplation* came from the pen of a monk whose flight from the world had been tempered by his realization that if he wished to be an authentic contemplative, then he must learn to share with people outside the monastery "their joys, their sufferings, their ideas, their needs, their desires" (*New Seeds of Contemplation*, 77). Indeed, he goes so far as to say that "contemplation is out of the question for anyone who does not try to cultivate compassion for other men" (77).

Photograph by Thomas Merton

New Seeds of Contemplation was published January 30, 1962, by New Directions. It was not as widely reviewed as its predecessor, though later critics referred to it as "a spiritual classic." Donald Grayston, who has done a singularly valuable and exhaustive analysis of the several versions of *Seeds*,[1] calls the final published work an "encheiridion," a traditional term for a handbook that would tell you all you wanted to know about spirituality. "It is," he says, "comprehensive enough to be a spiritual handbook for the serious and intelligent Christian of today." "It is wide-ranging, covering everything from creation to recreation, from sexuality to television, from war to solitude." "Unlike any of the older encheiridia, it can speak directly to the believer who deeply desires *both* to remain in touch with 'what has been valid' in the Christian past and who is also struggling to work out the dimensions of his or her contemplative vocation in the present world of potential nuclear holocaust."[2] Grayston's variorum edition of *Seeds/New Seeds* spells out in detail the additions, the omissions, the expansions that entitle the last version of *Seeds* to be called *New*.

Chapters 1 ("What Is Contemplation?") and 2 ("What Contemplation Is Not") are key to the book's themes and have no parallel in the earlier version. In language far removed from the manuals of spirituality that Merton had studied in his preparation for the priesthood, they spell out what contemplation had come to mean to him. The language and tone are existential, experiential, nondualistic, and clearly touched by the spirit and even the vocabulary of Zen. A key word is "awareness" (it appears nine times in the first chapter). "Awakening," "realization," and "enlightenment" are appropriate synonyms. Thus, the book begins, "Contemplation is the highest expression of man's intellectual and spiritual life. It is that life itself, fully awake, fully active, fully aware that it is alive" (1). "Contemplation reaches out to the knowledge and even to the experience of the transcendent and inexpressible God" (2). Yet, paradoxically, it is beyond all our knowledge and all our possible explanations. We do not bring God down to our level; rather, God raises us to the divine level. "Contemplation does not simply 'find' a clear idea of God...and hold Him there as a prisoner to Whom it can always return. On the contrary, contemplation is carried away by Him into His own realm, His own mystery and His own freedom" (5).

In chapter 2, and in a number of other places in the book,[3] Merton develops more fully an approach to spirituality that he had hinted at in *Seeds of Contemplation* and expanded somewhat in "The Inner Experience": the distinction between the true self and the false self. "There is an irreducible opposition," he tells us, "between the deep transcendent self that awakens only in contemplation, and the superficial, external self which we commonly identify with the first person singular" (7). The self that appears on the surface is not the hidden, mysterious self that alone is real in the eyes of God; rather, it is a prison from which we must escape. "The only true joy on earth is to escape from the prison of our own false self, and enter by love into union with the Life Who dwells and sings within the essence of every creature and in the core of our own souls" (25).

All through the book one finds the many ways in which Merton attempts to speak about the ineffable reality of God. "So much," he says, "depends on our idea of God! Yet no idea of Him, however pure and perfect, is adequate to express Him as He really is" (15). He adds the important point that our ideas of God tell us more about ourselves than about God. Yet Merton never gives up. Page after page he keeps trying to name the Unnamable, knowing all the while that if he is to talk about God, then he must listen. "Unless [God] utters Himself in you, speaks His own name in the center of your soul, you will no more know Him than a stone knows the ground upon which it rests in its inertia" (39).

Grayston's description of *New Seeds of Contemplation* as an encheiridion of spirituality suggests several possible ways for a profitable reading of the book. An unhurried reading from beginning to end will offer a fairly comprehensive picture of the spirituality of Thomas Merton. Another possible approach is to seek out the chapter that meets the reader's need at the time. Yet a third approach might involve searching the book for enlightenment about significant elements of the spiritual life. The three realities already mentioned, (1) contemplation, (2) true and false self, and (3) speaking about God — themes that thread their way through the book — are good starting points.

Faith, solitude, detachment, distractions, tradition, purity of heart, wisdom, contemplation and the world, and still others can be researched with real profit. Nor should any reader miss the breathtaking concluding chapter, "The General Dance." It integrates many of the themes mentioned above. More than that, it is a poetic bit of prose that ranks with "The Fire Watch" in *The Sign of Jonas* and the little booklet *Day of a Stranger* as vintage Merton.

New Seeds of Contemplation is a book that one can return to again and again as a help and encouragement to spiritual growth. WHS

SEE ALSO *SEEDS OF CONTEMPLATION.*

Notes

1. See Donald Grayston, *Thomas Merton: The Development of a Spiritual Theologian* (Lewiston, N.Y.: Edwin Mellen, 1985); idem, ed., *Thomas Merton's Rewritings: The Five Versions of Seeds/New Seeds of Contemplation as a Key to the Development of His Thought* (Lewiston, N.Y.: Edwin Mellen, 1989).

2. Grayston, *Spiritual Theologian*, 159–60.

3. See, e.g., pp. 21, 25, 26, 31, 33, 34, 38, 48, 57, 60, 109, 279–84, 295–97.

NHAT HANH, THICH

This Vietnamese Buddhist monk, poet, and peacemaker was forced to flee his own country during the Vietnam War. He lives in France in a monastic community known as Plum Village. He has lectured regularly in the United States and has written many books that deal with Buddhism and with peace. He has helped many who knew nothing of Buddhism to understand the teachings of the Buddha and their meaningfulness even for people who profess another religion. Thomas Merton had no difficulty in relating to this extraordinary monk. On May 28, 1966, John Heidbrink, head of the Fellowship of Reconciliation, brought Nhat Hanh to Gethsemani. Merton was impressed by this visit and wrote an article called "Nhat Hanh Is My Brother." "He is more my brother than many who are nearer to me by race and nationality, because he and I see things exactly the same way.... We are both monks, and we have lived the monastic life about the same number of years. We are both poets, existentialists. I have far more in common with Nhat Hanh than I have with many Americans, and I do not hesitate to say it. It is vitally important that such bonds be admitted. They are the bonds of a new solidarity and a new brotherhood which is beginning to be evident on all the five continents and which cut across all political, religious and cultural lines to unite young men and women in every country in something that is more concrete than an ideal and more alive than a program. This unity of the young is the only hope of the world" (*Passion for Peace*, 260–62). WHS

> SEE ALSO MYSTICS AND ZEN MASTERS; VIETNAM; VOID.

NICHOLAS OF CUSA:
Dialogue about the Hidden God

Translated by Thomas Merton. *Lugano Review* (Switzerland), summer 1966, pp. 67–70; also published in a limited edition of one hundred copies, New York: Dim Gray Bar Press, 1989. 14 pp. (unnumbered).

In 1961 Thomas Merton suggested to Victor and Carolyn Hammer a small work of Nicholas of Cusa for a special printing. This never happened. The work was published in the *Lugano Review* five years later. Eventually, the limited edition was published in 1989 by Dim Gray Bar Press. The work is a dialogue between a Christian and a pagan (Gentile). On New Year's Day of 1964 Merton sent a mimeograph of his translation to R. J. Zwi Werblowsky. He tells him, "One of the things that strikes the alert reason is that the 'pagan' is really a 'Christian' of the superficial type" (*Hidden Ground of Love*, 587). The basic theme of Nicholas of Cusa's book is the absolute unknowability of God. Through a series of paradoxes he leads the pagan to an understanding that God eludes every concept that affirms anything. God is not nothing and not something. For God is All. "God cannot be said to be this rather than that, since all things are from him" ([9]). The dialogue ends with a prayer: "May God therefore who is hidden from the eyes of the wise men of the world, be blessed forever" ([12]). WHS

"NIGHT BEFORE THE BATTLE, THE"

> SEE ALSO NOVELS, UNPUBLISHED.

NILES–MERTON SONGS, THE:
Opus 171 and 172

Music by John Jacob Niles; poetry by Thomas Merton. Champaign, Ill.: Mark Foster Music Company, 1981. xv+95 pp.

This book presents the collaboration between composer John Jacob Niles and poet Thomas Merton. In late summer 1967 Carolyn Hammer took John Jacob and Rena Niles to Gethsemani to visit with Merton. In "As I Remember," published, by way of introduction, in *The Niles–Merton Songs*, Rena Niles recalls that Niles and Merton "met no more than a half-dozen times," and yet when John and Rena heard of Merton's death in December 1968, they felt that they "both had lost an old and close friend" (*Niles–Merton Songs*, v).

Merton visited with John Jacob and Rena Niles at Gethsemani and at their home at Boot Hill Farm. It was on his first visit to the farm, in October 1967, that Merton heard the first of the songs. In his journal he writes about the visit. He found the Niles home "a fascinating place" and hearing the first of the songs "a moving experience" (*Other Side of the Mountain*, 7). He described it this way: "As we were finishing dinner the singer and pianist arrived and had coffee. Then the songs. John has set Messenger, Carol, Responsory (1948) and is working on Evening. I thought the settings very effective and satisfactory. In fact was very moved by them. But above all by this lovely girl, Jackie Roberts, who put her whole heart into singing them. What was most beautiful was that! I do think John Niles has brought out a lot of what I wanted to say and made me value my own poems more. It was to me a very intense experience" (7).[1] He added that John Niles was "a character" and that he liked him (7). Rena Niles recalled Merton's enthusiasm that evening: "Had Merton's response been anything but unrestrained enthusiasm, it is unlikely that other songs would have been written" (*Niles–Merton Songs*, v). Niles completed Opus

NO MAN IS AN ISLAND 327

171 by the fall of 1968, when, according to Rena Niles, Merton visited the Niles home for the second time and heard Jacqueline Roberts perform the first group of songs.[2] Niles composed the twelve songs in Opus 172 in 1969 and 1970, after Merton's death.

Opus 171 includes ten songs: "The Messenger," "The Nativity (Carol)," "A Responsory, 1948," "Sundown," "When You Point Your Finger," "The Weathercock on the Cathedral of Quito," "Evening," "Great Prayer," "Love Winter When the Plant Says Nothing," and "Lament of a Maiden for the Warrior's Death." Opus 172 includes twelve songs: "O Sweet Irrational Worship," "Autumn," "Wisdom," "The Mirror's Mission," "For My Brother: Reported Missing in Action, 1943," "The Greek Women," "Cana," "The Ohio River — Louisville," "Original Sin (A Memorial Anthem for Father's Day)," "Birdcage Walk," "Jesus Weeps into the Fire," and "Mosaic: St. Praxed's."

Rena Niles ends her reminiscence by quoting some lines from John Jacob Niles's last book, *Brick Dust and Buttermilk*.[3] The lines are a fitting tribute to John Jacob Niles and Thomas Merton and to their artistic collaboration: "When I am just a whisper in the wind, /... Even then my song will never die, / Even then my song will swirl and spin / And find men's hearts to rest therein" (*Niles–Merton Songs*, v). CMB

Notes

1. In "As I Remember" Rena Niles notes that Merton heard only "The Messenger" and "The Nativity" (entitled "Carol" in *Selected Poems*) — "the only songs composed" (*Niles–Merton Songs*, v). Perhaps they were the only songs completed at the time.

2. Merton mentions visiting the Nileses in Lexington in June 1968 and listening to John Jacob Niles's setting for his poems and for his translations of Cuadra, Cortes, and Carrera (see *Other Side of the Mountain*, 128). But Merton does not mention the meeting in fall 1968 that Rena Niles reports.

3. Frankfort, Ky.: Boone Tolliver Press, 1977.

NO MAN IS AN ISLAND

New York: Harcourt, Brace, 1955.

xxiii+264 pp.

The title of this work, a well-known and somewhat overworked sentence from John Donne, hardly captures the book's main thrust. The sense of community we have with one another, which the title suggests, is clarified in the prologue; and while it casts its light over the rest of the chapters, it is not, for all that, their principal emphasis. The book is about "some of the basic verities on which the spiritual life depends" (*No Man Is an Island*, x). It is dedicated (in Latin) to the scholastics and newly ordained priests of the Abbey of Gethsemani for whom Thomas Merton had been spiritual master, and may well have emerged from lectures given to these monks. There are times when clearly he seems to be talking to monks. This characteristic of some of his earlier writings can be irritating to nonmonastic readers. It may well suggest an impatience on his part to do the proper editing that a careful writer would do.

No Man Is an Island grew out of an earlier text of thirty pages that Merton called "Sentences," about which he wrote to Sr. Therese Lentfoehr in 1959, telling her that it was probably better than "the long-winded finished book." Merton sees the book as a sequel to his earlier work, *Seeds of Contemplation*. It returns to the material in the earlier work, but his intention is to make that material simpler, more fundamental, and more detailed.

Fundamental to the faith Merton professed is tradition that gives intelligibility to that faith. *No Man Is an Island* offers a much more mature understanding of tradition than does *Seeds of Contemplation*. In chapter 12 of the earlier book, entitled "Tradition and Revolution," he writes, "The reason why Catholic tradition is a tradition is because there is only one living doctrine in Christianity: there is nothing new to be discovered" (*Seeds of Contemplation*, 84). Hardly a revolutionary statement! By contrast, in the later book he says, "I do not intend to divorce myself at any point from Catholic tradition. But neither do I intend to accept points of that tradition blindly" (*No Man Is an Island*, xiv). In chapter 8 he writes, "Tradition, which is always old, is at the same time ever new because it is always reviving — born again in each new generation, *to be lived and applied in a new and particular way.... * Tradition is creative. Always original, it always opens out *new horizons for an* old journey.... [I]t teaches us how to love, because it develops and expands our powers, and shows us how to give ourselves to the world in which we live" (151 [italics added]).

No Man Is an Island has an author's note (ix–x), a prologue (xi–xxiii), and sixteen chapters (3–264). The topics of the chapters all relate to the spiritual life, but each stands pretty much on its own; no effort is made to link them together. These are the chapter titles: (1) "Love Can Be Kept Only by Being Given Away," (2) "Sentences on Hope," (3) "Conscience, Freedom and Prayer," (4) "Pure Intention," (5) "The Word of the Cross," (6) "Asceticism and Sacrifice," (7) "Being and Doing," (8) "Vocation," (9) "The Measure of Charity," (10) "Sincerity," (11) "Mercy," (12) "Recollection," (13) "My Soul Remembered God," (14) "The Wind Blows Where It Pleases," (15) "The Inward Solitude," and (16) "Silence."

Many of these topics are discussed in other essays in this encyclopedia—for example, asceticism, conscience, freedom, mercy, prayer, silence, and solitude. For further insights, see entries on these and similar topics. WHS

NONDUALISM

The word "nondualism" is seldom found in Thomas Merton's writings, but the notion of nondualism is the understood background of much of his writing on contemplation, especially in his later works. Nondualism is a rejection of the dualism that has so strongly influenced much of Western thought. The term "dualism" is not an easy one to define. It appears in Plato's teaching about two worlds (one of ideas and one of particulars), in the Manichaean teaching about two equal principles at work in the world (one of good and one of evil), in Descartes's understanding of the opposition of mind and matter, and in Kant's distinction between the world of phenomena and the world of noumena. Nondualism is not to be confused with monism, which holds that there is only one being that exists.

For Thomas Merton nondualism is the authentic way of seeing all of reality, that is, in nonseparateness. This vision, however, is not reflected in Merton's autobiography. *The Seven Storey Mountain* is heavily dualistic in tone. There is a clear separateness between God and creation, natural and supernatural. This is true also of *Seeds of Contemplation*. When the latter book was published, a reviewer from *The London Times Literary Supplement*, while praising the book, wrote nevertheless, "There is so sharp a break and so deep a gulf between 'natural' and 'supernatural' that those who refuse the leap must be pardoned."[1]

Nondualism appears definitively in "The Inner Experience." Merton writes about the apophatic experience of "knowing God in the darkness of unknowing." "The inner self of the mystic, elevated and transformed in Christ, united to the Father in the Son, through the Holy Spirit, now knows God not so much through the medium of an objective image, as through its own divinized subjectivity.... Intuition reaches [God] by one final leap beyond itself, an ecstasy in which it sacrifices itself and yields itself to His transcendent presence. In this last ecstatic act of 'unknowing' the gap between our spirit as subject and God as object is finally closed, and in the embrace of mystical love we know that we and He are one" ("Inner Experience," 68–69). Note the use here of the distinction between the true self ("the inner self," "its own divinized subjectivity") and the false or exterior self (the self that is yielded to God's transcendent presence). The discovery of the true self is the end of the experience of duality.

This same nondualism is present in numerous places and in various contexts in *New Seeds of Contemplation*. Thus, Merton writes of contemplation that it is "the experiential grasp of reality as *subjective*, not so much 'mine' (which would signify 'belonging to the external self'), but 'myself' in existential mystery. Contemplation does not arrive at reality after a process of deduction, but by an intuitive awakening in which our free and personal reality becomes fully alive to its own existential depths, which open out into the mystery of God" (*New Seeds of Contemplation*, 8–9). Similar passages abound in *New Seeds of Contemplation*. The final chapter, "The General Dance," speaks movingly about the way in which God raises us above the dualities of life and makes us one with God (294).

In the last ten years of his life Merton read deeply in Zen Buddhism and was strongly influenced by the nondualism that is so central to Zen. This influence can be found in his essay on "Mystics and Zen Masters" in his book of the same title, as well as in his extensive probing of Zen in *Zen and the Birds of Appetite*. In the initial essay in the latter work he discusses how Cartesian thought has adversely affected the Western understanding of human consciousness and even of God. He writes, "Modern man, in so far as he is still Cartesian..., is a subject for whom his own self-awareness as a thinking, observing, measuring and estimating 'self' is absolutely primary.... The more he is able to develop his consciousness as a subject over against objects... the more he tends to isolate himself in his own subjective prison, to become a detached observer cut off from everything else in a kind of impenetrable alienated and transparent bubble which contains all reality in the form of purely subjective experience." Imprisoned in his or her own consciousness, the Cartesian person is "isolated and out of touch with other such selves, in so far as they are all 'things' rather than persons" (*Birds of Appetite*, 22). Such a mentality, Merton insists, inevitably leads to "the death of God." Cartesian thought tries to reach God as an object by beginning with the thinking self. "But when God becomes object, he sooner or later 'dies,' because God as object is ultimately unthinkable" (23).

Merton would have us understand a different kind of consciousness: one that begins not from the thinking self-aware subject, but from Being, "ontologically seen to be beyond and prior to the subject-object division. Underlying the subjective experience of the individual self there is an immediate experience of Being.... It is completely nonobjective. It has in it none of the split and alienation that occurs when the subject becomes aware of itself as a quasi-object" (23–24). In such an understanding of consciousness "the self is not its own center and does not orbit around itself; it is centered on God, the one center of all, which is 'everywhere and nowhere,' in whom all are en-

countered, from whom all proceed. Thus from the very start this consciousness is disposed to encounter 'the other' with whom it is already united anyway 'in God'" (24).

In *Mystics and Zen Masters* Merton writes that Zen enlightenment "results from the resolution of all subject-object relationships and oppositions in a pure void" (*Mystics and Zen Masters*, 13). He points out that Zen is by no means a simple withdrawal from an outer world of matter into an inner world of spirit. "The first and most elementary fact about Zen is its abhorrence of this dualistic division between matter and spirit" (13).

In 1967 Merton responded to a group of students at Smith College who, under the tutelage of Dr. Amiya Chakravarty, had engaged in an afternoon and evening of reading and discussing Merton's writings. Chakravarty wrote to Merton telling him how enjoyable the sessions had been. Some of the students also wrote to him. In his response of April 13, 1967, Merton told them that nothing is more rewarding to a writer than to be understood and appreciated. He expresses his belief that they had indeed understood his writings; but more than that, they had come to see something most precious and most available too: "the reality that is present to us and in us." While we may call it different names (e.g., Being, Atman, Pneuma, Silence), what really matters is "the simple fact that by being attentive, by learning to listen (or recovering the natural capacity to listen which cannot be learned any more than breathing), we can find ourself engulfed in such happiness that it cannot be explained: the happiness of being at one with everything in that hidden ground of Love for which there can be no explanations" (*Hidden Ground of Love*, 115). Happiness, Merton is saying, can be found only by going beyond the dualities of life (no easy task, for these dualities seem so real to us) and being at one with everything. This oneness is no pantheistic or impersonal experience, for it springs from a "hidden ground," and that ground is personal, for it is "the ground of Love."

It was of this oneness that Thomas Merton spoke on October 23, 1968, to a group of religious leaders at the Temple of Understanding Meeting in Calcutta. "The deepest level of communication is not communication, but communion. It is wordless. It is beyond words, and it is beyond speech, and it is beyond concept. Not that we discover a new unity. We discover an older unity. My dear brothers, we are already one. But we imagine that we are not. And what we have to recover is our original unity. What we have to be is what we are" (*Asian Journal*, 308).

Before he left for Asia, Merton conversed with Br. David Steindl-Rast at Our Lady of the Redwoods Abbey in Whitethorn, California. Merton spoke about intercessory prayer. "We are not rainmakers, but Christians," Merton said. "In our dealings with God he is free and so are we. It's simply a need for me to express my love by praying for my friends. . . . If you love another person, it's God's love being realized. One and the same love is reaching your friend through you, and you through your friend." Br. David asked, "But isn't there still an implicit dualism in all this?" Merton replied, "Really there isn't, and yet there is. You have to see your will and God's will dualistically for a long time. You have to experience duality for a long time until you see it's not there. . . . Any moment you can break through to the underlying unity which is God's gift in Christ. In the end, Praise praises. Thanksgiving gives thanks. Jesus prays. Openness is all."[2] These words have the ring of autobiography. Merton realized that it is not a question of talking yourself out of duality or reasoning your way into unity; rather you must take the time to open yourself to experience — the experience of oneness with God and in God oneness with all that is. WHS

SEE ALSO CONTEMPLATION; GOD; MYSTICISM; SELF; THEOLOGY.

Notes

1. *The London Times Literary Supplement*, December 25, 1949, 845.
2. David Steindl-Rast, "Recollections of Thomas Merton's Last Days in the West," in *Monastic Studies* 7 (Pine City, N.Y.: Mt. Saviour Monastery, 1969 reprint), 10.

NONVIOLENCE

The breadth of Thomas Merton's vision of nonviolence is evident above all in his conviction

that war depends precisely on narrowness of vision, a deliberately limited range of identification, the division of humanity into "us" and "them." The roots of violence are found in a denial of the common human condition, a distorted, dualistic perception of self and society that projects one's own unadmitted evil upon "the other" (see *Ishi Means Man*, 26–27). Conversely, the peacemaker is one who is committed to the unity of the human race, to the search for a common ground that transcends division even as it respects legitimate differences. "Christian non-violence is not built on a presupposed division, but on the basic unity of man. It is not out for the conversion of the wicked to the ideas of the good, but for the healing and reconciliation of man with himself, man the person and man the human family" (*Faith and Violence*, 15). Nonviolence rejects the presupposition that the fullness of goodness and truth is possessed exclusively by one side or the other. Therefore the process of transformation, of conversion, must be mutual, arising from a dialogue in which all parties can deepen their perception of truth, both by recognizing what they have in common and by finding in each other not merely errors but valuable insights missing in themselves. "A test of our sincerity in the practice of non-violence is this: are we willing to *learn something from the adversary?* . . . Our readiness to see some good in him and to agree with some of his ideas (though tactically this might look like a weakness on our part), actually gives us power, the power of sincerity and of truth" (23–24).

This is by no means a sentimental, uncritical benevolence, as the examples of Gandhi and King, among others, testify; rather, it is a commitment to a more comprehensive perspective than self-interest and the "party line." Nonviolence is resistance to injustice and untruth, but to be consistent it must resist these tendencies as they are present within oneself and one's own group as well; otherwise it degenerates into a sterile pharisaism (see *Guilty Bystander*, 64–65), an exercise in self-righteousness and self-justification that cannot bring about peace and reconciliation. If the oppressor betrays his or her own humanity in denying that of the opponent, the true peacemaker affirms the common humanity of both by refusing to respond in kind. Nonviolence means commitment to liberation of the oppressed, but it must include the liberation of the oppressor as well. "The key to non-violence is the willingness of the non-violent resister to suffer a certain amount of accidental evil in order to bring about a change of mind in the oppressor" (*Faith and Violence*, 27–28). The measure of the peacemaker's success is not found in the response of the opponent, but in one's own fidelity to this fundamental truth.

If the breadth of Merton's vision of nonviolence is found in his conviction of "the total solidarity of all" (*Nonviolent Alternative*, 257), its length is revealed in his appropriating and transmitting the largely disregarded history and tradition of Christian peace witness. For Merton the redemptive love of Jesus signifies that nonviolence is not a peripheral aspect of Christian faith but the normative way of sharing in the paschal mystery: "The Christian is and must be by his very adoption as a son of God, in Christ, a peacemaker (Matt. 5:9). He is bound to imitate the Savior who, instead of defending Himself with twelve legions of angels (Matt. 26:55), allowed Himself to be nailed to the Cross and died praying for His executioners" (*Breakthrough to Peace*, 95). This basic truth was clearly understood by the first generations of Christians. The growth and development of the church in the era of persecution was fundamentally a consequence of this willingness to live and die in conformity with the example of Christ and in reliance on the power of Christ. Merton writes, "Christian non-violence and meekness imply a particular understanding of the power of human poverty and powerlessness when they are united with the invisible strength of Christ.... The early history of the Church, the record of the apostles and martyrs remains to testify to this inherent and mysterious dynamism of the ecclesial 'event' in the world of history and time. Christian non-violence is rooted in this consciousness and this faith" (*Faith and Violence*, 17–18).

Merton is also aware, of course, of the decline of the original nonviolent ideal: "Christianity overcame pagan Rome by nonviolence. But when Christianity became the religion of the Empire, then the stoic and political virtues of the Empire began to supplant the original theological virtues of the first Christians. The heroism of the soldier supplanted the heroism of the martyr" (*Guilty Bystander*, 87). Merton looks elsewhere for inspiration and enlightenment: to the steadfast witness of the early church, the largely forgotten testimony to nonviolence of Clement of Alexandria and Justin Martyr, of Origen and Maximus the Confessor; to the "deep, simple, all-embracing love" of Francis of Assisi, who thought "that the best way to turn men's minds to peace was to remind them of the goodness of life and of the world" (*Seeds of Destruction*, 182–83); to the Christian humanism of Erasmus, whose claim that one "can overcome evil by taking it upon oneself" is nothing but "the wisdom of the Gospels" (*Gandhi on Non-Violence*, 15); to the clarity of vision and depth of commitment shown by Franz Jägerstätter, the Austrian conscientious objector martyred by the Nazis (see *Faith and Violence*, 69–75); to Dorothy Day, whose "social action ... is far more significantly Christian than the rather subtle and comfy positions of certain casuists" (*Passion for Peace*, 91). It is the tradition of gospel nonviolence manifested through the ages by the "cloud of witnesses" such as these that Merton believes is most needed to deal creatively with the crises of the present day.

But Merton situates nonviolence in relation not only to the past but also to the future: "The Christian attitude to war and peace is fundamentally eschatological" (*Seeds of Destruction*, 129). More accurately, for the Christian the present moment must at once recapitulate the past, the redemptive events of Christ's life, death, and resurrection, and anticipate the future, the completion of the drama of salvation, for the eschatological dimension is present not only beyond but within history. "Christian nonviolence is nothing if not first of all a formal profession of faith in the Gospel message that the Kingdom has been established and that the Lord of truth is indeed risen and reigning over his Kingdom" (*Faith and Violence*, 18). God's rule has entered into history in the person of Jesus, and in every age must be incarnated, actualized, in the lives of the disciples of Jesus. The vocation of the Christian, and especially of the Christian community, is to be "a witness to an entirely new dimension in man's life" (*Seeds of Destruction*, 127); the church is called to be a sign, a "sacrament," that manifests the new order instituted by Christ: "Christian discipleship entails a certain way of acting, a *politeia*, a *conversatio*, which is proper to the Kingdom" (*Faith and Violence*, 16). Central to this way of acting is the renunciation of hatred, of violence. From this perspective nonviolence is simply one name given to authentic Christianity, to "life in Christ."

Such a stance is not, of course, a naive belief that everything will "work out" if one remains calm and serene. Gospel nonviolence is a sign of contradiction to a world fixated on power, wealth, and force, a world that may not only reject and ridicule but also try to destroy such a sign, as it did on Calvary; yet faith testifies that this "fierce combat which marshalls all the forces of evil and darkness against the still invisible truth . . . is already decided by the victory of Christ over death and over sin" (18). The Christian is empowered by the Spirit to forgo the satisfactions of immediate results because of this ultimate victory, or rather is able to leave the question of results in the hands of God: "The Christian can renounce the protection of violence and risk being humble, therefore *vulnerable*, not because he trusts in the supposed efficacy of a gentle and persuasive tactic that will disarm hatred and tame cruelty, but because he believes that the hidden power of the Gospel is demanding to be manifested in and through his own poor person" (18). Here is Merton's interpretation of the traditional ascetic ideal of "submission to the will of God." Far from being passive and resigned to one's "fate," it means being receptive to the divine energy, becoming a channel of God's power and love; it is active in the highest sense, because Pure Act is its source.

The depth of Merton's outlook on peacemaking is evident in his conviction that the nonviolence of the gospel corresponds to the deepest needs, desires, and hopes of the human spirit. Merton is profoundly aware of the tangled roots of violence, hatred, and the will to power that so often prevent the seeds of peace from germinating. He frequently explores and lays bare the illusions, the self-deceptions, the perversions of language that have enabled human beings to "make a desert and call it peace." Yet despite the innate tendency toward sin and the degree of evil imposed or freely chosen, each person is created good, in the image of God, and one can never presume that the spark of goodness has been extinguished in anyone, that anyone is beyond the reach of divine grace. Hence the Christian operates not from a naive optimism, an assurance that "the system" will set things right sooner or later, but with a mature hope, based on responsible human action in conformity with the salvific will of God, which appeals to the capacity for truth and love that makes one human. Such a consistent stance requires a spiritual discipline, a contemplative awareness, a receptiveness to "that peace which the world cannot give," without which even those formally committed to peace and love risk becoming participants in the very attitudes and actions they oppose. A compulsive activism that relies on its own resources and finds its satisfaction in its own successes is considered to be "cooperation in violence" by Merton: "The frenzy of the activist neutralizes his work for peace. . . . It destroys the fruitfulness of his own work, because it kills the root of inner wisdom which makes work fruitful" (*Guilty Bystander*, 73). In contrast, the figure of Gandhi, whose "non-violence was effective in so far as it began first within himself" (*Seeds of Destruction*, 224), provides a model for the integration of being and doing, worship and action. For Merton, as for Gandhi, "The first and fundamental truth is to be sought in respect for our own inmost being, and this in turn implies the recollectedness and the awareness which attune us to that silence in which alone Being speaks to us in all its simplicity" (232). Contemplation, the experiential awareness of union with God, is not a withdrawal from the concerns of the wider world, not a renunciation of activity, but an essential prerequisite and accompaniment, the inner leaven, to any authentically Christian social action. This recognition of the integral link between prayer and action, this sense of the relevance to the struggle for peace and justice of detachment (from power, possessiveness, jealousy, pride, even from results) and recollection (of the scattered consciousness into unity with itself and union with its Ground), is perhaps Merton's most profound contribution to a contemporary spirituality of nonviolence. As he writes in what was probably his final essay on the topic, "Nonviolence is not for power but for truth. It is not pragmatic but prophetic. It is not aimed at immediate political results, but at the manifestation of fundamental and crucially important truth. Nonviolence is not primarily the language of efficacy, but the language of *kairos*. It does not say 'We shall overcome' so much as 'This is the day of the Lord, and whatever may happen to us, *He* shall overcome'" (*Nonviolent Alternative*, 75). POC

SEE ALSO FAITH AND VIOLENCE; GANDHI ON NON-VIOLENCE; JUST WAR, THEORY OF; NONVIOLENT ALTERNATIVE; PASSION FOR PEACE; PEACE; SEEDS OF DESTRUCTION; WAR.

NONVIOLENT ALTERNATIVE, THE

Revised edition of *Thomas Merton on Peace*. New York: Farrar, Straus, and Giroux, 1980. xli+270 pp.

The revision of *Thomas Merton on Peace* consists in a new title and the replacement of one essay, "Message aux amis de Gandhi," by Merton's poem "Chant to Be Used in Processions around a Site with Furnaces." WHS

SEE ALSO THOMAS MERTON ON PEACE.

NOVELS, UNPUBLISHED

In the time between his baptism and his entrance into the Abbey of Gethsemani, Thomas Merton wrote one novel that eventually was published, *My Argument with the Gestapo* (though it was not published until 1969, the year after his death), and three novels (that are basically the same novel) that remain unpublished. Merton was working on them in the summer of 1939 at the Marcus cottage near Olean, New York, where he spent the summer with his college friends Robert Lax and Edward Rice. During that summer all three

were working on their separate novels. Merton writes, "The thing I got started on grew longer and longer and eventually it was about five hundred pages long, and was called first 'Straits of Dover' and then 'The Night Before the Battle,' and then 'The Labyrinth.' In its final form, it was shorter, and had been half rewritten, and it went to several publishers but to my great sorrow never got printed" (*Seven Storey Mountain*, 240). He describes it as partly autobiographical but mixed with a number of imaginary characters that he introduced when the story seemed to be getting dull. The autobiographical parts, he informs us, took in some of the ground covered in *The Seven Storey Mountain*, but much more of the ground that he had avoided in that book (241).

Sections of the "Straits of Dover" and "The Labyrinth" exist. There are also parts of a novel entitled "The Man in the Sycamore Tree." It appears that nothing is extant of "The Night before the Battle." Since Merton did not hesitate to change titles, it is possible that "The Man in the Sycamore Tree" is a variation of "The Night Before the Battle." Either title actually could fit the text that is extant. The main character in "The Man in the Sycamore Tree" is Jim Mariner, a thinly disguised name for Merton himself.[1] For some while after his confirmation he used the name he had been given at confirmation, signing himself Thomas James Merton. In the novel, Mariner is Zacchaeus of Luke's Gospel seeking a better view of Jesus' role in his life. He moves about New York City (the Messalina Hotel, Butler Hall at Columbia, the Church of Our Lady of Guadalupe), overwhelmed by the impending doom that is about to happen: the Second World War. Scattered through the text are apocalyptic verses from the New Testament that create an eerie sense of coming doom. Thoughts about becoming a priest and an encounter with a poor beggar who challenges his charity appear as disparate episodes in the story of a young man who feels bewildered and helpless in a world that he sees headed for destruction. In September 1939, on his way to church, Mariner hears the distressing news that Hitler has bombed Warsaw and the war has begun. The text of "The Man in the Sycamore Tree" concludes with these sobering words: "It was war. Already hundreds of people were dead" (38).[2]

"Straits of Dover" tells the story of Thomas Merton's life at Oakham, starting with the autumn of 1930, when he was fifteen and in his second year at the school. The narrative begins with a comparison of Oakham and other English public schools and a description of the environs of Oakham. He is especially fascinated by the roads leading out of Oakham: each "led to something of peculiar and individual interest." His favorite was the road to Brooke Hill. He went there often, sometimes with a friend, but more often alone. In one place, the words partially written over to delete them but still easy enough to read, he writes, "Nobody ever said anything to me about it. But it was rather unusual for one to go for walks alone, and I must have had the reputation of a rather solitary fellow." He mentions a week's trip, alone, to Rome during Easter time in 1931 but gives no details. He was a young man searching for maturity and meaning in life. "I knew that there was something tremendous I was living for, and it was good, and beautiful and irresistible: I didn't bother about knowing exactly what it was, because I would find out sooner or later." Perhaps, he conjectures, he will find it when he leaves Oakham to go to Cambridge.

Some Cambridge days are described. He writes of a class of seven students who met for Professor Bullough's lectures on Dante. "This was by far the best class we had, but unfortunately it came early in the morning, and if you got the big leather armchair, right in front of the fire, you were likely to go to sleep." At Cambridge he kept up his relationships with some of his Oakham schoolmates: Ray Dickens at St. John's College and Andrew Winser at St. Catherine's. The book concludes with the story of his grandfather's visit in 1932 and a description of Aunt Maud, his great aunt who was more or less his guardian during most of his years at Oakham. He expresses his love and gratitude for her and all she had meant to him. "Straits of Dover" is helpful in filling in the gaps in *The Seven Storey Mountain*.

So too is "The Labyrinth." The narrative begins in autumn 1931 with Merton boarding

Lax/Marcus cottage, Olean, New York

ship to return to Oakham after a month-and-a-half stay in America with his grandparents, Pop and Bonnemaman. They drove him to the ship in their big Buick, with his trunk strapped to the top. He brought back with him records of American jazz unavailable in a small town like Oakham. This was his third year at Oakham. He was a house prefect in Hodge Wing, where he had charge of some of the younger students. The remaining year and a half at Oakham are passed over rather briefly. More detailed is the description of his journey to the continent, following his graduation. With a generous gift from his guardian, Tom Bennett, he started out on February 1, 1933, the day after his eighteenth birthday. From Paris he traveled to southern France and then into Italy. He arrived in Florence with a boil throbbing on his elbow, a toothache, and a bad cold. Fortunately, he had a letter of introduction to a Mr. S., an English sculptor and brother of a former headmaster at Oakham. After a bit of tea and some hot compresses on his arm, he felt well enough to accept his host's invitation to a movie, where Greta Garbo was playing in *Grand Hotel*. When he arrived in Rome, the toothache was worse. After two trips to the dentist, the tooth at last was removed, and he returned to his hotel room feeling miserable and "spitting blood into a pail." The next day he felt much better and began his Roman adventure.

It was during this visit that he discovered not the Rome of a dimly remembered history enshrined in ruins, but a Rome that was very much alive: Christian Rome. He writes, "I suddenly began to find out about Byzantine mosaics: things that before I had scarcely looked at, for being clumsy and ugly and brutally stupid, suddenly revealed themselves to be full of sophistication at once with innocence of feeling. The things had a depth and complication and subtlety and wisdom in them that I had never seen anywhere." One day he found in the ruins of Caligula's palace the remains of an old church, "a couple of columns holding up a brick arch and on the wall a Byzantine fresco of the crucifixion . . . I was suddenly very awed and surprised to find that this was something I recognized and understood. Something I had been looking for." He began visiting church after church. He purchased a copy of the Latin Vulgate version of the Bible. One day he visited a Trappist monastery (the Tre Fontane). He writes, "I thought for about twenty minutes in my Protestant heart that I would like to be a Trappist monk, and never open my mouth except to confess or to pray or to sing those ancient Gregorian hymns."

A conversion experience[3] (and this it seems was what was happening to him) is not always joy and peace. As a convert, one has to face oneself. Sometimes, doing so can be a searing experience. Merton's self-respect, he tells us, completely collapsed. "I fell into the middle of a great depression. . . . I could actually feel myself go sour. I could feel myself turning to ashes inside. . . . I was convinced that I was an unbearable person, my ideas were impossible, my desires were beastly, my vanity an offense, my pride monstrous." In his visit to one of the churches he said the only prayer he knew, the Lord's Prayer. "I began to feel healed inside again. I asked God to let me be better than I had been so far, and to forgive me for being the kind of person I had wanted to be in the last three or four years."

The "conversion" was short-lived. He returned to America for spring and summer 1933. For a while he continued his prayers and reading of the Gospels. Then, on Easter Sunday, he attended an Episcopal service in Douglaston. He was shocked when the priest managed to give an Easter sermon without mentioning Christ. "After that Easter," he writes, "I reached the conclusion that I had been despondent in Rome, because I was simply lonely there. . . . By

the middle of the summer I was absorbed in a book about psychoanalysis and had forgotten about my gospels."

Chapter 2 of "The Labyrinth" tells of his return to England and his entrance into Clare College, Cambridge. He had lodgings in an old house on Bridge Street. Among the pictures he put on his wall was "one of my father's paintings of some homes in the south of France." Chapter 3 is missing. Chapter 4 has the title "The Party in the Middle of the Night." The night was November 14, 1933. The details of the party have been eliminated from the extant typescript of the book. He describes his year in Cambridge in general as the fall of a symbolic night. If Rome was the high point of this period in his life, Cambridge was a big low. "From Rome, as Zenith, you could take your compasses and draw the track of my sun about in a sweeping half circle that falls and falls to this nadir: Cambridge." Eventually he was called in by his guardian, who demanded an accounting of the way he was wasting his life. He tried to explain that he was sorry about not going to lectures, spending too much money, and the mix-up about girls. Curiously, he says about these things, "I was not really responsible for them." He tried to convey a sense of sorrow to his guardian: "I am sorry for everything." "He neither believed that nor did I mean it, as much as I thought I did."

After a mediocre showing in the examinations, he returned to America. The year was 1934. His grandfather suggested that he go to Columbia. With his entrance into Columbia the story begins to change and lighten up a bit. He discovered the Columbia library and a new-found happiness in making his way through the tiers and tiers of books that beckoned to him.

Chapter 4 is followed by chapter 17 and then an epilogue. Much of the material in these last two sections is fictional, and, with the skip from chapter 4 to 17, it would appear that much material is missing.

Reading these novels, even in the form in which they now exist, makes it easy to understand the judgment made by Robert Giroux, editor at Harcourt, Brace, that the problem with the novels was simply that "They got nowhere." For this reason he rejected them.[4] Later he would accept *The Seven Storey Mountain* because it actually did get somewhere! WHS

SEE ALSO *MY ARGUMENT WITH THE GESTAPO.*

Notes

1. Paul Pearson has pointed to Merton's use of "mariner" in his poem "Landfall" (*Figures for an Apocalypse,* 88; *Collected Poems,* 190): "O Mariner, what is the name of this unchartered Land? / On these clean shores shall stand what sinless voyager? / What angels breathe the music of this atmosphere?" See Paul Pearson, "Thomas Merton in Search of His Heart: The Autobiographical Impulse of Merton's Bonaventure Novels," *The Merton Annual* 9 (1996): 74–89.

2. The page reference is to the extant text of "The Man in the Sycamore Tree" as it appears in *The Merton Annual* 5 (1992): 8–38.

3. Interestingly, though the Roman narrative is longer in "The Labyrinth" than in *The Seven Storey Mountain,* it does not tell the story that is so prominent in *The Seven Storey Mountain:* the experience he had of his deceased father in his hotel room.

4. See Robert Giroux's article in *Columbia College Today* (spring 1969): 69.

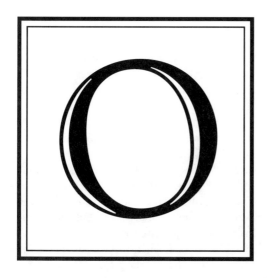

ORIGINAL CHILD BOMB
points for meditation to be scratched on the walls of a cave
THOMAS MERTON

OAKHAM

This market town in Rutland County in the English Midlands is home to the public school that Thomas Merton attended from 1929 to 1932. Rutland was the smallest county in England until its incorporation into Leicestershire. WHS

OAKHAMIAN, THE

The Oakhamian is the school paper for Oakham School. In 1931 Thomas Merton returned from America as editor. He wrote a number of articles and did some drawings for the paper. One of his drawings shows the ghost of a Latin poet against the background of the school courtyard. An editorial in the Christmas 1931 issue on "The City without a Soul" is the sophisticated writing of a young author who quite self-consciously assumes a cosmopolitan air as he writes about New York City, the city that he knows better than any of his schoolmates. "It is beautiful and terrifying. It is immense and unbelievable. It is a city of steel and concrete, of movie palaces and chewing gum, of mass-production and quick-lunch bars, of speakeasies and soda fountains. The home of

Oakham Chapel, Rutland, England

Duke Ellington and Jack Diamond, of Ziegfield and Al Smith. A city of skyscrapers and cereal breakfasts. The city without a soul." For most of the articles in *The Oakhamian* the authors are not named, but quite a number of them are not difficult to identify as clearly or probably from the pen of Thomas Merton, a young author beginning to flex his literary muscles. WHS

Cover for *Original Child Bomb* reprinted with the permission of Unicorn Press. Cover design and art by Emil Antonucci.

OAKHAM SCHOOL

Oakham School, located in the town of Oakham, is an English public school (public schools in England are privately endowed schools). It has a long history, having been founded in 1584 by Robert Johnson, archdeacon of Leicester, under royal charter from Queen Elizabeth I. Thomas Merton entered Oakham School in the autumn of 1929 and completed his studies there at the end of 1932. In the autumn of 1931 he became editor of the school journal, *The Oakhamian.* WHS

OBEDIENCE

Abbot James Fox is reported to have said to many that Fr. Louis (Thomas Merton) was "a most faithful monk, a most obedient monk."[1] Surprising as this may sound to those who recall that Fr. Louis and Dom James had their differences and that Thomas Merton was "something of a rebel,"[2] Dom James's observation offers a starting point for understanding how Thomas Merton regarded obedience. As a young Trappist monk, Merton understood that the three vows — obedience, stability, and conversion of manners — were "given to the monk as a means of consecrating his life to God" (*Sign of Jonas*, 9). Obedience means more than compliance to rules or directives; it requires that a monk set aside his own will and obey his abbot, and in so doing, he will be obeying God. The monk obeys the abbot because the voice of the abbot represents the voice of God. Merton knew that the practice of obedience was integral to the monastic vocation, and throughout his life as a monk he remained faithful to the vow of obedience that he took as a Trappist monk. But he also struggled to discern what obedience demanded of him at particular times in his monastic life. As a young and pious monk, Merton articulated his appreciation of the centrality of obedience in the monastic life and recorded his attempts to live up to its challenge. In later writings Merton reflected on obedience with a more critical perspective as he viewed obedience within the context of the renewal of monastic life, but he never wavered from his commitment to

obedience as an essential aspect of the monastic life. Merton's journal entries reflect this process of maturation in his understanding of obedience.

In March 1947 Merton wrote in his journal that "it is best to take this obedience business as literally and as universally as possible because as soon as it is divided with conditions and solicitudes, there is no longer any possibility of being a true contemplative, because a contemplative is undivided" (*Entering the Silence*, 44). Already Merton has discovered that the price of obedience may mean sacrificing "for a time" what he most longs for: contemplation. A few months later he confesses that he is "very imperfect" in his motives for obedience, which are "largely natural," and admits that he is willing enough to do the things he agrees with but that he experiences "interior rebellion at decisions that seem ... imperfect or unwise" (140). During this time Merton was tempted to leave Gethsemani and become a Carthusian. As he wrestled with stability, he also struggled with the demands of obedience. He confessed to "a certain spirit of independence" that led him to want to run his own life. "I have somehow acquired a notion that I can pick and choose in the kind of advice that my superiors and directors give me" (140). He devotes two days of entries to sorting out the demands of obedience, and on the third day, December 6, 1947, he offers a prayer to the Blessed Mother in which he renounces his will, judgment, and desires and he promises "to obey my superiors without criticism, believing that their commands and wishes are part of God's work, not for my own sanctification, but for the good of this Order and of the Church" (142). In June 1948 Merton asked himself, "What is more worth desiring than to be perfect in obedience? In the last weeks God has been working on me a lot and His grace has been softening up that interior toughness, and I am getting a kind of hunger to do things for Reverend Father, for God through him, and listen to his way of looking at things. I want to give up all the reserves of independence in me, all the last lines of defense" (214).

But Merton's promise to Mary did not resolve the matter of obedience once and for

all. Over the years Merton continued to grap-
ple with and refine his understanding of what
obedience meant and entailed. Writing in his
journal in 1958, Merton distinguished between
obedience and fidelity. Obedience is owed to
a superior in light of the superior's function.
Fidelity is owed to persons. Although the monastic vow calls for "a relationship that implies
fidelity to one's abbot as well as obedience" —
the Rule of Benedict states that monks "will
love the abbot with a sincere heart" — Merton
notes that the vow "stops short of the special self-surrender and self-consecration which
I have never been able to give to any man or
to any institution, even to my own Order. I
hope I believe I have consecrated myself thus
to Christ" (*Search for Solitude*, 180).

In 1959 Merton was considering and even
making plans to go to Latin America to live
there as a monk. In the midst of this crisis
of stability Merton wondered, "How it would
ever be possible to fully and interiorly obey
if this plan fails" (*Entering the Silence*, 343).
And yet when the indult that he was seeking
was denied, Merton did obey, and did so with
apparent equanimity.

By 1960 he was more critical in his understanding of obedience in the monastery and
struggling to balance obedience and freedom.
"I can no longer accept the superficial verbalism (going in circles) which evades reality by
simply saying the will of the Superior is the
will of God and the will of God is the will of
the Superior" (*Turning toward the World*, 46).
The "will of the Superior simply defines and
points out the way in which I am to try to
act intelligently and spiritually, and thus clarify the meaning of my own life ('giving glory to
God')" (46). He began to see more clearly that
"real obedience" meant obeying "Him on the
way in order to reach Him in Whom I have
begun, Who is the Way and the End — (the
Beginning)" (101).

As Merton was becoming more critical of
obedience in the monastic life, he also was
recognizing the dangers and abuses of obedience in the world around him. Above all, he
recognized the role played in the Holocaust
by the "blind obedience" and *Kadavergehorsam*
(corpselike obedience) of Eichmann and all the

others who, in obedience and with a sense of
duty, committed heinous atrocities (307).

In the last few years of life, as Merton wrote
to promote monastic renewal, he became increasingly critical of obedience that was "formal
and trivial" (*Water of Life*, 226). Renewal "must
mean above all a recovery of the sense of *obedience to God* — in all things, and not just —
obedience to rules and Superiors where demanded, and after that go woolgathering where
you may" (226). What really matters is obeying
God freely.

Merton was not alone in facing issues of
authority and obedience during the 1960s.
Writing in February 1966 to Daniel Berrigan,
Merton observed that the "moment of truth
will come when you will have to resist the
arbitrary and reactionary use of authority in
order to save the real concept of authority
and obedience, in the line of renewal. This
will take charismatic grace" (*Hidden Ground
of Love*, 91). He wondered what obedience
would require if one were silenced on some important social issue (139). Yet in 1962, when
Merton was ordered to stop writing about
war, he obeyed, recognizing that to do otherwise would "backfire" and damage the peace
movement (267).

One thing is clear: Merton recognized that
authority and obedience were not ends in
themselves. When he himself was given authority over other monks, first as master of
scholastics and then as master of novices, Merton recognized with even greater clarity the
complex role of obedience in the monastic
life. Merton was master of scholastics when,
in 1954, he wrote to Erich Fromm and shared
his understanding of the function of obedience
in the monastic life. He was convinced that it is
possible to take "the true Benedictine idea" of
"a long period of formation in which the whole
spiritual life is summed up in the two words
'obedience' and 'humility'" and make "it the
foundation of a life of spiritual freedom and
'humanism' and 'mysticism' in the best sense.
I am sure that is what St. Benedict intended.
The function of obedience in his context is not
merely to bring the monk into submission to
authority as if the authority were everything.
It simply presupposes that in the beginning he

does not know how to go about living the monastic life and needs to be told, and that the more he is willing to be open to suggestion and formation, the better off he will be. But if we consider the rule closely we find that the mature monk is a very capable and many-sided person, completely integrated, leading a life of freedom and joy under the guidance of the Holy Spirit rather than out of servile fear. In fact, servility is the exact opposite of the Christian and monastic spirit" (310). Perhaps it was because he was not talking about himself but about the young monks he was forming that Merton was able to grasp and express, with such clarity, his understanding of the role of obedience in the life of the monk. Writing to Fromm in 1954, Merton anticipated the vision of obedience and authority that would drive his later efforts for monastic renewal and that would inform his own life as a monk.

Some ten years later, in an article entitled "The Place of Obedience," published in the *American Benedictine Review* in September 1965 (359–68) and reprinted in *Contemplation in a World of Action*, Merton elaborated a vision of obedience and authority — consistent with personal integration, freedom, and joy — in light of the ecclesiology of the Second Vatican Council. Merton begins by noting that the Council's Constitution on the Church (*Lumen Gentium*) represents a shift from viewing the church "primarily and principally as a hierarchical society and a strictly organized institution" to seeing the church as "the community of the faithful, the Mystical Body of Christ, the people of God" (*World of Action*, 117/135). This move from a "static" to a "dynamic" ecclesiology creates the context for the renewal of religious life *and* for a renewed understanding of obedience and authority.

"The obedience which is vowed by a religious is not the obedience of a child to a parent, not the obedience of a citizen to civil authority, nor is it properly understood merely as the obedience of a subject to juridically constituted authority" (118/136). For the religious and particularly for the monk obedience is not an end in itself but "a means to closer union with God. It is, in fact, the chief way by which the monk

returns to God, as St. Benedict says in the opening sentences of his Prologue" (118/136). What is needed, Merton insists, is not "merely external and juridical obedience" but "the obedience of faith" viewed in the "context of love and discipleship" (118–19/136–37). A monk must obey not because he is a subject but because he is a disciple. "Obedience of love rooted in faith becomes at once a sign and a principle of living unity in Christ, and a way of 'returning to the Father' in and with the loving obedience of Christ" (122/139). This view of obedience is grounded in a "Eucharistic" concept of religious life as contrasted with religious life viewed "almost exclusively in terms of sacrifice and immolation" (121/139). In this view, obedience "becomes an expression of the new life and the new creation which restores the simplicity and peace of paradise" (122/140), and the "end of Christian obedience" is "not merely order and organization . . . but God Himself, the epiphany of God in his Church, and in the microcosm of the new creation which is the monastic community" (122/140). Such a theology of obedience has implications for both subject and superior: the "work of obedience implies a loyal collaboration between superior and subject, in which *both* strive, each according to his function, to understand and carry out the will of God" (123/141). Both subject and superior are called to service, and their relationship is actually "a dialogue between two forms of *service*" (124/141). CMB

SEE ALSO ABBOT; CAMALDOLESE; CARTHUSIANS; CENSORSHIP; LATIN AMERICAN WRITERS; VOWS.

Notes

1. Michael Mott, *The Seven Mountains of Thomas Merton* (Boston: Houghton Mifflin, 1984), 279.
2. See William H. Shannon, *"Something of a Rebel": Thomas Merton, His Life and Works* (Cincinnati: St. Anthony Messenger Press, 1997).

O'CALLAGHAN, THOMASINE

Thomasine ("Tommie") O'Callaghan, wife of Frank O'Callaghan, had attended the College of the Sacred Heart at Manhattanville, Purchase, New York, where Daniel Walsh was one of her teachers. It was he who first introduced

Tommie O'Callaghan

Thomas Merton to the O'Callaghan family. Merton became a welcome friend and was a frequent visitor at the O'Callaghan residence in Louisville. To the seven children of Tommie and Frank he soon became "Uncle Louie." It was his first experience in many years with any sort of family life. When Merton chose the members of his legacy trust, he wanted someone from Louisville, and Tommie O'Callaghan was the ideal choice. She has continued to be an active member of the Merton Legacy Trust. (She is the one remaining original trustee; the other two, Naomi Stone and James Laughlin, have been replaced by Robert Giroux and Anne McCormick, respectively.) WHS

OPENING THE BIBLE

Collegeville, Minn.: Liturgical Press, 1970.
84 pp.

Opening the Bible is an essay that originally was commissioned for the projected *Time-Life Bible* and was published posthumously as a separate volume when that project was canceled. Merton's approach is guided by the fact that the original intended audience would be a broad one, including believers and nonbelievers. Consequently, Merton draws on a wide variety of sources in a relatively short compass

to answer his opening question, "What kind of book is this?" (*Opening the Bible*, 1).

He begins by noting that not only nonbelievers but also believers often approach the Bible in an "alienated" way, as a source of meaning for others rather than for oneself. He states that part of the reason for this is that it has too often been interpreted in a dualistic fashion, as pertaining to a supernatural realm with little or no connection to earthly realities. He also notes that its strictly literary merits are open to question, so that reading it simply from an aesthetic perspective is likely to remain unsatisfying. For the full power of the Scripture as the word of God to be released, it must be encountered in an existential way, not as a source of information but as a power for transformation, as, in Pauline terms, spirit rather than letter. The Bible is the locus of encounter with "an ultimate Freedom which is at once the ground and source of man's being, the center of his history and the guide of his destinies" (15). The Bible, then, challenges the reader to confront the deepest issues of one's own identity and affirms that this identity is intrinsically related to the reality of God in Christ and the reality of Christ in other people, particularly the poor and marginalized, and in the whole creation.

Merton draws on the kerygmatic theology of the great Protestant theologians Bonhoeffer and Barth in taking this approach to the Bible, but he also looks beyond the confines of the church for evidence of this encounter with God's word. He points to Marxist filmmaker Pasolini's *Gospel of St. Matthew* as an example of a fresh, convincing encounter with the gospel, and he cites psychoanalyst Erich Fromm's nontheistic reading of the Scripture as providing valid and valuable insight into the "radical humanism" of the Bible (36), which stresses both the centrality of human freedom and the unity of the human race. He reflects on Dilsey's response to the sermon of Rev. Shegog in Faulkner's *The Sound and the Fury* as a prime example of hearing God's word as an experience of *kairos*, of the time of decision and transformation that transcends the quantitative approach to time as measured by the clock.

After a brief comparison of the Bible to other

religious texts (Hindu, Taoist, Buddhist), Merton sets forth six central aspects of the biblical experience: (1) the Bible is centered on events rather than on concepts or theories, and therefore is addressed to the whole person, not just to the intellect; (2) these events are characterized as breakthroughs that shatter existing human frameworks and demand a new understanding of and response to life; (3) unaided human efforts are inevitably marred by error and dishonesty, products of a reliance on a shallow self rather than on the transcendent will that is both within and beyond each person; (4) the confrontation and interplay of human and divine freedom is a dynamic process throughout history, characterized by the experience of covenant, a relationship of intimacy in which divine freedom does not overwhelm human freedom but enhances it; (5) this dynamic enhancement of freedom reveals the relationship between the two Testaments as a process of development in which the law is definitively fulfilled by emancipation from the law; (6) the full revelation of God is found in the *kenosis*, the self-emptying of God in the person of Christ, who calls not just for adherence to his message but for commitment to his person in a relationship of shared self-surrender.

According to Merton an authentic encounter with the word of God in the Bible leads both to a recognition of the need for redemption and to an experience of that redemption. Here he engages again the question of ultimate identity: the perennial temptation to settle for a superficial self that affirms its own unity "by shutting out other persons and by closing off the deepest area of inner freedom where the ego is no longer in full conscious control" (72). The power of God's word is precisely that it "breaks through this comfortable little system and shatters all its precarious selfish values, challenging us to risk a higher and more fundamental freedom" (73). To accept this challenge is to be brought into a new relationship with oneself, with the human community, with history, and with the transcendent.

This response of faith cannot be reduced to "religion" as defined by a secure and precisely defined set of beliefs and rituals. Drawing again on Barth and Bonhoeffer, Merton notes that the Bible is filled with challenges to a religious establishment that substitutes external practices and group identity for an encounter with the divine that transforms both the inner and outer world. Thus, Merton claims, there is a fundamentally eschatological thrust to biblical revelation, which continually challenges the self-sufficiency of the present with a call to deeper commitment, with the demands of *kairos*, "a time of breakthrough, convergence, the destruction of the old, the invasion by the new and unforeseen...*a time of decisive response*" (83). Merton concludes by reminding his readers that they live in such a time when the old answers no longer seem adequate, a time of questioning but also a time of possibilities and challenges that can lead to a renewed experience of the meaning of salvation.

In *Opening the Bible* Merton reveals how a number of key themes that run throughout his writings — above all, the search for the true self, for authentic identity — are grounded in the Scriptures. In a work dating from the final year of his life he makes clear that his interests in Eastern wisdom, contemporary culture, and the struggles for a more just society have not attenuated his own commitment to the Bible. While empathizing with his contemporaries' difficulties in grasping the significance of a work completed almost two millennia before, he aims to show that its message is no less meaningful to modern readers than it was to its original audience. POC

SEE ALSO BIBLE.

ORIGINAL CHILD BOMB
New York: New Directions, 1962.

This prose poem on the dropping of the first atomic bomb, on Hiroshima, is among the earliest of Thomas Merton's writings on the issues of war and peace. It originally appeared in Robert Lax's little magazine *PAX* in 1961 and was issued in book form the following year with illustrations by Emil Antonucci. It consists of forty-one numbered sections, ranging in length from a single sentence to three paragraphs, with most sections one paragraph long.

In large part the work provides a detailed

factual description of the series of events that culminated in the use of the bomb, from the accession to the presidency of Harry Truman on April 12, 1945, through the end of the Second World War on August 14, eight days after Hiroshima was destroyed. Twenty-eight of the sections open with a chronological reference. Principal incidents include: the initial briefing of the new president on the development of the bomb (*Original Child Bomb*, 2); the formation of a committee to advise the president on the feasibility of using the bomb (3) and the decision to drop the bomb (5) on the city of Hiroshima (7); the successful testing of the bomb (13–14); the Potsdam Conference, where Truman (17) and the British (18) (but not the Soviets) were informed of the results of the test, and where the ultimatum of unconditional surrender was made to the Japanese (20); the transport of the fissionable material to Tinian Island (19) and its assembly there into the bomb (22); the final preparations for the bombing run (25–28) and the details of the mission itself (29–34); the aftermath of the bombing and the surrender of the Japanese (35, 38). The impression of detached objectivity is reinforced by repeated use of quantitative statistics — in the initial presidential briefing (2): time spent in researching the bomb (six years), total cost (two billion dollars), destructive power (twenty thousand tons of TNT), number of bombs needed to destroy a city (one); in the description of the test (14): width of fireball of first bomb test (one mile), radius of visibility of flash (250 miles), height of smoke cloud (forty thousand feet); and in the details of the bombing itself (30, 32): height of bomber over Hiroshima (thirty-one thousand feet), distance of dropped bomb from aiming point (one hundred feet), fireball width (eighteen thousand feet), temperature at center of fireball (one hundred million degrees), number of people dead immediately or within a few hours (seventy thousand). Intercut with these details of the American preparation and attack is information on the efforts of the Japanese to arrange a negotiated surrender through Russian mediation (4, 12, 21, 24), and on the Russian decision, in the aftermath of Hiroshima, to declare war on Japan rather than to serve as intermediary (37, 39). Also

interspersed throughout the first part of the text are repeated expressions of doubt about whether the bomb would work (2, 10, 16, 23), and objections, first by some committee members (3), then by atomic scientists (9, 19), to using the bomb, but notable by its absence is any process of sustained moral evaluation; the "philosophy" expressed by President Truman is summed up by the statement "We found the bomb . . . and we used it" (40).

The author's attitude toward the events he describes is conveyed not through direct commentary but through irony and understatement, which are present in nearly every individual section. For example, the statement that the new president "knew a lot less about the war than many people did" implies both a contrast with those who experienced the war firsthand as combatants and victims and with those who had been involved in the research and preparation of the powerful weapon of which the second-highest elected official in the United States was previously unaware (2). The description of the decision to drop the bomb as "a demonstration of the bomb on a civil and military target" leads to a deconstruction of the bureaucratic language, in which "demonstration" is made equivalent to "show," and thus appropriated to the "civilian" part of the use of the bomb, while "the 'destructive' aspect of the bomb would be 'military'" (5). The decision not to reveal the existence of the bomb to "America's friendly ally" the Soviets, even though it would make them "even more friendly," is justified on the supposition that they are "now friendly enough" (6). Hiroshima is called "Lucky" because it had escaped all bombing up until that point, and so could compress the experience of four years of war into a single day (7). The list of Hiroshima entities to be "put . . . out of business" by the bomb includes five companies and "most of the inhabitants" (8). Instructions on board the U.S.S. *Indianapolis* "were that if the ship sank, the Uranium was to be saved first, before any life" (19). The fact that the pilot of the *Enola Gay*, Col. Tibbets, did not have a nervous breakdown after dropping the bomb is presented as evidence of his being "well-balanced . . . not sentimental" (25), while some of the other crew members are described as "not perfectly happy" with the outcome of the bombing mission (33). The irony extends also to the other combatants: the Japanese military leaders "believed that the war should continue until everybody was dead" because they "were professional soldiers" (4); likewise, the military governor of Hiroshima, who "issued a proclamation full of martial spirit" to "all the people without hands, without feet, with their faces falling off, with their intestines hanging out, with their whole bodies full of radiation . . . was a professional soldier" (36). The Soviets' decision to continue to fight in Asia after the Japanese surrender is described as a display of "good will in Manchuria, or even in Korea" (39).

But the principal focus of the irony centers on two clusters of images already present in the historical record. The first of these, which identifies the bomb with a child, as in the title, has two sources. The name "Original Child," given by the Japanese, is first mentioned in the opening section, before the object so named has been identified; the ominous overtones of their recognition "that it was the first of its kind" will reappear only at the poem's conclusion. A similar image had already been used by the Americans in the coded message, "Babies satisfactorily born" (18), sent to Potsdam after the initial test, and recurs in the name, "Little Boy," given to the bomb by its assemblers, whose "care for the Original Child" is described as "devoted and tender" (22). The naming of the bomber after the pilot's mother leads to the expansion of the child imagery to mention of "the womb of Enola Gay" in which " 'Little Boy' was . . . tucked away" (26). A concluding reference to "the Original Child that was now born" (40) recalls the wording of the opening section at a point when the perverse incongruity of associating an image of innocence and new life with an instrument of mass destruction has become fully evident.

The other cluster of images has religious associations, beginning with the code names of the original test ("Trinity" [13]) and of Tinian Island ("Papacy" [34]). These religious associations are found in the "reverent tone" in which one of the president's aides describes the bomb's potential to destroy the world (2); in

the quasi-miraculous ability of a blind woman to perceive its light from miles away when the first test is made (14); in the "religious terms" with which those attending the text expressed their satisfaction, the "atmosphere of devotion" that surrounded the event, the "act of faith" of observers (15), as well as the attitude of the "doubting Thomas," Admiral Leahy, whose predictions that the bomb would not work are described as "his own variety of 'hope' " (16); in the "quick prayer" said on Sunday, August 5, the day before the bombing run, and in the pilot's "baptiz[ing]" the plane after his mother (25); in the "procession" by which the bomb is brought forth and "devoutly" tucked in the plane's "womb"; and in the anticipation the night before the run in which the airmen are "as excited as little boys on Christmas Eve" (26). With this last image the religious and the child imagery converge, suggesting that the bomb to be "born" from the "womb" of the *Enola Gay* on the following day is a kind of demonic antitype of the true "Original Child," a nativity bringing ruin rather than redemption.

The contemporary implications of Hiroshima are reserved for the final section, which echoes Truman's evasive description of the bomb's development in the laconic observation that since that time "many other bombs have been 'found' " (41), but concludes by noting, "At the time of writing . . . men seem to be fatigued by the whole question" (41). The unrecognized dangers of such apathy already have been indicated in the poem's subtitle, "Points for meditation to be scratched on the walls of a cave," which situates the entire work in a post–nuclear war time frame. But the subtitle also suggests a possible antidote to apathy by pointing to the authentically religious dimension of the nuclear issue, which is a subject for meditation as surely as a biblical passage or a spiritual text. In this context the numbered sections of *Original Child Bomb* recall the similar arrangement of works such as "Notes for a Philosophy of Solitude" and the chapters of *No Man Is an Island*, which function as "points for meditation" in a more traditional sense and suggest Merton's conviction that the actual and potential use of atomic weaponry is an appropriate, indeed an essential, topic for religious reflection, which might possibly lead to a change in perspective and in behavior before it is too late and the horrors of Hiroshima have been multiplied over the entire earth. POC

SEE ALSO HIROSHIMA.

ORIGINAL SIN

Thomas Merton discusses the fall of humanity at some length in *The New Man* and in the dialogue with D. T. Suzuki in part 2 of *Zen and the Birds of Appetite*. He sees the fall as the archetypal symbol of the state of unfreedom into which we are born and from which we must be delivered. Humans have lost paradise and must recover it (yet paradoxically the possibility of that recovery is always within us). Original sin is not so much an inherited sin passed on from one generation to the next as it is the loss of that original blessing (or innocence) in which the human person was able to see reality as it is. Original sin, the total alienation from the "inmost ground of our identity" (*Birds of Appetite*, 12), is the accumulation of veils of illusion that cover reality and make it appear to be what it is not.

The fall so alienates us from the Real that the true God becomes an idol, the true self becomes a false self and created nature is grasped not in the unity that expresses its true status, but in isolation and separateness. The fall, in other words, is the loss of the contemplative vision and the nondualism that this vision brings. By reason of the fall human persons have acquired a pair of discriminating eyes that project a false dualism on reality.

The mercy of God, incarnated in the atoning grace of Christ, makes it possible for humans to leave these regions of unreality and return to the center of their being, where they find the true God, their true selves, and the vision of reality that is one and unseparated. The condition of this "return to paradise" is the unmasking of illusions, the removal of the veils that hinder us from seeing what is. This unmasking of illusions is no easy task, nor is it a Promethean struggle whereby I remake myself by my own unaided natural powers; rather, it is something I can achieve only by responding to the call of God's Spirit uttered in the depths of my being and inviting me to become a new person in Christ. This means experiencing the power of his resurrection, in which I die to my old self and clothe myself "with the new self created according to the likeness of God in true righteousness and holiness" (Eph. 4:24).

Experiencing the paschal mystery in my life and being reborn in Christ means a number of things. First of all, however, it means coming to see my life as one whole, not as a fragmented existence, in which the powers of my being are being pulled in so many directions and by so many claims on my attention that I do not know where I am going or even who it is that goes. This means that I must avoid the temptation to see my life in Christ as another compartment in an overly compartmentalized existence; instead, my life in Christ must become the center around which all else revolves and the point of unification in which my total life finds the meaning by which I live and the goal toward which I move (see the introduction in "The Inner Experience").

On September 5, 1962, John Whitman Sears, a licensed psychologist, wrote to Merton asking for clarification of what he had written about original sin in his dialogue with Suzuki. He asked if original sin was related to neurotic or psychotic disorders. In his reply (Cold War Letter 89) Merton makes clear that original sin belongs to a different order than psychology. "It is not a matter of subjective experience, conscious or unconscious. It is something ontological and objective" (*Witness to Freedom*, 304). Original sin does not vitiate the basic goodness of human nature. A person in the state of original sin can be perfectly well adjusted psychologically, for original sin is not an action that a person performs. Rather, "It is a condition in which people are conceived to be born. Here we are not in the realm of science at all, but very close to that of myth (if you will permit me to hold that a myth can somehow express a reality conceived to be objective, yet invisible and inexplicable). Hence the need to explain it in a parable, like that of the Prodigal Son.... The experience of alienation, pardon and return, reintegration, etc., is a symbol of a deeper metaphysical reality which is below the level of feeling or moral action" (305).

Merton goes on to explain how this understanding is a point of basic agreement between Suzuki and himself in their dialogue on Christianity and Buddhism. They agreed that humans, no matter how well balanced, healthy and sane as they may be, are still alienated from their "true self." They are in exile from their true spiritual country. According to Buddhists they may have basically deceptive and illusory views of life, and according to Christians they do not "see God" or have access to the ultimate meaning of life. They are not united with God. "In both religions there tend to be degrees of perfection, an ascent to enlightenment, to union, and to fulfillment in self-transcendence." Both religions call for inner discipline and development, as people work toward a "breakthrough into a different mode of being, and a transformation of one's whole attitude toward life, indeed of one's whole being itself" (305). WHS

SEE ALSO FALL; REDEMPTION; SALVATION; SELF.

OTHER SIDE OF THE MOUNTAIN, THE:
The End of the Journey
The Journals of Thomas Merton, vol. 7: 1967–68. Edited by Patrick Hart. New York: HarperSanFrancisco, 1998. xix+348 pp.

The title of this seventh, final volume of the Thomas Merton journals derives from a dream Merton had while making a retreat at the Mim Tea Estate near Darjeeling in India. In the dream he saw the beauty of Mt. Kanchenjunga as he had never seen it before. He reflects that every mountain has another side: the side that is never photographed and hence never gets turned into postcards. "The full beauty of the mountain," he says, "is not seen until you too consent to the impossible paradox: it is and is not. When nothing more needs to be said, the smoke of ideas clears, the mountain is SEEN" (*Other Side of the Mountain*, 286). This happens, however, not on *this* side of the mountain, but on the *other* side, the side that alone is worth seeing and that, when you finally see it, you realize really is not there.

This title is an excellent choice for the last volume of a series of journals that began with a volume called *Run to the Mountain*. It suggests progress and movement in the direction of fulfillment. The man who ran to the mountain and wrote about the "seven storey mountain" came at last to see the other side of the mountain.

This volume includes some material previously published. Pages 92–113 appeared as *Woods, Shore, Desert*; pp. 179–99 as *Thomas Merton in Alaska*; pp. 205–329 as *The Asian Journal of Thomas Merton*. The book's content is divided as follows: introduction (xiii–xix); part 1, "The Election of a New Abbot (October 1967–May 1968)" (1–88); part 2, "Woods, Shore, Desert (A Notebook, May 1968)" (89–114); part 3, "Preparing for Asia (May–September 1968)" (115–68); part 4, "New Mexico, Alaska, California (September–October 1968)" (169–202); part 5, "The Far East: The Last Days (October–December 1968)" (203–330). There is a five-page glossary of Asian terms and an index of twelve pages. (The glossary of terms and the index are significantly smaller than these items in *The Asian Journal*.)

Part 1: "The Election of a New Abbot (October 1967–May 1968)"
A number of themes, experiences, and issues run through these eighty-eight pages: Merton's lectures to the monks on Sufism; his concern to set up a trust to administer his works and thus relieve the monastery of this responsibility; his condemnation of the war in Vietnam; his anxiety about who would be elected to succeed Dom James as abbot; the cooling of his relationship with M. (a topic that had been so prominent in the previous volume of the journals); his severe critique of Dom James and of his fellow monks (he upbraids them as wanting only security and routine), then (when to his joy Fr. Flavian Burns was elected abbot) his realization of "how seriously I misjudged the community the other day — saying they were all conservatives and wanted security above all" (42); his regrets about his failures to live the hermit life as he felt he ought (having too many visitors, taking too many trips into town); hearing the news of the assassination of Martin

Luther King Jr.; preliminary talks with the new abbot about the meeting of monastics in Asia and the invitation he received to speak there; his December retreat for superiors of contemplative orders of women, leading him to change his superficial views of the vitality of the contemplative orders, coming to see how much it was alive among these women; the sad news of the death by shipwreck of his aunt Kit; the completion of the chapel addition to his hermitage.

Part 2: "Woods, Shore, Desert (A Notebook, May 1968)"

This recounts visits to the Redwoods Abbey, the California shore, and the monastery of Christ in the Desert. See the book *Woods, Shore, Desert* and see WOODS, SHORE, DESERT in this encyclopedia.

Part 3: "Preparing for Asia (May 1968–September 1968)"

Merton reminisces fondly of his visit to New Mexico and California, a pilgrimage of memories that kept coming back to him "in recurrent flashes and impressions" (118): the vast silence of California's redwood trees and the beauty of the Pacific, the liturgies at the Redwoods Abbey, the hospitality of the monastery of Christ in the Desert in New Mexico. Back at Gethsemani, he hears of the race riots in Louisville and the civil disobedience of the Berrigans, and in May 1968 he gives a second retreat for the superiors of contemplative orders and discusses further with Fr. Flavian a possible trip to Asia to speak at a meeting of Asian abbots. Reflecting on such a trip, he writes, "What I really want is, however, to meet Buddhists" (132). Several times he expresses his regrets for his failures as a monk. "It is a wonder I haven't lost my vocation to solitude by trifling and evasion" (137). Still, he feels he must face the fact that solitude is not possible for him at Gethsemani. On August 22, 1968, he sorts out papers in his hermitage. Coming upon the letters to M., he burns them without even glancing at one of them, as he laments the "incredible stupidity in 1966" (157). Near the end of August he travels to Washington, D.C., to visit the Indonesian embassy to arrange for that part of his Asian journey. On his return he stays overnight

Thomas Merton just before leaving for Asia, October 1968

at the Franciscan friary in Louisville, where he watches pro football (see pp. 160–61 for what probably is his only written comment on football!). On September 9 he spends his last night at Gethsemani and the next day celebrates a Mass at the hermitage. He speaks of his departure: "I go with a completely open mind, I hope without special illusions. My hope is simply to enjoy the long journey, profit by it, learn, change, and perhaps find something or someone who will help me advance in my own spiritual quest" (166).

Part 4: "New Mexico, Alaska, California (September–October 1968)"[1]

See the journal section of the book *Thomas Merton in Alaska* and see THOMAS MERTON IN ALASKA in this encyclopedia.

Part 5: "The Far East: The Last Days (October–December 1968)"

See the book *The Asian Journal of Thomas Merton* and see ASIAN JOURNAL OF THOMAS MERTON in this encyclopedia. WHS

Notes

1. On October 3, 1968, Merton made a brief informal presentation at the Center for the Study of Democratic Institutions in Santa Barbara. See Walter Capps, *Thomas Merton: Preview of the Asian Journey* (New York: Crossroad, 1989).

OX MOUNTAIN PARABLE OF MENG TZU, THE

Lexington, Ky.: Stamperia del Santuccio, 1960. 7 pp.

In his journal for July 10, 1960, Thomas Merton writes of his excitement in reading I. A. Richards's *Mencius on the Mind*, an analysis of the thought of the early Confucian master Meng Tzu (372–289 B.C.E.), and goes on to discuss one of the literal translations in the appendix, "The Ox Mountain Parable": "Importance of 'night-spirit' and 'dawn-breath' in the restoration of the trees to life. Men cut them down, beasts browse on the new shoots, no night spirit and no dawn breath — no rest; no renewal — and then one is convinced at last that the mountain *never had* any trees on it" (*Turning toward the World*, 19).[1] He soon reworked Richards's version in a more poetic form,[2] similar to what he would do with excerpts from Chuang Tzu, whom he had begun to read at the same time. A limited edition of Merton's rendering, with a brief introduction, was printed by his friend Victor Hammer on his hand press and appeared in September of the same year. In the introduction Merton stresses Meng Tzu's belief in the basic goodness of human nature, which had been perverted by evil acts but could be restored by a properly "humane" education. He reads the story of the destroyed mountain as "a parable of mercy" suggesting that as it is possible for the "night spirit" to restore the exhausted mountain if given the chance, so humankind can be restored to a "right mind" by "the merciful / pervasive and mysterious influence of unconscious nature." The translation and a slightly revised version of the introduction are included as the final section of Merton's essay "Classic Chinese Thought" (*Mystics and Zen Masters*, 65–68). POC

SEE ALSO CONFUCIANISM.

Notes

1. See also the expanded version of this passage in *Conjectures of a Guilty Bystander*, in which Merton concludes, "Without the night spirit, the dawn breath, silence, passivity, rest, man's nature cannot be itself. In its barrenness it is no longer *natura*: nothing grows from it, nothing is born of it any more" (123).

2. Richards's text (actually provided by collaborators) is simply an interlinear listing of the English equivalent beneath each Chinese character and its transliteration, so that Merton is responsible for creating a readable English text. See I. A. Richards, *Mencius on the Mind: Experiments in Multiple Definition* (New York: Harcourt, Brace, 1932), appendix, 9–12.

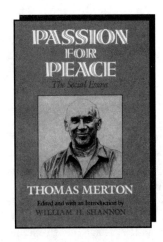

PARADISE

Among the myths — the imaginative patterns that convey a truth transcending literal facts — that Thomas Merton finds most powerful in conveying the wisdom of the Christian message is the return to paradise. Salvation is imaged as the restoration of that primordial unity and harmony of all creation in God that had been shattered by sin. It is this traditional image of the mysterious journey forward to the beginning, the reversal of the fall, that Merton repeatedly invokes in his efforts to describe what it means to be an authentic Christian, an authentic contemplative, an authentic human being.

By usurping the role of God rather than participating in it, by the futile desire to substitute himself for God as the center of his own being and of his world, Adam denied his own deepest identity as formed in the image of God, as well as his vocation to participate in the creative work of God. His refusal to accept his own contingency, his denial of his radical dependence upon his Creator was, in Merton's familiar terminology, the preference for the false self of egotistical desires over the true self loved into being by God, a

state of self-division and alienation from reality. "Man is created for peace, delight, and the highest spiritual happiness. . . . But man's weakness and superficiality, his inordinate love of a self metaphysically wounded with contingency, makes the Paradise life impossible" (*Literary Essays*, 254).

But the salvation brought by Christ reverses the effects of the fall. Christ, the new Adam, restores the paradisal unity disrupted by the first Adam's act of self-glorification, which was simultaneously an act of self-alienation. "In the beginning, Adam was 'one man.' The Fall had divided him into 'a multitude.' Christ had restored man to unity in Himself. The Mystical Christ was the 'New Adam' and in Him all men could return to unity, to innocence, to purity, and become 'one man.' *Omnes in Christo unum*" (*Birds of Appetite*, 117). Of course, this return to unity is possible only if one is willing to let go of one's self-created, self-centered identity by entering into the mystery of the cross. The false self must be surrendered to death in order for the true self to live in Christ. "This meant, of course, living not by one's own will, one's own ego, one's own limited and selfish spirit, but being 'one spirit' with Christ. . . . The individual has 'died' with Christ to his 'old man,' his exterior, egotistical self, and 'risen' in Christ to the new man, a selfless and divine being, who is the one Christ, the same who is 'all

Cover for *Passion for Peace* reprinted with the permission of Crossroad. Cover art by Pamela Keating; cover design by Paul Chevannes.

in all'" (117). By being one with Christ, one returns with Christ to the unity of God's original design for creation. Like the good thief, one hears the words of Christ, "This day you shall be with me in paradise" (Luke 23:43). To be in paradise, Merton writes, is to recover one's true self, to find oneself in Christ by losing oneself in Christ: "Paradise is simply the person, the self, but the radical self in its uninhibited freedom. The self no longer clothed with an ego" (*Love and Living*, 8). This emptying of self, the *kenosis* of which Paul speaks in Philippians 2, is actually the fullness of the divine Presence. In a sense, Merton says, we do not merely "reenter" paradise; we become the new paradise, the dwelling place of God with humanity: "We see that we ourselves are Adam, we ourselves are Christ, and that we are all dwelling in one another, by virtue of the unity of the divine image reformed by grace, in a way that is analogous to the circumincession of the Three Divine Persons in the Holy Trinity. God Himself dwells in us and we in Him. We are His new Paradise. And in the midst of that Paradise stands Christ Himself, the Tree of life" (*New Man*, 161).

Inner reintegration, therefore, is inseparable from the reformation of community. Union with the risen Christ is communion with all humanity, indeed all creation, that shares in the new life brought by Christ's victory over the divisions of sin and death. In Christ the "'mirror' of the divine nature," which "was shattered into millions of fragments by that original sin which alienated each man from God, from other men and from himself... becomes once again a perfectly united image of God in the union of those who are one in Christ" (149). Likewise, the power of the resurrection extends "not only into man's spirit but also, ultimately, into all the material creation as well" (150).

Merton makes clear that this paradise is not the final destination of humanity. It is a foretaste of eternal life but not its full fruition. "Paradise is not 'heaven.' Paradise is a state, or indeed a place, on earth. Paradise belongs more properly to the present than to the future life. In some sense it belongs to both. It is the state in which man was originally created to live on earth" (*Birds of Appetite*, 116). Nevertheless, it

is an experience of oneness not only with creation but also with the Creator because it is not merely a return to the state of the first Adam but a participation in the infinitely richer life of the new Adam, the risen Christ, who has ascended to the Father: "For in my soul and in your soul I find the same Christ Who is our Life, and He finds Himself in our love, and together we all find Paradise, which is the sharing of His Love for His Father in the Person of Their Spirit" (*New Seeds of Contemplation*, 66).

The realization of such an awareness is, of course, neither automatic nor instantaneous; the journey to Eden is a lifetime process of becoming what one is, of actualizing this recognition of renewed creation and living it out, of claiming the unity one has been given in Christ: "The recovery of this paradise, which is always hidden within us at least as a possibility, is a matter of great practical difficulty... a way of temptation and struggle" (*Birds of Appetite*, 123–24). The process of conformation to the new Adam and rejection of the old is undertaken by the series of deaths and resurrections that make up the life project of the Christian. One is simultaneously in paradise and in the desert, already saved and still working out one's salvation in fear and trembling. Yet paradoxically, Merton maintains, simply by accepting the desert, the state of emptiness, of dependence, of selflessness, one becomes aware that one has been in paradise all the while.

Such trust and freedom are discovered, according to Merton, in contemplation. To be a contemplative is to realize that the gates of paradise have been reopened; it is to enter the new creation, to know the new life brought by Christ not just by report but by experience. Merton writes, "The situation of the soul in contemplation is something like the situation of Adam and Eve in Paradise. Everything is yours, but on one infinitely important condition: that it is all *given*" (*New Seeds of Contemplation*, 229). Contemplation, therefore, is a liberation, a release from enslavement to idols, above all the idol of self. Freed from obsession with the narrow concerns of a particular individual, the contemplative is likewise free from the desire to control and exploit others, free to see them as they are seen by God and to love them as they are loved by God: "The contemplative, who had restored in his own soul the image of God, was the truly free man: for he alone could walk with God, as Adam had walked with Him in Paradise. He alone could stand and speak freely to God His Father, with complete confidence" ("Inner Experience," 8:345).

Contemplation, as Merton explains it, transcends all dualisms, between God and self, between the natural and the supernatural, between action and rest. "The Recovery of Paradise ... is the recovery of man's lost likeness to God in pure, undivided simplicity" (*Birds of Appetite*, 102). In this context contemplation is not opposed to action. Purifying activity leads to contemplation, and contemplation overflows into activity that is a participation in the creative work of God. Knowing the good by doing good leads to knowing God as the source and fullness of all goodness: "By turning away from the experiential knowledge of moral evil, by seeking only that existential knowledge of good which is the exclusive right of those who know good by doing it, we reenter the spiritual paradise of God and prepare ourselves to realize His presence within us by contemplation" (*New Man*, 185). The action that leads to contemplation is complemented by the action that springs from contemplation: "In Paradise there was no opposition between action and contemplation. We too, if we recover, in Christ, the paradisiacal life of Adam which He has restored to us, are supposed to discover that the opposition between them vanishes at last" (77). From this perspective, the return to paradise is not an escape from the world of space and time but the acceptance of a responsibility to share in God's continuing creative and redemptive work in and for the world; it is to become a sign and instrument of the unity intended by God and restored by Christ. To dwell in Eden is to be a sign of contradiction and a sign of attraction to a world that is largely unaware of its true form; it is to be energized by the Spirit of God to renew the face of the earth. The contemplative recognizes and affirms the unity of all humanity and the dignity of every human being. "If we instinctively seek a paradisiacal and special place on earth," Merton writes, "it is because we know in our inmost hearts that the earth was given us in order that we might find meaning, order, truth, and salvation in it.... Paradise symbolizes this freedom and creativity, but in reality this must be worked out in the human and personal encounter with the stranger seen as our other self" (*Mystics and Zen Masters*, 111).

Likewise, a respect for the created world as "sacrament," a revelation of God's creative love, is evidence of an authentically contemplative awareness. Writing of the great fourteenth-century English mystics, Julian of Norwich and her contemporaries, Merton finds in them "a 'paradise spirituality' which recovers in Christ the innocence and joy of the first beginnings and sees the world — the lovely world of moors and wolds, midland forests, rivers and farms — in the light of Paradise, as it first came from the hand of God" (152). The recovery of such an awareness is particularly important in the present age, when the power of technology and the profitability of exploiting natural resources make the recovery of a holistic appreciation of the natural world a matter of utmost urgency. Paradise consciousness is ecological consciousness, and the work of paradise is the protection of creation.

The intuition of paradise is also a bond that unites the contemplative and the poet. Intrinsic to the vocation of the literary artist is the "Edenic office of the poet" (*Literary Essays*, 29), the responsibility to call things by their right names and so to affirm the goodness and unity of reality, as well as to protest against the violation and denial and rejection of that unity. "All really valid poetry (poetry that is fully alive and asserts its reality by its power to generate imaginative life) is a kind of recovery of paradise," Merton claims. "Not that the poet comes up with a report that he, an unusual man, has found his own way back into Eden: but the living line and the generative association, the new sound, the music, the structure, are somehow grounded in a renewal of vision and hearing so that he who reads and understands recognizes that here is a new start, a new creation. Here the world gets another chance" (128). POC

SEE ALSO FALL; ORIGINAL SIN; REDEMPTION; SALVATION.

PASSION FOR PEACE:
The Social Essays

Edited and with an introduction by
William H. Shannon. New York: Crossroad,
1995. vii+338 pp.

This volume contains Thomas Merton's principal writings on war and peace, nonviolence,
and racism. It contains many of the essays
found in *Thomas Merton on Peace* and in *The
Nonviolent Alternative*. It differs from these two
earlier works in three ways: (1) it includes Merton's writings on racism; (2) it arranges all
these social essays in chronological order; and
(3) it places each article in its proper context.
The editor notes in his introduction, "Properly situated historically, the articles in this
book are a kind of autobiography of Merton
the social critic. They portray his frequent run-
ins with the censors, his concern not to be
misunderstood, his ongoing fear that he had
not expressed himself clearly and accurately,
his compulsion to rewrite articles to make his
meaning more intelligible. This background
knowledge helps to make these articles come
alive" (7).

Following the editor's seven-page introduction (showing how Merton entered the peace
movement and then the civil rights movement), the articles are arranged in two parts.
Part 1, "The Year of the *Cold War Letters*
(October 1961 to October 1962)"(11–123) includes eleven articles in all: (1) "The Root
of War Is Fear," (2) "The Shelter Ethic,"
(3) "Target Equals City," (4) "Nuclear War
and Christian Responsibility," (5) "Red or
Dead: The Anatomy of a Cliché," (6) "Testament to Peace: Father Metzger's Thoughts
about the Duty of a Christian," (7) "Christian Ethics and Nuclear War," (8) "Religion
and the Bomb," (9) "Christian Action in World
Crisis," (10) "*Breakthrough to Peace*: 'Introduction,'" (11) "*Breakthrough to Peace*: 'Peace: A
Religious Responsibility.'"

Part 2 (125–325), simply called "Following
the Year of the *Cold War Letters*," is arranged
by years:

> 1963, five articles: (12) "The Christian
> Failure: A Review" (written under the

pseudonym of Benedict Monk), (13) "Introduction to *Prison Meditations of Fr. Delp*,"
(14) "Danish Nonviolent Resistance to
Hitler," (15) "The Black Revolution: Letters to a White Liberal," (16) "The Legend
of Tucker Caliban";

> 1964, two articles: (17) "A Devout Med-
> itation in Memory of Adolf Eichmann,"
> (18) "Gandhi: The Gentle Revolutionary";

> 1965, five articles: (19) "From Nonviolence
> to Black Power," (20) "Religion and Race
> in the United States," (21) "Pacifism and
> Resistance in Simone Weil," (22) "An En-
> emy of the State," (23) "St. Maximus the
> Confessor on Nonviolence";

> 1966, two articles: (24) "Blessed Are the
> Meek: The Christian Roots of Nonviolence,"
> (25) "Nhat Hanh Is My Brother";

> 1967, four articles: (26) "Ishi: A Medita-
> tion," (27) "The Meaning of Malcolm X,"
> (28) "Auschwitz: A Family Camp," (29) "The
> Hot Summer of Sixty-Seven";

> 1968, three articles: (30) "War and the Cri-
> sis of Language," (31) "The Vietnam War:
> An Overwhelming Atrocity," (32) "Note
> for *Ave Maria*: Nonviolence Does Not...
> Cannot...Mean Passivity."

The appendix is Merton's "Prayer for Peace,"
read in Congress on April 12, 1962. The book
has an index of eight pages.

Part 1: "The Year of the Cold War Letters (October 1961 to October 1962)"

Merton's first article on war and peace was a
chapter from the manuscript of *New Seeds of
Contemplation*, chapter 16, entitled "The Root
of War Is Fear." It was published in the October
1961 issue of the *Catholic Worker*. In sending
this article to Dorothy Day, Merton mentioned
that he had added a page or two "to situate
these thoughts in the present crisis" (*Hidden
Ground of Love*, 140). This addition of three
long paragraphs, not seen by the censors, was
highly inflammatory, calling all peoples to work
for the total abolition of war, "the one task
which God has imposed upon us in the world
today" (*Passion for Peace*, 12). This was a crucial

step for Merton to take. Many of his contemporaries could not understand why this monk, so long known and admired for his writings on spirituality, suddenly had chosen to cast his lot with the social activists of the time. But this was only a beginning. Many more articles on social issues were to follow.

The article that is central to Merton's war-peace essays is "Nuclear War and Christian Responsibility," written for the Christmas 1961 issue of *Commonweal*, but, because of troubles with the censors, not published until February 9, 1962. Merton rewrote this article at least four times. One quite lengthy rewrite, which appeared in the *Catholic Worker*, eventually grew into a book (that Merton was forbidden to publish), *Peace in the Post-Christian Era*. Another appeared as a chapter of *Breakthrough to Peace* under the title "Peace: A Religious Responsibility."

Part 2: "Following the Year of the Cold War Letters"

Covering the years 1963 to 1968, this part contains further articles on war and peace and on civil rights. A number of them discuss the principles of nonviolence, especially those on Gandhi, Simone Weil, and "Blessed Are the Meek: The Christian Roots of Nonviolence" (one of his finest essays). There are also a number of articles on racism, especially as it affects African Americans and Native Americans — for example, "The Black Revolution: Letters to a White Liberal," "The Hot Summer of Sixty-seven," and "Ishi: A Meditation."

The background of all these essays is a mystical one: Merton's contemplative vision of the human family united at a level of reality that all too often we fail to appreciate. Reading this book leaves us with the unmistakable impression of essays written by Thomas Merton, monk and contemplative. WHS

SEE ALSO *THOMAS MERTON ON PEACE*

PASTERNAK, BORIS

Boris Leonidovich Pasternak (1890–1960), Russian poet and translator who became an international symbol of the moral courage of an artist at odds with the political establishment of Russia, was the son of artist parents. His father, a celebrated painter, and his mother, a concert pianist, were of Jewish descent. At first, Boris Pasternak embraced the revolution of 1917 but soon became disaffected by the Bolshevik restrictions on artistic freedom. He wrote several books of poetry, an autobiographical work titled *Safe Conduct* (1931), and excellent translations of Shakespeare, Goethe, and others. He managed to survive the Stalinist purges of the 1930s. He proved to be a source of courage to other Russian intellectuals. It was after Stalin's death that he began the novel that won international popularity, *Dr. Zhivago*. Publication of the novel in Russia was forbidden, and it appeared first in 1957 in an Italian translation. In 1958 it was translated into English, and that same year it won the Nobel Prize in literature. Pasternak accepted the award but then, under strong political pressures and the fear that he would not be allowed to return to Russia, retracted his acceptance. He was allowed to stay in Russia but was expelled from the Soviet Writers Union.

Thomas Merton had begun writing to Pasternak in August 1958, before he read *Dr. Zhivago*. In his first letter Merton praised Pasternak's autobiography and said, "With other writers I can share ideas, but you seem to communicate something deeper. It is as if we met on a deeper level of life on which individuals are not separate beings. In the language familiar to me as a Catholic monk, it is as if we were known to one another in God" (*Courage for Truth*, 87–88). Merton read *Dr. Zhivago* with enthusiasm. Deeply disturbed that Pasternak had been forced to give up the Nobel Prize, Merton wrote a letter to Aleksei Surkov, head of the Soviet Writers Union, protesting Pasternak's expulsion from that union. Merton's letters to Pasternak are found in *The Courage for Truth*. Both sides of the correspondence are available in a limited edition, *Six Letters: Boris Pasternak, Thomas Merton*. The first part of *Disputed Questions* is called "The Pasternak Affair," and is composed of three essays. Another essay, "Pasternak's Letters to Georgian Friends," is found in *The Literary Essays of Thomas Merton*. WHS

PEACE

When Thomas Merton discusses peace in his earlier writings, the focus usually is on peace as a spiritual quality, an interior state. In *Seeds of Contemplation* he emphasizes that interior peace requires detachment, even from the desire for peace itself. To seek God's will alone will bring peace even in the midst of conflict and upheaval, while to seek some sort of inner tranquility as an end in itself, to cling to some "feeling" or "experience" of peace, is to risk misinterpreting God's will. Peace is present because God is present, but it may not always be experienced as present. Sensible consolations, feelings of peace, may be signs of contact with God, but they are "accidental," not essential to authentic union, and by becoming preoccupied with them one may "lose the one important reality, union with the will of God, without which true peace is completely impossible" (*Seeds of Contemplation*, 132). Here, as elsewhere in his writings on inner peace, Merton's emphasis on the connection between the divine will and peace recalls Dante's famous line from the *Paradiso*, "In His will is our peace." As he writes in his pamphlet *Praying the Psalms*, "Peace in the will of God . . . is the foundation on which the psalmists build their edifice of praise . . . *the peace that comes from submission to God's will and from perfect confidence in Him*" (*Praying the Psalms*, 17).

The relationship between inner peace and the peace of society is suggested in *No Man Is an Island*, where Merton points out that it is important to be at peace within oneself if one is to contribute to a peaceful world. "A man who is not at peace with himself necessarily projects his interior fighting into the society of those he lives with, and spreads a contagion of conflict all around him" (*No Man Is an Island*, 120–21). Even the good such a person attempts to do will be spoiled because it is being done not as a fruit of peace but as an attempt to achieve or accomplish some good work and so escape one's own unhappiness by one's own efforts. His point here is very similar to one he will make later in *Conjectures of a Guilty Bystander*, when he discusses the temptation to a kind of demonic activism and overwork as

a form of violence: "The frenzy of the activist neutralizes his work for peace. It destroys his own inner capacity for peace. It destroys the fruitfulness of his own work, because it kills the root of inner wisdom which makes work fruitful" (*Guilty Bystander*, 73).

The true solution, Merton believes, is to "learn to be detached from the results of our own activity. . . . It is only when we are detached from ourselves that we can be at peace with ourselves" (*No Man Is an Island*, 121). This is a lesson that he will find exemplified above all in Gandhi, who shows with clarity the connection between inner and outer peace. For Gandhi the way of peace is the way of truth, and the "first and fundamental truth is to be sought in respect for our own inmost being, and this in turn implies the recollectedness and the awareness which attune us to that silence in which alone Being speaks to us in all its simplicity" (*Seeds of Destruction*, 232). True peacefulness therefore requires a certain distance and detachment from the busyness and overstimulation of a society that measures worth by achievement, and thus requires, in the classic Hindu formulation, detachment from the fruits of one's actions (227). Thus, in the development of Merton's own thought on peace there is a recognition of an intrinsic and crucial connection between inner and outer peace, between peace as gift and peace as task. The idea of working, or even "fighting," for peace can readily lead to justification of virtually any form of violence and coercion in the name of making peace. Merton suggests, "If you are yourself at peace, then there is at least *some* peace in the world. Then share your peace with everyone, and everyone will be at peace" (*Guilty Bystander*, 181). He recognizes that such a program may sound simplistic, but it emphasizes the primacy of the spiritual rather than the political in peacemaking; political action is certainly necessary (see *Seeds of Destruction*, 171), but it is insufficient, indeed counterproductive, if not rooted in a commitment to peace as a spiritual reality.

This recognition of the importance of grounding the political in the spiritual is particularly evident in the opening section of Merton's pamphlet *Monastic Peace*, published in the watershed year of 1958, the year of his "Fourth and Walnut" experience. He emphasizes that authentic peace is found in the hearts of those "who are wise because they are humble, humble enough to be at peace in the midst of anguish, to accept conflict and insecurity and overcome it with love, because they realize who they are, and therefore possess the freedom that is their true heritage" (*Monastic Journey*, 39–40).[1] True peace is found only by those who renounce all egotism and so rediscover their own true selves in Christ, for the peace that the world cannot give, the peace that Christ breathes out upon his disciples, "is not a thing, or a practice, or a technique: it is God Himself, in us. It is the Holy Spirit" (40). All those united to Christ are given the privilege and the duty to be peacemakers. The layperson "should build peace in his home, but he should spread peace in the community in which he lives and dedicate himself, as far as possible, to the cause of peace and order in his nation" (42). The monastic is called to create an image of peace, a sign of the heavenly city, by forming authentic community and so providing a "vision of peace, a window opening on the perspectives of an utterly different realm, a new creation, an earthly paradise in which God once again dwells with men and is almost visibly their God, their peace and their consolation" (43). Within a couple of years of writing this hymn to the peace of the cloister Merton will come to find that his monastic vocation involves not only being a sign of Christ's peace but also an instrument of that peace, by raising his voice to call upon Christians and all people of goodwill to incarnate the biblical vision of peace in a world moving inexorably toward the catastrophe of war.

In his essay "Peace: A Religious Responsibility" he emphasizes that "Christ Himself is our peace (Eph. 2:14)" and that every "Christian is and must be by his very adoption as a son of God, in Christ, a peacemaker (Matt. 5:9)" (*Breakthrough to Peace*, 94, 95). The vocation and task of Christian discipleship is "to struggle in the world of violence to establish His peace not only in their own hearts but in society itself," and to do so by following in the footsteps of the Master, who resisted evil to the point of death with no weapons but those of the Spirit (95). Peacemaking for the Christian is not quietistic inertia, not passive acceptance of injustice, but fidelity to the example of Christ, who made peace by the blood of the cross (96). The peace of the risen Christ is "an eschatological gift … a fruit of the Spirit (Galatians 5:22) and a sign of the Divine Presence in the world" (*Seeds of Destruction*, 127). By witnessing to the gift of Christ's peace, the church is called to be a sign of contradiction and a sign of invitation to a world that depends on coercion and domination to establish order. For Merton commitment to the peace of Christ expressed in opposition to the immorality of modern warfare is an intrinsic, indeed a central, dimension of authentic Christian living. It is a sign that the reign of God, the kingdom of *shalom*, has already begun in Christ and is being lived out by those who profess faith in Christ. The willingness to confront evil with no weapons but those of Jesus, the power of truth and love, is rooted in a profound trust that despite all evidence to the contrary, the Prince of Peace reigns: "Above all our confusions, our violence, our sin," Merton writes in his journal on Christmas Eve in 1961, "God established His kingdom no matter what 'the world' may do about it" (*Turning toward the World*, 188). It is this eschatological hope, not some naively optimistic belief that enemies will become friends if only they are treated kindly, that is the true basis for Christian peacemaking: "The message of Christians is not that the kingdom 'might come, that peace might be established, but that the kingdom is come, and that there will be peace for those who seek it'" (188). POC

SEE ALSO *FAITH AND VIOLENCE*; GANDHI ON NON-VIOLENCE; JUST WAR, THEORY OF; NONVIOLENCE; *NONVIOLENT ALTERNATIVE*; PASSION FOR PEACE; *SEEDS OF DESTRUCTION*; WAR.

Notes

1. *Monastic Peace* is included in *The Monastic Journey*, the posthumous collection of a number of Merton's monastic essays.

PEARCE, BENJAMIN

Benjamin Pearce (1856–1936) was the husband of Thomas Merton's great aunt Maud (Owen Merton's maternal aunt). During their first two years in England Owen and Tom stayed with the Pearces in Ealing, a suburb of London. Uncle Ben recently had retired as headmaster of Durston Preparatory School for Boys. It was he who suggested that Tom should go to Oakham School. WHS

PEARCE, MAUD GRIERSON

Maud Grierson Pearce, sister of Gertrude Hanna Grierson Merton and wife of Benjamin Pearce, was Owen Merton's maternal aunt, Thomas Merton's great aunt. In May 1928 Owen and Tom crossed the channel to England, where they stayed with Aunt Maud and Uncle Ben at 18 Carlton Road, Ealing, on the outskirts of London. Tom attended classes at Ripley Court and in the fall of 1929 entered Oakham School. The Pearces' home continued to be Tom's address and the place to which he returned during holiday time. Aunt Maud played a significant role in Tom's adolescent years. Later he saw her as a model and a symbol of the years of his innocence. After Owen Merton died in 1931, Tom Izod Bennett replaced Aunt Maud as Tom's guardian, and it was to his London residence rather than to Aunt Maud's that he returned during time off from school. Aunt Maud died in November 1933. Merton wrote, "They committed the thin body of my poor Victorian angel to the clay of Ealing, and buried my childhood with her.... She it was who had presided in a certain sense over my most innocent days. And now I saw those days buried with her in the ground" (Seven Storey Mountain, 121). WHS

PERSON

"The person must be rescued from the individual" (New Seeds of Contemplation, 38). This contrast is another way in which Thomas Merton expresses the difference he sees between the true self and the false self. It also leads to his contraposing of the community to the collectivity. The community is the "place" of persons, the collectivity the "place" of individuals.

In using this vocabulary Merton was influenced by the personalism of neoscholastic writers such as Jacques Maritain. In Scholasticism and Politics Maritain quotes Pascal as saying: "The ego is hateful.... This is a commonplace expression of Pascalian literature.... As a counterpart of the words of Pascal, we must remember the words of St. Thomas: The person is that which is noblest in the whole of nature" (46).

What is meant here is that we all live in the midst of people; we belong to human society. But that society may move in one of two directions. It may develop into community, where persons are respected for who they are and where freedom and responsibility are highly prized. On the other hand, it may degenerate into the collectivity: a conglomerate of individuals feeling their separateness, each motivated by self-serving concerns, all moving in disharmony toward what are often different, and even conflicting, societal goals. This is to say that the individual is a unit of society that is definable only in a negative way, for it exists in separateness and isolation. Individuals are at best only superficially united. They form a mass society that is constructed "out of empty and alienated human beings who have lost their center and extinguished their own inner light in order to depend in abject passivity upon the mass in which they cohere without affectivity or intelligent purpose" (Disputed Questions, x). Individuals are drowned in the nameless isolation and the unredeemed alienation of the collectivity. They surrender their freedom of thought and action and become part of a system that does all their thinking for them and formulates the opinions they should live by. "[The individual] does not think, he secretes clichés" (New Seeds of Contemplation, 55). The collectivity does not understand solitude and its absolute necessity for true human living. Instead, individuals turn to what Pascal calls divertissement, "diversion" or "distraction," by which one escapes from life's problems (but also its invitations) into meaningless activities: superficial enterprises that enable one to avoid having to face the true realities of human life. "The function of diversion," Merton says, "is simply to anesthetize the individual as individual and to plunge him in the warm, apathetic stupor of a collectivity which, like himself, wishes to remain amused" (*Disputed Questions*, 178). Today's television, with its "situation comedies" and "soap operas," may be seen as a contemporary example of such diversion.

What is perhaps most telling about such isolated individuals is that they have lost the sense of transcendence and therefore their natural capacity of contemplation. In his essay "Rain and the Rhinoceros" (in *Raids on the Unspeakable*) Merton draws on Eugene Ionesco's play *Rhinoceros* to describe the sickness of the collectivity. In this theater-of-the-absurd drama all but one person give up the sense of their own identity and surrender it to the collectivity: all become rhinoceroses. This one person, though tempted to join the herd, remains human in a world that has become a world of monsters. Merton's essay and Ionesco's play deserve a careful reading, as both show what society can become when people lose all sense of their human identity.

Far different from the individual is the "person," who sees the need for real solitude — "all the more real today when the collectivity tends more and more to swallow up the person in its shapeless and faceless mass" (*New Seeds of Contemplation*, 53). The person is a center of love and freedom, linked with sisters and brothers in all that makes them human and in a sharing of all that makes them one in Christ. It is only persons that can create the fullness of community. Persons are able to say with St. Paul, "I live, now not I [the isolated individual], but Christ [the archetypal person joined together with other persons] lives in me" (Gal. 2:20).

Persons find in community the place for solitude and therefore for contemplation. Renouncing the call to live by diversion, they assume responsibility for their own inner lives and for the society in which they live. They refuse to walk away from reality. They are ready to face life as it is, with all its complexities and absurdities. But this is possible only in a person who values solitude, who realizes that "with-

out solitude of some sort there is and can be no maturity" (*Disputed Questions*, 206). "Unless one becomes empty and alone, he cannot give himself in love because he does not possess the deep self which is the only gift worthy of love. And this deep self, we immediately add, cannot be *possessed*. My deep self is not 'something' which I acquire, or to which I attain after a long struggle. It is not mine and cannot become mine. It is no 'thing' — no object. It is 'I....'" "This inner 'I,' who is always alone, is yet always universal." For "in this inmost 'I' my own solitude meets the solitude of every other man and the solitude of God. Hence it is beyond division, beyond limitation, beyond selfish affirmation. It is only this inmost and solitary 'I' that truly loves with the love and the spirit of Christ. This 'I' is Christ Himself, living in us: and we, in Him, living in the Father" (207). WHS

SEE ALSO ALIENATION; SELF.

PHILOTHEUS, FR.

SEE BOEHNER, PHILOTHEUS.

PHOTOGRAPHY

Photography became one of Thomas Merton's most significant interests during the last three or four years of his life. The collection of his photographs in the Thomas Merton Center archives includes over twelve hundred prints. Journal entries from the early 1960s give little indication that this interest would develop. On October 10, 1961, he comments on the absurdity of taking color photographs at the hermitage — "Or any photographs at all" — and justifies it only as a way of letting nun friends who could not visit the place see the hermitage. Later in the same entry he sardonically comments on the image monks have of themselves as "'enriched' with all kinds of synthetic colors...full of spiritual plastics....Kodacolor" (*Turning toward the World*, 169). In reflecting on a winter landscape as seen from the novitiate window he contrasts the flat realism of nineteenth-century Western painters with the suggestiveness of the Chinese masters who "painted...not landscapes

358   PHOTOGRAPHY

Photograph by Thomas Merton

but Tao" and comments, "Nothing resembles reality less than the photograph. Nothing resembles substance less than its shadow. To convey the meaning of something substantial you have to use not a shadow but a sign, not the imitation but the image. The image is a new and different reality, and of course it does not convey an impression of some object, but the mind of the subject: and that is something else again" (*Guilty Bystander*, 134). It was not until Merton discovered that the camera could be an instrument for capturing not shadow but sign, not imitation but image, that he became fascinated by photography.

By late 1963 this interest had begun to manifest itself. He wrote in his journal for October 7, "Am planning to have enlargements made of some of my photos of Shakertown [taken as early as January 1962 — see *Turning toward the World*, 194] and Dant Station, and for some reason this is very satisfying" (*Water of Life*, 23), and on December 22 he writes of "taking pictures . . . down at 'The Point' in Louisville" as a way "to keep honestly situated" (48). But a main catalyst for this deeper involvement evidently came in September 1964 when he was equipped with a Kodak Instamatic as part of a project to provide photographs for a new illustrated book on the monastery that the abbot had decided to have published (which eventually appeared as *Gethsemani: A Life of Praise*

in 1966). Characteristically, the first thing he reports photographing is scarcely useful for the picture book: "a fascinating old cedar root I have on the porch" of the hermitage (147). Two days later, before the "dream camera" malfunctioned, he was taking pictures of "a mad window in the old tool room of the woodshed" and describing his surroundings as "a mine of Zen photography" (147). Within a few days he is writing of "Love affair with camera" (149). His interest clearly was in a more contemplative rather than a documentary use of the camera, as a tool for meditation rather than for more utilitarian purposes (though he does mention that during the following February he met with two other monks to look over contact sheets for the photo book and found there to be "much good stuff" [210; see also 297], so he didn't neglect his responsibilities in that line).

For some time after the project was completed his access to a camera apparently was somewhat sporadic, depending on the use of cameras borrowed from visitors, as when he mentions taking "a bunch of probably useless pictures" with Naomi Burton Stone's Nikon during her visit in April of 1967 (*Learning to Love*, 221). By early August he was using a Rolleiflex to take photos that might be used for the cover of what was to become his long poetic sequence *Cables to the Ace* — "roots again," he notes (274). His skill improved over time and was complemented by the "marvelous" Canon FX lent to him by John Howard Griffin in March 1968 (*Other Side of the Mountain*, 73), which he was to bring with him on his spring trip to the West Coast and on his Asian journey. His friendship with Griffin — novelist, civil rights activist, and photographer — was a major source of encouragement and advice, and from August 1967 until the time of Merton's death Griffin's son Gregory was the principal developer of Merton's photographs. Not surprisingly, Merton was not adept at the more technical side of photography: in a January 1967 letter to Griffin he comments, "I see no reason why an occasional picture taker like myself, who doesn't even know how to develop a film, can be considered a photographer" (*Road to Joy*, 134–35), and in September he writes, "I know nothing of such mysteries as ASA speeds. Never use a meter. So I presume everything I did was 'standard'" (137). Apparently he became somewhat more proficient with the loan of the Canon FX, which was "all full of happy suggestions: 'Try this! Do it that way!' Reminding me of things I have overlooked, and cooperating in the creation of new worlds" (141).

Merton photographed almost exclusively in black and white (not surprisingly, given his comments on Kodacolor). He typically focused on the play of light and shadow on landscapes and ordinary objects, on views of the hermitage and the surrounding woods, on the simple beauty of Shaker architecture and furniture, on the stark "suchness" of both natural and humanmade objects — roots, trees, weeds, stones, baskets, benches, buckets; numerous photographs are framed by windows, looking both in and out. In a letter to Griffin, Merton describes his interests: "Obviously I am not covering the Kentucky Derby etc. But I do like a chance at fast funny out of the way stuff too. The possibility of it in case. But as I see it I am going to be on roots, sides of barns, tall weeds, mudpuddles, and junkpiles until Kingdom come" (140). He describes a photo he took of Needle Rock on the Pacific coast as both "an interior landscape" and "there" in the outside world, the camera as mediating between observer and observed (*Other Side of the Mountain*, 110). Later, on his Asian trip, the camera is very much a part of what he called his "quarrel" with the Himalayan peak of Kanchenjunga in November during his retreat at the Mim Tea Estate. He first describes his photographing the mountain as an "act of reconciliation," then reconsiders, reminding himself that a camera cannot capture reality but only reflect limited perceptions of reality. "Hence the best photography is aware, mindful, of illusion and uses illusion, permitting and encouraging it — especially unconscious and powerful illusions that are not normally admitted on the scene" (284). Photographs from this final journey are among his most striking, including scenes of his visits to the New Mexico deserts, the Pacific coastline, and Asia, which include a number of portraits — of Tibetan monks and children — otherwise a rarity, and the evocative photos of

the Buddhas at Polonnaruwa. Griffin recounts learning that the Canon FX with eighteen undeveloped pictures was found among Merton's effects after his death, and his own careful developing of these final images, which Merton never saw, including the one of Bangkok harbor that recalls a dream Merton had of his own death (see *Guilty Bystander*, 170–71).

Two significant collections of Merton's photographs have been published: Griffin's *A Hidden Wholeness: The Visual World of Thomas Merton* (Boston: Houghton Mifflin, 1970), which also includes many of Griffin's photographs of Merton along with a helpful text (where the comment noted above is found [pp. 144, 146]), and Deba Patnaik's *Geography of Holiness: The Photography of Thomas Merton* (New York: Pilgrim Press, 1980), a collection of a hundred Merton photographs with the editor's introduction and afterword. Merton photographs also are included in *The Asian Journal of Thomas Merton*; *Day of a Stranger*; *Woods, Shore, Desert*; *Thomas Merton in Alaska*; and *The Thomas Merton 1981 Appointment Calendar.* POC

SEE ALSO CALLIGRAPHIES; DRAWINGS, REPRESENTATIONAL.

PLASSMAN, THOMAS BERNARD

Born in Avenwedde, Germany, Thomas Plassman (1879–1959) came to the United States in 1894 and in 1898 joined the Franciscan order at Paterson, New Jersey. He was ordained a priest in 1906. After studying in Rome for advanced degrees, he came to teach at St. Bonaventure College. He became president of the college in 1920, a position he held until 1949, when he was chosen provincial of the New York province. In 1940 Thomas Merton, in need of a job because his application to join the Franciscan order had been rejected, was hired by Fr. Plassman to teach English at the college. He was given three classes of sophomore English. It was in his first year of teaching, during Holy Week of 1941, that Merton visited Gethsemani — a visit that would lead to his ardent desire to enter the monastery. On December 9, 1941, toward the end of the first semester of his second year of teaching, that desire finally was brought to fulfillment as he boarded the train that would take him on his way to the Trappist monastery of Gethsemani.

Merton had a strong affection for Fr. Plassman. In his journal, under the date of February 4, 1941, he wrote, "I don't know how many people I ever knew it was possible to really revere. Father Thomas is one.... He is a man of the most immense and unshakeable calm I ever saw, and underneath his calm is this tremendous simplicity and pleasant humor" (*Run to the Mountain*, 304). WHS

POETRY, THEORY OF

Thomas Merton not only wrote poetry, but also wrote about poetry, particularly in its relation to the spiritual life. His essay "Poetry and the Contemplative Life" appeared in *Commonweal* on July 4, 1947, and was reprinted in *Figures for an Apocalypse*. A revised version of this essay, now entitled "Poetry and Contemplation: A Reappraisal," was published in the same magazine some eleven years later, on October 24, 1958, and is reprinted in *The Literary Essays of Thomas Merton* and elsewhere. A comparison of the two versions of his essay reveals not only how his ideas on artistic creativity had evolved, but also how this evolution is characteristic of the broader transformation that would mark Merton's life and writing in the 1960s.

The structure of "Poetry and the Contemplative Life" consists of a lengthy introduction followed by a three-part central section and a brief conclusion. The introduction focuses on "the contemplative life" as "the normal term of the Christian life even on earth" (*Figures for an Apocalypse*, 96), though it remains a pure gift beyond what can be achieved by human effort, and though relatively few are actually ready to receive the gift in their earthly lives. Having provided this overview, Merton then turns to the relationship of contemplation and art. His first point is that contemplation has much to offer the poet, since "it brings us into the closest contact with the one subject matter that is truly worthy of a Christian poet: God as He is seen by faith, in revelation, or in the intimate experience of the soul illumined

by the gifts of the Holy Ghost" (97). He encourages Catholic writers and poets to lead lives of active contemplation that will draw them closer to Christ through the disciplines of liturgy, penance, prayer, and spiritual reading.

After demonstrating that contemplation has much to offer poetry, Merton makes the case that the converse is also true, that poetry has something valuable to offer contemplation: "the poetic sense may be a remote disposition for mystical prayer" (101) because an authentic aesthetic experience is much deeper than mere sensual stimulation, and in fact goes beyond even rational apprehension.

But while aesthetic intuition and artistic creativity can play an important role in spiritual growth, beyond a certain point poetry and contemplation can begin to pull in different directions. This is the third and final point Merton makes in the article: when contemplation begins to become more passive, even the activity of art can become a hindrance. "It is precisely here," Merton states, "that the esthetic instinct changes its colors and, from being a precious gift becomes a *fatal handicap*" (108). The problem is a conflict of ends: "The artist enters into himself in order to work.... But the mystic enters into himself, not in order to work but to pass through the center of his own soul and lose himself in the mystery and secrecy and infinite, transcendent reality of God living and working within him" (108). Whereas the infused contemplative experience is passive and receptive, allowing God to do transformative work within the soul, the artistic experience remains active and creative, interested in what happens within the artist, however significant it may be in itself, primarily as raw material for the art. The higher good risks being sacrificed for the lower, the perfecting of the soul for the perfecting of the work.

Merton's conclusion, then, is that while poetry can be of great assistance during the early stages of contemplative life, to cling to poetic activity as one moves toward the higher levels of infused contemplation is to risk arresting further spiritual development. "In such an event," he states, "there is only one course for the poet to take, for his own individual sanctification: the *ruthless and complete sacrifice of his art*" (109–10). Merton does, however, leave some room for flexibility at the very end of the essay: personal moral certainty, or the desire of a religious superior, that one should continue to write for the benefit of others could be a sign that in a particular case this "ruthless sacrifice" is not called for; and while this will make for a continued painful struggle between the demands of art and the demands of contemplation, since such an exceptional situation "will not take away distractions, or make God abrogate the laws of the spiritual life" (111), Merton concludes that some comfort may be taken from the teaching of St. Thomas that sharing the fruits of contemplation is more meritorious than simply enjoying them oneself, and there is no one better prepared than the artist to articulate "what is essentially inexpressible" (111).

When he returned to the essay more than ten years later, Merton was at another turning point in his life as both monk and writer, when the clear-cut certainties that had marked his early years in the monastery no longer seemed adequate as advice to others or as a description of his own experience. Life in its existential richness and messiness did not conform neatly to the categories and distinctions of well-defined theories, however logical and intellectually satisfying they might be in the abstract. As Merton stated in the headnote to the revised version of his essay, "*The confident pronouncements made in my early writing lay more and more heavily on my conscience as a writer and as a priest*" (*Literary Essays*, 338), and prompted him to revisit his earlier argument, which he now saw as having "*stated a 'problem' and tried to apply a rather crude 'solution'*" (338). By tending to present contemplation "*as a separate department of life*" rather than as "*the very fullness of a fully integrated life*," the "problem" of the earlier version of the essay Merton now considers to be "*largely, an illusion, created by this division of life into formally separate compartments of 'action' and 'contemplation'*" (339).

It is to rectify this misapprehension that Merton rewrites his essay and arrives at a strikingly different conclusion about the relationship between artistic creativity and contemplative realization. The overall structure and much of the actual content of the two versions of the essay remain the same, but by significant additions and judicious alterations in each of the major sections, "Poetry and Contemplation: A Reappraisal" contrasts markedly with its predecessor both in its tone and in its main point. The change already is evident in the introductory description of contemplation, which begins with seven paragraphs of completely new material that situate the topic firmly in the context of contemporary life. The change in tone, and even in terminology, from the earlier version of the essay is immediately apparent: the framework of scholasticism has given way to a more existential outlook, an emphasis on the concrete situation of daily experience: "To the true Christian poet, the whole world and all the incidents of life tend to be sacraments — signs of God, signs of His love working in the world" (345). By recasting his explanation of contemplation in terms of the contemporary search for meaning and authenticity, Merton makes the links between contemplation and art more readily evident. Though not all poets are mystics in the strict sense, the genuine poet shares a " 'prophetic' intuition" (345) that perceives the inner spiritual dimension of ordinary events and objects. Merton rejects a disincarnate, "spiritual" conception of religious poetry as detached from "worldly" concerns in favor of "a fully integrated vision of our time and of its spirit" (346), a vision that penetrates but is not limited by its physical, intellectual, social, political, and cultural surroundings.

In the revised version Merton does not minimize the problem he had raised in "Poetry and the Contemplative Life." The temptation for the poet to sacrifice spiritual growth for the sake of artistic productivity is still quite evident, though it is now described as "a real danger" (350) rather than as the more absolute "*fatal handicap*" (*Figures for an Apocalypse*, 108). While the description of the tension between being and doing is retained from the earlier version, Merton now adds almost a full paragraph that considers the problem in terms of the tendency to objectify, to "withdraw from the mystery of identification with Reality beyond forms and objectivized concepts, and . . . return to the realm of subject and object" (*Literary Essays*, 351). In his less doctrinaire conclusion, the continuity between poetry and contemplation is not inevitably ruptured by a call to divine union. Merton does at first seem to have reached the same point in this version as in the original essay: despite the helpful role of poetry in the earlier stages of the contemplative journey, "when we are entering the realm of true contemplation," he writes, "where eternal happiness is tasted in anticipation, poetic intuition may ruin our rest in God 'beyond all images'" (352). But the operative word here is "may," not "will" or "must": if abstract logic leads to one conclusion, the particular circumstances of concrete lived reality may reveal a very different one, or rather many different ones.

Merton voices a healthy suspicion of any position — particularly his own of ten years before — that claims there is "an absolute clean-cut 'either/or' choice between 'art' and 'mystical prayer'" (352). He has let go of the security, which is also the confinement, of abstract certitudes. He now is able to envision a whole range of possibilities, only one of which is that an artist might be called to stop writing to enter more deeply into prayer. While Merton brings the essay to a close by affirming that spiritual gifts are "infinitely greater" than art, and that if an artist "is called upon to make an exclusive choice of one or the other" (354), art should give way to prayer, the whole thrust of his conclusion is that the necessity of such a choice is by no means inevitable or even normative; in rethinking the issue he had raised a decade earlier, Merton takes a position that is perhaps less self-assured but more reassuring in its affirmation of art, and by extension all authentic human activity, as compatible with and contributing to even the deepest relationship with God.

About midway between the two versions of this essay Merton included a discussion of poetry in his book on the psalms, *Bread in the Wilderness* (1953). The chapter "Poetry, Symbolism and Typology" (also included in *Literary Essays*) makes four main points. First, the purpose of a poem is not to convey information but to induce an experience unique to each particular poem, with its own irreducible form. Its language is not primarily conceptual but associative, with affective and spiritual connotations. Therefore, to read the psalms properly is to participate in the experience of their authors (*Bread in the Wilderness*, 53–54). Second, religious poetry must be distinguished from devotional verse. The latter does not convey an experience but communicates a formulaic content by rearranging standard devotional materials. Religious poetry, preeminently the psalms, draws the reader into a religious experience. In the case of the psalms, the experience of God that is presented is supremely personal, neither one of detached transcendence, nor of an immanent life force, nor of an anthropomorphic projection (55–56). Third, the psalms are filled with cosmic symbolism, the primitive revelation of the Creator in nature, purified and reappropriated in the context of the revelation to Israel (58–59). Fourth, Merton finds in the psalms typological symbolism, in which the pattern of experience conveyed here (and throughout the Old Testament) is seen to foreshadow the pattern of Christ's redemptive activity and its completion at the final judgment (62–64).

A final discussion of poetry comes in the "Message to Poets" of 1964, written for a gathering of young, mainly Latin American, writers in Mexico City, included in *Raids on the Unspeakable* (155–61). It is a kind of manifesto, an exhortation to resist the debasement of language. Merton opposes any "calculating" use of language for some predetermined end and calls on the poets to retain their "innocence," by which he means an immediacy of experience that resists formalities and abstractions (*Raids on the Unspeakable*, 156). He rejects the idea of words as "magical," able to produce effects on others without inner consent, which is the technique of propaganda and advertising (159). He calls on the poets either to deride this incantatory use of language (i.e., through antipoetry) or to prophesy, by which he means to bring out the hidden meaning beneath the surface of everyday life (159). He calls for words that seek not to persuade but to point toward the silence beyond words. He encourages the poets to accept their marginality, the insecurity and abjection of a "dervish" existence, and concludes by urging them to strip away all secondhand ideas for the sake of the immediacy of an experience of the "water of life" (160–61). POC

SEE ALSO ART, THEORY OF; CREATIVITY.

POINT VIERGE, LE

Thomas Merton's most prominent use of the phrase *le point vierge* (literally, "the virgin point") occurs in the well-known account of his experience on March 18, 1958, at the corner of Fourth and Walnut in the business district of Louisville (*Guilty Bystander*, 140–42/156–58). Although the phrase does not appear in the original journal account of the experience, it is a significant element in the expanded account that Merton wrote on September 20, 1965: "It was as if I suddenly saw the secret beauty of their hearts, the depths of their hearts where neither sin nor desire nor self-knowledge can reach, the core of their reality, the person that each one is in God's eyes.... Again, that expression, *le point vierge* (I cannot translate it) comes in here. At the center of our being is a point of nothingness which is untouched by sin and by illusion, a point of pure truth, a point or spark which belongs entirely to God, which is never at our disposal.... This little point of nothingness and of *absolute poverty* is the pure glory of God in us. It is so to speak His name written in us, as our poverty, as our indigence, as our dependence, as our sonship. It is like a pure diamond, blazing with the invisible light of heaven" (158).

Merton was struck and moved by the idea of the "*point vierge, où le désespoir accule le coeur de l'excommunié*" ("the virgin point, where despair corners the heart of the outsider") when he read an issue of *Les Mardis of Dar es Salaam*, sent to him by Louis Massignon. "What a very fine analysis, and how true," Merton wrote to Massignon on July 20, 1960 (*Witness to Freedom*, 278). When he read Massignon's piece, almost two months earlier, he had noted the phrase in his journal entry for May 30, 1960: "Deeply moving prayer of Louis Massignon on the Desert, on the tears of Agar, on the

Moslems, the '*point-vierge*' [the virgin point] of the Spirit seemingly in despair, encountering God" (*Turning toward the World*, 5). He reworked the journal entry for *Conjectures of a Guilty Bystander*, where he described "the '*point vierge*' of the spirit, the center of our nothingness where, in apparent despair, one meets God — and is found completely in His mercy" (*Guilty Bystander*, 151).

A few days later, on June 5, 1960, Merton used the phrase in a different, though related, context: "The first chirps of the waking birds — *le point vierge* of the dawn, a moment of awe and inexpressible innocence, when the Father in silence opens their eyes and they speak to Him, wondering if it is time to 'be?' And He tells them 'Yes.' Then they one by one wake and begin to sing.... With my hair almost on end and the eyes of the soul wide open I am present, without knowing it at all, in this unspeakable Paradise, and I behold this secret, this wide open secret which is there for everyone, free, and no one pays any attention" (*Turning toward the World*, 7). An expanded version of this entry concludes this way: "Here is an unspeakable secret: paradise is all around us and we do not understand. It is wide open" (*Guilty Bystander*, 118/132). As is often the case, Merton's description of the natural landscape mirrors a glimpse into his inner landscape. Merton had appropriated Massignon's phrase and made it his own.

Massignon's usage of the phrase *le point vierge* "has it roots in the mystical psychology of Islam, especially as one finds it in the thought of al-Hallâj. Massignon was fond of quoting a saying of al-Hallâj to the effect that our 'our hearts are a virgin that God's truth alone opens.'"[1] For al-Hallâj and for Massignon "'the virgin' is the innermost, secret heart (*as-sirr*) — the deep subconsciousness of a person."[2] Muslim mystics also speak of "the primordial point" (*an-nuqtah al-asliyyah*), "the apophatic point of the mystic's deep knowledge of God."[3] *Le point vierge*, the virgin point, is the secret center of the human heart where the person knows God.

It is not surprising that the phrase *le point vierge* resonated with Merton. In *Seeds of Contemplation* (1949) he had written, "There exists some point at which I can meet God in a real

and experimental contact with His infinite actuality: and it is the point where my contingent being depends upon His love. Within myself is a metaphorical apex of existence at which I am held in being by my Creator" (*Seeds of Contemplation*, 31; also *New Seeds of Contemplation*, 37). Massignon, with his deep knowledge and appreciation of the mystical tradition of Islam, offered Merton another way of speaking about a Reality that he himself had come to know and attempted to express in his own writings. CMB

SEE ALSO "FOURTH AND WALNUT" EXPERIENCE.

Notes

1. Sidney H. Griffith, "Merton, Massignon, and the Challenge of Islam," in *Merton and Sufism: The Untold Story*, ed. Rob Baker and Gray Henry (Louisville, Ky.: Fons Vitae, 1999), 64. The article, which offers a detailed discussion of *"le point vierge"* in the thought of Massignon and Merton, previously was published in *The Merton Annual 3* (1990): 151–74.
2. Ibid., 65.
3. Ibid.

POLONNARUWA

This ancient city, now in ruins, is in Sri Lanka (Ceylon). In the third century C.E. it was the residence of the Sinhalese kings and was their capital from the eighth to the twelfth centuries. There are ruins of palaces and of temples, both Hindu and Buddhist. Four huge figures survive: a large seated Buddha on the left of a cave, a reclining Buddha on the right, an Ananda (the Buddha's favorite disciple, standing by the head of the reclining Buddha), and in the cave another seated Buddha. Thomas Merton visited Polonnaruwa on December 2, 1968. He was deeply moved: "Looking at these figures I was suddenly, almost forcibly, jerked clean out of the habitual, half-tied vision of things, and an inner clearness, clarity, as if exploding from the rocks themselves, became evident and obvious. . . . I don't know when in my life I have ever had such a sense of beauty and spiritual validity running together in one aesthetic illumination. . . . I know and have seen what I was obscurely looking for. I don't know what else remains but I have now seen and pierced through the surface and have got beyond the shadow and the disguise" (*Asian Journal*, 233, 235–36; *Other Side of the Mountain*, 323). WHS

PRADES

This French town in the eastern Pyrenees, near the Spanish border, is where Thomas Merton was born on January 31, 1915. *The Seven Storey Mountain* opens with these words: "On the last day of January 1915, under the sign of the Water Bearer, in the year of a great war, and down in the shadow of some French mountains on the borders of Spain, I came into the world" (3). WHS

PRAYER

Thomas Merton offers two ways of thinking about prayer:[1] (1) as raising mind and heart to God, and (2) as the discovery of God within, in the course of which one discovers one's own true self, the importance of awareness of God's presence, and the realization that true prayer always involves an entrance into mystery — the mystery of a God we never can name. Very often when he speaks about prayer, Merton

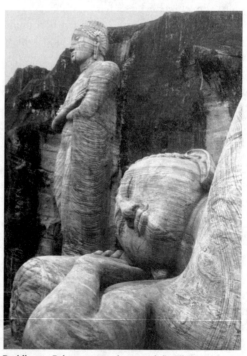

Buddhas at Polonnaruwa, photograph by Thomas Merton

actually means contemplation or contemplative prayer. Thus, in *The Climate of Monastic Prayer* (also published as *Contemplative Prayer*) he prefers to use the term "meditation" (perhaps because it was popular in the mid-1960s?), though much of what he says is about contemplation. One possible way of distinguishing prayer and contemplation is to see prayer as the wider term that would include, besides contemplation, vocal prayer, liturgical prayer, discursive meditation, and so forth. Yet even this distinction is not quite adequate, because Merton would want all prayer to be informed by a contemplative spirit.

In 1955 Merton was appointed master of novices at Gethsemani Abbey. In this role he was expected to teach the novices about prayer. He certainly would have taught them about *lectio divina* as part of the Benedictine spirit. Yet he was careful not to try to offer them specific methods of prayer. As he wrote to Etta Gullick on September 12, 1964, "I try to make them love the freedom and peace of being with God alone in faith and simplicity, to abolish all divisiveness and diminish all useless strain and concentration on one's own efforts and all formalism: all the nonsense of taking seriously the apparatus of an official prayer life, in the wrong way (but to love liturgy in simple faith as the place of Christ's sanctifying presence in the community)" (*Hidden Ground of Love*, 368).[2]

In March of 1966 Etta Gullick had suggested to him that he write an article or book on "progress in prayer." He expressed a hesitant willingness to write something on the subject, yet he warned of the danger involved in even thinking about "progress" in prayer. The chief obstacle to such progress is self-awareness, watching oneself praying, so to speak, so that one can assess the progress achieved. "I think progress in prayer comes from the Cross and humiliation and whatever makes us really experience our total poverty and nothingness, and also gets our mind off ourselves" (376).

In some of his earlier writings, such as *The Seven Storey Maintain* and *The Sign of Jonas*, Merton is moved to write various prayers into his text. Apart from these written prayers he tended to be quite reticent about his own prayer. There is a letter, however, to Abdul Aziz

in which, after repeated requests from Aziz, he does speak of his "ordinary way of prayer." "I have a very simple way of prayer. It is centered entirely on attention to the presence of God and to His will and His love. That is to say that it is centered on *faith*, by which alone we can know the presence of God. One might say this gives my meditation the character described by the Prophet as 'being before God as if you saw Him.'" Yet he warns that this should not be taken to mean imagining anything or conceiving a precise image of God. For this he would see as a kind of idolatry. "On the contrary," he goes on, "it is a matter of adoring Him as invisible and infinitely beyond our comprehension, and realizing Him as all." It is somewhat like what Sufis would call *fana*. "There is in my heart this great thirst to recognize totally the nothingness of all that is not God. My prayer is then a kind of praise rising up out of the center of Nothing and Silence. If I am still present 'myself,' this I recognize as an obstacle about which I can do nothing unless He Himself removes the obstacle. If He wills He can then make the Nothingness into a total clarity." In other words, he says that his prayer is "not 'thinking about' anything, but a direct seeking of the Face of the Invisible, which cannot be found unless we become lost in Him who is Invisible" (*Hidden Ground of Love*, 63–64).

Before his departure for Asia, Merton met with a group of men and women, staying at Our Lady of the Redwoods Abbey, who were searching for new ways of renewing religious life. They asked Merton to speak about prayer. His first remark was, "Nothing that anyone says will be that important. The great thing is prayer. Prayer itself. If you want a life of prayer, the way to get to it is by praying."[3] We have to start where we are. "We were indoctrinated so much into means and ends that we don't realize that there is a different dimension in the life of prayer. In technology you have this horizontal progress, where you must start at one point and move to another and then another. But that is not the way to build a life of prayer. In prayer we discover what we already have. You start where you are and you deepen what you already have, and you realize that you are already there. We already have everything, but we don't know it and we don't experience it. Everything has been given to us in Christ. All we need is to experience what we already possess."

Our trouble, he suggests, is that so often we are in a hurry. We do not take the time to experience life, to savor it, to let life fully come to itself in us. If we want to pray, then we must slow down to a tempo that is truly human. Then we shall begin to have time to listen. But we need to free ourselves from the imaginary claims that time places on us. We live in the fullness of time. "Every moment," Merton said, "is God's own good time, his kairos. The whole thing boils down to giving ourselves in prayer a chance to realize that we have what we seek. We don't have to rush after it. It is there all the time and if we give it time, it will make itself known to us."

During this conversation the topic of intercessory prayer came up. Merton expressed himself very simply: "We are not rainmakers, but Christians. In our dealings with God, he is free and so are we." He went on to say that when we pray for another person, it is a way of responding to a need in ourselves. We need to express our love by praying for our friends. "If you love another person, it's God's love being realized. One and the same love is reaching your friend through you, and you through your friend." Br. David Steindl-Rast raised an objection: "But isn't there still an implicit dualism in all this?" Merton replied, "Really there isn't, and yet there is. You have to see your will and God's will dualistically for a long time. You have to experience duality for a long time until you see it's not there.... Any moment you can break through to the underlying unity which is God's gift in Christ. In the end, Praise praises. Thanksgiving gives thanks. Jesus prays. Openness is all." WHS

SEE ALSO CONTEMPLATION; MEDITATION.

Notes

1. Much of what Merton had to say about prayer is discussed in this encyclopedia under the entry CONTEMPLATION.

2. The entire correspondence between Merton and Etta Gullick is worth reading for their discussion of prayer and spirituality.

3. This and the remaining quotations in this article are from David Steindl-Rast, "Recollections of Thomas Merton's Last Days in the West" in *Monastic Studies* 7 (Pine City, N.Y.: Mt. Saviour Monastery, 1969 reprint), 1–10.

PRAYER OF CASSIODORUS, A: From the Treatise De Anima

Preface and translation by Thomas Merton. Worcester, England: Stanbrook Abbey Press, 1967. 15 pp.

This second collaboration between Thomas Merton and the Benedictine nuns of Stanbrook Abbey in England (after the 1963 translation of Guigo the Carthusian's *The Solitary Life*) is a limited edition printed on handmade paper, and it includes a five-page preface (set by machine) followed by the prayer itself (set by hand), with the translation on the left-hand pages, justified right and printed in red, and the original Latin on the facing pages, justified left and printed in black. Though prose, both the original and the translation are printed in sense lines rather than continuous paragraphing (with no punctuation and only capitalization indicating new sentences in the translation, though the original is punctuated).

Merton first writes in his journal for June 7, 1962, of "The serene, pure music of Cassiodorus's prayer at the end of his *De Anima* [*On the Soul*]! What nobility of mind. Christian and classic nobility, simplicity, harmony. And what depth of religion" (*Turning toward the World*, 225). On July 3 he writes of translating the prayer while fasting in the morning (229).[1] On September 9, 1964, he sends the translation to Dame Hildelith Cumming, the Stanbrook printer, as a possible text for a limited edition (*School of Charity*, 234); the process moved along slowly (see 289), but Merton declared himself very pleased with the result when the volume finally appeared in early 1967 (331).

In his preface Merton gives a short summary of the life of Cassiodorus (b. 485), including his diplomatic service to the Ostrogothic emperor Theodoric and his eventual retirement to his estate at Vivarium, where he established a monastic community devoted to prayer and study, especially the copying of manuscripts. He points out Cassiodorus's importance in preserving classical manuscripts (though that importance had been exaggerated by earlier scholarship) and in teaching the significance of the liberal arts as a foundation for theological study. He discusses the composition of *De*

Anima, written after Cassiodorus's retirement from public life but before the foundation at Vivarium, and finds in the treatise a description of the soul in dynamic, almost existential terms, as "a substance whose full and final identity depends on a decision, a choice, a commitment" (*Prayer of Cassiodorus,* 3). He notes the author's focus on the body as a temple of God, which should be subordinated to the soul as the soul is to God, and comments on his vivid word portrait of a truculent politician as the "alienated" man, an indication of the chaotic period in which the treatise was composed. He points out the sobriety and light of the prayer that concludes the treatise, which reveals "the reality of Christ the Redeemer to the mind of this Roman patrician of the Dark Ages" (5), a "lay theologian," he reminds the reader, not a cleric or a monk even though the founder of a monastic house.

The prayer itself, addressed to Christ, asks that Christ not allow to perish that which he had saved by becoming human; that he protect humankind from "the savage hate" of "the gliding snake" who comes to deceive and destroy; that "I may know the nothingness I am without Thee / yet ... know what I may be with Thee." It asks for forgiveness and restoration and prays, "O good Craftsman / so tune the instrument of our body / that it may ring in harmony with our mind / let it not become so strong as to vaunt in pride / nor so weak as to fail," and it concludes by recognizing that Christ alone is aware of what is "truly to our measure" and thus able to "fill Thy vessels with favorable gifts" and so to keep "frail flesh" from offending God. POC

Notes

1. See also the quotation from *De Anima* on June 10 (*Turning toward the World,* 226), translated in *Conjectures of a Guilty Bystander* (208–9) as part of an appreciative comment on Cassiodorus.

PRAYING THE PSALMS

Collegeville, Minn.: Liturgical Press, 1956.
32 pp.

Praying the Psalms is Thomas Merton's second book on the psalms. In the first, *Bread in the*

Wilderness, written in 1950 and published in 1953, Merton explored the relationship between the psalms and contemplation, showing how praying the psalms can open one to receive God's gift of contemplation. In *Praying the Psalms,* a book of only thirty-two pages published by Liturgical Press in 1956, Merton offers a more popular treatment of the subject.[1] The book serves as a kind of introduction to the use of the psalms in prayer. In a series of seven reflections (neither numbered nor named) Merton explains why all should pray the psalms, offers suggestions on how to pray the psalms, and identifies some central themes in the psalms. The first edition of *Praying the Psalms* included drawings by the Grailville Art Center.

The church considers the psalms to be the perfect form of prayer. "To put it very plainly: the Church loves the Psalms because in them she sings of her experience of God, of her union with the Incarnate Word, of her contemplation of God in the Mystery of Christ" (9). The passion that moved the psalmists to praise God and to love God is awakened anew in the hearts of those who pray the psalms. The psalms form their minds and move their hearts. Merton reminds his readers that although the church considers the Psalms to be the "ideal" prayer for clerics and religious, they also are the "perfect" form of prayer for the laity. "It would be quite wrong to imagine that the prayer life of the Church is divided into two distinct halves, separated by a gap that is rarely bridged, as if the Psalter and the Missal were reserved for clerics and the rosary and other extraliturgical devotions were for the laity" (15). Prayed privately, the psalms nevertheless become part of the church's prayer. "It is by singing the Psalms, by meditating on them, loving them, using them in all the incidents of our spiritual life, that we enable ourselves to enter more deeply into that active participation in the liturgy which is the key to the deepest and truest interior life" (9).

Merton recommends reading the psalms slowly to savor them, meditating on their meaning, allowing their meaning to become one's own.[2] To illustrate the "serious use of the Psalms" Merton cites the example of Paul

Claudel, who internalized the psalms and then rendered them in his own words. The psalms *"entered* into the poet's whole life and being" (23). Claudel's experience illustrates how the meaning of the psalms can resonate in our own experience. Praying the psalms requires no special gifts: "All that we need is the ability to understand the meaning of the Psalms, their literal meaning as poems, and to 'echo' or answer their meaning in our own experience" (24). We need only to "recognize, in the Psalms, our own experience lived out and perfected, orientated to God and made fruitful" (25). To understand the words that spring from the heart of the ancient psalmists, "we must experience the sentiments they express in our own hearts" (13). It is not enough simply to acknowledge the psalms as a perfect form of prayer in order to recognize their value in one's own life. We must *"know by experience"* that in the psalms Christ himself prays in us (21).

The psalms range across the entire gamut of human experience of the divine: delight in the law of the Lord and peace in God's will (Psalm 1); submission to God (Psalm 14); confidence in God (Psalms 119–133);[3] suffering injustice (Psalm 25); affliction (Psalm 27); spiritual trial (Psalm 62); mystical joy (Psalm 41); society's sufferings (Psalm 2); sorrow for offending God (Psalm 129); joyful praise and adoration of God (Psalm 117). There also are the psalms that speak to Christians of the suffering of Jesus Christ (Psalm 21) and those psalms that anticipate the coming of God's reign (Psalm 95). "There is no aspect of the interior life, no kind of religious experience, no spiritual need of man that is not depicted and lived out in the Psalms" (44).

This book reveals something about its author and about the time in which it was written. Being a monk, Merton knew the psalms well. He had prayed the Psalter until the words of the psalmists resounded in his heart and their prayer became his own. Hearing the psalms again and again, Merton came to know the God whom they praised. It is this familiarity and intimacy that Merton invites others to experience. It should be noted that Merton was writing at a time when the Catholic Church was growing in its appreciation of the centrality of

Scripture in the life of the whole church. The biblical movement was well underway, liturgical renewal was beginning, and there was a growing appreciation of laity in the church. The influence of this pre–Vatican II ferment is evident in this book.[4] CMB

SEE ALSO *BREAD IN THE WILDERNESS.*

Notes

1. References in this entry are to the reprinted edition of *Praying the Psalms* (Collegeville, Minn.: Liturgical Press, 1956), 45 pp.
2. What Merton is advocating, though he does not use the term here, is the practice of *lectio divina.*
3. Known as the "Gradual Psalms."
4. *Praying the Psalms* first appeared in the Popular Liturgical Library Series.

PRIESTHOOD

Thomas Merton's most extensive comments about priesthood are found in *The Sign of Jonas* and in the corresponding sections of the second volume of his journals, *Entering the Silence.* It is the theology of the pre–Vatican II Catholic Church that sees the priest as primarily a cultic figure who does what no one else can do: "the one thing that saves the world and brings health into it and makes men capable of being happy" (*Sign of Jonas,* 186). Ordination wrought an ontological transformation in the one ordained. To be a priest was a unique honor. To "say Mass" privately at a side altar (as all the Gethsemani priests did at this time) was a special joy. Priestly involvement with a community of believers at Mass (so important in the theology of Vatican II), if it was thought of at all, was a very general understanding of the *ex opere operato* effects of the sacrament: the Mass by its very reality brought grace and help to people for whom the priest prayed and even, it might be, to people unknown to the priest whom the power of the Mass could reach.

Merton was ordained a priest on Ascension Thursday, May 26, 1949. He seems emotionally staggered by "the marvelous grace of ordination." He has the feeling of being transformed. "At last I have found the place in the universe that has been destined for me by the mercy of God" (*Road to Joy,* 193). He sees the grace of ordination as giving him his true identity. "The priestly character, unworthy as I am to receive

Thomas Merton's ordination

it, is so much 'mine,' in the designs of God and Our Blessed Lady, that I feel as if I had at last awakened to discover my true name and my true identity, as if I had never before been a complete person" (193). A week or so after his ordination he writes, "The Mass is the most wonderful thing that has ever entered into my life. When I am at the altar I feel that I am at last the person that God has truly intended me to be" (*Sign of Jonas*, 195).

It is worth noting that he seems to be saying about the effects of ordination what he says elsewhere about contemplation: it awakens him, enables him to discover his true identity and to become fully a person, to become what God always intended him to be. In a letter written to Dom James Fox just before his ordination he speaks about what he hopes being a priest will mean for him. "I ask Jesus to make me a purely contemplative priest. He has plenty of active workers, missionaries, preachers, spiritual directors, masters of novices, etc. But He has so few who are concerned with Him alone, in simplicity, silence, recollection and constant prayer. I beg Him daily that I may always be one of those few, and that I may live the life of pure union with Him that was led by the forgotten saints" (*School of Charity*, 11–12). This is a devotional approach to priesthood that sees it as an honor for the priest and a way of offering praise and honor to God and bringing salvation to "souls." At the time Merton was ordained, it was not uncommon for priests to speak of "my Mass." Thus, Merton writes the day before his ordination, "I can go to the altar with confidence and great joy and know that my Mass is going to make a tremendous difference to the happiness and salvation of the world, not only *in spite of* the fact that it is my Mass, but even *because* it is my Mass, that is, because of the special mercy of Christ to those who have nothing of their own to offer, nothing except weakness and misery and sin" (*Entering the Silence*, 317). This expresses well the understanding of priesthood that sees the priest as *alter Christus*.

Without doubt Merton was on an emotional high at the time of his ordination — one that could hardly be sustained. He himself recognized this. A week after the ordination, writing to Sr. Therese Lentfoehr, he says that he is probably in danger of "spiritual gluttony, . . . but I wish I could stand all day at the altar and be, most fully, Christ, and taste the magnificence of His power swimming through my veins for His Father's infinite glory and for the salvation of the world" (*Road to Joy*, 193). Thus, his ordination and the days following it may be viewed as one of those flash floods of emotional enthusiasm that from time to time seemed to overwhelm him. There would be other similar occasions.

After the flurry of reflections around the time of his ordination, there is little that Merton says about priesthood until the Second Vatican Council, though it should be said that he was devoted to daily Mass. His story about the Asian trip makes it clear that wherever and whenever possible he made arrangements to say Mass.

The new liturgical directions taken by the Second Vatican Council changed Merton's thinking about the Mass, as it did for countless other priests. The Mass, from being "my Mass" becomes "our Mass." In an article originally published in the *Critic* magazine he writes, "The best thing about the 'new Mass' is the real opening up of opportunities for participation. . . . Communication being consciously established and maintained, priest and people can more easily become aware that they are together *celebrating* the mystery of our Redemption in the Eucharistic Sacrifice and the Lord's Supper" (*Seasons of Celebration*, 232). Notice how it is no longer just the priest who is the celebrant, but priest and people celebrating together.

Radical changes in liturgy are not always comfortable, especially for those set in their ways and reluctant to do things differently. The move from silent spectator to active participant will be exciting for some and resented by others. Merton suggests that if an open approach to the liturgy is beyond the capacity of "those of us who have grown old in 'closed' and rigid forms," then it will be the children who will profit most from liturgical change. "Why not let them, in the simplicity and inspired spontaneity which are their special gift, and guided by sensitive and alert adults, begin to sketch out the creative and original forms of the future liturgy for which we are all waiting?" (247). He also suggests that the renewal be carried out *in a spirit of play*. In play humans are involved, open, joyous, serious, and self-forgetful. "The open, thoughtless, hieratic self-forgetfulness of play is more likely than anything else to provide a substitute for the self-concerned engrossment of subjective concentration that has so far provided the worshipper with his chief ground for seriousness in worship" (248). As an example of a form of play that might be used in worship, he mentions the ancient art of the dance (see the final chapter of *New Seeds of Contemplation*, "The General Dance"). WHS

SEE ALSO CELIBACY; EUCHARIST; LITURGY.

PROMETHEUS: A MEDITATION

Lexington, Ky.: King Library Press, 1958. 9 pp. (unnumbered).

On February 28, 1958, Thomas Merton was visited by Victor Hammer, the Austrian-born artist and printer, and his wife, Carolyn (*Search for Solitude*, 175). Some days later he writes of the visit, "I like them both, they are wonderful people, with great integrity and great love for honest work in art and anything else. Hence their printing. They are doing *Prometheus* for me and it is my favorite kind of project. Nice printing and no one inquiring about publicity or money or sales or anything. Doing something good for the sake of its own worth and therefore for the glory of God. 250 copies '*pro manuscripto*' [limited edition] in which I say something which I firmly believe" (178).[1]

What Merton "firmly believe[s]" is articulated in his reflections on the Prometheus myth, developed in seven numbered paragraphs. The theft of fire from the gods is described as an act of despair, a failure to recognize that one's true identity and hence one's infinite worth is a free gift of a loving God, not an achievement of one's own power, which is an effort doomed to failure because it seeks to seize transcendence as a right, and an expression of idolatry that creates a god in one's own self-seeking image and then both rebels against and abases oneself before that god. The meditation concludes by contrasting the illusory heroism of Prometheus, who "thought he had to ascend into heaven to steal what God had already decreed to give him," with the genuine heroism of Christ, who "came down with the fire Prometheus needed / hidden in His Heart . . . in order to show him that in reality God cannot seek to keep anything good to Himself alone" (*Prometheus*, [8]). The false gods of Prometheus are antagonistic to humanity, but the Living God of Jesus has an infinite love for all that creation and desires above all to share divine life and love with people. And yet, Merton ruefully notes, all too often those who claim to believe in and worship the Living God in fact confuse God with the petty, jealous gods of Prometheus and fail to realize that "there is nothing we can steal from Him at all / because before we can think of stealing it / it has already been given" ([9]).[2]

When the printing — done at the University of Kentucky's King Library Press, of which Carolyn Hammer, the curator of rare books, was director — had been completed, Merton sent copies of the volume to a number of literary figures, including Pablo Antonio Cuadra (*Courage for Truth*, 183), Czeslaw Milosz (*Striving towards Being*, 19), and Boris Pasternak (*Courage for Truth*, 88). Pasternak responded enthusiastically to the meditation, prompting Merton to reply, "I was so happy that you liked the best parts of *Prometheus*, and were able to tell me so" (90). Milosz, on the other hand, wrote, "In *Prometheus* you are unjust, it seems to me. If one is for Dante, one cannot be against Prometheus as fire in Heraclitus, probably in the Promethean myth, in Dante, has a symbolic meaning and is the same as the fiery pneuma of the New Testament" (*Striving towards Being*, 31). Merton tries to clarify his point in his letter to Milosz of May 21, 1959: "About Prometheus — I wonder if you interpreted it correctly? I have nothing against fire. Certainly it is the fire of the spirit: my objection is that it does not have to be stolen, and that it cannot be successfully stolen. It has been already given, and Prometheus's climb, defeat and despair is all in his own imagination. That is the tragedy. He had the fire already" (42–43). Nevertheless, Milosz's objections apparently

prompted Merton to further consideration of the figure of Prometheus. His meditation was based on the myth as presented by Hesiod, but in a journal entry of January 17, 1960, he writes of the experience of reading the *Prometheus Bound* of Aeschylus: "Shattered by it. I do not know when I have read anything so stupendous and so completely contemporary. . . . A great religious experience. Prometheus, archetypal representation of the suffering Christ. . . . Prometheus startles us by being more fully Christ than the Lord of our own cliches" (*Search for Solitude*, 370). When Merton comes to reprint *Prometheus* the next year in *The Behavior of Titans* (and later in *Raids on the Unspeakable*),[3] he will add a prefatory note entitled "The Two Faces of Prometheus" that will contrast the Prometheus of Hesiod, whose "view of life is cold, negative and odious" and "implicit in the atheism of the world into which I was born and out of which, by Christ's grace and the gift of God, I have been reborn," with the Prometheus of Aeschylus, hero of "one of the purest and most sacred of tragedies" and "the exact opposite" (*Raids on the Unspeakable*, 81)[4] of Hesiod's figure: "The Prometheus of Hesiod is Cain. The Prometheus of Aeschylus is Christ on the Cross" (*Behavior of Titans*, 14; *Raids on the Unspeakable*, 83). In a December 17, 1960, letter to James Laughlin, Merton admits, "Of course my commentary on Prometheus is a little confusing. It is certainly not a critique of the Prometheus of Aeschylus (rather of his Zeus). I tried to say that in a little note which will only leave the reader confused, I am afraid" (*Thomas Merton and James Laughlin*, 160). The confusion comes only if the reader expects the Prometheus of Aeschylus to make an appearance in the "Meditation" proper, which had been written before Merton's close acquaintance with the drama of Aeschylus. The Aeschylean Prometheus is also absent from the chapter on "Promethean Theology" in *The New Man*, which is a considerably expanded discussion of Prometheus as a representative of the false self that shares the outlook and occasionally the wording of *Prometheus: A Meditation*. POC

SEE ALSO *BEHAVIOR OF TITANS*; *RAIDS ON THE UNSPEAKABLE*.

Notes

1. In fact, only 150 copies eventually were printed.

2. See also the similar comment on Prometheus in *Monastic Peace*, published in the same year as *Prometheus*: "Christian sanctity is not a Promethean exploit. We do not have to storm the walls of heaven and bring down the fire of God, we do not have to raid His treasure rooms in order to obtain the good things He has reserved for us. Prometheus was a hero in a myth which expressed the ultimate despair of all the pagan religions. But Christ really descended from heaven, taking on our flesh, reuniting the human race in Himself, giving all men light in His light, sending us His Spirit to unite us to the Father" (in *Monastic Journey*, 47–48).

3. The revised text of the meditation in *The Behavior of Titans* and *Raids on the Unspeakable* includes about two dozen alterations, ranging in length from a single word to a sentence in length. There are only a couple of minor differences between the text of the meditation in *The Behavior of Titans* and that in *Raids on the Unspeakable*.

4. There are a number of textual differences between the prefatory note in *The Behavior of Titans* and that in *Raids on the Unspeakable*. Here, the earlier version reads: "view of life is utterly horrible" and "One of the most heartrending, pure and sacred of tragedies" (*Behavior of Titans*, 13).

PROPHECY

Thomas Merton finds biblical prophecy rooted in the vocation of Israel, the covenant intimacy offered at Sinai with "the austere, unseen yet ever-present and all merciful Lord of the desert" (*Disputed Questions*, 224). The role of the prophet was less to foretell the future than to recall the past, "the age of Israel's nuptials with the Lord" (224). The prophetic summons to an Israel easily seduced by the ready availability of the gods of the Canaanites was consistently a call to rediscover its roots, to recommit itself to the covenant made in the wilderness with its demands for fidelity, justice, and steadfast love. The prophetic message was unvarying in its core meaning: "Return to the spirit of your days in the desert! Recovery of the spirit of the desert meant a return to fidelity, to charity, to fraternal union; it meant the destruction of the inequalities and oppressions dividing rich and poor; conversion to justice and equity meant the return to the true sabbath. For the law of the desert was the law of the sabbath, of peace, direct dependence on the Lord, silence and trust, forgiveness of debts, restoration of unity, purity of worship" (224–25). It is a call to reintegration, to wholeness, a recovery of unity with the Lord, with one another, with creation.

But prophecy is a desert vocation in another sense as well. In calling the community to accountability and repentance, the prophet stands against the prevailing ethos, speaks the truth to power, and is often ignored or ridiculed or rejected or persecuted. The prophet is, almost perforce, a solitary, a desert figure, a voice crying in the wilderness. "In the Old Testament," Merton points out, "what happens to Elijah the prophet? He has to stand completely alone against the whole structure. . . . Something similar happens to Saint Francis. For him, too, there's a radical break with the world into a prophetic and free life where he made his own choices" (*Springs of Contemplation*, 132–33). But because the prophet is essentially a witness, this freedom is never for the sake of the individual prophet alone, but for the very people he has been called away from, to testify to a different way of life, a different source and goal, "to be to them a sign of contradiction which reminds them of a freedom they've forfeited" (134).

Merton finds that this prophetic tradition culminates in the person and work of Jesus, who is led by the Spirit into the wilderness to confront the power of evil, who preaches good news to the poor and liberation to captives, and who finally is rejected and led outside the city to be executed by religious and political authorities (81). Incorporation in Christ, then, means sharing in this prophetic mission. "A prophet is one who lives in direct submission to the Holy Spirit in order that, by his life, actions and words, he may at all times be a sign of God in the world of men. Christ the Incarnate Word was of course the supreme Prophet, and all sanctity participates in this prophetic quality" (*Disputed Questions*, 223). Prophecy, therefore, is not a relic of the past but a responsibility of the present; it is a participation in the identity and mission of Jesus, an intrinsic dimension of what it means to be called to a life of discipleship.

Merton conceives the role of prophecy in the contemporary world to be essentially what it was in the biblical world: the identification and denunciation of idolatry. If anything, the need for prophets is greater today because the false gods in which people place their faith and their hopes are less easily recognized as idols, yet no less divinized and worshiped, and no less enslaving. "If, in fact, we live in a society which is par excellence that of the *simulacrum*, we are the champion idolators of all history.... The things that we do, the things that make our news, the things that are contemporary, are abominations of superstition, of idolatry, proceeding from minds that are full of myths, distortions, half-truths, prejudices, evasions, illusions, lies.... ideals that claim to be humane and prove themselves, in their effects, to be callous, cruel, cynical, sometimes even criminal" (*Faith and Violence*, 152–53). Here Merton condemns not only worship of wealth and comfort and material possessions and political or even religious power, but also a more insidious appeal to concepts such as patriotism or freedom or justice, which, however valid they may be in the abstract, are frequently disguises for self-serving and oppressive policies in actual practice. Ideologies easily become gods to which people offer their time, devotion, and unquestioning loyalty, and to which they are all too often willing to sacrifice the lives of others, especially those who worship comparable idols at different shrines (154).

The first task of the prophet, then, is to see reality as it actually is, to distinguish substance from illusion. "To live prophetically, you've got to be questioning and looking at factors behind the facts. You've got to be aware that there are contradictions. In a certain sense, our prophetic vocation consists in hurting from the contradictions in society. This is a real cross in our lives today. For we ourselves are partly responsible" (*Springs of Contemplation*, 157). Note that for Merton authentic prophecy does not involve self-righteousness, a condemnation of others that simultaneously is an assertion of one's own innocence. The prophet must begin by recognizing and exorcising his or her own illusions and idolatries, his or her own complicity in acquiescing to, perhaps even promoting, a social structure built on deception and oppression. Prophets recognize their own liberation as a gift, a grace, which becomes the substance

of their witness. True prophecy is founded not in arrogance but in humility.

It is precisely this humility, rooted in the recognition of God's presence, that gives the prophet the courage to speak and act prophetically. Prophecy for Merton is simply the recovery of one's true identity as grounded in Christ and filled with the Spirit: what one says or does to challenge the powers and principalities is simply the logical consequence of being one's authentic self. "We just let Christ be faithful to us. If we live with that kind of mind, we are prophetic. We become prophetic when we live in such a way that our life is an experience of the infallible fidelity of God. That's the kind of prophecy we are called to, not the business of being able to smell the latest fashion coming ten years before it happens. It is simply being in tune with God's mercy and will" (73). The witness of prophecy is a matter of presence before it is a matter of words; its testimony is made by the orientation of one's entire life: "Prophecy is not a technique, it is not about telling someone else what to do. If we are completely open to the Holy Spirit, then the Spirit will be able to lead us where God wants us to go. Going along that line, our lives will be prophetic" (74).

Merton realizes, of course, that "going along that line" will inevitably bring one into conflict with a society that demands conformity and is heading in a different direction. When the wisdom implanted in the created world has been obscured and distorted by efforts to exploit creation, and particularly other human beings, for selfish purposes, those who share the prophetic vocation of Christ are called to be signs of contradiction: "The real challenge to Christianity today is ... above all the recovery of a creative and prophetic iconoclasm over against the idols of power, mystification and super-control" (*Faith and Violence*, 255). The freedom of the prophet also is exercised by standing with those who are not free, by "actual human solidarity and communion" with those victimized by idolatries of race and class and power and money and comfort (256). Thus, the first task of prophecy is denunciation, a clear-sighted critique of various forms of illusory meaning, for the sake of a defense of the human person as made in the image of God and therefore possessed of an inalienable dignity and liberty.

But the prophetic charism is not only denunciation, but also annunciation, the proclamation of the good news that the idols are indeed illusions, phantoms, and that the true Lord is a God of love and justice and liberation. The prophet is called not merely to predict what will happen in the future but to live God's plan for the future here and now. "This way of living is prophetic, not in the sense of sudden illuminations as to what is going to happen at some future moment, but in the sense that we are so one with the Holy Spirit that we are already going in the direction the Spirit is going" (*Springs of Contemplation*, 49). The prophetic charism is to live out the reign of God, to be sign and instrument of *shalom* and justice and love in the midst of a world of hatred and oppression and division. The prophet is so committed to the vision of God's kingdom that God's rule becomes visible, incarnate, in his or her own life. "The great historical event, the coming of the Kingdom, is made clear and is 'realized' in proportion as Christians themselves live the life of the Kingdom in the circumstances of their own place and time" (*Faith and Violence*, 16). This is the authentic prophetic charism, to allow the present moment at once to recapitulate the past, the redemptive events of Christ's life, death, and resurrection, and to anticipate the future, the completion of the drama of salvation.

Merton suggests, then, that the prophetic charism is to recognize and reveal the *kairos*, the acceptable time, the time of decision, the time of the inbreaking of God's reign (*Nonviolent Alternative*, 75). But this is properly understood as the gift and responsibility of the Christian community as a whole. "Not just individuals but the community itself should be prophetic. That's an ideal, of course. But that's our task: not to produce prophetic individuals who could simply end up as a headache, but to be a prophetic community" (*Springs of Contemplation*, 134). It is the task of the church, as the body of Christ and thus the heir to the prophets, to counter the "claim to complete autonomy," to self-constituted meaning, which passes for

a value system in the contemporary world. "Christianity sees that a society that justifies its behavior and bases its existence on this supposed autonomy of man does, in fact, devote to destruction and death the very resources and energies which it claims to be using for the affirmation and improvement of life. . . . It was the task of the prophets . . . to discover this kind of meaning in the events of the history of Israel. And it remains the prophetic task of the Church to interpret events of our own time in this same kind of way" (*Guilty Bystander*, 100). The church is called both to affirm what is authentic and good in human aspirations and to dissociate herself from all that can degrade and undermine these aspirations. The burden of prophecy is not an option but an obligation for Christians today, who must either "face the anguish of being a true prophet" or "enjoy the carrion comfort of acceptance in the society of the deluded by becoming a false prophet and participating in their delusions" (*Faith and Violence*, 68). Prophetic witness is central to the very identity and vocation of the church, which is to model and promote the unity God intended for all humanity. POC

PROVERB

"Proverb" is the name of a young Jewish girl of "the same race as St. Anne" who appears to Thomas Merton in a dream on February 28, 1958. Merton dreams that she embraces him "with determined and virginal passion" on the porch at Douglaston (the home of Merton's maternal grandparents) (*Search for Solitude*, 176). She is "a nice kid in a plain, sincere sort of way" who tells Merton that her name is Proverb (176). On March 4, 1958, Merton writes what can only be described as a love letter to "Dear Proverb." After noting the differences between them — particularly the "great difference in our ages" — Merton writes, "How grateful I am to you for loving in me something which I thought I had long ago entirely lost, and someone who, I thought, I had ceased to be" (176). Words cannot sufficiently express love and gratitude for "your lovely spontaneity, your simplicity, the generosity of your love," for "the revelation of your virginal solitude," and for your name with "its mystery, its simplicity and its secret" (176). Although he wonders if he will ever be worthy of her love, he pledges his love to her: "I will give you everything" (176).

On March 19, 1958, he describes his vision at the corner of Fourth and Walnut the day before. Struck by the "secret beauty" and "womanness" of the women he sees in the street, Merton observes, "For the woman-ness that is in each of them is at once original and inexhaustibly fruitful bringing the image of God into the world. In this each one is Wisdom and Sophia and Our Lady" (182). Again he writes to "Dear Proverb," speaking of their "meeting yesterday," which he shall never forget (182). "The touch of your hand makes me a different person. To be with you is rest and truth. Only with you are these things found, dear child sent to me by God" (182).

Merton speaks of Proverb in a letter to Boris Pasternak written in October 1958 and in a letter to Jacques Maritain written in December 1962. He tells Pasternak that he has met Lara (a character in Pasternak's novel *Dr. Zhivago*) and knows her, and then he describes in detail his dream of Proverb and his meeting with her on the Louisville street corner (*Courage for Truth*, 90). "I was walking alone in the crowded street and suddenly saw that everybody was Proverb," though they did not know it (90). "And they did not know their real identity as the Child so dear to God who, from before the beginning, was playing in His sight all days, playing in the world" (90). The child of God of whom Merton writes is Wisdom, begotten by God, with God before the earth was made, and beside God as God created the world, playing before God (see Proverbs 8).

Reading Raïssa Maritain's *Journal* puts Merton in mind of Proverb: "What moves me most is that in each line I see and I hear this 'child' of Proverbs 8:27–31 'ludens in orbe terrarum' [playing on the surface of the earth], *ludens* too in Raïssa" (33). Merton tells Jacques Maritain that he dreamed of this child a few times and, on a Louisville street, "saw suddenly that everyone was Proverb, without knowing it" (33). Raïssa is Proverb, he tells his friend. CMB

SEE ALSO "FOURTH AND WALNUT" EXPERIENCE; WOMEN.

PURITY OF HEART

Thomas Merton writes about "purity of heart" especially in *The Wisdom of the Desert* and in *The Climate of Monastic Prayer* (= *Contemplative Prayer*). The biblical basis of purity of heart is in the Beatitude "Blessed are the pure in heart, for they will see God" (Matt. 5:8). Its monastic basis is in the Egyptian desert and the pursuit by the desert fathers and mothers for *apatheia*. This Greek word means "passionlessness," and it is not to be confused with the modern term "apathy" with its meaning of insensitivity or indifference. In a very early book Merton describes "simplicity" (which could be a synonym for *apatheia*) as "getting rid of everything that does not help the monk to arrive at union with God by the shortest possible way" (*Spirit of Simplicity*, iii). Another term for *apatheia* is the more positive term used by John Cassian: "purity of heart."

In *The Wisdom of the Desert* Merton sees the monk as one who dies to the values of transient existence, "as Christ had died to them on the Cross and rises from the dead with him in the light of an entirely new wisdom" (*Wisdom of the Desert*, 7). That new wisdom is the clarity of vision that the Beatitude promises to the pure of heart. Merton describes it as "a clear unobstructed vision of the true state of affairs, an intuitive grasp of one's own inner reality as anchored, or rather lost, in God through Christ" (8). The life's goal of the monk is the kingdom of God, but the proximate objective of all his monastic observances — solitude, prayer, fasting, penances, charity — is "purity of heart."

By overcoming of the divisions within ourselves, "purity of heart" gives us a single-minded, unified grasp of our own identity. It is, Merton says, "the enlightened awareness of the 'new man,' as opposed to the complex and perhaps disreputable fantasies of the 'old man'" (*Climate of Monastic Prayer*, 93). This is possible only when we (1) have renounced all exaggerated notions of our own capacities; (2) give an unconditional and totally humble surrender of ourselves to God; and (3) totally and unambiguously accept ourselves and our situation as willed by God.

This acceptance of ourselves and our situation is no stoical acceptance of whatever is. There is no question of indifference toward the world or unconcern for people. Rather, such acceptance means standing before God naked and defenseless "in our nothingness, without explanation, without theories, completely dependent upon his providential care, in dire need of his grace, his mercy and the light of faith." Realizing our nothingness and helplessness in the presence of God need not be a mournful or discouraging experience. "On the contrary, it can be deeply tranquil and joyful, since it brings us in direct contact with the source of all joy and all life" (95–96).

Purity of heart enables us to know God, not speculatively, but through the realization that our very being is penetrated with God's knowledge and love for us. It is in proportion as we are known by God that we find our real being and identity in Christ. "Our knowledge of God is paradoxically a knowledge not of him as the object of our scrutiny, but of ourselves as utterly dependent on his saving and merciful knowledge of us" (113–14). WHS

SEE ALSO DETACHMENT; HUMILITY; SELF.

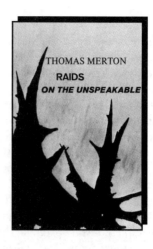

RACISM

One thread that links Thomas Merton's mature concerns for the Holocaust, the American civil rights movement, mistreatment of Native Americans, the Vietnam War, Latin American culture, Melanesian Cargo cults, and the relation of Christianity to other religious traditions is that the myth of racial superiority is a key element in all these areas. Merton sees "the error of racism" as a "logical consequence of an essentialist style of thought" prevalent in Western culture, which reduces others to neat categories as a means of objectifying and controlling them: "finding out what a man is and then nailing him to a definition so that there can be no change" (*Water of Life*, 200). Racism is a way of turning people into things, a process that the Nazis undertook with horrifying literalness, as Merton points out in his "Letter to Pablo Antonio Cuadra Concerning Giants": "For the sake of a name, a classification, you can be marched away with your pants off to be shot against a wall. For the sake of a name, a word, you can be gassed in a shower-bath and fed to the furnace to be turned into fertilizer. For the sake of a word or even a number they will tan your skin and make it into lampshades" (*Collected Poems*, 375). Racism also is evidence of a

Cover for *Raids on the Unspeakable* reprinted with the permission of New Directions. Cover photograph by Thomas Merton; cover design by David Ford.

fundamental insecurity and uncertainty about one's own identity that causes one group to project its fears onto another group. This scapegoating certainly was evident in Hitler's malign fantasies about Jewish conspiracies, but Merton finds it also in the compound of guilt, fear, and bad faith that characterizes racial prejudice in the United States. "Blaming the Negro," Merton suggests, "gives the white a stronger sense of identity, or rather it *protects* an identity which is seriously threatened with pathological dissolution. It is by blaming the Negro that the white man tries to hold himself together" (*Guilty Bystander*, 23).

What blacks are blamed for above all is the refusal any longer to accept the identity and conform to the stereotypes assigned to them by whites. Thus, Merton endorses the idea that the racial crisis in the United States is a manifestation of the global "colonial crisis" of the postwar era (*Faith and Violence*, 134–35), in which peoples throughout the world assert their right to determine their own destiny. The colonialist mentality is inherently racist because it claims to be bestowing the gifts of civilization on "inferior" races, which demonstrate their own inferiority either by gratefully accepting the proffered bounty or by rejecting it and so proving that "they cannot appreciate the superior benevolence and culture of the white race" (*Guilty Bystander*, 21). For Merton "the

377

greatest sin" of the ostensibly Christian West has been *"its unmitigated arrogance towards the rest of the human race,"* which led both to the conquest of other cultures and to a moral blindness that blocked an awareness *"that the races they conquered were essentially equal to themselves and in some ways superior"* (*Collected Poems*, 380–81). This "white Western myth-dream" (*Love and Living*, 94) of moral, cultural, and religious superiority that was responsible for the subjugation and even obliteration of other cultures has never been sufficiently recognized and repudiated and so is still operative, still wreaking havoc, in the present. The same mythology that led to the wholesale destruction of Native Americans Merton sees operative in the war in Southeast Asia: "Viet Nam seems to have become an extension of our old western frontier, complete with enemies of another 'inferior' race" (*Ishi Means Man*, 32). Even where it is less a matter of physical coercion than of psychological and spiritual reductiveness, the Western attitude of complacent superiority is inherently violent because it uses its own material affluence and technological mastery as evidence to buttress the validity of its own distorted perspectives; it seduces "the other," more or less effectively, into accepting the myth of his or her own inferior status: "The ultimate violence which the American white man, like the European white man, has exerted in all unconscious 'good faith' upon the colored races of the earth (and above all on the Negro) has been to impose on them *invented identities*, to place them in positions of subservience and helplessness in which they themselves came to believe only in the identities which had thus been conferred upon them" (11). Thus, the Cargo cults of the South Pacific that so fascinated Merton in his last years were at once a capitulation to the Western myth that one's worth was measured by one's possessions, and a desperate attempt to assert the equality, the essential humanity, of one's own group by obtaining "cargo": "The real message of the Cargo myth," according to Merton, "is the demand that the white man meet all peoples on a basis of moral equality and reciprocity" (*Love and Living*, 93–94). But this is a message that the West finds difficult if not

impossible to hear because it entails not only a surrender of a belief in its own superiority but also, ultimately, a relinquishing of the material basis on which that superiority is based, both by a recognition of the priority of spiritual wisdom to material wealth and by the actual redistribution of material resources (see *Seeds of Destruction*, 48).

Merton sees Gandhi as the great modern prophet of resistance to the mentality of subservience, and Gandhian noncooperation as a refusal to accept not only oppressive political and economic policies but also the presumptions about racial and cultural superiority that undergirded these policies. "Gandhi knew enough to see that to be 'civilized' by force was in reality to be reduced oneself to barbarism, while the 'civilizer' himself was barbarized" (*Gandhi on Non-Violence*, 20). In affirming the common humanity of oppressed and oppressor alike by his exercise of *satyagraha*, the power of truth, Gandhi intended not merely to effect a political liberation of his country but to rescue both the colonized and the colonizer from the "barbarism" of racist illusion and intolerance. For Merton the only genuine solution to the sin of racism is a repentance that recognizes that in fact there is only a single race, the human race, all of which is made in the image and likeness of God, all of which are brothers and sisters to the Word made flesh, who shared a common human life with every person who ever has been or ever will be and laid down his life for the sake of each of them. "Our task now," Merton declares, "is to learn that if we can voyage to the ends of the earth and there find *ourselves* in the aborigine who most differs from ourselves, we will have made a fruitful pilgrimage.... We have to come to the end of a long journey and see that the stranger we meet there is no other than ourselves — which is the same as saying that we find Christ in him" (*Mystics and Zen Masters*, 112). The same discovery needs to be made close to home as well: "The root of the answer is the love of Christ," Merton claims, the willingness to face reality, to look into "the sinful heart of sinful man as he really is — as we really are, you, and I, and our disconcerting neighbor" (*Faith and Violence*, 164), the recovery of "that Christian sense which sees every other man as Christ and treats him as Christ" (143). POC

SEE ALSO CIVIL RIGHTS MOVEMENT; *FAITH AND VIOLENCE*; *SEEDS OF DESTRUCTION*.

RAIDS ON THE UNSPEAKABLE

New York: New Directions, 1966. 182 pp.

This is a collection of thirteen pieces, on disparate topics and in somewhat disparate genres, all of which relate in some way to the theme of authentic freedom, and most of which represent some convergence of the spiritual, the literary, and the sociopolitical; all but one of the pieces previously had been published in other venues between 1958 and 1965. Fifteen of Thomas Merton's abstract drawings are placed between the essays and are described in a final note in which they are called "simple signs and ciphers of energy, acts or movements intended to be propitious" (*Raids on the Unspeakable*, 180) but "transcending all logical interpretation" (182). The title apparently is a variant of T. S. Eliot's description of poetry as "a raid on the inarticulate" ("East Coker," stanza 5, line 8), with the substitution of "the Unspeakable" emphasizing the horrors of an age of apocalyptic violence. In his prologue, addressed to the book itself, Merton distinguishes the book from its more "devout" predecessors, though he claims it has been "meditating in [its] own way" (1), more poetic and less "churchy" than the others, and while not repudiating them, he writes, "In some ways, *Raids*, I think I love you more than the rest" (2). He finds that its central message is "Be human in this most inhuman of ages, to guard the image of man for it is the image of God" (6).

The opening essay, "Rain and the Rhinoceros," is certainly the best-known section of the book. It is a meditation written from Merton's hermitage, though before the time when he was living there permanently. He presents the rain as an image of natural renewal and a countersymbol to the world of quantity and consumption that has intruded even into the hermitage in the slogan of the Coleman lantern: "*Stretches day to give more hours of fun*" (13). The insights of the sixth-century hermit Philoxenos, who writes of solitude as

essential for the discovery of a true self not defined by social myths and prejudices, are compared to those of the absurdist playwright Ionesco in *Rhinoceros*, in which the difficulty of maintaining one's own identity in the face of totalitarian demands for conformity and obedience is dramatized. The conclusion applies the theme to the contemporary political situation, as the speaker comments, "Even here the earth shakes. Over at Fort Knox the Rhinoceros is having fun" (23).

The two following essays both have a literary focus. "To Each His Darkness" is a reflection on a novel by the American-French Catholic author Julien Green, in which Green's pessimism is countered by Merton's awareness of the mercy of God, which breaks through a godless "consistency" and "liberates from all the rigid and deterministic structures" (32). "Flannery O'Connor: A Prose Elegy" praises the Catholic novelist of the South for her ironic depiction of people's illusions and self-deceptions, and concludes by comparing her with Sophocles for "the craft with which she shows man's fall and his dishonor" (42).

"A Devout Meditation in Memory of Adolf Eichmann" is placed in ironic juxtaposition with the memorial elegy for O'Connor. It centers on the reports of the Nazi death camp organizer's "sanity" and declares that psychological sanity cannot be equated with being in one's "right mind" (47), which requires a foundation in love. Adjustment to a society in which torture and mass murder are legal and normal may be "sane" but it is neither Christian nor authentically human.

"Letter to an Innocent Bystander" continues the focus on moral and political commitment by rejecting the notion that intellectuals can remain detached from social and political issues that have a moral dimension. Not to respond to injustice, Merton claims, is to be an accomplice; one must identify with "the others" (56), the marginalized, rather than the powerful. As Merton will suggest in the title of his published journal from this period, *Conjectures of a Guilty Bystander*, no one can remain both innocent and a bystander in an era when people are in danger of having their dignity and humanity stripped from them.

"The Time of the End Is the Time of No Room" is a Christmas meditation in which Christ's identity with the excluded is recognized as an eschatological sign that signals the end of the old world and the inbreaking of a radically different vision of justice and love, a time both "of great tribulation" and "certainly and above all the time of The Great Joy" announced by the angelic choir (74).

Like "Letter to an Innocent Bystander," the two following pieces previously were published in *The Behavior of Titans*. "Prometheus: A Meditation" rejects the image of God as a jealous tyrant from whom fire must be stolen in favor of a God of unlimited mercy incarnated in Christ, who empties himself even to the point of death so that all that belongs to God may belong to humanity as well. "Atlas and the Fat Man" is a prose poem in which Atlas, a personification of the goodness of the natural world, is challenged by the Fat Man, that ultimately illusory force that tries to control the world for the sake of its own self-assertion and self-gratification. "Martin's Predicament or Atlas Watches Every Evening" is, as Merton points out in his headnote, an earlier version of the Atlas myth with an "intentionally trifling" tone (111). It is made up largely of dialogue, in which Martin expresses the point of view taken by the Fat Man and is opposed by the sound perspective of John, who sees nature as beyond quantifying and human control, but who is ignored because he "is speaking in a foreign accent" (120).

"The Early Legend," subtitled "Notes for a Cosmic Meditation," is a six-part prose poem (with some sections in verse) that in some ways foreshadows the more elaborate experiments of *Cables to the Ace* and particularly *The Geography of Lograire*. It is a call to "recover your original name" (126), which is opposed by efforts to impose a socially constructed identity, presented through the piece in several different cultural guises, but countered by the presence of "God Who plays among His own children" (133).

"Readings from Ibn Abbad" is a poetic reworking of material by and about a fourteenth-century Sufi from Spain, somewhat akin, in much briefer compass, to Merton's renderings of Taoist texts in *The Way of Chuang Tzu*. The ten sections of the "Readings from Ibn Abbad" emphasize Ibn Abbad's simplicity and dedication to the Sufi way and his commitment to an apophatic spirituality of coming to Allah "In darkness, in emptiness, / In loss, in death of self" (146).

The final two pieces in the book have an aesthetic focus. "Message to Poets" was written for a gathering of Latin American poets in Mexico in 1964 and emphasizes the power and responsibility of art to resist the lies and half-truths of political and cultural establishments. Merton calls for poets to be prophets, that is, "to seize upon reality in its moment of highest expectation and tension toward the new" (159). He calls for poets to be "dervishes" (i.e., Sufi mystics, a subtle link to the previous piece) who are to dance in "the water of life" from which true poetry is born (161). "Answers on Art and Freedom" is a series of responses to questions asked by a South American literary journal, defending the "useless" (i.e., nonpragmatic) nature of art and warning against a pseudofreedom of nonconformism that in fact is a reduction of art to the level of propaganda just as surely as selling out to the system would be. He resists any reduction of the artist to a predetermined role, even that of rebel, and defends an aesthetic that finds true art in the perfection of the work itself, which then "becomes accidentally a work of love and justice" (172). POC

SEE ALSO *BEHAVIOR OF TITANS*; POETRY, THEORY OF; *PROMETHEUS: A MEDITATION*.

REDEEMING THE TIME
London: Burns & Oates, 1966. 187 pp.

This retitled and rearranged British edition of Thomas Merton's *Seeds of Destruction* omits the two chapters of part 1, "Black Revolution" ("Letters to a White Liberal" and "The Legend of Tucker Caliban"), which may have been considered less relevant to an English audience or perhaps somewhat dated, almost two years after the two articles' appearance in book form and close to three years after their initial periodical publication. It also omits "A Tribute to Gandhi" (part 2, section 3) and "Letters in a Time of Crisis" (part 3), and prints "The Christian in

World Crisis" (part 2, section 1) and "The Christian in the Diaspora" (part 2, section 2) in reverse order as parts 2 and 3. Part 1 consists of completely new material entitled "The Church and the 'Godless World,'" which includes six sections: "The 'World'"; "'Godless Christianity?'"; "God and the World"; "The Protest of Vitalism"; "Christian Humanism in the Nuclear Era"; "The Road Ahead." The two longest sections later were published in book form in America: "Godless Christianity?" which looks at the "Death of God" theologians and appears in revised and expanded form as the final chapter in *Faith and Violence* (259–87); "Christian Humanism in the Nuclear Era," a commentary on the personalism of the Vatican II Constitution on the Church in the Modern World (*Gaudium et Spes*), is published (along with the first two paragraphs of the following section, "The Road Ahead") in the posthumous *Love and Living* (151–70). The rest of the material from this section remains available only in *Redeeming the Time*.

"The 'World'" situates the Vatican II Constitution on the Church in the Modern World, the major focus of all of part 1, in the context of contemporary events, particularly the Vietnam War; it finds the meaning of the human person to be the principal topic of the document, explains that the Council fathers see the church as "ontologically separate from the world in which she is on pilgrimage" yet "identifie[d] . . . with the world by love and compassion" (*Redeeming the Time*, 10), and notes that the term "world" is multivalent, referring in different contexts to creation as it comes forth from God, the fallen realm darkened by human sinfulness, and the new creation redeemed by Christ. Section 3, "God and the World," provides a largely positive evaluation of Teilhard de Chardin's role as a bridge to scientific humanism, further discussion (carried over from section 2) of Bonhoeffer's rejection of using God as hypothesis to explain facts within the created order, and a defense of the traditional philosophical understanding of God as subsistent Being, which is rooted not in a logical argument of cause and effect but in "a *religious and metaphysical insight into the nature of Being, of ultimate reality as grasped*

by intuition in and through our own metaphysical ground" (47). Section 4, "The Protest of Vitalism," provides a critical yet sympathetic discussion of various currents of thought that reject scientist positivism in the name of an immanent spirit or life force that may or may not be identified with God; Merton maintains that self-transcendence, an affirmation of the person beyond the ego, ultimately requires an acceptance of divine transcendence, as is clearly expressed in the description of Christian humanism in the Council's Constitution on the Church in the Modern World. The final section, "The Road Ahead," considers the optimism of the Council's Constitution in the light of the critical situation of the modern world, and maintains that the role of the church must be one of critical engagement with political and scientific movements, but one that is not seduced by "worldly" power and that consistently defends the dignity of the human person. Merton concludes, "The Church must try to save modern man from his Faustian tendencies, and not become a sorcerer's apprentice herself while doing so. Such is the message of the Constitution on the Church in the Modern World" (92). POC

SEE ALSO *SEEDS OF DESTRUCTION.*

REDEMPTION

"Christian faith," according to Thomas Merton, "is not just a habit by which we are inclined to give assent to certain dogmatic information; it is a conversion of our whole being, a surrender of the entire person to Christ in His Church" (*Love and Living*, 230). It requires not just a change of beliefs but a change of identity, which is effected by participation in the mystery of Christ's passion and resurrection. Thus, his understanding of redemption is profoundly paschal: "Our knowledge of God through Christ depends on our spiritual union with Christ in the central mystery of our Redemption — His death and resurrection. This is not only a truth which we accept as historical, not only a dogma which we believe: it is a redemptive fact which we must make the center of our own spiritual life" (*New Man*, 232). For Merton, as for St. Paul, the Christian life is most fundamentally a "sharing of the death and resurrection of Christ" (167), a death to sin and the gift of new life "in Christ," which leads to discovery of the true self, to realization of authentic community, to contemplative union with God.

Spiritual transformation depends on identification with the crucified and risen Savior, which is possible only because the Savior first identified completely with the rest of humanity. God shared fully, in the person of Jesus, in the human condition, endured even the suffering and pain of human death, so that human persons might share fully in the life of God. Merton writes, "The sufferings of all men became His own sufferings; their weakness and defenselessness became His weakness and defenselessness; their insignificance became His. But at the same time His own power, immortality, glory and happiness were given to them and could become theirs" (*New Seeds of Contemplation*, 294). But this new life is available only by passing through death with Christ. Christ's compassion, his "suffering with" humanity, must be reciprocated by humanity's compassion, their "suffering with" Christ. Only in this way will the false self, "the self-centered and self-sufficient ego," captivated by the illusion of its own autonomy, disappear in order that "a new and liberated self who lives and acts 'in the Spirit'" (*Contemplative Prayer*, 110) might live. This paschal journey "is the passage through non-being into being, the recovery of existence from non-existence, the resurrection of life out of death" (*New Man*, 247).

Two supremely important consequences for the spiritual life follow from an identification of the true self with the risen Christ. First of all, it is the basis for genuine community. Union with Christ is at the same time communion with everyone else who is united with Christ: "Our Christian life is in fact the life of the risen Christ active and fruitful within all of us" (*Life and Holiness*, 81). The true self has passed, through the cross, from isolation to communion, from alienated individualism to loving solidarity with all who share the new life of faith in the risen Lord. "After all," Merton writes, "transformation into Christ is not just an individual affair: there is only one Christ, not many. He is not di-

vided. And for me to become Christ is to enter into the Life of the Whole Christ, the Mystical Body made up of the Head and the members, Christ and all who are incorporated in Him by His Spirit . . . so that the whole Christ is Christ and each individual is Christ" (*New Seeds of Contemplation*, 156–57).

Because in society, as in individual persons, the effects of the redemption are not yet fully realized, because Christ's victory over sin and death will reach its fulfillment only with the final revelation of God's reign, in a certain sense Christ continues to suffer throughout the course of history (*New Man*, 155). Therefore, to be one with Christ is to continue to share in the cross, though always in the context of hope grounded in experience of the risen Lord. The mission of the church to make the redemptive power of Christ available to the world depends upon the willingness of Christians to be signs and instruments of the divine compassion: "Life in Christ is life in the mystery of the cross. It is . . . a participation in a divine mystery, a *sacred action* in which God Himself enters into time and, with the co-operation of men who have answered His call and have been united in a holy assembly, the Church, carries out the work of man's redemption" (*New Seeds of Contemplation*, 163). The crucified Jesus also is to be encountered in all those who suffer, as he did, from the sins of others. "Murder, massacres, revolution, hatred, the slaughter and torture of the bodies and souls of men, the destruction of cities by fire, the starvation of millions, the annihilation of populations and finally the cosmic inhumanity of atomic war: Christ is massacred in His members, torn limb from limb; God is murdered in men" (71). It is with these least ones, the victims of injustice, the persecuted and afflicted, that Christ identifies in his own suffering, so that to be united to him is to be united with them in a special way. Therefore, Christian action on behalf of the poor and oppressed, in pursuit of justice and peace, has an essentially paschal character. It is rooted in the compassion of Christ, which must be incarnated in the compassion of Christians.

Such action is itself a participation in the redemptive work of Christ, and as such it is governed by the norms of that work. As Christ triumphed over sin and death through the un-armed power of suffering love, so those who are "in Christ" testify to that victory by confronting evil equipped only with the gifts of the Spirit. "If the Cross is God's 'No' to worldly arrogance, then our decision for Christ must be a renunciation of all reliance on worldly power" (*Love and Living*, 231). To believe in the non-violent power of the cross is to believe that the kingdom of God, the reign of truth and justice and love, has been definitively established, and that "the Lord of truth is indeed risen and reigning over his Kingdom" (*Faith and Violence*, 18). One lives the redeemed life not by avoiding or evading darkness and death, but by holding fast to the hope at the center of the paschal mystery: "From the darkness comes light. From death, life. From the abyss there comes, unaccountably, the mysterious gift of the Spirit sent by God to make all things new, to transform the created and redeemed world, and to re-establish all things in Christ" (*Contemplative Prayer*, 28).

If identification with Christ crucified and resurrected is the basis for human community, it is also the basis for union with God. Merton writes, "But if my true spiritual identity is found in my identification with Christ, then to know myself fully, I must know Christ.... The beginning of self-realization in the fullest Christian sense is therefore a sharing in the orientation which directs Christ, as Word, entirely to His Father" (*New Man*, 170). To know God, in other words, is to enter into the mystery of Trinitarian love, to be one with the Father as the Son is one with the Father, in the Holy Spirit, who is the mutual love of Father and Son. Such knowledge is a direct result of participation in the paschal mystery. One enters into God with and in the risen Jesus because one has left behind the self that cannot know God, the sinful self that has been put to death with Christ.

This passing over into God is experienced in two forms: the ultimate act of self-surrender and self-transcendence in physical, temporal death, and the foretaste of eternal life in the mystical death of contemplative union with God. For the true self, death is simply the ultimate ratification of the choice to die and live

Drawing by Thomas Merton

with Christ, the last in the series of paschal surrenders. The redemptive death of Christ transforms the meaning of death, or rather gives meaning to what is otherwise meaningless and absurd. The linkage between sin and death is broken; the cross makes death a liberation from sin, that is, from the self-absorbed isolation and self-divided alienation that are, quite literally, a hell. "For a Christian, this sublimation of death by freedom and love can only be the result of a free gift of God in which our personal death is united with the mystery of Christ's death on the Cross. The death of Christ is not simply the juridical payment of an incomprehensible ransom which somehow makes us acceptable at the gate of heaven. It has radically transformed the sinful death of man into a liberating and victorious death, a supreme act of faith and love, because it also transforms man's life by faith and love. The obedience of Christ transforms the death of man into an act of glad acceptance and of love which transcends death and carries him over into eternal life with the Risen Christ" (*Love and Living*, 103). This eternal life is not merely immortality but God's own life, the fullness of life that had no beginning and will have no end, the life that the Son shares with the Father, and that all the redeemed experience because they are identified with the Son.

But eternal life, "to know you the only true God, and Jesus Christ whom you have sent" (John 17:3), does not begin with physical death but with "the Christian's metanoia, his participation in the death and resurrection of Christ.... This death to the 'old self' and new life in the Spirit sent by Christ 'from the Father' means not only a juridical salvation 'in heaven' and 'in the hereafter' but much more a new dimension of one's present life" (*Love and Living*, 192). Contemplation is the full experiential awareness of this new dimension, of God's own life. "Christian contemplation gives a certain intuitive appreciation or savor of the divine inner life in so far as it is a personal participation, by grace, in that life itself" (*World of Action*, 179). That is, in the traditional phrase, we become by grace what Christ is by nature, a transformation that is brought about by the redemptive power of the cross: "We recognize the unseen Father in so far as we are sons, in and with Christ. The Spirit utters in us the cry of recognition that we are sons in the Son (Romans 8:15). This cry of admiration, of love, of praise, of everlasting joy is at once a cry of glad self-annihilation on the part of our transient human ego, and an exultant shout of victory of the New Man raised from the dead in Christ by the Spirit who raised Christ himself from the dead" (179). POC

SEE ALSO ALIENATION; BAPTISM; CHRISTOLOGY; FALL; ORIGINAL SIN; SALVATION; SIN.

REDWOODS ABBEY

Our Lady of the Redwoods Abbey is a community of Cistercian nuns at Whitethorn, California. Thomas Merton visited the abbey in May 1968, gave lectures to the nuns, and from there explored the Pacific coast looking for a possible site for a hermitage. He returned there briefly before leaving for Asia. WHS

REINHARDT, ADOLPH (AD)

Though he graduated from Columbia in 1935, a few months after Thomas Merton's arrival there, Ad Reinhardt (1913–67) continued to provide illustrations for *Jester*, the campus humor magazine, and so was an important part of the circle Merton joined. At Columbia, Reinhardt studied art history under Meyer Schapiro, who also encouraged his early creative work, strongly influenced by the cubists and Mondrian. In *The Seven Storey Mountain*, Merton calls Reinhardt "certainly the best artist that had ever drawn for *Jester*, perhaps for any other college magazine" (154). In a journal entry from early January 1940, after an evening at Reinhardt's he had written, "I think Ad Reinhardt is possibly the best artist in America. Anyway the best whose work I've seen." Even though Reinhardt considered himself a communist at the time, Merton went on to describe his work as "pure and religious. It flies away from all naturalism, from all representation to pure formal and intellectual values" (*Run to the Mountain*, 128). Reinhardt went on to become one of the most rigorous and committed abstract artists of the mid-twentieth century, progressively limiting his palette to a more and more restricted range of color, eventually working only in black from around 1960 until his death. In November 1957 Reinhardt sent Merton a small black-on-black painting, an "almost invisible cross on a black background," which Merton treasured as a kind of icon of emptiness and silence, "a very 'holy' picture — helps prayer — an 'image' without features to accustom the mind at once to the night of prayer — and to help one set aside trivial and useless images that wander into prayer and spoil it" (*Search for Solitude*, 139–40). Reinhardt also provided support, as well as art supplies, for Merton's own experimental calligraphies (*Road to Joy*, 281; *Water of Life*, 58). Reinhardt died suddenly on August 31, 1967, the beginning of a series of deaths of the old Columbia crowd that would include John

Slate, Seymour Freedgood, and Merton himself before the end of the following year. In a note for the first issue of *Monks Pond*, accompanying Reinhardt's 1962 manifesto "Art-as-Art," Merton wrote of his friend, "A classicist and a rigorous contemplative, he was only just beginning to be recognized as prophetic by a new generation. He was called the 'black monk' of abstract art, a purist who made Mondrian look problematic, who referred to himself as a 'quietist' and said: 'I'm just making the last paintings which anyone can make'" (*Monks Pond*, 62). Merton's letters to Reinhardt are found in *The Road to Joy* (279–83). POC

RELIGION

Merton recognizes and explores throughout his writings, particularly in the final decade of his life, the ambiguities inherent in the modern understanding of religion. When religion is recognized and practiced as an orientation toward the sacred that leads to inner transformation and to an attitude and acts of compassion, it is seen as crucially important for authentic human existence. When it is adherence to a formalized system of cult and dogma that domesticates the divine and is directed toward a comfortable acceptance of a current social or economic system, it must be challenged.

Merton declares himself "deeply in sympathy with, and I think inbued with, the traditional religious culture of the West" (*Guilty Bystander*, 293), and extends that sympathy to the traditional religious cultures of the East as well, which have retained a sense of the sacred as pervading all the actions of everyday life. Gandhi's "fundamentally religious view of reality, of being and of truth" is what enabled him to commit himself to the right in total disregard of the consequences, a faith that God will bring good results in God's own good time, a perspective that Merton considers the West, with its pragmatism and cult of success, to have lost (102–3). The irreligious mind is easily seduced by a scientistic reductivism that quantifies all reality and reduces the immediate world of struggle and growth to pallid abstractions, though Merton notes that "the fatal drive to adoration" cannot easily be banished entirely

(280) and that the rejection of an authentic religion generally leads to the fabrication of one's own myth-system, "with consequences that are only too well known" (*Faith and Violence*, 102). Genuine religious belief, Merton maintains, is "inevitably also a principle of freedom," a liberation from control of all that is "less than man, or entirely exterior to man," whether it be the forces of nature, or bodily and emotional needs, or the exterior dictates of society, or the tyranny of dictatorships (*Guilty Bystander*, 75). To submit to God is to refuse allegiance to all that is not God, and to submit to God is to become free of all illusions because one accepts one's identity as made in the image of God, who is absolute love and absolute freedom.

Yet Merton emphasizes repeatedly that in practice religion often has functioned in ways that inhibit rather than promote the human capacity to perceive and respond creatively to God and creation. The inherent temptation of religion is always to try to control the sacred, to reduce transcendent mystery to psychological comfort and spiritual reassurance, to substitute formal ritual for interior transformation. Religion easily can become the opium of Marx or the illusion of Freud when it is co-opted for ulterior purposes, used as a facade for justifying a social or economic system, an ideology of nation or class or race (*Contemplative Prayer*, 140–41). Merton points out that the critique of religion in this sense is at the heart of biblical revelation itself, in which the prophets inveigh against a system of worship reduced to "an external formality and a façade for exclusiveness, cruelty and injustice," and Paul preaches a faith by which one is "liberated from merely human religious obligations, ritual customs, taboos . . . based on adherence to a special 'pure' and 'chosen' group" (*Opening the Bible*, 79). Merton sees a need for this same "prophetic" challenge to a religious establishment that "abdicates its mission to disturb man in the depths of his conscience, and seeks instead simply to 'make converts' that will smilingly adjust to the status quo" (*Mystics and Zen Masters*, 273). Religion too often has turned God into a product to be marketed (*Faith and Violence*, 117) and made its goal to protect and expand its own "market share"; institutional survival and the purveying of superficial consolations have substituted for engagement with the deeper needs of individuals and society, "the great issues which compromise the very survival of the human race" (56). The insularity of organized religion may make it attractive to people who feel threatened and overwhelmed by the threats and challenges of the contemporary world, but religion as refuge ultimately is fraudulent and irresponsible, an abdication of religious responsibility to defend human dignity wherever and however it is threatened. Religion, Merton claims, too often strains out gnats and swallows camels (117), choosing irrelevant or marginal issues to set itself apart from the prevailing culture but conforming in areas that are in fact most deeply at odds with authentic spiritual values. "One of the grave problems of religion in our time," Merton writes, "is posed by the almost total lack of protest on the part of religious people and clergy, in the face of enormous social evils" (*Passion for Peace*, 127).

Following Karl Barth, Merton rejects "religion" insofar as it is understood as "something emanating from man's nature and tending to God . . . for a religion that starts in man is nothing but man's wish for himself" (*Guilty Bystander*, 138), a desire to preserve the self invented by oneself at the expense of the true self created by God. This is the level on which religiosity operates too often (though Merton is not so uncompromising as Barth in his relegation of "religion" to the sphere of the human in contrast and opposition to revelation as divine initiative and faith as human response). He is responsive likewise to Bonhoeffer's critique of religion and its irrelevance in the context of Nazi Germany, though he is skeptical of the "religionless religion" of many of Bonhoeffer's followers, which typically simply endorses the myths and illusions of secular culture as a substitute for what it regards as the myths and illusions of supernaturalism (259–60).

The recovery of authentic religious consciousness, Merton believes, needs to go beyond "endless definition, endless verbalizing," by which "words have become gods." Religion is not found in words but in the commitment of one's whole self: "My whole being must be a yes and an amen and an exclamation that is not heard. . . . One's acts must be part of the same silent exclamation" (*Courage for Truth*, 225). Religion without this contemplative depth, Merton believes, inevitably sacrifices its consistency and its inner truth (*Contemplative Prayer*, 142). "We must now learn to distinguish between 'religiosity' and 'discipleship of Christ.' . . . What is of importance today is not to get modern man to accept *religion* as a human or cultural value (he may do so or he may not) but to let him see that we are witnesses of Christ, of the new creation, of the Resurrection, of the Living God: and that is something that goes far beyond the cultural phenomenon of religion" (*World of Action*, 134). POC

RESURRECTION OF JESUS CHRIST

In September 1967 in his hermitage Thomas Merton was recording a tape for the Carmelite monastery in Savannah, Georgia. On September 15 he told them that he had been asked to write an Easter homily that was to be recorded (by someone else). He decided to read it onto the tape he was preparing for them. The homily eventually was published (1975) by Argus Communications (Niles, Illinois) in a small booklet, with contemporary colored photos, called *He Is Risen*. This booklet-homily is Merton's most extensive reflection on the resurrection of Jesus, though references to the resurrection are found here and there in his writings, most notably in *The New Man*, where he highlights the importance of the resurrection for understanding the role of the "Second Adam" and the meaning of life in Christ.

Fundamental to Merton's thinking is the Pauline insistence that the resurrection is not simply an event that happened to Jesus; it also is something that happens to us: we are called to experience it in our own lives "by following Christ who lives in us. . . . Christ lives in us if we love one another" (*He Is Risen*, 8). Christ lives in us and ushers us into a new future that we build together with him. That future is called the kingdom of God and, because of the resurrection, that future has already begun to exist.

In the coming of the kingdom Merton sees the significance of the Adam-Christ parallel drawn by St. Paul. "Just as Adam is the one chosen by God to preside over the first creation, Christ is sent by Him to institute and govern an entirely new spiritual Creation. For with the death and resurrection of Christ, we are in a new world, a new age. The fullness of time has come. The history of the world has achieved an entirely new orientation. We are living in the Messianic Kingdom" (*New Man*, 148).

The first creation of the world and of humans was simply the foreshadowing of a far greater reality, that of Christ and his kingdom. "[The] first creation is entirely secondary and subordinated to the new spiritual creation effected in and by Christ. *The new creation begins with the Resurrection of the Lord* and will be perfected in the end of time" (150 [italics added]). When the kingdom comes in its fullness, all of creation will share in the transformation. At the parousia "Christ will not only appear on the clouds of heaven in judgment, but will also at the same time shine forth through the transfigured trees and mountains and seas of a world divinized through its participation in the work of His Kingdom" (150–51).

In building the kingdom Christians are working toward that divinization of the world. In his letter to John and June Yungblut where he speaks about "Christ of the icons" (see CHRISTOLOGY), Merton makes clear that the icons represent that transfigured world. The light of Christ in the icons is the light of Christ penetrating everything. Monasticism went wrong, he suggests, when that light appeared over and against the world to repudiate it, not to transfigure it. He writes, "Monastic world denial is originally a denial of a world that has not been penetrated with the light of the Resurrection, in order to see the world that *has* been transfigured and illuminated. But it later becomes denial of the world, period, and the affirmation of the Resurrection as a proof of pure transcendence" (*Hidden Ground of Love*, 644). The resurrection in such a perspective takes the risen Christ out of the world instead of making him present in the world in a new transformed and transforming way.

The Christian encounters the risen, trans-forming Christ, as Paul encountered him on the road to Damascus. "Such an encounter does not have to be dramatic, but it has to be personal and real. Baptism is, of course, the seal and sign of this encounter" (*He Is Risen*, 12). This initial encounter with the living Christ is the beginning of many encounters with the Risen One: in the other sacraments, in the word of God, which awakens us to the hidden depths of our being, and in our daily involvement with people. "True encounter with Christ liberates something in us, a power we did not know we had, a hope, a capacity for life, a resilience, an ability to bounce back when we thought we were completely defeated, a capacity to grow and change, a power of creative transformation" (15). Since Christ is risen and lives in us, we cannot experience defeat. The living Christ has overcome anything that might seem to block our human and spiritual growth.

This is not to suggest that the Christian life is always an easy life. The presence of the resurrection in our lives means the presence of the cross. To rise with Christ, we first need to die. It is the cross that enables us to enter into the dynamism of transformation, which is the dynamism of unconditional love. But if participation in Jesus' risen life calls for the cross, it is important to remember that it likewise brings the freedom that Paul writes about with great passion. That freedom enables us to make decisions in accord with the gospel and to think and act differently from the crowd. It liberates us from passive domination by other people's ideas. Merton speaks of Jesus as a "freedom fighter," not in the false sense in which this term is often used, but as the one who liberates us from all forms of tyranny and domination, from anyone or anything except the Spirit of God.

Merton's homily on Easter in *He Is Risen* is based on chapter 16 of Mark's Gospel, wherein the women come to the tomb seeking for what they can only think is a dead Christ. He warns that Christianity all too easily can become simply a cult of the dead body of Christ. When it ceases to be a faith that is really alive and becomes a mere legalistic and ritualistic formality, "Christianity is no longer life in the Risen Christ but a formal cult of the dead Christ considered not as the Light and Savior of the world but as a kind of divine 'thing,' an extremely holy object, a theological relic" (50). In Jerusalem is the Church of the Holy Sepulchre. It is a valid place of worship for Christians only if we realize that it marks the place where Christ is no longer to be found. The Risen One goes before us into Galilee, and Galilee is wherever people are. Following him to Galilee is following him to where we are not yet, but one day will be, as the fullness of the kingdom comes into full realization. Merton concludes his homily, "Come, people of God.... He has risen.... He is going before us into his Kingdom! Alleluia!" (59).

An illustration of one of a number of passing references to the resurrection that may be found here and there in his writings is the following conclusion to a letter he wrote to Czeslaw Milosz:

> Milosz, life is on our side. The silence and the Cross of which we know are forces that cannot be defeated. In silence and suffering, in the heartbreaking effort to be honest in the midst of dishonesty (most of all our *own* dishonesty), in all these there is victory. It is Christ in us who drives us through darkness to a light of which we have no conception and which can only be found by passing through apparent despair. Everything has to be tested. All relationships have to be tried. All loyalties have to pass through fire. Much has to be lost. Much in us has to be killed, even much that is best in us. But Victory is certain. The Resurrection is the only light, and with that light there is no error. (*Courage for Truth,* 57–58; also, *Striving towards Being,* 19–20) WHS

REVOLUTION

The word "revolution" is, of course, a protean one, and Thomas Merton uses it in ways that are not always consistent with one another, though his underlying attitude is basically coherent. He repeatedly calls the era of the 1960s a time of revolution, in fact (with characteristic hyperbole) "the greatest revolution in history" (*Guilty Bystander,* 54), "the greatest revolution [our] world has ever seen" (*Love and Living,* 150). By this he is referring not exclusively,

or even primarily, to political upheaval, as significant as that was in the early postcolonial period, the time of the Vietnam War and the American civil rights movement, but to what would later come to be called a paradigm shift, affecting "scientific, technological, economic, demographic, cultural, spiritual" dimensions (150). "It is a far-reaching, uncontrolled, and largely unconscious revolution pervading every sphere of [human] existence and often developing new critical tendencies before anyone realizes what is happening" (*Witness to Freedom,* 316). The most marked characteristic of this revolutionary turmoil, in Merton's view, is its ambiguity. It is impossible to determine at this point whether ultimately it will be beneficial or destructive. "The great question is whether it can truly be directed to ends that are fully compatible with the authentic dignity and destiny of man" (*Love and Living,* 150). His answer is negative if the revolution is limited to economic or political or technological forces, and certainly if it is controlled by those committed to violence, whether the violence of the guerilla or the violence of nuclear threats (150). He views the revolutionary ferment above all as "a profound spiritual crisis of the whole world," a vast confusion about human identity and purpose. "We do not know if we are building a fabulously wonderful world or destroying all that we have ever had, all that we have achieved!" (*Guilty Bystander,* 55).

In this broad context Merton considers two opposed responses perhaps to be equally catastrophic. One is a reactionary refusal to recognize the genuine human values and hopes underlying at least some of the impetus toward revolutionary change, and the consequent fanatical determination to maintain the status quo. He examines this response at length in his discussion of the racial tension of the 1960s, in which he criticizes not merely conservatives who try to preserve the system of black subordination but self-styled liberals who want change, but only if it does not affect themselves and their lifestyle, who hope "the Negroes... will gradually and quietly 'fit in' to white society exactly as it is, with its affluent economy, the mass media, its political machines, and the professional inanity of its middle class suburban folkways" (*Seeds of Destruction,* 29). Merton sees the rise of the Black Power movement in the mid-1960s and large-scale rejection of the nonviolence of Martin Luther King as a judgment on this inadequate response to demands for social change that is more than cosmetic. Merton sees a fundamentally similar mind-set operative in America's role as world policeman: "The obsessive efforts of the U.S. to *contain* by violence all revolutionary activity anywhere in the world only precipitate revolution. And guarantee that it has to be violent" (*Other Side of the Mountain,* 51). The refusal to recognize and respond to legitimate needs radicalizes dissent and turns it revolutionary.

The other inadequate response is simply to allow the revolution to create and maintain its own logic and its own momentum, with no moral criteria other than the triumph of its own agenda. Merton returns repeatedly to the analysis of Camus, who rejects the absolutism of the revolutionary because it leads to "a facile justification of mass murder" (*Literary Essays,* 199). This critique is directed specifically against Marxism but also applies to any situation in which revolution becomes its own justification. Camus refuses to acquiesce in the oppressive structures of political tyranny but he also refuses to see any advantage in replacing one set of oppressors by another. He rebels on behalf of human values and human dignity common to all. As Merton summarizes Camus's position, "Revolt has to be perpetually renewed to prevent revolution from hardening into a tyranny which inexorably contradicts all of its own first principles" (221). Revolution in this sense is abstract: it considers not the worth of particular people but humanity as a concept, an ideal to be fulfilled as the culmination of a revolutionary process that is willing to sacrifice people to a program. "The nature of revolt, as opposed to the rigid authoritarianism of a totalist revolution directed from above by 'the Party,' is that it springs from the warmth and authenticity of human solidarity and compassion" (243).

Merton viewed the general "cultural" and "spiritual" revolution as to a great extent spasmodic and directionless, "manifested largely in desperation, cynicism, violence, conflict, self-contradiction, ambivalence, fear and hope, doubt and belief, creation and destructiveness, progress and regression, obsessive attachments to images, idols, slogans, programs" (*Guilty Bystander,* 55). As for the political dimension of this commotion, he considered that there could be "a semblance of world peace and order" only if there were a revolution in America itself that would realign the country in support of Third World revolution, but he concluded that "such a revolution cannot possibly succeed" (*Other Side of the Mountain,* 51) unless some sort of economic or military catastrophe (e.g., a nuclear attack) were to take place (*Faith and Violence,* 176). Hence he seemed to foresee an ongoing social, political, and cultural upheaval with no clear resolution in sight.

The role of the Christian in such a revolutionary situation is fidelity to values of the gospel no matter who is in power. In his conversation at the Center for the Study of Democratic Institutions two months before his death, Merton expressed skepticism about a radical Christianity that sees "the revolutionary mystique as the only valid discipline," calling this mystique "a complete illusion" (*Preview of the Asian Journey,* 56), though of course he is even more critical of those Christians who align themselves with oppressive social and political structures. In the context of the nuclear threat Merton described the Christian mission "in an epoch of revolution" as "not to contribute to the blind forces of annihilation" but to "orient [one's] efforts towards world unity and not towards world division" (*Breakthrough to Peace,* 115–16). He answers his question about whether revolutionary forces can be life-giving by concluding that "the one hope of their successful coordination remains the deepest and most unifying insight that has been granted to man: the Christian revelation of the unity of all men in the love of God as His One Son, Jesus Christ" (*Love and Living,* 150). He perhaps expresses his own position most clearly in a letter to a Latin American friend in 1958, the year of his decisive "turn toward the world," when he writes, "Basically, also, I am a revolutionist — in a broad, non-violent sense of the word. I believe that those who have used violence have betrayed all true revolution, they have changed nothing, they have simply enforced with greater brutality the anti-spiritual and anti-human drives that are destructive of truth and love in man. I believe that the true revolution must come slowly and painfully, not merely from the peasant, etc., but from the true artist and intellectual . . . from the thinker and the man of prayer" (*School of Charity*, 112). POC

SEE ALSO CIVIL RIGHTS MOVEMENT; COMMUNISM; MARXISM; VIETNAM.

RÉVOLUTION NOIRE, LA

Translated by Marie Tadié. Paris: Casterman, 1964. 125 pp.

This book consists of translations of the two articles ("Letters to a White Liberal" and "The Legend of Tucker Caliban") that would comprise part 1, "Black Revolution," of Thomas Merton's *Seeds of Destruction*, published later that same year, along with a preface that appears only in the French and subsequent foreign-language editions. This preface, written in early December 1963, less than two weeks after the assassination of President Kennedy, uses that event to frame the discussion of the violence and upheaval that marked the current crisis in America: "The President's assassination was simply one in a series of murders which had recently taken place in the South and which were all manifestations of the same confusion, irresponsibility, malice, lawlessness and hatred" (*Honorable Reader*, 74). Merton's focus is, of course, on racial oppression, but he links this kind of injustice to "the insecurity, the brutality, the hatred, the stupidity, the frank inhumanity which are so close to the surface of all social life everywhere in the world today" (76). Merton considers the causes of the current disorder to be not only economic and sociological but also "symptoms of a world-wide spiritual crisis that may soon reach apocalyptic dimensions" (76) and that are evident in totalitarian movements and in the nuclear arms race as well. He affirms that there are "forces of life" (77) that counter the movements toward violence and oppression but cautions against a naive optimism that believes that the good will prevail without efforts to resist evil, a tendency he identifies in the emerging neo-

pentecostal movement, which "has very little to do with present social realities" (78). He concludes with an emphatic statement of his conviction that Christians, even Christian contemplatives, must witness to the truth of the dignity and equality of all human beings in a society where this truth is being undermined: "In a day when the moral and physical destinies of man are at the mercy of the politician, it is not licit for a so-called 'contemplative' willfully to ignore the major problems of his age" (80). POC

SEE ALSO *SEEDS OF DESTRUCTION*.

RICE, EDWARD

Edward Rice (1918–2001) was a close friend of Thomas Merton at Columbia and his godfather at the time of his baptism on November 16, 1938, at Corpus Christi Church in New York City. A freelance photographer and writer, Rice founded and edited the avant-garde Catholic magazine *Jubilee*. He became the first biographer of Merton with *The Man in the Sycamore Tree: The Good Times and Hard Life of Thomas Merton: An Entertainment* (Garden City, N.Y.: Doubleday, 1970). Besides telling the Merton story, the book contains fine photographs of Merton at Gethsemani and also some of Merton's drawings done for the *Jester*, the Columbia humor magazine, as well as examples of his later calligraphic drawings. Merton's letters to Rice are published in *The Road to Joy*. WHS

Edward Rice

ROAD TO JOY, THE: The Letters of Thomas Merton to New and Old Friends

Edited by Robert E. Daggy. New York: Farrar, Straus, and Giroux, 1989. xvi+383 pp.

This is the second of five volumes of Thomas Merton's letters, published under the general editorship of William H. Shannon. Not all, or even most, of the letters Merton wrote to his many "friends" are included here, but all the letters in this volume document and celebrate the significance of relationship and friendship in Merton's life. Some of Merton's friendships began and grew through an exchange of letters. There were some correspondents — some "friends" — whom he never actually met in person. Writing letters to old friends was a way to keep in touch between visits. Arranged by correspondent, the letters also offer a glimpse of Merton in the context of various relationships with old and new friends, revealing what he was like and what mattered to him. These letters show him to be at once serious and insightful, witty and playful. The volume also includes ten of the 111 "Cold War Letters," which Merton wrote between October 1961 and October 1962 on the urgent issues of war and peace facing the nation and the world (see "COLD WAR LETTERS").

The title of the volume is taken from a phrase inspired by one of Merton's young correspondents. In 1962 Merton received a picture of a house drawn by five-year-old Grace Sisson. Merton described the picture, in careful detail, in a poem entitled "Grace's House," which ended with the line "Alas, there is no road to Grace's house!"[1] Five years later she sent another drawing. This one was entitled "The Road to Joy." Thanking her for the drawing, Merton wrote, "I hope you and I together will secretly travel our own road to joy, which is mysteriously revealed to us without our exactly realizing. When I say that, I don't want you to start thinking about it. You already know it without thinking about it" (*Road to Joy*, 352–53). Robert Daggy concludes his introduction to the volume with the thought that Merton "might well have invited all his friends to join him in traveling the 'road to joy'" (xiv).

The volume includes a preface by William H. Shannon. In addition to an introduction, Robert E. Daggy provides brief notes on each of Merton's correspondents and occasional clarifying comments. The volume is divided into five parts: (1) "To Mark Van Doren"; (2) "To Family and Friends"; (3) "Circular Letters to Friends"; (4) "To Some Special Friends"; and (5) "To and About Young People."

The letters to Mark Van Doren, Merton's favorite teacher at Columbia University, span almost thirty years: the first was written on March 24, 1939, when Merton was living on Perry Street in New York, and the last was a brief note mailed from Darjeeling, India, in November 1968.[2] A poet himself, Van Doren encouraged and supported Merton's writing. It was Van Doren who selected the poems for Merton's first collection of poems and lobbied James Laughlin at New Directions for the publication of *Thirty Poems*. Merton's affection for Van Doren is evident throughout these letters and especially on the occasion of Van Doren's retirement from Columbia in 1959: "You are certainly one of the joys of life for all who have ever come within a mile of you . . . you have become a kind of sacrament, which is what every man should be. You are certainly one of the most Christian people I have ever seen" (34).

Part 2, dedicated to Merton's letters "to and about family," begins with a letter that Merton wrote on the day of his father's funeral, January 20, 1931, to Owen Merton's art teacher, Percyval Tudor-Hart. Daggy notes that it is the earliest extant letter written by Merton. This section includes also Merton's letters to Aunt Kit (Agnes Gertrude Stonehewer Merton) and Aunt Ka (Beatrice Katherine Merton) — two of Owen's sisters — and other members of the Merton and Jenkins families, as well as a letter to Iris Weiss Bennett, wife of Merton's guardian, Tom Bennett. Hearing from family members and family friends sparked memories of his childhood and youth and reminded him of the passing of generations.

Part 3 includes seventeen letters that Merton wrote and mimeographed for circulation. The first letter, written ca. 1963, was a form letter that Merton wrote to send out in response to the many inquiries he received about his life and writings, particularly from high school students. Merton included a brief biography and explained what the contemplative life meant to him: "the search for truth and for God." He explained how he wrote poetry ("I just write it"), commented on his interest in art and politics, and urged attention to "extremely serious" issues: "the race issue" and "the question of nuclear war" (88–91). One circular letter was written at Christmas 1965, two in 1966, and the rest in 1967 and 1968, when Merton was finding it increasingly difficult to answer personally all the letters he received. The last of the circular letters, written from New Delhi, India, on November 9, 1968, concludes with these words: "I wish you all the peace and joy in the Lord and an increase of faith: for in my contacts with these new friends [the Dalai Lama was one] I also feel consolation in my own faith in Christ and His indwelling presence. I hope and believe He may be present in the hearts of all of us" (121). Merton's circular letters enabled him to let his friends know what he was doing and also thinking. Circular letters also provided him with a way to raise issues that he believed demanded urgent attention.

Part 4, comprising almost half the book, contains letters "To Some Special Friends." In his introduction Daggy explains that the title needs "further explanation" (xi). Merton's letters to some "special friends," such as Catherine de Hueck Doherty, Dorothy Day, James Forest, and W. H. Ferry, already had been published in the first volume of the letters, *The Hidden Ground of Love*. Letters to other special friends, such as Ernesto Cardenal, Jacques Maritain, Sister Mary Luke Tobin, and Naomi Burton Stone, would appear in the remaining volumes of the series. Included in this volume are Merton's letters to "special friends" he made while he was at Columbia University (Robert Lax, Mahanambrata Bramachari, Seymour Freedgood, Ad Reinhardt, Edward Rice, John H. Slate, and Dan Walsh) and at St. Bonaventure College (Fr. Joseph Vann, O.F.M; Fr. Thomas Plassman, O.F.M.; and Fr. Irenaeus Herscher, O.F.M.). The remaining letters in this section were written to persons who became Merton's friends after he became a monk: Tommie O'Callaghan, Beatrice Olmstead, John Howard

Griffin, and Sr. Therese Lentfoehr. Selections from Merton's letters to Sr. Therese, written over the course of two decades, fill some seventy-five pages of the book. Sr. Therese typed for Merton and carefully preserved all the manuscripts he sent her, assembling an extensive private collection of Merton materials (now housed at Columbia University). Daggy suggests that writing to Sr. Therese became for Merton "an alternate form of journal keeping" (xii). At the very least, the letters provide a window on twenty years of Merton's life as a monk and writer.

Part 5 includes a selection of letters "To and About Young People," beginning with seven letters Merton wrote to Suzanne Butorovich, who was sixteen and a half when she wrote to Merton in June 1967. Describing himself as "an underground hippie monk" (309), Merton wrote with enthusiasm about subjects of mutual interest: their writing and publishing projects, the music of Bob Dylan, Zen. Merton met Suzanne when he visited California in 1968. Responding to a host of other inquiries about his writing and his life, Merton offered interpretations of his work and thoughts on a host of spiritual and moral issues: faith, prayer, religion, ecumenism, the Vietnam War, racism, and nonviolence.

The Road to Joy reveals the many faces of Merton. Merton emerges in all his complexity and passion as a man ever grateful for the gifts so generously bestowed on him: "There are three gifts I have received, for which I can never be grateful enough: first, my Catholic faith; second, my monastic vocation; third, the calling to be a writer and share my gifts with others" (89). Had Merton mentioned a fourth gift, perhaps it would have been the gift of friendship — the gift celebrated in this volume of letters and in the others as well. *The Road to Joy* highlights a particular dimension of Merton's interests and relationships. Its celebration of friendship serves as a reminder that this monk, living a life of silence and solitude in a monastery in rural Kentucky, very much valued relationships with old friends and family members and, through his correspondence, built and maintained relationships with many who were and became his friends. CMB

Notes

1. Originally published in 1963 in *Emblems of a Season of Fury*, the poem was reprinted in 1977 in *Collected Poems*, 330–31.
2. For Van Doren's letters to Merton, see *The Selected Letters of Mark Van Doren*, ed. George Hendrick (Baton Rouge: Louisiana State University Press, 1987).

ROME

Thomas Merton twice visited the Eternal City: first, a week's visit at Easter time 1931, when he visited the ruins of ancient Rome; second, in 1933, when he discovered early Christian Rome. This was a Rome that was very much alive, as he saw it in the churches and basilicas with their mosaics and frescoes. He underwent a brief conversion experience and began reading the Latin Vulgate Bible. What happened to bring about this conversion is not completely clear. In *The Seven Storey Mountain* he speaks about some kind of experience of his deceased father, though his autobiographical novel, "The Labyrinth," while describing the Roman conversion, makes no mention of such a "vision." At any rate, whatever the nature of the experience, it was not long-lasting. He returned to America and New York City in the summer of 1933, where his interest in Christian faith gradually weakened and then simply disappeared — for a time. WHS

RUETHER, ROSEMARY RADFORD

Rosemary Radford Ruether, born in St. Paul, Minnesota, did her undergraduate studies at Scripps College and went on to receive, in 1965, a doctoral degree in classics and patristics at the Claremont Graduate School in Claremont, California. The following year she and her husband and three children moved to Washington, D.C., where she joined the faculty of Howard University, teaching there for ten years. She was actively involved in urban churches working on issues of racism, poverty, and militarism. In 1976 she joined the faculty of Garrett Evangelical Theological Seminary in Evanston, Illinois.

It was while she was in Washington that she corresponded with Thomas Merton. The correspondence (*Hidden Ground of Love*, 497–516; *At Home in the World*, 1–100) extended over a relatively short period of time: August 1966 to February 1968. Still, there was an intensity about it and evidence of much reflection going into the letters on both sides. It began with an offer on the part of Ruether to send him the manuscript of her forthcoming book, *The Church against Itself*. This exchange of letters gave Ruether an opportunity to express her views on church, authority, and monasticism. It enabled Merton to sort out some of the issues he had to deal with that involved his own personal integrity as a monk. They disagreed sharply about the monastic life. Ruether challenged him to leave the safety of the cloister and enter the world where the real demons are. Merton listened to her, yet still held undauntedly to a sense of the importance of the monastic life, in the church probably, but certainly in his own life. While protesting that in reality he is not the kind of monk people expect him to be, he is convinced that he is where God wants him to be. "I am now convinced that the first way to be a decent monk is to be a non-monk or an anti-monk, as far as the 'image' goes; but I am certainly quite definite about wanting to stay in the bushes (provided I can make some sort of noises that will reach my offbeat friends)" (*Hidden Ground of Love*, 511; *At Home in the World*, 66). WHS

RUN TO THE MOUNTAIN: *The Story of a Vocation*

The Journals of Thomas Merton, vol. 1: 1939–41. Edited by Patrick Hart. San Francisco: HarperSanFrancisco, 1995. xvii+478 pp.

This first of the seven volumes of Thomas Merton's journals actually comprises three journals that Merton kept, all of them prior to his entrance into the Abbey of Gethsemani. The first deals with his life while he lived on Perry Street in New York City, the second with his trip to Cuba (with a stop off at Miami), the third with his life at St. Bonaventure College (where he taught for a year and a half). "The Cuban Interlude" (February 18–May 30, 1940) is the shortest of the three (seventy-six pages) and contains some of the best descriptive writing in the book. The Perry Street journal (150 pages) covers the period from May 2, 1939, to February 13, 1940, and, among other things, his acceptance (later to be rescinded) into the Franciscan order. The final journal in this volume, the St. Bonaventure years (1940–41) is the longest (240 pages); it details the story of his life as a teacher at the college, reaches a high point in his Holy Week visit to the Trappist Abbey of Gethsemani, and brings the reader to the threshold of his entrance into the monastic life at Gethsemani.

Together, these three journals make up a remarkable book. In them we see a young, unproven writer (he was in his midtwenties and unpublished except for articles in school papers and a few book reviews) flexing his literary muscles to his own obvious delight. There can be no question that Thomas Merton loved to write and was not sure from one day to the next what he might write about. At one point in the Perry Street journal he asks himself, "Why do I write so much about things about which I know so little?" (*Run to the Mountain*, 144).

The style of *Run to the Mountain* is not easy to describe; it varies considerably from one part to another. It is, one can safely say, quite uniformly good writing. It can be clever, casual, breezy; witty, sprightly, dynamic, enthusiastic; frivolous, conceited, arrogant, dogmatic, overly erudite. But often it is serious, pensive, impressive, insightful, and profound. There are splendid passages of reflection that touch deeply into the human soul and there are passages of fun and humor when he plays with ideas and words and sentences and shows a sharp eye for the foibles in human nature, including his own. His penchant for superlatives is here, as it will be in his later writings. Thus, "Lorca is easily the best religious poet of this century" (106); and not many pages later, "[Joyce] happens to be the best writer in this century" (153); and still later, "*Robinson Crusoe* is one of the best books ever written" (317).

These journals present us with a writer who had a prodigious memory. In reading this book one is fascinated by the many events of his past that he recalls, as something happening on the day he is writing reminds him of an event of yesteryear. On January 18, 1940, for instance, thinking of picnics, he recalls the afternoon at Oakham when Tom and Iris Bennett came to visit him and they went to tea, taking with them one of his schoolmates, Tabacovici, the Rumanian (140–41). Or again, he mentions a day in 1928 at St. Antonin "when Father and I ran a race up the middle of the street and I was astonished that he beat me so badly" (290). Recalling a sign he had seen on the Long Island Railroad, he asks, "What is this terrific importance that memory seems to have for me?" (58). In response we might quote back at him what he quotes about St. Augustine: "Walsh quotes Gilson or someone saying [that] what Augustine is interested in is his own religious experience: he narrates it over and over" (183).

By 1939, when *Run to the Mountain* begins, Merton's reception into the Roman Catholic Church was half a year behind him, but the influence of it remained strong and colored much of what he wrote. In a variety of ways he does, like Augustine, "narrate it over and over." He muses on the relationship of this wonderful power of recall to spirituality, and tells us, somewhat ruefully, that St. John of the Cross says that the memory must be completely darkened (35). That would be no easy task for Thomas Merton.

This book often is wonderfully descriptive. Merton always was fond of guidebooks, he tells us. While he may have used a guidebook for the details of his descriptions, his narrative picture of Havana, for instance, as he disembarked from the ship and entered the city, is a gem of descriptive writing. Similar descriptive passages abound.

A good bit of the narrowness of Roman Catholic thought of the early 1940s is painfully evident in *Run to the Mountain*. There are the stereotypes of Jews and Protestants so typical of the Catholicism of that time. He tells us that purgatory burns with the same fires as those of hell, the one difference being that the souls in purgatory burn with love not with hate. Even the recent, quite conservative, catechism of the Catholic Church has pretty much put out those fires. But Merton was writing in 1941.

Without doubt, the climactic event of *Run to the Mountain* is Merton's visit to the Trappist Monastery of Gethsemani during Holy Week of 1941. He was ecstatic. "This is the center of America. I had wondered what was holding this country together. . . . It is this monastery . . . the only real city in America in a desert" (333). His journal entries are full of love for the monastic life and joy at being at Gethsemani. There are many quotations from St. Bernard's *De Diligendo Deo.* Little could he have realized then that one day his own writings would be compared favorably with St. Bernard's.

There still remained the fear that his past had created an impediment that would debar him from the priesthood. Back at St. Bonaventure, he finally summoned up the courage to ask one of the friars, Fr. Philotheus, who promptly told him that no such impediment existed. He writes to Gethsemani and awaits the answer. It is on this note of expectancy, and with a prayer that he may renounce everything and belong entirely to the Lord, that this impressive volume concludes. WHS

SEE ALSO *SECULAR JOURNAL OF THOMAS MERTON.*

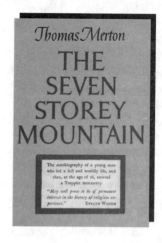

SACRAMENT

According to Thomas Merton, "To say that the Christian religion is mystical is to say that it is also *sacramental*" (*Life and Holiness,* 76). Reception of the sacraments, particularly baptism and the Eucharist, both symbolizes and effects union with God with and through Christ: "They signify a spiritual reality, and at the very same time produce the reality which they signify" (*New Man,* 202). The symbolism of the sacraments makes the most profound mysteries of faith available to the senses. As early as *The Seven Storey Mountain* Merton had written, "All our salvation begins on the level of common and natural and ordinary things. (That is why the whole economy of the Sacraments, for instance, rests, in its material element, upon plain and ordinary things like bread and wine and water and salt and oil.)" (*Seven Storey Mountain,* 178). The sacraments integrate the material with the spiritual (*New Man,* 86); they bring sensible things into the life of faith and the spirit (*Contemplative Prayer,* 105); they are signs of the work of divine love (*Life and Holiness,* 76), signs of faith (*New Man,* 201). But of course the visible sign of the sacrament points beyond itself to a reality transcending the sensible: "The sacraments . . . manifest something more

Cover for *The Seven Storey Mountain* reprinted with the permission of Harcourt, Brace and Company.

than themselves, something hidden. Indeed, a sacrament is at once something visible and something hidden" (201). Merton points out that the Latin *sacramentum* is the equivalent of the Greek *mysterion,* the "mystery" of God's hidden design made manifest in the person and work of Christ. The sacraments are essentially paschal; they draw Christians into a participation in the saving events of Christ's death and resurrection and foreshadow the final consummation of the process of salvation on the last day. "Every sacrament therefore unites in itself the past, the present and the future. It makes 'present' in some way, the whole 'mystery of Christ' by virtue of its own, proper sacramental signification" (202).

While Merton acknowledges that the sacrament does not depend on the worthiness of the administrator or the subjective feelings of the recipient, that it operates *ex opere operato,* as the traditional phrase has it, he stresses that no sacrament functions magically, without the cooperation and commitment of the one receiving the sacrament (*Life and Holiness,* 79). The power of the sacrament is objective, but it is not automatic. (Merton does not deal with the issue of infant baptism, but no doubt he would see the community and its representatives as making the commitment in the child's name and would maintain that at some point each baptized person must personally ratify this commitment.) Merton warns against the danger of the sacraments becoming simply formal transactions, "signs of a consecrated impersonality and of business-like despatch" (*Seasons of Celebration*, 234). The celebration of the sacraments should itself be a sign of that richness of life in the Spirit that the sacraments themselves communicate.

The sacraments are the source of ongoing transformation, deeper identification with the person of Christ: "The sacramental order is meant to be fulfilled by our application of the graces of the Sacraments to our own lives. This means that we share in Christ's Passion and Resurrection not merely in a hidden and mystical sense, but also by active imitation of His virtues" (*Bread in the Wilderness*, 82). Sacramental grace is energizing and empowering, extending into the ordinary events of one's everyday life and filling them with the presence of the divine. "The grace of the sacraments is given us not merely to be enjoyed but used. It is not merely to be thought about or looked at: it must be put to work. Only then do we begin to appreciate what we have received because only then does grace take hold upon our spirit, in the exercise of our interior freedom" (*New Man*, 233–34).

In addition to discussing sacraments in the strict sense, Merton occasionally uses the word "sacrament" in a more analogous way, similar to the traditional description of certain objects as "sacramentals" (*New Man*, 86). For example, he speaks of the saint as a "sacrament," both a sign and an instrument, of divine mercy (*Disputed Questions*, 274), and he follows St. Bernard in discussing the "sacrament" of Advent: the season is a revelation of the "mystery" of God's plan to unite all things in the person of Christ, whose birth is about to be celebrated (*Seasons of Celebration*, 63). As sacraments are symbols, participating in the reality they signify, so a true symbol, as distinguished from conventional signs, can be described as sacramental, not merely pointing toward but "contain[ing] in itself a structure which in some way makes us aware of the inner meaning of life and of reality itself" (*Love and Living*, 54). Any authentic religious symbol is "an *embodiment*" of the mystery of faith, "a

'sacrament,' by which one participates in the religious presence of the saving and illuminating One," rather than simply indicating the sacred as an object (74). For one who has eyes to see, creation itself has a sacramental quality, a capacity to serve as a window on the divine: "To the true Christian poet," Merton writes, "the whole world and all the incidents of life tend to be sacraments — signs of God, signs of His love working in the world" (*Literary Essays*, 345). POC

SEE ALSO BAPTISM; EUCHARIST; MARRIAGE; PRIESTHOOD.

ST. ANNE'S "HERMITAGE"

In January 1953 Dom James Fox gave Thomas Merton permission to use as a place for solitude a toolshed that had been used in the monastery building projects and that had been relocated in the woods beyond the horse barn. Merton fixed it up as a kind of hermitage. Subsequently Dom James gave him permission to stay there to collation time. Merton called this "hermitage" St. Anne. The solitude he experienced at St. Anne's is the solitude he wrote about in *Thoughts in Solitude*, which was written at St. Anne's. WHS

SEE ALSO HERMITAGE.

ST. BONAVENTURE UNIVERSITY

St. Bonaventure University is a private, Catholic, Franciscan, coeducational residential center of learning. It was founded in 1858 by the Franciscan Friars of the Holy Name Province. Located in the southwest corner of New York State between the city of Olean and the village of Allegany, the campus covers some five hundred acres with academic buildings and residence halls. In the fall of 1940 Thomas Merton was hired by Fr. Plassman, president of what at that time was a college for men only, to teach English. He was given three classes of sophomore English. He lived in a student resident hall, Devereaux Hall. In this first year of teaching, during Holy Week of 1941, he visited Gethsemani — a visit that would lead to his

St. Theresa's Shrine, St. Bonaventure University

ardent desire to become a monk. On December 9, 1941, toward the end of the first semester of his second year of teaching, he was able to bring that desire to fulfillment as he boarded the train that would take him on his way to the Trappist monastery of Gethsemani. WHS

SALVATION

Thomas Merton emphasizes that salvation is not exclusively or primarily to be equated with one's fate after death, but is a profound spiritual and even ontological transformation that takes place in the present when one accepts the gift of new life in Christ. "It is a pity," he writes, "that the beautiful Christian metaphor 'salvation' has come to be so hackneyed and therefore so despised" (*New Seeds of Contemplation*, 37). He criticizes as an "all-too-familiar oversimplification" the idea that the Christian behaves well and puts up with sufferings in this world in order to gain acceptance in the next. Authentic conversion "means not only a juridical salvation 'in heaven' and 'in the hereafter' but much more a new dimension in one's

present life" (*Love and Living*, 192). Salvation entails not merely a change of attitude or a change in habits but a change of identity, or rather, a restoration of true identity. "Salvation," according to Merton, is "first of all the full discovery of who [one] really is" (*No Man Is an Island*, xv). Yet it is not simply a subjective, psychological self-awareness and self-realization, but a discovery of the true self in God and the fulfillment of one's God-given powers in the love of God and of other people (xv).

One is saved from illusion, above all the illusion of self-sufficiency that is the essence of sinfulness, an estrangement from our own reality due to a rejection of the divine Ground of all reality, including our own. "To be 'lost' is to be left to the arbitrariness and pretenses of the contingent ego, the smoke-self that must inevitably vanish. To be 'saved' is to return to one's inviolate and eternal reality and to live in God" (*New Seeds of Contemplation*, 38). This return is, of course, brought about not by one's own efforts, not by ritual acts or ascetic techniques or religious observances (*Seasons of Celebration*, 146), but by the free gift of new life that comes through Christ's acceptance and transcendence of death. "Our salvation is not to be found in asceticism alone but in the Cross of Christ. Self-denial, however rigorous, lacks all Christian meaning apart from the Cross and Resurrection of Christ" (142). One cannot be saved by one's own efforts, one's own "works," yet once the gift of salvation has been accepted, "once the sacrifice of the cross is seen as our true salvation, then even the smallest act of charity becomes valuable and precious in the sight of God" (*Monastic Journey*, 20). One is saved, then, by faith, but there is a danger that faith itself may be regarded as a "thing" one does, so that the "act" of faith itself becomes a work. Convincing oneself that one really believes and therefore has been saved, Merton warns, "is pathological Christianity. And a Christianity of works." It is not faith as our act, and thus faith *in* our act, that saves. "Only Christ is the key, the way, and salvation itself." To say we are saved by faith is a shorthand way of saying "we are saved by Christ, whom we encounter in faith" (*Water of Life*, 285).

Salvation is a profoundly personal experience: "In the New Testament, the message of salvation is addressed not to a group or a totality but to individuals.... In the New Testament salvation is a matter of a free personal decision to accept and to follow Christ" (*Disputed Questions*, 134–35). One is not saved by conforming to "the customs and dictates of any social group," as the first desert solitaries realized when the Roman world suddenly became Christian, at least in name (*Wisdom of the Desert*, 3). Yet, to be saved is to be drawn into a profoundly communal experience, to be reunited to all humanity and all creation in "the mystery of the recapitulation, the summing up of all in Christ" (*No Man Is an Island*, xvi). To discover one's true identity in Christ is to say with St. Paul, "It is no longer I who live but Christ who lives in me" (Gal. 2:20), and so to encounter Christ as the common center of all reality. "We seek Jesus not only as our personal, individual salvation, but as the salvation and the unity of all mankind" (*Monastic Journey*, 21–22). Acceptance of the gift of salvation is acceptance of the vocation to make that salvation visible and tangible to others, and so to become a kind of sacrament, a sign and instrument, of Christ's saving work. Discipleship is "not simply the decision to accept one's personal salvation from the hands of God, in suffering and tribulation, but the decision to become *totally engaged in the historical task of the Mystical Body of Christ*, for the redemption of man and the world" (*Faith and Violence*, 64).

The "scandal" of Christianity, according to Merton, is precisely the proclamation that salvation is a present event. The Christian "must live to God in Christ, not only as one who seeks salvation but as one who *is saved*" (*Seasons of Celebration*, 147). This claim is a scandal to outsiders because of the failure of Christians to live redeemed lives, to incarnate God's love and compassion; and it is a scandal to Christians themselves because they are hesitant to accept the full meaning of salvation as a participation in new life, the eternal life of God's own love, here and now. But, Merton affirms, that is the good news proclaimed by Jesus, the inbreaking of salvation now, not as a static, once-and-for-all decision but as a dynamic, constantly renewed invitation and response, "not a perma-

nent possession but an ever present gift of God's love" (148). Thus, this experience of salvation is not an assurance that promotes complacency, a security that avoids "dread" (*Contemplative Prayer*, 127–28), but a continual summons to radical trust, as Merton emphasizes in his reflection on the word of God to Staretz Sylvan: "Keep your heart in hell and do not despair." To be saved is not to be released from the anguish of the human condition, "apparent rejection and darkness," but to be firmly grounded in something, someone, deeper than the anguish. "To have the flames of hell around me like Sylvan and to hope I *shall* be saved. Thus I *am* saved, but no need to insist on myself. Jesus, Savior" (*Turning toward the World*, 45). POC

SEE ALSO REDEMPTION.

SANCTITY

"What do you want to be anyway?" Robert Lax asked Thomas Merton. "I guess what I want to be is a good Catholic," Merton replied. "What do you mean you want to be a good Catholic?" Lax responded, adding, "What you should say is that you want to be a saint." When Merton replied that he "can't be a saint," Lax assured him, "All that is necessary to be a saint is to want to be one" (*Seven Storey Mountain*, 237–38). As he immersed himself in Catholic culture, Merton deepened his understanding of saints and sanctity. In his autobiography he reports that while he was teaching at St. Bonaventure College, he was doing "a lot of spiritual readings — Lives of Saints — Joan of Arc, St. John Bosco, St. Benedict" as well as the writings of St. John of the Cross (352). Merton soon learned that there was more to the saints than the stereotypes perpetuated in popular imagination. For example, he found that St. Thérèse of the Child Jesus, the Little Flower, was "a saint, and not just a mute pious little doll in the imaginations of a lot of sentimental old women" (353). But when he tried his hand at hagiography, he learned just how difficult it was to write saints' lives. In addition to writing a series of short accounts of the lives of Cistercian saints (a project in which he was quite successful), during the 1940s, Merton wrote book-length lives of two Cistercian women, St. Lutgarde

(*What Are These Wounds?*) and Mother Berch-mans (*Exile Ends in Glory*), which he ranked as his worst writing.

What does it mean to be a saint? What is sanctity? Merton's responses to these questions emerge in the context of his writings about contemplation, notably in *Seeds of Contemplation* (1949) and *New Seeds of Contemplation* (1961). Chapter 1 of *Seeds of Contemplation*, entitled "Everything That Is, Is Holy," opens with the statement "It is not true that the saints and the great contemplatives never noticed created things, and had no understanding or appreciation of the world and its sights and sounds and the people living in it" (*Seeds of Contemplation*, 20). Merton demythologizes a stereotypical image of saints as he introduces an important theme in his understanding of both sanctity and contemplation: neither sanctity nor contemplation involves a rejection of created things. "It was because the saints were absorbed in God that they were truly capable of seeing and appreciating created things" (20). Saints can talk about the world "without any explicit reference to God" in a way that nevertheless gives glory to God (21). In chapter 2 Merton writes, "A tree gives glory to God first of all by being a tree" (24). Things give glory to God in their very identity. "Their inscape is their sanctity" (25). The sanctity of trees, colts, dogwood flowers, and leaves lies in being what they are intended to be. The "great, gashed, half-naked mountain is another of God's saints. There is no other like it. It is alone in its character; nothing else in the world ever did or ever will imitate God in quite the same way. And that is its sanctity" (25–26). It is much the same for humans. "For me to be a saint means to be myself. Therefore the problem of sanctity and salvation is in fact the problem of finding out who I am and of discovering my true self" (26). But while trees and animals simply are what they are, humans are "free to be whatever we like" (26). The "problem" of sanctity stems from freedom. *"The seeds that are planted in my liberty at every moment, by God's will, are the seeds of my own identity, my own reality, my own happiness, my own sanctity"* (27). The saint is one who has discovered the secret of his or her identity, which lies "hidden

in the love and mercy of God" (29). The saint has exposed the illusions of the false self to realize the true self, discovered in God. These fundamental insights about the self, so central to Merton's understanding of contemplation, provide the key to Merton's understanding of sanctity. Simply put, the saint is one who knows himself or herself in God.

Observing that "God does not give us graces of talents or virtues for ourselves alone," Merton explains that *"the gift of sainthood"* is not given in order to separate saints from others or to place them above others. "Their sanctity is given them in order that they may help us and serve us" (*New Seeds of Contemplation*, 57). The gift of sainthood "gives them a clarity of compassion that can find good in the most terrible criminals. It delivers them from the burden of judging others, condemning other men. It teaches them to bring the good out of others by compassion, mercy and pardon. A man becomes a saint not by conviction that he is better than sinners but by the realization that he is one of them, and that all together need the mercy of God" (57). And yet the saints were not free of faults, imperfections, blind spots, and eccentricities, nor was their sanctity obvious to them or to those who lived with them. "If the holiness of all the saints had always been plainly evident to everybody, they would never have been polished and perfected by trial, criticism, humiliation and opposition from the people they lived with" (59).

It is God who leads a person to sanctity by paths that he or she may not understand (60). It is God who is holy, and "to enter into His sanctity I must become holy as He is holy" (61). But God's holiness is "utterly mysterious" and "inscrutable." Thus, if "I am to be 'holy' I must therefore be something that I do not understand, something mysterious and hidden, something apparently self-contradictory; for God, in Christ, 'emptied Himself.' He became a man" (61). Christ was tried and condemned "because He did not measure up to man's conception of His Holiness.... He was not holy enough, He was not holy in the right way, He was not holy in the way they had been led to expect. Therefore he was not God at all" (62). In his death Christ manifested God's holiness, and that holiness was "the complete denial and rejection of all human ideas of holiness and perfection" (62). If we want to be holy, then we need to "renounce our own way and our own wisdom" and "empty ourselves" as Christ did (62). "But if He sends His own Love, Himself, to act and love in me and in all that I do, then I shall be transformed, I shall discover who I am and shall possess my true identity by losing myself in Him. And that is what is called sanctity" (63).

In *Life and Holiness* (1963), a collection of essays, most of which were previously published in *Sponsa Regis*, Merton makes it clear that "the Christian striving for holiness" (*Life and Holiness*, xi/10) is essential to the Christian life. Anticipating the "universal call to holiness" that became a hallmark of the Second Vatican Council, Merton challenged Christians to become holy in the fullest sense by realizing their full humanity. What the world needs is not "plaster saints" but "human saints." Sanctity "is not a matter of being *less* human, but *more* human." Sanctity is most fully manifest in Jesus Christ, who was "the most deeply and perfectly human being who ever lived" (20–21/22–24). The gospel of Jesus marks the path to sanctity; it is a path of rebirth and *metanoia*, a path of ongoing conversion of life, a path that invites an "endless series of large and small 'conversions,' inner revolutions" that lead to "our transformation in Christ" (159/117). But holiness "is not a mere matter of ethical perfection" (70/57). It is "life in Christ." Nor is "our transformation in Christ" simply a matter of personal sanctification. Christians are called to transform the very structures of the society in which they live and the places in which they work. "Holiness is not and never has been a mere escape from responsibility and from participation in the fundamental task of man to live justly and productively in community with his fellow men" (xii/10). Holiness means the discovery and recovery of our hidden wholeness, and even though it always is a gift, "we can dispose ourselves to receive it by fortitude, humility, patience, and, above all, by a simple fidelity to his will in every circumstance of our ordinary life" (162/119). As Lax said to Merton, "All that is necessary to be a saint is to want to

be one" (*Seven Storey Mountain*, 238) — and, Merton would add, openness to the gift. CMB

SEE ALSO CONTEMPLATION; *LIFE AND HOLINESS.*

SCHOOL OF CHARITY, THE: *The Letters of Thomas Merton on Religious Renewal and Spiritual Direction*
Edited by Patrick Hart. New York: Farrar, Straus and Giroux, 1990. xii+434 pp.

The title of this third volume of Thomas Merton's letters is taken from St. Bernard's description of a monastery as "a school of charity." It is an appropriate title, as the book is made up of letters addressed to monks, to nuns, and to scholars who, though not monks, are interested in the monastic life. The subtitle suggests the tenor of the letters: they deal in one way or another with monastic life, monastic renewal, and spiritual direction.

The format of this volume differs from the other letter volume in that the letters are arranged in chronological order, and this is for two reasons: (1) most of the correspondents would not be well known to readers; (2) reading the letters in sequence helps readers to see the growth in Merton's understanding of the monastic life. The book is divided into three parts: (1) "The Early Monastic Years, 1941–1959"; (2) "The Middle Formative Years, 1960–1964"; and (3) "The Later Solitary Years, 1965–1968." There also is an appendix, "Two Private Vows."

Part 1: "The Early Monastic Years, 1941–1959"

The initial three letters are to Dom Frederic Dunne, abbot of Gethsemani: the first, written before Merton's entrance into the monastery, reflects on his Holy Week retreat at the abbey; the second, written at the suggestion of the novice master, tells his life story (anticipating *The Seven Storey Mountain*); the third is about his profession and his desire to offer himself fully to God. This last letter is preceded by a will that Merton made before profession. Of special interest is his leaving of funds to his guardian, Thomas Izod Bennett, to be given "to the person mentioned to him by me in my letters, if that person can be found" (*School of Charity*, 8). There also are letters to the next abbot of Gethsemani, Dom James Fox, in which Merton's desire for more solitude begins to surface, and letters to the abbot general, Gabriel Sortais, regarding, among other things, publication problems with his books (especially *The Sign of Jonas*). This part of the journal marks, among others, the beginning of correspondences with Dom Jean Leclercq and also Dom Gregorio Lemercier, both of whom will figure prominently later in his life.

Part 2: "The Middle Formative Years, 1960–1964"

These years could be described as years of new and wider relationships for Merton: a new position in the order (as novice master, putting him in contact with the young men coming to the monastery), involvement in ecumenical dialogues, and increased concern for the social issues of the time. As the introduction points out, it was during this time that "more women were now admitted to his world" (xi) — for example, Mother Angela Collins of the Louisville Carmel; Sr. Mary Luke Tobin, who had been an observer at the Second Vatican Council; Mother Myriam Dardenne, from Belgium, who founded Our Lady of the Redwoods Abbey in California; and two English Benedictine nuns, Dame Hildelith Cumming and Dame Marcella van Bruyn. Correspondence with the abbot general, Dom Gabriel Sortais, often dealt with problems of censorship regarding his writings. He ran into difficulties over an article on solitude (131–32) and over his several articles on war. In April 1962 he was forbidden by the abbot general to write anything further on war and peace, including *Peace in the Post-Christian Era*. There are many insightful letters to various monastic persons about the need for growth and change in religious life. He sounds a constant concern of his when he writes to Archbishop Paul Philippe, secretary of the Congregation for Religious, "One of the problems of all religious in this country is the fact that *opportunities to grow and develop along the true lines of one's vocation,* especially in its contemplative aspect, are generally lack-

ing" (164). He calls for greater flexibility and a more honest discussion of monastic authenticity, a topic often evaded, in Merton's view. There is a lengthy and lively correspondence on monastic life and reform with Benedictine Fr. Ronald Roloff and several polite but spirited letters to a new abbot general, Dom Ignace Gillet, on the monastic life in general and on the hermit life in particular (234–35, 245–47).

Part 3: "The Later Solitary Years, 1965–1968"

These were the years of Merton's residence in the hermitage, with 1968 as the year of his travels: those preparatory for his Asian journey and finally that journey itself. He began living full-time in the hermitage in August 20, 1965. In one of his first letters from the hermitage, addressed to Dame Hildelith Cumming, he writes, "As to life in the hermitage, it is beyond all expectations: for the first time I really know and experience all that I came to the monastery for" (289). He continues to struggle with his role "in the world." To Nora Chadwick he writes, "The whole question of relations with the 'world' is in ferment today and it has to be treated even, and perhaps especially, by a hermit" (308). In November of 1967 he held the first of two conference sessions with superiors of orders of religious women. Sr. Elaine M. Bane, a Franciscan sister from Allegany, was one of the organizers of this conference. The question Merton proposed to them was this: "Suppose that tomorrow all religious communities were dissolved by law and you had to go elsewhere: what would you do?" (352–53). (The tapes of this conference and also of the one held in the spring of 1968 have been transcribed and published as *The Springs of Contemplation.*) In January 1968 Fr. Flavian Burns was elected as abbot. Jean Leclercq invited Merton to a meeting of Asian monastic superiors in Bangkok, Thailand. Fr. Flavian gave his permission. A series of trips preceding the Asian journey took him to Redwoods Abbey in California and the Abbey of Christ in the Desert in New Mexico. The last letters come from Asia: Calcutta, New Delhi, Dharamsala, Darjeeling, Madras, Colombo, Singapore, and finally, Bangkok. The final letter, bringing this collection to a close, was written just two days before his untimely death. It affirms his commitment to the monastic life and to his monastery. To Br. Patrick Hart, his secretary, he wrote, "I think of you all on this feast day [Immaculate Conception]. Also with Christmas approaching I feel homesick for Gethsemani.... Best love to all, Louie" (417). WHS

SEARCH FOR SOLITUDE, A:
Pursuing the Monk's True Life

The Journals of Thomas Merton, vol. 3: 1952–60. Edited by Lawrence S. Cunningham. San Francisco: HarperSanFrancisco, 1996. xviii+406 pp.

This is the third volume of Thomas Merton's private journals and includes entries written between July 25, 1952, and May 23, 1960. When Merton began this journal, he had been living at the Abbey of Gethsemani for more than a decade, had been a finally professed monk for five years, and an ordained priest for three. Merton wrote in his journal occasionally during the second half of 1952 and 1953, not at all during 1954 and 1955, and quite regularly beginning in 1956. The editor divided this volume into two parts: part 1, "Master of Students" (July 1952–March 1953), and part 2, "Master of Novices" (July 1956–May 1960); this division reflects Merton's responsibilities in the monastery during these years. As master of scholastics, Merton was in charge of monks preparing for ordination to the priesthood; as master of novices, he was responsible for the formation of men preparing to become monks. In his introduction Lawrence S. Cunningham suggests that the entries written between 1956 and 1960 "must be read against his role as novice master" whose "thought constantly focused on who and what a monk was" (*Search for Solitude*, xiii).

Cunningham notes that Merton published ten books during this period and alerts readers to the fact that reflections that appear "in raw form" in this journal find their way into published works. For example, "A not insignificant portion of *Conjectures of a Guilty Bystander*" is drawn from this journal. "Seeds" of Merton's essays on Pasternak, *The Wisdom of the Desert*, and *Thoughts in Solitude* also "appear on these pages as embryonic projects struggling to mature" (xv). What Cunningham finds especially striking in this journal are "the wonderful passages where Merton lets his poetic eye capture the natural environment," the passages in which Merton turns his "fiction writer's sharp eye and ear" to "the beauties as well as the idiosyncrasies of his brethren" and to the monasticism itself, and the passages that reveal Merton's "rather original angle" on ecumenism (xv–xvi).

Although part 1 opens with an account of a drive to Ohio to view a possible site of a monastic foundation — it was one of Merton's rare forays outside the monastery — Merton quickly turns his attention inward as he begins to describe, in depth and detail, his life in the monastery. Merton's longing for ever greater solitude is quite apparent: "I am now almost completely convinced that I am only really a monk when I am alone in the old toolshed Reverend Father gave me" (14). The interludes of solitude during which he enjoyed reading, writing, and praying in the toolshed (which he affectionately named St. Anne's) sustained him and, at least in part, made it possible for him to resist the temptation to leave Gethsemani and join the Carthusians or the Camaldolese. Merton's struggle with the vow of stability is as apparent from the opening pages of this volume as it is near the journal's end, when in the late 1950s, Merton's considers going elsewhere — this time it is to Latin America — to live as a monk. Merton's attention to his role as master of scholastics is evident in notes he makes on the subject of spiritual direction during a day of recollection in 1952. These notes later found their way into *Spiritual Direction and Meditation*.

Part 2 begins with an entry written on July 17, 1956, and ends almost four years later with one written on May 23, 1960. The subtitle of the journal (vii), "Pursuing the Monk's True Life," points to a unifying theme in the next 350 or so pages. As novice master, Merton is about the work of initiating men into monastic life and forming them in the tradition that informs the life of a monk. At the same time, he is deepening his own understanding of the monastic life and what it means for him to be a monk. It is apparent in these pages that Merton is discovering the meaning of his own vocation in solitude. As an epigraph for the journal (vii), the editor chose these lines: "What it [all] comes down to is that I shall certainly have solitude but only by miracle and not at all by my own contriving. Where? Here or there makes no difference. Somewhere, nowhere, beyond all 'where.' Solitude outside geography or in it. No matter" (359). Merton wrote these lines on December 17, 1959, after his request for an indult that would have permitted him to leave Gethsemani and live as monk in Latin America had been denied. Months of consideration, letter writing, and planning had ended in the denial of the request. Merton accepted the decision in obedience with equanimity, and perhaps relief. He was learning an important lesson about solitude, a lesson he would come to appreciate more deeply in the coming years. While one door had closed, other doors were opening, and he was taking steps that would define his solitary life as a monk in radically new ways. While the next volume of Merton's journals is entitled *Turning toward the World,* and appropriately so, it is already obvious in *A Search for Solitude* that the turn is well under way.

Part 2 of *A Search for Solitude* documents Merton's changing experience and understanding of solitude in at least three important ways. First, Merton is beginning to enjoy contacts with writers and religious leaders all over the world. Not only is he reading writers such as D. T. Suzuki, Boris Pasternak, and Czeslaw Milosz, but also he is corresponding with them and crossing over into their worlds and returning enriched. Suzuki draws him into the wisdom of the East, and Merton begins to realize that what the world's wisdom traditions share is as important, and perhaps more important than what divides them. His contact with Boris Pasternak, however brief, reinforces his sense of kinship beyond geography. His friendship with Czeslaw Milosz, which began in 1958 with Merton's reading of *The Captive Mind,* makes him confront the very real threats of totalitarian regimes. There were other contacts as well. Nicaraguan poet Ernesto Cardenal, who was for a time his novice, taught him about Latin American life and culture and

introduced him to a host of Latin American poets and writers. There were contacts with Christians and with Jews, and Merton was learning about Islam as well.

Second, Merton is experiencing important turning points in his own self-understanding. The most dramatic, though by no means the only, experience of this sort was symbolized by his experience at Fourth and Walnut in Louisville on March 18, 1958. In the middle of the Louisville business district Merton realized how his sense of difference and superiority had been an illusion, how he really was "a member of the human race." Merton's journal account (181–82) became the basis for an enlarged and enriched rendering of the experience, published in *Conjectures of a Guilty Bystander.* On May 5, 1958, in a less well-known but nevertheless important passage, Merton writes, "Thinking of the new and necessary struggle in my interior life. I am finally coming out of chrysalis. The years behind me seem strangely inert and negative, but I suppose that passivity was necessary. Now the pain and struggle of fighting my way out into something new and much bigger. I must see and embrace God in the whole world. (It is all very well to say I have been seeing God in Himself. But I have not. I have been seeing Him only in a very small monastic world. And this is much too small.)" (200). His expansive idea of his own calling is also evident in these lines: "To be a man of the church I have to be fully myself — and fully responsible and free before God — not a 'unit' or a mere 'member'" (221).

Third, Merton is realizing that his monastic commitment is not only compatible with, but even requires, engagement in the issues of the world and the church. He is reading Gandhi's letters himself and sharing what he is reading with the community. On September 22, 1958, he notes that a Filipino postulant objected when he spoke of Gandhi. "Said nonviolence was 'not-natural.' No, I guess maybe it isn't. And yet without some more of it, what is going to happen to human nature?" (218). He is writing a letter to the leader of the Soviet Writers Union to protest the treatment of Boris Pasternak. He is envisioning his vocation in terms of the world: "My vocation and task in this world is to keep alive all that is usefully individual and personal in me, to be a 'contemplative' in the full sense — and to share it with others — to remain as a witness of the nobility of the private person and his primacy over the group" (221), he wrote in October 1958. A few months earlier he had expressed his vocation as an American, "not just an American of the U.S.": "My vocation is American — *to see and to understand and to have in myself the life and the roots and the belief and the destiny and the Orientation of the whole hemisphere* — as an expansion of something of God, of Christ, that the world has not yet found out — something that is only now after hundreds of years of coming to maturity!" (168).

Merton's search for solitude indeed was leading to his pursuit of a monk's true life. CMB

SEASONS OF CELEBRATION: Meditations on the Cycle of Liturgical Feasts

New York: Farrar, Straus and Giroux, 1965.
vii+248 pp.

In an author's note written in August 1965 Thomas Merton explains that all but two of the fifteen "essays and addresses on the Liturgy" included in this book actually had been delivered to various groups at Gethsemani, a fact that accounts for "certain changes of tone and tempo" (*Seasons of Celebration*, vii). While Merton was working on the "Liturgy book" in October 1963, he wondered whether the material was worth revising (*Water of Life*, 21). In February 1964 he had finished going over the material to be typed for the book (77). In July 1964 he mentioned in his journal that he still had "to proofread the typescript of *Seasons of Celebration* which has been lying around for several months. The job does not appeal" (127)! One censor who read the manuscript had said that Merton was "written out" (144). With an advance copy of the book in hand, Merton found the book club blurb "completely idiotic" and remarked, "As usual I see the defects when the book is finally in print" (309).

The unevenness of the essays did not escape the notice of reviewers, some of whom criticized the book before going on to praise it. One reviewer found the title "misleading" but noted that "the book is full of useful, helpful, valuable, penetrating comments."[1] Another suggested that although the collection might have benefited from being "trimmed to the next six most recent essays," the book "hits a new tone: a quiet joy echoes from its pages, the alleluia of a man who has sensed the glory of the coming of the Lord."[2]

That these essays and addresses were written over a period of fourteen years (between 1950 and 1964) is worth noting. Five essays were written in the early and mid-1950s: "Christian Self-Denial" (1950), "The Sacrament of Advent in the Spirituality of St. Bernard" (1952), "Time and the Liturgy" (1955), "In Silentio"[3] (1955), and "The Nativity Kerygma" (1956). Two essays date from the late 1950s: "Ash Wednesday" (1958) and "Easter: The New Life" (1959). The remaining essays were written in the 1960s: "Church and Bishop in St. Ignatius of Antioch" (1961), "The Good Samaritan" (1961), "A Homily on Light and the Virgin Mary" (1962), "The Name of the Lord" (1962), "Advent: Hope or Delusion?" (1963), "The Community of Pardon" (1963), "Liturgy and Spiritual Personalism" (1963), and "Liturgical Renewal: The Open Approach" (1964). But the essays do not appear in chronological order in the book. Instead, articles on liturgy and liturgical renewal frame a selection of pieces on Advent and Christmas, Lent and Easter, and assorted scriptural themes and readings. Merton notes that the most recent articles "come closer to saying what the author really wants to say" and he identifies three essays as representing "most articulately his current concerns": "Liturgy and Spiritual Personalism" (1963), "Easter: The New Life" (1959), and "The Good Samaritan" (1961) (*Seasons of Celebration*, vii).

In the opening essay, "Liturgy and Spiritual Personalism," written in final form in 1963, Merton addresses the subject of liturgical reform. Merton originally published "Liturgy and Spiritual Personalism" in *Worship* in October 1960. The version included in *Seasons of Celebration* is a version expanded in the light of the Second Vatican Council's Constitution on the Sacred Liturgy (*Sacrosanctum Concilium*). The essay "is concerned with the meaning of liturgical renewal not only as participation in new modes of worship, but as the creative joint effort of all Catholics to attain a new understanding of worship itself" (2). Drawing on the Greek concept of liturgy as the "public work" that is the free citizen's contribution to the *polis*, Merton defines liturgical celebration as "a sacred and public action in which the community, at once religious and political, acknowledges its identity in worship" (4). Only insofar as liturgy is "the activity of free and mature persons" can it be "genuinely *communal*" (5–6). Liturgy is not performance; the members of the assembly are not "passive spectators" (6). The liturgy is the people's work. "In the sacred liturgy, therefore, the faithful act not as mere spectators, as inert and passive figures, or as servants and slaves. The liturgy everywhere implies awareness that we are the friends and collaborators with Christ in His great work of Redeeming and sanctifying the entire cosmos" (10–11). Although Merton clearly distinguishes between the role of the priest and that of the faithful, he advocates for the full participation of the faithful. The people of God are a royal priesthood. Active participation in the liturgy is "a spiritual co-operation in the very work of God Himself" (14). In the concluding section of the essay Merton defines Christian personalism as "the sacramental sharing of the inner secret of personality in the mystery of love. . . . Christian personalism is the discovery of one's inmost self, and of the inmost self of one's neighbor, in the mystery of Christ: a discovery that respects the hiddenness and incommunicability of each one's personal secret while paying tribute to his presence in the common celebrations" (22). It is in the public and communal celebration of the liturgy that a person "finds himself and his brother" (22). Merton concludes, "It is precisely because it is public in the classical or 'political' sense of the word, that the liturgy enables us to discover and to express the deepest meaning of Christian personalism" (25).

The second essay, "Church and Bishop in St. Ignatius of Antioch," explores the second-century bishop's ecclesiology as "a theology of *kerygma* and proclamation" that emphasizes "the reality of Christ, flesh and spirit, in His historical presence, in His eucharistic presence, and His real presence in His Body the Church" in which Christ unites all peoples (29). In "Time and the Liturgy" Merton discusses the ways in which Christ is present anew in the liturgy and the liturgical cycle.

"The Sacrament of Advent in the Spirituality of St. Bernard" elaborates on Advent as "the 'sacrament' of the PRESENCE of God in His world, in the Mystery of Christ at work in History through His Church, preparing in a hidden, obscure way for the final manifestation of His Kingdom" (61). When Merton returned to the theme of Advent more than a decade later in "Advent: Hope or Delusion?" he was mindful of "the tragedy of contemporary disorders and injustice" that "prevent men from becoming one in Christ" and rend humankind "in pieces when, in the Advent Mystery, Man already *is* at least inchoatively, one in Christ!" (99). "The Nativity Kerygma" is a proclamation of Christ's birth. Christ is "light of light," and Christians are called to manifest Christ's light by "witness" and "charity" (104–5). "This one day is the day of His birth, but every day of our mortal lives must be His manifestation, His divine Epiphany, in the world which He has created and redeemed" (112).

The next three essays address the movement from Lent to Easter. In "Ash Wednesday" Merton explains the original meaning of Lent as the church's "holy spring," in which catechumens were prepared for baptism and public penitents were restored to life in the community. "Lent is . . . not a season of punishment so much as one of healing" and of *metanoia* (113–14). "Christian Self-Denial" explores the purpose and meaning of Christian asceticism. "The function of penance and self-denial is . . . the 'breaking up' of that hardness of heart which prevents us from understanding God's command to love, and from obeying it effectively" (130). Christian asceticism is not an escape from the world but a way of entering into its confusion "bearing something of the light of Truth in our hearts, and capable of exercising something of the mysterious, transforming power of the Cross, of love and of sacrifice" (132). Christian asceticism "is characterized by wholeness and by balance," and its purpose is liberation (141). In "Easter: The New Life," one of the essays in *Seasons of Celebration* that Merton liked best, he observes, "Easter . . . does not merely recall the act by which we are liberated, it revives our freedom itself, in the renewal of the mystery in which we become free" (144). Thus, it is fittingly celebrated not once a year but every day. Easter celebrates our freedom from enslavement to sin and to the law. The Christian "has no Law but Christ" (147). "Why do we secretly keep cherishing a spirituality that is based on the Law rather than on Christ?" Merton asks (151).

The next five essays focus on a variety of themes. "A Homily on Light and the Virgin Mary" honors Mary as "the perfect rekindling of the pure light . . . extinguished by the sin of Adam" (163). "The Good Samaritan" grapples with the question "Who, then, is my neighbor?" in the context of *chesed,* the mercy and power of God that call us to "be to ourselves and to others signs and sacraments of mercy" (179). In "The Name of the Lord" Merton reflects on the revelation of God's name "Yahweh." "In Silentio," a note on monastic prayer, explores the meaning of the monastic vocation in the context of wisdom and silence. "The monk is called to enter into the hiddenness and the silence of God" (212). "The Community of Pardon" presents the church as "an epiphany of the Divine Love, Agape" (217) insofar as it is a church of pardon responsive to the gospel imperative of reconciliation. "We all need the mercy of God, we all need the pardon and love of our neighbor" (221).

"Liturgical Renewal: The Open Approach," the final essay in *Seasons of Celebration,* is an expanded and revised version of an article that appeared in *The Critic* in December 1964. Writing a year after the initial implementation of liturgical reform that began to introduce such changes as the increased use of the vernacular, the altar facing the people, the presence of a lay commentator, concelebration, and communion under both species, Merton observes that the church is in "a period of transition." Much remains to be done. Biblical translations prepared for private use are poorly suited for public proclamation. Bible readings *are* in English — "But what English!" (233). And, "What

difference does it make if the priest says the whole canon out loud if it still means something like this: 'I am the priest, you are the laity. . . . You have your place and I have mine. I am here to confect valid sacraments for you to receive and you are there because if you were not there I would not be here confecting sacraments' " (234). Merton denounces "validism," an outlook according to which "what matters is not that the ceremonies have meaning, or that the sacraments eloquently speak the grace which they signify. . . . All that matters is the sacraments be valid, the formulas correct, and the gestures rubrically exact" (235). Above all, he calls for a new outlook, "a new spirit of openness, in which the priest is open to his people, and they are open to him and one another. This means that the words of the liturgy should be spoken by a person to persons, and not just uttered abstractly in a sacred void" (236). This spirit of openness is essential to renewal. Renewal must be more than "saying the formulas of prayer in a familiar language and with the intonations of colloquial and rotarian togetherness" (236).

Renewal means "discovering a *new* sense of sacred space, of community, of oneness in the Spirit, as a result of a communication on a deep level with which we have long ceased to be familiar: it means learning to experience the mystery of oneness in grace" (236). "The words, songs, ceremonies, signs, movements of worship are all designed, by their very nature, to open the mind and heart of the participant to this experience of oneness in Christ. But this sacramental consciousness depends first of all on human sympathy, relatedness, and on some degree of mutual understanding" (237). Remembering his own experience at Corpus Christi Church in the late 1930s, Merton reveals that what kept him going to Mass was that "everything was well done, not out of aestheticism or rubrical obsessiveness, but out of love for God and His truth" (237). At Corpus Christi, Merton experienced the openness that must characterize Christian worship if it is to be a "communion in love" and not merely a "communion in correctness" (238). Both progressives and conservatives need to be mindful that renewal means "the replacement of constraint by the openness of simple and joyous participation" (243). The world needs "forms of worship that are dynamic, colorful, rhythmic and full of disciplined and expressive movement," and "the new nations, the more primitive societies which are the children in the family of nations" may be our teachers (248).

An abridged version of *Seasons of Celebration* was published in Great Britain in 1976 under the title *Meditations on Liturgy,* with an introduction by Basil Hume, archbishop of Westminster. CMB

> SEE ALSO LITURGY; *MEDITATIONS ON LITURGY; NATIVITY KERGYMA; SILENCE IN HEAVEN.*

Notes

1. Robert W. Hovda, review of *Seasons of Celebration,* by Thomas Merton, *Critic* 24 (February–March 1966): 74–75.
2. Michael Glazier, review of *Seasons of Celebration,* by Thomas Merton, *The Catholic World* 202 (February 1966): 311–12.
3. "In Silentio" is an abridged version of material published in *Silence in Heaven* in 1955.

SECULAR JOURNAL OF THOMAS MERTON, THE

New York: Farrar, Straus and Cudahy, 1959. xv+270 pp.

The preface of this book, one of several journals that Thomas Merton himself edited and prepared for publication, serves several purposes. In addition to identifying the sources from which the selections were drawn, describing the circumstances surrounding publication of the journal, and informing the reader about what to expect in the book, Merton pays tribute to Catherine de Hueck Doherty, founder of Friendship House and of a secular institute called Madonna House in Combermere, Ontario.

Merton first met Catherine de Hueck in the summer of 1941 when she spoke at St. Bonaventure College, where he was teaching. Later that summer Merton spent a few days at Friendship House in Harlem.[1] He writes of this in *The Secular Journal.*

The story of Catherine de Hueck Doherty is intimately tied to that of *The Secular Journal* in another way. In 1941 Merton produced a typed manuscript of selections taken from the "diary" he kept between 1939 and 1941. Before leaving for Gethsemani in December 1941, he gave the manuscript to Catherine de Hueck, with the understanding that any proceeds from the publication of the book would be hers to use in support of her apostolate. In 1955 she wrote to Merton to ask if the offer still stood, and Merton replied that it did. Neither of them anticipated the reaction of the censors (*Search for Solitude,* 147), which would delay publication of the book for several years, during which time Merton pleaded his case to Dom Gabriel Sortais. Writing to inform the abbot general that Catherine de Hueck accepted the decision not to permit publication of the journal, Merton nevertheless was clear about what a decision not to publish the book would cost her: "They could have bought a new car to transport the nurses in the abandoned country where there are poor farmers that she helps; they might also have made a little building for those who come and join their institute; they might even have helped a family in distress."[2] In the same letter Merton suggested, "One might perhaps change the expressions here and there, suppress the overly shocking sentences, without damaging the substance of the book" (*School of Charity,* 106–7). Merton went ahead and made changes in manuscript. On February 15, 1958, he wrote in his journal, "Have been editing the *Secular Journal* — still like it. Have written to Fr. Irenaeus at St. Bonaventure's for the original mss. To add more. The cuts suggested by the most critical of the 4 censors have, perhaps, been wise" (*Search for Solitude,* 166). In April 1958 Merton was granted permission to publish the book as long as he revised the text and made it clear that this was a premonastic journal written *before* his entrance into the Abbey of Gethsemani. In addition to noting in the preface that the manuscript required some editing without "destroying or notably altering the artless spontaneity of the original" and while keeping "its somewhat naïve essence" (*Secular Journal,* viii), Merton added a caveat of his own, warning readers about "the careless style, the callow opinions and all the other defects...of a writer much younger and even more unwise that I am at present" as well as some "youthful sarcasms" (viii, ix).

The Secular Journal consists of selections from three premonastic journals. The first began on May 2, 1939, and ended on February 13, 1940; the second, known as the "Cuban Journal," began on February 13, 1940, and ended on October 19, 1940; and the third, known as the "St. Bonaventure Journal," began on October 19, 1940, and ended on December 5, 1941. The three monastic journals have been published in their entirety in the first volume of Merton's complete journals, *Run to the Mountain*, edited by Br. Patrick Hart. *The Secular Journal*, which Merton himself edited, represents a very small selection from the premonastic journals.

Merton divided *The Secular Journal* into five parts, identifying each according to the location(s) in which it was written — part 1: Perry Street, New York (winter 1939–40); part 2: Cuba (spring 1940); part 3: New York and St. Bonaventure (1940–41); part 4: interlude, Abbey of Our Lady of Gethsemani (Holy Week 1941); and part 5: St. Bonaventure, Harlem, and Our Lady of the Valley.

The entries that Merton selected for part 1 portray him as a young intellectual interested in literature and writing. He was living in Greenwich Village while attending Columbia University, where he received his M.A. in English in February 1939, continuing studies for the Ph.D., and teaching in the university extension. There are entries on William Blake and Dante, on a biography of James Joyce and a novel by Graham Greene, on art and travel, and on religion. Merton's Good Friday 1940 reflection on the woman who poured ointment over the body of Jesus (Matt. 26:12) proclaims her action an act of "perfect charity." "Without love," Merton observes, "almsgiving is no more important an action than brushing your hair or washing your hands...but love does not merely give money, it gives itself" (34).

Part 2 recounts Merton's visit to Cuba in the spring of 1940. Merton evokes a sense of Cuba with colorful descriptions of landscape and city life and he reveals a deep affection for the Cuban people. Included in passages Merton chose from the "Cuban Journal" are descrip-

tions of the churches he visited, La Reina and Nuestra Señora del Carmen, and a moving account of Mass at the Church of St. Francis, where the "strong and clear voices" of children crying out "Yo creo" ("I believe") triggered an intense experience of God's presence. The "knowledge that heaven was right in front of me, struck me like a thunderbolt and went through me like a flash of lightning and seemed to lift me clean up off the earth" (76–77).[3]

Merton wrote the entries in part 3 while he was living in New York, vacationing in Olean, and teaching at St. Bonaventure College. He continued to write about what he was reading: novels by Thomas Mann and Léon Bloy, poems by Dylan Thomas; and about his own writing: his novel "The Labyrinth," which he thought was "not so bad" despite the fact that it continued to be rejected by the publishers (158). He reports that he tore pages out of last year's journals and that he experimented with writing dialogues in which he responded to questions he posed to himself with witty and revealing replies. The war casts a shadow over these pages as Merton wrestles with what war says about God, the dehumanized destruction reported in a film on the war in Poland, the price of fighting Hitler ("If we fight Hitler, we will become like him, too, we will turn into something just as dirty as he is. If we are going to beat him, we will have to" [130]). On March 19, 1941, he wrote about reporting to the draft board for his physical.[4] Seeds of his later thinking are apparent in passages in which he draws perspective from his faith — for example: "We have no peace because we have done nothing to keep peace, not even prayed for it! We have not even *desired* peace except for the wrong reason: because we didn't want to get hurt, we didn't want to suffer.... If we are ever going to have peace again, we will have to hate war for some better reason than that we fear to lose our houses, our refrigerators, our cars, our legs, our lives" (121–22). Eight months later, on February 22, 1941, Merton wrote, "when I pray for peace I pray for the following miracle. That God move all men to pray and do penance and recognize each one his own great guilt, because we are all guilty of this war, in a way" (164).[5]

The entries in part 4 offer a glimpse of Merton's first visit to the Abbey of Gethsemani, where he made a retreat during Holy Week 1941. Merton's unbridled enthusiasm for Gethsemani is evident in the opening lines of the first entry written on April 7: "I should tear out all the other pages of this book, and all the other pages of anything else I have ever written, and begin here. This is the center of America . . . keeping the universe from cracking in pieces and falling apart" (183). Writing in Douglaston, New York, a little more than a week later, he confesses, "Leaving Gethsemani was sad" (204). As he made the Stations of the Cross on Easter Sunday, he wished he were going to stay.

Part 5 consists of selections written between May 12, 1941, and November 27, 1941, less than two weeks before Merton entered the Abbey of Gethsemani. The most significant entries recount Merton's first encounters with Baroness Catherine de Hueck. She spoke to the nuns and clerics enrolled in the summer session at St. Bonaventure. A week later, inspired by the baroness's moving example, Merton arrived at Friendship House "full of Hail Marys" (234). A few months later she was back, and as they drove from Buffalo to Olean, the baroness pressed Merton about working at Friendship House, as he had anticipated that she would. As The Secular Journal ends, Merton is torn between going to Harlem and going to Gethsemani. "I return to the idea again and again: 'Give up everything, give up everything!'" (270).

The Secular Journal drew mixed reviews. While some reviewers praised the book, others compared it to The Seven Storey Mountain and found it wanting. Perhaps these reviewers would have responded more positively to the whole of the premonastic journals now published in Run to the Mountain. But The Secular Journal remains the sampling of entries that Merton himself selected as a young man — already a writer, not yet a monk. CMB

SEE ALSO RUN TO THE MOUNTAIN.

Notes

1. For a description of his meeting with Catherine de Hueck and his visit to Friendship House, see The Seven Storey Mountain, 344–52. For Merton's letters to Catherine de Hueck Doherty, see The Hidden Ground of Love, 3–24.

2. See the letter to Dom Gabriel Sortais, dated January 27, 1958 (School of Charity, 106). Compare to this the statement in the preface to The Secular Journal: "The sale of this volume may mean many things to the workers at Combermere: a new car in which nurses can reach outlying farms, or perhaps a new building, to house the novices of the Institute. It may mean the difference between life and death to someone in Canada, in the Yukon, in Arizona. It may mean the difference between bitterness and peace, to many souls who will be helped by Catherine and her workers. It may mean the salvation of many souls who cannot be reached until their bodily needs are first taken care of" (xv).

3. Merton elaborates on this experience in The Seven Storey Mountain, 285.

4. As Michael Mott notes, there are passages in Merton's premonastic journals that are more personally revealing than those that he chose to include in The Secular Journal — for example, his account of imagining the devastation of a London he knew (see Run to the Mountain, 244–46). See Michael Mott, The Seven Mountains of Thomas Merton (Boston: Houghton Mifflin, 1984), 161–65.

5. See "The Root of War Is Fear" (New Seeds of Contemplation, 112–22) for Merton's later take on these themes.

SEEDS OF CONTEMPLATION
New York: New Directions, 1949. 201 pp.

Published on March 2, 1949, in the wake The Seven Storey Mountain, Seeds of Contemplation achieved instant popularity. In four months it sold forty thousand copies. It was acclaimed as a modern-day Imitation of Christ. Thomas Merton had been admonished by his confessor to write about contemplation and let people know that it was accessible, not just to an elite, but to all (Sign of Jonas, 20). Seeds of Contemplation was Merton's response to that admonition.

The title is derived from the Scriptures: the Parable of the Sower and the Seed, which all three of the Synoptic Gospels narrate (Matthew 13; Mark 4; Luke 8). While generally called the Parable of the Seed, it really is about the different kinds of soil that receive the seed. Merton realized this and initially titled the book The Soil and the Seeds of Contemplation. The application of the parable to contemplation already had appeared in Merton's earlier book What Is Contemplation? There he had written, "The seeds of this perfect life [contemplation] are planted in every Christian soul at Baptism. But seeds must grow and develop before you reap the harvest" (What Is Contemplation? 17).

Perhaps the most important thing that can be said about *Seeds of Contemplation* is that for many people it opened a door that they had hitherto thought was closed to them, the door to a new spirituality: the way of contemplation. Merton invites people "to read [this book] in communion with the God in Whose presence it was written" (*Seeds of Contemplation*, 15).

Seeds of Contemplation is not easily summarized, since, as its author tells us, it is a volume of "more or less disconnected thoughts and ideas and aphorisms about the interior life" (13). Written by a young monk (he was thirty-two years old and just seven years in the monastic life when it was published), it contains many notable passages but displays all too often the naivete that marks his earlier works. He had left the world and seems to wish that everyone could follow his example. Those who cannot do so are advised to live as much like a monk as possible (see, e.g., 60–61, a passage that impresses more by its earnestness than its practicability). The book also is marred by a dualism (see, e.g., 21–22, 133) that would separate God and creation, the natural and the supernatural, though there are signs of his beginning to move in a different direction. This movement is evident in a passage that comes near the end of the book, "where contemplation becomes what it is really meant to be, it is no longer something poured out of God into a created subject, so much as God living in God and identifying a created life with His own Life so that there is nothing left of any significance but God living in God" (196).

In all, besides the author's note and the explanation of the title, there are twenty-seven chapters. Many of them foreshadow topics that Merton would write more about in his later works — for example, "Everything That Is, Is Holy" (ch. 1), "Things in Their Identity" (ch. 2), "Pray for Your Own Discovery" (ch. 3), "Solitude" (ch. 6), "Integrity" (ch. 8), "The Root of War Is Fear" (ch. 9), "Faith" (ch. 11), "Humility against Despair" (ch. 15), "Freedom under Obedience" (ch. 16), "Detachment" (ch. 18), "Distractions" (ch. 20), "The Gift of Understanding" (ch. 21), "Contemplata Tradere" (ch. 26), and "Pure Love" (ch. 27). Especially significant is the begin-

ning of the development of a theme that will become increasingly important in his later writings: the distinction between the false self, which is nothing but an illusion, and the true self, which we find only in God (28–29). This notion will be developed considerably especially in "The Inner Experience" and in *New Seeds of Contemplation*, but also in other later writings.[1] It is a key theme for understanding what spirituality means to Merton.

Merton's own evaluation of *Seeds of Contemplation* is somewhat negative. True, a fairly positive statement does appear in a letter to James Laughlin written in the spring of 1949: "Really I am happy about *Seeds*. That is the kind of stuff I ought to be writing. It has its faults, no doubt, but I can see my way more clearly in that direction" (*Thomas Merton and James Laughlin*, 52). He was not, however, in such a happy mood when he wrote on March 6, 1949, "It lacks warmth and human affection.... I don't see how the book will ever do any good" (*Sign of Jonas*, 165).[2] Indeed, on July 9, 1949, he told Jacques Maritain that he was revising the book. Many statements in it, he said, "are hasty and do not express my true meaning" (*Courage for Truth*, 25). He promised to do a revision in August. A revised edition did appear on December 19, 1949. It was not a large-scale revision. It does, however, carry a new preface that sets forth an important methodological statement: "In this book the author is talking about spiritual things from the point of view of experience rather than in the concise terms of dogmatic theology or of metaphysics" (*Seeds of Contemplation*, xii). Apart from the new preface, a few things are omitted (e.g., a statement about the Sufis [87] that later had embarrassed him), and a few additions were made. But the extensive rewrite had to wait until 1962, when *New Seeds of Contemplation* was published.

Although *Seeds of Contemplation* was replaced by *New Seeds of Contemplation*, in 1986 New Directions issued a facsimile edition of the original work. WHS

SEE ALSO *NEW SEEDS OF CONTEMPLATION*.

Notes

1. See, for example, "Notes for a Philosophy of Solitude," in *Disputed Questions*.
2. See also *Entering the Silence*, 287.

SEEDS OF DESTRUCTION

New York: Farrar, Straus and Giroux, 1964.
xvi+328 pp.

"The contemplative life is not, and cannot be, a mere withdrawal, a pure negation, a turning of one's back on the world with its sufferings, its crises, its confusions and its errors," Thomas Merton wrote in the author's note for *Seeds of Destruction* (xiii). Dated July 1964, the note expressed what Merton had come to see as "a solemn obligation of conscience" (xv) to speak out on issues of justice. When he entered the monastery in 1941, he readily embraced withdrawal from the world as essential to the monastic life. But in the early 1960s he recognized that engagement in the world's issues had a place in the contemplative life. The concluding lines of his author's note reflect this shift in his thinking: "To have a vow of poverty seems to me illusory if I do not in some way identify myself with the cause of people who are denied their rights and forced, for the most part, to live in abject misery. To have a vow of obedience seems to me to be absurd if it does not imply a deep concern for the most fundamental of all expressions of God's will: the love of His truth and of our neighbor" (xvi).

Seeds of Destruction is divided into three parts: (1) "Black Revolution," (2) "The Diaspora," and (3) "Letters in a Time of Crisis." The two essays in part 1 represent Merton's thinking on the growing crisis of racism and on the civil rights movement. "Letters to a White Liberal" was written in the early summer of 1963, revised during the following fall, and published as "The Black Revolution: Letter to a White Liberal" in the Christmas 1963 issue of *Ramparts*, dedicated to the memory of the four girls who were killed when Ku Klux Klansmen bombed a church in Birmingham, Alabama, in 1963.[1] "The Black Revolution" was also published in England in the November and December 1963 issues of *Blackfriars*, and in August 1964 in *Black Digest*. In his introductory note Merton observes that events which occurred in 1964 have "substantiated" (3) the message expressed in "Letters to a White Liberal." Yes, the Civil Rights Act was passed, but legislation is "*only the beginning of a new and more critical phase in*

the conflict" (4). The situation remains critical and urgent. "Though it is quite true that the vast majority both of whites and Negroes want to solve this problem without force and bloodshed, their 'wanting' and their good intentions are no longer enough" (6–7). The assassination of President John F. Kennedy exposed a truth that the majority of Americans cannot believe: "*Where minds are full of hatred and where imaginations dwell on cruelty, torment, punishment, revenge and death, then inevitably there will be violence and death*" (7).

"I believe that Christianity is concerned with human crises, since Christians are called to manifest the mercy and truth of God in history," Merton writes in the opening paragraph of "Letters to a White Liberal" (10). If Christians are obligated to respect the dignity of all persons, "How then do we treat this other Christ, this person who happens to be black?" (17). Christian believers in the South accept the personhood of the Negro "only with serious qualification" (17). "Not a few of these Christians . . . absolutely refuse to worship Christ in the same congregations as Negroes" and some Catholics refuse "to receive the Body of Christ together with Negroes" (18). For their part, Northern Christians act as though the Negro is invisible. They grant Negroes rights on paper but not in reality. While insisting that he was not questioning the sincerity or the generosity of those who marched in Washington, Merton charged that white liberals "once again obscured the real issue, which is that American society *has to change* before the race problem can be solved. The atmosphere of congenial fraternity and nobility which marked the great demonstration, and certainly made it edifying from many points of view, seemed once again to indicate that liberal optimism and fair weather principles would be enough, and that the Negro would move into the place that belongs to him in white American society. But to the Negro, that is only a liberal myth. He knows that there is at present no *place for him* whatever in American society, except at the bottom of the totem pole" (34–35). White liberals marched because they "*needed to be there*," Merton wrote. "Instead of seeing the Negro revolution as a manifestation of a deep disorder that is eating away the inner substance of our society, because *it is in ourselves,* do we look at it only as a threat from outside ourselves — as an unjust and deplorable infringement of our rights by an irresponsible minority, goaded on by Red agitators?" (38). The very structure of society has to change, and the change needs to be a revolutionary one that will be felt by Negroes and whites alike. The change, however, must be accomplished not by whites but by Negroes themselves. "The liberation of the Negro and the redemption of the white man" represent a struggle for truth (43). A purpose of nonviolent protest is "to awaken the conscience of the white man to the awful reality of his injustice and of his sin, so that he will be able to see that the Negro problem is really a *White* problem: that the cancer of injustice and hate which is eating white society and is only partly manifested in racial segregation with all its consequences, *is rooted in the heart of the white man himself*" (46).

"The Legend of Tucker Caliban" is a review of William Melvin Kelley's novel *A Different Drummer.* The review was first published in the September 1963 issue of *Jubilee.* Merton summarizes the plot of the novel this way: "The book opens as the loafers on the porch of a general store, in a small town of the deep South, watch a truckload of rock salt pass through on its way to the farm of a Negro called Tucker Caliban. It ends as the same loafers, after watching all the Negroes, mysteriously and without explanation, clear out of the state, lynch the last Negro available to them, a potentate from the North, and founder of a black racist movement" (76). Tucker sterilizes his field with rock salt, shoots his animals, sets his house on fire, and leaves during the night with his pregnant wife. "He simply vanishes" (79). All the other Negroes leave too. Merton interprets their departure as "a symbolic statement." It is the Negro's "final refusal to accept paternalism, tutelage, and all different forms of moral, economic, psychological and social servitude wished on them by the whites. In the last analysis, it is the final rejection of the view of life implied by white culture. It is a definitive NO to White America" (79). The whites are bewildered by the departure of the

Negroes. They do not understand. Merton concludes that we "need to listen very seriously" to the Negro. "I for one, am absolutely ready to believe that *we need him to be free, for our sake even more than for his own*" (90).

In the three essays included in part 2 — "The Christian in World Crisis," "The Christian in the Diaspora," and "A Tribute to Gandhi" — Merton turns to the subject of war and peace. In "The Christian in World Crisis" Merton reflects on the moral climate of the 1960s in light of the teaching of Pope John XXIII's encyclical *Pacem in Terris.* There are five parts to this essay: "Can We Choose Peace?" "The Christian as Peacemaker," "War in Origen and St. Augustine," "The Legacy of Machiavelli," and "The Reply of *Pacem in Terris.*" The first four parts were included in *Peace in the Post-Christian Era,* the book Merton wrote in 1962 but was not permitted to publish. Raising the question "Can We Choose Peace?" Merton observes that in a climate of violence, hatred, and power politics, the "more important question is not 'What is going to happen to us?' but 'What are we going to do?' or more cogently, *'What are our real intentions?'* " (94–95). The question needs to be answered in the context of our obligations, as Christians, to God and to the whole of humankind. *Pacem in Terris* provides a framework in which to examine those obligations. While it actually says little about war, "the encyclical concentrates on basic principles: the dignity of the human person and the primacy of the universal common good over the particular good of the political unit" (101). Thus, Pope John XXIII calls attention to the fundamental ideas on which peace depends and that are the antidote to "the general climate of thought (or thoughtlessness)" in which moral and social epidemics — of panic, hatred, and destruction — take their origin (100). Countering such a climate of opinion requires a new way of thinking: it requires "peace-thinking." In "The Christian as Peacemaker" Merton explains that there will be no peace without "a climate favorable to peace" (117), which will involve, as Pope John XXIII realized, *"new methods of relationships in human society"* (*Pacem in Terris,* no. 163 [118]). Pope John said "that we had reached a point in history where it was clearly no longer reasonable to make use of war in the settlement of international disputes, and that the important thing was not merely protest against the latest war technology, but the construction of permanent world peace on a basis of truth, justice, love and liberty" (123).

In the next two sections of "The Christian in World Crisis" Merton outlines three views of war: Origen's view that Christians are united against war in their obedience to Christ, Augustine's view that there are conditions under which a war may be "just," and Machiavelli's view that the conduct of war is to be governed by the ruthless use of power. In the last section Merton explains that "the power for peace" of which *Pacem in Terris* speaks resides "in the profound and optimistic Christian spirit with which the Pope lays bare the deepest roots of peace, roots which are placed in man by God Himself and which man himself has the mission to cultivate" (180).

"The Christian in the Diaspora" consists of three parts: "Rahner's Diaspora," "The Monk in the Diaspora,"[2] and "Monastic Thought in the Russian Diaspora." Merton's reading of Karl Rahner's *The Christian Commitment* inspired these essays. The German Catholic theologian proposed that the church needed to come to terms with its "diaspora situation." Christians find themselves in the midst of an increasingly secular culture and are called to manifest Christ in their situations. Christians "must intervene in the social life of our world, and we must do so as Christians, guided by Christian principles, indeed moved and led by the Holy Spirit.... We cannot propagate our social ideas precisely in the name of the church, invoking her hierarchical authority" (192). The diaspora challenges Christians to live their commitment in new ways, discovering values in the secular world and manifesting the gospel message in the world. In "The Monk and the Diaspora" Merton explores the implications of Rahner's book for monastic orders. In this essay, originally written as a review of Rahner's *Christian Commitment*, Merton recognizes that the diaspora situation of the Church is relevant not only to lay Christians but also to monks. "The effectiveness of the monk's presence in the

world and of his monastic witness to the Gospel of Christ will depend on his ability to see his own place in relation to the world correctly. He too must learn to understand his monastic calling in the general diaspora situation of the whole Church" (203). Rather than merely reshaping itself into a "a new contemporary mode," monasticism needs to distinguish between "what is really essential to monasticism and what is not" and learn to preserve even accidentals that have "a serious importance of their own," such as Gregorian chant (206–7). Fruitful contact with the world will not be achieved "by diminishing the seriousness" of the monastic vocation. "The monk who simply confronts the world of the diaspora with a polite curse, a formula of reprobation and disdain, or even a tear of genuine pity, will not justify his existence in it and will probably cease to exist" (210). Although the monastery is not organized for dialogue with the world, Merton sees the value of a "*fruitful sense of polarity* in which the monk and, say, the atheist intellectual, are able to discover not only that they can treat one another politely, but that *they are indeed brothers*, and that they share many of the same concerns, for example in the area of world peace, racial justice, and indeed everything that concerns the well-being and development of man" (210–11). In the final piece of this section, "Monastic Thought in the Russian Diaspora," Merton points to Fr. Zossima in Dostoevski's *The Brothers Karamazov* as an embodiment of the ideal *staretz*. "The monk of the diaspora is, then, the charismatic man of God, distinguished from the world only by his humility and his dedication, by his fidelity to life and to truth, rather than by his garments, the cloister in which he lives, by his hieratic gestures and ascetic practices" (217).

"A Tribute to Gandhi" also appeared in *Ramparts* in December 1964. Merton begins the essay by recalling Gandhi's visit to England in 1931 and remembering how he argued about Gandhi in the dormitory at Oakham. "How could Gandhi be right when he was *odd*? And how could I be right if I was on the side of someone who had the wrong kind of skin, and left altogether too much of it exposed?" (222). Years later Merton continued to be moved by the witness of this nonviolent man whose dedication to the service of truth and the way of nonviolence exemplified what Merton saw to be at the very core of the Christian gospel. Gandhi understood the message of the gospel better than many Christians did. "He is one of the very few men of our time who applied Gospel principles to the problems of a political and social existence in such a way that his approach to these problems was *inseparably* religious and political at the same time" (226). For Merton, Gandhi is a model to be imitated.

Part 3, "Letters in a Time of Crisis," consists of thirty-five letters that Merton selected for publication from among the "Cold War Letters," a mimeographed collection of letters on war and peace that Merton wrote between October 1961 and October 1962. Merton's "Cold War Letters" appear not as a complete collection but scattered throughout the five volumes of Merton's letters, published under the general editorship of William H. Shannon. Each of the "Cold War Letters" is labeled and numbered as it appears in the volumes. Although the letters cover a range of topics and themes, all reveal Merton's sense of urgency in the face of impending global crisis. Unfortunately, not all the recipients of the letters included in *Seeds of Destruction* are identified, nor are the letters dated.[3] Among those included in the book are letters that Merton wrote to James Baldwin, Dorothy Day, Catherine de Hueck Doherty, Jacques Maritain, and Mark Van Doren.

There were problems with the publication of *Seeds of Destruction*. On June 2, 1964, Merton noted in his journal that Robert Giroux wrote to the abbot general and "got a settlement. One essay on war may be printed if I will 'transform' it" (*Water of Life*, 107). Ten days later Merton noted that he had finished rewriting "the peace section" of *Seeds of Destruction* (108). On July 14 Merton wrote that "the long section on peace for *Seeds of Destruction* had been passed without change by the General! Thus the real heart of the forbidden book, *Peace in the Post-Christian Era*, is to be published after all" (127). While the section on peace had created problems with the order, the essay on racism drew negative responses from

some readers. "Reviews on the new book come in and I am beginning to think it is my most non-understood book. The essay on race is not according to the liberal party line at all, and people read it, get miffed, and then don't read the rest" (*School of Charity*, 264). One of those most "miffed" was Martin Marty, historian of American religion at the University of Chicago. At the time, Marty strongly criticized Merton for questioning the sincerity of white liberals, but in August 1967 Marty apologized, in print, for his failure to recognize the prophetic truth of what Merton had written.[4] CMB

> SEE ALSO CIVIL RIGHTS MOVEMENT; "COLD WAR LETTERS"; NONVIOLENCE; PEACE; RACISM; WAR.

Notes

1. See Merton's poem "Picture of a Black Child with a White Doll," in *Collected Poems*, 626–27.

2. An earlier version of this article appeared as a review of Karl Rahner's *The Christian Commitment* in *Commonweal* (March 20, 1964), *Blackfriars* (July–August 1964), and *Ramparts* (October 1964).

3. For a listing of the "Cold War Letters," see *The Hidden Ground of Love* and *Witness to Freedom*.

4. See William H. Shannon, *Silent Lamp* (New York: Crossroad, 1993), 228–29.

SELECTED POEMS OF THOMAS MERTON

This collection was issued in two editions. The first (New York: New Directions, 1959 [xvii + 140 pp.]) includes an introduction by Mark Van Doren, seventy-two poems (sixty-eight from Thomas Merton's first five collections plus four additional poems), and his essay "Poetry and Contemplation: A Reappraisal," which first appeared in *Commonweal* in 1958. The contents, selected by Merton himself, include sixteen of the *Thirty Poems* (1944), all but two of which date from before Merton entered Gethsemani (printed according to the slightly different order found in the appendix to *A Man in the Divided Sea*); twenty-six of the fifty-six poems in *A Man in the Divided Sea* (1946) (sixteen of which are premonastic); three of the eight sections from the title sequence of *Figures for an Apocalypse* (1948), along with seven of the remaining twenty-six poems; eight of the seventeen poems from *The Tears of the*

Blind Lions (1949); eight of the twenty-two pieces from The Strange Islands (1957) (these are printed in an order different from that of the original volume); and four poems previously unpublished in book form (the first of these, "A Practical Program for Monks," does not appear in any other volume of Merton's verse before the Collected Poems [where it is included in appendix 3, "Humorous Verse"]; the other three were later included in Emblems of a Season of Fury). This edition of Selected Poems includes just over 42 percent of the poems from Merton's first five collections (counting the eight sections of "Figures for an Apocalypse" individually), sixty-eight poems of a possible 159 pieces; of these, thirty (of a possible fifty-two) were written before Merton entered Gethsemani (almost 58 percent), an indication of how highly Merton thought of his early work; thirty-eight monastic poems (of a possible 107) were included (35.5 percent).

The enlarged edition (New York: New Directions, 1967) omits the concluding essay and substitutes sixteen additional poems (for a total of nineteen out of thirty) from Emblems of a Season of Fury (1963) (the number of poems added apparently was determined by the amount of space made available by the removal of the essay; the total number of pages in the two editions remains the same). The percentage of monastic verse included in this edition rises to slightly over 41.5 percent (fifty-seven poems of a possible 137, not counting "A Practical Program for Monks"). Except for a slight change to Van Doren's introduction (in reference to "Poetry and Contemplation"), it is otherwise identical in its contents with the first edition.

Almost all of Merton's best-known poems can be found in the Selected Poems, including, for example, "Song for Our Lady of Cobre," "For My Brother, Reported Missing in Action, 1943," and "The Trappist Abbey: Matins" from Thirty Poems; "The Ohio River — Louisville," "Aubade — Harlem," and "The Trappist Cemetery — Gethsemani" from A Man in the Divided Sea; "On the Anniversary of My Baptism," "Freedom as Experience," and "The Sowing of Meanings" from Figures for an Apocalypse; "The Reader" and "Senescente Mundo" from

The Tears of the Blind Lions; "Elegy for the Monastery Barn," "The Guns of Fort Knox," and "Wisdom" from The Strange Islands; "O Sweet Irrational Worship," "Grace's House," "Love Winter When the Plant Says Nothing," "Chant to Be Used in Processions around a Site with Furnaces," "Night-flowering Cactus," and "A Song for Nobody" from Emblems of a Season of Fury. Among the relatively few exceptions, these can be mentioned: "The Quickening of St. John the Baptist" from The Tears of the Blind Lions; "In Silence," "Stranger," and particularly "Elias — Variations on a Theme" from The Strange Islands; and "Song: If you seek . . ." and especially the prose poem "Hagia Sophia" from Emblems of a Season of Fury. The lengths of the Baptist poem, "Elias," and "Hagia Sophia" may have been at least partially responsible for their omission.

An unrelated British edition also entitled Selected Poems was published by Hollis and Carter (London) in 1950 with a foreword by Robert Speaight. It includes sixty-six poems, selected by Speaight, not Merton: fifteen from Thirty Poems (these are listed under A Man in the Divided Sea rather than separately); twenty-four from A Man in the Divided Sea; fifteen from Figures for an Apocalypse; and eleven from The Tears of the Blind Lions (a twelfth poem, "Sports Without Blood," listed under this volume, originally was intended to be included in it but in fact was published in book form only in The Strange Islands: [see Merton's comment on the poem in the preface to The Strange Islands]; Speaight may have been working from a prepublication text of The Tears of the Blind Lions in which "Sports Without Blood" was still included; his ordering of the poems from this volume also differs from the text as published).

The British edition includes 55 percent of the poems in Merton's first four collections (counting "Figures for an Apocalypse," none of which appears, as a single poem, and not including "Sports Without Blood"). Although Speaight makes only indirect reference to Merton's work in verse before entering Gethsemani, exactly half the poems included are in fact premonastic (thirty-three of a possible fifty-two, over 63 percent), while slightly less than 42 percent of the available monastic poems are included (thirty-three of seventy-nine, again counting "Figures for an Apocalypse" as a single poem, but including "Sports Without Blood"); only a single monastic poem (of a possible six) from *Thirty Poems* ("For My Brother, Reported Missing in Action") is included, and only five (of a possible twenty-eight) from *A Man in the Divided Sea*; fifteen are taken from *Figures for an Apocalypse* (of a possible twenty-seven), and twelve (of a possible seventeen) from *The Tears of the Blind Lions*, which Speaight considers Merton's best collection.

It is interesting to note that fully half of the poems included in this edition are not found in the American *Selected Poems*. Notable among these are "Iphigenia — Politics" and "An Argument — of the Passion of Christ" from *Thirty Poems*; "The Bombarded City" "Aubade — The Annunciation," and "Ode to the Present Century" from *A Man in the Divided Sea*; "Song: Contemplation," "St. John's Night," and "Theory of Prayer" from *Figures for an Apocalypse*; and "Christopher Columbus" and "The Quickening of St. John the Baptist" from *The Tears of the Blind Lions*. Among better-known poems from the first four collections not selected are "The Trappist Abbey — Matins" from *Thirty Poems*; "Aubade — Harlem" and "Trappists, Working" from *A Man in the Divided Sea*; "The Sowing of Meanings" (as well as any section of the title sequence) from *Figures for an Apocalypse*; and "A Psalm" and "*Senescente Mundo*" from *The Tears of the Blind Lions* (all of which appear in the American *Selected Poems*). POC

SELF

A central theme that weaves its way through Thomas Merton's writings is that sanctity consists in discovering our true identity. The essence of the spiritual quest is our search for our true, or real, self. In an early work (1949) he writes, "For me to be a saint means to be myself. Therefore the problem of sanctity and salvation is in fact the problem of finding out who I am and of discovering my true self" (*Seeds of Contemplation*, 26). In the same chapter he identifies what is at the heart of the problem of discovering one's identity: "every one of us is shadowed by an illusory person: a false self"

(28). Thus, very early in his writings, Merton introduces two terms (that will recur repeatedly in his later writings) that we must understand if we are to grasp what he has to say about the achievement of personal identity. The goal in the quest for self-identity is the "true self"; the villain who obstructs the way is the "false self." How does Merton understand these terms?

First, what does he mean by the term "false self"? He does not, it seems, intend primarily to see the false self as "false" in a moral sense, as if the false self were untruthful, sinful, immoral. No doubt it can, and perhaps often does, have that meaning. But such a meaning is derivative and does not catch the primary sense in which he uses the term "false self." Merton is thinking more in ontological terms. This is to say that the adjective "false" conveys the notion of unsubstantiality, of lacking in any fullness of being. The false self is deficient in being — deficient especially in the sense that it is impermanent, not enduring. Thus Merton writes, "This outer self [a synonym for 'false self'] is nothing but an evanescent shadow. Its biography and its existence both end together at death" (*New Seeds of Contemplation*, 279). He explicitly states that the "the self that exists only in my ego-centric desires" has "no substance." It is "hollow," destined by its very contingency to be destroyed (35).

That the false self has this ontological meaning for Merton is also borne out by reflection on the adjectives he uses in his writings as substitutes for "false" — for example, "superficial," "empirical," "outward," "exterior," "alienated," "shadow," "smoke," "contingent," "imaginary," "private," "illusory," and "petty." All these adjectives suggest, in various ways, that we are dealing with a self that is "real," but only at a very limited level of reality. The false self keeps us for the most part on the surface of reality: both its joys and its fears are superficial. It is limited *by* time and space and *to* time and space. This means that it has a biography and a history, both of which we write by the actions we perform and the roles we play and both of which are destined to cease with death. This is why Merton calls it an "evanescent" self or a "smoke" self that will disappear like smoke up a chimney. Its well-being needs to be fed constantly by accomplishments and by the approval and admiration of others. It is the ego-self, the self as object, or, in Merton's words, "The self which we observe as it goes about its biological business, the machine which we regulate and tune up and feed with all kinds of stimulants and sedatives, constantly trying to make it run more and more smoothly, to fit the patterns prescribed by the salesman of pleasure-giving and anxiety-allaying commodities" (*Faith and Violence*, 112).

The false self is a self of changing emotions — now up, now down. It exists not at any deep level of reality, but only in our egocentric desires: the desire to manipulate, to be recognized, to be praised, to possess, to accumulate. "The tragedy of a life centered on 'things,' on the grasping and manipulation of objects, is that such a life closes the ego upon itself, as though it were an end in itself, and throws it into a hopeless struggle with other perverse and hostile selves competing together for the possession, which will give them power and satisfaction" (*Birds of Appetite*, 82). Such a false self has no voice of its own; it speaks the voice of the anonymous collectivity. In our time the media generally are the source from which it derives its judgments and opinions. It has objectified itself; that is, it has made itself into an object that can be talked about and described. This means that it has lost touch with its own subjectivity and therefore, quite literally, does not (and cannot ever) know itself.

This does not mean that we limit the false self to the realm of the conscious. In "The Inner Experience" Merton reflects on the false self using the synonym "exterior self": "Those recesses of the unconscious, in which neurotic and psychotic derangement have their center, belong in reality to man's exterior self. ... Freud's concept of the super-ego as an infantile and introjected substitute for conscience fits very well my idea of the exterior and alienated self. It is at once completely exterior and yet at the same time buried in unconsciousness. So too with the Freudian concept of the 'id,' insofar as it represents an automatic complex of drives toward pleasure or destruction, in response to external stimuli" ("Inner Experience," 22).

Life's most pressing task is to unmask this false, illusory self and become "aware of the presence within us of a disturbing stranger, the self that is both 'I' and someone else. The self that is not entirely welcome in his own house because he is so different from the everyday character that we have constructed out of our dealings with others — and our infidelities to ourselves."[1]

What must we do to move beyond this empirical ego, this ego-self, which alienates us from our true being, and recover that true and substantial self, which is beyond and above the level of mere empirical individuality with its superficial enjoyments and fears? The Christian answer (and there are similar answers in other religions) is that there must be death and rebirth. "In order to become oneself, one must die. That is to say, in order to become one's true self, the false self must die" (*Love and Living*, 196). This means, Merton tells us, "a deepening of the new life, a continuous rebirth, in which the exterior and superficial life of the ego-self is discarded like an old snake skin and the mysterious, invisible self of the Spirit becomes more present and more active" (199). In discarding our false self we are born again. Yet this new birth does not mean that we become someone else. We become ourselves. We become the true self that God willed us to be. (Merton uses a number of descriptive adjectives in his writings to describe this self — for example, "true self," "inner and hidden self," "creative mysterious inner self," "inner self," "inmost self," "real self," "deepest most hidden self.")

This process of rebirth is not a single event, but a continuous dynamic of inner renewal. It is a transformation in which we are "progressively liberated from selfishness and not only grow in love, but in some sense 'become love,' The perfection of this new birth is reached where there is no more selfishness, there is only love. In the language of the mystics, there is no more ego-self, there is only Christ; self no longer acts, only the Spirit acts in pure love" (199).

How do we arrive at this state of pure love? How do we transcend the ego-self and discover (or, better, recover) our true self? Merton's answer would be that this consummation is reached either in death or in contemplation, which is to say that it is either an eschatological experience or an in-depth prayer experience that transforms our consciousness. For death is better understood not as the separation of the soul from the body, but as the disappearance of the false self and the emergence of the true self, "that mysterious and unknown 'self' whom most of us never discover until we are dead" (*New Seeds of Contemplation*, 7). Death is not a "passion" (something that happens to us); rather, it is an action (something that we do). What this means is that at last we are able to act with the fullest degree of freedom. No longer bound by the limitations of space and time, we are able to cast aside the illusions that once were so captivating and, in an emptiness never heretofore experienced, we are enabled at last to affirm our true identity. We discover in death what was always true, but which we were not conscious of: we are and always have been in God. What we never come to know in our mortal life, but in death come to know with full attentive awareness, is that we are and always have been in paradise.

On this side of the eschatological awakening, the only way we can realize our true identity is in contemplation, for contemplation is the awakening of the true self. This awakening means death in order to achieve life. "To enter into the realm of contemplation one must in a certain sense die: but this death is in fact the entrance into a higher life" (2). For "contemplation is the highest expression of man's intellectual and spiritual life. [It] is that life fully awake, fully active, fully aware that it is alive." It is "a vivid realization . . . that life and being in us proceed from an invisible, transcendent and infinitely abundant Source. . . . It is, above all, awareness of the reality of that 'Source'" (1) in a simple spiritual vision that goes beyond reason and beyond simple faith. Contemplation does not mean finding a clear concept of God and limiting God to that concept; rather, "contemplation is being carried away by Him into His own realm, His own mystery and His own freedom" (5). We do not bring God down to our own level; instead, God raises us to the divine level, where we are "at one with everything in that hidden ground of Love for which

there can be no explanations" (*Hidden Ground of Love*, 115).

One problem needs to be discussed. What has been said thus far easily could lead to the impression that there are three entities involved in our achieving our true identity. For example, it was said that we must move beyond our empirical self and recover our true and substantial self. Who is the "we" that must do this moving and recovering? Does this suggest that when we talk about true self and false self, somehow there is a third party that *has* these two selves and in whom they battle to see who will win out? This problem clearly is present in a text in which Merton writes about the spiritual journey of the desert fathers of Egypt, a journey that is an inner journey and far more important than a journey into outer space. "What can we gain by sailing to the moon, if we are not able to cross the abyss that separates us from ourselves?" (*Wisdom of the Desert*, 11). He is saying that we have to cross the abyss that separates our surface consciousness from the deep realms of the spiritual unconscious. Only when we cross over do we become our true self. Now if my true self is on the other side of the abyss, who is it that crosses over the abyss? At this point dualistic language simply breaks down. No one crosses over and there is no crossing over. The true self simply *is*, in all its grandeur and in all its littleness. The true self was always there. It had to be awakened.

The awakening of the true self marks the end of dualism, for the true self is my own subjectivity united to the subjectivity of God. My experience of God is an experience of total and radical dependence on God, but at the same time an experience of the God upon whom I am so totally and radically dependent. It would be a mistake, however, to think of these as two different experiences. No, coming to know God in the divine selfhood and coming to know our true selves converge in a single intuition: our awareness of our total dependence on God. When we know God, we know ourselves; when we know ourselves, we know God. As Merton puts it, "Our knowledge of God is paradoxically a knowledge not of him as the object of our scrutiny, but of ourselves as utterly dependent on his saving and merciful knowledge of us" (*Contemplative Prayer*, 103–4). WHS

SEE ALSO CONTEMPLATION; FREEDOM; NONDUALISM.

Notes

1. "Creative Silence," *The Baptist Student* (June 1968). This also appears in *Love and Living*, 40. In *Love and Living* the last phrase in the quotation is "our infidelities in ourselves," instead of "to ourselves."

"SENSATION TIME AT THE HOME AND OTHER NEW POEMS"

This collection of twenty-nine pieces was never published as a separate volume; it is included as appendix 1 of *The Collected Poems of Thomas Merton* (611–65). The bulk of the material originally was to be published as part 2 of what was to be called "Edifying Cables and Other New Poems," dated September 1966. When "Edifying Cables" was expanded to become *Cables to the Ace* and eventually published by itself, the shorter poems of part 2 were set aside to be issued at a later date in a somewhat expanded and revised edition. Of the original twenty-three pieces, one ("The Prospects of Nostradamus") was incorporated into the revised *Cables to the Ace*, and another ("Long Enough," the final poem in the collection) was omitted — whether intentionally or inadvertently; the rest are included in almost exactly the same order in the retitled "Sensation Time at the Home," with the addition of eight more pieces, two at the beginning and the other six interspersed toward the end. Because of the publication of *Cables to the Ace* and then of *The Geography of Lograire,* the appearance of this collection of shorter poems was postponed, and due to Merton's death and the subsequent process of preparing the *Collected Poems* for publication, it was never issued separately.

The tone and even the style of much of the volume is very close to that of *Cables to the Ace,* with its sometimes ironic, sometimes blatant critique of the violence and spiritual bankruptcy of contemporary society. The opening poem, "The Originators" (no. 1; 24 ll.) provides an appropriate, and appropriately enigmatic, warning about the possible impact of what is to follow: "every morning / At about four ... influence goes out of my windows / Over the suburbs / Get out of the way of my ideas" (ll. 15–18); the concluding lines provide a prediction and an anticipation of the wild course that is to follow: "O Brothers and Sisters here we go again / Flip-flopping all over the circus / With airs of invention" (ll. 22–24).

The title poem (no. 12; 43 ll.), with its recycling of advertising clichés ("Save $$$$$ / (For a limited time) / In a smashing program / To resettle limbs and renew skin" [ll. 9–12]) and reduction of meaning to a succession of sensual stimuli ("Spasms are guaranteed / To relax giant smiles" [18–19]), is an updated equivalent of Pascal's critique of *divertissement* ("Free of ennui / On the sensation farm / For the whole family" [ll. 21–23]). "First Lesson About Man" (no. 9; 43 ll.) considers the consequence of a reductively materialist anthropology (no "joy / Except in zoology" [ll. 18–19]) to be a restlessness without direction or purpose, an anxiety that has now expanded into space: "He flies his worries / All around Venus / But it does him no good" (ll. 30–32). The loss of a mythic consciousness is also evident in "The Lion" (no. 20; 35 ll.), in which the stars have been reduced to "glistening points / Of exasperation" (ll. 8–9) and "All classic shapes have vanished / From alien heavens" (ll. 12–13). Likewise, "Tonight There Is a Showing of Champion Lights" (no. 11; 38 ll.) implicitly contrasts the emptiness of a sterile scientism ("two thousand billion years of *nada*" [l. 29]) with the fertile "nothingness" of a St. John of the Cross, and a passionless analysis of the universe with the conviction of cosmic vitality of a Gerard Manley Hopkins ("'O look, look up at all the firefolk' sitting in the mind / Of the champion blackboard" [ll. 34–35]). In "A Tune for Festive Dances in the Nineteen Sixties" (no. 14; 47 ll.) the dehumanization of man the questioner, the removal of any "sign of doubt or double desire" (l. 5), is seen as crucial for the triumph of a truly "orderly" world in which "the machine / Will stand out trim because it likes / All the numbers of the strong white spikes" (ll. 15–17).

"Man the Master" (no. 17; 85 ll.) presents a kind of collective human personality in which the intent to be "master" proves both self-contradictory and self-destructive: "Here comes . . . / The all-time winner / To lead his squad against himself / Into the fiery question / (Each is his own question / Each pumps deadly lights / In honor of his own answer / Each is his answer)" (ll. 22–29). This intersection of identity confusion with violence is found also in "Hopeless and Felons" (no. 24; 35 ll.), in which the felons of the title, who claimed that "they were friends of all men / Regardless of color etc." (ll. 14–15), nevertheless "design war / Games against innocent owners / Stained so dark / They do not recognize / Their own faces" (ll. 2–6) — that is, they fail to see their shared humanity in those they oppress and attack, both Southern blacks and Southeast Asians. The irrationality of war also is central to "Secular Signs" (no. 22; 27 ll.), in which the religious sanction given to war is represented by the "Three lost lights" (l. 1), "A long fire" (l. 7), "Darkness" (l. 13), and "The proverbs of mistaken counsel" (l. 26), all described as having been "blest by priests" (ll. 1, 7, 13, 27). In "Fall '66" (no. 21; 28 ll.) the legendary expectation of the return of King Arthur becomes a nightmarish vision of an eruption from the underworld in which "Infernal smoke / Fills Washington and Camelot [an ironic echo of the Kennedy years?] / And ashes cut the sight of red-eyed intelligence" (ll. 7–9) — that is, the CIA and similar agencies that can see only a threat of communism and announce, "There, in the Far East, are the malefactors" (l. 16). In "The Great Men of Former Times" (no. 8; 42 ll.) the link between war and business is highlighted as the military theorist Clausewitz and great generals of the past repeatedly are encountered haunting the stock exchange because they "have nowhere else to go / Nowhere else to go" (ll. 5–6) and threaten to prove ("By killing you" [l. 21]) their disbelief that the era of war is over because "It is sufficient to 'deter'" (l. 18). The final piece, the deliberately enigmatic prose text "Ben's Last Fight" (no. 29; 3 parts), provides vivid descriptions of "Ben's" three successive fights, only to challenge the reader to make sense of "the fable with the conclusion," with the implication that the search for winners and losers is in the end futile and meaningless.

Two of the poems deal in very different ways with the civil rights movement. "Picture of a Black Child with a White Doll" (no. 10; 41 ll.) is a reflection on a photograph of Carole Denise McNair, the youngest of the four children killed in the September 1963 Birmingham church bombing. It juxtaposes the "experience" of the speaker, who sees the doll (a Barbie or the like) that the child holds in the picture as an image of the artificiality, blindness, and crass commercialism of the dominant white culture, with the innocence of the child, who responds with love, nurture, and caring to the doll not despite but because of the fact that it is "plastic glass-eyed / Merchandise" (ll. 3–4). The speaker's bitter loathing thus is countered by the child's own compassion, not simply a pitiable ignorance of the harsh reality of white hatred but an instinctive recognition of white need, white failure, white inability to love. The child becomes an icon of "risen and Christian / Africa" (ll. 31–32), a sign of the redemptive Christ that, like Christ, has been rejected and destroyed by a world that has refused to recognize the time of its salvation. "Plessy vs. Ferguson: Theme and Variations" (no. 28), a prose "anti-poem" of twenty-one sections, takes a very different approach to the question of racial injustice, providing testimony to the distortion of language in the service of oppressive power by drawing out the absurd implications of the actual text of the 1896 "separate but equal" court decision and concluding that the current ideology of "black power" is the "logical" consequence of the Plessy statute.

Contemporary disregard for oppression is projected back into an earlier era in "A Baroque Gravure" (no. 4; 37 ll.), which describes a portrait "From a 17th-century Book of Piety" in which a "devout and plump, but not happy" (l. 1) woman's preoccupation with "Her own cross" (l. 32) makes her totally unresponsive, indeed insensible, to the sufferings of the "blackamoors / In chains" (ll. 7–8) depicted in the background of the picture. "Welcome" (no. 23; 30 ll.) suggests the classic scenario of invasion and conquest as a ship with its "forest of guilty masts / And climbing animals" (ll. 1–2) is metamorphosed into a modern "cruiser" with its "sunken mischief" that "Fills the bay with chances" (ll. 25–26) and once again sets its sights on the "fortunes" and "elegant memories" of "The Inca city of stone" (ll. 27–29). In another historical tableau with current relevance, the prose poem "Rites for the Extrusion of a Leper" (no. 28; 11 secs.), readers are invited to recognize that society continues to practice its own rituals for casting out "lepers," the marginalized, the unacceptable, that in fact "This very day the long-hanjed meazel [sic] is the one who is eating our breakfast" (prefatory "Note").

A small group of poems focuses on other writers. "Seneca" (no. 5; 22 ll.) contrasts the experience of the Roman stoic philosopher, who "promenades / Within his own temple / Master and censor / Overseeing / His own ways" (ll. 9–13), with that of his wife, who "waits in darkness / For the Night Bird's / Inscrutable cry" (ll. 20–22); in view of the ultimate fate of Seneca, forced to commit suicide by his erstwhile pupil Nero, the wife's vague forebodings are more prescient than her husband's confident self-possession. "Rilke's Epitaph" (no. 6; 18 ll.) rings changes on the actual inscription on the gravestone of one of Merton's favorite poets, in which the experience of the *"Music"* of Rilke's verse finally transcends death and *"nobody's / Sleep"* (ll. 3–4 [from the actual epitaph]) is transformed into *"Everybody's / Vision"* (ll. 17–18). "For the Spanish Poet Miguel Hernandez" (no. 19; 32 ll.) likens the treatment of the tormented poet to that of a bull in the ring, when "Every man's last truth / Shines red like a rag / Snatched on the blade's end" (ll. 29–31). "Reading Translated Poets, Feb. 1" (no. 7; 57 ll.) describes this experience first in terms of fragmentary impressions and evidence left behind like "the precise ruin / Of an eaten kill" (ll. 49–50), but finally as one of renewal and coherence, "an incredible local Easter. / A warmer season" (ll. 56–57).

Two of the poems are directly autobiographical, reflective of Merton's experience of back surgery in March 1966. "With the World in My Bloodstream" (no. 3; 97 ll.), originally the opening poem of the collection (and also the first of the *Eighteen Poems* published in 1985), depicts the speaker's immersion in "The world's machinery" (l. 15) and consequent loss of a sense of personal identity during his hospital stay, which leads ultimately to the awareness that his deepest truth is found in what Meister Eckhart called the spark of the soul, "the accurate little spark / in emptiness" (ll. 75–76). In realizing that "Only the spark is now true" (l. 86), the speaker finds his true self in Christ: "I am Christ's lost cell / His childhood and desert age / His descent into hell" (ll. 91–93). In "A Carol" (no. 25; 31 ll.), a more sardonic treatment of the same experience, the speaker presents his "broken back" (l. 1) to Jesus as a Christmas gift, juxtaposing the birth of Christ both with the awareness of his own mortality ("So Juniors see my borrowed body in the stable / Cutting one more cold night out of the funeral's domain" [ll. 23–24]) and with death as a result of war, suggested by the parenthetical insertions "Never trust / The military sun" (l. 7), "... The military air" (l. 14), "... The military rain" (l. 31).

Explicitly religious or spiritual poems make up a smaller percentage of this volume than of any previous collection. "Origen" (no. 18; 47 ll.) celebrates and defends the controversial legacy of the church's first great theologian, noting that "His sin was to speak first / Among mutes" (ll. 1–2); after tracing his condemnation by various ecclesiastical officials, particularly for his doctrine of universal salvation, the poem concludes by focusing on his continued influence on the great figures of the High Middle Ages, "Bernards and Abelards together" (l. 42), attracted above all by the all-embracing "compassion in this man / Who thought he heard all beings / From stars to stones, angels to elements, alive / Crying for the Redeemer with a live grief" (ll. 44–47). A more contemporary celebration is "Elegy for a Trappist" (no. 13; 35 ll.) (originally titled "Elegy for Father Stephen"), an affectionate tribute to a rather eccentric fellow monk whose passionate love for flowers was his (not always appreciated) way of responding to and reflecting the divine presence: "Master of the sudden enthusiastic gift / In an avalanche / Of flower catalogues / And boundless love" (ll. 11–14).

Two poems draw on the Islamic tradition that Merton was exploring with increasing interest in his final years. "Lubnan" (no. 2; 28 ll.)

(based on the writings of the Sufi mystic Ibn al' Arabi) reflects Merton's continued fascination with the figure of Elijah; drawing on a tradition that identifies Idris (i.e., Enoch) and Ilyas (Elias), the two biblical figures taken up to heaven while still alive, the poem traces their/his descent into the chaos of human sinfulness and subsequent ascent to the heavens, and foresees a future return, an eschatological revelation "When the vision / Will be total" (ll. 27–28). In "The Night of Destiny" (no. 15; 31 ll.), a meditation on the conclusion of Ramadan, the darkness suggests the apophatic way to God and intimates a unity of spiritual experience inaccessible to the rational mind: "My love is darkness! / Only in the Void / Are all ways one: / Only in the night / Are all the lost / Found" (ll. 25–30).

"Early Blizzard" (no. 26; 33 ll.) presents a snowstorm experienced at the hermitage as a contemplative immersion in which "It feels good to be without hearing / In the lone house. . . . / Or out following the hidden ways / The ways of instinct" (ll. 4–5, 7–8), and advises the reader to "Sink in the hidden wood / And let the weather / Be what it is" (ll. 26–28). But the most deeply contemplative poem of the collection is the one written (in rhymed dimeter quatrains) in French, "Le Secret" (no. 16; 56 ll.), in which the naked heart is said to hide nothing, keep nothing, know nothing, dream nothing (ll. 13–18), an experience of total emptiness that is at the same time complete fullness, so that in the depths of night the poet is both no one and everyone ("Dans la nuit / La plus profonde / Je suis personne / Et tout le monde" [ll. 37–40]), a figure who has surrendered all identity except that of "un oiseau / Enchanté" (ll. 53–54) ("an enchanted bird"), "Amour que Dieu / A inventé" (ll. 55–56) ("Love which God has devised"). POC

SEVEN STOREY MOUNTAIN, THE

New York: Harcourt, Brace, 1948. 429 pp.[1]

The Seven Storey Mountain is Thomas Merton's narrative of his life story from the year of his birth (1915) to the year in which he made his solemn vows as a monk at the Abbey of Our Lady of Gethsemani (1947). This story of aimlessness finding peace in faith became an instant bestseller (some six hundred thousand copies sold in its first year of publication). It has drawn hundreds of thousands of people to Thomas Merton — people of different backgrounds, religions, races, countries, and continents. And after more than half a century it remains in print.

The book came at just the right time. In 1948 people were recovering from the havoc of the Second World War. This story of one man's search for meaning and purpose in life struck a responsive chord in the hearts of countless women and men who, like Merton, were looking for a significance to life that went beyond the superficial and the temporal. They found Merton putting into words what they were experiencing but not able to articulate. They also discovered insights that helped make sense out of life's confusion. The reviewer for the *Chicago Sun* put it well: the book is "a hymn of positive faith sung in the midst of a purposeless world searching for purpose, a book that can be read by men of any faith or none at all."[2]

This is not to say that the book is without faults. Its pages are marked by the triumphalism of pre–Vatican II Roman Catholicism, excessive moralizing, and a dualistic understanding of reality that separated creation from God and divided the secular from the sacred. The immanence of God gets absorbed into the divine transcendence.

Yet the story is compellingly told. The personal magnetism of the author is engaging. The book is the work of someone born a writer. It is so vivid and alive that his shortcomings are transcended and the reader is swept along by the power of this young man's story as he tries to make sense out of a hitherto undisciplined life. *The Seven Storey Mountain* captivated a generation of readers when it was published and continues to do so after more than half a century. Readers see the mystery of their own story mirrored in his. They can begin to identify with what he says toward the end of the story: "The life of each [one of us] is part of a mystery. . . . In one sense we are always travelling, and travelling as if we did not know where we were going. In another sense we have already arrived" (*Seven Storey Mountain*, 419). Perceptive readers will realize that there are three levels of meaning to think about in dealing with this book: (1) the level of history, what actually happened; (2) the level of memory, what he recalled and chose to write; and (3) the level of interpretation, the meaning given to Thomas Merton's story by the Trappist monk, Fr. Louis.

Merton took his title from the seven-circled mountain of Dante's *Purgatorio*.[3] The theme of the book is the gradual purification of desires, as Merton moves away from the false loves that had attracted him in his youth to the love of God and of the things of the spirit.

He made no attempt to follow the order of *Purgatorio*. Structurally, the book has three parts. There are four chapters each in parts 1 and 3, and two chapters in part 2. The book concludes with an epilogue and has an index.

Part 1 (pages 3–165)

Part 1 covers twenty-two years of his life: from his birth (1915) to the death of his maternal grandmother (1937).

Chapter 1, "Prisoner's Base," narrates the story of his childhood up to the age of ten. The title takes its name from a child's game, played by two teams, in which each team tries to capture members of the other team and bring them to a base, where they have to stay as prisoners. At the beginning of the chapter he speaks of himself as "the prisoner of my own violence and my own selfishness" (3). He sees his parents as "captives" in a world they did not really belong to. His mother, Ruth (Jenkins), died when he was six. He continued to "play the game of 'Prisoner's Base,'" as he was "tagged" and brought by his father to places not of his own choosing — Bermuda and France, for example. The chapter concludes with his father's announcement that they were going to France. "And on August the twenty-fifth of that year [1925], the game of Prisoner's Base began again, and we sailed for France" (28–29).

Chapter 2, "Our Lady of the Museums," tells his story during the years in France. He and his father, Owen, settled in the medieval town of St. Antonin, where Owen made plans to build a house. But, as he was more interested in painting than in building, Owen spent much of his time traveling the countryside looking for good subjects for pictures, leaving little time for construction work. Young Tom tagged along and often found himself wandering in the ruins of ancient chapels and monasteries (the reason for this chapter's title). But he was young and needed schooling. In 1926 he was enrolled in the Lycée Ingres at Montauban. He was not happy there (it was yet another prisoner's base[4]), though he adjusted and eventually became involved with a group of young writers, furiously writing novels and critiquing one another's works. In May 1928 his father arrived at the school with what his son saw as a message of freedom: they were leaving for England. It is sad though, he remarks, that they never got to live in the house that Owen had begun to build but never finished (60).

Chapter 3 is titled "The Harrowing of Hell." In autumn 1929 Thomas Merton entered the Oakham public school in Rutland County in the English Midlands. He was reasonably happy at Oakham, a happiness shadowed by his father's terminal illness. In January 1931 Owen died, leaving Tom an orphan at the age of sixteen, albeit under the care of his guardian, Tom Izod Bennett. He graduated from Oakham in January of 1933. A trip to Rome brought a momentary conversion as he fell in love with the mosaics in the churches of Rome. The conversion did not last. He returned to America in the summer, and in the autumn of 1933 he entered Clare College, Cambridge, quite likely an unbeliever at the time. The year proved a disaster: too much drinking, too little study, too much "womanizing." His guardian advised him to return to America to his maternal grandparents. The whole year had been, as the title of this chapter suggests, a "harrowing," distressing experience for him. Toward the end of the chapter there are a number of references to "hell." He speaks of "burning in the flames of my own hell," rotting "in the hell of my own corrupt will," and seeing "the door to a deeper pit in Hell" (123). These references evoke the chapter's title. The "Harrowing of Hell" refers to a statement in the Creed: "[Christ] descended into hell" (i.e., Hades, the lower regions). There, Christ despoils ("harrows") hell of the souls of the righteous who had been detained there since the beginning of time. The reference to Merton's life is clear: he had fallen into a "hell" from which only Christ could deliver him — something he did not know at the time, but could realize only in retrospect.

Chapter 4 is titled "The Children in the Market Place." Tom returned to America and began his studies at Columbia, where teachers (Mark Van Doren, Daniel Walsh) and significant books (Aldous Huxley's *Ways and Means* and Etienne Gilson's *Spirit of Medieval Philosophy*) moved him toward a more disciplined life and helped to prepare the way for his eventual baptism into the Catholic Church. The title alludes to Matt. 11:16, in which Jesus describes the different reactions of people to himself and to John the Baptist. John was a man of great austerity, and they accused him of having a demon; Jesus ate and drank with all sorts of people, and they called him a drunkard and a friend of sinners. They are, Jesus says, like "children in the marketplace" who are never satisfied. "We played the flute for you and you did not dance; we wailed and you did not mourn."

The title aptly describes Merton's up-and-down life at Columbia in the early years. He delighted in university life, yet at the same time he experienced an inner emptiness. Thus, at one point he could say, "I had discovered in myself something of a capacity for work and for activity and for enjoyment that I had never dreamed of" (153). Then a few pages later, the reader comes upon this graphically grim statement of his deep anguish of spirit: "I was bleeding to death" (164).

Part 2 (pages 167–255)

Part 2 covers only two and a half years of his life: February 1937 to September 1939.

Chapter 1, "With a Great Price," deals with events leading up to and concluding with the moving account of his baptism into the Catholic Church. The title is part of a verse from Paul's first epistle to the Corinthians, wherein Paul reminds the people of Corinth that they are temples of the Holy Spirit. "For you were bought," he says, "with a price" (1 Cor. 6:20). Merton adds the adjective "great," which is not found in the Greek text, but is in the Latin Vulgate and also in the Rheims New Testament, the only English translation approved for use by Catholics at that time. The title is an expression of Merton's gratitude for the gift of faith bought for him by Christ at the price of Christ's own blood.

Chapter 2, "The Waters of Contradiction," covers the period from after his baptism, through the challenges he faced in his efforts to live up to the demands of this new life of baptism, and concludes with his desire to be a priest. The chapter title comes from Num. 20:13: "These are the waters of Meribah where the people quarreled with the Lord and by which he showed his holiness." Again Merton uses the Rheims translation of the Vulgate, in which the text becomes "waters of contradiction." The context of these words from Numbers is the murmuring of the Israelites against Moses for having brought them out of Egypt. Experiencing the hardships of life in the desert, they look back and begin to feel that life in Egypt was not so bad after all. Their temptation is to want to return to their former life.

After his baptism Merton sees himself as making only half-hearted efforts to live the commitments of his baptism. He fears that he might slip back into the old ways of willfulness and irresponsibility. He was taken up with his desire to be a writer and to see his name in print. Then one day he was caught up short by his friend Robert Lax, who asked him what he wanted to be. The best he could think of was, "I guess what I want is to be a good Catholic" (238). Lax chided him and told him he should have said that he wanted to be a saint. These words had a strong impact. Some weeks later at a holy hour in the Jesuit Church of St. Francis Xavier, he looked at the eucharistic host: "Yes, I want to be a priest, with all my heart I want it. If it is Your will, make me a priest" (255).

Part 3 (pages 257–404)

Part 3 covers almost four years of his life: September 1939 to April 17, 1943.

Chapter 1 is titled "Magnetic North." His desire to be a priest finds expression in his application to join the Franciscan friars. He is accepted as candidate, by Fr. Edmund Mur-phy, to begin his novitiate in September 1940. During the summer, while at Olean, beset with scruples about his past life, he takes the train to New York City to unburden himself to Fr. Murphy. He is advised to withdraw his application. He was crushed, heartbroken. He went across Seventh Avenue to the Capuchin church. "I could not keep back the tears. . . . So I prayed before the Tabernacle and the big stone crucified Christ above the altar" (298).

"Magnetic north" is north as indicated on a compass. It differs from what is geographi-cally the North Pole. Magnetic north always is a bit off from true north. Merton is being led in the right direction: toward a religious commu-nity. But the Franciscan community was not the right one.

Chapter 2 is titled "True North." Having taken a teaching position at St. Bonaventure College, Merton, during Holy Week of 1941, makes a retreat at a monastery that Daniel Walsh had told him about, the Trappist Abbey of Our Lady of Gethsemani, near Bardstown, Kentucky. To say that he was deeply moved by this experience would be a gross understate-ment. "This is the center of all the vitality that is in America. This the cause and reason why the nation is holding together" (325). He left with an ardent desire to return as a postulant. He had discovered "true north."

Chapter 3, "The Sleeping Volcano," cov-ers a brief but extremely significant period in his life: July to December 1941. The longing to be a Trappist smoldering in his heart (the "sleeping volcano") erupts at last when he sum-mons the courage to ask the question he so long feared to ask and receives the assurance (from Franciscan friar Philotheus Boehner) that no impediment exists to his becoming a priest. On December 9, 1941, he took the evening train out of Olean and began his journey toward Gethsemani and his new life.

Chapter 4, "The Sweet Savor of Liberty," narrates his initial years in the monastery and concludes with a poem on the death of his brother, John Paul (April 17, 1943). After years of willfulness and self-centeredness Merton felt he had finally found what it really meant to be free. "Brother Matthew locked the gate behind

me and I was enclosed in the four walls of my new freedom" (372) — an unusual way of de-scribing freedom, but at the time, it was right for this young postulant. He was given the reli-gious name of Louis, and he remembered that it was on the Feast of St. Louis (August 25) that he and his father had set sail for France in 1925. One of the initial problems he strug-gled with in these early years was his desire to write. "I brought all the instincts of a writer with me into the monastery, and I knew that I was bringing them too" (389). It was not a case of smuggling them in either, as Father Master as well as the abbot approved of his writing, even encouraged him when he wrote poems and other reflections.

In July 1942 his brother, John Paul, now a sergeant in the Royal Canadian Air Force, came to visit. The brothers talked and remi-nisced. They also discussed baptism and John Paul's desire for it. On the Feast of St. Anne, July 26, he was baptized in the nearby parish church at New Haven. He departed the next day, and in November he wrote from England. On Easter Monday 1943 Tom received the let-ter in which John Paul told of his marriage. Tom wrote immediately, but he never sent the letter. That very day the abbot summoned him to his room and read him the telegram saying that Sergeant J. P. Merton was missing in action. His plane had crashed in the English Chan-nel. The other members of the crew survived the crash. John Paul did not. He was buried at sea on April 19, 1943. Merton's poem on the death of his brother originally concluded the autobiography.

Epilogue

The epilogue, a later addition, incorporated disparate material: his struggle as a writer ("this shadow, this double, this writer who had followed me into the cloister" [410]), the adaptation of his article on religious life ("Ac-tive and Contemplative Orders," *Commonweal* [December 5, 1947]),[5] and his final prayer (composed on the Feast of the Sacred Heart in 1947).[6]

Merton received the first copy of the book on July 11, 1948, from the hands of his abbot, Dom Frederic Dunne, though the official publication date was October 4, 1948. It was the book that would make him the most famous monk in America. WHS

Notes

1. There have been numerous reprints of *The Seven Storey Mountain*, several paperback editions, and a number of foreign-language translations. On October 4, 1998, a special fiftieth anniversary edition was published by Harcourt, Brace.

2. James O. Supple, *Chicago Sun*, December 28, 1948.

3. There are two references to Dante in *The Seven Storey Mountain*: p. 122 (a class at Cambridge) and p. 221 (the story of his baptism).

4. On p. 49 he calls the Lycée a "prison."

5. This was a very late inclusion (March 1948). It had been suggested to the publisher, Robert Giroux, by Dr. Francis X. Connolly, of Fordham University.

6. See Merton's letter of November 12, 1949, to Sr. Therese Lentfoehr, in which he describes how the epilogue came to be (*Road to Joy*, 197).

SEXUALITY

On the vigil of his fiftieth birthday, Thomas Merton's thoughts turned from the present to the past. "So one thing on my mind is sex, as something I did not use maturely and well, something I gave up without having come to terms with it" (*Water of Life*, 198). Recalling his "last adultery," twenty-five years ago, he is struck by the "madness and futility" (198). At fifty, Merton was recognizing and, perhaps, beginning to come to terms with his past. "I suppose I am the person that lived for a while at 71 Bridge Street, Cambridge, had Sabberton for my tailor (he made me that strange Alphonse Daudet coat, and the tails I wore perhaps twice — once to the boat race ball where I was very selfish and unkind to Joan). And Clare was my College, and I was a damned fool, sitting on the steps of the boat house late at night with Sylvia, when the two fairies came down expecting to get in the boat house, saw us there, turned and hurried away.... All things like that. Adventures" (198). Not all his activities could be termed "adventures." His behavior at Cambridge was promiscuous, and apparently he impregnated a woman that year. None of this is mentioned in *The Seven Storey Mountain*, but Merton's account of Cambridge bears the mark of a time that, in retrospect, filled him with regret. He describes the atmosphere

of Cambridge as "dark" and "sinister," and so it was for him (*Seven Storey Mountain*, 118).

The subject of sex had surfaced in other journal entries. In December 1962 he had admitted that his "sexual adventures were always seductions — I wanted them to be conquests in which in reality I gave nothing, only 'took'" (*Turning toward the World*, 278). In retrospect, he could recognize his "failure to really trust another person enough to give himself completely to her" (278).

In April 1966 Merton met and fell in love with M., a student nurse in her midtwenties who had been assigned to care for him while he was in the hospital for back surgery. With M. he experienced an intimacy that had been lacking in his earlier encounters with women — encounters driven by sexual desire and lacking in love. Merton's feelings for M. were deeply passionate, but perhaps more important is the fact that Merton was speaking of sex *and* love. "Our depths really communicate.... It is the real root and ground of everything, and of this sexual love can only be at best a sign," he wrote on April 25, 1966 (*Learning to Love*, 45). He struggled to act responsibly and to reconcile his love for M. with his monastic vocation and his commitment to a life of solitude. Both love and solitude were "root facts" of his existence. The intensity of his passion and his love spilled onto the pages of his journal during the spring and summer of 1966. In June he also wrote "A Midsummer Diary for M.," which he gave to M.[1] By his own admission, it is the poems inspired by their love that he felt best expressed what was in his heart.[2] The journals and the poems show Merton coming to terms with strong sexual feelings, within the context of his monastic commitment.

Merton was very much aware of how different this relationship was from previous "relationships" he had when he had been in a hurry (66). He was accepting his sexuality in a way he never had before. "Instead of feeling impure I feel purified (which is in fact what I myself wrote the other day in the 'Seven Words' for Ned O'Gorman). I feel that somehow my sexuality has been made real and decent again after years of rather frantic suppression (for though I thought I had it all truly controlled, this was an illusion). I feel less sick, I feel human, I am grateful for her love which is so totally mine. All the beauty of it comes from this that we are *not* just playing, we belong totally to each other's love (except for the vow that prevents the last complete surrender)" (67). Yet, that same afternoon, Merton revealed that there was more ambiguity in his response to the relationship than he had admitted to that morning: "Nevertheless, as always, I end up impatient of sex, backing away from domination by it, suspicious of its tyranny, and this afternoon I am turning with all my being toward freedom. I love her but do not want to think of her. I want to get to work, to write my conference for Sunday, to read, to meditate, to get the heaviness of passion off my mind" (67).

These entries reveal a relationship marked by tension. And although Merton appears to be coming to terms with his sexuality, his very circumstances preclude resolution. While Merton is experiencing an intimacy he has never experienced before, he recognizes that he and M. "do *not* meet completely in our love: it is partial, not whole" (69). Although he feels that some sides of their selves come together in harmony, other sides do not. He is aware that his own "ambiguities" come into play. "My deepest self evades this and is jealous of absolute freedom and solitude" (69–70). There was an inherent tension between love and solitude, and although he tried to reconcile his love for M. with his life of solitude, in the end he chose solitude. CMB

SEE ALSO CELIBACY; *EIGHTEEN POEMS*; *LEARNING TO LOVE*; WOMEN.

Notes

1. "A Midsummer Diary for M." is published in *Learning to Love*, 301–48.
2. See *Eighteen Poems*, five of which are published in *Learning to Love*.

SHAKERS

Thomas Merton first visited the site of the Shaker community at Pleasant Hill, Kentucky, in June 1959, when he and James Laughlin were on their way back from Lexington. Once a thriving community, it was now uninhabited and "the big old dormitories stood among

the weeds in desolation" (*A Search for Solitude*, 286). Among Merton's first impressions, as recorded in his journal, was the observation, "There is a lot of Shakertown in Gethsemani." The two communities, located only fifty miles apart, "had much in common" and "were born of the same Spirit" (287). And, in a comment that said more about Merton's own dissatisfaction with developments at Gethsemani than it did about the Shakers, Merton noted that if Shakertown had survived, the "prim ladies in their bonnets would have been driving tractors and the sour gents would have advertised their bread and cheese" (287).

Three days before Christmas 1959, following a visit to the University of Kentucky Library, a stop at the bookstore, and a "wonderful" lunch at the Hammers', Merton returned to Shakertown. The guesthouse was open, and Merton climbed the "marvelous double winding stair" to discover that the third-floor bedroom walls had been desecrated with "scribbles" (362). Merton tried to get into the center family house, but it was locked, and so he did not get to see the Shaker furniture stored there. But he was allowed to borrow a copy of the *Sacred Roll*, "the Shaker Bible, full of inspirations" (362). Even in its abandoned state, Shakertown spoke to Merton. "The empty fields, the big trees — how I would love to explore those houses and listen to that silence. In spite of the general decay and despair there is joy there still and simplicity." The Shakers "fascinate me," he continued. "Mother Ann Lee thought she was Sophia. The role of the sexes in their mysticism. The pure, entranced, immaculate dancing, shaking the sex out of their hands. And the whirling. God, at least, they had the sense to dance. I want to study them" (362).[1]

And study them he did. He ordered books and contacted photographer Shirley Burden about the possibility of doing an article and photo essay on the Shakers. Burden was enthusiastic about the idea and suggested sources for Merton to study.[2] In March 1960 Merton received a "charming" letter and a leaflet from a Shaker eldress in New Hampshire in response to an inquiry he had sent her. Merton agreed with the position expressed in the leaflet: Shakerism is not a failure. Rather, Merton thought, it is "something of a sign — mystery…pure and good, though in many ways absurd" (378).[3] Merton was moved by the loyalty of the Shakers to their vision and haunted by "the atmosphere and spirit, the image they created, the archetype" (379).

By December 1960, when Merton received a letter from Edward Deming Andrews, he was already familiar with Andrews's writings on the Shakers and had two of Andrews's books on his shelves: *The People Called Shakers* and *Shaker Furniture*. Andrews was a renowned authority on Shakers, and it is not surprising that Merton's interest led him to read the best on the subject. Edward Deming Andrews and his wife, Faith Andrews, had studied Shakers, collected their work, and promoted appreciation of their legacy. In his letters to Andrews, Merton expressed, in personal terms, as he did in his journal, how deeply touched he was by the Shaker spirit, and he surfaced ideas and insights that later he refined in two essays on the Shakers.[4]

Merton sensed an affinity between the Shaker and Cistercian spirits. "Certainly a Cistercian ought to be in a good position to understand the Shaker spirit" (*Hidden Ground of Love*, 33). Although the earliest settlers of Gethsemani and Pleasant Hill never met, despite their geographical proximity, they had much in common. Merton was especially moved by the "integration of the spiritual and physical" that informed "the silent eloquence of Shaker craftsmanship" (32). The Shakers realized that "their work was a cooperation in the same will that framed and governed the cosmos: and more governs history" (37–38). When Andrews sent Merton a booklet on herbs and herbalists, Merton observed another example of "the similarity of ideals and practices which bring Shakers and Cistercians closer together," recalling that St. Bernard wanted the monks of Tre Fontane "to 'use common herbs such as they are used by the poor'" (33). Merton included one of his letters to Andrews, written on December 21, 1961, in the collection he designated the "Cold War Letters."[5] Andrews later quoted from this letter in chapter 2 of *Religion in Wood*: "The Shakers remain as witnesses to the fact that only humility keeps man in communion with

truth, and first of all with his own inner truth. This one must know without knowing it, as they did. For as soon as a man becomes aware of 'his truth' he lets go of it and embraces an illusion" (36).[6]

Pleasant Hill, Kentucky, photograph by Thomas Merton

Even Merton's critical observations of Shaker life were tempered by his empathy for the Shaker spirit. For example, Merton notes "the mystery of Shaker 'absolutism' which in many ways appears to be 'intolerant' and even arbitrary," but adds, "there is an underlying gentleness and tolerance and understanding that appears not in words but in life and in work" (37).[7] Merton took delight in the presence of Shaker work in his own life: a desk, modeled on an old Shaker school desk, which a friend made for him and which he used in the hermitage; a print of *The Tree of Life*, which Andrews had sent him and which Merton hung in the hermitage kitchen; the Shaker song "Decisive Work" Merton sung to himself "from time to time" when he was alone (37); the photographs he took at Pleasant Hill in January 1962, when he returned to Shakertown, this time with camera in hand, on a day so cold his finger could not feel the shutter release. "Cold, pure light, and some grand trees. . . . Some marvelous subjects. How the blank side of a frame house can be so completely beautiful I cannot imagine. A completely miraculous achievement of forms" (*Turning toward the World*, 194).[8] The Shaker spirit continued to speak to Merton: "The moments of eloquent silence and emptiness in Shakertown stayed with me more than anything else — like a vision" (194).

Although Merton never completed the photographic essay he proposed in 1960, he published two essays on the Shakers. He wrote the first of the two on October 22, 1963, and called it "The Shakers: American Celibates and Craftsmen Who Danced in the Glory of God." The article was published in *Jubilee* (January 1964). Merton's journal entry for October 23, 1963, addresses the question that was uppermost in his mind as he was writing the piece: "Why were the Shakers first hated so much, then loved so much? Probably for their celibacy, or their mixture of celibacy and common life (both sexes in the same communities). And loved for their work? Not only that, for their angelic gentleness which, after all, was traced to their celibacy. Perhaps what underlay it all was the pioneers' panic at the thought of a kind of loss of virility involved in a man's living chastely with women and in a state of exaltation at that! 'Unnatural!' " (*Water of Life*, 26).

The article was reprinted as "Pleasant Hill: A Shaker Village in Kentucky" in *Mystics and Zen Masters*. Merton acknowledges that he relied "heavily" on Andrews's work, especially on *Shaker Furniture* and *The People Called Shakers* (*Mystics and Zen Masters*, 300).[9] "Pleasant Hill" serves as an introduction to the United Society of Believers in Christ's Second Appearing, as the Shakers had named themselves, and to the community at Pleasant Hill. Merton describes the Shakers as simple working-class people living celibate lives in community. They believed that the end of the world was imminent and that they "had been completely regenerated and were living the perfect risen life in and with Christ" (195). Their celibacy was a sign of their regeneration. "The most eloquent witness to the Shaker spirit is the fruit of their labor" (196). They were consummate craftsmen who made beautiful, simple, useful things that reflected the spiritual purity of their lives. They viewed their work as the work of God and labored attentively and deliberately — resisting hurry and overwork — and so experienced "a kind of wholeness and order and worship

that filled the whole day and the whole life of the working community" (198). Mother Ann Lee's sayings had set the tone for their labors and their lives. " 'Put your hands to work and your hearts to God' " (198). In work as in life, the Shakers were devoted to *truth*. "A thing or a person is perfect insofar as it is what it is meant to be." Although "the Shakers had no unrealistic dreams about utter perfection," they "strove in all things for truth, and made a point of simply *being themselves*" (199–200).[10]

Turning his attention to the Shakers at Pleasant Hill, Merton cites John Dunlavy, one of the first chief ministers, who "explicitly compared" the common life of the Shakers with that of Catholic monks. He approved of their "professing greater sanctity than the Church in general" and "their freedom from marital ties" but "felt that their dependence on vow instead of 'conscience alone' was a weakness, and their reliance on alms led them to be 'patronized by public approbation and authority,' whereas the Shakers were regarded as outcasts" (200–201). Merton was quite certain that Dunlavy must have known something of the first Trappists in Kentucky. During the century the Shakers were in Kentucky, from 1806 until 1910, when the United Society of Believers at Pleasant Hill was dissolved, they were "maligned" (201), but now, Merton noted, there is "a general awareness that the Shakers made a unique and original contribution to American culture" (202).

Merton wrote the introduction to Andrews's *Religion in Wood* on July 18, 1964, having just heard of the unexpected death of Edward Deming Andrews. The introduction takes the form of "a meditation on the Shaker aesthetic," in which Merton attempts "to capture something of its deep religious and 'monastic' quality" by looking at the Shakers in the light of William Blake and particularly Blake's idea of imagination.[11] "The Shaker's 'religion in wood' (surely an inspired title) is an expression of a profoundly religious creativity very like that which moved Blake to write and engrave."[12] Merton celebrates the religious and creative imagination of the Shakers, inspired by their communal life and expressed in craftsmanship that is a witness to Shaker faith. The Shakers were "simple, joyous, optimistic people whose joy was rooted in the fact that Christ *had* come, and that the basic Christian experience was the discovery of Christ living in us all now."[13] Theirs was "the wholly new vision of the children of the Resurrection for whom creativity and worship became prayer and their work was an embodiment of 'form' . . . an expression of spiritual force."[14] Believing that Mother Ann Lee was "Christ reincarnated as a woman," they witnessed to the " 'maternal' aspect of God's love."[15] The Shaker spirit gave expression to Blake's conviction that "creative and religious imagination plays an extremely important part in the life of man."[16] It is through the imagination that humans penetrate mystery. "For Blake, as for the Shakers, creative imagination and religious vision were not merely static and contemplative. They were active and dynamic" and expressed in creative work.[17]

For Merton, the Shakers embodied an essential element of the American spirit — at its best. CMB

Notes

1. A few weeks later Merton talked to the Hammers about Shakertown and learned that there was talk of the state turning Pleasant Hill into a monument. No doubt pleased by the possibility of its renovation, Merton determined to write to the governor about the matter.

2. See Michael Mott, *The Seven Mountains of Thomas Merton* (Boston: Houghton Mifflin, 1984), 343.

3. Also see *Guilty Bystander*, 118–19/132–33.

4. Edward Deming Andrews and Faith Andrews visited Merton at Gethsemani on November 6, 1961. See *Turning toward the World*, 178.

5. This letter to Andrews is no. 12 in the collection of "Cold War Letters." A portion of this letter was published in *Seeds of Destruction*, 259–61.

6. See also Edward Deming Andrews and Faith Andrews, *Religion in Wood: A Book of Shaker Furniture* (Bloomington: Indiana University Press, 1966), 13.

7. It is worth noting that Merton was much less accepting of what he saw to be the absolutism and arbitrariness of Cistercian life.

8. Merton included a revised version of the passage in *Conjectures of a Guilty Bystander* (200/220).

9. Merton notes that *The People Called Shakers* (New York: Oxford University Press, 1953) is "the best introduction to Shaker history and thought."

10. Merton expressed a similar ideal in "Things in Their Identity," chapter 5 of *New Seeds of Contemplation* (29–36).

11. In Andrews and Andrews, *Religion in Wood*, viii.

12. Ibid., vii.

13. Ibid., ix.

14. Ibid., x.

15. Ibid.

16. Ibid., xiii.

17. Ibid., xiv.

SIGN OF JONAS, THE

New York: Harcourt Brace Jovanovich, 1953. 362 pp.

The Sign of Jonas, the first journal that Thomas Merton himself edited and published, covers the period from December 1946 to July 1952.[1] He selected and revised entries, including less than half of the original journal, which he had entitled "The Whale and the Ivy."[2] The book has a prologue, "Journey to Nineveh," followed by six parts: (1) "Solemn Profession" (December 1946–December 1947); (2) "Death of an Abbot" (March 14, 1948–October 10, 1948); (3) "Major Orders" (October 15, 1948– April 29, 1949); (4) "To the Altar of God" (May 1, 1949–August 31, 1949); (5) "The Whale and the Ivy" (September 1, 1949– April 18, 1950); (6) "The Sign of Jonas" (October 9, 1950–June 1952). There also is an epilogue, "Fire Watch, July 4, 1952." Each of the six parts is preceded by a brief, italicized introductory note that expresses Merton's own retrospective reading of his personal journals and reveals what Merton saw to be the defining events and experiences of the period.

In the prologue Merton lays out the basic elements of monastic life and shares something of life at Gethsemani. Monks live "lives of silence, prayer, labor, penance, and constant union with God in solitude" (*Sign of Jonas*, 4). Cistercian monks make five vows: poverty, chastity, obedience, stability, and conversion of manners (*conversio morum*) (9).[3] A monk's life is physically demanding and highly regimented, and the life of a Cistercian monk is especially austere. In the late 1940s and early 1950s numbers at Gethsemani swelled, and there were 270 men living in buildings designed for seventy. It was difficult to experience silence and solitude in those circumstances, and the crowding was especially trying for Merton. His longing for solitude prompted a struggle with stability, evident in the pages of *The Sign of Jonas*. Should he remain a monk at Gethsemani, as he had vowed to do, or should he join a religious order, such as the Carthusians or the Camaldolese, in which he would be able to live a life of deeper solitude as a hermit? The biblical story of Jonah, carried to Nineveh in the belly of a whale, provided Merton with a metaphor to express his struggle with stability. He likened himself to Jonas carried in the belly of a whale where God wanted him to go. For Merton, stability was "the belly of a whale" (10).

Merton explains that this was a book written "not in the language of speculation but in terms of personal experience" (8). It was precisely the personal nature of the book that stood in the way of its publication. Although the American censors had accepted the book, the English-speaking censor of the order objected to its publication, after the book was already in galleys, declaring it inappropriate and full of "trivialities." Permission to publish the book was granted after Jacques Maritain wrote a letter to Robert Giroux in support of publication of *The Sign of Jonas*. Giroux forwarded the letter to Dom Gabriel Sortais. *The Sign of Jonas* was published in English with the approval of the order on February 5, 1953 (*Courage for Truth*, 26).

Merton experienced several milestones as a monk between December 1946, when *The Sign of Jonas* opens, and July 1952, when it ends. He made his solemn profession, was admitted to major orders, ordained a priest, and in 1951 appointed master of scholastics, responsible for teaching and directing student monks preparing for the priesthood. He also experienced his defining moment as a writer: the publication and phenomenal success of his autobiography, *The Seven Storey Mountain*. If *The Seven Storey Mountain* inaugurated Merton's writing career, *The Sign of Jonas* established his reputation as a spiritual writer. *The Sign of Jonas* was reviewed enthusiastically in the *New York Times* and *Newsweek*, and its publication was noted in *Time*. *The Seven Storey Mountain* had traced Merton's journey to Gethsemani. *The Sign of Jonas* documented Merton's struggle with his dual identity as a monk *and* a writer, and in the introduction to each section of the journal Merton looks back and tells his story. These italicized introductions are Merton's guide to readers of *The Sign of Jonas*.

Part 1 opens on December 10, 1946, the fifth anniversary of Merton's entrance into the monastery, and draws the reader into Merton's monastic world, as he moves toward solemn profession on March 19, 1947 — a world of prayer and liturgy, cells and general chapters, saints and holy days — and into the monk's mind and heart, revealing the earnestness and piety of the young monk who was convinced that if "we would find God in the depths of our souls we have to leave everybody else outside, including ourselves" (*Sign of Jonas*, 48). But the entries also portray a writer deeply immersed in his work. Already in the second entry, Merton notes how he is trying to be deliberate about his work: taking things one at a time and going over each slowly and patiently, and how many projects he has underway. And just before the beginning of the New Year, when he learns that *The Seven Storey Mountain* has been accepted for publication, he is writing another book, *The Waters of Siloe*.

Looking back, Merton described 1948 as "*a year of transition.*" Two events made it so: the publication of *The Seven Storey Mountain* and the death of Abbot Frederic Dunne, the latter being the inspiration for the title of the second part of the journal. The publication of *The Seven Storey Mountain* changed Merton's life: the "*obscure Trappist*" became "*an author*" and an "*author in a Trappist monastery is like a duck in a chicken coop*" (89). Not only had the aspiring writer become a published author, but also his work had become a bestseller. Acknowledging Dom Frederic Dunne's encouragement and recalling the delight with which the abbot handed him the book, the young monk clearly felt supported, both as a monk and a writer, by Dom Frederic. "*A few days later, he was telling me to go on writing, to love God, to be a man of prayer and humility, a monk and a contemplative, and to help other men penetrate the mystery of the love of God. It was the last time I ever spoke to him or saw him alive, because that night he died*" (91). The abbot died on August 3, 1948, and Dom James Fox was installed on August 25, 1948. One era at Gethsemani had ended and another had begun.

"Major Orders," the title of part 3, marks Merton's ordination to the subdiaconate and the diaconate in the winter and Lent of 1949. While Merton was making progress toward his ordination to the priesthood, he was experiencing difficulties in his writing. He was working on *The Ascent to Truth*. He was frustrated by the "paralysis" he was experiencing and "*decided to stop trying to be a poet any more*" since he "*had never really been a good poet anyway*." But he quickly tempered his resolve by admitting that he had continued to write where "*charity demanded or permitted it*" (127).

Merton's ordination to the priesthood is the dominant theme of part 4. "*My priestly ordination*," he wrote in the introduction to this section of the book, "*was, I felt, the one great secret for which I had been born*" (181). Celebrating "*the grace*" of his priesthood, Merton wrote, "*After my first Mass I understood perfectly and for the first time in my life that nothing else in the world is important except to love God and to serve Him with simplicity and joy*" (182).

Introducing part 5, Merton noted that ordination is "*only the beginning of a journey, not its end*" (229). The journey was somewhat troubled for Merton as he experienced a period of depression during which he found it very difficult to write and even tore up pages of his journal. Between April and December 1950 he stopped keeping a journal. He surfaced from this period of darkness with the realization that "*the essence of a solitary vocation is that it is a vocation to fear, to helplessness, to isolation in the invisible God*" (231).

In the introduction to part 6 Merton noted that the peace he had found during "*the solitude of the winter of 1950, deepened and developed in me beyond measure*" (303). After several hospitalizations between September and November of 1950, Merton's "*impotence as a writer*" disappeared in December 1950, and he finished *The Ascent to Truth* in three months. In May 1951 he was appointed master of scholastics, and in June he became an American citizen (303).

The epilogue, "Fire Watch, July 4, 1952," is a meditation, a prose poem in which Merton, the night watchman, makes his way through the monastery buildings and, along the way, retraces his life as a monk. Each stop is a reminder of what has been and a call to prayer. Memories and descriptions alternate with prayers as Merton makes his way from the cellar to the kitchen, to the furnace room, to the choir novitiate. "It is when you hit the novitiate that the fire watch begins in earnest. Alone, silent, wandering on your appointed rounds through the corridors of a huge, sleeping monastery, you come around the corner and find yourself face to face with your monastic past and with the mystery of your vocation. The fire watch is an examination of conscience in which your task as watchman suddenly appears in its true light: a pretext devised by God to isolate you, and to search your soul with lamps and questions, in the heart of darkness" (352). Moving on through the guesthouse, library, dormitory, and infirmary, Merton ascends to the top of the belfry of the church, "the top of this religious city" (359). Once again he prays: "You, Who sleep in my breast, are not met with words, but in the emergence of life within life and of wisdom within wisdom. You are found in communion: Thou in me and I in Thee and Thou in them and they in me." And God reassures him: "*I have always overshadowed Jonas with My mercy. . . . Have you had sight of Me, Jonas, My child? Mercy within mercy within mercy*" (362).

The Sign of Jonas is nothing less than an exercise in contemplative spirituality by Merton — defined by silence, solitude, awareness of God's presence within him, and attentiveness to the beauty of God's creation around him. CMB

SEE ALSO *ENTERING THE SILENCE*.

Notes

1. In 1941, before he entered the monastery, Merton selected entries from his premonastic journals and entrusted the manuscript to Catherine de Hueck. It was published in 1959 as *The Secular Journal*.

2. The complete journal that Merton kept during this period has been published in *Entering the Silence: Becoming a Monk and Writer*. In his introduction to that volume, Jonathan Montaldo notes that in a letter to Naomi Burton Stone, dated January 14, 1950, Merton reports that he was typing up the journal for Robert Giroux (see *Entering the Silence*, xvi).

3. Cistercian monks actually take three vows: obedience, stability, and conversion of manners, the vow that embraces poverty and chastity. See VOWS, MONASTIC.

SILENCE

Thomas Merton was a man who spoke out of the silence of a Trappist monastery a word that struck a responsive chord in a world of busyness and noise. He was born into that world in 1915 and into the new world of Gethsemani in

1941, a world of silence.[1] The story of the steps that led him to Gethsemani is told in his autobiography, *The Seven Storey Mountain*, which significantly, in its British edition, was given a new title: *Elected Silence*.

We live in an age of words. They smother us as they relentlessly bombard us from radios, televisions, newspapers, and the Internet. Our lives are so cluttered with words that we no longer know how to handle silence. We live in a society where silence is simply a futile pause between words rather than a creative silence out of which deep and authentic words can emerge. We are starved for silence because we are sated with words. Words and noise conspire to block silence out of our lives, and all too often we are parties to the conspiracy. Merton writes, "If our life is poured out in useless words, we will never hear anything, will never become anything, and in the end, because we have said everything before we had anything to say we shall be left speechless" (*Thoughts in Solitude*, 91).

Merton discusses the fear of silence that our world of noise and clutter all too readily foists upon us. Why are we afraid to be alone? It may be, he suggests, because of "our secret despair of inner reconciliation. If we have no hope of being at peace with ourselves in our own personal loneliness and silence, we will never be able to face ourselves at all: we will keep running and never stop. And this flight from the self is, as the Swiss philosopher Max Picard pointed out, 'a flight from God.' After all, it is in the depths of conscience that God speaks, and if we refuse to open up inside and look into those depths, we also refuse to confront the invisible God who is present within us. This refusal is a partial admission that we do not want God to be God any more than we want ourselves to be our true selves."[2] In speaking of monastic silence, Merton writes, "The chief function of monastic silence is then to preserve the *memoria Dei*, which is much more than memory. It is total consciousness and awareness of God which is impossible without silence, recollection, solitude, and a certain withdrawal" (*Come to the Mountain*, 46).

Merton's message for today's world is that silence is a basic need, not just for monks, but for anyone who wishes to live his or her humanness at its authentic best. "Words stand between silence and silence: between the silence of things and the silence of our own being. Between the silence of the world and the silence of God. When we have really met and known the world in silence, words do not separate us from the world nor from other men nor from God, nor from ourselves, because we no longer trust entirely in language to contain reality" (*Thoughts in Solitude*, 86). Silence alone gives us access to a dimension of reality that lies too deep for words. When you speak out of silence, there is always silence left over. You cannot put into words the totality of your silence. That is why the solitary life (whether lived in the monastery or, with greater difficulty and adaptation, outside monastic walls) thrives on silence. "The solitary life, being silent, clears away the smoke-screen of words that man has laid down between his mind and things. In solitude we remain face to face with the naked being of things" (85). This unimpeded contact with the reality of things leads to a sense of communion and love. "The world our words have attempted to classify, to control, and even to despise (because they could not contain it) comes close to us, for silence teaches us to know reality by respecting it where words have defiled it. When we have lived long enough alone with the reality around us, our veneration will learn how to bring forth a few good words about it from the silence which is the mother of Truth" (86).

Silence also is the mother of speech. For human life has its own proper rhythm — not the cacophonous rhythm of an uninterrupted flow of words, but rather, a rhythm that "develops in silence, comes to the surface in moments of necessary expression, returns to deeper silence, culminates in a final declaration, then ascends quietly into the silence of Heaven which resounds with unending praise" (*No Man Is an Island*, 261).

When Merton speaks of silence, he has in mind an exterior silence (the silence of the tongue) and an interior silence (the silence of the heart) (256). The first is important because it removes the barrier between us and the world of things, things like the sky and the clouds and the trees — things that exist not for themselves but for the praise of God. Even when noise defiles the silence of things, their silence is never lost. "The silence of the sky remains when the plane has gone" (257).

The silence of the heart (which is interior silence), by ridding us of inordinate desires, dissolves the barrier between God and us (256). It prepares us for the final word of yielding self to God that terminates mortal life, as it ushers into the eternal silence of God. WHS

SEE ALSO SELF; SILENCE IN HEAVEN; SOLITUDE; THOUGHTS IN SOLITUDE.

Notes

1. When Merton entered Gethsemani in 1941, it indeed was a world of silence. The monks communicated with one another only through sign language. In the 1960s this silence was somewhat relaxed and monks could speak when necessary.

2. "Creative Silence," *The Baptist Student* (June 1968). Also published in *Love and Living*, 41.

SILENCE IN HEAVEN:
A Book on the Monastic Life
New York: Thomas Y. Crowell, 1956. 70 pp.

This book was produced by L'Abbaye de la Pierre-Qui-Vire, a Benedictine abbey in France well known for its artistic work. It was first published in French in 1955 under the title *Silence dans le Ciel*, with Marie Tadié translating Thomas Merton's introduction. The English edition appeared in 1956.

It is a handsome volume with a foreword by a monk of the monastery, an introduction by Thomas Merton, and ninety impressive photographs whose intent is to give visitors to a monastery something more than a superficial picture of the daily life of monks. The photographs are accompanied by texts from spiritual classics (principally Scripture or the Rule of St. Benedict). Besides these texts there are nine numbered brief sections (or chapters) that precede each set of photos. The author of these sections is not named. The first photograph shows a road leading into dark wilderness; the last, stone steps leading upward into light. In between is the way from darkness into light: superb photos illustrating the prayer and work that make up the simple daily life of the mon-

astery. As readers peruse the photos and their accompanying texts, it is as if the monastery gate has opened wide and they have been invited in to roam about freely wherever they please.

Thomas Merton had nothing to do with the photographs. His role in this book was to write an introduction that would lead the reader to a deeper insight into the meaning of the photos. This introduction of fourteen pages, with the title *In Silentio*,[1] offers a remarkable interpretation of the monastic life. Merton turns to Scripture and its narrative of two beginnings. He starts with the world's first beginnings and sees the first humans symbolized as "the void and emptiness," waiting for the creative Spirit of God to hover over them and pour into their emptiness the perfect light of the word of God (*Silence in Heaven*, 7). Thus, they came into being filled with the presence of God. They knew their identity: they came from God and were destined always to be in God.

As children of God they had no need to know evil, since God did not know evil. But when they freely chose evil, they embraced illusion. Night descended upon them. They cried out for help, for light, for the recovery of their true identity.

Then, in the fullness of time, the Spirit of God once again moved over the waters — this time, the waters of the Jordan. But more, the Spirit overshadowed Christ as he emerged from those waters. His coming among people enabled them to hear God's word as spoken to them too: "This is my beloved Son" (48). It was another beginning, the new creation. Humans reacquired, radically at least, what was their own, what they were supposed to be. But Scripture makes clear that, as he came out of the waters, the scene of the new creation, Jesus was led by the same Spirit into the desert.

This is the meaning of vocation, especially of the monastic vocation. By penance, renunciation, silence, and solitude, the monk waits on the Spirit of Wisdom, which is the wisdom of the desert. This wisdom enlightened the mind not by speculative science, but by obscure, existential understanding begotten of love. This desert wisdom is a hidden wisdom; yet paradoxically it is a wisdom that cries out in the streets, waiting for people to recognize it. So often people do not recognize it, because they do not know that the word of wisdom that God utters is full of silence.

Snatched from the world by the silence of God into the desert of their new life, monks experience the world transformed from within. They do not expect people to understand them; in fact, they do not fully understand themselves. The monastic life cannot be defined by any of its parts, nor can it be reduced to any one of its aspects. "The monk is one who goes out to the frontiers of the Absolute, seeking the impossible, seeking the vision which no man can see without dying" (24). Then in the deep silence, Wisdom begins to sing her song in the monk, "the unique irreplaceable song that each soul sings for himself with the unknown Spirit, as he sits on the doorstep of his own being, the place where his own existence opens out into the abyss of God" (24).

It is the silence of God that is the power that moves nature and makes possible the products of human industry. God's silence forms the floor on which we live and act. If God's silence were to give way beneath us, we would fall back into oblivion and nothingness. It is the silence of God that speaks in the prayer of the monks. The value of their public prayer comes not so much from the sound of song as from the sound of silence, for the deep silence of God "enters into that sound and gives it actuality, value and meaning" (26).

When Merton wrote this piece, he was master of novices at Gethsemani. He lived in community yet longed for solitude. A couple of years before writing this preface he had been given a small building on the grounds of the monastery where he could retire for solitude for several hours each day. He readily agrees that most monks live in the cenobium, the cloister, and rightly so; a few, however, are called to the hermit life. But whether in the cloister or the hermitage, the monk's vocation is essentially the same. It is always "a call to sink deep roots in the silence of God" (29). At the same time, the monk's love embraces the world, for "he feels within him the silence of God expanding into a tremendous smile." It is the infinite Word present in the world and claiming possession of

humanity, "a possession due to Him not only as Head of the human race but by right of conquest. He has won the right to exult in our hearts by the triumph of His Cross" (30). WHS

SEE ALSO *NEW MAN.*

Notes

1. This introduction was reprinted in abridged form in *Seasons of Celebration*, 204–15.

SILENT LIFE, THE:

New York: Farrar, Straus and Cudahy, 1957. xiv + 178 pp.

Thomas Merton describes *The Silent Life* as "a meditation" on the monastic life by one who knows the life from the inside (*Silent Life*, xii). Merton's perspective, colored by his lived experience as a monk of Gethsemani and by a strong and persistent attraction to a life of deeper solitude, is very much in evidence in this book, as are his enthusiasms for a more primitive form of Benedictine life and for the hermit life of the Carthusians and the Camaldolese.

This book, like many others Merton wrote, had its seeds in earlier work. In 1954, Merton wrote an introduction for *Silence dans le Ciel* (published in France in 1955), a collection of photographs depicting the life of monks at the Benedictine monastery, L'Abbaye de la Pierre-Qui-Vire.[1] In 1955, he rewrote the introduction adding some new chapters on religious orders.[2] When the Italian and French editions of *The Silent Life* appeared in 1957 (the same year the English edition was published), Merton found himself in trouble with the Superior General. Dom Gabriel Sortais was displeased that the Italian version (apparently published without Merton's knowledge, although he knew it had been sent to Camaldoli) had not been passed by the censors. Merton was also required to submit a page of corrections for the French edition. When he wrote to Dom Gabriel to explain the situation, Merton's tone was once again apologetic and conciliatory.[3]

The Silent Life has three sections as well as a prologue, epilogue, and index. The original cloth edition includes sixteen pages of photographs that portray a number of monasteries and offer readers a glimpse of the lives of the monks who lived there. A photo on the book jacket pictures Cistercian monks at the Abbey of Hauterive (Fribourg, Switzerland) and a photo reproduced on both inside covers depicts a hooded monk, with his back to the camera, walking toward Gethsemani's entrance, over which are inscribed the words "Pax intrantibus."[4]

The Silent Life introduces readers to common aspects of the monastic life and to the variety of ways in which the monastic spirit finds expression in particular monastic communities. In the prologue, entitled "What Is a Monk?" Merton defines the monk as one who devotes his life to "seeking God." One cannot understand what that seeking entails unless one "is enlightened, at the same time, by the Spirit speaking within his own heart," and the one who finds God has already been found by God (vii).

Part I, entitled "The Monastic Peace," consists of five short chapters: (1) "*Puritas Cordis* [Purity of Heart]," (2) "*In Veritate* [In Truth]," (3) "*In Laboribus Multis* [In Many Labors]," (4) "*In Tabernaculo Altissimi* [In the Tabernacle of the Most High],"[5] and (5) "*In Unitate* [In Unity]." Each explores a theme Merton sees as essential to the spirit and practice of the monastic life. Monks are called to become pure of heart; to live in truth; to take joy in created things and work productively and creatively; to build the monastic community as a new Jerusalem; and to live in unity, which is promoted and symbolized by the abbot.

Merton develops these themes in a way that not only describes monastic practice but also introduces ideas that are significant to his spirituality. For example, Merton notes that purity of heart is the beginning of a monk's unity within himself and with his brother monks (19). Purity of heart "is not so much a psychological state as a new level of reality" in which one is lifted out of oneself and becomes "a new being," a new creation (11–12). The pure heart becomes transparent to the image of God within. Purity of heart is the "light of God shining in the humble soul that is empty of self" (10).

Merton also introduces the contrast between the "imaginary self" with its "illusory projects" (4) and the "real" self (13),[6] as he elaborates on the monk's calling to live in truth. The monk's mission is "to become so real, under the action of the Spirit of Him Who is, that his own life is a pure 'amen,' a conscious echo, freely replying 'Yes' to the infinite reality and goodness of God" (22). The monk says "Yes" in work as well as in prayer. There is a place for manual labor and also for intellectual work, but the work done by monks should never obscure the fact "that silence, solitude, recollection and prayer are the most important elements in the monastic life" (33). The monk lives "in the secret of God's face" and the monastery is "a tabernacle in the desert" where God's presence is experienced (34). But it is also in the "silence of the forest, the peace of the early morning wind moving the branches of the trees, the solitude and isolation of the house of God" that God is revealed (38).

In Part II, "The Cenobitic Life," Merton shows how the monastic spirit, described in Part I, is embodied in various Benedictine communities. This part of the book consists of three chapters: (1) "St. Benedict," (2) "The Benedictines," and (3) "The Cistercians." While the Rule of Benedict, with its emphasis on simplicity and balance in monastic observance, provides the framework for all Benedictines, "the accidental variations" that distinguish one order from another are "profound enough to constitute specific differences in their spirituality" (59). Again Merton's own preferences come through especially as he describes the Benedictines of the Primitive Observance at La Pierre Qui-Vire: "It is a cenobitic life, in which the monk can still enjoy the privacy of his own cell" (87). "There is at the same time an apostolate of writing and of art, at La Pierre qui Vire: but this apostolate is integrated into the monk's contemplative life, so that it enables him to nourish his spirit by contact with all that is living in the present and in the past. It keeps him conscious of the developments in art, letters and thought, without dragging him into the whirlpool of controversies and intellectual fashions. It is good for the monk to be able to take intelligent note of what is going on in the intellectual and artistic world outside the monastery, and to offer his own discrete and Christian comment, from the vantage point of his solitude" (87). This passage expresses Merton's own dream as a monk *and* a writer.

When, in Part III, Merton directs his attention to "The Hermit Life," specifically the Carthusians and the Camaldolese, he is describing a way of life that very much appealed to him. Merton's "Carthusian temptation" was already a leitmotif in his thinking in the late 1940s.[7] His attraction for the hermit life reached a critical point in 1952 when he actually wrote to a superior of a Carthusian foundation in Vermont "to ask you if there is any chance of my being accepted as a Carthusian."[8] In the summer of 1955, he "had come to the decision to go to Camaldoli."[9] Though none of these plans materialized, Merton's longing for the hermit life was realized, at least in part, when in 1965 he was finally granted permission to live in a hermitage on Gethsemani's grounds.

Merton describes in some detail the lives of Carthusian and Camaldolese monks. The Carthusians "occupy a place of special eminence among the monastic Orders not only because of the intrinsic perfection of their Rule of life, but also because of the extraordinary fidelity of the Order to that Rule" (130). Merton describes in great detail the small cottages that along with the common cloister make up the Charterhouse: the hermitages, each with its own garden, woodshed and workshop, porch, and cell with "a bedroom and sitting room with two alcoves, one an oratory and the other a study" (131). He even imagines the books he might find on the shelf — some reflecting special interests and light reading along with the expected spiritual classics. He also describes in detail the daily schedule of prayer, work, and study in which nineteen or twenty hours are spent alone. It is this "single-minded insistence on silence and solitude" that appealed to Merton (134). Exterior solitude is the way to interior solitude. Turning to the Carthusian foundation at Whitingham, Vermont ("Sky Farm"), Merton cautions that Carthusians will have to resist "the great temptations" of American culture — "publicity, technology, popularity, commercialism, machines and the awful impulse to throw everything overboard for the sake of fame and prosperity" (144),

and he concludes that the "whole monastic structure in America may eventually depend on their doing so successfully" (144).

Like the Carthusians, the Camaldolese view exterior solitude as a way to foster interior silence. Merton summarizes the history of this Benedictine offshoot and describes in detail the Camaldolese way of life. He also notes that the Camaldolese hermit may become a recluse and live "absolutely alone" — joining the community only several times a year (153). Such a life makes "real" solitude possible. The hermit's life becomes a "return to 'paradise'" (169) and a way to experience the reality of the Living God.

In the Epilogue, Merton addresses a theme to which he often returns in later years and which offers a counterpoint to monastic withdrawal: "The Monk and the World." The monastery is "neither a museum nor an asylum." The monk "remains in the world from which he has fled" and is "inextricably involved in [its] suffering and problems" (172).

Merton himself places *The Silent Life* in context. Looking back on his writings in 1962, Merton observed that there had been "a slight evolution in my thought about the monastic life from *The Waters of Siloe* (which I regard now as a rough and immature essay) to *The Silent Life* and even more recent essays, such as some of those in *Disputed Questions*."[10] *The Silent Life* is a record, in progress, of Merton's thinking on monasticism and on his own monastic life. CMB

Notes

1. The introductory essay appeared in the English edition of *Silence in Heaven: A Book on the Monastic Life* (New York: Thomas Y. Crowell, 1956) and was reprinted in part as *"In Silentio"* in *Seasons of Celebration* (New York: Farrar, Straus and Giroux, 1965).

2. See letter to Dom Gabriel Sortais, February 7, 1957 (*School of Charity*, 100). In this letter, Merton tries to explain the "mix-up" with the Italian edition in which the new chapters were omitted and which was published without approval of the censors. Merton ends the letter with reassurances: "I am trying to be a monk. I am not writing and I do not think of writing anything whatsoever. True, I still have two or three manuscripts that are going to be published, but after that the name of Thomas Merton can be forgotten. So much the better" (101).

3. See letters to Dom Gabriel Sortais, February 7, 1957, and April 16, 1957 (*School of Charity*, 99–102). In the second letter, Merton invokes his state of mind to help explain the mess: "When I was writing this work, at the moment of a crisis in my religious life, I was not looking at things in an altogether normal way" (101).

4. No photos appeared in the paperback edition except for the original book jacket photo, which was reproduced on the cover of the paperback edition.

5. "In the Highest Tabernacle," the incorrect translation included in the Table of Contents, could not have come from Merton, who was an excellent Latinist.

6. Merton later develops these themes, which are so integral to his theology of the self, in the opening chapters of *New Seeds of Contemplation*.

7. See *The Sign of Jonas*, in which Merton published selections from personal journals kept in the period 1946–52.

8. Letter to Dom Humphrey Pawsey, September 11, 1952 (*School of Charity*, 41).

9. Letter to Dom Gabriel Sortais, February 7, 1957 (*School of Charity*, 100). Later, in 1959, he requested an indult that would permit him to live as a monk in Latin America. The indult was not granted, and Merton remained at Gethsemani. For an account of Merton's "Carthusian temptation" and his Latin American temptation, see William H. Shannon, *Silent Lamp* (New York: Crossroad, 1992), 148–60. See also *Witness to Freedom*, 200–230.

10. Letter to Ronald Roloff, O.S.B., September 26, 1962 (*School of Charity*, 147).

SIN

Thomas Merton links sin with the abuse of human freedom. Human freedom can be abused by coercion — that is, by physical force that prevents me from doing what I choose. It also can be abused, even falsified, by sin. Sin often is thought of as the breaking of an external law. This is a superficial understanding that in no way penetrates to the deepest meaning of sin as a betrayal of my inner freedom, as a failure to respond to my inner truth. Merton writes in "The Inner Experience": "[The sense of sin] is not merely a sense of guilt referred to the authority of God. It is a sense of evil in myself. Not because I have violated a law outside myself, but because I have violated the inmost laws of my own being, which are, at the same time, the laws of God Who dwells within me." This means that the sense of sin is the experience of "having been deeply and deliberately false to my own inmost reality, my likeness to God." It is the realization that I am dead, not only morally but also spiritually. "Moral death would savor rather of guilt — I have been 'killed' by the violation of a law. But spiritual death is the sense of having separated myself from truth by complete inner falsity, from love by selfishness, from reality by trying

to assert as real a will to nothingness. The sense of sin is then something ontological and immediate." It does not spring from reflecting on my actions and comparing it with a moral code. "It springs directly from the evil that is present in me: it tells me not merely that I have done wrong, but that I *am* wrong, through and through. That I am a false being. That I have destroyed myself" (*Cistercian Studies* offprint vi, 148).

Sin, therefore, amounts to illusion. It offends against truth. It is "a conscious and deliberate disloyalty to ethical truth and rectitude" (*Witness to Freedom*, 305). It is the failure (or the refusal) to see reality as it truly is, as God sees it. "Sin is the will to do what God does not will, to know what He does not know, to love what He does not love" (*No Man Is an Island*, 84). Sin also is delusion in the literal sense of the word *deludere*, which means "to play false with"; it is playing the game of life falsely. I not only do what is false, but also I become, in a sense, a false being. It is a false self that appears on the stage of life.

Sin frustrates the inner journey toward God and my true self. The inner journey is the return to paradise. It is a journey wherein I move toward the center of reality, where I find my true self and God as the ground of my being. I enter into the circulation of love that is God's life and in doing so I discover the inner laws of my own being and the will of God. My actions flow from that center, so that in all I do I love what God loves and will what God wills.

Sin reverses that movement toward the center; indeed, it is a withdrawal, permanent or temporary, from that center into "the multiplicity and confusion of exterior things" (*New Man*, 114). God is dethroned from God's rightful place in my heart. I seek freedom in a total independence, whereas the very condition of my freedom is dependence on God. I become Prometheus seeking to possess on my own what I can possess only as gift.[1] WHS

SEE ALSO CONSCIENCE; FALL; FREEDOM; ORIGINAL SIN.

Notes

1. "Prometheus thought he had to ascend into heaven to steal what God had already decreed to give him" (*Raids on the Unspeakable*, 87; see 83–88).

SIX LETTERS:
BORIS PASTERNAK,
THOMAS MERTON

Edited by Naomi Burton Stone and Lydia
Pasternak Slater. Lexington, Ky.: King Library
Press, 1973. xx+28 pp.

Published in a limited edition of 150 copies,
this book represents a labor of love. It was
edited jointly by Naomi Burton Stone, for the
trustees of the Merton Legacy Trust, and by
Lydia Pasternak Slater, on behalf of the sons
of Boris Pasternak. The book was printed at
the King Library Press, with the composition,
press work, and binding done by apprentices
to Carolyn Hammer at the King Library Press.
Carolyn and her husband, Victor Hammer,
were close friends of Merton's.

Six Letters consists of a foreword by Naomi
Burton Stone, an introduction by Lydia Pasternak Slater, and, as the title states, six letters:
three letters of Merton to Pasternak (August 22, 1958; October 23, 1958; December 15,
1958) and three letters of Pasternak to Merton (September 27, 1958; October 3, 1958;
February 7, 1960). Writing for the trustees of
the Merton Legacy Trust, Naomi Burton Stone
notes that Merton had asked that his trustees
arrange for the publication of his letters "at such
a time as seemed to them appropriate" (*Six Letters*, iii). Mindful of the challenge of doing so
in a fitting way, the trustees responded positively to Carolyn Hammer's desire to publish
the letters under the King Library imprint.[1]
"The exchange seemed to us to fulfill what
we had been looking for, a rounded view of
Thomas Merton as a letter writer" (iv).[2] As
Merton's literary agent for more than two decades, Stone appreciated the significance of
this exchange "about publishing and peace and
social justice and the inner life" (iv).

The introduction, by Lydia Pasternak Slater,
sister of Boris Pasternak, establishes a context
for the correspondence that follows. Observing that Boris Pasternak's English vocabulary
was "somewhat archaic and unidiomatic" (for
years he had been translating Shakespeare) and
that he was "far less familiar with contemporary
colloquial English," she notes that his letters,
"written in extreme haste and under enormous

pressure ... were meant for Thomas Merton,
and for him *alone*: Boris knew that the man to
whom he was writing would get his message —
whatever the words and sentences expressing
it" (ix). Slater quotes, at some length, from
several sources as she traces the exchange of letters, which was truly "a meeting in spirit" that
was "significant and important" to both writers:
Merton's own account of his correspondence
with Pasternak[3] and his preface to *Disputed
Questions*; Merton's first letter to Pasternak
(August 22, 1958); two letters (originally written in German and dated September 18, 1958,
and May 12, 1959) from Pasternak to his friends
Kurt and Helen Wolff, through whom Pasternak communicated, indirectly, with Merton;[4]
a letter that Slater wrote to *Encounter*, August 1959; and a letter from Merton, dated
April 3, 1961, that Lydia Pasternak Slater received when she wrote to Merton after reading
Disputed Questions and sending him "a book of
her translations of her brother's poems and two
small recordings of my reciting these" (xviii). In
that letter Merton expressed his gratitude for
the books and for the recordings, noting that
he played them for the novices, and that the experience of hearing her read the poems brought
him "closer to Boris in understanding and love"
(xix). Slater was moved by Merton's tribute to
her brother: "It was my conviction that he was
a truly spiritual man in an age when even apparently religious people are seldom spiritual.
His religion, his belief, was more than conformity to accepted norms. He obeyed God in his
own way, and for this he had to pay dearly,
but he realized the meaning of his actions."
Merton continued to say, "That a man of such
integrity should arise, and not help everyone
else to be honest! But surely he helped many,
and he certainly helped me. I am sure that the
many he helped were the right ones, and the
right ones do not have to be either eminent or
famous" (xix–xx).

Merton initiated the correspondence with
Pasternak with his letter of August 22, 1958,
which began this way: "Although we are separated by great distances and even greater
barriers it gives me pleasure to speak to you
as to one whom I feel to be a kindred mind."
Merton wrote, "I feel much more kinship with

you, in your writing, than I do with most of the great modern writers in the West.... With other writers I can share ideas, but you seem to communicate something deeper. It is as if we met on a deeper level of life on which individuals are not separate beings. In the language familiar to me as a Catholic monk, it is as if we were known to one another in God" (3–4). Merton went on to express his deep admiration for Pasternak's work: "A voice like yours is of great importance for all mankind in our day" (5). He told Pasternak that he was sending him a copy of *Prometheus: A Meditation,* and that he planned to learn Russian.

Boris Pasternak responded with two letters. In the first, written on September 27, 1958, Pasternak thanked Merton for his "warm, congenial letter . . . wonderfully filled with kindred thoughts as having been written half by myself" (7). Pasternak's halting English did not obscure the fact that the deep sense of kinship Merton had felt was reciprocated. Pasternak wrote a second letter on October 3, 1958, thanking Merton for *Prometheus* and pronouncing strophes 4 and 7 the most successful. And, as in the first letter, he insisted that, of all his writings, only *Dr. Zhivago* was worth Merton's attention. He initialed the letter; he had left his earlier letter unsigned to increase its chances of reaching Merton.

In his letter of October 23, 1958, Merton expressed his great joy in receiving Pasternak's letters. Recognizing the significance of their exchange, Merton wrote, "The great business of our time is this: for one man to find himself in another one who is on the other side of the world. Only by such contacts can there be peace, can the sacredness of life be preserved and developed and the image of God manifest itself in the world" (9). Merton had read *Dr. Zhivago* with deep appreciation and found the book to be "a world in itself, a sophiological world, a paradise and a hell, in which the great mystical figures of Yurii and Lara stand out as Adam and Eve and though they walk in darkness walk with their hand [*sic*] in the hand of God" (10). Merton confessed that he already knew Lara and told Pasternak about his dream of Proverb, "a very young Jewish girl of fourteen or fifteen" who "suddenly manifested

a very deep and pure affection for me and embraced me so that I was moved to the depths of my soul."[5] A few days later, "I was walking alone in the crowded street and suddenly saw that everybody was Proverb and that in all of them shone her extraordinary beauty and purity and shyness" (12).[6]

Merton wrote again on December 15, 1958, to express concern and support. After being chosen to receive the Nobel Prize for literature in October, Pasternak had been expelled from the Soviet Writers Union. When he heard that news, Merton had written a letter of protest to Aleksei Surkov on October 29, 1958.[7] Pasternak declined the prize. Aware that Pasternak's situation was becoming increasingly difficult, Merton encouraged his friend with this blessing: "May you find again within yourself the deep lifegiving silence which is genuine truth and the source of truth: for it is a fountain of life and a window into the abyss of eternity and God" (17). Merton reported that he was reading *Essai Autobiographique* "with great pleasure" and that he was sending Pasternak a copy of *The Sign of Jonas.* He added that he was learning Russian.

Pasternak wrote the last letter in the exchange on February 7, 1960. He apologized for his "long silence" and confessed that he was in a "sad state of mind." "I am perishing of the forced unproductiveness that is worse than pure idleness. But I shall rise, you will see it" (21). "Don't write me," he added in a postscript. "The next turn to renew the correspondence will be mine" (22). Boris Pasternak died on May 30, 1960.

Although their correspondence was brief, there is no question that it was significant to both of them. For Merton, the "encounter" with Pasternak came at a critical time in his own life. Merton was "turning toward the world." His epiphany at Fourth and Walnut, in March 1958, had symbolized a transformation that already was well under way. The monk who had withdrawn from the world in 1941 to enter the monastery was, in 1958, viewing that world in a new light. He was "returning to the world" that he had left behind and embracing his responsibility to it. In addition to his correspondence with Boris Pasternak, Merton was establishing contacts with Latin American writers — contacts facilitated by one of his novices, Ernesto Cardenal, a Nicaraguan poet. At the end of the year he began what would be an important correspondence with Lithuanian-born Polish writer Czeslaw Milosz, who then was living in exile in France. The following year he would begin corresponding with Japanese Zen scholar D. T. Suzuki. Merton felt himself called to a mission. He put it this way in a letter he wrote, on November 10, 1958, to Pope John XXIII: "It seems to me that, as a contemplative, I do not need to lock myself into solitude and lose all contact with the rest of the world. . . . I also have to think in terms of a contemplative grasp of the political, intellectual, artistic and social movements in this world — by which I mean a sympathy for the honest aspirations of so many intellectuals everywhere in the world and the terrible problems they have to face. I have had the experience of seeing that this kind of understanding and friendly sympathy, on the part of a monk who really understands them, has produced striking effects among artists, writers, publishers, poets, etc., who have become my friends without my having to leave the cloister" (*Hidden Ground of Love*, 482). Boris Pasternak was one of those friends. CMB

Notes

1. Merton sent to Pasternak a copy of *Prometheus: A Meditation*, also published in a limited edition of 150 copies by the King Library Press in 1958.

2. The project of publishing Merton's letters in earnest was launched in 1985 with the publication of *The Hidden Ground of Love: Letters on Religious Experience and Social Concerns*. It was the first of five volumes of Merton's letters published under the general editorship of William H. Shannon. Merton's letters to Pasternak were published in the fourth volume of the letters, *The Courage for Truth: Letters to Writers* (87–93).

3. From "Appendix A: Postscript to the Pasternak Affair," in *Disputed Questions*, 291–94. Part 1 of the book was entitled "The Pasternak Affair" and consisted of three items: "In Memoriam," "The People with Watchchains," and "Spiritual Implication."

4. For Merton's letters to Helen Wolff, see *The Courage for Truth*, 96–109. Merton also received news from Boris Pasternak through another friend, John Harris. See Merton's letters to Harris in *The Hidden Ground of Love*, 384–401.

5. For another account of this dream, see Merton's letter to Jacques Maritain, dated December 16, 1962, in *The Courage for Truth*, 33–34.

6. For an account of Merton's epiphany at Fourth and Walnut, in the business district of Louisville, see *Conjectures of a Guilty Bystander*, 140–42. For Merton's journal account of the experience, see *Search for Solitude*, 181–82.

7. The letter is published in *The Courage for Truth*, 93–95.

SLATE, JOHN

A member of Merton's circle of Columbia friends (see *Run to the Mountain*, 74, 313; *Seven Storey Mountain*, 233), John Slate (1913–67) became an attorney, specializing in aviation law. Like most of Merton's group, he also had literary interests and wrote a number of articles for various quality magazines, including one on his own hospital stay that Merton comments on in his journal (*Learning to Love*, 293). When Merton decided to set up the Merton Legacy Trust to oversee his literary affairs, he contacted Slate in March 1967 to ask him to draw up the necessary legal documents. Preliminary work was done when Slate visited the monastery in early April 1967 (*Learning to Love*, 212). Plans for a return visit by Slate with his wife were never realized because of his sudden death from a heart attack on September 19, 1967, his fifty-fourth birthday. POC

SOLITARY LIFE, THE

Thomas Merton wrote two different works that bear this title.

The first of the two works was an essay published by Victor Hammer in 1960 in a limited edition.[1] In 1977 Br. Patrick Hart included it as a section of *The Monastic Journey*. The essay grew out of one published in 1955 in the French journal *Temoignages*, titled *Dans le desert de Dieu*.[2] This essay, in turn, grew into a larger one, "Notes for a Philosophy of Solitude," published in 1960 in *Disputed Questions*.

The French essay and its expanded form are spirited defenses of the hermit life. They explain the meaning of the hermit life: it is not so much a withdrawal from people as a "refusal to accept the myths and fictions with which social life is always full — and never more than today" (*Monastic Journey*, 152). Merton discusses the trials of the hermit, his prayer, and his doubts, but also the riches of his life. He is rich because his solitude contains God, surrounds him with God.

The second of the two works, a small booklet of eleven pages, was published by the Stanbrook Abbey Press in Worcester, England, in 1963. It is Merton's translation of a letter written by Guigo (1083–1136), the fifth prior of the Carthusian monastery the Grande Chartreuse. In a brief introduction Merton praises Guigo as one of the great spiritual lights of his time. Writing to an unidentified friend, Guigo urges him to give up honors and worldly dignities and "undertake our observance." "Take care," he advises him, "to save the little bit of life that remains still unconsumed, snatch it from the world, light under it the fire of love to burn up as an evening sacrifice to God" (*Solitary Life,* 10).

It is not difficult to see why Merton was attracted to this little work, extolling, as it does, the solitary life. The dedication of the book, "For J-B-P," indicates his continuing fondness for the Carthusians. In a letter to Dom Jean-Baptiste Porion, procurator general of the Carthusians, Merton writes that he had dedicated this small booklet to him. "Out of deference for your love of hiddenness I have put only your initials in the dedication, but it will be enough to express my friendship, long silent, and my gratitude for your past sharing in my own concerns for solitude" (*School of Charity,* 210).

This same booklet, but without Merton's introduction, was published in a limited edition of 240 copies by the Banyan Press in Pawlet, Vermont, during January 1977. It was given a slightly different title: *On the Solitary Life.* WHS

SEE ALSO CARTHUSIANS; *DISPUTED QUESTIONS*; SOLITUDE.

Notes

1. There is a manuscript of this work, which Merton called "Vocation to Solitude."

2. Also published in Italian, *Nel deserto.* The first English translation appeared in the spring 1993 issue of *The Merton Seasonal.*

SOLITUDE

Solitude may be thought of as time when and space where a person can be alone in conscious awareness of the presence of God. Some ele-

ment of solitude is essential to any authentic spirituality.

The word "solitude" looms large in the vocabulary of Thomas Merton. He seems to have had a natural disposition for solitude, even a need for it. It may be that circumstances of his life moved him in this direction. His mother died when he was six, and after that he often was left alone — with family members or in boarding school — by his father, whose artistic projects too often took precedence over his fatherly responsibility. At times young Tom was desperately lonely; at other times he embraced the solitude that life often thrust on him. At Oakham School he was popular among his classmates, but on vacation time he often traveled alone.

It is not surprising, then, that when he became a Roman Catholic in 1938, he found himself attracted to a life in the church that emphasized solitude. At the time he entered the Abbey of Gethsemani in December 1941, it was a Trappist monastery dedicated to silence (the monks communicated with one another through sign language), though the monks lived in community. Yet Merton admitted that the Trappist order was second choice for him. Had it not been for the war, which prevented him from going to Europe, he would have chosen to become a Carthusian (*Seven Storey Mountain,* 383), for they were an order of hermits, each one living alone in his own hermitage. This desire to be a Carthusian continued to surface in his life, especially during the early years, when he quite literally wore out his confessor and abbot with requests to transfer to a Carthusian monastery. In his later years at Gethsemani, it was more generally the desire for greater solitude that he continued to seek.

In 1953, Dom James Fox, his abbot, gave him an abandoned toolshed out in the woods and allowed him to spend time there in solitude. He embraced this gift of a space and time for solitude with great enthusiasm, naming this "hermitage" St. Anne's. It was at St. Anne's that he wrote *Thoughts in Solitude.* In 1965 he was given as his hermitage a building in the woods, about a mile from the monastery, which originally had been built for ecumenical dialogue. Thus, in August of 1965 he shattered tradition by entering upon the life of a hermit in the Trappist order.

He enjoyed the solitude of his hermitage but squandered it to some degree, as he allowed (and, let it be said, enjoyed) all too many visits from friends and acquaintances. When he left for Asia, one of his hopes was to find a place of more secure solitude, where he could live apart from the monastery, but still as a monk of Gethsemani. That hope was short-circuited by his untimely death.

Merton wrote a great deal about solitude. There is much about it scattered throughout his letters and journals. His best sustained writing on the topic is found in *Thoughts in Solitude* and in a long essay in *Disputed Questions*. The essay, entitled "Notes for a Philosophy of Solitude," represents his most detailed and knowledgeable study of solitude. Several times in later writings he singled out this essay as of special importance (see, e.g., *Hidden Ground of Love*, 624, 642). This essay got him into difficulties with the censors of the order. The heart of the censors' problem with him concerned the distinction between interior solitude and exterior solitude. Merton was in complete agreement with them that the heart of any true solitude is solitude of the heart. Interior solitude is essential. Exterior solitude without the inner reality of an undivided, silent heart is simply a mockery of solitude. Interior solitude is essential for an authentic living of the monastic life.

What they disagreed about was whether or not exterior solitude, the actual physical separation from others, had its place in the Cistercian tradition for some few who are called to it. After all, the Cistercians were a cenobitic community; living together in community was an essential part of their lives. Merton was quite willing to accept this understanding of Cistercian life. Still, he believed that the monastic tradition allowed that, once a monk had proved himself in community, he could experience a call to the solitary life of the hermit, even while belonging to a community whose basic lifestyle was cenobitic. To disallow such a call to the solitary life to Trappists who feel thus called was an unwarranted restriction on their freedom to follow the will of God. Merton made the

statement, "It is cruel and unjust to force these people on to the Procrustean bed of a conventional, institutional vocation." This was a bit much for the censors. He was forced to withdraw this statement from his essay "Notes for a Philosophy of Solitude." After several rewrites, however, the essay finally was accepted for publication. Merton's basic position was sustained, though he had been forced to remove some of his most forceful statements in defense of the solitary life. He narrates the story of his frustrations with the censors in a somewhat explosive letter of May 30, 1960, to Sr. Therese Lentfoehr (*Road to Joy*, 235–36). WHS

SEE ALSO HERMIT; *THOUGHTS IN SOLITUDE*; *DISPUTED QUESTIONS*.

SORTAIS, GABRIEL

Dom Gabriel Sortais (1902–63), who had served as a chaplain in World War II and been taken prisoner by the Germans, was elected abbot general of the Cistercians of the Strict Observance in 1948. Earlier that year, as vicar general of the order, he had visited Gethsemani. Acting as his interpreter, Thomas Merton had an opportunity to get acquainted with him. His political leanings were decidedly conservative and royalist.

There is an extended correspondence with Dom Gabriel (in *The School of Charity*) that covers most of his time as abbot general. The correspondence dealt with Merton's writings, the censorship of his writings, and his vocational crises. Three works that especially created tensions between Merton and his abbot general were *The Sign of Jonas*, *The Wisdom of the Desert*, and the essay in *Disputed Questions* "Notes for a Philosophy of Solitude." There also was trouble over his writings on war and peace, leading in early 1962 to an order from the abbot general absolutely forbidding him to publish anything further on the subject. Regarding the essay on solitude, Merton wrote an embittered letter to Sr. Therese Lentfoehr, saying, among other things, "The Abbot General picked this up [a statement about hermits and the will of God] and flew into one of his rages, which can be very stormy, and I was all but consigned to the nether regions as a contumacious heretic" (*Road to Joy*, 236). Merton eventually ironed out the difficulties with the censors. In April of 1963 Pope John XXIII published his encyclical *Pacem in Terris*. That same month Merton wrote to Dom Gabriel, "Now the Holy Father clearly says that war can no longer be used as an instrument of justice in a world where nuclear arms are possessed. Fortunately he does not have to be approved by the censors of the Order in America, for they said very energetically last year that this thesis, when I proposed it myself, was wrong, scandalous and I don't know what more" (*School of Charity*, 166). WHS

> SEE ALSO CENSORSHIP; "COLD WAR LETTERS"; *DISPUTED QUESTIONS*; *SIGN OF JONAS*; *WISDOM OF THE DESERT*.

SOUL OF THE APOSTOLATE, THE

Jean-Baptiste Chautard
Translated by a Monk of Our Lady of Gethsemani. Trappist, Ky.: Abbey of Gethsemani, 1946. xxii+290 pp.

This is a new translation by Thomas Merton of a work by the Trappist abbot of the French monastery of Sept-Fons (1858–1935). It replaced an earlier translation first done in 1912 (though evidently not published until 1927) that had been reissued by Gethsemani in 1941. The improvement in style and comprehensibility can be gauged from the opening paragraph of part 1. The earlier version reads, "To be sovereignly liberal is an attribute of the Divine Nature. God is infinite goodness. Goodness longs to give and to make others share the wealth it enjoys"; Merton's translation reads, "Sovereign liberality is inseparable from the divine Nature. God is infinite goodness. Goodness seeks nothing except to *give itself* and to communicate the riches which it enjoys."

The Soul of the Apostolate reached its final form in the years immediately following World War I. Though written by a Trappist, it is intended not for members of contemplative orders but for those, particularly priests, in active apostolates, stressing the necessity of a deep spiritual life as a foundation for communicating the gospel. It is divided into five sections:

(1) "Active Works and the Interior Life; What They Mean" explains its basic terms and warns against a busyness in the active life that loses touch with the Source of its energy by a neglect of prayer; (2) "Union of the Active and Interior Lives" emphasizes the interdependence of the two dimensions of Christian life; (3) "Danger of the Active Life without Interior Life" warns against substituting activity for prayer instead of allowing activity to flow from prayer; (4) "Action Made Fruitful by the Interior Life" emphasizes the positive results that flow from intimacy with and dependence upon God; (5) "Principles and Counsels for the Interior Life" provides practical advice for mental prayer, liturgical prayer, and what Chautard calls "custody of the heart," a solicitude to preserve purity of intention for apostolic activity from being corrupted by more self-centered motives.

In addition to translating the work, Merton provides an introductory biographical note on Dom Chautard, in which he discusses the future abbot's conversion as a university student from a nominal to a fervent Catholic, principally as a result of contact with a youth group in Marseilles; his entrance into the Trappist monastery at Aiguebelle in 1877, his providential role in saving the abbey from financial ruin due to a "chance" meeting after being sent to Paris, and his subsequent very busy life as abbot of two monasteries, Chambarand and Sept-Fons; his role in the repurchase of Cîteaux as the motherhouse of the order; and his defense of the Cistercians against anticlerical French regimes. Merton details the development of *The Soul of the Apostolate* from a 1907 pamphlet to its final form, and while recognizing that its audience is nonmonastic, he sees its spirit as being characteristically Cistercian, marked by the maxim "God Alone" written over the doors of many Trappist monasteries (including Gethsemani): "Not contemplation, not action, not works, not rest, not this or that particular thing, but God in everything, God in anything, God in His will, God in other men, God present in his own soul.... It is the spirit of St. Bernard, and the spirit of the While Monks" (*Soul of the Apostolate*, xiv).

On December 13, 1960, Merton writes in his journal, "Had to revise for Image Books, preface to *The Soul of the Apostolate* ... written when I was a different person fifteen years ago. I am not concerned now with the same things in the same way" (*Turning toward the World,* 74). A new, paperback edition of the book, published by Doubleday, appeared in September 1961, with Merton now listed as translator and author of the introduction, which in fact includes the whole of the earlier biographical note on Chautard, lightly revised and preceded by three pages of new material that identify the "great problem of the modern world" as "the problem of rush, confusion, preoccupation with all those endless and profoundly absorbing activities which alienate a man from himself, distract him from God, and plunge him into a maelstrom in which it is no longer possible for him to retain his full stature as a free and rational human being, made in the image and likeness of God" (9). Thus, Merton relates his own characteristic themes of the early 1960s to Chautard's book, which he judges to be "slightly 'dated'" yet insistent on "the basic truth that, without supernatural roots in grace, Christian activity will be a dry and fruitless plant.... Unless our apostolate is a communication of the Life and Spirit of Jesus Christ, it is without value, and it is not even worthy of the name of Christian, no matter how many pious Christian formulas may be called upon to deck it out" (11). POC

SPIRIT OF SIMPLICITY, THE

Trappist, Ky.: Abbey of Our Lady of Gethsemani, 1948. vi+139 pp.

Though issued anonymously, this is the first published prose work to which Thomas Merton made a substantial contribution. The full description of the volume on the title page provides some indication of the nature of that contribution: "The Spirit of Simplicity Characteristic of the Cistercian Order. An Official Report, demanded and approved by the General Chapter. Together with Texts from St. Bernard of Clairvaux on Interior Simplicity. Translation and Commentary by A Cistercian Monk of Our Lady of Gethsemani." The work has two major parts. The first, "The Spirit

of Simplicity" proper, is Merton's annotated translation from the French of an official report on simplicity in Cistercian life approved by the general chapter of the order in 1925; the second, "St. Bernard on Interior Simplicity," consists of the translation and discussion by Merton of selected texts from the sermons and treatises of St. Bernard on the topic of simplicity. These two parts are framed by a brief foreword and an even briefer conclusion. While Merton calls himself "the translator and editor" of the volume in an introductory note, his extensive discussion of Bernard in part 2 qualifies him to be given the title of author as well, as is indicated by the reprinting of this material as the second part of the posthumously published *Thomas Merton on St. Bernard* (Kalamazoo, Mich.: Cistercian Publications, 1980).

In his six-page foreword Merton characterizes simplicity as a central quality of Cistercian life, though one easily liable to vagueness or sentimentality. The report to the general chapter gives official recognition to this centrality, but its concentration on the externals of simplicity (in clothing, buildings, liturgy, etc.) has prompted Merton to provide a discussion of interior simplicity based on the teaching of Bernard as a complement to the report. He summarizes the meaning of simplicity in the Cistercian tradition as *"getting rid of everything that did not help the monk to arrive at union with God by the shortest possible way"* (*Spirit of Simplicity,* iii), and explains that this means discarding, first, all that is opposed to charity, since the shortest possible way to God is through love, and second, all indirect ways to God through nonessential active works, since union with God's person is found through "silence, prayer, penance, sacrifice and contemplation" (iv).

The official report consists of an introduction and five chapters. Chapter 1, "Interior Simplicity," emphasizes that the monk seeks the one thing necessary, union with God, which also produces unity in the monastic community. Chapter 2, "Let Us Be True to the Ideal of Our Founders," is a general exhortation to fidelity to the original Cistercian charism, with particular emphasis on the figure of St. Stephen Harding. Chapter 3, the longest chapter, "Simplicity in the *Little Exordium,*" applies this admonition to St. Stephen's 1119 document, in which the basic aspects of Cistercian simplicity with regard to clothing, work, enclosure, and worship are described in detail. Chapter 4, "Anxiety of the General Chapters to Preserve the Spirit of Simplicity," surveys subsequent efforts, not always successful, to retain a simple lifestyle up through the French Revolution. Chapter 5, "Let Us Die in Our Simplicity," focuses on modern efforts to return to the primitive sources and the original spirit of Cîteaux and its monastic forebears, to humility, poverty, solitude, and, of course, simplicity.

In addition to translating this material, Merton adds a considerable number of explanatory notes throughout, in some cases explaining practical details (e.g., for meals [34]) or furnishing descriptive information on sources (e.g., Bernard's *Apologia ad Guillielmum* [44]). At times he provides more evaluative comments, as with the long note on following the spirit rather than the letter of original regulations (39–40), or the reference to the architecture of a particular church as "a flagrant example of what a Cistercian church should *not* be" (42). He even engages in somewhat controversial discussions, as when he disputes G. C. Coulton's description of Cistercian simplicity as "puritanism" (45). In one instance he even adds a somewhat dissenting note to the official document, when he comments on the statement that "Monks who were afflicted with the mania for writing poetry were to be sent to another house" by pointing out that "there was, as a matter of fact, both in the twelfth and thirteenth centuries, a flourishing Cistercian school of poets," and cites as a possible explanation of the strictures against poets the fact that "a misguided Cistercian" had written a long epic in praise of Frederic Barbarossa, a longtime foe of the order and the papacy (56). Thus, part 1 furnishes evidence of Merton's interaction with the text he is translating.

Part 2 provides a more spiritual and even theological approach to the subject of simplicity by its quotation and reflection on key texts of St. Bernard. Merton begins by providing an overview of Bernard's theology of image and likeness, which identifies natural simplicity as one of the three aspects of the divine image

in the human person, and sees the true greatness of human nature in its ability "*to rise to a participation* in the infinitely perfect simplicity of the Word*" (78), a union that for Bernard is "the *normal term* of the Cistercian life of simplicity" (80). Thus, Merton emphasizes Bernard's teaching that simplicity is intrinsically and dynamically oriented toward contemplation. After this introduction Merton provides four series of texts from Bernard. The first series, taken from Sermons 81 and 82 on the Song of Songs, emphasizes "Man's Original Simplicity" (81ff.); here as throughout part 2, Merton provides both extensive running commentary in his annotations and a summary analysis of the texts following their translation. Here he stresses the Cistercian father's emphasis on the centrality of self-knowledge, of discovering one's "real self, in the image of God" as well as on the necessity "to get rid of . . . the overlying layer of duplicity that is *not* ourselves" (90); the roots of Merton's own understanding of the true and false self can be recognized here.

The second series of texts, from Sermons 35–38 on the Song of Songs, focuses on "Intellectual Simplicity," in which knowledge is seen as oriented toward love, which alone makes possible that union with God which is the highest knowledge. Merton stresses that this position is far from anti-intellectual: it calls not for "a kind of holy blindness and stupidity" (100) but a learned ignorance, which renounces vain striving after useless knowledge but promotes a "harmony between knowledge and love" (101).

The third series of texts, on "The Simplification of the Will" (complementing the previous section on simplification of the intellect), is divided into two subsections, the first emphasizing obedience, seen in the context of charity and the common life, as the key for overcoming self-will, the second focusing on the danger of relying on one's own judgment, both for one's own salvation and for the peace of the community.

Finally, the last set of texts, based on Bernard's treatise *On the Love of God* and headed "Perfect Simplicity — Unity of Spirit with God," focuses on the full restoration of one's likeness to God in a union not of substance but of wills, in which the soul can be said "*to become God*" (131) insofar as it loses itself in God. This is the perfection of simplicity as it transcends multiplicity to become one spirit with God.

In concluding the volume, Merton calls for a deeper acquaintance on the part of Cistercians with the sources of their tradition, ideally through reading of the texts themselves, not for the sake of a "stuffy intellectualism" (138) but as a way to foster the humility, charity, and simplicity that will lead to unity and peace in the community and to union with the Source and Goal of all genuine simplicity. He sets up a goal that will continue to absorb much of his attention as a writer, teacher, and monk over the course of the final two decades of his life. POC

SPIRITUAL DIRECTION AND MEDITATION

Collegeville, Minn.: Liturgical Press, 1960.
108 pp. (paperback)

Thomas Merton himself noted that this short book — he called it a "booklet" — contains "a revised and considerably expanded version of material" (*Spiritual Direction and Meditation*, 5) that appeared in installments in *Sponsa Regis*.[1] As the title suggests, *Spiritual Direction and Meditation* actually is two books in one. At the time of its writing, the section on spiritual direction would have been of interest to priests and religious. Given the contemporary interest in spiritual direction, the book now may be of wider interest. The section on meditation appealed and may still appeal to a broader audience. The articles on spiritual direction were published in the magazine between July and November 1959, and those on meditation between February and June 1960. Merton's ideas on spiritual direction had been taking shape for almost two decades. As a monk, he had been experiencing spiritual direction for more than ten years when, on August 13, 1952, he reflected in his journal on the relationship between the spiritual director and the "penitent." While the director must be prepared to listen "with untiring patience" and "to observe and to advise and to guide" the penitent, it is necessary that the penitent "really can and does rely" on the director, sensing that the director is "one who can discover God's ways in their particular soul" (*Search for Solitude*, 8). In May 1951 Merton was named the master of scholastics and given responsibility for the formation of men preparing for ordination and final vows. This work gave him another perspective on direction. In a journal entry, written in February 1953, Merton prayed with gratitude for the scholastics and observed that "direction is sometimes an experiment in recognition: they recognize something new in themselves and I in myself: for God recognizes Himself in us" (30). By October 1958, when he was writing the articles on direction[2] published in *Spiritual Direction and Meditation*, Merton had been novice master since 1955. In August 1959 Merton explained to Fr. Killian McDonnell, editor at Liturgical Press, that he was sending him a new version of the articles, considerably lengthened with additions and corrections.[3]

The five sections on spiritual direction that comprise the first part of the book are numbered: (1) "The Meaning and Purpose of Spiritual Direction," (2) "Is Direction Necessary?" (3) "How to Profit by Direction," (4) "Manifestation of Conscience and Direction," and (5) "Special Problems." In the first section Merton explains how spiritual direction began, defines its nature and purpose, and describes the role of a spiritual director. Spiritual direction began with the "first religious" (*Spiritual Direction and Meditation*, 12): Christians who withdrew into the desert, where, separated from the Christian community, they discovered "the need for 'discernment of the spirits' — and for a director" (*Spiritual Direction and Meditation*, 12). Merton defines spiritual direction as "a continuous process of formation and guidance, in which a Christian is led and encouraged *in his special vocation,* so that by faithful correspondence to the graces of the Holy Spirit he may attain to the particular end of his vocation and to union with God" (13). Direction "is not mere ethical, social, or psychological guidance. It is spiritual" (14). It speaks to the whole person in the particular circumstances of his or her life. Its purpose is to encourage persons "to penetrate beneath the surface" (16), to come to know "our inmost self, our *real* self," not as we are in the eyes of others or in our own eyes but "as we are in the eyes of God" (39). The spiritual director, whom Merton likens to "a spiritual father" and "a kind of 'sacrament' of the Lord's presence in the ecclesiastical community" (17), helps a person "to recognize and to follow the inspirations of grace" in his or her life and to discern where God is leading (17). Merton quotes seventeenth-century Benedictine mystic Dom Augustine Baker to drive home the point that spiritual direction requires "a normal, spontaneous human relationship" (19). Baker wrote, "The director is not to teach his own way, nor indeed any determinate way of prayer, but to instruct his disciples how they may themselves find out the way proper to them.... In a word, he is only God's usher, and must lead souls in God's way, and not his own" (20–21).

"Is direction necessary?" is the question addressed in the second section. For many, contact with a pastor or confessor will suffice. "But certainly, wherever a layman has a special work to do for the Church, or is in a situation with peculiar problems, he certainly ought to have a director" (22). As examples, Merton identifies college students, "professional men," and couples preparing for marriage, but quickly he focuses on religious, for whom direction is "a much more serious matter" (22). Spiritual direction is integral to the formation of religious and it must not be limited to a formation focused merely on rules, rites, and observances. Religious need "a really interior and sensitive direction" (23). Noting that "spiritual directors are not easy to find" (26), Merton explains that the first duty of "an effective director" is "to see to his own interior life and take time for prayer and meditation, since he will never be able to give to others what he does not possess himself" (28).[4] Profiting by spiritual direction involves recognizing that direction is a gift of God that requires a combination of gratitude (spiritual direction is a gift of God), realism (spiritual directors do not work wonders), and humility to accept direction.

The "manifestation of conscience" is "*absolutely necessary*" (31) to spiritual direction, we learn in the fourth section. Those "being

directed must bring the director into contact with [their] real self, as best [they] can, and not fear to let him see what is false in [their] false self" (33). Directors, for their part, must be interested in "the basic attitudes of our soul, our inmost aspirations, our way of meeting difficulties, our mode of responding to good and evil" and must respect "the mystery of personality" (34). Rather than getting lost in verbiage about prayer and contemplation, spiritual directors need to help those they direct to "reintegrate their whole existence, as far as possible, on a simple, natural and ordinary level on which they can be fully *human*." Then, God's grace "can work on them" (45).

Among the problems that Merton addresses in the last section, on "special problems" in spiritual direction, are these: the temptation to reject and disregard the advice of the director, particularly when what the director says is disturbing; changing directors with whom one does not "click" (this should not be done hastily); direction by mail (it is "seriously handicapped" by "the lack of direct personal contact");[5] obedience to the director (one does not owe "strict obedience" as one does to one's superior); the distinction between direction and psychoanalysis ("the director is not a psychoanalyst") (45–50).

The second half of the book is devoted to the subject of meditation and consists of five unnumbered sections, entitled "What Is Meditation?" "Meditation in Scripture," "Meditation — Action and Union," "How to Meditate," and "Temperament and Mental Prayer." In the introduction to the book Merton explains that he wrote these notes in 1951 "as a kind of companion to *What Is Contemplation?*" (6).[6]

Although Merton sometimes used the terms "contemplation" and "meditation" interchangeably in the later 1960s,[7] in this book he distinguishes between meditation and contemplation. Meditation is the first step in a process of mental prayer that ends in contemplation and communion with God. "To meditate is to exercise the mind in serious reflection" (52). However, meditation is not "a purely intellectual activity"; it is not "mere reasoning" (52). It involves the whole person — mind and heart. One enters into reality not merely by studying it, but by living it. Mental prayer is "something like a sky-rocket," streaking heavenward to "new and unsuspected heights." When intelligence reaches its limits and the mind acknowledges its limitations, then "love again takes the initiative and the rocket 'explodes' in a burst of sacrificial praise" (56). Surrendering to that praise, the soul rests in God in silence.

In "Meditation in Scripture" Merton suggests meditating on God's law and God's mercy as revealed in Scripture, especially in the psalms. One should "savor" them and "absorb" their meaning. Although he does not use the term at this point, what he is recommending is the practice of *lectio divina* ("divine reading"). Reading the Hebrew Scriptures through a Christian lens, Merton sees Christ as being everywhere in the psalms (63). He also recommends meditating on the Eucharist, "the memorial of Christ's sacrifice" (63).

In "Meditation — Action and Union" Merton cautions against expecting meditation to be "colorful or spectacular" or to culminate "in a burst of emotion" (65–66). While "sentiments of fervor" may be helpful at the beginning, they may become obstacles to progress in the interior life. "A good meditation may well be quite 'dry,' and 'cold,' and 'dark'" (67). The "power of meditation" is generated "by *faith*" which can bring "light" to prayer if we allow the "words of salvation" to "sink deeply into our hearts" (68–69). Although meditation may deepen understanding of truth, strengthen resolve, or solve a spiritual problem, "the ultimate end of all mental prayer is communion with God," that is, contemplation (71). To illustrate how meditation may achieve this end, Merton offers the example of meditating on the passion of Christ to increase patience and explains how becoming "*spiritually* identified with Christ in His Passion" is essential (73). He concludes in this way: "Unless our mental prayer does something to awaken in us a consciousness of our union with God . . . it has not achieved the full effect for which it is intended" (76).

Merton begins the section "How To Meditate" by observing, "Meditation is really very simple" (77). Although he insists that there

is no need to follow a simple system, there are "certain universal requirements" (77). One needs to bring to meditation the following: recollection, which Merton describes as "living in an atmosphere of faith . . . with occasional moments of prayer and attention to God" and resisting the noise and distraction that are so much a part of ordinary life (78); "a sense of indigence," or awareness of one's own neediness and spiritual poverty; sincerity, or never saying "anything . . . that we do not really mean, or at least sincerely desire to mean" (88); and concentration on a single objective: "union with God" (92). One also needs an atmosphere that is conducive to prayer: "we can best meditate in silence and retirement — in a chapel, in a garden, a room, a cloister, a forest, a monastic cell" (82). Again Merton recommends meditation on the mysteries of the Christian faith — for example, the incarnation. However, other subjects appropriate for meditation are our own lives and problems — our vocation, our response to God and to others as well as the events of history. On the latter point Merton observes that he "would be inclined to say that a nun who has meditated on the Passion of Christ but has not meditated on the extermination camps of Dachau and Auschwitz has not yet fully entered into the experience of Christianity in our own time. For Dachau and Auschwitz are two terrible, indeed apocalyptic, presentations of the *reality* of the Passion renewed in our time" (97). Merton urges his reader to "*create a religious perspective* in which to view everything that happens" (99) in light of the passion, death, and resurrection of Christ. *Lectio divina*, "the meditative reading of Sacred Scripture" (100), is the foundation for the interior life. Merton concludes this section with "an outline [of] the simple essentials of meditative prayer": recollection, vision ("the attempt to see, to focus, to grasp what you are meditating on"), aspiration ("desires, resolutions to act in accordance with one's faith," to live one's faith), communion (resting in the presence of God), and thanksgiving (101).

In the brief section "Temperament and Mental Prayer" Merton explains that how a person meditates depends on his or her own temperament and gifts. For the majority, meditation is "rooted in the senses" and involves creating a mental picture by placing oneself in the presence of Christ (104).

In the "Summary and Conclusion" Merton states that meditation is "almost all contained in this one idea: the idea of *awakening* our interior self and attuning ourselves inwardly to the Holy Spirit, so that we will be able to respond to His grace" (107). CMB

Notes

1. The articles on spiritual direction were "considerably revised and expanded," but the material on meditation in *Sponsa Regis* and *Spiritual Direction and Meditation* is essentially the same. References in this entry are to the paperback edition: *Spiritual Direction and Meditation* (Collegeville, Minn.: Liturgical Press, 1960) (108 pages).

2. *Search for Solitude*, 222, 225. See the entries for October 7 and 23, 1958, in which Merton expresses his doubts about the value of writing these short articles. He asks himself whether he would be making better use of his time to write articles on Pasternak and resolves that he will go on doing both.

3. See the letter dated May 31, 1960, in *The School of Charity*, 133.

4. Although earlier in the book Merton noted that "a wise prioress or a good novice mistress should be capable of some direction" (24), he seems to assume that normally the spiritual director is a priest.

5. Among Merton's many correspondents were persons who sought his advice and direction, including some of his friends. Merton was careful to explain that one "cannot really get direction by mail," as he observed in a letter to his friend Etta Gullick. See *Hidden Ground of Love*, 365.

6. Also see Merton's letter to Sr. Therese Lentfoehr, dated June 15, 1962, in *The Road to Joy*, 241.

7. See, for example, *Contemplative Prayer* (also published as *Climate of Monastic Prayer*).

SPRINGS OF CONTEMPLATION, THE: A Retreat at the Abbey of Gethsemani

Edited by Jane Marie Richardson. New York: Farrar, Straus and Giroux, 1992. xvi+285 pp.

In December 1967 and again in May 1968 Thomas Merton hosted small gatherings of superiors of cloistered convents to assist their efforts toward renewing religious life for contemplative women, in the spirit of the Second Vatican Council. In his journal for December 7, 1967, he writes of the first of these retreats, attended by fifteen contemplative nuns: "The last four or five days have been quite fantastic: among the most unusual in my life." After providing short descriptions of a number of the

sisters, he adds, "I am completely confident in the contemplative orders once again. There is a lot that needs changing, but our life is fundamentally one of the soundest and most healthy things in the Church, and I am sure has all kinds of promise.... These four days have been very moving and I feel completely renewed by them: the best retreat I ever made in my life" (*Other Side of the Mountain*, 20–21). His comments of May 28, 1968, on the second gathering, which took place shortly after his return from California and New Mexico, are more sober, focusing on the difficulties of renewal in women's orders with little autonomy, though the tone also may reflect to some extent his own weariness after a busy trip: "Once again, realization of the paralyzing problems of these contemplative convents and of their need.... Although it does not seem to be my 'line' to think in institutional terms, still there are *people* involved who badly need help. And those who are concerned enough to come here are really alert and well informed and want to do something" (123).

The Springs of Contemplation consists of edited transcripts of Merton's conferences at these two retreats: seven talks from the first retreat and nine from the second[1] (as well as a reprinting of Merton's 1962 pamphlet *Loretto and Gethsemani*, written to mark the 150th anniversary of the founding of the Congregation of Loretto, included as an appendix). The conferences, which are given titles by the editor that reflect the main focus of each presentation, typically begin with Merton's informal introductory remarks on a topic, but usually more than half the time is spent responding to questions and comments from the retreatants. This relaxed, collegial atmosphere highlights Merton's ability to keep the major issue in focus without needing to control or dominate the discussion. (On one occasion when the conversation threatens to get off the track — he had mentioned a flying squirrel that had come down the hermitage chimney — he answers the question "Did it really fly?" and then steers the group back to the topic [the balance between prayer and work] by asking, "Well, do we have any other questions about karma?" [*Springs of Contemplation*, 221].)

The wide range of topics discussed in the sixteen conferences all touch in some way on the point of intersection between contemplative commitment and contemporary church and society. Merton cites Martin Buber and Herbert Marcuse along with magazine advertisements and a science fiction story; he draws on insights from Zen masters and yogis as well as Teresa of Avila and his own Cistercian fathers. Charlie Chaplin and Che Guevara, Marshall McLuhan and Malcolm X, the Taizé brothers and the rituals of Native American rites of passage all make their contribution. The tension between demands of solitude and community, the priority of charism over structure and of communion over institution, the call for simultaneous fidelity to living tradition and to the need for flexibility and adaptability, the distinction between obedience and subservience, the place of sexuality in a celibate life, detachment from the results of one's actions as a sign of trust in God, issues of racism and nonviolence — these are but some of the key aspects of the process of renewal that Merton discusses. A central point to which Merton repeatedly returns throughout the retreats is the prophetic dimension of the contemplative vocation. The very "irrelevance" of the monastic life, what Merton elsewhere calls its "marginal" status, gives it the potential, beyond that even of more obviously dissident groups, to avoid being co-opted, to be a sign of true liberation in a world where fewer and fewer choices are not predetermined.

Perhaps the most significant (and, in its own way, the most prophetic) conference is one that deals with a topic not discussed elsewhere by Merton in any detail: the role of women in the church and in society. At a time when relatively few other Catholics, men and women, were aware of this issue, Merton could begin his reflections by remarking, "Underlying this feminine mystique is the fact that women take an awful beating and have a very tough time in the Church." He finds this "idealization of supposed special feminine qualities which are put up on a pedestal and made much of" a particular problem for cloistered religious, who are turned into a kind of icon of "passive" and "mysterious" womanhood, and who are almost completely under the control of male clerical authorities (161). Merton's recommendation to his audience, those "officially" designated to live out this stereotype, is quite explicit: "I think you have an absolute duty to rebel, for the good of the Church itself.... If you're going to liberate yourselves, you have to break out of this image, this view that you can't make your own decisions because you're passive and mysterious and veiled and different" (162–63). He confesses that he does not know about women priests, though he adds significantly, "I leave that to you to figure out" (175). (He does see optional priestly celibacy as part, though not a major part, of a solution.) More important than giving women access to the existing power structure is transforming the structure itself: "I think we need to develop a whole new style of worship in which there is no need for one hierarchical person to have a big central place, a form of worship in which everyone is involved" (175–76).

In her introduction Merton's friend Sr. Mary Luke Tobin, who participated in the retreats, summarizes the key themes of the conferences as "authentic autonomy, the overcoming of alienation,... the value of the contemplative life in general, and of the lives of these sisters in particular" (xi), and adds, "So well did Merton discern... the impact of culture and events on our times that I believe we have not caught up with him yet" (xii). POC

SEE ALSO *LORETTO AND GETHSEMANI;* WOMEN.

Notes

1. One of the conferences included in the first set, "Contemporary Prophetic Choices" (79–90), actually belongs with the second, since it makes reference both to the assassination of Martin Luther King (86–87) and the Catonsville Nine draft board raid (79), events of April 4 and May 19, 1968, respectively.

STONE, NAOMI BURTON

Naomi Burton was born in England and came to America in 1939. She became a literary agent for aspiring writers, among them Thomas Merton. In 1951 she married Melville E. (Ned) Stone. Early on she recognized Thomas Merton's literary gifts but initially was unsuccessful in selling his novels to any publisher. The big

Naomi Burton Stone

break came in 1946 when she sent the manuscript of *The Seven Storey Mountain* to Robert Giroux, an editor at Harcourt, Brace. The book became a bestseller and won instant fame for its author. Naomi Stone was more than a literary agent for Merton. They became close friends. Merton valued her counsel, which she was quite ready to give when she thought he needed it. She was a "sister" to him, and sometimes a "mother" who did not hesitate to "scold" him when she felt he needed it. When Merton set up the Merton Legacy Trust to administer his estate on behalf of the monastery, she was one of the three trustees. There is a selection of Merton's letters to her in *Witness to Freedom*. WHS

"STRAITS OF DOVER"

SEE NOVELS, UNPUBLISHED.

STRANGE ISLANDS, THE

New York: New Directions, 1957. 102 pp.

This is Thomas Merton's fifth published book of verse, the first since 1949. Most of the poems, as Merton himself notes in the preface, come from the two previous years, when he had returned to writing verse after almost completely abandoning it. Though not quoted in the volume itself, the source of the title is the thirteenth stanza of the "Spiritual Canticle" of St. John of the Cross: "My Beloved is the mountains, / And lonely wooded valleys, / Strange islands, / And resounding rivers, / The whistling of love-stirring breezes," and particularly in the final section of the book, the poems become records of voyages to these islands, which are identified with the God who is loved and is Love. Both in style and in subject matter this is a transitional volume: a number of its poems are marked by the simpler diction that critic George Woodcock called "the poetry of the desert," as contrasted with the more ornate "poetry of the choir" typical of his verse from the previous decade;[1] suggestions of the greater openness toward the world, an identification with and compassion for its people, that would characterize the writing of his final decade also begin to become evident here.

The Strange Islands is arguably the most carefully organized of all Merton's books of shorter poems (although the ordering is due not to Merton himself but to James Laughlin, his publisher at New Directions). It is arranged in three sections, the first consisting of nine poems, the second of the verse play "The Tower of Babel — A Morality," published in a limited edition the same year, and the third of twelve poems. As the play focuses on the theme of the "two cities," corresponding to the two kinds of love, *cupiditas* and *caritas*, mentioned in the second epigraph (from Augustine, *City of God* 14.28) and corresponding to the two halves of the play, "Part I — The Legend of the Tower" and "Part II — The City of God," so the poems in part 1 are largely concerned with failed attempts to discover social and personal wholeness, while those in part 3 describe movement toward and experiences of authentic integration.

The opening poem, the five-part "How to Enter a Big City" (no. 1; 89 ll.) presents the city (presumably Louisville) as a place of alienation, "Centered in its own incurable discontent" (l. 43), where pedestrians "Cannot agree to be at peace / With their own images, shadowing them in windows / From store to store" (ll. 56–58). While there are signs of hope with the coming of night, they are associated principally with leaving the city, as "Branches baptize our faces with silver / Where the sweet silent avenue escapes into the hills" (ll. 80–81). This poem is followed by "The Guns of Fort Knox" (no. 2; 30 ll.), perhaps the earliest of Merton's "antiwar" statements, reminiscent both of the opening scene of *Hamlet*, with its observation that "Wars work under the floor" (l. 4), and of Hardy's "Channel Firing," with its closing address to the guns not to wake the dead "to do death's work once more" (l. 22) for "this is not / The right resurrection" (ll. 23–24).

"Nocturne" (no. 3; 21 ll.) is a dream poem, suggesting that sleep frequently unlocks anxieties, particularly about lack of direction ("all / Must miss some train, be late at school, / Found without money in the strange hotel" [ll. 7–9]), but also that it has the potential to be revelatory as it "Explores all countries where the soul has gone" (l. 11); the ambivalence culminates with an awareness that night asks "one prophetic question" (l. 19), the unknown answer to which might either bring "your tides and histories" to an end, or else "begin all storms" (ll. 20, 21). It is the latter result that is the focus of "Spring Storm" (no. 4; 19 ll.), in which the torrential rains reveal "How unsubstantial is our present state" (l. 4), yet also suggest the possibility for genuine renewal, but one from which "the woolen hundreds" (l. 19) mindlessly flee — a flock of sheep without a shepherd.

The focus takes a personal, indeed confessional turn with "Whether There Is Enjoyment in Bitterness" (no. 5; 30 ll.), in which the speaker demands the right "To be sick of myself" (l. 4) like other people, and to "break my bones (within me) / In the trap set by my own / Lie to myself" (ll. 7–9). He asks to be left in peace to "enjoy" (l. 23) the agony of

life and death contesting for victory within him, but finally asks for prayers "for in my bitterness / I hardly speak to Him: and He / while He is busy killing me / Refuses to listen" (ll. 27–30).

"Sports Without Blood — A Letter to Dylan Thomas" (no. 6; 121 ll.) is the earliest of the poems in the volume (dated 1948), a four-part reflection on Cambridge, where both Thomas and Merton attended university in the interwar period ("a spell between two bombs" [l. 43]). It is depicted as a place of death, above all death by drowning, in waters that turn everything upside down. He concludes by addressing his fellow poet and urging, "Come, let us die in some other direction / Sooner than the houses in the river quiver and begin their dance / And fall in the terrible frown" (ll. 119–21).

"Exploits of a Machine Age" (no. 7; 30 ll.) (dedicated to Robert Lax) describes the mindless routines of industrial work, in which some apocalyptic upheaval is both feared and desired but "Once again the explosion was / Purely mental.... / The machines were safe. Nothing / At all had happened. / Literally nothing" (ll. 18–19, 21–23). The irony of the final line, "Better luck tomorrow!" (l. 30), suggests that even catastrophe would be preferable to the dissatisfactions of meaningless work. "The Anatomy of Melancholy" (no. 8; 41 ll.) is a mordant portrait of a man who initially lives by clichés ("kept his head" [l. 5]; "heart was not / On his sleeve" [ll. 9–10]; "ready / With a civil answer" [ll. 10–11]), but when he fails to conform (losing his balance when "he could not find his feet" [l. 12]), he is stripped of all his possessions ("He kept a stiff upper lip but no / Money and no social standing" [ll. 34–35]) and finally is arrested when he goes off "in no direction" (l. 37) with his dog ("man's best friend" [l. 38]) "For romping as they walked / And barking as they spoke" (ll. 40–41).

The final poem of the first part, "Elias — Variations on a Theme" (no. 9; 178 ll.), marks a turning point in the development of the volume. The biblical figure, envisioned as both prophet and solitary, represents the tensions and ambiguities, but also the rich possibilities, of the relationship between contemplation and action. His flight from the wrath of Queen Jezebel leads him to silence, stillness, patience, in order to listen and to learn, to renounce a spurious sense of superiority and self-righteousness to the world he had judged and to acknowledge his own complicity in the wrongs he had denounced. By surrendering his own projects, his own will, his own image of himself, he is able to take the crucial step toward discovering the authentic and lasting fulfillment of an identity at once contemplative and prophetic: like the bird who "sings no particular message" (l. 138), like "the seed, the salt, / The snow, the cell, the drop of rain" (ll. 142–43), Elias (and the speaker who comes to identify with him) realizes that the genuine prophet is one who has discovered his oneness with all reality, who resonates with the needs and hopes of others because he has found these very needs and hopes in his own depths, who has been made aware that because the center of the self is not the self but God, to experience one's true center is to pass beyond the self without leaving the self, to be "surrounding the Spirit / By which he is himself surrounded" (ll. 176–77).

This greater openness toward the world becomes a predominant theme in the poems of part 3. "Birdcage Walk" (no. 11; 42 ll.), based on an actual childhood experience (see *Run to the Mountain*, 38), contrasts innocence with experience as the bishop ("this old pontifex" [l. 28] — literally "bridge builder") declares there is no bridge, "No crossing to the cage / Of the paradise bird!" (ll. 31–32), yet the young boy nevertheless goes and "open[s] all the palace aviaries" (l. 40) and frees the caged birds. The following poem, "Landscape" (no. 12; 44 ll.), though written in a much starker style, shares the same theme, contrasting the imagination of "the Child" which enables him to draw pictures of cosmic realities, with the perspective of the adult "Personage," whose picture of the beginning of the world is perceived by the Child as actually depicting "its end" (l. 26), and who at the poem's conclusion indeed "crosses out the sun" (l. 44).

The brief and enigmatic "Wisdom" (no. 13; 8 ll.) reveals the paradox that it is beyond objective knowledge and therefore "is well known / When it is no longer seen or thought of" (ll. 6–7); to seek to possess wisdom is to discover that one knows "nothing" (l. 1), yet it is this "no-thing" that intuitively is recognized by one who no longer craves it as a possession to be the fullness of reality and transcendent knowledge. A similar insight is found more concretely expressed in "When in the Soul of the Serene Disciple" (no. 14; 23 ll.), for whom "Poverty is a success" (l. 3) and who therefore has let go of all possessiveness, even the desire for reputation: "his halo" has been blown away "with his cares" (l. 12), and "His God lives in his emptiness like an affliction" (l. 19).

Photograph by Thomas Merton

"In Silence" (no. 15; 33 ll.) raises the question of ultimate identity, suggesting that it is a mystery beyond definition but not beyond experience. Creation, represented by "the stones of the wall" (l. 2), calls the listener to "Be what you are (but who?) be / The unthinkable one / You do not know" (ll. 19–21). This is possible only by being still and becoming attentive to the revelatory Word speaking through all creatures, to "the Unknown / That is in you and in themselves" (ll. 27–28), but the poem ends with acknowledgment of the difficulty of doing this when, like the burning bush, "The whole / World is secretly on fire. . . . / All their silence / Is on fire" (ll. 31–32, 37–38).

The subtitle of "Early Mass" (no. 16; 29 ll.), ("*St. Joseph Infirmary — Louisville*"), is an important clue to the poem's significance. In inviting people to the Eucharist, to "the Cross and Wedding" (l. 4), the speaker focuses on the liturgy as the act by which Christ builds "His sacred town" (l. 7). But the emphasis is not, as often in Merton's earlier poems, on the contrast between the city of God and the earthly city, but on their congruency. Celebrating Mass in the city itself, the speaker finds the presence of the eschatological kingdom hidden in the midst of ordinary reality: "Gather us God in honeycombs, / My Israel, in the Ohio valley!" (ll. 15–16). The facile dualism of transcendent and earthly, or of abbey and world, is overcome as "These mended stones shall build Jerusalem" (l. 20); after distributing communion he invites his congregation to "Open the doors and own the avenue / For see: we are the makers of a risen world" (ll. 26–27).

"A Prelude: For the Feast of St. Agnes" (no. 17; 28 ll.), which dates back to 1950 (see *Entering the Silence*, 400), also is a eucharistic poem, in which the Mass is seen as an event that transcends both time, as the martyrs of the Roman canon, including Agnes, are summoned to be present at the celebration (ll. 1–9), and space, as "No lines, no globes, / No compasses" (ll. 17–18) are of any use, or any need, in effecting the presence of the saint.

"The Annunciation" (no. 18; 45 ll.) is a poem of renewal, in which the destructive fires of passion give way to the "Sparks of His Spirit" (l. 12) that are one day to burst into pentecostal flame but now are hidden in the simple girl in a simple room (unlike the elaborate settings of many paintings of the scene), whom "seven pillars of obscurity / Build . . . to Wisdom's house, and Ark, and Tower" (ll. 19–20). Through her the expulsion from "Eden's wood" (l. 36) is reversed, and "Suddenly we find ourselves assembled / Cured and recollected under several green trees" (ll. 37–38).

"Sincerity" (no. 19; 33 ll.) initially appears to belong to the first rather than the third part of the volume, and indeed its incisive critique of self-deception could fit there well, but placed toward the end of the volume it is a reminder that the struggle for a self-surrender that does not entail self-righteousness is an ongoing one. The same theme is personalized in "To a Se-

vere Nun" (no. 20; 30 ll.), in which the sister's quest for self-justification and her attempt to leave behind all companions in her ascent of "A path too steep for others to follow" (l. 3) is critiqued as an approach that alienates her from the Christ who identifies with weakness and "seems glad to suffer in another" (l. 26); the poem concludes with the hope that eventually she may recognize her own weakness and so become open to the power of the suffering Christ.

The penultimate poem, "Elegy for the Monastery Barn" (no. 21; 41 ll.) (from 1953), begins by comparing the burning barn to the finery of a dying woman, who reveals a beauty previously unnoticed, but who also "has another legacy" (l. 20), as the past years, "Fifty invisible cattle" (l. 29), return to testify to the transience of all temporal reality and so to serve as a kind of sacrament, an outward sign of the "gentle doom" (l. 41), the end of all things; the fire itself finally is an epiphany, a manifestation of "the Holy / One sitting in the presence of disaster" (ll. 39–40).

If the "Elegy" has an eschatological, even an apocalyptic, flavor, the final poem, "Stranger" (no. 22; 39 ll.), balances it with a more contemplative perspective, albeit one that itself looks forward to "the first morning / Of a giant world / Where peace begins / And rages end" (ll. 8–11). The "One bird" who "sits still / Watching the work of God" (ll. 11–12), ordinary events of the natural world that nevertheless are filled with the divine presence, becomes the paradigm of contemplative awareness and prompts the speaker to turn within and attend to the "inward Stranger / Whom I have never seen" (ll. 26–27) but who is an incomparably better teacher "Than any wordy master" (l. 25), and who discloses the revelation of unity beyond time and space, beyond subject and object, with which the poem and the volume concludes: "Look, the vast Light stands still / Our cleanest Light is One!" (ll. 38–39). POC

SEE ALSO *TOWER OF BABEL*.

Notes

1. George Woodcock, *Thomas Merton: Monk and Poet* (New York: Farrar, Straus and Giroux, 1978), 51, 62.

STRIVING TOWARDS BEING:
The Letters of Thomas Merton and Czeslaw Milosz
Edited by Robert Faggen. New York: Farrar, Straus and Giroux, 1997. xii+178 pp.

This collection of letters between Thomas Merton and Czeslaw Milosz is one of several volumes published to date that present Merton's exchange of letters with individuals who were friends and correspondents. Each of these collections contributes to a deeper understanding of Merton's person and interests as revealed in the exchange. This volume is no exception. In these letters, written over the course of a decade, readers glimpse something of Merton, of Milosz, and of the friendship they shared. *Striving towards Being* includes forty letters: twenty-one by Merton and nineteen by Milosz between December 6, 1958, and November 21, 1968. The first and the last (a card from Asia) are Merton's. Merton's letters to Milosz were published previously in *The Courage for Truth* (1993). Milosz's letters to Merton are published here for the first time.

Robert Faggen's introduction characterizes the correspondence, to highlight the similarities between the two men and to preview the exchange. Faggen notes that the correspondence between Merton and Milosz "represents a mutually edifying dialogue, a *concerto grosso*, between two powerful voices seeking to maintain faith in some of the most turbulent years of the late twentieth century. They recognized totalitarianism, scientism, atomic war, and racism as among the greatest threats to mankind's ability to sustain belief in a just God and in Providence" (*Striving towards Being*, v). While the two lived very different lives — Merton a French-born American monk living in Kentucky and Milosz a Lithuanian-born Polish poet living in France and then Berkeley — there were significant similarities between them. Both were writers who recognized the value of solitude and the demands of social responsibility. Both engaged serious issues of faith. "Both men were poets who valued literature as a way to revelation" (vi). And although they met only twice, at Gethsemani in 1964 and in Berkeley in 1968 as Merton was on

his way to Asia, "their letters reveal a powerful relationship of mutual spiritual guidance" (vi). In Merton, Milosz found a "spiritual father" (vii); in Milosz, Merton found "a mentor" (viii).

When Merton initiated the correspondence in December 1958, he was at an important juncture in his own life. He was "turning toward the world," and Milosz — along with other writers and intellectuals such as Ernesto Cardenal and Boris Pasternak — offered Merton a window on that world. Merton had just finished reading Milosz's "remarkable" and "important" book *The Captive Mind*, and he was excited, enthusiastic, and encouraged (3). "I find it especially important for myself in my position as a monk, a priest and a writer. It is obvious that a Catholic writer in such a time as ours has an absolute duty to confine himself to reality and not to waste his time in verbiage and empty rationalizations" (3). Merton found *The Captive Mind* "frankly 'spiritual,' that is to say, as the inspiration of much thought, meditation and prayer about my own obligations to the rest of the human race, and about the predicament of us all" (3–4). Merton recognized in Milosz "a kindred mind" and was ready for the dialogue that would follow. He ended that first letter by peppering Milosz with questions about the writers of whom he wrote in *The Captive Mind*. Milosz responded at length and in earnest, answering Merton's questions and sharing his own ideas about the book. And Milosz revealed something of himself in a postscript to his letter: "My road is and was more torturous than it seems from this letter. Forgive me its external, informative character" (13).

In the letters that followed during the next few years they explored ideas, read and criticized each other's work, wrestled with issues of war and peace and with challenges to freedom and human dignity, critiqued American society, and explored a host of theological issues. They questioned and encouraged each other and sometimes they disagreed.

These letters document the differences in viewpoint that emerged between the two men. One subject on which they differed was nature. After reading *The Sign of Jonas*, Milosz criticized Merton's romantic, one-sided view of nature. "Every time you speak of Nature, it appears to you as soothing, rich in symbols, as a veil or a curtain. You do not pay much attention to torture and suffering in Nature" (64). Merton responded with equal candidness and conviction: "Not that there is not plenty of resentment in me: but it is not resentment against nature, only against people, institutions and myself.... I am in complete and deep complicity with nature, or imagine I am: that nature and I are very good friends, and console one another for the stupidity and the infamy of the human race and its civilization. We at least get along, I say to the trees....I don't find it in myself to generate any horror for nature or a feeling of any evil in it. Or myself" (69–70).

Milosz also was critical of Merton's writings on war and peace. In an undated letter (probably written early in 1962 — Merton responds on March 14, 1962) Milosz stated his disagreement without mincing words: "I am completely puzzled by your papers on duties of a Christian and on war. Perhaps I am wrong. My reaction is emotional: no. Reasons: (1) My deep skepticism as to moral action which seems to me Utopian. (2) My distrust of any peace movements, a distrust shared probably by all the Poles, as we experienced to what use various peace movements served (the slogan *mourir pour Danzig* in 1939, the peace movement of Stalin, which started in 1948 with a congress in Poland). (3) Noble-sounding words turning around the obvious, because nobody would deny that atomic war is one of the greatest evils.... Any peace action should take into account its probable effects and not only a moral duty. It is possible that every peace manifesto for every 1 person converted throws 5 persons to the extreme right, by a reaction against 'defeatism'" (138–39). Merton assuaged Milosz's worry that his words had offended him and reassured Milosz that he did "not feel at all disturbed or unsettled" by what Milosz had to say. Merton explained, "The chief reason why I have spoken out was that I felt I owed it to my conscience to do so. There are certain things that have to be stated clearly" (146). In his journal, however, Merton's response was not so measured. There he wrote, "A very im-

portant letter from Milosz, in reaction to the articles on peace I sent him. It touches me deeply because I respect his judgment more than that of anyone I know, on this question. For he has been through it. And we have not. And yet, merely 'having been through it' is not enough either. The history of the last twenty years has been one immense brainwashing of everybody. And he is a graduate" (*Turning toward the World*, 200–201). On this subject, they remained divided.

Despite their differences — or perhaps, in part, because of them — their correspondence documents, in a most compelling way, a dialogue between two men in conversation with each other and with their world as both strive toward being. CMB

SUFISM

Although Thomas Merton never published an essay on Sufism, much less a book, he found the study of Sufism both intellectually rewarding and spiritually meaningful. It was much more than a passing enthusiasm and merits the scholarly attention it is receiving. In recent years Merton scholars have been documenting the development of Merton's interest in Sufism and exploring the breadth and depth of his exploration of the mystical tradition of Islam and, in so doing, fleshing out a significant dimension of Merton's thought. In 1999 a compendium of articles and a selection from Merton's writings on Sufism were published in *Merton and Sufism: The Untold Story*.[1]

Merton's interest in Sufism was sparked and nurtured by a series of personal contacts. Herbert Mason, a young American writer who began corresponding with Merton in May 1958, told Merton about Louis Massignon and sent Merton an offprint of an article by Massignon on the "Seven Sleepers of Ephesus." Merton was fascinated by the piece. Then Mason showed Massignon a copy of Merton's article on Boris Pasternak, and on September 3, 1959, Massignon wrote to Merton to thank him for the Pasternak article.[2] Merton's appreciation for Massignon's work in making the wisdom of Islam available to him is evident in Merton's letter of March 18, 1960, expressing both his gratitude for the book of prayers and exhortations *Akhbar al-Hallaj*, which Massignon had published with a French translation, and his resonance with al-Hallaj. "I think it is tremendous. In many ways the rude paradoxes are striking in the same way as Zen. But there is the added depth and fire of knowledge of the one God. There is the inexorable force of sanctity. The sense of the Holy, that lays one low: as in Isaias. To read Hallaj makes one lament and beat his breast. Where has it gone, this sense of the sacred, this awareness of the Holy? What has happened to us? How true it is that in the light of such blinding sincerity, our ordinary prayers and protestations of faith are acts of impiety" (*Witness to Freedom*, 276).

It was Massignon who put Merton in touch with Abdul Aziz, a student of Sufism living in Pakistan. Merton and Aziz shared a correspondence rich in detail and substance.[3] In response to Aziz's first letter Merton wrote, "As one spiritual man to another (if I may so speak in all humility), I speak to you from my heart of our obligation to study the truth in deep prayer and meditation, and bear witness to the light that comes from the All-Holy God into this world of darkness where He is not known and not remembered. . . . May your work on the Sufi mystics make His name known and remembered, and open the eyes of men to the light of His truth" (*Hidden Ground of Love*, 45–46). Merton's sense that they were meeting on a deep spiritual plane was validated in the letters that followed as both men shared openly about their religious faith and practice.[4] A few months later Merton wrote, "I am tremendously impressed with the solidity and intellectual sureness of Sufism. There is no question but that here is a living and convincing truth, a deep mystical experience of the mystery of God our Creator Who watches over us at every moment with infinite love and mercy. I am stirred to the depths of my heart by the intensity of Moslem piety toward His Names, and the reverence with which He is invoked as the 'Compassionate and the Merciful'" (48).

Through the 1960s Merton read widely on Sufi mysticism, as evidenced in his journal and in his letters. Merton was well acquainted with scholarly writings on Islam and Sufism. In addition to Massignon and Aziz, Merton had read Arberry, Arasteh, Burckhardt, Corbin, Foucauld, Iqbal, Lings, Nasr, Nwyia, and Schuon.[5] But Merton not only read about Sufism, he also immersed himself in the actual writings of Sufi mystics and saints. "A list of the Islamic saints mentioned in Merton's writings reads like a 'who's who' of classical Islamic philosophy and Sufi thought. . . . Ibn Abbad, al-Hallâj, Rûmî, Imâm Riza, al-Ghazâlî, Avicenna, Ibn Arabî, al-'Alawî, al-Junayd, al-Hujwîrî, and Averroës."[6] On occasion Merton responded to what he was reading by writing poetry inspired by Islamic and Sufi themes: "The Moslems' Angel of Death (Algeria 1961)," "The Night of Destiny," "Song for the Death of Averroës," "Lubnan," "Tomb Cover of Imam Riza," "Readings from Ibn Abbad" (all are reprinted in *Collected Poems*).

In October 1966 Sidi Abdeslam, a Sufi master from Algeria, came to Gethsemani. Merton wrote in his journal about what he termed a "momentous visit" with this "true man of God," who told Merton that he was "very close to mystical union" (*Learning to Love*, 152). "A real experience of Sufism. I now see exactly what it is all about. Close to monastic spirit. Very close indeed in simplicity, spontaneity, joy, truth," he noted in some points that he jotted down after the visit. "Above all," he continued, "importance of knowing and following the voice of one's own heart, one's own secret: God in us" (153).

Merton lectured on Sufism — its wisdom and insights about the mystical life — in the conferences that he gave to the novices in the late 1960s. The conferences, taped and made available to other monks in the community, reveal much about Sufism that appealed to Merton. What spoke to him most deeply was the Sufi realization of the centrality of the awareness of one's oneness with God. The human person is called to union with God. That insight, valid for all believers, is absolutely central to the monastic life. The monk is not called simply to live an ascetic life but also to open himself to the mystical life. In one of the conferences Merton said, "The basic thing in

Sufism then is ... the awakening to total awareness and to a real deep sense of the Reality of God. Not ... a sense of God as object, not a sense of God as thing," but rather, "an awareness of God as Subject, an awareness that God is within my own subjectivity, that He is the root of my own personality so that I do not see Him as somebody else entirely, and yet He is Totally Other ... the awareness that one is totally penetrated by God's knowledge of us ... a sense not only that God is listening when we pray but that we are known and seen through and through by Him and penetrated by Him."[7] In the conferences Merton spoke from his own heart: he had read and reflected on the wisdom of the Sufis and, as was very much his style, he shared what had touched him as a Christian monk. He probed the Sufi masters not only to understand them as best he could, but also to glean those insights that enriched his own understanding of the contemplative life. It is these insights that he shared with the novices. The themes that surface in the conferences have a special relevance for persons committed to nurturing the inner life: union with God, the names of God, the mercy of God, mercy, the dissolution or extinction of the self, peace.

As he traveled in summer and fall 1968, to California and Alaska during the summer and back to California and then on to Asia in the fall, Sufism continued to be on Merton's mind. He spoke about Sufism to women religious in Alaska and at Redwoods in California and in talks that he gave in Asia. References to Sufism are sprinkled throughout *The Asian Journal* as he made notes on his reading and reported on conversations. CMB

Notes

1. Rob Baker and Gray Henry, eds., *Merton and Sufism: The Untold Story* (Louisville: Fons Vitae Press, 1999). Included in the book are seminal essays on Merton and Sufism by Sidney H. Griffith, Erlinda Paguio, Bonnie Thurston, and Burton Thurston. Also included is Merton's essay "Final Integration: Toward a 'Monastic Therapy,'" in which Merton discusses Dr. Reza Arasteh's idea of the breakthrough to final integration, which Arasteh describes in the language of Sufism.

2. See Sidney H. Griffith, "Merton, Massignon, and the Challenge of Islam," in Baker and Henry, eds., *Merton*

and Sufism, 51–78, for an account of the correspondence between Merton and Massignon. Six of Merton's letters to Massignon have been published in *Witness to Freedom,* 276–81.

3. For a detailed discussion of this correspondence, see Sidney H. Griffith, "'As One Spiritual Man to Another': The Merton-Abdul Aziz Correspondence," in Baker and Henry, eds., *Merton and Sufism,* 101–29.

4. It was to Abdul Aziz that Merton wrote candidly about his own way of meditation or contemplative prayer. See *Hidden Ground of Love,* 63.

5. Bonnie Thurston, "The Example of Dhikr," in Baker and Henry, eds., *Merton and Sufism,* 49 n. 12.

6. Ibid., 42.

7. Transcribed by Bernadette Dieker in "Merton's Sufi Lectures to Cistercian Novices, 1966–68," in Baker and Henry, eds., *Merton and Sufism,* 160.

SURVIVAL OR PROPHECY?
An Exchange of Letters,
Thomas Merton and Jean Leclercq
Edited with foreword by Patrick Hart.
Introduction by Rembert Weakland. New York: Farrar, Straus and Giroux, forthcoming.

This volume of letters, spanning nearly twenty years, contains all the extant letters exchanged between the two best-known monks of the twentieth century: Jean Leclercq (1911–93) and Thomas Merton. One was a Benedictine monk from Luxembourg, a scholar of the medieval, who spent thirty years working on the critical edition of the works of St. Bernard of Clairvaux, while the other was a Trappist cloistered monk at the Abbey of Gethsemani in rural Kentucky in the United States. Monasticism underwent extraordinary changes during this period, which coincided with the Sec-

Jean Leclercq, O.S.B., and Thomas Merton

ond Vatican Council and the following years of adaptation and change. What we have in this volume is a microcosm of the history of monastic renewal in the mid-twentieth century. Bernard McGinn, well-known medievalist, has written, "When the history of twentieth-century monasticism comes to be written, it is hard not to think that two monks will dominate the story: Thomas Merton and Jean Leclercq" (book jacket).

The first exchange of this volume concerned a microfilm of some texts from St. Bernard discovered among the manuscripts and incunabula in Gethsemani's Obrecht Collection, which were then housed in the vault that Merton used for his office as master of scholastics. Merton took advantage of the occasion to invite Leclercq to visit Gethsemani the next time he was in the United States. Thus began a lifelong friendship between a Benedictine monk of Europe and a Cistercian (Trappist) monk from the United States.

The correspondence continued for nearly twenty years and developed beyond early monastic texts to the burning questions of the monk in the modern world, to ecumenical forays among fellow Christians as well as non-Christian monastics of the Far East. Both monks developed and matured in their thinking throughout their entire lives. Vatican II was a stimulant for them, but they always were great explorers of the spirit from the beginning of their monastic lives.

The last letter by Thomas Merton to Jean Leclercq has this memorable line, which bears repeating because it succinctly sums up the content of the book: "The vocation of the monk in the modern world is not survival but prophecy." Both monks were in agreement that it was not simply a matter of survival but of prophetic vision if monasticism was to flourish in the years ahead.

(This preview of a book not yet published at the time of this writing was kindly furnished by Br. Patrick Hart, O.C.S.O.)

SUZUKI, DAISETZ T.

A Zen scholar who taught at leading universities not only in Japan but also in Europe and in the United States, Daisetz T. Suzuki (1870–1966) served as a bridge between East and West. Proficient in English, he introduced many English-speaking people to Zen with his lectures and books, especially his *Essays on Zen Buddhism* (three volumes). Thomas Merton deeply admired his works and wrote to him in 1959. Merton had hoped to collaborate with him on a book dealing with the desert fathers and the Zen masters, but this was frowned upon by Merton's Order. The two did collaborate on a dialogue that appeared in *New Directions Annual* (vol. 17, 1961). It was called "Wisdom in Emptiness" and moved from the topic of the desert fathers to a discussion of knowledge and wisdom with special references to the Genesis narrative of the creation of man and woman. This dialogue was published in *Zen and the Birds of Appetite* (1968).

Merton paid a brief visit to Suzuki at Columbia University in June of 1964, one of the rare occasions when he was absent from Gethsemani. He was much impressed by this Zen scholar, who soon was to be ninety-four years of age. Merton remarks in his journal how important it had been for him to see and experience the deep understanding that existed between himself and "this extraordinary and simple man whom I have been reading for about ten years with great attention" (*Water of Life*, 116). When Suzuki died in 1966, Merton wrote a tribute to him that appeared first in *The Eastern Buddhist* (Otani University, Kyoto, Japan, August 1967) and later in *Zen and the Birds of Appetite* (1968) with the title "D. T. Suzuki: The Man and His Work." Merton's letters to Suzuki are printed in *The Hidden Ground of Love*. The book *Encounter: Thomas Merton and D. T. Suzuki* brings together the Merton-Suzuki letters and the journal account of their meeting in New York City in 1964. WHS

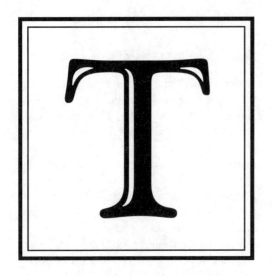

TALBOTT, HAROLD

While a student at Harvard, Harold Talbott became a Catholic. Later he was confirmed at the Abbey of Gethsemani, where he made his first contact with Thomas Merton. He became a student and an admirer of Dom Aelred Graham. Traveling to India, he became acquainted with the Dalai Lama and studied Buddhism under his direction. Talbott met Merton at New Delhi and brought him to the bungalow at Dharamsala that the Dalai Lama had made available to Talbott. It was from here that Merton went to his three meetings with the Dalai Lama. Talbott accompanied Merton to Darjeeling. They parted company on November 24, a grateful Merton bidding his friend goodbye. WHS

TAOISM

Thomas Merton's attraction to and affinity for classic Taoist thought is evident in his discussions of the *Tao Te Ching* of Lao Tzu and particularly in *The Way of Chuang Tzu*, Merton's collection of poetic reworkings of material from the book named after the fourth-century B.C.E. Taoist master. As Merton points

Cover for *Thomas Merton in Alaska* reprinted with the permission of New Directions. Cover photograph by Thomas Merton; cover design from Turkey Press adapted by Sylvia Frezzolini.

out, the word "tao," meaning "way," is not unique to Taoism; it is found in Confucianism as well (*Way of Chuang Tzu*, 20). Both religious philosophies date from the same general era, the so-called axial period of the sixth–fifth centuries B.C.E. (*Mystics and Zen Masters*, 47–48), but the "way" of Confucianism can be distinguished from that of Taoism in that the former focuses on "the ethical *Tao*, the way of man, rather than the metaphysical *Tao* or the inscrutable way of God" (58). The Tao of Taoism is not simply a set of directions for properly virtuous behavior, as in Confucianism, but the Great Tao, the Eternal Tao, "the nameless and unknowable source of all being" (*Way of Chuang Tzu*, 20). The ethical Tao is still linked to observable achievement, to measurable success, but living according to the Eternal Tao means living in harmony with the inscrutable order of the cosmos, an uncalculated goodness "without self-conscious reflection, or self-congratulation" (*Mystics and Zen Masters*, 49). Like Confucianism, Taoism is profoundly traditional, looking to the past for its model, but it turns its gaze back even further than Confucius to the archaic past, to small, primitive communities integrated with their natural environment and made up of people not competing with one another (48). Merton even suggests that the Taoist perspective has strong affinities "to immemorial modes of vision go-

462

ing back into the prehistoric past. I don't know if it can be proved, but Chuang Tzu, for instance, and Lao Tzu, even more, seem to be fighting to preserve an essentially Stone Age view of the world and of society, in which all that man now needs from his inventions was once attained and realized in himself" (*Guilty Bystander*, 281).

The true "Man of Tao" is one who rejects all self-assertion and self-aggrandizement, who is content to live in obscurity and solitude, as did the legendary founder of Taoism, Lao Tzu. Merton points out that the ideogram for "Tzu" carries connotations not only of "master," as it is usually translated, but also, paradoxically, of "child," because the true master is the heir of the wisdom of past generations, and in the case of Lao Tzu is best described as a child of "his 'mother' the Tao . . . born to his wisdom by the mysterious all-embracing and merciful love which is the mother of all being" (*Mystics and Zen Masters*, 72–73). Here one may recognize Merton's implicit linking of the Tao with "Hagia Sophia," the creative and nurturing "Holy Wisdom" of Proverbs 8.

The basis for an authentically Taoist life is "wu-wei," usually translated as "non-action" but better interpreted, according to Merton, as "non-activism" (54), or following the translation of his friend and mentor John Wu, as "non-ado" (75). "Wu-wei" is not passivity or inertia or quietism; it is a renunciation of "conscious striving" (*Way of Chuang Tzu*, 24) in favor of spontaneous action in harmony with the Eternal Tao. It is not independent activity but the action of the Tao through oneself, "action that seems both effortless and spontaneous because performed 'rightly,' in perfect accordance with our nature and with our place in the scheme of things" (28). It is action flowing from a cosmic humility, "a tranquillity which transcends the division between activity and contemplation" (26), that is aligned with "the dynamism of the whole" (28).

This humble refusal to dogmatize, Merton notes, sometimes can be mistaken as a kind of ethical relativism that rejects a clear division between good and evil. But what is rejected, Merton points out, is an inadequate perspective that attempts to substitute a part for the whole:

"When a limited and conditioned view of 'good' is erected to the level of an absolute, it immediately becomes an evil, because it excludes certain complementary elements which are required if it is to be fully good" (30). Only the Eternal Tao is completely good, but the Eternal Tao is beyond conceptualizing and defining; it can be reached only by a kind of intuitive identification that cannot be reduced to a system of unvarying principles. Far from being antinomian, Taoism is rooted in an eternal "Law" that transcends the limitations of human laws and leads to "genuine virtue which is 'beyond virtuousness'" (24). Though he points out that an imperfect understanding of Taoism can and has led to irresponsible escapism in the face of social and political oppression (*Seeds of Destruction*, 112), Merton believes that at its authentic best Taoist insight provides the proper detachment that allows one to discern that "*kairos*" moment "when action makes a great deal of sense" and is willing to wait patiently for that decisive moment to arrive (*Guilty Bystander*, 156). The contemplative "in harmony with the *Tao*" is in a better position to recognize and respond to the genuine needs of the world than "the politician who thinks himself in command" ("Inner Experience," 8:341).

Merton, following the lead of his friends D. T. Suzuki and John Wu, sees Zen, the result of the encounter of Taoism with Mahayana Buddhism, as the true heir of the tradition of Lao Tzu and Chuang Tzu, rather than the "hodgepodge of quasi-magical rites, folklore, and superstition" that goes by the name of popular Taoism (*Mystics and Zen Masters*, 46). Zen, Merton remarks, transmits the wisdom of the *Tao Te Ching* without the "*Ching*" (the authoritative book) (73). He also finds Taoism to have many analogies with Christianity, with parallels to the spiritual liberty of St. Paul (*Way of Chuang Tzu*, 25) and to the cosmic kinship of Francis of Assisi (27). He refers approvingly to John Wu's Chinese translation of "Logos" as "Tao" in the opening verse of John's Gospel (*Mystics and Zen Masters*, 72), and finds parallels in the *Tao Te Ching* to the focus on mercy and humility in the Gospels, going so far as to say, "The power of the sage is then the very power which has been revealed in the Gospels as Pure Love" (76) and that "the sapiential awareness of the hidden patterns of life . . . in Taoism, foreshadowed their fulfillment in the Gospel of Christ" (70). He even writes to John Wu, "The wisdom of Chuang Tzu demands the Resurrection, for the Resurrection goes beyond all moralities and moral theories, it is a totally new life in the Spirit" (*Hidden Ground of Love*, 614). Considering the Taoist classics in the context of a discussion of the Christian Scriptures, he sums up his understanding of Taoism as "a full awareness of the transcendent dimensions of everyday life in its very ordinariness" (*Opening the Bible*, 51), and elsewhere he maintains that such an awareness, recalling that of the Sermon on the Mount, "is absolutely necessary for us not only to progress but even to survive" (*Mystics and Zen Masters*, 70). POC

SEE ALSO CONFUCIANISM; WAY OF CHUANG TZU.

TEARS OF THE BLIND LIONS, THE

New York: New Directions, 1949. 32 pp.

Thomas Merton's fourth published book of verse, coming five years after his initial volume, *Thirty Poems* (1944), and two years after his third, *Figures for an Apocalypse* (1947), this thirty-two page volume is the shortest book of Merton's poetry published in his lifetime, containing just seventeen poems, ranging in length from the twenty-line "Je crois en l'Amour" (Merton's first published poem in French) to the ninety-five lines of "Christopher Columbus." It was the last book of his verse to appear for eight years, until *The Strange Islands* of 1957. In his 1967 evaluation of his writings Merton ranked *The Tears of the Blind Lions* as "better," the highest category for any of his books (none are ranked "best"), shared only by *Thirty Poems* and *Emblems of a Season of Fury* (1963) among the poetry volumes.

The title is taken from a sentence of Léon Bloy used as the book's epigraph: "When those who love God try to talk about Him, their words are blind lions looking for springs in the desert." The desert setting, the blindness, and the inadequacy of verbal expression all point toward

Merton's preference for the apophatic way to God, the *via negativa* of darkness and emptiness, and perhaps suggest part of the reason why he was to fall silent, in verse at least, over the coming years. It should be noted that the tears of Merton's title are not taken from the Bloy quotation; they perhaps were suggested by, and are intended to symbolize, the poems themselves, virtually all of which contain water imagery; they may be intended to represent the tears of compunction traditionally associated with desert spirituality, though repentance is not a prominent theme in the volume, or tears of sorrow at the perilous state of a world estranged from the love of God, which certainly is a central focus throughout.

The majority of the poems are concerned directly or obliquely with the monastic life. The simplest and most straightforward, "The Reader" (no. 4; 21 ll.), is a prayer of the monk appointed to read to his brothers during their meal, as he awaits their arrival. The poem is one of anticipation, the readiness of the speaker to provide the monks with spiritual nourishment being implicitly likened to the "red cheeses" (l. 5) and bowls of milk on the tables. The poem itself, "this my psalm" (l. 21), is compared to the "little pearls of water" (l. 21) with which the entering monks bless themselves: as they prepare to listen to the word by that gesture of reverence, so he has prepared to speak it by this act of attentiveness and recollection.

"On a Day in August" (no. 6; 46 ll.) presents the speaker as one of the community of monks sweating in the fields on a day so hot that "Our souls are trying to crawl out of our pores" (l. 16). The natural world, usually a source of revelation for Merton, here is analogized to the silence of the saints who speak no word to the monks. The poem ends with an appeal to the clouds to turn from "blowsy cotton" (l. 36) to dark stormy purple, to "Summon the punishing lightning" (l. 38) that represents a death to self but also makes possible a rebirth, as "thoughts come bathing back to mind with a new life" (l. 44). Here the work routines of the abbey provide the setting for an exploration of the analogy between natural and spiritual states — a favorite Merton strategy.

The opening poem of the volume, simply

entitled "Song" (26 ll.), is a strong expression of the poet's desire for silence and solitude, and perhaps of his restlessness in the current monastic atmosphere where these are in short supply. In the midst of a rainstorm that "has devoured my house" (l. 1) the speaker contrasts his own position with that of "others," who may, or may not, be his monastic confreres: "In the rude door, my shelter / . . . I eat my air alone / With pure and solitary songs / While others sit in conference" (ll. 5–8). The "speech" (l. 11), "conversations" (l. 15), and "pale expressions" (l. 17 — perhaps both visual and aural) of the others are distinguished from the speaker's attitude of abandonment and openness to the uncontrollable natural world around him, which enables him both to "Distinguish poems" (l. 19) and to "speak to God, my God, under the doorway" (l. 24). A similar situation (without the comparison to the "others") is described in "In the Rain and the Sun" (no. 11; 46 ll.), where a storm brings "Dogs and lions . . . to my tame home, . . . my Cistercian jungle" (ll. 22–23) and makes the "Songs of the lions and whales" audible in his verse: "With my pen between my fingers / Making the waterworld sing!" (ll. 26–28); thus, a kind of return to Eden is experienced, in which "Adam and Eve walk down my coast / Praising the tears of the treasurer sun" (ll. 43–44).

Three of the poems make connections to the monastic liturgical office. "The Captives — A Psalm" (no. 9; 34 ll.) has as its epigraph the Vulgate Latin of Psalm 136 [137]:4, and is a modernized version of that psalm, with the Babylonian captivity analogized to enslavement to modern urban materialism, and the familiar verse "If I forget you, O Jerusalem, let my right hand wither" (v. 5) rendered "May my bones burn and ravens eat my flesh / If I forget thee, contemplation" (ll. 28–29). "A Responsory, 1948" (no. 15; 32 ll.) is a rare example of rhyme in Merton's verse, eight quatrains patterned x-a-y-a, with the first, fourth, and eighth stanzas the repeated refrain: "Suppose the dead could crown their wit / With some intemperate exercise, / Spring wine from their ivory / or roses from their eyes?"; the poem counterpoints the faith in resurrection implied in the refrain with a bleak vision of history in the intervening stan-

zas, as "The tides of new wars / Sweep the sad heavens" (ll. 20–21). "A Psalm" (no. 16; 29 ll.) describes the progression from the singing of the divine office, "When psalms surprise me with their music" (l. 1), through a resultant experience of the harmony of all creation, as "Choirs of all creatures sing the tunes / Your Spirit played in Eden" (ll. 9–10), to a deep contemplative silence and emptiness in which "God sings by Himself in acres of night" (l. 28); this poem foreshadows a vein that Merton will explore in many of the poems of the 1950s and 1960s.

"Je crois en l'Amour" (no. 13; 20 ll.) also is a deeply monastic and liturgical poem, perhaps written in French to provide a certain distancing for what is a very intimate profession of faith. The "Love" of the title is Christ, hidden in the seed ("caché dans les sémences" [l. 2]), but emerging in the spring when the speaker is moved by the heights of the liturgy ("des sommets liturgiques" [l. 4]) to the depths of his being ("au plus profond / De mon être mortel" [ll. 6–7]), and harvested in the summer by "chant" (both his own poetry and the communal divine office), which is his true wealth ("mon capital" [l. 12]). The poem concludes with an invitation to his brothers to join him in drinking the wine of Melchisedec (ll. 14–15), and with the declaration, modeled on the "cleft of the rock" image from the Song of Songs (2:14) (and implicitly compared to the germination of the seed earlier in the poem), that poems are born from his cleft human heart ("Dans le creux de mon coeur d'homme" [l. 19]).

Four of the poems have saints as their focus. "Hymn for the Feast of Duns Scotus" (no. 2; 51 ll.) (certainly regarded by Merton as a saint, though uncanonized) is filled with the Trinitarian paradoxes of the "Three Who is One Who is Love" (l. 11) and finally modulates into a prayer in which "my life becomes Thy Life" (l. 45) and Word, Father, and Spirit are invoked successively (ll. 46–47) as filling and transcending the created universe. "From the Legend of St. Clement" (no. 5; 43 ll.) describes the martyrdom of saints on the shore of the Black Sea as "poetry [that] shall grow in distant places . . . / . . . hymns [that] shall stand like vineyards / And swing with fruit in other worlds, in other centuries" (ll. 28, 30–31). "St. Malachy" (no. 8; 42 ll.) describes the twelfth-century Irish bishop (whose life was written by St. Bernard) as a kind of mythic figure, "bearded / With all the seas of Poseidon" (ll. 5–6), who visits Gethsemani on his feast day (November 3) in (or as) a rainstorm, and in departing brings down the autumn leaves and so brings the season to an end. "The Quickening of St. John the Baptist" (no. 3; 70 ll.), probably the best-known poem of the volume, has as its subtitle "On the Contemplative Vocation," and compares the unborn child who recognizes its Savior even in the darkness and silence of the womb to "Mother Church's hidden children," vowed contemplatives, "Planted in the night of contemplation, / Sealed in the dark and waiting to be born" (ll. 42, 47–48).

A number of the poems take a rather dour, pessimistic view of the state of the world, specifically the Cold War world of the late 1940s. The longest and most ambitious poem of the volume, "Christopher Columbus" (no. 7; 95 ll.), surveys the history of America as a tragedy of lost opportunities, in which Columbus is presented as a St. Christopher figure, a giant walking through the Atlantic, "head and shoulders above the horizon" (l. 14), bearing Christ to the pristine New World; but he is all too soon succeeded by "the devils … sailing for your harbors" (l. 69) bent on gold and domination, harbingers of a future of materialism and exploitation. "The City After Noon" (no. 10; 37 ll.) contrasts natural landscape with urban blight and imagines the disappearance of a city (evidently, Louisville) where "the fathers of destitution run / With horse, bottle and gun" and "the Little One dies of hunger in His manger" (ll. 16–17, 21), so that "there were nothing left in the world / But fields, water and sun / And space went on forever to eternity, without a rim" (ll. 33–35). "Dry Places" (no. 12; 37 ll.) pictures an abandoned mining town as a contemporary equivalent to the demon-haunted deserts of monastic Egypt, literally a "ghost town" where the bones of the dead try to seize the souls of the living; the scene by metonymy suggests the fallen world in toto, contrasted with the remembrance of

"Adam our Father's old grass farm" (l. 33), the paradisal world for which "Christ was promised first without scars [a clear expression of Merton's Scotist belief that the incarnation was not exclusively a consequence of the fall] / When all God's larks called out to Him / In their wild orchard" (ll. 35–37). "To the Immaculate Virgin, On a Winter Night" (no. 14; 28 ll.) is a somber prayer to Mary in which the cold and darkness represent the spiritual deadness of "a land without prayer" and "a year that wants more war" (ll. 26, 28); the words of the speaker's prayer are first imaged as "turn[ing] to ice in my dry throat" (l. 25) but then, in a displacement of the ice imagery that provides at least a modicum of hope, as "Walking to you on water all winter" (l. 27).

Merton's recent ordination to the priesthood is a major element in the last poem of the volume, "Senescente Mundo" ["As the world grows old"] (no. 17; 36 ll.), which unites, or rather contrasts, the volume's major themes of evil world and Christian, more specifically monastic, redemption. The first half of the poem (ll. 1–17) presents an apocalyptic scenario of the world's end when everything, whether valuable or vicious, is to be indiscriminately destroyed: "Beauty and ugliness and love and hate / Wisdom and politics are all alike undone" (ll. 6–7). This vision is countered by a sudden awareness of the power of the Eucharist that the speaker is now able to celebrate, which can "Revers[e] … all things / That now go on with fire and thunder" (ll. 24–25), and which is the foretaste of that "whole new universe, a great clean Kingdom" (l. 30) that one day will "rise up" (l. 31). The resurrected Jesus encountered in the Eucharist thus promises a cosmic resurrection, but is also a sign of hope for "my companions whom the wilderness has eaten" (l. 35), described in the final line of the poem and of the volume, in an image that anticipates its much more famous use in the journal to be published four years later, as "Crying like Jonas in the belly of our whale" (l. 36). POC

TECHNOLOGY

It probably is true that technology became a problem to Thomas Merton when Dom James began to modernize the monastery and its activities. Replacing horses and wagons with motorized vehicles troubled Merton, as he saw the silence and quiet of the monastery being invaded by noise and busyness. It is fair to say, however, that it was not until 1964 that technology became a subject of serious reflection for him. A quick look at the Merton journals confirms this. In volume 3 (1952–60) one finds but a single reference to technology; the same is true of volume 4 (1960–1963). In volume 5 (1963–65) a number of references to technology and to some of the literature on the subject shows an intensification of Merton's interest. A number of these references in volume 5 are found also in *Conjectures of a Guilty Bystander.*

In March of 1964 Wilbur H. Ferry sent Merton a copy of "The Triple Revolution," a publication of the Center for the Study of Democratic Institutions (based at Santa Barbara, California). The three revolutions were (1) the cybernation revolution (new ways of communication made possible by computer and automated, self-regulating machines); (2) the weaponry revolution (the creation of weapons of mass destruction that could destroy the human family); and (3) the human rights revolution (a worldwide effort to establish social and political equality of peoples of all races). Merton was deeply impressed by this booklet. Ferry also introduced him to a number of social philosophers, such as Lewis Mumford and Jacques Ellul.

Ellul's book *La Technique* (published in 1954), dealing especially with the cybernation revolution, became available in English in 1964. The book grabbed Merton's interest. He wrote in his journal under the date of October 30, 1964, "Reading Jacques Ellul's book, *The Technological Society.* Great, full of firecrackers. A fine provocative book and one that really makes sense" (*Water of Life*, 159). He expressed the hope that the fathers of the Second Vatican Council were aware of its contents as they struggled with the document "The Church in the Modern World."

In November of 1964 a group of peace activists (among them Daniel Berrigan, A. J. Muste, Jim Forest, and John Howard Yoder)

met at Gethsemani to discuss "Our Common Grounds for Religious Dissent in the Face of Injustice and Disorder." Much of the time was devoted to discussion of the nature of a technological society and what hopes and fears it held for the future of humanity. Was such a society oriented by its very nature to self-destruction or could it become a source of hope for a new "sacral" order in which God would be manifested and praised and people would become free and enlightened? The participants agreed that whatever the eventual answer might be, "technology at present is not in a state that is morally or religiously promising" (*Nonviolent Alternative*, 260).

It was Merton's excitement with Ellul's book that moved the discussion in this direction. On December 28, 1964, he wrote to a French Franciscan priest in Bordeaux, Hervé Chaigne, about the meeting, "There was much discussion of a book which I at the time had just read, Jacques Ellul's great work on technology. Do you know Ellul? You must, I am sure. I admire his work and find it entirely convincing and indeed it has the stamp of prophecy which so much Christian writing on that subject seems to lack" (*Witness to Freedom*, 109).

In the December 4, 1964, issue of *Commonweal* Merton wrote a brief but hard-hitting review of Ellul's book, describing it as "one of the most important books of this mid-century." Technology can be disruptive of human community because, as Merton argues, "it has produced a world in which means determine ends and become ends in themselves." This mentality all too frequently produces a false ethic that gives priority to material progress over moral growth and efficiency in getting things done over social responsibility. The overriding imperative of technology is that what can be done must be done. Merton writes, "Technology has its own ethic of expediency and efficiency. What *can* be done efficiently *must* be done in the most efficient way" (*Guilty Bystander*, 63/73). This easily leads to a subversion of fundamental human values and the disintegration of human culture. "It does us no good to make fantastic progress if we do not know how to live with it, if we cannot make good use of it, and if, in fact, our technology becomes nothing more than an expensive and complicated way of cultural disintegration" (60/73).

Technology all too easily may set false priorities that endanger human values and divide people from one another. Power tends to be concentrated in the hands of a few, often at the expense of the many. Profit-oriented endeavors tend to enrich even more the already wealthy and increase the poverty of the already poor. We have put a man on the moon and eventually will land someone on Mars, but does this enhance human dignity when it is done at a time when "four-fifths of the human race remain in abject misery, not properly clothed or fed, subject to arbitrary and senseless manipulations by politicians, or violence at the hands of police, hoodlums or revolutionaries" (203/223)? In his *Commonweal* review of Ellul's book Merton makes the point: "To assume that our massive technology is fully under the rational control of human intelligence orienting it toward a flowering and fulfillment of man is not only naïve but perilous. Ellul does not say that it *cannot* be brought under such control. But he thinks the situation is desperate and that we have not yet begun to do anything serious about it."

Technology, as Ellul says, "desacralizes the world," for it cannot tolerate mystery. The world we live in is not restricted to our ordinary daily experiences. There exists, as Merton often points out, a world of spiritual reality below and above and indeed all around our ordinary daily experiences. This is a world of mystery. There is much that we do not know and much that is unknowable. We live in a context of mystery, and yet mystery is not a part of technology's vocabulary. For technology there are no mysteries; there are only problems. It has the hubristic conviction that it has never met a problem that eventually it could not solve. What it envisions is a world without grace or, as Merton put it in an article that seems whimsical enough but actually is in deadly earnest, a world without angels. Entitled "The Angel and the Machine,"[1] the article suggests that the angels, once thought to be our helpers in carrying out God's plans, have been replaced by the machine. "Technological civilization is . . . a civilization without angels . . . in which we have chosen the machine instead of the angel: that is to say, that we have placed the machine where the angel used to be: at the limit of our own strength, at the frontier of our natural capacity."

The machines, Merton notes, are our angels. We made them. They become extensions of our own intelligence and power. They create our weather for us and even abolish day and night as we dwell in our windowless buildings "surrounded by angels of chromium and steel." Foolishly we have convinced ourselves that our machines are able to satisfy all our needs, that there is nothing they cannot accomplish. "It is in our anxiety to make our machine world completely self-sufficient and autonomous [something which is no fault of the innocent machine!] that we render it spiritually unlivable for ourselves." We need the angels, he tells us, not to replace the machines, but to teach us how to live with them. For they will teach us how to rest, how to relax in silence, how to "let go" and abandon ourselves, not in self-conscious fun, but in self-forgetful faith. We need the angels to remind us of the contemplative dimension in our lives that we so easily can neglect. Restoring that dimension can help us to see that we can get along without so many goods and satisfactions that burden our lives instead of lightening them.

We need the wisdom that comes from God, a wisdom that earlier ages personified in the form of superhuman beings. Without needing to explain precisely what our ancestors meant by these angelic beings, we need the wisdom that they personify, the wisdom that was their message from God. A technological society can be enlightened by this wisdom, but only if it is ready to renounce its obsession with the triumph of the isolated individual and the collective will to power in order to adopt a different view of reality — one that springs from solitude and contemplation and is directed toward the building of true community, where all are respected for their inherent dignity and where all share both gifts and responsibilities. Technology can build community not by mechanizing the person, but by personalizing the machine. That, Merton suggests, is the choice we have to make.

It should be clear from all this that Merton was not opposed to technology and the wondrous advances it has made for human welfare and better living. Thus, he welcomes the inside plumbing added to his hermitage in early 1968. He counted it a distinct advantage that he no longer had to face regular encounters with the "Bastard," as he had "affectionately" named the snake that had staked equal claim to the outhouse that served Merton's needs in the early years in the hermitage (*Day of a Stranger*, 53). He also enjoyed the typewriter for his voluminous writing and the refrigerator to keep his food from spoiling.

In a circular letter sent to his friends in Lent of 1967 Merton replied to those who thought that his remarks about technology in *Conjectures of a Guilty Bystander* were overly negative.

> Obviously I am not maintaining that we ought to get rid of matches and go back to making fires by rubbing sticks together.... Nor am I maintaining that modern transportation, medicine, methods of production and so on are "bad." I am glad to have a gas heater this winter, since I can't cut wood. Yet I am not saying I am a better human being this winter, when I have more "leisure," than I was last winter when I did a lot of chopping. Nothing wrong with chopping either. What I question is the universal myth that technology infallibly makes everything in every way better for everybody. It does not. (*Road to Joy*, 98)

He goes on to show how technology can be used to help people or to destroy them. "Thank God," he says, "for the fact that penicillin saves thousands of lives. But let's also face the fact that penicillin saves lives for people whom society then allows to starve because it is not set up to feed them. If it used its technological resources well, society could certainly feed them. In fact, it doesn't" (98).

He speaks too of the adverse impact technology can have on the developing countries of the world. Multinational corporations have gone into financially backward countries with technological skills that may work well in affluent countries but can be disastrous in countries that are poor. These corporations bring huge profits back to their own country but often bring about the dislocation of people of the "backward" countries, with many going to the city seeking work and finding themselves living in abject poverty because technology, by developing labor-saving methods of production, has reduced instead of increased the number of jobs available. This, Merton says, is a technology in the service of profit, not people (98).

The illusion that technological progress inevitably leads to human improvement alienates us from reality. "It is precisely because we are convinced that our life, as such, is better if we have a better car, a better TV set, better toothpaste, etc., that we contemn and destroy our own reality and the reality of our natural resources. Technology was made for man, not man for technology" (*Guilty Bystander*, 202/222).

For vast numbers of people technology has dulled the creativity of the human spirit, for it has made work boring, routine, monotonous — so much so that the workers' sense of their own worth and of their own creative powers has been diminished by the very work that they do. There is a deadening of spirit and of sensibility and a blunting of perception. Work ceases to be a challenge and a source of joy, becoming instead something to escape from as quickly and as often as possible. Workers thus are drawn into the vortex of what Pascal calls *divertissement*,[2] or distraction, where they lose themselves in activities that are mindless and without any real human significance. The television soap opera has become the stereotype of this kind of soporific activity.

Merton's thoughts on technology perhaps can be summed up in these words from *Conjectures of Guilty Bystander*: "Technology can elevate and improve man's life only on one condition: that it remains subservient to his *real* interests; that it respects his true being; that it remembers that the origin and goal of all being is in God.... But when [it] merely exploits and uses up all things in the pursuit of its own ends, and makes everything, including man himself, subservient to its processes, then it degrades man, despoils the world, ravages life, and leads to ruin" (230/253). WHS

Notes

1. "The Angel and the Machine," *Season* 5 (1967) (a small Dominican journal out of Berkeley that was short-lived). The article was republished thirty years later in *The Merton Seasonal* 22, no. 1 (spring 1997): 3–6.

2. On *divertissement*, see DISPUTED QUESTIONS.

THEOLOGY

Thomas Merton entered Gethsemani with the desire to be not only a monk but also a priest. In preparing for the priesthood, he would have been expected to study the theology texts in current use in seminaries in the 1940s. Thus, he studied Tanquerey (for dogmatic theology) and Sabetti-Barrett (for moral theology). In his journal notes for September 21, 1947, he speaks of Fr. Anthony "expounding to us Sabetti's *Moral Theology* and Tanquerey's *Dogma*" (*Entering the Silence*, 119). This neoscholasticism influenced some of his early writing, though his one venture to write a full-length book in that idiom (*The Ascent to Truth*) was not very successful.[1] Indeed, at the very time he was struggling to complete *The Ascent to Truth*, he was, as he indicated in the revised edition (December 1949) of *Seeds of Contemplation*, already moving toward a more experiential approach to God: "The author is talking about spiritual things from the point of view of experience rather than in the concise terms of dogmatic theology or of metaphysics" (*Seeds of Contemplation*, xii). In the same vein, in the prologue to *The Sign of Jonas*, he says, "I have attempted to convey something of a monk's spiritual life and of his thoughts, not in the language of speculation, but in terms of personal experience" (*Sign of Jonas*, 8). If Merton was in any sense a "theologian" (a designation he certainly would have disclaimed[2]), he was preeminently a theologian of experience.

Merton was more comfortable with the understanding of "theology" that he found in the Greek fathers. They distinguished between "natural contemplation (*theoria physike*) and theology (*theologia*) or the contemplation of God." Merton explains,

> *Theoria physike* is the intuition of divine things in and through the reflection of God in nature and in the symbols of revelation.

It presupposes a complete purification of heart by a long ascetic preparation which has delivered the soul from subjection to passion and, consequently, from the illusions generated by passionate attachment to exterior things.... This is a mystical grace from God.... The word "natural" in connection with this kind of contemplation, refers not to its origin but to its object. *Theoria physike* is contemplation of the divine *in nature*, not contemplation of the divine *by our natural powers*. (MS., 67, *Cistercian Studies* offprint, 298)

He goes on to say that this may be called "mystical," in that it is a gift of God, but it still involves effort on the part of contemplatives. They have to look about, see the created world and the symbols it embodies. They have to receive in Scripture and liturgy words of God, which transform their inner life. It is "a contemplation which man seeks and prepares by his own initiative, but which, by a gift of God, is completed in mystical intuition" (67/298).

> *Theologia*, or pure contemplation ("mystical theology" in the language of Pseudo Denis), is a direct, quasi-experiential contact with God beyond all thought, that is to say, without the medium of concepts. This excludes not only concepts tinged with passion, or sentimentality, or imagination, but even the simplest intellectual intuitions that require some sort of medium between God and the spirit. Theology in this sense is a direct contact with God. (67/298)

For the Greek fathers, then, the theologian was the holy person who experienced God directly. The theologian was the saint. However, the term "theologian" could apply especially to those who not only experienced this direct contact with God, but also were able to articulate the experience — not only their own, but also the experience of God going on in the community.

If Merton is to be called a theologian, it surely would be in the way it was understood by the Greek fathers: one who talks or writes about God with the authority of experience. This is not to deny that a theologian must have a clear and accurate grasp of the dog-mas taught by the church. "But God gives true theologians a hunger born of humility, which cannot be satisfied with formulas and argu-ments, and which looks for something closer to God than analogy can bring you" (*New Seeds of Contemplation*, 147–48). This approach to God is essential for the well-being of the church. "It is by deepening this Christian conscious-ness and developing the capacity for mystical understanding and love that the Christian con-templative keeps alive in the Church that pure and immediate experience without which the-ology will always lack one of its most important dimensions" (*World of Action*, 180/193–94).

Toward the end of his life Merton was moving in the direction of a theology of experi-ence that would incorporate the experience of religions beyond the pale of Christian faith. Thus, in notes prepared for a talk that he was to deliver at the Temple of Understand-ing meeting in Calcutta (October 23, 1968), he says: "I think we have now reached a stage of (long-overdue) religious maturity at which it may be possible for someone to remain perfectly faithful to a Christian and Western monastic commitment, and yet to learn in depth from, say, a Buddhist or Hindu discipline and experience" (*Asian Journal*, 313). This in-sight of Merton anticipates what has become a dominant theological concern in the early twenty-first century, namely, the theology of religious pluralism. WHS

SEE ALSO CONTEMPLATION; DOCTRINES; INTERRELIGIOUS DIALOGUE; MYSTICISM.

Notes

1. In his 1967 graph evaluating his books, he listed *The Ascent to Truth* as only "fair."

2. In a letter to Rosemary Radford Ruether he writes, "I am not a pro at anything except writing: I am no theologian" (*Hidden Ground of Love*, 509).

THIRTY POEMS

Norfolk, Conn.: New Directions, 1944.
29 pp. (unnumbered).

This was the first of Thomas Merton's pub-lished books. Merton himself continued to regard it as a quite successful work, rating it

"better" (the highest level any volumes were given) on his 1967 graph of his books. An appropriate starting point for understanding and appreciating *Thirty Poems* is the awareness that it is rightly attributed to the authorship of Thomas Merton rather than M. Louis Mer-ton, O.C.S.O. (thus setting a precedent that would be followed for the dozens of books to come). The vast majority of the poems in-cluded in the volume, twenty-four of the thirty, were composed before Merton became a Cis-tercian. Though the best-known, and arguably the best, poem in the collection, the elegy "For My Brother: Reported Missing in Action, 1943" (no. 12; 28 ll.), was, of course, written in the monastery, the majority of the poems date from his time as a teacher at St. Bonaventure College in upstate New York; even the one explicitly monastic piece, "The Trappist Abbey: Matins" (no. 22; 24 ll.), was written not after entrance into Gethsemani but shortly after his initial visit there during Holy Week, 1941. (In addition to the elegy, the only poems written after Merton joined the order, according to dates appended to Merton's personal copy of his second vol-ume of verse, *A Man in the Divided Sea* [which included *Thirty Poems* in an appendix], were "The Evening of the Visitation" [no. 20; 27 ll. (1942)], "The Blessed Virgin Mary Compared to a Window" [no. 23; 42 ll. (1942)], "The Holy Sacrament of the Altar" [no. 26; 35 ll. (1943)], "Saint Agnes: A Responsory" [no. 28; 27 ll. (1943)], and "The Holy Child's Song" [no. 29; 45 ll. (1943)].) Therefore the poems mainly offer insight into Merton's preoccupations, in-terests, and attitudes during the crucial period leading up to his decision to become a monk and suggest both continuities and changes be-tween the premonastic and monastic years. In some cases the themes and ideas even seem closer to those of the mature Merton in the last decade of his life than to the more restricted focus of the early monastic years.

It should be noted that the contents of *Thirty Poems* represent a selection of Merton's early verse made principally not by Merton himself but by his Columbia mentor, Mark Van Doren (*Road to Joy*, 17). To get a complete picture of Merton as poet in this period one needs also to examine his next volume, *A Man in the Divided*

Sea, which contains poems written between 1939 and 1946, the generally less religious verse of *Early Poems, 1940–42*, which did not appear until 1971, and even the remaining early poetry (six poems from 1939) included in the alphabetically arranged "Uncollected Poems" section of *The Collected Poems*. Thus, *Thirty Poems* provides a view, but not a definitive view, of the early Merton as poet. But it can be said safely that Van Doren chose wisely and perceptively, resulting in a volume that does provide a representative if incomplete picture of Merton's central concerns, as poet and as Christian, during the months that led up to his decision to become a Trappist and his early days in the monastery.

The influence of some of Merton's favorite poets is evident in the volume. The tetrameter quatrains and couplets of "An Argument: Of the Passion of Christ" (no. 27; 62 ll.) (the only poem in the volume consistently to use rhyme and meter) recall Merton's model here, Andrew Marvell, and the "argument" itself is in the metaphysical tradition, with more than a dash of Dylan Thomas as well. "The Sponge Full of Vinegar" (no. 30; 17 ll.) is an almost Protestant look at the inadequacies of even one's good deeds, closest in tone to John Donne of all the poems in the volume, but also echoing Gerard Manley Hopkins in its final line, "Reeks of the death-thirst manlife found in the forbidden apple" (l. 27). Hopkins's influence is evident also in "The Blessed Virgin Mary Compared to a Window," which recalls the earlier poet's "The Blessed Virgin Mary Compared to the Air We Breathe." William Blake's "Mercy, Pity, Peace and Love" from "The Divine Image" reappear in the final verse paragraph of "The Holy Sacrament of the Altar," while the Edenic vision of poems such as "Evening" (no. 18; 23 ll.) and "Aubade: Lake Erie" (no. 11; 22 ll.) exemplify Merton's own "Songs of Innocence." The influence of Federico García Lorca is evident not only in the elegy dedicated to his memory (no. 21; 26 ll.) but also in the quasi-surrealist imagery of poems such as "Lent in a Year of War" (no. 1; 16 ll.), "The Night Train" (no. 6; 27 ll.), and "Saint Jason" (no. 7; 20 ll.).

In considering the principal themes that emerge from a careful reading of *Thirty Poems*, one does not find much evidence, to use critic George Woodcock's terms,[1] either of "The Poetry of the Choir" (verse with a monastic focus) or of "The Poetry of the Desert" (except for "The Flight into Egypt" [no. 2; 13 ll.] and "Prophet" [no. 3; 18 ll.]); nor does the *via negativa*, the way of emptiness and silence, play a major role in this collection (only the frame verses of "The Holy Child's Song," beginning "When midnight occupied the porches of the Poet's reason" [ll. 1, 43] and perhaps the refrain of "The Communion" [no. 17; 21 ll.], "O sweet escape! O smiling flight!" [ll. 1, 6, 7, 12, 13, 18, 21], with its echo of St. John of the Cross, suggest this more "mystical" approach).

The predominant impression of the volume as a whole is of a poet vividly aware of the spiritual dimensions of the natural world; it is a collection saturated with an awareness of nature as sacrament, as epiphany of the divine. Thus, the cycle of the seasons repeatedly is aligned with the patterns of the liturgical year: in "The Messenger" (no. 8; 19 ll.) the coming of spring is juxtaposed to and implicitly aligned with the coming of the angel Gabriel to the Virgin Mary; in "The Vine" (no. 19; 27 ll.) the pruning process and eventual flowering are recognized as analogues of the passion and resurrection of Christ; in "The Evening of the Visitation" the "evening journey" of the "full moon, wise queen" parallels the journey of Mary to "the house of Zachary" (ll. 3, 2, 5). In a number of the poems reference is made specifically to the eucharistic elements in their natural setting, as in "the shining vineyards" and "hills of wheat" (ll. 3, 4) of "The Communion"; the "growing bread" and "sweet, wounded vine" (ll. 11, 12) of "Aubade: Lake Erie"; the "gay wheatfields" and "glances . . . as good as wine" (ll. 9, 27) of "The Holy Child's Song." "The Regret" (no. 9; 19 ll.) reverses the dominant pattern of the volume by presenting a failure of vision, a missed epiphany, a lack of correspondence between the seasonal cycle and the movements of the spirit; it includes the most complex use of the imagery of prisons and captivity that pervades the collection. A similar lack of correspondence between the human and the natural world is found in "Dirge for the Proud World" (no. 25; 27 ll.), while in "Poem (Watching among the rifled branches...)" (no. 10; 24 ll.) the initial sense of natural unity and clarity in the classical past has given way to disruptions and blocked vision in the present. (Classical myth, also evident in "Iphigenia: Politics" [no. 13; 27 ll.] and "Ariadne at the Labyrinth" [no. 24; 23 ll.], is a favorite resource for Merton's premonastic poetry that will be more in evidence in his second volume, *A Man in the Divided Sea*.)

Frequently the sacramental vision is associated specifically with the innocence of children. In "Aubade: Lake Erie," an evocation of Merton's Franciscan sensibility, it is the "innocent children" who recognize "the hay-colored sun" as "our marvelous cousin" and issue an invitation to wholeness, while the busy but aimless world of adults, represented by the tramps, "A hundred dusty Luthers," is unheeding of the inner meaning of the landscape (ll. 5, 9, 19). In "The Winter's Night" (no. 14; 21 ll.) the children's expectation of a revelation is satisfied at the poem's conclusion as the moon and stars are perceived as heavenly visitors. In "Evening" the children are able to respond with simplicity and wonder to the beauty of the twilight world in a way that adults cannot. The delicate balance between white girls and black girls that structures the first three sections of "Song for Our Lady of Cobre" (no. 5; 13 ll.) gives way to the poignancy of the final lines, "And all the pieces of the mosaic, earth, / Get up and fly away like birds" (ll. 12–13), which suggest how fleeting the vision of authentic unity and complementarity often is.

There is also apparent a kind of "spiritual geography" in many of the poems, a sense of cosmic unity represented by the compass points, as in "In Memory of the Spanish Poet Federico Garcia Lorca": "In the four quarters of the world, the wind is still" (l. 21); in "The Evening of the Visitation": "Go, roads, to the four quarters of our quiet distance" (l. 1); and in "St. Agnes: A Responsory": "Her charity has flown to four horizons" (l. 25). Another pattern is that of contrast between sacred and profane landscapes, as most memorably in "The Trappist Abbey: Matins," where the orderly departure of the "pilgrim moon" up the "long avenue of trees" (ll. 3, 5) leading from the mon-

astery is juxtaposed with the train that "runs, lost,... / Where fire flares, somewhere, over a sink of cities" (ll. 7, 9); a similar contrast structures "The Flight into Egypt," where the deadly threats of "the wintry city" are contrasted with the safety of "the singing desert" (ll. 1, 11); in "Holy Communion: The City" (no. 16; 22 ll.) "the jungles of our waterpipes and iron ladders" (l. 6) are countered by the interior landscapes in which "massbells" transform the "wounds" of "our dry and fearful spirit" into "vineyards" (ll. 10, 11).

Another major theme of these poems is the interpenetration of biblical and contemporary events. Sometimes this is indirect, as in "The Flight into Egypt," where the implications for the present are only suggested by such details as "the dark steps of the tenements" that "Herod's police / Make shudder" (ll. 3–4) as they search for the Christ Child. More frequently the connections are explicit, as with the application of the passage on the wise and foolish virgins (part of Merton's broader fascination with images of light), which is present in no fewer than three of the poems: "The Winter's Night," where the expectant children are compared to "sleepy virgins" who "stir, and trim their lamps" (l. 17); "The Trappist Abbey: Matins," in which the soul awakened by the bells summoning the monks to prayer is told, "Burn in the country night / Your wise and sleepless lamp" (ll. 12–13); and "The Holy Sacrament of the Altar," where the intellect is commanded, "Be kindled" even though "your strongest lamps are night-lights" (l. 19) before the radiance of the Lamb, the church's Bridegroom.

It is, of course, the events of Christ's passion that evoke most strongly this sense of participation in the scriptural drama: at times the identification is with the oppressors of Christ, as in "Lent in a Year of War," where the figures ask, "What if it was our thumbs put out the sun / When the Lance and Cross made their mistake?" (ll. 8–9); more directly, the speaker in "An Argument: Of the Passion of Christ" recognizes in Christ's sufferings "the work my hands had made" (l. 39), while in "The Sponge Full of Vinegar" the speaker pictures his offering of prayer, like the drink given to the crucified Jesus, as soured, "Reek[ing] of the death-thirst manlife found in the forbidden apple" (l. 17). In "The Trappist Abbey: Matins" the contrast between the peace of the monastic landscape and the chaos of the city is both scripturalized and personalized as the soul is offered two alternatives: to identify either with the wise virgins carrying their lamps or with the mob bringing smoky torches to seize Christ in Gethsemani (both garden and abbey). This pattern of involvement in the passion is most crucial in the two elegies, for Federico García Lorca and John Paul Merton, whose deaths are identified with the redemptive death of Christ, and so offer the hope of resurrection; it is present also in the final two lines of "Death" (no. 15; 18 ll.), whose power is finally overcome by the seemingly fragile forces of a child's prayer and the light of a candle symbolizing the risen Jesus.

These last three poems are also part of a broader group that confronts the issue of war, particularly the war currently raging in Europe: this topic is found in the opening poem, "Lent in a Year of War," which concludes with the apocalyptic vision of "the north-south horizon parting like a string!" (l. 16); it is evident in "The Dark Morning" (no. 4; 12 ll.), which finds evil not just in the external enemy but in "the prisoner's" inner self (l. 4), presumably imprisoned by his own selfish desires, "Whose heart is his Germany / Fevered with anger" (ll. 7–8); "The Night Train" laments "the deaths of the cathedrals" (l. 14) in wartime France; "Iphigenia: Politics" seems to refer to the fall of France in 1940 in particular (note the line about "Our minds . . . bleaker than the hall of mirrors" [l. 26], an allusion to Versailles, where the surrender took place), but has a more universal application to the sacrifice of innocence and truth, symbolized by the figure of the daughter of Agamemnon, in pursuit of political ends, with its dire conclusion, "And the world has become a museum" (l. 27).

These prominent themes — the revelatory power of nature, the innocent vision of the child, the geography of the spirit, participation in the events of the Gospels, particularly the passion, the religious dimensions of political and social issues — all are concerns that will continue, or reemerge, in Merton's later writings, both prose and poetry, sometimes in quite different form or with a new focus, but not without elements of similarity as well. POC

Notes

1. George Woodcock, *Thomas Merton: Monk and Poet* (New York: Farrar, Straus and Giroux, 1978), 51, 62.

THOMAS MERTON AND JAMES LAUGHLIN: *Selected Letters*
Edited by David D. Cooper. New York: Norton, 1997. xxiii+398 pp.

This volume of selected letters has the following sections: (1) an introduction, (2) some notes on the text, (3) acknowledgements, (4) the letters, (5) an epilogue, (6) an appendix, and (7) a selected bibliography.

A valuable introduction shows the parallels and contrasts between the Merton story and the Laughlin story. Up to the time of their first contact (in the 1940s), their lives sharply contrast one another. Laughlin's life was one of emotional stability and financial security. Born in 1914 into an upper-class family that made its wealth in the thriving steel business, Laughlin attended private schools (in Pittsburgh, Switzerland, and Massachusetts), with higher education at Harvard. Thomas Merton, born in 1915, attended good schools and had reasonable financial security but clearly lacked emotional stability and family warmth. His mother died when he was six, his father when he was almost sixteen. He never really had a family home, living much of his childhood and youth in boarding schools and finally living on his own when, in 1935, he entered Columbia University (Laughlin was accepted at Harvard in 1932). In 1933 (the year that Merton was making a mess of his life at Clare College, Cambridge) Laughlin went to Italy, where he met Ezra Pound. Pound was to prove an important influence on his future, as he convinced Laughlin that he should give up a career as a poet and become a publisher. Laughlin accepted his advice and launched the New Directions Publishing Corporation in an unused building donated by an aunt. From the very beginning New Directions published young poets who invested their talents in the modernist literary revolution in America.

Meanwhile, Thomas Merton had undergone a deep religious conversion, had become a Roman Catholic, and then in 1941 a Trappist monk in the Abbey of Gethsemani in rural Kentucky.

Their paths crossed when Mark Van Doren, Merton's mentor at Columbia, brought Laughlin a collection of Merton's poems, which he published in 1944 as *Thirty Poems*.

The exchange of letters, as presented in this volume, begins with Merton's letter of May 27, 1945, in which he looks forward to Laughlin's visit, and concludes with Merton's letter of November 28, 1968, from Madras, India, and Laughlin's letter of December 4, 1968, which may never have reached Merton, since his death occurred just six days later. The many letters between 1945 and 1968 are very revealing. They show a remarkable affection between these two men of such different backgrounds and lifestyles. It is interesting to note how Merton signs his letters: first he uses his religious name, "Fr. Louis"; then it becomes "Tom," with "Fr. Louis" written below; by 1956 it is simply "Tom."

Some of the earlier letters tend to display Merton's piety and devotion, as he invites Laughlin to pray and to cultivate tranquillity and purity of heart. This attempt at "catechesis" soon disappears, as Merton becomes more and more fascinated by the various poets who are being published in the *New Directions Annual*. At one point Merton expressed his moral reservations about some of the material New Directions was publishing. This concern seems to have disappeared as Merton became more and more enthusiastic about the young American poets with whom Laughlin put him in contact.

Laughlin encouraged Merton to continue writing poetry. He, as well as the many other poets he put Merton in touch with, exercised a strong influence on the direction in which Merton's poetry began to move in the late 1950s and the 1960s. "From the drafts of new poems Merton began sending him in 1956, Laughlin sensed an important new direction in the writing, the beginning of what he considered the secularization of Merton's poetry.... Merton combusted into an experimental poet *par ex-*

cellence" (*Thomas Merton and James Laughlin*, xx–xxi).

The letters are the biography of a relationship, as they discuss authors being published by New Directions and share their comments on literary, social, and political events of the day. In addition, the letters show the genesis and growth of the various Merton books published by New Directions.

The epilogue of the book is a three-page letter from Laughlin to "S,"[1] the young woman with whom Merton had been in love. The letter, written July 25, 1970, speaks about Merton's untimely death and his writings to her, including a short journal, a copy of which Merton had sent to Laughlin. After speaking of the affection that Merton had for her, he writes, "But you know, in one way, Tom didn't belong to this world that you and I live in, that is something we have to understand and accept" (371).

The appendix, a portrait of Thomas Merton by James Laughlin, is taken from Paul Wilkes's interview with Laughlin in preparation for the documentary on Merton that Wilkes produced. It appeared in Paul Wilkes, ed., *Merton, by Those Who Knew Him Best* (San Francisco: Harper & Row, 1984). WHS

Notes

1. See "M."

THOMAS MERTON IN ALASKA: The Alaskan Conferences, Journals and Letters

New York: New Directions, 1988. xvii+162 pp.

In addition to a preface by David D. Cooper and an introduction by Robert E. Daggy, this book consists of two parts. Part 1 contains the prologue, itinerary, Alaskan journal, Alaskan letters, notes, and photographs that document Thomas Merton's trip to Alaska (and then on to San Francisco and Santa Barbara), from September 17 to October 3, 1968. Part 1 also has been published as *The Alaskan Journal of Thomas Merton* (Isla Vista, Calif.: Turkey Press, 1988) in a limited deluxe edition of 150 copies. Eleven photos, which Merton took during his

Alaskan journey, and one photo of Merton, dressed in a clerical suit and wearing a Roman collar, were added to part 1 in *Thomas Merton in Alaska*.[1]

Part 2 consists of edited transcriptions of the Alaskan conferences: eight conferences that Merton gave to women religious and priests during his stay in Alaska. From September 18 to September 21 he conducted a workshop (six conferences) for the sisters of the Monastery of the Precious Blood in Eagle River: "This Is God's Work," "Prayer, Personalism, and the Spirit," "Building Community on God's Love," "Community, Politics, and Contemplation," "Prayer, Tradition, and Experience," and "Prayer and Conscience." On September 29 he preached a day of recollection for sisters of the diocese at Providence Hospital in Anchorage on "The Life That Unifies." On October 1 he addressed the priests of the diocese on the topic of "Prayer and the Priestly Tradition" at a day of recollection held at the Monastery of the Precious Blood. All the conferences were taped. The seven conferences that Merton gave to the sisters were transcribed by Br. Patrick Hart, edited for publication in *Sisters Today* by Naomi Burton Stone,[2] and edited further by Robert E. Daggy for publication in this book. The last conference, given at the day of recollection for priests, was taped by Fr. Bartholomew Egan, C.S.Sp., transcribed by Fr. Brian Cogan, C.S.Sp., and published in *The Priest* (*Thomas Merton in Alaska*, 69).

Conversational and engaging in style, the Alaskan conferences address a number of themes that Merton recognized as essential to the renewal of religious life, most especially contemplation, prayer, and community. In "This Is God's Work" Merton insists that contemplatives must recognize that they are "completely in God's hands" (71). The contemplative life is about "the action of God's grace in our life," which is "a very, very deep call which is heard in silence in the deepest part of our being" (71–72). The contemplative life, the Christ life, is "a covenanted life" (73) marked by a call and a promise. "A contemplative is someone who has a direct relationship with God in the depths of his heart and who speaks to God" (75).

In "Prayer, Personalism, and the Spirit" Merton takes up the subject of meditation, that is, praying "with your heart or with the depths of your being" (81). Drawing on the work of Eastern Orthodox theologian Vladimir Lossky (whose work Merton was reading at the time), Merton focuses on the work of the Holy Spirit, an aspect of theology neglected by the Western church. "The Holy Spirit is central and primary in our present stage of existence because it is he who is carrying on the work of forming the new creation and of transforming all in Christ and restoring all in Christ. Prayer must be seen in that context" (89).

"Building Community on God's Love" is inspired by Merton's reading of German Anabaptist theologian Eberhard Arnold, whose writings included a book entitled *Living in Community*. Arnold stresses that "community is not built by man, it is built by God. It is God's work and the basis of community is not just sociability but faith" (97). The church is "God's community," the body of Christ. Religious are called to build real community not only among themselves but also beyond their own communities. Merton quotes Arnold as saying, "Only faith in the ultimate mystery of good in God is able to build community" (104).

In the fourth conference, exploring the themes of "Community, Politics, and Contemplation," Merton suggests that people are tempted to look for community in political movements. Again he draws on Eberhard Arnold, who cautions, "All revolutions, all voluntary associations of idealists and life-reformers have given proof both of their longing for community and their incapacity for community" (110). It is in prayer, Merton insists, that "we are truly and fully ourselves" and are free of "any other power, authority, or domination" (113).

In the fifth conference for the sisters at the Monastery of the Precious Blood, Merton spoke about "Prayer, Tradition, and Experience," insisting that we need a theology that "supports prayer" (115), that is, a biblical theology. Merton is critical of those who equate revolutionary action with prayer and say, "What I do is *it* — it is my prayer" (116). But he also is critical of a view of prayer that is mechanical and directed toward a God who is "a great big machine, an impersonal, loveless kind of thing" (117). Monastic formation that nurtures the contemplative life of prayer and silence is essential and requires "education for experience" (126).

In his last conference for the sisters at the Monastery of the Precious Blood, Merton focused on "Prayer and Conscience." He explained that prayer and identity "go together" (129). Conscience is "very close to our identity." Conscience, according to some of the Rhineland mystics, is "the place you experience union with God" (130). "The deepest level of conscience is beyond both consciousness and moral conscience; it is beyond thinking and self-awareness and decision. It is the conscience of God in us; it is where the Holy Spirit operates" (130). Consequently, prayer is "opening up this deepest conscience and consciousness, a mystical conscience and a mystical consciousness, in which God and I work together" (131). Building on this understanding of conscience, Merton develops the idea of the self not as an individual but as a person "defined by a relationship with others." The Christian conscience is not just "an individual conscience," but "a kind of collective conscience" (134). Prayer is not merely an action of an individual, but a communal act. "All prayer is communion, not only between Christ and me but also between everybody in the Church and myself. All prayer takes us into the communion of saints" (136).

The talk that Merton gave at the day of recollection for sisters in the Diocese of Anchorage examined "The Life That Unifies," by which he meant the contemplative life. "The contemplative life and the monastic life 'unify,' both in terms of community — a unity of persons in a community — and also unity within myself" (145). This unification is what the Persian writer Reza Arasteh called "final integration" — an integration that occurs in love, as one is taken out of oneself.[3] The real meaning of the contemplative life is "to develop people who really love God and who radiate love" (149). Consequently, the education of a contemplative is "the education of the heart" (153).

Merton's final conference in Alaska ex-plored "Prayer and the Priestly Tradition," during a day of recollection for priests. Again, as during his previous conferences in Alaska, he focused on prayer. "Today, the only way we priests can live and keep our sanity amidst all the complications of life is by breaking through to the deeper level of simplicity. The real level of course is the level of death, and that can only be reached by prayer" (157). In a second session Merton focused on the story of Emmaus (Luke 24:13–35). We are like the disciples on the way to Emmaus, so absorbed with our own problems that we fail to see Jesus walking with us. But the risen Christ is with us. We have only to recognize him. CMB

SEE ALSO ALASKAN JOURNAL OF THOMAS MERTON.

Notes

1. For a description of part 1 of *Thomas Merton in Alaska*, see ALASKAN JOURNAL OF THOMAS MERTON.
2. These conferences were published in *Sisters Today* between August/September 1970 and April 1971.
3. See Thomas Merton, "Final Integration: Toward a 'Monastic Therapy'" in *Contemplation in a World of Action* (205–17).

THOMAS MERTON ON PEACE

Edited and with an introduction by Gordon C. Zahn. New York: McCall, 1971. xli+269 pp.

This book contains a series of essays written by Thomas Merton in the 1960s on the issue of war and peace. It begins with a lengthy introduction (thirty-nine pages) by sociologist and pacifist Gordon C. Zahn, followed by thirty-nine articles by Thomas Merton, most of them originally published in journals (including the *Catholic Worker, Commonweal, Jubilee, Ramparts, Fellowship, Blackfriars, Saturday Review, Peace News, Pax*). The Merton articles are arranged in three parts: (1) "Principles of Peace" (3–162), (2) "The Nonviolent Alternative" (163–253), and (3) "Incidental Writings" (255–69). There is no index.

Merton had made the initial contact with Zahn, inviting him to write an article for a book that Merton and James Laughlin were planning on the issue of war and peace. The book, *Breakthrough to Peace*, was published in September 1962 and did contain an article by Zahn entitled "The Case for Christian Dissent."

The breadth of Merton's correspondence, Zahn suggests, matches the breadth of his social concerns. Much of Merton's writing was prophetic — for example, his "Letter to White Liberals." Eschewing a chronological approach (because so many of the articles were undated), Zahn chose to arrange the articles under the rubric of principal themes.[1] One of those themes, "The Nonviolent Alternative," is given special prominence with its own separate section.

Merton, Zahn tells us, recognized the importance of dissent and civil disobedience but counseled against protests that were "too ambiguous or too threatening" (*Thomas Merton on Peace*, xiv). The 1960s were not easy years for Merton, as he faced opposition from bishops and from his own religious superiors. By April 1962 he had been forbidden by the abbot general of his order to write any longer on war and peace. Yet he continued to reach people with mimeographed articles that spelled out his position.

Merton refused to be labeled a "pacifist." Zahn suggests that he was a relative pacifist in that he allowed, in theory at least, the possibility of a war of defense, even nuclear defense. Merton was not entirely consistent and his tendency always was in the direction of pacifism; for example, he admired Dorothy Day's brand of peace activity, and she was unequivocally pacifist. Merton may well have been "hung up" on the just war theory that for centuries had guided the Catholic approach to war. Merton, Zahn contends, was a pacifist in that "he rejected the legitimacy of war in the actuality" (xx), for he was convinced that total war was immoral and that any war was bound to escalate into nuclear war. His assessment of the Cold War confrontation tended to be pessimistic. "In an arresting image he spoke of everyone walking backwards toward a precipice they know is there, insisting all the while that they are going forward" (xxi).

His moving words about a Vietnamese monk, Thich Nhat Hanh, as his brother, are the opposite side of his opposition to the war in Vietnam. In his preface to the Vietnamese edition of *No Man Is an Island* he sees the war in Vietnam as "a bell tolling for the whole world,

warning the whole world that war may spread everywhere, and violent death may sweep over the entire earth" (*Honorable Reader*, 124).

As a priest and a highly esteemed writer of spirituality, as one whose words reached many people, Merton's contribution to the peace movement was twofold. First, he gave the movement the respectability of his name. Second, he set forth clearly the gospel principles that must direct nonviolent action. "Nonviolence is not for power but for truth. It is not pragmatic but prophetic...." It is "not primarily the language of efficacy but the language of *Kairos*. It does not say 'We shall overcome' so much as 'This is the day of the Lord, and whatever may happen to us, He shall overcome'" (*Thomas Merton on Peace*, xxix, also 75).

Part 1, "Principles of Peace," has eighteen essays. It is not possible to discuss all of them here. The first, "Original Child Bomb," is a powerful reflection on the bombing of Hiroshima, narrated in the form of forty-one brief "news bits" telling the story in an "objective way," which by its very matter-of-factness evokes powerful emotions. The second essay, "Peace: Christian Duties and Perspectives," is a key essay, actually a rewrite of an important article that *Commonweal* published, February 9, 1962. The third essay, "The Christian in World Crisis: Reflections on the Moral Climate of the 1960s," is a rewrite of portions of a book that in 1962 Merton was forbidden to publish ("Peace in the Post-Christian Era"). "Breakthrough to Peace" and "Peace: A Religious Responsibility" are taken from the book, mentioned above, that Merton and James Laughlin put together, *Breakthrough to Peace*. The remaining essays in part 1 are briefer and develop aspects of the essays already mentioned.

Part 2, "The Nonviolent Alternative," has fourteen essays (most of them relatively short) on that subject. An essay on Gandhi is of prime importance for understanding Merton's view of nonviolence; so also the two longer essays: "Blessed Are the Meek: The Christian Roots of Nonviolence" and "War and the Crisis of Language."

Part 3, "Incidental Writings," includes Merton's words accepting the Pax Medal in 1963; notes for a retreat for peace activists held at

Gethsemani in 1964; a message of January 31, 1965 (in French), to the group known as the "friends of Gandhi"; a tribute to Nhat Hanh, who visited Gethsemani May 28, 1966; notes for a statement on aid to civilian war victims in Vietnam; and a prayer for peace read in the U.S. House of Representatives on April 12, 1962.

Note that this book, published in 1971 by McCall, was republished by Farrar, Straus and Giroux in 1980. The two editions are identical except that the 1980 edition has a new title (*The Nonviolent Alternative*) and has replaced the "Message aux amis de Gandhi" with Merton's "Auschwitz poem," "Chant to Be Used in Processions around a Site with Furnaces." Up to page 260, the pagination is identical in both editions. WHS

SEE ALSO *PASSION FOR PEACE*.

Notes

1. For a chronological arrangement of Merton's social essays, see *Passion for Peace*, which publishes much the same articles, but in the order in which they were written.

THOMAS MERTON ON ST. BERNARD

Kalamazoo, Mich.: Cistercian Publications, 1980. 241 pp.

This volume consists of three separate studies by Thomas Merton of the thought of St. Bernard (1090–1153), the greatest of the early Cistercians. "Action and Contemplation in St. Bernard" first appeared in the order's journal, *Collectanea Ordinis Cisterciensium Reformatorum*, in three parts in 1953–54 and subsequently was published in somewhat expanded form in French as *Marthe, Marie et Lazare* (1956);[1] "St. Bernard on Interior Simplicity" originally was part 2 of *The Spirit of Simplicity* (1948), supplementing Merton's translation of an official Cistercian document on the topic; "Transforming Union in St. Bernard of Clairvaux and St. John of the Cross" also appeared in the *Collectanea* as a five-part series between April 1948 and January 1950. The ordering of the pieces, therefore, is not chronological but thematic, moving from the broader topic of the relationship between contemplation and action, to the more specific discussion of simplicity, to a comparison of the teaching of the twelfth-century French Cistercian and the sixteenth-century Spanish Carmelite John of the Cross.

"Action and Contemplation in St. Bernard," though published in three sections, actually consists of five parts. The first, "Action and Contemplation in the Mystery of Christ," surveys the topic from the New Testament up to the time of Bernard. Focusing particularly on John's Gospel, Merton presents Jesus as the model for both contemplation and action and shows that the two dimensions complement one another in Jesus and in his disciples. Jesus' intimate union with his Father is the foundation for his ministry, and his ministry is to lead others into that same intimate union. The role of the apostle is to do likewise, which is possible only if it is based in an authentic experience of God. "An apostolate that does not spring from contemplation and end in contemplation is not the christian apostolate" (*Thomas Merton on St. Bernard*, 26). While the Johannine emphasis is on love of God manifesting itself in the two forms of contemplative abiding in God and active witness to others, the apostle Paul stresses that members of the body of Christ have different functions, some more active, some more contemplative (29–30). The early monastic literature teaches the superiority of the contemplative life to the active, respectively represented by the figures of Mary and Martha, though both are seen as necessary, and Merton cites Cassian's statement "that Martha's active and cenobitic life has a peculiar excellence of its own which even the solitary life of contemplation cannot duplicate" (34). Thus, Bernard is seen as building on a long tradition of evangelical and monastic teaching in the East and West in his exploration of the paradoxical relation of action and contemplation in the Christian life.

The three central sections of the essay look at "Action in the Monastic Life," "The Contemplative Life," and "The Apostolate." Merton notes that Bernard typically considers not two types of monastic life but three, including Lazarus with his two sisters as models: Lazarus represents the penitents, Mary the contemplatives, and Martha the active administrators or preachers (43). Bernard teaches that the way of contemplation is to be preferred as more conducive to peace and rest in God, but that "the 'mixed' life, composed of action and contemplation together, is in a certain sense more necessary to the Church than contemplation alone, and therefore it has a higher dignity than the life of pure and unmixed contemplation" (60). However, because of its difficulty the mixed life is not a way that should be chosen for oneself but only accepted as an obligation by one who "is first of all both a penitent and a contemplative" (44). No "apostolic" work (a term not used by Bernard but accurately representing his thought) that does not flow from deep contemplative realization can be fruitful (52), but on the other hand there is a certain "sterility" in contemplative rest that does not communicate the love of the Bridegroom to others (58). Thus, Bernard paradoxically can maintain "that contemplation is, in itself, superior and preferable to action, while on the other hand action is 'more necessary' and 'better' than contemplation" (63), considering action not as the ascetical discipline of Lazarus but the apostolic charity of Martha (69). For most monks the life of penance in itself or a life of penance that leads to contemplation is the road to sanctification, but for some the further dimension of care for others becomes the completion of their vocation. "Hence the apostolic vocation . . . is not *substituted* for contemplation. It is *added* to contemplation, and becomes an integral part in the interior, contemplative life of the soul perfectly united to the Word" (71).

The final section of the essay presents Bernard's teaching that the Virgin Mary is the perfect model of both contemplation and action, receiving the Word into her soul and body in intimate union and offering him to the world in an act of supreme love. Thus, the Mother of God combines the vocations of Mary and Martha, though not of Lazarus, since she has no need of repentance. As the embodiment of supreme wisdom and of spiritual maturity and fruitfulness, Mary is both the model and the cause of sanctity in others, leading Merton to exhort his readers "to seek, by prayer

and ardent desire, for a charity that will bring us to that spiritual maturity in Christ which will, to some extent, unite both action and contemplation in our own souls" (87).

The other essay that had not appeared previously in book form, "Transforming Union in St. Bernard of Clairvaux and St. John of the Cross," also consists of five parts, introduced by a brief preface indicating that the purpose of the essay is to show that while their terminology differs so radically that some commentators see the teaching of the two saints as being irreconcilable, in fact "the same goal lies at the end of both their journeys" (161). In part 1 Merton focuses on the two saints' respective views of human nature as "The Subject of Transforming Union." Whereas Bernard stresses that it is "natural" to love God and that divine union is the fulfillment of human potential, John emphasizes that such union is beyond all natural human capacity and that the natural operations of the soul must be "annihilated" in order to receive the divine indwelling. Merton responds that there is no inherent contradiction: "St. Bernard is talking about nature in its essential definition, in itself. St. John is talking about nature as it finds itself, *per accidens,* in its present, actual, fallen condition" (169).

In part 2, "The Ontology of the Transformation," Merton compares Bernard's description of the process of stripping away the false garments of sin that obscure the "naked" natural dignity of the human person to John's doctrine of emptiness and annihilation in the experience of the dark night, and concludes that despite the difference in imagery the experience described is the same, and indeed that using Bernard as a context for viewing John's teaching "makes it thoroughly understandable" (181).

Part 3, "Spiritual Betrothal and Marriage," notes that John of the Cross makes a distinction between two phases of the unitive life: the deep yet transient experiences of the divine presence in the spiritual betrothal and the incomparably greater state of transforming union that he calls the spiritual marriage. Bernard's descriptions in his early works of the visits of the Bridegroom seem to refer to John's "betrothal," whereas in Bernard's view "the perfect union with God described by St. John of the Cross as mystical marriage was only to be attained in the next life" (200).

But in part 4, "Mystical Marriage in St. Bernard," Merton suggests that in the final sermons on the Song of Songs, Bernard is speaking of "a perfect union of wills, a perfect union of love with God, perfect likeness to God . . . and therefore mystical marriage even on earth" (206), a description that Merton considers to be based on personal experience (211).

Part 5, "The State of Pure Love," deals with what Merton considers to be the biggest difficulty of all in reconciling the teaching of the two saints: is the pure love that Bernard describes a permanent state, a union that has permanently and irrevocably transformed the soul? According to Étienne Gilson it is an experience and not a permanent state, but Merton maintains that Bernard himself "no longer has any hesitation in calling this union of love a permanent and habitual state" (215), though he makes the necessary distinction between "the union of the *faculties*" of the soul, which cannot be continual, and the "uninterrupted union" of the "substance of the soul," which is marked by *"an uninterrupted joy"* (217). Here Merton actually touches on the topic of the other (later) essay, for the union of the faculties in times of contemplation results in the fruitful activity of apostolic service in which the uninterrupted union of the soul and God is manifested in the sharing of the fruits of contemplation with others. "It is thus God who rests in the soul and God who works in the soul" (220).

In his introduction to the volume, Merton's friend Jean Leclercq, O.S.B., the editor and preeminent modern scholar of St. Bernard, notes his initial skepticism as to whether these essays of Merton's early career, the product of "poet become monk, who had not been trained in historical and theological studies" (11), were worth republishing. His conclusion that "these texts have lost nothing of their value or timeliness" (11) came as a surprise even to him, he writes, and is due, in his judgment, to the fact that Merton "was more than an historian: he was a witness to the living tradition. . . . This early Merton, already full of love and enthusiasm, still marked to

some degree by ingenuousness, was building the solid foundation upon which would rise Merton the activist and social critic of the following decades" (14). POC

SEE ALSO *LAST OF THE FATHERS; SPIRIT OF SIMPLICITY.*

Notes

1. See the preface published with this edition in *Honorable Reader,* 13–22, which emphasizes that the purpose of the essay is to correct partial and therefore distorted readings of St. Bernard that overemphasize either his statements on contemplation or those on action.

THOMAS MERTON:
Preview of the Asian Journey
Edited by Walter Capps. New York: Crossroad, 1989. 114 pp.

This work contains an introduction that explains the three parts of the book: (1) "The Center Dialogue," (2) "The Sacred City,"[1] and (3) "The Wild Places." The last two are articles that Thomas Merton wrote for the Center for the Study of Democratic Institutions at Santa Barbara, California. The first item (the only one to be discussed here) is the transcription of a dialogue between Merton and Center members and guests. Wilbur H. Ferry introduced Merton, and a spirited discussion followed. Merton explained why he was at Santa Barbara and offered a preview of what he hoped to experience in Asia.

"The Center Dialogue" is a helpful preparation for reading of *The Asian Journal,* for it gives some preliminary understanding of what Merton's expectations were for the trip that then lay ahead of him. He describes his itinerary, as much of it as he knew then: Bangkok meeting of Christian monks; Darjeeling and "Summit Meeting of Religions"; Mim Tea Estate near Mt. Kanchenjunga; November meeting with the Dalai Lama, arranged by Harold Talbott. His goal is an exchange (he is not yet ready to call it a dialogue) between Eastern and Western religious experience. He speaks of the relationship of Catholicism to Buddhism, carefully pointing out that Buddhism is not really a religion but a way of experiencing reality. In response to questions, he discusses monastic renewal, making clear that it is not simply institutional reform. At the heart of this renewal is the recovery of the depth of purpose that brings a person to a monastery. The monastic life is "an unconditional breaking through the limitations that are imposed by normal society. You become a completely marginal person in order to break through the inevitable artificiality of social life" (*Preview of the Asian Journey*, 42). In this process monks must avoid the danger of constructing another artificial society. Responding to questions, he makes clear that he is talking about transformation of consciousness that is essential to both Eastern and Western monasticism. He discusses the problem of becoming socially active while preserving the solitude necessary for such transformation. "How do you remain involved and detached at the same time?" (69). How does one combine a quiet, mystical spirituality with a prophetic stance?

There is something unique about this dialogue between Merton and a group of intellectuals. It is the only such recorded event that we possess in such great detail. Merton appears at ease, wanting to listen to others and at the same time eager to share his own insights with them. For readers it is an appropriate preparation for understanding the exchange that would take place during his Asian journey. whs

Notes

1. "The Sacred City" is also included in *Ishi Means Man*.

THOMAS MERTON READER, A

Edited by Thomas P. McDonnell. New York: Harcourt, Brace & World, Inc., 1962. xix+553 pp.

This was the first anthology of Thomas Merton's writings to be published in the English language.[1] Merton actually worked with McDonnell on the book. "I am keeping my fingers in the selection process to make sure it does not become either too dull or too frivolous," Merton wrote to Mark Van Doren on June 21, 1961 (*Road to Joy*, 42). Merton was happy with the book: "It gathers together all sorts of diverse bits of writing that might add up to some kind of a clear picture in the end" (*Witness to*

Freedom, 306). He was, however, disappointed that it did not include all the material that he would have liked to include. Nevertheless, he judged the selection to be representative. But by 1964 he already was thinking about other things that "ought to be in the book rather than much that is in the big *Reader*."[2]

Writing a preface for *A Thomas Merton Reader* provided Merton with an opportunity to review his writing and to characterize his development as a writer. The value of the preface is not limited to its usefulness to readers of the anthology. Entitled "First and Last Thoughts: An Author's Preface" (*Thomas Merton Reader*, vii–xiii), Merton's essay not only serves to present an overview of his writing but also to provide a revealing glimpse of the writer himself.

Although the anthology includes some of Merton's early work — two reviews published in the *New York Herald Tribune Books* in 1938 — and some poems written when Merton was living in Greenwich Village and later when he was teaching at St. Bonaventure College, most of what is published in the volume was written at Gethsemani. Merton's writing is so intimately connected with his life as a monk that he divides his work as a writer into four periods related to his life in the monastery. First, during his novitiate (1942–44) he wrote what he was "appointed to write" and to translate French books. The period from his first vows to ordination to the priesthood (1944–49) constitutes the second stage. The books written during this time (*The Seven Storey Mountain*, *Seeds of Contemplation*, *The Waters of Siloe*) are "most widely known and read." After a time during which he was "almost incapable of writing," he was appointed master of scholastics in 1951. That began the third period (1951–54), during which he wrote *The Ascent to Truth* and *Bread in the Wilderness* and completed *The Sign of Jonas*, *The Living Bread*, *No Man Is an Island*, and *The Silent Life*. In 1955 he became master of the choir novices and wrote little during the next year. The year 1957 marked the beginning of the fourth period, during which Merton produced books such as *Disputed Questions*, *The Wisdom of the Desert*, *The Behavior of Titans*, and *New Seeds of Contemplation*. It was during this last period, 1957–62, that he began writing on war and peace and on Eastern religions, as well as on liturgy and on solitude. The books of this last period seemed "most significant" to Merton.[3]

Merton's preface reveals much about him — his self-understanding and his approach to life. "It is possible to doubt whether I have become a monk (a doubt I have to live with), but it is not possible to doubt that I am writer, that I was born one and will most probably die as one" (*Thomas Merton Reader*, x). Being a monk *and* writer shaped the way in which he viewed life. Being a monk taught the writer to let go of his work: "When something has been written, publish it, and go on to something else" (x). Accept "life and everything in life as a gift . . . clinging to none of it" (x). Recognize that all life grows "in mystery inscaped with paradox and contradiction, yet centered, in its very heart, on the divine mercy" (x–xi). Know that it is God's grace that unifies. "Without the grace of God there could be no unity, no simplicity in our lives: only contradiction" (xi). The paradoxes and contradictions in his life were "signs of God's mercy" (ix) to Merton, and his life and work are a "witness" to that mercy: "Whatever else it may do, this book should bear witness to the fact that I have found what I sought and continue to find it" (xi–xii).

The book is divided into seven parts: (1) "The Unreal City"; (2) "Magnetic North"; (3) "The Monastery"; (4) "Mentors and Doctrines"; (5) "Love"; (6) "Vision"; and (7) "The Sacred Land." Each part contains writings from a variety of genres, such as his autobiography, journals, poetry, essays, and excerpts from his many books. The variety and mix of genres serve to underscore Merton's versatility as a writer. McDonnell's nonchronological ordering of selections serves to highlight the thematic consistency in Merton's work over time. Merton himself remarked in the preface that much that is "spelled out in later books and articles is already implied" (vii) in his autobiography, *The Seven Storey Mountain*, published in 1948. And so Merton found it fitting that the *Thomas Merton Reader* begins and ends with selections from *The Seven Storey Mountain*, and the numerous selections from the autobiography included in the book create

a unifying narrative thread. In addition to the numerous selections from *The Seven Storey Mountain*, the book includes selections from books such as *The Waters of Siloe*, *The Ascent to Truth*, *The Sign of Jonas*, *No Man Is an Island*, *The Wisdom of the Desert*, and *New Seeds of Contemplation*, as well as more than forty poems and excerpts from various essays. In 553 pages McDonnell succeeds in demonstrating the depth and breadth of Merton's thought and writing on prayer and contemplation, on monasticism, on living in love, on the horrors of war, and on living faithfully in modern times.

A *Thomas Merton Reader*, Revised Edition

Six years after Merton's death (1968), McDonnell brought out *A Thomas Merton Reader*, revised edition (New York: Doubleday Image, 1974). While retaining "the essential concept and structure of the original," the revised edition includes "significant revisions" (9). While some selections were cut, others chosen from Merton's later writings (1962–68) were added. In the editor's note written for the revised edition McDonnell explains that "the image of the journey, as a way of seeking, had a compelling force" in Merton's spiritual life and work and so defines the direction of the book. The "physical journey as well as the spiritual one" and "the psychological and cultural modes of searching," reflected in the *Thomas Merton Reader*, constitute "important ways" of looking at Merton's life and thought (9). McDonnell observes that Merton's journey from "The Unreal City" (the title of part 1) to "The Sacred Land" (the title of part 7) illustrates his changing view of things from an early "disdain" for the world to a recognition of himself as "a member of the human race" called to "prophetic witness" (9–10).

Among the additions to the revised edition are the well-known account of Merton's epiphany at the corner of Fourth and Walnut in downtown Louisville (the description of an experience that Merton had in 1958 and shared with his readers in *Conjectures of a Guilty Bystander*, published in 1966), "Day of a Stranger" (an essay written in response to a request from a Latin American publisher who asked Merton to describe a day in his life as a poet), and the closing prayer Merton offered in Calcutta, shortly before his death. CMB

Notes

1. A one-volume edition of *The Complete Works of Thomas Merton* was published in Argentina as *Obras Completas* (Buenos Aires: Editorial Sudamericana, 1960). It included the complete texts of seven books and an introduction by Merton. Additional projected volumes never were published. See *Honorable Reader*, 35–44.

2. Letter to José Coronel Urtecho, dated April 17, 1964 (*Courage for Truth*, 173). Merton lists some of the pieces that he thinks should be included, among them: "Preface to Japanese Edition of *The Seven Storey Mountain*," "Classic Chinese Thought," "Message to Poets," and "Meditation on Adolf Eichmann."

3. Compare these four periods with the three periods into which he divides his work in a letter he wrote in 1968 to Sr. J. M.: (1) the years 1938–47, the "'first fervor' stuff," which he characterized as reflecting "a highly unworldly, ascetical, intransigent, somewhat apocalyptic outlook"; (2) the period during the 1950s, when he "began to open up again to the world"; and (3) the years after 1960, when he produced books such as *Seeds of Destruction, Raids on the Unspeakable, Conjectures of a Guilty Bystander, Emblems of a Season of Fury*, and *The Way of Chuang Tzu*. He added, "It appears that I am now evolving further, with studies on Zen and a new kind of experimental creative drive in prose poetry, satire, etc." (*School of Charity*, 384).

THOMAS MERTON'S FOUR POEMS IN FRENCH

Translated by Rupert E. Pickens, with an afterword by Robert E. Daggy. Lexington, Ky.: Anvil Press, 1996. 53 pp.

This is the last of the collaborations between Thomas Merton and his friends the printers Victor and Carolyn Hammer. In 1966 Merton had sent his French poem "Le Secret" to the Hammers with the suggestion that they might be interested in printing it on their hand press under the imprint of Stamperia del Santuccio.[1] While nothing came of the proposal at the time, almost three decades after the death of both Merton and Victor Hammer "Le Secret" and the three other known poems written by Merton in French were published in a limited edition of one hundred copies by Carolyn Hammer. The earliest of the poems, "Je crois en l'Amour" ("I believe in the Love . . ."), first appeared in *The Tears of the Blind Lions* (1949); the other three all date from 1966: "Le Secret" is one of the poems included in

"Sensation Time at the Home," a volume of Merton's shorter poems from the mid-1960s that never was published as a separate volume and appears as appendix 1 of *Collected Poems*; "Cable no. 35" is a section of *Cables to the Ace* in the style of the French poet René Char, whom Merton was reading extensively at the time;[2] "Les Cinq Vierges," a humorous variation of the Parable of the Wise and Foolish Virgins written for Jacques Maritain shortly after his visit to Merton's hermitage, appears by itself as appendix 4 of *Collected Poems*. The four poems are provided with new translations by Rupert E. Pickens that replace the rather unsatisfactory prose renditions in *Collected Poems*. Robert E. Daggy's afterword provides information on Merton's youthful immersion in French language and culture and on the circumstances of composition of the individual poems. POC

Notes

1. See the headnote to Robert E. Daggy's expanded version of his afterword to the volume in *The Merton Seasonal* 21, no. 2 (1996): 19–26.

2. See Merton's letter of March 10, 1967, to Cid Corman (*Courage for Truth*, 250).

THOMAS MERTON STUDIES CENTER, THE

By Thomas Merton, John Howard Griffin, and Monsignor [Alfred] Horrigan. Santa Barbara, Calif.: Unicorn Press, 1971. 25 pp.

This booklet includes three brief essays published to commemorate the inauguration of the Thomas Merton Studies Center at Bellarmine College (now University) in Louisville, Kentucky. The first, by Msgr. Alfred Horrigan, then-president of Bellarmine, is simply entitled "Thomas Merton Studies Center" (7–11). It relates the history of the developments that led to the formation of the Center: the proposal that the college establish a Thomas Merton Collection as part of its library, which was approved both by Bellarmine and by the Abbey of Gethsemani and Merton himself and which led to the formal inauguration of the collection on November 10, 1963; the dedication of the library's Thomas Merton Room[1] a year later on November 8, 1964; the stipulation in Merton's 1967 document establishing the Merton

Legacy Trust that all materials not otherwise assigned should be deposited in the Bellarmine Merton Collection; and the announcement on November 9, 1969, of the development of the Merton Room and Collection into the Thomas Merton Studies Center as a research and educational facility dedicated to scholarly research on Merton and his work and to furthering interest in "the great themes which absorbed Father Merton — peace, freedom, interracial justice, ecumenism, and East-West relations" (*Thomas Merton Studies Center*, 9).

The second essay, by Merton himself, is a statement entitled "Concerning the Collection in the Bellarmine College Library" (13–15); it was read in his absence by Daniel Walsh on the occasion of the inauguration of the Bellarmine Merton Collection on November 10, 1963. In addition to paying tribute to Walsh himself, his Columbia philosophy professor who had first suggested that Merton visit Gethsemani and who had eventually come to Kentucky himself to teach at the monastery as well as at Bellarmine, Merton describes the collection as both a sign and a means of his own relationship to and participation in the local church, the Diocese of Louisville. He also uses the occasion to provide a succinct summary of his own work: "Whatever I may have written, I think it all can be reduced in the end to this one root truth: that God calls human persons to union with Himself and with one another in Christ, in the Church which is His Mystical Body" (14). He goes on to add that his work "is also a witness to the fact that there is and must be, in the Church, a contemplative life which has no other function than to realize these mysterious things, and return to God all the thanks and praise that human hearts can give Him" (14–15), and that "if I have written about interracial justice, or thermonuclear weapons, it is because these issues are terribly relevant to one great truth: that man is called to live as a son of God . . . to live in peace with all his brothers in the One Christ" (15).

The final essay, "In Search of Thomas Merton," by John Howard Griffin, who had been appointed Merton's official biographer,[2] is the presentation delivered on the occasion of the formal announcement of the Merton Studies Center in November 1969 (17–24). Griffin provides a brief overview of his preliminary work on the biography and reads excerpts from the journal he himself was keeping during the one week each month that he stayed at Merton's hermitage while researching the biography.[3] Among the details he relates is Merton's response after his presentation in Thailand on the final day of his life to a question about direct evangelizing of non-Christians: "What we are asked to do at present is not so much to speak of Christ as to let Him live in us so that people may find him by feeling how He lives in us" (22).

The booklet was published by Merton's friend Teo Savory at her Unicorn Press in a limited edition of 1500 copies, five hundred of which were hand-printed and hand-bound. The inclusion of "Volume One" on the initial page suggests that this was intended to be the first in a series, but no further volumes appeared. In 1976 the Center itself began publishing *The Merton Seasonal,* currently a joint publication of the Center and the International Thomas Merton Society.

The Merton Center soon outgrew its room in the Bellarmine Library and moved to the lower level of Bonaventure Hall on the Bellarmine campus, where over the course of more than two decades it developed into a major research facility under the leadership of its longtime director, the late Dr. Robert E. Daggy. On October 10, 1998, the new quarters of the Thomas Merton Center (as it is now known), on the second floor of the recently completed W. L. Lyons Brown Library, were dedicated by Archbishop Thomas Kelly of Louisville, fulfilling hopes already voiced by Msgr. Horrigan in 1969 (10). The largest collection of Merton materials in the world, with more than 45,000 items, the Center is currently directed by Dr. Paul M. Pearson.[4] POC

Notes

1. For Merton's own comments on the Bellarmine Merton Room, see *Learning to Love,* 296–97.

2. Griffin was prevented by illness from completing the biography; one section has been published as *Follow the Ecstasy: Thomas Merton, The Hermitage Years, 1965–1968* (Fort Worth, Tex.: Latitudes Press, 1983).

3. For the complete journal see John Howard Grif-

fin, *The Hermitage Journals* (Kansas City: Andrews and McMeel, 1981).

4. The Thomas Merton Center is located at Bellarmine University, 2001 Newburg Road, Louisville, KY 40205; its web site is www.merton.org.

THOUGHTS IN SOLITUDE

New York: Farrar, Straus and Cudahy, 1958. 124 pp.

In 1953, when Thomas Merton was begging for more solitude, Dom James Fox allowed him to use an abandoned toolshed in the woods behind the monastery, where he was able to stay for some hours each day. He fixed it up as a hermitage and named it St. Anne's. It was here that he wrote *Thoughts in Solitude*.[1] It is not thoughts *about* solitude, but *in* solitude. The "solitude" in the title indicates the place of the book's writing. There is, however, a great deal about solitude in the book; in fact, part 2 is called "The Love of Solitude."

It is a small book (124 small pages) in the style of *Seeds of Contemplation* and *No Man Is an Island*: brief meditations in thirty-seven mini-chapters of two or three pages each (its initial title was simply *37 Meditations*). In a brief preface Merton tells us that the book is made up of "thoughts on the contemplative life, fundamental intuitions" (11) that seemed to be of particular importance at the time he wrote.

Part 1 is called "Aspects of the Spiritual Life." He points out that the spiritual life is indeed life, the totality of one's life, a life that is unified, a life that is always new. It is a turning of our whole self to God with the will simply to be one's real self and nothing more. This calls for listening to God and responding. In an interesting metaphor he speaks of the "inner ears" that alone can listen to God. "The ears with which one hears the message of the Gospel are hidden in man's heart, and those ears do not hear anything unless they are favored with a certain interior solitude and silence" (*Thoughts in Solitude*, 13). He also uses the more familiar metaphor of the "inner eye." He speaks of the Presence of God and our awareness of that Presence in prayer. "The 'eye' which opens to His presence is in the very center of our humility, in the very heart of our freedom, in the

very depths of our spiritual nature. Meditation is the opening of this eye" (51).

Part 2^2 is called "The Love of Solitude." Some of what he says was inspired by his reading of *The World of Silence*, by Swiss philosopher Max Picard. Merton deals with a theme that much occupied him in the mid-1950s, as he sought for greater solitude and as he saw the introduction of much machinery into the monastery, with the consequent increase of the level of noise, an obstacle to solitude. One of the important themes is the need of silence for true solitude and for true communion with reality. "The solitary life, being silent, clears away the smoke-screen of words that man has laid down between his mind and things. In solitude we remain face to face with the naked being of things. . . . When we have really met and known the world in silence, words do not separate us from the world nor from other men, nor from God nor from ourselves, because we no longer trust entirely in language to contain reality" (85–86). Much of this second part can be read as a defense of exterior solitude, the solitude of the hermit. It was a topic that eventually would get Merton into trouble with the censors of his order.

In 1955, three years before the publication of *Thoughts in Solitude*, Merton had written in French an article defending the hermit life. Entitled *Dans le desert de Dieu*, it appeared in *Temoignages* 48 (March 1955): 32–36. See "Notes for a Philosophy of Solitude" (in *Disputed Questions*) for the subsequent fate of this article. WHS

SEE ALSO SILENCE; *SILENCE IN HEAVEN;* SOLITUDE.

Notes

1. Merton indicates that he wrote this work in 1953–54. It was not published, however, until 1958.

2. The one-page second chapter of part 2 (p. 83) is the well-known prayer that has been duplicated thousands and thousands of times: "My Lord God, I have no idea where I am going. . . ."

TIME

"Time," according to Thomas Merton, "is *quality* not *quantity*" (*Learning to Love*, 352). Yet this is not generally how it is experienced by the people of contemporary society, "when everyone is obsessed with lack of time, lack of space, with saving time, conquering space, projecting into time and space the anguish produced within them by the technological furies of size, volume, quantity, speed, number, price, power and acceleration" (*Raids on the Unspeakable*, 70).[1] Unlike people in traditional societies, who were integrated (and also, from a certain perspective, trapped [*Seasons of Celebration*, 49]) in the cycle of the seasons, modern people are on a "linear flight into nothingness" (51), a temporal journey with no sense of a goal or even of a direction. Thus, the first stage in a genuinely Christian response to time is to rediscover a sense of time that is not measured by the clock, to "recover the rhythm and order of man's real nature" (51). This is the message of Merton's "myth" of "Atlas and the Fatman," in which Atlas juxtaposes the patterns and rhythms of nature, the unmeasurable "time of the sea" from which all life emerges, with the spurious technical efficiency and actual destructiveness of the Fatman, "faithless mad son of clocks and buzzers" (*Raids on the Unspeakable*, 100–101). It is the revelation of the rain, whose speech "no clock . . . can measure," in "Rain and the Rhinoceros" (14), which is in stark contrast to the message on the box of the Coleman lantern, a promise, as Merton sardonically notes, to increase the quantity of time available for its owner: "*Stretches days to give more hours of fun*" (13). The biblical experience of time is incompatible with time as quantity but builds on the natural experience of temporal rhythms, as Merton symbolically expresses at the conclusion of the famous "Fire Watch" passage when he emerges into the open air on the church tower and puts down the watch he has been carrying, and suddenly discovers that the "things of Time are in connivance with eternity," and that "Eternity is in the present. Eternity is in the palm of the hand. Eternity is a seed of fire, whose sudden roots break barriers that keep my heart from being an abyss" (*Entering the Silence*, 487).

Christianity is not a flight from time but a redeeming of time, a recognition of time and history as the arena of God's saving action (*Seeds of Destruction*, xiv). The incarnation is the pivotal event of the fullness of time, the acceptable time, the time of salvation, the fullness of time (*Raids on the Unspeakable*, 66–67). Salvation is not a victory over time, for time is not the enemy, or rather, is no longer an enemy when transiency and mortality are no longer to be regarded as absolutes (*Seasons of Celebration*, 46–47). "The freedom of the Christian contemplative," Merton says, "is not freedom *from* time, but freedom *in* time" (*Seeds of Destruction*, xiv). It is the recognition and acceptance of *kairos*, the "moment of breakthrough toward which history itself, with all the good and evil that are in man, has gradually been maturing" (*Opening the Bible*, 82), which is also and "above all *a time of decisive response*" (83), an obedience to the Lord's command to "repent and believe the good news" because "the time is fulfilled and the reign of God is at hand" (Mark 1:14–15).[2]

Merton warns that there is always a danger of simply canonizing and sacralizing accepted temporal and social patterns and institutional structures as though they were manifestations of *kairos*, of redeemed time (*Seasons of Celebration*, 60) — a temptation that he at least at times thought his own monastery had succumbed to (see *Turning toward the World*, 151). Hence, there is a need to link *kairos* with *kenosis*, a recognition of the fullness of time in Christ with an awareness of our own emptiness, as a guard against complacency and self-congratulation: "The fullness of time is the time of His emptiness in us. The fullness of time is the time of our emptiness, which draws Christ down into our lives, so that in us and through us He may bring the fullness of His truth to the world" (*Seasons of Celebration*, 94–95).

The recognition of time as transcending chronology is particularly evident in the liturgy, in which the natural patterns of seasonal renewal are transmuted into "*a cycle of salvation*" in which "each new season renews an aspect of the great Mystery of Christ living and present in His Church" (51–52). Even more significantly, in the liturgy there is a convergence of past and future in the present, a re-presentation of the saving mysteries of cross and resurrection that also is an anticipation, a foretaste, of the fulfillment of these mysteries in the final consummation of the eschatological banquet

(56–57); "we believe that He who has come and will come is present here and now" (92).

This sense of the present as the time of salvation has profound social consequences, as it demands that "some evidence of the presence and action of Christ, some visible manifestation of the *Pneuma*" (93) be made visible and tangible by those claiming to be disciples of the Christ whose salvific power is present now. Merton explores this sense of the present as *kairos* particularly with respect to the nonviolent civil rights movement, which he views as "the providential 'hour,' the *kairos* not merely of the Negro, but of the white man. It is, or at any rate it can be, God's hour...the hour of vocation, the moment in which, hearing and understanding the will of God as expressed in the urgent need of our Negro brother, we can respond to that inscrutable will in a faith that faces the need of reform and creative change, in order that the demands of truth and justice may not go unfulfilled" (*Seeds of Destruction*, 65). He soon came to believe, however, that white Christians had failed to recognize and respond to this *kairos*, had ignored or rejected the invitation to live out the biblical image of the "Beloved Community" offered by Martin Luther King (*Faith and Violence*, 130). What is still available is the opportunity for repentance, for a humble and salutary recognition "that our faith does not exempt us from facing the mysterious realities of the world with the same limitations as everybody else, and with the same capacity for human failure" (142).

It is not merely a failure in action but a failure in contemplation that undermines the church's response to "the time of urgent and providential decision" (130), a failure to see as well as, and at the root of, a failure to act. Thus, in his final extended comment on the mystery of time, little more than a month before his death, Merton called for the contemplative life to "create a new experience of time, not as stopgap, stillness, but as '*temps vierge*' — not a blank to be filled or an untouched space to be conquered and violated, but a space which can enjoy its own potentialities and hopes — and its own presence to itself." Such an experience of "virgin time" would not be marked by introversion or solipsism, but would be "open

to others — *compassionate* time, rooted in the sense of common illusion and in criticism of it" (*Other Side of the Mountain*, 262). It would have the insight to perceive redeemed time as essentially unviolated by the stupidities and crimes of humanity, and so continue to call humanity, despite its attraction to "common illusion," to the vision of the final page of *New Seeds of Contemplation*, where Merton affirms that "the world and time are the dance of the Lord in emptiness" (*New Seeds of Contemplation*, 297). POC

Notes

1. Merton's discussion of the contrast between secular, quantitative time and biblical time in Faulkner's *The Sound and the Fury* vividly expresses these differences (*Opening the Bible*, 48–49; *Literary Essays*, 499–512).

2. For the influence of the Orthodox view of time as *kairos* on Merton, as expressed particularly by Olivier Clément, see *Turning toward the World*, 39, 42; see also *Search for Solitude*, 354, for Berdyaev's notion of the reign of antichrist as "a total tyranny of mere *duration*."

TOBIN, MARY LUKE

Born in 1908, Mary Luke Tobin entered the Sisters of Loretto at the age of nineteen. She made her perpetual vows in 1932. Quickly recognized as a leader, she was elected president of the Sisters of Loretto in 1958 and served in that position until 1970. The motherhouse of the Loretto sisters at that time was in Nerinx, Kentucky, just a short distance from the Abbey of Gethsemani. In August 1964 she was elected president of the Conference of Major Superiors of Women. Two sessions of the Second Vatican Council had already taken place. Members of the executive committee of the Conference suggested that Mary Luke go to Rome to learn what she could about what was happening at the Council. While she was en route to Rome by boat, she received the exciting news that she had been invited to be one of fifteen women (the only one from the United States) to be auditors at the Council. In her book *Hope Is an Open Door*, Sr. Mary Luke saw this invitation as an offering of hope to women, though she remarked wryly, "True, fifteen women among twenty-five hundred bishops was hardly a 'quota,' but it was a beginning."[1] During the third and fourth ses-

Mary Luke Tobin

in Nerinx, Kentucky, which is now a retirement home for the sisters. WHS

Notes

1. Mary Luke Tobin, *Hope Is an Open Door* (Nashville: Abingdon, 1981), 20.

"TOM'S BOOK"

**Unpublished. Thomas Merton Archives.
Louisville, Ky.: Thomas Merton Center.**

Thomas Merton's first journal-biography was written by his mother, Ruth. It covered the period from February 1, 1915, to January 31, 1917, and was called "Tom's Book" (Ruth insisted that his name be "Tom," not "Thomas"). Ruth had taken note of virtually everything that Tom said and did. These notes (some made in France, others in America) were transcribed and sent to Tom's paternal grandmother (Gertrude Hannah Merton), who visited Ruth, Owen, and their two children in 1920. On the first page of this transcribed book is the title and dedication: "TOM'S BOOK TO GRANNY with Tom's best love, 1916."

The book records something new about him for each month of 1915. "At four weeks he held his head erect, and was very active from the beginning, always kicking and waving his arms while he was awake" (p. 1). "On the twentieth of June he made a desperate effort to creep and screamed with rage that he did not succeed" (p. 2). "When he was called he came with joyous shouts to announce himself" (p. 3 [September 1915]). "He stood up in his pram, especially to see the river when we went on the bridge" (p. 3). Ruth records that in December 1915 he was circumcised by Tom Bennett (p. 5). (There is no mention of baptism.) He did not always fit the presuppositions for children of his age that she discovered in the child psychology books she read (p. 6). On November 1, 1916, she recalls, "He will look for hours at pictures in books, recognizing all the objects he knows, and sometimes pretending to read.... When we go out he seems conscious of everything.... Sometimes he put up his arms and cried out: 'Oh Sui! Oh joli!' Often it is to the birds or trees that he makes these pagan hymns of joy.... Before we left

sions of the Council she was present at every session and was appointed to a subcommittee working on "Schema 13," which in its final form became the Constitution on the Church in the Modern World (*Gaudium et Spes*).

In several places in his journals (see vols. 5 and 6), Thomas Merton writes of Sr. Mary Luke reporting to him and some of the monks about the workings at the Second Vatican Council. In December of 1967 and the spring of 1968 Merton gave retreats to contemplative nuns. He invited Sr. Mary Luke to come to the retreats and also to help with the transportation. (The account of these retreats is found in *The Springs of Contemplation*.)

Sr. Mary Luke moved to Denver when the headquarters of the Loretto sisters was transferred there. She was in residence with several other Loretto sisters and from this residence she set the agenda for the Thomas Merton Center for Creative Exchange. She organized retreats and much activity for peace and justice. She was one of the founding members of the International Thomas Merton Society and has been active in the Call to Action movement. At present she resides at the former motherhouse

Prades, he had already begun to wave his arms toward the landscape, crying out 'Oh color!' ('Color' is the word he used to mean landscape, his father's pictures and all the paraphernalia of painting.)" (7).

In the November 1, 1916, entry (which is quite long) she gives us an insight into a person who, when grown to adulthood, each day would want to record everything that happened. "Before going to bed or just when he is getting up, he often tells over to himself all the things which have happened" (p. 9). In the same vein: "We never know when he learns these things, but he must see and notice everything that takes place, for everyday he surprises us by some proof of knowing all that goes on" (p. 12).

Pages 15 and 16 detail his daily schedule and the kinds of foods he ate at breakfast, lunch, dinner, and supper. Pages 18–20 list the quite extensive vocabulary he possessed at the age of two.

Michael Mott, in speaking about "Tom's Book," offers the interesting and insightful comment that the book "reveals as much of Merton's first biographer as it does of her subject."[1] WHS

Notes

1. Michael Mott, *The Seven Mountains of Thomas Merton* (Boston: Houghton Mifflin, 1984), 7.

TOWER OF BABEL, THE:
A Morality
New York: New Directions, 1957. 30 pp.

The only published work of Thomas Merton in dramatic form, *The Tower of Babel* originally appeared[1] as part 2 of *The Strange Islands* (1957) and subsequently was published in a limited edition of 250 copies, with four woodcuts, printed on a hand press by Richard von Sichowsky of Hamburg. It has its origin in a short poem from the early 1940s entitled "Tower of Babel" and subtitled "The Political Speech" (later included in *Early Poems* [1971]); reordered and slightly rewritten, these lines become part of the speech of the Professor in part 1, scene 2, of the longer work. They focus on the misuse of language to conceal, distort, and manipulate reality rather than reveal the

truth, and conclude with the ominous transformation of the image of the web, from "The backward-forward working of the web" (l. 18) by which words are said to create the only reality there is, to "The movement into the web" (l. 19), which implies the ultimate purpose of the web and the ultimate fate of those trapped by it.

In 1953, at the request of composer Paul Hindemith, Merton wrote "A Responsory" (*Collected Poems*, 672–78) as a text to be set to music by Hindemith. This text had no reference to Babel, but a short time later Merton wrote a longer text entitled "Tower of Babel: Oratorio," a six-part work that incorporated the material from the early poem into part 2 and much of the "Responsory" (in revised form) into parts 3–5. When Hindemith decided not to set the text, Merton revised it extensively as "The Tower of Babel: A Morality," which on January 27, 1957, was performed (condensed and adapted by Richard J. Walsh) on the *Catholic Hour* on the NBC television network.

The published version of the text consists of two parts, each with two scenes. It is preceded by three epigraphs: the original Genesis story of the Tower of Babel (11:1–9); an excerpt from St. Augustine's *City of God* describing the two cities, the heavenly city built by love of God and the earthly city built by love of self (14.28); and a passage from the Apocalypse (Revelation) about the fall of Babylon (18:21, 23–24).

Part 1, "The Legend of the Tower," opens with Thomas and Raphael, the two characters who continue throughout the play, discussing "The Building of the Tower," as scene 1 is called. Thomas, whose name, of course, suggests that of the author, is presented initially as somewhat naive and obtuse; his companion, whose name recalls the angelic guide in Tobit, is much wiser and more insightful and instructs Thomas as to the real meaning of what they see. While Thomas suggests that they join the builders, Raphael warns that the workers' apparent unity is an illusion. After the builders profess their unquestioning loyalty to the Leader, who then appears and proclaims the tower "perfect and eternal," Raphael exposes the builders' busyness as "their substitute for faith. Instead of believing in themselves, they seek to convince themselves, by their activity, that they exist." Life is not gift but accomplishment, not community but competition. This is why the Leader promises war as a diversion after the tower is completed. However, before this can occur, nature itself, "Wind with a thousand fingers," brings the tower down. While Thomas sees this fall as "Babylon's end," Raphael calls it "Babylon's beginning," since the seeds of disunity will be spread throughout the world.

Scene 2, "The Trial," takes place in the ruined city square, where blame for the fall of the tower is initially placed on language. But after the first witness, the Professor, asserts that words have only a utilitarian function (in a speech expanded from the original "Tower of Babel" poem, given to the King of Babylon himself in the "Oratorio" version), the Leader is ready to acquit words and call Silence to the bar. However, the Captain first draws the distinction between three types of speech, Truth, Falsehood, and Propaganda, each of which is called to the stand in turn. Truth declares that the people destroyed their own tower, and rouses the crowd to a fury, but is "defended" by a Second Philosopher, a relativist who claims Truth should not be killed since in fact there is no truth. Propaganda is then called to the stand to fasten responsibility for the destruction of the tower on the impossibly eclectic group of "The religious warmongers, the clergy, the freemasons, the Pope, the millionaires, the Elders of Zion, the Young Men's Christian Association, the Jesuits and the Legion of Mary." As reward he is given "exclusive freedom of speech and worship in every part of the world" and commissioned to form the minds of the young. Finally, Falsehood is called to the stand and identifies himself as Truth, who will split each of his followers in half so that they "become two angels," and reveals that the tower has not been destroyed at all, since it "is a spiritual reality and so am I." Once Falsehood has been duly recognized, by the Leader himself, as "Divine and omnipresent Majesty," the final witness, Silence, is disregarded and sent to be crucified, at which point part 1 concludes.

Scene 1 of part 2, "The City of God," is entitled "Zodiac." Raphael and Thomas come upon a wasteland where a great city once stood, but they encounter the Prophet, who reminds them that "The city under the sand / Lives everywhere," that "the same Babylon" is present throughout the world. The rest of the scene consists of alternating sections of verse by a chorus of children who chant in quatrains about the passing of time, symbolized by the signs of the zodiac, and prose commentary by the Prophet (in one instance, perhaps a mistranscription, by Raphael) revealing the original divine plan for authentic human unity, to be restored by the speaking of the true Word of God, who will create the "perfect city" of which Babylon was the distorted image, "built by the thought and the silence and the wisdom and the power of God."

In the final scene, entitled "The Exiles," Thomas, Raphael, and the Prophet encounter a group of exiles who have lost a sense of their own identity, deprived of names and reduced to numbers. The newcomers encourage them to continue their pilgrimage, and together they come upon a village festival in which the dancers sing of primordial unity of body and soul and of friend with friend. The Prophet identifies the villagers as those "who have never been conquered by the builders of the ancient tower . . . the children of God," for whom language brings both communication and communion. As the Ancient, leader of the exiles, asks why "the whole world is not like this," Raphael, Thomas, and the Prophet announce that it will be, as Babylon has fallen, doomed by its own untruth to be destroyed by "one Word uttered in silence." The play culminates with the chorus singing in Latin the prologue to John's Gospel, alternating with explanatory words of the Prophet, joined by Raphael and Thomas, identifying the Word as the power of salvation throughout history, culminating in the ultimate revelation of the "*Verbum crucis, / Verbum pacis*" — the Word of the cross which is the Word of peace, who is to be the final Word leading time into eternity. POC

SEE ALSO LANGUAGE AND PROPAGANDA.

Notes

1. The earliest published version of the play appeared in the October 1955 issue of *Jubilee* magazine, and subsequently was made available as a reprint.

TRADITION

Tradition is the process whereby the teachings, the rituals, and the life of the church are transmitted from the past to the present. The word "tradition" also can be used to designate the content of what is transmitted. In the 1960s Thomas Merton wrote a great deal about the monastic tradition. He realized that this tradition had been shaped in part by cultural elements that in themselves have nothing to do with monasticism or Christian faith. While he believed that the authentic wisdom drawn from the ages in which monasticism was fully lived must not be lost, he also thought that monasteries in the present needed to be more democratic and less authoritarian. Monks should have more initiative in running their own lives. Superiors no longer should arrogate to themselves the right to do all the thinking and make all the decisions for their subjects.

He sees tradition not as "passive submission to the obsessions of former generations," but rather, as "a living assent to a current of uninterrupted vitality." He continues, "What was once real in other times and places becomes real in us today. And its reality is not an official parade of externals. It is a living spirit marked by freedom and by certain *originality*. Fidelity to tradition does not mean the renunciation of all initiative, but a new initiative that is faithful to a certain spirit of freedom and of vision which demands to be incarnated in a new and unique situation" (*World of Action*, 22/41–42).

This understanding of tradition was something Merton grew into over the years. In *Seeds of Contemplation* (1949) he seems to see tradition as a strict adherence to dogmatic formulas handed down from the past. He feels constrained in the introduction of the book to say, "We sincerely hope it does not contain a line that is new to Catholic tradition or a single word that would perplex an orthodox theologian" (*Seeds of Contemplation*, 14).

In 1955 *No Man Is an Island* appeared, in which a new notion of tradition is emerging. Speaking of the monastic tradition, Merton writes that it is "rooted in the wisdom of the distant past, and yet is living and young, with something peculiarly new and original to say

to the [people] of our own time" (*No Man Is an Island*, 148). What he says about monastic tradition easily can be said about the notion of tradition in general and of the tradition of Christian faith. He writes,

> Tradition is living and active.... [It] does not form us automatically, we have to work to understand it.... [It] teaches us to live and shows us how to take full responsibility for our own lives.... *Tradition which is always old, is at the same time ever new because it is always reviving — born again in each generation, to be lived and applied in a new and particular way....* Tradition is creative. Always original, it always opens out new horizons for an old journey.... Tradition teaches us how to love, because it develops and expands our powers, and shows us how to give ourselves to the world in which we live. (150–51 [italics added])

This maturing understanding of tradition makes it possible for Merton to expand the statement about tradition in *Seeds of Contemplation* (quoted above) to the "sincere hope that [this book] does not contain a line that is new to Christian tradition" (*New Seeds of Contemplation*, xiv). He no longer is worried about perplexing orthodox theologians, and the substitution of "Christian" for "Catholic" indicates that he had a wider audience in view for *New Seeds of Contemplation*.

In *Conjectures of a Guilty Bystander* Merton makes clear that he has no desire to be seen as the "answer man." "I do have questions," he says, "and, as a matter of fact, I think a person is better known by his questions than by his answers" (*Guilty Bystander*, v/5). In fact, he suggests that one of the reasons that his writings appeal to many people "is precisely that I am not so sure of myself and do not claim to have all the answers.... In fact I often wonder quite openly about these 'answers' and about the habit of always having them ready. The best I can do is to look for some of the questions" (38/49).

In this same work he describes himself as being like Pope John XXIII: "a progressive with a deep respect and love for tradition." He wants to "preserve a very clear and marked continuity with the past" and at the same time to be "completely open to the modern world, while retaining the clearly defined, traditionally Catholic position" (285–86/312).

Merton had a strong sense of the responsibility he had as a monk and as a writer not only to respect tradition but also to help in its proper transmission. In a passage in *Conjectures of a Guilty Bystander* that may have been written in August 1961, he writes of his conviction that "my job is to clarify something of the tradition that lives in me, and in which I live: the tradition of wisdom and spirit that is found not only in Western Christendom but in Orthodoxy and also, at least analogously, in Asia and in Islam. Man's sanity and balance and peace depend, I think, on his keeping alive a continuous sense of what has been valid in his past" (176/194).[1] WHS

Notes

1. I date this entry to August 1961 because there is a somewhat similar statement in volume 4 of the journals, *Turning toward the World*, 155. This appears to be the source of the *Conjectures of a Guilty Bystander* passage.

TRAPPIST LIFE: A Guide to the Order of Cistercians of the Strict Observance called Trappists

Trappist, Ky.: Abbey of Our Lady of Gethsemani, 1953. 63 pp.

This illustrated pamphlet, with no author designated, is an updated version of *Cistercian Contemplatives* (1948), and like its predecessor provides an introduction to Cistercian life in general and to Gethsemani and its daughterhouses in particular; although it does not appear in the standard bibliographies, its relation to the earlier version, which is by Thomas Merton (see *Entering the Silence*, 96), makes its authorship evident.

The opening pages (3–5) include a dedication of the booklet to St. Bernard on the eighth centenary of his death, accompanied by an illustration of Bernard with Mary and Christ and a quotation from Bernard on the three degrees of charity (from *The Steps of Humility and Pride*, though not identified). The opening section, new to this edition, is entitled "Havens

of Peace" (7–8) and summarizes the new period of vitality at Gethsemani that had led to four foundations in the previous decade, with eight hundred men currently living in the five monasteries of the Gethsemani filiation. The second section, "The Contemplative Life" (9–11), is taken from *Cistercian Contemplatives* and focuses on Cistercian monasticism as a life for God alone, which moves from multiplicity to unity through the cross and finds perfection in an all-absorbing love for God alone. It defines true contemplatives as those who have forgotten and lost themselves in God beyond all experiences. The third section,[1] "History of Gethsemani" (13–23), updates the earlier pamphlet's "A Hundred Years of History" by including the death of Dom Frederic Dunne and the first years of Dom James Fox's abbacy. It looks at the problem of expansion, which had brought the population of the monastery up to 290, and the new foundations in South Carolina and upper New York State, the remodeling of Gethsemani, and the passing of the "crisis" through these internal and external solutions. Then follow short descriptions of the four daughterhouses, "Our Lady of the Holy Ghost" (Georgia), "Our Lady of the Holy Trinity" (Utah), "Our Lady of Mepkin" (South Carolina), and "Our Lady of the Genesee" (New York) (25–32). These are briefer than the corresponding sections on the Georgia and Utah monasteries in *Cistercian Contemplatives*. "A Visit to Gethsemani" (33–41) is a revised version of a similar section in the earlier pamphlet, but with detailed descriptions (with photographs) of the new buildings and additions to the monastery. The section now entitled "The Trappist Formula" (43–54) corresponds closely to "Summary of the Cistercian Observance" in the previous version, providing descriptions of the three major elements of Trappist life, "Opus Dei" (subtitled "Liturgy" in the first edition), "Manual Labor," and "Lectio Divina." The final sections, "Joy in Austerity" (55–58), "Admission to a Trappist Monastery" (59), and "A Monk's Average Day" (60–61) are found in *Cistercian Contemplatives* as well. Thus, *Trappist Life* brings the Gethsemani story up to date for visitors and prospective entrants to the monastery, a necessity after five brief but eventful years since the publication *of Cistercian Contemplatives.* POC

SEE ALSO *CISTERCIAN CONTEMPLATIVES.*

Notes

1. The section of *Cistercian Contemplatives* entitled "The Cistercian Ideal," which precedes the capsule history of Gethsemani, is dropped in the new version, presumably for reasons of space.

TRIER, GWYNEDD FANNY MERTON

Owen Merton's sister Gwyn, Thomas's aunt, was born in 1885 and died in 1986. When Thomas was on holidays from Ripley Court, he stayed with Aunt Maud (actually Owen's aunt) at Ealing or with Aunt Gwyn at "Fairlawn" in West Horsley. At Aunt Gwyn's he quickly established himself as a favorite with his younger cousins, delighting them with the adventure stories he composed for their enjoyment. WHS

TRINITY, THE BLESSED

The focal point of Thomas Merton's reflection on God is the supreme transcendent unity of God. To his correspondent Abdul Aziz, a Sufi Muslim, he makes clear that there is no other God besides God. Creation and salvation are entirely God's work alone. When we speak of Christ as Savior, we are not talking about a being outside of God as God's helper. Merton tries (not entirely successfully) to draw a parallel between the Muslim notion of God manifesting the divine Self in and through the prophet Muhammad and the Christian understanding of the working of God in and through Christ. He makes clear, though, that the Christian doctrine of the incarnation makes an enormous difference. Still, he suggests that the Christian view of the Trinity may be seen as similar to the Muslim notion of Allah as Rahman (the mercy of God limitless in God) and Rahim (the mercy of God as manifested in creation). "Just as Allah remains 'one' while being compassionate and merciful, and His compassion and mercy represent Him in different *relations* to the world, so the Father and Son and Holy Spirit are perfectly One, yet represent different relations" (*Hidden Ground of Love,* 56). But the parallel breaks down when it becomes clear that Rahman and Rahim are attributes or names of God, not subsisting relations.

At the heart of the problem of discussing the Trinity is a notion strenuously debated in the early centuries of the Church: the meaning of the term "person." For most people today "person" means a separate, individual human being. Thus, the notion of three persons in God conjures up the image of three separate individuals. We tend to think of "person" in psychological terms, whereas the tradition views it in ontological terms. The persons of the Trinity are seen as subsistent relations. The Son is what the Father is; the Spirit is what Father and Son are. There is one nature (*ousia*), but three persons (*hypostases*) who are that one nature.

When Merton attempts to describe the Trinity, he does so in terms readily available to him in the Christian tradition. It is the teaching of Chalcedon, later formulated at the Council of Florence (1442), in these words: "Everything in God is one except where there is opposition of relationships."[1]

In *New Seeds of Contemplation* Merton speaks of the Trinity in the context of the human creature's union with the triune God in contemplation. When we rid ourselves of selfishness, we find ourselves and one another as we truly are; and in contemplation we share in the life of one God in three persons. "God in His Trinity of subsistent relations infinitely transcends every shadow of selfishness. For the one God does not subsist apart and alone in His nature; He subsists as Father and as Son and as Holy Ghost. These three Persons are one, but apart from them God does not subsist also as One. He is not Three Persons *plus* one nature, therefore four! He is three persons, but one God. He is at once infinite solitude (one nature) and perfect society (Three Persons). One infinite Love in three subsistent relations" (*New Seeds of Contemplation,* 68).

God is a circle of relations in which divine Love is always beginning, always renewed, always perfectly shared. "But if you follow Love forward and backward from Person to Person, you can never track it to a stop, you can never corner it and hold it down and fix it to one of the Persons, as if He could appropriate to Himself the fruit of the love of the others. For the One Love of the Three Persons is an infinitely rich giving of Itself which never ends and is never taken, but is always perfectly given, only received in order to be perfectly shared" (68–69). The three selves of God are three subsistent relations of complete selflessness. This means that the divine Love never terminates in any one self that is able to halt it or absorb it. In the context in which Merton is here discussing the Trinity, he makes clear that contemplation makes it possible to enter into that circle of love.

In *The New Man* Merton speaks of the Trinity as the hidden, unknowable, mystery of God's inner life. Only the incarnation can reveal God's deep hidden darkness. "This darkness is forever impenetrable unless the Father reveals Himself to us in the Son. But the Son manifests Himself and His Father in the Holy Spirit Whom He gives to us.... He Who alone has power to enter into the depths of our being, into those depths which lie far beyond our own domination, can there unlock an ontological abyss that opens out within us upon the darkness of the Beginning, the Source, the Father" (*New Man*, 174).

Thus, it should be clear that the revelation of the triune life of God is not given to us simply to satisfy our curiosity about the mystery of God's inner life; rather, it is God's gift to us, enabling us to understand something of what it means to experience God and through Christ to participate in the divine life. We are not "outsiders," peering, so to speak, into God's house and seeing how God lives. Quite the contrary, through Christ we have been brought "inside" the life of God. Only when we are "inside" can we realize that in speaking about the Trinity, we are not "subjects" talking about "three objects" that we can experience in a speculative way.

In a letter to an Anglican friend, Merton warns of the danger of objectifying our experience of God's life and thus falsifying it — something we tend to do when we try to explain too much. Thus, "The ancient way of looking at it, 'to the Father in the Son by the Holy Spirit,'[2] reminds us of the *unity* and the

un-objective character of it. And yet they are Three, or we are in their Three and One in the Three. The authenticity of the experience depends on the dissolution of the apparent 'I' that can seem to stand outside all this as subject and observe it from somewhere else. Of course we fall back into this when commenting and explaining and that is the trouble with commenting and explaining" (*Hidden Ground of Love*, 369).

In an intriguing passage in "The Inner Experience" — a passage that fascinates by its insightfulness, though some might see it tipping the scales of orthodoxy — Merton comments on the "names" of the three persons of the Trinity. While we know the name of the first person and the second, we cannot name the third. Is this perhaps, Merton asks, because the third person's name is our secret name that the Spirit takes when uniting us to the Father and the Son, a name that we learn only when we receive from the Spirit the revelation of our own identity in that same Spirit?

> The Father is a Holy Spirit, but He is named Father. The Son is a Holy Spirit, but He is named Son. The Holy Spirit has a name which is known only to the Father and the Son. But can it be that when He takes us to Himself, and unites us to the Father through the Son, He takes upon Himself, in us, our own secret name? Is it possible that His ineffable Name becomes our own? Is it possible that we can come to know, for ourselves, the Name of the Holy Spirit when we receive from Him the revelation of our own identity in Him? I can ask these questions, but not answer them. ("Inner Experience," 35–36)

Is Merton perhaps saying in this enigmatic paragraph that the "Breath" of God is our own "breath," and that, however we name it, the mystery of the Spirit is the mystery of selfless love flowing from the Spirit to us, from us to one another, and back to the Spirit again? The Spirit "breathes" that divine reality into us and we "breathe" the Spirit into others in the outgoing of our love, so that there is, not only in God but also in us, a circulation of receiving and giving that never ends. As Merton puts it, "We receive from God, in the Spirit, and in the same Spirit we return our love to God through our brothers" (*New Seeds of Contemplation*, 159). WHS

Notes

1. Norman P. Tanner, ed., *Decrees of the Ecumenical Councils*, 2 vols. (Washington, D.C.: Georgetown University Press, 1990), 1:570–71.

2. Regarding this Trinitarian formula, Merton corrects himself at the end of the letter: "I should rather say: 'in the Father through the Son by the Spirit.'" Should he perhaps have said "to the Father through the Son in the Spirit"?

TRUTH

"Truth, in things, is their reality" (*No Man Is an Island*, 189). This succinct and simple definition is a key to the meaning of truth in Thomas Merton's spirituality and social vision as expressed in the many references to truth threaded throughout Merton's published writings, including his letters and journals.

God is Truth and therefore is the source of all truth. In using this image of God, Merton draws on biblical sources. Jesus names the Spirit of God as the Spirit of Truth. Jesus Christ himself is the Truth. "Those who are quickened to a divine life in Christ, by His Spirit, enter into intimate communion with the Truth" (*Seasons of Celebration*, 127). Propositions or "truths" about God, Merton insists, are conceptual expressions and are not to be confused with the Reality of the God who is Truth.

Truth is a matter of identity. The human search for authentic identity is the struggle to realize who we already are. Merton realized that it is difficult to grasp "even the smallest bit of the enormous truth about ourselves." In a world rife with illusion, sham, and lies we confuse "self" with reality and image with truth (*Courage for Truth*, 245–46). Merton knew this in his own life. In a journal entry written in 1961 he characterized his life as "a struggle to seek the truth" (*Turning toward the World*, 146). In a letter to Jacques Maritain, written two years later, Merton confessed, "There are great illusions to be got rid of, and there is a false self that has to be taken off.... There is still much to change before I will really be living in the truth" (*Courage for Truth*, 39). This "false self" is the ego or external self. It is like a mask or dis-guise that obscures the authentic self. The real self is the true self. Buried and hidden within, the true self is who we really are. The true self knows its Source in the God who is Truth and in so doing recognizes its unity with others whom it meets "on a common ground of spiritual Truth" (*Search for Solitude*, 273). Fidelity to Truth means fidelity to "the light that is in us from God" (*Courage for Truth*, 73).

Having a true identity "means having a belief one stands by; it means having certain definite ways of responding to life, of meeting its demands, of loving other people, and in the last analysis, of serving God. In this sense, identity is one's witness to truth in one's life" (*World of Action*, 59/78). True identity is formed and expressed in action. "We make ourselves real by telling the truth" (*No Man Is an Island*, 188).

Truth-telling does not simply mean avoiding falsehood in speech; truth-telling demands that we speak out in truth. Recognizing that it takes a discerning eye to see through "the obsessive fictions of the establishment everywhere," Merton saw truth-telling as a special vocation of writers. This is especially evident in Merton's letters to writers published in *The Courage for Truth*. Note especially Merton's letters to Czeslaw Milosz, Boris Pasternak, James Baldwin, and Ernesto Cardenal and other Latin American writers who modeled the courage for truth and yet were in need of "en-couragement," as Merton himself was. Merton's own writing on social issues — war and peace, violence and racism — had shown him that establishments, both social and ecclesiastical, resisted the truth and the truth-teller both. Sooner or later, Merton wrote to Ernesto Cardenal, telling the truth "brings us into confrontation with system and power which seek to overwhelm truth for the sake of particular interests.... Sooner or later this human duty presents itself in a form of crisis that cannot be evaded. At such a time it is very good, almost essential, to have at one's side others with a similar determination, and one can then be guided by a common inspiration and a communion in truth" (*Courage for Truth*, 159).

Merton was as keenly aware of the power of language to distort and conceal reality as he was of its ability to express and reveal it. He decried the language of advertisement and the illusions it proffered. He was appalled by the manipulation of language to obscure violence and deadly actions. He condemned the "illness of political language" characterized by "double-talk, tautology, ambiguous cliché, self-righteous and doctrinaire pomposity, and pseudoscientific jargon that mask a total callousness and moral insensitivity, indeed a basic contempt for man" (*Passion for Peace*, 313).[1]

For Merton, living in truth entails the practice of inner and outer truth. "We must be true inside, true to ourselves, before we can know a truth that is outside us. But we make ourselves true inside by manifesting the truth as we see it" (*No Man Is an Island*, 188). The inner truth is an encounter with Truth itself. Merton expressed this conviction in words of blessing that he shared with Boris Pasternak: "May you find again within yourself the deep life-giving silence which is genuine truth and the source of truth: for it is a fountain of life and a window into the abyss of eternity and God" (*Courage for Truth*, 92). CMB

Notes

1. From "War and the Crisis of Language," reprinted in *Passion for Peace*. See also *Guilty Bystander*, 78–79.

TURNING TOWARD THE WORLD: *The Pivotal Years*

The Journals of Thomas Merton, vol. 4: 1960–63. Edited by Victor Kramer.
San Francisco: HarperSanFrancisco, 1996.
xix+360 pp.

The introduction to this book, "Toward Crisis and Mystery,"[1] clarifies the title and sets forth the critical questions and issues that surfaced in Thomas Merton's life during this crucial period. These early years of the 1960s were times of profound change in society and in the Catholic Church: the civil rights movement in America and the Second Vatican Council in the Catholic Church. These stirrings in society and church awakened in Merton a deep sense of social and ecclesial responsibility at the very time that he was most aggressively seeking a far greater degree of solitude in his life. This paradox (engagement and disengagement), which

stalked him all his monastic life, reached in this volume an intensity unparalleled in his earlier journals. This journal furnishes the background for the "Cold War Letters" (October 1961– October 1962) as well as his correspondence with Rome seeking approval to enter into greater solitude (specifically at Cuernavaca in Mexico). Readers will recognize in this volume the raw material for many of the reflections in *Conjectures of a Guilty Bystander*.

The volume is divided into four parts. Part 1, "The Promise of a Hermitage" (May 1960– December 1960), is appropriately titled. While many issues are discussed, the consistent theme running through this part is the building of a "retreat center" that would be used for ecumenical dialogues, though Merton clearly had in mind from the start that this would be a "hermitage." Thus, plans are mentioned as a possibility (June 21, 1960), and soon after as definitely drawn up for a "retreat house" (August 14). Then, actual work starts on "the Mount Olivet *hermitage*" (September 29). The plans are scaled down to a cottage with two rooms and a porch: "Clearly it is a hermitage rather than a place for conferences" (October 3). The completion of the foundation takes place on October 9. The roof is raised on what Merton is now calling the hermitage of St. Mary of Carmel (October 29), and shortly thereafter the work is completed (December 1). Merton spends time at the hermitage (through the month of December), though he is not yet allowed to sleep there.

Many other themes are discussed in this first part: Merton's ongoing struggle about the meaning of solitude; his disillusionment with Gethsemani linked with an admission of his own failures as a monk; his mounting criticism of Dom James; a further appeal to Rome for permission to go elsewhere where he could have more solitude; the wide variety of his reading (Chuang Tzu, Olivier Clément, Teilhard de Chardin, Karl Barth, Abraham Heschel, Ananda Coomaraswamy, to name but a few).

Part 2 is "The Continuing Need to Question" (January 1961–December 1961). During the year of 1961 Merton underwent a great deal of introspection: insisting that he must cut back on his writing (but never quite managing it); struggling with the ambiguities in his life; his realization of God's goodness to him and his refusal to be content; his critical stance toward the monastery, especially the abbot, yet his need to love them; his responsibility to speak out against the danger of nuclear war that threatened the world; his concern that his speaking out will be misunderstood.

In a moment of enlightenment he sees himself called "to clarify the living content of spiritual traditions, especially the Christian, but also the Oriental, by entering myself deeply into their disciplines and experience, not for myself only, but for all my contemporaries who may be interested and inclined to listen" (*Turning toward the World*, 155).

There are comments on his own writings (e.g., *The New Man*) as well as reflections on his correspondence with Erich Fromm, Etta Gullick, Abdul Aziz, Czeslaw Milosz, and others, and on his voluminous reading (Karl Barth, F. X. Durwell, Mohandas Gandhi, Karl Rahner, Christopher Dawson, and more). He expresses his affection for Clement of Alexandria ("certainly one of the Fathers I like best and with whom I feel the closest affinity" [154]).

In June 1961 Dom Jean Leclercq visited Gethsemani and Merton. During their conversations Leclercq suggests that Merton is a pessimist, too anxious, too negative (124). This bothers Merton, but a reading of this part of the journal does offer some support for Leclercq's judgment. A good bit of negativity — about the world, the church, the monastic life, Gethsemani, his own life as a monk — does surface in these pages.

This period saw the revision of *Seeds of Contemplation* into *New Seeds of Contemplation*, the beginning of the "Cold War Letters," and Merton's articles on war and peace (appearing first in the *Catholic Worker*). Very important to this section of the journal is the dawning of ecological concern (which will continue to grow), as Merton, now spending more time in the hermitage, is more in touch with nature.

Part 3 is "Seeking the Right Balance" (January 1962–December 1962). Merton is strongly convinced of his obligation to speak out against nuclear war and the threat that it poses to the very existence of the human race. He

speaks out in the *Catholic Worker, Commonweal, Jubilee,* and other journals. He is stung by the criticisms of his writings and uncomfortable with his role as practically the only priest and surely the only monk taking so decisive a stand on war (yet, one may wonder whether he subconsciously enjoys his position). His conviction that nonviolence is the only way to peace moves him to examine his own frequent failure to practice in his actions his commitment to this Gandhian principle. "Energy wasted in contempt, criticism and resentment is thus diverted from its true function, *insistence on truth*" (239). On April 27, 1962, the axe falls. The abbot general directed Dom James in January to inform Merton that he is forbidden to publish anything more on war. Merton notes that for some *unaccountable* reason Dom James waited three months to inform him of this decision. He does not seem to give any thought to the possibility that Dom James's reason may have been to give him as much time as possible to say what he needed to say about war and peace. (Is this a blind spot in Merton's attitude toward his abbot?) Merton expresses some concerns about the Catholic peace movement, though still he supports it.

A theme that seems to run through all the journals keeps coming up: his own failure as a monk. On May 11, 1962, he writes of "laxity and lack of direction in my interior life" (218). He laments his rash judgments of fellow monks and his lack of compassion for them (197, 278).

Reflections on ecclesiology are found in parts of the journal. One instance links with his reading of Hans Küng's *The Council, Reform and Reunion* (209). As with the other journal volumes, one is hard put to keep abreast of Merton's wide, eclectic reading: Karl Rahner, John Howard Griffin, Olivier Clément, Gordon Zahn, Tertullian, St. Cyprian, Lactantius, John Wu, D. T. Suzuki, *The Cloud of Unknowing,* Jacob Boehme, J. F. Powers, and more. It was during this period that the *Thomas Merton Reader* was put together by Thomas McDonnell, with an important preface by Merton.

Part 4 is "Gifts of Quiet and Nature" (January 1963–July 1963). Able to spend more time in the quiet and natural surroundings of the hermitage, Merton struggles with his attitude toward the Gethsemani community and especially the abbot. On January 6, 1963, he speaks of his woundedness: "He [the abbot] despises me, uses me (outwardly respects me) and fears me because I am different from him, and have no part in his kind of image!" (287). Nine days later his attitude changes: "They have need of me and I have need of them.... My attitude toward the abbot is changing. Of course it is obvious that my complaints and discontent have been absurd.... He is what he is, and he means well, and in fact does well. He is the superior destined for me in God's Providence and it is absurd for me to complain" (288–89). In May some of the old hurts reemerge when a meeting of abbots and novice masters is scheduled for Gethsemani and he is expected to speak. "When the canary is asked to sing, well, he is expected to sing merrily....It is true that I have a nicer cage than any other canary in the Order.... Everyone can come and see me in my cage, and Dom James can modestly rejoice in the fact that he is in absolute control of a bird that everyone wants to hear sing" (320). The next day, after a good night's sleep, he writes, "I realize how sick were my thoughts yesterday." Admitting the complexity of his relationship with the abbot, he acknowledges the goodwill and genuine sincerity that he must recognize in him.

At a January 1963 retreat Merton struggles once more with his compulsion to publish and determines especially to avoid writing books on "the spiritual life" (293). He laments the lack of meaning in his life. "How much I am still the same self-willed and volatile person who made such a mess of Cambridge" (294).

There is a bit of ecclesiology in this section, "the Church considered less as an organization than as a living body of interrelated freedoms" (290), and further reflections on a favorite Merton theme: the difference between the true self and the false self (299). Merton expresses his love and admiration for Pope John XXIII. He praises Martin Luther King Jr. as "one of the few really great Christians in America" (325). There are references to his reading of St. Anselm, Erasmus, Karl Rahner, and Cesar Vallejo ("the most truly 'Catholic' in the sense of universal poet of our century" [335]).

It was during this time that Merton got into trouble with his publishers, giving a manuscript to Macmillan when he was under contract with Farrar, Straus and Giroux. Under threat of a suit for breach of contract, he withdrew the manuscript.

Near the end of the volume Merton evaluates the role that the solitude of the hermitage has played in his life. "The greatest thing has been a recovery of the real dimensions of the mystery of Christ....A recovery so to speak of a deep and primitive faith — with the realization that it is a pure gift. What a renewal and how thankful I am. My spirit is once again breathing after a long time of stuffiness and suffocation" (329). WHS

Notes

1. This title is taken from an entry in the journal for August 16, 1961. Merton is concerned about the specter of war that threatens the human race. He writes, "Inexorably life moves on toward crisis and mystery" (152).

UNCONSCIOUS, THE

Erich Fromm, a psychoanalyst who corresponded with Thomas Merton over a period of twelve years, invited him in 1962 to comment on a booklet he had written for the American Friends Service Committee on the psychological causes of violence and war. His chief concern was with the alienation existing in modern society. In his booklet he analyzed the psychological roots of destructiveness and the existence of certain types of personalities dominated by a death-loving orientation: "a perversion which occurs necessarily when the primary, life-favoring potentialities fail to develop."[1] Fromm sent his essay to six persons, including Thomas Merton,[2] asking for their comment. Merton took the issue very seriously and wrote the only response of any length. After reading the six responses, Fromm made his own comments on each. He found Merton's most to his liking. Merton had written, "I fully accept Fromm's analysis of alienation as it is hinted at here and developed more fully in his other books. But I think the concept needs a great deal of further exploration, beyond the limits of sociology and psychology, even of depth psychology. I think it has been too often forgotten that there are *two*

Drawing by Thomas Merton.

aspects of that vast mysterious area of our being which we call the unconscious" (*Faith and Violence*, 111–12).[3]

The two aspects that Merton refers to are (1) the psychosomatic area rooted in our biological substratum, and (2) "an infinitely more spiritual and metaphysical substratum in man's being, which the Rhenish mystics called 'the ground' or 'base' of the soul, and which the Zen Masters continually point to, but which they refuse to describe except by incomprehensible and paradoxical terms like 'your original face before you were born.'...I would like to suggest," Merton goes on, "the overwhelming and almost totally neglected importance of exploring this spiritual unconscious of man. There is no real love of life, unless it is oriented to the discovery of one's true, spiritual self, beyond and above the levels of mere empirical individuality, with its superficial enjoyments and fears" (112).[4]

In his reflections on the comments of his respondents Fromm singles out Merton's and expresses his complete agreement with Merton's call to explore the depths of one's spiritual unconscious. This exploration was a topic of great interest to Merton and important to his understanding of spirituality. In a letter to Etta Gullick written March 5, 1961, he says, "We are too rational. We do not permit anything to remain unconscious. Yet all that is best is unconscious or superconscious" (*Hidden Ground of Love,* 341).

This letter was written at the time when Merton was revising *Seeds of Contemplation.* Chapter 19 of *New Seeds of Contemplation,* "From Faith to Wisdom," contains what is perhaps Merton's most detailed discussion of the realm of the conscious and the unconscious. Faith, he says, is not an act of assent to truths; it is acceptance of God that leads to communion with God. With faith's growth, communion with God becomes all-pervasive in our lives; it gives a dimension of depth to all our experiences. This dimension of depth is "the incorporation of the unknown and of the unconscious into our daily life.... Faith brings together the known and the unknown so that they overlap or rather that we are *aware* of their overlapping" (*New Seeds of Contemplation,* 135–36). Life is a mystery because so very little of what constitutes that life comes to our conscious understanding. When we accept only what we consciously can reason about, we severely limit the horizons of our lives. Faith not only teaches us "about God," but even "reveals to us the unknown in our own selves, in so far as our unknown and undiscovered self actually lives in God" (137). Faith is life; it takes us to regions of ourselves that are mysterious and unknown.

Merton warns us that we should not be thinking of a conscious realm that is "above" and a subconscious realm that is "below." Rather, "the conscious mind of man is *exceeded in all directions* by his unconscious. There is darkness not only below our conscious reason, but also above it and all around it" (137). The unconscious may be below or above our conscious mind. What is below is what is less than human; what is above is spiritual, even divinizing. Faith accepts what is below, insofar as it is willed by God; at the same time, it subjects our minds to the hidden spiritual forces that are above. Thus, it integrates all of the unconscious into our lives. "In this superconscious realm of mystery is hidden not only the summit of man's spiritual being (which remains a pure mystery to his reason) but also the presence of God, Who dwells at this hidden summit, according to traditional metaphor. Faith then brings man into contact with man's own inmost spiritual depths and with God Who is 'present' within those same depths" (138–39).

The spiritual life, then, is a balanced life in which the body with its passions and instincts and the mind with its reasonings are subject to a higher principle: the human spirit directed by and united with the Spirit of God. As Merton writes, it is "a life neither of dionysian orgy nor of apollonian clarity; it transcends both. It is a life of wisdom, a life of sophianic love" (141).[5] WHS

SEE ALSO ALIENATION; AWARENESS; CONTEMPLATION; GOD; SELF.

Notes

1. Erich Fromm, *War within Man: A Psychological Enquiry into the Roots of Destructiveness* (Philadelphia: Peace Literature Service of the American Friends Service Committee, 1963), 5. His original title had been *The Psychological Causes of War.*

2. The others were Jerome Frank, Roy Menninger, Hans Morgenthau, Paul Tillich, and Pitirim Sorokin.

3. See Fromm, *War within Man,* 45.

4. See ibid.

5. See ibid.

UNQUIET CONSCIENCE, THE

By Piero Bargellini. Translated by Thomas Merton. Lexington, Ky.: Stamperia del Santuccio, 1958. 4 pp.

This is an early collaboration between Thomas Merton and Victor Hammer, a single sheet (title page and three pages of text) printed by Hammer on his hand press. The selection, translated from the Italian of Bargellini (1897–1980), a prolific Florentine historian and man of letters, is a reflection on the familiar story of Aloysius Gonzaga, Jesuit novice and scion of a great Italian noble family, who was asked during a recreation period what he would do if he were to learn that he was to die within a minute; his response that he would "keep on playing" is for the author a sign of a conscience at peace with God, for whom all actions, even play, were prayers, done for the glory of God. Bargellini's response is to ask, "What about us?" What response could we — writers, lawyers, artists, doctors, laborers — give to the same question? He answers for himself, "If I realized that in a minute I would have to die / could I go on writing? No / because my writing is not a sincere prayer to God / and my pen does not serve the Lord with undivided dedication." For most people, even while performing a good work, "a little grain of self love" is mixed in with their actions — for example, "the writer / even the best intentioned of writers / ruins his words of praise for God with the desire that he himself may be praised." For the most part, the author concludes, unlike Gonzaga, we would have to throw ourselves on our knees at the news of approaching death and "cry out with the threefold plea for mercy: Lord / have mercy on us! Lord / have mercy on us sinners! Lord / have mercy on us poor sinners!" With its theme of mixed motives, highlighting especially the self-interest of the writer, in particular the religious writer, and its concluding threefold prayer for mercy, it is evident why this short meditation would have appealed to Thomas Merton as a text for translation and setting in this special format. It is noteworthy that the abbreviation "a+m+d+g" concludes the text, standing for the words *Ad majorem Dei gloriam* ("For the greater glory of God") — a motto particularly associated with the Jesuits but also very apropos to the subject of Bargellini's reflections. POC

VAN DOREN, MARK

Mark Van Doren (1894–1972), a distinguished American poet, was professor of English at Columbia College from 1920 to 1959. His classes and his person were a strong influence on Thomas Merton. He figures prominently in *The Seven Storey Mountain*. After Merton entered Gethsemani, Van Doren visited him several times. On one occasion he returned to New York with a book of Merton's poems, which he persuaded James Laughlin at New Directions to publish. This was Merton's first published book and it appeared under the title *Thirty Poems*. In 1959 Van Doren wrote an introduction for Merton's *Selected Poems*. The correspondence penned between Merton and Van Doren is extensive. Merton's last letter to him came from Darjeeling, India, in November 1968, a month before Merton's death. When Van Doren heard of that death, he wrote to Fr. Flavian Burns, expressing his deep sorrow at the news. "He was one of the great persons of our time or of any time. I shall mourn for him as long as I live."[1] Merton's letters to Van Doren are published in *The Road to Joy*. WHS

Notes

1. Quoted in *Road to Joy*, 55.

Cover for *A Vow of Conversation* reprinted with the permission of Lamp. Cover design by Jack Harrison.

VATICAN COUNCIL, THE SECOND

Perhaps the most significant religious event of the twentieth century, the Second Vatican Council brought together in Rome Catholic bishops from all over the world in four separate sessions (all held in St. Peter's Basilica): October–December 1962, September–December 1963, September–November 1964, and September–December 1965.

Thomas Merton took an active interest in the Council from the very beginning. He prepared himself for the Council by reading Hans Küng's *The Council, Reform and Reunion* as soon as he could get his hands on it. He admired it as a straightforward and courageous book. "The vigor and honesty of the message was tremendous" (*Road to Joy*, 242). He was concerned that it might raise vain hopes that the Council probably could not measure up to, yet it was important to hope for the best. "That Council! Such hopes and such fears! But the Holy Spirit really is in command there, though He may not be at the Pentagon" (*Witness to Freedom*, 283). At the same time, he admitted to certain fears about what the Council might do, especially the fear that new obligations would be authoritatively imposed, "without freeing the heart to receive the Holy Spirit in abundance" (*Turning toward the World*, 209). The Council would be a disaster if it simply reaffirmed disciplinary rules that had been in place for centuries. What was needed was reform and renewal. "This is not the world of Gregory VII or Innocent III or Pius V, or even Pius X. To be a perfect Christian, even a saint, according to their pattern, is no longer enough. On the contrary, it is apt to be terribly dangerous, even fatal" (*Witness to Freedom*, 45).

Very early on, Merton foresaw some of the issues that the Council must face: major liturgical reforms, clarification of the role of the bishops, peace in the world, reforming the Roman curia. He especially expressed his concern about the Roman curia, "who know and have known for years how to make a lot of fuss and tighten up a lot of bolts in lieu of real reform" (*Turning toward the World*, 209). In a letter to Erich Fromm several months before the Council met he wrote, "The irony of it is that the integrist faction in Rome, which is most insistent on papal infallibility, is actually against the Council, which gives more importance to the ideas of the bishops as a body.... A paradoxical development of Vatican centralism" (*Hidden Ground of Love*, 317). "The 'pessimists' whom the Pope criticized in his opening address . . . are the integrists, the conservatives, who think the Church has to condemn everything modern. This is the great struggle at the Council" (*Turning toward the World*, 260). It was a struggle between those who opposed change and those who wanted the Catholic Church to respond to the "signs of the times." The danger in all this maneuvering by the curial officials, Merton points out in a letter of July 2, 1964, to Gordon Zahn, is that it almost appears as if "the charism of infallibility [has been] transferred to the Curia. It thus becomes anonymous and institutional. It is no longer a charism. It is a bureaucratic procedure" (*Hidden Ground of Love*, 653). The day before, he had written in a similar vein to Wilbur H. Ferry, "The Holy Office crowd is serenely convinced that it has to arrogate to itself all the powers of the Pope, . . . becoming in the end the real seat of infallibility" (218).

Merton followed the workings of the Council with great interest. He read Xavier Rynne's chatty, informal summaries of the events of the Council as well as Michael Serafian's *The Pilgrim*.[1] The most dramatic event of the Council's first session was the refusal of the bishops, led by Cardinal Liénart of Lille, to accept the list of names of the heads of the various conciliar commissions that the curia had proposed. On October 23, 1962, Merton wrote in his journal, "French and Germans not willing to accept proposed lists.... Most important! Card. Liénart rallied a group together for action rather than passive and automatic acceptance, and apparently it worked" (*Turning toward the World*, 260).

No documents were promulgated in the first session. Liturgy, revelation, and the church were discussed. The original draft on the church was sent back by the bishops for redrafting. The bishops of the world had come of age, as it were. They knew now the role that they must play in subsequent sessions of the Council. Merton wrote on December 20, 1962, to Sr. Therese Lentfoehr, "The Council was tremendous, wasn't it? (Isn't it?) Really Pope John has been a great gift from God to all of us. What a superb Pope, and what a heart. The past few months have made me realize the greatness of the Church as I had never realized it before, not the stuffed shirt pompous greatness that some of the Curia people evidently want it to be, but the charity and the real concern for all men, the *cura pastoralis*" (*Road to Joy*, 243).

Nevertheless, he warns that there are critical junctures yet to be reached, such as the issue of what stand the Catholic Church would take on nuclear war and on peace. "The great problem," he writes to E. I. Watkin, "is the fact that the Church is utterly embedded in a social matrix that is radically unfriendly to genuine spiritual growth, because it tends to stifle justice and charity as well as genuine inner life" (*Hidden Ground of Love*, 581).

In the interim between the first and second sessions of the Council, on Holy Thursday, April 11, 1963, Pope John XXIII published his encyclical on peace, *Pacem in Terris*. Merton was delighted. It said so many things he had been trying to say.[2] "I am happy," he writes to James Forest, "about the encyclical saying clearly that it is 'impossible for war to be an instrument of justice' in the context of nuclear armaments"

(273–74). Merton could hardly wait to contact the abbot general in France. In a letter dated Easter 1963 he writes to Dom Gabriel Sortais, "Now the Holy Father clearly says that war can no longer be used as an instrument of justice in a world where nuclear arms are possessed. Fortunately he does not need to be approved by the censors of the Order in America, for they said very energetically last year that this thesis, when I proposed it myself, was wrong, scandalous, and I don't know what more" (*School of Charity*, 166).[3]

Clearly, of all the issues discussed at the Council, these most concerned Merton: war, peace, deterrence, conscientious objection, and nonviolence. He wrote to E. I. Watkin, "My *Peace* manuscript [*Peace in the Post-Christian Era*] has gone to one of the bishops most concerned with lay affairs and he may be very sympathetic" (*Hidden Ground of Love*, 581). That bishop was John J. Wright, then bishop of Pittsburgh. In February 1964 Merton wrote to Bishop Wright, thanking him for making his "peace writings" available to the *periti* at the Council (609). He also sent him a copy of *Breakthrough to Peace*.

The Council document that discussed these issues of war and peace originally was called "Schema 13" and eventually became the Pastoral Constitution on the Church in the Modern World (*Gaudium et Spes*). In the autumn of 1965, as the fourth and last session of the Council was about to convene, Merton wrote an article for *Worldview* with the title "Schema Thirteen: An Open Letter to the American Hierarchy."[4] In his open letter Merton calls on the Council fathers to make an unequivocal statement calling for the renunciation of force in favor of reasoned negotiation and other peaceful means of settlement. The indiscriminate slaughter of combatants and noncombatants must be condemned. "The common man, the poor man, the man who has no hope but in God, everywhere looks to the Church as a last hope of protection against the unprincipled machinations of militarists and power politicians" (*Witness to Freedom*, 90). "It is surely reasonable to applaud the prudence of those who, at the time of the third session, thought that the Council ought to say *more* against the use of

force than modern Popes have said, and *not less*" (91). Merton concludes his letter to the American bishops with a challenging charge: "What matters is for the Bishops and the Council to bear witness clearly and without any confusion to the Church's belief in the power of love to save and transform not only individuals but society. Do we believe or do we not that love has this power? If we believe it, what point is there in splitting hairs about the superior morality of killing a thousand defenseless non-combatants rather than a million?" (92).

He sent copies of this letter and some of his other peace writings to some of the bishops, but also to Dorothy Day, Hildegard Goss-Mayr, and a number of women who had banded together to lobby the bishops for a strong statement of condemnation against war, especially nuclear war. To Hildegard Goss-Mayr he wrote, as early as December 17, 1962, "It is most important for the Church to recognize clearly that the presence of nuclear weapons in the world has *essentially* changed the whole problem of war. . . . It is of no use discussing the traditional ideas of the just war in a situation where the whole concept of war has been fundamentally altered. To treat this *merely* as a new means of self-defense is tantamount to suicide on a global scale" (*Hidden Ground of Love*, 330). As early as 1963 Merton had sent a packet of mimeographed articles to Dorothy Day with the hope that this group of women would be able to get his papers to the bishops and the *periti* at the Council.

It is tantalizing to ask whether Merton's peace writings influenced the attitude that the Council finally took toward war in *Gaudium et Spes*. The document confirmed a number of positions that Merton had taken, as the following selection of texts will indicate. "The horror and perversity of war are immensely magnified by the multiplication of scientific weapons." Such weapons, with their ability to inflict massive and indiscriminate destruction, "compel us to undertake an evaluation of war with an entirely new attitude." "An act of war aimed indiscriminately at the destruction of entire cities or of extensive areas along with their population is a crime against God and man himself. It merits unequivocal and unhesitating condemnation" (art. 80). "The arms race is an entirely treacherous trap for humanity" (art. 81). "It is our clear duty to strain every muscle as we work for the time when all war can be completely outlawed by international consent" (art. 82). The Council praises "those who renounce the use of violence in the vindication of their rights and who resort to methods of defense which are otherwise available to weaker parties too" (art. 78), and also sanctions the right of conscientious objection (art. 79).

In general, Merton was pleased with the documents that had come out of the Council. Though his writings do not indicate that he had had the time to assimilate all of them thoroughly and incorporate them into his own thinking and writing, there are several articles, as well as statements here and there in his writings, that show his understanding of the basic directions in which the Council was seeking to move the Catholic Church. In 1965 he wrote of the remarkable shift of emphasis emanating from the Council's Constitution on the Church (*Lumen Gentium*): "Instead of considering the Church primarily and principally as a hierarchical society and a strictly organized institution, [the Constitution] affirms that the Church is the community of the faithful."[5] The implications of this change are far-reaching, for it affirms the primacy of the spiritual life and its fruitfulness over organizational rigidity and institutional power. This is not a denial that the Church is an organized institution, but an affirmation that its laws and institutional workings exist for the sake of love and life. They must not become ends in themselves. "They exist to safeguard the freedom of the Spirit within the framework of earthly society" (*World of Action*, 117/135). The true end of the Church is the transformation of its members and of society and the consecration of all life to God. The static concept of the Church that prevailed since the Council of Trent is replaced by "a dynamic concept of the Church as a living Body moved by the invisible and divine Spirit of Truth and Love imparted to her by the Risen Christ" (135).

Earlier, Merton had written two essays on the first document to come out of the Council, the Constitution on the Sacred Liturgy

(*Sacrosanctum Concilium*): "Liturgy and Christian Personalism"[6] and "Liturgical Renewal: The Open Approach."[7] In the first article he reflects on the words of *Sacrosanctum Concilium* that see the liturgy as the chief means "whereby the faithful may express in their lives and manifest to others the mystery of Christ and the real nature of the true Church" (art. 2). He sees the liturgical renewal as the greatest development in liturgy since the patristic age. In the second article he discusses some aspects of the renewal that he sees as especially significant: the departure from rubricism (where all that was needed was to make sure that the priest did everything correctly); the active involvement of the people in the liturgy; communion under both kinds; and a new spirit of openness between priest and people. He also saw problems ahead: the need for a translation of the Scriptures that was meant for public proclamation and the need for good music. On April 25, 1964, he wrote to Canon A. M. Allchin, an Anglican friend at Oxford, that he thought it would be helpful for Roman Catholics, as they move into the vernacular, to learn from the Anglican tradition (*Hidden Ground of Love*, 26).

A discussion of Merton's involvement in the workings of the Council would not be complete without a mention of the fact that his friendship with the well-known Jewish theologian Rabbi Abraham Heschel moved him to speak out about what the Council was planning to say about the Catholic Church's relationship with the Jews. A truly prophetic statement dealing with that relationship had been discussed at the Council's third session. Before the fourth session convened, rumor spread that the statement on the Jews would be modified because of the concerns of bishops in Arab countries.

On July 13, 1964, Heschel visited Merton at Gethsemani. He expressed his anguished concerns. Merton was deeply moved. The very next day he wrote a long letter to Cardinal Augustine Bea expressing his deep concern yet still hoping that the Council would not miss "this opportunity for repentance and truth which is being offered her and which so many are ready to reject and refuse" (*Hidden Ground of Love*, 433). Merton points out that it is especially the Church that would gain from this statement on the Jews. "I am personally convinced that the grace to truly see the Church as she is in her humility and in her splendor may perhaps not be granted to the Council Fathers, if they fail to take account of her relation to the anguished Synagogue." This is not, he suggests, simply a "gesture of magnanimity"; rather, "the deepest truths are in question." "The very words themselves should suggest that the *ecclesia* is not altogether alien from the *synagogue* and that she should be able to see herself to some extent, though darkly, in this antitypal mirror.... Yet she has the power to bring mercy and consolation into this mirror image, and thus to experience in herself the beatitude promised to the merciful."

He goes on to remind the cardinal that the Church has on more than one occasion yielded its prophetic role for motives of a temporal and political nature. Merton does not hesitate to say that the Council might, at this juncture, be in the very position in which Pius XII found himself and might be accused, as Pius has been, of acting for diplomatic and political reasons rather than for the truth of the gospel. Thus, he writes, "If [the Church] foregoes this opportunity out of temporal and political motives (in exactly the same way as a recent Pontiff is accused of having done), will she not by that very fact manifest that she has in some way forgotten her own true identity? Is not then the whole meaning and purpose of the Council at stake?" (*Hidden Ground of Love*, 433).

He suggests that one way of dealing theologically and diplomatically with the fears of the bishops in Arab countries would be the realization that Jews, Muslims, and Christians all are Abrahamic peoples as well as "people of the book." "Perhaps this common theological root in the promises made to Abraham might bear fruit in a Chapter on anti-Semitism, oriented to peace with *all* Semites and then with special emphasis on the relation of the Church and the Synagogue and at least an implicit recognition of the long-standing sin of anti-Jewish hatred among Catholics" (434).

In September of that same year Heschel, quite upset, wrote a letter to Merton telling him that the original Council statement, which had been in almost all respects a monumental declaration, had been — he had been told — replaced by a watered down text that was offensive to Jews, even expressing the desire that the Jewish people would seek union with the Catholic Church.[8] Heschel wrote that he had told Pope Paul VI, "I am ready to go to Auschwitz any time if faced with the alternative of conversion or death" (see *Hidden Ground of Love*, 434). Merton responded immediately, saying that he was stunned by what Rabbi Heschel had told him. "My latent ambitions to be a true Jew under my Catholic skin" (434) surely will be realized, he said, if he had to continue to go through experiences of this kind. He expressed his confidence in Cardinal Bea.

That confidence was not misplaced. In the fourth session of the Council a statement was incorporated into the Declaration on the Relationship of the Church to Non-Christian Religions (*Nostra Aetate*). Though it did not have the prophetic vision of the earlier statement, it had eliminated the offensive aspects of the document that Heschel had feared. Thus, the final statement might have been hailed as a noteworthy document had it not been preceded by a far better one that lost out, it would seem, to the demands of expediency. The text of *Nostra Aetate* was approved by the Council fathers in October 1965. WHS

Notes

1. Merton was more impressed by Serafian's book than by Xavier Rynne's letters from Rome. He described the latter as "gossip." See the letter to Daniel Berrigan in *Hidden Ground of Love*, 82.

2. On November 11, 1961, Merton had written to Pope John about the link between the military and the economic-industrial complex that compromised any efforts for peace. Pope John's secretary, Msgr. Capovilla, wrote to Merton saying that the Holy Father had been "impressed" by this letter. Merton's possible influence on the writing of *Pacem in Terris* might prove an interesting topic for research.

3. On January 15, 1963, Merton had written of the abbot general to Hildegard Goss-Mayr: "I do hope that his participation in the Council has made our General realize at least dimly that the whole Church is not clinging in desperation to rigid and conservative positions, and that those who seek renewal and strive for a spiritual awakening are not necessarily all heretics and rebels" (*Hidden Ground of Love*, 331).

4. This letter to the American bishops was published in September 1965, as the bishops were preparing to return to Rome for the final session of the Council. It is reprinted in *Witness to Freedom*, 88–92.

5. *American Benedictine Review*, 1965; published also in *World of Action*, 117/135.

6. This essay is published in *Seasons of Celebration*, whose subtitle is "Meditations on the Cycle of Liturgical Feasts" (1965). At the end of the article it is indicated that it was published previously in 1963, but does not say where. The comprehensive bibliography by Breit and Daggy says that it was published in *Worship* 34 (October 1960): 494–507. I found this quite puzzling, for the article begins with references to and quotations from the Constitution on the Sacred Liturgy, which was not promulgated by the Council until December 1963. The mystery cleared up when I checked the article as it appeared in *Seasons of Celebration*. It is the same as the *Worship* article, except that Merton has added two pages at the beginning in which he does indeed quote from the Council document on the liturgy. Thus, these two pages are the only part of this article that belongs to 1963!

7. *Seasons of Celebration*, 231–48 (first appeared in *Critic* 33 [December 1964]: 10–15).

8. Merton commented in his journal on the text that Heschel sent him (*Water of Life*, 142–43). This text, it should be remembered, was not the one accepted by the Council.

VIETNAM

Thomas Merton's opposition to the Vietnam War was early, constant, insistent, and forthright. He first refers in his journal to Vietnam on November 7, 1963, describing the assassination of President Ngo Dinh Diem as a "sickening affair," particularly since he was a flagrant example of "these corrupt 'Catholic' bosses" operating through a combination of church power and American weaponry. His comment "What an appalling scandal and symptom of our own decay!" (*Water of Life*, 32) sets the tone for his attitude toward American involvement in Vietnam throughout the rest of his life. In May 1964 he wrote to Lyndon Johnson "to add my voice to the voices of all those who have pleaded for a peaceful settlement in Vietnam" (*Hidden Ground of Love*, 439), and he objects to the war not only on humanitarian and moral grounds but also in the belief that the war can only strengthen the appeal of communism in Asia — a point he will continue to make in the coming years. He is skeptical of the growing scope of the war in the months that follow, particularly of the Tonkin Gulf incident, which he suspects of having political motivations in that election year (*Water of Life*, 133). After the crisis has blown over, he notes that the situation has returned to "normal": "guerrilla warfare, napalm bombs, helicopters, etc." (133). By the end of the year, as the Congo also heats up, he sees

the danger of a repetition of "the madness of Viet Nam" as the Americans move to fill the "vacuum" left by the withdrawal of European colonial powers, and decries as a "demonic illusion" the "technological hubris" that believes human problems can be fixed by sophisticated weaponry (177).

The increasingly bold Vietcong incursions into the cities of South Vietnam in February of 1965 lead to Merton's most detailed reflection on the situation to date. He sees a fourfold problem inevitably contributing to the "stupid failure" of American policy: first, there is no understanding of the country and its culture; second, the Americans rely on slick "operators" who manipulate their patrons by telling them what they want to hear in order to accumulate wealth and power for themselves; third, by committing themselves to these corrupt figures the Americans make reform impossible and drive authentic reformers into the arms of the enemy; fourth, military force is ineffective in such a situation because the population itself is pushed into opposition, yet the only "solution" the outsiders know is to escalate military action. His conclusion is that "we are doing more than anyone else, China included, to make Asia effectively Communist" (204). Part of the problem is "a false eschatology" that trusts in science and technical "progress" to solve all problems (228); this is combined with the premise that the United States has a divine mission to destroy communism in Southeast Asia, a premise that Merton rejects as reminiscent of the justification of fascism in the years leading up to World War II (231).

By April, Merton describes the war, in tandem with the murders of civil rights workers, doubts about the Kennedy assassination, and the rise of various fanatical fringe groups, as creating "a moral landscape of damnation" in America (235). The next month he describes the war as a kind of mocking of God and rejecting of God's lordship of history, and comments, "In the end, an accounting will be demanded" (250). Increasingly he views the conflict in Vietnam and elsewhere in the underdeveloped world as "an enormously equipped and self-complacent white civilization in combat with a huge, sprawling, colored and mestizo world (a majority!) armed with anything they can lay hands on" (253). With the turn toward separatism and violence in the struggle for racial justice in the American South, Merton sees the domestic repercussions of the underlying assumptions that motivate the war in Asia. "The Vietnam war has had a great deal to do with the new trend to Black Power. The Negroes have been more keenly aware than anyone else of the war's ambiguities. They have ... seen the Vietnam war as another manifestation of whitey's versatility in beating down colored people" (*Faith and Violence*, 122).

In response to Pope Paul VI's plea for peace at the United Nations in October 1965, Merton writes in "Peace and Protest" of the need to break the "addiction" to war (41), of the need to develop not merely new policies but "an entirely new attitude towards war" (43). He warns against protest that is ambiguous and perhaps self-contradictory, calling for "dissent that recalls people to their senses, makes them think deeply, plants in them a seed of change, and awakens in them the profound need for truth, reason and peace which is implanted in man's nature" (44), a call to overcome rather than to give expression to "the desperation and hopelessness" felt in response to the "unjust suffering inflicted on the innocent largely as a result of our curious inner psychological needs, fomented by the climate of our technological culture" (45–46).

The escalation of the war in the spring of 1966 brings a reflection on the distorted vision of Americans: "men with incredible technical skill and no sense of human realities in Asia — lost in abstractions, sentimentalities, myths, delusions, Narcissism and the Great Mania fixation of America!" (*Learning to Love*, 41). The visit of Vietnamese Buddhist monk and dissident Thich Nhat Hanh to Gethsemani in late May leads Merton to write the short reflection "Nhat Hanh Is My Brother," a declaration of human solidarity with those suffering in the war. "He represents the young, the defenseless, the new ranks of youth who find themselves with every hand turned against them except those of the peasants and the poor, with whom they are working.... If I mean something to you, then let me put it this way; do for Nhat

Hanh whatever you would do for me if I were in his position. In many ways I wish I were" (*Faith and Violence*, 106, 108). This same commitment to people rather than to a political ideology marks Merton's contribution (written in September 1966 and published in 1967) to the volume *Authors Take Sides on Vietnam*, in which his "side" is that of "the people who are being burned, cut to pieces, tortured, held as hostages, gassed, ruined, destroyed. They are the victims of both sides" (109–10). In his preface to the Vietnamese translation of *No Man Is an Island*, also written in September, he refers to the source of his title in the *Devotions* of John Donne and declares, "The war in Viet Nam is a bell tolling for the whole world, warning the whole world that war may spread everywhere, and violent death may sweep over the entire earth" ("*Honorable Reader*," 124), and he prays that as the sickness of the entire world is erupting there, the healing of the entire world may begin there as well (126). His foreword, written in late October, to Nhat Hanh's *Vietnam: Lotus in a Sea of Fire* stresses the need to reject the "comic-strip mythology" surrounding the Asian war and face the truth of the tragic consequences of this distorted vision.[1]

As the war escalates with the bombing of Haiphong in the spring of 1967, Merton notes the economic benefits of an economy geared to war as a prime motivation for continuing the destruction (*Learning to Love*, 224–25). This wartime prosperity is matched by the corruption in Vietnam itself, where "the people are simply and mindlessly making the best of the American glut while it lasts" and are "rotting in consequence" (277). In the face of this pragmatism and profiteering Merton stresses in a statement on aiding war victims the "grave moral responsibility" of Christians to aid innocent victims of the war, and so to show sorrow for the harm done as well as reparation both to the victims and to God, who identifies with the poor and oppressed; he therefore presses for the removal of all obstacles to sending aid to the war zone (*Nonviolent Alternative*, 266). In his review essay "Ishi: A Meditation," published in the March issue of the *Catholic Worker*, Merton finds disturbing analogies between the extermination of Native Americans and the destruction of the Vietnamese. "Here again, one meets the same myths and misunderstandings, the same obsession with 'completely wiping out' an enemy regarded as diabolical" (*Ishi Means Man*, 31), the same spiral of violence in which eventually "it is the civilians that are killed in the ordinary course of events, and combatants only get killed by accident" (32). In November, Merton is attracted by an invitation from the Quakers to participate in an unofficial peace delegation that would meet with Vietcong representatives in an effort to arrive at concrete peace proposals (*Other Side of the Mountain*, 12). His request to participate was of course turned down by the abbot, leading him once again to question the restrictiveness of his situation (*Hidden Ground of Love*, 638; *School of Charity*, 360). He ends the year in his Advent/ Christmas circular letter by calling the war "one of the greatest and most stupid blunders in American history" (*Road to Joy*, 107).

Merton prophetically saw the Tet Offensive in February of 1968 as the beginning of the end for America in Vietnam, an expression of the victory of people over machines, of the failure of power and the victory of spirit, even if in this case spirit was ruthless and totalist; because of what he calls the "stupidity and inefficacy of the technical ideas of Americans," he concluded that "the war *cannot* be won by the U.S. now. Or the military objectives of the U.S. *cannot* be attained" (*Other Side of the Mountain*, 53). The following month his most vehement public statement about the war appeared in the *Catholic Worker*, with a title that summed up his view over the past four years: "Vietnam — An Overwhelming Atrocity" (*Faith and Violence*, 87–95). The same month he was vilified for supporting the application of Joseph Molloy for conscientious objection (*Other Side of the Mountain*, 65), and he wrote to correspondents that his books were being burned in Louisville because of his opposition to the war (*Courage for Truth*, 85, 161; *When Prophecy*, 38). While he saw some hope for a resolution to the war with Johnson's decision not to run for reelection (*Other Side of the Mountain*, 76), he was skeptical of Johnson's motives (88), and he saw little to choose from in the prospective candidates, Humphrey and Nixon (*Witness to*

Freedom, 119). He heard of the complete bombing halt and scheduling of peace talks while in Dharamsala for his meetings with the Dalai Lama, and he was torn between hope for lasting peace and suspicion of the motivation as "last-minute expediency for the election" (*Other Side of the Mountain*, 243–44).

In his final, ironic notice of the war, he quotes a rather garbled account in the business section of the local English-language newspaper, in which economic developments once again emerge as paramount, as indicated by the headline: "BOMBING HALT IMPARTS FIRMNESS TO SHARES" (250). In a final twist of fate, of course, Merton's body was flown back to the United States in a U.S. Air Force jet, along with the bodies of soldiers killed in the war he opposed so vigorously. POC

SEE ALSO JUST WAR, THEORY OF; NONVIOLENCE; PEACE; WAR.

Notes

1. Foreword to Thich Nhat Hanh, *Vietnam: Lotus in a Sea of Fire* (New York: Hill and Wang, 1967), viii, x.

VOID

Thomas Merton occasionally uses the term "void" in a negative way, denoting a kind of meaningless emptiness, as in the prologue to *Raids on the Unspeakable* when he equates the latter term in his title with the abyss of absurdity lying beneath the apparent good sense and rationality of most official discourse, "the void that gets into the language of public and official declarations at the very moment when they are pronounced" (*Raids on the Unspeakable*, 4). In Faulkner's "Old Man" he finds the flooded Mississippi a natural symbol for the threat of ultimate meaninglessness that underlies normal human existence and occasionally reveals itself: "the River as the Void, from which comes inexhaustible, malignant power" (*Learning to Love*, 173–74) but which also calls forth unexpected and hitherto unrecognized resources of human resiliency and solidarity. Even this apparent chaos, empty of all meaning, is at least potentially the arena of divine action: "The void itself, when hovered over by the

Spirit, is an abyss of creativity" (*Raids on the Unspeakable*, 71).

But Merton's more typical use of the term is as the English equivalent of the Buddhist term *sunyata*, the emptiness that is ultimate reality. He emphasizes repeatedly that although this term appears to be negative, what is negated is limitation and partial views of reality caused by a dualistic perspective that divides subject and object. The void is a pure emptiness that refuses to conceptualize, and so to "possess," even the notion of emptiness. He remarks, "It would be more helpful for Western minds to call it *a pure affirmation* of the fullness of positive being, though Buddhists would prefer to stick to their principle, neither affirming nor negating" (*Mystics and Zen Masters*, 27).

For Zen, "the Void itself [is] an inexhaustible source of creative dynamism at work in the phenomena that are seen before us and constitute the world around us" (284). It is not simply a psychological but an ontological or metaphysical state, and the experience of enlightenment is "an intuition of the metaphysical ground of all being and knowledge as void" (39), an infinite emptiness that also is infinite fullness, because in infinity there are no bounds to distinguish one from the other: "Experience is full because it is inexhaustible void" (*Other Side of the Mountain*, 234).

Merton sees in this awareness a striking analogy to the "pure consciousness" of apophatic Christian mystics such as John of the Cross; while the theological emphasis on being drawn into the darkness of naked faith by grace is absent (though not denied) in the Buddhist understanding of the void, for Christian and Buddhist alike there is a similar need for "a 'death' of that ego-identity or self-consciousness which is constituted by a calculating and desiring ego" (*Mystics and Zen Masters*, 242). Hence, it is not the individual empirical self that experiences the void, but "the *void itself*, the Unconscious as manifest and conscious in us" (28). It is precisely by surrendering all desire to possess fullness, by entering into the desert, the emptiness of the void, by letting go of a separate self, "by plunging through the center of [one's] own nothingness and coming out in the All which

is the Void and which is if you like the Love of God" (*Learning to Love*, 324), that one discovers that zero equals infinity, that the *nada* of a self stripped of all limited identity has become "the *todo*, the All, in which the freedom of personal love discovers itself in its transcendent Ground and Source which we are accustomed to call the Love of God and which no human name can ever account for or explain" (*Mystics and Zen Masters*, 269). Thus, Merton considers the void to be not only compatible with but very useful in understanding the Christian belief in union with God, despite the obvious difference in the avoidance or acceptance of personal language for the Absolute. He even finds in D. T. Suzuki's consideration of the void "a kind of trinitarian" analogy: "intelligence coming forth from the void and . . . love and wisdom in the void" (*Springs of Contemplation*, 223; see also *Mystics and Zen Masters*, 39–40).

Like so much else about his encounter with Buddhism, Merton's experience of the void culminated during his Asian pilgrimage before the statues at Polonnaruwa: "The rock, all matter, all life, is charged with *dharmakaya* — everything is emptiness and everything is compassion" (*Other Side of the Mountain*, 323), a profoundly realized recognition both of the Buddhist belief in "the ultimate emptiness, the unity of *sunyata* and *karuna*" (278) and of the Christian belief that *kenosis*, the self-emptying of God in Christ, is the ultimate revelation of divine compassion and love. POC

SEE ALSO BUDDHISM; ZEN.

VOW OF CONVERSATION, A: *Journal, 1964–1965*

Edited with a preface by Naomi Burton Stone. New York: Farrar, Straus and Giroux, 1988. 212 pp.

This Thomas Merton journal covers the period from January 1, 1964, to September 6, 1965. It parallels, though in much abbreviated form, the section from pages 52 to 291 in the journal volume *Dancing in the Water of Life*. A *Vow of Conversation* was edited by Merton himself, but not published until 1988. The title of the book derives from the vow of *conversio* (or *conversa-*

tio) morum taken by all Trappists. It is a vow to grow continually toward perfection in the living out the Christian life as a monk. The title is appropriate: it shows a Merton more mature than the Merton of the 1950s, as he strives seriously and most humanly to work toward the goal set by this vow. This volume shows Merton's humanness in its heights and depths, its struggles, its defeats, its victories, and, always at last, in total dependence on God.

A Vow of Conversation is as probing and insightful as *Conjectures of a Guilty Bystander,* but more personal; and as personal as *The Sign of Jonas,* but more mature. There are bits of autobiography, such as the June 1964 visit to New York City to see the ninety-four-year-old D. T. Suzuki, whose books Merton had read for so many years. Returning to New York was nostalgic. He writes, "The first thing about New York was that I was delighted to see it again" (*Vow of Conversation,* 55). This despite the fact that a few days earlier he had written, "I can think of nowhere I would less like to go than New York.... The mere thought of New York gives me stomach spasms" (54–55).

Photograph by Thomas Merton

There was, in July of 1964, the memorable visit from Abraham Heschel, their discussion of Heschel's books and of their mutual fear of a watering down, for political reasons, of the Second Vatican Council's statement on the Jews. Merton was prompted by this visit to pen a strong statement to Cardinal Bea. He remarks in the journal, "But if Rome simply declares herself complacently to be the mouthpiece of God and perfect interpreter of God's will for

the Jews, with the implication that He in no way ever speaks to them directly, this is simply monstrous!" (76).

November 1964 was the occasion for a retreat at Gethsemani for people involved in the peace movement. The Berrigans were there, and for the first time Merton met A. J. Muste, who for so many years had been closely identified with the struggle for peace. Merton remarks, "A. J. Muste is impressive in real wisdom, modesty, gentleness" (101).

The book's climactic event — one that surely in its significance for him rivals his entrance nearly twenty-four years earlier into the monastery — was Merton's moving definitively to the hermitage on August 20, 1965. The journal entry for this day is relatively brief and curiously detached: a short reflection on Hebrews 11 and the saints of old who witnessed to the faith. "I enter into this other close-knit society of invisible witnesses and I'm very aware of their presence" (206).

One finds in *A Vow of Conversation* comment after comment on Merton's reading: Bultmann, Jaspers, Walker Percy, Jacques Ellul, Abelard, Anselm, Vladimir Lossky, Sartre, Chuang Tzu, Simone Weil, and numerous others. There are comments too on some of his own writings: his misgivings about parts of *Seeds of Destruction* and his obvious delight in *The Way of Chuang Tzu.*

One also finds here dark reflections on obedience and Merton's often troubled relationship with his abbot; at the same time, there is a growth in his perception of obedience and his understanding of his abbot, Dom James. Perhaps typical: "[When] I think of the power that authority has to be most unreasonable in our lives and see how that power is sometimes used so arbitrarily, I am filled with frustration and resentment. Yet it is precisely this that I must accept. This should be all the easier when he has, in fact perhaps also unreasonably, given me so much latitude in other matters" (87).

There is much reflection on the meaning of solitude. No topic is spoken of more frequently. What he says about solitude here rivals in its perceptiveness what he earlier wrote in *Thoughts in Solitude* and in "Notes for a Philosophy of Solitude." One feels that here, even more than in those other justly valued works, he is talking out of his experience. Thus, "My one job as a monk is to live this hermit life in simple direct contact with nature, primitively, quietly, doing some writing, maintaining such contacts as are willed by God, and bearing witness to the value and goodness of simple things and ways, loving God in all of it" (174). Another example: "It seems to me that solitude rips off all the masks and all the disguises. It tolerates no lies. Everything but straight and direct affirmation or silence is mocked and judged by the silence of the forest" (204).

A *Vow of Conversation* concludes with one of Merton's most moving meditations. Occasioned by the sight of two does and two stags in the woods, it needs to be read in its entirety to be fully appreciated. Here is the conclusion: "The deer reveals to me something essential, not only in itself, but also in myself. Something beyond the trivialities of my everyday being, my individual existence. Something profound. The face of that which is both in the deer and in myself. The stags are much darker than the does. They are mouse-gray, or rather a warm gray-brown, like flying squirrels. I could sense the softness of their brown coat and longed to touch them" (208). WHS

SEE ALSO *DANCING IN THE WATER OF LIFE*.

VOWS, MONASTIC

In *Basic Principles of Monastic Spirituality*[1] Thomas Merton says that the monk consecrates his whole life to God by his five monastic vows: conversion of manners (*conversatio morum*), stability, obedience, poverty, and chastity (*Monastic Spirituality*, 86–87). The last two are not specifically mentioned in the Rule of St. Benedict, but they are included in conversion of manners. It is possible therefore to speak of three vows: stability, obedience, and conversion of manners.

The vow of stability binds a monk to one monastery until death. It involves the renunciation of the freedom to travel about from place to place, from one monastery to another. Merton considers the vow of stability as one of St. Benedict's original contributions to monasticism. At a time when laxity in monastic life led to wandering monks who were not subject to a regular superior or attached to a particular monastery, Benedict saw the importance of permanent, lifelong commitment to the monastery of one's profession. Stability is one of the foundations of monastic peace, for it protects the monk against the pull of a natural restlessness. The monk's journey becomes spiritual, not spatial (*Monastic Journey*, 67).

Merton sees obedience as the greatest of the vows, for by it "the monk renounces not his possessions, nor his body, but the inmost sanctuary of his spirit" (*Monastic Journey*, 64). This inmost sanctuary never can be invaded from the outside, unless one permits. A person can be forced to *do* something, but can never be forced to *will* something. Obedience, then, is giving up the right to exercise freedom as one pleases. "To surrender our own will and judgment to another is to surrender that which is most personal and inviolable in ourselves" (64). It is the surrender of one's own judgment and will "in order to be guided and governed by the 'common will' (voluntas communis) of the monastery, which is ordinarily determined by the Rule and the Abbot" (82). Resisting the common will cuts the monk off from the life-giving flow of grace, "which circulates in the monastery under the impulsion of the Holy Spirit, who is the 'soul' of the monastic community, as he is the soul of the Church herself" (82).

Stability, then, is *foundational*, for without it the other vows cannot be lived out. Obedience is *the greatest* of the vows, because one gives up what is most deeply personal. The vow of conversion of manners (*conversio morum*) is the *essential* vow: it is at the heart of everything the monk does. For it means changing one's attitudes "from those of the world to those of the cloister" (*Monastic Spirituality*, 86). In 1966 Merton wrote an entire article in *Cistercian Studies* on *conversio morum*. It was republished in *The Monastic Journey* (107–20). While the term[2] seems archaic and quaint, it expresses "the monk's essential task" (*Monastic Journey*, 107). It has been defined as an explicit commitment to make constant progress in virtue. "It is a vow of renunciation and penance, a vow to abandon the world and its ways, in order to seek God in the solitude, *ascesis*, obedience, prayer, poverty and labors of the monastic way" (110). *Conversio morum* is so essential to the life of the monk that it may be seen to include the other two vows; or, as Merton puts it, "The *promissio* of stability, *conversio morum,* and obedience is in fact regarded simply as one inclusive promise, not as 'three vows'" (112). WHS

Notes

1. Citations from *Basic Principles of Monastic Spirituality* all from the 1996 Templegate edition.

2. The older term for this vow was *conversatio morum.* The monk leaves the "conversation" of the world for that of the cloister. This leads to obedience to the voice of Christ and the will of God; hence, conversion (*conversio morum*). The term generally used today is *conversio morum.*

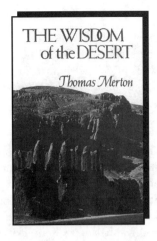

WALSH, DANIEL

On November 10, 1963, the Thomas Merton Collection at Bellarmine College was officially dedicated. Merton was not present, but a statement from him was read by his friend Daniel Walsh. Merton said,

> It is more than strange that the man who will read these words to you, Dan Walsh, is the one who first told me of the Abbey of Gethsemani. It is he, therefore, who first turned my thoughts in this direction. It is partly due to him that I came to this diocese and to this state twenty-two years ago. But he is no more a native Kentuckian than I am, and if he is here now, it is partly because of me. I am quite sure that neither he nor I were ever able to foresee that he would one day be speaking here, on such an occasion as this. One of awesome things about this event, then, is that it indicates to me that, when Dan and I were talking together over a couple of glasses of beer in a New York City hotel, God was present there and was doing his work in us. Therefore, we can trust he still continues to be just as present and just as active here in all of us now.[1]

Daniel Walsh was born on November 3, 1907, in Scranton, Pennsylvania. On November 7 he was baptized Daniel Cyril at St. Peter's Cathedral in Scranton. In 1930 he was awarded a B.A. degree in philosophy at the University of Toronto, and an M.A. the following year in philosophy and Latin paleography at the same university. He received the degree of Ph.D. in philosophy and history from the Pontifical Institute of Medieval Studies, also at the University of Toronto, where he studied with Etienne Gilson. He was professor of philosophy at Manhattanville College in Purchase, New York, from 1934 to 1960. From 1936 to 1955 he was a visiting professor of philosophy at Columbia College, and in 1955 he became an adjunct professor of philosophy.

In 1939 Merton took a graduate course on St. Thomas Aquinas from Walsh. In *The Seven Storey Mountain* Merton is lavish in his praise of his mentor. "He, like Gilson, had the most rare and admirable virtue of being able to rise above the petty differences of schools and systems and seeing Catholic philosophy in its wholeness, in its variegated unity and in its true Catholicity" (*Seven Storey Mountain*, 220). Walsh was a forceful person: a little, stocky man with a square jaw and "something of the appearance of a good-natured prizefighter, smiling and talking with the most childlike delight and cherubic simplicity about the *Summa Theologica*" (219). Walsh and Merton became friends, and it was Walsh who introduced him to Jacques Maritain. In September 1939 Merton arranged to meet Walsh at the Biltmore Hotel. He asked his advice about a vocation to the priesthood. They talked about several religious congregations. They agreed that Merton would apply to the Franciscans. This never worked out, and eventually Merton entered an order that Walsh was enthusiastic about: the Trappists in Kentucky.

In 1960 Walsh came to Kentucky at the behest of Dom James Fox, abbot at the Abbey of Gethsemani. The abbot had invited him to help in the reorganization of the philosophy program at the abbey's seminary, which had been set up for the instruction of the monks who were studying for the priesthood. Walsh also lectured at the motherhouse of the Loretto Sisters. Soon after, he became a visiting professor at Bellarmine College in Louisville and took up residence in Lenahan Hall on the campus.

In 1967 Archbishop John Floersh took the unexpected step of inviting Walsh to be ordained as a priest of the Louisville Diocese. The sixty-year-old Walsh was stunned and overjoyed. The ordination took place at St. Thomas Seminary on Pentecost Sunday, May 14, 1967. Merton notes in his journal that at the party after the ordination at the O'Callaghans' residence, "I talked too much, drank too much champagne, and generally misbehaved" (*Learning to Love*, 236).

Daniel Walsh's death came suddenly on August 28, 1975. He is buried in the cemetery just outside the monastic enclosure at Gethsemani. Some of his writings have been preserved, but it was as a teacher rather than a writer that he excelled. Merton wrote in his autobiography, "I pray to God that there may be raised up more like him in the Church and in our universities" (*Seven Storey Mountain*, 220). WHS

Notes

1. Alfred F. Horrigan, Thomas Merton, and John Howard Griffin, *The Thomas Merton Studies Center* (Santa Barbara, Calif.: Unicorn Press, 1971), 13–14.

WAR

In the special introduction to his chapter on war from *New Seeds of Contemplation*, published in the October 1961 issue of the *Catholic Worker*, Thomas Merton declared, "The one task which God has imposed upon us in the world today . . . is to work for the total abolition of war" (*Passion for Peace*, 12). The unique significance he assigns to this task indicates not only the critical danger in which he found the world at the beginning of the 1960s but also his conviction that opposition to war, particularly nuclear war, was an intrinsic dimension of an authentically Christian moral and spiritual life. A failure to confront the issue of war was for Merton an abdication of Christian responsibility to affirm the human dignity of every person and to love one's neighbor as oneself.

Merton's life was framed by the wars of the twentieth century. He was born in the south of France "in a year of a great war" (*Seven Storey Mountain*, 3). His entrance into the Abbey of Gethsemani coincided with America's entrance into the second "great war," in which his only brother was killed, the event with which he concludes his autobiography, *The Seven Storey Mountain* (401–4). His body, as has often been noted, was flown back to America from Southeast Asia in the company of servicemen who had been killed in a war that he had strenuously opposed. While his major writings on war come from the final eight years of his life, they are the fruit of a concern that predated even his conversion (144–45), and led him to seek noncombatant conscientious objector status as a Catholic in the early months of World War II (311–13; *Run to the Mountain*, 316–17).

Merton's early writings on war emphasize the notion of personal responsibility for creating the kind of immoral society that makes war possible; not only are the Germans "proud and conceited and violent and pompous and cruel and cowardly," Merton writes in his journal, but also "because of all these things in our hearts, too, we get wars and revolutions all over the earth, and that is what it means to say the wars are punishments from heaven upon us for our own sins because, if we loved God more and

violence less, we would not have wars and revolutions" (*Run to the Mountain*, 186; see also *My
Argument with the Gestapo*, 76–77, 119; *Seven
Storey Mountain*, 248). But he also recognizes
economic, political, and ideological motives for
warfare (*Run to the Mountain*, 231–32), and he
reflects that opposition to war simply on the
basis of its horrors or its economic devastation
will not provide strong enough motivation to
preserve peace (403).

In his only extended published reflection on
war, aside from the autobiography, in the early
period of his writing, the chapter "The Root
of War Is Fear" in *Seeds of Contemplation*, Merton emphasizes that only love for and trust in
God can bring lasting peace, "for only love —
which means humility — can cast out the fear
which is the root of all war" (*Seeds of Contemplation*, 72), and he again emphasizes the personal
moral responsibility dimension of opposition to
war: "Instead of hating the people you think
are warmakers, hate the appetites and the disorder in your own soul, which are the causes
of war" (73). When he returns to the topic
of war in *New Seeds of Contemplation* twelve
years later these passages are preserved (*New
Seeds of Contemplation*, 119, 122), but they are
part of a much expanded chapter that emphasizes also the collective myths that demonize
the enemy (114), as well as the hypocrisy, or
at least moral blindness, that can reconcile the
slogan "pray for peace" used to cancel stamps
with the "utterly fabulous amount of money,
planning, energy, anxiety and care which go
into the production of weapons which almost
immediately become obsolete and have to be
scrapped" (120). He stresses the importance of
praying for peace, praying "not only that the
enemies of my country may cease to want war,
but above all that my own country will cease to
do the things that make war inevitable" (121),
but also points out the need to work for peace,
by opposing the "fictions and illusions" that undergird the modern state, whether communist
or capitalist (122).

Although the appearance of *New Seeds of
Contemplation* marks the entry of Merton into
the public forum, at least for a time, on issues
of war and peace, it does not signal any radical shift in his convictions on war. As early

as April 1948 he deplored the failure of moral
theologians to speak out against the threat of
nuclear war (*Entering the Silence*, 197), and in
a March 1955 letter to Erich Fromm he wrote,
"It seems to me that there are no circumstances
that can make atomic war legitimate. The ax-
iom *non sunt facienda mala ut eveniant bona* (evil
must not be done even for a good end) applies here more than ever before. . . . Therefore,
I am entirely with you on the issue of atomic
war. I am opposed to it with all the force of
my conscience" (*Hidden Ground of Love*, 311–
12). At the time, however, he thought that his
position as a cloistered religious "out of the
world" would not permit him to sign the antiwar petition that Fromm had forwarded. But by
October 1959 he is asking in his journal, "How
many Christians have taken a serious and effective stand against atomic warfare?" (*Search for
Solitude*, 337), and by July 1960 (on the same
day that plans for the building that will become
his hermitage are first seriously discussed) he
is critiquing American complacency and infidelity to professed values in connection with
the arms race and concluding, "I feel I ought to
use my voice to say something, in public, and I
don't know where to begin. By the time it got
through the censors it would have lost most of
its meaning" (*Turning toward the World*, 21).

Nevertheless, between October 1961, when
"The Root of War Is Fear" appeared in the
Catholic Worker, and September 1962, when the
collection of essays by various hands assembled
by Merton and entitled *Breakthrough to Peace*
was published, Merton did "use [his] voice to
say something, in public," until the censors, or
rather the abbot general, silenced the voice, for
a time. In a series of articles published during
this period and subsequently, after the ban was
lifted, he has at least three principal goals.

First, he argues strenuously against nuclear
war and the mindset that makes nuclear war
thinkable. He applies traditional ethical principles of the just war to the current threat of
nuclear destruction and maintains that nuclear
war cannot be morally justified. A nuclear first
strike, he argues, would be "clearly unjust and
utterly unacceptable to a Christian moralist"
both because it initiates aggression and because
it would result in the death or maiming of mil-

lions of innocent people (*Passion for Peace*, 22). He critiques the idea that total war and the destruction of the Soviet Union is a "lesser evil" than what is presented as the only other alternative, capitulation to communist domination; besides dissenting from this simplistic either/or thinking, Merton insists that such a conclusion is in fact a surrender to godlessness far more serious than a communist takeover would be: "Even for the best of ends it is not permitted to do evil. Total war is nothing but mass murder" (52). While he allows for the theoretical possibility that a "counter-force" nuclear strike could meet just war norms, he maintains that in actual fact such a strike almost certainly would result in massive civilian casualties and escalate into full-scale nuclear annihilation, and hence is morally unacceptable (89). He considers the notion of nuclear deterrence to be largely illusory, since it has not prevented numerous conventional wars (*Breakthrough to Peace*, 8), and the development of a first-strike capacity that could wipe out the enemy's weapons before they could be launched creates a further destabilizing factor that makes deterrence even more problematic (8). Merton recommends "the rejection of nuclear deterrence as a basis for international policy" and increased efforts for genuine disarmament (91).

Second, he maintains that conventional war likewise is morally unacceptable, both because it regularly violates norms of justice and because in the modern age it always includes the threat of escalation to mass destruction. In "Target Equals City" (an article never published in Merton's lifetime due to censors' objections) he points out how in World War II the gradual erosion of moral restraints led to acts of "pure terrorism" such as obliteration bombing and eventually to the use of atomic weapons, even though such tactics were totally incompatible with long-accepted moral principles on warfare, so that at present "the traditional doctrine of the just war has been so profoundly modified that it is almost unrecognizable" (*Passion for Peace*, 29). In a later discussion of war he points to the destruction of Dresden in World War II, in which more people were killed than in the atomic bombing of Hiroshima and Nagasaki, as an example of the immorality of so-called conventional weapons and concludes, "Anyone who willingly participates in modern warfare sooner or later commits himself to cooperation in acts like this" (*Love and Living*, 130). In his later writings on the immorality of the Vietnam conflict he will protest against what he will call the "overwhelming atrocity" of American policy and conduct in a particular instance of "conventional" warfare (*Faith and Violence*, 87–95).

Third, he writes to strip away the mystique of war and to delegitimize resort to war as a valid way of responding to social and political conflicts. He writes, "There is only one winner in war. That winner is not justice, not liberty, not Christian truth. The winner is war itself" (*Passion for Peace*, 36). In a letter entitled "To a Statesman's Wife" (Ethel Kennedy [see *Hidden Ground of Love*, 444–46]), published in *Seeds of Destruction*, he emphasizes that war itself is the principal enemy and suggests that it is such a problem because the facade of morality is too often "a front for organized selfishness and systematic irresponsibility" (*Seeds of Destruction*, 251). He later compares war to an addiction and concludes, "Man is so addicted to war that he cannot possibly deal with his addiction. And yet if he does not learn to cope with it, the addiction will ruin him altogether" (*Love and Living*, 129). In his preface to the privately distributed "Cold War Letters" he aligns himself with "the modern Popes, particularly Pius XII and John XXIII, who have repeatedly pleaded for rational and peaceful ways of settling disputes, and who have forcefully declared that the uninhibited recourse to destructive violence in total war, nuclear or conventional, is 'a sin, an offense and an outrage' (Pius XII)" (*Witness to Freedom*, 21).

By the time *Breakthrough to Peace* was published, Merton had been forbidden to publish further on the issue of war, on the grounds that it was inappropriate to the vocation of a monk. He heeded this ban, although he strenuously disagreed with "the thought that a monk might be deeply enough concerned with the issue of nuclear war to voice a protest against the arms race, is supposed to bring the monastic life into *disrepute*" (*Hidden Ground of Love*, 267) — evidence to him of how out of touch the monastic institution was with the crucial moral and spiritual issues of the day. When the ban finally was lifted and *Seeds of Destruction* appeared in 1964, the emphasis in the section on "The Christian in World Crisis" is more on creating a climate of peace than on the specifics of the morality of nuclear, or conventional, war, but Merton frames the discussion, which draws extensively on John XXIII's *Pacem in Terris*, by focusing on what he calls the twofold task of the Christian to struggle against totalitarian dictatorship and against war, pointing out that the first aspect is directed not simply against communism "but also against our own hidden tendencies towards fascist or totalist aberrations," and the second "not only against the bellicosity of the Communist powers, but against our own violence, fanaticism and greed" (*Seeds of Destruction*, 97–98).

In one of his major later statements on war, his "open letter" to the American bishops before the final session of the Second Vatican Council, he voices his conviction that "the modern world is one which still believes in war, from guerrilla warfare to total and even nuclear war, while cold war and deterrence by terroristic threat of violence seemingly remain with us as permanent features of our civilization" (*Witness to Freedom*, 89). He pleads that the Council fathers, in the final version of the Constitution on the Church in the Modern World (*Gaudium et Spes*), do not resort to "fine moral distinctions that would savor of evasion and pharisaism" (91) and thereby leave room for interpretations that would allow for the use or threatened use of nuclear weapons. He calls "for the Bishops and the Council to bear witness clearly and without any confusion to the Church's belief in the power of love to save and transform not only individuals but society" (92) by "stating *the Church's view of modern war in the light of the eschatological message of salvation*" rather than simply in the context of great-power politics (91). In his subsequent article on *Gaudium et Spes* he cites with approval "the Council's condemnation of total war in the clearest and most unequivocal language" (*Love and Living*, 167) and endorses its call for "a whole new attitude toward war" and its affirmation "that all men must take seriously and

personally the obligation incumbent on the entire human race to abolish war" (168). While Merton recognizes that the struggle to develop this "whole new attitude" had only begun, he could take some comfort and satisfaction in the fact that what had been a controversial and in his own case even an officially impermissible position a few short years before had now become in large part the official teaching of the Catholic Church. POC

SEE ALSO JUST WAR, THEORY OF; HIROSHIMA; HOLOCAUST; NONVIOLENCE; *PASSION FOR PEACE*; *THOMAS MERTON ON PEACE*; PEACE.

WATERS OF SILOE, THE
New York: Harcourt, Brace, 1949.
xxxviii+377 pp.

This is the second book that Thomas Merton published with Harcourt, Brace, appearing the year after *The Seven Storey Mountain*. The title is a reference to Isaias's (Isaiah's) image of "*the waters of Siloe* [Siloam] *that flow in silence*" (Isa. 8:6), which Merton uses as a symbol of the life of contemplation (*Waters of Siloe*, xxix) and associates with the "fountain of water, springing up into life everlasting" that Jesus promises in John 4:14 (vii). The work consists of two parts, the first a survey of the history of the Cistercian Order, with a particular focus on its foundation and development in the United States; the second, considerably shorter section an examination of the central characteristics of Cistercian life. The two parts are structurally independent but they share a focus on what might be considered Merton's central theme: the essentially contemplative character of Cistercian monasticism — a focus lost for much of its history but being recovered in the twentieth century.

After a helpful listing of the daily schedule of a Cistercian, the prologue provides a brief introduction to Trappist life and an overview of the historical survey to follow, highlighting the suggestion "that the reason why there is such a ferment of new life and spiritual energy in the Trappist monasteries of the world today is that they have become something more than just 'Trappist'" (xxii); that is, that they have recovered an emphasis on "contemplation in this strict sense" that was "the atmosphere in which the Cistercians of the Middle Ages lived and breathed" (xxv). This is followed by a short "Note on the Function of a Contemplative Order," in which the author points out and defends the distinction between contemplative communities and active orders engaged in preaching and teaching: "The Order has recovered its full strength in proportion as it has withdrawn from fields of endeavor into which it never had any business to go" (xxxii). (Note that both the prologue and the note are included in part 1 in the table of contents but precede part 1 in the text itself.)

Part 1 consists of eleven chapters. Chapter 1 moves rapidly from the foundations of monastic life in the fourth century, through the rise of Benedictine monasticism in the West and its influence throughout the Middle Ages, to the beginnings of Cistercianism as a reform movement aimed at restoring the original Benedictine spirit. The emphasis is on the necessity for "fidelity to the contemplative ideal" (29) in order to preserve the vitality of the order, a fidelity that was soon lost as the order became influential and consequently wealthy. Chapter 2 focuses on the Trappist reform instituted by de Rancé in the seventeenth century, with its return to austerity but not to a focus on contemplation. Chapter 3 considers the suppression of the order during the French Revolution and its reconstitution at La Val Sainte in Switzerland by Dom Augustin de Lestrange and companions in a form that "allowed their latent activism to run away with them" (61). The initial heroic but eventually unsuccessful efforts of La Val Sainte to plant Cistercian life in America, first in Kentucky then in Illinois, are described in chapter 4, followed by a chapter on the more lasting efforts in Nova Scotia and Canada. Merton's skill in weaving together dramatic incident and anecdote is particularly evident in the stories of these rather eccentric efforts. The foundation of the Abbey of Gethsemani in 1848 finally is effected in chapter 6, which includes an interesting comparison of the emigrant monks with the founders of the utopian Icarian community that sailed for America on the same ship. Chapter 7 takes the Gethsemani foundation

through much of the nineteenth century under its first three abbots and looks at other Cistercian foundations at New Melleray in Iowa, and in Canada. Chapter 8 begins with the crucial formation of the Order of Cistercians of the Strict Observance from various reform groups, the rebuilding of the mother abbey of Cîteaux, and the long reign at Gethsemani of the dynamic Dom Edmond Obrecht, who brought the abbey back from the brink of dissolution and reestablished it on firm spiritual and economic foundations. Chapter 9 surveys "Eight American Foundations" of Cistercian houses in the early twentieth century, notably including the Abbey of Our Lady of the Valley in Rhode Island and the foundation in Canada of the first two women's Cistercian abbeys in North America. Chapter 10, "A Contemplative Order in Two World Wars," focuses particularly on the tribulations of European monasteries caught in the middle of war (the Spanish Civil War as well as the First and Second World Wars) but also describes the final years of Dom Edmond Obrecht and the election of his successor, Dom Frederic Dunne, the first American-born Cistercian abbot (and Merton's own first abbot). Chapter 11, the last in part 1, brings the story up to date by juxtaposing the growth of the order in the United States with its brutal suppression in newly communist China, seeing the transformation of a New Mexico dude ranch into a monastery as a countermovement to the destruction of Yang Kia Ping abbey, "the quiet and effective way Christian communism has of liquidating capitalist institutions and replacing them with something more healthy and fruitful in the moral order" (262).

The final eighty or so pages of the book, the three chapters of part 2, return to the early days of Cistercianism to find a model for authentic monastic contemplative life. Chapter 12, "Cistercian Life in the Twelfth Century," considers the location, physical structure, and daily organization of a typical early Cistercian monastery as reflecting the atmosphere of simplicity, community, and contemplative love characteristic of Cistercian spirituality in the first generations. Chapter 13, "The Cistercian Character and Sanctity," discusses the loss of the original Cistercian charism in later periods, the tendency to consider contemplation "something you measured by the clock" (301), and the efforts of the recent past to recover "some sense of the scope and depth and beauty, as well as the sane and healthy simplicity, of Cistercian mystical theology" (317) by a return to the teachings of the great Cistercian fathers of the twelfth century. Finally, chapter 14, *"Paradisus Claustralis"* (which can be translated "The Enclosed Garden" or "Paradise of the Cloister"), comes full circle by returning to the focus of the opening sentence of chapter 1: "A monk is a man who has given up everything in order to possess everything" (3). Here Merton expands on this thought by declaring that "the key to the Cistercian life" of renunciation is the monk's recognition that "when he owns nothing, God becomes his fortune, and he owns and enjoys all things in God, their Creator" (333). The focus on spiritual growth, on the paradoxical life of solitude in community, is seen to be directed, in language that Merton takes from St. Bernard and that he will make uniquely his own in subsequent writings, at the discovery of the "real self, ... concealed under the 'disguise' of a false self, the *ego* whom we tend to worship in place of God" (349). Merton ends on a note of great hope that by drinking from the waters of its own well, "the waters of contemplation, whose mystery fascinated and delighted the first Cistercians" (351), the order can and will recover that "integrity of the Cistercian life in its letter and spirit" (350) that once gave renewed spiritual vitality not only to its individual members but also to the entire church. POC

WAUGH, EVELYN

This well-known British author (1903–66) edited Thomas Merton's *The Seven Storey Mountain* (giving it a new title, *Elected Silence*, for the British edition) and also his *Waters of Siloe* (which Merton dedicated to him). Merton's letters to Waugh are published in *The Courage for Truth*. WHS

SEE ALSO *COURAGE FOR TRUTH; ELECTED SILENCE.*

WAY OF CHUANG TZU, THE
New York: New Directions, 1965. 159 pp.

This is Thomas Merton's collection of what he calls "imitations" of "characteristic passages" (*Way of Chuang Tzu*, 9) from the fourth-century B.C.E. Chinese Taoist master. Since Merton had minimal knowledge of Chinese, he worked from existing translations in English, French, and German, and created what he described as "ventures in personal and spiritual interpretation" (9). Most of the selections, which range in length from seven lines to six pages, are rendered into verse, though the originals (and the translations from which he worked) are in prose. In the introduction to his own translation of *The Complete Works of Chuang Tzu*, Burton Watson recommends that "readers interested in the literary qualities of the text" consult Merton's adaptations, which "give a fine sense of the liveliness and poetry of Chuang Tzu's style, and are actually almost as close to the original as the translations upon which they are based."[1]

Following a prefatory note to the reader in which Merton explains his methodology, mentions his own attraction, as a monk and solitary, for a kindred spirit "concerned ... with the direct existential grasp of reality in itself" (11), expresses his gratitude for the encouragement of his friend John C. H. Wu, to whom the book is dedicated, and declares that he "enjoyed writing this book more than any other" he could recall (9–10), the book consists of two sections. The first, "A Study of Chuang Tzu," is an essay setting Chuang Tzu in the context of the currents of classic Chinese thought and exploring his particular characteristics. The second, "Readings from Chuang Tzu," includes sixty-two passages from the Chuang Tzu Book.

In his essay Merton highlights the "humor, the sophistication, the literary genius, and philosophical insight of Chuang Tzu" (15). He contrasts him with the more social and formalized approach of Confucianism, as well as with the superstitions of popular Taoism, and follows D. T. Suzuki in seeing the early Chinese Zen masters as the true heirs of Chuang Tzu. Merton defends the sage against charges of antinomianism, pointing out that

Chuang Tzu's religious and mystical perspective transcends external rules and standards by centering not on the ego but on the Tao, the mysterious "Way" that is beyond all formulation but is at the heart of all reality. He claims Chuang Tzu as a true personalist, not a self-centered individualist, but he contrasts the Taoist's respect for the human person with the traditional personalism of Confucian "Ju" philosophy, in which the duties of the virtuous person can be clearly defined and punctiliously observed.

The authentic "man of Tao" as described by Chuang Tzu acts not by conscious calculation but with an intuitive sense of harmony with all reality, "according to the divine and spontaneous mode of wu wei, which is the mode of action of Tao itself, and is therefore the source of all good" (24). The characteristic Taoist notion of "wu wei," or "non-action," is thus not passive inactivity but a way of taking part in the ongoing single act of the cosmos. It is a self-forgetfulness, an "ontological" humility that accepts one's own nothingness as an independent entity, that empties the self of its distinctness and so is able to be filled with the "boundless vitality and joy" (27) of life shared by all reality. To live in harmony with the Tao is to realize that one is still in paradise, "living at peace with himself, with Tao, and with all other creatures" (27). It is to recognize the provisional and partial character of all programs and systems, all regulations and abstract principles, and to be constantly receptive to new insights, new revelations. The "man of Tao" lives and acts with a freedom that Merton compares to the spiritual liberty of St. Paul that transcends righteousness based on one's own efforts. For Merton it is this suppleness, this willingness to respect the uniqueness of each experience without superimposing artificial classifications and abstract conceptualizations, that makes Chuang Tzu's teaching both profound and practical, "at home on two levels: that of the divine and invisible Tao that has no name, and that of ordinary, simple, everyday existence" (32).

Merton includes somewhat less than 20 percent of the material that makes up the traditional thirty-three chapters of the Chuang Tzu Book. Sixteen sections are adapted from six of the seven "inner chapters" of the work, usually considered the oldest and most significant material in the book; thirty-one sections from nine of the fifteen "outer chapters," which extend and rework the preceding material; and fifteen sections from six of the eleven "miscellaneous" chapters that conclude the work, some of which apparently come from a considerably later period. Merton supplies his own titles for the selections, though in some cases (e.g., "Autumn Floods," "Perfect Joy," "When Knowledge Went North," "Keng Sang Chu") they are borrowed from the traditional title of the chapter from which the selection is taken. Occasionally the title chosen is intended to provide an implicit connection to a more familiar Western source: Merton probably uses "Perfect Joy" rather than "Perfect Happiness" as the title for this selection to recall the famous story, with a very similar message, from *The Little Flowers of St. Francis;* "In My End Is My Beginning" (75) is directly borrowed from the last line of T. S. Eliot's "East Coker."

A number of the stories feature Chuang Tzu as a character, while other selections are presented as words of Chuang Tzu, and still others feature other characters or are spoken by other figures. In some cases Merton provides the narrative context for the passage selected, while in others, particularly some of the shorter selections, the passage is allowed to stand on its own: for example, the selection "Great and Small" (87–90) actually is a continuation of instruction of the Ocean God to the River God begun in the previous section, "Autumn Floods" (84–86), but the speaker is not identified; the penultimate selection, "Flight from the Shadow" (155), is spoken to Confucius by a mysterious stranger, but neither is mentioned. Merton's intent evidently is to highlight what he finds particularly apposite in a passage rather than to provide information that might distract from the particular focus he has chosen; he feels the freedom to "crop" the picture in accordance with his own designs. He occasionally chooses a rendering that suggests a contemporary reference, as when he concludes the selection "Three Friends" (54–55), in which a Confucian criticizes two friends for what he considers improper behavior at a third friend's funeral, with the friends' comment, "Poor fellow, . . . he doesn't know the new liturgy!" In "Cracking the Safe" (67–69) a "rich man" who "steals a whole state" is said to be "acclaimed / As statesman of the year." In "Flight from Benevolence" the three classes of men to be avoided are described as "yes-men, blood-suckers, and operators" (147). But generally the distances of time and space are given due recognition, yet transcended by an awareness of spiritual or simply human affinities.

Slightly over half of the selections are narratives of one sort or another. Some focus on Chuang Tzu himself, as does "The Turtle" (93–94), in which Chuang Tzu turns down an invitation to become prime minister by comparing himself to a turtle, which is better off in the mud of the river than as an empty shell that has become a cult object; or the final story of Chuang Tzu's death, when he disregards his disciples' desires to bury him, and so to protect him from scavenging birds, by pointing out that underground he will be eaten by ants and worms, and ironically concludes (in a twist that seems to be Merton's own "take" on the story), "Why are you so partial to birds?" (156). Others focus on Confucius, Lao Tzu, the "Yellow Emperor," and other famous figures, or on more obscure folk such as the cook who is able to find "the secret opening, the hidden space" (46) within an ox and so effortlessly to dissect it; or the woodcarver who fasted until all thought fell away except that of the work to be done, and so was able to see the finished bell stand already present in a particular tree (110–11); or the exile Lin Hui, who leaves behind his precious jade but takes his infant child because "My bond with the jade symbol . . . / Was the bond of self interest. / My bond with the child / Was the bond of Tao" (116). A few of the stories are allegorical, as when Science, Analysis, and Logic fail to find the emperor's lost pearl, which could be found only by Nothingness (74); or when Knowledge, looking for Tao, questions "Non-Doing" about a "system of thought / And . . . technique of meditation" that will "apprehend Tao," only to receive no answer at all (118).

The other selections are more discursive

than narrative yet typically point beyond the words to that which cannot be spoken: for example, "Action and Non-Action" identifies "perfect Tao" with "Emptiness, stillness, tranquillity, tastelessness, / Silence, non-action" (80); "The Man of Tao" concludes that " 'No-Self' / Is 'True-Self.' / And the greatest man / Is Nobody" (92); "Wholeness" declares that the "eternal place" of rest "is no-place" (105), while "Where Is Tao?" issues the invitation "come with me / To the palace of Nowhere / Where all the many things are One" (124); "The Tower of the Spirit" cautions against self-display and promises that true peace is to be found when one "act[s] rightly, unseen, / In his own solitude, / In the tower of his spirit" (135). In these and similar passages Merton sets out the fruits of his "five years of reading, study, annotation, and meditation" and shows why in *Day of a Stranger* he says of Chuang Tzu that his "climate is perhaps most the climate of this silent corner of woods" (35). POC

SEE ALSO TAOISM.

Notes

1. Burton Watson, trans., *The Complete Works of Chuang Tzu* (New York: Columbia University Press, 1968), 28.

WHAT ARE THESE WOUNDS?
The Life of a Cistercian Mystic, Saint Lutgarde of Aywières
Milwaukee: Bruce Publishing Company, 1950. xi+191 pp.

Dedicated to Cistercian nuns in America, this biography of thirteenth-century Flemish Cistercian mystic St. Lutgarde of Aywières began "as an anonymous pamphlet," which Thomas Merton wrote in 1945 "at the earnest wish" of Dom Frederic Dunne, abbot of Gethsemani (*What Are These Wounds?* x).[1] In the preface to *What Are These Wounds?* Merton offers a tribute to his first abbot, who had a special devotion to St. Lutgarde. He writes,

> Her life expresses many of the themes that were dearest to Dom Frederic's heart and which, indeed, must always be dear to the heart of every contemplative monk: the love

of God, penance and reparation, intercession for souls. But it cannot be too much stressed that in St. Lutgarde, as in all the early Cistercians, the love that embraces penance and hardship for the sake of Christ is never merely negative, never descends to mere rigid formalism, never concentrates on mere exterior observance of fasts and other penitential rigors. The fire of love that consumed the heart of St. Lutgarde was something vital and positive and its flames burned not only to destroy but to rejuvenate and transform. It was this love that Christ came to cast upon the earth and which Dom Frederic did so much to enkindle in the Cistercian (Trappist) monasteries of America that came under his influence. (x–xi)

In the preface Merton introduces St. Lutgarde, highlighting her devotion to the Sacred Heart of Jesus, some four hundred years before St. Margaret Mary popularized devotion to the Sacred Heart and advanced the institution of the Feast of the Sacred Heart, and noting that she received a "mystical wound" (vii) in her heart and thus was one of the earliest stigmatics. Merton also comments on her strength and her beauty: "She was a great penitent, but she was anything but a fragile wraith of a person. Lutgarde, for all her ardent and ethereal mysticism, remained always a living human being of flesh and bone" (viii). Merton notes that she was "remarkably attractive" and "more than merely pretty," imagining that she "must have had one of those marvelously proportioned Flemish faces, full of a mature and serious beauty" (viii). In a simple line drawing, one of many images of women's faces that Merton drew in the late 1940s and in the 1950s, he portrays St. Lutgarde. His "portrait" of St. Lutgarde[2] is strikingly different from the image of the saint that appeared on the book jacket: "a nun adoring the feet of Christ nailed to the cross." "What a cover!" Merton wrote to Naomi Burton on March 28, 1950. "Please inform me as soon as it receives the golden raspberry award from all the critics" (Witness to Freedom, 128).[3] It was not only the cover that displeased Merton. When, in 1967 he ranked his books, Merton declared

What Are These Wounds? "awful." Years before, in a 1949 letter to Evelyn Waugh, he had proclaimed it "an atrocious" book (Courage for Truth, 14). It should be noted, however, that the book generally was well received by critics.

Merton's primary source was Vita Lutgardis, written by Thomas of Cantimpré, a Dominican friar and theologian who had studied at Cologne under St. Albert the Great and was a classmate of St. Thomas Aquinas. Thomas of Cantimpré, who also wrote the life of Bl. Christine the "admirable," had known St. Lutgarde for sixteen years and wrote the story of her life shortly after she died. Although he had been Lutgarde's director, Thomas of Cantimpré was also Lutgarde's "spiritual son," seeking and following her guidance (What Are These Wounds? 90). Merton pronounced the Vita Lutgardis "a minor masterpiece," "fresh and full of life," rich in "vivid little details that stamp his whole record of the saint's life with authenticity" (ix).

What Are These Wounds? includes nine chapters followed by a one-page bibliography. Chapter titles serve to summarize Lutgarde's life and to reveal Merton's attempt to place her story in context and to analyze her impact. The titles are (1) "Childhood. Student in the Benedictine Convent. Two Suitors. Her First Mystical Graces"; (2) "Prioress at St. Catherine's"; (3) "Aywières. The Albigensians. Her First Seven Year Fast"; (4) "The Souls in Purgatory. Her Power over Demons. Her Power of Healing"; (5) "Sinners"; (6) "The Spirituality of St. Lutgarde. Her Mysticism"; (7) "St. Lutgarde's School of Mysticism at Aywières. Her Relations with the Order of Preachers"; (8) "Last Years and Death of St. Lutgarde"; and (9) "After Her Death. Miracles. Cult."

Born in 1182, Lutgarde lived her adult life in the thirteenth century, "an age of conflict and contradiction . . . a century of great saints and great sinners, great greed and great charity, great mercy and great cruelty" (1). As Christian spirituality "became more imaginative, affective and individual," the humanity of Jesus "became a reality to which saints of the thirteenth century were passionately, romantically, almost extravagantly devoted" (2). St. Lutgarde was one of these saints. Her bourgeois father had arranged for her marriage while she was still a child. When he lost his daughter's dowry, Lutgarde's mother, a noblewoman, refused to furnish a dowry, "saying that if she had to put up money at all she would only do so in order to get Lutgarde into a convent." Lutgarde's mother sensed the "deep seeds of spirituality beginning to germinate in the child's pure soul" (4). Lutgarde went to the Benedictine convent of St. Catherine's at St. Trond. It is not clear whether she, at first, lived there as a student or entered the novitiate. But it is clear that she continued to have contacts outside the convent, among them a young man who fell in love with Lutgarde and visited her frequently. "One day, while the simple girl was sitting behind the grille in the parlor listening to the whisperings of her admirer, Christ in His humanity suddenly appeared, blazing before her astonished eyes. He revealed the spear-wound in His side, and said to her: 'Seek no more the pleasure of this unbecoming affection: behold, here, forever, what you should love, and how you should love: here in this wound I promise you the most pure of delights'" (6). When another disappointed suitor tried to seize Lutgarde while she was traveling to her sister's house, she managed to escape. After wandering through the woods all night, she made her way to a friend's house. Embarrassed and afraid to show herself in town, she took courage from the thought of how Christ suffered, was mocked and scourged, stripped and crucified. Returning to the convent, Lutgarde imposed upon herself "a voluntary rule of enclosure and solitude in order to give herself entirely to God" (8). As she fasted, prayed, and took on many penances, the other sisters resented her, especially as her intimacy with God deepened. When Jesus asked her what favor she desired, she asked for his heart. "'What do you mean: you want My Heart?' said Jesus: 'I want *your* heart.' Lutgarde replied: 'Take it, dear Lord. But take it in such a way that Thy Heart's love may be so mingled and united with my own heart that I may possess my heart in Thee, and may it ever remain there

Drawing of St. Lutgarde by Thomas Merton

secure in Thy protection'" (13). This was, Merton observes, a mystical marriage. Lutgarde left St. Catherine's and entered the Cistercian convent at Aywières, where she lived and, on June 16, 1246, died.

Merton recounts the story of Lutgarde's life in considerable detail: he writes of her visions, her seven-year fasts (there were three), her gift of healing, her determination to make reparation for sinners, and her stigmata. Devotion to the suffering Jesus was at the center of her spiritual life. "'What are these wounds in the midst of Thy hands?' Lutgarde was to cry, in spirit, to her Christ, and all her years at Aywières were to be amazed and filled with sorrow at His reply: 'With these was I wounded in the house of them that loved Me!'" (71).

St. Lutgarde's spirituality contrasted sharply with the spirituality of some in her own time, such as the Albigensians, who strove "to 'annihilate' human nature" (95). Her devotion to the Sacred Heart framed a spirituality centered upon the humanity of Jesus and inspired by his passion. As a weekly communicant Lutgarde defied the custom of infrequent communion.

Although Merton reports Lutgarde's extraordinary mystical experiences, he points to the significance of the ordinary elements of Cistercian spirituality in Lutgarde's life. Her life was centered "upon the Word of God, through whom we come to the Father" (119) and nourished by the liturgical cycle, the divine office, and devotion to Our Lady and the saints.

Blind for the last eleven years of her life, Lutgarde continued acts of penance, including a final seven-year fast, begun in 1239, "to save the Church from the power-politics of Emperor Frederick II" (161). While she lived a life apart from the world, she interceded on its behalf though prayer and penance. And, as is clear from the cult, encouraged by miracle, that developed after her death, she was known and honored for her life and witness.

What Are These Wounds? is an exercise in hagiography, typical of the genre and of the time in which it was written. But in addition to making known St. Lutgarde's story, the book reveals much about Merton: his interest in and knowledge of Cistercian history, spirituality, and mysticism; his familiarity with mystics of this period, including women mystics; and his own regard for Cistercian saints. The book also reveals Merton's ambivalence about Lutgarde. On the one hand, he reclaims her story and situates it in the larger tradition of Cistercian history and spirituality, underlining the ways in which St. Lutgarde's example underscores the essentials of Cistercian life; on the other hand, he has to conclude that St. Lutgarde (and some other thirteenth-century Cistercian mystics[4]) does not represent "the pure Cistercian spirituality that characterized the first century of the Order's history" (158).

In St. Lutgarde we find practically nothing of that beautiful and simple zeal which was the very foundation stone of the Order — the zeal for the Rule of St. Benedict in its purity, the zeal for labor in the fields, silence, solitude, community life, monastic simplicity, and that concern with doing ordinary things quietly and perfectly for the glory of God, which is the beauty of pure Benedictine life. Of course, St. Lutgarde was

Cistercian and Benedictine in her spirituality, in her love of the Divine Office, in her love of Christ above all else; but she lacks this Benedictine *plainness*, and this Cistercian technique of humility which consists in a kind of protective coloring, by which the monk simply disappears into the background of the common, everyday life, like those birds and animals whose plumage and fur make them almost indistinguishable from their surroundings. (158–59)

Nevertheless, as he ends the book, Merton insists that St. Lutgarde's story has something to teach Cistercians and others as well: "If Jesus has raised up saints like Lutgarde in the Church," it has been to remind people "to embrace the Cross, in order to follow Him to true peace and true joy of heart. St. Lutgarde is there, wounded with the wounds of Christ's love, sharing in His Passion, for our sakes, that we may learn, from her, to despise our own wills, renounce that mean and petty preoccupation with ourselves which freezes and contracts the heart, and keeps us living, all our days, in the shadows of worry, and jealousy, and fear. She is there, with her own bleeding heart, to inspire us to take up arms against our selfishness, and storm heaven with love and abnegation" (190).

It is not surprising that Merton ranked this book "awful" in the late 1960s. In the 1950s and 1960s Merton would discover genres better suited to him as a writer than hagiography, and he would give expression to his own vision of spirituality and monasticism. CMB

Notes

1. The short biography has been reprinted as "Saint Lutgarde: Nun of Aywières, Belgium (Edited with a Note by Patrick Hart, OCSO)," *Cistercian Studies Quarterly* 35, no. 2 (2000): 217–30. Merton's piece on Lutgarde was one of a selection of short biographies of Cistercian saints that Merton was asked to write. The collection, which included biographies of Alberic, Robert, Stephen Harding, and William of Saint-Thierry, was mimeographed and circulated as "Modern Biographical Sketches of the Cistercian Blessed and Saints."

2. Merton's drawing, dedicated to Dom Frederic Dunne, is reproduced in *Cistercian Studies Quarterly* 35, no. 2 (2000): 218. The dedication reads, "Dear Rev. Father — As you will probably have many notes to read tomorrow I am sending St. Lutgarde to wish you a happy feast, instead of writing a note. She will tell you all my

good wishes and prayers for you on this day. Your devoted child in Jesus. Fr. M. Louis."

3. Michael Mott declares the book "the worst writing he could do," citing examples he found particularly poor (*The Seven Mountains of Thomas Merton* [Boston: Houghton Mifflin, 1984], 257).

4. Merton identifies a number of thirteenth-century Cistercian mystics as belonging to St. Lutgarde's "school of mysticism," including Bl. Ida of Louvain, Bl. Ida of Léau, Bl. Ida of Nivelles, Bl. Simon of Aulne, and Bl. Alice, or Aleyde, of La Cambre.

WHAT IS CONTEMPLATION?
Notre Dame, Ind.: St. Mary's College, 1948.
25 pp.

This book (perhaps more properly a pamphlet) was written as Thomas Merton's response to a student from St. Mary's College, Notre Dame, Indiana, who put to him the question that became the book's title. It has been reprinted a number of times by different publishers.[1]

Apart from a brief section in the epilogue of *The Seven Storey Mountain*, this represents Merton's initial attempt to write about a topic that would become central to much of what he later would write.[2] In this work he breaks no new ground. His approach is very close to the tradition about contemplation that was standard fare in the books on spirituality of the first half of the twentieth century. As resources he draws on the Scriptures, St. Thomas Aquinas, and St. John of the Cross.

The book is divided into eight sections: (1) "What Is Contemplation?" (2) "The Promises of Christ," (3) "St. Thomas Aquinas," (4) "Kinds of Contemplation," (5) "Infused Contemplation," (6) "The Test," (7) "What to Do — The Teaching of St. John of the Cross," and (8) "The Danger of Quietism."

Merton expresses the belief that contemplation is a gift of God that everybody can desire, but all too many Christians confine their spirituality to routine acts of piety and never develop a true interior life. Yet "the seeds of this perfect life are planted in every Christian soul at Baptism" (*What Is Contemplation?* 17).[3] But in so many cases they lie dormant and never germinate. Such people allow God "to maintain His rights over the substance of their souls, but their thoughts and desires do not belong to Him" (18).

In the strict sense of the term, there is only one kind of "contemplation": infused or mystical contemplation. Active contemplation is experiencing God in one's daily life. The liturgy is a form of active contemplation, as is the search for God in the activities of one's life. Such persons, Merton suggests, may be called *"quasi-contemplatives,"* "because of the great purity of heart maintained in them by obedience, fraternal charity, self sacrifice and perfect abandonment to God's will in all that they do and suffer" (32).

Infused contemplation is a supernatural gift of God that makes possible a direct and experiential contact with God. It is the perfection of pure charity. While it is true that contemplation always brings peace and strength to the soul, there are times when that peace seems "almost buried under pain and darkness and aridity." "The experience of God in infused contemplation is a flat contradiction of all the soul has imagined concerning him.... Infused contemplation then sooner or later brings with it a terrible interior revolution" (42). The light of God that illumines the soul becomes a "ray of darkness" (45). "The surest sign of infused contemplation behind the cloud of darkness is a *powerful, mysterious and yet simple attraction which holds the soul prisoner in this darkness and obscurity*" (51). Though afflicted and filled with a sense of defeat, the soul has no desire to withdraw from this obscurity and aridity. The conviction grows that true joy and peace "are *to be found somewhere in this lonely night of aridity and faith*" (52).

The concluding section of the book deals with the danger of quietism, a topic much discussed in the mid-twentieth century. The quietist is the opposite of the true contemplative. Such a person seeks "to empty himself of all love and all knowledge and remain inert in a kind of spiritual vacuum" (71). Whereas Christian contemplation is the perfection of love, quietism is the exclusion of all love. The quietist wants to depend on himself or herself. It is an attitude of selfishness. The contemplative lets go of all care and trusts not in self but in God, praying, "*Purify our minds not only of sin but of all the vanity of earthly wisdom and make us docile instruments of Thy all-Holy will in simplicity and truth, that the brightness of thy son Jesus may shine in our lives and give Thee glory"* (78–79). WHS

Notes

1. Burns and Oates of London published it in 1950 with minor revisions. The St. Mary's version concluded with a prayer to the Virgin Mary; the Burns and Oates edition, being in their *Pater Noster* series, concludes with a prayer to the Father. Templegate published the Burns and Oates edition in the United States in 1951 and again in 1960. In 1978 Templegate did another edition in a different (somewhat clumsy to handle) edition, which included a series of woodcuts. In 1981 Templegate produced still another edition in more conventional and manageable size and illustrated with some of Merton's drawings.

2. In *Cistercian Contemplatives*, written about the same time, Merton speaks briefly about contemplation.

3. In this article, quotations from *What Is Contemplation?* are taken from the Templegate edition of 1981. The mention of "seeds of contemplation" in this text will offer Merton the title for his next work on contemplation: *Seeds of Contemplation* (1949).

WHAT OUGHT I TO DO?
Sayings of the Desert Fathers

Lexington, Ky.: Stamperia del Santuccio, 1959. 35 pp.

Thomas Merton's original collection of sayings of the desert fathers, which later was expanded into *The Wisdom of the Desert* (1960), is a beautiful volume printed in a limited edition by Merton's friend Victor Hammer on his hand press, consisting of a short introduction by Merton and one hundred sayings taken from volume 73 of Migne's *Patrologia Latina*. The compilation is closely associated with Merton's novitiate conferences on early monastic sources; the collection is referred to extensively in Merton's notes to the conferences on "Cassian and the Fathers."

The first seventy-five sayings are taken from the most authoritative Latin collection of the *Verba Seniorum* (*Words of the Elders*), book 5 of the *Vitae Patrum* (*Lives of the Fathers*), reprinted by Migne; these include about 650 sayings and stories, arranged in eighteen *libelli* (booklets or chapters) according to topic. Merton's collection follows the order of the chapters, with some rearrangement of material within the individual *libelli*. He draws most heavily from the chapters on discretion (sixteen sayings) and

humility (ten sayings) and the opening chapter concerning the monastic way of life (nine sayings). Other sayings are taken from chapters on self-control (six sayings); patient courage and vigilance (five sayings each); lack of ostentation and refusal to judge (four sayings each); quiet, unceasing prayer, and patience (three sayings each); nonpossessiveness and generosity (two sayings each); and compunction, obedience, and charity (a single saying each). None of the sayings is drawn from the fifth chapter, on temptations against chastity, and none from the last, which initially might seem surprising since its title is *"De praevidentia sive contemplatione"* ("On Foresight or Contemplation"), until one notices that the stories generally are about various kinds of miraculous insights, whereas Merton's stress in the collection is on the ordinariness of the desert fathers and the down-to-earth qualities of their spirituality.

The final twenty-five entries are somewhat more heterogeneous. They include a group of five (nos. 76–79, 81) from book 7, a collection of forty-four chapters organized principally according to vices to be combated, with a saying from book 5 inserted (no. 80); and one following (no. 82) from book 6, a short collection of four chapters that is a kind of appendix to book 5; eight more (nos. 83–89, 96) come from book 3, a collection that is not divided into chapters; and ten more are taken from book 5 (nos. 90–95, 97–100). It should be noted that the various collections overlap and frequently one of the sayings selected is found in more than one collection, but in virtually every case the version translated by Merton can be determined by the variants in the versions and/or by the sequence in which it appears.

There are two basic types of *verba*. First, there are sayings proper, usually though not always brief, of the elder (the *abba* or *senex*), either presented by itself or in response to the request of a disciple for a "word of salvation," or occasionally for advice on a particular situation. This type of saying is exemplified in its purest form in the first of the sayings translated (the second in book 5 of Migne), the source of the title of Merton's collection: The appealing character of Abbot Pambo asks Abbot

Anthony, "What ought I to do?" and Anthony responds, "Have no confidence in your own virtuousness. Do not worry about a thing once it has been done. Control your tongue and your belly" (*What Ought I to Do?* 7). (It is worth noting that in the final selection Bishop Theophilus of Alexandria comes to this same Pambo for a word, but the elder tells his disciples, "If he is not edified by my silence, there is no hope that he will be edified by my words" [36], a conclusion that both provides a kind of symmetry to the collection and ends the series of "words" by emphasizing the monastic priority of silence over speech.) The second category of *verba* consists of stories about the desert fathers, generally illustrating the practice of some virtue, though occasionally a failure in practice, with particular emphasis on the dangers of spiritual pride, often manifested in imprudent asceticism. The two categories are not rigidly separable, as often a narrative will include a "word" from one of the fathers that solves a difficulty within the story or clarifies its meaning. About 60 percent of the *verba* selected by Merton for this collection belong to the first category and about 40 percent to the second.

The sayings and stories sometimes are about particular fathers (and mothers) referred to by name, sometimes about anonymous elders.[1] Slightly over half of the selections in this collection refer to particular figures: Anthony, Arsenius, and the rest. In some cases little more is known about the person than the name, but in others an individual personality emerges vividly, as with Abbot Moses, who appears at an assembly called to pass judgment on an erring brother and compares his own sins to the sand running out behind him from a basket filled with holes (no. 32 [15]); or John the Dwarf, who wishes to become an angel needing no food or shelter and has to repent for his presumption (no. 36 [16–17]); or Isaac, who flees when he is sought for ordination, only to have his hiding place discovered by an ass (no. 84 [30]). The appealing character of Abbot Pastor (or Poemen, as he is known in Greek, retained in book 3 and so occasionally here) is revealed through the sheer number of the sayings attributed to him and the gentle humanity that they exemplify.

The sayings and stories that Merton chooses show both variety and consistency. They emphasize simplicity, as in Pastor's saying that the two things a monk must hate are an easy life and vainglory (no. 5 [8]); stability, as in the anonymous saying that as a transplanted tree cannot bear fruit, neither can a monk who frequently moves (no. 24 [12]); flexibility, as in an anonymous elder's reference to different biblical figures exemplifying different virtues (no. 3 [7]); realism, as in Pastor's saying that virtue is exhibited in temptations (no. 23 [12]); tough-mindedness, as when Theodore of Pherme refuses to give a "word" to a particular monk whom he recognizes as "a trader in words, [who] seeks to glory in the words of another" (no. 27 [12]); refusal to judge, as when an elder warns the chaste not to judge fornicators, for the same Lord who said not to be unchaste also said not to judge (no. 33 [15]); humility, exemplified by Pambo's statement at the point of death that he had scarcely made a beginning in following the Lord (no. 6 [8]); true asceticism, as when Ammonas tells a severe brother that reciting the prayer of the publican (the source of the "Jesus Prayer") is more efficacious than feats of spiritual athleticism (no. 35 [16]). There are occasional flashes of humor, as when the devil appears to one monk and claims to be the angel Gabriel, only to be told that he must have come to the wrong person as the monk had done nothing to deserve an angelic visit (no. 70 [25]). There also are rare glimpses of spiritual elevation, as when the dying Abbot Bessarion says, "The monk should be all eye, like the cherubim and seraphim" (no. 52 [21]); or when Abbot Joseph, raising his hands to heaven with fingers like ten flaming lamps, says to Abbot Lot, "Why not be totally changed into fire?" (no. 55 [21]). POC

SEE ALSO DESERT; *WISDOM OF THE DESERT.*

Notes

1. In the Greek collections of the *Apophthegmata,* these categories are kept separate: the Alphabetical collection groups the sayings according to the figure named, while a separate Anonymous collection includes sayings and stories not attached to a particular person; the Latin collections, organized by topic, mix the two groups, though generally in each chapter *verba* associated with named elders precede those that are anonymous.

WHAT THINK YOU OF CARMEL?

**Trappist, Ky.: Abbey of Gethsemani, 1962.
11 pp.**

This small booklet (6″ x 3″) discusses Carmelite sanctity for the Carmel of the Most Holy Incarnation in Durham, North Carolina. It was written to commemorate the 400th anniversary of the reform of Carmel by St. Teresa of Avila that began August 24, 1562. Thomas Merton plunges directly into the question: "Is the desire for sanctity compatible with Christian humility and self-forgetfulness?" (*What Think You of Carmel?* 1). The presumption is that a young woman entering a Carmelite convent must have, somehow or other, the desire to be a saint. But can such a desire be free from unconscious self-seeking and spiritual pride? Assuming that the desire to be a saint is a desire for moral perfection, does not such a desire contain a hidden temptation to pride: the implicit desire to be better than other people? Can the demon of hidden pride be exorcised by the plea that one is in Carmel to save others through prayer? Even then, it must still be asked: Does this presuppose that precisely because one's prayer for them has a special efficacy, one is so much better than others?

The only answer to these questions is an existential one: actual acquaintance with "the joyous, humble, thoroughly simple nuns who live in these convents, with their abundant common sense, their unfailing humor, their generous and self-effacing love" (2). It is true that the cloistered life may attract women not properly adjusted to a full social life who see the cloister as a shelter from worldly cares. What they soon find out, however, is that convent life intensifies the difficulties of social adjustment. "The common life of a cloistered community demands constant attentiveness, politeness, charity, humility, self-sacrifice and thoughtfulness of others" (3). There is a kind of built-in selective process in convent life: the four years before final vows can help an unfit person, as well as her superiors, discover that this is not the life for her.

Merton points out that the Carmelite convent is not a place for seeking out extraordinary graces from God. "The life of the Carmelite nun is nothing but the life of the Gospels, lived under certain very definite and specialized conditions" (4). Prayer and self-denial are central. The liturgy (the monastic office and the Mass) is at the heart of Carmelite life, but so too is interior, meditative, contemplative prayer. Contemplative prayer is a mystery of God's grace, unattainable by mere human efforts. The life of Carmel disposes one toward such prayer, though not all receive that gift. What is most important for a Carmelite is the ability to forget and renounce her own self in order to live by a rule, by obedience, by love. Love is the most powerful force that exists. "The love of God for His creation, and the responding love of those creatures of His, is the inner secret of the universe" (7). "The Carmelite nun offers herself to the fire of God's merciful love, that He may kindle that fire in the 'hearth' of the convent, and so give light and warmth to all those who, albeit, secretly and spiritually, are within the radius of that convent's action" (7).

The aim of Carmelite life is to become not "something," but "nothing," with an emptiness that can be transformed into the fullness of Christ. This brings Merton back to the question posed at the beginning of the booklet about the "desire to be a saint." The paradox, he suggests, is that one who aspires to be a saint in Carmel "must from the very beginning renounce even the most secret desire *to see herself* as a saint or to be acknowledged as one" (10). Her interior life is life in Christ. "The guiding star of her life is a total, uncompromising faith and trust in Him which shows her, at every moment, that *love is enough*" (11). WHS

WHEN PROPHECY STILL HAD A VOICE: *The Letters of Thomas Merton and Robert Lax*

Edited by Arthur W. Biddle. Lexington: University Press of Kentucky, 2001. xx+448 pp.

This volume of the complete extant correspondence between Thomas Merton and Robert Lax, a record of Merton's longest and deepest friendship, consists of a total of 346 letters dating from June 17, 1938, the year the two men graduated from Columbia, through December 8, 1968, two days before Merton's death. The title is taken from a November 25, 1957, letter from Merton to Lax, then back in Olean, New York, advising him to "Visit all the haunts, stamp in all the snows, pause beneath all the trees & drive back & forth to Bradford as in the days of old when prophecy still had a voice" (*When Prophecy*, 139). Of the total of 346 letters, 191 by Merton and 155 by Lax, 237 had not previously appeared in print. Some of these are brief notes but the majority are substantial and add significantly to knowledge of the relationship. In particular, the 102 letters (forty-seven by Merton) between 1950 and December 1961 cover a gap not represented at all in *A Catch of Anti-Letters* (which begins with letters of 1962) or in *The Road to Joy*, the second volume of Merton's collected letters, which includes forty-three letters to Lax but none from this period. *When Prophecy Still Had a Voice* restores omissions found in a considerable number of the letters in the two previous collections, all helpfully marked by the editor, who also provides a brief introduction, headnotes to the major sections of the volume and to individual letters, a detailed chronology for both men, and a wide-ranging interview with Lax that closes the volume. It is now possible to get a reasonably comprehensive picture of this mutually enriching friendship, which was maintained largely through correspondence.

The correspondence is arranged in five periods. The first consists of sixty letters (forty-four by Merton) beginning in the summer of 1938, as the two friends try to settle into life after college. The letters are filled with references to friends, books, movies, various writing projects, political events, especially the early phases of the Second World War, and eventually on Merton's part, religious concerns. The letters are slangy and allusive from the start, and in late 1940 begin to show the influence of James Joyce in their punning and double-talk, which will be a standard feature of the friends' later correspondence — though the final letter in the group, dated December 6, 1941, in which Merton announces his plans to enter Gethsemani, reverts to a style of grammatical as well as thematic sobriety: "It is time to stop arguing with the seven guys who argue inside my own head and be completely quiet in front of the face of Peace" (84).

The second section, covering Merton's first ten years in the monastery, consists of only twenty letters, just eight of them by Merton, whose correspondence during this period was restricted by the Cistercian rule that limited sending and receiving mail to four times a year. Merton's letters, generally one per year at most (two from 1948, the year of *The Seven Storey Mountain*), mainly focus on his twin themes of life as a writer and life with God, with reflections both on the congruence and the tension between them. Lax's letters, generally briefer, and almost all from the latter half of the period, after he too had become a Catholic in 1943, detail his own geographical and spiritual odyssey, from the *New Yorker* and Friendship House, to a Hollywood studio, to western Canada and the Cristiani Family Circus, back to Olean for a period of intense work on what would become *Circus of the Sun*, and eventually to France, where he would spend a good part of the early 1950s. Though less explicitly and less frequently than does Merton, Lax also articulates his maturing spiritual vision during this period, as when he declares that "finding the Living God in the Scriptures . . . finding Him in the teacher and the student; the good performer and the beholder" is "the only way to teach" (111).

The third section consists of sixty-seven letters, almost evenly divided between the two correspondents, from mid-1956 through the end of 1960 (as well as two 1953 letters from Lax, at that time still in France). The increased volume is due largely to Lax's return to America and involvement with *Jubilee*, the magazine founded by their mutual friend Ed Rice, for which Lax had been serving as "roving editor" in Europe, as well as with his own offbeat poetry broadside *Pax*. Merton was a frequent contributor to both publications, and much of the correspondence is concerned with poems and articles submitted and requested, though in the process the friends discuss an increasingly broad range of topics: illnesses, personal encounters, mutual friends and friends of one or the other, world events, reading, and writing. Merton's first letter to Lax during this period, dated April 19, 1956, is addressed to "Oh Lax," signed "Lv — in the Lord. Merton" (121–22), and is written in standard grammar, but the next, from early June, begins "First of all it comes soon for Rice the paperish manuscrib I have wrought concerning the secret harps" and is signed "Uncle Pete" (122–23). From this point onward the two will match one another's inventiveness with wacky names, fractured syntax, and wildly extravagant, sometimes semicoherent language — obviously a delightfully welcome form of release from routine for both men, Merton especially, perhaps, since his routines were the more restrictive. Even when they were being most serious, the form they had adopted would keep them from taking themselves, each other, and their own problems or those of the world too seriously. This period is marked by significant turning points for both men, as Merton is drawn both toward greater solitude and deeper involvement with the world, and Lax finds his poetic voice in *Circus of the Sun*, which Merton praises as "one of the few if only religious books of any value that has skidded off the slides in these United Steaks for many years" (182).

Well over half the letters in the collection (199 of them) date from the last eight years of Merton's life, divided into two sections of four years each. While eighty-two of these, completely or in part, have already appeared in print, the majority now are available for the first time (though a number of these, especially from Lax, are brief notes). The fourth section consists of seventy-six letters, thirty-seven by Merton (eighteen previously published). Merton's interest in issues of war and peace emerges very prominently in these letters, three of which eventually were included by Merton in his mimeographed collection of "Cold War Letters," privately circulated among his friends as a way of circumventing the Trappist censorship. Merton also reports on his health, his reading, and events both ordinary (Fr. Innocent preaching on Sartre on the Feast of the Holy Innocents: "an interesting sermon and nobody slept," although "Fr Innocent hasn't read Sartre any more than any body else around here and kept calling him 'Sarter'" [234]) and extraor-

dinary (particularly his clandestine trip to New York City to meet D. T. Suzuki in July 1964 — a letter filled with references to the friends' old Columbia haunts [279–81]). Lax, meanwhile, has returned to Europe, first temporarily and then permanently, spending time on a number of Greek islands and finally settling on Kalymnos. (He would move to Patmos, where he remained until almost the end of his life, only after Merton's death.) Much of the correspondence from this period concerns this relocation. There is as well a good deal of discussion of the relationship between Catholicism and Orthodoxy. Also included are samples of Lax's later minimalist poetry, a style that prompts Merton's enthusiastic comment that "the book is so good that the typewriter ribbon gets darker with enthusiasm" (261).

The final section of the letters, from the period 1965–68, includes 123 letters, more than one-third of the total. Of these, forty-eight come from the last year of Merton's life, during most of which Lax was back in America, which made for a faster turnaround time between letters. The two writers continue to exchange literary work, with more poetry than prose coming from Merton. Merton's permanent move to the hermitage is related, prompting from Lax this response: "it is good to be a hermit. i too am a hermit. it is best. always be one" (313). A shared sense of the absurdities of contemporary life is illustrated by the exchange of various photos and advertisements clipped from newspapers and magazines, as well as by the increasingly surreal style of the letters, which often are tinged, especially on Merton's part, with bitterness at the immorality of the war in Southeast Asia and at some of the inanities of monastery and church, both the conservative reaction to conciliar reforms and some of the more superficial manifestations of "updating." The successive deaths of Columbia friends Ad Reinhardt, John Slate, and (in a house fire) Seymour Freedgood in late 1967 and early 1968 bring a heightened awareness of mortality and prompt perhaps the only letter in the final decade of the correspondence not written in double-talk, a brief note addressed to "oy, Merton," signed "Lax," and concluding, "We must pray for old Freedgood who was up in the flames & makes Slate & Reinhardt seem blessed in their birthdays. and always, every minute take care" (379). The year would end, of course, with the death of another member of the old Columbia crowd, in a guesthouse room in Thailand. In his last letter to Lax, now returned to Greece, Merton writes from Calcutta that the abbot has sent permission for "estencion of le voyage" and adds, "I bear in mente the winds of spring from Tokyop wafting the passengers to Athens and Mount Arthritis" (417). But the projected visit was not to be: on December 8, 1968, Lax wrote back, in a letter Merton would never receive, "learn as many breathings as possible from the meditative monks & whatever else can be done for recollection," and adds, "send me anyway your next address" (420). POC

SEE ALSO CATCH OF ANTI-LETTERS.

WILLIAMS, ROBERT LAWRENCE

Robert Williams, a young African-American tenor, wrote to Thomas Merton in March 1964 asking him to write a series of poems that Williams hoped to have set to music. He planned to hold a benefit concert on behalf of the National Foundation for African Students in which he himself would sing these songs. Merton wrote the poems ("Freedom Songs"), but Williams never got to sing them. Merton's letters to Williams are published in The Hidden Ground of Love. WHS

SEE ALSO "FREEDOM SONGS."

WISDOM

The ability to perceive the sacredness of the ordinary, the unity of the disparate, is regularly associated by Thomas Merton, especially in the last decade of his life, with the gift of wisdom. In his essay "Gandhi and the One-Eyed Giant" he describes wisdom as a way of knowing "which transcends and unites, . . . which dwells in body and soul together and which, more by means of myth, of rite, of contemplation, than by scientific experiment, opens the door to a life in which the individual is not lost in the cosmos

and in society but found in them" (Gandhi on Non-Violence, 1). This "sapiential" or "sophianic" consciousness responds to the world not as a detached, "objective" observer, but with an intuitive, participatory awareness of the "hidden wholeness" (Collected Poems, 363) of all reality, and with a willingness to allow this "transfigured, spiritualized and divinized cosmos" to become aware of itself and to "[utter] its praise of the Creator" (Disputed Questions, 20–21) in and through oneself — a vocation shared particularly by the contemplative and the poet.

Wisdom becomes an increasingly important category for Merton's thought in the last decade of his life for at least four reasons: it firmly roots him in his own Christian contemplative tradition; it serves as a point of contact and dialogue with the great traditions of the East; it provides a theological grounding for a sacramental view of creation; and it provides an alternative perspective to the analytical, quantitative, exploitative approach characteristic of scientific rationalism.

While Merton certainly is familiar with the association of the scriptural term "wisdom" (sophia, sapientia) with maxims of practical behavior such as those found in Proverbs, his customary use of the term is based on other biblical texts and contexts: wisdom as the first, and particularly in the Cistercian tradition the most exalted, of the seven gifts of the Holy Spirit listed in Isaiah 11; the Pauline contrast between human and divine wisdom in 1 Corinthians; and especially the personified figure of Wisdom as the creative agent of God in Proverbs 8 and the Wisdom of Solomon, a figure identified implicitly in the New Testament and explicitly by the church fathers with the Logos of John's Gospel, the preexistent Word of God through whom all things were made and who takes on human nature in the person of Jesus. From this standpoint, growth in wisdom is a process of more and more complete conformation to Christ, divine Wisdom incarnate, through sharing in the paschal mystery, "the wisdom given by His Spirit to those who have left all things to follow Him — the wisdom of the Cross" (Silence in Heaven, 20). It culminates in "an experience of God, an existential communion in His own intimate life which is Love Itself" (*New Man*, 109). For Merton, "Contemplative wisdom is...a living contact with the Infinite Source of all being, a contact not only of minds and hearts, not only of 'I and Thou,' but a transcendent union of consciousness in which man and God become, according to the expression of St. Paul, 'one spirit'" (*Faith and Violence*, 222).

Without in any way relinquishing or compromising this explicitly Christian, and christocentric, view of wisdom, Merton gradually comes to recognize a similar process operative in non-Christian contemplation. He writes, "In all religions it is more or less generally recognized that this profound 'sapiential' experience, call it gnosis, contemplation, 'mysticism,' 'prophecy,' or what you will, represents the deepest and most authentic fruit of the religion itself" (*Mystics and Zen Masters*, 204). This discovery of a comparable focus, especially in the religions of the East, on a concrete, intuitive, existential illumination that is at once perfect self-realization and a union beyond subject and object with the ground of all reality, opens the way to a fruitful dialogue focused not on abstract concepts and conflicting doctrines but on contemplative experience. Thus, Merton finds wisdom terminology particularly useful for articulating some of the common, or at least analogous, elements found in diverse traditions. While sensitive to the particular nuances of the various forms of Eastern thought, and careful to point out their differences with Christianity and among themselves, Merton is able to show how a sapiential orientation invariably is present in all authentic spiritual paths. It is with Buddhism, specifically with Zen, that the fruitfulness of Merton's method of correlation becomes most apparent, as Merton defines "the true purpose of Zen" as "awakening a deep ontological awareness, a wisdom-intuition (*Prajna*) in the ground of the being of the one awakened" (*Zen and the Birds of Appetite*, 48).

While the use of wisdom terminology has distinct advantages as a bridge between East and West, it also raises questions about the intrinsic relationship, if any, between Christian and non-Christian wisdom. Can the Christian identification of wisdom with Christ be reconciled with the non-Christian perception of wisdom? Though he is clear that there are significant differences in experience and articulation between Christian and non-Christian wisdom, Merton's whole approach to the issue suggests that this question can be answered affirmatively because creation itself is a manifestation of divine wisdom. For Merton, the very existence, order, life, and beauty of the universe, and of each creature within it, reflects the image of the Logos, the divine Wisdom, who made it: "The forms and individual characters of living and growing things, of inanimate beings, of animals and flowers and all nature, constitute their holiness in the sight of God. Their inscape is their sanctity. It is the imprint of His wisdom and His reality in them" (*New Seeds of Contemplation*, 30). This is the aspect of wisdom that Merton eventually liked to call the "sophianic," the epiphany of wisdom in creation and the corresponding human response, "the central wisdom that comes in tune with the divine and cosmic music" (*Guilty Bystander*, 3). Thus, there is a pattern of order, a revelatory dimension, within the structure of reality itself, prior to but in harmony with the positive revelation of Scripture and incarnation. This "cosmic revelation" is the key for integrating explicitly Christian wisdom with that not only of Eastern religions but also of pre-Christian Western thought and even of artists who may not be Christian but who share a fundamental sapiential consciousness. Merton's understanding of wisdom unites a deeply christocentric, incarnational faith with an openness to insights from all sources, a true catholicity, because the same mystery of Being that finds its definitive manifestation in Christ also is disclosed in many different forms through the natural or cosmic revelation available to all. From this Christian humanist perspective, all authentic human insight into reality is intrinsically related to Christ, for all truth participates in the infinite wisdom of the Logos, who became flesh in Jesus.

As important as this transcultural, transconfessional communion in wisdom is for Merton in and of itself, it assumes even greater significance in light of the present critical state of human development. One aspect of wisdom to which Merton returns again and again is the figure of Wisdom "at play" in creation, from Proverbs 8. He describes her memorably in "Hagia Sophia": "Sophia, the feminine child, is playing in the world, obvious and unseen, playing at all times before the Creator. Her delights are to be with the children of men. She is their sister. The core of life that exists in all things is tenderness, mercy, virginity, the Light, the Life considered as passive, as received, as given, as taken, as inexhaustibly renewed by the Gift of God. Sophia is Gift, is Spirit, *Donum Dei*. She is God-given and God Himself as Gift" (*Collected Poems*, 368). This association of wisdom with play and with the feminine is contrasted with the deadly seriousness of a pragmatic, utilitarian, "masculine" approach to life, in which everything is to have a clearly defined purpose. Wisdom celebrates the realm of delight, spontaneity, joy, freedom. It is pure gift, the antithesis of personal achievement, as Merton notes in describing theologian Karl Barth's love of Mozart in the opening pages of *Conjectures of a Guilty Bystander*, suggesting that Barth may have been "unconsciously seeking to awaken, perhaps, the hidden sophianic Mozart in himself, the central wisdom that comes in tune with the divine and cosmic music and is saved by love, yes, even by *eros*" (*Guilty Bystander*, 3).

Scientific knowledge, which basically is objective, analytical, abstract, and quantitative, has a legitimate, indeed indispensable, role to play in human life. When it is properly balanced with wisdom, there is personal, social, and cosmic harmony. The problem comes when science usurps the role of wisdom and claims to have all the answers or, rather, declares the questions raised by a sapiential perspective to be meaningless. This spiritual disorientation and restlessness always has been an inescapable part of the human condition, but in traditional societies has been held in check by the respect accorded to the sapiential dimension. Modern Western technological society, however, has tended to erode or even actively suppress such a respect, to emphasize control over rather than appreciation of and unity with what is known. Knowledge becomes a mode of power, and power the primary motive for knowledge.

Merton writes, "Without wisdom, without the intuition and freedom that enable man to return to the root of his being, science can only precipitate him still further into the centrifugal flight that flings him, in all his compact and uncomprehending isolation, into the darkness of outer space without purpose and without objective" (*Faith and Violence*, 224). Hence comes the urgent need to draw on all available resources of wisdom to counteract the distorted and dangerous preeminence of manipulative, self-aggrandizing knowledge by keeping alive "a kind of knowledge by identification, an intersubjective knowledge, a communion in cosmic awareness and in nature . . . a wisdom based on love" (*Literary Essays*, 108). POC

SEE ALSO CONTEMPLATION; *HAGIA SOPHIA*.

WISDOM OF THE DESERT, THE
New York: New Directions, 1960. ix+81 pp.

This is an expanded version of Thomas Merton's collection of sayings of the desert fathers, first published in a limited edition as *What Ought I to Do?* (1959). The introduction is rewritten and much expanded, and the number of sayings is increased from one hundred to 150. Merton placed it in the "better" category in his own evaluation of his works, the highest rank given.

Originally, Merton had asked Zen scholar D. T. Suzuki to write the introduction (*Hidden Ground of Love*, 562), as Merton saw remarkable points of comparison between the sayings and stories of these fourth-century monks and those of the Zen tradition, but the idea was vetoed by the censors of the order (*School of Charity*, 128). (Suzuki's commentary on this material, with a response by Merton, appeared separately as "Wisdom in Emptiness" in the *New Directions Annual* 17, and later was republished as part 2 of *Zen and the Birds of Appetite*.) Merton's own introduction conveyed his appreciation for the desert fathers as models for monastics and for Christians in general. He emphasized the social context of their solitary vocation as a sign of contradiction to the conformism and passivity of secular society (even, or especially, Christian secular society);

WISDOM OF THE DESERT

their withdrawal was, he writes, not an avoidance but a response to the problems of their time, a "personalism" that emphasized spiritual identity and relationships in opposition to a pragmatic individualism and a herd mentality. Refusing either to rule over others or to be ruled themselves, they sought a life of spiritual equality marked by "the charismatic authority of wisdom, experience and love" (*Wisdom of the Desert*, 5). Theirs was a search for true identity, the true self in Christ, a life of freedom discovered in conformity to the will of God; such a way of life required maturity, the renunciation of the ego, a search for purity of heart based in practical, unassertive wisdom. Despite their reputation in later eras, they emerge as the antithesis of wild-eyed fanatics in the simple proverbs and tales that make up the *Verba Seniorum*, from which Merton draws his selections. The sayings and stories emphasize the importance of experienced spiritual guidance, the integration of manual labor and spiritual aspiration, the centrality and superiority of charity to all the other virtues, the simplicity of their prayer, and the down-to-earth ordinariness of the solitaries who nevertheless were unreservedly committed to living the gospel. Merton concludes by seeing the desert fathers as models, not in specifics but in spirit, for another age with its own radical need "to ignore prejudice, defy compulsion and strike out fearlessly into the unknown" (24).

This expanded edition includes all of the sayings published the year before in the earlier collection, with the following changes and additions: In sixteen instances Merton rearranges the order of the sayings to correspond to the order as found in the original source in volume 73 of Migne's *Patrologia Latina*; in only two cases does he fail to correct the sequence to conform to Migne, and in both cases it is simply a case of two successive entries placed in reverse order. In only one instance does Merton reorder the original arrangement except to restore the original sequence (three sayings from near the end of the collection are moved back toward the middle). Within the original group of one hundred Merton inserts thirty additional sayings, occasionally singly (nos. 8, 17, 121, 123), more usually in groups (nos. 32–38, 58–

60, 67–70, 89–90, 113–18). Of these, thirteen are taken from book 5 of the *Vitae Patrum*, the collection Merton relied on most heavily in the original selection (eight of these from the chapter on discretion, already the most frequently excerpted), and seventeen from book 3. Then twenty additional sayings are added at the end of the new collection: four (nos. 131–33, 144) from book 7, six (nos. 134–39) from book 6 (otherwise represented by a single saying), eight (141–48) from book 5 (three more from the chapter on discretion), and the two final sayings (nos. 149–50) from book 3.

Slightly more than half of the new material consists of sayings; the rest are stories, some of them quite long, which make a significant contribution to the overall tone of the collection. Among the noteworthy additions in this expanded collection are these: the saying of Anthony that a highly praised monk who could not bear to be insulted was like a house with a strong gate but unlocked windows (no. 58 [46]); the saying of Abbess Syncletica that the struggles and successive joys of the spiritual life are like a fire that is at first smoky but finally full of light and heat (no. 89 [55]); the saying of Abbot Pastor that the way to avoid conflict is to ask oneself, "Who am I?" and to judge no one (no. 105 [63]); the advice to Abbot Evagrius not to speak until asked, which Evagrius called learning greater than any found in books (no. 117 [69–70]); the humorous story of the cenobites who were treated hospitably by a hermit and then criticized him for his high living, only to be put to a severe regimen by the next hermit they visited, to whom they conveyed the message from the first, "Be careful not to water the vegetables" (no. 8 [27–28]); the story of Abbot Anastasius, who appraised a book stolen from him at a high rate without revealing his ownership and thus converted the thief (no. 17 [30–31]); the story of the visiting monk who criticized monks working "for bread that perisheth" until he was left without a meal (no. 33 [36–37]); the story of a monk who resisted the temptations of a woman who came to his cell to seduce him (no. 90 [55–56]); the story of the monk who took the handles off his own baskets and gave them to another monk whose baskets had no handles (no. 121 [71]); the story of Macarius, who endured without complaint the accusations that he had fathered the child of a village girl but fled when the truth was discovered and he became an object of praise (no. 150 [79–81]). POC

SEE ALSO DESERT; *WHAT OUGHT I TO DO?*

WITNESS TO FREEDOM:
The Letters of Thomas Merton in Times of Crisis

Edited by William H. Shannon. New York: Farrar, Straus and Giroux, 1994. xiii+352 pp.

This is the fifth and final volume of the Thomas Merton letters. The dominant, recurring theme, as suggested by the title and in the introduction, is Merton's ongoing struggle to achieve authentic freedom in his life amidst a number of crises that he faced in the process. Outstanding among the crises that he dealt with were the struggle against war and his unsuccessful effort in the period from 1959 to 1960 to leave Gethsemani for what he hoped would be a more solitary life. The frustrations engendered by these struggles are evident in many of the letters.

The volume is divided into four sections, though with the realization that Merton's letters are like a river continually overflowing its banks — few of them can be restricted to a single topic. The first section deals with "art and freedom" and contains the remarkable letter to Victor Hammer explaining the meaning of "Hagia Sophia" (Holy Wisdom) and preparing the way for his long poem of that name.

The second section is about war and freedom, and among other things has a list of all the "Cold War Letters," and includes the text of all the "Cold War Letters" that did not appear in the four earlier volumes of the letters. (See "COLD WAR LETTERS.")

The third section, "Merton's Life and Works," has letters to his literary agent, Naomi Burton Stone, as well as letters to people at the various schools he attended. The correspondence with Stone is striking, as Merton moves from a strictly professional relationship to much more personal revelations of himself — his fears, his needs, his concerns. In their correspondence two strong personalities meet; the sparks fly at times, when they do not agree, but the sparks only helped to deepen their friendship. This section includes the letters centering on his vocational crisis of 1959–60 (when he almost was desperately begging for permission to leave Gethsemani for a place of greater solitude). There also is an unusual set of letters to fellow monk and fellow author Fr. Raymond Flanagan.

The fourth section, "Religious Thought and Dialogue," covers a wide range of topics. There are a number of single letters to individuals, some identified only by a first name. Also in this section one finds Merton's letters to Canadian author Leslie Dewart and to renowned scholar of Islam Louis Massignon, as well as his letters to a friend of Massignon, Herbert Mason.

The last of the letters is followed by a summarizing quotation from one of Merton's poems in *Figures for an Apocalypse*, intended to give a final articulation to the book's central theme, freedom: "And all the hopes that seem to founder in the shadows of the cross / Wake from a momentary sepulchre, and they are blinded by their freedom!" (*Witness to Freedom*, 340).

The book, completing, as it does, the five volumes of the published letters, concludes with a parody on the ending of *The Seven Storey Mountain: "Sic finis scribendi, non finis legendi."* WHS

WOMEN

The publication of the sixth volume of Thomas Merton's journals, *Learning to Love*, called attention to Merton's relationship with M., a student nurse assigned to care for him while he was hospitalized for back surgery in the spring of 1966. They fell in love, and for a short time in the spring and summer of 1966 their relationship absorbed Merton. With M., Merton seemed to experience, for the first time in his life, the intimacy of loving and letting himself be loved. Although their relationship was short-lived, it focuses attention, as do Merton's own observations, on the unsatisfactoriness of his earlier relationships with women as well as the complexity of his relationship with M. But there is more to be said about the subject of Merton and women.[1] And the importance of the subject did not escape Merton himself: "Man is most human, and most proves his humanity (I did not say his virility) by the quality of his relationship with woman" (*Guilty Bystander*, 172/190).

His mother, Ruth Jenkins Merton, died on October 3, 1921, when he was only six years old. Merton's memories of his mother, as recorded in *The Seven Storey Mountain*, are less than positive, perhaps colored by the abandonment he must have felt during her illness and at her death. Even years later, Merton was harsh in his judgment of his mother when he observed that "in the natural order, perhaps solitaries are made by severe mothers" (*Sign of Jonas*, 262).[2] After Ruth's death, Owen Merton became involved with Evelyn Scott, a writer, with whom Owen and Thomas lived for a time in Bermuda. In his autobiography, Merton glossed over the interlude in Bermuda, as he later glossed over his time at Cambridge, but it has come to light that the young Merton suffered at the hands of Evelyn Scott, who was said to have been cruel in her treatment of him. For her part, Scott reported, "Tom hated me. What was there to do?"[3] However, not all of Merton's early interactions with women were unsatisfactory. He remembered with affection his maternal grandmother, his aunts Maud, Kit, and Ka, and Madame Privat, with whom he stayed as a child in France (*Seven Storey Mountain*, 55–59). He also remembered the sister of a fellow student at Oakham, Anne Winser: "She was the quietest thing . . . dark and secret child. One does not fall in love with a child of thirteen, and I hardly remember even thinking of her. Yet the other day I realized that I had never forgotten her. . . . Actually, I think she is a symbol of the true (quiet) woman with whom I never really came to terms in the world, and because of this there remains an incompleteness that cannot be remedied" (*Water of Life*, 259). He also remembered friends such as Ginny Burton, who "was the symbol of the girl I ought to have fallen in love with but didn't (and she remains the image of one I really did love, with a love of companionship, not of passion)" (259).[4]

Some months earlier, on the vigil of his fiftieth birthday in January 1965, in a moment

Drawing by Thomas Merton

of reverie, as Merton looked back at his life, he had reflected on, among other things, his relationships with women — mindful of "relationships" gone sour — relationships driven by sexual urgency rather than love. "I suppose I regret most my lack of love, my selfishness and glibness (covering a deep shyness and need of love) with girls who, after all, did love me I think, for a time. My great fault was my inability really to believe it, and my efforts to get complete assurance and perfect fulfillment" (198). Continuing, he wrote in his journal, "So one thing on my mind is sex, as something I did not use maturely and well, something I gave up without having come to terms with it" (198). He was remembering the summer of 1940, his "last adultery" during the "blinding, demoralizing summer heat of Virginia . . . what madness and what futility. I remember walking on the beach with her the next day and not wanting to talk to her, talking only with difficulty, and not wanting to share *ideas,* or things I really loved" (198). The memory of that sexual encounter twenty-five years earlier was imprinted on Merton's memory, as were memories of himself at Cambridge, where he was "very selfish and unkind" to one woman and "a damned fool" with another. There were other memories of that year at Cambridge (1933–34) that must have haunted Merton: heavy drinking, promiscuous sex, and apparently getting a woman pregnant. The details remain unclear. If a child was born, nothing is known about the child or about the child's mother. What is known is this: upon entry into the monastery, each candidate was required to provide character references from places where he had lived. The headmaster at Oakham School wrote to the bishop of Nottingham that Merton left Cambridge with a possible paternity suit hanging over his head. Before monks make a simple profession, the order requires them to make a will. In his will Merton left assets in a saving shares account to be divided between his sister-in-law and his guardian, T. Izod Bennett, Esq. M.D., stipulating "this second half to be paid by him to the person mentioned to him by me in my letters, if that person can be found" (*School of Charity*, 8). Could this perhaps be a reference to the woman with whom Merton had conceived a child?

In November 1941, three years after his conversion and a few weeks before he entered the monastery, Merton admitted that he found being with women difficult. Considering the pros and cons of working at Friendship House in Harlem, Merton wrote this in his journal:

> There are a lot of things that would make it hard for me to serve God — First of all, being with girls: I might be the only man on the staff — with five or six girls, and that situation is, to me personally, intolerable. To someone else it might not be. To me, it is. It inevitably means you are a sort of center of a certain obscure kind of attention, and if you are not, you feel you are, or at any rate, I would either be so, or have to fight like a tiger with myself in order not to *try* to be. When I was there before, only for a few days, I got into a lot of situations where I was talking loud and asserting myself just because there were women around. I had eyes in the back of my head that followed the women around the room. But I don't want to get mixed up in such situations; I can't take them. If I am with women, I know they are women, every minute: and when I was in the world altogether, that was

what I liked to be aware of. Now I cannot dare to. When I am away from women, I do not think about them, however, and can be at peace to pray. (*Run to the Mountain*, 464–65)

This candid passage gives new meaning to the title given to the first volume of Merton's journals, *Run to the Mountain*, as the young Merton concludes that one way to deal with the problem of women is to get away from them.

But Merton did not get away from women by becoming a monk. Certainly his memories of earlier experiences and unresolved issues went with him into the monastery, only to resurface later, as illustrated by his wrestling with his past as his fiftieth birthday approached. Merton continued to notice women, as his journal entries illustrate. Poet Lawrence Ferlinghetti, who met Merton in San Francisco as he was on his way to Asia in 1968, recalls that "as [they] sat at a table in the front window of Malvina Coffee Shop, [Merton] was quite interested in any beautiful woman who walked by." "A natural Trappist interest — why not?" Ferlinghetti quips.[5]

Natural Trappist interest or not, it is a fact that Merton continued to notice and comment on women. One particularly significant example of Merton's attentiveness to the women he sees occurs in his original account of his experience at Fourth and Walnut:

> It is not a question of proving to myself that I either dislike or like the women one sees in the street. The fact of having a vow of chastity does not oblige one to argument on this point — no special question arises. I am keenly conscious, not of their beauty (I hardly think I saw anyone really beautiful by special standards) but of their humanity, their woman-ness. But what incomprehensible beauty is there, what secret beauty that would perhaps be inaccessible to me if I were not dedicated to a different way of life. It is as though by chastity I had come to be married to what is most pure in all the women of the world and to taste and sense the secret beauty of their girl's hearts as they walked in the sunlight — each one secret and good and lovely in the sight of God —

never touched by anyone, nor by me, nor by anyone, as good as and even more beautiful than the light itself. For the woman-ness that is in each of them is at once original and inexhaustibly fruitful bringing the image of God into the world. In this each one is Wisdom and Sophia and Our Lady — (my delights are to be with the children of men!). (*Search for Solitude*, 182)

What follows this revealing entry is a note to Proverb, the young Jewish girl, belonging to the same race as St. Anne, who appeared to him in a dream earlier that month. Merton had written a letter to her in his journal on March 4, 1958, in which he said, "How grateful I am to you for loving in me something which I thought I had entirely lost, and someone who, I thought, I had long ago ceased to be.... I treasure, in you, the revelation of your virginal solitude" (176). Merton wrote to Proverb again after "meeting" her at Fourth and Walnut, where he "saw" her "in a different place, in a different form, in the most unexpected circumstances" (182). Merton's encounter with woman was taking another form, a spiritual form, symbolized by Proverb, at once Wisdom and Sophia and Our Lady.

Merton's relationship with M. was neither an encounter with a dream figure nor an experience of "woman-ness" in the abstract. M. was real and unique and responsive. With her, Merton was able to share not only deep passion but also what was in his heart *and* mind, if only for a brief time, as *Learning to Love* shows. *Learning to Love* (as well as *The Other Side of the Mountain*, with its few but highly significant references to his relationship with M.), "A Midsummer Diary for M." (published in *Learning to Love*), and *Eighteen Poems* tell the story — from Merton's perspective, of course — of their relationship and offer some insight into the meaning it had for Merton.

A discussion of Merton and women would be unbalanced if it did not reflect, even if all too briefly, on Merton's many other friendships with women. As a monk, Merton enjoyed long-lasting working relationships and deep friendships with women. Merton's relationship with Naomi Burton Stone began as a relationship between literary agent and client and over

the years grew into a warm, although occasionally heated, relationship. Her candid appraisal of his work — she did not spare a critical word when it was needed — was matched by strong personal affection and, on occasion, a readiness to dispense some motherly advice. Writing in his journal in 1965, Merton noted that he had gotten "a very fine letter" from Naomi: "Full of mature realistic understanding, and feminine comfort — the warmth that cannot come from a man, and that is so essential." That insight led to an admission: "Psychologically, my doubt is based in this giant, stupid rift in my life, the *refusal* of woman which is a fault in my chastity (and in the chastity of so many religious!). But I am learning to accept this love (of Naomi, for instance) even if it means admitting a certain loss" (*Water of Life*, 281).

Almost as long-lasting was Merton's relationship with Sr. Therese Lentfoehr, with whom Merton shared a correspondence that began in 1948 and continued until his death, although Sr. Therese's overly ardent admiration for Merton hardly made for a true friendship. Nevertheless, he shared much about his work with her. Sr. Therese read his work with appreciation and carefully preserved it as Merton sent and she saved his manuscripts. There were other women too, strong women whose vision and witness inspired and challenged Merton and supported him in friendship: Catherine de Hueck Doherty, Dorothy Day, and Mary Luke Tobin, S.L. There were women with whom he corresponded who became friends: Etta Gullick, Hildegard Goss-Mayr, and Sr. Emmanuel. There was Rosemary Radford Ruether, with whom Merton enjoyed a short but very intense correspondence. And, of course, there was Tommie O'Callaghan, who welcomed Merton into her home and circle of family and friends, and who visited him often with food and friends in tow. Merton appointed Tommie O'Callaghan and Naomi Burton Stone (as well as Jay Laughlin) as his literary trustees.

Although this by no means exhausts the list of women with whom Merton shared ideas and friendship, it does illustrate Merton's capacity for friendship with women. At different times in his life they offered him perspective, inspiration, counsel, support, concern, challenge, and affection. Certainly Merton continued to learn some things about women that he did not know when, in 1941, he "ran to the mountain."

In the late 1960s Merton, like many others, began to reflect on women's roles. His reflections focused on the situation of women religious, and in conferences and retreats in Kentucky and California he talked about the "feminine mystique." At Gethsemani in May 1968 he challenged the male and female stereotypes. Women are not "passive" and "mysterious." Stereotypes of gender and race are "not true" (*Springs of Contemplation*, 162). "I think you have an absolute duty to rebel, for the good of the Church itself. Otherwise, you are creating and perpetuating this image of the mysterious, veiled, hidden woman who is an 'enclosed garden.' The truth is not that there's all this 'femininity' locked up in a convent. The truth is that there are *people* loving God" (163). In the beginning, religious life was "a real liberation" for women, "a chance to be a *person*," but that no longer was the case (164). Merton was only beginning to work out the ideas expressed here. One wonders what he would say about women today. CMB

> SEE ALSO *EIGHTEEN POEMS*; *LEARNING TO LOVE*; *SEXUALITY*; *SPRINGS OF CONTEMPLATION*.

Notes

1. Two issues of *The Merton Seasonal* have explored the subject of "Merton and Women": vol. 15, no. 1 (winter 1990); vol. 17, no. 1 (winter 1992). Especially notable is Bonnie B. Thurston, "'I Never Had a Sister': Merton's Friendships with Women," *The Merton Seasonal* (winter 1992): 4–8. Thurston takes her title from Merton's comment to Etta Gullick: "I never had a sister, and really I have felt this as a kind of lack" (*Hidden Ground of Love*, 353). Thurston contends that Merton's friendships with women, particularly in the 1950s and 1960s, helped to fill this lack of a feminine perspective in Merton's life.

2. See also *Entering the Silence*, 392.

3. Michael Mott, *The Seven Mountains of Thomas Merton* (Boston: Houghton Mifflin, 1984), 26.

4. It is worth noting that the same month (June 1965), when Merton was remembering and writing in his journal about Anne Winser and Ginny Burton, he also was reading Karl Stern's *Flight from Woman*: "Some fascinating material (loaded word—*mater!*) especially in the chapter on Descartes" (*Water of Life*, 260). He not only mentions Stern's book in his journal but also writes about it to Sr. Mary Luke Tobin.

5. "Lawrence Ferlinghetti," in Paul Wilkes, ed., *Merton, by Those Who Knew Him Best* (San Francisco: Harper & Row, 1984), 31.

WOODS, SHORE, DESERT: A Notebook, May 1968

Santa Fe, N.Mex.: Museum of New Mexico Press, 1982. xiv+58 pp.

This is the last selection of journal writing, which Thomas Merton himself prepared for publication. In doing so, Merton drew from two sources: a small notebook that he kept during a visit to California and New Mexico, May 6–20, 1968, and two additional journal entries that he made after returning home and continuing to reflect on an "experience, a pilgrimage, memories of which keep coming back in recurrent flashes and impressions" (*Other Side of the Mountain*, 118). Later, Merton dictated onto tape the notebook entries he made during his trip (May 6–20, 1968) and the two journal entries (May 22 and 30, 1968). During the summer Merton prepared a "manuscript" comprised of a cut-and-pasted version of "Day of a Stranger," which had been published in the *Hudson Review* (summer 1967), and the typescript of "Woods, Shore, Desert." Though Merton planned to publish the two works in one volume, both remained unpublished for more than a decade after Merton's death in 1968. *Day of a Stranger* was published as a book in 1981, and in 1983 *Woods, Shore, Desert* appeared, with a foreword by Br. Patrick Hart and an introduction and notes by Joel Weishaus.[1] Both books included a selection of Merton's photographs. *Woods, Shore, Desert* opens with a "Prelude" consisting of four quotations (three from the Astavakra Gita and one from the Orthodox writer Yelchaninov) as well as several pages of brief notes and talking points for the conferences that Merton was about to give at Redwoods Abbey. This is followed by notebook entries and journal entries that recount Merton's memories of his visit to Redwoods.

An itinerary of Merton's trip, drawn up by Br. Patrick Hart and Robert E. Daggy, is included in the book. On May 6, Merton had traveled to Eureka, California, and Our Lady of the Redwoods Abbey in Whitethorn, California, where he gave a set of conferences to the Trappist nuns living there. On May 15, he traveled to San Francisco, where he visited briefly with Lawrence Ferlinghetti, and then flew to

Albuquerque, New Mexico, on May 17. There he visited the Monastery of Christ in the Desert in Abiquiu, New Mexico. On May 20, Merton returned to Albuquerque and flew back to Louisville. The trip was the first of several that Merton would make in 1968 before his death in Bangkok, Thailand, on December 10, 1968.

Pacific shoreline, photograph by Thomas Merton

Interspersed throughout the book are photographs that Merton took during the trip, including several shot from the plane. It was John Howard Griffin who first introduced Merton to photography and who observed, "The camera became in his hands, almost immediately, an instrument of contemplation."[2] The photographs in *Woods, Shore, Desert*, together with vivid verbal descriptions, offer striking evidence of Merton's attention to his surroundings. Throughout his journey he was looking around and recording what he saw on film, in his notebook, and in his memory. Flying out of O'Hare, on the second leg of his trip to California, in a "big fish with tail fins elevated in light smog" (*Woods, Shore, Desert*, 6), Merton looked out to see the snow-covered mountains and the "dark profile of a river in snow," and found himself reading the "calligraphy of snow and rock from the air" as he flew over Idaho, Utah, Nevada, and California (7). Some days later, as he is flying to Albuquerque, he notes that the "snow suddenly gives place to a copper colored desert" (21). In words and photos Merton captures the vistas of California's forests and coastlines, the grandeur of New Mexico's rocky canyons, and the beauty of ordinary things everywhere: leaves, tree trunks, a

stretch of beach littered with washed-up debris. Among the shots of landscape and still lifes is a photo of Georgia O'Keeffe and Peter Nabokov, taken in New Mexico. Merton's photos and entries reveal his sense of place — betraying an awareness nurtured during many years in the monastery and then in his hermitage.

Merton not only was looking around, but also was looking ahead, keeping an eye out for a suitable site for a hermitage. Merton's longing for ever deeper solitude together with the apparent ease with which visitors found him at Gethsemani combined to produce an interest in finding another site. California appealed to him. More immediately on his mind was his trip to Asia. He already was preparing for the journey in his reading, which included Hindu sages and Chinese poets.

Merton also was continuing to look within and to record insights, as was his way. On May 16, a traveling day, Merton writes, "I am the utter poverty of God. I am His emptiness, littleness, nothingness, lostness. When this is understood, my life in His freedom, the self-emptying of God in me is the fullness of grace. A love for God that knows no reason because He is the fullness of grace. A love for God that knows no reason because He is God; a love without measure, a love for God as personal" (24). On May 30, back at Gethsemani, Merton reflects on monasticism and on his own calling:

> In our monasticism, we have been content to find our way to a kind of peace, a simple undisturbed thoughtful life. And this is certainly good, but is it good enough? I, for one, realize that now I need more. Not simply to be quiet, somewhat productive, to pray, to read, to cultivate leisure — *otium sanctum!* There is a need of effort, deepening, change and transformation. Not that I must undertake a special project of self-transformation or that I must "work on myself." In that regard, it would be better to forget it. Just to go for walks, live in peace, let change come quietly and invisibly on the inside. But I do have a past to break with, an accumulation of inertia, waste, wrong, foolishness, rot, junk, a great need of clarification of mindfulness, or rather of no mind — a re-

turn to genuine practice, right effort, need to push on to the great doubt. Need for the Spirit. Hang on to the clear light! (48) CMB

SEE ALSO *DAY OF A STRANGER; OTHER SIDE OF THE MOUNTAIN.*

Notes

1. The text of the notebook "Woods, Shore, Desert" has been published in its entirety in *The Other Side of the Mountain*, 89–114. A comparison of the original notebook and the book *Woods, Shore, Desert* shows little difference, just a few minor revisions.

2. John Howard Griffin, "Les Grandes Amitiés," *Continuum* 7 (summer 1969): 29 (cited by Joel Weishaus in his introduction to *Woods, Shore, Desert*, xi).

WORLD

In traditional Christian teaching as commonly understood, "the world" was something to be avoided, part of the unholy trinity, along with the flesh and the devil. To "leave the world," as one would by entering a monastery, was to escape from a host of snares, threats, and temptations. Such an outlook tended to draw a sharp distinction between the natural and the supernatural, the material and the spiritual. It also had the effect of relegating laypeople to a necessarily second-class spirituality, if not worse, since they unavoidably were in contact with the world on a regular basis. In more recent times a reaction to this negative depiction of the world has developed, taking the form of a strong affirmation of this-worldly existence, a celebration of the secular, the physical, the mundane, the world of the senses. This new attitude perhaps is epitomized by the comment that the most numinous place in America — the spot most filled with divinity — is the bargain basement at Macy's.

Thomas Merton's response to these divergent attitudes is quite indicative of his entire spiritual teaching. Its starting point can be found in the title of the fourth chapter of *New Seeds of Contemplation*, "Everything That Is, Is Holy." In this chapter he writes, "In His love we possess all things and enjoy fruition of them, finding Him in them all. And thus as we go about the world, everything we meet and everything we see and hear and touch, far from defiling, purifies us and plants in us something

more of contemplation and of heaven" (*New Seeds of Contemplation*, 25). In this profoundly sacramental vision, so characteristic of Merton, creation is a sign of the Creator, an epiphany of the transcendent, and earthly things are windows through which one may catch a glimpse of God. Moreover, Merton repeatedly points out that this is the genuine teaching of Christian tradition, which consistently has opposed any Manichaean rejection of material reality. He traces this "natural contemplation, which beholds the divine in and through nature" ("Inner Experience," 4:298), back to the Greek fathers of the fourth century, and elsewhere speaks of the great contemplative theologians and artists of the High Middle Ages — Aquinas, Scotus, Bonaventure, Dante — as having "a basically world-affirming and optimistic view of man, of his world and his work"; for them, "the created world itself is an epiphany of divine wisdom and love" (*World of Action*, 147). In his rejection of a negative view toward the material world, Merton certainly could be considered an advocate of what has come to be called "creation spirituality."

However, this does not mean that Merton simply embraces a glorification of the secular without reservation. He comments, "The stereotype of world rejection is now being firmly replaced by a collection of equally empty stereotypes of world affirmation in which I, for one, have very little confidence" (149). Having shown that the tradition is basically world-affirming, he goes on to examine the more negative elements that undeniably also are to be found in traditional teaching, to see what they could mean, if and how they can be reconciled with a sacramental view of the world, and what value they might still be able to convey if properly interpreted.

Merton is no unqualified apologist for the church of the past. He can be, and often is, fiercely critical of the compromises, evasions, and even betrayals of the gospel that mark Christian history. He is well aware that hostility toward the world often has been a mark of complacent arrogance or of timid insecurity. But he also realizes that this is not always the case. There is a healthy wariness toward the world as well. The problem, he finds, is not in created reality itself but in our attitude toward it, our relationship to it. "The fulfillment we find in creatures belongs to the reality of the created being, a reality that is from God and belongs to God and reflects God. The anguish we find in them belongs to the disorder of our desire which looks for a greater reality in the object of our desire than is actually there: a greater fulfillment than any created thing is capable of giving. Instead of worshipping God through His creation we are always trying to worship ourselves by means of creatures" (*New Seeds of Contemplation*, 26).

The danger is basically one of substituting a means for an end, of absolutizing what is relative, which is a good working definition of idolatry. The term "the world" as it is frequently used in the tradition is thus a kind of shorthand for a flawed perception of reality, a distorted view that sees the world not as it comes forth from the hand of God but as we try to reorder it to suit ourselves; it is a world of egocentric desires in which we try to force reality, including other persons, to revolve around ourselves; when it refuses to do so, in frustration we maltreat and foul and profane it, transforming it into an image of our interior disorder. It is that world which is to be fled — a false, unreal mockery of God's creation. Merton writes, "It is not Christianity, far from it, that separates man from the cosmos, the world of sense and of nature. On the contrary, it is man's own technocratic and self-centered 'worldliness' which is in reality a falsification and a perversion of natural perspectives, which separates him from the reality of creation, and enables him to act out his fantasies as a little autonomous god, seeing and judging everything in relation to himself" (*Guilty Bystander*, 269).

It is not the world itself, then, that must be rejected, but this seductive pseudoreality of self-sufficiency and Godlike control. It entails a change in perspective, above all about oneself. Merton comments, "As far as I can see, what I abandoned when I 'left the world' and came to the monastery was the *understanding of myself* that I had developed in the context of civil society — my identification with what appeared to me to be its aims" (36). But this means that leaving the world does not involve

abandoning the world to its fate. Rather, it is to enter into a new relationship with reality; it is not sufficient to recognize the abyss between the world as sacrament and the world as mirror of sinful, self-deluded humanity. This recognition also is a summons to responsible action, to work toward bringing the second into conformity with the first: "To choose the world . . . is first of all an acceptance of a task and a vocation in the world, in history and in time. In my time, which is the present. To choose the world is to choose to do the work I am capable of doing, in collaboration with my brother, to make the world better, more free, more just, more livable, more human. And it has now become transparently obvious that mere automatic 'rejection of the world' and 'contempt for the world' is in fact not a choice but the evasion of choice. The man who pretends that he can turn his back on Auschwitz or Viet Nam and act as if they were not there is simply bluffing" (*World of Action*, 149).

Here we have a further instance of that incarnational dimension of Merton's thought. The Christian vocation is a call to be a sign and instrument of God's kingdom, of God's world as it was meant to be, in the midst of the concrete forces and events that block and contradict this vision. Such a response is possible only because it already has been accomplished definitively in Christ. In what is perhaps his most complete statement about the world, Merton says,

Do we really choose between the world and Christ as between two conflicting realities absolutely opposed? Or do we choose Christ by choosing the world as it really is in him, that is to say created and redeemed by him and encountered in the ground of our own personal freedom and of our love? Do we really renounce ourselves and the world in order to find Christ, or do we renounce our alienated and false selves in order to choose our own deepest truth in choosing both the world and Christ at the same time? If the deepest ground of my being is love, then in that very love itself and nowhere else will I find myself, and the world, and my brother and Christ. It is not a question of either-or but of all-in-one. (155–56) POC

WU, SR., JOHN C. H.

Born in Ningpo, China, in 1899, John C. H. Wu authored a number of books on jurisprudence, literature, and philosophy. He was both a scholar and a diplomat, serving for thirteen years as a member of the National Legislature of the Republic of China and for three years as China's ambassador to the Vatican. He taught for a time at Seton Hall University in South Orange, New Jersey. His books include *Beyond East and West,* his autobiography, and *The Golden Age of Zen,* for which Thomas Merton wrote an introduction.

Wu assisted Merton in preparing his "translation" of some of the poems of the Chinese Taoist philosopher Chuang Tzu. He sent Merton four translations of Chuang Tzu, as well as his own literal translation of the selections of Chuang Tzu that Merton had chosen to make his own. Wu was delighted with Merton's versions. "Only a man like yourself," he wrote, "steeped in the works of the great Christian mystics can know what Lao Tzu and Chuang Tzu were pointing at and how utterly honest and correct they were." Wu visited Merton in late June of 1962. Later he wrote, "I swear that I am not flattering when I say that this is exactly what Chuang Tzu would write had he learned English."[1] On December 17, 1965, Wu wrote telling Merton that his name in Chinese was Mei Teng, which means "silent lamp." Merton's letters to Wu are published in *The Hidden Ground of Love.* WHS

SEE ALSO *HIDDEN GROUND OF LOVE.*

Notes

1. For the two John Wu quotations, see *Hidden Ground of Love,* 612, 632.

WYGAL, JAMES

This Louisville psychologist was recommended to Thomas Merton by Gregory Zilboorg. In 1960 Merton started visiting him, and they became good friends. Gradually their sessions turned into friendly conversation rather than counseling visits. In 1966 he sometimes used Wygal's office as a meeting place with the young student nurse with whom he was in love. Wygal was put in a difficult situation. He tried to play the role of a helpful friend; at the same time, he warned Merton of the dangers of his situation. At one point (June 15, 1966) Wygal told him, "You are on a collision course" (*Learning to Love,* 85; see also 95). Merton realized that he was right, yet found it hard to act, at least immediately, on that realization. WHS

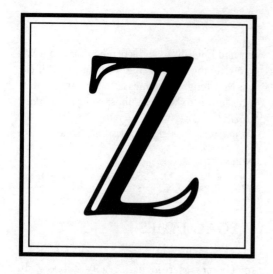

Zen and the Birds of Appetite
Thomas Merton

ZEN

Thomas Merton expresses an interest in Zen Buddhism as early as August 1938 (*When Prophecy*, 12), though there is no evidence of serious study of Zen until the summer of 1956, when he speaks of Zen as an important instrument of his "apostolate" (*Search for Solitude*, 48) and mentions his reading of D. T. Suzuki, probably the foremost interpreter of Zen in the West (57). His direct contact with Suzuki, which led to a meeting in 1964 (*Water of Life*, 115–17), began with an invitation to write a preface to Merton's translations from the desert fathers (*Hidden Ground of Love*, 561–62), which developed into a dialogue that was not permitted to be published with the translation but later appeared in *Zen and the Birds of Appetite* (99–138). Merton's personal contacts with John Wu, for whose book *The Golden Age of Zen* he wrote an introduction (33–58), and with Jesuits working at Sophia University in Tokyo (*Hidden Ground of Love*, 170–74, 439–43) were also important for his interest in Zen; an invitation in 1964 from one of the Jesuits, Heinrich Dumoulin, to visit Japan and experience Zen firsthand was vetoed by Merton's abbot (173), but Merton hoped to include Japan on his itinerary

<hr>

Cover for *Zen and the Birds of Appetite* reprinted with the permission of New Directions. Cover art by Sesshu; cover design by David Ford.

during his 1968 trip to the Far East, which ended prematurely with his death. Merton's writings on Zen, found in *Mystics and Zen Masters* (1967) and *Zen and the Birds of Appetite* (1968), date mainly from the last five years of his life, though he already had included a discussion of Zen enlightenment in his manuscript of "The Inner Experience," dating from the late 1950s.

In trying to explain Zen to a Western audience Merton is careful to delineate what Zen is not: a religion, a philosophy, a method or system, a doctrine (*Mystics and Zen Masters*, 12). "Zen is the ontological *awareness of pure being beyond subject and object*, an immediate grasp of being in its 'suchness' and 'thusness'" (14). It is pure awareness, not awareness of... — consciousness without an object, prior to all differentiation between observer and observed. "Zen insight is not *our* awareness, but Being's awareness of itself in us" (17). The purpose of the *koan*, the enigmatic question, characteristic of the Rinzai school of Zen, which is impervious to a logical solution, is to break through the limited awareness of the empirical consciousness and make possible a direct intuition of reality, "a spontaneous and immediate grasp of being" (251), without the filter of conceptual thought. The experience of enlightenment (*satori*) in Zen is one that destroys all illusions of the self as an independent center of consciousness, "the sudden, definitive, integral realization of the nothingness of the exterior self and, consequently, the liberation of the real self, the inner 'I,'" though even this terminology, Merton points out, can be misleading, as "the real self, in Zen language, is beyond the division between self and not-self" ("Inner Experience," 1:7). Enlightenment is an experience of absolute emptiness (*sunyata*), "the pure void [that] is also pure light, because it is void of all (limited) mind" (*Mystics and Zen Masters*, 39). The negative terminology is used as a guard against misunderstanding, not as the description of a negative experience: "The great 'emptiness' of *Sunyata* ... is described as emptiness only because, being completely without any limit of particularity it is also perfect fullness" (*Birds of Appetite*, 85). Hence, in Suzuki's characteristic formulation, "zero equals infinity" (65).

Merton traces the development of Zen (Ch'an) in China to the convergence of Mahayana Buddhism with Taoism (*Way of Chuang Tzu*, 15–16; *Birds of Appetite*, 2). It is deeply experiential, depending on "mind-to-mind transmission" of its teaching from master (*roshi*) to disciple rather than any rigid "reliance upon the authority of the scriptures" (*Mystics and Zen Masters*, 219). Though in practice Zen uses various Buddhist sutras, it elevates the spirit above the letter: "Enlightenment ... demands a certain freedom with respect to the authority of any literal canonical text" (282). Merton emphasizes, with Suzuki, that the authentic line of Chinese Zen is associated with the southern school of Hui Neng and Shen Hui, which rejects the "mirror-wiping" approach of the northern patriarch Shen Hsiu because it retained a duality between the mind (the mirror) and its reflection (reality), in which "*'emptiness' itself is regarded as a possession and an 'attainment'*" (23). According to the approach of Hui Neng, "There is no mirror to be wiped. What we call 'our' mind is only a flickering and transient manifestation of *prajna* — the formless and limitless light" (25). From this perspective Zen was not to be identified with specialized techniques or experiences of meditation, for "*all life was Zen*" (21) and "Zen is your everyday mind" (33). Merton also fa-

vored the Rinzai (Lin-Chi) sect of Japanese Zen, with its emphasis on the *koan* and the sudden breakthrough to enlightenment, over the Soto sect, with its focus on *zazen*, sitting in meditation, which seems to emphasize introversion (35–36), though it might be argued that what Dōgen, the chief representative of Soto, means in saying that enlightenment already is present in *zazen* is what Hui Neng meant in "refus[ing] to separate meditation as a means (*dhyana*) from *enlightenment as an end (prajna)*" (21), and identical to his successor "Shen Hui's teaching ... not that the mind *must be* emptied, but that it is empty in the first place."[1]

Merton was skeptical and somewhat bemused by the faddishness of interest in Zen in the West, which he considered "a symptom of western man's desperate need to recover spontaneity and depth in a world which his technological skill has made rigid, artificial, and spiritually void" (*Way of Chuang Tzu*, 16), but which was too often a superficial and undisciplined search for spiritual experience precisely as an attainment and possession — antithetical to the authentic spirit of Zen. Nevertheless, he saw Zen as a salutary challenge to the dualism of Western analytical consciousness, "a healthy reaction of people exasperated with the heritage of four centuries of Cartesianism: the reification of concepts, idolization of the reflexive consciousness, flight from being into verbalism, mathematics, and rationalization. Descartes made a fetish out of the mirror in which the self finds itself. Zen shatters it" (*Guilty Bystander*, 260).

He saw the infusion of Zen into Christian life as a particularly promising development. While Zen developed from and within Buddhism, Merton sees it as ultimately "a trans-cultural, trans-religious, trans-formed consciousness" (*Birds of Appetite*, 4) that is not exclusive to Buddhism, and agrees with Suzuki that the "perfect poverty" of Meister Eckhart, in which there is no "place" for God to work, and therefore no separation between the self and its divine Ground, is an expression of a Zenlike awareness. Insofar as Zen is considered as "direct and pure experience on a metaphysical level, liberated from verbal formulas and lin-

548 ZEN AND THE BIRDS OF APPETITE

guistic preconceptions" (44), a "metaphysical intuition of the ground of being" (47), it is compatible with Christianity and indeed can be said to "prepare the way" for Christian revelation. Zen may be at odds with speculative, theoretical theologizing, but not with a deep personal experience of oneness with the Trinity through perfect identification with Christ. In Merton's judgment, "They can well complement each other, and for this reason Zen is perfectly compatible with Christian belief and indeed with Christian mysticism (if we understand Zen in its pure state, as metaphysical intuition)" (47). POC

SEE ALSO BUDDHISM; ENCOUNTER: THOMAS MERTON AND D. T. SUZUKI; INTERRELIGIOUS DIALOGUE; MYSTICS AND ZEN MASTERS; TAOISM; ZEN AND THE BIRDS OF APPETITE.

Notes

1. Thomas Merton, "The Zen Insight of Shen Hui," *The Merton Annual* 1 (1988): 10.

ZEN AND THE BIRDS OF APPETITE

New York: New Directions, 1968. ix+141 pp.

Zen and the Birds of Appetite was published on October 31, 1968. At the time, Thomas Merton was in New Delhi in the middle of his journey to the East. An important work, it shows how deeply he had immersed himself in Zen not just as a subject to write about, but as a way to a direct, unmediated experience of reality.

The book is divided into two parts, though part 2 is the earlier and might well be read before proceeding to the essays of part 1. Part 1 brings together eight articles on Zen, all of which were published in the last three years of his life. The first, "The Study of Zen," originally was published in *Cimarron Review* of Oklahoma State University in June 1968. The second, "The New Consciousness," appeared in a journal of McGill University, *The R. M. Bucke Memorial Society Newsletter* (vol. 2, no. 1 [April 1967]). The third article actually is a preface that Merton contributed to *The Golden Age of Zen*, written by his Chinese friend John C. H. Wu. Wu's book was published in 1967, though Merton wrote his preface in July of 1966. The

fourth article is about Merton's mentor in the study of Zen, "D. T. Suzuki: The Man and His Works." This was first published by the Eastern Buddhist Society of Otani University (Kyoto, Japan) in *The Eastern Buddhist* (n. s.) 2, no. 1 (August 1967). The fifth article is about a Japanese scholar of Zen Buddhism who died in 1945 (when Merton had been at Gethsemani for only four years and had not yet made any deep connection with Zen). The article, "Nishida: A Zen Philosopher," actually is a review of a book by Kitaro Nishida (*A Study of Good*) written for the Cistercian journal, *Collectanea Cisterciensia* (vol. 29 [1967]). The sixth article, "Transcendent Experience," appeared in *The R. M. Bucke Memorial Society Newsletter* 1, no. 2 (1966). The seventh article, simply titled "Nirvana," was written as a foreword to a dissertation by a Smith College student, Sally Donnelly. The dissertation was called "Marcel and Buddha: A Metaphysics of Enlightenment." Merton's essay was published in *Journal of Religious Thought* 24 (1967/68). The eighth article, "Zen in Japanese Art," was a review of a book by that name written by Totshimitsu, Hasumi, translated from the German by John Petrie (1962). Merton's review was published in the *Catholic Worker* (July/August 1967). The eight articles are followed by an appendix in which Merton defends Buddhism against the charge that it is world-denying.

Part 2 of *Zen and the Birds of Appetite* appeared earlier than the eight articles of part 1. It grew out of Merton's interest in the sayings of the desert fathers; he had written a book about them, *The Wisdom of the Desert*, in 1959. He was struck by the fact that the *Verba* ("Words") of the desert fathers bore a remarkable resemblance to some of the stories told of the Japanese Zen masters. He sent his manuscript to D. T. Suzuki with the hope that they might enter into a dialogue about the wisdom of the desert fathers and the Zen masters. Suzuki accepted the invitation, but Dom Gabriel Sortais, the French abbot general of the Cistercians, refused to give his approval for such a joint publication, fearing that Catholics might be confused and misled by the inclusion of a Zen master's reflections in a book about early Catholic monastics. He did say, however, that the Merton-Suzuki dialogue might be published in some American journal. This happened in 1961, when "Wisdom in Emptiness: A Dialogue," by Daisetz Suzuki and Thomas Merton, was published in *New Directions* 17. In 1968 it became part 2 of *Zen and the Birds of Appetite.*

A reader would find it helpful to approach *Zen and the Birds of Appetite* by reading the longest essay of part 1, "A Christian Looks at Zen." It contains much of what Merton has to say about Zen. What baffles most Westerners about Zen is finding out that it is in essence nonverbal. It makes no statements about life. It offers no explanation of reality. Quite literally, it has nothing to say. It is content to be. Hence, it is not a religion or a philosophy or a worldview. While it is possible to speak of Zen Buddhism, Zen is not confined to Buddhism or its religious structure. In fact, Zen is outside of all structures. It is simple attentiveness to reality. It "simply sees what is right there and does not add any comments, any interpretation, any judgment, any conclusion. It just *sees*" (*Birds of Appetite*, 53).

Because Zen is not confined to any particular structure or system, "it can shine through this or that system, religious or irreligious, just as light can shine through glass that is blue, or green, or red, or yellow. If Zen has any preference it is for glass that is plain, has no color, and is 'just glass'" (4). Thus, it is possible to speak of Christian Zen or Zen Catholicism.[1]

Zen is about experience, but experience that is unmediated by the preconceived structures into which Western people so often strive to fit their experiences (thus often missing what the experience actually is). To quote Merton, "The convenient tools of language enable us to decide beforehand what we think things mean and tempt us all too easily to see things only in a way that fits our logical preconceptions and our verbal formulas" (48). By contrast, "The whole aim of Zen is not to make foolproof statements about experience but to come to direct grips with reality without the mediation of logical verbalizing" (37).

Zen is about enlightenment, which is transformed consciousness of reality. Enlightenment has to do with awareness: not the self-conscious awareness whereby a reflecting, knowing subject is aware of some object, but rather, pure awareness. Pure awareness does not mean abstraction; it grasps reality in its existential concreteness, which is to say that it is experienced in the daily realities of life. Zen simply is receptivity to what is. *Nirvana* (enlightenment) is *samsara* (the daily flow of life). And it is here, in the ordinariness of everyday life, that enlightenment is to be experienced. This explains why Zen teachers can say that when enlightenment is attained, nothing is attained.

It is a mistake to turn to Zen in order to achieve "something," whether that be enlightenment or spirituality or peace of mind. Those who do so are like birds of prey hovering over a corpse that is not there. "Zen enriches no one. There is no body to be found. The birds may come and circle for a while in the place where it is thought to be. But they soon go elsewhere. When they are gone, the 'nothing,' the 'no-body' that was there suddenly appears. That is Zen" (ix).

The path to enlightenment is the path of self-emptying. Our ego-consciousness must be left behind. Here Merton is dealing with the distinction, so fundamental to his writing, between the false self (the self-serving ego) and the true self (the person). The ego-self, instead of being realized in its limited selfhood, simply vanishes. This does not mean that the person loses his or her identity, but rather, that it becomes clear that our real status is quite different from what it appears to be empirically. This kenotic[2] experience can be identified in Zen and in Christian spirituality. Commenting on the emptying of Christ and at the same time his exaltation by God (as expressed in Philippians 2), Merton writes, "This dynamic of emptying and of transcendence accurately defines the transformation of the Christian consciousness in Christ. It is a kenotic transformation, an emptying of all the contents of the ego-consciousness to become a void in which the light of God or the glory of God, the full radiation of the infinite reality of His Being and Love are manifested" (75).

The Buddhist experience of *sunyata* (the void) is similar to the kenotic experience of the Christian. The individual ego is completely emptied and takes on the mind of the Buddha. Are the experiences of the Christian putting on the mind of Christ and of the Buddhist taking on the mind of the Buddha simply the same experience articulated differently because each religious system uses its own framework of expressed belief? Merton does not believe that we are in a position as yet to answer this question in any definitive way, yet he sees it as an issue that can lead to fruitful, ongoing dialogue between the West and the East.

Fittingly, this book is dedicated to Amiya Chakravarty, the Indian poet, philosopher, and world scholar who corresponded with Merton, helped him in his planning for the Asian journey and was with him during part of that journey. WHS

Notes

1. William Johnston has written a book entitled *Christian Zen* (New York: Harper & Row, 1971), and Aelred Graham one called *Zen Catholicism* (New York: Harcourt, Brace & World, 1963).

2. The Greek word *kenosis* means "emptying." In Philippians 2, Paul writes that Jesus "emptied himself, taking the form of a slave." The text goes on to say that because of this self-emptying, even to death on the cross, God exalted Jesus and gave him the name above all names.

ZILBOORG, GREGORY

Gregory Zilboorg (1891–1959) was a well-known psychiatrist whose conversion to Catholicism made him something of an unusual phenomenon among Catholics. In July of 1956 at St. John's Abbey in Collegeville, Minnesota, he spoke with Thomas Merton and his abbot (John Eudes also was there). Zilboorg maintained that Merton's desire to be a hermit was pathological: "You want a hermitage in Times Square with a large sign over it saying 'HERMIT.'"[1] Merton was stunned and moved to tears — tears of rage. He soon recovered, however, and found in Louisville a more congenial therapist in Dr. James Wygal. It is questionable whether Zilboorg, who resented Merton's attempts to write about psychological issues, was capable of an unbiased analysis of Merton's psychological stability. It has been suggested that what occurred was a conflict between two men whose conversion to Catholicism had made them prominent figures in the Catholic community. WHS

Notes

1. See Michael Mott, *The Seven Mountains of Thomas Merton* (Boston: Houghton Mifflin, 1984), 297.

Acknowledgments

Reprinted by permission of Ave Maria Press:

Excerpts from *The Springs of Contemplation: A Retreat at the Abbey of Gethsemani* by Thomas Merton, 1997.

Reprinted by permission of Cistercian Publications:

Excerpts by Thomas Merton from *The Climate of Monastic Prayer*, 1969, and *Thomas Merton on Saint Bernard*, 1980.

Reprinted by permission of The Crossroad Publishing Company:

Excerpts by Thomas Merton from *Passion for Peace: The Social Essays* edited by William H. Shannon. Copyright © 1995 by the Trustees of the Merton Legacy Trust.

Reprinted by permission of Doubleday, a division of Random House, Inc.:

Excerpts from *Conjectures of a Guilty Bystander* by Thomas Merton. Copyright © 1966 by The Abbey of Gethsemani.

Reprinted by permission of Farrar, Straus and Giroux, LLC:

Excerpts from *The Courage for Truth: The Letters of Thomas Merton to Writers* by Thomas Merton, edited by Christine M. Bochen. Copyright © 1993 by the Merton Legacy Trust.

Excerpts from *Disputed Questions* by Thomas Merton. Copyright © 1960 by The Abbey of Our Lady of Gethsemani. Copyright renewed 1988 by Alan Hanson.

Excerpts from *The Hidden Ground of Love: The Letters of Thomas Merton on Religious Experience and Social Concerns* by Thomas Merton, edited by William H. Shannon. Copyright © 1985 by the Merton Legacy Trust.

Excerpts from *The Living Bread* by Thomas Merton. Copyright © 1956 by The Abbey of Our Lady of Gethsemani, Inc. Copyright renewed 1984 by the Trustees of the Merton Legacy Trust.

Excerpts from *Love and Living* by Thomas Merton. Copyright © 1979 by the Merton Legacy Trust.

Excerpts from *Mystics and Zen Masters* by Thomas Merton. Copyright © 1967 by The Abbey of Gethsemani. Copyright renewed 1995 by Robert Giroux, James Laughlin, and Tommy O'Callaghan as trustees of the Merton Legacy Trust.

Excerpts from *The New Man* by Thomas Merton. Copyright © 1961 by Thomas Merton. Copyright renewed 1989 by Farrar, Straus & Giroux, Inc.

Excerpts from *The Nonviolent Alternative*. Copyright © 1980 by the Merton Legacy Trust.

Excerpts from *The Road to Joy: The Letters of Thomas Merton to New and Old Friends* by Thomas Merton, selected and edited by Robert E. Daggy. Copyright © 1989 by the Merton Legacy Trust.

Excerpts from *The School of Charity: The Letters of Thomas Merton on Religious Renewal and Spiritual Direction* by Thomas Merton, edited by Brother Patrick Hart. Copyright © 1990 by the Merton Legacy Trust.

Excerpts from *Seasons of Celebration* by Thomas Merton. Copyright © 1965 by The Abbey of Gethsemani. Copyright renewed 1993 by Robert Giroux, James Laughlin, and Tommy O'Callaghan.

Excerpts from *Seeds of Destruction* by Thomas Merton. Copyright © 1964 by The Abbey of Gethsemani. Copyright renewed 1992 by Robert Giroux, James Laughlin, and Tommy O'Callaghan.

Excerpts from *The Silent Life* by Thomas Merton. Copyright © 1957 by The Abbey of Our Lady of Gethsemani. Copyright renewed 1985 by the Merton Legacy Trust.

Excerpts from *The Springs of Contemplation: A Retreat at the Abbey of Gethsemani* by Thomas Merton. Edited by James M. Richardson, 1992.

Excerpts from *Striving towards Being: The Letters of Thomas Merton and Czeslaw Milosz* by Thomas Merton and Czeslaw Milosz, edited by Robert Faggen. Copyright © 1997 by the Merton Legacy Trust. Copyright © 1997 by Czeslaw Milosz.

Excerpts from *Thoughts in Solitude* by Thomas Merton. Copyright © 1958 by The Abbey of Our Lady of Gethsemani. Copyright renewed 1986 by the Trustees of the Merton Legacy Trust.

Excerpts from *A Vow of Conversation* by Thomas Merton and excerpts from *Journals 1964–1965* by Thomas Merton. Copyright © 1988 by the Merton Legacy Trust.

Excerpts from *Witness to Freedom* by Thomas Merton, edited by William H. Shannon. Copyright © 1994 by the Merton Legacy Trust.

Reprinted by permission of Harcourt, Inc.:

Excerpts from *The Seven Storey Mountain* by Thomas Merton. Copyright © 1948 by Harcourt, Inc. and renewed 1976 by the Trustees of the Merton Legacy Trust.

Excerpts from *The Sign of Jonas* by Thomas Merton. Copyright © 1953 by The Abbey of Our Lady of Gethsemani and renewed 1981 by the Trustees of the Merton Legacy Trust.

Excerpts from *The Last of the Fathers* by Thomas Merton. Copyright © 1954 and renewed 1982 by the Trustees of the Merton Legacy Trust.

Excerpts from *The Waters of Siloe* by Thomas Merton. Copyright © 1949 by Thomas Merton and renewed 1977 by the Trustees of the Merton Legacy Trust.

Reprinted by permission of HarperCollins Publishers Inc.:

Excerpts from *Run to the Mountain: The Journals of Thomas Merton, Volume One 1939–1941* by Thomas Merton and edited by Patrick Hart. Copyright © 1995 by the Merton Legacy Trust.

Excerpts from *Entering the Silence: The Journals of Thomas Merton, Volume Two 1941–1952* by Thomas Merton and edited by Jonathan Montaldo. Copyright © 1995 by the Merton Legacy Trust.

Excerpts from *A Search for Solitude: The Journals of Thomas Merton, Volume Three 1952–1960* by Thomas Merton and edited by Lawrence S. Cunningham. Copyright © 1996 by the Merton Legacy Trust.

Excerpts from *Turning toward the World: The Journals of Thomas Merton, Volume Four 1960–1963* by Thomas Merton and edited by Victor A. Kramer. Copyright © 1996 by the Merton Legacy Trust.

Excerpts from *Dancing in the Water of Life: The Journals of Thomas Merton, Volume Five 1963–1965* by Thomas Merton and edited by Robert E. Daggy. Copyright © 1997 by the Merton Legacy Trust.

Excerpts from *Learning to Love: The Journals of Thomas Merton, Volume Six 1966–1967* by Thomas Merton and edited by Christine M. Bochen. Copyright © 1997 by the Merton Legacy Trust.

Excerpts from *The Other Side of the Mountain: The Journals of Thomas Merton, Volume Seven 1967–1968* by Thomas Merton and edited by Patrick Hart. Copyright © 1998 by the Merton Legacy Trust.

Reprinted by permission of King Library Press:

Excerpts from *Six Letters: Boris Pasternak, Thomas Merton*, 1973.

Excerpts from *Unquiet Conscience*, 1958.

Excerpts from *What Ought I to Do?* 1959.

Reprinted by permission of Liturgical Press:

Excerpts by Thomas Merton from *Praying the Psalms*. Copyright © 1956 by the Order of St. Benedict.

Excerpts by Thomas Merton from *Spiritual Direction and Meditation*. Copyright © 1960 by the Order of St. Benedict, Inc.

Reprinted by permission of the Merton Legacy Trust:

Excerpts from *Cistercian Contemplatives* © 1948 by The Abbey of Gethsemani.

Excerpts from *Gethsemani: A Life of Praise* © 1966 by The Abbey of Gethsemani.

Excerpts from *Gethsemani Magnificat* © 1949 by The Abbey of Gethsemani.

Excerpts from *Guide to Cistercian Life* © 1948 by The Abbey of Gethsemani.

Excerpts from *The Life and Kingdom of Jesus in Christian Souls* (translated by Thomas Merton) © 1948 by The Abbey of Gethsemani.

Excerpts from *Loretto and Gethsemani* © 1962 by The Abbey of Gethsemani.

Excerpts from *The Soul of the Apostolate* (translated by Thomas Merton) © 1946 by The Abbey of Gethsemani.

Excerpts from *Trappist Life* © 1953 by The Abbey of Gethsemani.

Excerpts from *What Think You of Carmel?* © 1962 by The Abbey of Gethsemani.

Reprinted by permission of New Directions Publishing Corporation:

Excerpts from *The Asian Journal of Thomas Merton* by Thomas Merton. Copyright © 1975 by the Trustees of the Merton Legacy Trust.

Excerpts from *The Behavior of Titans* by Thomas Merton. Copyright © 1961 by The Abbey of Gethsemani, Inc.

Excerpts from *Bread in the Wilderness* by Thomas Merton. Copyright © 1953 by Our Lady of Gethsemani Monastery.

Excerpts from *Breakthrough to Peace* (Introduction and essay) by Thomas Merton. Copyright © 1962 by Thomas Merton.

Excerpts from *The Collected Poems of Thomas Merton* by Thomas Merton. Copyright © 1977 by the Trustees of the Merton Legacy Trust, © 1944, 1949 by Our Lady of Gethsemani Monastery © 1946, 1948 by New Directions Publishing Corporation, © 1957, 1962, 1963, 1968 by The Abbey of Gethsemani, Inc.

Excerpts from *Eighteen Poems* by Thomas Merton. Copyright © 1977, 1985 by the Trustees of the Merton Legacy Trust.

Excerpts from *Gandhi on Non-Violence* by Thomas Merton. Copyright © 1964, 1965 by New Directions Publishing Corp.

Excerpts from *The Geography of Lograire* by Thomas Merton. Copyright © 1968, 1969 by the Trustees of the Merton Legacy Trust.

Excerpts from *The Literary Essays of Thomas Merton* by Thomas Merton. Copyright © 1960, 1966, 1967, 1968, 1973, 1975, 1978, 1981 by the Trustees of the Merton Legacy Trust. Copyright © 1959, 1961, 1963, 1964, 1965, 1981 by The Abbey of Gethsemani, Inc. Copyright © 1953 by Our Lady of Gethsemani Monastery.

Excerpts from *My Argument with the Gestapo* by Thomas Merton. Copyright © 1969 by The Abbey of Gethsemani, Inc., © 1968 by Thomas Merton.

Excerpts from *New Seeds of Contemplation* by Thomas Merton. Copyright © 1961 by The Abbey of Gethsemani, Inc.

Excerpts from *Raids on the Unspeakable* by Thomas Merton. Copyright © 1966 by The Abbey of Gethsemani, Inc.

Excerpts from *Thomas Merton in Alaska* by Thomas Merton. Copyright © 1989 by the Merton Legacy Trust.

Excerpts from *The Way of Chuang Tzu* by Thomas Merton. Copyright © 1965 by The Abbey of Gethsemani, Inc.

Excerpts from *The Wisdom of the Desert* by Thomas Merton. Copyright © 1960 by The Abbey of Gethsemani, Inc.

Excerpts from *Zen and the Birds of Appetite* by Thomas Merton. Copyright © 1968 by The Abbey of Gethsemani, Inc.

Reprinted by permission of W. W. Norton & Company:

Excerpts from *Thomas Merton and James Laughlin: Selected Letters* edited by David Cooper, 1997.

Reprinted by permission of Templegate Publishers:

Excerpts from *What Is Contemplation?* by Thomas Merton, 1981.

Excerpts from *Basic Principles of Monastic Spirituality* by Thomas Merton, 1996.

Reprinted by permission of University of Notre Dame Press:

Excerpts from *Faith and Violence* by Thomas Merton. Copyright © 1984 by University of Notre Dame Press.

CREDITS FOR PHOTOS AND DRAWINGS

**Courtesy of the Merton Legacy Trust
and the Thomas Merton Center at Bellarmine University:**

Thomas Merton in Bangkok, p. 15

Standing Buddha at Polonnaruwa, photograph by Thomas Merton, p. 34

Calligraphy by Thomas Merton, p. 39

Drawing of Christ by Thomas Merton, p. 52

Merton as a Columbia University student, p. 69

The Dalai Lama and Abbot Timothy Kelly, O.C.S.O., p. 99

Cross and wagon wheel near Thomas Merton's hermitage, p. 101

John Paul and Tom Merton, p. 119

Photograph by Thomas Merton, p. 126

Plaque at Fourth and Walnut site, photograph by Paul M. Pearson, p. 159

Drawing of Gethsemani by Thomas Merton, p. 175

Merton's desk in the hermitage, p. 230

Jacques Maritain, p. 280

Owen Merton, p. 296

Ruth Jenkins Merton, p. 297

Monastery of Christ in the Desert, photograph by Thomas Merton, p. 299

Drawing by Thomas Merton, p. 307

Photograph by Thomas Merton, p. 320

Photograph by Thomas Merton, p. 324

Thomas Merton just before leaving for Asia, p. 347

Photograph by Thomas Merton, p. 358

Buddhas at Polonnaruwa, photograph by Thomas Merton, p. 364

Thomas Merton's ordination, p. 369

Drawing by Thomas Merton, p. 383

Pleasant Hill, Kentucky, photograph by Thomas Merton, p. 429

Naomi Burton Stone, p. 453

Photograph by Thomas Merton, p. 455

Jean Leclercq, O.S.B., and Thomas Merton, p. 460

Photograph by Thomas Merton, p. 512

Drawing by Thomas Merton, p. 538

Pacific shoreline, photograph by Thomas Merton, p. 542

Courtesy of William H. Shannon:

A. M. Allchin, p. 6

Photograph of a watercolor by Owen Merton, p. 9

Abbot John Eudes Bamberger, O.C.S.O., p. 22

Clare College Court, p. 41

Altar in Thomas Merton's hermitage, p. 142

Brother Patrick Hart, O.C.S.O., p. 193

Thomas Merton's hermitage, p. 199

Lax/Marcus cottage, Olean, New York, p. 334

Oakham Chapel, Rutland, England, p. 337

St. Theresa's Shrine, St. Bonaventure University, p. 398

Photograph of drawing of St. Lutgarde by Thomas Merton, p. 525

Courtesy of the Estate of John Howard Griffin: Thomas Merton, cover and p. ii.

Courtesy of the archives of Clare College: Entering class, Clare College, 1933, p. 62

Courtesy of The Abbey of Our Lady of Gethsemani: Dom James Fox, O.C.S.O., p. 161

Courtesy of Arthur Wang: Robert Giroux, p. 179

Courtesy of King Library Press, Lexington: woodcut of Hagia Sophia, by Victor Hammer, p. 192

Courtesy of Brother Patrick Hart: William H. Shannon, p. 219

Courtesy of Marcia Kelly: Robert Lax, p. 249

Courtesy of John Stanley, who was given the photograph by the late Marilyn Miscall Eighmey: John Paul Merton, p. 294

Courtesy of Chris Rice: Edward Rice, p. 390

Courtesy of the archives of Loretto Motherhouse: Mary Luke Tobin, p. 489